Kaplan SCHWESER™

2024 CFA® Notes 备考笔记三级

第一册（全五册）

SCHWESERNOTES™ 2024 CFA® PART III

BOOK 1

Capital Market Expectations and Asset Allocation

美国开普兰公司 著

中信出版集团 | 北京

图书在版编目（CIP）数据

Kaplan SCHWESER 2024 CFA®; Notes 备考笔记 = SCHWESERNOTES™; 2024 LEVEL Ⅲ CFA®; 三级 : 全五册 : 英文 / 美国开普兰公司著 . -- 北京 : 中信出版社 , 2023.8

ISBN 978-7-5217-5649-4

Ⅰ . ① K… Ⅱ . ①美… Ⅲ . ①金融－分析－资格考试－自学参考资料－英文 Ⅳ . ① F83

中国国家版本馆 CIP 数据核字 (2023) 第 083168 号

Kaplan SCHWESER 2024 CFA® Notes 备考笔记三级第一册（全五册）
著者：　美国开普兰公司
出版发行：中信出版集团股份有限公司
（北京市朝阳区东三环北路 27 号嘉铭中心　邮编　100020）
承印者：　河北鹏润印刷有限公司

开本：889mm×1194mm 1/16　　印张：74.5　　字数：2130 千字
版次：2023 年 8 月第 1 版　　印次：2023 年 8 月第 1 次印刷
书号：ISBN 978-7-5217-5649-4
定价：1599.00 元（全五册）

Kaplan Schweser's Path to Success

Level III CFA® Exam

CFA®

Welcome

As the head of Advanced Designations at Kaplan Schweser, I am pleased to have the opportunity to help you prepare for the CFA® exam. Kaplan Schweser has decades of experience in delivering the most effective CFA exam prep products in the market and I know you will find them to be invaluable in your studies.

Our products are designed to be an integrated study solution across print and digital media to provide you the best learning experience, whether you are studying with a physical book, online, or on your mobile device.

Our core product, the SchweserNotes™, addresses all of the Topics, Learning Modules, and LOS in the CFA curriculum. Each reading in the SchweserNotes has been broken into smaller, bite-sized modules with Module Quizzes interspersed throughout to help you continually assess your comprehension. Online Topic Quizzes appear at the end of each Topic to help you assess your knowledge of the material before you move on to the next section.

All purchasers of the SchweserNotes receive online access to the Kaplan Schweser online platform (our learning management system or LMS) at www.Schweser.com. In the LMS, you will see a dashboard that tracks your overall progress and performance and also includes an Activity Feed, which provides structure and organization to the tasks required to prepare for the CFA exam. You also have access to the SchweserNotes, Module Quizzes, and Topic Quizzes content as well as the Module Videos (if purchased), which contain a short video that complements each module in the SchweserNotes. Look for the icons indicating where video content, Module Quizzes, and Topic Quizzes are available online. I strongly encourage you to use the dashboard to track your progress and stay motivated.

Again, thank you for trusting Kaplan Schweser with your CFA exam preparation. We're here to help you throughout your journey to become a CFA charterholder.

Regards,

Derek Burkett

Derek Burkett, CFA, FRM, CAIA
Vice President (Advanced Designations)

Book 1: Capital Market Expectations and Asset Allocation

SchweserNotes™ 2024

Level III CFA®

KAPLAN SCHWESER

SCHWESERNOTES™ 2024 LEVEL III CFA® BOOK 1: CAPITAL MARKET EXPECTATIONS AND ASSET ALLOCATION

Published in 2023 by Kaplan, Inc.

ISBN: 978-1-0788-3750-7

CONTENTS

CAPITAL MARKET EXPECTATIONS

ASSET ALLOCATION

LEARNING OUTCOME STATEMENTS (LOS)

1. Capital Market Expectations, Part 1: Framework and Macro Considerations

The candidate should be able to:

a. discuss the role of, and a framework for, capital market expectations in the portfolio management process. (page 1)
b. discuss challenges in developing capital market forecasts. (page 2)
c. explain how exogenous shocks may affect economic growth trends. (page 8)
d. discuss the application of economic growth trend analysis to the formulation of capital market expectations. (page 9)
e. compare major approaches to economic forecasting. (page 11)
f. discuss how business cycles affect short- and long-term expectations. (page 13)
g. explain the relationship of inflation to the business cycle and the implications of inflation for cash, bonds, equity, and real estate returns. (page 15)
h. discuss the effects of monetary and fiscal policy on business cycles. (page 18)
i. interpret the shape of the yield curve as an economic predictor and discuss the relationship between the yield curve and fiscal and monetary policy. (page 21)
j. identify and interpret macroeconomic, interest rate, and exchange rate linkages between economies. (page 22)

2. Capital Market Expectations, Part 2: Forecasting Asset Class Returns

The candidate should be able to:

a. discuss approaches to setting expectations for fixed-income returns. (page 33)
b. discuss risks faced by investors in emerging market fixed-income securities and the country risk analysis techniques used to evaluate emerging market economies. (page 37)
c. discuss approaches to setting expectations for equity investment market returns. (page 38)
d. discuss risks faced by investors in emerging market equity securities. (page 38)
e. explain how economic and competitive factors can affect expectations for real estate investment markets and sector returns. (page 46)
f. discuss major approaches to forecasting exchange rates. (page 49)
g. discuss methods of forecasting volatility. (page 51)
h. recommend and justify changes in the component weights of a global investment portfolio based on trends and expected changes in macroeconomic factors. (page 55)

3. Overview of Asset Allocation

The candidate should be able to:

a. describe elements of effective investment governance and investment governance considerations in asset allocation. (page 67)
b. formulate an economic balance sheet for a client and interpret its implications for asset allocation. (page 70)
c. compare the investment objectives of asset-only, liability-relative, and goals-based asset allocation approaches. (page 71)
d. contrast concepts of risk relevant to asset-only, liability-relative, and goals-based asset allocation approaches. (page 72)
e. explain how asset classes are used to represent exposures to systematic risk and discuss criteria for asset class specification. (page 73)
f. explain the use of risk factors in asset allocation and their relation to traditional asset class–based approaches. (page 75)
g. recommend and justify an asset allocation based on an investor's objectives and constraints. (page 76)

h. describe the use of the global market portfolio as a baseline portfolio in asset allocation. (page 78)
i. discuss strategic implementation choices in asset allocation, including passive/active choices and vehicles for implementing passive and active mandates. (page 79)
j. discuss strategic considerations in rebalancing asset allocations. (page 81)

4. Principles of Asset Allocation

The candidate should be able to:

a. describe and evaluate the use of mean–variance optimization in asset allocation. (page 91)
b. recommend and justify an asset allocation using mean–variance optimization. (page 97)
c. interpret and evaluate an asset allocation in relation to an investor's economic balance sheet. (page 100)
d. recommend and justify an asset allocation based on the global market portfolio. (page 97)
e. discuss the use of Monte Carlo simulation and scenario analysis to evaluate the robustness of an asset allocation. (page 101)
f. discuss asset class liquidity considerations in asset allocation. (page 101)
g. explain absolute and relative risk budgets and their use in determining and implementing an asset allocation. (page 103)
h. describe how client needs and preferences regarding investment risks can be incorporated into asset allocation. (page 104)
i. describe the use of investment factors in constructing and analyzing an asset allocation. (page 104)
j. describe and evaluate characteristics of liabilities that are relevant to asset allocation. (page 106)
k. discuss approaches to liability-relative asset allocation. (page 107)
l. recommend and justify a liability-relative asset allocation. (page 107)
m. recommend and justify an asset allocation using a goals-based approach. (page 109)
n. describe and evaluate heuristic and other approaches to asset allocation. (page 111)
o. discuss factors affecting rebalancing policy. (page 112)

5. Asset Allocation with Real-World Constraints

The candidate should be able to:

a. discuss asset size, liquidity needs, time horizon, and regulatory or other considerations as constraints on asset allocation. (page 121)
b. discuss tax considerations in asset allocation and rebalancing. (page 127)
c. recommend and justify revisions to an asset allocation given change(s) in investment objectives and/or constraints. (page 130)
d. discuss the use of short-term shifts in asset allocation. (page 132)
e. identify behavioral biases that arise in asset allocation and recommend methods to overcome them. (page 134)

READING 1

Capital Market Expectations, Part 1: Framework and Macro Considerations

EXAM FOCUS

Combining capital market expectations with the investor's objectives and constraints leads to the portfolio's strategic asset allocation. A variety of economic tools and techniques are useful in forming capital market expectations for return, risk, and correlation by asset class. Unfortunately, no one technique works consistently, so be prepared for any technique and its issues as covered here.

MODULE 1.1: FORMULATING CAPITAL MARKET EXPECTATIONS

Video covering this content is available online.

LOS 1.a: Discuss the role of, and a framework for, capital market expectations in the portfolio management process.

Capital market expectations are risk and return expectations regarding classes of assets. Investors should establish long-term expectations for each allowable asset class specified in the investment policy statement. They can also create short-term expectations for making active investment decisions. Using a disciplined approach to set short- and long-term expectations leads to more effective security selection, asset allocation, and risk management.

Achieving long-term investment objectives is largely dependent on constructing proper asset allocations. Although projecting asset class returns may be subject to forecasting errors, investors should ensure that portfolios are internally consistent. **Cross-sectional consistency** refers to consistency across asset classes regarding portfolio risk and return characteristics. **Intertemporal consistency** refers to consistency over various investment horizons regarding portfolio decisions over time.

To formulate capital market expectations, an analyst should use the following seven-step process:

Step 1: Determine the specific capital market expectations needed according to the investor's allowable asset classes and investment horizon(s). Time horizon is particularly important in determining the set of capital market expectations that are needed.

Step 2: Investigate assets' historical performance to determine the drivers that have affected past performance and to establish some range for plausible future performance. With the drivers of past performance established, the analyst can use these to forecast expected future performance as well as compare the forecast to past results to see if the forecast appears reasonable.

Step 3: Identify the valuation model to be used and its requirements. For example, a comparables-based, relative value approach used in the United States may be difficult to apply in an emerging market analysis.

Step 4: Collect the best data possible. The use of faulty data will lead to faulty conclusions. Financial publications and commercial databases are likely the best sources for reliable information on asset classes.

Step 5: Use experience and judgment to interpret current investment conditions and decide what values to assign to the required inputs. Verify that the inputs used for the various asset classes are consistent across classes.

Step 6: Formulate capital market expectations. Any assumptions and rationales used in the analysis should be recorded.

Step 7: Monitor performance and use it to refine the process for setting expectations. If actual performance varies significantly from forecasts, the process and model should be refined.

Information needed to support the investment process includes:

- Geography—individual countries, economic blocks (e.g., EU), non-domestic vs. domestic, regional, and global.
- Major asset classes such as fixed income, equity, and real assets.
- Sub-asset classes:
  - Equity—industries, sectors, size, style
  - Fixed income—nominal vs. TIPS, floating vs. fixed, credit quality, maturities
  - Real assets—commodities, real estate, timber

Good forecasts are unbiased, objective, well researched, efficient (small forecasting error), and internally consistent. A general guideline is that at least 30 observations are needed to test a hypothesis.

Problems in Forecasting

LOS 1.b: Discuss challenges in developing capital market forecasts.

Poor forecasts can result in inappropriate asset allocations. Analysts should be aware of potential problems in data, models, and the resulting capital market expectations.

Nine problems encountered in producing forecasts are (1) limitations to using economic data, (2) data measurement error and bias, (3) limitations of historical estimates, (4) the use of ex-post risk and return measures, (5) non-repeating data patterns, (6) failing to account for conditioning information, (7) misinterpreting of correlations, (8) psychological bias, and (9) model uncertainty.

1. There are several **limitations to using economic data:**
   - The time lag between collection and distribution is often quite long. The International Monetary Fund, for example, reports data with a lag of as much as two years.
   - Data are often revised and the revisions are not made at the same time as the publication. Additionally, data definitions and methodology change over time. For example, the basket of goods in the Consumer Price Index (CPI) is updated every few years.
   - Data indexes are often rebased over time (i.e., the base upon which they are calculated is changed). Although a rebasing is not a substantial change in the data itself, the unaware analyst could calculate changes in the value of the indexes incorrectly if she does not make an appropriate adjustment.
2. There are numerous possible **data measurement errors and biases**. *Transcription errors* are the misreporting or incorrect recording of information and are most serious if they are biased in one direction. *Survivorship bias* commonly occurs if a manager or a security return series is deleted from the historical performance record of managers or firms. Deletions are often tied to poor performance and bias the historical return upward. *Appraisal data* for illiquid and infrequently priced assets makes the path of returns appear smoother than it actually is. This biases downward the calculated standard deviation and makes the returns seem less correlated (closer to 0) with more liquid priced assets. This is a particular problem for some types of alternative assets such as real estate.
3. The **limitations of historical estimates** can also hamper the formation of capital market expectations. Values from historical data must often be adjusted going forward as economic, political, regulatory, and technological environments change. This is particularly true for volatile assets such as equity. These changes are known as *regime changes* and result in *nonstationary* data. For example, the global financial crisis in 2007–2009 resulted in returns data that were markedly different than those from the previous five years. Nonstationarity would mean different periods in the time series have different statistical properties and create problems with standard statistical testing methods.

   Two questions can be used to help resolve the issue of which time period to select:

   a. Is there a reason to believe the entire (longer) time period is not appropriate?
   b. If the answer to the first question is yes, does a statistical test confirm there is a regime change and the point in the time series where it occurs?

   If both answers are yes, the analyst must use judgment to select the relevant subperiod.

Historical data are a starting point for estimating expected returns, standard deviations, and correlations. A long time period is preferable for several reasons:

- It may be statistically required: To calculate historical covariance (and correlation), the number of data points must exceed the number of covariances to be calculated.
- A larger data set (time period) provides more precise statistical estimates with smaller variance to the estimates.
- Using a short time period creates a temptation to use more frequent data, such as weekly data, rather than monthly data points in order to have a larger sample size. Unfortunately, more frequent data points are often more likely to have missing or outdated values (this is called *asynchronous* data) and can result in distorted correlation calculations. Also, it has been found that more frequent data will not improve the precision of expected returns.

However, long time periods also create the potential problem of including regime changes, which are shifts in underlying fundamentals. Each regime change creates a subperiod with distinctly different characteristics.

In addition to selecting time periods, caution should be exercised when data are assumed to be normally distributed. Asset returns have historically exhibited "fat tails" and skewness, which adds complexity to statistical tests. In some cases, the benefits of accounting for non-normality might not outweigh the costs of introducing complexity to a model.

4. Using **ex post data** (after the fact) to determine **ex ante** (before the fact) risk and return can be problematic. For example, suppose that several years ago investors were fearful that the Federal Reserve was going to have to raise interest rates to combat inflation. This situation would cause depressed stock prices. If inflation abated without the Fed's intervention, then stock returns would increase once the inflation scenario passed. Looking back on this situation, the researcher would conclude that stock returns were high while being blind to the prior risk that investors had faced. The analyst would then conclude that future (ex ante) returns for stocks will be high. In sum, the analyst would underestimate the risks that equity investors face and overestimate their potential returns.

   This issue could also lead to an overestimation of risk when sample data include rare negative events. Using a data subset that includes outliers will likely distort the estimation of value at risk (VaR). This would suggest that rare negative events are expected with more frequency than would be observed in practice.

5. Using historical data, analysts can also uncover patterns in security returns that are unlikely to occur in the future and can produce biases in the data. One such bias is *data mining*. Just by random chance, some variables will appear to have a relationship with security returns, when, in fact, these relationships are unlikely to persist. For example, if the analyst uses a 5% significance level and examines the relationship between stock returns and 40 randomly selected variables, two (5%) of the variables are expected to show a statistically significant relationship with stock returns just by random chance. Another potential bias results from the time span of data chosen (*time period bias*). For example, small-cap U.S. stocks are widely thought to outperform large-cap stocks, but their advantage disappears when data from 2000 to 2010 are excluded.

To avoid these biases, an analyst should first ask if there is any economic basis for the variables found to be related to stock returns. Second, he should scrutinize the modeling process for susceptibility to bias. Third, the analyst should test the discovered relationship with out-of-sample data to determine if the relationship is persistent. This would be done by estimating the relationship with one portion of the historical data and then reexamining it with another portion.

6. Analysts' forecasts may also fail to account for **conditioning information**. The relationship between security returns and economic variables is not constant over time. Historical data reflect performance over many different business cycles and economic conditions. Thus, analysts should account for current conditions in their forecasts. As an example, suppose a firm's beta is estimated at 1.2 using historical data. If, however, the original data are separated into two ranges by economic expansion or recession, the beta might be 1.0 in expansions and 1.4 in recessions. Going forward, the analyst's estimate of the firm's beta should reflect whether an expansion is expected (i.e., the expected beta is 1.0) or a recession is expected (i.e., the expected beta is 1.4).
7. Another problem in forming capital market expectations is the **misinterpretation of correlations** (i.e., causality). Suppose the analyst finds that corn prices were correlated with rainfall in the midwestern United States during the previous quarter. It would be reasonable to conclude that rainfall influences corn prices. It would not be reasonable to conclude that corn prices influence rainfall. Rainfall is an exogenous variable (i.e., it arises outside the model), whereas the price of corn is an endogenous variable (i.e., it arises within the model).

   It is also possible that the correlation between two variables is spurious or that a third variable influences both variables. In addition, two variables may have a nonlinear relationship that is missed by the correlation statistic, which measures linear relationships.
8. Analysts are susceptible to **psychological biases:**
   - In the **anchoring bias** (cognitive), the first information received is overweighted. If, during a debate on the future of the economy, the first speaker forecasts a recession, that forecast is given greater credence.
   - In the **status quo bias** (emotional), predictions are highly influenced by the recent past. If inflation is currently 4%, that becomes the forecast, rather than choosing to be different and potentially making an active error of commission.
   - In the **confirmation bias** (cognitive), only information supporting the existing belief is considered, and such evidence may be actively sought while other evidence is ignored. To counter these tendencies, analysts should give all evidence equal scrutiny and seek out contrary opinions.

- In the **overconfidence bias** (emotional), past mistakes are ignored, the lack of comments from others is taken as agreement, and the accuracy of forecasts is overestimated. To counter this bias, consider a range of potential outcomes.
- In the **prudence bias** (cognitive), forecasts are overly conservative to avoid the regret from making extreme forecasts that could end up being incorrect. This bias can also be mitigated by considering a range of potential outcomes.
- In the **availability bias** (cognitive), what is easiest to remember (often an extreme event) is overweighted. Many believe that the U.S. stock market crash of 1929 may have depressed equity values in the subsequent 30 years. To counter this bias, base predictions on objective data rather than emotions or recollections of the past.

PROFESSOR'S NOTE

Five of these six biases are the same as in the behavioral readings; the prudence bias is the same as the conservatism bias in the behavioral readings.

9. **Model uncertainty** refers to selecting the correct model. An analyst may be unsure whether to use a discounted cash flow (DCF) model or a relative value model to evaluate an expected stock return. *Parameter uncertainty* refers to estimation errors in model parameters. *Input uncertainty* refers to knowing the correct input values for the model. For example, even if the analyst knew that the DCF model was appropriate, the correct growth and discount rates are still needed. Among the three types of uncertainty, model uncertainty is the most serious given that an incorrect model will likely lead to invalid conclusions.

MODULE QUIZ 1.1

1. An analyst uses a variety of valuation approaches for different asset classes and collects the necessary data from multiple sources. The analyst does not make any effort to systematically compare the data used. As a result, the analyst uses relatively low discount rates for equity analysis (overestimating theoretical value) and high discount rates for fixed income (underestimating theoretical value). **Discuss** the likely effect on the analyst's asset allocation recommendations.

2. An analyst would like to forecast U.S. equity returns. He is considering using either the last 3 years of historical annual returns or the last 50 years of historical annual returns. **Provide** an argument for and against each selection of data length.

3. **Explain** why smoothed data may be present for some types of alternative investments and the consequences for their risk and correlation with other assets from using such data.

Video covering this content is available online.

MODULE 1.2: THE TREND RATE OF GROWTH

LOS 1.c: Explain how exogenous shocks may affect economic growth trends.

Identifying problems in developing forecasts is important when setting capital market expectations. However, a far greater concern is the connection between investment outcomes and economic output. In general, economic growth can be partitioned into cyclical variations and growth trends. The former is more short-term focused whereas the latter is more relevant for determining long-term return expectations. Later in this topic review, we will discuss how the business cycle influences short- and long-term expectations. In this section, we will discuss the application of growth trends when formulating expectations.

Economic growth trends are subject to unexpected surprises or shocks that are exogenous to the economy. Many shocks and their impact on capital markets cannot be predicted. For example, turmoil in the Middle East may change the long-term trend for oil prices, inflation, and economic growth in the developed world. Shocks may also arise through the banking system. An extreme example is the U.S. banking crisis of the 1930s, when a severe slowdown in bank lending paralyzed the economy.

Exogenous shocks are unanticipated events that occur outside the normal course of an economy. Because the events are unanticipated, they are not already built into current market prices, whereas normal trends in an economy, which would be considered endogenous, are built into market prices. Note that the impact of these events will likely produce statistical regime changes. Exogenous shocks can be caused by several factors:

- **Changes in government policies.** Government policies that can encourage long-term growth include sound fiscal policy, minimal government interference with free markets, facilitating competition in the private sector, development of infrastructure and human capital, and sound tax policies.
- **Political events.** Geopolitical tensions that divert resources to less productive uses may lead to decreases in growth. Conversely, cuts in defense spending due to higher levels of world peace may lead to increases in growth.
- **Technological progress.** The creation of new and innovative markets, products, and technologies has the potential to improve growth.
- **Natural disasters.** Natural disasters likely reduce short-term growth, but may (arguably) encourage long-term growth if more efficient capacity replaces previous capacity.

PROFESSOR'S NOTE

The counterargument here is that the owners of capital already replace old facilities with newer and more efficient ones when the time is right.

- **Discovery of natural resources.** Production of new natural resources or the introduction of new ways to recover existing resources can enhance growth. In addition, decreases in resource production costs will improve growth while decreases in resource supply will restrict growth.

- **Financial crises.** Shocks to the financial system will lead to a crisis of confidence among market participants. Financial crises may reduce the level of economic output in the short term and may also decrease the trend rate of growth.

LOS 1.d: Discuss the application of economic growth trend analysis to the formulation of capital market expectations.

The trend rate of growth is an important input when setting capital market expectations. Some of the key considerations of economic growth trend analysis are as follows:

- Forecasting returns with DCF models incorporate the trend rate of growth. The need to keep these forecasts consistent with long-term economic growth imposes discipline on the models. The trend rate of growth acts as an anchor for long-term bond and equity returns.
- Higher trend growth rates may lead to higher stock returns assuming the growth is not already reflected in stock prices.
- When we speak of higher trend growth rates, we mean the economy can grow at a faster pace before inflation becomes a major concern. This consideration influences monetary policy and the level of bond yields.
- Higher trend growth rates tend to generate higher government bond yields.

Overall, the trend rate of growth is relatively stable in developed economies. In emerging economies, that growth rate can be less predictable and include longer periods of rapid growth as those economies catch up with developed economies.

A basic model for forecasting the economic growth rate focuses on the following:

- *Labor input,* based on growth in the labor force and labor participation. Growth in the labor force depends on population growth and demographics. Labor participation refers to the percentage of the population working and is affected by real wages, work/leisure decisions, and social factors.
- *Capital per worker,* which increases labor productivity.
- *Total factor productivity,* which is reflected in technological progress and changes in government policies.

EXAMPLE: Forecasting the long-term economic growth rate

Assume that the population is expected to grow by 2% and that labor force participation is expected to grow by 0.25%. If spending on new capital inputs is projected to grow at 2.5% and total factor productivity will grow by 0.5%, what is the long-term projected growth rate?

Answer:

The sum of the components equals 2% + 0.25% + 2.5% + 0.5% = 5.25%, so the economy is projected to grow by this amount.

Asset Returns and the Trend Rate of Growth

The trend rate of growth can also provide an estimate for long-term equity returns. The market value of equity can be expressed as the product of three terms: nominal GDP, earnings/GDP (which is the share of profits in the economy), and the P/E ratio.

Over long periods, the share of profits in the economy (earnings/GDP) and the P/E ratio cannot continually increase or decrease thus, in the long-term, the growth rate of the total value of equity in an economy is linked to the growth rate of GDP.

This applies to the capital appreciation component of equity returns but not the dividend yield. The dividend yield (annual dividends/market value) can be derived from the dividend payout ratio (dividends/profit) divided by the profit multiple (market value/profit).

EXAMPLE: Forecasting long-run equity return

Cindy Navaro is an equity analyst for Evergreen Asset Management. She has been asked to produce capital market expectations for asset classes in several different markets relevant to the company's Renewable Green Energies fund. Navaro is aware that long-term GDP trend forecasting is considered the starting point to form capital market expectations. In order to make a forecast of trend GDP growth in the domestic economy, Navaro collects the following data displayed in Exhibit 1.

Exhibit 1: Domestic Economy Information

Annual labor input growth	0.4%
Annual labor productivity growth	1.4%
Annual inflation	3.8%
Dividend yield	2.6%
Long-term change in profits as a share of GDP	0%
Long-term change in PE multiples	0%

Based on the data in Exhibit 1, the projected long-term domestic market equity return is *closest* to:

- 4.4%.
- 5.6%.
- 8.2%.

Explanation:

The correct answer is 8.2%.

Real GDP growth = labor input growth + labor productivity growth = 0.4% + 1.4% = 1.8%

Nominal GDP growth = real GDP growth + inflation = 1.8% + 3.8% = 5.6%

Long-term capital gains in equity markets = %Δ nominal GDP + %Δ profits/GDP + %Δ PE = 5.6% + 0% + 0% = 5.6%

Long-term total domestic market equity return = capital gains + dividend yield = 5.6% + 2.6% = 8.2%

High rates of growth in capital investment are associated with high rates of growth in the economy. However, these high growth rates are not necessarily linked to favorable equity returns. This may be the case because growth rates are already factored into equity prices. An additional explanation is that the source of equity returns is related to the rate of return on capital. If the rate of growth of capital is faster than the rate of economic growth, return on capital may decrease and equity returns may become less attractive.

Market Forecasting

LOS 1.e: Compare major approaches to economic forecasting.

Three approaches to economic forecasting are econometric modeling, use of economic indicators, and a checklist approach.

Econometric analysis uses statistical methods to explain economic relationships and formulate forecasting models. *Structural models* are based on economic theory while *reduced-form models* are compact versions of structural approaches. These types of models range from being quite simple to very complex, involving several or hundreds of relationships. For example, an analyst may want to forecast GDP using current and lagged consumption and investment values. Ordinary least squares regression is most often used, but other statistical methods are also used to develop these models.

Advantages:

- Modeling can incorporate many variables.
- Once the model is specified, it can be reused.
- Output is quantified and based on a consistent set of relationships.

Disadvantages:

- Models are complex and time-consuming to construct.
- The data may be difficult to forecast and the relationships can change.
- Output may require interpretation or be unrealistic.
- It does not work well to forecast turning points.

Economic indicators are available from governments, international organizations (e.g., the Organization of Economic Cooperation and Development), and private organizations (e.g., the Conference Board in the United States).

Many analysts use a combination of publicly available indicators and their own proprietary indicators. The most useful indicators are **leading indicators** that move ahead of the business cycle with a reasonable stable lead time. These can be used to predict what will happen next. The leading indicators can be used individually or as a **composite**. For example, the Conference Board provides 10 leading indicators for the United States, which they combine into an index. Traditionally, three consecutive months of increase (decrease) for the index are expected to signal the start of an economic expansion (contraction) within a few months. A composite can also be interpreted as a **diffusion index** by observing the number of indicators pointing toward expansion versus contraction in the economy.

There are also **coincident** and **lagging indicators** that move with and after changes in the business cycle. These can be used to confirm what is happening in the economy.

Advantages:

- Economic indicators are simple, intuitive, and easy to interpret.
- Data are often readily available from third parties.
- Indicator lists can be tailored to meet specific forecasting needs.

Disadvantages:

- Forecasting results have been inconsistent.
- Economic indicators have given false signals.
- Indicators are revised frequently, which can make them appear to fit past business cycles better than they did when the data were first released.

A **checklist approach** is more subjective. In this approach, an analyst considers a series of questions. For example, to forecast GDP, the analyst may consider, "What was the latest employment report? What is the central bank's next move, given the latest information released? What is the latest report on business investment?" Then the analyst uses judgment and perhaps some statistical modeling to interpret the answers and formulate a forecast. Judgment is required both in determining which factors to consider and how to interpret them.

Advantages:

- Less complex than econometrics.
- Flexible in mixing objective statistical analysis with judgment to incorporate changing relationships.

Disadvantages:

- Subjective.
- Time-consuming.
- Complexity must be limited due to manual process.

MODULE 1.3: THE BUSINESS CYCLE

Video covering this content is available online.

LOS 1.f: Discuss how business cycles affect short- and long-term expectations.

As mentioned, the trend rate of growth provides guidance on setting long-term expectations. Any deviations from this trend tend to cancel out over the long run; however, identifying these deviations can be very useful when making shorter-term projections. Fluctuations in economic growth over short to intermediate time horizons are often associated with the business cycle.

A fundamental reason why economic activity is cyclical is the nature of business decisions. Decision makers allocate resources to what they believe are their highest valued uses, but can only do so with imperfect information. Adjustments to unexpected events take time to implement and reversing incorrect decisions can be costly.

Understanding business cycle phases is important for forming capital market expectations, but their relationship is not straightforward for the following reasons:

1. Business cycles vary in duration and intensity, and their turning points are difficult to predict. Their variations may be thought of as resulting from the interactions of many subcycles with a wide range of frequencies.
2. Although we typically think of and model economic activity in terms of cycles fluctuating around a long-term trend, it can be difficult to distinguish which effects result from shorter-term factors that arise from the business cycle and which are related to longer-term factors that affect the trend rate of economic growth.
3. Returns in the capital market are strongly related to activity in the real economy, but they also depend on factors such as investors' expectations and risk tolerances.

Business cycle analysis is most useful for identifying opportunities within the time horizon of a typical business cycle. For longer investment horizons that are likely to include one or more full business cycles, information about the current state of the economy is less valuable.

Business Cycle Phases

> **For the Exam:** Have a working knowledge of, and be able to explain, the general relationships between interest rates, inflation, stock and bond prices, et cetera, as you progress over the business cycle. For example, as the peak of the cycle approaches, everything is humming along. Confidence and employment are high, but inflation is starting to have an impact on markets. As inflation increases, bond yields increase and both bond and stock prices start to fall.

The business cycle can be subdivided into five phases: (1) initial recovery, (2) early expansion, (3) late expansion, (4) slowdown, and (5) contraction. The phases have the following characteristics:

Initial Recovery

- Duration of a few months.
- Business confidence rising.
- Government stimulus provided by low interest rates and/or budget deficits.
- Decelerating inflation.
- Large output gap.
- Low or falling short-term interest rates.
- Bond yields bottoming out.
- Rising stock prices.
- Cyclical, riskier assets such as small-cap stocks and high yield bonds doing well.

Early Expansion

- Duration of a year to several years.
- Increasing growth with low inflation.
- Increasing confidence.
- Rising short-term interest rates.
- Output gap is narrowing.
- Stable or rising bond yields.
- Rising stock prices.

Late Expansion

- High confidence and employment.
- Output gap eliminated and economy at risk of overheating.
- Increasing inflation.
- Central bank limits the growth of the money supply.
- Rising short-term interest rates.
- Rising bond yields.
- Rising/peaking stock prices with increased risk and volatility.

Slowdown

- Duration of a few months to a year or longer.
- Declining confidence.
- Inflation still rising.
- Short-term interest rates at a peak.
- Bond yields peaking and possibly falling, resulting in rising bond prices.
- Possible inverting yield curve.
- Falling stock prices.

Contraction

- Duration of 12 to 18 months.
- Declining confidence and profits.
- Increase in unemployment and bankruptcies.
- Inflation topping out.
- Falling short-term interest rates.
- Falling bond yields, rising prices.
- Stock prices increasing during the latter stages, anticipating the end of the recession.

Inflation Implications

LOS 1.g: Explain the relationship of inflation to the business cycle and the implications of inflation for cash, bonds, equity, and real estate returns.

Inflation means generally rising prices. For example, if the CPI increases from 100 to 105, inflation is 5%. Inflation typically accelerates late in the business cycle (near the peak).

Disinflation means a deceleration in the rate of inflation. For example, if the CPI then increases from 105 to 108, the rate of inflation decreases to approximately 3%. Inflation typically decelerates as the economy approaches and enters recession.

Deflation means generally falling prices. For example, if the CPI declines from 108 to 106, the rate of inflation is approximately –2%. Deflation is a severe threat to economic activity for the following reasons:

- It encourages default on debt obligations. Consider a homeowner who has a home worth $100,000 and a mortgage of $95,000; the homeowner's equity is only $5,000. A decline of more than 5% in home prices leads to negative equity and can trigger panic sales (further depressing prices), defaulting on the loan, or both.
- With negative inflation, interest rates decline to near zero and this limits the ability of central banks to lower interest rates and stimulate the economy. Following the financial crisis of 2007–2009 and the resulting very low interest rates, several central banks tried a new monetary policy of **quantitative easing (QE)** to stimulate the economies of their countries. Traditionally, central banks have used open market operations to increase the money supply and decrease short-term interest rates on a temporary basis by buying high quality fixed-income instruments. QE was different in that it was larger in scale, the purchases included other security types such as mortgage-backed securities and corporate bonds, and the intent was a long-term increase in bank reserves.

Monetary policy and inflation levels will vary over the business cycle. In general, moderate levels of inflation only create moderate costs for the economy. As a result, central banks tend to target a slightly positive inflation rate. Investors generally expect that equity and bond prices will reflect some level of positive inflation.

Figure 1.1 summarizes the relationship of inflation to the business cycle. Figure 1.2 describes the typical behavior of asset class returns in different inflation scenarios.

Figure 1.1: Inflation and the Business Cycle

The Business Cycle	Inflation	Economic Policy	Markets
Initial recovery	Initially declining inflation	Stimulative	Short-term rates low or declining Long-term rates bottoming and bond prices peaking Stock prices increasing
Early expansion	Low inflation and good economic growth	Becoming less stimulative	Short-term rates increasing Long-term rates bottoming or increasing with bond prices beginning to decline Stock prices increasing
Late expansion	Inflation rate increasing	Becoming restrictive	Short-term and long-term rates increasing with bond prices declining Stock prices peaking and volatile
Slowdown	Inflation continues to accelerate	Becoming less restrictive	Short-term and long-term rates peaking and then declining with bond prices starting to increase Stock prices declining
Contraction	Real economic activity declining and inflation peaking	Easing	Short-term and long-term rates declining with bond prices increasing Stock prices begin to increase later in the recession

Figure 1.2: Inflation Expectations and Asset Classes

Inflation within expectations	Cash equivalents: Earn the real rate of interest Bonds: Shorter-term yields more volatile than longer-term yields Equity: No impact given predictable economic growth Real estate: Neutral impact with typical rates of return
Inflation above or below expectations	Cash equivalents: Positive (negative) impact with increasing (decreasing) yields Bonds: Longer-term yields more volatile than shorter-term yields Equity: Negative impact given the potential for central bank action or falling asset prices, though some companies may be able to pass rising costs on to customers Real estate: Positive impact as real asset values increase with inflation
Deflation	Cash equivalents: Positive impact if nominal interest rates are bound by 0% Bonds: Positive impact as fixed future cash flows have greater purchasing power (assuming no default on the bonds) Equity: Negative impact as economic activity and business declines Real estate: Negative impact as property values generally decline

PROFESSOR'S NOTE

These generalizations will not hold in every case. They are a good starting point for a forecaster taking a macro approach. Even if the generalizations always held, it is not easy to determine when a business cycle phase starts, how long it will last, or when it ends.

MODULE QUIZ 1.2, 1.3

1. An analyst believes that GDP is best forecasted using a system of equations that can capture the fact that GDP is a function of many variables, both current and lagged values. Which economic forecasting method is she *most likely* to use?

2. The phase of the business cycle in which we *most likely* expect to observe rising short-term interest rates and stable bond yields is:
   A. late expansion.
   B. initial recovery.
   C. early expansion.
3. **Describe** how bonds and equities typically perform during deflationary periods.

MODULE 1.4: MONETARY AND FISCAL POLICY

Video covering this content is available online.

LOS 1.h: Discuss the effects of monetary and fiscal policy on business cycles.

Monetary Policy

Central banks often use monetary policy as a countercyclical force, attempting to optimize the economy's performance. Most central banks strive to balance price stability against economic growth. The ultimate goal is to keep growth near its long-run sustainable rate, because growth faster than the long-run rate usually results in increased inflation. As discussed previously, the later stages of an economic expansion are often characterized by increased inflation. As a result, central banks usually resort to restrictive policies toward the end of an expansion. The risk at this stage is that they may overtighten and cause a recession.

To spur growth, a central bank can take actions to reduce short-term interest rates. This results in greater consumer spending, greater business spending, higher stock prices, and higher bond prices. Lower interest rates also usually result in a lower value of the domestic currency, which is thought to increase exports. In addition to the direction of change, the level of interest rates is important. If, for example, rates are increased to 4% to combat inflation, but this is still low compared to the average of 6% in a country, then this absolute rate may still be low enough to allow growth while the rise in rates may begin to dampen inflation. The equilibrium interest rate in a country (the rate at which a balance between growth and inflation is achieved) is referred to as the neutral rate. It is generally thought that the neutral rate is composed of an inflation component, a real growth component, and judgment from policy makers. If, for example, inflation is targeted at 3% and the economy is expected to grow by 2%, then the neutral rate would be 5%.

The neutral rate is the rate that most central banks strive to achieve as they attempt to balance the risks of inflation and recession. If inflation is too high, the central bank should increase short-term interest rates. If economic growth is too low, it should decrease interest rates. The **Taylor rule** embodies this concept. Thus, it is used as a prescriptive tool (i.e., it states what the central bank should do). It also is fairly accurate at predicting central bank action.

The Taylor rule determines the target interest rate using the neutral rate, expected GDP relative to its long-term trend, and expected inflation relative to its targeted amount. It can be formalized as follows:

$$n_{target} = r_{neutral} + i_{expected} + [0.5(GDP_{expected} - GDP_{trend}) + 0.5(i_{expected} - i_{target})]$$

where:

n_{target} = target nominal short-term interest rate

$r_{neutral}$ = neutral real short-term interest rate

$GDP_{expected}$ = expected GDP growth rate

GDP_{trend} = long-term trend in the GDP growth rate

$i_{expected}$ = expected inflation rate

i_{target} = target inflation rate

EXAMPLE: Calculating the short-term interest rate target

Given the following information, **calculate** the nominal short-term interest rate target.

Neutral rate	3%
Inflation target	2%
Expected inflation	4%
GDP long-term trend	2%
Expected GDP growth	0%

Answer:

$$n_{target} = 3\% + 4\% + [0.5(0\% - 2\%) + 0.5(4\% - 2\%)]$$

$$= 7\% + (-1\% + 1\%) = 7\%$$

In this example, weak projected economic growth would call for cutting interest rates if inflation were not a consideration. If the central bank was only concerned with growth, the target interest rate would be 1% lower than the neutral rate. However, the higher projected inflation overrides the growth concern because projected inflation is 2% greater than the target inflation rate. In net, the target rate is 7% because the concern over high inflation overrides the weak growth concern.

PROFESSOR'S NOTE

The Taylor rule can also be expressed in terms of the real inflation-adjusted target rate by moving expected inflation to the left-hand side of the equation.

$$n_{target} - i_{expected} = r_{neutral} + [0.5(GDP_{expected} - GDP_{trend}) + 0.5(i_{expected} - i_{target})]$$

Negative Interest Rates

Negative interest rates were generally considered a hypothetical curiosity before the 2007–2009 financial crisis. A *negative rate* is defined as a net payment made to keep money on deposit at a financial institution or payment of a net fee to invest in short-term instruments.

Zero was regarded as the sustainable lower rate of interest because investors could hold physical cash instead (earning no interest). As investors withdrew funds from banks to hold cash, bank balance sheets would shrink as they paid out funds and stopped making loans. Simple supply and demand analysis should dictate that with a smaller supply of funds available to lend, the price paid (interest rate) to borrow increases.

The flaw in this analysis was that negative interest rates did not cause the expected large move into physical cash. The daily exchange of funds in modern economies is too large. The implicit advantages of being able to quickly transfer large amounts of money held on deposit to settle transactions outweighed the explicit cost of holding those deposits at negative rates. Without the exit of funds from the banking system, it turned out that negative interest rates were sustainable for extended periods.

As mentioned earlier, the slowdown in economic activity during the crisis and already very low interest rates led some central banks to experiment with less-tested monetary policy—QE approach. QE led to larger injections of funds by central banks into the commercial banking system with the announced intent that these injections were long term in nature. The hope was this would stimulate bank lending and increase economic activity.

Negative interest rates should, in theory, have similar effects. Holders of funds would find it more desirable to spend the money, stimulating economic activity; or, they would invest in longer-term stocks and bonds, driving up prices and creating a wealth effect. Or, negative rates would lead consumers and businesses to borrow at zero or negative rates to spend now.

How these new policies actually end up working remains to be seen. For the policies to work, consumers, investors, and businesses have to believe the risk of spending now is worth it. Purchases and investments made now provide positive economic benefit in the future. But negative interest rates also signal uncertainty as to what the future holds.

Negative interest rates complicate the process of forming capital market expectations:

- The risk-free rate is the starting point for buildup models used to estimate long-run returns for asset classes. When the risk-free rate is negative, a sustainable expected risk-free rate, such as the policy neutral rate in the Taylor rule, is more appropriate as that starting point. That rate is generally not regarded as fully risk free, so a modest default premium can be removed.

- Forming capital market expectation over shorter time horizons is further complicated by a need to forecast the time path over which negative rates will converge to a long-run sustainable risk-free rate. Multiple path projections should be considered to allow for uncertainty regarding how the convergence will occur.
- Another approach to shorter-term projections of asset class returns is to interpret negative risk-free rates as being consistent with contraction or early recovery stages of the business cycle.
- Using historical data as a starting point for forecasting is more problematic because few comparable periods exist, and the negative rates suggest significant structural economic changes are occurring. This kind of regime change makes statistics based on historical data less reliable, requiring more subjective assessments. Anticipating the effects of negative rates when combined with less-tested QE makes forecasting even more challenging.

Fiscal Policy

Another tool at the government's disposal for managing the economy is fiscal policy. If the government wants to stimulate the economy, it can implement loose fiscal policy by decreasing taxes or increasing spending, thereby increasing the budget deficit. If they want to rein in growth, the government does the opposite to implement fiscal tightening.

There are two important aspects to fiscal policy. First, it is not the level of the budget deficit that matters—it is the change in the deficit. For example, a deficit by itself does not stimulate the economy, but increases in the deficit are required to stimulate the economy. Second, changes in the deficit that occur naturally over the course of the business cycle are not stimulative or restrictive. In an expanding economy, deficits will decline because tax receipts increase and disbursements to the unemployed decrease. The opposite occurs during a recession. Only changes in the deficit directed by government policy will influence growth.

The Yield Curve

LOS 1.i: Interpret the shape of the yield curve as an economic predictor and discuss the relationship between the yield curve and fiscal and monetary policy.

The yield curve demonstrates the relationship between interest rates and the maturity of debt securities. The curve is sensitive to government actions as well as current and expected economic conditions. When both fiscal and monetary policies are expansive, for example, the yield curve is sharply upward sloping (i.e., short-term rates are lower than long-term rates), and the economy is likely to expand in the future. When fiscal and monetary policies are restrictive, the yield curve is downward sloping (i.e., it is *inverted*, as short-term rates are higher than long-term rates), and the economy is likely to contract in the future.

Fiscal and monetary policies may reinforce or conflict with each other. If the policies reinforce each other, the implications for the economy are clear. In all cases, there are likely implications for the yield curve:

- If both policies are stimulative, the yield curve is steep and the economy is likely to grow.
- If both policies are restrictive, the yield curve is inverted and the economy is likely to contract.
- If monetary policy is restrictive and fiscal policy is stimulative, the yield curve is flat and the implications for the economy are less clear.
- If monetary policy is stimulative and fiscal policy is restrictive, the yield curve is moderately steep and the implications for the economy are less clear.

In terms of the business cycle, the yield curve is typically steep at the bottom of the cycle. As the cycle moves toward expansion, the curve tends to flatten. At the top of the cycle, the yield curve will likely be flat to inverted. During contraction, the curve will begin to re-steepen. Given these expectations, analysts can use the yield curve as a predictor of the state of the economy as well as the future path of interest rates. However, analysts should also exercise caution that these relationships may not always hold.

International Considerations

LOS 1.j: Identify and interpret macroeconomic, interest rate, and exchange rate linkages between economies.

Economic links between countries have become increasingly important with globalization, especially for small countries with undiversified economies. Larger countries with diverse economies, such as the United States, are less affected but still influenced by globalization.

Macroeconomic links can produce convergence in business cycles among economies. International trade produces one such link, as a country's exports and economy are depressed by a slowdown in a trading partner's economy and level of imports. International capital flows produce another link if cross-border capital investing by a trading partner declines as its economy contracts.

A country's current account and capital account are measures of macroeconomic linkages. The current account largely consists of a country's net exports while the capital account reflects net investment flows. The two accounts are opposites of each other in that a surplus in one account will produce a deficit in the other.

A useful relationship for understanding how the current account influences economic activity is the following formula:

net exports = net private saving + government surplus

$$(X - M) = (S - I) + (T - G)$$

where:

X = exports
M = imports
S = private saving
I = investment spending
T = tax
G = government spending

Interest rates and currency exchange rates can also create linkages. A strong link is created when a smaller economy "pegs" its currency to that of a larger and more developed economy. The peg is a unilateral declaration by the pegging country to maintain the exchange rate. In general, the linkage between the business cycles of the two economies will increase, as the pegged currency country must follow the economic policies of the country to which it has pegged its currency. If not, investors will favor one currency over the other and the peg will fail.

Generally, the interest rates of the pegged currency will exceed the interest rates of the currency to which it is linked, and the interest rate differential will fluctuate with the market's confidence in the peg. If confidence is high, the rate differential can be small. If there is doubt the peg will be maintained, investors will require a larger interest rate differential as compensation for the risk of holding the pegged currency. A common problem arises if investors begin to lose confidence in the pegged currency and it begins to decline in value. The pegging country must then increase short-term interest rates to attract capital and maintain the value of the currency at the peg.

In the absence of pegging, the relationship of interest rate differentials and currency movement can reflect several factors:

- If a currency is substantially overvalued and expected to decline, bond interest rates are likely to be higher to compensate foreign investors for the expected decline in the currency value.
- Relative bond yields, both nominal and real, increase with strong economic activity and increasing demand for funds.
- Savings and investment decisions as well as capital productivity drive the level of real rates. Although real rates may differ across countries, there is a tendency for them to move up and down together given that global savings and investing are linked through the current account.

PROFESSOR'S NOTE

The relationship between currency values and interest rates is complicated. You may recall a theory from earlier levels that if real interest rates are equal and the movement of currency value consistently reflects the difference in inflation rates, then the forward exchange rate is a good predictor of what will happen in the currency market. The Level III material will not support those assumptions and does not support the use of the forward exchange rate as a predictor of what will happen. This is addressed in multiple readings.

MODULE QUIZ 1.4

1. During an economic expansion, an analyst notices that the budget deficit has been declining. She concludes that the government's fiscal policy has shifted to a more restrictive posture. **Comment** on her conclusion.

2. **Calculate** the nominal short-term interest rate target given the following information.

Neutral real rate	2%
Inflation target	3%
Expected inflation	5%
GDP long-term trend	3%
Expected GDP	4%

3. A forecaster notes that the yield curve is steeply upwardly sloping. **Comment** on the likely monetary and fiscal policies in effect and the future of the economy.

4. An analyst is evaluating two countries. Maldavia has a GDP of $60 billion and an economy that is dominated by the mining industry. Ceania has a GDP of $1.2 trillion and an economy that sells a variety of items. He is predicting a global economic slowdown. Which country is at greater risk?

5. At a conference, Larry Timmons states that a pegged exchange rate allows a less developed country to achieve greater currency and economic stability, as well as relatively lower and more stable interest rates, and to pursue the fiscal and economic policies to maximize the country's real economic growth. **Explain** what is correct and incorrect in Timmons's statement.

KEY CONCEPTS

LOS 1.a

Capital market expectations help in formulating the strategic asset allocation. They can also assist in detecting short-term asset mispricings exploitable through tactical asset allocation. Asset allocations should display both cross-sectional and intertemporal consistency.

To formulate capital market expectations, use the following process:

- Determine the relevant capital market expectations given the investor's allowable asset classes and investment horizon(s).
- Investigate assets' historical performance as well as the determinants of their performance.
- Identify the valuation model used and its requirements.
- Collect the best data possible.
- Use experience and judgment to interpret current investment conditions.
- Formulate capital market expectations.
- Monitor performance and use it to refine the process.

LOS 1.b

Limitations in the use of economic data for forecasting include the following:

- Data are reported with a lag, subject to revision, and defined inconsistently in different countries.
- Data are subject to biases and errors such as transcription errors, survivorship bias, and smoothed (appraised) data estimates.
- Using historical data is less appropriate when economic conditions change (regime change and nonstationary issues).
- Ex-post risk generally understates ex-ante risk, as surviving the past does not guarantee the future cannot be worse.
- Data mining or selection of time periods may introduce biases.
- Models should be conditioned for the likely state of the economy.
- Correlation does not imply causation. Does A cause B, does B cause A, or are both associated with some other factor C?
- Psychological biases and cognitive errors may affect an analysis.
- Models, parameters, and inputs are subject to uncertainty.

LOS 1.c

Exogenous shocks are unanticipated events that occur outside the normal course of an economy and may have either a positive or negative impact on growth. They can be caused by different factors, such as changes in government policies, political events, technological progress, natural disasters, discovery of natural resources, and financial crises.

LOS 1.d

In forecasting a country's long-term economic growth trend, the trend growth rate can be decomposed into two main components and their respective subcomponents:

- Changes in employment levels, which are related to population growth and labor force participation.
- Changes in productivity, which are related to capital inputs and technological advancement.

LOS 1.e

Econometric analysis uses statistical methods to formulate forecasting models. These models range from being quite simple to very complex, involving several data items of various time period lags to predict the future.

Economic indicators attempt to characterize an economy's phase in the business cycle and are separated into lagging indicators, coincident indicators, and leading indicators. Analysts prefer leading indicators because they help predict the future path of the economy.

In a checklist approach, the analyst checks off a list of questions that should indicate the future growth of the economy. Given the answers to these questions, the analyst can then use her judgment to formulate a forecast or derive a more formal model using statistics.

LOS 1.f

Understanding business cycle phases is important for forming capital market expectations, but their relationship is not straightforward. Business cycles vary in duration and intensity, and their turning points are difficult to predict. It can be difficult to distinguish among factors that arise from the business cycle and factors that affect the trend rate of growth. Returns in the capital market are strongly related to activity in the real economy, but also depend on factors such as investors' expectations and risk tolerances.

The business cycle can be subdivided into five phases: (1) initial recovery, (2) early expansion, (3) late expansion, (4) slowdown, and (5) contraction.

LOS 1.g

Inflation varies over the business cycle, rising in the latter stages of an expansion and falling during a recession and the initial recovery. Deflation reduces the value of investments financed with debt (e.g., real estate) because leverage magnifies losses.

Bond prices will rise during a recession when inflation and interest rates are declining. In a strong expansion, bonds tend to decline in price as inflation expectations and interest rates rise.

Equities provide an inflation hedge when inflation is moderate. High inflation can be problematic because slow growth may result from central bank action to combat inflation. Deflation is harmful because it encourages defaults and limits the scope for monetary policy.

LOS 1.h

Central banks often use monetary policy as a countercyclical force. The goal is to keep growth near its long-run sustainable rate because growth faster than the long-run rate usually results in increased inflation. To spur growth, a central bank can take actions to reduce short-term interest rates.

The Taylor rule determines the target interest rate using the neutral rate, expected GDP relative to its long-term trend, and expected inflation relative to its targeted level:

$$n_{target} = r_{neutral} + i_{expected} + [0.5(GDP_{expected} - GDP_{trend}) + 0.5(i_{expected} - i_{target})]$$

- A central bank can use the Taylor rule to determine the appropriate level for short-term interest rates.
- An investment strategist who expects unanticipated changes in the inputs to the Taylor rule can use the rule to anticipate changes in short-term interest rates by the central bank.

Another tool at the government's disposal for managing the economy is fiscal policy. If the government wants to stimulate the economy, it can implement loose fiscal policy by decreasing taxes or increasing spending, thereby increasing the budget deficit. If they want to rein in growth, the government does the opposite to implement fiscal tightening.

LOS 1.i

The yield curve demonstrates the relationship between interest rates and the maturity of debt securities. The curve is sensitive to government actions as well as current and expected economic conditions.

When both fiscal and monetary policies are expansive, the yield curve is sharply upward sloping, which indicates that the economy is likely to expand in the future. When fiscal and monetary policies are restrictive, the yield curve is downward sloping, indicating that the economy is likely to contract in the future.

When fiscal and monetary policies are in disagreement, the shape of the yield curve is less definitively formed. If monetary policy is expansive while fiscal policy is restrictive, the yield curve tends to be upward sloping, though less steep than when both policies are expansive. If monetary policy is restrictive while fiscal policy is expansive, the yield curve tends to be flatter.

LOS 1.j

Macroeconomic links refer to similarities in business cycles across countries. Economies are linked by both international trade and capital flows so that a recession in one country dampens exports and investment in a second country, thereby creating a slowdown in the second country.

Exchange rate links are found when countries peg their currency to others. The benefit of a peg is that currency volatility is reduced and inflation can be brought under control. Interest rates in the pegging country often reflect a risk premium relative to the country to which it pegs.

Interest rate differentials between countries can also reflect differences in economic growth, monetary policy, and fiscal policy.

Reading 1

ANSWER KEY FOR MODULE QUIZZES

Module Quiz 1.1

1. The analyst has not been systematic and has used inconsistent assumptions. In this case, the result is overstating the attractiveness of equity and understating the attractiveness of fixed income. The result would be allocating too much to equity. (LOS 1.a)

2. Pro: The recent three-year period is more likely to reflect the current economic and political environment.

   Con: The recent shorter period does not reflect the full course of a business cycle or a variety of possible economic conditions.

   Pro: The longer period is more likely to reflect various economic conditions that can occur.

   Con: The longer period is more likely to be subject to regime change, be nonstationary, and reflect conditions that are no longer relevant.

   (LOS 1.b)

3. Some types of alternative investments are not regularly traded, and only infrequent prices (smoothed data) are available. This makes the calculated standard deviation lower because there are no actual periodic changes in value (there are no prices to examine). The smoothed return data also appears to be less correlated with the more erratic pricing of other asset classes that have and report actual trading prices. The correlation will appear closer to zero. (LOS 1.b)

Module Quiz 1.2, 1.3

1. Econometric analysis would be the best approach to use. It can model the complexities of reality using both current and lagged values. Ordinary least squares regression is most often used, but other statistical methods are also available. (Module 1.2, LOS 1.e)

2. **C** *Early Expansion*: In this period of the business cycle, we expect to observe rising short-term interest rates and stable or rising bond yields.

   The expectations of short-term and long-term yields for the other phases are listed as follows:

   Late Expansion: Both short-term and long-term rates increase.

   Initial Recovery: Low or falling short-term rates, and bond yields have bottomed out. (Module 1.3, LOS 1.f)

3. Bonds tend to perform well during periods of falling inflation or deflation because interest rates are declining. This holds true as long as credit risk does not increase. Equities do poorly in periods of declining inflation or deflation due to declining economic growth and asset prices. (Module 1.3, LOS 1.g)

Module Quiz 1.4

1. Her conclusion may not be warranted. In an economic expansion, the budget deficit will decline naturally because tax receipts increase and disbursements to the unemployed decrease. The changes she is observing may be independent of the government's fiscal policy.

   Note that only government-directed changes in fiscal policy influence the growth of the economy. Changes in the deficit that occur naturally over the course of the business cycle are not stimulative or restrictive. (LOS 1.h)

2. $$n_{target} = 2\% + 5\% + [0.5 \times (4\% - 3\%) + 0.5 \times (5\% - 3\%)]$$
   $$= 7\% + [0.5\% + 1\%] = 8.5\%$$

   In this example, the higher-than-targeted growth rate and higher-than-targeted inflation rate argue for a targeted nominal interest rate of 8.5%. This rate hike is intended to slow down the economy and inflation. (LOS 1.h)

3. If the yield curve is steeply upwardly sloping, then it is likely that both fiscal and monetary policies are expansive. The economy is likely to expand in the future. (LOS 1.i)

4. A global economic slowdown would affect smaller countries with undiversified economies more because economic links are more important for these types of countries. Larger countries with diverse economies are less affected by events in other countries. (LOS 1.j)

5. Greater currency and economic stability: true. The peg is likely to create a more stable currency that provides confidence for investors and business, both of which promote economic stability. Maintaining the peg prevents excessive money creation, which holds down inflation and also promotes economic stability. The peg is a commitment to follow the policies needed to maintain the value of the currency.

   Relatively lower and more stable interest rates: partially true (or partially false). Interest rates will be related to but higher than the country to which the currency is pegged. The interest rate premium will reflect the investor's perception of the country's commitment and ability to maintain the peg. If that comes into question, the country will likely have to increase interest rates in order to maintain the currency value. The goal of the peg is lower and more stable rates, but if the peg fails, the opposite can occur.

   Pursue the fiscal and economic policies to maximize the country's real economic growth: false. The country must largely follow the economic policies of the country to which it is pegged. These may or may not be optimal for the country's growth. (LOS 1.j)

READING 2

Capital Market Expectations, Part 2: Forecasting Asset Class Returns

EXAM FOCUS

This reading builds on the preceding capital markets section and expands it for setting expectations for the various asset classes. The section begins with an overview of tools used for forecasting capital market returns. Forecasting the returns of different asset classes is next: fixed income, equities, real estate, and currencies. Make sure you are able to distinguish between risk analysis techniques used for developed and emerging market economies. The final two sections focus on forecasting volatilities, including the variance-covariance matrix, followed by a discussion on how an analyst can make recommendations for adjusting an asset portfolio. Several of the concepts have been consistently tested in past Level III exams, including the Grinold-Kroner and Singer-Terhaar models.

Introduction

PROFESSOR'S NOTE

While this is a longer introduction, it contains necessary information to understand the subsequent sections on forecasting returns. It is also a synthesis of many of the valuation approaches discussed in this reading.

Forecasting returns requires not only assessing expected returns, variances, and correlations, but also understanding that time horizons are important. Investment opportunities, and therefore investment decisions, can change over time. At their core, investment techniques assume that investments tend to return to their fundamental levels over time, knows as *central tendency*. There are three approaches to forecasting capital market expectations: formal tools, surveys, and judgments.

Formal Tools

The use of **formal tools** helps the analyst set capital market expectations. When applied to reputable data, formal tools provide forecasts replicable by other analysts. The formal tools we examine are statistical methods, discounted cash flow models, and risk premium models.

Statistical methods involve sample statistics, shrinkage estimation, and time series estimation. Sample statistics use well-known data, including means, variance, and correlation, to forecast future data. This is the clearest approach in forecasting, but it can be imprecise. Alternatively, a *shrinkage estimate* can be applied to the historical estimate if the analyst believes simple historical results do not fully reflect expected future conditions. A shrinkage estimate is a weighted average estimate based on history and some other projection. A *time series estimate* can also be used to make forecasts. A time series estimate forecasts a variable using lagged values of the same variable and combines it with lagged values of other variables, which allows for incorporating dynamics (volatilities) into the forecasts.

Discounted cash flow models express the intrinsic value of an asset as the present value of future cash flows. The advantage of these models is their correct emphasis on the future cash flows of an asset and the ability to back out a required return.

An alternative to estimating expected return is a **risk premium** or buildup model. Risk premium approaches can be used for both fixed income and equity. The approach starts with a risk-free interest rate and then adds compensation for *priced risks*, or risks for which an investor would want to be compensated. Risk premium models include equilibrium models (e.g., the Capital Asset Pricing Model), a factor model, and building blocks.

Surveys and Judgment

Capital market expectations can also be formed using **surveys**, which can be the most useful ways to gauge consensus. In this method, a poll is taken of market experts, such as economists and analysts, for their opinions regarding the economy or capital market. For example, the U.S. Federal Reserve Bank of Philadelphia conducts an ongoing survey regarding the U.S. consumer price index and GDP.

Judgment can also be applied to project capital market expectations by using qualitative information based on experience. Although quantitative models provide objective numerical forecasts, there are times when an analyst must adjust those expectations using experience and insight to improve upon those forecasts.

MODULE 2.1: FORECASTING FIXED INCOME RETURNS

Video covering this content is available online.

LOS 2.a: Discuss approaches to setting expectations for fixed-income returns.

Forecasting fixed income returns can be done through the **discounted cash flow (DCF) method**, the **risk premium approach**, or the **equilibrium model**. We previously introduced the basics of the DCF and risk premium approaches. The equilibrium approach assumes that supply and demand in global asset markets are in balance.

DCF Analysis

The DCF analysis of fixed income securities is useful when there are known future cash flows, or when cash flows can be estimated reasonably accurately. The DCF analysis supports the use of yield to maturity (YTM) as an estimate of expected return. As you recall, the YTM is the discount rate that makes the present value of future bond cash flows equal to the bond's price. The YTM is an IRR calculation and, like any IRR calculation, it will be the realized return earned if the cash flows are reinvested at the YTM and the bond is held to maturity. For zero-coupon bonds, there are no cash flows to reinvest, though the held-to-maturity assumption still applies. For bond portfolios, the YTM is the weighted average of the portfolio bonds' individual YTMs, which is generally considered a good approximation.

The assumption of holding the bond to maturity does not factor in optionality, which may result in cash flows not being received as expected. However, even if all expected cash flows are received, there are several reasons why the bond's realized return may deviate from the initial YTM. First, an investor may sell the bond prior to maturity, generating a capital gain or loss. Second, rising or falling interest rates may result in not only changing bond prices, but changing reinvestment returns. For example, falling (rising) interest rates will decrease (increase) reinvestment returns. The overall gain or loss to the investor will depend on the investment horizon. For an investment horizon that is shorter than the Macaulay duration, the capital gain/loss impact will be more dominant than the reinvestment impact, meaning for example that falling (rising) interest rates will result in a higher (lower) realized return. For an investment horizon longer than the Macaulay duration, the reinvestment risk dominates, meaning that falling (rising) interest rates will result in a lower (higher) realized return.

> **For the Exam:** Remember that the Macaulay duration can be calculated from modified duration (i.e., by multiplying modified duration by the bond's YTM).

EXAMPLE: Forecasting bond investment returns

Jordan Turk manages a $200 million bond portfolio. The portfolio has a YTM of 5.5 and a modified duration of 6.25. Turk has an investment horizon of four years and expects bond yields to fall by 25 bps each year over the investment horizon. Will Turk likely realize a higher or lower overall return than the initial YTM?

Answer:

No detailed calculations are required. The Macaulay duration is 6.6 (= 6.25 × 1.055). Given that the investment horizon (four years) is shorter than the Macaulay duration, a decline in bond yields will result in a realized return that is higher than the YTM because the gain on the bond price will outweigh the decline in reinvestment yield.

The Risk Premium (Building Block) Approach

The building block approach starts with a risk-free rate and then adds compensation for additional risks. The required return will include the one-period default-free rate, a term premium, a credit premium, and a liquidity premium.

1. *The short-term default-free rate*

   The short-term default-free rate matches the forecast horizon and is calculated from the most liquid instrument. As a result, it is closest to the government zero-coupon yield and is closely tied to the central bank policy rate. The observed risk-free rate is typically sufficient as the default-free rate, although it may be necessary to normalize this rate. When the investment horizon is much longer than the maturity of the short-term instrument, alternative approaches may be optimal, either by using the yield of a longer maturity zero-coupon bond, or taking the return that could be realized by rolling over the short-term instrument over the investment horizon. Futures contract rates provide useful proxies for this expected path of short-term interest rates.

2. *Term premium*

   While the rates implied from the spot yield curve gives us useful information about the term premium, the real term premium cannot be derived from the yield curve alone. Empirical evidence suggests that the term premiums are positive and are related to duration. There are four primary drivers of the term premium:

   - *Inflation uncertainty*: Higher inflation levels typically correspond to higher inflation uncertainty, causing nominal yields to rise and the term premium to increase.
   - *Recession hedge*: When inflation is caused by strong aggregate demand, nominal bond returns are negatively correlated with growth, corresponding to low term premiums. When inflation is caused by aggregate supply, nominal bond returns are positively correlated with growth, corresponding to higher term premiums.

- *Supply and demand*: The relative supply of short- and long-term default-free bonds determines the slope of the yield curve, which influences the level of term premiums.
- *Business cycles*: The slope of the yield curve and level of term premiums are also related to the business cycle.

Other indicators also influence the term premium forecasts:

- *Ex ante* (forecast) real yield.
- *Cochrane and Piazzesi curve factor*: a measure that captures both the slope and curvature of the yield curve.
- *Kim and Wright premium*: a three-factor model of the term structure.
- *Slope of the yield curve*.
- *Supply indicator*: proportion of debt with a maturity greater than 10 years.
- *Cyclical proxies*: corporate profit-to-GDP ratio, business confidence, unemployment rate.

3. *Credit premium*

The credit premium compensates for the expected level of losses and for the risk of default losses, both of which are components of the credit spread.

Empirical evidence suggests that while average yield spreads include a small return premium, the premiums earned tend to be uneven and are subject to significant clustering of persistent high and low default rates. As a result, the yield spread is typically not considered a good predictor of future default rates. Spreads are affected primarily by financial market conditions and the credit premium, but only to a lesser extent by expected default losses. The financial market variables with the strongest predictive power of the credit spread are stock returns, stock volatility, and the risk-free rate, while GDP growth and default rate changes do not have strong predictive capabilities.

Bonds with very high credit quality (AAA and AA) have extremely low default rates, and their credit premium and spreads are mainly driven by *downgrade bias*—this is an asymmetrical risk indicating that a downgrade is more likely than a credit improvement or an upgrade. The credit premium and spreads of low(er) rated bonds, especially non-investment grade bonds, reflect much higher compensation for credit risk.

Historical evidence for U.S. investment grade corporate bonds suggests that high corporate option-adjusted spreads correspond to a higher credit premium, and steep Treasury curves correspond to declining default rates. Overall, steep yield curves indicate both high credit and term premiums, both of which are bullish indicators because they imply larger compensation for credit losses. However, it is interesting to note that credit premiums are not positively related to maturity. In fact, credit premiums tend to be higher at shorter maturities, possibly due to *event risk* (defaults are large credit negative events, but a bond will not pay more than its face value), and illiquidity (bonds with a short time left to maturity tend to be illiquid older bonds that are not actively traded). To take advantage of these credit features, portfolio managers often use a barbell strategy, in which they take on credit risk from shorter maturity bonds and take duration risk from long maturities.

Reading 2

4. *Liquidity premium*

   Liquidity tends to be the highest at the earliest stages of a bond's life, typically during the first few weeks only. Securities with the highest liquidity are the newest sovereign bond issues, current coupon mortgage-backed securities, and some high quality corporate bonds. As a general rule, liquidity is higher for bonds that are (1) issued at close to par or market rates, (2) new, (3) large in size, (4) issued by a frequent and well-known issuer, (5) simple in structure, and (6) of high credit quality. An analyst could gauge the "true" liquidity premium by comparing the yield spread between the highest quality issuer (usually the sovereign) and the next highest quality issuer. The analyst can then make adjustments to this spread as he moves further away from the features described previously.

MODULE QUIZ 2.1

1. An investor has a bond portfolio with a yield to maturity (YTM) of 4 and a modified duration of 5. The investor expects to hold on to the bond portfolio for at least the next six years but expects that bond yields will gradually rise over the investment horizon by a total of 100 bps. **Determine** whether the investor will realize a higher or lower overall yield than the initial YTM.

Use the following information to answer Questions 2 and 3.

Lou Bee is looking to add two new securities to his fixed income portfolio and considers the following bonds (both noncallable):

- One-year government bond
- Five-year AA rated corporate bond

Bee has also gathered the following information:

Risk-free interest rate (one year)	2.5%
Term premium (five-year vs. one-year government bond)	60 bps
Credit premium (five-year AA corporate bond vs. five-year government bond)	30 bps
Liquidity premium on five-year AA corporate bonds	25 bps

2. The expected return of an equal-weighted investment in the two securities will be *closest* to:
   A. 2%.
   B. 3%.
   C. 4%.
3. The expected total risk premium of the two securities will be *closest* to:
   A. 0.6%.
   B. 1.2%.
   C. 1.7%.

MODULE 2.2: EMERGING MARKET BOND RISK

Video covering this content is available online.

LOS 2.b: Discuss risks faced by investors in emerging market fixed-income securities and the country risk analysis techniques used to evaluate emerging market economies.

Emerging market debt offers the investor high expected returns at the expense of higher risk. Many emerging countries are dependent on foreign borrowing, which can later create crisis situations in their economy, currency, and financial markets.

Many emerging countries also have unstable political and social systems. Their undiversified nature makes them susceptible to volatile capital flows and economic crises. The investor must carefully analyze the risk in these countries. For the bond investor, a significant risk is credit risk—does the country have the ability and willingness to pay back its debt? Economic, political, and legal risks are also important.

Signs that an emerging market is more susceptible to risk include:

- Wealth concentration.
- Income concentration and less diverse tax base.
- Greater dominance of cyclical industries, including commodities and less pricing power.
- Restrictions on capital flows and trade; currency restrictions.
- Inadequate fiscal and monetary policies.
- Poor workforce education and infrastructure and weak technological advancement.
- Large amounts of foreign borrowing in foreign currencies.
- Less developed and smaller financial markets.
- Exposure to volatile capital flows.

There are several guidelines that look at the health of an emerging market. Potential bond investors should look at these factors before committing to invest funds in these markets:

- To gauge fiscal policy, most analysts examine the *deficit-to-GDP ratio*. Ratios greater than 4% indicate substantial credit risk. Most emerging counties borrow short term and must refinance on a periodic basis. A buildup of debt increases the likelihood that the country will not be able to make its payments. The *debt-to-GDP ratio* of 70% to 80% has been troublesome for emerging countries.
- To compensate for the higher risk in these countries, investors should expect a *real growth rate* of at least 4%. Growth rates less than that may indicate that the economy is growing slower.
- A *current account deficit* exceeding 4% of GDP has been a warning sign of potential difficulty.

- Although emerging countries are dependent on foreign financing for growth, too much debt can eventually lead to a financial crisis if foreign capital flees the country. These financial crises are accompanied by currency devaluations and declines in emerging market asset values. *Foreign debt levels* greater than 50% of GDP indicate that the country may be overleveraged. *Debt levels* greater than 200% of the current account receipts also indicate high risk.
- *Foreign exchange reserves* relative to short-term debt is important because many emerging country loans must be paid back in a foreign currency. Foreign exchange reserves less than 100% of short-term debt is a sign of trouble (greater than 200% is considered strong).

The government's stance regarding structural reforms and property rights is important. If the government is supportive of structural reforms necessary for growth, then the investment environment is more hospitable. When the government is committed to responsible fiscal policies, competition, and the privatization of state-owned businesses, there are better prospects for growth. Weak enforcement laws, property rights laws, nationalization of property, and corruption are hazard signs. Coalition governments are also seen as riskier because of the inherent political, and therefore policy, instability.

MODULE QUIZ 2.2

1. An analyst is evaluating an emerging market for potential investment. She notices that the country's current account deficit has been growing. Is this a sign of increasing risk? If so, **explain** why.

Video covering this content is available online.

MODULE 2.3: FORECASTING EQUITY RETURNS

LOS 2.c: Discuss approaches to setting expectations for equity investment market returns.

LOS 2.d: Discuss risks faced by investors in emerging market equity securities.

When looking at a very long time horizon—over 100 years—mean real returns of equity markets in various countries do not show statistically meaningful differences. These sample averages tend to be imprecise, unless the volatility of the data is small. As we saw, shrinkage estimators are typically more reliable as predictors of equity returns.

Discounted Cash Flow Approach

A second tool for setting capital market expectations is **DCF models**. These models say that the intrinsic value of an asset is the present value of future cash flows. The advantage of these models is their correct emphasis on the future cash flows of an asset and the ability to back out a required return. The models are most suitable for long-term valuation.

Applied to equity markets, the most common application of DCF models is the Gordon growth model, or constant growth model. It is most commonly used to back out the expected return on equity and is often applied to entire markets. In this case, the growth rate is proxied by the nominal growth in GDP, which is the sum of the real growth rate in GDP plus the rate of inflation. The growth rate can be adjusted for any differences between the economy's growth rate and that of the equity index.

Grinold and Kroner (2002) take this model one step further by including a variable that adjusts for stock repurchases—which companies use to transfer cash to shareholders—and changes in market valuations as represented by changes in the price-earnings (P/E) ratio. The **Grinold-Kroner model** states that the expected return of a stock is its dividend yield, plus the inflation rate, plus the real earnings growth rate, minus the change in stock outstanding, plus changes in the P/E ratio:

$$E(R_e) \approx D/P + (\%\Delta E - \%\Delta S) + \%\Delta P/E$$

where:
$E(R_e)$ = expected equity return
D/P = dividend yield
$\%\Delta E$ = expected percentage change in total earnings
$\%\Delta S$ = expected percentage change in shares outstanding
$\%\Delta P/E$ = expected percentage change in the P/E ratio

PROFESSOR'S NOTE

Candidates often get confused by the variable %ΔS, and when to deduct or add as a number within the GK model.

Remember, a share repurchase is a reduction in shares outstanding, which means the company buys back shares and pays cash to investors. This cash payment is a form of positive return and increases cash flow to investors, EPS, and expected return (mathematically, a share repurchase is a negative %ΔS term, so subtracting a negative term becomes a positive number).

The variables of the Grinold-Kroner model can be regrouped into three components: the expected income return, the expected nominal growth in earnings, and the expected repricing return.

1. The **expected cash flow return** (income return):

   $$D/P - \%\Delta S = \text{income return}$$

   D/P is the current yield as seen in the constant growth dividend discount model. It is the expected dividend expressed as a percentage of the current price. The Grinold-Kroner model goes a step further in expressing the expected current yield by considering any repurchases or new issues of stock.

2. The **expected nominal earnings growth** is the real growth in earnings plus expected inflation:

   expected nominal earnings growth return = $\%\Delta E$

3. The **expected repricing return** is captured by the expected change in the P/E ratio:

   expected repricing return = $\%\Delta P/E$

It is helpful to view the Grinold-Kroner model as the sum of the (1) expected cash flow return, (2) expected nominal earnings growth rate, and (3) expected repricing return.

$$E(R_e) \approx (D/P - \%\Delta S) + \%\Delta E + \%\Delta P/E$$

It is important to understand that the assumptions of the Grinold-Kroner model may lead to irrational results. Because the model assumes an infinite time horizon, it ignores an investor's time horizon. For example, an investor may assume that the P/E ratio would revert to its long-term average. However, by selecting any positive growth rate for the P/E ratio, the model would assume an infinitely rising P/E ratio, an implausible result. For very long-term time horizons, the theoretically appropriate $\%\Delta P/E = 0$ (and also $\%\Delta S = 0$).

EXAMPLE: Calculating expected equity return using the Grinold-Kroner model

Suppose an analyst uses the Grinold-Kroner model to estimate the stock market return. The analyst estimates a 2.1% dividend yield, real earnings growth of 4.0%, long-term inflation of 3.1%, a 0.5% increase in shares outstanding, and an expansion of the P/E multiple of 0.3%.

What is the implied return on the stock market given these assumptions?

Expected *cash flow* (income) return = dividend yield – increase in shares outstanding

= 2.1% – 0.5% = 1.6%

Expected nominal earnings growth = real earnings growth + inflation

= 4.0% + 3.1% = 7.1%

Expected repricing return = change in P/E ratio

= 0.3%

The total expected return on the stock market is 1.6% + 7.1% + 0.3% = 9.0%.

It is relatively easy to observe the inputs of the model, which can be obtained from published statistical data. It is more challenging to estimate the change in the P/E ratio. The assumption of the P/E ratio (or price relative to other metrics including cash flow or sales) is that it has an observable long-term mean and the ratio will revert to this mean. Empirical evidence suggests that this is true in the long term, but not in the short term.

MODULE QUIZ 2.3

1. At the beginning of the fiscal year, Tel-Pal, Inc. stock sells for $75 per share. There are 2 million shares outstanding. An analyst predicts that the annual dividend to be paid in one year will be $3 per share. The expected inflation rate is 3.5%. The firm plans to issue 40,000 new shares over the year. The price-to-earnings ratio is expected to stay the same, and nominal earnings will increase by 6.8%.

   Based upon these figures, **calculate** the expected return on a share of Tel-Pal, Inc. stock in the next year.

2. An analyst uses the Grinold-Kroner model and assumes an infinite time horizon and a P/E growth rate of 2%. **Discuss** *one* shortcoming of the P/E growth assumption.

MODULE 2.4: THE RISK PREMIUM APPROACH

Video covering this content is available online.

The equity risk premium is generally defined as the amount by which the equity return exceeds the risk-free rate. An alternative way is to think about the equity premium as the amount by which the equity return exceeds the expected return on a default-free bond. Whereas the approach relative to the risk-free rate looks at a single premium for equity, the approach relative to bonds uses a building block approach.

Forecasting the equity premium is generally quite challenging, regardless of the approach selected. An analyst must therefore supplement her forecasts with other methods of analyses.

The Equilibrium Approach

The financial equilibrium approach assumes that financial models will value securities correctly. The **Singer-Terhaar model** is based on two versions of the international *Capital Asset Pricing Model* (CAPM): one in which global asset markets are fully integrated, and another in which markets are fully segmented. The model then looks at the expectations of actual segmentation/integration and takes a weighted average of the two assumptions to calculate returns. The Singer-Terhaar approach begins with the CAPM:

$R_i = R_f + \beta_{i,M}(R_M - R_f)$, or alternatively $RP_i = \beta_{i,M} \times RP_M$

where:

R_i = expected return on asset *i*

R_f = risk-free rate of return

$\beta_{i,M}$ = sensitivity (systematic risk) of asset *i* returns to the global investable market

R_M = expected return on the *global* investable market

RP_i = the asset's risk premium

RP_M = the market's risk premium

Think of the global investable market as consisting of all investable assets, traditional and alternative. We can manipulate this formula to solve for the risk premium on a debt or equity security using the following steps:

Step 1: $$\beta_{i,M} = \frac{Cov(R_i, R_M)}{Var(R_M)} = \rho_{i,M}\left(\frac{\sigma_i}{\sigma_M}\right)$$

where:

$\rho_{i,M}$ = correlation between the returns on asset *i* and the global market portfolio

σ_i = standard deviation of the returns on asset *i*

σ_M = standard deviation of the returns on the global market portfolio

$Cov(R_i, R_m)$ = covariance of asset *i* return with the global market portfolio return

Step 2: Rearranging the CAPM, we arrive at the expression for the risk premium for asset *i*, RP_i:

$$RP_i = \beta_{i,M} RP_M = \rho_{i,M}\sigma_i\left(\frac{RP_M}{\sigma_M}\right)$$

This expression states that the risk premium for an asset is equal to the product of its correlation with the global market portfolio and the standard deviation of the asset, multiplied by the Sharpe ratio for the global portfolio (in parentheses). From this formula, we forecast the risk premium and expected return for a market.

EXAMPLE: Calculating equity and bond risk premiums

Given the following data, **calculate** the equity and debt risk premiums for Country X:

	Expected Standard Deviation	Correlation With Global Investable Market
Country X bonds	10%	0.40
Country X equities	15%	0.70
Market Sharpe ratio = 0.35		

Answer:

$RP_{bonds} = 10\% \times 0.40 \times 0.35 = 1.40\%$

$RP_{equities} = 15\% \times 0.70 \times 0.35 = 3.68\%$

The Singer-Terhaar model then adjusts the CAPM for market imperfections, such as segmentation. When markets are segmented, capital does not flow freely across borders. The opposite of segmented markets is integrated markets, where capital flows freely. Government restrictions on investing are a frequent cause of market segmentation. If markets are segmented, two assets with the same risk can have different expected returns because capital cannot flow to the higher return asset. The presence of investment barriers increases the risk premium for securities in segmented markets.

In reality, most markets are neither fully segmented nor fully integrated. Investors have a preference for their own country's equity markets, which prevents them from fully exploiting investment opportunities overseas. Developed world equity markets have been estimated as 75% to 90% integrated, whereas emerging market equities have been estimated as 50% to 75% integrated. In the example that follows, we will adjust for partial market segmentation by estimating an equity risk premium assuming full integration and an equity risk premium assuming full segmentation, and then taking a weighted average of the two. Under the full segmentation assumption, the relevant global portfolio is the individual asset as its own market portfolio, meaning that the asset is perfectly correlated with itself ($\beta_{i,M} = \rho_{i,M} = 1$).

Step 3: Calculate the risk premium for asset *i* assuming a fully segmented market:

$$\text{if } \rho_{i,M} = 1 \rightarrow RP_i^S = \sigma_i\left(\frac{RP_i^S}{\sigma_i}\right)$$

If no local market Sharpe ratio is given, then use the global market Sharpe ratio.

Step 4: The last piece is to take a weighted average of the two risk premiums (calculated under full integration and full segmentation) to calculate the asset's risk premium:

$$RP = \phi RP^G + (1 - \phi)RP^S$$

where ϕ measures the degree of the asset's integration with the global markets, and the superscripts are G (globally integrated) and S (segmented).

Reading 2

EXAMPLE: Calculating the risk premium using the Singer-Terhaar model

Suppose an analyst is valuing two equity markets. Market A is a developed market, and Market B is an emerging market. The investor's time horizon is five years. The other pertinent facts are as follows:

	Market A	Market B
Sharpe ratio	0.29	0.40
Volatility (standard deviation)	17%	28%
Correlation with global market	0.82	0.63
Degree of integration	80%	65%
Illiquidity premium	0%	2.3%
Risk-free rate is 5.0%		
Sharpe ratio of the global market is 0.29		

Calculate the risk premiums and expected returns for each market.

Answer:

First, we calculate the risk premium for both markets assuming full integration. Note that for the emerging market, the illiquidity risk premium is included:

$$RP_i = \rho_{i,M}\sigma_i(\text{market Sharpe ratio})$$
$$RP_A = (0.82)(0.17)(0.29) = 4.04\%$$
$$RP_B = (0.63)(0.28)(0.29) + 0.0230 = 7.42\%$$

Next, we calculate the equity risk premium for both markets assuming full segmentation:

$$RP_i = \sigma_i(\text{market Sharpe ratio})$$
$$RP_A = (0.17)(0.29) = 4.93\%$$
$$RP_B = (0.28)(0.40) + 0.0230 = 13.50\%$$

Note that when we calculate the risk premium under full segmentation, we use the local market as the reference market instead of the global market and thus, the correlation between the local market and itself is 1.0.

We then take a weighted average of the integrated and segmented risk premiums by the degree of integration and segmentation in each market to arrive at the weighted average risk premium:

$$RP_i = (\text{degree of integration of } i)(\text{ERP assuming full integration}) + (\text{degree of segmentation of } i)(\text{ERP assuming full segmentation})$$

$$RP_A = (0.80)(0.0404) + (1 - 0.80)(0.0493) = 4.22\%$$

$$RP_B = (0.65)(0.0742) + (1 - 0.65)(0.1350) = 9.55\%$$

Finally, the expected return in each market also incorporates the risk-free rate:

$$\hat{R}_A = 5\% + 4.22\% = 9.22\%$$

$$\hat{R}_B = 5\% + 9.55\% = 14.55\%$$

Emerging Market Equity Risk

Emerging markets are often characterized by fragile economies, political and policy instability, and weaker legal protections, including weak property rights, and weak disclosure and enforcement standards. They tend to exhibit idiosyncratic risks where local country effects tend to be more important than global effects. Emerging markets tend to be less fully integrated than developed markets.

MODULE QUIZ 2.4

Use the following data to answer the questions below:

Sharpe ratio of the global portfolio	0.29
Standard deviation of the global portfolio	8.0%
Risk-free rate of return	4.5%
Degree of market integration for Market A	80%
Degree of market integration for Market B	65%
Standard deviation of Market A	18%
Standard deviation of Market B	26%
Correlation of Market A with global portfolio	0.87
Correlation of Market B with global portfolio	0.63

1. **Calculate** the risk premiums for Market A and Market B.

2. **Calculate** the expected return for each market.

Video covering this content is available online.

MODULE 2.5: FORECASTING REAL ESTATE RETURNS

LOS 2.e: Explain how economic and competitive factors can affect expectations for real estate investment markets and sector returns.

Unlike traditional asset classes (think equities, bonds, and cash or cash equivalents), real estate is generally immobile and illiquid, and each property is part of a heterogeneous group with its unique characteristics. Managing real estate also requires maintenance and, therefore, operating costs can be significant. Calculating returns is often done through appraisals, which are subject to time lags and data smoothing given that they are done infrequently, so appraised values may differ significantly from market values.

Real Estate Cycles

As a general asset class, real estate values are subject to business cycle movements, but they also drive business cycles. Given that supply is fixed at any given point in time, property values exhibit *cyclicality*, and demand will be strongly influenced by the quality and type of property available. High quality properties tend to fluctuate less with business cycles, while low quality properties will show more cyclicality. When looking at real estate and business cycles, we observe the following characteristics:

- *Boom*: Increased demand will drive up property values and lease rates, which induces construction activity. This higher activity translates to stronger economic activity.
- *Bust*: Falling demand leads to overcapacity and overbuilding, driving values and lease rates down. Because leases lock in tenants for longer terms and moving costs are high, excess supply can't be quickly absorbed.

A recent study suggests that the U.S. commercial real estate collapse following the global financial crisis was caused by leverage and speculation rather than business cycle movements.

Capitalization Rates

The **capitalization rate**, or **cap rate** for short, is a commercial real estate property's earnings yield, and is calculated by dividing current **net operating income (NOI)** by the property value. The cap rate is similar to the denominator of the Gordon Growth model, looking at expected return less the NOI growth rate. When an infinite time period is assumed, the cap rate can be calculated as:

$$\text{cap rate} = E(R_{re}) - \text{NOI growth rate}$$

$$E(R_{re}) = \text{cap rate} + \text{NOI growth rate}$$

During stable periods, the long-run NOI growth rate should be close to GDP growth. If an investor has a finite time period, the formula changes by subtracting from expected return the change in the cap rate:

$$E(R_{re}) = \text{cap rate} + \text{NOI growth rate} - \%\Delta\text{cap rate}$$

As you likely observed, this formula has similarities with the Grinold-Kroner model, noting that NOI growth is also a nominal measure, incorporating real growth plus inflation.

The cap rate is quite sensitive to competitive pressures. With the rapid growth of online retailers, the difference in the cap rates of malls in the United States with high and low productivity grew from 1.2% in 2008 to 3.2% in 2018.

Similar to the expected return net of growth rate for equities, the cap rate is used as a long-term measure of risk discount rate for real estate property valuations. Hence, cap rates are positively related to changes in interest rates and vacancy rates. Lenders are less willing to extend credit due to perceived higher risk resulting in cap rates that are inversely related to the availability of credit and the availability of debt financing. Credit spreads, which are countercyclical, mitigate the cyclical sensitivity of cap rates.

Risk Premiums on Real Estate

Real estate assets require several risk premiums to compensate for their higher risk. These include a term premium for holding long-term assets, a credit premium to compensate for the risk of tenant nonpayment, and an equity risk premium above corporate bond returns for the fluctuation in real estate values, leases, and vacancies. Overall, the combined risk premium is higher than that of corporate bonds but lower than equities.

Liquidity risk is also important for real estate. For publicly traded real estate, including REITs, the liquidity risk is the risk that the asset cannot be sold quickly at a reasonable price. For real estate as an asset group, liquidity risk reflects an inability to sell the asset except at periodic times. The liquidity premium is considered to be between 2% and 4% for commercial real estate.

Once the appropriate risk premiums are calculated, real estate can be used in equilibrium models including Singer-Terhaar. However, analysts must make two adjustments: the impact of smoothing must be removed from the data, and the analyst should adjust for illiquidity by incorporating a liquidity premium. The local, rather than global, nature of real estate should also be considered.

Public vs. Private Real Estate

Wealthy individuals and large institutional investors can create diversified real estate portfolios. Investors with less wealth can choose publicly traded real estate, including REITs, to benefit from diversification. REITs are generally strongly correlated with equities in the short term, while direct real estate shows low correlation. However, the low correlation is partly due to the smoothing of return data. Over long time horizons, REITs have a relatively high correlation with direct real estate.

Given that REITs use significant leverage, their returns and risks must be first unlevered to provide the appropriate comparison with direct real estate holdings. When adjusted for leverage, REITs as an asset class historically show higher returns and lower volatility than direct real estate. This difference may be due to investors capturing much of the liquidity risk premium of direct investments, while also profiting from professional management.

However, there are significant differences between apartment, office, industrial and retail classes. Retail REITs had the highest return and second lowest volatility. Industrial REITs had the lowest return and highest volatility. Within directly owned real estate, apartments had the highest return while office had the lowest.

Residential Real Estate Returns

Residential real estate is the largest class of developed properties, accounting for 75% of global values. Overall, residential real estate outperformed equities on an inflation-adjusted basis with lower volatility. Nevertheless, their return performance differed before and after World War II, with relatively weaker postwar returns. The strongest postwar period returns were during 1950–1980 when residential real estate generally outperformed equities, but had comparably weaker returns during 1980–2015. However, and important for diversification, residential real estate returns were uncorrelated across countries after the war, while equity returns showed rising correlations.

MODULE QUIZ 2.5

1. **List** *two* adjustments that analysts must make to the risk premiums calculated using equilibrium models.

2. **Discuss** how cap rates are related to vacancy rates and the availability of debt financing.

MODULE 2.6: EXCHANGE RATE FORECASTING

Video covering this content is available online.

Reading 2

LOS 2.f: Discuss major approaches to forecasting exchange rates.

Currency exchange rate forecasting is particularly difficult, causing investment managers to either fully hedge currency exposure, or accept the volatility. Currencies are units of account in which asset prices are quoted. Movements in exchange rates change the value of all assets denominated in one currency relatively to all other currencies. Exchange rates are determined by factors influenced by trading, governments, financial systems, and geographies, as well as by laws, regulations, and customs of a country.

Trade in goods and services affects exchange rates through (1) trade flows, (2) purchasing power parity, and (3) competitiveness and sustainability of the current account.

- *Trade flows*: The impact of net trade flows (gross trade flows less exports) tends to be relatively small on exchange rates assuming they can be financed. Large trade flows without large financing flows in foreign exchange markets likely indicates a crisis.
- *Purchasing power parity (PPP)*: PPP implies that the prices of goods and services in different countries should reflect changes in exchange rates. As a result, the expected exchange rate movement should follow the expected inflation rate differentials. Furthermore, the expected change in real exchange rates should be zero, if real exchange rates are the ratio of price levels converted through a common exchange rate. PPP does not work well in explaining short-term exchange rate changes, but works better in the long term and when inflation differences are large and are determined through money supply.

  Actual real exchange rates may differ from those predicted through PPP. For example, there could be trade barriers or certain goods may not be traded. PPP does not account for capital flows, which may exert significant influence on exchange rates. Exchange rates may also be influenced by economic development independent of PPP.

- *Current account and exchange rates*: When restrictions are placed on capital flows, exchange rate sensitivity tends to increase relative to the current account (trade) balance. Current account balances will have the largest influence on exchange rates when they are persistent and sustained. However, it is not the size of the current account balance that matters as much as the length of the imbalance.

  Structural imbalances in the current account can exist from (1) fiscal imbalances that persist over time, (2) demographics and trade preferences that impact savings decisions, (2) how abundant or scare resources are, (4) availability (or lack) of viable investment opportunities, and (5) the terms of trade.

Adjustments to capital flows will place substantial pressure on exchange rates. Three important considerations to look at are the implications on capital mobility, uncovered interest rate parity, and portfolio balances and compositions.

1. *Capital mobility*: The expected percentage change in the exchange rate can be computed as the difference between nominal short-term interest rates and the risk premiums of the domestic portfolio over the foreign portfolio:

   $$E(\%\Delta S_{d/f}) = (r^d - r^f) + (\text{Term}^d - \text{Term}^f) + (\text{Credit}^d - \text{Credit}^f) + (\text{Equity}^d - \text{Equity}^f) + (\text{Liquid}^d - \text{Liquid}^f)$$

   When there is a relative improvement in investment opportunities in a country, the currency initially tends to see significant appreciation but "overshoots" and eventually depreciates. There are three phases of the response to stronger investment opportunities: (1) the exchange rate will initially significantly appreciate, (2) following an extended level of stronger exchange rates in the intermediate term, investors will start to expect a reversal, and (3) the exchange rate in the long run will tend to start reverting (depreciate) once the investment opportunities have been realized. The third phase is shown in the equation above with a positive $E(\%\Delta S_{d/f})$, indicating the domestic currency will depreciate by that amount in percent.

2. *Uncovered interest rate parity (UIP)*: UIP states that exchange rate changes should equal differences in nominal interest rates. UIP implies that in the previous equation, only the interest rate differential matters and not the premium differentials. In contrast to UIP, *carry trades* involve borrowing in a low-rate currency and lending in a high-rate currency. Carry trades are considered to be successful because they include a risk premium, confirming the validity of the risk premiums in the equation.

   When capital flows into a country given exchange rate differentials, this is referred to as *hot money*. Hot money creates monetary policy issues. First, central banks' ability to use monetary policy effectively is limited. Second, firms use short-term financing to fund long-term investments, which increases financial market risk. Third, exchange rates tend to overshoot, creating business disruption. Central banks may try to counter the effects of hot money flows through intervention in the currency markets, including selling government securities or maintaining interest rate targets.

3. *Portfolio balance and composition*: Strong economic growth in a country tends to correspond to an increasing share of that country's currency in the global market portfolio. Investors need to be induced to increase their allocations to

that country and currency, which weakens the currency and increases the risk premiums. However, a few factors could mitigate this impact:

- Investors tend to have a strong home country bias, which leads them to absorb a larger share of the new assets.
- If growth is due to productivity gains, investors may fund it with financial flows and foreign direct investment.
- Countries that experience high trend rates tend to be smaller, emerging markets. Increasing the weight in these countries generally does not weaken their currency.

Similarly, large current account deficits also weaken exchange rates, but several mitigating factors exist:

- Current account deficits due to large investment spending are easier to finance if they are expected to be profitable.
- Small current account deficits in global reserve currencies, including the U.S. dollar, help provide global liquidity and are beneficial to the financial system.

MODULE QUIZ 2.6

1. Assume that Japanese inflation is projected to be a cumulative 8.2% over the next five years, while U.S. inflation is 13.2% over the same period. U.S. inflation is thus projected to be 5% higher. Stock prices have just started to rise and will continue to do so for some time. **Explain** which asset class should an investor in Japanese assets favor assuming PPP holds true.

MODULE 2.7: VOLATILITY FORECASTING

Video covering this content is available online.

LOS 2.g: Discuss methods of forecasting volatility.

Estimating the variance for a single asset is relatively easy. Estimating variances for many assets is more complex, and requires the use of a **variance-covariance (VCV) matrix** or other forecasting tools.

The VCV Matrix

Sample VCV Matrix

Estimating a constant VCV matrix can most easily be done from deriving variances and covariances from sample statistics. However, choosing the appropriate sample size for large portfolios will be critical. If the sample size is small relative to the number of assets (i.e., the number of assets cannot exceed the number of historical observations), the outcomes may be meaningless; for example, it may show that a large portfolio is riskless. It is recommended that the number of observations should be at least 10 times larger than the number of portfolio assets.

PROFESSOR'S NOTE

There are a large number of formulas in this section. They are included primarily to explain the underlying concepts, but it is unlikely that you would be required to do these calculations on the exam. The LOS only asks you to *discuss* methods of volatility forecasts.

Factor-Based VCV Matrices

The main advantage of using multifactor models for VCV matrices is that it significantly reduces the number of required observations. Correlations can be estimated from a few common factors, while variances require factors related to specific assets.

The return of the *i*th asset in a multifactor model can be calculated as:

$$r_i = \alpha_i + \sum_{k=1}^{K} \beta_{ik} F_k + \varepsilon_i$$

where K represents the number of common factors, α_i is the intercept, β_{ik} is the *i*th asset's sensitivity to the *k*th factor, F_k is the *k*th factor return, and ε_i is a factor term unique to asset *i* with a zero mean.

The variance of the *i*th asset can be derived as:

$$\sigma_i^2 = \sum_{m=1}^{K} \sum_{n=1}^{K} \beta_{im} \beta_{in} \rho_{mn} + \nu_i^2$$

where ρ_{mn} is the covariance between the *m*th and *n*th factors, and ν_i^2 is the variance of the ε_i unique factor.

The last step is to look at the covariance between the *i*th and *j*th asset:

$$\sigma_{ij} = \sum_{m=1}^{K} \sum_{n=1}^{K} \beta_{im} \beta_{jn} \rho_{mn}$$

Assuming these factors are not redundant and do not have zero terms will help us ensure that the matrix outcomes are not meaningless and that portfolios do not incorrectly appear riskless.

The factor model also helps simplify the number of calculations used in the VCV matrix. For example, whereas the VCV matrix would need ($N(N-1) / 2$) covariances, the factor model would need only ($N \times K$) factor sensitivities and ($K(K + 1) / 2$) factor elements. For $N = 50$ and $K = 6$, the VCV matrix would need (50(49) / 2) = 1,225 sensitivities, whereas the factor model would need only (50 × 6) = 300 sensitivities and (6 × 7 / 2) = 21 elements.

Despite their significant advantages, factor-based VCV matrices have several shortcomings:

1. The matrix is *biased*: Matrix inputs need to be estimated and will be misspecified. As a result, the matrix will be biased, meaning it will not be a predictor of the true returns, not even on average.
2. The matrix is *inconsistent*: As the sample size increases in the factor-based VCV matrix, the model does not converge to the true matrix. In contrast, the sample VCV matrix will be both consistent and unbiased.

Shrinkage Estimates

Combining information in the sample VCV matrix with a target matrix (e.g., the factor-based VCV matrix) will result in more precise data and reduced estimation error. The shrinkage estimate is a weighted average estimate of the sample and target (e.g., factor-based) matrix, with the same weights used for all elements of the matrix, including the variance and covariance factors. The resulting figures will be more efficient because they will have smaller error terms. Even though shrinkage estimates may be biased, more precise (less biased) target matrices will result in greater improvement.

For example, suppose that the sample covariance between two assets is 180 and the target (from a factor-based model) estimated covariance is 220. If the analyst weights the historical covariance by 60% and the target by 40%, the shrinkage estimate would be 196 (= 180 × 0.60 + 220 × 0.40). If conditions of the model and weights are well chosen, the shrinkage estimate covariances are likely to be more accurate.

Smoothed Returns to Estimate Volatility

Smoothing of data leads to underestimating risk and overstating returns and diversification benefits. Not adjusting for smoothing tends to lead to distorted portfolio analysis and suboptimal asset allocation decisions. As a result, it is important that analysts adjust the data for the impact of smoothing, by taking a weighted average of the current "true" returns and previously observed returns:

$$R_t = (1 - \lambda)r_1 + \lambda R_{t-1} \text{ where } \lambda \text{ is a weight between 0 and 1}$$

The portfolio variance is then calculated as:

$$\text{var}(r) = \left(\frac{1+\lambda}{1-\lambda}\right)\text{var}(R) > \text{var}(R)$$

For example, if $\lambda = 0.6$, then the true variance is 1.6 / 0.4 = 4× the variance and 2× the standard deviation of the observed data.

One shortcoming of this model is that the true current return is not directly observable. Proxies for estimating the true return include using an asset index.

ARCH Models

PROFESSOR'S NOTE

You previously encountered the concept of ARCH in Level II. Use that knowledge to your advantage.

Asset returns generally show periods of high and low volatilities, leading to **volatility clustering**. These volatilities can be addressed through autoregressive conditional heteroskedasticity (ARCH) models. ARCH models can be used for portfolios with multiple assets in VCV matrix estimations. The simplest ARCH formula can be written as:

$$\sigma_t^2 = \gamma + \alpha\sigma_{t-1}^2 + \beta\eta_t^2 = \gamma + (\alpha + \beta)\sigma_{t-1}^2 + \beta\left(\eta_t^2 - \sigma_{t-1}^2\right)$$

where α, β, and γ are nonnegative parameters and $(\alpha + \beta) < 1$, and η_t is a random variable indicating the unexpected return component.

Higher $\alpha + \beta$ terms indicate higher emphasis on past information, leading to volatility clustering.

MODULE QUIZ 2.7

1. A portfolio manager determines that in order to estimate the variance-covariance matrix used in the portfolio's asset allocation, the matrix will need 17 asset classes. The manager has obtained weekly sample return data over the last 6 months. The manager decided to also use the factor-based matrix approach, but does not use shrinkage estimation. **Determine** the strengths and shortcomings of the manager's approach.

2. **Discuss** *one* potential remedy to the manager's shortcomings.

MODULE 2.8: GLOBAL PORTFOLIO ADJUSTMENTS

Video covering this content is available online.

LOS 2.h: Recommend and justify changes in the component weights of a global investment portfolio based on trends and expected changes in macroeconomic factors.

> **For the Exam:** This LOS asks you to use much of what you have learned here and apply it to portfolio management. Given that the emphasis of the Level III exam is portfolio management, you need to be able to pull all this material together.

In this section, we apply what we have learned so far to adjust portfolio allocations. The main focus here is *how* to adjust a portfolio rather than get caught up in the particular forecast details. For example, if the starting point is a typical portfolio of equities and bonds, we may want to consider changing the weighting between equities and bonds, changing the weights between domestic and international investments, or adjusting the credit quality, duration, yield curve positioning or currency exposures of the underlying assets. To aid this decision-making process, it is helpful to keep in mind the following questions:

- Have the drivers of trend growth changed significantly?
- Are markets becoming more or less integrated?
- Where is the country positioned within the business cycle, and are fiscal and monetary policies consistent with the business cycle phase?
- What is the trend in current account balances?
- Are currencies strong or weak, and how are currencies affecting economic growth and competitiveness?

Trend growth is generally favorable to equities because it implies long-term earnings growth. Trend growth is unfavorable to bonds because it typically results in higher interest rates. The analyst can use country-specific and global expectations through VCV matrices to adjust the allocations between equities and bonds.

As markets become more integrated globally, required returns will fall. We saw this relationship in the Singer-Terhaar model. The analyst should increase allocations towards emerging markets that are expected to see increased integration, and away from those markets that are already highly integrated.

When the economy is at the *trough* of the business cycle, equities perform well, and valuation ratios and earnings growth are expected to increase. The analyst could also use the Grinold-Kroner model to compute the required equity risk premium and increase the portfolio's equity weights. At this stage, the yield curve is steep with high credit and term premiums. However, the expectation of rising interest rates means that bonds tend to underperform, and the analyst should reduce the portfolio's bond allocation. The overall bond duration should also be reduced, and a barbell strategy may be optimal (increased short-term and long-term exposure and reduced medium-term exposure). If the economy is at its peak, the reverse strategy should be followed (i.e., reduce the equity exposure and increase bond exposure and durations).

Monetary and fiscal policy changes can also be important considerations. The analyst should focus less on monetary and fiscal policy activities, which are expected to be already reflected in asset values, but rather on structural changes in policy direction. For example, changes in the tax code or changes from standard interest rate targeting to other policies, including quantitative easing, can influence the direction of portfolio reallocation changes.

Current account balances fluctuate with business cycles. It is the long-term trend in current account balances that is more important in setting portfolio expectations. Rising current account deficits tend to be associated with rising required returns (and therefore falling asset prices), and increased capital flows to the deficit country to fund its deficit. Capital flows also influence currencies. If assets in a particular currency offer higher risk-adjusted return potential than in other currencies, capital will flow to that country and put upward pressure on its currency. The analyst will need to determine whether the currency still has potential to appreciate, or whether it is at its peak.

MODULE QUIZ 2.8

A portfolio manager has a global portfolio invested in several countries and is considering other countries as well. The decisions the manager faces and the economic conditions in the countries are described in the following. In each case, the portfolio manager must reallocate assets based on economic conditions.

1. The portfolio manager has noticed that the yield curve is downward sloping in Country A. The current portfolio in this country is 60% stocks and 40% bonds.

   Determine the appropriate reallocation within Country A. **Suggest** changes to the portfolio based on this information.

2. Country B has experienced declining prices and this trend is expected to continue. The manager has no funds invested in this country yet but is considering investments in bonds, equity, and real estate.

   Determine the appropriate reallocation within Country B. In which assets should the manager invest?

3. The manager is considering the purchase of government bonds in either emerging Country C or Country D. The countries have the following characteristics:

   Characteristics of Countries C and D

	Country C	Country D
Foreign exchange/short-term debt	147%	78%
Debt to GDP	42%	84%

   Determine the appropriate reallocations within emerging Country C and Country D.

KEY CONCEPTS

LOS 2.a

The three approaches to forecast fixed income returns are the DCF method, the risk premium approach, and the equilibrium model.

The DCF method is used to estimate the required return of an asset. It is the most precise method for fixed income securities. It includes analysis of the YTM and the Macaulay duration. The Macaulay duration will determine whether an expected yield change will generate positive or negative returns (by looking at its impact on prices vs. return from reinvestment of cash flow).

The risk premium (or building block) approach starts with the risk-free rate and adds on different risk premiums, including the term premium, credit premium, and liquidity premium.

The short-term risk-free rate can be estimated from government zero-coupon yields. The term premium is positively related to duration and the slope of the yield curve, and is influenced by inflation uncertainty, recession hedges, supply and demand of bonds, and business cycle movements.

Credit premiums compensate for the expected level of losses and for the risk of default losses, and are also positively related to the slope of the yield curve.

Steep yield curves generally indicate both high credit and term premiums, both of which are considered bullish indicators.

Liquidity tends to be highest for bonds that are (1) issued at close to par or market rates, (2) new, (3) large in size, (4) issued by a frequent and well-known issuer, (5) simple in structure, and (6) of high credit quality. Liquidity premiums can be established by comparing the yield spread between the highest quality issuer (usually the sovereign) and the next highest quality issuer.

LOS 2.b

Investors in emerging market debt face higher risks associated with the foreign government's ability and willingness to repay its obligations, and are exposed to other political, legal, and economic risks.

Indicators of heightened credit risk in emerging market bonds include (1) deficit-to-GDP ratio greater than 4%; (2) debt-to-GDP ratio greater than 70%–80%; (3) real growth rate less than 4%; (4) a current account deficit exceeding 4% of GDP; (5) foreign debt levels greater than 50% of GDP or debt levels greater than 200% of the current account receipts; and (6) foreign exchange reserves less than 100% of short-term debt.

LOS 2.c

Equity market returns can be estimated using the DCF analysis, a risk premium approach, and the equilibrium approach.

The DCF analysis can also be used for equity valuation and establish the intrinsic value of an asset as the present value of its future cash flows.

The Grinold-Kroner model calculates the expected equity return as its dividend yield plus the inflation rate plus the real earnings growth rate minus the change in stock outstanding plus changes in the P/E ratio.

The Grinold-Kroner model can also be viewed as the (1) expected cash flow return (dividend yield minus change in shares outstanding), (2) nominal earnings growth (real earnings growth plus inflation), and (3) expected repricing return (change in the P/E ratio).

The risk premium approach looks at the equity risk premium as the amount by which the equity return exceeds the expected return of a default-free bond. However, forecasting the equity premium can be challenging.

The Singer-Terhaar model combines two versions of the international CAPM: one in which global asset markets are fully integrated and another in which markets are fully segmented.

The Singer-Terhaar model calculates the risk premium for an asset in a fully integrated market as the product of its correlation with the global market portfolio and the standard deviation of the asset, multiplied by the Sharpe ratio of the global portfolio. The model calculates the risk premium for an asset in a fully segmented market as the product of the standard deviation of the asset and its Sharpe ratio plus any illiquidity premium.

The Singer-Terhaar model then calculate the asset's overall risk premium as the weighted average of the risk premiums calculated under full integration and full segmentation.

LOS 2.d

Emerging equity markets tend to be characterized by political and policy instability, weaker legal protections, and weak disclosure and enforcement standards. Emerging markets tend to be more segmented than developed markets.

LOS 2.e

Real estate values are subject to business cycle movements, including boom (higher demand drives up property values) and bust (falling demand drives values and lease rates down).

Real estate valuation is measured by the cap rate, which is calculated by dividing current NOI by the value of a commercial real estate property.

Real estate returns include a term premium for holding long-term assets, a credit premium to compensate for the risk of tenant nonpayment, and an equity risk premium above corporate bond returns for the fluctuation in real estate values, leases, and vacancies.

REITs are generally strongly correlated with equities in the short term, while direct real estate shows low correlation, although the low correlation is partly due to the smoothing of return data.

Over the very long run, residential real estate outperformed equities on a real basis with lower volatility, although their return has been relatively weak over the last 40 years.

LOS 2.f

Trade in goods and services affects exchange rates through trade flows, purchasing power parity (PPP), and competitiveness and sustainability of the current account.

Net trade flows have small impacts on exchange rates; large trade flows without large financing flows in foreign exchange markets likely indicate a crisis. PPP does not work well in explaining short-term exchange rate changes but works better in the long term and when inflation differences are large and are determined through changes in the money supply. Current account balances will have the largest influence on exchange rate when they are persistent and sustained.

Adjustments to capital flows place substantial pressure on exchange rates. Three important considerations include the implications on capital mobility, UIP, and portfolio balances and compositions.

Under ideal capital mobility conditions, the expected percentage exchange rate change will equal the "excess" risk-adjusted expected portfolio return denominated in the domestic currency relative to the foreign currency. However, the exchange rate may overshoot in the short run, which results from hot money chasing higher returns.

Carry trades tend to be profitable, but this contradicts the assumptions of UIP, which states that exchange rate changes should equal differences in nominal interest rates.

Looking at the portfolio balance and composition, exchange rates tend to adjust given changes in the relative sizes and compositions of the aggregate portfolios denominated in each currency.

LOS 2.g

A sample variance-covariance matrix is a popular tool to estimate the true VCV structure. Problems with the sample VCV matrix is that it cannot be used for large numbers of asset classes and it is subject to sampling error.

Factor-based (multifactor) models allow the VCV matrix to handle large numbers of asset classes. However, the factor-based VCV matrix is biased and inconsistent.

The shrinkage estimate is a weighted average estimate of the sample and target (e.g., factor-based) matrix, with the same weights used for all elements of the matrix.

Smoothing of data leads to underestimating risk and overstating returns and diversification benefits. Not adjusting for smoothing tends to lead to distorted portfolio analysis and suboptimal asset allocation decisions.

ARCH models can be used for portfolios with multiple assets to address volatility clustering of financial asset returns.

LOS 2.h

Be able to discuss how the relationships covered in the previous LOS can be used in assessing the relative attractiveness of asset classes (i.e., estimating expected return and risk through the VCV matrices, using the Singer-Terhaar model or the Grinold-Kroner model, phases of the business cycle, capital flows, and expectations of currency movements).

ANSWER KEY FOR MODULE QUIZZES

Module Quiz 2.1

1. The investor will realize a gain. The portfolio's Macaulay duration is 5.2 (= 5 × 1.04). Given that the investor's investment horizon of six years is longer than the Macaulay duration, a rise in bond yields will result in a return that is higher than the YTM because the increase in reinvestment yield will outweigh the fall in the bond price. (LOS 2.a)

2. **B** The expected annual return of the one-year government bond is 2.5% (no risk premiums). The expected one-year return of the corporate bond is 3.65% (= 2.5% + 0.6% + 0.3% + 0.25%). The estimated weighted average return of an equal-weighted investment in the two securities is 3.08% (= (2.5% + 3.65%) / 2). (LOS 2.a)

3. **A** The average spread (vs. one-year government bond) is 0.58% (= [0 + (0.6 + 0.3 + 0.25)] / 2). (LOS 2.a)

Module Quiz 2.2

1. When exports are less than imports, a current account deficit usually results. This can be problematic because the deficit must be financed through external borrowing. If the emerging country becomes overleveraged, it may not be able to pay back its foreign debt. A financial crisis may ensue where foreign investors quickly withdraw their capital. These financial crises are accompanied by currency devaluations and declines in emerging market asset values. (LOS 2.b)

Module Quiz 2.3

1. The equation for expected return on Tel-Pal, Inc. using these inputs is:

$$E(R_e) \approx D/P + (\%\Delta E - \%\Delta S) + \%\Delta P/E)$$

$$\widehat{R}_T = \left(\frac{\$3}{\$75} \times 100\right) + 6.8\% - 2\% + 0 = 8.8\%$$

The expected return is 8.8%. The expected dividend yield is 4%, and the expected percentage increase in the number of shares is 2% (= 40,000 / 2,000,000). Nominal earnings of 6.8% includes expected inflation of 3.5%, which would be subtracted from the nominal earnings forecast to get the forecast of real earnings growth of 3.3%. The change in P/E is expected to stay the same for a value of 0. (LOS 2.c)

2. An infinite time horizon ignores the fact that the P/E ratio would likely revert to its long-term average. A 2% constant growth rate of the P/E ratio would result in an infinitely rising P/E ratio, which is considered an implausible outcome. (LOS 2.c)

Module Quiz 2.4

1. First, we calculate the risk premium assuming full integration.

   $RP_i = \rho_{i,M}\sigma_i(\text{market Sharpe ratio})$

   $RP_A = (0.87 \times 0.18 \times 0.29) = 4.54\%$

   $RP_B = (0.63 \times 0.26 \times 0.29) = 4.75\%$

   Then, we calculate the risk premium assuming full segmentation.

   $$RP_i = \sigma_i\left(\frac{RP_M}{\sigma_M}\right)$$

   $RP_A = (0.18 \times 0.29) = 5.22\%$

   $RP_B = (0.26 \times 0.29) = 7.54\%$

   Finally, weight the integrated and segmented risk premiums by the degree of integration and segmentation:

   $RP_A = (0.80 \times 0.0454) + [(1 - 0.80) \times 0.0522] = 4.68\%$

   $RP_B = (0.65 \times 0.0475) + [(1 - 0.65) \times 0.0754] = 5.73\%$

   (LOS 2.c)

2. The expected return in each market is then:

   $R_A = 4.68\% + 4.50\% = 9.18\%$

   $R_B = 5.73\% + 4.50\% = 10.23\%$

   (LOS 2.c)

Module Quiz 2.5

1. Once an analyst estimates the risk premiums using equilibrium models, the analyst should (1) remove the impact of smoothing from the data, and (2) adjust for illiquidity using a liquidity premium. (LOS 2.e)

2. Cap rates are positively related to changes in interest rates and vacancy rates. They are inversely related to the availability of credit and the availability of debt financing. (LOS 2.e)

Module Quiz 2.6

1. The PPP relationship states that countries with high inflation will see their currency depreciate, so the manager should invest in Japan. Within Japan, the investor should invest in stocks because stock prices have just started to rise and will continue to do so for some time. Bond yields will soon rise and their prices will fall as the economy expands. (LOS 2.f)

Module Quiz 2.7

1. The manager can use the sample VCV matrix because the sample size (26 weeks) exceeds the number of assets (17). However, this will be subject to large sample errors unless the number of observations is at least 10 times the number of assets. This condition is not satisfied. The factor matrix approach in this regard is superior because it can be used for any number of assets. However, the factor model is biased and inconsistent. (LOS 2.g)

2. The manager could have avoided these issues by using shrinkage estimation of the weighted averages of the sample and factor-based VCV matrices. (LOS 2.g)

Module Quiz 2.8

1. The downward sloping yield curve indicates that the economy is likely to contract in the future. In recessions, bonds outperform stocks because inflation and interest rates decrease and economic growth is slow. Assuming the accuracy of the yield curve forecast and that interest rates will fall further, the portfolio manager should consider reallocating from stocks into bonds. (LOS 2.h)

2. The manager should invest in bonds. In periods of declining prices or deflation, bonds perform well because there is no inflation and interest rates are declining. Stocks usually perform poorly during deflationary periods because economic growth is slowing. Real estate also performs poorly during deflationary times, particularly when the investment is financed with debt. (LOS 2.h)

3. The manager should purchase the bonds of Country C. Many emerging market bonds are denominated in a hard currency, so less risky countries have greater foreign currency reserves. Low levels of leverage are also preferred. One measure of leverage is the debt-to-GDP ratio. (LOS 2.h)

TOPIC QUIZ: CAPITAL MARKET EXPECTATIONS

You have now finished the Capital Market Expectations topic section. On your Schweser online dashboard, you can find a Topic Quiz that will provide immediate feedback on how effective your study of this material has been. The test is best taken timed; allow three minutes per question. Topic Quizzes are more exam-like than typical QBank questions or module quiz questions. A score less than 70% suggests that additional review of the topic is needed.

READING 3

Overview of Asset Allocation

EXAM FOCUS

Strategic asset allocation is often considered the most important decision in the portfolio management process. This reading provides a big picture overview of asset allocation and its relationship to the investor's objectives and constraints. It discusses issues related to an investor's overall financial situation and use of an economic balance sheet. It also provides an overview of three major asset allocation approaches (asset-only, liability-relative, and goals-based), passive versus active approaches to implementing the asset allocation, and key issues to consider when rebalancing the asset allocation.

MODULE 3.1: INVESTMENT GOVERNANCE

Video covering this content is available online.

LOS 3.a: Describe elements of effective investment governance and investment governance considerations in asset allocation.

Investment governance ensures that appropriate individuals or groups make informed investment decisions and conduct oversight activities on behalf of investors. The objective of effective governance is to match the investor's objectives with their constraints while ensuring that investment decisions comply with relevant laws and regulations. Investment governance also seeks to improve investment performance by aligning asset allocation with implementation.

Effective investment governance models:

1. Establish long-term and short-term investment objectives.
2. Allocate rights and responsibilities within the governance structure.
3. Specify processes for creating an investment policy statement (IPS).
4. Specify processes for creating a strategic asset allocation.

5. Apply a reporting framework to monitor the investment program's stated goals and objectives.
6. Periodically perform a governance audit.

Investment Objectives

Long-term and short-term objectives articulate what the investor would like to achieve. Some examples of investment objectives are as follows:

- The objective for a pension fund is for plan assets to meet current and ongoing plan liabilities.
- The objective for an endowment is to achieve a rate of return that exceeds the return required to fund current and ongoing distributions.
- The objective for an individual investor is to have sufficient assets for retirement while adhering to constraints and risk preferences.

At the core of the investment objective statement is the return requirement. Additional information that provides context to this required return includes the investor's willingness and ability to tolerate risk, the obligations that require funding, and how cash flows transfer into and out of the fund. The overall goal of the investment objective is to discover the optimal risk/return combination that accounts for the investor's constraints and risk tolerance.

Effective investment governance should also evaluate the liquidity aspects of investments. An allocation that has a relatively high number of illiquid assets will make it difficult to fund obligations during periods of market stress. In addition to liquidity risk, risks to consider include volatility risk and the risk of selling at the worst possible time. Investors should understand that asset allocations that provide high expected returns with high risk will lead to greater price swings. Overall, investors making asset allocation decisions must consider how risk sensitivities influence their required return.

Rights and Responsibilities

Investment governance assists with allocating the rights and responsibilities of the investment program. This allocation will vary depending on the investment program size; the availability of internal staff members; and the knowledge, skills, and abilities of internal staff. Effective governance aims to delegate investment decision-making to the best-qualified individuals. These individuals should have the knowledge and experience to make informed investment decisions. They should also have the capacity to manage the investment program responsibilities and be able to execute the investment program in a timely fashion.

Resource availability will impact the allocation of rights and responsibilities as well as investment program complexity. For example, smaller investment programs will likely have less complex investment options due to smaller asset sizes and fewer internal staff for managing those assets. On the other hand, large investment programs may pursue more complex strategies as long as a robust internal control process exists and the internal staff has appropriate knowledge and experience. However, large investment programs may run into governance issues due to capacity constraints where too many managers are involved in the investment decision-making process.

Investment Policy Statement

An effective investment program begins with a well-developed investment policy statement (IPS). The IPS serves as a roadmap for portfolio management and provides confidence to stakeholders that the investment program will be managed with due diligence and care.

Strategic Asset Allocation

The investment committee, which is the highest level of the governance structure, will typically approve the strategic asset allocation decision. A proposed asset allocation will be developed after (1) the IPS is constructed, (2) investment results are simulated over the appropriate time horizon(s), and (3) the risk and return attributes of all possible asset allocation strategies are considered. In addition to approving the asset allocation, good governance should also specify rebalancing decisions and responsibilities.

Reporting Framework

A reporting framework allows stakeholders to evaluate performance, investment guideline compliance, and the investment program's progress toward achieving its stated goals and objectives. The framework should outline the current status of the program, where it is in relation to its goals and objectives, and how management decisions have added or subtracted value. Proper benchmarking is important for evaluating the performance of investment managers and staff. Also, management reporting is needed for determining which sections of the portfolio are ahead or behind schedule. In addition, governance reporting should be conducted regularly to address investment program strengths and weaknesses.

Governance Audit

An independent third party should audit the effectiveness of the governance structure, policies, and procedures. The auditor examines governing documents, determines the organization's capacity to effectively execute decisions based on those documents, and reviews portfolio efficiency given any governance constraints. Effective investment governance aims to minimize *decision-reversal risk*, which is the risk of reversing investment decisions at the worst possible time (i.e., creating the maximum loss). This action helps the investment program survive unexpected periods of market stress. Effective investment governance also aims to provide durability by evaluating the turnover of the investment program staff and the investment committee as well as any overreliance on one staff member. New investment committee and staff members should be properly trained on investment documentation, policies, procedures, and decision-making skills to ensure the continued success of the investment program.

MODULE 3.2: ECONOMIC BALANCE SHEET

Video covering this content is available online.

LOS 3.b: Formulate an economic balance sheet for a client and interpret its implications for asset allocation.

The traditional accounting balance sheet encompasses an organization's assets, liabilities, and owner's equity. It is used by accountants to illustrate the financial position of an organization. In contrast, an **economic balance sheet** contains an organization's financial assets and liabilities, as well as any nonfinancial assets and liabilities that are applicable to the asset allocation decision. These nonfinancial assets and liabilities are referred to as **extended portfolio assets and liabilities** because they are not included on traditional balance sheets.

Investors making appropriate asset allocation decisions should recognize assets and liabilities in both the financial portfolio and the extended portfolio. Extended portfolio assets may include the present value of expected earnings (i.e., human capital) and the present value of pension income (for individual investors) as well as the present value of expected intellectual property royalties and underground mineral resources (for institutional investors). Extended portfolio liabilities may include the present value of expected consumption (for individual investors) and the present value of expected foundation payouts (for institutional investors). An example of an economic balance sheet for an institutional investor can be seen in Figure 3.1.

Figure 3.1: Economic Balance Sheet

Assets		**Liabilities and Net Worth**	
Financial Assets		*Financial Liabilities*	
Domestic equity	400	Short-term borrowing	100
Real estate	250	Mortgage obligations	200
Extended Assets		*Extended Liabilities*	
PV of expected royalties	150	PV of expected payouts	300
		Economic Net Worth	
		Economic assets – Economic liabilities	200
Total	800	**Total**	800

A practical application of an investment that includes human capital is a life-cycle balanced fund (i.e., target retirement fund). These funds consider the changing levels of human capital and financial capital for an individual investor over time. When an individual enters the workforce, human capital will be much greater than financial capital. However, as the individual ages, financial capital will begin to outweigh human capital because the present value of expected future earnings will gradually decline. At retirement, an individual's total wealth will be made up of financial capital.

Life-cycle balanced funds adjust asset allocations for individual investors over time by taking into account both financial assets and extended portfolio assets. For example, at age 25, a target-date fund may be invested in 85% equity and 15% bonds. This considers the fact that human capital has significant bond-like characteristics. As the investor ages, the equity/bond mix will increase its allocation to bonds as human capital decreases. At retirement (e.g., age 65), the target-date fund may be invested in an asset mix that is closer to 50% equity and 50% bonds.

MODULE 3.3: APPROACHES TO ASSET ALLOCATION

Video covering this content is available online.

LOS 3.c: Compare the investment objectives of asset-only, liability-relative, and goals-based asset allocation approaches.

There are three types of asset allocation approaches: (1) asset-only, (2) liability-relative, and (3) goals-based. In this section, we will discuss the investment objectives of each approach. These asset allocation approaches attempt to match investors' goals with their optimal level of risk.

Asset-only approaches make asset allocation decisions based solely on the investor's assets. An example of an asset-only approach is *mean-variance optimization* (MVO), which incorporates the expected returns, volatility, and correlations of asset classes. The investment objective for this approach is to maximize the expected return per unit of risk (e.g., maximize the Sharpe ratio). The chosen investments should consider investor constraints (stated in the IPS) as well as investor risk tolerance.

Liability-relative approaches involve asset allocation decisions based on funding liabilities, with the objective of paying liabilities when they come due. An example of a liability-relative approach is *surplus optimization*, which is based on principles from mean-variance asset allocation. The surplus is computed as the investor assets value minus the present value of investor liabilities. Modeling liabilities may be achieved by shorting an amount of bonds that matches the duration and present value of liabilities. Liabilities may also be modeled by creating a portfolio designed to hedge the liabilities. Asset allocation focused on funding liabilities is also known as *liability-driven investing* (LDI).

Goals-based approaches are geared toward asset allocations for subportfolios, which help individuals or families achieve lifestyle and aspirational financial objectives. For example, goals could involve maintaining a current lifestyle or donating money to a university at some point in the future. In order to achieve the stated goals, it is necessary to specify the type of cash flows needed (e.g., even, uneven, or bullet payment), the time horizon(s), and the level of risk tolerance in terms of the probability of attaining a certain goal. Each sub-portfolio will have a unique asset allocation designed to meet the stated goals. Summing these asset allocations will produce the investor's overall portfolio strategic asset allocation. Asset allocation focused on investor's goals is also known as *goals-based investing* (GBI).

Both liability-relative and goals-based asset allocation approaches are based on meeting liabilities. The main difference is that liability-relative approaches focus on the liabilities of institutional investors while goals-based approaches focus on the liabilities of individual investors. Institutional investors have legal obligations or debts, whereas individual investors wish to meet specific lifestyle goals. This suggests that penalties for not meeting liabilities are much higher for liability-relative approaches. In addition, the type and number of obligations will differ between approaches. Institutional investor obligations are constant and numerous (e.g., life insurance and pension benefit payments are the future liabilities of insurance companies and defined benefit pension plans), while individual investor goals are much less predictable. This suggests that institutional liabilities can be more confidently forecasted since the average of a large number of obligations is more certain than the uncertain time horizon needs of one individual investor.

Relevant Risk Concepts

LOS 3.d: Contrast concepts of risk relevant to asset-only, liability-relative, and goals-based asset allocation approaches.

Risk concepts associated with asset-only approaches focus on asset class risk as well as constructing effective asset class combinations. The relevant risk measure for MVO, the most popular asset-only approach, is the standard deviation of portfolio returns, which incorporates asset class volatilities and asset class return correlations. Other risk sensitivities, such as relative risk and downside risk, can also be measured with a mean-variance framework. For example, the risk relative to a benchmark can be modeled with tracking error, and downside risk can be modeled with value at risk (VaR), semivariance, or maximum drawdown.

Monte Carlo simulation is a statistical modeling tool often used to complement MVO. For example, a manager could begin by selecting several optimal portfolios using MVO that have acceptable risk and return for the client and then use Monte Carlo simulation to generate multiple simulated paths, which display how these portfolios would perform over time. This action would provide useful information on downside risk when portfolios encounter a market stress scenario. These results can then be used to refine asset allocation decisions.

Risk concepts associated with liability-relative approaches focus on not having enough assets to pay liabilities when they come due. The volatility of contributions used for funding liabilities is also a risk. The standard deviation of the surplus may be used as the relevant risk measure. In general, the differences between asset and liability characteristics (e.g., size, sensitivity to interest rate changes) are the main drivers of risk for liability-relative asset allocation approaches.

Risk concepts associated with goals-based approaches focus on the risk of not being able to achieve the stated financial goals. If an investor has multiple goals, then the risks will encompass multiple future time periods. Thus, portfolio risk under a goals-based approach is the weighted sum of the risk that is attached to each goal.

MODULE QUIZ 3.1, 3.2, 3.3

1. Which of the following investment objectives would *most likely* be associated with a defined benefit pension fund?
   A. Plan assets should meet current and future plan liabilities.
   B. Assets should provide for retirement subject to each investor's constraints and risk tolerance.
   C. The rate of return should meet the current distribution rate plus future inflation.
2. Which of the following investments would *most likely* be part of the extended portfolio of the assets and liabilities sections on an economic balance sheet?
   A. Human capital.
   B. Financial assets.
   C. Financial liabilities.
3. Which of the following asset allocation approaches is focused on achieving lifestyle and aspirational financial objectives?
   A. Asset-only approach.
   B. Goals-based approach.
   C. Liability-relative approach.
4. The asset allocation approach that is concerned with the risk of not having enough assets to pay liabilities when they come due is known as:
   A. asset-only.
   B. goals-based.
   C. liability-relative.

MODULE 3.4: ALLOCATION BY ASSET CLASS OR RISK FACTOR

Video covering this content is available online.

LOS 3.e: Explain how asset classes are used to represent exposures to systematic risk and discuss criteria for asset class specification.

An asset class is a group of assets that have similar investment characteristics. Each asset class has its own quantifiable systematic risk, and strategic asset allocation is a conscious effort to gain the desired exposure to systematic risk via specific weights to individual asset classes. Exposure to specific asset classes in specific proportions enables portfolio managers to effectively monitor and control their systematic risk exposure. In other words, strategic asset allocation reflects the investor's desired systematic risk exposure.

In a generic sense, there are three categories of "super asset classes": (1) capital assets, which provide a continuous source of value (e.g., dividends), (2) consumable or transformable assets, which can be consumed or transformed into a source of value (e.g., commodities), and (3) store-of-value assets, which provide value when exchanged or sold (e.g., currencies, art).

For the purposes of asset allocation, it is necessary to define asset classes. With this information, investors and managers can better distinguish among asset classes when developing an investment strategy. For example, combining emerging market equities and domestic equities into a single asset class labeled *equities* would be appropriate only from a general description standpoint; their risk and return characteristics are obviously different. The following criteria can be used to specify asset classes:

- *Assets in an asset class should have similar attributes from both a descriptive and statistical perspective.*
- *Assets cannot be classified into more than one asset class.* If it can be legitimately argued that assets can be placed in more than one class, the descriptions of the classes are too vague.
- *Asset classes should not be highly correlated in order to provide desired diversification.* A high correlation between classes would indicate that the classes are related from a risk and return standpoint. This would defeat the purpose of holding separate classes in an allocation.
- *Asset classes should cover all possible investable assets.* This factor not only increases the set of investable assets, but also pushes up the efficient frontier (i.e., increases expected return at all levels of risk).
- *Asset classes should contain a sufficiently large percentage of liquid assets.* If liquidity and transaction costs are significant, the asset class may not be ideal for investment because it lacks sufficient liquidity.

Some well-accepted asset classes include domestic equity, domestic fixed income, global equity, global fixed income, cash and equivalents, and alternative investments, which may be further divided into classes such as real estate, private equity, et cetera.

Too much granularity (number of subdivisions of classes used) in the asset allocation can make it difficult to construct an optimal portfolio based on an investor's required level of return and risk. Within each asset class, sub–asset classes can be created that are less distinct than their corresponding broad asset classes. For example, Figure 3.2 shows how the asset class of global equity can be broken down into U.S. and non–U.S. equity securities. The sub–asset class of U.S. equities can be further segmented into large-cap and small-cap equities.

Figure 3.2: Asset Classes and Sub–Asset Classes

Asset Classes	Sub-Asset Classes	
Global equity	U.S. equities	Large-cap equities
		Small-cap equities
	Non–U.S. equities	Developed countries
		Emerging countries
Global fixed income	U.S. debt	Investment-grade debt
		High-yield debt
	Non–U.S. debt	Developed countries
		Emerging countries

Strategic asset allocation should focus primarily on the asset class divisions that have distinctly different characteristics and will provide diversification (i.e., global equity versus fixed income). As you move down in granularity (level of subdivision) the differential between classes will shrink (i.e., U.S. and non–U.S. equity will be less distinctly different from each other than global equity versus global fixed income). However, when progressing from strategic asset allocation to policy implementation and tactical asset allocation, decisions may focus more on the sub–asset classes.

Common Risk Factors

LOS 3.f: Explain the use of risk factors in asset allocation and their relation to traditional asset class–based approaches.

Asset classes have traditionally been used as units of analysis when making asset allocation decisions. This process is known as *asset-based asset allocation*. For example, MVO incorporates expected return, volatility, and correlation estimates from the selected asset classes. However, using asset classes in this fashion may be problematic due to overlapping risk factors among asset classes.

An investor selects asset classes based on their desired exposure to common risk factors. Examples of risk factors include volatility, liquidity, inflation, interest rates, duration, foreign exchange, and default risk. As mentioned, risk factor exposures may overlap across multiple asset classes. For example, the asset classes of domestic equity and domestic fixed income will both share exposures to foreign exchange (in the sense that changes in value of the domestic currency can affect profitability of issuers and return on investments in their debt and equity), liquidity, and volatility risk factors. Examining these overlapping risk factors can help investors identify the correlations among asset classes.

Due to overlapping risk factors, it may be insightful to focus on risk factors rather than traditional asset classes as units of analysis. This is accomplished by identifying the risk factors as well as the desired exposure to each factor. Multifactor models can then be used for asset allocation by creating factor portfolios, which isolate systematic risk exposures (i.e., nondiversifiable risks). This process is known as *factor-based asset allocation*.

This does not mean risk factor analysis is inherently more useful. It has its own limitations. For example investors may not be able to directly invest in all risk factors. But risk factor analysis may offer additional insight, and risk factors often correspond to expected return premiums. Some risk factors may be investable with spread positions, which take long and short positions in assets, or by using derivatives. For example, to isolate inflation risk, an investor would go long Treasuries (which reflect compensation for consensus-expected inflation) and short inflation-linked bonds (which will adjust and compensate for actual future inflation); or an investor would invest in volatility index (VIX) futures with payoffs based on actual change in volatility.

Reading 3

Strategic Asset Allocation

LOS 3.g: Recommend and justify an asset allocation based on an investor's objectives and constraints.

Strategic asset allocation combines capital market expectations (expected return, volatility, and correlation) with an investor's risk, return, and investment constraints (from the IPS). Strategic asset allocation is long term in nature, and the weights are called *targets* and the portfolio represented by the strategic asset allocation is a *policy portfolio*, *target portfolio*, or *benchmark*.

Most quantitative approaches to asset allocation are based on utility theory. This framework uses a utility function that incorporates investor risk aversion. Expected utility for a certain asset allocation is determined with a distribution of ending wealth values, which is based on asset class weights, asset class returns, and beginning wealth values. The maximum level of utility, subject to asset class constraints, will represent the investor's optimal asset association given the investment horizon.

Selecting and justifying a strategic asset allocation based on investor objectives and constraints is outlined in the following steps:

1. *Determine investor objectives.* Relevant questions include the following: How will the investor use these assets? What would the investor like to achieve? What are the investor liabilities and goals? How should the objectives be measured?
2. *Determine investor tolerance for risk.* Relevant questions include the following: What are the investor's sensitivities to risk? How should risk be measured in terms of asset allocation?
3. *Determine investor time horizon(s).* Relevant questions include the following: What investment horizon should be used to evaluate investor objectives? What investment horizon should be used to evaluate investor risk tolerance?
4. *Determine investor constraints.* Relevant questions include the following: What is the investor's tax situation? Are there any social, environmental, or governance considerations? Are legal, regulatory, and political issues a consideration? Does the IPS indicate any additional constraints?
5. *Select the asset allocation approach.* This is the asset allocation that is most ideal for the investor's situation (e.g., asset-only, liability-relative, goals-based).
6. *Specify the asset classes.* Once the asset classes are appropriately specified, capital market expectations can be established.
7. *Develop potential asset allocations.* With optimization procedures, a number of asset allocation choices can be constructed for investor consideration.
8. *Simulate results of potential asset allocations.* The potential asset allocations should be tested to see if the results align with the investor's objectives and risk tolerance for the chosen investment horizon.
9. *Repeat Step 7 until the optimal asset allocation is discovered.*

Once the strategic allocation has been implemented, it should be monitored regularly as specified in the IPS. The monitoring process should contain a feedback loop so that changes in long-term market factors can be incorporated back into the model. An assessment can then be made to determine whether adjustments to the strategic allocation are justified. If the market changes are only short term in nature, the manager should consider implementing tactical allocation measures, as will be discussed elsewhere.

MODULE QUIZ 3.4

1. Which of the following statements identifies one criterion for specifying an asset class when making asset allocation decisions?
   A. Assets may be classified into more than one asset class.
   B. Asset classes cover all possible investable assets.
   C. Asset classes should be highly correlated in order to provide desired diversification.
2. Duration and convexity would *most likely* be risk factors for which type of asset class?
   A. Domestic equities.
   B. Domestic real estate.
   C. Domestic fixed income.

MODULE 3.5: EXAMPLE: STRATEGIC ASSET ALLOCATION

Video covering this content is available online.

PROFESSOR'S NOTE

The following example provides a general overview of constructing a strategic asset allocation.

EXAMPLE: Strategic asset allocation

Nathan Tillman is a 50-year-old entrepreneur who plans to retire in five years. He is considering purchasing an annuity for retirement. He has a $5 million portfolio with $1 million in real estate and $700,000 in mortgage debt. He would like to eliminate all mortgage debt before retirement. His son, David, is 18 years old and starting college this year with eventual plans for medical school. Tillman estimates he will contribute $500,000 to his son's education. Tillman is generally conservative with his investments, does not like portfolio volatility, and does not have any social or environmental investment constraints. For Asset Allocation A and then for Asset Allocation B:

- **State** whether it is most consistent with (1) an asset-only, (2) a liability-relative, or (3) a goals-based approach to asset allocation.

- **Give** *one* reason based on Tillman's situation that the approach is appropriate for Tillman.

Do not draw any conclusion as to the optimal overall approach to allocation for Tillman.

Asset Allocation	Cash	Global Equities	Global Fixed Income	Diversifying Strategies
A	45%	15%	35%	5%
B	5%	50%	20%	25%

Answer:

Asset Allocation A is consistent with a goal-based approach because:

- It has more than sufficient cash for liquidity needs of $1.2 million to pay the mortgage and education expense. The cash can also be used for the possible annuity purchase.
- The high allocation to cash would reduce portfolio volatility.
- It fits his conservative investment views.

Asset Allocation B is consistent with an asset-only approach because:

- It emphasizes higher growth equity.
- It provides diversification with alternative investments and some fixed income.

Note that you were directed not to draw any final conclusion. This was an initial step that illustrates the need to develop a complete IPS and consider additional asset allocations that may best meet those objectives.

MODULE 3.6: OTHER APPROACHES AND ISSUES

Video covering this content is available online.

LOS 3.h: Describe the use of the global market portfolio as a baseline portfolio in asset allocation.

Financial theory proposes that the first asset allocation to consider should be the **global market portfolio**. This portfolio contains all available risky assets (i.e., global equity, global fixed income, real estate, etc.) in proportion to their total market values. It is also the portfolio that minimizes diversifiable risk since it is the most diversified portfolio possible. The market portfolio is found on the efficient frontier by drawing a line from the risk-free asset that is tangent to the efficient frontier (known as the capital market line). The point of tangency is the location of the global market portfolio.

The asset class weights within the global market portfolio serve as a good starting point for asset allocation. The portfolio's weights can then be adjusted to meet specific investor objectives, constraints, and desires (e.g., a home-country or small-cap basis).

Note that it's challenging to invest in some asset classes within the global market portfolio. For example, investments in residential real estate or private equity may not be practical for individual investors. For this reason, investors often use a proxy to represent the global market portfolio, such as a portfolio of exchange-traded funds (ETFs).

PROFESSOR'S NOTE

Recall that nondiversifiable risk can also be called market, priced, or systematic risk. Diversifiable risk can also be called non-market, non-priced, company-specific, or unsystematic risk. Remember that you should expect compensation in the form of higher expected return for taking nondiversifiable risk but not for taking diversifiable risk.

Strategic Implementation Choices

LOS 3.i: Discuss strategic implementation choices in asset allocation, including passive/active choices and vehicles for implementing passive and active mandates.

Once the strategic asset allocation has been constructed, implementation choices must be made regarding passive/active management for both asset class weights and allocations within asset classes. The first aspect of passive/active choices is to determine if the investor should deviate from the strategic asset allocation by adjusting the asset mix. The second aspect is to decide how investors should make allocations within selected asset classes. Managing and monitoring the portfolio in terms of a client's changing needs is an important element of portfolio management.

Passive/Active Choices for Asset Class Weights

Tactical asset allocation (TAA) is an active management strategy that deviates from the strategic asset allocation (SAA) to take advantage of perceived *short-term* opportunities in the market. TAA introduces additional risk, seeking incremental return, often called alpha. These deviations from the SAA weightings by asset class should be restricted by risk budgets or rebalancing ranges that control the amount of deviation. The deviations may be based on forecasted asset class valuation, business cycle state, or stock price momentum. A multiperiod view of the investment horizon is sometimes referred to as **dynamic asset allocation (DAA)**. DAA recognizes that asset (and liability) performance in one period affects the required rate of return and acceptable level of risk for subsequent periods. Changes to the SAA may be limited to simply adjusting the mix between stocks, bonds, and cash. Conversely, global TAA may involve a broader and more complex multiasset approach.

Reading 3

With tactical asset allocation, there is a tradeoff between potential outperformance and tracking error. A key limitation of this approach is the additional trading and monitoring costs as well as possible capital gains taxes. Thus, the decision to implement a tactical asset allocation should be evaluated under a cost-benefit approach.

Passive and Active Choices Within Asset Classes

Passive and active management choices can also be made regarding the allocations within asset classes. Under **passive management**, investor insights or expectations do not impact the composition of the portfolio. Examples of a passive approach include indexing or holding bonds to maturity. With indexing, the portfolio may add or drop positions based on the index holdings, but it would not react to the changing expectations of investors regarding valuations. In contrast, under **active management**, the portfolio composition changes when investor insights or expectations change. The goal of active management is to earn risk-adjusted returns that exceed an associated passive benchmark.

To better understand the degree of passive/active management in a portfolio, we can view decisions along a spectrum from most passive to most active. The most passive approach would include buying and holding a self-rebalancing, broad index of risky assets, such as the global market portfolio. Tilting the allocation toward a certain investment style index (e.g., growth equity index) is slightly more active given that it involves an active decision, but it still uses the passive implementation of indexing. The next step toward a more active approach would involve taking a growth investment approach while using security selection to enhance returns. The most active approach would include unconstrained mandates where the portfolio is not managed with regard to traditional benchmarks.

In general, indexing is considered a low-cost means of investing. However, some transaction costs are involved when the portfolio must adjust positions based on the changing composition of the index. Furthermore, if the index is tracked with a different weighting approach, such as equally weighted rather than market-cap weighted, additional transaction costs will apply. Portfolios that follow a fixed-income index will also incur transaction costs as bonds reach maturity, are called, or default. As a portfolio moves from passive to active, tracking error and expected active return relative to a benchmark will increase. These measures quantify the degree of active management within a portfolio.

The decision of where to invest along the active/passive spectrum depends on the following factors:

- Availability of appropriate investments (e.g., a relevant index).
- Active management scalability in terms of value added from each active decision.
- Investor constraints, such as social and environmental concerns, when using a passive approach.
- An investor belief in efficient markets, which would discourage the use of active management.

- The cost-benefit tradeoff where additional transaction costs are needed for achieving excess returns.
- The tax status of investors, which differs between taxable and tax-exempt investors.

Risk Budgeting

Asset allocation can also be conducted with a risk perspective. The types of risk to take, as well as the amount of risk to take, is addressed with **risk budgeting**. Measuring risk may differ depending on the risk focus, such as volatility of returns or tail risk. In these cases, risk would be quantified with the standard deviation of returns and value at risk (VaR), respectively. Risk budgets can be established in either relative or absolute terms and stated in either money or percentage terms (e.g., 10% return volatility). These risk budgets specify how risk should be distributed among portfolio assets without regard to asset expected returns.

In the context of making passive/active asset allocation choices, active risk budgeting determines how much additional risk the investor is willing to take relative to the benchmark. The objective of this approach is to outperform the benchmark while sticking to the investor's risk budget. Regarding passive/active choices for the asset class mix, active risk is determined relative to the strategic asset allocation benchmark. Regarding passive/active choices for allocation within asset classes, active risk is determined relative to the asset class benchmark.

Rebalancing

Reading 3

LOS 3.j: Discuss strategic considerations in rebalancing asset allocations.

Strategic asset allocation responds to the interaction of the investor's long-term strategic (policy) needs and long-run capital market expectations. The investor's goals are expressed in terms of IPS objectives and constraints. The allocation itself is typically specified in a range of percentages (e.g., a strategic allocation for domestic equity of 30% to 40%), and if the actual percentage wanders outside that range, the portfolio needs to be rebalanced. Rebalancing can be triggered by normal asset price changes, which cause the asset mix to fluctuate from its target weights.

The primary benefit of rebalancing is maintaining the investor's desired exposure to systematic risk factors. If the portfolio is allowed to simply drift, the riskier assets in the portfolio tend to take over. For example, as the value of the equities in a portfolio increases, the equities become an ever larger percentage of the portfolio and the risk of the portfolio increases accordingly. Only by rebalancing the portfolio (e.g., selling equities and buying debt) will the portfolio return to its original risk and return characteristics as specified in the investor's IPS.

Rebalancing also provides discipline. Often the investor will see significant gains in the equity portion of the portfolio and want to "let it ride." Successful performance may lead the client to react to temporary market conditions rather than follow a long-term, disciplined approach. But "letting it ride" can also lead to the failure to realize the gains from temporarily overvalued securities before they fall back to their true values. This could be considered a potential cost of not rebalancing.

Of course, when equities become too large of a portion within the portfolio and we sell them to rebalance, there is an associated tax liability. In addition, the investor will face transaction costs. The costs of rebalancing can be affected by the conditions under which the trade is made (i.e., whether the trade requires liquidity from or provides liquidity to the market). If the manager is selling when other managers are selling, the trade requires liquidity and the associated transaction cost (bid-ask spread) can be substantial. If the trade provides liquidity, on the other hand (e.g., selling when others are buying), the costs may be minimal.

Rebalancing Approaches

Rebalancing an allocation to its precise target weight requires more or less constant trading. With constant analysis and trading come the associated transaction costs and the inability to time trades. Rather than set strict target allocations, managers will set allowable ranges that they consider optimal for the asset classes. In order to provide discipline to portfolio rebalancing, managers can adopt either calendar-based rebalancing or range-based balancing.

Calendar rebalancing. As its name implies, calendar rebalancing is rebalancing the portfolio to its strategic allocation on a predetermined, regular basis (e.g., monthly or quarterly). Generally, the frequency of rebalancing depends on the volatility of the portfolio, but sometimes rebalancing is scheduled to coincide with review dates.

The primary benefit to calendar rebalancing is that it provides discipline without the requirement for constant monitoring. The drawback is that the portfolio could stray considerably between rebalancing dates and return to its strategic allocation ranges on the rebalancing date. In other words, rebalancing is related to the passage of time rather than the value of the portfolio.

Percentage-range rebalancing. With this approach, rebalancing is triggered by changes in value rather than calendar dates. The manager sets what are called tolerance bands or corridors that are considered optimal for each asset class. For example, a corridor of 50% ± 5% would indicate that the related asset class must stay within a band of 45% to 55%. If the asset class wanders outside that corridor, which would no doubt mean other classes have violated their corridors also, the portfolio is rebalanced.

By not waiting for specified rebalancing dates, range-based rebalancing provides the benefit of minimizing the degree to which asset classes can violate their allocation corridors. Cost is increased by the time and expense of constantly monitoring the portfolio (as compared to only checking valuations on the specified calendar dates) and by potentially more frequent trading.

When applying range-based rebalancing, the following four questions need to be addressed:

- Who is ultimately responsible for rebalancing the portfolio?
- How frequently should the portfolio be monitored for rebalancing decisions?

- What is the size of the rebalancing corridors?
- Should rebalancing to target weights be fully or only partially corrected?

Strategic Considerations

The optimal width of the corridor for an asset class will depend on the following:

- **Transaction costs.** Obviously, the more expensive it is to trade, the less frequently you should trade. If an asset is particularly illiquid, for example, trading can be quite expensive. In that case, the corridor for the class should be wide. In general, the more illiquid the asset, the wider the corridor.
- **Risk tolerance.** More (less) risk-averse investors will have tighter (wider) rebalancing corridors.
- **Correlations.** The more highly correlated the assets (allocations) in a portfolio, the less frequently the portfolio will require balancing. If all assets tend to move together, their values will tend to stay within acceptable ranges. For example, if stocks and bonds both increase 20% in value (assuming only stocks and bonds in the portfolio), their weights in the portfolio will probably stay within acceptable limits. However, if stocks increase 20% while bonds decrease 20%, they will probably both violate their corridors.
- **Momentum.** If investors believe that current trends will continue, an argument can be made for using wider rebalancing corridors. Conversely, if investors anticipate mean reversion, tighter rebalancing corridors should be applied.
- **Liquidity.** Illiquid investments, such as private equity and real estate, are typically associated with larger trading costs. These liquidity costs encourage the use of wider rebalancing corridors.
- **Derivatives.** Rather than selling underlying assets, a derivatives overlay strategy can be used to synthetically rebalance a portfolio. This approach results in lower transaction costs, lower taxes, and can be executed quicker and easier compared to rebalancing with only the underlying stock and bonds. The tradeoff is that derivatives require additional risk management when used as a rebalancing tool.
- **Taxes.** When making rebalancing decisions, taxes must be considered since realized capital gains and losses will impact investor taxes. Therefore, taxable portfolios will typically have wider rebalancing corridors than tax-exempt portfolios. The corridors may also be asymmetric due to tax savings (i.e., loss harvesting). This suggests that the range may be less below a certain target weight than above (e.g., the tolerance band may go from 48% to 55% for a 50% target weight).

Asset class **volatility** also has an impact on optimal corridor width. In the simplest situations, higher volatility *most likely* calls for narrower corridors in order to control risk. But the impact of volatility can be more complex than that. **Higher volatility** (in the absence of high positive correlation between classes) will lead asset class weights to shift more quickly.

- But more frequent rebalancing increases transaction costs. This argues for wider corridors to control transaction costs, particularly when those costs are substantial.

- This argues for narrower corridors to control risk exposure. (Consider this the most likely conclusion.)

Ultimately the choice of corridor width depends on a trade-off between risk control, transaction costs, and correlations between classes. In complex situations, a quantified cost-benefit analysis will be required.

MODULE QUIZ 3.5, 3.6

1. Jack Manning, CFA, and Tess Brown, CFA, have just joined a financial planning firm. They will work as a team assessing and managing the portfolios of individual clients. Manning will specialize in forming long-term capital market expectations. Brown focuses on relative value models to assess shorter-term over- and undervaluation. Based on this information, we would define the focus of:
   A. both Manning and Brown as tactical asset allocation.
   B. both Manning and Brown as strategic asset allocation.
   C. Manning as strategic asset allocation and Brown as tactical asset allocation.
2. Which of the following statements is *most correct* regarding the global market portfolio as the baseline portfolio in asset allocation?
   A. The market portfolio contains most investable risky assets.
   B. The market portfolio minimizes total risk since it is the most diversified portfolio.
   C. Investors can use a proxy to represent the market portfolio, such as a portfolio of exchange-traded funds (ETFs).
3. Deviation from strategic asset allocation due to short-term capital market expectations is *most correctly* called:
   A. active management.
   B. tactical asset allocation (TAA).
   C. alpha management.
4. Which of the following asset allocation rebalancing techniques provides discipline without need for constant monitoring?
   A. Range-based balancing.
   B. Corridor-based rebalancing.
   C. Calendar-based rebalancing.

KEY CONCEPTS

LOS 3.a

Investment governance models should:

- Establish long-term and short-term investment objectives.
- Allocate the rights and responsibilities of all the involved parties.
- Specify processes for creating an investment policy statement (IPS).
- Specify processes for creating a strategic asset allocation.
- Apply a reporting framework to monitor the investment program's stated goals and objectives.
- Include periodic review of the governance policies by an independent third party.

LOS 3.b

An economic balance sheet contains an organization's financial assets and liabilities, as well as any nonfinancial assets and liabilities that are applicable to the asset allocation decision. These nonfinancial assets and liabilities are referred to as extended portfolio assets and liabilities because they are not included on traditional balance sheets. A practical application of an investment that includes human capital (an extended portfolio asset) is a life-cycle balanced fund. These funds consider the changing levels of human capital and financial capital for an individual investor over time.

LOS 3.c

There are three types of asset allocation approaches: (1) asset-only, (2) liability-relative, and (3) goals-based. Asset-only approaches make asset allocation decisions based on the investor's assets. Liability-relative approaches involve asset allocation decisions based on funding liabilities. Goals-based approaches are geared toward asset allocations for subportfolios, which help an individual achieve lifestyle and aspirational financial objectives.

LOS 3.d

Risk concepts associated with asset-only approaches focus on asset class risk as well as constructing effective asset class combinations. The relevant risk measure is the standard deviation of portfolio returns. Risk concepts associated with liability-relative approaches focus on not having enough assets to pay liabilities when they come due. The relevant risk measure is the standard deviation of the surplus. Risk concepts associated with goals-based approaches focus on the risk of not being able to achieve the stated financial goals.

LOS 3.e

Asset classes have been appropriately specified if:

- Assets in an asset class have similar attributes from both a descriptive and statistical perspective.
- Assets cannot be classified into more than one asset class.

- Asset classes are not highly correlated.
- Asset classes cover all possible investable assets.
- Asset classes contain a sufficiently large percentage of liquid assets.

LOS 3.f

Investors select asset classes based on their desired exposure to common risk factors. Examples of risk factors include volatility, liquidity, inflation, interest rates, duration, foreign exchange, and default risk. Risk factor exposures may overlap across multiple asset classes. Examining these overlapping risk factors can help investors identify the correlations among asset classes.

LOS 3.g

Strategic asset allocation is long term in nature; hence, the weights are called *targets* and the portfolio represented by the strategic asset allocation is called the *policy portfolio*.

Selecting and justifying a strategic asset allocation based on investor objectives and constraints is outlined in the following nine steps:

1. Determine investor objectives.
2. Determine investor tolerance for risk.
3. Determine investor time horizon(s).
4. Determine investor constraints.
5. Select the asset allocation approach.
6. Specify the asset classes.
7. Develop potential asset allocations.
8. Simulate results of potential asset allocations.
9. Repeat Step 7 until the optimal asset allocation is discovered.

LOS 3.h

Investors may consider the global market portfolio as a baseline asset allocation. It will minimize (eliminate) diversifiable risk. Because it's challenging to invest in some asset classes within the market portfolio, investors often use a proxy, such as a portfolio of exchange-traded funds (ETFs).

LOS 3.i

The SAA can be implemented with passive or active management for both asset class weights and allocations within asset classes.

- TAA introduces active decisions to deviate from the SAA in an effort to add value, but it is likely to increase error.
- Active management security selection is based on investor insights or expectations.

Risk budgeting specifies which risks and how much of each risk can be taken. Active risk budgeting specifies risk as allowable deviations from the portfolio's benchmark.

LOS 3.j

Calendar rebalancing is done on a periodic basis, and percentage-range rebalancing is done when a corridor is breached.

Wider optimal corridors are associated with:

- Higher transaction costs (including costs due to tax and illiquidity).
- Increased investor risk tolerance.
- Higher correlations among asset classes.
- Belief in momentum and that trends persist.
- Less volatile asset classes.

Derivatives may allow synthetic rebalancing at a lower cost.

Capital gains taxation suggests setting asymmetric rebalancing corridors (e.g., a 28% to 35% range around a 30% target weight).

ANSWER KEY FOR MODULE QUIZZES

Module Quiz 3.1, 3.2, 3.3

1. **A** The objective for a defined benefit pension fund is for plan assets to meet current and ongoing plan liabilities. Choice B is generally appropriate but phrased more for an individual investor, and Choice C is appropriate for a foundation or endowment fund (and sometimes for individuals). Defined benefit plan inflation issues are already reflected in the actuary provided present value of the liabilities (PVL). (Module 3.1, LOS 3.a)

2. **A** An economic balance sheet contains all of an organization's financial assets and liabilities, as well as any nonfinancial assets and liabilities that are applicable to the asset allocation decision. Extended portfolio assets may include the present value of expected earnings (i.e., human capital). The others are already part of a more traditional balance sheet. They are part of the economic balance sheet but not the extended section. (Module 3.2, LOS 3.b)

3. **B** Goals-based approaches are geared toward asset allocations for subportfolios, which help individuals or families achieve lifestyle and aspirational financial objectives. (Module 3.3, LOS 3.c)

4. **C** Risk concepts associated with liability-relative asset allocation approaches focus on not having enough assets to pay liabilities when they come due. (Module 3.3, LOS 3.c)

Module Quiz 3.4

1. **B** As a group, asset classes cover all possible investable assets. Assets cannot be classified into more than one asset class. Also, asset classes should not be highly correlated. (LOS 3.e)

2. **C** The asset class of domestic fixed income would most likely include default risk, duration, and convexity risk factors in addition to foreign exchange, liquidity, and volatility risk factors. (LOS 3.f)

Module Quiz 3.5, 3.6

1. **C** Manning is using longer-term capital market expectations to form strategic asset allocation, while Brown is looking at shorter-term indicators, which is TAA. (Module 3.6, LOS 3.i)

2. **C** The global market portfolio contains *all* available risky assets in proportion to their total market values. It is also the portfolio that minimizes *diversifiable* risk since it is the most diversified portfolio possible. The total risk (standard deviation) of the market portfolio is not the lowest possible. Over any specific time period the risk-free asset has zero standard deviation. It's challenging to invest in some asset classes within the global market portfolio. For this reason, investors often use a proxy to represent the global market portfolio, such as a portfolio of ETFs. (Module 3.6, LOS 3.h)

3. **B** Short-term deviations from the strategic asset allocation to take advantage of short-term capital market expectations is called TAA. The motives for TAA may well include active management and adding alpha, but they are less accurate labels for what was described. (Module 3.6, LOS 3.i)

4. **C** The primary benefit to calendar rebalancing is that it provides discipline without the requirement for constant monitoring. Range- or corridor-based rebalancing provides the benefit of minimizing the degree to which asset classes can violate their allocation corridors, but it can be more costly in that it requires continual monitoring of the portfolio. (Module 3.6, LOS 3.j)

READING 4

Principles of Asset Allocation

EXAM FOCUS

The reading reviews the mean-variance optimization (MVO) approach to strategic asset allocation (SAA) that has been taught at Levels I and II. The focus then shifts to MVO pitfalls and how MVO can be more practically applied to real-world portfolios.

The mathematics behind many of these discussions is beyond the scope of the exam or a typical charterholder. Do not try to learn details that are not covered in the material. If you want to pursue some of these for personal interest after the exam, a Google search is a good starting point.

MODULE 4.1: BASIC MEAN-VARIANCE OPTIMIZATION

Video covering this content is available online.

LOS 4.a: Describe and evaluate the use of mean–variance optimization in asset allocation.

Creating a diversified portfolio with allocations to multiple asset classes requires:

- Asset allocation decision: using the investors' objectives and constraints to identify the appropriate portfolio weights for the various asset classes.
- Implementation decisions: identifying the specific assets within each asset class according to the weights specified in the first step.

Mean-variance optimization (MVO) is the most common approach to asset allocation. It assumes investors are risk averse, so they prefer more return for the same level of risk. Given an opportunity set of investable assets, their expected returns and variances, as well as the pairwise correlations between them, MVO identifies the portfolio allocations that maximize return for every level of risk. If the MVO analysis includes all investable risky assets, the result is the familiar "efficient frontier" (at least it should be familiar to the Level III candidate!), as shown in Figure 4.1. The analysis can also be constrained by an investor's objectives and constraints to some subset of assets suitable to that investor.

Figure 4.1: Mean-Variance Efficient Frontier

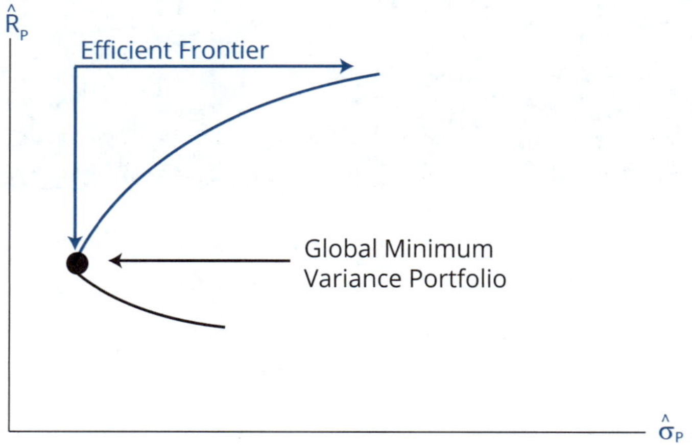

One approach to finding the optimal point on the efficient frontier for a given investor is to maximize that investor's utility:

Utility maximization: $U_m = E(R_m) - 0.005 \times \lambda \times Var_m$

U_m = the investor's utility from investing in a portfolio with asset allocation m

$E(R_m)$ = the expected return of the portfolio with asset allocation m (expressed as a %)

λ = the investor's risk aversion coefficient ("lambda")

$Var_m = \sigma^2_m$ = the variance of the portfolio with asset allocation m (expressed as a %)

PROFESSOR'S NOTE

The investor's utility function as shown assumes the expected return and variance are expressed in percentage terms (e.g., 8% is input as 8.00) so that the appropriate coefficient is 0.005. If the expected return and variance are expressed in decimal terms (e.g., 0.08), you should use the coefficient 0.5.

Lambda captures each individual investor's preference for trading off risk and return. If you look closely at the formula, you'll see that higher expected return for the same level of risk will increase the investor's utility, while a higher risk for the same level of return will decrease the investor's utility. This is consistent with a risk-averse investor, as it imposes a "penalty" for risk. U_m is also referred to as the *certainty-equivalent return.*

Lambda is unique to each individual and is based on the investor's willingness and capacity to take on risk. A risk-neutral investor will have a lambda of 0, although in practice it is typically assumed to be between 1 and 10 with an average level of 4.

Maximization problems in general usually also have constraints. In other words, the objective function is maximized subject to one or more constraints. These are restrictions on the variables in the objective function. In MVO, the constraints typically involve the portfolio weights, but they can also reflect restrictions on portfolio expected return, variance, or both.

The most common constraint in MVO is called the *budget constraint* or the *unity constraint*, which means the asset weights must add up to 100%. The next most common constraint used in MVO is the *nonnegativity constraint*, which means all weights in the portfolio are positive and between 0% and 100% (there are no short positions in the SAA). We will discuss other common constraints throughout this topic review.

A graphical depiction of MVO is shown in Figure 4.2.

Figure 4.2: MVO Process

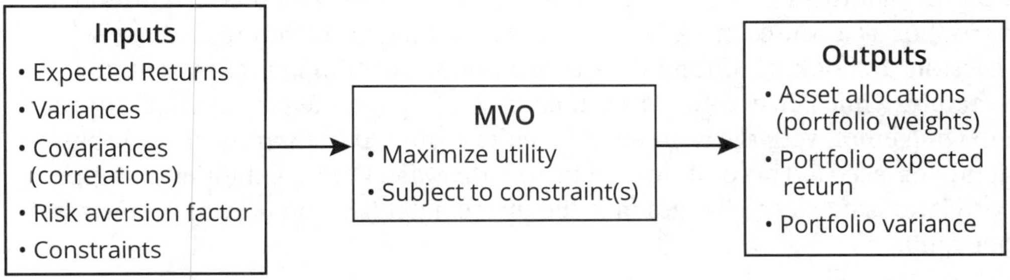

Levels I and II focused on a more academic treatment of MVO. That approach assumed:

- All tradable assets were included in the optimization and efficient frontier.
  - We will no longer assume all assets are used or that the efficient frontier constructed from all assets is necessarily optimal for a given investor.
- That a true risk-free asset exists and the optimal allocation line between the risk-free asset and the efficient frontier identifies an optimal (the market) portfolio that all investors should use (allocating between the tangent portfolio and risk-free asset). That optimal tangent portfolio is the portfolio on the efficient frontier with the highest Sharpe ratio.
  - We will no longer assume a true risk-free asset exists where risk-free means the variance of return is zero and return is uncorrelated with the return of other assets (correlation = 0).

Criticisms of MVO

There are a number of criticisms of MVO that we will address throughout this reading.

1. **GIGO**: The quality of the output from the MVO (portfolio allocations) is highly sensitive to the quality of the inputs (i.e., expected returns, variances, and correlations). In other settings, this is often called the "garbage-in-garbage-out" (GIGO) problem. Although all three inputs are a source of estimation error in MVO, expected returns are particularly problematic, so we focus here on addressing the quality of the expected return inputs.

2. **Concentrated asset class allocations**: MVO often identifies efficient portfolios that are highly concentrated in a subset of asset classes, with zero allocation to others; in other words, lowest calculated standard deviation is not the same thing as practical diversification.
3. **Skewness and kurtosis**: MVO analysis, by definition, only looks at the first two moments of the return distribution: expected return and variance; it does not take into account skewness or kurtosis. But empirical evidence suggests quite strongly that asset returns are not normally distributed: there is significant skewness and kurtosis in actual returns.
4. **Risk diversification**: MVO identifies an asset allocation diversified across asset classes but not necessarily the sources of risk. For example, equities and fixed-income securities are two different asset classes, but they are driven by some common risk factors, and diversifying across the two classes won't necessarily diversify those risk factors.
5. **Ignores liabilities**: MVO also does not account for the fact that investors create portfolios as a source of cash to pay for something in the future: individual investors are looking to fund their consumption spending in retirement, for example, while pension funds are focused on funding the pension liability and repaying employees the retirement benefits promised to them. A more robust approach needs to account for the factors that affect these liabilities and the correlations between changes in value of the liabilities and returns on the asset portfolio.
6. **Single-period framework**: MVO is a single-period framework that does not take into account interim cash flows or the serial correlation of asset returns from one time period to the next. This means it ignores the potential costs and benefits of rebalancing a portfolio as capital market conditions change and asset allocations drift away from their optimal starting point.

We address critiques 1 through 4 in this LOS; critique 5 in LOS 4.j, 4.k, and 4.l; and critique 6 in LOS 4.g and 4.o.

The first two criticisms of MVO—GIGO and concentrated asset class allocations—can be addressed by improving the quality of the inputs, particularly expected return.

MODULE 4.2: REVERSE OPTIMIZATION AND BLACK-LITTERMAN

Video covering this content is available online.

Improving the Quality of the Inputs

Reverse optimization (Black-Litterman is an extension of this) can be used to improve the return estimates.

Reverse optimization is just what it sounds like: instead of starting with expected returns (and the other inputs) and deriving optimal portfolio weights, start with what we assume to be "optimal" portfolio weights from the global market portfolio and derive the expected returns consistent with those weights. Then we use these return estimates (called implied returns) to do a traditional MVO and derive optimal portfolio weights for our particular investor. This process is depicted in Figure 4.3.

Figure 4.3: Reverse Optimization

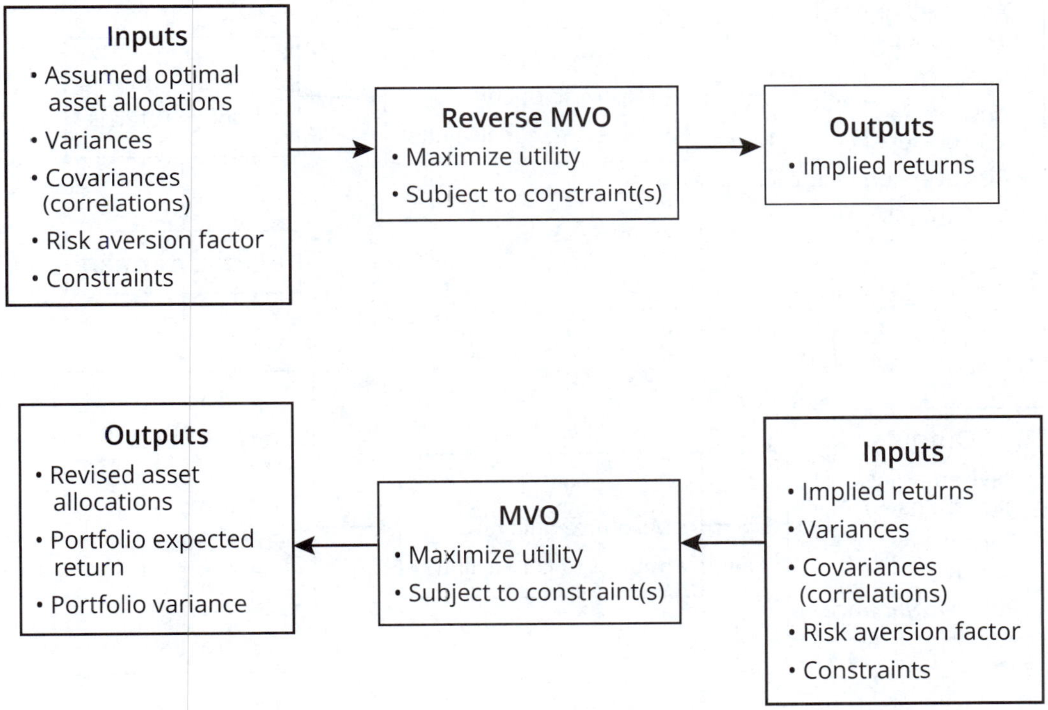

It is common to assume the world market portfolio provides optimal diversification and is therefore the appropriate starting point for weights to use in reverse optimization. The advantage of this is the derived returns already reflect a highly diversified portfolio and you avoid the tendency of MVO to come up with highly concentrated (in a few asset classes) allocations. Other starting points are possible, such as the weights from an existing IPS of the client.

The **Black-Litterman model** is an extension of reverse optimization in which the implied returns (actually implied excess returns) from a reverse optimization are subsequently adjusted to reflect the investor's unique views of future returns. For example, if reverse optimization:

- Derives an expected return for emerging market equities of 6.5% and you believe this is too low, you could adjust the expected return by 75 basis points to 7.25%. You can then rerun the MVO using your adjusted return estimates.
- Projects a return for U.K. large-cap equities of 8.2% and U.S. large-cap equities of 8.0% (a return differential of 20 basis points) and you believe that U.S. large-cap equities will outperform U.K. large-cap equities by 100 basis points, adjust the differential. Figure 4.4 displays a schematic view of the Black-Litterman model.

Figure 4.4: Black-Litterman Model

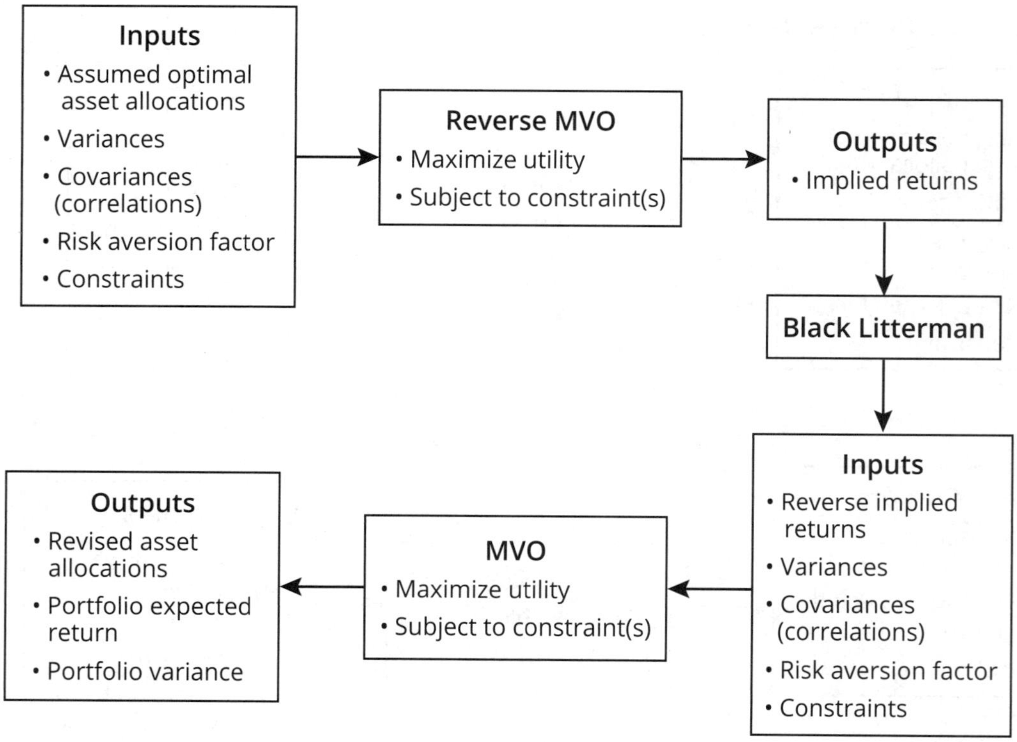

MODULE 4.3: EXAMPLE

Video covering this content is available online.

LOS 4.b: Recommend and justify an asset allocation using mean–variance optimization.

LOS 4.d: Recommend and justify an asset allocation based on the global market portfolio.

EXAMPLE: Recommending and justifying an asset allocation using MVO

Marsha Bronsten has come to her investment adviser for help to determine an appropriate asset allocation. The adviser discerns in conversations with Bronsten that her risk tolerance is average ($\lambda = 4$) and that she would also like to minimize the chance of earning less than 3%. The available asset allocations are as follows:

	Expected Return	Variance
Allocation 1	8%	0.0225
Allocation 2	6%	0.0144
Allocation 3	4%	0.0025

Recommend which of the three strategic asset allocations is appropriate for Bronsten.

Answer:

The first step is to calculate the certainty-equivalent return for each allocation using the equation $U_m = E(R_m) - 0.5 \times \lambda \times Var_m$.

$$U_1 = 0.08 - 0.5 \times 4 \times 0.0225 = 0.0350 = 3.50\%$$
$$U_2 = 0.06 - 0.5 \times 4 \times 0.0144 = 0.0312 = 3.12\%$$
$$U_3 = 0.04 - 0.5 \times 4 \times 0.0025 = 0.0350 = 3.50\%$$

Based solely on the criteria of the certainty-equivalent return, Bronsten is indifferent between Allocations 1 and 3, but prefers them both to Allocation 2.

The second step is to calculate Roy's safety-first criterion, which is equal to $\frac{R_P - R_L}{\sigma_P}$ and identifies the portfolio with the highest probability of exceeding

the threshold return of $R_L = 3\%$.

$$\text{Allocation 1: } \frac{0.08 - 0.03}{\sqrt{0.0225}} = 0.33$$

$$\text{Allocation 3: } \frac{0.04 - 0.03}{\sqrt{0.0025}} = 0.2$$

Reading 4

Allocation 1 has a higher probability of exceeding the threshold return than Allocation 3, so the adviser should recommend Allocation 1 to Bronsten.

Note that the data was given in a mixture of percent and decimal forms. The solution converted all data to decimal form. You could have also converted everything to percent form. For example:

$$U_1 = 8.00 - 0.005 \times 4 \times 225 = 3.50\%$$

$$\text{Allocation 1: } \frac{8-3}{\sqrt{225}} = 0.33$$

The ranking and conclusions will be the same. The approach you take is just personal preference.

EXAMPLE: Recommending and justifying an asset allocation using MVO

The Plowshare University endowment fund has an annual return objective of 9%, which is sufficient to cover its spending rate, expected inflation, and cost of earning investment returns. Its risk objective is to minimize risk (as measured by standard deviation of returns) while meeting its minimum expected return objective. The table provides the output from an MVO with a budget constraint and a nonnegativity constraint. Allocations AA, BB, CC, and DD can also be referred to as corner portfolios.[1]

	Expected Return	Standard Deviation of Returns
Allocation AA	15%	24%
Allocation BB	18%	27%
Allocation CC	12%	20%
Allocation DD	10%	14%

The risk-free rate is 3%. If the client and manager believe a true risk-free asset exists and can be used to construct the SAA, **identify** the appropriate asset allocation for Plowshare and **calculate** the risk of the optimal allocation.

Answer:

The first step is to calculate the Sharpe ratio for each allocation.

$$\text{Sharpe ratio AA} = \frac{15\% - 3\%}{24\%} = 0.5$$

$$\text{Sharpe ratio BB} = \frac{18\% - 3\%}{27\%} = 0.56$$

$$\text{Sharpe ratio CC} = \frac{12\% - 3\%}{20\%} = 0.45$$

$$\text{Sharpe ratio DD} = \frac{10\% - 3\%}{14\%} = 0.5$$

[1] See Level III CFA Curriculum Reading "Principles of Asset Allocation," footnote 6.

The optimal risk allocation is BB as it has the highest Sharpe ratio.

The second step is to calculate the mix between BB and the risk-free asset assuming the return objective is 9%. Allowing w_{BB} to be w is calculated as follows:

$$9\% = 18\%(w) + 3\%(1 - w)$$

$$9 = 18w + 3 - 3w$$

$$6 = 15w; \text{ therefore, } w_{BB} = 0.40$$

The optimal portfolio invests 40% in Allocation BB and 60% in the risk-free asset.

The risk (standard deviation) of the optimal portfolio is as follows:

$$\sigma_{BB} \times w_{BB} = 27\% \times 0.40 = 10.8\%$$

MODULE QUIZ 4.1, 4.2, 4.3

1. Which of the following methods is *most appropriate* for addressing highly concentrated allocations in portfolios?
   A. Reverse optimization.
   B. Monte Carlo simulation (MCS).
   C. Liability-relative MVO.

2. Jane Cullis is considering three potential asset allocations. She wishes to earn a nominal return of no less than 4%, and she has a high risk tolerance with a lambda of 2.

   The following asset allocations are available:

	Expected return	Variance
Allocation 1	6%	0.02
Allocation 2	8%	0.03
Allocation 3	10%	0.04

   Based on the information provided, which of the following allocations should Cullis choose?
   A. Allocation 1.
   B. Allocation 2.
   C. Allocation 3.

Reading 4

3. Melody Chan is considering three potential asset allocations. She wishes to earn a nominal return of no less than 4% and maximize her chances of exceeding a 4% return.

   The following asset allocations are available:

	Expected return	Variance
Allocation 1	6%	0.02
Allocation 2	8%	0.09
Allocation 3	10%	0.16

   Based on the information provided, which of the following allocations would Chan *most likely* choose?

   A. Allocation 1.
   B. Allocation 2.
   C. Allocation 3.

Video covering this content is available online.

MODULE 4.4: ISSUES FOR INDIVIDUALS

LOS 4.c: Interpret and evaluate an asset allocation in relation to an investor's economic balance sheet.

So far, we have only considered tradable financial assets such as equities and bonds. However, a significant portion of the typical investor's asset portfolio is human capital, as well as the residential real estate property the investor owns and lives in. We can adapt the MVO framework to incorporate these kinds of assets into the analysis.

For investors who have stable jobs with consistent wages that increase with inflation, we can model the cash flows associated with human capital (future wages) as an inflation-linked bond. For individuals with less certain and more volatile future wages, we could model their human capital as a mix of inflation-linked bonds, equities, and corporate bonds. By including this source of economic value in the investor's portfolio, the individual's capacity to take on additional risk is increased. Because human capital is not tradable, one of the constraints must be to set the percentage allocation to human capital at whatever it is currently valued at in relation to the investor's total portfolio value.

Residential real estate owned by the investor can be treated in a similar fashion, with return and risk inputs estimated using a residential real estate property index for the investor's geographic region. Once again, the allocation to the property must be constrained to its current value as a percentage of the investor's total portfolio.

Because human capital and residential real estate property are two large but often overlooked components of an investor's total investment portfolio, including them in the analysis along with traditional investment vehicles increases the investor's capacity to bear risk.

LOS 4.e: Discuss the use of Monte Carlo simulation and scenario analysis to evaluate the robustness of an asset allocation.

MCS can be used to:

- Address the limitations of MVO as a single-period model and the related issues of rebalancing and taxes in a multiperiod framework. In a single-period model, taxes are easy to incorporate into the analysis, and rebalancing the portfolio is irrelevant. However, in a multiperiod framework, rebalancing to move toward a strategic allocation target will involve buying and selling investments that trigger taxable capital gains and losses. Also, investors will save (add) money into and spend money out of their portfolio, resulting in interim cash flows. It is relatively straight-forward to do this at each future point in an MCS.
- Guide individual investors to identify their risk tolerance level. MCS can be useful in illustrating the range and likelihood of possible outcomes given various assumptions. Clients planning for retirement can visually see how often and when they are likely to run out of money.

PROFESSOR'S NOTE

Monte Carlo simulation (MCS) has multiple uses. It is essentially a random number generator, but random means random within user-defined boundaries. We saw MCS used in resampling to generate a range of possible inputs for MVO where the range was around the best guess of inputs. Here, MCS is being used another way—to simulate multiple future return paths for a portfolio over time. The various paths are based around a best guess of expected return and risk for the portfolio.

LOS 4.f: Discuss asset class liquidity considerations in asset allocation.

Less-liquid asset classes like direct real estate, infrastructure, and private equity require a liquidity return premium to compensate the investor for the additional liquidity risk. However, these asset classes are difficult to include in MVO because:

- There are few indexes available that accurately track these illiquid investments, making it harder to find data to use for estimating return, risk, and correlations.
- Even where indexes exist to provide return data, they are generally not investable as a passive alternative to active management of these asset classes.
- The risk-return characteristics of a specific real estate, private equity, or infrastructure investment are different from those of its asset class. For example, investing in the infrastructure asset class (assuming it is possible) should reflect the characteristics of a portfolio of all infrastructure, with only systematic risk priced. However, any one infrastructure fund is not fully diversified and, therefore, its risk and return characteristics reflect both systematic and nonsystematic risk.

Reading 4

To address these issues:

- Exclude illiquid asset classes when running an MVO, but use them to meet separately set target asset allocations.
- Include the illiquid asset classes in MVO and model the inputs of the specific (not asset class) investments you plan to use (i.e., the risk estimate will be based on both nonsystematic and systematic).
- Include the illiquid asset classes in MVO using highly diversified asset class inputs, recognizing that the actual investments made may have different characteristics. The input estimates for this approach are normally made using reported alternative investment indexes. Such indexes are usually not pure representations of the asset class but include characteristics of other asset classes as well. This violates the requirement that asset classes be mutually exclusive and biases the reported correlations upward.

MODULE QUIZ 4.4

1. Louise Davey is 26 years old and has just paid off her student loans from college and hopes to begin saving to accumulate a portfolio. She is currently set to begin a career as a licensed insurance salesperson, working primarily on a commission-based pay structure. Louise is an only child and will be the sole beneficiary of her parents' substantial estate, which she estimates she will receive in about 30 years.

   Based on the information provided, which of the following statements is *most accurate*?
   A. Louise's human capital could likely be modeled as an inflation-linked bond.
   B. Louise's capacity to bear investment risk is relatively high.
   C. Louise's human capital is a small component of her total economic worth.
2. When dealing with illiquid assets, such as the investor's personal residence or a private company he owns, it is *most accurate* to say:
   A. a liquidity premium reduces the assets' expected return.
   B. the positions can be excluded when running mean variance optimization for the client.
   C. use data on publicly available funds to model the specific characteristics of the client's holdings when running mean variance optimization for the client.
3. Which of the following methods is the *least appropriate* way of incorporating client risk preferences into asset allocations?
   A. Specify additional constraints.
   B. Specify a maximum return.
   C. Use MCS.
4. Which of the following statements regarding MCS is *most accurate*?
   A. MCS replaces mean variance optimization (MVO) by addressing the limitations of MVO.
   B. There is a high level of consistency between the MCS tools available in the marketplace.
   C. MCS is not necessary to model taxes and portfolio rebalancing in a single period.

MODULE 4.5: A RISK BUDGETING APPROACH

Video covering this content is available online.

LOS 4.g: Explain absolute and relative risk budgets and their use in determining and implementing an asset allocation.

The goal of risk budgeting is to maximize return per unit of risk, where we can define risk as total portfolio risk, active risk, or residual risk.

The marginal contribution to portfolio risk is the change in total portfolio risk for a small change in the asset allocation to a specific asset class. For those of you with calculus backgrounds, it's the partial derivative of risk with respect to changes in portfolio allocations. Absolute contribution to total risk (ACTR) is the asset classes' contribution to portfolio volatility.

By estimating each asset classes' marginal contribution to total risk (MCTR), we can (1) see what happens to portfolio risk as we change individual allocations, (2) identify optimal allocations, and (3) develop a risk budget.

Here are some useful formulas:

Marginal contribution to total risk: $MCTR_i$ = (beta of asset $class_i$ with respect to the portfolio)(total portfolio risk as measured by standard deviation)

Absolute contribution to total risk: $ACTR_i$ = ($weight_i$)($MCTR_i$)

% of risk contributed by $position_i$ = $ACTR_i$ / total portfolio risk

The optimal allocations to each asset class occur when the ratio of excess return to MCTR is equal for all asset classes and is equal to the portfolio Sharpe ratio.

A simple example of a portfolio with an optimal risk allocation is shown in Figure 4.5.

Figure 4.5: Optimal Risk Allocation Example

	Weight	Excess Return	Beta	MCTR	ACTR	% Contribution to Risk	Ratio of Excess Return to MCTR
U.S. equities	60%	6.50%	1.300	15.60%	9.36%	78.03%	0.417
U.S. bonds	30%	3.66%	0.732	8.78%	2.64%	21.97%	0.417
Cash	10%	0.00%	0.000	0.00%	0.00%	0.00%	
Total portfolio	100%	5.00%	1.000		12.00%	100.00%	

Note that the portfolio excess return is 5% (the weighted average of the excess returns of each asset class) and the portfolio standard deviation is 12%. Here are the calculations for U.S. equities:

$MCTR_{equities} = 1.300 \times 12.00\% = 15.60\%$

$ACTR_{equities} = 0.60 \times 15.60\% = 9.36\%$

$\%$ contribution to total $risk_{equities} = 9.36\% / 12.00\% = 78.00\%$

ratio of excess return to $MCTR_{equities} = 6.5\% / 15.60\% = 0.417$

Note also that the portfolio Sharpe ratio of 5% / 12% = 0.417 is equal to the ratio of excess return to MCTR for both U.S. equities and U.S. bonds. Therefore, the 60/30/10 allocation is optimal from a risk-budgeting perspective.

LOS 4.h: Describe how client needs and preferences regarding investment risks can be incorporated into asset allocation.

We have discussed a number to ways to incorporate client risk preferences into the asset allocation:

- Specify additional constraints, such as setting limits on allocations to risky asset classes or setting a ceiling on portfolio risk. We did this in the Plowshare example.
- Specify a risk aversion factor for the investor, as we did in the first example with Marsha Bronsten when we assumed she was an average investor and her risk aversion factor was 4.
- Use MCS to illustrate to the investor the various wealth outcomes possible from assuming allocations with different levels of risk.

LOS 4.i: Describe the use of investment factors in constructing and analyzing an asset allocation.

Up to this point, our opportunity set of investments consisted of asset classes, such as equities, fixed income, REITs, etc. Another approach is to define the opportunity set as factors, such as market exposure, size, valuation, momentum, liquidity, duration, credit, and volatility.

This approach is consistent with fundamental factor return models, such as the Fama-French model, in which the factors are the market portfolio, size, and value-growth.

The factors themselves are zero-dollar investment portfolios that are long the better performing attribute and short the underperforming attribute. For example, there are three factors in the Fama-French model:

- A zero-dollar portfolio long in small stocks and short in large stocks (the size factor).
- A zero-dollar portfolio long in value (high book-to-market) stocks and short growth (low book-to-market) stocks (the value-growth factor).
- The market portfolio.

Because of the way the factors are formed, they are not highly correlated with each other or the market portfolio, which improves the risk-return tradeoff from the optimal portfolios and expands the efficient frontier.

Once the factor portfolios, their expected returns, variances, and covariances are identified, MVO can be used in the same manner as we've previously discussed to identify portfolios with optimal allocations to the factors.

Research comparing the results of MVOs using asset class exposures versus factor exposures indicates that when the two opportunity sets broadly reflect the same exposures (underlying assets), the resulting efficient frontiers are not significantly different (i.e., one approach is not clearly superior). The choice of approach depends on how you form capital market expectations (i.e., the space in which you operate). If you collect data and think in terms of asset class, allocate risk by asset class. If you collect data and think in terms of risk factors, allocate risk by risk factor.

MODULE QUIZ 4.5

1. The following portfolio is being analyzed. The data is incomplete and does not show other asset classes held in the portfolio.

	Weight	Excess Return	Beta
Canadian equities	50%	8.25%	1.19
Canadian bonds	15%	2.75%	0.88

The portfolio standard deviation is 10%.

Which of the following amounts is *closest* to the ratio of excess returns to marginal contribution to total risk (MCTR) for the Canadian equities within the portfolio?

A. 0.313.
B. 0.595.
C. 0.693.

2. Regarding the use of investment factors in forming an asset allocation, it is *most accurate* to say:

A. this method is superior to asset class–based allocations for institutional portfolios.
B. this method will replicate the allocations produced by asset class–based allocations for institutional portfolios.
C. factor exposures may be investable by forming a series of zero-dollar long/short portfolios.

MODULE 4.6: AN ALM APPROACH

Video covering this content is available online.

Liability-Relative Asset Allocation

In this section, we address critique 5 of MVO, that MVO as discussed so far does not address the relationship between the asset investment portfolio and the liabilities that the investor will repay using the cash flow from the asset portfolio. We will focus our attention here on institutional investors such as pension funds, insurance companies, and banks. All three have liabilities they are obligated to meet at some point in the future, and they face strict regulatory rules and penalties for failure to meet those obligations.

Let's use the example of a defined benefit (DB) pension plan to illustrate the key issues and provide some definitions. There are two components to a DB pension plan: the pension liability and the investment portfolio that is managed to meet the cash flow requirements of the liability. A pension plan promises workers a stream of payments upon retirement that is usually dependent on how long the employee has worked for the company, as well as the worker's salary in the last few years before retirement. The pension liability represents the present value (calculated at the appropriate discount rate) of those future retirement obligations of the plan.

The plan surplus and the funding ratio are calculated as follows:

plan surplus = market value of investment portfolio assets – present value of the pension liabilities

funding ratio = market value of assets / present value of liabilities

A pension plan is fully funded if the funding ratio = 1 (which means the plan surplus is 0). An underfunded plan has a funding ratio less than 1, and an overfunded plan has a funding ratio greater than 1.

The characteristics of the pension liability drive the return and risk requirements of the investment portfolio and ultimately the asset allocation decision. Furthermore, the analysis should recognize that the value of the assets and the liabilities are driven by some of the same factors, so the correlations between changes in value of the two are important.

LOS 4.j: Describe and evaluate characteristics of liabilities that are relevant to asset allocation.

The following characteristics of liabilities are relevant to the asset allocation decision:

- Fixed versus contingent: Fixed liabilities have cash flows whose amount and timing are specified in advance, such as a fixed-rate corporate bond. Contingent liabilities have cash flows that depend on uncertain future events, such as the pension liability associated with a defined pension plan.
- Legal versus quasi-legal: Legal liabilities are obligations defined in a legal agreement. Quasi-legal liabilities are not legal obligations but are cash outflows expected to occur in the future and are essential to the mission of the institution. University endowments can be considered to have quasi-legal liabilities.

- Duration and convexity measure the change in value of a liability for a given change in interest rates. In the CFA curriculum, we typically talk about duration and convexity in relation to fixed-income securities, but the concept can be applied to any liability.
- Liability value versus size of sponsoring organization: A large liability in relation to the size of the sponsoring organization will necessarily be accounted for in the asset allocation decision; a small liability can usually be ignored as its effect on the optimal asset allocation is minimal.
- Factors that affect future cash flows: These factors include inflation, interest rates, risk premiums, and other economic conditions. DB pension obligations are influenced by the choice of the discount rate, for example.
- Timing considerations, including longevity risk.
- Regulations affecting the determination of the liability's value, typically found in the insurance industry.

LOS 4.k: Discuss approaches to liability-relative asset allocation.

LOS 4.l: Recommend and justify a liability-relative asset allocation.

We will discuss three approaches to liability-relative asset allocation. They are summarized here and then discussed in more detail:

- Surplus optimization: This is an extension of MVO in which we determine an efficient frontier based on the surplus with its volatility as our measure of risk, stated either in money or percentage terms.
- Two-portfolio approach: In this approach, we separate the asset portfolio into two subportfolios: a hedging portfolio and a return-seeking portfolio.
- Integrated asset-liability approach: This approach integrates both the assets and the liabilities in a joint optimization method.

Reading 4

Surplus Optimization

We can define the surplus return as:

$R_{s,m}$ = surplus return = (change in asset value − change in liability value) / initial asset value

Then the objective function to maximize is:

$$U_m = E(R_{s,m}) - 0.005 \times \lambda \times Var_{s,m}$$

where:
$E(R_{s,m})$ = expected surplus return
$Var_{s,m}$ = variance of surplus return

We then proceed with the same MVO as previous, except we also include the expected returns and variances of the liabilities. The correlations reflect the extent to which the assets are useful to hedge the liabilities.

There are a number of ways to estimate the expected returns and variances of the liabilities. The first is to make the assumption that the liabilities behave like corporate bonds and the liability inputs can be estimated using the expected return and volatility of corporate bonds. The second is to use a factor approach and identify the common factors that affect both the asset classes and the liabilities.

Two-Portfolio Approach (Also Known as the Hedging or Return-Seeking Approach)

Conceptually this is a straight-forward approach. We create an asset portfolio that hedges the liabilities, and the remainder is managed independently using MVO to maximize utility and identify the optimal risk-return tradeoff.

The hedging portfolio can be created using the various techniques outlined elsewhere in the Level III curriculum fixed-income readings: cash flow matching, duration matching, and immunization.

This approach is most often used for insurance companies and overfunded pension plans that want to minimize the risk of underfunding.

This approach can be modified by (1) only partially hedging the liabilities and allocating more capital to the return-seeking portfolio or (2) increasing the allocation to the hedging portfolio as the funding ratio and the surplus increase. Both of these approaches are more aggressive than completely hedging the liabilities, as they trade off higher expected return for higher risk.

There are two limitations of this approach:

- If the funding ratio is less than one, it's difficult to create a hedging portfolio that completely hedges the liabilities.
- A hedging portfolio may not be available to hedge certain kinds of risk (like earthquakes).

Integrated Asset-Liability Approach

The distinctive feature of the previous two approaches is that the composition of the liabilities is already in place when the asset allocation decisions are made, so the two decisions are made independently. Banks, hedge funds with short positions, and insurance companies, however, make decisions about the composition of their liabilities jointly with their asset allocation decisions. There is a continuous feedback loop between the two, which requires a multiperiod model. This is often referred to as an integrated asset-liability approach.

For example, a key risk faced by large global banks, which are very highly leveraged, is whether the bank's capital is sufficient to absorb losses when their asset values decline, their liability values increase, or both. And as both bank assets (loans) and liabilities (deposits) are affected by changes in interest rates, although to varying degrees, stress testing requires a framework that can simultaneously account for both sides of the balance sheet. An integrated asset-liability approach is therefore necessary for banks to identify the optimal mix of assets and liabilities to meet their return and risk objectives.

MODULE QUIZ 4.6

1. Which of the following items is *best* described as a contingent liability?
   A. A company's fixed-coupon debt.
   B. An insurance company's obligations to pay policyholders.
   C. Planned distributions by a foundation.
2. A bank is *most likely* to use which of the following approaches to liability-relative asset allocation?
   A. Surplus efficient frontier approach.
   B. Integrated asset-liability approach.
   C. Two-portfolio approach.

MODULE 4.7: GOALS-BASED AND MISCELLANEOUS APPROACHES

Video covering this content is available online.

LOS 4.m: Recommend and justify an asset allocation using a goals-based approach.

The **goals-based approach** to asset allocation is useful for individual investors, who typically have a number of (sometimes conflicting) objectives, with different time horizons and different levels of urgency, which we will measure as specified required probabilities of success. For example, an individual investor might define one goal as saving enough for college tuition in 10 years and specify that she requires a 90% probability of success, while another goal is having $1,000,000 in 30 years to set up a foundation when she retires, with a 60% probability of success. The first goal in this case is more urgent than the second goal.

In this approach:

- The investor's portfolio is composed of subportfolios, and each investment goal is addressed individually with these subportfolios.
- Taxable and tax-exempt investments are part of the opportunity set.
- Instead of expressing an investment goal as an expected average return on the portfolio, we identify and document "minimum expectations" for each goal, which is the minimum expected return necessary to provide a specified minimum required probability of success over the given time horizon.

Often, the advisor will select from a set of pre-established subportfolios (modules) to meet specific goals of a client rather than create new subportfolios for each client. The modules are distinguished by differences in risk-return tradeoffs, liquidity requirements, and the inclusion or exclusion of certain asset classes.

The asset allocation is determined by identifying, for each goal, the module that provides the highest expected return with the specified probability of success over the required time horizon. Then the size of the investment in that module is simply the present value of the future goal discounted at the expected return of that module. The portfolio allocation is then the sum of all of the individual investments necessary to achieve each goal.

EXAMPLE: Goals-based approach

An investor has a goal of having $500,000 to fund his daughter's undergraduate and graduate education beginning in 10 years with a 90% required probability of success. He also has a goal of transferring $6,000,000 to his daughter in 30 years with a required probability of success of 75%.

The modules in the table are available to the adviser to implement each of these goals.

	Module A	Module B	Module C
Expected return	5%	6%	8%
Expected volatility	4%	7%	14%

The annual minimum expectation returns at various probabilities of success over the 10-year time horizon are as follows:

Required Success	Module A	Module B	Module C
90%	3.0%	2.4%	–2.2%
75%	3.6%	3.8%	1.7%

The annual minimum expectation returns at various probabilities of success over the 30-year time horizon are as follows:

Required Success	Module A	Module B	Module C
90%	4.0%	4.3%	4.7%
75%	4.1%	4.8%	5.2%

Determine the module to use and **calculate** the amount to invest in that module to meet each goal. Treat each goal separately.

Answer:

For the first goal, Module A has the highest return given a 90% required probability of success of 3.0% over the 10-year time horizon. The investment necessary today in Module A to fund the $500,000 college tuition in 10 years is the present value of $500,000 discounted at 3.0% for 10 years, or $372,047.

For the second goal, Module C has the highest return given a 75% required probability of success of 5.2% over the 30-year time horizon. The investment necessary today in Module C to fund the $6,000,000 transfer in 30 years is the present value of $6,000,000 discounted at 5.2% for 30 years, or $1,311,231.

LOS 4.n: Describe and evaluate heuristic and other approaches to asset allocation.

There are additional approaches to optimal asset allocation that are ad hoc and not based on theoretical models and don't require sophisticated mathematics, but also don't necessarily lead an optimal allocation in the way in which we have defined it up to this point.

120 Minus Your Age

This one is easy. It relates your age to your allocation to equities so that 120 – age = % allocation to equities, with the remainder going to fixed incomes. That means a 40-year-old woman would have an 80/20 split between stocks and bonds, and when she is 50, it would be 70/30.

It's consistent with the idea that as the value of human capital declines as we age, our capacity to bear risk in the rest of the portfolio declines, suggesting that we move from equities into fixed incomes. What's interesting about this approach is that it seems to come close to mimicking the allocations of target-date retirement funds.

60/40 Split

This one is even easier than the 120-minus-your-age rule. You simply maintain your asset allocation at 60% stocks and 40% bonds. This is not nearly as off-the-wall as it sounds, as the global financial asset portfolio has historically been split approximately 60/40 between stocks and bonds.

PROFESSOR'S NOTE

I guess the assumption with this method is that you are 60 years old throughout your entire life!

Endowment Model or Yale Model

Under this approach, you allocate larger amounts to alternative investment asset classes (private equity, real estate, or natural resources) than is typically recommended by a strict MVO. Presumably these markets are less-than-perfectly informationally efficient, so investment managers with expertise in these markets can outperform expectations. Also, they are less liquid, and certain institutional investors are positioned to take on additional liquidity risk in return for a liquidity premium because of their longer time horizons. The approach is popular with university endowment funds.

Risk Parity

The idea with the risk parity asset allocation approach is that diversification is achieved by ensuring that each asset class contributes the same amount to the total portfolio risk. This addresses critique 4 of MVO that diversification across asset classes does not guarantee diversification across risk sources. The criticism of this approach is that it ignores expected returns and focuses only on risk.

1/N Rule

If we create an equally weighted portfolio in which we allocate the same percentage to each asset class, we have in effect weighted each class by 1/N, where N is the number of classes. For example, with 8 asset classes, this approach suggests we invest 1/8 = 12.5% in each class. One common method is to rebalance to equally weighted each quarter. Although it sounds very simple, there is some empirical evidence that this type of approach actually performs better than we would expect.

Video covering this content is available online.

MODULE 4.8: REBALANCING POLICY

LOS 4.o: Discuss factors affecting rebalancing policy.

Investment managers rebalance portfolios for a number of reasons, including in response to changing client goals and capital market expectations or changes in tactical allocations. Here we will stick to the CFA curriculum definition: adjusting asset allocations to move toward the originally defined strategic allocation goal. Percentage range rebalancing involves setting trigger points around the optimal percentage allocation and rebalancing back to the target allocation or partially correcting when those trigger points are hit.

The key factors that impact the optimal corridor width (or the rebalancing range) of an asset class include transaction costs, risk tolerance, correlations with the rest of the portfolio, and the volatility of the rest of the portfolio.

The higher the transaction costs, the wider the optimal corridor, as the benefits of rebalancing have to "pay" for higher costs to rebalance. The higher the investor's risk tolerance, the wider the corridor, because the investor is less concerned about deviations from the optimal allocation. The higher the correlation of the asset class with the rest of the portfolio, the wider the corridor, because a portfolio tends to move with the asset class, and the allocations tend to stray more slowly from the target. Finally, the higher the volatility of the asset classes, the narrower the optimal corridor. This is because higher volatility increases the likelihood that the actual allocation will diverge over time from the target allocation.

Ultimately, the choice of corridor width depends on a trade-off between risk control, transaction costs, and correlations between classes. In complex situations, a quantified cost-benefit analysis will be required.

MODULE QUIZ 4.7, 4.8

1. Which of the following statements regarding subportfolios within the context of the goals-based approach to asset allocation is *most accurate*?
   A. The most significant difference between the subportfolios is the return-risk tradeoff.
   B. Higher priority goals require higher return assets.
   C. The size of the investment in a particular subportfolio is the present value of the future goal discounted by the risk-free rate.
2. Which of the following statements regarding the "120 minus your age" heuristic is *most correct*?
   A. A 70-year-old individual should have 50% of the investment portfolio invested in equity securities.
   B. A 60-year-old individual should have 60% of the investment portfolio invested in fixed-income securities.
   C. The approach generally does a poor job of mimicking the allocations of target-date retirement funds.
3. A portfolio has invested in Asset Class Z and the manager is setting the optimal rebalancing corridor. The corridor will be wider if:
   A. the rest of the portfolio is highly volatile.
   B. the correlation of Z with the rest of the portfolio is highly positive.
   C. transaction costs are low.

KEY CONCEPTS

LOS 4.a

Given an opportunity set of investable assets, their expected returns and variances, as well as the pairwise correlations between them, MVO identifies the portfolio allocations that maximize return for every level of risk. If we assume the opportunity set includes all assets, the result is the efficient frontier.

MVO is criticized for:

1. **GIGO:** The quality of the output from the MVO (portfolio allocations) is highly sensitive to the quality of the inputs.
2. **Concentrated asset class allocations:** MVO often identifies efficient portfolios that are highly concentrated in a subset of asset classes.
3. **Skewness and kurtosis:** These are ignored.
4. **Risk diversification:** MVO identifies an asset allocation diversified across asset classes, but not necessarily the sources of risk.
5. **Ignores liabilities:** MVO also does not account for the fact that investors create portfolios as a source of cash to pay for something in the future.
6. **Single-period framework:** MVO is a single-period framework that does not take into account interim cash flows or the serial correlation of asset returns from one time period to the next.

LOS 4.b, 4.d

MVO provides an efficient frontier of asset allocation choices. However, the allocation selected will depend on the specific investor:

- How do they quantify return to risk?
- Do they require specific assets or asset classes to be excluded or included?
- Do they use an asset-only, liability-relative, or goals-based approach?

Variations on MVO may be used:

- Reverse optimization solves for expected return by asset class based on the classes' weights in the world market portfolio and uses those consensus return expectations to determine asset allocation for an investor.
- Black-Litterman allows the manager to view adjust those consensus return expectations.
- MCS complements MVO; MCS is covered later.

LOS 4.c

A significant portion of the typical investor's asset portfolio is human capital and also the residential real estate property the investor owns and lives in. We can adapt the MVO framework to incorporate these kinds of assets into the analysis by estimating the expected return and risk inputs for these assets and constraining the allocations to match current values.

LOS 4.e

Monte Carlo simulation can be used to (1) address the limitations of MVO as a single-period model and the related issues of rebalancing and taxes in a multiperiod framework and (2) guide individual investors to identify their risk tolerance level.

LOS 4.f

Less-liquid asset classes like direct real estate, infrastructure, and private equity require a liquidity return premium to compensate the investor for the additional liquidity risk.

LOS 4.g

The goal of risk budgeting is to maximize return per unit of risk, where we can define risk as total portfolio risk, active risk, or residual risk.

LOS 4.h

Ways to incorporate client risk preferences into asset allocation include:

- Specifying additional constraints.
- Specifying a risk aversion factor for the investor.
- Using Monte Carlo simulation.

LOS 4.i

Investment factors can be used in asset allocation by defining the opportunity set as risk factors that affect expected return. Such factors include market exposure, size, valuation, momentum, liquidity, duration, credit, and volatility.

LOS 4.j

The following characteristics of liabilities are relevant to the asset allocation decision:

- Fixed versus contingent.
- Legal versus quasi-legal.
- Duration and convexity.
- Liability value versus size of sponsoring organization.
- Factors that affect future cash.
- Timing considerations.
- Regulations affecting the determination of the liability's value.

LOS 4.k, 4.l

There are three common approaches to liability-relative asset allocation.

- Surplus optimization: Use MVO to determine an efficient frontier based on the surplus with its volatility as our measure of risk, stated either in money or percentage terms.
- Two-portfolio approach: Separate the asset portfolio into two subportfolios: a hedging portfolio and a return-seeking portfolio.
- Integrated asset-liability approach: Jointly optimize the selection of both the assets and the liabilities.

LOS 4.m

The goals-based approach is useful for individual investors, who typically have a number of (sometimes conflicting) objectives, with different time horizons and different levels of urgency.

- The investor's portfolio is composed of subportfolios, and each investment goal is addressed individually with these subportfolios.
- Taxable and tax-exempt investments are part of the opportunity set.
- Minimum expectations are specified for each goal.

LOS 4.n

Additional ad hoc approaches to asset allocation include:

- 120 minus your age.
- 60/40 split.
- Endowment model or Yale model.
- Risk parity.
- 1/N rule.

LOS 4.o

The following indicate wider corridors for asset classes:

- Higher transaction costs.
- Higher investor risk tolerance.
- Higher correlation of the asset class with the rest of the portfolio.
- Higher volatility of asset classes indicates a narrower corridor to control risk.

Ultimately, the choice of corridor width depends on a trade-off between risk control, transaction costs, and correlations between classes. In complex situations, a quantified cost-benefit analysis will be required.

ANSWER KEY FOR MODULE QUIZZES

Module Quiz 4.1, 4.2, 4.3

1. **A** Reverse optimization is most likely to produce a more diversified portfolio because it starts with the weights of all assets in the global world market portfolio and solves for the consensus expected returns consistent with that highly diversified portfolio. MCS does not address this issue at all because it is used to model behavior over time of any one specific asset allocation. Liability-relative MVO is focused on the change in value of the surplus (PVA − PVL). Resampled MVO is another way to address the concentration issue, but that was not a choice. (Module 4.2, LOS 4.a)

2. **C** Step 1 is to exclude any portfolios that do not meet the 4% minimum return objective. Next, calculate the certain equivalent returns:

   Allocation 1: $0.06 - (0.5 \times 2 \times 0.02) = 0.04$

   Allocation 2: $0.08 - (0.5 \times 2 \times 0.03) = 0.05$

   Allocation 3: $0.10 - (0.5 \times 2 \times 0.04) = 0.06$

   Allocation 3 has the highest certainty-equivalent return, so it should be chosen by Cullis. (Module 4.1, LOS 4.a)

3. **C** Step 1 is to exclude any portfolios that do not meet the 4% minimum return objective. Next, calculate the safety-first ranking to determine highest probability of exceeding the 4%:

   Allocation 1: $(0.06 - 0.04) / (0.02)^{1/2} = 0.141$

   Allocation 2: $(0.08 - 0.04) / (0.09)^{1/2} = 0.133$

   Allocation 3: $(0.10 - 0.04) / (0.16)^{1/2} = 0.150$

   Allocation 3 has the highest probability of exceeding the threshold return. (Module 4.3, LOS 4.d)

Module Quiz 4.4

1. **B** She is young, starting a job, and apparently debt free. A high ability to take risk is plausible. She appears to have no financial capital, so human capital (the new job) appears to be her only capital. Her HC is somewhat riskier and uncertain, so not at all like an inflation-linked bond, which would require her income to be linked directly to changes in inflation. (LOS 4.c)

2. **B** Ignoring the positions and running MVO for the rest of the client's portfolio is a method of dealing with such preexistent positions. This essentially recognizes the client will not sell such positions. Two other methods exist. Include the positions in MVO by (1) modeling the specific characteristics of what that client actually owns, or (2) using data on

public funds but realizing that such data will not reflect the specific characteristics of the client's positions. However, you cannot use public data to model the highly specific characteristics of what the client owns. Also, a liquidity premium increases expected return. (LOS 4.f)

3. **B** The reading lists three methods: specifying additional constraints, specifying a risk aversion factor for the investor, and using MCS. (LOS 4.e)

4. **C** In a single-period model, taxes are easy to incorporate into the analysis, and rebalancing the portfolio is irrelevant. Therefore, MVO can address taxes in a single-period model and MCS is not necessary. MCS becomes useful in dealing with a multi-period framework, where the analysis of taxes and rebalancing becomes much more mathematically challenging otherwise.

   MCS *complements* (does not replace) MVO by addressing the limitations of MVO as a single-period framework.

   MCS tools can be quite different. They vary significantly in their ability to model non-normal returns, serial correlations, tax rates, and non-traditional investments, for example. (LOS 4.e)

Module Quiz 4.5

1. **C** $MCTR_{equities} = 1.19 \times 10\% = 11.9\%$

   Ratio of excess return to $MCTR_{equities} = 8.25\% / 11.9\% = 0.693$

   (LOS 4.g)

2. **C** Not all factors are replicable, but the ones that are can be obtained with a position that is long the desired factor (e.g., growth) and short the undesired factor (e.g., value). Neither asset class–based allocation nor factor-based allocation is superior. It is a matter of which method better resonates with how the manager looks at investing, not the kind of client. (LOS 4.i)

Module Quiz 4.6

1. **B** Insurance company obligations to policyholders are typically contingent (uncertain in timing, amount, or both) liabilities (a legal obligation to pay). Fixed-coupon debt is a fixed obligation to pay, and foundation distributions are not legal liabilities (but may be regarded as quasi liabilities). (LOS 4.j)

2. **B** A bank can typically vary the nature of both its assets and liabilities. A joint optimization (deciding how to set up both) is common. The other approaches take the liabilities as a given and only focus on managing the assets. (LOS 4.l)

Module Quiz 4.7, 4.8

1. **A** The priority of the goal determines the amount of risk taken. Thus, you expect significant differences in risk and return between subportfolios. The allocation to a subportfolio is the future need discounted by the expected return of the assets used in that subportfolio, not by risk-free rates. High-priority goals require more certainty and would be funded by lower, not higher, risk and return assets. (Module 4.7, LOS 4.m)

2. **A** The percentage allocation to equities is based on 120 minus your age. Such an approach has been found to come close to mimicking the allocations of target-date retirement funds. (Module 4.7, LOS 4.n)

3. **B** High correlation allows wider corridors because if the assets move in sync, divergence between them is less likely. Low transaction costs allow narrower corridors because the cost of rebalancing is reduced. High volatility in either Z or the rest of the portfolio increases risk and calls for narrower corridors. (Module 4.8, LOS 4.o)

READING 5

Asset Allocation with Real-World Constraints

EXAM FOCUS

Asset allocation is not an exercise in abstract math. This reading continues the discussion of practical considerations that may arise. Be prepared to recognize the potential impact of the issues discussed on a particular client's asset allocation.

MODULE 5.1: REAL WORLD ISSUES

Video covering this content is available online.

LOS 5.a: Discuss asset size, liquidity needs, time horizon, and regulatory or other considerations as constraints on asset allocation.

Additional Constraints When Choosing an Optimal Asset Allocation

Asset Size

Smaller funds often lack the expertise and governance structure to invest in complex strategies, and therefore, often face a problem of how to achieve an adequate level of diversification. In addition, many capital markets impose local legislation, restricting investment in some assets to investors with a given level of capital or experience. Smaller funds may use commingled investment accounts (pooling money from a small group of investors) to achieve adequate size to diversify. To enable investment in assets where local legislation requires minimum investment levels, families may pool their assets to qualify.

Larger portfolios can generally access greater management expertise in the governance capacity, allowing them to consider complex strategies that smaller funds cannot. Their larger capital base also enables investment in accounts with relatively high minimum investment requirements. This allows large funds to achieve higher levels of diversification.

Large portfolios benefit from economies of scale via cost savings regarding internal management and greater negotiating power regarding management fees, allowing higher allocations to alternative investments. As the size of the fund increases, the *per-participant* cost of the internal governance infrastructure decreases, giving the fund a competitive advantage in private equity, hedge fund, and infrastructure investing.

Funds that are too large may not be able to take advantage of asset classes that lack the capacity to absorb large amounts of funds. For example, active equity strategies involving small-cap stocks may be less suitable because the size of investment can be too large for an external manager to take on. A small-cap manager may suffer diseconomies of scale as: larger trades have increased price impact, the inflow of capital may encourage managers to abandon their core strategies, and the need for increased numbers of staff may slow the decision-making process. A potential solution is to split the allocation among several managers, but identifying and monitoring suitable managers is an added burden and cost. The result is that large funds often take a passive approach in such situations.

Very large funds may find that there are not enough alternative investments (e.g., too few hedge funds) available and may choose a fund-of-funds (FoF). But this carries a double fee structure for the FoF manager and the underlying fund managers. In addition, the strategies of one hedge fund manager may be offset by strategies of another manager.

Liquidity Needs

The key to successfully addressing the liquidity constraint for a portfolio is to integrate the needs of the owner and the characteristics of the asset class. Some owners require extremely high levels of liquidity and hence typically invest in high-quality, short-term, liquid assets. Other owners with lower needs and much longer time horizons can take advantage of the illiquidity premium inherent in alternative investments, such as real estate and infrastructure.

The following table summarizes the typical liquidity needs of a range of portfolio owners.

Portfolio Owner	Typical Liquidity Needs
Banks	High liquidity needed to support day to day operations and stand ready to repay deposits
Sovereign Wealth Funds, Endowments, Pension Plans, Foundations	Longer time horizons and lower liquidity needs
Property and Casualty Insurance	Relatively high due to unpredictability of claims
Life and Auto Insurance	Relatively low due to predictability of claims
Individuals	Varies by individual circumstance

But there are always case-specific exceptions, such as a bank with highly liquid loan assets that can provide necessary liquidity that is normally provided by the investment portfolio or a foundation supporting research that requires high liquidity to fund potential but unpredictable breakthrough research opportunities.

The possibility of extreme market conditions should also be considered when planning liquidity levels. Investor behavior changes during times of stress, and a successful allocation should take account of the resulting change in cash flows. Portfolio governance is also important in this context. In times of stress, unsophisticated investors may panic sell assets, leading to permanent losses and lower total returns from the capital base when returns revert to precrisis levels.

Time Horizon

A portfolio's time horizon is defined by a liability to be paid or a goal to be funded at a future date. Asset allocations must consider the horizons defined by each liability and goal, as well as adapting to the changing mix of assets and liabilities as time progresses. The value of human capital, for example, declines over time. As a result, the asset allocation will likely shift towards lower risk asset classes such as fixed income.

The changing nature of liabilities over time also requires changes in asset allocation. A pension fund catering for a young workforce, for example, would be heavily invested in long-term bonds. A more mature scheme would move towards intermediate and short-term bonds.

The time horizon is also associated with the ability to take on risk. Portfolios with longer time horizons are often invested in assets with higher risk. There is evidence that risky asset returns mean revert over time, evening out below and above average levels of return. This concept is known as time diversification.

Asset allocations for individual investors also change over time, as illustrated in the following examples.

EXAMPLE: Older retired individual

Barry Garland is 70 years old and recently retired. He has two goals that require funding from his current portfolio:

- Goal 1: To maintain a constant standard of living to age 85.
- Goal 2: To maintain a constant standard of living from age 85 to 100.

Goal 1 is fully funded, but Goal 2 is only partially funded. Barry's life expectancy at age 70 is 17.5 years.

Goal 1 will have the higher priority as his chances of living decline as he ages. Goal 1 is fully funded and higher priority so the subportfolio will emphasize more conservative investments.

Goal 2 is of a lower priority and currently not fully funded. This subportfolio can be invested more aggressively with more growth potential.

EXAMPLE: Families with multiple funding goals

Jane and Arthur Bigstone are both 52 years old and work as lawyers in their home town. The Bigstones have a daughter, Alice, age 16, who they intend to send to college, and a son Mark, a promising young politician, age 27, who aims to run for mayor of the nearest city in 8 years. If their financial situation allowed it, they would like to make a donation to any campaign he ran. They would also like to set up a scholarship at the local school to fund talented children from underprivileged neighborhoods. Ideally, they would like to do this when they are 80 years old to celebrate the 40th anniversary of Arthur setting up his own practice.

The Bigstones have four goals for their portfolio:

1. Funding lifestyle and consumption needs.
2. Funding Alice's college education.
3. Donating to Mark's mayoral campaign.
4. Funding the scholarship.

A typical allocation could split the lifestyle/consumption goal into a worst-case scenario of reduced standard-of-living, a baseline case maintaining standard-of-living, and an aspirational case where the standard-of-living improves. This would mean the Bigstones would have 6 subportfolios with risk preferences similar to those shown in Figure 5.1.

Figure 5.1: Subportfolios

Goals	Risk	Allocation	% of Total Portfolio
Minimum	Conservative	100% Bonds & Cash	65%
Maintain	Moderate	60% Equity & 40% Bonds	12%
Aspirational	Aggressive	100% Equity	8%
College Fund	Conservative	100% Bonds & Cash	6%
Campaign Donation	Aggressive	100% Equity	6%
Scholarship	Aggressive	100% Equity	3%
Aggregate		25% Equity & 75% Bonds	100%

In another 15 years, the allocation for the Bigstones would look very different. With fewer years of consumption to fund, the assets required to fund future consumption are much lower. The college and mayoral campaign have been funded and only the scholarship remains as an aspirational goal. The allocation may now look similar to Figure 5.2, assuming the goals as defined earlier have not changed. Clearly, as the Bigstones' children grow up and pursue careers, it is entirely possible that new goals (e.g., a run for congress for Mark) would replace the aspirational goal of the scholarship.

Figure 5.2: Subportfolios 15 Years Later

Goals	Risk	Allocation	% of Total Portfolio
Minimum	Conservative	100% Bonds & Cash	60%
Maintain	Moderate	60% Equity & 40% Bonds	10%
Aspirational	Aggressive	100% Equity	6%
Scholarship	Aggressive	100% Equity	24%
Aggregate		35% Equity & 65% Bonds	100%

PROFESSOR'S NOTE

It should be evident the specific allocations shown are somewhat arbitrary. There is no formula to determine the numbers. Your task is to see the logic behind choosing a higher or lower allocation to equity, bond, and cash in one subportfolio relative to another.

Regulatory and Other External Constraints

Each portfolio faces its own set of regulatory and other external constraints. Several of these portfolios are addressed in the following.

Insurance Companies

Investment returns are a large contributor to the performance of an insurance company. The asset class with the largest allocation will be fixed income, reflecting the need for the insurer to match assets to the projected cash flows of the risks being insured. Local accounting laws often require fixed income investments to be stated at book value, so the insurer can focus primarily on the pattern of cash flow receipts rather than the volatility of market value.

The main risk considerations are the need to maintain enough capital to meet claims made by policyholders, along with factors that directly affect the company's financial strength metrics. These include:

- Risk-based capital measures.
- Liquidity.

- Yield levels.
- Credit ratings.
- Potential to liquidate assets to meet claims.

Local legislation often limits the allocation insurance companies can make to asset classes. Equity investment maybe limited to as little as 10%, with caps also placed on allocations to private equity investments and high-yield bonds.

Pension Funds

As well as capping the allocation to certain asset classes, local legislation often places a wide range of tax, accounting, reporting, and funding constraints on pension funds. There may be tax incentives offered to invest in domestic assets. Accounting rules may allow deferred recognition of losses.

These factors will be considered in the fund's decision on the level of risk exposure. The final asset allocation is likely to consider the anticipated funding cost, and the implication for the pension expense that is likely to be reported in the financial statements.

When considering funding as a constraint, the pension fund will compare the risk of funding cost exceeding a given threshold for the asset allocation (a risk the fund would like to minimize), to the present value of expected contributions (which the fund would also like to minimize).

For example, higher allocations to equities rather than bonds will increase the volatility of returns. In turn, this increases the risk that low returns increase the required contributions. However, there is a benefit in that the higher expected return would decrease the present value of expected contributions.

The fund will need to decide on the optimal combination of risk (that contributions exceed a given level) and return (as measured by the PV of expected contributions) while taking into account the external regulatory requirements and allocation limits.

Endowments and Foundations

Endowments and foundations are both assumed to have an infinite time horizon and are subject to very few regulatory constraints compared to other entities. In some countries, there may be a minimum required annual distribution or socially responsible investment required to maintain a tax-exempt status. The long time horizon usually allows investment in risky assets, but if the endowment is part of the funding of an organization, covenants placed on the organization by lenders may constrain the activities of the portfolio.

Sovereign Wealth Funds

Sovereign wealth funds are government-owned entities investing on behalf of the state, and are typically not looking to match assets and liabilities. They are, however, subject to scrutiny from the citizens of that state which may reduce the level of risk that their long time horizon would otherwise allow them to take on.

In addition, each fund self-governs by capping the allocation of funds to certain assets. The aim of these constraints may include:

- Minimum investment requirements in socially or ethically acceptable assets.
- Maximum investments in risky assets such as alternative investments.
- Limits on the investment allowed in certain currencies.

Investing in ethically acceptable assets involves considering environmental, social, and governance goals. This is usually not part of the initial asset allocation process. Rather, an allocation will be set aside and invested in acceptable assets.

LOS 5.b: Discuss tax considerations in asset allocation and rebalancing.

In the presence of taxation, pre-tax, after-tax risk, and return characteristics may be significantly different. For this reason, taxable entities should consider after-tax characteristics during the allocation process. Adjusting for taxes after allocations have been made may lead to suboptimal allocations.

Although each country has its own unique tax legislation, there are several common characteristics that should be noted.

- Interest income is usually taxed at a higher rate than dividends or capital gains, and often at progressively higher rates. As a result, tax-exempt bonds (such as munis in the United States) may form a large part of a taxable investor's fixed income allocation.
- Dividends are usually taxed at a lower rate than interest. Some investors may invest in preferred stocks in place of bonds for this reason.
- Capital gains are usually taxed at a lower rate than income, and capital losses can be used to offset capital gains elsewhere in the portfolio.
- Certain investment accounts may be tax deferred or tax exempt. The least tax-efficient (most heavily taxed) assets should be placed in the most tax-advantaged accounts.

Taxes complicate the portfolio optimization process. Return and risk need to be considered on both a pre- and after-tax basis, although correlations will be unaffected by taxes.

EXAMPLE: After-tax return

An investor subject to income tax on interest earned at a rate of 40% is considering investing in a bond with a 5% coupon that is expected to be held to maturity. What return should the investor use as an input into the asset allocation process?

Answer:

As the investor is taxable, the after-tax return of $0.05(1 - 0.4) = 0.03$ or 3% should be used.

Equity returns include both dividend income and capital gains. Therefore, the after-tax calculation must adjust for income tax and capital gains tax.

Reading 5

EXAMPLE: Multi-step after-tax return calculation

An investor is subject to income tax at a rate of 30% on dividend income and 20% on capital gains. One potential investment under consideration is a stock with an estimated pre-tax return of 16%. Ten percent of this return is expected be realized in the form of dividend income and 90% as price appreciation (capital gains are assumed to be realized annually). What is the after-tax return to be used in the asset allocation process?

Answer:

Pre-tax dividend income:	16% × 0.1	= 1.6%
After-tax divided income:	1.6% (1 – 0.3)	= 1.12%
Pre-tax capital gain:	16% × 0.9	= 14.4%
After-tax capital gain:	14.4% (1 – 0.2)	= 11.52%
After-tax return:	**1.12 + 11.52**	**= 12.64%**

When an asset has a cost basis (for tax purposes) that differs from the market value, it has an existing unrealized gain (cost basis is below market value) or loss (cost basis is above market value). Unrealized gains imply an embedded tax liability and losses imply an embedded tax asset. There are three potential ways in which the current market value may be adjusted to reflect the liability or asset.

1. Subtract the value of the embedded capital gains tax from the current market value of the asset as if it were to be sold today.
2. Assume the asset is to be sold in the future and discount the tax liability to its present value using the asset's after-tax return as a discount rate.
3. Assume the asset is to be sold in the future and discount the tax liability to its present value using the after-tax risk-free rate.

Risk, as measured by standard deviation, must also be adjusted in the presence of tax. Capital gains tax reduces the gains realized on price appreciation, and the ability to use capital losses to offset those gains also reduces the losses realized from price declines. A post-tax standard deviation should therefore be used as an input into the asset allocation process.

EXAMPLE: After-tax standard deviation of return

A security has an expected pre-tax standard deviation of 12% and is under consideration for purchase by an investor who suffers capital gains tax at a rate of 20%. What is the after-tax standard deviation?

Answer:

after-tax standard deviation = 12%(1 – 0.2) = 9.6%

The use of both after-tax returns and after-tax risk can have significant impacts on the efficient frontier. Notably, allocations to tax inefficient assets such as high yield bonds will usually decrease. Such assets can, however, still play a part in the optimal allocation assuming they have low correlations with other assets in the portfolio.

Portfolio Rebalancing

To maintain the strategic asset allocation, all portfolios must periodically rebalance. Taxable asset owners will realize taxable gains at each rebalancing, so they must balance the need to maintain the strategic asset allocation with the desire to avoid taxable gains through frequent rebalancing.

Rebalancing should occur less frequently in taxable portfolios due to the reduction in volatility caused by taxation (while correlations remain unaltered). The acceptable rebalancing range after-tax can be calculated by first finding the allowable deviation from target: after-tax deviation = pre-tax deviation / (1 – t).

PROFESSOR'S NOTE

Be careful not to confuse the impact of taxes on after-tax standard deviation (of return) with the impact of taxes on allowable after-tax deviation from target weight for an asset class.

- Taxes cushion the pretax upside and downside of an asset's return and therefore **decrease** after-tax standard deviation of the asset (compared to its pretax standard deviation).

  $\sigma_{AT} = \sigma_{PT}(1 - t)$

- Because taxes lower return volatility, they **increase** the allowable deviation from target allocation weight (compared to pretax deviation).

  $\text{deviation from target weight}_{AT} = \text{deviation from target weight}_{PT} / (1 - t)$

EXAMPLE: Pretax vs. after-tax deviation from target allocation weight

A tax-exempt investor's strategic asset allocation calls for a 40% investment in fixed income, ±5% for a range of 35–45%. If fixed income returns are subject to a 30% tax rate, **calculate** the equivalent after-tax rebalancing range.

Answer:

pretax allowable deviation from target weight = 45% – 40% (or 40% – 35%) = 5%

post-tax deviation from target weight = 5% / (1 – 0.30) = 7.14% for a range of 32.86–47.14%

There are two strategies that can be employed to reduce the impact of taxation:

- Tax loss harvesting.
- Strategic asset location.

Tax loss harvesting involves deliberately realizing losses to offset gains elsewhere. Strategic asset location involves making the most efficient use of tax advantageous accounts. There are two types of accounts that offer tax advantages:

- Tax exempt accounts: assets in these accounts are not subject to taxation.
- Tax deferred accounts: assets can appreciate in these accounts tax free but are taxed upon distribution.

Assets placed in tax-exempt accounts need no adjustment to their market value before being included in the asset allocation process. However, the value of assets in tax-deferred and taxable accounts should be reduced by the tax burden.

The portfolio optimization process should consider both the asset classes available and the asset location. For example, if an investor has two accounts available: one taxable and one tax deferred—and two potential asset classes: fixed income and equities, the process should use four account types. It should use two for each asset class, depending on whether they are placed in the taxable or tax-deferred accounts.

The risk and return inputs for equities and fixed income assets to be located in the tax-deferred vehicle (which are allowed to grow tax-free) should be pre-tax. Risk and return inputs for each asset class to be located in the taxable vehicle should be after-tax.

Although liquidity needs for consumption should always be considered (e.g., assets allocated to pension accounts may not be accessible without incurring financial penalties), the following general rules should be applied when considering asset location:

- Assets subject to the lowest tax rates (typically equity) should be first allocated to taxable accounts.
- Assets subject to frequent trading and high tax rates should be allocated to tax-advantaged accounts.

MODULE QUIZ 5.1

1. An extremely large fund seeking to make a large allocation to an asset class will *most likely* face a liquidity constraint when investing in:
   A. hedge funds.
   B. global equity.
   C. investment-grade bonds.
2. A fund manager oversees a tax-exempt fund and a taxable fund. The strategic asset allocation for both funds is 60% equity and 40% fixed income, with an after-tax rebalancing range of ±12.5%, assuming a tax rate of 20%. The current allocation in both funds is 71% equity and 29% fixed income. Which of the following statements is *most accurate*?
   A. Only the tax-exempt fund is outside its applicable rebalancing range.
   B. Both funds are outside their respective rebalancing ranges.
   C. Neither fund is outside its applicable rebalancing range.

MODULE 5.2: ADJUSTING THE STRATEGIC ASSET ALLOCATION

Video covering this content is available online.

LOS 5.c: Recommend and justify revisions to an asset allocation given change(s) in investment objectives and/or constraints.

It is unlikely that the initial optimal asset allocation will be applicable for the entire lifetime of any portfolio. In practice, it is common to reevaluate the allocation annually or if a change in goals, constraints, or beliefs suggests it is required.

Change in Goals

For (some) institutions, the business cycle may trigger changes in goals.

A downturn in business, for example, may necessitate increased cash flows from the portfolio. For instance, as airlines face competition from low-budget competitors, and because of uncertain revenue streams, they may reduce the level or risk exposure in their pension fund in order to smooth the volatility of contributions. Pension funds themselves have faced increasing deficits in recent years, which also triggers a reexamination of the asset allocation.

Changes in personal circumstances for the individual investor will also impact the allocation decision. Changes in employment status or starting a family, could both impact an investor's willingness and ability to take on risk.

Change in Constraints

A change in any of the constraints discussed earlier in this reading would also necessitate a review of the current allocation. Examples include:

- Government regulations requiring increased distributions to maintain tax-exempt status.
- Large unexpected cash flows to cover one-off events.
- Increased funding requirements for the beneficiary of an endowment.
- Forced early retirement of an investor due to illness.

Any change in constraint that leads to a requirement for increased cash outflows is likely to necessitate a shift to more liquid assets. Conversely, a large inflow (such as a donation to a foundation) is likely to give the portfolio more flexibility to take on risk.

Change in Beliefs

The investment activities of the asset owner are guided by a set of principles, or beliefs. Just as with goals and constraints, there is no guarantee that these beliefs will not change over time.

For a portfolio run by an investment committee, for example, a change in the makeup of that committee could change beliefs. New members are typically walked through an asset allocation study to make sure they understand the investing approach that had been adopted.

Changes in the economic environment are also likely to have a major impact on the optimization process.

The key inputs when optimizing the asset allocation are expected returns, volatility, and correlation of assets. If macroeconomic forecasts for any major asset class change, then the optimal allocation will likely change. An allocation exercise undertaken in the interest rate environment pre-2008 would have very different expectations for fixed income performance than one undertaken post-2008.

Asset allocations may also change at predetermined dates without the need for a detailed reexamination. Target-date mutual funds, for example, adjust allocations for individual investors depending on their age. Such funds use a *glide-path* and shift from equity to more conservative investments (nominal and inflation-protected bonds) as the target date of the fund approaches.

LOS 5.d: Discuss the use of short-term shifts in asset allocation.

The long-term asset allocation specified in an investment policy statement is known as the *strategic asset allocation (SAA).* This represents the target asset weightings for the portfolio.

Short-term deviations, known as *tactical asset allocations (TAAs),* are typically used to take advantage of cyclical conditions in the market or a perceived mispricing in a given asset class.

Objective

The objective of TAA is to increase risk-adjusted returns by exploiting these short-term opportunities. It should be noted that this strategy assumes short-term returns are predictable (rather than a random walk as for long-term returns), and its success is dependent on market or factor timing, not individual security selection.

The TAA will still take into account the risk constraint specified in the investment policy statement, but will not consider specific goals or liabilities.

Constraints

The success of the TAA should be judged against the benchmark of the SAA. The size of deviations may often be limited to a range around this allocation. There may also be an allowable range of predicted volatility or a tracking error budget versus the SAA.

Evaluation

There are several common methods of measuring the success of a TAA decision.

- Comparing the Sharpe ratios under the TAAs and the SAAs.
- Calculating the information ratio or t-stat of the excess realized returns relative to the SAA.
- Comparing the realized risk and return of the TAA to portfolios lying on the SAA's efficient frontier. It may be less optimal than other portfolios on that frontier.
- Perform attribution analysis on the excess return to identify the contribution of specific under- or over-weightings.

Drawbacks

The use of TAA incurs additional trading costs and taxation in the case of taxable investors. Overweighting an asset class also concentrates risk within the portfolio and reduces diversification benefits.

Approaches to Tactical Asset Allocation

Discretionary TAA relies on qualitative interpretation of macroeconomic variables. A skillful manager will aim to enhance returns in a rising market and hedge risks in falling markets by successfully forecasting short-term deviations from expected returns for an asset class. A manager may use a combination of macroeconomic data, fundamental data, and sentiment indicators to assist with forecasting.

Macroeconomic data will focus on bond yields and credit spreads, monetary policy, GDP growth, earnings and inflation predictions, and other leading economic indicators. Fundamental data such as the deviation of P/E, P/B ratios and dividend yield from their historic means may also be used. Economic sentiment can be gauged using a consumer confidence index.

Market sentiment can be assessed using:

1. Margin borrowing: Increasing purchases on margin drives up prices and indicates investors are bullish, although if the level of margin buying gets too high, it can be a bearish sign and indicates investors are overenthusiastic.
2. Short interest (aggregate amount of short selling): This is essentially the opposite. Increasing short interest drives down prices and indicates investors are bearish, although very high levels could indicate the market is at or near a low.
3. Volatility indices: These indicate the level of fear in the market. It can be calculated using the bid-ask spread on index options. It increases with more purchases of puts and decreases with more purchase of calls.

Although the range of data used in discretionary TAA is quantitative in nature, the individual manager decides which indicators to use and how to prioritize and interpret them.

A systematic approach takes a more quantitative view. It attempts to capture excess returns using strategies that have historically been predictable and persistent. Two of the main factors that may be exploited are value and momentum.

A value approach aims to exploit the excess return of value stocks over growth stocks. Value in equities is most commonly measured using dividend or cash flow yields. Shiller's earnings yield (E/P) uses a 10-year average inflation-adjusted earnings figure compared to market price. Value currencies may be identified using short-term interest rate differentials, and commodities may be identified using roll yields. Commodity markets in backwardation will provide positive roll yields to the long, and those in contango negative. Yield spreads over risk free rates can be used to identify value in fixed income.

A momentum strategy assumes that trends will persist, which is why recent price movements are used to indicate whether to overweight or underweight an asset class. Indicators used include:

- Most recent 12-month trend: a momentum strategy assumes this trend will persist for the next 12 months.
- Moving-average crossover: shorter-term moving averages crossing above longer-term moving averages indicate an uptrend and vice versa.

Video covering this content is available online.

MODULE 5.3: BEHAVIORAL ISSUES

LOS 5.e: Identify behavioral biases that arise in asset allocation and recommend methods to overcome them.

Behavioral biases can cause problems during the asset allocation process. An awareness that behavioral bias exists is crucial to dealing with every bias.

Loss aversion is a bias in which investors dislike losses more than they like gains. This makes it difficult for investors to maintain discipline when returns are negative. There is a strong temptation to alter the asset allocation. Goals-based investing can help overcome the loss aversion bias. Goals are prioritized and subportfolios are used. High priority goals are funded with less risky assets, and riskier assets can be used in each subportfolio as the goal priority declines. Risk analysis typically focuses on downside measures such as shortfall risk.

Illusion of control is a tendency to overestimate the ability to control events. Combined with overconfidence, it typically leads to investors failing to diversify, trading too frequently, or both. Some common signs of this bias include:

- Frequent trading and tactical allocation shifts in an attempt at market timing. Investors who correctly call the reversal of a trend have too much confidence in their ability to repeat.
- Active security selection by institutional investors who believe the level of resources at their disposal gives them superior asset selection skills.
- Above average use of short selling and leverage.
- Shifting asset allocations despite a lack of consensus opinion as an individual trustee believes they know better than the market.
- Concentrated positions that expose the portfolio to diversifiable risk.
- Use of biased risk and return forecasts in the asset allocation framework that result in allocations that are inappropriately different from the market portfolio.

To counter the illusion of control, the market portfolio derived from the basic CAPM mean-variance framework should be used as the starting point for the allocation, and shifts in allocation away from this position should be subject to a formal review process.

Mental accounting involves separating assets and liabilities into different "buckets" based on **subjective criteria**. Mental accounting often leads to suboptimal asset allocations and less chance of meeting the goals. Individuals, for example, may spend their tax refund on luxury goods even when their savings are inadequate, or they may maintain low-interest savings accounts while paying high interest on large credit card balances. Entrepreneurs may form an emotional attachment to a company they founded and irrationally hold it in their high risk aspirational risk bucket, even when they no longer have any control at the company. Goals-based investing can help overcome mental accounting bias.

PROFESSOR'S NOTE

Notice that mental accounting is not the same thing as goals based even though goals-based investing has some elements of mental accounting in it. Goals-based investing is primarily a rational effort to differentiate the priority of goals and then use subportfolios in an effort to increase the chances of meeting the goals.

Representative bias, or *recency bias*, occurs when investors attach more importance to recent data than old data. The most common result is for an investor to shift allocations towards assets that have performed well recently. The popularity of purchasing and "flipping" (planning to sell it quickly at a profit) real estate property in the 1990s, can be traced back to a generation who had only experienced rising house prices. The problem was the past trend can and did change. Strong governance and objective asset allocation process are the best methods of defense against representative bias.

Framing bias occurs when the way information is presented affects the resulting decision. This is a common problem in asset allocation. If risk is presented as standard deviation, most investors prefer the lower risk. But downside risk measures may be more useful in specific situations. These include:

- VaR indicates amount of loss at some probability over a time.
- Conditional VaR quantifies the average loss within the VaR tail.
- Shortfall probability directly states the probability of some adverse outcome occurring.

The best way to overcome framing bias is to provide a full range of relevant information and not selectively frame only some pieces of the information.

Availability bias occurs when personally experienced or more easily recalled events disproportionately influence decisions. For example, an investor who suffered significant losses when the tech bubble burst won't buy tech or high P/B ratio stocks ever again. Investors make availability bias mistakes if they benchmark their portfolio performance to that of other investors, without regard to whether those other investors have comparable goals and constraints.

- *Familiarity bias* may be considered an offshoot of availability in that what is familiar or easy to recall is given too much importance in the decision process.
- *Home bias* can be considered another offshoot and is often seen in portfolios that over allocate to domestic securities, missing the opportunity to diversify with international securities.

Starting the allocation process with the global market portfolio can help to mitigate availability biases in the asset allocation process.

Investment Governance

Effective governance is essential to keeping behavioral bias under control. An effective framework should incorporate:

- Clearly stated long-term and short-term objectives.
- Logical allocation of responsibility for asset allocation decisions based on skills and workload.
- Documented processes for developing and approving the investment policy statement.
- Documented process for developing and approving the strategic asset allocation.
- Framework to monitor and report performance relative to specified goals and objectives.
- Periodic audits.

MODULE QUIZ 5.2, 5.3

1. A target date mutual fund being used by an individual with a goal of retiring at age 65 will *most likely*:
   A. increase the allocation to inflation-protected bonds later in the glide path.
   B. have a larger allocation to nominal bonds earlier in the glide path as opposed to later.
   C. allocate more of the portfolio to cash in the early phases of the glide path.
2. Which of the following statements regarding the relative success of a tactical asset allocation (TAA) against the strategic asset allocation (SAA) is *most likely* correct?
   A. The TAA is successful if it has a positive Sharpe ratio.
   B. The TAA is unsuccessful if the information ratio is negative.
   C. The TAA is successful if it has a lower standard deviation than that of the SAA.
3. Ellie Rotheram is a 42-year-old real estate broker. Through patient saving, she has accumulated a retirement portfolio worth $720,000. Her investment approach is very conservative, with 88% allocated to fixed income and 12% to equity. She does not want to take the higher risk of equity in this retirement portfolio.

   Recently, Rotheram inherited $500,000 and placed this in a separate portfolio. She realizes she has been very conservative in her retirement portfolio and plans to invest this portfolio more aggressively, in an effort to improve her lifestyle. So far, she has invested $225,000 in real estate investment trusts with holdings in her home state. She also invested $50,000 in the equity of a property development company, because she used to work there several years ago.

   Which of the following behavioral biases is Rotheram *most clearly* exhibiting?
   A. Mental accounting.
   B. Familiarity bias.
   C. Framing bias.

KEY CONCEPTS

LOS 5.a

Portfolios that are too small may be unable to invest in alternative investment vehicles that have minimum investment or qualification requirements.

Large portfolios have the skill, governance structure, and capital resources to invest in complex strategies and achieve diversification levels that smaller portfolios may be unable to achieve.

Portfolios that are too large may find it difficult to invest in niche strategies as the asset pool or managers available are quickly exhausted.

The asset owner's liquidity needs should be matched to the liquidity characteristics of an asset when optimizing asset allocation.

Investor behavior often changes during periods of negative returns, so any liquidity analysis should include an evaluation of liquidity requirements in times of market stress.

Longer time horizons typically allow for greater risk exposure due to the time diversification of risk.

Changes in goals, liabilities, and human capital as time passes mean the asset allocation process is a dynamic one that must be regularly revisited.

LOS 5.b

Investors subject to regulatory and tax requirements must factor those constraints into the asset allocation process.

Taxation reduces the risk and return of assets but leaves asset correlations unaltered.

Lower after-tax risk levels lead to wider rebalancing ranges for taxable investors. Frequent rebalancing leads to realized taxable gains.

Assets taxed at higher effective rates should be allocated first to tax advantaged accounts.

LOS 5.c

Asset allocations should be reviewed in the light of changing goals, beliefs, or other constraints.

Asset allocations may change automatically along a predetermined glide path in reaction to milestones or predictable events that change an investor's risk ability and willingness to take risk.

LOS 5.d

Short-term alterations to the long-term strategic asset allocation are known as tactical asset allocations (TAAs). The permitted size of alterations is likely to be dictated by the investment policy statement.

TAAs aim to enhance returns by altering asset classes, sectors, or risk-factor premium weightings.

The performance of TAAs can be measured by comparing realized portfolio results with TAA implemented to what would have happened under strategic asset allocation (SAA). Success is indicated by a better Sharpe ratio, information ratio, or t-stat of the excess returns. Actual TAA results that plot on the efficient frontier also indicate success.

TAAs can result in excessive trading and tax costs and in the concentration of risk in specific assets in the portfolio.

Systematic TAA uses quantitative signals to dictate shifts in weightings, whereas discretionary allocation relies on qualitative interpretation of data and manager skill in identifying shorter-term trends.

LOS 5.e

- Loss aversion occurs when a dislike of losses and preference for gains distorts rational decision making. Use goals-based investing to mitigate.
- Illusion of control is an overestimation of ability to control events. Start with the CAPM market portfolio and use sound corporate governance to mitigate.
- Mental accounting subjectively (not rationally) treats different pools of funds differently and often leads to suboptimal asset allocation. Use goals-based investing to mitigate.
- Representative (recency) bias overemphasizes the importance of the most recent events and can lead to trend following, assuming what is currently happening will continue. Use sound corporate governance to mitigate.
- Framing bias can result in suboptimal decisions when the way information is presented affects the decisions made. Start with a full range of relevant information to mitigate.
- Availability, familiarity, and home bias are closely related. What is easily recalled or available is given too much importance in the decision process. Start with the CAPM market portfolio to mitigate.

A strong governance process guards against most behavioral biases and should include clearly defined objectives (short and long term), responsibilities, and decision-making process along with a framework for monitoring, reviewing, and performing periodic internal audits.

ANSWER KEY FOR MODULE QUIZZES

Module Quiz 5.1

1. **A** Hedge funds are likely the smallest and least liquid class of the three choices. (LOS 5.a)

2. **A** The after-tax rebalancing deviation specified is 12.5% using a tax rate of 20%. The pretax deviation is therefore 12.5% × 0.8 = 10%. This means the tax-exempt portfolio is outside its applicable range. The range for the tax-exempt fund is 50% to 70% for equity and 30% to 50% for FI. The range for the taxable fund is 47.5% to 72.5% for equity and 27.5% to 52.5% for FI. Note that the effect of taxes on allowable deviation from target allocation weight was directly covered in our write up.

   $$\text{deviation from target weight}_{AT} = \text{deviation from target weight}_{PT} / (1 - t)$$

   In this case, you must work from deviation AT backwards to deviation PT, so the relationship is:

   $$\text{deviation from target weight}_{AT} (1 - t) = \text{deviation from target weight}_{PT}$$

   (LOS 5.b)

Module Quiz 5.2, 5.3

1. **A** Target date funds are intended for individuals who plan to retire on the fund's target date. The glide path ends on the target date. As the fund moves from early to late on the glide path, the asset allocation is shifted from equity towards more fixed income and cash. (Module 5.2, LOS 5.e)

2. **B** None of these are perfect answers in that we'd like to know how return to risk for the fund after TAA compares to what would have happened if the SAA (no TAA) had been followed. A negative IR certainly indicates failure as the goal of TAA is positive value added (the numerator of the IR ratio should be positive not negative). A positive Sharpe ratio alone says nothing about how SAA would have done, and lower risk with no idea of return earned provides little information. (Module 5.2, LOS 5.d)

3. **B** She exhibits familiarity bias when investing in equity of a company because she used to work there and a REIT because it has holdings in her home state. She is also using goals-based investing and while that has elements of mental accounting in it, the motivations are quite different. Using subportfolios to address different priority goals can be quite rational and is not by itself a bias. There is no indication that framing of information is a factor here. (Module 5.3, LOS 5.e)

TOPIC QUIZ: ASSET ALLOCATION

You have now finished the Asset Allocation topic section. On your Schweser online dashboard, you can find a Topic Quiz that will provide immediate feedback on how effective your study of this material has been. The test is best taken timed; allow three minutes per question. Topic Quizzes are more exam-like than typical QBank questions or module quiz questions. A score less than 70% suggests that additional review of the topic is needed.

FORMULAS

Target interest rate using the neutral rate:

$$n_{target} = r_{neutral} + i_{expected} + [0.5(GDP_{expected} - GDP_{trend}) + 0.5(i_{expected} - i_{target})]$$

Grinold-Kroner model:

$$E(R_e) \approx D/P + (\%\Delta E - \%\Delta S) + \%\Delta P/E$$

Singer-Terhaar model:

risk premium assuming full integration:

$$RP_i = \rho_{i,M}\sigma_i(\text{market Sharpe ratio})$$

risk premium assuming full segmentation:

$$RP_i = \sigma_i(\text{market Sharpe ratio})$$

weighted average risk premium:

RP_i = (degree of integration of *i*)(ERP assuming full integration) + (degree of segmentation of *i*)(ERP assuming full segmentation)

Capitalization rate (with infinite time period):

$$\text{cap rate} = E(R_{re}) - \text{NOI growth rate}$$
$$E(R_{re}) = \text{cap rate} + \text{NOI growth rate}$$

Capitalization rate (with finite time period):

$$E(R_{re}) = \text{cap rate} + \text{NOI growth rate} - \%\Delta\text{cap rate}$$

Expected percentage change in the exchange rate:

$$E(\%\Delta S_{d/f}) = (r^d - r^f) + (\text{Term}^d - \text{Term}^f) + (\text{Credit}^d - \text{Credit}^f) + (\text{Equity}^d - \text{Equity}^f) + (\text{Liquid}^d - \text{Liquid}^f)$$

Return of the *i*th asset in a multifactor model:

$$r_i = \alpha_i + \sum_{k=1}^{K} \beta_{ik}F_k + \varepsilon_i$$

Variance of the *i*th asset:

$$\sigma_i^2 = \sum_{m=1}^{K} \sum_{n=1}^{K} \beta_{im}\beta_{in}\rho_{mn} + \nu_i^2$$

Covariance between the *i*th and *j*th asset:

$$\sigma_{ij} = \sum_{m=1}^{K} \sum_{n=1}^{K} \beta_{im}\beta_{jn}\rho_{mn}$$

Smoothed returns to estimate volatility is the weighted average of the current "true" returns and previously observed returns:

$R_t = (1 - \lambda)r_1 + \lambda R_{t-1}$ where λ is a weight between 0 and 1

Portfolio variance = $\text{var}(r) = \left(\frac{1+\lambda}{1-\lambda}\right)\text{var}(R) > \text{var}(R)$

ARCH model:

$$\sigma_t^2 = \gamma + \alpha\sigma_{t-1}^2 + \beta\eta_t^2 = \gamma + (\alpha + \beta)\sigma_{t-1}^2 + \beta\left(\eta_t^2 - \sigma_{t-1}^2\right)$$

where α, β, and γ are nonnegative parameters and $(\alpha + \beta) < 1$, and η_t is a random variable indicating the unexpected return component.

Higher $\alpha + \beta$ terms indicate higher emphasis on past information, leading to volatility clustering.

$U_m = E(R_{s,m}) - 0.005 \times \lambda \times Var_{s,m}$

where:
$E(R_{s,m})$ = expected surplus return
$Var_{s,m}$ = variance of surplus return

After-tax *standard deviation* = pretax standard deviation (1 – t)

After-tax *deviation from midpoint of target asset allocation* = pretax deviation / (1 – t)

INDEX

Notes

LEVEL III SCHWESER'S QuickSheet

CRITICAL CONCEPTS FOR THE 2024 CFA® EXAM

CAPITAL MARKET EXPECTATIONS

Long-term economic growth rate:
pop growth + labor force part. + new cap. spending + TFP

Taylor rule:

$n_{target} = r_{neutral} + i_{expected} + [0.5(GDP_{expected} - GDP_{trend}) + 0.5(i_{expected} - i_{target})]$

n_{target} = target nominal short-term interest rate
$r_{neutral}$ = neutral real short-term interest rate
$GDP_{expected}$ = expected GDP growth rate
GDP_{trend} = long-term trend in the GDP growth rate
$i_{expected}$ = expected inflation rate
i_{target} = target inflation rate

Risk premium approach to expected bond return:
risk-free rate + term premium + credit premium + liquidity premium

Grinold-Kroner model:
$E(R_e) \approx D/P + (\%\Delta E - \%\Delta S) + \%\Delta P/E$
$E(R_e)$ = expected equity return
D/P = dividend yield
$\%\Delta E$ = percentage change in earnings
$\%\Delta S$ = percentage change in shares outstanding
$\%\Delta P/E$ = expected repricing return

Singer-Terhaar model:
Risk premium assuming full integration:
$RP_i = \rho_{i,M}\sigma_i$(market Sharpe ratio)
Risk premium assuming full segmentation:
$RP_i = \sigma_i$(market Sharpe ratio)

Weighted average risk premium:
RP_i = (degree of integration of i) (ERP assuming full integration) + (degree of segmentation of i) (ERP assuming full segmentation)

Commercial real estate:
Cap rate = NOI / (property value)
$E(R_{re})$ = cap rate + NOI growth rate
For a finite time period: $E(R_{re})$ = cap rate + NOI growth rate − %Δcap rate

ASSET ALLOCATION

Asset Allocation Approaches
- **Asset-only:** focuses on asset return and standard deviation.
- **Liability-relative:** focuses on growth of the surplus and standard deviation.
- **Goals-based:** uses subportfolios to meet specified goals.

Asset classes:
- Assets within a class are similar and don't fit in more than one class.
- Classes have low correlation to other classes, cover all investable assets, and are liquid.

Calendar rebalancing is done at a set frequency.

Percentage range rebalancing is when a band is violated. Wider bands for: higher transaction cost and correlations between classes, higher risk tolerance, momentum markets, and less volatile asset classes.

MVO use E(R), σ, and correlations to solve for the efficient frontier (EF) and asset allocation.

Pitfalls of MVO analysis include: estimating the inputs, concentrated allocations, and a single period analysis.

Utility maximization: $U_m = E(R_m) - 0.005 \times \lambda \times Var_m$

U_m = the investor's utility from investing in a portfolio with asset allocation m
$E(R_m)$ = the expected return of the portfolio with asset allocation m (expressed as a %)
λ = the investor's risk aversion coefficient ("lambda")
$Var_m = \sigma^2_m$ = the variance of the portfolio with asset allocation m (expressed as a %)

- Reverse optimization solves for the E(R)s based on market weights.
- Black-Litterman view adjusts these returns and then resolves for an EF.
- Monte Carlo simulation models how an allocation may perform over time.

DERIVATIVES AND CURRENCY MANAGEMENT

Option Strategies

Know the inherent payoff patterns of the option combinations, then:
- Calculate profit/loss at any ending price for the underlying as sum of initial investment versus ending value of the positions held.
- Max gain and loss: examine the payoff pattern and, from that underlying's price, sum the initial investment versus ending value of the positions held.
- Breakeven(s): examine the payoff pattern and, from either max gain or loss, determine how much the underlying must increase or decrease.

Synthetic long forward = long call + short put. Both options are short the underlying.

- **Covered Call**

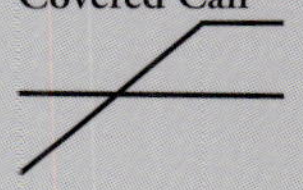

Protective Put

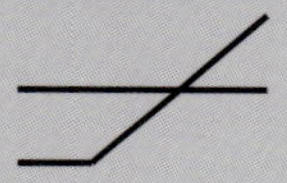

- **Bull Spread**

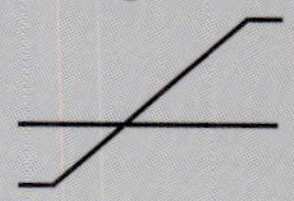

Collar: Payoff pattern is identical to a bull spread but includes owning the underlying.

- **Bear Spread**

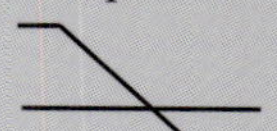

Straddle

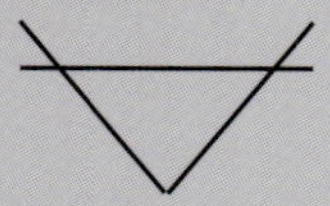

- **Calendar spread**—Options have different expirations.
- **Volatility smile**—Further-from-ATM options have higher implied volatilities resulting in a U-shaped (smiling) curve when implied volatility is plotted against strike price.
- **Volatility skew**—Implied volatility increases for more OTM puts, and decreases for more OTM calls. Explained by OTM puts being desirable as insurance against market declines while the demand for OTM calls is low.
- For an expected increase in equity market volatility buy an ATM call on volatility index (VIX) futures and sell an OTM put on VIX futures.

Choosing Options Strategies Based on Direction and Volatility of the Underlying Asset

		Outlook on the Trend of Underlying Asset		
		Bearish	*Neutral*	*Bullish*
Expected move in implied volatility	Decrease	Write calls	Write straddle	Write puts
	Remain unchanged	Write calls and buy puts	Calendar spread	Buy calls and write puts
	Increase	Buy puts	Buy straddle	Buy calls

Interest rate swaps

Converting fixed-rate and floating-rate exposures:

Existing Exposure	*Converting*	*Interest Rate Swap Required*	*Beneficial When:*
Floating-rate liability	Floating to fixed	Payer swap	floating rates expected to rise
Fixed-rate liability	Fixed to floating	Receiver swap	floating rates expected to fall
Floating-rate asset	Floating to fixed	Receiver swap	floating rates expected to fall
Fixed-rate asset	Fixed to floating	Payer swap	floating rates expected to rise

The notional principal of the interest rate swap.

$$NP_S = \left(\frac{MD_T - MD_P}{MD_S}\right)(MV_P)$$

where:
NP_S = notional swap principal
MD_T = target modified duration
MD_P = current portfolio modified duration
MD_S = modified duration of swap
MV_P = market value of portfolio

Forward rate agreements are typically used to hedge the uncertainty about a future short-term borrowing or lending rate.

Hedging Interest Rate Risk Using Treasury Futures

To hedge the interest rate risk of a long bond portfolio the fund manager will use Treasury bond futures.

A duration-based hedge ratio (BPV HR) is calculated to determine the number of futures contracts required for a hedge.

$$BPVHR = \frac{-BPV_{portfolio}}{BPV_{CTD}} \times CF$$

Basis point value (BPV) is the expected change in value of a security or portfolio given a one basis point (0.01%) change in yield.

$BPVHR$ = number of short futures
$BPV_{Portfolio} = MD_{Portfolio} \times 0.01\% \times MV_{Portfolio}$
MD = modified duration
$BPV_{CTD} = MD_{CTD} \times 0.01\% \times MV_{CTD}$
MV_{CTD} = CTD price / 100 × \$100,000

To achieve a target duration, the formula can be amended to:

$$BPVHR = \frac{BPV_{target} - BPV_{portfolio}}{BPV_{CTD}} \times CF$$

$BPV_{Target} = MD_{Target} \times 0.0001 \times MV_{Portfolio}$

Currency forwards and futures allow users to exchange a specified amount of one currency for a specified amount of another currency on a future date. Forwards are customized while futures are standardized contracts.

The hedge ratio for futures can be calculated as:

$$HR = \frac{\text{amount of currency to be exchanged}}{\text{futures contract size}}$$

Equity swaps can be used to create a synthetic exposure to physical stocks, allowing market participants to increase or decrease their exposure to equity returns.

continued on next page...

The three main types of swaps:
1. Pay fixed, receive equity return
2. Pay floating, receive equity return
3. Pay another equity return, receive equity return

Equity Futures and Forwards

Equity futures are exchange-traded, standardized, require margin, have low transaction costs, and are available on indexes and single stocks. They enable market participants to:

- Implement tactical allocation decisions (alter the exposure to equity of a portfolio).
    - Selling futures (short position) reduces equity exposure.
    - Buying futures (long position) increases equity exposure.
- Achieve portfolio diversification.
- Gain exposure to international markets.
- Make directional bets on the direction of the market.

Forwards provide the same advantages but lack liquidity, are not subject to mark-to-market margin adjustments, counterparty credit risk exists, major advantage is they can be customized.

Achieving a target portfolio beta:

$$\text{number of futures required} = \left(\frac{\beta_T - \beta_P}{\beta_F}\right)\left(\frac{MV_P}{F}\right)$$

where:
β_T = target portfolio beta
β_P = current portfolio beta
β_F = futures beta (beta of stock index)
MV_P = market value of portfolio
F = futures contract value = futures price × multiplier

Note that to fully hedge the portfolio from market risk $\beta_T = 0$.

VIX Futures

- Negative correlation between the VIX and stock returns which becomes more pronounced during equity market downturns.
- An equity holding can be protected from extreme downturns (tail risk) by buying VIX futures. If volatility increases the equity portfolio will decline in value but VIX futures should increase in value.
- VIX futures will increase in value when the market's expectation of future volatility at contract maturity increases.

Position	*Term structure*	*Roll yield*
Long futures position	Contango	Negative
Short futures position	Contango	Positive
Long futures position	Backwardation	Positive
Short futures position	Backwardation	Negative

VIX Options

- Call options gain in value if expectations of volatility at maturity of the option increase.
- Put options gain in value if expectations of volatility fall.

Variance swaps are based on variance (σ^2) rather than volatility (standard deviation).

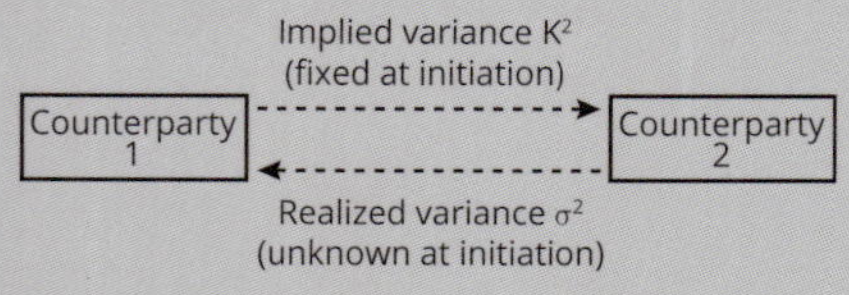

There is no initial exchange of notional principal, no interim settlement periods, and a single payment at the expiration of the swap based on the difference between actual and implied variance over the life of the swap.

$\text{Settlement amount}_T$ = (variance notional)(realized variance − variance strike)

Long (purchaser) describes the counterparty who receives the realized variance (actual) and pays the swap's variance strike (implied volatility).

Realized volatility	>	strike	Buyer (long) of swap makes a profit
Realized volatility	<	strike	Buyer (long) of swap makes a loss

The notional amount for a variance swap can be expressed as either variance notional (N_{VAR}) or vega notional (N_{VEGA}).

$$\text{variance notional} = \frac{\text{vega notional}}{2\times\text{strike price (K)}}, \text{ so}$$

$$\text{profit or loss} = N_{VAR} \times (\sigma^2 - K^2) = N_{vega} \times \left(\frac{\sigma^2 - K^2}{2K}\right)$$

where:
σ = realized volatility
K = strike volatility (implied volatility)

Both the actual (σ) and the implied volatility (K) on the swap are quoted in standard deviations, but remember that this is a variance swap; therefore, we must square the volatility.

The market convention is to quote the notional on a swap as vega notional (N_{VEGA}) rather than variance notional (N_{VAR}). Recall that vega refers to the change in option premium per a 1% change in volatility, $\frac{\Delta\text{premium}}{\Delta\text{volatility}}$, a natural way to think about the return for volatility.

Foreign Currency Equations

$$R_{DC} = (1 + R_{FC})(1 + R_{FX}) - 1 = R_{FC} + R_{FX} + (R_{FC})(R_{FX})$$

$$R_{DC} \approx R_{FC} + R_{FX}$$

R_{FC} = return on the foreign asset and
R_{FX} = return on the foreign currency

$$\sigma^2(R_{DC}) \approx \sigma^2(R_{FC}) + \sigma^2(R_{FX}) + 2\sigma(R_{FC})\,\sigma(R_{FX})\,\rho(R_{FC},R_{FX})$$

If R_{FC} is a risk-free asset:

$$\sigma(R_{DC}) = \sigma(R_{FX})(1 + R_{FC})$$

Currency Management Strategies

- **Passive hedging:** eliminates currency risk relative to the benchmark.
- **Discretionary hedging** allows the manager to deviate modestly from passive hedging. The goal is risk reduction.
- **Active currency management** allows a manager to have greater deviations from passive hedging. The goal is adding value.
- **Currency overlay** is the outsourcing of currency management to another manager.

Factors That Shift the Strategic Decision Toward a Benchmark Neutral or Fully Hedged Strategy

- A short time horizon for portfolio objectives.
- High risk aversion.
- Little weight given to the opportunity costs of missing positive currency returns.
- High short-term income and liquidity needs.
- Significant foreign currency bond exposure.
- Low hedging costs.
- Clients who doubt the benefits of discretionary management.

Tactical Currency Management

- **Economic fundamentals:** in the long term, relative currency values will converge to their fair values. Increases in currency values are associated with currencies:
    - That are undervalued relative to their fundamental value.
    - That have the greatest rate of increase in fundamental value.
    - With higher real or nominal interest rates.
    - With lower inflation relative to other countries.
    - Of countries with decreasing risk premiums.
- **Carry trade:** borrow in a lower interest rate currency and invest in a higher interest rate currency.
- **Volatility trading:** profit from predicting changes in currency volatility. If volatility is expected to increase, purchase an at-the-money call and put (long straddle). Sell volatility by selling both options (a short straddle).

Forward Premiums or Discounts and Currency Hedging Costs

If the hedge requires:	$F_{P/B} > S_{P/B}$, $i_B < i_P$ The forward price curve is upward sloping.	$F_{P/B} < S_{P/B}$, $i_B > i_P$ The forward price curve is downward sloping.
A long forward position in currency B the hedge earns:	Negative roll yield, which increases hedging cost and discourages hedging.	Positive roll yield, which decreases hedging cost and encourages hedging.
A short forward position in currency B the hedge earns:	Positive roll yield, which decreases hedging cost and encourages hedging.	Negative roll yield, which increases hedging cost and discourages.

The **minimum-variance hedge ratio** (MVHR): a regression of past changes in value of the portfolio to past changes in value of the foreign currency. The hedge ratio is the beta (slope coefficient) of that regression.

- Strong positive correlation between R_{FX} and R_{FC} increases the volatility of R_{DC} resulting in a hedge ratio > 1.0.
- Strong negative correlation between R_{FX} and R_{FC} decreases the volatility of R_{DC} resulting in a hedge ratio < 1.0.

FIXED INCOME

Liability-based mandates:

- Cash flow matching directly funds liabilities with coupon and par amounts.
- Duration matching requires:
    - PVA = PVL; there are exceptions when asset and liability discount rates differ.
    - $D_A = D_L$ or $BPV_A = BPV_L$
    - Minimize portfolio convexity but make it greater than that of the liabilities.
- Derivatives overlays:
    - involving the use of futures or swaps contracts, can be used to implement duration matching or contingent immunization strategies.

Regularly rebalance the portfolio:

- $BPV_{futures} \approx BPV_{CTD} / CF_{CTD}$
- $BPV = MD \times V \times 0.0001$
- $N_f = (BPV_L - \text{current BPV}) / BPV_{futures}$
- Nonparallel yield curve shifts can be a problem, match key rate durations: $\%\Delta\text{ value} = -MD_{\text{key rate n}}\,\Delta y_n$
- Contingent immunization: active management if the surplus is positive.

$$\text{Effective duration} = \frac{(PV_-) - (PV_+)}{2(\Delta\text{Curve})(PV_0)}$$

$$\text{Effective convexity} = \frac{(PV_-) + (PV_+) - 2(PV_0)}{(\Delta\text{Curve})^2(PV_0)}$$

where:
PV_0 = current value of the portfolio
PV_- = value of portfolio when benchmark curve is shifted down
PV_+ = value of portfolio when benchmark curve is shifted up
ΔCurve = change in benchmark curve

Return can be projected (or actual return decomposed) as the sum of:

1. Coupon income: annual coupon amount / current bond price
2. Rolldown return, assuming no change in yield curve: (projected ending bond price (BP) – beginning BP) / beginning BP

- Property risk: Loss in value of physical property (FC). Use property insurance (homeowner's and automobile).
- Liability risk: If legally responsible for damages. Use liability insurance.
- Health risk: Direct loss of FC to pay illness or injury related expenses and may reduce HC. Use health and medical insurance.

Asset allocation based on investor's total economic wealth, FC and HC:

- Individual employed in a high risk profession would choose lower risk FC.
- If HC is positively correlated with the stock market then best to select asset classes other than equity for risky assets used.
- Avoid FC tied directly to employer.

Risk Management Decision Matrix

Characteristic of the Loss	*Occurs Regularly*	*Infrequent*
Very severe	Risk avoidance	Risk transfer
Not severe	Risk reduction	Risk retention

INSTITUTIONAL INVESTORS

Stakeholders and key elements of the IPS for defined benefit (DB) pension plans vs. defined contribution (DC) pension plans:

	DB Plan	*DC Plan*
Stakeholders	Employers, plan beneficiaries, investment staff, investment committee/ board, governments, shareholders	Employers, plan beneficiaries, investment staff, investment committee/ board, governments
Liabilities	Present value of future benefits promised to plan participants. Higher when: • Employees work longer • Salaries are higher • Participants live longer • Lower employee turnover leads to higher vesting • Discount rate is low	No liability to plan sponsor once required contribution to plan has been met
Investment time horizon	Longer if proportion of active lives is higher	Dependent on the age of participant: longer if younger
Liquidity needs	Higher with: • More retired lives • Older workforce • Higher funded status (may reduce contributions) • Flexibility of participants to switch plans	Higher with: • Older workforce • Flexibility of participants to switch plans
External constraints	• Regulations vary by country: IORP II in Europe, ERISA in U.S. • Tax treatment favorable • Accounting rules: ASC 715 requires funded status to be shown on balance sheet (U.S. GAAP); public pension plans follow GASB	• Regulations vary by country: IORP II in Europe, ERISA in U.S. • Sponsor must offer appropriate default option to disengaged participants • Plans are tax deferred
Investment objectives	Achieve a long-term target return over a specified horizon with appropriate risk to meet contractual liabilities.	Prudently grow assets to meet spending needs in retirement.

Stakeholders and key elements of the IPS for the five types of sovereign wealth funds (SWF):

	Budget Stabilization	*Development*	*Savings*	*Reserve*	*Pension Reserve*
Stakeholders	Country's citizens, the government, external and internal investment management				
Liabilities	Uncertain: linked to commodity prices/ economic cycle	Linked to socio-economic investments	Spending on future generations	Yield promised on central bank/ government bonds	Future pension Payments
Investment time horizon	Short term	Long/medium term dependent on investment projects	Long term	Long term	Long term
Liquidity needs	Highest	Generally low	Lowest	Intermediate	Varies: low during accumulation stage, higher during decumulation stage
External constraints	Established by national legislation. Best practice set by ISWF's Santiago Principles. Generally tax exempt.				
Investment objectives	Capital preservation	Real growth higher than real GDP growth	Maintain real perpetual spending	Grow faster than yield on central bank/ government bonds	Earn returns to meet future unfunded government pension payments

Stakeholders and key elements of the IPS for university endowments and private foundations:

	University Endowments	*Private Foundations*
Stakeholders	Current and future students, alumni, university employees	Founding family, donors, grant recipients and broader community, governments
Liabilities	Set by the future spending promised to the university. Spending policy should consider (1) ongoing donations, (2) reliance of university on spending, (3) ability to issue debt. Spending may use a spending rule which takes a weighted average of last period's spending adjusted for inflation and a fixed spending rate applied to average AUM.	U.S. tax rules require minimum spending of 5% of assets plus investment expenses. Must also spend donations in the same year they are received.
Investment time horizon	Perpetual	Typically perpetual, but shortened for limited-life foundations
Liquidity needs	The spending rate net of donations is very low at 2%–4% of assets.	Higher than endowments—legally required to spend 5% of assets. Reliance on spending by foundation is usually higher than the reliance of a university on endowment spending.
External constraints	Typically tax exempt. Regulation varies by jurisdiction but generally requires a total return approach and prudence in investing (UPMIFA in U.S., The Trustee Act in the U.K.).	
Investment objectives	Generate a total real return after inflation measure by the HEPI of about 5% on a 3–5 year rolling basis, with reasonable annual volatility in the range of 10%–15%	Generate a real return over consumer price inflation of the spending rate (minimum 5%) plus investment expenses on a 3–5 year rolling basis, with reasonable annual volatility in the range of 10%–15%

Stakeholders and key elements of the IPS for banks and insurers:

	Banks	*Insurers*
Stakeholders	External: shareholder, depositors, borrowers, creditors, credit ratings agencies, regulators, and communities. Internal: employees, management, and board	External: shareholders, policyholders, derivatives counterparties, creditors, regulators, credit ratings agencies. Internal: employees, management, and board
Liabilities	Primarily deposits which are short term	Life insurers: long duration contract payouts. P&C insurers: shorter and less certain contract payouts
Investment time horizon	While perpetual organizations, investments are run on a short/medium term LDI basis.	
Liquidity needs	Driven by deposit withdrawals and potential need to raise liquidity in adverse market conditions. Regulators apply liquidity coverage ratios and net stable funding ratios.	Varies by product line—P&C liquidity needs generally higher than life. Liquidity needs will increase in times of high interest rates due to policyholders surrendering in search of high yields elsewhere.
External constraints	Highly regulated due to importance to real economy and systemic risk, particularly SIFIs. Main goal of regulators is to ensure the institution holds sufficient risk-based capital to absorb losses. Three different types of accounting systems apply: 1. Standard financial reporting (GAAP or IFRS) 2. Statutory accounting for regulators (more conservative than financial reporting) 3. True economic accounting (marked-to-market) Banks and insurers are fully taxable.	
Investment objectives	Manage liquidity and risk mismatches between the institution's non-investment assets and liabilities. This needs to be done in the context of the institution's overall profit maximization objective.	

The change in the market value of equity for banks and insurers:

$$\%\Delta E = \%\Delta A(M) - \%\Delta L(M - 1)$$

where:

$\%\Delta E$ = percentage change in the value of equity
$\%\Delta A$ = percentage change in the value of assets
$\%\Delta L$ = percentage change in the value of liabilities
M = leverage multiplier, A / E

The duration of the equity of a bank or insurer:

$$D_E = D_A(M) - D_L(M - 1)\left(\frac{\Delta i}{\Delta y}\right)$$

where:

D_E = modified duration of the institution's equity capital
D_A = modified duration of the institution's assets
D_L = modified duration of the institution's liabilities
M = leverage multiplier, A / E
$\frac{\Delta i}{\Delta y}$ = estimated change in yield of liabilities, *i*, relative to a unit change in yield of assets, *y*

The expected volatility (i.e., standard deviation) of the percentage change in the market value of equity capital for a bank or insurer:

$$\sigma_E^2 = M^2\sigma_A^2 + (M - 1)^2\sigma_L^2 - 2(M)(M - 1)\sigma_A\sigma_L\rho_{AL}$$

where:

σ_E = standard deviation of percentage change in the market value of equity
σ_A = standard deviation of percentage change in the value of assets
σ_L = standard deviation of percentage change in the value of liabilities
M = leverage multiplier, A / E
ρ_{AL} = correlation of percentage value changes in assets and liabilities

TRADING, PERFORMANCE EVALUATION, AND MANAGER SELECTION

Implementation shortfall (IS) at the highest level the absolute value is:

IS = paper return − actual return

IS can be decomposed into the following parts:

- *Execution cost* occurs due to executing shares at a less favorable price than the original decision price. Execution cost can be further broken down into:
  - *Delay cost* occurs due to adverse price movements in the time between the portfolio manager submits the order to the trader and the time the trader releases the order to the market. For a buy order: delay cost = shares executed × (arrival price − decision price)
    - Decision price = price when manager decides to buy (or sell).

b. *Insurance/reinsurance* strategies:
    - *Insurance strategy*—An insured person sells their insurance policy (through a broker) to a hedge fund.
    - *Reinsurance* strategies—Insurance companies sell off some of their risk to reinsurance companies who may then sell the risk to hedge funds in exchange for capital.

c. **Multimanager** strategies use other hedge fund strategies as building blocks, combining different strategies together, rebalancing exposures over time.

Drawdown:
Defined as the percentage peak-to-trough decline for a portfolio.
High-water mark refers to the maximum value the portfolio has ever reached.

Estimating investor cash flows to and from a private investment:
Capital contribution in period t = percentage to be called in period t × (committed capital − capital previously called)
Distributions in period t = percentage to be distributed in period t × [NAV in period t − 1 × (1 + growth rate)]
- NAV in period t = [NAV in period t − 1 × (1 + growth rate)] + contributions in period t − distributions in period t

PRIVATE WEALTH MANAGEMENT

OVERVIEW OF PRIVATE WEALTH MANAGEMENT

Behavioral Biases Associated with Retirees:
- *Increased loss aversion.* Affects return assumptions and asset allocation decisions in retirement.
- *Consumption gaps.* Consumption spending tends to be *lower* than what economic studies forecast, can be attributed to *loss aversion* and *uncertainty about future retirement spending.*
- *The "annuity puzzle".* Individuals tend to avoid buying annuities, possible explanations include: (a) clinging to hope of funding a better retirement lifestyle, (b) a desire to keep control of assets, and (c) the high cost of annuities.
- *Mental accounting and lack of self-control.* Retirees prefer to *meet their spending needs from investment income rather than liquidating securities.*

IPS for a Private Clients:
- **Client Background** obtained from relevant *personal, financial* and *tax* information. **Investment Objectives** may be *planned, unplanned, ongoing,* or *one-off.* Multiple objectives should be prioritized into *primary* and *secondary* objectives.
- **Key Investment Parameters:**
    - *Risk tolerance*—willingness and ability, low risk tolerance usually associated with *high priority* goals and *near-term* goals.
    - *Time horizon*—described as a *range* (e.g. in excess of 15 years for a long horizon and less than 10 years for a short horizon). If *multiple* objectives, a *different time horizon* for each objective.
    - *Other investment parameters*—include *asset class preferences, liquidity preferences* (including a cash reserve), *unique investment preferences.*
    - *Constraints*—restricting investments for client's portfolio.
- **Asset Allocation**—*Strategic* long-term target asset allocation for each asset class and *tactical* asset allocation as an active management strategy specifying a range for each asset class.
- **Portfolio Management and Implementation** guidelines for *discretionary authority, portfolio rebalancing, tactical asset allocation changes,* and acceptable *investment vehicles.*
- **Wealth Manager Duties and Responsibilities** include; formulating/reviewing the client's IPS, constructing the portfolio, monitoring and rebalancing the portfolio, monitoring portfolio costs and third-party providers, and reporting portfolio performance.
- **IPS Appendix** includes modelled portfolio performance and capital market expectations.

Portfolio Construction:
- Traditional Approach—views risk in an *overall portfolio* context.
- Goals-based investing—*separate portfolios are created for each of the client's goals.* Mean-variance optimization used to maximize expected returns for a given level of risk or to meet a specified probability of success is carried out for each goal portfolio rather than for the entire portfolio.

TOPICS IN PRIVATE WEALTH MANAGEMENT

- Main categories of taxes: income tax, capital gains tax, wealth/property tax, stamp duties, wealth transfer tax.
- General equation for capital gains: net sales price − tax (cost) basis = capital gain/loss.
- Three main types of investment accounts: taxable, tax-deferred (TDA), and tax-exempt (TEA).

Common metrics used in examining tax efficiency:
1. After-tax holding period return $R' = [(value_1 - value_0) + income - tax] / value_0$
   Alternatively, $R' = R - (tax / value_0)$.
2. After-tax post-liquidation return (R_{PL}) involves deducting the implied tax:
   $R_{PL} = [(1 + R'_1)(1 + R'_2)\ldots(1 + R'_n) - (\text{liquidation tax/final value})]^{1/n} - 1$. Liquidation tax = (final value − tax basis) × tax rate on capital gains
3. After-tax excess return (x') is computed as the after-tax return of the portfolio (R') minus the after-tax return of the benchmark (B'):
   $x' = R' - B'$. In this regard, the **tax alpha** would be defined as after-tax excess return (x') minus the pretax excess return (x): $\alpha_{tax} = x' - x$
4. Tax-efficiency ratio (TER) is calculated as after-tax return (R') divided by pretax return (R): $TER = R' / R$

Taxable accounts involve one or more tax rates on income (e.g., interest, dividends) or return (e.g., realized capital gains) to determine R': $FV_{AT} = (1 + R')^n$

Tax exempt accounts (TEAs), after-tax funds are deposited so no tax is due on the returns earned or on withdrawals: $FV_{AT} = (1 + R)^n$

Tax deferred accounts (TDAs), pretax funds are deposited and the investor may take a tax deduction for the amount contributed thereby reducing taxable income and taxes due. All tax is deferred until withdrawal allowing tax-deferred compounding: $FV_{AT} = (1 + R)^n(1 - t)$

Tax-efficient assets (e.g., equities that generate capital gains are often subject to lower tax rates) should be placed in taxable accounts. **Tax-inefficient assets** (e.g., taxable bonds that generate taxable interest, which is often subject to higher tax rates) should be placed in tax-exempt or tax-deferred accounts.

Four common investment vehicles include:
- Partnership
- Mutual fund
- Exchange-traded fund (ETF)
- Separately managed account (SMA)

Tax loss harvesting involves the sale of securities with embedded losses to offset gains, which will lower the tax liability for the current year.
- Highest in, first out (HIFO) is generally optimal
- In case future tax rates are expected to be *higher* than current tax rates, first in, first out (FIFO) may be better
- In case future tax rates are expected to be *lower* than current tax rates, last in, first out (LIFO) may be better

Strategies for managing a concentrated position in public equities:
- Staged diversification strategy over multiple years to spread out tax liability
- Completion portfolio using other assets to complement/complete the concentrated position
- Equity monetization by hedging a large part of the risk in the position using derivatives and then borrow using the hedged position as collateral
- Zero-cost collars are used to lower initial cost by giving up some stock upside. The put premium paid and call premium received are equal.
- Covered call writing is possibly a staged diversification assuming the share price appreciates sufficiently
- Exchange fund with a pooling of investments on a tax-free basis
- Charitable remainder trust to benefit both beneficiaries and a designated charity

Strategies for managing concentrated positions in privately owned businesses:
- IPO
- Direct sale to another investor
- Sale of non-essential business assets
- Personal line of credit secured by company shares (owner borrows from company or from a third-party lender)
- Leveraged recapitalization (e.g., private equity firm)
- Sale to employee stock ownership plan

Lifetime Gifts vs. Testamentary Bequests
Basic form of the relative value (RV) ratio: FV after-tax to the receiver if gifted now / FV after-tax to the receiver if bequeathed at death:

Two tax scenarios to consider:
- The gift now is tax free to both the receiver and the donor
- The gift is taxable with tax paid by the receiver

Relevant tax factors to consider:
- r_g and t_g are the pretax return earned and the applicable tax rate on those earnings for assets held by the gift receiver
- r_e and t_e are the pretax return earned and the applicable tax rate on those earnings for assets held by the gift giver
- T_e is the estate tax rate and would be paid from the estate
- T_g is the gift tax rate and is assumed to be paid by the receiver
  $FV_{gift} = [1 + r_g(1 - t_g)]^n$
  $FV_{bequest} = [1 + r_e(1 - t_e)]^n(1 - T_e)$
- RV of a tax-free gift, $T_g = 0$
- $RV_{\text{Tax Free Gift}} = \dfrac{FV_{\text{Gift}}}{FV_{\text{Bequest}}} = \dfrac{[1+r_g(1-t_g)]^n}{[1+r_e(1-t_e)]^n(1-T_e)}$
- RV of a taxable gift, T_g paid by receiver
- $RV_{\text{Taxable Gift}} = \dfrac{FV_{\text{Gift}}}{FV_{\text{Bequest}}} = \dfrac{[1+r_g(1-t_g)]^n(1-T_g)}{[1+r_e(1-t_e)]^n(1-T_e)}$

RISK MANAGEMENT FOR INDIVIDUALS

- Total wealth is composed of both human capital (HC) and financial capital (FC). HC is the discounted present value of expected future labor income. FC is the sum of all the other assets of an individual.
- Net wealth is the sum of the individual's FC and HC less any liabilities owed by the individual.
- The economic (holistic) balance sheet extends the traditional balance sheet assets to include HC. Liabilities can also be extended to include consumption and bequest goals.
- Earnings risk: Use disability income insurance.
- Premature death risk: Use life insurance.
- Longevity risk of living too long: Use annuities.

continued on next page...

3. Price change due to investor yield change predictions: $(-MD \times \Delta Y) + (\frac{1}{2}C \times \Delta Y^2)$
4. Price change due to investor spread change predictions: $(-MD \times \Delta S) + (\frac{1}{2}C \times \Delta S^2)$
5. Currency G/L: projected change in value of foreign currencies weighted for exposure to the currency

Coupon income + rolldown return may be referred to as rolling yield.

Leveraged return $= r_I + [(V_B / V_E) \times (r_I - r_B)]$.
where:

r_p = return on portfolio
r_I = return on invested assets
r_B = rate paid on borrowings
V_B = amount of leverage
V_E = amount of equity invested

Active management for a stable upward sloping yield curve:

- Buy and hold: extend duration to get higher yields.
- Roll down the yield curve: portfolio weighting highest for securities at the long end of the steepest yield curve segments, maximize gains on securities from declines in yield as time passes.
- Repo carry trade: borrow at lower rates to purchase securities with higher rates.
- Long futures position
- Receive-fixed swap

Active management for a changing yield curve:

- Increase (decrease) portfolio duration if rates are expected to decrease (increase).
- Add call options on either a bond price or a bond futures contract to *increase* duration.
- Add put options on either a bond price or bond futures contract to decrease duration.
- A payer swaption (right to enter a pay-fixed swap decreases duration.
- A receiver swaption (right to enter a receive-fixed swap) increases duration.

$$\text{KeyRateDur} = -\frac{\text{change in portfolio value}}{\text{portfolio value} \times \text{change in key rate}}$$

- Increase portfolio convexity (decreasing yield) when large changes in rates are expected.
- Bullet portfolios have more yield, but barbells have more convexity and also tend to outperform in curve-flattening environments.

Curvature of the yield curve can be measured through the butterfly spread: butterfly spread = −(short-term yield) + (2 × medium-term yield) − long-term yield

- $\% \Delta \text{ value} = -MD\Delta y$
- $\%\Delta\text{relative value} = -SD\Delta s$ where spread duration (SD) measures a portfolio's percentage sensitivity to a 1% change in credit spreads (Δs).
- spread $= y_{\text{higher yield}} - y_{\text{government}}$
- credit spread ≈ POD × LGD
- $\text{EffRateDur}_{FRN} = \dfrac{(PV_-)-(PV_+)}{2(\Delta MRR)(PV_0)}$
- $\text{EffSpreadDur}_{FRN} = \dfrac{(PV_-)-(PV_+)}{2(\Delta DM)(PV_0)}$
- effective spread duration $= \dfrac{(PV_-)-(PV_+)}{2(\Delta\text{spread})(PV_0)}$
- effective spread convexity $= \dfrac{(PV_-)+(PV_+)-2(PV_0)}{(\Delta\text{spread})^2(PV_0)}$
- %Δprice = (−EffSpreadDur × Δspread) + (½ × EffSpreadCon × Δspread^2)
- Expected excess spread = spread − (EffSpreadDur × Δspread) − (POD × LGD)
- Effective spread for a buy order = trade size × (trade price − midquote)
- Effective spread for a sell order = trade size × (midquote − trade price) where: midquote = (bid + ask) / 2
- CDS price ≈ 1 + [(fixed coupon − CDS spread) × $\text{EffSpreadDur}_{CDS}$]

EQUITY

Constructing and maintaining the index involves:

- The weighting method to construct the index: (1) market-cap weighting, (2) price weighting, (3) equal weighting, or (4) fundamental weighting.
- Considering the level of stock concentration. The "effective number of stocks" can be determined as the reciprocal of the Herfindahl-Hirschman index (HHI):

$$HHI = \sum_{i=1}^{n} w_i^2$$

$$\text{effective number of stocks} = \frac{1}{HHI}$$

Common equity risk factors: growth, value, size, yield, momentum, quality, and volatility.

Factor-based strategies: return oriented, risk oriented, and diversification oriented.

Common approaches to passive equity investing use: (1) pooled investments, such as open-end mutual funds and ETFs, (2) derivatives-based strategies, and (3) separately-managed index-based portfolios.

Three methods of constructing passively managed index-based equity portfolios: (1) full replication, (2) stratified sampling, often based on cell matching, (3) technical and quantitative approach (optimization)

Fundamental managers use discretionary judgment vs. **quantitative managers** use rules-based (systematic) data-driven models.

Fundamental law of active management:

$$E(R_A) = IC\sqrt{BR}\sigma_{RA}TC$$

Active share measures the degree to which the number and sizing of the positions in a manager's portfolio differ to those of a benchmark:

$$\text{Active share} = \frac{1}{2}\sum_{i=1}^{n}\left|W_{p,i} - W_{b,i}\right|$$

Active risk (tracking error), is the standard deviation of active returns (portfolio returns minus benchmark returns).

The contribution of Asset *i* to portfolio variance (CV_i) is given by the equation:

$$CV_i = \sum_{j=1}^{n} w_i w_j C_{ij} = w_i C_{ip}$$

where:

w_j = Asset *j*'s weight in the portfolio
C_{ij} = the covariance of returns between Asset *i* and Asset *j*
C_{ip} = the covariance of returns between Asset *i* and the portfolio $\left(=\sum_{j=1}^{n} w_j C_{ij}\right)$

The contribution of Factor *i* to portfolio variance is given by the formula:

$$CV_i = \sum_{j=1}^{n}\beta_i\beta_j C_{ij} = \beta_i C_{ip}$$

where:

β_i = sensitivity of portfolio to Factor *i* (regression coefficient)
C_{ij} = the covariance of Factor *i* and Factor *j*
C_{ip} = the covariance of Factor *i* and the portfolio $\left(=\sum_{j=1}^{n}\beta_j C_{ij}\right)$

Long extension portfolios guarantee investors 100% net exposure with a specified short exposure. A typical 130/30 fund will have 130% long and 30% short positions.

Market-neutral portfolios aim to remove market exposure through offsetting long and short positions. Pairs trading is a common technique in building market-neutral portfolios, with quantitative pair trading referred to as *statistical arbitrage*.

Benefits of long/short strategies include the ability to better express negative views, the ability to gear into high-conviction long positions, the removal of market risk to diversify, and the ability to better control risk factor exposures.

Drawbacks of long/short strategies include potential large losses since share prices are not bounded above, negative exposures to risk premiums, potentially high leverage for market-neutral funds, and the costs of borrowing securities and collateral demands from prime brokers. Being subject to a short squeeze on short positions is also a risk.

ALTERNATIVE INVESTMENTS

Hedge Funds Strategies:

1. **Equity related** with the primary source of risk being equity risk.
   a. *Long/short equity*—The fund manager takes long positions in stocks that they think will rise in value, and takes short positions in stocks that they believe will fall in value.
   b. *Dedicated short bias funds*—These seek overpriced securities to sell short.
   c. *Equity market neutral*—These seek to attain a near-zero overall exposure to the stock market.
      - Take long positions in undervalued stocks and short positions in overvalued stocks with the betas of the positions summing to zero.
      - Alpha occurs through mean reversion.
2. **Event-driven** relate to corporate actions such as governance activities, mergers, acquisitions, bankruptcies, and other major business events. The main risk is event risk.
   a. *Merger arbitrage* earns a return from the uncertainty that exists in the market from when an acquisition is announced until completed (i.e., the fund manager purchases the stock of the target company and shorts the stock of the acquiring company, anticipating the deal will be completed).
   b. *Distressed securities* take positions in the securities of firms that are in financial distress, including firms that are in bankruptcy or near-bankruptcy.
3. **Relative value** strategies profit from the relative valuation differences between securities.
   a. *Fixed-income arbitrage* takes advantage of temporary mispricing of fixed-income instruments by going long undervalued securities and short overvalued securities.
      - *Yield curve trades* go long and short fixed-income investments in order to profit from the anticipated yield curve steepening or flattening.
      - *Carry trade* the portfolio manager shorts a low-yielding security and goes long a high-yielding security.
   b. *Convertible bond arbitrage* the manager purchases the convertible bond which is often underpriced and short sells the underlying equity.
4. **Opportunistic** strategies employ a top-down approach making macro investments on a global basis across regions, sectors, and asset classes.
   a. *Global macro* profits from making correct assessments and forecasts of various global economic variables.
   b. *Managed futures* strategies take long and short positions in derivatives contracts.
5. **Specialist** strategies require specialized market expertise or knowledge.
   a. *Volatility* strategies trade volatility-related assets globally.

- Arrival price = price when the order is placed by trader.
- *Trading cost*: due to the market impact of executing the trade.

  Trading cost = shares executed × (average purchase price − arrival price)

- *Opportunity cost* is the cost of *not* trading any unfilled part of the order. The paper portfolio assumes that all shares are executed immediately at the original decision price. The actual trade may have only filled part of the order and the lost profit on the unfilled portion is the opportunity cost. For a buy order:

  Opportunity cost = portion of order not filled × (closing price − decision price)

- *Fixed fees* are any explicit commissions or fees incurred in executing the trade.

  Fixed fees = Σ executed × commission per share

Total IS value ($) = delay cost + trading cost + opportunity cost + fixed fees

All of the components of and total IS can be expressed in terms of basis points (bps) of the original cost of the paper portfolio. A basis point is 1/100th of one percent. A decimal number is multiplied by 10,000 to convert it to basis points.

Trade costs represent costs relative to the benchmark, a positive value represents underperformance:

Absolute cost ($) = side × (execution price − benchmark price) × shares executed

Trade cost (bps) =

$$\text{side} \times \frac{(\text{execution price} - \text{benchmark price})}{\text{benchmark price}} \times 10{,}000$$

where:
side = +1 for a buy order, −1 for a sell order

Market-adjusted cost is used to remove the impact of market movements on trade cost which ensures a trader is not penalized or rewarded for general market movements over the trade horizon.

index cost (bps) =

$$\text{side} \times \frac{(\text{index VWAP} - \text{index arrival price})}{\text{index arrival price}} \times 10{,}000$$

Market-adjusted cost (bps) = arrival cost (bps) − β × index cost (bps)

where:
arrival cost is the arrival cost of the trade based on an arrival price benchmark
β = beta of the security vs. the index used to calculate index cost

Added value is a different method of trade cost analysis comparing the arrival cost of the trade with the estimated pre-trade cost.

Added value (bps) = arrival cost (bps) − estimated pre-trade cost (bps)

A negative cost is a benefit—the trader has added value through their trading decisions.

Micro Attribution vs. Macro Attribution

- *Micro attribution* analyzes the portfolio at the portfolio manager's level.
- *Macro attribution* analyzes investment decisions at the fund sponsor's level.

Returns-Based, Holdings-Based, and Transactions-Based Attribution

- *Returns-based attribution* uses regressions to analyze the portfolio returns over time and isolates the asset class components through indices that would have generated these returns.
- *Holdings-based attribution* uses beginning-of-period portfolio assets.
- *Transactions-based attribution* updates the beginning-of-period holdings-based attribution for any subsequent trades.

Brinson-Fachler and Brinson, Hood, Beebower (BHB) models quantify the portfolio returns into three attribution effects: allocation effect, security selection effect, and the interaction effect.

- *Allocation effect* refers to the portfolio manager's decision to overweight or underweight specific sector weightings versus the benchmark. Using the Brinson-Fachler model, the contribution to the *i*th sector is equal to the portfolio's sector weight minus the benchmark's sector weight, times the benchmark sector return minus the overall benchmark return: $A_i = (w_i - W_i)(B_i - B)$. For the BHB model, the contribution to the ith sector is equal to the portfolio's sector weight minus the benchmark's sector weight, times the benchmark sector return: $A_i = (w_i - W_i)B_i$
- *Security selection* is the portfolio manager's value added by selecting individual securities (stock picking) within the sector and weighting the portfolio differently compared to the benchmark's weightings. The contribution to selection in the ith sector is equal to the benchmark sector weight times the portfolio's sector return minus the benchmark's sector return: $S_i = W_i(R_i - B_i)$
- *Interaction effect* is a residual amount (e.g., plug) that ensures the arithmetic return minus the relative benchmark is fully accounted for in attribution analysis. The contribution to the ith sector is equal to the portfolio sector weight minus the benchmark sector weight, times the portfolio sector return minus the benchmark sector return: $I_i = (w_i - W_i)(R_i - B_i)$

Carhart model is a fundamental factor model calculating the excess return from active management decisions by determining the impact on the portfolio due to the following factors: (1) market index (RMRF), (2) market-capitalization (SMB), (3) book-value-to-price (HML), and (4) momentum (WML):

$$R_p - R_f = a_p + b_{p1}RMRF + b_{p2}SMB + b_{p3}HML + b_{p4}WML + E_p$$

Benchmark quality of a portfolio return can be broken up into three components: market, style, and active management.

P = M + S + A

where:
P = investment manager's portfolio return
M = return on the market index
S = B – M = excess return to style; difference between the manager's style index (benchmark) return and the market return (S can be positive or negative)
A = P – B = active return; difference between the manager's overall portfolio return and the style benchmark return

Performance Appraisal

Sharpe ratio

$$S_A = \frac{\bar{R}_A - \bar{r}_f}{\bar{\sigma}_A}$$

Treynor ratio

$$T_A = \frac{\bar{R}_A - \bar{r}_f}{\bar{\beta}_A}$$

Information ratio is used to measure a portfolio's performance against the benchmark accounting for differences in risk.

$$IR = \frac{E(r_P) - E(r_B)}{\sigma(r_P - r_B)}$$

Appraisal ratio is calculated as alpha divided by the standard deviation of the residual/unsystematic risk (the standard error of regression).

$$AR = \frac{\alpha}{\sigma_\varepsilon}$$

Sortino ratio only considers the standard deviation of the downside risk where r_T refers to the minimum acceptable return (MAR) and (σ_D) refers to target semistandard deviation.

$$SR_D = \frac{E(r_P) - r_t}{\sigma_D}$$

Capture ratios determine the manager's relative performance when markets are up or down. Capture is calculated as portfolio return divided by benchmark return. The capture ratio is calculated as upside capture divided by downside capture.

Type I and II errors in hiring managers and continuation decisions

- Null hypothesis (H_0) is that there is no value added.
- Type I error is when the null hypothesis is rejected when in fact there was no value added.
- Type II error is when the null hypothesis is not rejected when in fact there was value added.

CASES IN PORTFOLIO MANAGEMENT AND RISK MANAGEMENT

Calculating life insurance needs

Human life value method estimates the amount of future earnings that must be replaced.

1. Start with the current amount of after-tax income to be replaced
2. Subtract annual expenses attributable to the person passing away
3. Add any employee benefits such as contributions to pension plans that would not be earned
4. Gross up to a required pretax payout
5. Use the growth-adjusted discount rate (r*) to calculate the present value of the pretax annuity due. These calculations use the growth-adjusted discount rate (r*) entered as I/Y on your financial calculator to calculate a growing annuity due (beginning of period payments) with the calculator in BGN mode.

   r* = (1 + r)/(1 + g)

   where:
   r = annual discount rate
   g = annual growth rate
6. Subtract existing life insurance = additional life insurance needs

Needs analysis method estimates the amount needed to cover living expenses.

1. Determine the total cash needs (funeral, emergency fund, debts)
2. Plus the capital needs which are the PV of surviving spouse's annual living expenses minus PV of survivor's income until retirement using the growth-adjusted discount rate r* = total financial needs
3. Subtract the capital available (savings)
4. Less PV of vested retirement accounts attributable to the surviving spouse = additional life insurance needs

- Review the SchweserNotes™ and/or Module Videos.

ETHICS (INCLUDING GIPS)

Review the SchweserNotes™ and/or Module Videos and questions in the SchweserNotes™, CFA® text, and SchweserPro™ Qbank.

Kaplan SCHWESER™

2024 CFA® Notes 备考笔记三级

第二册（全五册）

SCHWESERNOTES™ 2024 CFA® PART III

BOOK 2

Derivatives and Currency Management

美国开普兰公司 著

中信出版集团 | 北京

图书在版编目（CIP）数据

Kaplan SCHWESER 2024 CFA®; Notes 备考笔记 = SCHWESERNOTES™; 2024 LEVEL Ⅲ CFA®; 三级 : 全五册 : 英文 / 美国开普兰公司著 . -- 北京 : 中信出版社 , 2023.8
ISBN 978-7-5217-5649-4

Ⅰ . ① K⋯ Ⅱ . ①美⋯ Ⅲ . ①金融－分析－资格考试－自学参考资料－英文 Ⅳ . ① F83

中国国家版本馆 CIP 数据核字 (2023) 第 083168 号

SCHWESERNOTES™ 2024 CFA® LEVEL Ⅲ

Kaplan SCHWESER 2024 CFA® Notes 备考笔记三级第二册（全五册）
著者：　美国开普兰公司
出版发行：中信出版集团股份有限公司
（北京市朝阳区东三环北路 27 号嘉铭中心　邮编　100020）
承印者：　河北鹏润印刷有限公司

开本：889mm×1194mm 1/16　　印张：74.5　　字数：2130 千字
版次：2023 年 8 月第 1 版　　印次：2023 年 8 月第 1 次印刷
书号：ISBN 978-7-5217-5649-4
定价：1599.00 元（全五册）

Book 2: Derivatives and Currency Management

SchweserNotes™ 2024

Level III CFA®

KAPLAN SCHWESER

SCHWESERNOTES™ 2024 LEVEL III CFA® BOOK 2: DERIVATIVES AND CURRENCY MANAGEMENT

Published in 2023 by Kaplan, Inc.

Printed in the United States of America.

ISBN: 978-1-0788-3752-1

CONTENTS

LEARNING OUTCOME STATEMENTS (LOS)

6. Options Strategies

The candidate should be able to:

a. demonstrate how an asset's returns may be replicated by using options. (page 10)
b. discuss the investment objective(s), structure, payoff, risk(s), value at expiration, profit, maximum profit, maximum loss, and breakeven underlying price at expiration of a covered call position. (page 12)
c. discuss the investment objective(s), structure, payoff, risk(s), value at expiration, profit, maximum profit, maximum loss, and breakeven underlying price at expiration of a protective put position. (page 17)
d. compare the delta of covered call and protective put positions with the position of being long an asset and short a forward on the underlying asset. (page 34)
e. compare the effect of buying a call on a short underlying position with the effect of selling a put on a short underlying position. (page 18)
f. discuss the investment objective(s), structure, payoffs, risk(s), value at expiration, profit, maximum profit, maximum loss, and breakeven underlying price at expiration of the following option strategies: bull spread, bear spread, straddle, and collar. (page 20)
g. describe uses of calendar spreads. (page 41)
h. discuss volatility skew and smile. (page 44)
i. identify and evaluate appropriate option strategies consistent with given investment objectives. (page 47)
j. demonstrate the use of options to achieve targeted equity risk exposures. (page 47)

7. Swaps, Forwards, and Futures Strategies

The candidate should be able to:

a. demonstrate how interest rate swaps, forwards, and futures can be used to modify a portfolio's risk and return. (page 65)
b. demonstrate how currency swaps, forwards, and futures can be used to modify a portfolio's risk and return. (page 78)
c. demonstrate how equity swaps, forwards, and futures can be used to modify a portfolio's risk and return. (page 84)
d. demonstrate the use of volatility derivatives and variance swaps. (page 92)
e. demonstrate the use of derivatives to achieve targeted equity and interest rate risk exposures. (page 102)
f. demonstrate the use of derivatives in asset allocation, rebalancing, and inferring market expectations. (page 104)

8. Currency Management: An Introduction

The candidate should be able to:

a. analyze the effects of currency movements on portfolio risk and return. (page 132)
b. discuss strategic choices in currency management. (page 136)
c. formulate an appropriate currency management program given financial market conditions and portfolio objectives and constraints. (page 139)
d. compare active currency trading strategies based on economic fundamentals, technical analysis, carry-trade, and volatility trading. (page 143)
e. describe how changes in factors underlying active trading strategies affect tactical trading decisions. (page 148)
f. describe how forward contracts and FX (foreign exchange) swaps are used to adjust hedge ratios. (page 150)
g. describe trading strategies used to reduce hedging costs and modify the risk–return characteristics of a foreign-currency portfolio. (page 155)
h. describe the use of cross-hedges, macro-hedges, and minimum-variance-hedge ratios in portfolios exposed to multiple foreign currencies. (page 157)
i. discuss challenges for managing emerging market currency exposures. (page 159)

READING 6

Options Strategies

EXAM FOCUS

The primary focus of this topic area is on the ways in which derivative contracts (instruments whose values derive from the economic performance of underlying securities, currencies, or other instruments or factors) may be used to hedge, or change the degree of exposure to, existing positions (for example a holding of a stock, or the exposure to a foreign currency caused by the ownership of an asset or liability in that currency). We will also see how derivatives, particularly options, can be used to obtain exposures to instruments and factors that cannot be obtained directly from the instruments and factors themselves (strategies such as straddles and spreads, for instance).

Reading 6 deals with options, mainly focusing on options on individual stocks, although the principles apply equally well to options on any other instruments. Reading 7 looks at the principles and uses of futures and forward contracts, while Reading 8 is concerned with currency management, beginning with the various approaches to currency along the passive-active spectrum, moving on to active currency strategies (including volatility trading via options), before considering currency hedging using futures and forwards (mainly the latter), and options.

The sequence of topics in our coverage of Reading 6 differs from the LOS order. We start by looking at the payoffs and profits associated with holding option positions to expiration. Since value at expiration is purely reflective of intrinsic value, the calculations involved are simple (but highly examinable, so worth getting clear before the complicating issue of time value is addressed). Only then do we move on to the more theory-heavy areas associated with time value—the option "Greeks" and strategies derived from them.

Video covering this content is available online.

MODULE 6.1: OPTIONS BASICS—VALUE AT EXPIRATION AND PROFIT AT EXPIRATION

PROFESSOR'S NOTE

Options have already been met at the previous levels, of course, so the material in this first module is largely revision. However, we recommend that you don't skip it, since it is vital to everything that follows.

In particular, distinguishing between option value and profit (respectively pre- and post-initial premium), and the graphical representation of how they vary with differing values of the underlying price, is very helpful when we move on to analyze more complex strategies.

A Refresher on Options Terminology

- A **call** is a right to **buy**
- A **put** is a right to **sell**

Each option contract will specify the **underlying** to which the right relates.

- Underlyings include stocks and stock indices, bonds and bond futures, currencies, commodities, and more abstract factors such as stock volatility.

The contract will specify the **exercise** (**strike**) price at which the right can be exercised, and the **expiration** (**expiry**) date (and time) at which the right can be exercised (or not).

- **European-style options** may only be exercised at the point of expiration, while **American-style options** may be exercised on any trading day up to and including the point of expiration.
  - Note that European- and American-style are just labels for the two main styles of option, and are nothing to do with where the options are traded (there are other, more exotic, styles, such as Bermudan, but the details of such exotics are beyond the scope of the syllabus).

The buyer of an option pays a **premium** (the value of the option) to the seller.

- The **buyer** (who takes the **long** position in the option) has the right.
- The **seller** (taking the **short** position) receives the premium as payment for taking on the contingent liability associated with the buyer's right:
  - In the case of a **call** option, the short has undertaken to deliver the underlying if the buyer chooses to exercise (receiving the strike price in exchange).
  - In the case of a **put** option, the short has undertaken to take delivery of the underlying if the buyer chooses to exercise (paying the strike price).

Symbols and Formulas

PROFESSOR'S NOTE

We must minimize the use of formulas, where possible. The curriculum text does include some formulas and, if they help your understanding, by all means learn and use them, but our experience is that it is more reliable to focus on the underlying principles embedded in the formulas. None of the strategies tested are greatly complex, and in all cases, answers can be determined from the basic principles of in/out the moneyness that follow in the next section.

When symbols are used, we will follow the notation in the curriculum:

- X = the e**x**ercise (strike) price.
- S = the underlying (**s**tock) price.
- p and c = the prices (premiums) of the **p**ut and **c**all options.
- Subscripts on S, p, and c will stand for time, with 0 = the point at which the position is entered and T = option expiration.

Intrinsic Value and Time Value

At any point in time any given option will have a value. This is set, as are all values, by supply and demand but is likely to be determined by reference to one of the many option pricing models, of which the Black-Scholes-Merton (BSM) was the first (introduced in 1973), and is still widely used.

The key determinants of an option's value are:

- The strike price.
- The current level of the underlying (e.g., stock price, currency rate, etc.).
- The remaining time to expiration.
- The volatility of the underlying (the **expected** annualized standard deviation of the underlying over the period to option expiration).
- The annualized risk-free interest rate over the period to expiration.
- The annualized yield expected from the underlying (if any) over the period to expiration.
- Whether it is European- or American-style (in principle the latter might be worth more because they give the right to exercise before expiration, in addition to at expiration).

Market participants may not agree on what an option is worth—most likely because they disagree on the appropriate figure to use for volatility. However, note that all options that trade on exchanges will have a value, which is reflective of the consensus at that point in time. The current value of an option can be used to infer the consensus estimate of volatility for the underlying, known as **implied volatility**. This is done by working backwards through a pricing model, given the other factors can be directly observed.

Note that implied volatility is not the same as **historical (realized) volatility**, which is the square root of the **actual** realized variance of returns to date.

It is important to note that the volatility that is used to determine the option value is an estimate of the volatility **looking forward**, which is not the same as actual movement in the stock price. For example, the implied volatility for a stock option could well rise, even though the stock price is currently stable, if the consensus view changes on the potential for price moves during the period to expiration.

The value of an option can be decomposed into its intrinsic value and its time value, the total premium being the sum of these two.

- **Intrinsic value** is the value of immediate exercise[1]. It reflects the degree to which the option is in the money (ITM).
- **Time value** is the additional value reflective of *what might happen* between now and the point of expiration (i.e., over the option's remaining life).

An option is ITM if the long would derive a benefit from immediate exercise.

- **A call option is ITM if the current price of the underlying > strike price**, so the long has the right to pay less than the current market price for the underlying.

  The intrinsic value in such a case equals the underlying price minus the strike price (the extent to which the underlying price exceeds the strike price, which is the amount the long could gain by exercising their right, then immediately selling the underlying in the market). Note that here, and throughout, we will ignore transaction costs.
- **A put option is ITM if the current price of the underlying < strike price**, so the long has the right to receive more than the current market price for the underlying.

  The intrinsic value in such a case equals the strike price minus the underlying price (the extent to which the strike price exceeds the underlying price, which is the amount the long could gain by buying the underlying in the market, then immediately exercising their right to sell at the strike price).

Note that the intrinsic value is not the same as the profit to the long, which would have to factor in the premium that the long originally paid for the option. This means that it is perfectly possible for an option to be ITM, but for exercise to result in a loss to the long (if the intrinsic value < initial premium paid).

Note also that we are not saying that the long will *choose* to exercise, just that (ignoring premium paid) exercise would lead to a gain.

An option that is not ITM will have zero intrinsic value. It could be at the money (ATM), with the underlying = strike price, or out of the money (OTM):

- **A call option is OTM if current price of the underlying < strike price.**
- **A put option is OTM if current price of the underlying > strike price.**

At any point before expiration an option also has time value, which reflects what might happen over its remaining life. This is a much more complex concept, which explains why the first option pricing formula only appeared in 1973. Time to expiry, volatility, the risk-free rate, and the yield on the underlying all have a part to play, in addition to the underlying price and the strike price.

---

[1] This can be computed for both European and American-style options, even though the former can only be exercised at expiration. It can be thought of as the base level for the option's value.

The details of pricing models are beyond the scope of the Level III curriculum—you will not be plugging figures into the BSM model, for example—but a couple of general principles are worth remembering, namely that with **all other factors held constant:**

- **Higher** volatility means **higher** option premiums (both for calls and puts).
- **Less** time to expiry means **lower** option premiums (both for calls and puts).

Data for Examples

For most of the examples in this reading we will use the following options on XYZ stock (current stock price = $52.14). The premiums are quoted as of "now" (assumed to be 20 March), and the April, May, and June expiration dates are respectively 31, 61, and 91 days in the future. The risk-free interest rate is 3%, and volatility has been assumed to be a constant 60% (we will see later that this is unrealistic, but this is not in itself a problem). The XYZ stock pays no dividends.

Each option contract is a right over 100 shares, but this table shows prices per share (in $), and we will work in per-share terms, unless otherwise stated:

Call Price			Strike	Put Price		
APR	MAY	JUN	Price	APR	MAY	JUN
4.80	6.26	7.40	**50**	2.53	3.87	4.88
3.53	5.05	6.22	**52.5**	3.75	5.14	6.19
2.52	4.02	5.20	**55**	5.24	6.61	7.65

We refer to the May expiry call with a strike price of 50 as the MAY 50 call, for instance.

PROFESSOR'S NOTE

We will initially be limiting ourselves to evaluating values and profits at expiration. This simplifies things since at expiration there will be no time value—only intrinsic value (which may be referred to as the option's payoff).

Basic At-Expiration Payoff Diagrams for Calls and Puts

Calls

Let us use the example of a long call to illustrate the way in which option values and profits can be depicted graphically.

Consider an investor who buys (goes long) an XYZ MAY 50 call, paying the $6.26 premium.

At the May expiration the option will either be ITM or OTM, dependent on whether the stock price then is above or below \$50. Below \$50 it will be OTM, with no (intrinsic) value, while above \$50 the intrinsic value will equal stock price—\$50:

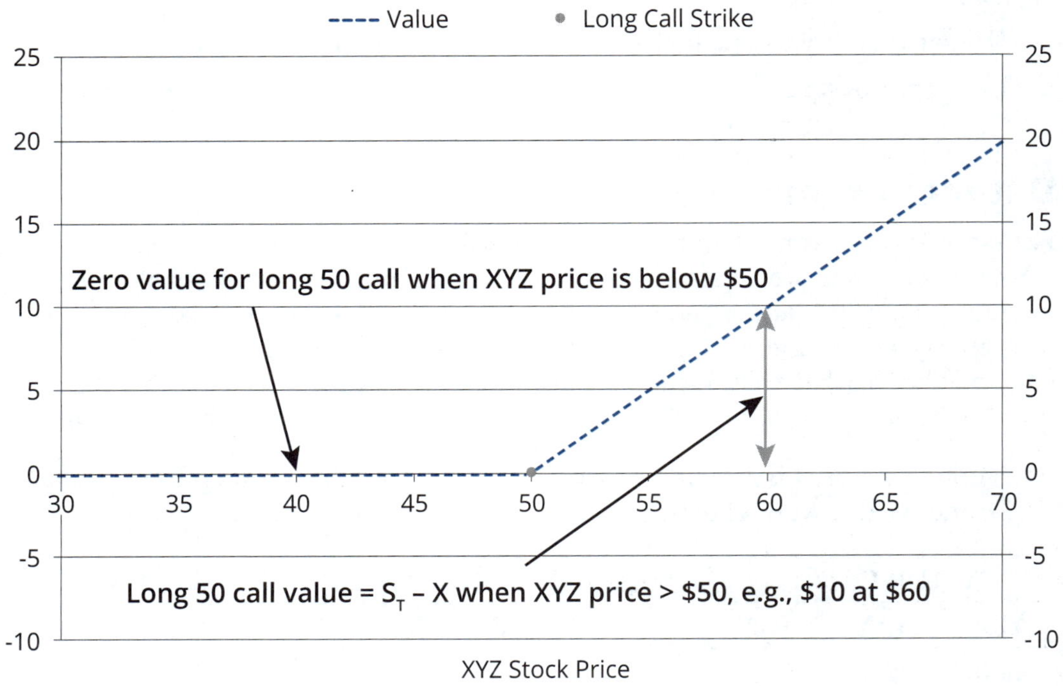

In all such diagrams, the horizontal axis represents the value of the underlying, while the vertical axis represents the value or profit of the position [which it is will be clear from the labelling of the line(s)] corresponding to that underlying value.

For example, if the XYZ stock price at expiry is \$40 then the 50 call will expire OTM, with zero value, while if the stock price at expiry is \$60 then the 50 call will expire ITM, with a value of \$60 – \$50 = \$10.

The initial cost of the option was \$6.26 (per the table), so the profit at expiration will equal the value of the call minus \$6.26, implying:

- If XYZ stock price = \$40, profit = \$0 – \$6.26 = loss of \$6.26.
- If XYZ stock price = \$60, profit = \$10 – \$6.26 = \$3.74.

Overall, the profit line will be the value line shifted downward uniformly by the \$6.26 initial premium.

As a rule, for each and every strategy we consider, the profit line will be the value line shifted:

- **Downward** by the amount of the (net) initial premium – if the (net) initial premium is an outflow (as here).
- **Upward** by the amount of the (net) initial premium – if the (net) initial premium is an inflow.

This means that if we know the shape of the value line for a strategy, the profit line will have exactly the same shape.

For the long XYZ MAY 50 call:

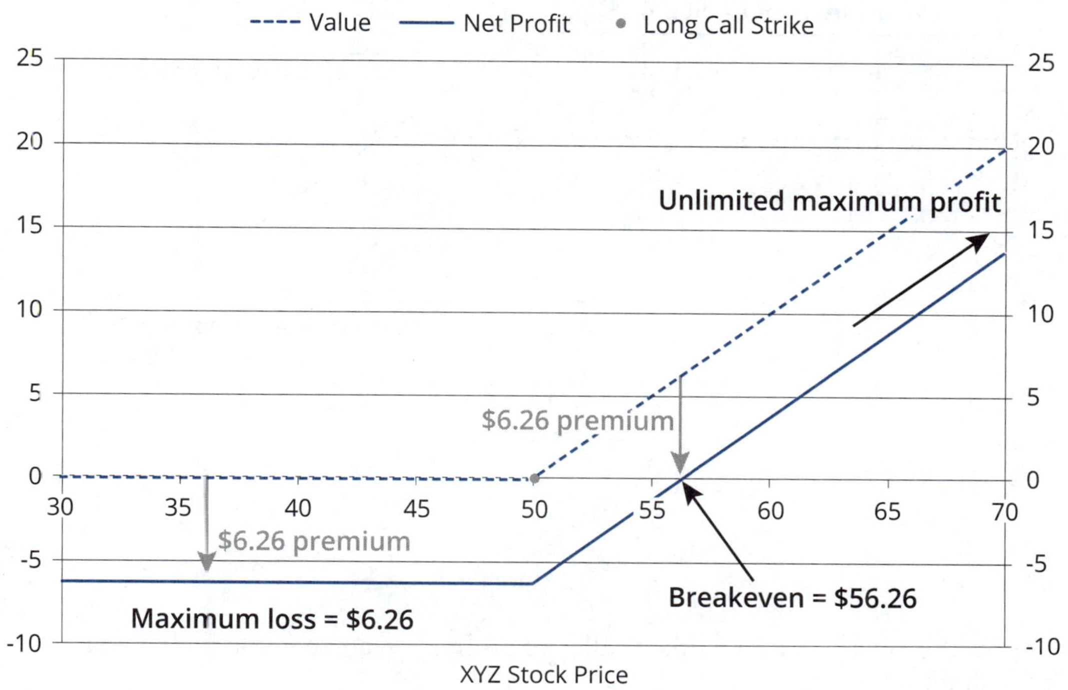

It is clear that the maximum loss from a long call occurs when the option expires OTM with zero value, thus equals the premium paid.

The long call position will break even at expiration if the value at expiration is exactly equal to the premium paid. This will happen when the stock price expires at the sum of the strike and the premium, $50 + $6.26 = $56.26 as shown on the previous diagram.

A long call has no maximum profit—the higher the stock price at expiry, the higher the profit on the call, with no upper limit.

The diagrams for a short call are identical, except that plus values, vertically, become minus, and vice-versa (since, in the absence of transaction costs, a positive result for the long is a negative result for the short, and vice-versa (in the jargon, it is a zero-sum game).

This means that equivalent long and short positions will have identical breakeven values for the underlying, while their maximum losses and profits will just swap around.

The short XYZ MAY 50 call has value and profit at expiration as here:

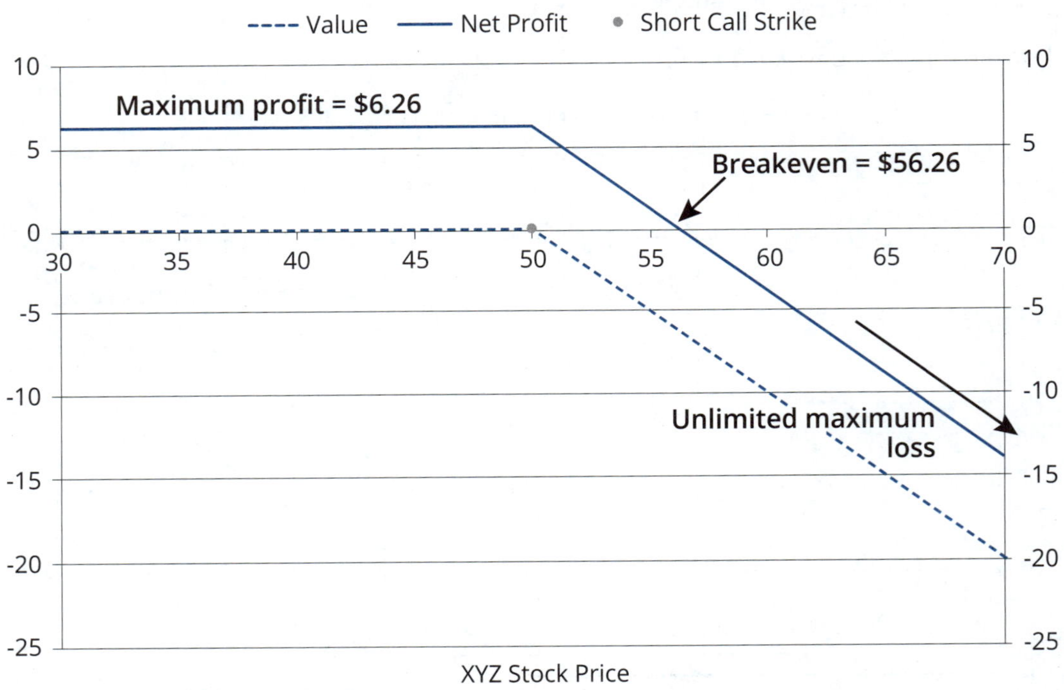

The basic motivation for buying a call is to profit from a rise in the underlying price, while limiting the downside.

When a call is sold (without any hedging position in place) then the position is described as a **naked** (uncovered) **call**, and limited upside from falls in the underlying price is balanced against unlimited potential losses from the underlying rising.

Puts

Puts are ITM on expiry when the underlying value ends below the strike price. This means that the graph for a put exposure will look like the call graph with left and right reversed.

For example, a long XYZ JUN 50 put (initial premium = $4.88) at expiration:

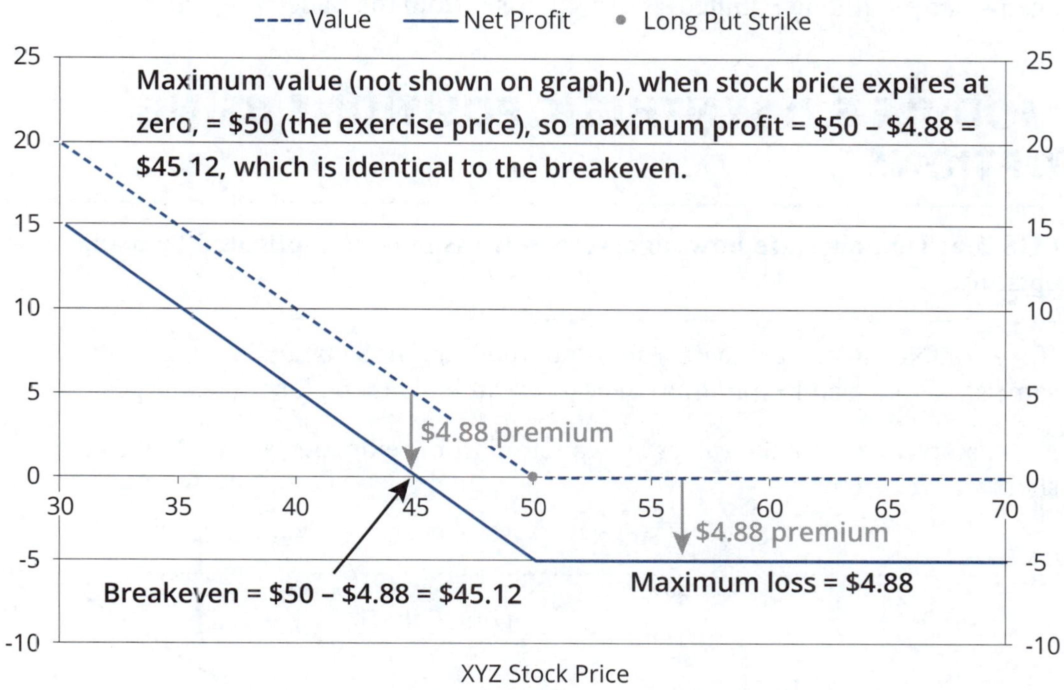

Here is the corresponding short XYZ JUN 50 put at expiration:

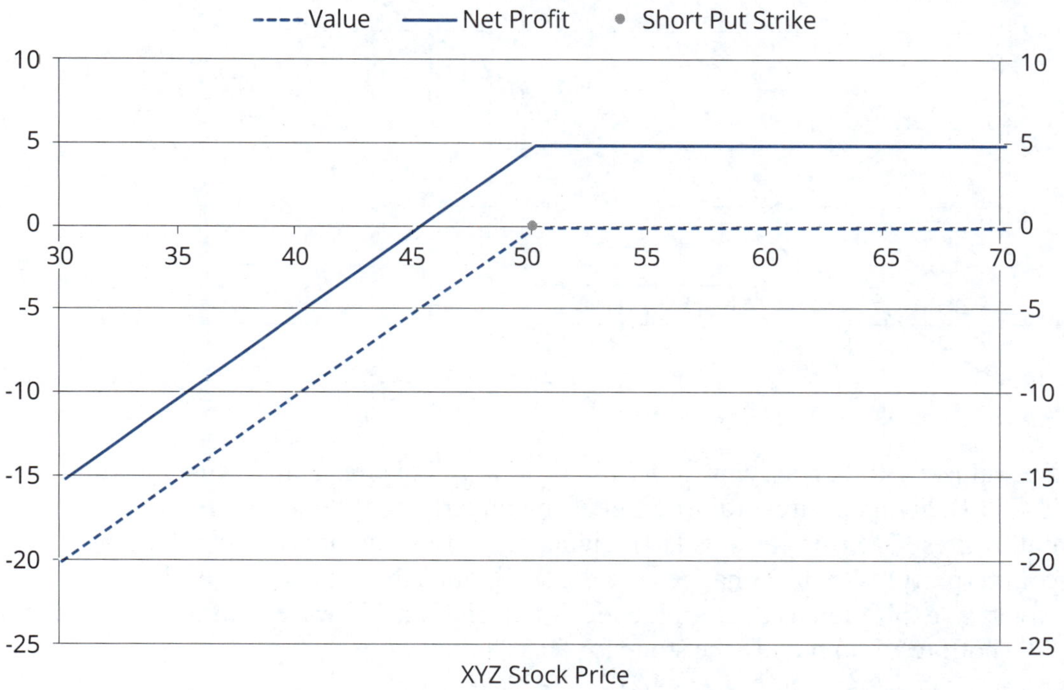

Confirm that you understand why the short XYZ JUN 50 put has maximum profit at expiration of $4.88, and breakeven = maximum loss = $45.12.

The basic motivation for buying a put is to profit from a fall in the underlying price, while limiting the downside.

When a put is **sold**[2] limited upside from rises in the underlying price is balanced against large (although limited) potential losses from the underlying falling.

Video covering this content is available online.

MODULE 6.2: SYNTHETIC POSITIONS USING OPTIONS

LOS 6.a: Demonstrate how an asset's returns may be replicated by using options.

If we combine a long call with a short put (both on the same underlying, with the same strike price and expiration) then we create a synthetic long forward position.

For example, here are the values at expiration from being long an XYZ 50 call and short an XYZ 50 put:

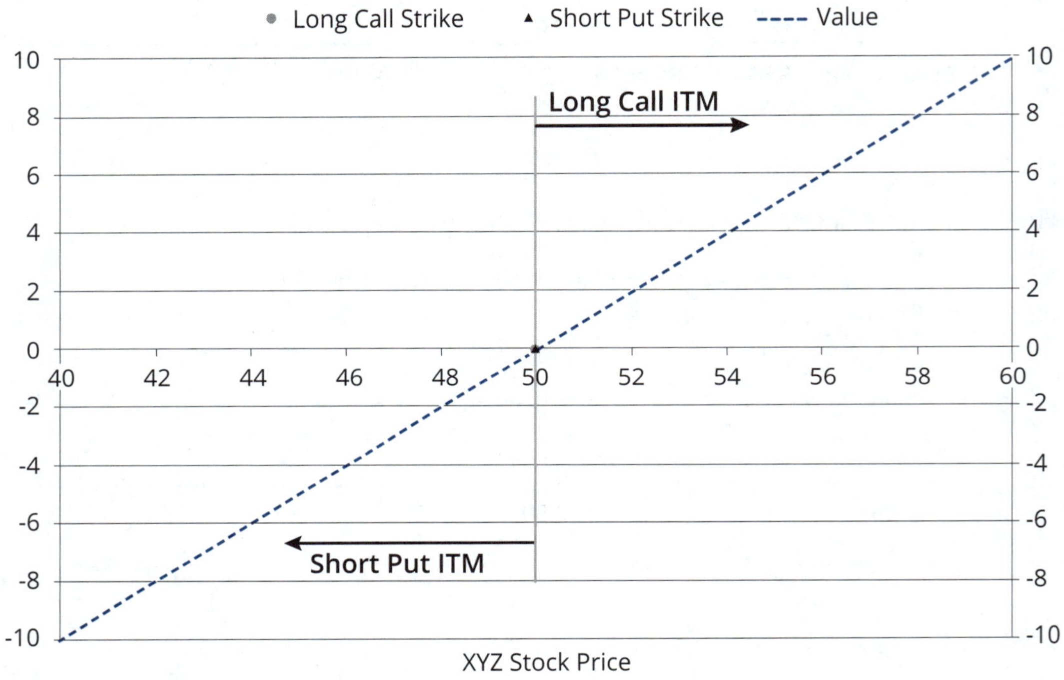

For values of the underlying above 50 the long call expires ITM (while the put is OTM), giving positive value, while if the underlying is below 50 the short put expires ITM (the call is OTM), giving negative value (it is exercised by the counterparty). Whatever happens to the stock price this position gives the same payoff at expiration as does an identical-maturity long forward contract on XYZ at 50—both result in buying the stock for 50.

- In symbols the value at expiration = $S_T - X$.

---

[2] Writing a put option and simultaneously depositing the exercise price into a designated account is called writing a **cash-secured** put, thereby the long is assured that the put writer would be able to purchase the stock, if called on to do so. Simply writing a put without doing this is called a **naked** put.

Suppose both options were for May expiration, then the premium paid for the call would have been \$6.26, while the premium received on the put would have been \$3.87, for a net initial payment of \$6.26 – \$3.87 = \$2.39. The profit line would thus be \$2.39 below the value line. The breakeven at expiration for the position is \$50 + \$2.39 = \$52.39 (the call would be \$2.39 ITM at this stock price, just covering the net premium paid).

This profit calculation has ignored the time value of money, as we do throughout this topic review when we calculate net profits, but in this section let us be a bit more accurate. The premiums are paid "now" (assumed to be 20 March), whereas the value at expiration is in May, 61 days later, so we should not really just net them off.

As an alternative to buying the call and selling the put, consider buying the underlying XYZ stock in March (for \$52.14) and holding it to the May expiration date. If we simultaneously borrow the PV of the strike price then at the May expiration date we will end up with a position with a net value exactly the same as the value of the long call + short put position we just examined: we will be able to sell the stock for the stock price at expiration and will have repay the borrowing (the amount to repay will be the strike price, since the amount borrowed was its present value), leaving us with $S_T - X$, as before.

Since these two positions end up with identical values, irrespective of the stock price at expiration, they must cost the same, so:

- Call premium (paid initially) – put premium (received initially) = initial stock price paid – PV(X) received
- In symbols, $\mathbf{c_0 - p_0 = S_0 - PV(X)}$, which can be rearranged to $\mathbf{S_0 + p_0 = c_0 + PV(X)}$.

This, of course, you will recognize as the **put-call parity** relationship. Note that this version of the put-call parity formula assumes that the underlying pays no yield (during the period to expiry).

In this case, we have $c_0 - p_0 = \$6.26 - \$3.87 = \$2.39$. The risk-free interest rate is 3%,

so $PV(\$50) = \$50/(1.03)^{61/365} = \$49.75$, and the equation works, since $S_0 - PV(X) = \$52.14 - \$49.75 = \$2.39$.

Were PV(X) exactly equal to S_0 then put-call parity tells us that the call and put should have identical premiums (because $c_0 - p_0$ would equal zero). X in that situation would be the fair price for a forward contract.

Put-call forward parity substitutes $\mathbf{PV(F_0(T))}$ in place of S_0, where $F_0(T)$ is the forward price for a contract that matures at the same time as the options expire, giving $\mathbf{PV(F_0(T)) + p_0 = c_0 + PV(X)}$. Given that cash-and-carry arbitrage means that the fair forward price for an underlying that pays no yield equals $FV(S_0)$, and $PV(FV(S_0)) = S_0$, this is just a restatement of standard put-call parity.

EXAMPLE: Synthetic Long Forward Position

Gavin Ennis is a dealer who has just sold a four-month forward contract on AlphaCo Stock to a client who will thereby purchase 1,000 shares of the stock for 179.59. AlphaCo's current share price is 179, and AlphaCo will not be paying a dividend during the next four months. The annualized interest rate is 1%, and AlphaCo 179.59 calls and puts are both currently trading at 16.34 per share.

Explain how Ennis could hedge his short forward position using a synthetic long forward position, and explain what happens at expiry if the AlphaCo share price is above or below 179.59.

Answer:

Ennis should purchase a 179.59 call and sell a 179.59 put (both on 1,000 shares) with expiration matching the maturity of the forward contract. The net premium for these options will be zero.

At forward contract maturity, whatever happens, Ennis will have to sell the 1,000 shares to his client and receive 179.59 × 1,000. This is also the expiry point of the options.

If the share price is above 179.59 then Ennis will exercise the call, which is ITM, and purchase 1,000 shares, whereas if the share price is below 179.59 then the put counterparty will exercise the put (ITM) and sell 1,000 shares to Ennis. In either case Ennis buys 1,000 shares for 179.59 per share, which precisely offsets his obligation under the forward contract.

MODULE 6.3: COVERED CALLS

Video covering this content is available online.

LOS 6.b: Discuss the investment objective(s), structure, payoff, risk(s), value at expiration, profit, maximum profit, maximum loss, and breakeven underlying price at expiration of a covered call position.

Covered Calls with Extra Yield the Main Focus

Suppose an investor has a long position in XYZ stock on 20 March. They think that the stock has limited upside over the next month, and are prepared to sell off upside above $55 ($2.86 above the 20 March stock price of $52.14).

The classic way of doing this is to sell a call (a **covered call**, because the risk of the short option position is hedged by ownership of the stock), in this case an XYZ APR 55 call. This will give premium income of $2.52 (per share) in March.

At expiration, if the XYZ stock price is above $55 then the call will be exercised by the counterparty and the investor will be obliged to sell the stock to them for $55. If the stock price is below $55 the call will expire OTM and unexercised, so the investor continues to hold the stock. Ignoring the call premium received, this means the gain/loss associated with holding the stock is capped for stock prices above $55:

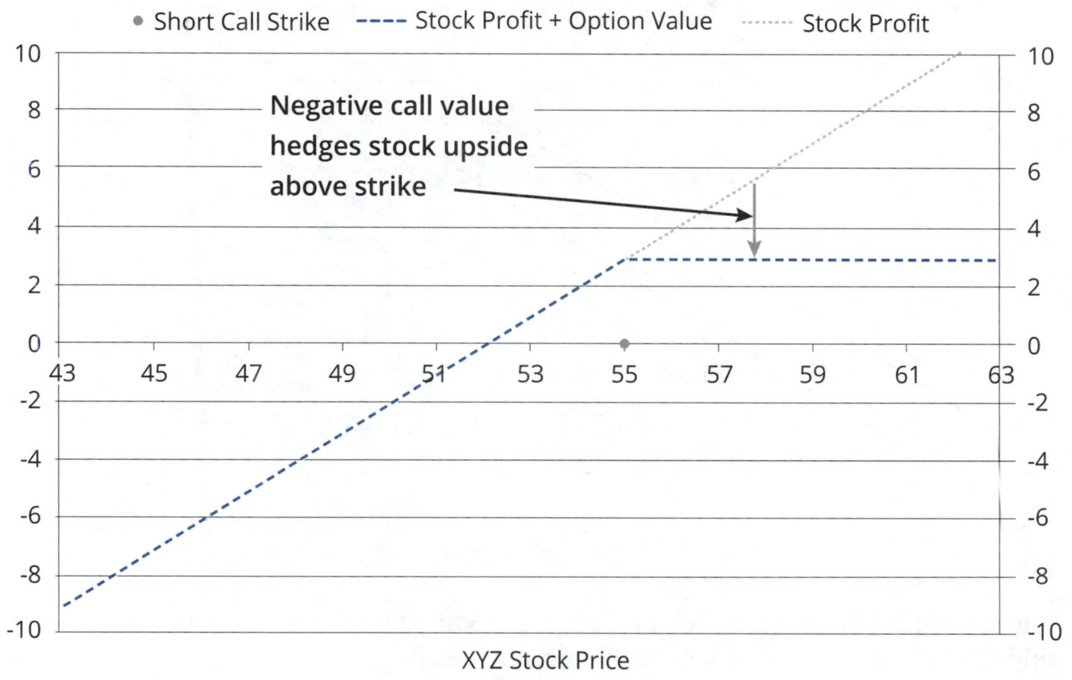

An equivalent way of thinking about it is that below $55 the call has zero intrinsic value, so adding this to the original stock gain/loss leaves us as we were, whereas above $55 the call's intrinsic value is the stock price minus the strike price (with a minus sign in front, since it is short), thus any gain on the stock above $55 is precisely offset by the increasing negative value of the short call.

At $55 the stock has risen by $2.86, and this is thus the maximum gain (ignoring the call premium). Note also that, ignoring the call premium, the breakeven point is the original stock price of $52.14.

Taking account of the \$2.52 call premium received takes us to the overall net profit/loss line:

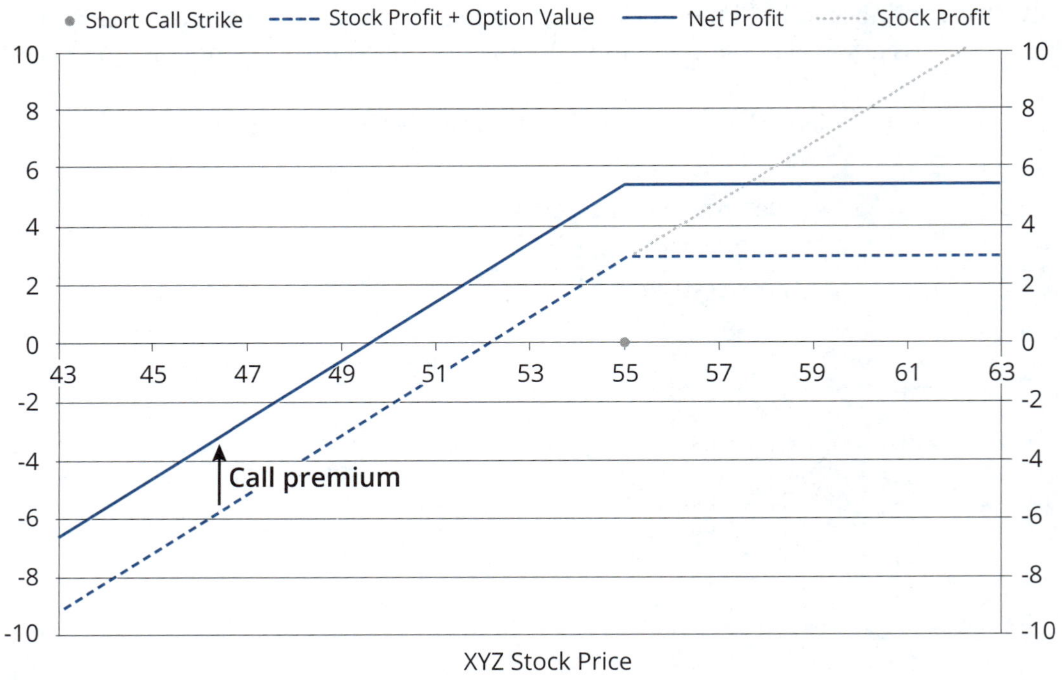

The net profit line is the stock gain/loss (as modified by the call intrinsic value) shifted uniformly upward by the call premium received.

The maximum profit equals \$2.86 + \$2.52 = \$5.38, while the breakeven is \$2.52 lower than it was without the premium received, which is at \$52.14 – \$2.52 = \$49.62 (up to a \$2.52 fall in the stock price is cushioned by the call premium).

Notice that the profit line has the same general shape as a short put and, as for a short put, the maximum loss is the same as the breakeven (since the loss increases one-for-one below breakeven, but the stock price cannot fall below zero). Thus maximum loss = \$49.62.

Since the investor holding the stock believed the stock had limited upside over the month, they have turned upside potential (which they did not need) into cash in hand. They will only end up worse off if the stock price at expiry exceeds \$55 + \$2.52 = \$57.52, which is the level at which the original stock gain/loss line cuts through the net profit line.

In general, for a covered call:

- maximum profit at expiry = $X - S_0 + c_0$
- breakeven stock price at expiry = maximum loss at expiry = $S_0 - c_0$

The motivation in the previous example of a covered call was earning extra yield (the focus was on the premium income).

There are two other likely motivations: reducing a position at a favorable price, and target price realization. Let us look at each in turn.

Reducing a Position at a Favorable Price

A second scenario where covered calls might be written is when an investor holds a position in a stock and intends to reduce that holding in the near future. For example Jenkins might hold 5,000 shares in XYZ on 20 March (share price = \$52.14), but plans to dispose of 1,500 of these. She might simply sell 1,500 shares at \$52.14, realizing \$78,210, but instead could write 15 exchange-traded XYZ April 50 call contracts (on 1,500 shares), receiving a total premium of 1,500 × \$4.80 = \$7,200. Note that the options are currently ITM.

Provided the share price at the April expiry is no lower than \$50, the options will get exercised, and Jenkins will be obliged to deliver 1,500 shares for 1,500 × \$50 = \$75,000. Adding the premium already received to this brings the total proceeds to \$75,000 + \$7,200 = \$82,200, which exceeds the proceeds had she simply sold at the market price on 20 March.

However, there is a risk: if the XYZ price at expiration is lower than \$50 then the calls will not be exercised and the shares will not be sold—the opportunity to sell at the current favorable price will have been missed.[3]

Target Price Realization

A third motivation is realizing a target price. In this case calls are written with a strike just above the current market price. The idea is that the investor believes the stock should be worth a bit more than its current price, and would be happy to sell it at that slightly-higher price. For example Perkins holds XYZ shares at \$52.14 and writes APR 52.5 calls, receiving \$3.53 per share. If the calls are exercised in April, then the shares are sold at the \$52.50 strike price, so a total per share of \$52.50 + \$3.53 = \$56.03 has been realized.

The dangers are twofold. First, the stock price may rise substantially, in which case Perkins would regret having to sell at \$52.50, rather than the higher market price. Second, the stock price might decline, and the opportunity to sell at the current level will have been missed.

Note that this use of covered calls is best seen as a hybrid of the previous two.

The observable difference between these three uses of covered calls is the value of the strike relative to the current stock price:

- For yield enhancement, the calls are OTM (possibly substantially so).
- For reducing a position at a favorable price, the calls are ITM.
- For target price realization, the calls are marginally OTM.

[3] If the strategy does work as intended, however, Jenkins will have captured the time value embedded in the option price (in this case \$4.80 – (\$52.14 – \$50) = \$2.66 per share, which corresponds to 1,500 × \$2.66 = \$3,990 (= \$82,200 – \$78,210).

MODULE QUIZ 6.1, 6.2, 6.3

1. Which of the following trades would create a synthetic short exposure to PQR stock? The options expire in 6 months, and the risk-free interest rate is 2%.
   A. Borrow 99, buy a PQR 100 put and sell a PQR 100 call.
   B. Borrow 101, buy a PQR 100 put and buy a PQR 100 call.
   C. Buy a PQR 100 call and sell a PQR 100 put, simultaneously selling a six-month forward contract on PQR at 100.

2. An investor purchases a stock for $43 and sells a call for $2.10 with a strike price of $45. At expiration of the call:

   a) **compute** the maximum profit and loss and the breakeven price.

   b) **compute** the profit or loss when the stock price is $0, $35, $40, $45, $50.

MODULE 6.4: PROTECTIVE PUTS

Video covering this content is available online.

Reading 6

LOS 6.c: Discuss the investment objective(s), structure, payoff, risk(s), value at expiration, profit, maximum profit, maximum loss, and breakeven underlying price at expiration of a protective put position.

For an investor who has a long position in an underlying, the classic options-based hedge is the protective put—buying a put option to protect against the underlying falling in value, while retaining upside.

Suppose that an investor has a holding of XYZ stock on 20 March, and purchases XYZ May 50 puts on an equal number of shares as a hedge. The puts will cost $3.87 per share, and the share price is $52.14.

The position at May expiry is as shown on the next graph (in per-share terms, as always):

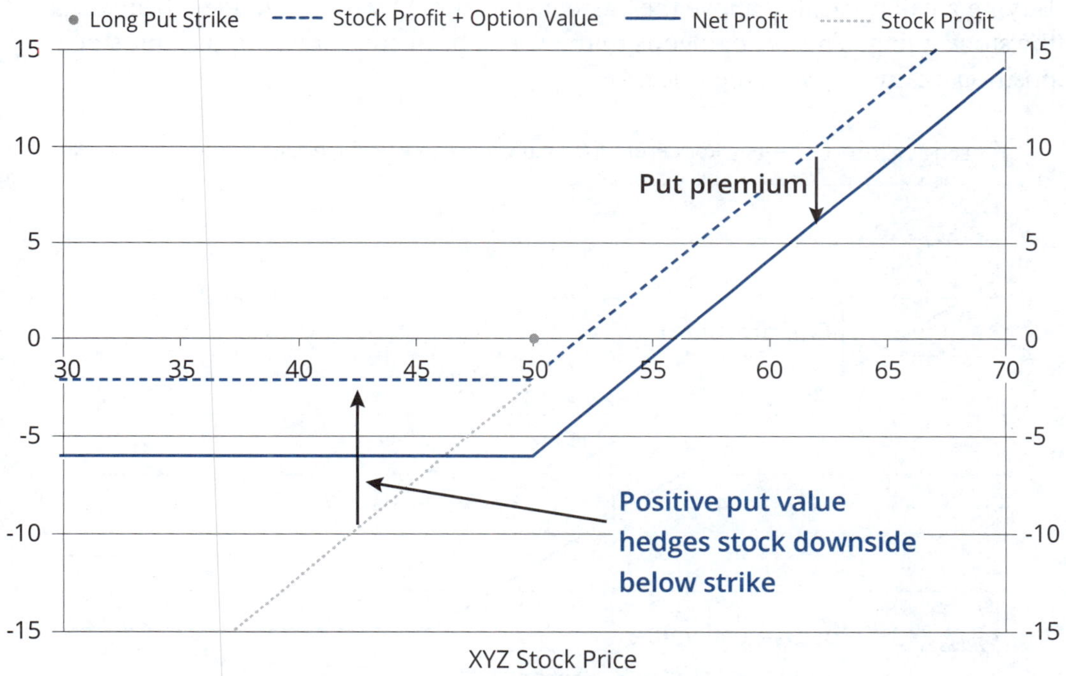

As with the covered call, when the initial option premium cost is ignored the breakeven is the same as for the unhedged stock, but this time we see that the stock loss is limited to the distance of the strike below the initial stock price ($52.14 – $50 = $2.14). Factoring in the initial premium, the net maximum loss is $2.14 + $3.87 = $6.01, while the breakeven is the premium added to the unhedged breakeven of $52.14, so $52.14 + $3.87 = $56.01. This breakeven can also be inferred from the fact that at 50 there is a loss of $6.01, so the underlying needs to expire $6.01 above that, at $56.01, to break even.

In general, for a protective put:

- Maximum loss at expiry = $S_0 - X + p_0$
- Breakeven stock price at expiry = $S_0 + p_0$
- Maximum profit = unlimited

Video covering this content is available online.

MODULE 6.5: OPTIONS AS A HEDGE OF A SHORT POSITION

LOS 6.e: Compare the effect of buying a call on a short underlying position with the effect of selling a put on a short underlying position.

If an investor starts with a short position in the underlying, they will gain if the price falls and lose if the price rises.

Buying a call (probably above the current stock price) would provide a hedge against the stock rising. This is analogous to the way a protective *put* hedges a *long* stock position against a *fall* in the price:

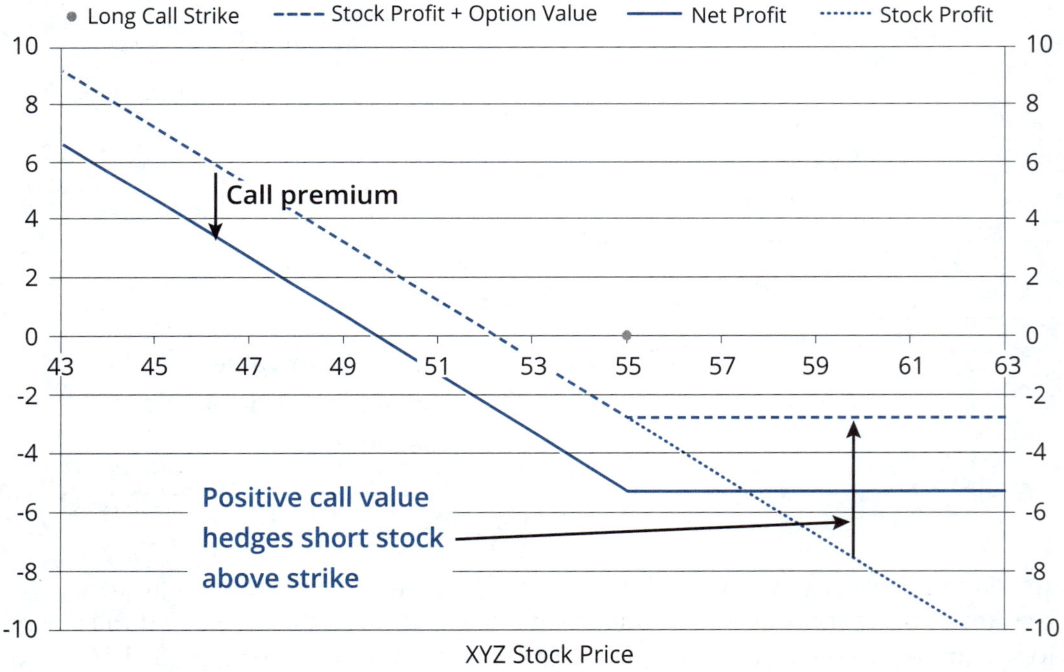

Similarly, the sale of a put (probably below the current stock price) sells off (part of) the benefit of the stock falling, in the same way a **covered *call*** sells off the upside of a ***long* stock** position:

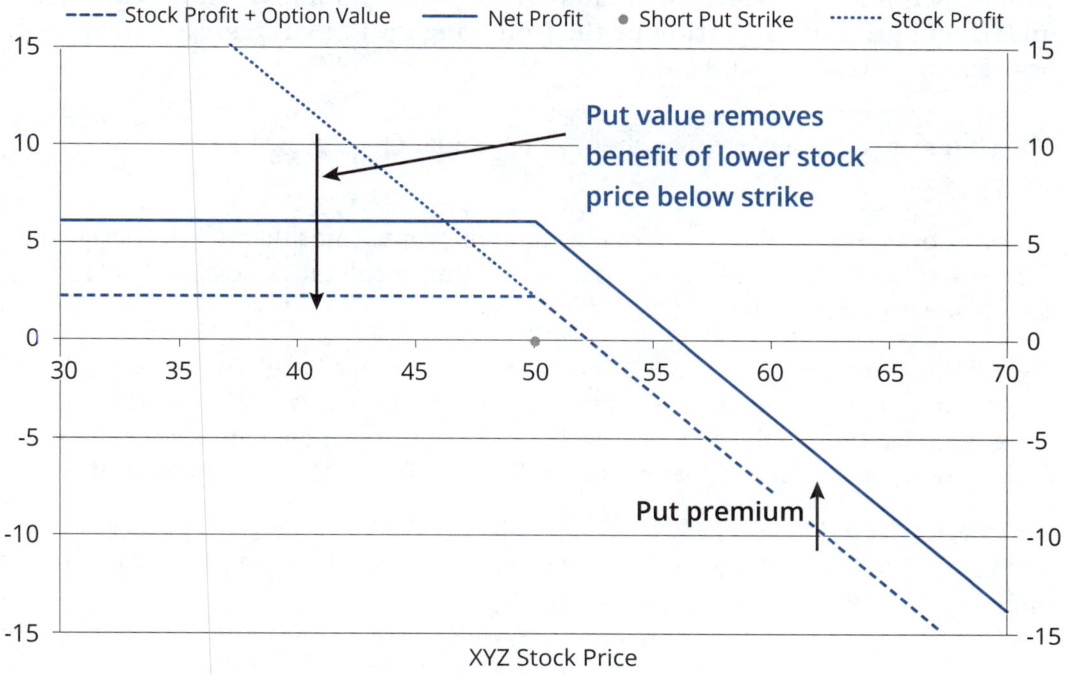

MODULE QUIZ 6.4, 6.5

1. An investor purchases a stock for $37.50 and buys a put for $1.40 with a strike price of $35. At expiration of the put:
   a) **compute** the maximum profit, maximum loss, and breakeven price.

   b) **compute** the profit or loss for when the stock price is $30, $35, $40, and $50.

2. It is September, and Jones has a short position in Alphacorp stock. The share price is currently 220 and Jones anticipates little movement in the price over the next month, although his long-term view is bearish. To increase his yield from the holding Jones would *most likely* sell:
   A. October 240 calls.
   B. October 240 puts.
   C. October 200 puts.

Video covering this content is available online.

MODULE 6.6: COLLARS

LOS 6.f: Discuss the investment objective(s), structure, payoffs, risk(s), value at expiration, profit, maximum profit, maximum loss, and breakeven underlying price at expiration of the following option strategies: bull spread, bear spread, straddle, and collar.

The **collar**[4] is probably best thought of as combination of protective put and covered call.

An investor who is long the underlying could buy a put (most likely OTM) to hedge the stock's downside, while at the same time selling a call (also most likely OTM) to sell off the upside and subsidize the cost of the put.

Usually the put strike is set, then an appropriate call strike is determined such that the call and put have the same premium. If the options are over-the-counter, rather than exchange-traded, this will be easy to do. In this case there will be no net inflow or outflow at initiation and the investor will have constructed a **zero-cost collar**.

For example, consider an investor with a holding of XYZ stock on 20 March (price = $52.14). They buy a June 50 put (premium = $4.88) and sell a June 55.87 call (premium = $4.88). At the June expiration:

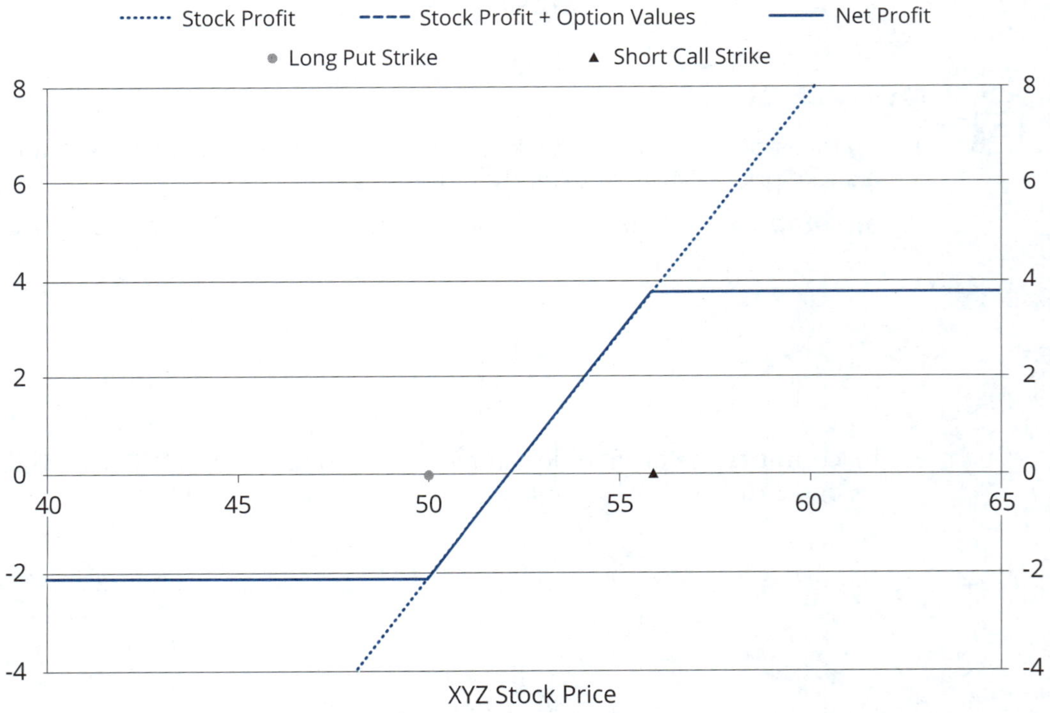

Notice, in this case, that the line for stock profit + option values is the same as the net profit line because of the zero net initial premium.

[4] Also known as a *fence* or a *hedge wrapper.*

The stock value is hedged beyond the strikes, with a maximum profit equal to the rise from the initial stock price up to the call strike ($55.87 – $52.14 = $3.73) and a maximum loss equal to the fall from the initial stock price down to the put strike ($52.14 – $50 = $2.14). The breakeven stock price is simply the initial stock price of $52.14, as when it was unhedged.

MODULE 6.7: STRADDLES

Video covering this content is available online.

The **straddle** is the classic volatility play. A **long straddle** involves the purchase of an equal number of calls and puts on a given underlying. The options all have the same expiry date and strike[5].

Notice that, unlike the strategies we have considered up to now, the straddle (and the spreads that follow) do not involve a position in the underlying—they just use options.

Keeping it simple, let us consider the purchase of a call and a put on one share of XYZ on 20 March. Typically the strike would be close to ATM, so given the stock price is $52.14, let us go long both the June 52.5 call and the June 52.5 put.

At expiration *either* the call *or* the put will be ITM, but not both. The call is ITM for stock prices above 52.50, while the put is ITM for stock prices below 52.50:

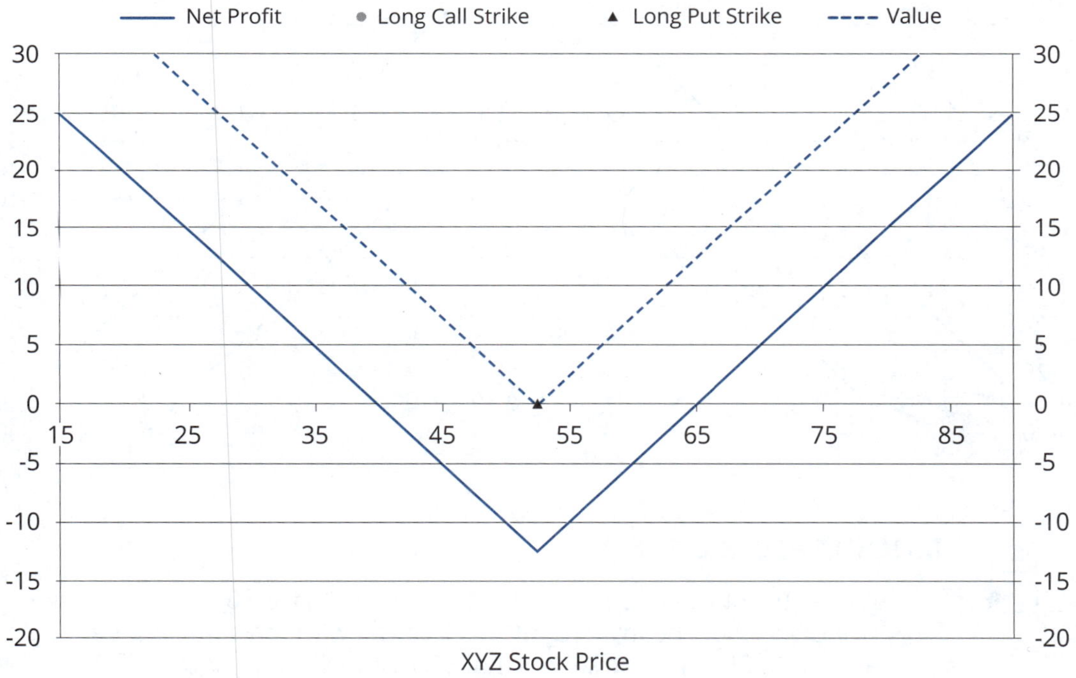

The value line for a long straddle is always V-shaped, centered on the strike, where both options expire worthless, so the total value is 0.

[5] **Strangles**, which we encounter in the currency reading, are like straddles, but the calls and puts have different strikes.

In this case, the premium for the call was $6.22, while the premium for the put was $6.19. Both were paid at initiation, so there was a total outlay of $6.22 + $6.19 = $12.41. This is thus the maximum loss (at the strike). The strategy breaks even at expiration when:

- either the call is $12.41 ITM at $52.50 + $12.41 = $64.91
- or the put is $12.41 ITM at $52.50 – $12.41 = $40.09

The strategy, if held to expiration, makes larger profits, the further from the strike the underlying ends up (i.e., the more the underlying moves, either way). There is no maximum profit.

A **short straddle** involves selling, instead of buying, and is a neutrality play. It makes more profit the closer to the strike the underlying ends up, with no limit on potential loss.

The at-expiration value and profit for the short XYZ June straddle is shown here:

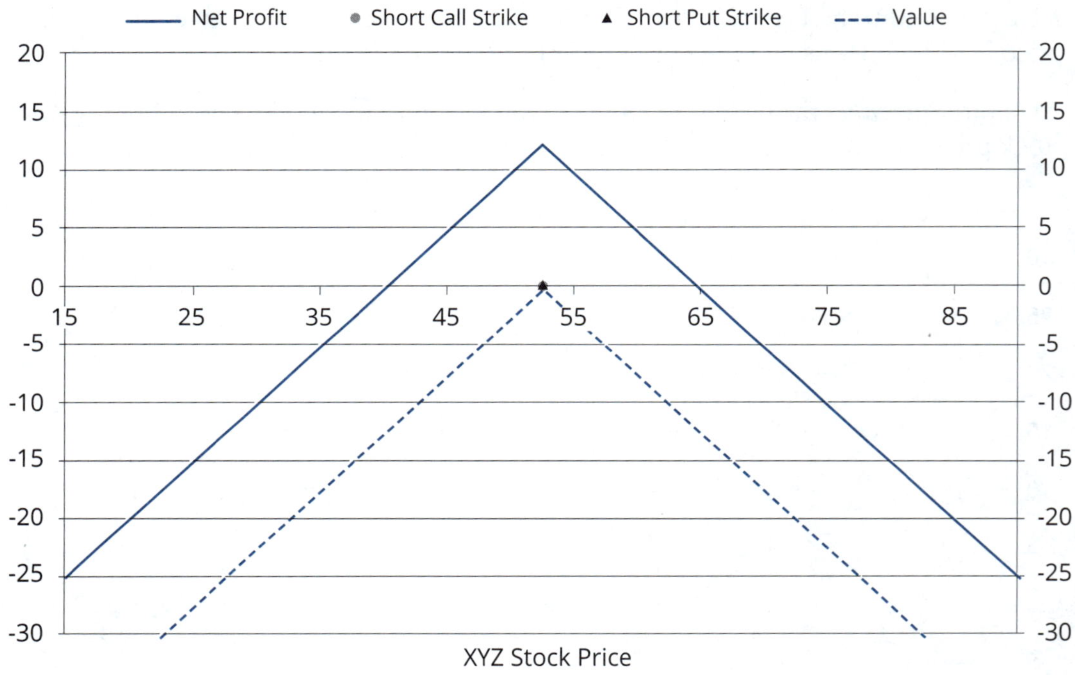

MODULE QUIZ 6.6, 6.7

1. An investor purchases a stock for $29 and a put for $0.20 with a strike price of $27.50. The investor also sells a call with the same expiration date for $0.20 with a strike price of $30. At expiration of the options:
   a) **Calculate** the maximum profit and loss and the breakeven price.

b) **Calculate** the profit or loss when the price is $20, $25, $28.50, $30, and $100.

2. An investor purchases a call on a stock, with an exercise price of $45 and premium of $3, and a put option with the same maturity that has an exercise price of $45 and premium of $2. At expiration of the options:

   a) **Compute** the maximum profit, maximum loss, and breakeven price.

   b) **Compute** the profit or loss when the price is $0, $35, $40, $45, $47, $55, and $100.

3. The EUR is trading at USD 1.035. A trader expects the EUR to become much more volatile than is reflected in current option prices. Puts and calls on the EUR are available. Puts with a strike of USD 0.98 are trading at USD 0.005 and with a strike of USD 1.04 are trading at USD 0.017. Calls with a strike of USD 0.98 are trading at USD 0.068 and with a strike of USD 1.04 are trading at USD 0.004. **Compute** the at-expiry breakeven price or prices of the correct option strategy.

MODULE 6.8: SPREADS

Video covering this content is available online.

Bull and bear spreads are positions that have equal numbers of long options on one strike and short options on a second strike. A spread will *either* be constructed using calls *or* using puts.

- **Bull** spreads use **long** options on the **lower** strike (**Bull** = **Buy** Low) and **short** options on the **higher** strike.
- **Bear** spreads use **short** options on the **lower** strike and **long** options on the **higher** strike.

Bear spreads are just short bull spreads, in fact.

Bull Call Spread

Suppose that on 20 March an investor buys an XYZ June 50 call for $7.40 and sells an XYZ June 55 call for $5.20. This will involve a net outlay of $7.40 – $5.20 = $2.20.

The following diagram shows the value of the position, and the net profit, for a range of stock prices at expiration:

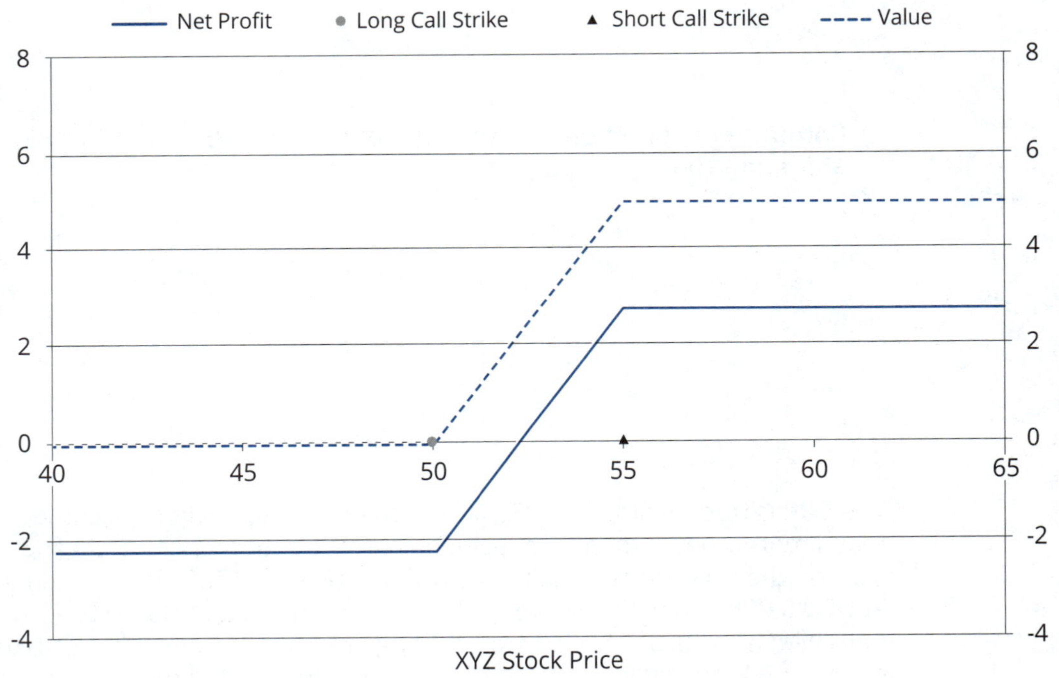

It is clear that the exposure is bullish, but limited, compared to just having a long call at 50.

We can think of the bull call spread as similar to a covered call, but with a long call taking the place of the stock.

Below the lower strike the position has zero value since both options expire OTM.

Between the strikes only the long call expires ITM, so the value is equal to the difference between the stock price and the lower strike.

At 55 the value will equal 5, the difference between the strikes. This is also the maximum value, since any further upside to the long call is hedged away by the short call, which goes ITM above 55.

The maximum loss (when value = 0) is the net premium paid, $2.20.

Breakeven occurs when the value of the long call exactly compensates for the net premium paid. This will be $2.20 above the lower strike, at $50 + $2.20 = $52.20.

The maximum profit is the maximum value of $5 less the net premium, thus $5 – $2.20 = $2.80.

In general, for a bull call spread:

- Maximum loss = net premium paid
- Breakeven = lower strike + net premium paid
- Maximum profit = difference between strikes – net premium paid

The bull call spread is an example of a **debit spread** since it entails a net outlay: the bought call, with a lower strike, is more valuable than the sold call.

The other debit spread is the bear put spread.

Bear Put Spread

Here we sell a lower strike put and buy a higher strike put.

Suppose that on 20 March an investor buys an XYZ May 55 put for $6.61 and sells an XYZ May 50 put for $3.87. This will involve a net outlay of $6.61 – $3.87 = $2.74.

Value and profit at May expiration:

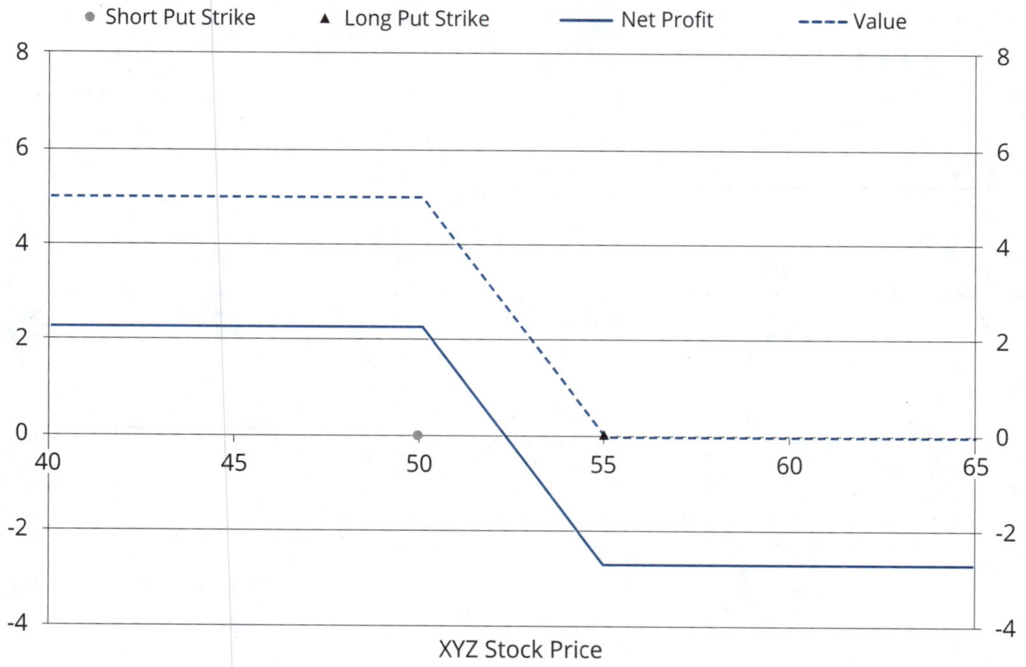

It is clear that the exposure is bearish, but limited, compared to just having a long put at 55.

Both options are OTM above the higher strike, for zero value.

Between the strikes the value reflects the moneyness of the long 55 put (how far the stock price is below the upper strike).

At the lower strike, the value is maximized and is hedged at that level for any lower stock price.

For a bear put spread:

- Maximum loss = net premium paid ($2.74 in this case)
- Breakeven = higher strike – net premium paid ($55 – $2.74 = $52.26)
- Maximum profit = difference between strikes – net premium paid ($5 – $2.74 = $2.26)

Bear Call and Bull Put Spreads

It is also possible, of course, to use calls to create a bear spread, or puts to create a bull spread. In both cases there would be a net inflow of premium (since the relatively more valuable option is sold) and they are referred to as **credit spreads**.

PROFESSOR'S NOTE

As a general rule, assume that a bull spread would be constructed using calls and that a bear spread would be constructed using puts (i.e., that debit spreads are to be preferred over credit spreads) unless a question states otherwise.

For example, a bear call spread could use a short XYZ June 50 call ($7.40) plus a long XYZ June 55 call ($5.20), with a net initial inflow of $7.40 – $5.20 = $2.20, which is the maximum profit at 50 and below. At 55 and above, the net intrinsic value is –$5, resulting in a maximum loss of $2.80.

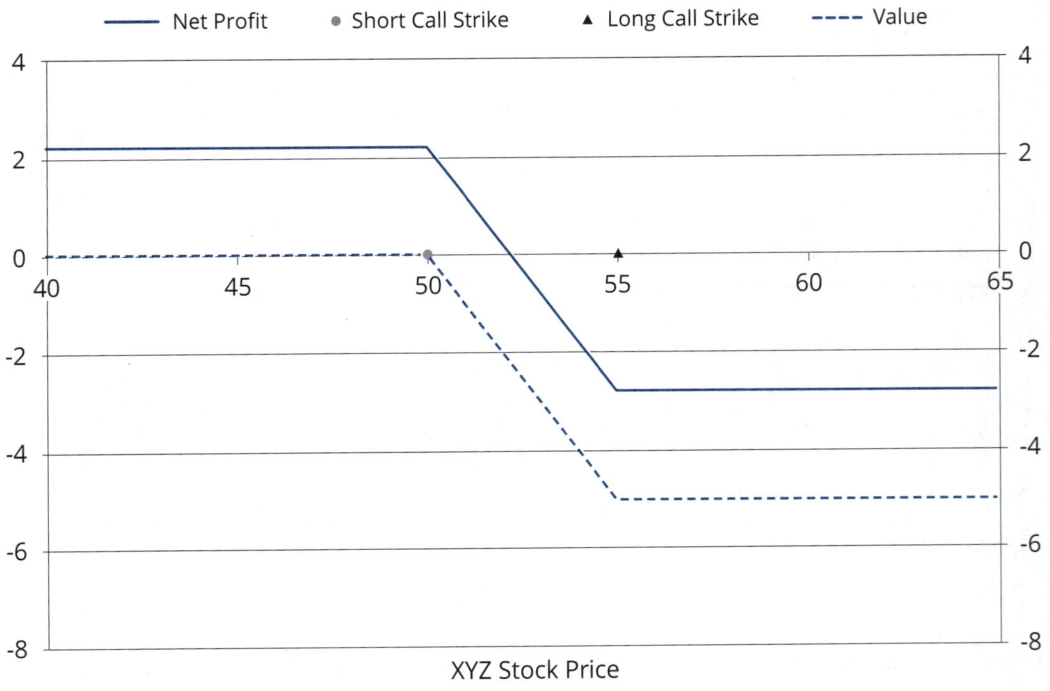

- Maximum profit = net premium received
- Breakeven = lower strike + net premium received
- Maximum loss = difference between strikes – net premium received

Similarly, a **bull put spread** is the reverse of a bear put spread, in this case a short XYZ May 55 put ($6.61) and a long XYZ May 50 put ($3.87). At expiration:

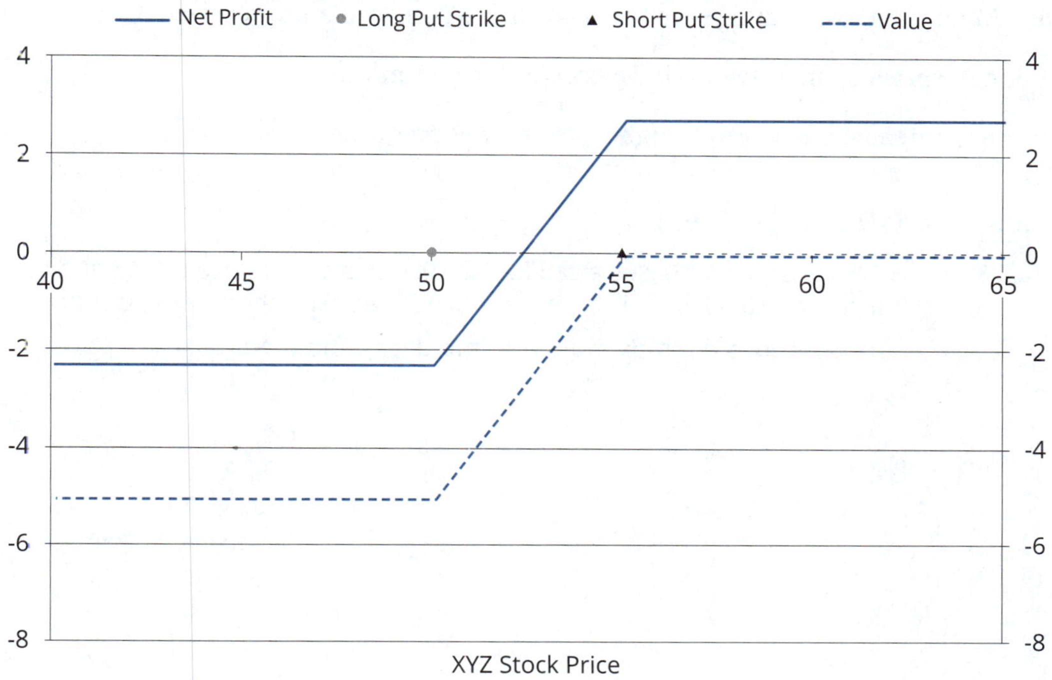

- Maximum profit = net premium received
- Breakeven = higher strike – net premium received
- Maximum loss = difference between strikes – net premium received

Beware of credit spreads using American-style options, where there is the possibility of the short option going ITM, while the long option is still OTM, in which case the counterparty might choose to exercise early, which would disrupt the strategy.

Adding a Short Leg to a Long Position

Both legs of the spread do not necessarily have to be established at the same time, or held for the same length of time. For instance, a trader might have gone long an October 30 call in August, when the stock price was 28, and by September the stock may have risen to 38.5, so that he is already sitting on a potential profit. If at that point he thinks it unlikely that the stock price will rise further, he might sell an October 40 call, effectively cashing in the upside potential he does not think he needs. This is similar to the motivation behind a covered call.

Generalized At-Expiration Formulas for Spreads

In these formulas, net premium means the absolute value of the difference between the premiums.

For **debit spreads** (bull call and bear put):

- Maximum loss = net premium paid
- Maximum profit = difference between strikes – net premium paid

For **credit spreads** (bear call and bull put):

- Maximum profit = net premium received
- Maximum loss = difference between strikes – net premium received

For **call spreads**, breakeven = lower strike + net premium

For **put spreads**, breakeven = higher strike – net premium

MODULE QUIZ 6.8

1. An investor purchases a call for $2.10 with a strike price of $45 and sells a call for $0.50 with a strike price of $50. At expiration of the options:

   a) **Compute** the maximum profit and loss and the breakeven price.

   b) **Compute** the profit or loss when the price is $35, $45, $48, $50, and $55.

2. An investor purchases a put for $4.00 with a strike price of $25.00 and sells a put for $1.80 with a strike price of $20.00. At expiration of the puts:
   a) **Compute** the maximum profit and loss and the breakeven price.

   b) **Calculate** the profit or loss when the price is $15, $20, $23.50, $25, and $30.

3. A stock trades at 51. Calls with strike prices of 47 and 53 are priced at 5.25 and 0.75, respectively. **Compute** the initial investment for a bear spread and the breakeven price or prices of the spread at options expiration.

Video covering this content is available online.

MODULE 6.9: DELTA AND GAMMA

So far, we have only considered values and profits at the point of option expiration; in so doing, we only had to worry about intrinsic value (thus simple one-for-one relationships).

During their lives, the way in which options respond to changes in the value of the underlying (and other factors) is more complicated, and we will now look at some aspects of this.

The Greeks

As you should recall, each is a ratio of absolute changes (in each case assuming only the named factor changes):

- **Delta** (Δ) = change in option **price** per +1 change in **stock price**.

  Delta is positive for (long) calls and negative for (long) puts.
- **Gamma** (Γ) = change in option **delta** per +1 change in **stock price.**

  Gamma is positive for (long) calls and for (long) puts.
- **Theta** (θ) = daily change in option **price** (effect of **time passing**).

  Theta is negative for (long) calls and (long) puts.
- **Vega** (ν) = change in option **price** per +1% change in **volatility.**

  Vega is positive for (long) calls and for (long) puts.

Like option premiums, you will not be asked to calculate the values of the Greeks—if needed in a question they would be provided. What is important is an appreciation of the meaning and significance of each one. We will see they help us more fully understand some of the options strategies met in the last few sections.

Recall that **delta** measures the change in the price of an option for a +1 change in the price of the underlying (all other factors held constant).

Taking the XYZ stock options as an example, below is the table of option premiums on 20 March (when the stock price was $52.14) as seen before, together with a table of deltas at the same point in time:

Call Price			Strike	Put Price		
APR	MAY	JUN	Price	APR	MAY	JUN
4.80	6.26	7.40	**50**	2.53	3.87	4.88
3.53	5.05	6.22	**52.5**	3.75	5.14	6.19
2.52	4.02	5.20	**55**	5.24	6.61	7.65

Call Delta			Strike	Put Delta		
APR	MAY	JUN	Price	APR	MAY	JUN
0.634	0.623	0.623	**50**	–0.366	–0.377	–0.377
0.525	0.546	0.560	**52.5**	–0.475	–0.454	–0.440
0.419	0.470	0.499	**55**	–0.581	–0.530	–0.501

For example, the MAY 55 call has a delta of 0.47, meaning that if the stock price rose by $1 to $53.14 then the MAY 55 call would rise, in principle, by $0.47, to $4.02 + $0.47 = $4.49. Note that all other factors are assumed held constant, in particular, time, so the change has to be *instantaneous*.

In fact, if we recompute the MAY 55 call premium for the $53.14 stock price, the pricing model gives us a figure of $4.51, slightly higher than the $4.49 predicted by delta. This is because the option price line is not a straight line (other than at expiration), with a curvature measured by **gamma**, so delta itself varies with the underlying.

The vertical distance between the (total) value line and the intrinsic value line corresponds to the time value, which is at its greatest around ATM, and diminishes the more the option is ITM or OTM[6]:

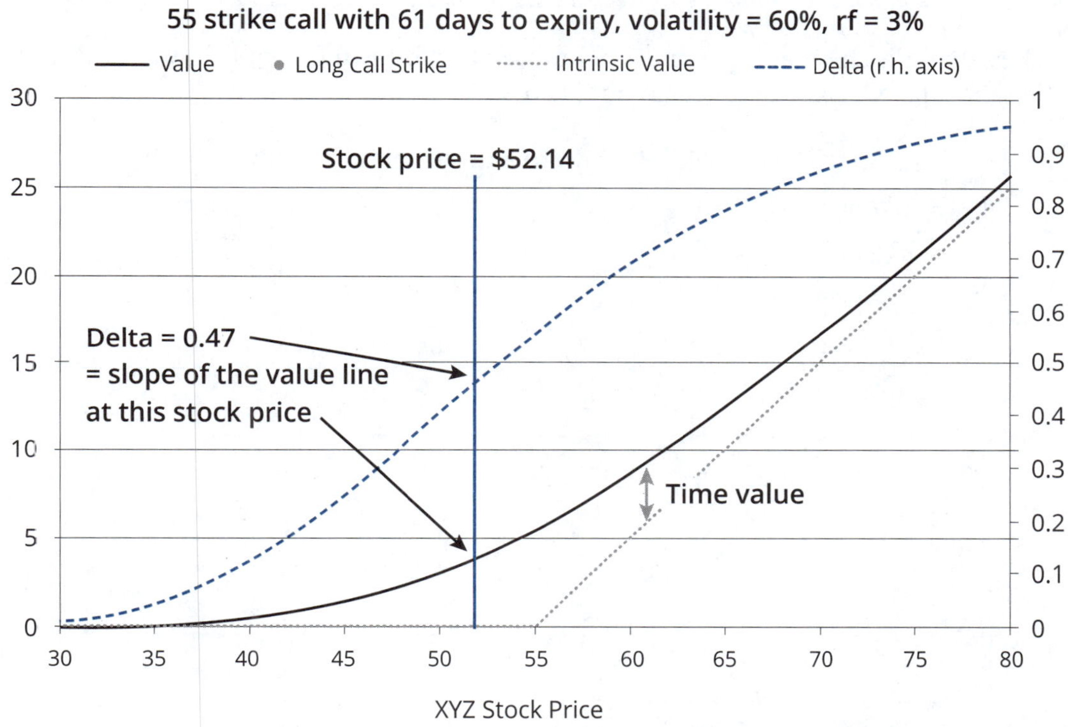

Here is the corresponding table for the option gammas on 20 March (at the original stock price of $52.14):

Call Gamma			Strike	Put Gamma		
APR	**MAY**	**JUN**	**Price**	**APR**	**MAY**	**JUN**
0.041	0.030	0.024	**50**	0.041	0.030	0.024
0.044	0.031	0.025	**52.5**	0.044	0.031	0.025
0.043	0.031	0.026	**55**	0.043	0.031	0.026

For example, the MAY 55 call has a gamma of 0.031, meaning if the share price were $1 higher, the call's delta would be 0.031 higher: 0.470 + 0.031 = 0.501.

[6] Time value is a reflection of the relative difficulty of hedging an option, and options are harder to hedge when it is unclear whether they are going to **expire** ITM or OTM. If they are already deeply ITM or OTM there is less uncertainty about this.

PROFESSOR'S NOTE

The gamma adjustment is an approximation, in that same way that delta is. They are both only accurate for infinitesimal changes in the underlying price. Delta is the slope of the option price line at the current underlying price (think of it as the slope of the tangent to the line at that point)—as soon as the underlying moves at all, the delta changes. Similarly gamma is the slope of the line representing delta, and this changes with the underlying, too.

Don't worry about having to do this calculation, but if delta at the $52.14 stock price is 0.470, while it is 0.501 at the $53.14 price, then the average delta between those stock prices is (0.470 + 0.501)/2 = 0.486, so we could predict that the call value $1 above $52.14 would be $4.02 + $0.486 = $4.506, which is much closer than when we just used the initial value of delta.

The same principles apply to puts, of course. The following graph shows value and delta for the XYZ APR 50 (long) put (also on 20 March):

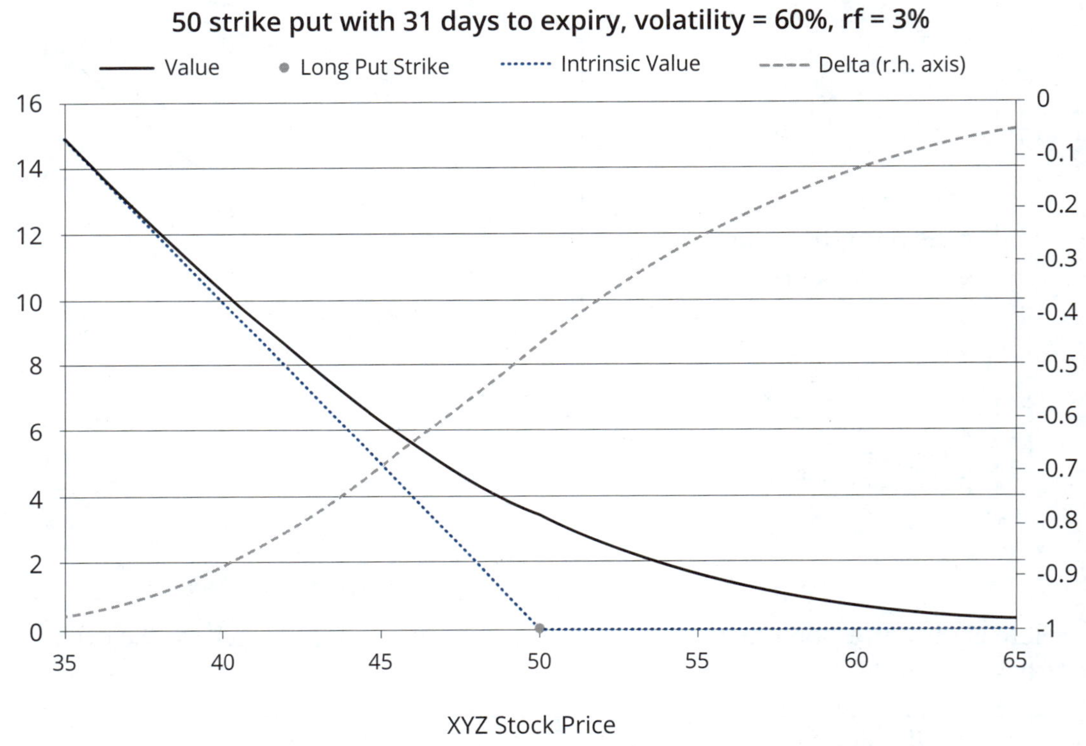

Puts (long) have negative delta, since the line slopes downward, but there is a simple rule that applies to both calls and puts regarding the absolute size of delta (i.e., ignoring the sign):

All other factors held constant:

- The **more ITM** is an option, the **higher** is its (absolute) delta (closer to 1).
- The **more OTM** is an option, the **lower** is its (absolute) delta (closer to 0).

The following diagram summarizes the ranges of values of delta for long and short calls and puts:

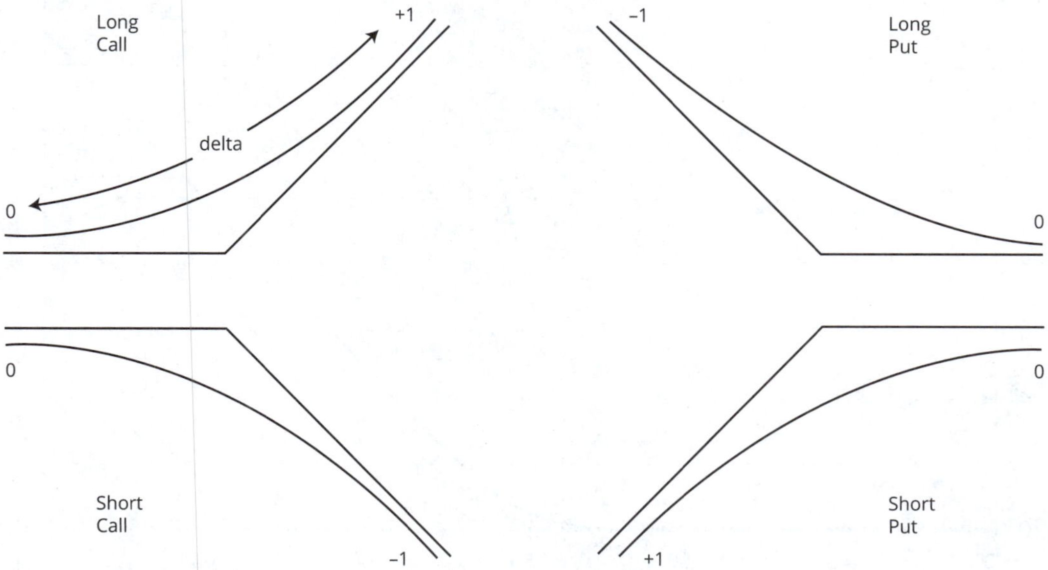

Gamma is trickier to generalize, but it tends to be higher the closer to ATM an option, **and is at its greatest for ATM options that are close to expiration**. For instance, the following graphs illustrate the same call, first with 20 days to expiration and then with one day to expiration when, with much less time remaining (so much less time value), the option premium line is crammed into a narrow range either side of the strike price, so gamma is highest over that range:

55 strike call with 20 days to expiry, volatility = 60%, rf = 3%

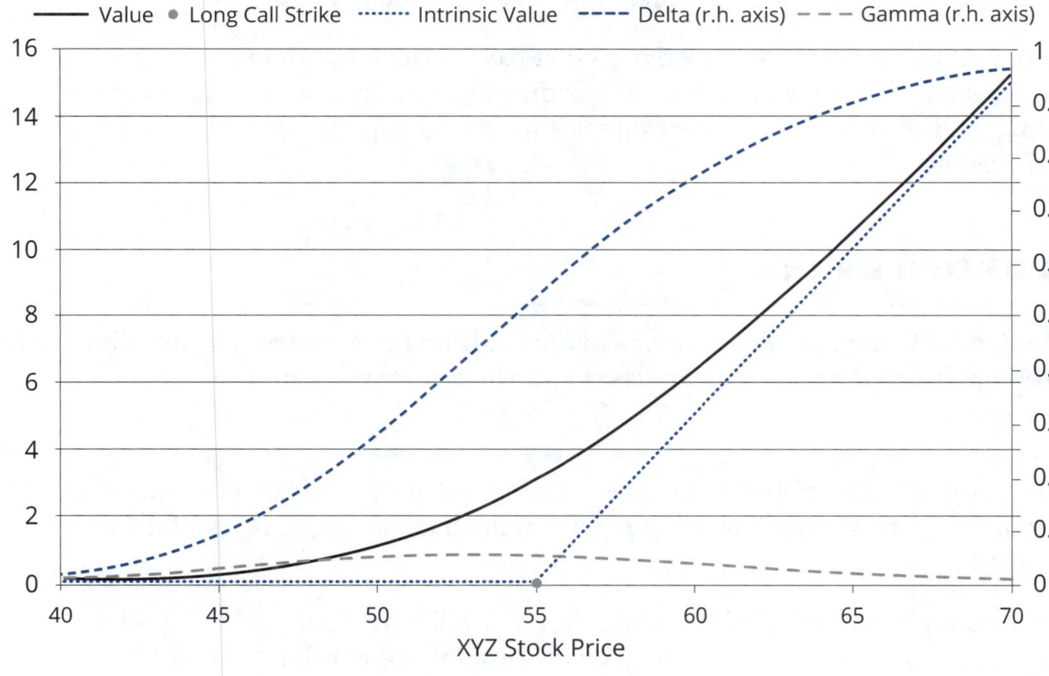

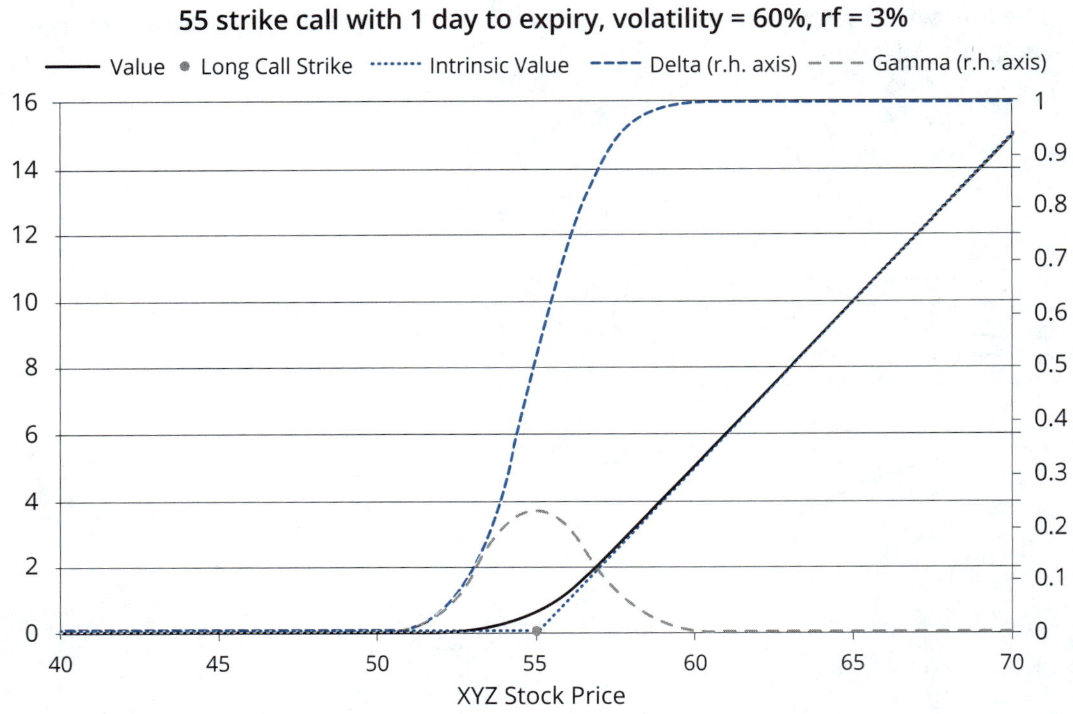

Deltas for the Underlying and for Futures and Forwards on the Underlying

It follows directly from the definition of delta that:

- The delta of a **long** position in one unit of the underlying is **+1**.
- The delta of a **short** position in one unit of the underlying is **–1**.

Futures and forwards on underlyings that pay no yield (e.g., nondividend paying stocks) are essentially proxies for the underlying, so they also have deltas of +1 (if long) and –1 (if short). All the examples we consider in this reading use underlyings of this sort.

Position Deltas

LOS 6.d: Compare the delta of covered call and protective put positions with the position of being long an asset and short a forward on the underlying asset.

The overall (or portfolio) delta for a combination of options and positions in the underlying is computed by adding up the individual deltas (being careful with the signs).

For example, a holding of 100 shares in XYZ will have a delta of 100 × +1 = +100. That is, if the stock price rises $1 then the position value will rise by $100.

Reading 6

PROFESSOR'S NOTE

Unless told otherwise, assume that a traded stock option contract is a right over 100 shares. So a long position in an XYZ call option contract, where the option delta is +0.65, would have a position delta of 100 × +0.65 = +65.

A holding of 1,000 shares in XYZ, plus a long position in 10 XYZ put contracts (delta = –0.6), has a position delta of (1,000 × +1) + (10 × 100 × –0.6) = 1,000 – 600 = 400. Some of the stock's exposure is being offset by the negative exposure given by the puts.

If the stock price falls $1, then the shares lose $1,000, but the net position value will only fall $400.

Protective Put Pre-Expiry

In the earlier section, where we concentrated on value at expiration, we thought of a protective put as a strategy that retains the full stock exposure above the strike price, but completely hedges below the strike price. For example a protective put on the XYZ stock, using the May 50 put (premium = $3.87), looks like this at expiration (assuming one share plus a long put on one share):

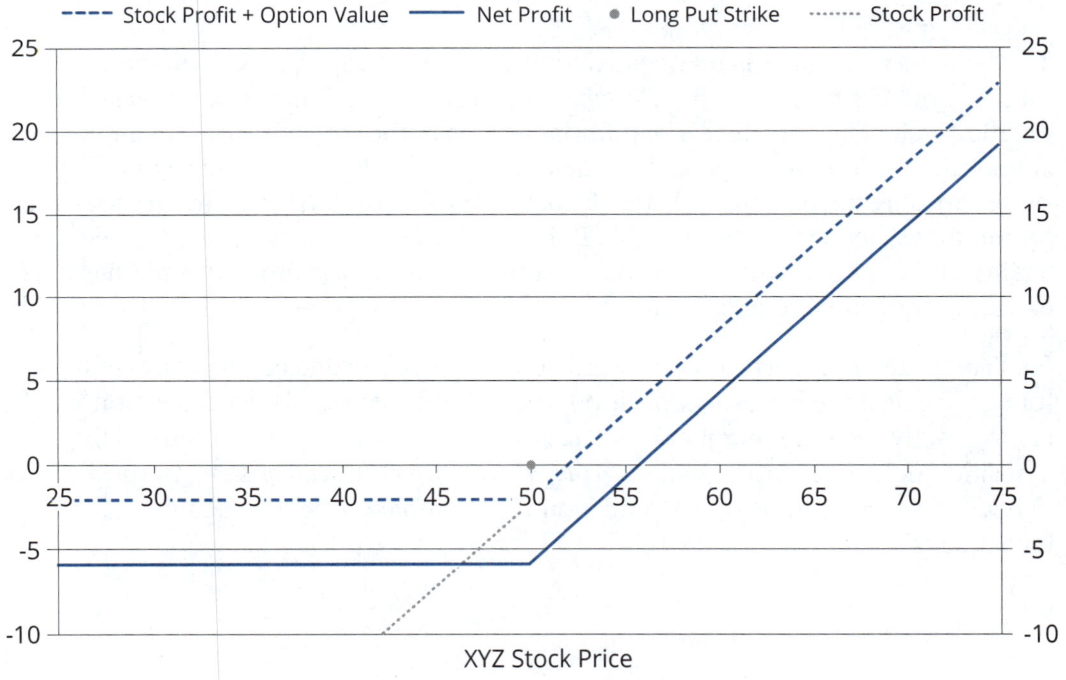

However, before expiration, the protective put is better thought of as modifying the delta of the long stock from its unhedged value of +1:

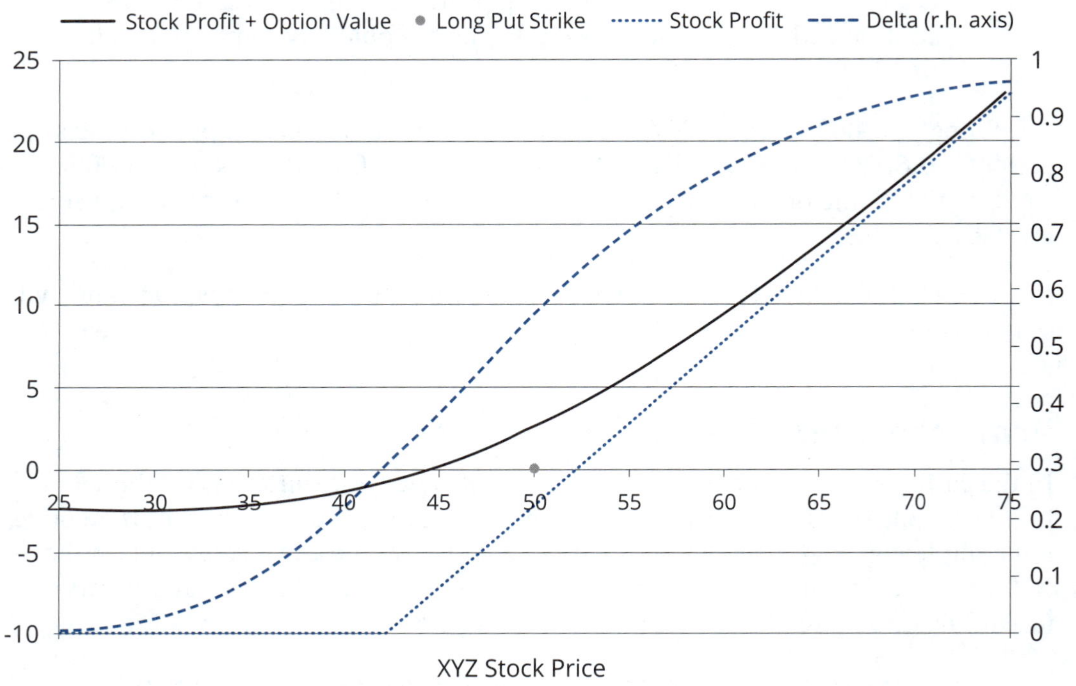

This graph shows the impact of the option value (ignoring the premium paid) on the gain/loss position for the stock at the point the option position was set up on 20 March. The net effect is that for large rises in the stock, the option moves substantially OTM, and the position delta tends toward +1 (so we have almost the same exposure as from the unhedged stock), whereas for large falls in the stock the option moves to being substantially ITM, and the delta tends toward 0 (protecting against the stock's downside). Notice that the stock plus the protective put has a net exposure equivalent to a long call.

Had we, instead, undertaken a forward contract-based hedge of the stock (selling forward against the long stock position) then, given that our forward position would be on exactly the same number of shares as we were holding, we would obtain a position delta of *number of shares* × *(delta of long stock + delta of short forward)* = *number of shares* × *(+1 + –1)* = *0*, and would be completely hedged against price movements.

Covered Call Pre-Expiry

Similarly, we can compare a covered call (XYZ June 55) at expiration and earlier in the option's life:

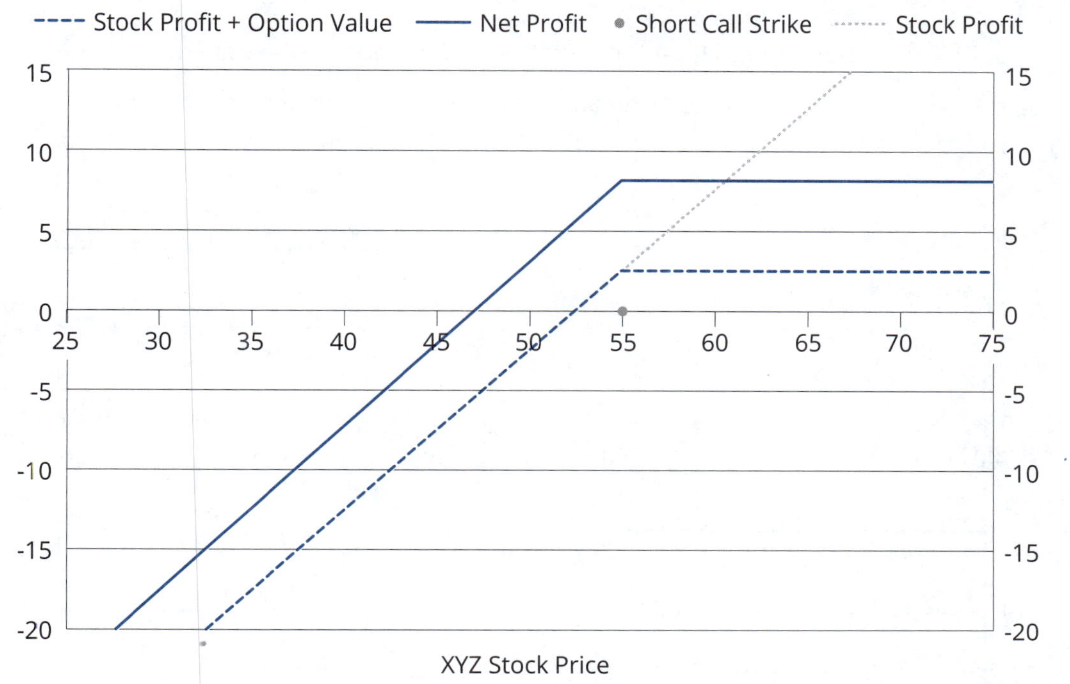

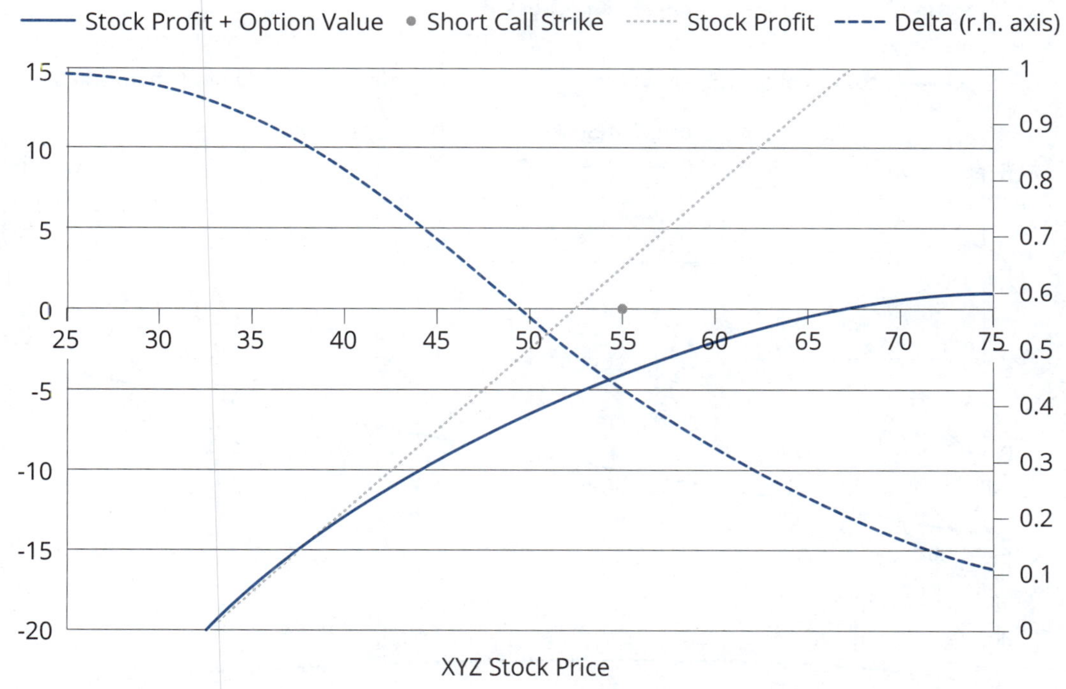

As with the protective put, the position delta varies from close to +1 (when the call is deeply OTM) to close to 0 (when the call is deeply ITM, and virtually all of the stock's upside is hedged away).

Collar Pre-Expiry

Here is a collar [XYZ stock, long June 50 put (premium = $4.88), short June 55.87 call (premium = $4.88)] shown in the same way, at expiration, and at initiation (91 days before expiration):

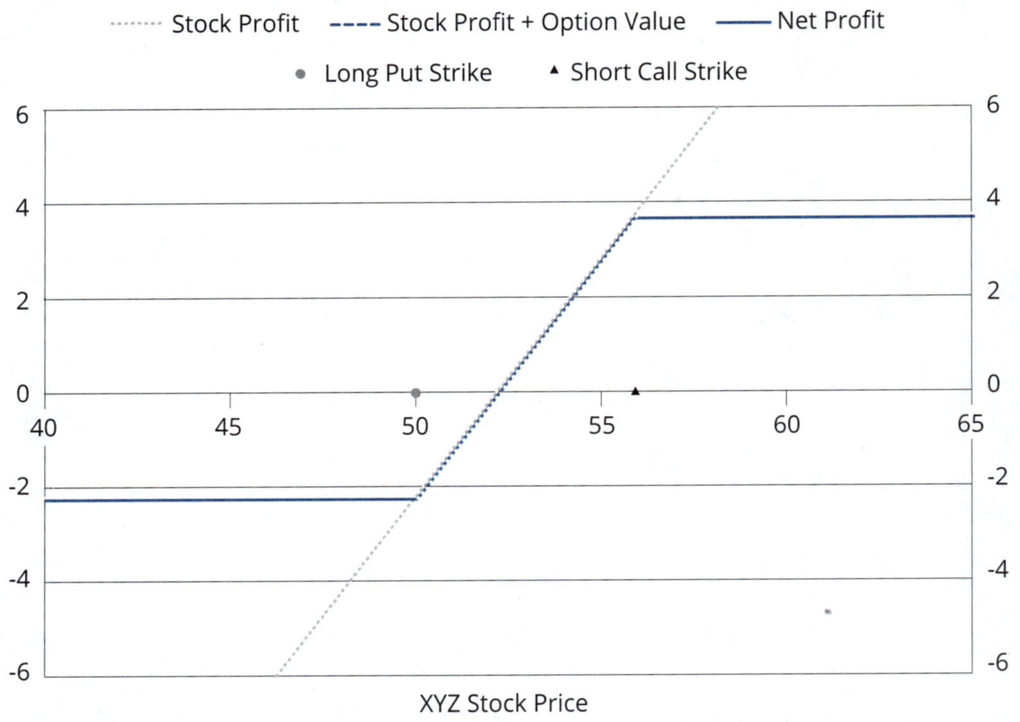

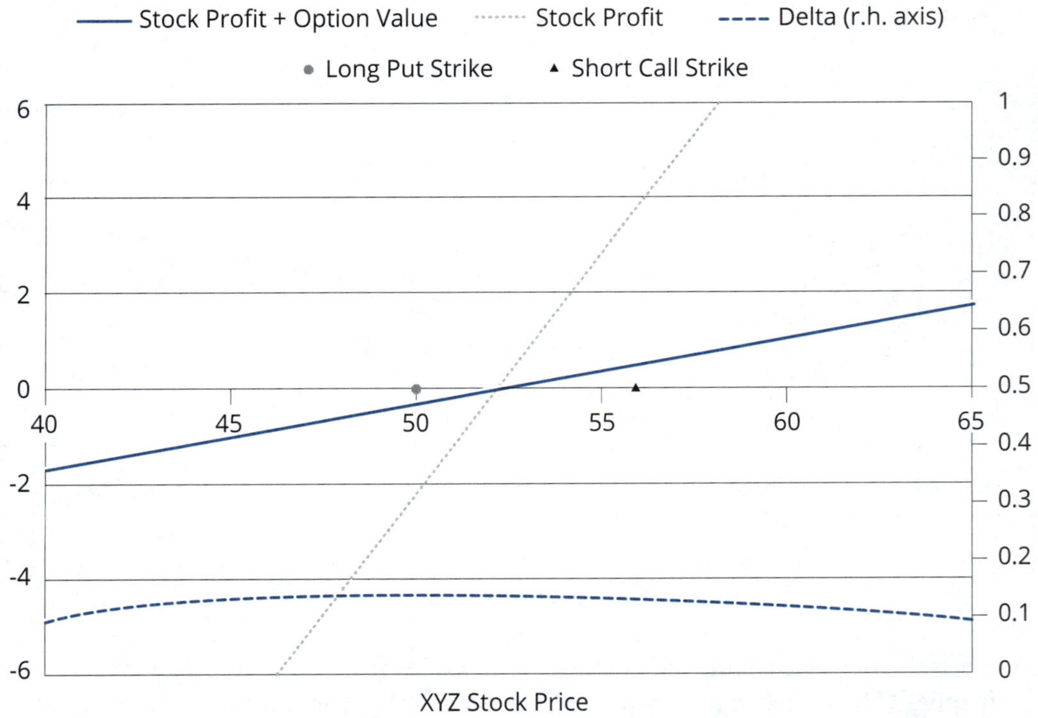

Pre-expiry the impact of the collar is to considerably dampen down the variability of the position (to about 15–20% of its unhedged level, in this case).

Bull Call Spread Pre-Expiry

Here is the value and delta for the XYZ bull call spread (long 50 call and short 55 call) at the point the strategy is initiated, 91 days pre-expiration:

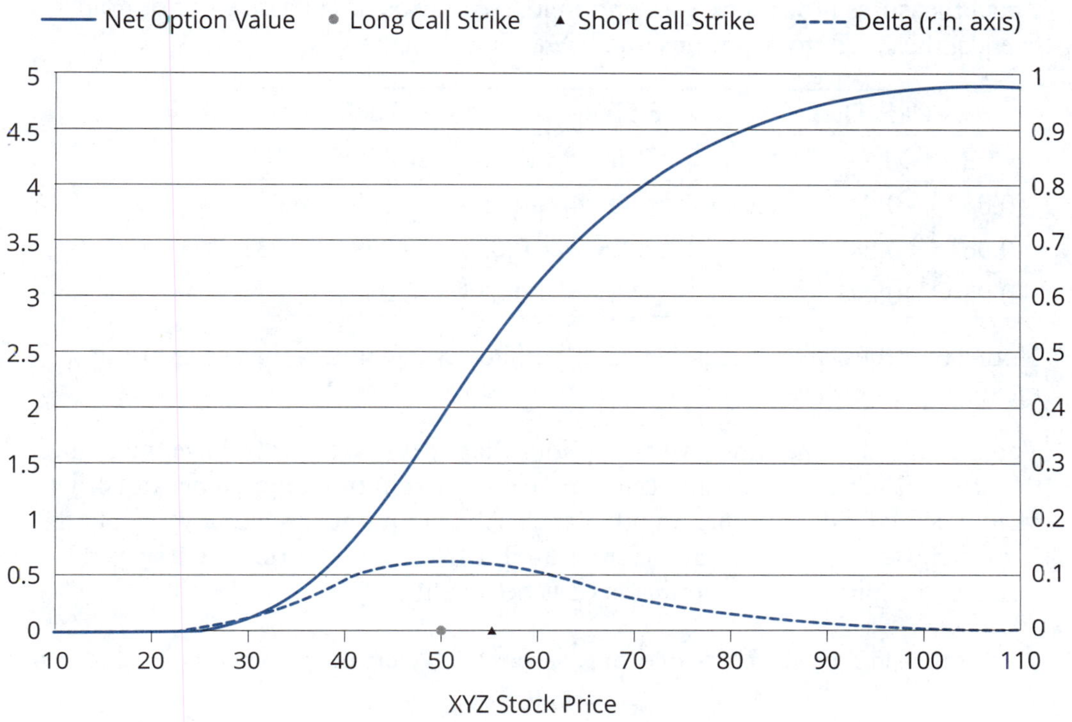

It is still clear why it is bullish in outlook, but the exposure is highly muted, compared to the position at expiration (look at the values for delta). Notice the resemblance to the position for the collared stock. Something very similar would be seen for the other bull and bear spreads.

PROFESSOR'S NOTE

Detailed calculation questions are extremely unlikely for pre-expiry scenarios such as these, given how complex is the behavior of the options during their lives, in contrast to the relatively simple at-expiration scenarios.

MODULE QUIZ 6.9

1. Which of the following would *most likely* be possible deltas for covered call and protective put positions, just after they were established with three months to expiration?
   A. Both have deltas of zero.
   B. The covered call has a delta of 0.4, and the protective put has a delta of 0.45.
   C. The covered call has a delta of 0.35, while the protective put has a delta of –0.4.

Video covering this content is available online.

MODULE 6.10: THETA AND VEGA

Theta

Theta measures how quickly an option loses value as time passes. For our old friends, the XYZ stock options on 20 March the thetas are:

Call Theta			Strike	Put Theta		
APR	MAY	JUN	Price	APR	MAY	JUN
–0.058	–0.042	–0.035	**50**	–0.054	–0.038	–0.031
–0.061	–0.043	–0.036	**52.5**	–0.056	–0.039	–0.031
–0.059	–0.043	–0.036	**55**	–0.055	–0.039	–0.031

Notice that they are all negative: all other factors equal, less time to expiration means less time value.

Theta changes as the time passes. Options that are close to ATM have the highest thetas (in absolute terms), and these increase as expiration approaches (all other factors being held constant). In other words ATM options lose time value at an increasing rate as they mature. Here is an illustration, the horizontal axis is number of days to expiry, and the vertical axis is time value:

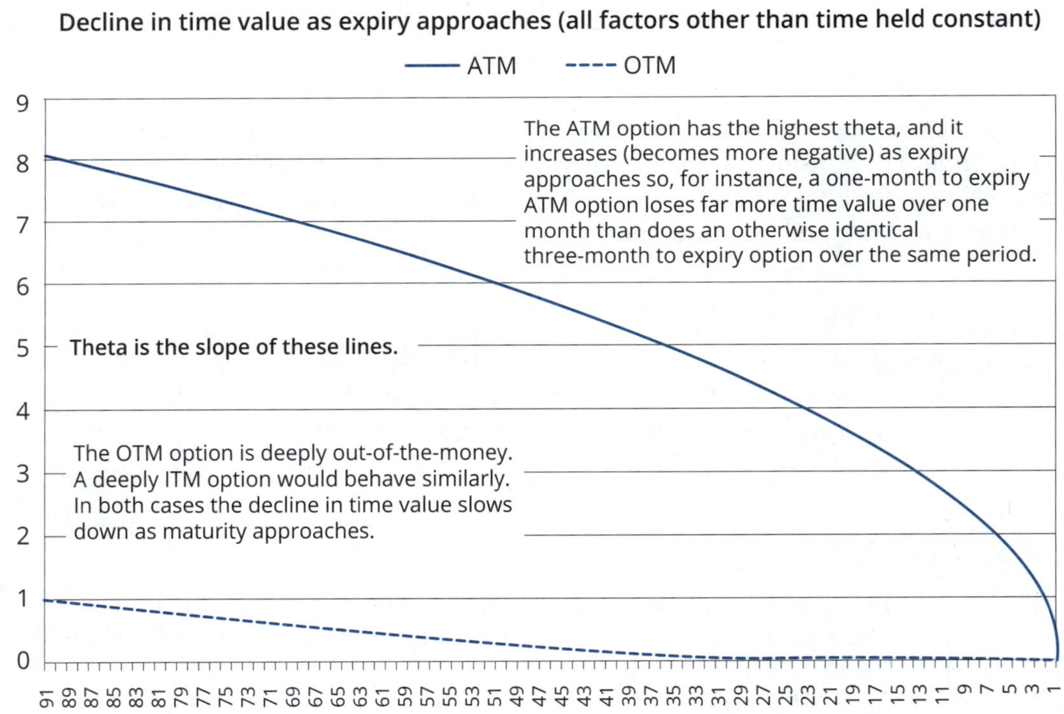

Calendar Spreads

LOS 6.g: Describe uses of calendar spreads.

In the spreads we have looked at so far, the options all expired at the same point (as well as being on the same underlying). **Calendar spreads** are the only examples we consider of option strategies where the options have different expirations.

The basic motivation with calendar spreads is to exploit the difference in **theta** between close-to-expiry and more-distant-from-expiry options.

For options that are near to ATM, the nearer-dated options will have a higher absolute value of theta (more negative) than longer-dated options.

A long calendar spread entails buying longer-dated options and selling shorter-dated options with the same strike and underlying. In principle the premium on the shorter-dated should fall faster than the premium on the longer-dated. Thus more value is gained on the short position than is lost on the long position, and a net profit is realized.

The options need to be close to ATM so the thetas are the right way around, and little movement should be anticipated in the underlying over the period to expiry of the nearer-dated option (large movement might undermine the profit from the strategy). Both options will either be calls or puts, and the choice between calls and puts will reflect the investor's view on the longer-term prospects for the stock (calls if bullish, puts if bearish).

EXAMPLE: Long calendar spread

Suppose that on 20 March, when the XYZ stock price is $52.14 Jenkins has a long-term bullish view on the XYZ stock price, but that over the next month he anticipates very little price movement.

He buys 4 XYZ June 52.5 call contracts (on 100 shares) at 6.22, and sells 4 XYZ April 52.5 call contracts for $3.53. The net premium outlay is $2.69 × 4 × 100 = $1,076.

If at the April call's expiry the stock price is still $52.14, both calls will be OTM and the April call will expire worthless. Assuming all other factors are unchanged, the June call will now be worth $5.00 (this is derived from the pricing model and, if needed, would be given in a question).

Jenkins will now have a position worth $5 × 400 = $2,000, having paid only $1,076 a month earlier. The profit would be even higher if implied volatility rose since that would drive the June call value higher.

A short calendar spread entails selling longer-dated options and buying shorter-dated options with the same strike and underlying. When options are sufficiently ITM or OTM the thetas are relatively higher for the longer-dated options, so this time the belief is that the longer-dated options will lose time value relatively more rapidly, thus the position as a whole should gain.

The short calendar spread strategy is vulnerable, however, to the underlying moving so the options end up ATM when the shorter-dated option expires (so the longer-dated option premiums rise, unless implied volatility also falls, and overall there is a loss since we are short). If the stock moves at all during the period of the strategy, it would be better for it to move a lot.

In both cases, the strategy is fundamentally the same: to sell the options that are expected to fall relatively faster as time passes.

In general:

- A long calendar spread will benefit from a stable market or an increase in implied volatility.
- A short calendar spread will benefit from a big move in the underlying market or a decrease in implied volatility.

Vega

Vega measures the effect of a 1% increase in volatility on the value of the option. The vegas for the XYZ stock options on 20 March are:

Call Vega			Strike	Put Vega		
APR	MAY	JUN	Price	APR	MAY	JUN
0.057	0.081	0.098	**50**	0.057	0.081	0.098
0.060	0.084	0.102	**52.5**	0.060	0.084	0.102
0.059	0.084	0.103	**55**	0.059	0.084	0.103

Vegas are always positive: a more volatile underlying makes all the options on it more valuable (because there is more uncertainly about how things will turn out at expiration, thus more time value).

All other factors constant, vega is higher the more time there is to expiry, but it diminishes the further ITM or OTM the option is. For example:

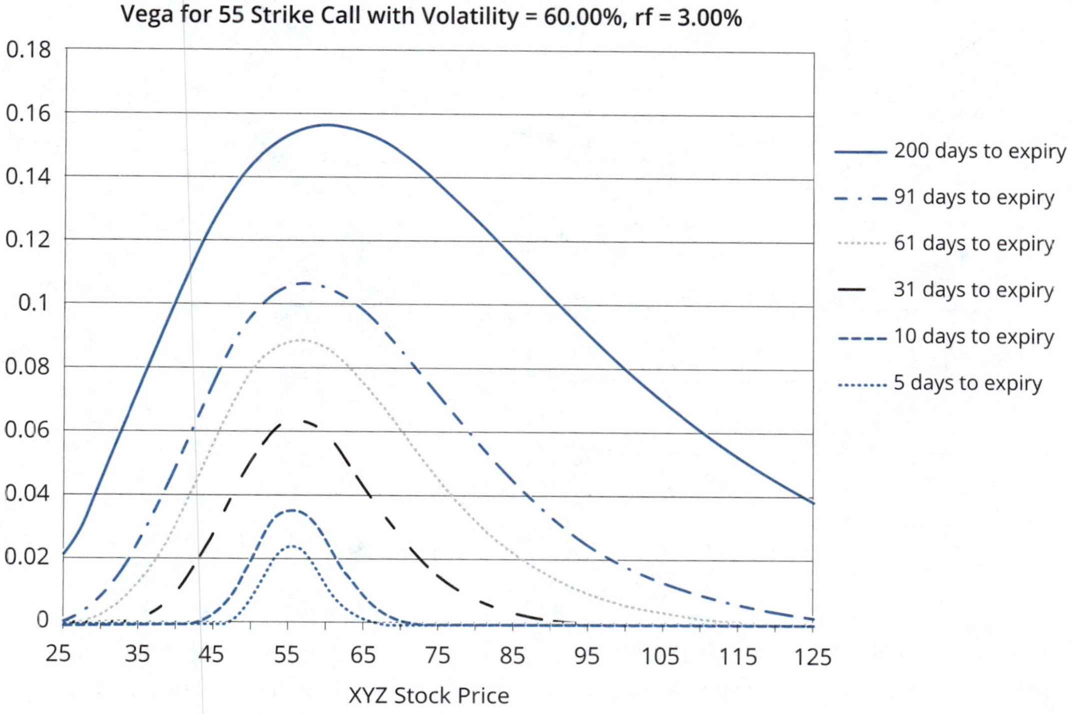

An Aside on Calculating Volatility

In converting between volatility (standard deviation) values for different time periods we multiply the volatility number by the **square root** of the ratio between the period lengths. For example, if we have used our pricing model to compute an annualized implied volatility of 57% from the value of an option expiring in two months (of, say, 42 trading days), then assuming a 252-day trading year we could derive an expected two-monthly volatility of $57\% \times \sqrt{\frac{42}{252}} = 23.27\%$.

Converting from monthly (21 days) to annual, on the other hand, would entail multiplying by $\sqrt{\frac{252}{21}}$.

Straddle Pre-Expiry

Earlier on we looked at the values and profits for long and short straddles at expiration. Let us now briefly look at the behavior of the value of a (long) straddle pre-expiration. We see that, at a given level of volatility the value varies with the underlying in a more subtle way than the V-shape we saw at expiry. It is still the case that value increases the further the underlying price is from the strike price, but the slope of the line (i.e., the delta) near the strike is close to zero, tending toward +1 as the underlying increases, and toward –1 as the underlying decreases. In particular note how, at a given point in the option's life, the level of volatility can have a dramatic effect on the value of the position:

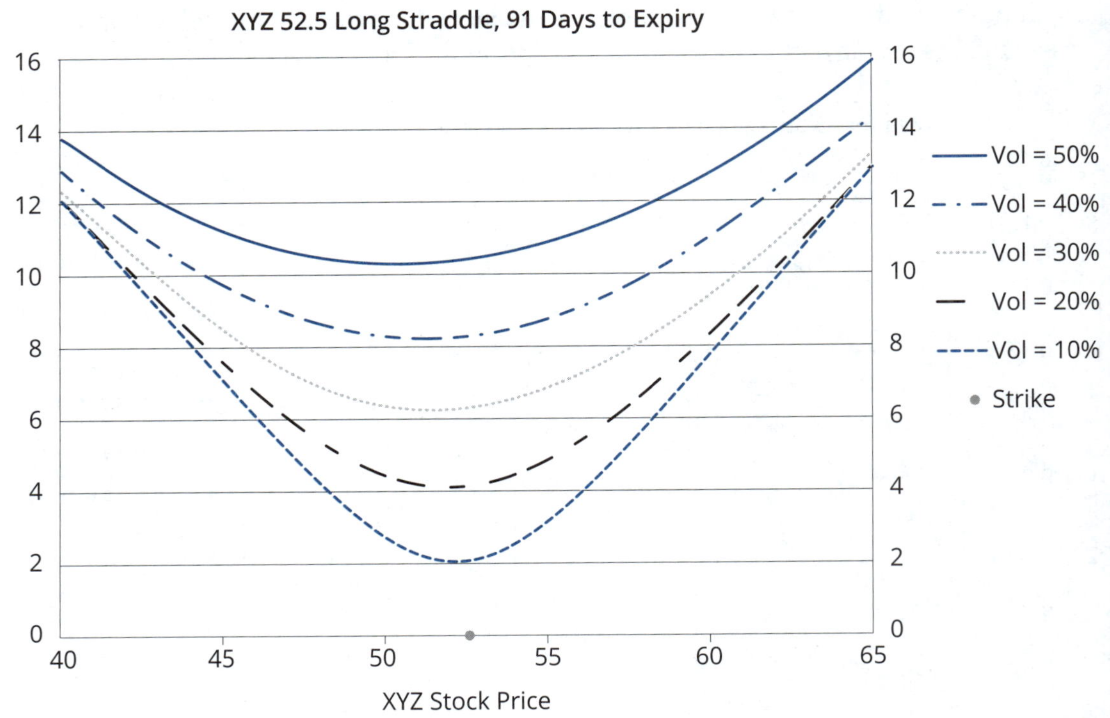

In particular this means that if a straddle is bought, and then volatility increases, the position is likely to rise in value, even if nothing happens to the price of the underlying. This is the real reason why we refer to a long straddle as going long volatility.

Having both a call (with positive delta) and a put (with negative delta) means that we can have a position with a delta close to zero (**delta-neutral**, so we do not care what happens to the underlying price, within reason) but with positive vega.

Beware, however, that with two long options we will have negative theta, which means that the value will fall over time. The volatility must rise quickly enough to compensate for this.

Similarly, a short straddle, where both options are sold, can be delta-neutral but vega-negative, which would be a bet on falling volatility.

MODULE 6.11: VOLATILITY SKEW AND SMILE

Video covering this content is available online.

LOS 6.h: Discuss volatility skew and smile.

The option prices that we have been using for the XYZ options were calculated assuming a volatility of 30% for all the expirations and strike prices. This was for simplicity.

In practice, if implied volatility is computed for actual traded options on a particular underlying (e.g., a stock) the option prices for different expirations and strike prices are likely to imply differing values of volatility (and implied volatilities likely differ between calls and puts, too).

Holding expiration date constant, there are two often-observed patterns in the relationship between implied volatility and strike price:

- A **volatility smile** is where the further-from-ATM options have higher implied volatilities, so we would see a U-shaped (smiling) curve if implied volatility were plotted against strike.

  This is less common, however, than volatility skew.
- A **volatility skew** is where implied volatility increases for more OTM puts, and decreases for more OTM calls. This is explained by OTM puts being desirable as insurance against market declines (so their values are bid up by higher demand, and higher values imply higher volatility), while the demand for OTM calls is low.

Deviations in the skew from historical levels can be used to draw conclusions about market sentiment:

- A sharp increase in the level of the skew, plus a surge in the absolute level of implied volatility, is an indicator that market sentiment is turning bearish.
- Higher implied volatilities (relative to historical levels) for OTM calls indicate that investors are bullish, so the demand for OTM calls to take on upside exposure is strong.

Deviations that are expected to correct could form the basis of trading strategies, which might involve the use of risk reversals.

A long (short) **risk reversal** combines long (short) calls and short (long) puts on the same underlying.

For example, if a trader believes that put implied volatility is relatively too high, compared to that for calls, a long risk reversal could be created by buying the OTM call (seen as relatively underpriced) and selling the OTM put (seen as relatively overpriced) for the same expiration. This would create a broadly long exposure to the underlying, which could be problematic.

The following diagram shows values and deltas for a risk reversal on PQR stock. The PQR price is currently 50 and the call is bought at a strike of 60, while the put is sold at 40. The call's implied volatility is 50%, while the put's implied volatility is 70%. Suppose that this differential is substantially greater than we have seen in the past.

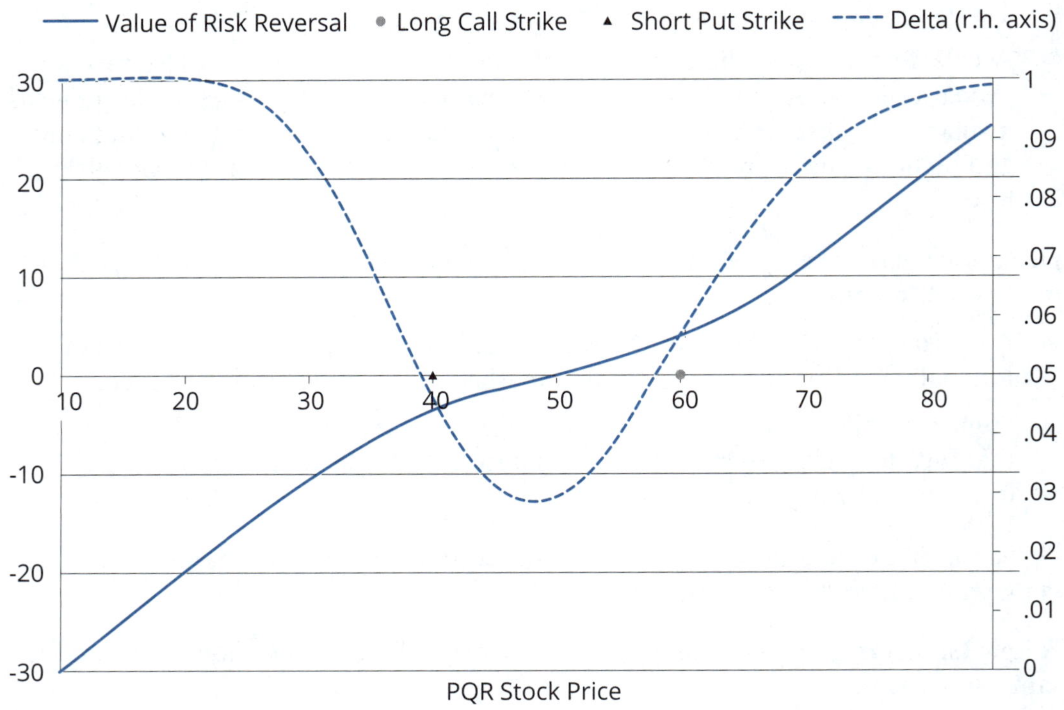

Do not worry about the precise details here, but notice that, at the current stock price of 50, the risk reversal has a delta considerably less than one. Suppose it equals 0.3, and the strategy involves 10 call contracts and 10 put contracts (each on 1,000 shares). For each $1 fall in the stock price the risk reversal will lose roughly $1 × 0.3 × 1,000 = $300.

The aim of the strategy is to make money if the anomalous relationship among the implied volatilities corrects (we went long the options that should gain value and short the options that should lose value if this happens). We were not aiming to bet on the stock price moving, but we have a net long exposure to the stock. To remove this exposure to the stock one further trade is necessary: the sale of 300 shares.

Why 300 shares? Because such a short position will experience equal and opposite gains/losses to the risk reversal, and will thus hedge the exposure to the stock price. This kind of hedge is called a **delta hedge** because the size of the position on one side of the hedge is adjusted to compensate for the delta of the position on the other side. 1,000 shares' worth of options with a delta of 0.3 are delta-hedged by 1,000 × 0.3 = 300 shares.

Note that the delta of the risk reversal will not stay constant (for example it changes as the stock price changes, and as time passes) and the size of the delta-hedge position will need to be adjusted (this is typical of delta hedges; they are **dynamic hedges** and require periodic rebalancing).

Finally, be aware of two further pieces of terminology:

- There is a **term structure of volatility**, where implied volatilities differ across option maturities (*contango* is quite common, with longer-dated options having higher implied volatilities).
- An **implied volatility surface** uses a three-dimensional graph, with implied volatility on the z-axis, to examine the joint influence of maturity (x-axis) and strike price (y-axis).

MODULE QUIZ 6.10, 6.11

1. An investor has a long-term bearish view on the Acme stock price, but over the next two months he anticipates very little price movement. An appropriate strategy to benefit from this view would be to:
   A. buy ATM calls on Acme with two months to expiry and simultaneously sell ATM calls on Acme with five months to expiry.
   B. sell ATM puts on Acme with two months to expiry and simultaneously buy ATM puts on Acme with five months to expiry.
   C. buy OTM calls on Acme with two months to expiry and sell OTM puts on Acme with two months to expiry.
2. Which of the following statements is *most correct*?
   A. A long straddle is a strategy based on the implied volatility smile, since the further the underlying moves from the strike by the expiration of the options, the greater the profit from the strategy.
   B. Volatility skew describes the empirical situation where implied volatility increases for more OTM calls, and decreases for more OTM puts.
   C. Volatility skew describes the empirical situation where implied volatility increases for more OTM puts, and decreases for more OTM calls.

MODULE 6.12: APPLICATIONS

Video covering this content is available online.

LOS 6.i: Identify and evaluate appropriate option strategies consistent with given investment objectives.

LOS 6.j: Demonstrate the use of options to achieve targeted equity risk exposures.

PROFESSOR'S NOTE

In the final section of the curriculum reading a sequence of scenarios are described, each of which illustrates a use of a particular option strategy. The following outlines each scenario, and explains the choice of strategy, highlighting key issues in each case.

Covered Call

SCENARIO

A client needs cash. Within their portfolio is a stock (current price = 169) that they are considering selling in the near future and on which their advisor has a bearish outlook over the next six months. Information is provided on 44-day exchange-listed options (calls and put premiums and deltas, plus vegas).

Solution

Sell calls on the stock to generate premium income (provides the required cash) and reduce delta of stock holding (reduce exposure given bearish outlook).

Considerations

The premium on chosen option must be high enough to meet cash target (assumes 50 contracts sold to match 5,000 shares held): ITM call would generate the most cash, but there is a danger of shares being called away, so choose 170 calls (just OTM). More OTM calls raise too little cash.

Risks

Stock may rise. If it is above 170 at expiry then sell at 170 and lose further gain.

Stock may fall over period to expiry, giving loss on long stock position (but cushioned by premium).

Other points

Position delta is calculated for covered call at point options written, but otherwise the focus is on at-expiry outcomes. Vegas are ignored.

Put Writing

SCENARIO

Investor OQ wants to purchase shares, but considers them too expensive at 169. OQ is prepared to pay no more than 165.

Solution

Write OTM puts (165 strike), and effectively gets paid to buy the stock.

If the stock is less than 165 at expiry then the put is exercised (by the counterparty) and OQ has to buy at 165.

Risks

Shares may fall below $X - p_0$ by expiry, in which case would have been better off buying them outright (cheaper than 165 by more than the premium).

The stock may rise to point where $S_T - 169 > p_0$. At that point it would have been better off buying shares at 169 since the rise in value since would exceed the premium received.

Long Straddle

SCENARIO

KH believes a stock price is about to rise or fall dramatically (at least ±10%), and considers a straddle.

Before KH makes the trade, a news story breaks that increases volatility, making the same straddle more expensive.

Solution

The straddle is no longer worthwhile, since to reach new breakeven points stock needs to move > ±12%. Therefore, do not enter into the long straddle.

Other points

KH uses vega of the straddle before the news story broke to predict the effect of the story on the price of the straddle (sum of put and call premiums). The implied volatility is higher by 15 percentage points × initial vega of 0.468 (given) = 7.02 ($) increase in straddle value. This is very close to actual rise in price of straddle, given earlier in the solution.

Collar

SCENARIO

A client has a long position in a low cost basis stock, which means that selling is ruled out. Need to protect against a decline in price.

Solution

Use a zero-cost collar. Short calls sell off right tail of return distribution (potential large gains) and subsidize the purchase of puts that eliminate the left tail (potential large losses).

Calendar Spread

SCENARIO

ID expects little price movement in Euro Stoxx 50 index over next month from the current level of 3,500, but has a bearish long-term view. The consensus is for a flat market. ATM options are available.

Solution

Sell a three-month 3,500 put option and buy a six-month 3,500 put option (a **long** calendar spread, since they are long the options with more time to expiry).

This requires a net initial payment because the longer-dated put is more valuable (€173 – €119 = €54).

If ID's expectation is correct, and the stock index is unchanged at the expiry of the short (so the options are still ATM) then the following is true:

- The short put expires worthless. The long put (which now has three months to expiry) will be worth less than when it was bought (less time value), but its value will be higher than the net premium paid initially.
- This is because the three-month put had higher (more negative) theta, so it fell in value by more. ID was short this put and long the other, so makes a net profit.
- ID could either sell the long put at this point, realizing the net profit, or keep it as a bet on the index subsequently falling (having paid less, net, compared to solely going long).

Considerations

A calendar spread could use calls or puts, so why puts in this case? Because once the near-dated option expires ID wants to be left with a bearish exposure to the index – hence long puts.

Risks

At the short put's expiry it will only have intrinsic value, whereas the long put will have both intrinsic and time value. At any expiry level of the index the two options will have identical (absolute) intrinsic values (same strike), and these will cancel out, but the long put will also have time value, which is thus the net value of the position. Subtracting the net premium from the time value gives us the net profit:

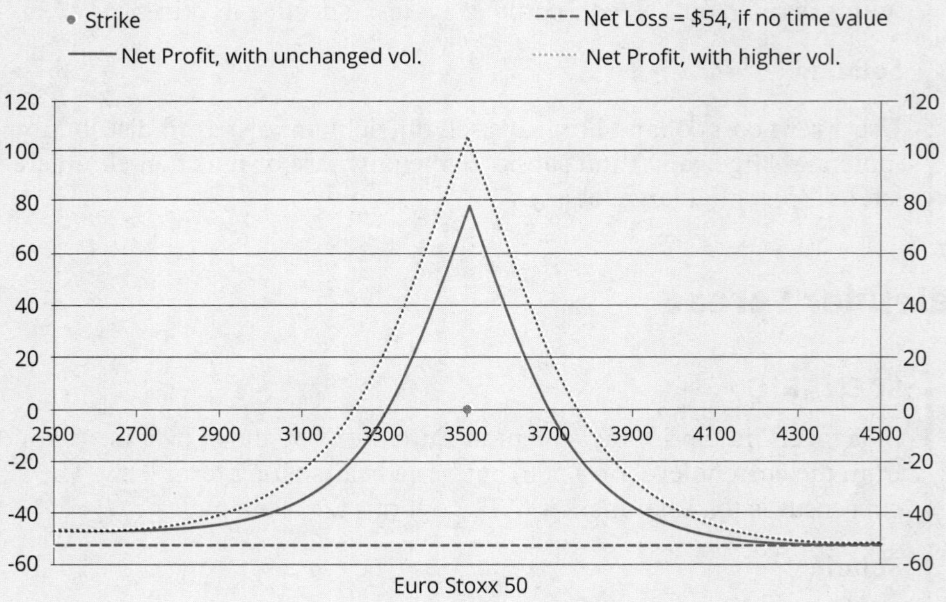

A rise or fall in the index would reduce the (time) value of the long put, reducing the profit. A sufficiently large move, either way, could lead to a loss.

The worst outcome would be the entire net premium being lost.

A rise in implied volatility could increase profit/reduce loss, by pumping-up the long put's time value. Vice-versa a fall in implied volatility would decrease profit/increase loss.

Hedging an Expected Increase in Equity Market Volatility

SCENARIO

JW has a stock portfolio and fears the market is due a correction (a fall), which will be accompanied by a rise in short-term volatility. He wants to set up a position that will benefit from higher volatility, while lowering the cost of this hedge.

Solution

Buy an ATM call on volatility index (VIX) futures (futures which rise or fall with an index of market volatility). If volatility rises then the call will expire ITM and he will receive a payoff.

However, such a call could be expensive, so he simultaneously sells an OTM put on VIX futures—selling off the benefit of a fall in volatility.

Considerations

A regression of the portfolio's historic profits/losses versus changes in volatility could be used to determine what value of options to trade (to balance the hedge).

Buying VIX futures would be an alternative, less flexible, hedge.

Other points

Given the apparent negative correlation between volatility and the level of the market JW is in effect short volatility, and the hedge can be seen as equivalent to a collar, but against a short, rather than a long exposure.

Long Calls as a Proxy for the Underlying

SCENARIO

AS anticipates a rise in a share's price from £60 to £70 over the next three months, with no change in the implied volatility of the associated stock options. He wants to recommend the three-month (long) call that will maximize profits if this happens.

Solution

Choose the call which maximizes the ratio of expected profit to cost (assuming the stock rises to £70):

$$\frac{\text{profit at expiration if stock} = £70}{\text{premium}} = \frac{70 - (X + c_0)}{c_0}$$

Note that we can automatically rule out any call where the breakeven ($X + c_0$) is above £70.

They also comment on delta, presumably because they are implicitly assuming that the position may not be held to call expiration, but could be closed out by selling the call once the rise in share price has happened. In that case the key issue is how the call value will change if the share price rises. The call that has the highest value for the profit to cost ratio has a lower (absolute) value of delta, suggesting that it is less responsive to rises in the underlying share price (bad), but it does have a higher gamma which, the answer claims, will more than compensate.

Risks

Not covered within the solution, but the obvious risk is that the share ends at a price other than £70, in which case a different call could have been preferable.

Protective Put

SCENARIO

EM holds shares that he expects will suffer a decline of up to 10% in one week. This would take the price down from €42 to €37.80. He wants to protect the position, while keeping the cost of the protection to a minimum. A range of one-month puts are presented.

Solution

Similarly to the previous example, they identify the put that maximizes the ratio of expected profit to cost (assuming the stock falls to €37.80):

$$\frac{\text{profit at expiration if stock} = €37.80}{\text{premium}} = \frac{(X - p_0) - 37.8}{p_0}$$

Note that we can automatically rule out any put with breakeven ($X - p_0$) below €37.80.

Since the put will not be held to expiration this breakeven calculation (based on intrinsic value) is not definitive (although it could be seen as providing a worst-case estimate, ignoring time value). In practice the hedge will be closed out by selling the put once the period in which the decline is

> likely has passed, thus the hedge is really based on how the premium on the put will change over the holding period.
>
> They thus go on to discuss delta, since the key issue is how the put value will change if the share price falls. The put that has the highest value for the profit to cost ratio has a lower (absolute) value of delta, suggesting that it is less responsive to falls in the underlying share price, but it does have a higher gamma which, the answer claims, will more than compensate.

For the following table, we suggest that you work out why the particular strategy is chosen in each case, given what you have read so far. Explanations are given below the exhibit on that same page if you want to check your conclusions:

Choosing Options Strategies Based on Direction and Volatility of the Underlying Asset

		Outlook on the Trend of Underlying Asset		
		Bearish	**Trading Range/ Neutral View**	**Bullish**
Expected Move in Implied Volatility	Decrease	*Write calls*	*Write straddle*	*Write puts*
	Remain Unchanged	*Write calls and buy puts*	*Calendar spread*	*Buy calls and write puts*
	Increase	*Buy puts*	*Buy straddle*	*Buy calls*

*Reproduced from Level III CFA Curriculum reading "Options Strategies," Exhibit 32, with permission from CFA Institute.

MODULE QUIZ 6.12

Use the following information to answer Questions 1 and 2.

Dennis Austin works for O'Reilly Capital Management and manages endowments and trusts for large clients. The fund invests most of its portfolio in S&P 500 stocks, keeping some cash to facilitate purchases and withdrawals. The fund's performance has been quite volatile, losing over 20% last year but reporting gains ranging from 5% to 35% over the previous five years. O'Reilly's clients have many needs, goals, and objectives, and Austin is called upon to design investment strategies for their clients. Austin is convinced that the best way to deliver performance is to, whenever possible, combine the fund's stock portfolio with option positions on equity.

1. Given the following scenario:
   - Performance to date: Up 3%
   - Client objective: To maintain a positive stock position and retain upside potential
   - Austin's scenario: Expect low stock price volatility between now and the end of year.

   Which is the *best* option strategy to meet the client's objective?
   A. Bull call.
   B. Protective put.
   C. Bull put.

2. Given the following scenario:
   - Performance to date: Up 16%
   - Client objective: Earn at least 15%
   - Austin's scenario: Good chance of large gains or large losses between now and end of year.

   Which is the *best* option strategy to meet the client's objective?
   A. Long straddle.
   B. Long calendar spread.
   C. Short straddle.

3. An investor believes that a stock they own will continue to oscillate in price and may trend downward in price. The *best* course of action for them to take would be to:
   A. sell call options on the stock.
   B. buy put options on the stock.
   C. enter into both a covered call and protective put strategy.

4. A short position in naked calls on an asset can be hedged by:
   A. buying a put.
   B. buying the underlying asset.
   C. shorting the underlying asset.

KEY CONCEPTS

LOS 6.a

Options can be used to replicate an asset's returns, or the returns from a forward contract.

- A long call plus a short put, with the same strikes and expiration, gives a synthetic long forward—equivalent to a long position in the underlying financed by borrowing at the risk-free rate.
- A short call plus a long put, same strikes and expiration, gives a synthetic short forward, which is equivalent to a short position in the underlying plus a long bond paying Rf.
- Put-call parity links all these positions together: $c_0 - p_0 = S_0 - PV(X)$ or $S_0 + p_0 = c_0 + PV(X)$.

LOS 6.b

An investor creates a covered call position by buying the underlying security and selling a call option.

- Covered call writing strategies can be used to generate additional portfolio income when the investor believes that the underlying stock price will remain unchanged over the short term. The calls are likely to be written OTM.
- ITM calls could be written when the investor aims to reduce a position at a favorable price.
- Marginally OTM calls could be used if the aim is to realize a target price.

LOS 6.c

A protective put is constructed by holding a long position in the underlying security and buying a put option (usually ATM, or somewhat OTM). You can use a protective put to limit the downside risk at the cost of the put premium.

- The purchase of the put provides a lower limit to the position at a cost of lowering the possible profit (i.e., the gain is reduced by the cost of the insurance). It is an ideal strategy for an investor who thinks the stock may go down in the near future, yet who wants to preserve upside potential.

LOS 6.d

The delta of a long (short) position in one unit of the underlying is +1 (–1). If a long position in an asset is hedged by a short forward, then the delta will be reduced to zero, whereas both covered call and protective put positions have (positive) deltas that are different than zero.

- In other words, the effect of the covered call and protective put, during the option's life, is to reduce the asset's delta, but not eliminate it.

LOS 6.e

If an investor has a short position in the underlying then they could:

- Hedge their exposure to the underlying *rising* by buying a call (analogous to hedging a long position with a protective put).
- Sell off some of the benefit from the underlying *falling* by selling a put (analogous to a covered call).

LOS 6.f

There are many strategies that combine option positions, all on a single underlying, having the same expiration date:

- A bull call spread strategy comprises a long call and a short call. The short call has a higher exercise price, and its (lower) premium subsidizes the long call. A bull spread offers gains if the underlying asset's price goes up, but the upside is limited.
- A bear put spread strategy comprises a long put and a short put. The short put has a lower exercise price, and its (lower) premium subsidizes the long put. A bear spread offers gains if the underlying asset's price goes down, but the upside is limited.
- Both bull call and bear put spreads are known as *debit* spreads, because they involve an initial net premium payment. Particularly with American-style options, where early exercise is possible, they are the most common bull and bear spreads.
- Bull put and bear call spreads are also possible, however. These are *credit* spreads, and are the short versions of the other two spreads.
- Before expiration, bull (bear) spreads are best seen as positions giving long (short) exposure to the underlying, but with a reduced level of (absolute) delta.
- A long straddle is a long call plus long put with the same exercise price. The greater the move in the stock price, the greater the payoff from a straddle at expiration (with no upper limit on profit). Before expiration, the prime focus is on volatility increasing, since a long straddle will have positive vega (but low delta, when ATM).
- A short straddle is a short call plus short put with the same exercise price. The closer the stock price ends to the strike the greater is the payoff from a short straddle at expiration (this is limited to the sum of the premiums). Before expiration, as with a long straddle, the prime focus is on volatility, this time falling—a short straddle has negative vega (but low delta, when ATM).

The spreads and straddles only use options, whereas the collar combines options with the underlying:

- A collar strategy is simply a covered call and protective put combined to limit the downside and upside values of the position at expiration. Before expiration the collar can be seen as a way of reducing delta.

LOS 6.g

A long calendar spread involves the sale of a shorter-dated ATM (or near-ATM) call and the purchase of a longer-dated call with the same strike (or both could be puts). The basic motivation is to profit from the higher theta of the closer-to-expiry ATM option. At expiration the position will have a net value equal to the long put's time value. If the options are still ATM this will exceed the net premium paid initially.

- The danger is that the underlying could have moved away from its initial level, and the long put's time value is below the initial premium, although an increase in implied volatility could offset this.
- A short calendar spread buys the shorter-dated and sells the longer-dated options. The options are either ITM or OTM, and now a large move in the underlying (so it ends up well away from the strike) is needed (and/or a decrease in implied volatility).

LOS 6.h

A volatility smile is where further-from-ATM options have higher implied volatilities.

The relatively more common situation is volatility skew, where implied volatility increases for more OTM puts, and decreases for more OTM calls.

- The skew is explained by OTM puts being desirable as insurance against market declines, while the demand for OTM calls is low.
- Deviations of the skew from historical levels could form the basis of trading strategies, e.g., a long (short) risk reversal combines long (short) OTM calls and short (long) OTM puts on the same underlying, delta-hedged using the underlying stock. A long risk reversal assumes the OTM calls are relatively underpriced (their implied volatility is relatively too low, compared to OTM puts).

LOS 6.i, LOS 6.j

See the examples toward the end of this reading for illustrations of the uses of the various strategies that have been covered in the reading.

ANSWER KEY FOR MODULE QUIZZES

Module Quiz 6.1, 6.2, 6.3

1. **A** Remember put-call parity: $\mathbf{c_0 - p_0 = S_0 - PV(X)}$, which can be rearranged to $\mathbf{-S_0 = p_0 - c_0 - PV(X)}$.

   This means that short stock equals long put plus short call plus borrowing at r_f.

   Given that X = 100, r_f = 2% and T = 0.5, we have $PV(X) = 100/(1.02)^{0.5} = 99.01 \approx 99$.

   The options position in B is a long straddle, whose profile is nothing like a short position in the stock.

   The options in C would create a synthetic long forward. (Module 6.2, LOS 6.a)

2. a) **Maximum profit** occurs at the strike, and above.

   Rise in stock value at strike = \$45 – \$43 = \$2, plus the premium received of \$2.10 = \$4.10

   Breakeven price = premium below the initial stock price = $S_0 - c_0$ = \$43 – \$2.10 = \$40.90

   Maximum loss = breakeven = \$40.90

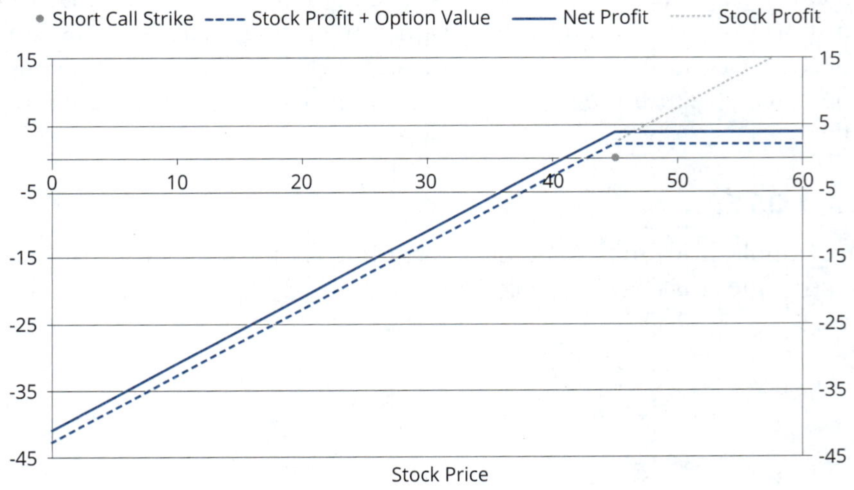

   b) Given breakeven = \$40.90, while maximum profit = \$4.10 at the \$45 strike and above:

   - Profit at \$0 (\$40.90 below breakeven) = loss of \$40.90 (= maximum loss)
   - Profit at \$35 (\$40.90 – \$35 = \$5.90 below breakeven) = loss of \$5.90
   - Profit at \$40 (\$0.90 below breakeven) = loss of \$0.90
   - Profit at \$45 = Profit at \$50 = maximum profit = \$4.10

   (Module 6.3, LOS 6.b)

Module Quiz 6.4, 6.5

1. a) **Maximum profit** = unlimited

   Maximum loss occurs at the strike, and below

   Fall in stock value to strike = $37.50 – $35 = $2.50, plus the premium paid of $1.40 = $3.90

   Breakeven price = premium above the initial stock price = $X + p_0$ = $37.50 + $1.40 = $38.90

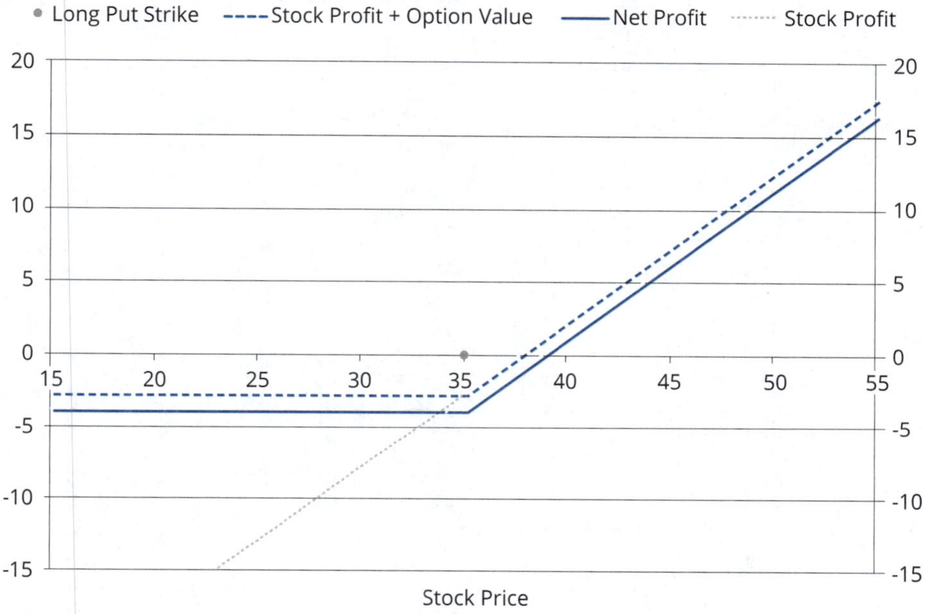

   b) Given breakeven = $38.90, while maximum loss = $3.90 at the $35 strike and below:

   Profit at $30 = Profit at $35 = loss of $3.90

   Profit at $40 ($40 – $38.90 = $1.10 above breakeven) = $1.10

   Profit at $50 = $50 – $38.90 = $11.10

   (Module 6.4, LOS 6.c)

2. **C** Jones has a short exposure to Alphacorp. Selling an OTM put is the best choice to enhance yield.

   October 240 calls would only be appropriate were his exposure long. October 240 puts are ITM puts, which would likely get exercised by the counterparty unless the share price rises, which Jones does not anticipate happening. Selling the 200 puts is a better choice than the 240 calls because the puts result in limited risk exposure whereas selling uncovered calls results in unlimited risk exposure if the stock price goes up. (Module 6.5, LOS 6.e)

Module Quiz 6.6, 6.7

1. a) Call and put premiums are identical, so this is a **zero-cost collar**. Between strikes the profit/loss is the same as for the stock alone, and **breakeven** = initial stock price = $29

   Maximum profit at call strike = gain on stock at $30 = $30 – $29 = $1

   Maximum loss at put strike = loss on stock at $27.50 = $29 – $27.50 = $1.50

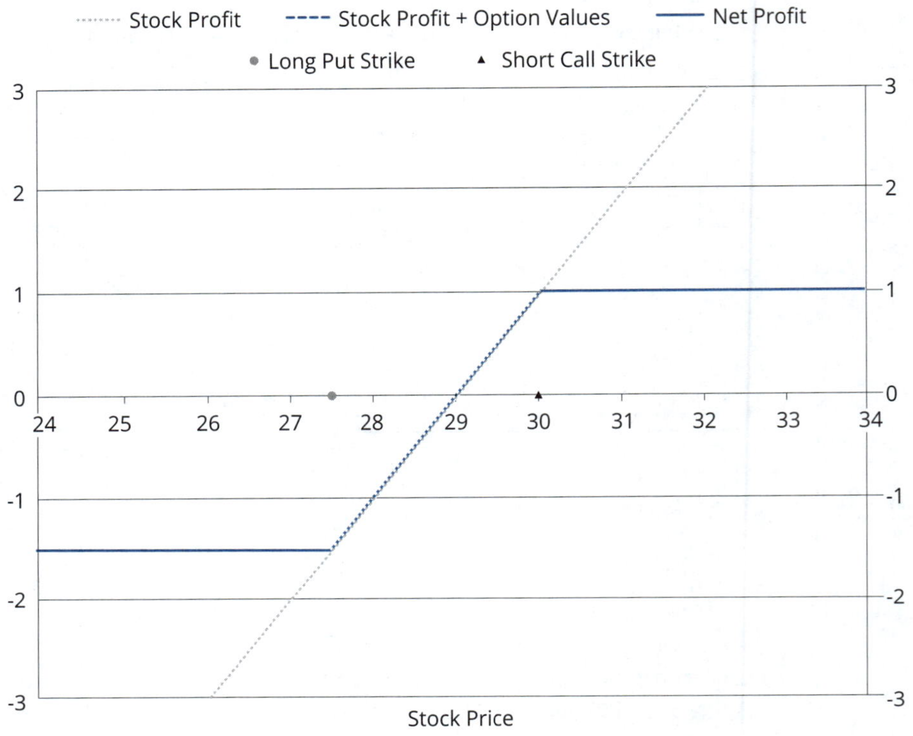

   b) $20 and $25 are both below put strike, so profit at $20 = profit at $25 = loss of $1.50 (= maximum loss)

   Profit at $28.50: between strikes, so the same as for stock alone. $0.50 below breakeven, so loss = $0.50

   Profit at $30 = profit at $100 = $1 (= maximum profit)

   (Module 6.6, LOS 6.f)

2. a) **Maximum profit** = unlimited

   Maximum loss occurs at the strike and equals the total premium paid = $3 + $2 = $5

   Breakeven prices = total premium below and above the strike = $45 ± $5 = $40 and $50

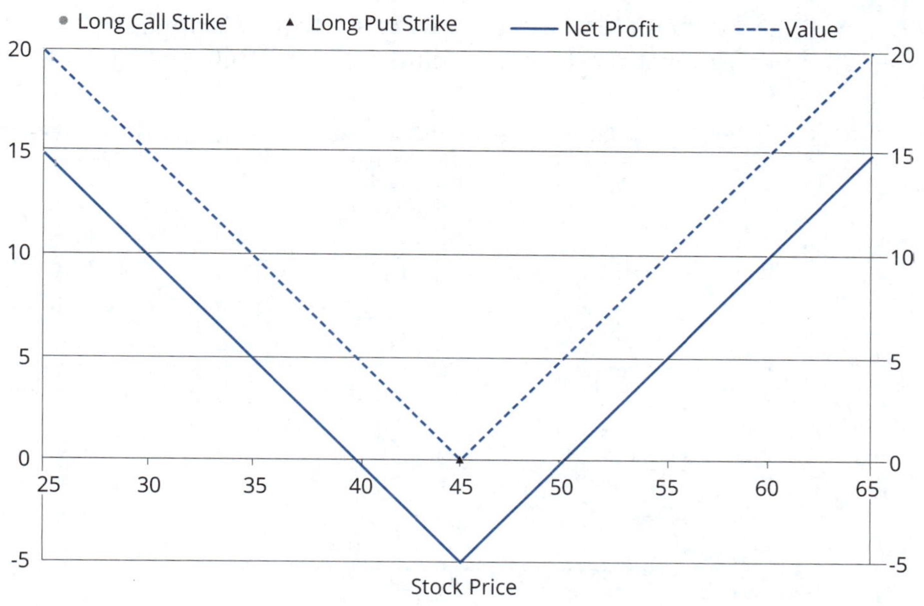

b) Profit at \$0: long put is \$45 ITM, so profit = \$45 – total premium = \$45 – \$5 = \$40 (= lower b/even)

Profit at \$35: long put is \$45 – \$35 = \$10 ITM, so profit = \$10 – \$5 = \$5

Profit at \$40 = \$0 (breakeven)

Profit at \$45 = loss of \$5 (maximum loss at strike)

Profit at \$47: long call is \$47 – \$45 = \$2 ITM, so profit = \$2 – \$5 = loss of \$3

Profit at \$55: long call is \$55 – \$45 = \$10 ITM, so profit = \$10 – \$5 = \$5

Profit at \$100: long call is \$100 – \$45 = \$55 ITM, so profit = \$55 – \$5 = \$50

(Module 6.7, LOS 6.f)

3. Buy ATM puts and calls on the EUR. The 1.04 strike price is the closest to ATM. Buying the call and put will cost: 0.004 + 0.017 = 0.021. This is the max loss and occurs if the EUR closes at 1.04. For breakeven prices, the EUR must decrease or increase 0.021 to USD 1.019 or 1.061. (Module 6.7, LOS 6.f)

Module Quiz 6.8

1. a) This is a bull call spread, which is a debit spread (net initial outlay).

For debit spreads, the **maximum loss** = net premium paid = \$2.10 – \$0.50 = \$1.60.

The difference between the maximum loss and the maximum profit is equal to the difference between the strikes, which is \$50 – \$45 = \$5, so the **maximum profit** = \$5 – \$1.60 = \$3.40.

Maximum loss occurs at lower strike (and below), so **breakeven price** = lower strike + net premium = $45 + $1.60 = $46.60

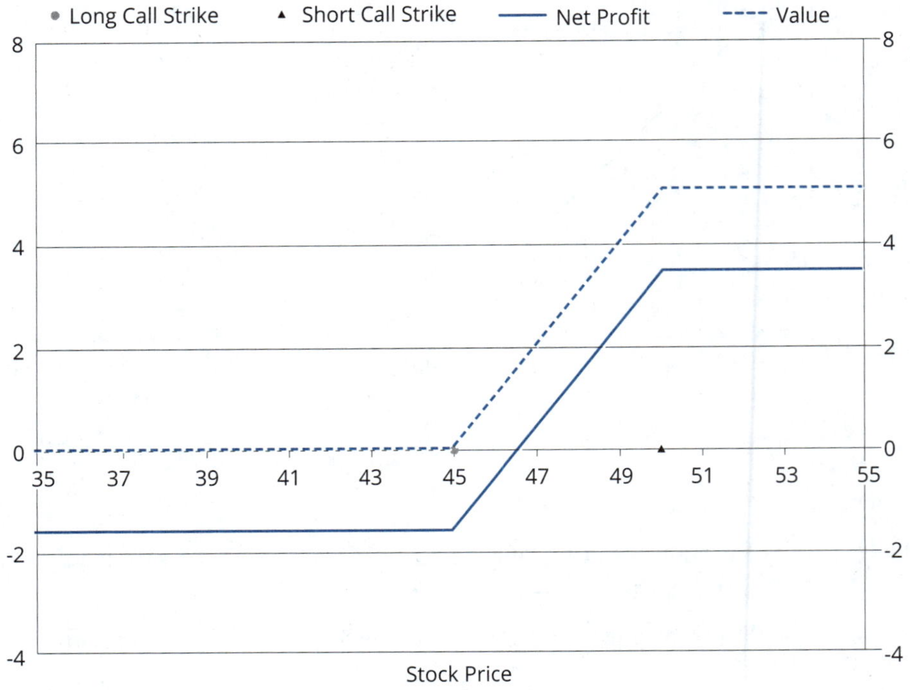

b) Given breakeven = $46.60, maximum loss = $1.60 at $45 and below, while maximum profit = $3.40 at $50 and above:

Profit at $35 = profit at $45 = loss of $1.60 (= maximum loss)

Profit at $48 ($48 – $46.60 = $1.40 above breakeven) = $1.40

Profit at $50 = profit at $55 = $3.40 (= maximum profit)

(LOS 6.f)

2. a) This is a bear put spread, which is a debit spread (net initial outlay).

For debit spreads the maximum loss = net premium paid = $4.00 – $1.80 = $2.20.

The difference between the **maximum loss** and the maximum profit is equal to the difference between the strikes, which is $25 – $20 = $5, so the **maximum profit** = $5 – $2.20 = $2.80.

Maximum loss occurs at upper strike (and above), so **breakeven price** = upper strike – net premium = $25 – $2.20 = $22.80.

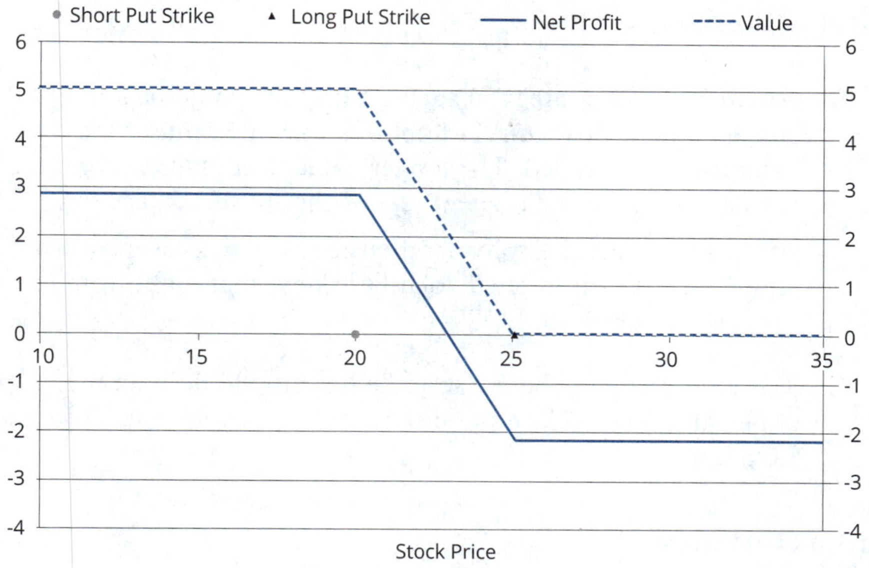

b) Given breakeven = \$22.80, maximum loss = \$2.20 at \$25 and above, while maximum profit = \$2.80 at \$20 and below:

Profit at \$15 = profit at \$20 = \$2.80 (= maximum profit)

Profit at \$23.50 (\$23.50 – \$22.80 = \$0.70 above breakeven) = loss of \$0.70

Profit at \$25 = profit at \$35 = loss of \$2.20 (= maximum loss)

(LOS 6.f)

3. In a bear spread the lower strike option is sold and the higher strike option is bought. Using calls this is a credit spread, since there is a net initial inflow of premium of 5.25 – 0.75 = 4.50.

Initial investment = –4.50 (per share).

The initial investment is also the maximum profit from the strategy. This occurs at and below the lower strike of 47, above which the profit falls one-for-one with rises in the underlying stock. Thus breakeven is 4.50 above the lower strike, at 47 + 4.50 = 51.50. (LOS 6.f)

Module Quiz 6.9

1. **B** Before expiration both covered calls and protective puts have positive deltas (short calls and long puts both have negative deltas, with absolute values less than 1, so they partially, but not fully, hedge the +1 delta of the long underlying). Neither fully eliminate the delta of the underlying. (LOS 6.d)

Module Quiz 6.10, 6.11

1. **B** An appropriate strategy in such a situation would be a long calendar spread, where close-to-ATM options with the same strikes but different expirations are traded. The longer-dated is bought and the shorter-dated is sold, to exploit the higher theta of the shorter-dated.

   A is a short calendar spread, whereas C is a risk reversal, which is a strategy to exploit implied volatility skews that differ from historical levels. (Module 6.10, LOS 6.g)

2. **C** A is incorrect because the straddle has little to do with the volatility smile, and B has calls and puts the wrong way around. (Module 6.11, LOS 6.g)

Module Quiz 6.12

1. **B** The client wants to stay positive on the stock and a protective put will retain the stock upside with limited down side risk. In addition volatility is low which will make option prices low. Both of the other strategies will compromise stock upside potential and involve selling options to reduce initial investment cost. Lowering initial investment was not a specific goal and it makes little sense to do so while option prices are low. (LOS 6.i)

2. **A** Long straddle produces gains if prices move up or down, and limited losses if prices do not move. Short straddle produces significant losses if prices move significantly up or down. (LOS 6.i)

3. **C** With a stock that is oscillating in price in which it is not trending upward, a covered call strategy is appropriate in which the investor owns the underlying asset and sells call options to enhance income. This strategy will work as long as the stock price does not go above the call strike price. In a downward trending market in which the investor believes the stock price will decrease, a protective put is appropriate in which they purchase a put on the underlying stock. The combination of the covered call and protective put is a collar. (LOS 6.i)

4. **B** Hedging a naked call can be accomplished by owning the underlying asset called a covered call strategy. (LOS 6.i)

READING 7

Swaps, Forwards, and Futures Strategies

EXAM FOCUS

The primary focus here is understanding how to use derivatives to (1) change the beta of an equity portfolio, (2) change the duration of a bond portfolio, (3) change portfolio exposure to various asset classes, (4) create synthetic positions, and (5) lock in an interest rate for anticipated future borrowing or lending. Understand how the risks of various derivative contracts offset existing portfolio risks. This material may be tested with either a constructed response question on the morning exam or an item set on the afternoon exam.

MODULE 7.1: MANAGING INTEREST RATE RISK—INTEREST RATE SWAPS, FORWARD RATE AGREEMENT, AND INTEREST RATE FUTURES

Video covering this content is available online.

LOS 7.a: Demonstrate how interest rate swaps, forwards, and futures can be used to modify a portfolio's risk and return.

Interest rate swaps can be used to alter the duration of a fixed-income portfolio by changing a fixed-rate exposure to a floating-rate exposure, or vice versa.

Interest Rate Swaps

A *payer swap* is a contract to make a series of fixed-rate payments and receive a series of floating-rate payments, both based on a specified *notional principal* (amount). If future floating rates are higher than rates expected at the initiation of a swap, a payer swap will increase in value. A payer swap will decrease in value if future floating rates are less than expected. The counterparty to a payer swap has a *receiver swap* and will receive the fixed-rate payments and make the floating-rate payments. In practice, the payments from each party to a swap are netted (the party that owes the larger amount pays the difference) to reduce credit risk.

The floating-rate payment for the first *settlement date* is known at contract initiation, but the floating-rate payments for future settlement dates are not. A quarterly pay swap, for example, has quarterly settlement dates with floating-rate payments based on a quarterly market reference rate (MRR). The risk-return characteristics of a swap can be replicated with a capital market trade. For example, issuing a fixed-rate bond and buying an otherwise identical floating-rate bond would generate the same payments as a payer swap.

Converting a Floating-Rate Exposure to a Fixed-Rate Exposure

A company with a floating-rate exposure can use a payer swap (pay fixed, receive floating) to change it into a fixed-rate exposure. The swap must have settlement dates that match the payment dates on the floating-rate liability.

Figure 7.1: Converting Floating to Fixed Using a Payer Swap

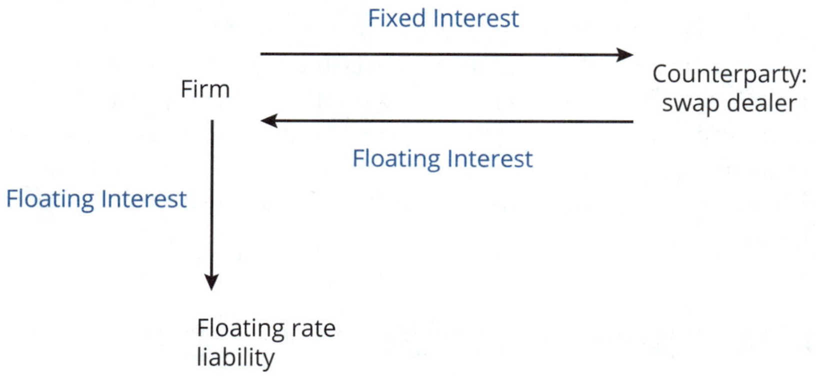

Note that the firm's floating-rate payments from the swap will just offset its floating-rate payments on the liability, so the firm has only its fixed-rate liability from the swap.

Figure 7.2: Converting Fixed-Rate and Floating-Rate Exposures

Existing Exposure	Converting	Interest Rate Swap Required	Beneficial When
Floating-rate liability	Floating to fixed	Payer swap	Floating rates expected to rise
Fixed-rate liability	Fixed to floating	Receiver swap	Floating rates expected to fall
Floating-rate asset	Floating to fixed	Receiver swap	Floating rates expected to fall
Fixed-rate asset	Fixed to floating	Payer swap	Floating rates expected to rise

EXAMPLE: Converting a floating-rate liability to a fixed-rate liability

ABC, Inc., has issued $30 million four-year, semiannual-pay, floating-rate notes (FRNs) with coupons equal to the six-month market reference rate (MRR) plus a 25 basis point margin. After one year, the firm expects interest rates to rise. ABC enters into a three-year payer swap with a fixed rate of 2%, semiannual payments, and a notional principal of $30 million. At initiation of the swap, the six-month reference rate was 1.5%. The FRN and the swap have the same settlement dates.

Settlement date 1 (180 days after swap initiation):

Swap: fixed payment = $30 million × 2% × 180 / 360 = $300,000
floating payment = $30 million × 1.5% × 180 / 360 = $225,000
net cash flow = $225,000 – $300,000 = –$75,000
FRN: floating payment = $30 million × (1.5% + 0.25%) × 180 / 360 = $262,500

ABC, Inc.: total payment = $262,500 + $75,000 = $337,500

The six-month reference rate at settlement date 1 = 3%

Settlement date 2 (360 days after swap initiation):

Swap: fixed payment = $30 million × 2% × 180 / 360 = $300,000
floating payment = $30 million × 3% × 180 / 360 = $450,000
net cash flow = $450,000 – $300,000 = $150,000
FRN: floating payment = $30 million × (3% + 0.25%) × 180 / 360 = $487,500

ABC, Inc.: total payment = $487,500 – $150,000 = $337,500

Note that, regardless of the realized MRR at the remaining settlement dates, the cash payments from ABC, Inc., will be $337,500—the fixed rate on the swap plus the margin above the reference rate on the FRN:

$30 million × (2% + 0.25%) × 180 / 360 = $337,500

The floating-rate payments of the FRN and the floating-rate payments from the payer swap just offset each other.

For the issuer of an FRN, the payer swap has converted the floating exposure to a fixed-rate exposure. This strategy eliminates both the downside and upside of exposure to floating rates.

Using Interest Rate Swaps to Alter Portfolio Duration

The cash flows on a payer swap can be replicated with two capital markets transactions: issuing a fixed-rate note and purchasing a floating-rate note (FRN). A receiver swap is equivalent to issuing an FRN and buying a fixed-rate note.

Because a fixed-rate note has a greater modified duration than an otherwise identical FRN, a payer swap has a negative duration (increasing in value when interest rates increase) and a receiver swap has a positive duration (decreasing in value when interest rates increase). Adding a payer swap to a fixed-income portfolio will reduce portfolio duration, while adding a receiver swap to a fixed-income portfolio will increase portfolio duration.

PROFESSOR'S NOTE

The analysis presented here is based on modified duration, one of several available measures of price sensitivity to changes in interest rates. Using modified duration implicitly assumes that the yield curve is flat and shifts in the yield curve are parallel.

The notional principal of the interest rate swap to increase (or reduce) portfolio duration (target duration) can be calculated as follows:

$$NP_s = \left(\frac{MD_T - MD_p}{MD_s}\right)(MV_P)$$

where:
NP_S = notional swap principal
MD_T = target modified duration
MD_P = current portfolio modified duration
MD_S = modified duration of swap
MV_P = market value of portfolio

EXAMPLE: Using an interest rate swap to alter portfolio duration

A fund manager has a portfolio of £120 million fixed-rate U.K. bonds. The fund manager believes that interest rates will fall over the next three years and wishes to increase the portfolio's modified duration (exposure to changes in interest rates). She decides to increase portfolio duration from 4.5 to 6. A payer swap has a modified duration of –2 and a receiver swap has a modified duration of +2.

What type of swap will achieve the desired portfolio duration, and what is the required notional principal of the swap?

Answer:

The fund manager wishes to increase duration, so she should add a receiver swap with a notional principal of:

$$NP_s = \left(\frac{6 - 4.5}{2}\right) \times £120 \text{ million} = £90 \text{ million}$$

Interest Rate Forwards and Futures

Forward Rate Agreements (FRAs)

FRAs are typically used to hedge the uncertainty about a future short-term borrowing or lending rate. Consider a firm that anticipates borrowing a lump sum for 60 days, 30 days from now. The 60-day interest rate 30 days from now is uncertain. To hedge this uncertainty, the firm could take a long position in an FRA.

The long position in an FRA will receive a payment at settlement if the market rate of interest rate is higher than the (forward) rate specified in the FRA. Thus, if the 60-day rate 30 days from now is greater than the forward rate, the firm receives a payment from the FRA (with notional principal equal to the anticipated loan amount) that offsets the firm's higher borrowing costs. If the 60-day rate 30 days from now is less than the forward rate, the firm must make a payment to settle the FRA. This payment offsets the decrease in the firm's borrowing costs. Thus, the firm's borrowing costs in the future are essentially fixed by the FRA hedge. A firm that anticipates lending in the future could hedge the uncertainty about the market interest rate of the loan by taking a short position in an FRA. The key point is that long FRA positions will increase in value when future interest rates rise, and short positions will increase in value when interest rates fall.

Figure 7.3: FRA Diagram

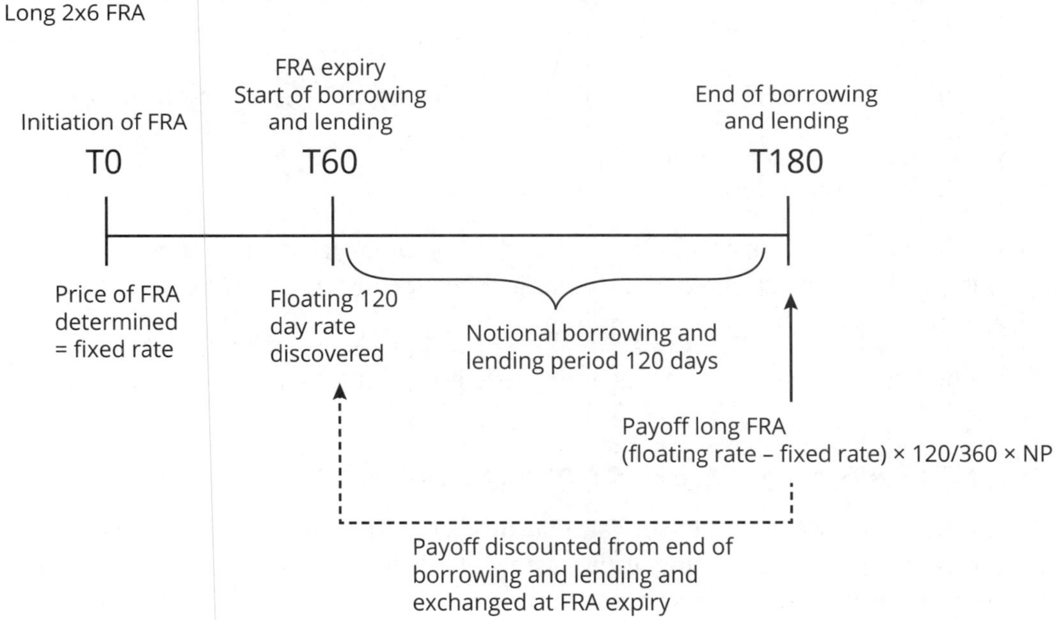

Figure 7.3 illustrates an FRA based on the future 120-day borrowing rate that settles 60 days from initiation. Note that the payment is made at the future borrowing or lending date and is equal to the present value of the difference in interest between a market-rate loan and a loan at the forward rate (rate specified in the FRA).

EXAMPLE: Using an FRA to hedge short-term future borrowing

Smithies Plc needs to borrow £1,000,000 for 180 days, 90 days from now, at the market reference rate (MRR) + 50 basis points (bp). The company is concerned that interest rates will rise over the 90-day period, increasing the cost of the 180-day loan. Smithies takes a long position in an FRA on the six-month reference rate, 90 days in the future with a forward rate of 5% (annualized) and a notional principal of £1,000,000.

Calculate the firm's borrowing costs on the loan net of the FRA payment for realized six-month reference rate values, 90 days from now of 7% and 3%.

Answer:

MRR 7% at FRA expiry:

Cost of loan: (7% + 0.5%) × 180 / 360 × £1,000,000 = £37,500

Long FRA receipt: (7% – 5%) × 180 / 360 × £1,000,000 = £10,000*

Net cost: £37,500 – £10,000 = £27,500

MRR 3% at FRA expiry:

Cost of loan: (3% + 0.5%) × 180 / 360 × £1,000,000 = £17,500

Long FRA payment: (3% – 5%) × 180 / 360 × £1,000,000 = –£10,000*

Net cost: £17,500 + £10,000 = £27,500

The total cost is fixed at 5% + 50 bp regardless of the direction of interest rates:

5.5% × 180 / 360 × £1,000,000 = £27,500

*Note this is the payoff at the end of the borrowing and lending period; it is typically discounted and exchanged between FRA counterparties at settlement at day 90.

The firm has effectively hedged its future borrowing costs.

Short-Term Interest Rate (STIR) Futures

STIR futures are conceptually very similar to FRAs. The futures price is forward interest rate on deposits starting at the expiry of the future and lasting for 90 days. The standardization of futures means that contracts are only available on specific maturities (typically quarterly). Users that are hedging interest rate risk will often need to enter an offsetting transaction to close their futures position out when the hedge is no longer needed.

Eurodollar futures ($-based STIR futures) are based on deposits of $1 million and are priced using the IMM Index convention (i.e., 100 – annualized forward rate). The pricing convention means that futures prices will rise when forward rates fall. The forward interest rate is calculated from current spot MRR in the same way the forward price of an FRA is established. One basis point change in the forward rate will cause the contract's value to change by $25 ($1 million × 0.0001 × 90 / 360 = $25).

Using this pricing convention, a long Eurodollar futures position will increase in value as forward rates decrease and decrease in value as forward rates increase. Note that this differs from a long FRA position, which increases in value as forward rates increase and decreases in value as forward rates decrease.

EXAMPLE: Using Eurodollar futures to hedge short-term future investing

Allan Luard is expecting to receive a $20 million inheritance in 120 days. Allan intends to invest the $20 million in a 90-day deposit account at the market reference rate (MRR) –25 bp. Currently, Eurodollar futures expiring in 120 days are trading at 95. Allan is concerned that short-term rates may fall before he makes his deposit and would like to lock in a guaranteed interest rate today. He takes a long position in 20 Eurodollar futures contracts.

A. After 120 days, the three-month reference rate is quoted at 3.5%. Allan closes out his future position and invests his inheritance in a 90-day deposit account at the market reference rate – 25 bp. What is Allan's $ return from depositing his inheritance combined with his futures position?

Answer:

Interest received on deposit: $20 million × (3.5% – 0.25%) × 90 / 360 = $162,500

Number of futures contracts: $20 million / $1 million = 20

Futures price at settlement: 100 – 3.5 = 96.5

Profit on futures: 96.5 – 95 = 150 bp; 150 bp × $25 × 20 contracts = $75,000

Total return: $162,500 + $75,000 = $237,500

Allan has locked in the 90-day forward rate of 5% – 25 bp:

$20 million × (5% – 0.25%) × 90 / 360 = $237,500

B. If the three-month reference rate is 6.5% in 120 days, what is Allan's $ return from depositing his inheritance combined with his futures position?

Answer:

Interest received on deposit: $20 million × (6.5% – 0.25%) × 90 / 360 = $312,500

Futures price: 100 – 6.5 = 93.5

Loss on futures: 93.5 – 95 = –150 bp; –150 bp × $25 × 20 contracts = –$75,000

Total return: $312,500 – $75,000 = $237,500

Both Eurodollar futures and FRA agreements allow lenders and borrowers to lock in rates for future borrowing and lending. While the pricing mechanisms are different, in both contracts, forward price is a forward rate of interest derived from current MRRs. The FRA forward price (based on a 90-day loan period) should be the same as the forward reference rate used to price the Eurodollar futures in order to prevent arbitrage between futures and an equivalent FRA. The major differences between the two, besides their pricing conventions, are that futures are standardized, exchange traded, and require a margin deposit that is marked to market, while

FRAs are customized contracts, created by dealers so that they are not liquid, and subject to counterparty risk.

Interest rate futures are available for many currencies. Euro interest rate futures, for example, are based on a euro floating reference rate.

Fixed-Income Futures

Interest rate futures can be used to hedge the interest rate risk of short-maturity bonds (2–3 years), but this requires the estimation of the sensitivity of the value of each of the bond's cash flows to changes in the corresponding forward rate. Liquidity of interest rate futures decreases for forward rates further in the future. Longer-maturity bonds are most often hedged with fixed-income futures (bond futures), which have very good liquidity.

Treasury futures are available on T-bills, Treasury notes and Treasury bonds and are traded on the CBOT (Chicago Board of Trade) and CME (Chicago Mercantile Exchange). In Europe, government bond futures are traded on the Eurex and ICE exchanges and are available for bonds of various maturities.

Mechanics of Fixed-Income Futures

In practice, the majority of bond futures are closed out prior to settlement (the delivery date) by entering an offsetting trade. For futures held until settlement, bond futures include delivery options for the short party. For example, with U.S. Treasury bond futures, the short party may deliver any U.S. Treasury bond with a maturity between 15 and 25 years at contract maturity. This practice ensures availability of government bonds for the short to deliver.

The price of Treasury bond futures is based on a notional government bond. The notional government bond is assumed to have a coupon rate of 6%. Each eligible bond that can be delivered by the short party is assigned a **conversion factor (CF)** to reflect its value relative to the notional bond in the contract.

CFs for eligible Treasury bonds are computed as the clean price of $1 face value of the eligible bond discounted at a yield to maturity of 6%. Note that bonds with a 6% coupon will automatically have a CF of one. Bonds with coupons higher than 6% will have CFs greater than one, and bonds with coupon rates less than 6% will have CFs less than one.

The short party will receive the principal invoice price on delivery:

principal invoice price = (futures settlement price / 100) × \$100,000 × CF

Settlement price is quoted with a par of \$100. \$100,000 is the face value of Treasury bond futures.

In practice, the bond delivered may be between coupon dates at the delivery date, so the short party will also receive any accrued interest on the bond delivered:

total invoice amount = principal invoice price + accrued interest

The process to compute the CF is imperfect largely because it assumes a flat interest rate term structure at 6%. The deliverable bonds have different coupons and maturities and, therefore, different durations. As a result, the shape of the term structure of interest rates does have an effect on the bond's value, which is ignored by the computation. If CFs were perfect, the short party would be indifferent between which of the eligible bonds to deliver. The bias in the computation of CFs means that one of the eligible bonds will generate the greatest gain (or smallest loss) to the short party at delivery. This bond is known as the **cheapest-to-deliver (CTD) bond**.

The cash-and-carry model is still used to price the future. The bond selected to price the future is the CTD. There are two methods to identify the CTD bond. The first method identifies the eligible bond that generates the highest return (implied repo rate) on a cash-and-carry trade. The second method is to find the eligible bond with the lowest basis. Basis is defined as the spot price minus the futures price.

The Treasury bond with the lowest basis will typically have the highest implied repo rate and be the cheapest to deliver.

PROFESSOR'S NOTE

Due to the mark-to-market feature in futures contracts, the short party does not receive the initial futures price at contract expiry. Daily futures settlement prices are used to compute the daily profit or loss on the futures contact with gains being added to the counterparties' margin accounts and losses being deducted. Daily profit or loss is calculated as $FP_t - FP_{t-1}$. To avoid double-counting profits and losses, the short party will receive the final settlement price multiplied by the CF at the maturity of the futures contract.

At delivery, the short party will deliver the CTD bond—with a value equal to the clean price plus accrued interest (the dirty or invoice price)—to the long party at the delivery date and receive the settlement price multiplied by the CF plus accrued interest. The CTD bond will be the bond that generates the greatest profit or lowest loss on delivery.

profit/(loss) on delivery = [(settlement price × CF) + AI_T] – (CTD clean price + AI_T)

EXAMPLE: Identifying the CTD bond at delivery

	Bond 1	Bond 2
Coupon	5.5%	5.75%
Time to maturity	20 years	19 years
Bond price	$141.13	$145.10
Accrued interest at delivery	$0	$0
CF	0.9422	0.9719
Futures settlement price	$148.75	$148.75

Answer:

	Bond 1	Bond 2
Settlement price × CF	$148.75 × 0.9422	$148.75 × 0.9719
= principal invoice amount	$140.15	$144.57
+ AI_T	$0	$0
= total invoice amount	$140.15	$144.57
Per $100,000 par	$140,150	$144,570
CTD clean price	$141.13	$145.10
+ AI_T	$0	$0
= CTD dirty price	$141.13	$145.10
Per $100,000	$141,130	$145,100
Delivery loss	–$980	–$530

Note that this example has assumed that delivery is immediately after a coupon payment and, therefore, accrued interest at delivery is zero. This is a simplifying assumption.

Bond 2 is the cheapest to deliver as it results in the smallest loss on delivery. Due to bias in the computation of CFs if yields are lower than 6%, there is a bias to short-duration (high coupon, low maturity) securities. If yields are greater than 6%, there is a bias to long-duration securities.

Hedging Interest Rate Risk Using Treasury Futures

To hedge the interest rate risk of a long bond portfolio, the fund manager will sell Treasury bond futures. As interest rates rise, bond prices fall and the futures price decreases, increasing the value of a short futures position. Futures contracts are typically used by portfolio managers to achieve a target duration. Short futures positions reduce portfolio duration, while long futures positions increase portfolio duration.

The starting point when hedging interest rate risk with Treasury futures is to identify the futures contract CTD security. Treasury futures prices will tend to correlate most closely with the CTD bond because the CTD has the lowest basis of any deliverable bond. The implication of this is that the change in the futures price will equal the change in the value of the CTD adjusted by its CF (i.e., the CTD and futures contract have the same duration).

$$\Delta \text{ futures price} = \frac{\Delta \text{CTD}}{\text{CF}}$$

To fully hedge (immunize) a portfolio's value against interest rate changes, the change in portfolio value must be offset by the change in the futures value:

$\Delta P = HR \times \Delta$ futures price

where:
ΔP = change in portfolio's value
HR = hedge ratio = Number of futures contracts

$$\Delta P = HR \times \frac{\Delta CTD}{CF}$$

$$HR = \frac{\Delta P}{\Delta CTD} \times CF$$

In practice, the CTD bond and the bonds in an investor's portfolio are unlikely to be perfect substitutes. The mismatch between the change in value of an asset or portfolio and the change in value of the derivative used to hedge it is referred to as basis risk or spread risk. The hedge ratio mentioned previously will be effective if the portfolio only contains the CTD bond. If the portfolio does not consist solely of the CTD bond, a duration-based hedge ratio (BPVHR) is calculated to determine the number of futures contracts required for a hedge:

$$BPVHR = \frac{-BPV_{portfolio}}{BPV_{CTD}} \times CF$$

Basis point value (BPV) is the expected change in value of a security or portfolio given a one basis point (0.01%) change in yield.

BPVHR = number of short futures

$BPV_{portfolio} = MD_{portfolio} \times 0.01\% \times MV_{portfolio}$

MD = modified duration

$BPV_{CTD} = MD_{CTD} \times 0.01\% \times MV_{CTD}$
MV_{CTD} = CTD price / 100 × \$100,000

To achieve a target duration, the formula can be amended to:

$$BPVHR = \frac{BPV_{target} - BPV_{portfolio}}{BPV_{CTD}} \times CF$$

$BPV_{target} = MD_{target} \times 0.0001 \times MV_{portfolio}$

The original formula is a special case where the BPV_{target} equals zero.

EXAMPLE: Immunizing a bond portfolio from interest rate risk

A fixed-income portfolio manager is holding a portfolio with a market value of £60 million and wants to fully hedge the portfolio value against parallel movements in the yield curve. The portfolio has a modified duration of 10.75. The portfolio manager will sell U.K. Government Long Gilt futures to hedge the portfolio.

U.K. Government Long Gilt Futures Specifications	
Futures price	£130.21
Futures contract size	£100,000
CTD	4.75% coupon, 12 years to redemption
CTD price	£139.56
CTD CF	1.0709
CTD modified duration	9.7

1. **Compute** the number of U.K. Government Long Gilt futures to be sold to immunize the portfolio.
2. **Compute** the number of Gilt futures that need to be sold to achieve a target duration of 8.7.

Answer:

1. *Step 1*: Compute the BPV of the portfolio ($BPV_{portfolio}$):

$$BPV_{portfolio} = 10.75 \times 0.0001 \times £60 \text{ million} = £64{,}500$$

Step 2: Compute the BPV of the CTD (BPV_{CTD}):

$$BPV_{CTD} = 9.7 \times 0.0001 \times [(£139.56 / 100) \times £100{,}000]$$

$$= £135.37$$

Step 3: Compute the BPV hedge ratio:

$$BPVHR = \frac{-BPV_{portfolio}}{BPV_{CTD}} \times CF = \frac{-£64{,}500}{135.37} \times 1.0709$$

$$= -510.25 \approx -510$$

The fund manager will need to sell 510 Long Gilt futures to fully hedge the portfolio.

2. $BPV_{target} = MD_{target} \times 0.0001 \times MV_{portfolio} = 8.7 \times 0.0001 \times £60$ million

$= £52{,}200$

$$BPVHR = \frac{BPV_{target} - BPV_{portfolio}}{BPV_{CTD}} \times CF$$

$$= \frac{£52{,}200 - £64{,}500}{£135.37} \times 1.0709 = -97.30 \approx -97$$

Selling 97 Long Gilt futures will achieve the portfolio's target modified duration of 8.7.

In practice, hedging results are not perfect due to three main factors:

1. The hedge was constructed using the CTD bond. If the level or slope of the term structure of interest rates changes significantly, the eligible bond, which is the CTD bond, may change. If the CTD bond changes, the duration of the Treasury bond future will also change.
2. Duration is not a perfect measure of how bond prices react to interest rate changes. Duration ignores the convexity of the bonds.
3. Modified duration only captures the impact of parallel movements in the term structure of interest rates. Shaping risk refers to nonparallel changes in the term structure, such as steepening, flattening, and changes in curvature.

MODULE QUIZ 7.1

1. Ben Root holds an interest rate swap with a tenor of one year and quarterly settlement dates. The variable reference rate is the floating market reference rate (MRR). The variable payment/receipt on day 270 will be determined by:
   A. 270-day MRR at initiation.
   B. 90-day MRR at day 270.
   C. 90-day MRR at day 180.
2. Virat Sharma, a high-net-worth individual, holds a four-year floating-rate note (FRN) with semiannual coupons at the six-month reference rate + 40 bp and a par value of $4 million. Sharma is concerned about falling interest rates and would like to hedge this risk.

   Four-year semiannual swaps are quoted at a swap rate of 4%; the six-month reference rate at initiation is 3.5% and the six-month reference rate at the first settlement date is 2.5%.

   What type of swap should Sharma use? **Compute** the net cash flow on the swap at the first and second settlement dates. **Compute** the net return on Sharma's combined positions.
3. Carlos Hendricks is a fixed-income fund manager. Hendricks is running a fund with a modified duration of 12 and a market value of $200 million. He is concerned that interest rates will increase and wants to reduce the duration of his portfolio to 8 using U.S. Treasury futures.

U.S. Treasury Future	
Futures price	$164.20
Contract size	$100,000
CTD	4%, 20 years to maturity
CTD price	$126.39
CF	0.7689
CTD modified duration	14.54

What Treasury future position is required to achieve a portfolio duration of eight?
A. Sell 335 contracts.
B. Sell 435 contracts.
C. Sell 1,004 contracts.

Video covering this content is available online.

MODULE 7.2: MANAGING CURRENCY EXPOSURE

LOS 7.b: Demonstrate how currency swaps, forwards, and futures can be used to modify a portfolio's risk and return.

Many investors have assets and liabilities denominated in foreign currencies (not their domestic, or local, currency). When exchange rates change, the domestic-currency value of assets and liabilities denominated in a foreign currency will change. The exposure of foreign-currency denominated assets and liabilities to changes in exchange rates is termed currency risk.

Currency Swaps

In a **currency swap**, one party agrees to make periodic interest rate payments on a notional amount in one currency, while the other party agrees to make period interest payments on a notional amount in another currency. The notional amounts are equivalent based on the exchange rate at the inception of the swap. Currency swaps allow borrowers requiring foreign currency to effectively borrow in a foreign currency. This may be advantageous to a company that will invest in a foreign asset that will generate foreign currency cash flows. The firm may not have good access to capital markets in the foreign country. A currency swap will allow the firm to hedge its currency risk from the foreign-currency cash flows. This is known as synthetic borrowing.

The parties to a currency swap may exchange only interest payments, but they may also exchange the notional amounts of each currency at the beginning and the end of the swap. This second case is known as a **cross-currency basis swap**. The periodic payments on a currency swap may be fixed or floating, but the typical swap is floating for floating.

EXAMPLE: Cross-currency basis swap

A euro-based company requires USD but does not have access to direct USD borrowing or finds it prohibitively expensive. The company decides to borrow in euros at the three-month euro reference rate and enter into a cross-currency basis swap to USD based on the three-month USD reference rate (a floating-for-floating swap). The swap has a tenor of two years with quarterly settlement. The principal on the euro loan is €50 million and the \$/€ exchange rate at initiation of the swap is \$1.1236.

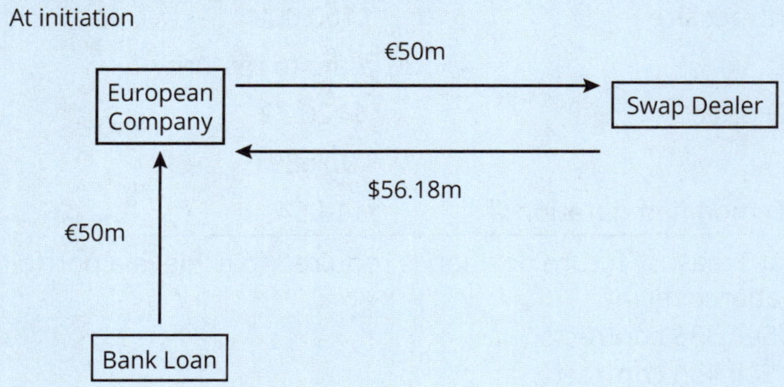

The euro-based company borrows €50 million and exchanges it for €50 million × 1.1236 = $56.18 million.

At quarterly settlement dates

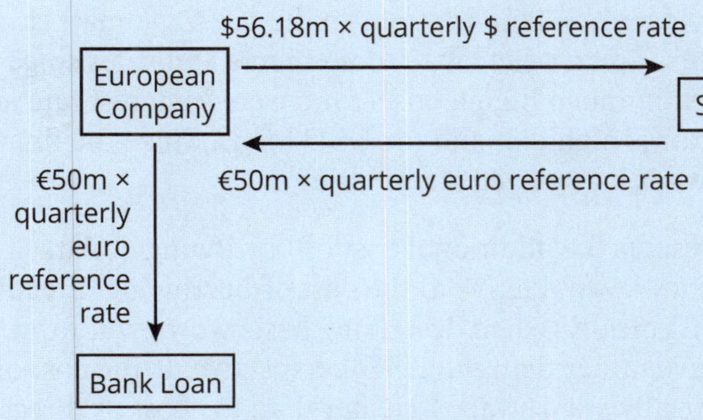

Each counterparty pays variable interest for the currency they initially received. The euro-based company will be paying USD interest to the swap dealer. The swap dealer will be paying the euro interest to the company, which will then use it to service the interest on its loan with the bank.

At swap maturity (2 years)

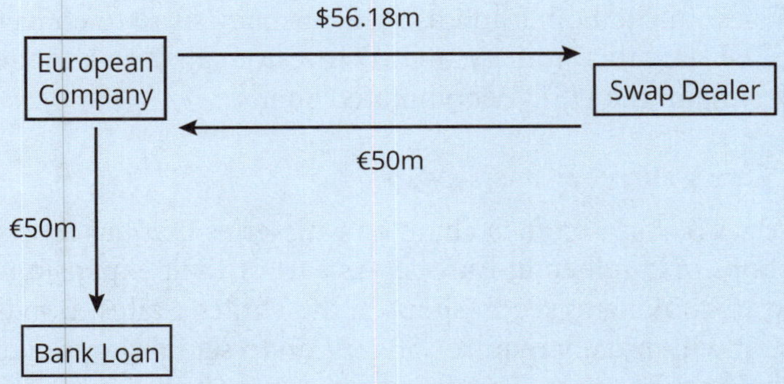

At the swap's expiration, the notional principal amounts are exchanged. The amounts are the same as those exchanged initially; changes in the exchange rate over the life of the swap do not affect these amounts, so there is no uncertainty (exchange rate risk) on the principal flows. The European company receives the €50 million and uses it to repay its bank loan.

In this swap, the European company is described as the dollar payer and the swap dealer as the euro payer (i.e., the description relates to the interest flows and final principal payment, not the swap of initial principal).

Cross-Currency Basis

For the three decades leading up to the great financial crisis in 2008–2009, the **covered interest rate parity (CIRP)** relationship held quite well. When CIRP holds, borrowing directly in USD should have the same cost as borrowing in a foreign currency and hedging exchange rate risk with a currency swap.

When the CIRP relationship does not hold, arbitrage profits are theoretically possible, and exploitation of any arbitrage profits should result in zero basis over time. In a frictionless market, cross-currency basis should not exist.

Since the financial crisis, basis has not been zero, indicating a failure of CIRP. The failure of CIRP to hold results from frictions in the arbitrage market. The introduction of stricter capital adequacy requirements and rules since the financial crash has resulted in much higher costs for covered interest rate arbitrage transactions. Another factor is high demand for USD loans. Since the financial crisis, USD lending via swaps has attracted a premium.

Cross-currency basis represents the additional cost of borrowing dollars synthetically with a currency swap relative to the cost of borrowing directly in the USD cash market. Typically, when describing basis we view it from the foreign-currency perspective rather than the USD perspective. If the cost of borrowing dollars synthetically via a swap is greater than the cost of direct USD borrowing, the foreign currency is said to be exhibiting negative basis. Most currencies have shown a negative basis against the dollar since the financial crisis. The implication is that the USD borrower must accept a lower interest rate on the foreign-currency interest payments it receives.

USD fixed-income investors can benefit when foreign currencies have a negative basis versus the USD by swapping USD for foreign currency and investing in foreign-currency denominated bonds and using a currency swap to convert the returns back to USD. Using this strategy, a USD investor can earn a higher return than by simply investing in the USD denominated bonds.

EXAMPLE: Cross-currency basis swap

Boivis Patisseries Sarl is a French chain of patisseries that has an extensive network of shops in continental Europe. As part of their expansion strategy, they are looking to set up shops in the United States. Boivis estimates that it will initially require $50 million to set up shops and cover working capital requirements. The finance directors at Boivis have looked at directly borrowing in USD but have found that costs would be the U.S. dollar reference floating rate + 100 bp. The decision is made to borrow for four years in euros at a rate of the euro reference floating rate + 60 bp with interest paid quarterly and enter a currency swap to exchange euros for dollars. Basis on the Eurodollar swap is being quoted at –20 basis points (–20 bp). The swap pays variable interest on both legs on a quarterly settlement basis. The current $/€ exchange rate is $1.1815.

The three-month euro reference rate is 1.5% and U.S. dollar reference rate is 2.0% at swap initiation. Three months later at the first settlement date, the three-month euro reference rate is 1.6% and the U.S. dollar reference rate is 1.9%.

Compute the principal flows exchanged at the start and end of the swap's tenor. **Compute** the interest payments at the first and second settlement dates on the swap and the cost to Boivis for its synthetic dollar loan.

Answer:

Principal flows:

$50,000,000 / $1.1815 = €42,319,086

Boivis will need to borrow €42,319,086 and exchange it for $50,000,000. These amounts will be swapped back at the maturity of the swap.

Interest payment at first settlement date

Pays:

€ interest on the loan: €42,319,086 × (0.015 + 0.006) × 90 / 360 = €222,175

$ interest on the swap: $50,000,000 × 0.02 × 90 / 360 = $250,000

Receives:

€ interest on the swap: €42,319,086 × (0.015 – 0.002) × 90 / 360 = €137,537

Cost of $ financing:

Cost of borrowing $ direct: $50,000,000 × (0.02 + 0.01) × 90 / 360 = $375,000 (U.S. dollar reference rate + 100 bp)

Cost of synthetic $ borrowing: $50,000,000 × (0.02 + 0.006 + 0.002) × 90 / 360 = $350,000 (U.S. dollar reference rate + 80 bp)

Net benefit of swap: $375,000 – $350,000 = $25,000

Net benefit of swap: $50,000,000 (1% – 0.8%) × 90 / 360 = $25,000

Interest payment at second settlement date

Pays:

€ interest on the loan: €42,319,086 × (0.016 + 0.006) × 90 / 360 = €232,755

$ interest on the swap: $50,000,000 × 0.019 × 90 / 360 = $237,500

Receives:

€ interest on the swap: €42,319,086 × (0.016 – 0.002) × 90 / 360 = €148,117

Cost of $ financing:

Cost of borrowing $ direct: $50,000,000 × (0.019 + 0.01) × 90 / 360 = $362,500 (U.S. dollar reference rate + 100 bp)

Cost of synthetic $ borrowing: $50,000,000 × (0.019 + 0.006 + 0.002) × 90 / 360 = $337,500 (U.S. dollar reference rate + 80 bp)

Reading 7

Net benefit of swap: \$362,500 – \$337,500 = \$25,000

Net benefit of swap: \$50,000,000 (1% – 0.8%) × 90 / 360 = \$25,000

Conclusion:

By borrowing in euros and entering a currency swap, Boivis has locked into a cost of the U.S. dollar reference rate + 80 bp for their USD borrowing, reflecting the 60 bp spread above the euro reference rate on the loan and the –20 bp on the swap.

Currency Forwards and Futures

Currency forwards and futures allow users to exchange a specified amount of one currency for a specified amount of another currency on a future date. Forwards are customized, while futures are standardized contracts. Consider, for example, a U.K. company exporting goods to Canada that expects to receive a payment of 30 million Canadian dollars (CAD) in 90 days. The risk to the U.K. company is that the exchange rate may change over the next 90 days, so the amount received when converted to British pounds (GBP) is uncertain. A forward contract to purchase a specific number of GBP for 30 million CAD effectively guarantees the future exchange rate in 90 days. The customization of forward contracts allows the contract to be tailored to both the specific quantity of CAD to be received and the expected date of receipt.

Currency futures are standardized in terms of quantity of currency to be exchanged and delivery dates, so a futures hedge may not exactly match the requirements of a hedger. The range of currency pairs on which futures are available is limited, although they are available on most major currency pairs. The greater liquidity of currency futures is attractive to many investors and currency dealers.

The hedge ratio for futures can be calculated as:

$$HR = \frac{\text{amount of currency to be exchanged}}{\text{futures contract size}}$$

EXAMPLE: Hedging exchange rate risk using futures

A U.S. firm is due to receive €20 million in 90 days for goods they sold. The firm is seeking to hedge this risk by selling EUR futures contracts maturing closest to date the euros will be received. The EUR-USD FX future contract size is €125,000. The futures price is 1.3150 USD/EUR. The firm will sell futures contracts (promising to deliver euros at the rate of 1.3150 USD per EUR).

Calculate the number of futures contracts required to hedge the asset and the amount of USD to be received at contract settlement.

Answer:

$$\text{futures position HR} = \frac{€20,000,000}{€125,000} = 160 \text{ EUR-USD futures}$$

At contract settlement, the firm will deliver €20 million and receive 20 million × 1.3150 = $26,300,000.

If the settlement date of the futures does not match the date that euros will be received, the hedge will not be perfect. If the futures settlement is prior to the receipt of the euros, the firm will have exchange rate risk from the settlement date until the euros are received. If the futures settle after the euros are received, the futures position will be closed prior to the futures settlement. In this case, the futures price when the futures are purchased (to close out the short position) will likely not equal the spot price, so the firm has basis risk. This difference could lead to the receipt of either more or less USD than delivery at the settlement of the futures contract would.

MODULE QUIZ 7.2

1. The New Zealand dollar (NZD) is trading at a positive cross-currency basis against the U.S. dollar (USD). Sterling (GBP) is trading at a negative cross-currency basis to the USD. Which of the following strategies would generate the greatest return?
   A. Swapping USD for NZD and investing in New Zealand government securities.
   B. Swapping NZD for USD and investing in U.S. government securities.
   C. Swapping GBP for NZD and investing in New Zealand government securities.

2. Barney Wood imports goods to the U.K. from the Eurozone. He is due to make a payment in 30 days of €20 million. Wood is concerned that the pound will depreciate against the euro over this period and would like to hedge his currency risk with futures. The current spot rate is £/€ = 0.8929.

Cross-Currency EUR-GBP Future	
Futures price* £/€	0.8989
Contract size	€125,000

*Expires in 40 days

Calculate the futures position needed to hedge Wood's liability.

In 30 days, the exchange rate is £/€ = 0.9034 and the futures price is £/€ 0.9054. **Calculate** the cost to Wood if he leaves his euro liability unhedged and if he hedges the position using the future.

3. ABC Robotics, Inc., a U.S. firm, will borrow £30 million to set up a subsidiary in the U.K. ABC can borrow GBP directly at a cost of the pound reference rate + 50 bp. ABC Robotics can borrow in USD at the dollar reference rate + 40 bp. A GBP-USD swap is quoted at –15 bp. The spot exchange rate at swap initiation is quoted as $/£ = $1.2000. The swap is a four-year semiannual swap where both the USD and GBP reference rates are based on six-month floating reference rates. The six-month U.S. dollar reference rate is 2.5% and pound reference rate is 1.5% at initiation of the swap. At the first settlement date, the six-month U.S. dollar reference rate is 2.25% and pound reference rate is 1%. **Calculate** the interest payments at the first and second settlement dates. How much better off is ABC Robotics from using the cross-currency swap rather than directly borrowing GBP?

MODULE 7.3: MANAGING EQUITY RISK

Video covering this content is available online.

LOS 7.c: Demonstrate how equity swaps, forwards, and futures can be used to modify a portfolio's risk and return.

Equity Swaps

Equity swaps can be used to create a synthetic exposure to physical stocks, allowing market participants to increase or decrease their exposure to equity returns. Equity swaps enable users to achieve the economic benefits of share ownership without the cost and expense of ownership.

The three main types of swaps include the following:

1. Pay fixed, receive equity return.
2. Pay floating, receive equity return.
3. Pay another equity return, receive equity return.

An example of paying another equity return and receiving an equity return would be paying the return on the Nasdaq Composite Index and receiving the return on the S&P 500.

The equity return may be based on:

- A single stock.
- A basket of equities.
- An equity index.

The equity return may be price return (typical) or total return (price + dividends).

A typical equity swap will involve a series of payments at periodic settlement dates over the tenor of the swap. Some equity swaps require each party to make a single payment at the end of the swap's life.

Figure 7.4: Equity Swap vs. Physical Stock

Advantages	Disadvantages
■ Gain exposure to equity when participation in physical market is restricted ■ Avoid tax on physical ownership (i.e., stamp duty) ■ Avoid custody fees on physical ownership ■ Avoid the cost of monitoring physical positions, which may increase due to corporate actions (i.e., dividend payments, stock splits, buy-backs, M&A, etc.)	■ Equity swaps typically require collateral ■ Swaps are illiquid ■ Swaps do not convey voting rights

EXAMPLE: Changing equity exposure using a swap

A German pension fund manager holds a €200 million portfolio of domestic stocks passively tracking the DAX 30 stock market index. The pension fund expects the index to rise in the next year and wishes to increase its exposure by 40%. The fund manager enters an equity swap with a notional principal of €80 million, agreeing to pay a floating interest rate + 30 bp and receive the return on the equity index. The swap has a tenor of one year and semiannual settlements. The DAX 30 at the time of swap initiation is 12,400 points.

Scenario 1:

The six-month floating reference rate relating to the first settlement date is = 6%.

The DAX 30 at the first settlement date = 13,020.

Scenario 2:

The six-month floating reference rate relating to the first settlement date is = 6%.

The DAX 30 at the first settlement date = 11,780.

Compute the gain or loss on the portfolio, the cash flows on the swap, and the net position for the fund manager in both scenarios.

Answer:

Scenario 1:

Return on DAX 30 = (13,020 / 12,400) – 1 = 5%

Increase in portfolio value = €200 million × 0.05 = €10 million

Equity leg of swap = €80 million × 0.05 = €4 million

Floating leg of swap = €80 million × (0.06 + 0.003) × 180 / 360 = €2.52 million

Net cash flow on swap = €4 million – €2.52 million = €1.48 million

This is the synthetic equivalent to borrowing €80 million in the money markets at the floating reference rate + 30 bp and investing €80 million in an index-tracking portfolio:

€80 million × [0.05 – (0.063 × 180 / 360)] = €1.48 million

Fund manager's position = €10 million + €1.48 million = €11.48 million

Scenario 2:

Return on DAX 30 = (11,780 / 12,400) – 1 = –0.05

Decrease in portfolio value = €200 million × –0.05 = –€10 million

Equity leg of swap = €80 million × –0.05 = –€4 million

Floating leg of swap = €80 million × (0.06 + 0.003) × 180 / 360 = €2.52 million

Net cash flow on swap = –€4 million – €2.52 million = –€6.52 million

Note that the equity return receiver pays both the floating rate of interest and the negative return on the equity index.

This is the synthetic equivalent to borrowing €80 million in the money markets at the floating reference rate + 30 bp and investing €80 million in an index-tracking portfolio:

€80 million × [–0.05 – (0.063 × 180 / 360)] = –€6.52 million

Fund manager's net position = –€10 million – €6.52 million = –€16.52 million

To reduce the exposure to equity, the fund manager would enter a swap to pay the equity return and receive a floating (or fixed) rate of interest. This synthetically creates a position equivalent to selling equity and investing the proceeds in the money markets.

Equity Futures and Forwards

Equity futures are exchange traded, standardized, require margin, have low transaction costs, and are available on indexes and single stocks. They enable market participants to do the following:

- Implement tactical allocation decisions (alter the exposure to equity of a portfolio).
  - Selling futures (short position) reduces equity exposure.
  - Buying futures (long position) increases equity exposure.
- Achieve portfolio diversification.
- Gain exposure to international markets.
- Make directional bets on the direction of the market.

Forwards provide many of the same advantages but lack liquidity and are not subject to mark-to-market margin adjustments. Because there is no clearinghouse, the credit quality of the counterparties is a concern. The major advantage of forward contracts is they can be customized.

Index futures have a multiplier. The actual futures price is the quoted futures price (in points) × the multiplier. For S&P 500 Index futures, the multiplier is $250; for FTSE 100 Index futures, the multiplier is £10.

EXAMPLE: Using index futures to hedge equity market exposure

A fund manager holds a £200 million equity portfolio, which is passively tracking the FTSE 100 Index. The fund manager wishes to hedge 30% of the portfolio against equity market risk.

Contract Details for FTSE 100 Index Futures	
Quotation	Index points
Multiplier	£10 per point
Delivery dates	March, June, September, December
Settlement price	FTSE 100 cash price on last day of trading
Futures price – September delivery	7,300

Compute the number of contracts required to hedge 30% of the portfolio's equity position. **Compute** the profit or loss if the FTSE 100 increases by 5% and the futures price is 7,665. **Compute** the profit or loss if the FTSE 100 falls by 5% and the futures price changes to 6,935.

Answer:

number of futures contracts needed

$$= \frac{\text{monetary value of position to be hedged}}{\text{futures price} \times \text{multiplier}}$$

$$= \frac{-£60{,}000{,}000}{7{,}300 \times £10} = -821.9 = 822 \text{ short futures}$$

FTSE 100 @ 7,665 at delivery (5% increase)

Futures gain/(loss): 7,665 − 7,300 = 365 points ∴ 365 points × £10 × −822 = −£3,000,300

Portfolio value: (1 + 0.05) × £200,000,000 = £210,000,000

Net position: £210,000,000 − £3,000,300 = £206,999,700

Impact of hedge	£
Future position	−3,000,300
Portfolio £60,000,000 × 0.05	3,000,000
Net gain	−300

The imperfection in the hedge is the result of rounding the hedge ratio.

FTSE 100 @ 6,935 at delivery

Futures gain/(loss): 6,935 − 7,300 = −365 points ∴ −365 points × £10 × −822 = £3,000,300

Portfolio value: (1 − 0.05) × £200,000,000 = £190,000,000

Net position: £190,000,000 + £3,000,300 = £193,000,300

Impact of hedge	£
Future position	3,000,300
Portfolio £60,000,000 × −0.05	−3,000,000
Net gain	300

Achieving a Target Portfolio Beta

Short equity futures positions can be used to decrease the beta of a portfolio, and long positions can be used to increase the beta of a portfolio. A portfolio's beta is the weighted average of the betas of the portfolio stocks. The number of contracts required to change the beta of an existing portfolio can be calculated with the following formula:

$$\text{number of futures required} = \left(\frac{\beta_T - \beta_P}{\beta_F}\right)\left(\frac{MV_P}{F}\right)$$

where:
β_T = target portfolio beta
β_P = current portfolio beta
β_F = futures beta (beta of stock index)
MV_P = market value of portfolio
F = futures contract value = futures price × multiplier

Note that to fully hedge the portfolio from market risk, $\beta_T = 0$.

EXAMPLE: Achieving a target portfolio beta using index futures

A fund manager has a $60 million portfolio of aggressive stocks with a portfolio beta of 1.2 relative to the S&P 500. The fund manager believes the market will decline over the next six months and wishes to reduce the beta of the portfolio to 0.8 using S&P 500 futures. S&P 500 futures currently have a contract price of 2,984 and a multiplier of $250. At the end of the six-month period, the S&P 500 Index has decreased by 1.5%. By definition, beta of the S&P 500 Index equals 1.

Calculate the number of futures contracts and **determine** whether they should be bought or sold to achieve the target portfolio beta. **Compute** the effectiveness of the strategy at the end of the six-month period.

Answer:

$$\text{number of futures required} = \left(\frac{0.8 - 1.2}{1}\right)\left(\frac{\$60{,}000{,}000}{\$746{,}000}\right) = -32.17$$

$$= -32 \text{ futures contracts}$$

futures contract value = 2,984 × $250 = $746,000

Because the calculated value of the number of futures contracts is negative, the futures contracts should be sold.

Value of portfolio in six months:

$60,000,000 × [1 – (0.015 × 1.2)] = $58,920,000

Note that if the market falls by 1.5%, the portfolio will fall by more than 1.5% because its beta is greater than 1.

Reading 7

Profit on futures contract:

Futures contract value in six months: 2,984 × (1 – 0.015) = 2,939.24 = 2,939 (rounded to the nearest 0.5 index point)

Futures profit: (2,984 – 2,939) × $250 × 32 = $360,000

Net position: $58,920,000 + $360,000 = $59,280,000

$$\text{return} = \frac{\$59{,}280{,}000}{\$60{,}000{,}000} - 1 = -0.012, \textit{ or} -1.2\%$$

$$\text{beta of portfolio} = \frac{\%\text{ change in portfolio}}{\%\text{ change in index}} = \frac{-0.012}{-0.015} = 0.8$$

Cash Equitization

Holding cash balances will typically reduce the return on a portfolio because cash typically yields a lower rate of return than equity or fixed income. Holding cash balances will therefore increase the risk that the portfolios will underperform the benchmark. **Cash equitization** refers to purchasing index futures to replicate the returns that would have been earned by investing the cash in an index with risk and return characteristics similar to those of the portfolio. The major advantages of futures, in this application, are their liquidity and low transaction costs relative to direct investment in the equity markets. Cash equitization is also known as cash securitization or cash overlay.

An alternative to purchasing futures would be to buy call options and sell put options on the appropriate stock index with the same strike and expiry to create a synthetic forward position.

EXAMPLE: Cash equitization

A U.S. fund manager runs a passive fund, which tracks the S&P 500. Cash balances have built up in the portfolio and the fund manager is concerned that the cash drag will lead to portfolio underperformance relative to the S&P 500. The fund currently holds $8 million in cash. S&P 500 futures currently have a contract price of 2,780, a multiplier of $250, and a beta of 1.

Calculate the number of stock index futures needed to equitize the portfolio's excess cash.

Answer:

$$\text{number of futures required} = \left(\frac{\beta_T - \beta_P}{\beta_F}\right)\left(\frac{MV_P}{F}\right)$$

where:

β_P = current portfolio beta of cash position = 0 (note cash has a beta of 0)

MV_P = cash position

$$\text{number of futures required} = \left(\frac{\beta_T}{\beta_F}\right)\left(\frac{MV_P}{F}\right)$$

where:

β_T = target portfolio beta (In this case, the target will be set to 1, as we want the beta of the synthetically invested cash to match the beta of the index.)

$$\text{number of futures required} = \left(\frac{1}{1}\right)\left(\frac{\$8{,}000{,}000}{\$695{,}000}\right) = 11.51$$

$$= 12 \text{ futures contracts}$$

$F = 2{,}780 \times \$250 = \$695{,}000$

MODULE QUIZ 7.3

1. A U.K. fund manager has a defensive equity portfolio with a market value of £20 million and a beta equals 0.8 relative to the FTSE 100. The manager believes that U.K. equity will perform strongly over the next year and wishes to increase the portfolio beta to 1.4. FTSE 100 futures are currently trading at 7,425 points with a multiplier of £10. How many futures contracts are required to achieve the desired beta?
   A. 162 FTSE 100 futures.
   B. 377 FTSE 100 futures.
   C. 1,620 FTSE 100 futures.
2. Hideko Kobayashi is an active fund manager running an equity portfolio benchmarked against the Nikkei 225. The funds market value is ¥4,350,000,000. Due to recent sales, Hideko is worried that cash balances have built up to 5% of the fund's value. Hideko is worried about the cash drag affecting her performance fees and wishes to temporarily invest the surplus cash in the Nikkei 225. The Nikkei future she is considering has a price of 21,624 and a multiplier of ¥1,000. How many Nikkei 225 futures will she require for this cash overlay?
   A. 10 futures.
   B. 100 futures.
   C. 201 futures.

Video covering this content is available online.

MODULE 7.4: DERIVATIVES ON VOLATILITY

LOS 7.d: Demonstrate the use of volatility derivatives and variance swaps.

Volatility is a measure of the magnitude of price movements over a certain period of time. The best known measure of market volatility is the CBOE Volatility Index (more commonly known as VIX). The VIX Index measures implied volatility in the S&P 500 Index over a forward period of 30 days. VIX computes a weighted average of implied volatility inferred from S&P 500 traded options (calls and puts) with an average expiration of 30 days. It is important to note that VIX is not a measure of actual volatility but rather the expected volatility that is priced into options. VIX is also known as the fear index or fear gauge as we can directly view the market's expectations of future volatility.

Specifically, the VIX Index value is the annualized standard deviation of the expected +/− percentage moves in the S&P 500 Index over the following 30 days. For example, if the VIX was at 20, we could interpret it as telling us that the market expects that the S&P will stay within a +/−20% range over one year with a 68% level of confidence. This implies a range $+/-\frac{20}{\sqrt{12}} = 5.77\%$ over the next 30-day period.

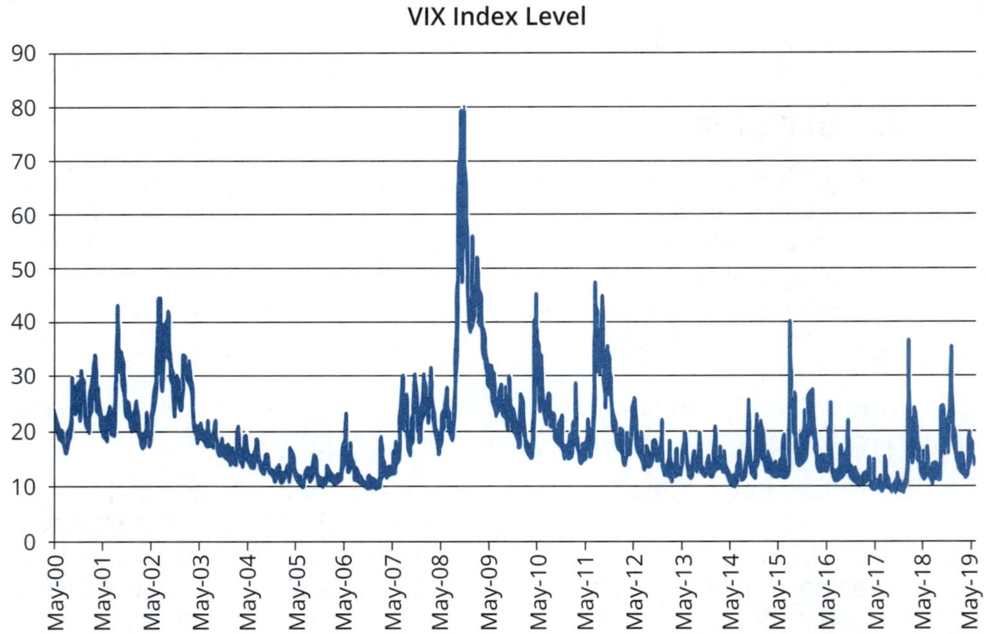

Source: "Historical Data for Cboe VIX® Index and Other Volatility Indices," Cboe, https://www.cboe.com/tradable_products/vix/vix_historical_data.

The graph of the VIX Index over the past 19 years shows large spikes in the index at times of great uncertainty—for example, in 2008 with the great financial crash, 2010 with the "flash crash" attributed to high-frequency traders, and 2011 with the S&P downgrade of U.S. sovereign debt. As a rule of thumb, a value lower than 20 represents a low-risk environment and values above 30 represent a high-risk environment. However, very low levels of the VIX Index can indicate an excessively bullish market, while very high levels can imply an excessively bearish market. The performance of VIX over this 19-year period also demonstrates the mean reversion of the index. Spikes in the index do not last, and the index reverts to more moderate levels soon after.

Importantly, empirical studies have shown a negative correlation between the VIX and stock returns, which becomes even more pronounced during downturns. This correlation allows derivatives based on the index to be used to offset the losses on an equity portfolio when volatility increases.

The following chart shows a rolling 252-day correlation between the VIX price and daily returns on the S&P 500.

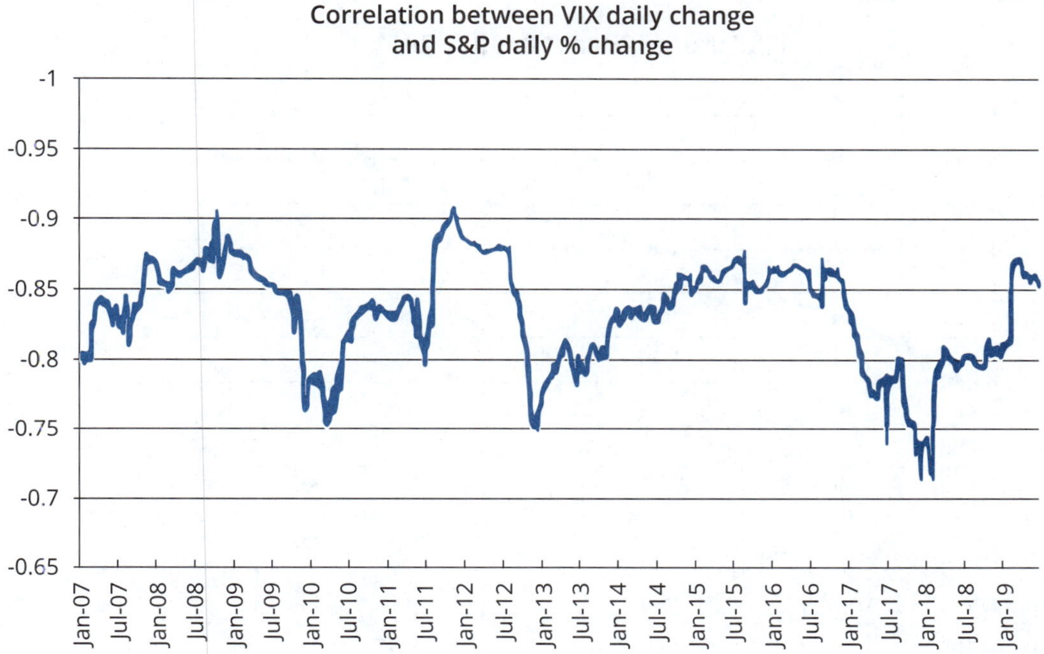

Source: Ibid.

While investors cannot directly invest in VIX, the CBOE introduced futures based on the VIX Index in 2004 and options in 2006. This has led to volatility being viewed as a separate asset class that can be bought and sold. VIX futures and options offer participants pure-play bets on market volatility.

VIX Futures

Unlike other futures contracts, the cost-of-carry model cannot be used to determine the fair value of the future because it is not possible to directly invest in spot VIX. The **VIX futures** price can be interpreted as the expected S&P 500 Index volatility in the 30-day period after the futures contract expiration date.

An equity holding can be protected from extreme downturns (tail risk) by buying VIX futures. Remember that VIX returns and equity returns are negatively correlated. If volatility increases, the equity portfolio will decline in value but VIX futures should increase in value. VIX futures will increase in value when the market's expectation of future volatility at contract maturity increases.

Selling VIX futures creates a short volatility position and captures the volatility risk premium embedded in S&P 500 options. Short volatility positions can result in large losses if expected volatility rises significantly.

The term structure of VIX futures can provide insights into the market's expectations of volatility over time. Contango and backwardation in the futures market are therefore driven by expected changes in volatility over time. The term structure of VIX futures is constantly changing, reflecting changes in expected 30-day volatility at future dates, current expected 30-day volatility, and VIX futures trading activity.

Contango Market

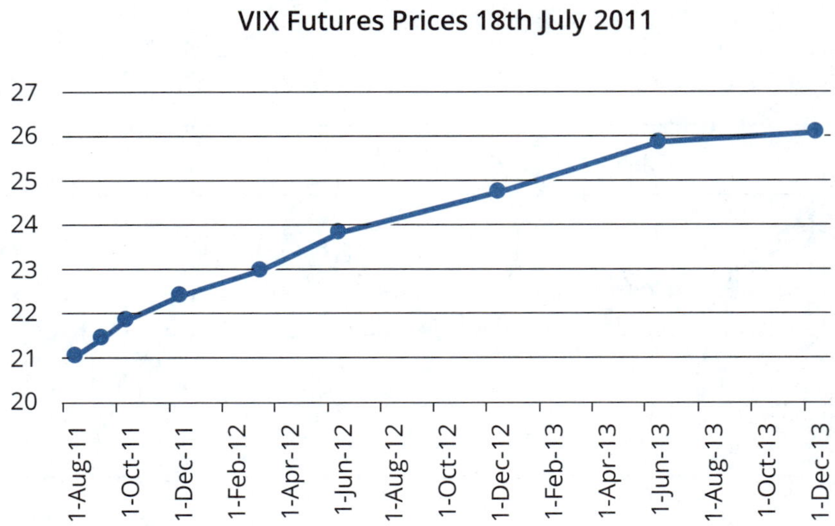

18 July, 2011; spot VIX = 20.95

Source: Ibid.

The chart shows futures prices on the y-axis and futures expiration dates on the x-axis. Looking at the data on 18 July, 2011, the VIX futures market is in contango. Negative basis defines contango, where basis is computed as spot minus futures price. Longer-dated futures contracts have higher prices than short-dated futures contracts. We can interpret this as market participants expecting 30-day volatility to increase from August 2011 until December 2013. When levels of the VIX Index are low, it is common for the futures market to be in contango.

Backwardation

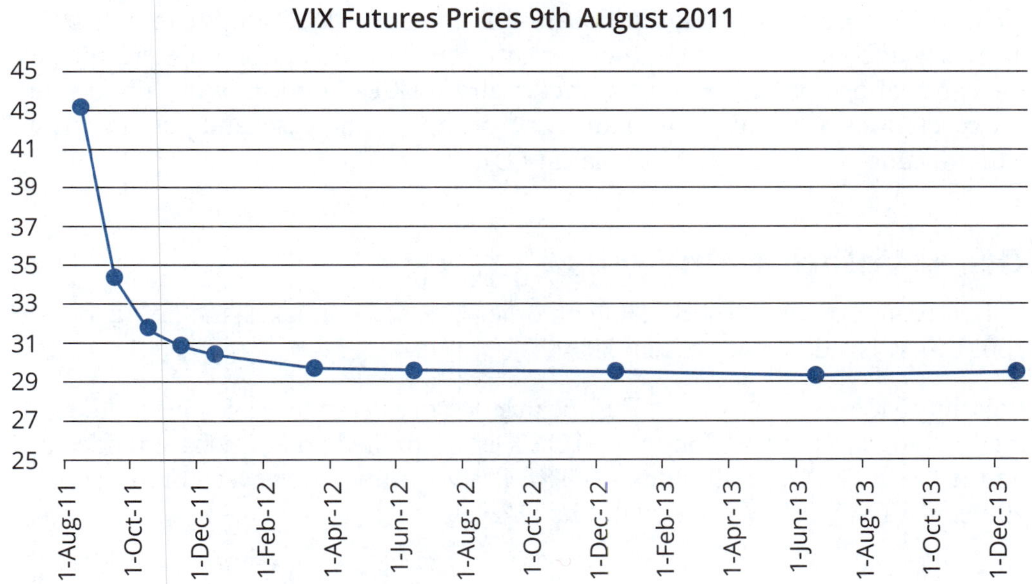

9 August, 2011; spot VIX = 35.06

Source: Ibid.

Less than one month later, the term structure of VIX futures has completely changed and is now in backwardation. We can interpret this shape as the market expecting 30-day volatility to decrease over the period. The cause of the sudden change from contango to backwardation was a sudden increase in the VIX Index caused by the S&P downgrade of U.S. sovereign debt from AAA to AA+ on August 5, 2011.

VIX futures prices and the VIX Index will converge at contract maturity because VIX futures settle against spot VIX at expiration. For a participant who purchases long-dated VIX futures when the market is in contango (the typical situation), the difference between the spot and futures price will decline over time as the futures price moves toward spot VIX at expiration. If the market is in backwardation, the futures price should rise over time as it moves toward spot VIX. The profit or loss generated as the basis moves toward zero over the life of the futures contract is referred to as roll yield. When the short end of the VIX futures curve is steeper than the long end, the roll yield will be magnified.

Position	Term Structure	Roll Yield
Long futures position	Contango	Negative
Short futures position	Contango	Positive
Long futures position	Backwardation	Positive
Short futures position	Backwardation	Negative

VIX Options

VIX options are cash-settled European-style options. VIX options can only be exercised at contract maturity; therefore, the value of the option is determined by the expectations of VIX at the contract expiry. VIX call options will gain in value if expectations of volatility at maturity of the option increase, and put options will gain in value if expectations of volatility fall.

Other Volatility Indexes

Volatility indexes are also available on other U.S. stock indexes, including the S&P 100, DJIA, Nasdaq, and Russell 2000.

Volatility indexes also exist on European stock market indexes. Using similar methodology to the VIX Index, VSTOXX is an implied volatility-based index based on the EURO STOXX 50 Index. VFTSE is a volatility index based on the FTSE 100, and VDAX-NEW is based on the DAX 30.

Variance Swaps

Variance swaps payoffs are based on variance rather than volatility (standard deviation). Variance is σ^2. These products are termed swaps as they have two counterparties, one making a fixed payment and the other making a variable payment. The fixed payment is typically based on implied volatility^2 (implied variance) over the period and is known at the initiation of the swap; this is referred to as the variance strike. The variable payment is unknown at swap initiation and is only known at swap maturity. It is the actual variance of the underlying asset over the life of the swap and is referred to as realized variance (σ^2).

The party receiving the variable payment (the purchaser) will gain on the contract when the realized variance is greater than the implied variance and will lose when the realized variance is less than the implied variance. A variance swap can, therefore, be viewed as a pure play on whether realized variance will be higher or lower than expected variance (implied variance) over the tenor of the swap.

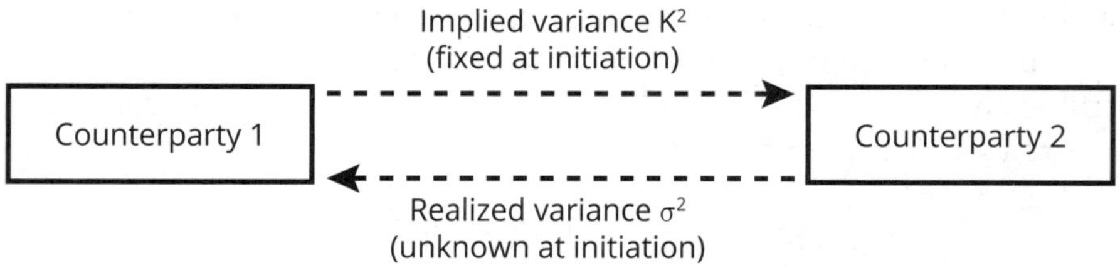

There is no exchange of notional principal at the initiation of the swap. A variance swap also has no interim settlement periods. With a variance swap, there is a single payment at the expiration of the swap based on the difference between actual and implied variance over the life of the swap:

$$\text{settlement amount}_T = (\text{variance notional})(\text{realized variance} - \text{variance strike})$$

The value of the swap is zero at initiation because implied volatility is the best ex ante estimate of realized volatility.

Long (purchaser) describes the counterparty who receives the realized variance (actual) and pays the swap's variance strike (implied volatility).

Realized volatility	>	strike	Buyer (long) of swap makes a profit
Realized volatility	<	strike	Buyer (long) of swap makes a loss

Realized variance is calculated by taking the natural log of the daily price relatives, the closing price on day *t*, divided by the closing price on day *t* – *1*:

$$R_i = \ln(P_t / P_{t-1})$$

If we have *N* days of traded prices, we can compute N – 1 price relatives (R):

$$\text{daily variance} = \left[\frac{\sum_{i=1}^{N-1} R_i^2}{(N-1)}\right]$$

annualized variance = daily variance × 252; 252 = assumed trading days in a year

PROFESSOR'S NOTE

This appears to be an unusual variance computation, as most computations we have seen deduct the mean from the numerator before squaring (i.e., $\frac{\sum_{i=1}^{N-1}(R_i - \bar{R})^2}{(N-1)}$). In this variance computation, the mean is not deducted. The logic is that we are calculating movement regardless of direction rather than movement around a mean. This has the advantage of making the variances perfectly additive (i.e., one-year variance can be split into two equal six-month periods). This concept will be used later for valuing variance swaps prior to maturity.

Variance swaps can be created for any underlying asset as long as it is traded and there is a record of daily prices.

The notional amount for a variance swap can be expressed as either variance notional (N_{VAR}) or vega notional (N_{vega}). Variance notional represents the profit or loss per point difference between implied variance (strike^2) and realized variance (σ^2). Variance notional can therefore be thought of as a multiplier that turns the point difference between σ^2 and K^2 into a monetary amount:

$$\text{profit/(loss)} = N_{VAR} \times (\sigma^2 - K^2)$$

where:
σ = realized volatility
K = strike volatility (implied volatility)

PROFESSOR'S NOTE

Both the actual (σ) and the implied volatility on the swap (K) are quoted in standard deviations but remember this is a variance swap and therefore we must square the volatility.

The market convention is to quote the notional on a swap as vega notional (N_{vega}) rather than variance notional (N_{VAR}). Recall that vega refers to the change in option premium per a 1% change in volatility, $\frac{\Delta Premium}{\Delta Volatility}$, a natural way to think about the return for volatility.

Given the relationship between N_{VAR} and N_{vega}, we can calculate the gains or losses on a variance swap with either of them. Using N_{VAR}, this calculation is more intuitive as it is multiplied by the difference between actual and implied variance:

$$\text{variance notional} = \frac{\text{vega notional}}{2 \times \text{strike price (K)}}, \text{ so profit/(loss)} = N_{VAR} \times (\sigma^2 - K^2)$$

$$= N_{vega} \times \left(\frac{\sigma^2 - K^2}{2K}\right)$$

Convexity

Because the payoffs on a variance swap are based on variance, while the strike price is expressed in terms of volatility, the payoffs for a variance swap are convex with respect to volatility. Compared to the payoffs on a volatility derivative with payoffs that are linear with respect to volatility, (1) when realized volatility is below the strike, the losses on the variance swap are smaller than the losses on the volatility derivative, and (2) when realized volatility is above the strike, the gains on the variance swap are greater than the gains on the volatility derivative. This convexity is similar in nature to the convexity of bond prices with respect to yield. With the variance swap, payoffs are increasing at an increasing rate when volatility rises and decreasing at a decreasing rate when volatility falls.

Convexity is an attractive feature to those who use variance swaps to hedge tail risk. When equity values fall sharply and volatility increases dramatically, decreases in portfolio value are offset by profits on a variance swap that increase at an accelerating rate.

Mark to Market

The value of a variance swap is zero at initiation, but over time, the swap will either gain or lose value as realized and implied volatility diverge. At any point, the expected variance at maturity is simply the time-weighted average of the variance realized over the time since swap inception and the implied variance over the remaining time to maturity.

Consider a one-year swap where three months have elapsed since inception:

Step 1: Compute expected variance at maturity (the time-weighted average of realized variance and implied variance over the remainder of the swap's life).

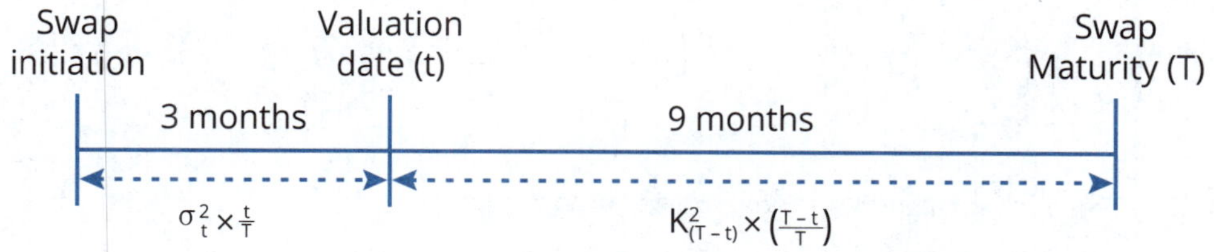

$$\text{expected variance to maturity} = \left(\sigma_t^2 \times \frac{t}{T}\right) + \left(K^2_{(T-t)} \times \frac{T-t}{T}\right)$$

where:

σ_t^2 = annualized realized volatility from initiation to valuation date squared

$K^2_{(T-t)}$ = annualized implied volatility from valuation date to swap maturity squared

$$\frac{t}{T} = \frac{3}{12}$$

$$\frac{T-t}{T} = \frac{9}{12}$$

Step 2: Compute expected payoff at swap maturity:

$$\text{payoff} = N_{VAR} \times (\text{expected variance to maturity} - \text{original strike}^2)$$

Step 3: Discount expected payoff at maturity back to the valuation date.

EXAMPLE: Valuing a variance swap during its life

Luke Amos, an equity fund manager, has purchased a one-year variance swap on the S&P 500 with vega notional of $100,000 and a strike of 20%.

Nine months have passed and the S&P has realized a volatility of 21%. The strike price for a three-month variance swap at this time is quoted at 22%, and the annual interest rate is 2%.

Compute the current value of the swap.

Answer:

Step 1: Compute the expected variance at maturity:

$$\left(21^2 \times \frac{9}{12}\right) + \left(22^2 \times \frac{3}{12}\right) = 330.75 + 121 = 451.75$$

Step 2: Compute the expected payoff at maturity:

$$\text{variance notional} = \frac{\text{vega notional}}{2 \times K} = \frac{\$100{,}000}{2 \times 20} = \$2{,}500$$

expected payoff at maturity = $(\sigma^2 - K^2) \times$ variance notional, where $K^2 = 20^2 = 400$

expected payoff at maturity = (451.75 – 400) × \$2,500 = \$129,375

Step 3: Discount expected payoff from maturity to the valuation date (3 months):

$$\text{unannualize the interest rate} = 2\% \times \frac{3}{12} = 0.5\%$$

$$\text{current value of swap} = \frac{\$129{,}375}{1.005} = \$128{,}731$$

This is a gain to the purchaser (long) and a loss to the seller (short).

MODULE QUIZ 7.4

1. Which of the following comments is *least* accurate regarding the VIX Index?
   A. Empirically, the VIX Index and equity returns are negatively correlated.
   B. VIX measures realized volatility over a 30-day period on the S&P 500.
   C. The VIX Index level is the annualized standard deviation of implied volatility on the S&P 500.
2. Which of the following comments is *most* accurate? The payoff on a variance swap can be calculated by multiplying the difference between actual variance and implied variance by:
   A. notional vega.
   B. notional variance.
   C. the expected return to volatility.
3. Quark Dealers sold a one-year FTSE MIB variance swap with a strike of 15 three months ago. Quark set the vega notional at €150,000. As part of their swap agreements, Quark requires the contract to be marked to market and subject to margining every three months.

   At the end of the first three-month period, realized volatility is 28. The strike on a nine-month variance swap is 32, and the annual interest rate is 0.6%.

   Compute the mark-to-market value of the swap.

Video covering this content is available online.

MODULE 7.5: USES OF DERIVATIVES IN PORTFOLIO MANAGEMENT

LOS 7.e: Demonstrate the use of derivatives to achieve targeted equity and interest rate risk exposures.

Using Equity Swaps

EXAMPLE: Using equity swaps to reduce equity exposure

Jennifer Seago has a concentrated holding of 80,000 shares in ABC Gmbh. Seago does not want to sell the shares—which she has held for many years—for tax reasons. ABC Gmbh is currently trading at €6.00 and she is concerned that the share price will decline over the next year as the company undergoes a restructuring. The one-year floating rate is 0.95% and ABC is expected to pay an annual dividend of €0.05.

Suggest a swap strategy that will address Seago's concerns and constraint. **Evaluate** the results of this strategy for both an increase of 5% and a decrease of 5% in the price of ABC.

Consider the use of a one-year annual-pay total return swap. The interest leg of the swap is the floating market reference rate. The notional principal is 80,000 shares × €6.00 = €480,000.

Scenario 1:

The stock price falls by 5% and ABC pays a dividend of €0.05:

$$\text{total return on ABC} = \frac{€5.70 + €0.05}{€6.00} - 1 = -4.1667\%$$

$$€6.00 \times (1 - 0.05) = €5.70$$

Seago receives interest and will pay positive returns on the stock and receive negative stock returns.

Seago receives:

$$[0.0095 - (-0.041667)] \times €480{,}000 = €24{,}560$$

Scenario 2:

The stock price rises by 5% and ABC pays a dividend of €0.05:

$$\text{total return on ABC} = \frac{€6.30 + 0.05}{€6.00} - 1 = 5.8333\%$$

$$€6.00 \times (1 + 0.05) = €6.30$$

Seago receives:

$$(0.0095 - 0.058333) \times €480{,}000 = -€23{,}440 \text{ (i.e., pays €23,440)}$$

Cash Equitization

EXAMPLE: Investing surplus cash using index futures

Yoann Barbet is the manager of an equities fund for which the investment universe is the FTSE 100. Currently, the fund holds £60 million in cash and £300 million in equities with a beta of 1.2 relative to the FTSE 100. The six-month rate earned on the cash will be 0.86% (annualized). Barbet does not want to commit the cash to specific equities over the next six months but is concerned about cash drag. If he wants to avoid cash drag and would like the beta of the portfolio to be 1.2, what strategy should be employed?

Barbet should gain exposure to equities with FTSE 100 futures over the next six months.

Six-month FTSE 100 futures are currently at 7,348.50 with a multiplier of £10. The beta of the FTSE 100 futures is 1.

$$\text{number of futures to purchase} = \left(\frac{\beta_T}{\beta_F}\right)\left(\frac{MV_P}{F}\right)$$

$$\text{number of futures to purchase} = \left(\frac{1.2}{1}\right)\left(\frac{£60{,}000{,}000}{£73{,}485}\right)$$

$$= 979.79 \text{ (i.e., 980 contracts)}$$

Scenario:

The FTSE 100 gains 6% over the six-month period, the six-month pound reference rate is 0.86%, and the futures price at the end of the period is 7,642.

value of equities invested = £300 million × [1 + (0.06 × 1.2)] = £321.6 million

return on equity portfolio = £321.6 million − £300 million = £21.6 million

Receives:

interest on cash holding = £60 million × 0.0086 × 180 / 360 = £258,000

futures profit = (7,642 − 7,348.50) = 293.5 points; 293.5 points × £10 × 980 contracts = £2,876,300

total return = £21,600,000 + £258,000 + £2,876,300 = £24,734,300

$$\text{return \%} = \frac{£24{,}734{,}300}{(£300{,}000{,}000 + 60{,}000{,}000)} = 6.87\%$$

Note that the underperformance of the portfolio relative to the 6% return on the index plus a beta of 1.2 (overall desired portfolio return of 7.2%) results from rounding in the number of contracts, and a basis change on the FTSE forward contract.

Note the change in the FTSE 100 futures $= \frac{£7{,}642}{£7{,}348.50} - 1 = 3.99\%$;

however, the FTSE 100 increased by 6%.

LOS 7.f: Demonstrate the use of derivatives in asset allocation, rebalancing, and inferring market expectations.

Asset Allocation Using Derivatives

EXAMPLE: Changing allocations between asset classes using futures

Mathieu Chausset is a French fund manager with €800 million assets under management. Currently, Chausset has 80% allocated to equity and 20% allocated to French fixed-income securities. Chausset currently splits his equity portfolio 50-50 between German and French stocks.

Chausset wishes to alter his asset allocation for the next six months. Firstly, he wishes to increase the fixed-income proportion to 40% and reduce the equity proportion to 60%. Secondly, he wishes to reduce the proportion of his equity holdings in German securities to 30% and increase the proportion in French equity to 70%. Chausset intends to achieve his new asset allocation by using index and government bond futures.

French government bonds = OATs

Chausset's German stock portfolio has a beta of 1.2 relative to the DAX 30, and the French stock portfolio has a beta of 0.95 relative to the CAC 40. The French government bonds (OATs) portfolio has a modified duration of 8.5.

Futures Contract Details (Equity Index)		
Index name	French CAC 40	German DAX 30
Futures price	5,500	12,200
Multiplier	€10	€25
Beta	1	1

Futures Contract Details (French OATs)	
Futures price	€163.84
Contract size	€100,000
CTD	€127.72
CF	0.7768
CTD modified duration	8.89

Determine how many long and short futures positions Chausset will need to use to implement his desired asset allocation.

Reading 7

Answer:

	Original	**New**	**Change in Exposure**
Equity	€640 million = 80%	€480 million = 60%	
German stocks	€320 million = 50%	€144 million = 30%	Decrease €176 million
French stocks	€320 million = 50%	€336 million = 70%	Increase €16 million
Fixed Income			
French OATs	€160 million = 20%	€320 million = 40%	Increase €160 million

German stocks: Alter exposure from €320 million to €144 million = decrease of €176 million

$$\text{number of futures required} = \left(\frac{\beta_T - \beta_P}{\beta_F}\right)\left(\frac{MV_P}{F}\right)$$

where:

β_T = target beta = 0 (the target beta is set to zero because we are reducing our exposure to German stock)
β_p = portfolio beta = 1.2
β_F = futures beta (i.e., beta of the index)
MV_P = reduction in portfolio exposure = €176 million
F = futures price × multiplier = 12,200 × €25 = €305,000

$$\text{number of futures required} = \left(\frac{0 - 1.2}{1}\right)\left(\frac{€176{,}000{,}000}{€305{,}000}\right) = -692.45$$

$$= -692 \text{ futures contracts}$$

Chausset needs to sell 692 DAX futures.

French stocks: Alter exposure from €320 million to €336 million = increase of €16 million

β_T = target beta = 0.95 (we need to create an additional €16 million exposure with a beta of 0.95)
β_p = portfolio beta = 0
β_F = futures beta (i.e., beta of the index) = 1
MV_P = increase in portfolio size = €16 million
F = futures price × multiplier = 5,500 × €10 = €55,000

$$\text{number of futures required} = \left(\frac{0.95 - 0}{1}\right)\left(\frac{€16{,}000{,}000}{€55{,}000}\right) = 276.36$$

$$= 276 \text{ futures contracts}$$

Chausset will need to purchase 276 futures on the CAC 40.

French OATs: Alter exposure from €160 million to €320 million = increase of €160 million

$$BPVHR = \frac{BPV_{target} - BPV_{portfolio}}{BPV_{CTD}} \times CF$$

$BPV_{target} = MD_{target} \times 0.0001 \times MV_{portfolio} = 8.5 \times 0.0001 \times €160$ million = €136,000

$BPV_{CTD} = MD_{CTD} \times 0.0001 \times$ (price / 100 × contract size) = 8.89 × 0.0001 × [(€127.72 / 100) × €100,000] = €113.54

$$BPVHR = \frac{€136,000 - €0}{€113.54} \times 0.7768 = 930.46 = 930 \text{ futures contracts}$$

Chausset will need to purchase 930 French OATs futures contracts.

Summary	Futures Position	Number of Contracts
German stock	Short DAX 30 futures	692
French stock	Long CAC 40 futures	276
French bonds	Long OATs futures	930

Assume that over the next six months, the German stock portfolio decreases in value by 4% while the French portfolio increases in value by 2%; at the end of the six-month period, the CAC 40 futures price is 5,616 and the DAX 30 futures price is 11,793.5. What is the impact on Chausset's portfolio after the asset allocation adjustments in the example have been made?

Answer:

German portfolio:

Original holding falls in value by €320 million × –0.04 = –€12,800,000

DAX futures gain = (11,793.5 – 12,200) × €25 × –692 = €7,032,450

net loss = –€12,800,000 + €7,032,450 = –€5,767,550

If the portfolio had been reduced to €144,000,000 by physically selling stock, the loss would have been €144,000,000 × –0.04 = –€5,760,000.

imperfection in hedge = –€5,767,550 – (–€5,760,000) = –€7,550 (caused by rounding in the hedge ratio and the basis change on futures position)

French portfolio:

Original holding increases in value by €320 million × 0.02 = €6,400,000

CAC futures gain = (5,616 – 5,500) × €10 × 276 = €320,160

net gain = €6,400,000 + €320,160 = €6,720,160

If the portfolio had been increased to €336 million by buying stock, the gain would have been €336,000,000 × 2% = €6,720,000.

imperfection in hedge = €6,720,160 – €6,720,000 = €160

Using the data from Chausset's asset allocation example, assume that the French yield curve undergoes a parallel downward shift of 50 bp. What is the impact on Chausset's portfolio after the asset allocation adjustments have been made?

Answer:

original holding gain = –8.5 × –0.005 × €160,000,000 = €6,800,000

bond futures gain/(loss) = BPV_F × change in yield × number of futures contracts

$BPV_F = BPV_{CTD}$ / CF = €113.54 / 0.7768 = €146.16

bond futures gain/(loss) = €146.16 × 50 × 930 = €6,796,440

net position = €6,800,000 + €6,796,440 = €13,596,440

If the portfolio had been increased to €320,000,000 by buying physical OATs, the gain would have been –8.5 × –0.005 × €320,000,000 = €13,600,000.

EXAMPLE: Rebalancing asset allocation using futures

Josh Birmingham is the fund manager for a portfolio that has a target asset allocation of 70% equity and 30% government bonds. The portfolio increased in value from $200 million to $210 million over the previous month. The following table shows the portfolio's current position and what is needed to maintain the target allocations:

Equity	Current	Target	Change in Exposure
U.S. large cap	$140 million (66.67%)	$147 million (70%)	+$7 million
Fixed Income			
U.S. Treasury bonds	$70 million (33.33%)	$63 million (30%)	–$7 million
Total	$210 million	$210 million	
Equity portfolio beta = 0.8			
Fixed-income portfolio modified duration = 9.5			

Reading 7

Birmingham intends to use the following futures contracts to hedge his position:

S&P 500 futures		Classic U.S. Treasury futures	
Futures price	2,930	Futures price	$135.00
Multiplier	$250	Contract size	$100,000
Beta	1	CTD	$110.25
		CF	0.8140
		CTD modified duration	8.5

Determine the futures positions Birmingham will need to use to rebalance the asset allocation.

Answer:

Equity portfolio:

Aim: increase exposure by $7 million

$$\text{Number of futures required} = \left(\frac{\beta_T - \beta_P}{\beta_F}\right)\left(\frac{MV_P}{F}\right)$$

$$\text{Number of futures required} = \left(\frac{0.8 - 0}{1}\right)\left(\frac{\$7{,}000{,}000}{\$732{,}500}\right) = 7.65$$

$$= 8 \text{ futures contracts}$$

$F = 2{,}930 \times \$250 = \$732{,}500$

Birmingham will need to purchase 8 S&P 500 futures.

Fixed-income portfolio:

Aim: decrease exposure by $7 million

$$\text{BPVHR} = \frac{\text{BPV}_{\text{target}} - \text{BPV}_{\text{portfolio}}}{\text{BPV}_{\text{CTD}}} \times \text{CF}$$

$\text{BPV}_{\text{portfolio}} = \text{MD}_{\text{portfolio}} \times 0.0001 \times \text{MV}_{\text{portfolio}} = 9.5 \times 0.0001 \times \$7$ million = $6,650

$\text{BPV}_{\text{CTD}} = \text{MD}_{\text{CTD}} \times 0.0001 \times [\text{price} / 100 \times \text{contract size}] = 8.5 \times 0.0001 \times [(\$110.25 / 100) \times \$100{,}000] = \$93.71$

$$\text{BPVHR} = \frac{\$0 - \$6{,}650}{\$93.71} \times 0.8140 = -57.76 = -58 \text{ futures contracts}$$

Birmingham will need to sell 58 Treasury futures contracts.

Changing Allocations Between Asset Classes Using Swaps

EXAMPLE: Altering asset allocation using swaps

Akasuki Weber is a portfolio manager running the Cross Bright Helper fund. The fund has a current value of ¥21,580,000,000. The portfolio is currently invested in Japanese equity and bonds. Within the equity portion, the fund is split into exposures to both growth and value stocks. Within the fixed-income portion, the fund is split into exposures to government and corporate bonds.

Weber wants to alter the allocation between fixed income and equity and alter the allocation to the subfunds. The following table summarizes the changes she would like to make:

Stock	Current	Target	Change in Exposure
Value stock portfolio	¥9,063,600,000 (60%)	¥3,884,400,000 (30%)	–¥5,179,200,000
Growth stock portfolio	¥6,042,400,000 (40%)	¥9,063,600,000 (70%)	+¥3,021,200,000
Total equity	¥15,106,000,000 (70%)	¥12,948,000,000 (60%)	
Fixed income			
Government bonds	¥3,237,000,000 (50%)	¥5,179,200,000 (60%)	+¥1,942,200,000
Corporate bonds	¥3,237,000,000 (50%)	¥3,452,800,000 (40%)	+¥215,800,000
Total fixed income	¥6,474,000,000 (30%)	¥8,632,000,000 (40%)	
Total fund	¥21,580,000,000	¥21,580,000,000	

To avoid transaction costs involved in physical changes to the fund's asset allocation, Weber decides to use equity and fixed-income swaps. She has identified the following indexes, which have the closest characteristics with her existing subportfolios:

- MSCI Japan Value Index
- MSCI Japan Growth Index
- S&P Japanese Government Bond Index
- S&P Japanese Corporate Bond Index

Answer:

Swap 1: Pay return on MSCI Japan Value Index, receive floating reference rate (– dealers margin bp), based on a notional principal of ¥5,179,200,000

Swap 2: Pay reference rate (+ dealers margin bp), receive return on MSCI Japan Growth Index, based on a notional principal of ¥3,021,200,000

Swap 3: Pay reference rate (+ dealers margin bp), receive return on S&P Japanese Government Bond Index, based on a notional principal of ¥1,942,200,000

Swap 4: Pay reference rate (+ dealers margin bp), receive return on S&P Japanese Corporate Bond Index, based on a notional principal of ¥215,800,000

The equity and fixed-income indexes used in the swaps are unlikely to match the performance of Weber's subportfolios unless her subportfolios are passive trackers of these indexes. In addition, the index funds track total return (i.e., price and cash flow return on the index). Take swap 1 where Weber is paying the return on the MSCI Japan Value Index—Weber's value portfolio will not generate the price-change element of index return unless capital gains are realized by selling securities. Additionally, the dealer's margin on the floating rates will also need to be paid.

Inferring Market Expectations

Market expectations are current expectations derived from market prices. In the event of a market shock, market expectations can change rapidly.

Typical applications:

Application	Derivative
Inferring expectations of FOMC moves	Fed funds futures
Inferring expectations of inflation	CPI swaps
Inferring expectations of future volatility	VIX futures and options

Using Fed Funds Futures to Infer the Expected Average Federal Funds Rate

Market participants can use Fed funds futures to infer the expected probabilities of upcoming Fed interest rate changes. Some terms and definitions used in the analysis include the following:

- **Federal funds rate.** This is the interest rate that deposit institutions (banks and credit unions) charge other deposit institutions for loans in the overnight interbank markets. The federal funds effective (FFE) rate is the weighted average of interest rates charged on overnight interbank loans.
- **Federal funds target rate.** This is the rate set by governors of the Federal Reserve in Federal Open Market Committee (FOMC) meetings. The FOMC meets eight times a year to set the target rate based on current and forecasted macroeconomic variables. The most important considerations when setting the target rate are inflation rates and GDP growth rates. When market participants refer to the central bank (Fed) changing interest rates, it is typically this target rate they are referring to. The target rate is typically set as a range (e.g., 2.25%–2.50%).

Note that the Fed does not directly control the FFE rate, but it influences the rate through its monetary policy tools with the goal of keeping it within the target range. The monetary policy tools are open-market operations and the interest rate paid on bank reserves held at the Fed. Many central banks function in a similar fashion.

Fed fund futures are traded on the CME. The futures price reflects the market expectation of the FFE rate at the time of contract maturity. The Fed funds futures price will reflect market expectations about future changes in the Fed funds target rate. Fed fund futures can have monthly maturity dates as far out as 36 months.

To determine the probability of a change in the Fed funds target rate, use the following equation:

$$\text{percent probability of rate change} = \frac{\text{effective rate implied by futures} - \text{current Fed funds target rate}}{\text{Fed funds rate assuming a rate change} - \text{current Fed target funds rate}}$$

Note that this can be expressed as

$$\frac{\text{implied Fed funds effective rate} - \text{current target rate}}{\text{expected size of rate change}}$$

EXAMPLE: Determining the markets expectation of a target rate increase

Joe Stokes works at a bank where the interest received on loans made is linked to the FFE rate. Stokes has been asked to compute the likelihood that the FOMC will increase the rate by 25 bp at the next FOMC meeting.

Stokes has collected the following market data:

Fed funds future price*	98.1625
Current Fed funds target rate	1.50%–1.75%

*Nearest futures contract after the date of the next FOMC meeting

Calculate the following:

1. The expected average FFE rate at the futures contract maturity
2. The probability of a 25 bp increase in target rate at the next FOMC meeting

Answer:

1. Expected average FFE rate at contract expiration: 100 – 98.1625 = 1.8375%

Reading 7

2. Current target rate midpoint: $\dfrac{1.5\% + 1.75\%}{2} = 1.625\%$

Target rate assuming a 25 bp rise: $1.625\% + 0.25\% = 1.875\%$

$$\text{Percent probability of a rate change} = \frac{1.8375\% - 1.625\%}{1.875\% - 1.625\%}$$

$$= \frac{1.8375\% - 1.625\%}{0.25\%} = 0.85 = 85\%$$

MODULE QUIZ 7.5

1. Elise Schwarz manages a €400 million fund that invests in German and Spanish equities and government bond futures. Currently, her portfolio has a 60% exposure to equity and a 40% exposure to government securities. Schwarz believes that the monetary policy of the ECB will provide a significant stimulus to European equity markets and would like to increase her equity exposure to 70% of the portfolio's value.

   Additionally, the current portfolio is 50% invested in Spanish stocks and 50% in German stocks. Schwarz would like to change the proportions to 60% Spanish stocks and 40% German stocks. She also wishes to change the asset allocation of her fixed-income portfolio—which is currently 50% invested in German Bunds and 50% in Spanish Obligaciones del Estado—to 70% German government debt and 30% Spanish government debt.

   Her current portfolios have the following details:

	Beta		Modified Duration
Spanish equity	β = 1.2	Spanish fixed income	7.34
German equity	β = 0.9	German fixed income	10.25

   Elise intends to use futures to achieve her new asset allocation, to avoid transaction costs involved with liquidating positions, and reinvesting.

   Elise has gathered the following futures information:

Equity Futures	German	Spanish
Index	DAX 30	IBEX 35
Futures price	12,500	9,200
Multiplier	€25	€10
Futures beta	1	1

Government Bond Futures	German Bund	Spanish Obligaciones del Estado
Contract size	€100,000	€100,000
CTD price	€105.44	€149.94
CTD CF	0.6095	0.9628
CTD modified duration	9.67	8.26

Calculate and **describe** the future positions that would achieve Elise's new target asset allocation.

2. Stuart Zackaman has been announced as the new chair of the Federal Reserve. In his inaugural speech, he mentions that it is time that the United States stopped punishing savers to bail out irresponsible lenders.

   Joe Bear works at a bank where the interest paid on deposits is linked to the Fed funds rate. Bear observes that Zackaman's speech caused Fed funds futures prices to fall.

   Joe has collected the following market data:

Fed funds future price*	97.925
Current Fed funds target rate	1.75%–2.00%

   *Nearest futures contract after the date of the next FOMC meeting

   What is the probability of a 50 bp increase in target rate at the next FOMC meeting implied from the current Fed funds future price?

   A. 20%.
   B. 40%.
   C. 80%.

KEY CONCEPTS

LOS 7.a

- Interest rate swaps can be used to convert floating-rate assets (or liabilities) into fixed-rate assets (or liabilities).
- Interest rate swaps can be used to alter a fixed-income portfolio's duration.
  - Payer swaps (pay fixed) have negative durations.
  - Receiver swaps (receive fixed) have positive durations.
- To compute the notional principal of a swap to achieve a target duration, use the following equation:

$$NP_S = \left(\frac{MD_T - MD_P}{MD_S}\right)(MV_P)$$

  where:

  NP_S = notional swap principal

  MD_T = target modified duration

  MD_P = current portfolio modified duration

  MD_S = modified duration of swap

  MV_P = market value of portfolio

- Forward rate agreements (FRAs) are OTC forward contracts that can be used to hedge short-term future floating lending or borrowing requirements (i.e., lock into a fixed interest rate). FRAs can also be used to speculate on the direction of interest rates.
  - Long FRA = pay fixed and receive floating, from FRA expiry to the end of a notional borrowing or lending period.
  - Short FRA = pay floating and receive fixed, from FRA expiry to the end of a notional borrowing or lending period.
  - The price of an FRA is a forward rate of interest determined from spot rates.
  - Long FRA increases in value when interest rates rise.
  - Short FRA increases in value when interest rates fall.
- Short-term interest rate (STIR) futures are exchange traded and, therefore, benefit from liquidity and no credit risk. Like FRAs, STIR futures can be used to hedge short-term future interest rate risk and speculate on interest rate direction.
  - STIR futures use IMM price convention = 100 – annualized interest rates.
  - Long STIR futures will increase in value when rates fall.
  - Short STIR futures will increase in value when rates rise.

- The forward rate in the STIR future is the same forward rate in an FRA (assuming the same expiry and borrowing/lending periods).
- STIRs are typically more liquid than bond futures.
- Strips of STIRs are often used to hedge bonds with 2–3 years to maturity.

■ Government bond futures are used to hedge fixed-income portfolios when the constituent bonds have more than 2–3 years to maturity.
- Treasury bond futures prices are based on a notional bond (typically with a 6% coupon).
- Short party to the contract can deliver a range of eligible government bonds.
- One of the government bonds will be cheapest to deliver (CTD).
- The CTD bond has the highest repo rate or lowest basis.
- Futures price is based on the CTD price divided by the CTD conversion factor (CF).
- Each eligible bond has a CF.
- Proceeds to short on delivery = (FP at settlement × CF of bond delivered) + AI_T.

■ Hedging with Treasury futures is determined as follows:

$$\text{BPVHR} = \frac{\text{BPV}_{\text{target}} - \text{BPV}_{\text{portfolio}}}{\text{BPV}_{\text{CTD}}} \times \text{CF}$$

where:
BPV hedge ratio = BPVHR = number of futures required

BPV of target = $\text{BPV}_{\text{target}} = \text{MD}_{\text{target}} \times 0.0001 \times \text{MV}_{\text{portfolio}}$

BPV of portfolio = $\text{BPV}_{\text{portfolio}} = \text{MD}_{\text{portfolio}} \times 0.01\% \times \text{MV}_{\text{portfolio}}$

MD = modified duration

BPV of CTD = $\text{BPV}_{\text{CTD}} = \text{MD}_{\text{CTD}} \times 0.01\% \times \text{MV}_{\text{CTD}}$

market value of futures contract = MV_{CTD} = CTD price / 100 × \$100,000

To fully hedge a portfolio against interest rate risk, set $\text{BPV}_{\text{target}}$ to zero.

LOS 7.b

■ Currency risk is the change in value of assets and liabilities denominated in overseas currencies when converted to the domestic currency and is caused by exchange rate fluctuations.

■ Cross-currency swaps = synthetic overseas borrowing.
- Borrow in cheap currency (often but not exclusively domestic).
- Use a cross-currency swap to exchange domestic borrowing for overseas currency.
- Principal exchanged using the spot rate at initiation at the start and end of the swap's life.
- Counterparties pay the interest on the currency received at initiation.

  - The breakdown of covered interest rate parity means many currencies trade at a negative basis to the dollar.
  - Negative basis means the cost of synthetic $ borrowing > the cost of direct $ borrowing (i.e., lenders of the $ receive a premium).
  - Negative basis means that the $ lender will pay less than the overseas floating reference rate on their interest payments (i.e., overseas floating reference rate – basis).
  - Negative basis allows U.S. fixed-income managers to lend dollars via a swap, invest the foreign currency in a foreign bond market, and generate a higher return (due to the basis) than if they invested domestically.
- Currency forwards allow a participant to lock in a guaranteed exchange rate for converting a fixed amount of one currency into another at a future delivery date.
- Currency futures are exchange-traded currency forwards:

$$HR = \frac{\text{value of risk exposure}}{\text{futures contract size}}$$

LOS 7.c

- Equity swaps can be used to create synthetic exposures to equity market return.
- There are three main types of equity swaps:
  - Pay fixed, receive equity return.
  - Pay floating, receive equity return.
  - Pay one equity return, receive another equity return.
- Equity return may be based on:
  - A stock index.
  - A basket of stock.
  - A single stock.

  Return may be computed as price return or total return (including dividends).
- The equity payer in an equity swap pays the return if positive and receives the return if negative.
- Equity futures are available for most major stock market indexes.
- Benefits of equity futures include:
  - Low transaction costs.
  - Implementing tactical asset allocation without transactions in the physical securities.
    - Selling futures: reduces equity exposure.
    - Buying futures: increases equity exposure.
  - Diversification of portfolios.
  - Gain exposure to a different equity market.

- To achieve a target beta, use the following:

  $$\text{number of futures required} = \left(\frac{\beta_T - \beta_P}{\beta_F}\right)\left(\frac{MV_P}{F}\right)$$

  where:

  β_T = target portfolio beta

  β_P = current portfolio beta

  β_F = futures beta (beta of stock index)

  MV_P = market value of portfolio

  F = futures contract value = futures price × multiplier

  – To reduce equity exposure $\beta_T = 0$ MV_P = market value of exposure to reduce

  – To equitize a cash position $\beta_P = 0$ MV_P = cash value to invest

LOS 7.d

- VIX = volatility index (CBOE Volatility Index):
  – Measures implied volatility of the S&P 500 over a forward period of 30 days.
  – Implied volatility computed from call and put options on the index.
  – Volatility mean reverts over time.
  – Market participants cannot directly invest in VIX.
- VIX level and equity returns are negatively correlated.
- VIX futures:
  – Term structure of futures allows us to view the market's expectation of volatility for different contract maturities.
  – Typically, the market is in contango when implied 30-day forward volatility is low.
  – VIX futures can be used to offset tail risk in equity portfolios.
- Variance swap payoff = $(\sigma^2 - K^2) \times N_{VAR}$
- Based on realized vs. implied volatility over the swap's life:
  – N_{vega} = profit or loss for a 1% change in volatility
  – N_{VAR} = multiplier that converts $(\sigma^2 - K^2)$ into a payoff
  – K = implied volatility over the swap period
  – σ = realized volatility over the swap period
  – $\text{variance notional} = \dfrac{\text{vega notional}}{2 \times \text{strike price (K)}}$
- Variance swaps have convex payoffs with respect to volatility.
- Volatility options and futures have linear payoffs with respect to volatility.

- Convexity makes variance swaps more attractive for hedging tail risk because, as volatility rises and equity returns fall, the payoffs on variance swaps increase at an increasing rate.
- Mark-to-market valuation of a variance swap:

  Step 1: Compute expected variance at maturity (the time-weighted average of realized variance and implied variance over the remainder of the swap's life):

  $$\text{expected variance to maturity} = \left(\sigma_t^2 \times \frac{t}{T}\right) + \left(K_{(T-t)}^2 \times \frac{T-t}{T}\right)$$

  Step 2: Compute expected payoff at maturity:

  $$\text{variance swap payoff} = (\text{expected variance} - K^2) \times N_{VAR}$$

  Step 3: Discount expected payoff from maturity back to the valuation date.

LOS 7.e

- Use an equity swap to reduce equity exposure by entering into a pay total return equity swap receive fixed.
- Invest surplus cash by purchasing equity index futures.

LOS 7.f

- Probability of FOMC rate changes can be inferred from Fed funds futures:

  percent probability of rate change

  $$= \frac{\text{effective rate implied by futures} - \text{current Fed funds target rate}}{\text{Fed funds rate assuming a rate change} - \text{current Fed target funds rate}}$$

  Note that this can be expressed as

  $$\frac{\text{implied Fed funds effective rate} - \text{current target rate}}{\text{expected size of rate change}}$$

ANSWER KEY FOR MODULE QUIZZES

Module Quiz 7.1

1. **C** The variable leg cash flow on an interest rate swap is determined by the floating market reference rate (MRR) rate determined at the previous settlement date. Remember, the MRR is an add-on yield with payment in arrears. (LOS 7.a)

2. Type of swap:

Schwarz is receiving a variable reference rate base cash flows on the FRN he holds. To hedge his interest rate risk, Schwarz will want to swap the floating rate he receives on the FRN for a fixed rate on a swap. Schwarz will use a receiver swap with a notional principal of $4 million, in order to pay floating and receive fixed.

Swap cash flow at settlement date 1:

Fixed leg = 4% × 180 / 360 × $4 million = $80,000

Floating leg = 3.5% × 180 / 360 × $4 million = $70,000

Net receipt = $80,000 – $70,000 = $10,000

Swap cash flow at settlement date 2:

Fixed leg = 4% × 180 / 360 × $4 million = $80,000

Floating leg = 2.5% × 180 / 360 × $4 million = $50,000

Net receipt = $80,000 – $50,000 = $30,000

Net return settlement date 1:

Interest received on FRN = (3.5% + 40 bp) × 180 / 360 × $4 million = $78,000

Net receipt on swap = $10,000

Total cash received = $78,000 + $10,000 = $88,000

$ return = $88,000 / $4,000,000 = 2.2%, annualized = 4.4%

Net return settlement date 2:

Interest received on FRN = (2.5% + 40 bp) × 180 / 360 × $4 million = $58,000

Net receipt on swap = $30,000

Total cash received = $58,000 + $30,000 = $88,000

$ return = $88,000 / $4,000,000 = 2.2%, annualized = 4.4%

Schwarz's annualized return is 4.4%, equal to the 4% rate on the swap and the 40 bp cost on the FRN. (LOS 7.a)

3. **A** $BPV_{target} = 8 \times 0.0001 \times \$200 \text{ million} = \$160{,}000$

$BPV_{portfolio} = 12 \times 0.0001 \times \$200 \text{ million} = \$240{,}000$

$BPV_{CTD} = 14.54 \times 0.0001 \times [(\$126.39 / 100) \times \$100{,}000] = \$183.77$

$$BPVHR = \frac{BPV_{target} - BPV_{portfolio}}{BPV_{CTD}} \times CF$$

$$= \frac{\$160{,}000 - \$240{,}000}{\$183.77} \times 0.7689 = -334.72 = -335$$

(LOS 7.a)

Module Quiz 7.2

1. **B** If the NZD is trading at a positive cross-currency basis to the USD, New Zealand investors can earn superior returns by lending NZD via a currency swap and investing in U.S. government bonds. There is an additional return because the interest rate on lending NZD is higher than the rate suggested by covered interest rate parity (CIRP). Note that when the NZD has positive basis against the USD and the GBP has negative basis to the USD, then the GBP must have negative basis against the NZD. Most currencies trade at a negative cross-currency basis to the USD, due to high demand for USD funds versus a shortage of supply and a failure of CIRP. The positive basis on NZD and AUD (Australian dollar) has led organizations such as the World Bank to issue bonds in NZD and AUD and swap back to USD, reducing borrowing costs compared to borrowing directly in USD. (LOS 7.b)

2. $$\text{Number of contracts needed to hedge} = \frac{€20{,}000{,}000}{€125{,}000} = 160 \text{ contracts}$$

Wood is converting from the price currency to the base currency and, therefore, will need to buy futures.

Unhedged position:

Cost at current exchange rate = €20,000,000 × 0.8929 = £17,858,000

Unhedged position in 30 days = €20,000,000 × 0.9034 = £18,068,000

Cost of euro strengthening = £18,068,000 – £17,858,000 = £210,000

Hedged position:

Cost of euro strengthening = £18,068,000 – £17,858,000 = £210,000

Profit on hedge = (£0.9054 – £0.8989) × €20,000,000 = £130,000

Note that when Barney enters the contract, he is agreeing to buy euros at £0.8989, and when he closes out, he is agreeing to sell euros at £0.9054.

Net position = £130,000 – £210,000 = loss £80,000

This loss on the hedge is the result of the change in basis:

	Spot	Future	Basis
At initiation £/€	0.8929	0.8989	0.006 or 60 pips
At close	0.9034	0.9054	0.002 or 20 pips

Change in pips = 60 to 20 = −40

−40 pips ÷ 10,000 × €20,000,000 = −£80,000

(LOS 7.b)

3. **Exchange of principal at initiation of swap:**

£30 million × $1.2/£ = $36 million

ABC Robotics, Inc., borrows $36 million domestically and uses the currency swap to exchange $36 million for £30 million.

At the first settlement date:

Pays:

£ interest on swap = £30 million × (1.5% – 0.15%) × 180 / 360 = £202,500

$ interest on loan = $36 million × (2.5% + 0.4%) × 180 / 360 = $522,000

Receives:

$ interest on swap = $36 million × 2.5% × 180 / 360 = $450,000

Total net payments:

£ interest on swap = £202,500

$ difference between the loan and swap = $522,000 – $450,000 = $72,000, which represents the 40 bp on the U.S. loan ($36 million × 0.4% × 180 / 360 = $72,000)

Direct £ borrowing cost = £30 million × (1.5% + 0.5%) × 180 / 360 = £300,000 (pound reference rate + 50 bp)

Cost of synthetic borrowing = £30 million × (1.5% + 0.4% – 0.15%) × 180 / 360 = £262,500 (pound reference rate + 25 bp)

Benefit of swap = £300,0000 – £262,500 = £37,500

Benefit of swap = (0.5% – 0.25%) × 180 / 360 = £37,500

At the second settlement date:

Pays:

£ interest on the swap = £30 million × (1% – 0.15%) × 180 / 360 = £127,500

$ interest on loan = $36 million × (2.25% + 0.4%) × 180 / 360 = $477,000

Receives:

$ interest on the swap = $36 million × 2.25% × 180 / 360 = $405,000

Total net payments:

£ interest on swap = £127,500

$ difference on loan and swap = $477,000 – $405,000 = $72,000, which represents the 40 bp on the U.S. loan ($36 million × 0.4% × 180 / 360 = $72,000)

Direct £ borrowing cost = £30 million × (1% + 0.5%) × 180 / 360 = £225,000 (pound reference rate + 50 bp)

Cost of synthetic borrowing = £30 million × (1% + 0.4% – 0.15%) × 180 / 360 = £187,500 (pound reference rate + 25 bp)

Benefit of swap = £225,000 – £187,500 = £37,500

Benefit of swap = (0.5% – 0.25%) × 180 / 360 = £37,500

Conclusion:

By borrowing in dollars and entering a currency swap, ABC Robotics has locked into a cost of the pound reference rate + 25 bp for their USD borrowing, reflecting the 40 bp spread above the U.S. dollar reference rate on the loan less the 15 bp received on the swap. (LOS 7.b)

Module Quiz 7.3

1. **A**

$$\text{Number of futures required} = \left(\frac{\beta_T - \beta_P}{\beta_F}\right)\left(\frac{MV_P}{F}\right)$$

$$\text{Number of futures required} = \left(\frac{1.4 - 0.8}{1}\right)\left(\frac{£20{,}000{,}000}{£74{,}250}\right) = 161.62$$

$$= 162 \text{ futures contracts}$$

Futures contract value = 7,425 × £10 = $74,250

(LOS 7.c)

2. **A** Cash element of fund = ¥4,350,000,000 × 5% = ¥217,500,000

$$\text{Number of futures required} = \left(\frac{\beta_T - \beta_P}{\beta_F}\right)\left(\frac{MV_P}{F}\right)$$

$$\text{Number of futures required} = \left(\frac{1-0}{1}\right)\left(\frac{¥217{,}500{,}000}{¥21{,}624{,}000}\right) = 10.06$$

$$= 10 \text{ futures contracts}$$

β_T = 1 (the beta of the future equals the beta of the index)

β_P = 0 (the beta of a cash position always equals zero)

Futures contract value = 21,624 × ¥1,000 = ¥21,624,000

(LOS 7.c)

Module Quiz 7.4

1. **B** VIX is a measure of expected volatility of the S&P 500 Index over the forthcoming 30 days. It is an annualized implied volatility calculation using an option-pricing model and the price of call and put options trading in the market. It suggests +/– range for the percentage change in the S&P 500, with a 68% level of confidence.

   Empirically, VIX and equity market performance is negatively correlated (i.e., when volatility spikes upward, equity returns fall dramatically). The convexity of variance swaps relative to volatility makes their returns attractive when volatility is rising and equity markets are falling. (LOS 7.d)

2. **B** The payoff on a variance swap can be calculated as notional variance × ($\sigma^2 - K^2$). Using notional vega, we must additionally divide by 2 times the strike price (implied volatility), K:

$$\text{payoff} = N_{vega} \times \left(\frac{\sigma^2 - K^2}{2K}\right)$$

   (LOS 7.d)

3. *Step 1*: Compute the expected variance at maturity as the time-weighted average of realized and implied volatility:

$$\text{expected variance at maturity} = \left(\sigma_t^2 \times \frac{t}{T}\right) + \left(K_{(T-t)}^2 \times \frac{T-t}{T}\right)$$

$$\text{expected variance at maturity} = \left(28^2 \times \frac{3}{12}\right) + \left(32^2 \times \frac{9}{12}\right) = 964$$

Step 2: Compute the expected payoff at maturity:

$$\text{variance notional} = \frac{\text{vega notional}}{2 \times K} = \frac{€150{,}000}{2 \times 15} = €5{,}000$$

$$K^2 = 15^2 = 225$$

$$\text{expected payoff at maturity} = (\sigma^2 - K^2) \times \text{variance notional}$$

$$\text{expected payoff at maturity} = (964 - 225) \times €5{,}000 = €3{,}695{,}000$$

Step 3: Discount expected payoff from maturity to valuation date (9 months):

$$\text{unannualize the interest rate} = 0.6\% \times \frac{9}{12} = 0.45\%$$

$$\text{current value of swap (purchaser)} = \frac{€3{,}695{,}000}{1.0045} = €3{,}678{,}447$$

This is the gain to the purchaser of the variance swap. Quark Dealers is a seller and, therefore, this is a loss. Note that this illustrates the risk of shorting variance. When volatility suddenly spikes upward, the losses increase at an accelerating rate. (LOS 7.d)

Module Quiz 7.5

1. *Step 1*: Set out current, target, and changes to asset allocations in percentages and monetary value.

Summary	Original	New	Change in Exposure
Equity	**€240 million (60%)**	**€280 million (70%)**	
German stocks	€120 million = 50%	€112 million = 40%	Decrease €8 million
Spanish stocks	€120 million = 50%	€168 million = 60%	Increase €48 million
Fixed Income	€160 million (40%)	€120 million (30%)	
German Bunds	€80 million = 50%	€84 million = 70%	Increase €4 million
Spanish Obligaciones del Estado	€80 million = 50%	€36 million = 30%	Decrease €44 million

Step 2: Compute each futures position.

German equity:

$$\text{Number of futures required} = \left(\frac{\beta_T - \beta_P}{\beta_F}\right)\left(\frac{MV_P}{F}\right)$$

β_T = target beta = 0 (the target beta is set to zero because we are reducing our exposure to German stock)

β_p = portfolio beta = 0.9

β_F = futures beta (i.e., beta of the index)

MV_P = reduction in portfolio size = €8 million

F = futures price × multiplier = 12,500 × €25 = €312,500

$$\text{Number of futures required} = \left(\frac{0 - 0.9}{1}\right)\left(\frac{€8{,}000{,}000}{€312{,}500}\right)$$

$$= -23.04 = -23 \text{ futures contracts}$$

Spanish equity:

β_T = target beta = 1.2 (the target beta is set to the beta of the existing portfolio)

β_p = portfolio beta = 0

β_F = futures beta (i.e., beta of the index)

MV_P = increase in portfolio size = €48 million

F = futures price × multiplier = 9,200 × €10 = €92,000

$$\text{Number of futures required} = \left(\frac{1.2 - 0}{1}\right)\left(\frac{€48{,}000{,}000}{€92{,}000}\right)$$

$$= 626.09 = 626 \text{ futures contracts}$$

German fixed income:

$$\text{BPVHR} = \frac{\text{BPV}_{\text{target}} - \text{BPV}_{\text{portfolio}}}{\text{BPV}_{\text{CTD}}} \times \text{CF}$$

$\text{BPV}_{\text{target}} = \text{MD}_{\text{portfolio}} \times 0.0001 \times \text{MV}_{\text{portfolio}} = 10.25 \times 0.0001 \times €4{,}000{,}000 = €4{,}100$

$\text{BPV}_{\text{CTD}} = \text{MD}_{\text{CTD}} \times 0.0001 \times [\text{price} / 100 \times \text{contract size}] = 9.67 \times 0.0001 \times [(€105.44 / 100) \times €100{,}000] = €101.96$

$$\text{BPVHR} = \frac{€4{,}100 - €0}{€101.96} \times 0.6095 = 24.51 = 25 \text{ futures contracts}$$

Spanish fixed income:

$$\text{BPVHR} = \frac{\text{BPV}_{\text{target}} - \text{BPV}_{\text{portfolio}}}{\text{BPV}_{\text{CTD}}} \times \text{CF}$$

$\text{BPV}_{\text{portfolio}} = \text{MD}_{\text{portfolio}} \times 0.0001 \times \text{MV}_{\text{portfolio}} = 7.34 \times 0.0001 \times €44{,}000{,}000 = €32{,}296$

$\text{BPV}_{\text{CTD}} = \text{MD}_{\text{CTD}} \times 0.0001 \times [\text{price} / 100 \times \text{contract size}] = 8.26 \times 0.0001 \times [(€149.94 / 100) \times €100{,}000] = €123.85$

$$\text{BPVHR} = \frac{€32{,}296}{€123.85} \times 0.9628 = -251.07 = -251 \text{ futures contracts}$$

Summary of Futures Positions	
German DAX 30 futures	Sell 23 futures
Spanish IBEX 35 futures	Buy 626 futures
German Bund futures	Buy 25 contracts
Spanish Obligaciones del Estado futures	Sell 251

(LOS 7.f)

2. **B** Expected average effective rate at contract expiration = 100 – 97.925 = 2.075%

Current target rate midpoint = $\frac{1.75\% + 2.00\%}{2}$ =1.875%

Target rate assuming a 50 bp rise = 1.875% + 0.50% =2.375%

$$\text{Percent probability of a rate change} = \frac{2.075\% - 1.875\%}{2.375\% - 1.875\%} = \frac{2.075\% - 1.875\%}{0.50\%}$$

$$= 0.4 = 40\%$$

(LOS 7.f)

READING 8

Currency Management: An Introduction

EXAM FOCUS

Globalization of financial markets is an important topic in portfolio management and for the CFA exam. This section reviews currency math and then discusses an extensive list of currency management tools and techniques.

MODULE 8.1: MANAGING CURRENCY EXPOSURE

Video covering this content is available online.

Introduction

PROFESSOR'S NOTE

Good technique always matters but particularly with currency. This material emphasizes (1) thinking of a currency quote as a base currency in the denominator and a pricing currency in the numerator, and (2) being prepared to interpret a currency quote from the perspective of either the base or pricing currency.

The Price and Base Currencies: The **base currency** is the denominator of the exchange rate and it is **priced** in terms of the numerator. Unless clearly identified otherwise, the terms "buy" and "sell" refer to the base currency. But remember, there are two currencies involved. For example, sell spot 1,000,000 at CAD/USD 0.9800 is assumed to mean sell for "immediate delivery" 1,000,000 U.S. dollars and buy 980,000 Canadian dollars. (The convention is settlement in two business days but this detail is ignored in most cases; the FX swap is an exception where the two business days are considered).

Buy 500,000 USD/CHF six months forward at 1.07 is assumed to mean buy 500,000 Swiss francs, settling in six months versus sell USD 535,000.

Bid/Asked Rules: Currencies are quoted with a **bid/offered** or **bid/asked price**. By convention, the smaller number is written first and the larger number is second. However, both the bid and the asked can be interpreted as the sale of one currency versus the purchase of the other currency. The difference is the dealer's profit margin to buy or sell the currencies. The customer pays the bid/ask spread, paying more and/or receiving less in the transaction. A quote of 0.9790/0.9810 CAD/USD has four interpretations.

Deliver more CAD can be phrased as:

- Buy 1.0000 USD and deliver (sell) 0.9810 CAD.
- Sell 0.9810 CAD and receive (buy) 1.0000 USD.

Receive less CAD can be phrased as:

- Sell 1.0000 USD and receive (buy) 0.9790 CAD.
- Buy 0.9790 CAD and deliver (sell) 1.0000 USD.

Spot Versus Forward: Spot exchange transactions are for immediate settlement and a **forward transaction** is a price agreed to on a transaction date for delayed (longer than spot) settlement. The forward quote can be given directly or in forward points (an adjustment from the spot quote).

Forward points are an adjustment to the spot price to determine the forward price. The points are interpreted based on the number of decimal places in which the spot price is quoted. The rule is to move the decimal in the points to the left by the same number of decimal places shown in the right for the spot price. For example:

Spot Quote	Forward Points	Points with Decimal Adjusted	Forward Price
1.33	1.1	1.1 / 100 = 0.011	1.33 + 0.011 = 1.341
2.554	–9.6	–9.6 / 1,000 = –0.0096	2.554 – 0.0096 = 2.5444
0.7654	13.67	13.67 / 10,000 = 0.001367	0.7654 + 0.001367 = 0.766767

There is a myth that the forward points are always divided by 10,000. That is only true if the spot quote is given to four decimal places. To continue the pattern, if the spot quote shows five decimals on the right, move the forward point decimal five places to the left (i.e., forward points / 100,000).

EXAMPLE: Spot and forward bid/asked quotes of the Australian dollar/euro

Maturity/Settlement	Spot Quote/Forward Points
Spot AUD/EUR	1.2571/ 1.2574
30 days	–1.0/–0.9
90 days	+11.7/+12.0

1. What is the 30 day forward bid/offered quote?
2. If a manager sells 1,000,000 AUD forward 90 days, **calculate** what the manager will deliver and receive. When will the exchange take place?

Answer:

1. The spot quote is given to four decimal places making the forward points for 30 days: –1.0 / 10,000 = –0.00010 and –0.9 / 10,000 = –0.00009, a four decimal place adjustment to match the spot quote. The 30-day forward bid/asked are: 1.2571 – 0.00010 = 1.25700 and 1.2574 – 0.00009 = 1.25731.
2. The exchange will be 90 days from the trade date, at contract expiration. The manager will deliver AUD 1,000,000.

   The 90-day forward quotes are 1.2571 + 0.00117 by 1.2574 + 0.00120, which is 1.25827/1.25860 for the AUD/EUR. The manager is delivering AUD and receiving EUR. The manager must deliver more AUD or receive fewer EUR. In this case, the bid/asked quotes are both for 1 EUR and the manager will deliver AUD.

   The manager must deliver at AUD/EUR 1.25860. The manager will receive EUR: AUD 1,000,000 / (1.25860 AUD/EUR) = EUR 794,533.61.

Offsetting Transactions and Mark to Market: While forward contracts do not require market to market cash flow exchanges prior to settlement, it is often desirable or required for regulatory purposes to mark the position to market value. The mark-to-market value is the present value of any gain or loss that would be realized if the contract were closed early with an offsetting contract position.

EXAMPLE: Offsetting transactions

Based on the initial quotes given in the previous example, a different manager entered into a trade to sell (deliver) 90 days forward, EUR 10,000,000 at the "all-in" forward quote of AUD/EUR 1.25827. Thirty days have passed and exchange rates are now the following:

Maturity/Settlement	Spot Quote/Forward Points	Market Reference Rates AUD
Spot AUD/EUR	1.3189/1.3191	
30 days	+1.1/+1.2	1.10%
60 days	+10.3/+10.5	1.20%
90 days	+15.3/+16.1	1.25%

1. **Identify** the offsetting position the manager would take to close the initial transaction and **calculate** the resulting gain or loss. When will this gain or loss be settled?
2. **Calculate** the mark to market the manager would report on day 30 of the original trade if the trade were not closed out early.

Answers:

1. Thirty days have passed and the initial trade to sell EUR 10,000,000 forward has 60 days until expiration. The offsetting transaction is to buy 10,000,000 EUR 60 days forward. The solution is done in steps.

Step 1: Thirty days have passed and the initial trade to sell EUR 10,000,000 forward has 60 days until expiration. The offsetting transaction is to buy 10,000,000 EUR 60 days forward. The solution is done in steps. Identify the forward exchange rate for the offsetting position. The manager must buy EUR 10,000,000 (which requires delivering AUD) 60 days forward at AUD/EUR 1.3191 + 0.00105, which is AUD/EUR 1.32015.

Step 2: In 60 days, the manager will do the following:

- On the original trade: sell EUR 10,000,000 and buy AUD at AUD/EUR 1.25827. The manager will receive AUD 12,582,700.
- On the offsetting trade: buy EUR 10,000,000 and sell AUD at AUD/EUR 1.32015. The manager will pay AUD 13,201,500.

The difference, a loss of AUD 618,800, will be settled and paid 90 days after the initial transaction and 60 days after the offsetting transaction.

Alternatively, this can be solved directly. The base currency (euro) is sold at 1.25827 AUD and then bought at 1.32015 AUD for a loss of 1.32015 – 1.25827 = 0.06188 AUD per euro. On the trade of 10,000,000 euros, this is a loss of AUD 618,800.

2. The current mark to market is the present value of the gain or loss that would be locked in with an offsetting transaction. That offsetting loss was calculated in Solution 1 as AUD 618,800. The 60-day market reference rate on the AUD is 1.20%.

   Mark-to-market loss = AUD 618,800 / {1 + [0.012 (60 / 360)]} = AUD 617,564.87

An FX Swap: The FX swap is not a currency swap or even a swap as that term is otherwise used. The FX swap rolls over a maturing forward contract using a spot transaction into a new forward contract. An existing forward is "swapped" for another forward transaction.

EXAMPLE: An FX swap

A manager purchased 10,000,000 South African rand (ZAR) three months forward at ZAR/USD 9.4518.

Two days before contract expiration the manager decides to extend the transaction for another 30 days. **Explain** the FX swap used to implement this decision.

Answer:

The manager sells spot ZAR 10,000,000 to offset the maturing contract. Both the initial forward and offsetting spot transaction will settle in two business days. The manager enters a new 30-day forward contract to buy ZAR 10,000,000 versus the USD to rollover the trade.

Option Basics: A call option is a right to buy the underlying and gains value as the underlying rises above the strike price; its delta approaches 1.00 (a 100-delta). The call loses value as the underlying falls below the strike price and its delta approaches 0.00 (a 0-delta).

A put is the right to sell the underlying and gains value as the underlying falls below the strike price; its delta approaches –1.00 (this can also be referred to as a 100-delta, the negative sign is assumed and not written). The put loses value as the underlying rises above the strike price and the delta approaches 0.00 (a 0-delta).

For a call and a put with identical parameters (time to expiration, strike price, and price of the underlying), the sum of the absolute deltas is 1.00 or 100-delta.

Currency Option Basics: Currency options require two currencies and a call on one currency is a put on the other currency. Unless otherwise specified, the option is from the base currency perspective. For example, a call option to buy 10,000,000 at a strike price of ZAR/GBP 14.56 is the right to buy 10,000,000 British pounds and sell 145,600,000 South African rand. It is also a put option—the right to sell 145,600,000 South African rand and buy 10,000,000 British pounds.

A put option to sell 100,000 at MXN/EUR at 20.1 is the right to sell 100,000 euros and buy 2,010,000 Mexican pesos. It is also a call option to buy 2,010,000 Mexican pesos and sell 100,000 euros.

The important relationships can be summarized as follows:

As the Price of the Base Currency Increases:	The Call Option to Buy the Base Currency:	The Put Option to Sell the Base Currency:
From 0 to the strike price	Is out-of-the-money and rising in value. Delta is shifting from 0.0 toward 0.5 (from a 0-delta to a 50-delta).	Is in-the-money and falling in value. Delta is shifting from –1.0 toward –0.5 (from a 100-delta to a 50-delta).
To the strike price	Is at-the-money. Delta is approximately 0.5 (a 50-delta).	Is at-the-money. Delta is approximately –0.5 (a 50-delta).
From the strike price upward	Is in-the-money and rising in value. Delta is shifting from 0.5 toward 1.0 (from a 50-delta to a 100-delta).	Is out-of-the-money and falling in value. Delta is shifting from –0.5 toward 0.0 (from a 50-delta to a 0-delta).

Reading 8

Effects of Currency on Portfolio Risk and Return

Domestic currency or **home currency** is the currency of the investor (or the currency in which portfolio results are reported and analyzed).

Domestic asset is an asset denominated in the investor's domestic currency.

Foreign currency and **foreign asset** are a currency other that the investor's domestic currency and an asset denominated in that foreign currency. These are sometimes called the local currency and local market, respectively.

Foreign-currency return (R_{FC}) is the return of the foreign asset measured in its local (foreign) currency. It can be called the local market return.

The **percentage change in value of the foreign currency** is denoted as R_{FX}. It can be called the local currency return.

Domestic-currency return (R_{DC}) is the return in domestic currency units considering both the foreign-currency return (R_{FC}) and the percentage change in value of the foreign currency (R_{FX}).

LOS 8.a: Analyze the effects of currency movements on portfolio risk and return.

An investment in assets priced in a currency other than the investor's domestic currency (a *foreign asset* priced in a *foreign currency*) has two sources of risk and return: (1) the return on the assets in the foreign currency and (2) the return on the foreign currency from any change in its exchange rate with the investor's *domestic currency*. These returns are multiplicative and an investor's returns in domestic currency can be calculated as:

Equation 1: $R_{DC} = (1 + R_{FC})(1 + R_{FX}) - 1 = R_{FC} + R_{FX} + (R_{FC})(R_{FX})$

$$R_{DC} \approx R_{FC} + R_{FX}$$

PROFESSOR'S NOTE

There are three ways to calculate R_{DC} that you will see and are responsible for. The choice of approach is dictated by the case facts and question.

- $R_{DC} \approx R_{FC} + R_{FX}$: This approach is an approximation of the more accurate compounded calculation. It emphasizes the two sources of return, R_{FC} and R_{FX}. It is acceptable when precision is not needed, such as selecting between three quite different multiple choice answers or discussing the theoretical sources of return.
- $R_{DC} = (1 + R_{FC})(1 + R_{FX}) - 1 = R_{FC} + R_{FX} + (R_{FC})(R_{FX})$: This approach is precise if the precise R_{FX} is known. I would generally use this approach, unless given clear reasons to do something else.
- However, there are cases where determining R_{FX} is not simple. If the currency is hedged, then a precise currency hedge must short the ending number of foreign currency units; however, that ending number is not knowable for a risky asset. You will see a naïve hedge is normally used and the beginning number of foreign currency units are sold forward. In that case, a simple comparison of F_0 and S_0 will not be the true R_{FX}. In that case, you will see a different set of calculations made. You would directly calculate beginning and ending value of the portfolio in the investor's domestic currency units. Then R_{DC} is (EV – BV) / BV.

EXAMPLE: Calculating domestic currency returns

Consider a USD-based investor who invests in a portfolio of stocks that trade in euros. Over a one-year holding period, the value of the portfolio increases by 5% (in euros) and the euro-dollar exchange rate increases from 1.300 USD/EUR to 1.339 USD/EUR.

The EUR has appreciated with respect to the USD, so the investor has positive returns from foreign exchange of:

R_{FX} = 1.339 / 1.300 – 1 = 0.03 = 3%.

The investor's return in domestic currency terms over the one-year holding period is:

R_{DC} = (1.05 × 1.03) – 1 = 0.05 + 0.03 + (0.05)(0.03) = 0.0815 = 8.15%

$R_{DC} \approx R_{FC} + R_{FX}$ = 5 + 3 = 8%

This example illustrates two important points. First, simply adding R_{FC} and R_{FX} (5% + 3% = 8%) yields an approximation of the domestic currency return. The approximation is closer to the actual return the smaller the values of the two sources of return.

Second, the exchange rate quotes must use the foreign currency (EUR) as the base currency (the denominator) to calculate the change in value of the currency (R_{FX}). To see why, consider what happens if the domestic currency (USD) had been the base currency.

FX Quotes	Foreign Currency as the Base Currency	1/X for Domestic Currency as the Base Currency
Beginning value	USD/EUR 1.300	EUR/USD 0.76923
Ending value	USD/EUR 1.339	EUR/USD 0.74683

0.74683/0.76923 – 1 = –0.02912 = –2.912%, which is depreciation of the USD relative to the EUR. The appreciation of the EUR is not simply the negative of the depreciation in the USD. R_{FX} is 3.000%, not 2.912%.

PROFESSOR'S NOTE

The message is to be careful when working with currency. Read the question and determine which is the foreign versus domestic currency. Label the numbers to determine if you are looking at domestic/foreign or foreign/domestic. Always use domestic/foreign (taking reciprocals if needed) and then solve as $EV / BV - 1 = R_{FX}$.

Calculating Portfolio Return for Multiple Investments in Foreign Assets

An investor may invest in multiple markets with different currencies. In that case, the domestic portfolio return is a weighted average of the domestic currency returns for each investment. Formally, we have the following.

Equation 2: $R_{DC} = \sum_{i=1}^{n} w_i \left(R_{DC,i} \right)$

where:

w_i = the proportion (in domestic currency terms) of the portfolio invested in assets traded in currency *i*

$R_{DC,i}$ = the domestic currency return for asset *i*

The following example illustrates this calculation.

EXAMPLE: Domestic currency returns on an investment in two foreign markets

A euro-based investor has a 75% position in GBP denominated assets and a 25% position in USD denominated assets. The results for the past year are the following.

R_{FC} for the GBP assets = 12%

R_{FC} for the USD assets = 5%

Beginning EUR/GBP exchange rate: 1.1666

Ending EUR/GBP exchange rate: 1.1437

Beginning USD/EUR exchange rate: 1.332

Ending USD/EUR exchange rate: 1.324

Calculate the investor's return over the period in domestic (EUR) currency terms.

Answer:

First, calculate the R_{DC} (in EUR) for each investment.

For the investment denominated in GBP, we have:

$$R_{DC} = 1.12 \times (1.1437 / 1.1666) - 1 = (1.1200 \times 0.9804) - 1 = 9.80\%.$$

The foreign currency (GBP) has depreciated approximately 2% relative to the euro. The negative currency return reduces the 12% return of the foreign market.

For the investment denominated in USD, the exchange rates were given with the foreign currency (USD) in the numerator. These can be inverted to make the investor's currency (the euro) the price currency and the foreign currency (USD) the base currency.

1 / 1.332 = 0.7508 EUR/USD
1 / 1.324 = 0.7553 EUR/USD

> Allowing the investment denominated in USD R_{DC} (in EUR) to be calculated as:
>
> $R_{DC} = [1.05 \times (0.7553 / 0.7508)] - 1 = (1.0500 \times 1.0060) - 1 = 5.63\%$
>
> The foreign currency (USD) has appreciated approximately 0.6% relative to the euro. The positive currency return increases the 5% return of the foreign market.
>
> The investor's total portfolio return is the weighted average of the R_{DC} for each market:
>
> $(0.75 \times 9.80\%) + (0.25 \times 5.63\%) = 7.35 + 1.41 = 8.76\%$

Risk

An investor investing in a foreign denominated asset has two sources of risk: the fluctuation of the foreign currency and the fluctuation in foreign currency price of the foreign asset. Both will affect the standard deviation of R_{DC}.

The variance of R_{DC} can be calculated using a variation of the basic formula for variance of a two asset portfolio:

$$\sigma^2(R_{DC}) \approx w^2(R_{FC})\sigma^2(R_{FC}) + w^2(R_{FX})\sigma^2(R_{FX}) + 2w(R_{FC})w(R_{FX})\sigma(R_{FC})\sigma(R_{FX})\rho(R_{FC},R_{FX})$$

where:
ρ = the correlation between R_{FC} and R_{FX}

However, this basic two asset variance formula can be simplified when a domestic investor holds a single foreign currency denominated asset. The exposures (weights) to R_{FC} and R_{FX} are each 100% with the weights in the formula expressed as 1.0. The formula becomes:

Equation 3: $\sigma^2(R_{DC}) \approx \sigma^2(R_{FC}) + \sigma^2(R_{FX}) + 2\sigma(R_{FC})\sigma(R_{FX})\rho(R_{FC},R_{FX})$

The standard deviation of R_{DC} is the square root of this variance. Examining the equation indicates risk to our domestic investor:

- Depends on the standard deviation of R_{FC} and R_{FX}.
- May be higher for our domestic investor because standard deviation of R_{FX} is an additive term in the equation.
- However, correlation also matters. If the correlation between R_{FC} and R_{FX} is negative, the third component of the calculation becomes negative. The correlation measures the interaction of R_{FC} and R_{FX}.
  - If the correlation is positive, then R_{FC} returns are amplified by R_{FX} returns, increasing the volatility of return to our domestic investor.
  - If the correlation is negative, then R_{FC} returns are dampened by R_{FX} returns, decreasing the volatility of return to our domestic investor. (This is discussed further under this reading's topic of minimum variance hedge ratio).

Reading 8

PROFESSOR'S NOTE

The variance formula in Equation 3 is only an approximation but appropriate. It is based on the simple addition of R_{FC} and R_{FX} and ignores the cross product of $(R_{FC})(R_{FX})$. The use of an approximate variance formula relates to the number of correlations that would be required for true variance. Consider a portfolio of two foreign assets that has four variables, two foreign assets, and two foreign currencies resulting in six correlation pairs. With three foreign assets, there are six variables resulting in a total of 15 correlation pairs. A precise variance calculation would require accurately estimating all possible correlation pairs. That is considered unrealistic and the exact formula would create a false impression of precision. The approximation method is used for the CFA text. A special case is discussed in the following. Think of this special case as risk depends on end of period exposure to the foreign asset.

If R_{FC} is a Risk-Free Return: In this case, its standard deviation and correlation with R_{FX} are zero. When R_{FX} is the only source of risk for the domestic investor in the foreign asset, a direct and precise calculation of the standard deviation of R_{DC} is practical.

Equation 4: $\sigma(R_{DC}) = \sigma(R_{FX})(1 + R_{FC})$

where:
R_{FC} = the return on a foreign currency denominated risk-free asset

PROFESSOR'S NOTE

Equation 4 is a special case when the foreign asset (R_{FC}) is a risk-free asset and cannot be derived from equation 3.

Strategic Decisions

LOS 8.b: Discuss strategic choices in currency management.

PROFESSOR'S NOTE

This is a lengthy discussion of factors to consider. The next LOS summarizes the conclusions.

Neither academic nor empirical analysis support firm conclusions on currency risk management. Opinions range from doing nothing to active management.

- Arguments made for not hedging currency risk include:
  - It is best to avoid the time and cost of hedging or trading currencies.
  - In the long-run, unhedged currency effects are a "zero-sum game;" if one currency appreciates, another must depreciate.
  - In the long-run, currencies revert to a theoretical fair value.

- The argument for active management of currency risk is that, in the short run, currency movement can be extreme, and inefficient pricing of currencies can be exploited to add to portfolio return. Many foreign exchange (FX) trades are dictated by international trade transactions or central bank policies. These are not motivated by consideration of fair value and may drive currency prices away from their fair value.

Currency management strategies for portfolios with exchange rate risk range from a passive approach of matching benchmark currency exposures to an active strategy that treats currency exposure independently of benchmark exposures and seeks to profit from (rather than hedge the risk of) currency exposures. Different approaches along this spectrum include:

- **Passive hedging** is rule based and typically matches the portfolio's currency exposure to that of the benchmark used to evaluate the portfolio's performance. It will require periodic rebalancing to maintain the match. The goal is to eliminate currency risk relative to the benchmark.
- **Discretionary hedging** allows the manager to deviate modestly from passive hedging by a specified percentage. An example is allowing 5% deviations from the hedge ratio that would match a currency's exposure to the benchmark exposure. The goal is to reduce currency risk while allowing the manager to pursue modest incremental currency returns relative to the benchmark.
- **Active currency management** allows a manager to have greater deviations from benchmark currency exposures. This differs from discretionary hedging in the amount of discretion permitted and the manager is expected to generate positive incremental portfolio return from managing a portfolio's currency exposure. The goal is to create incremental return (alpha), not to reduce risk.
- A **currency overlay** is a broad term covering the outsourcing of currency management. At the extreme, the overlay manager will treat currency as an asset class and may take positions independent of other portfolio assets. Seeking incremental return, an overlay manager who is bearish on the Swedish krona (SEK) for a portfolio with no exposure to the SEK would short the SEK. The manager is purely seeking currency alpha (incremental return), not risk reduction. Overlay managers can also be given a pure risk reduction mandate or restricted to risk reduction with modest return enhancement.

The IPS: The account's policy on whether to hedge or not to hedge currency risk should be recorded in the client's investment policy statement (IPS). Sections of the IPS that will be particularly relevant in reaching this strategic decision include investor objectives (including risk tolerance), time horizon, liquidity needs, and the benchmark to be used for analyzing portfolio results. The IPS should also specify:

- The target percentage of currency exposure that is to be hedged.
- Allowable discretion for the manager to vary around this target.
- Frequency of rebalancing the hedge.
- Benchmarks to use for evaluating the results of currency decisions.
- Allowable (or prohibited) hedging tools.

Reading 8

EXAMPLE: Choosing a hedging approach

A client with a USD based portfolio has little need for liquidity and is focused on short- term performance results. The client evaluates performance relative to a global equity index, which fully hedges currency exposure back to the USD and rebalances the hedge monthly.

1. **Discuss** how this information would affect the manager's views on hedging currency exposure in the portfolio.
2. **Explain** why rebalancing of currency exposure could be needed even if no changes are made to asset holdings.

Answers:

1. The client information leads to two possible strategies. (A) If the manager lacks currency expertise, the manager should also fully hedge currency risk and rebalance monthly, then focus on other areas such as asset selection to add value. (B) If the manager does have views on currency movement, the manager can instead increase exposure to currencies expected to appreciate and decrease exposure to currencies expected to depreciate.

   Given the client's focus on short-term results, the manager must consider the currency exposure of the index and either match it or deliberately deviate. A long-term assumption that "currency does not matter" is not appropriate. The lack of liquidity needs reduces the need for currency hedging as it reduces the likelihood of liquidations of foreign asset positions at depressed values.
2. Suppose both the U.S. client and the index allocate 10% to U.K. equities and sell the GBP forward to fully hedge the currency risk. Then over the course of the month, the U.K. stocks in the benchmark fall in value ($-R_{FC}$) while the U.K. stocks in the portfolio rise in value ($+R_{FC}$). The index will reduce the short GBP position to reflect the decreased GBP asset value. In contrast, the manager needs to increase the GBP short position to reflect increased GBP market value. Rebalancing the hedge must consider not only explicit transactions by the manager but also differentials in R_{FC} between the index and the portfolio.

Strategic Diversification Issues

- In the longer run, currency volatility has been lower than in the shorter run, reducing the need to hedge currency in portfolios with a long-term perspective.
- Positive correlation between returns of the asset measured in the foreign currency (R_{FC}) and returns from the foreign currency (R_{FX}) increase volatility of return to the investor (R_{DC}) and increase the need for currency hedging. Negative correlation dampens return volatility and decreases the need to hedge.
- Correlation tends to vary by time period, providing diversification in some periods and not in others, suggesting a varying hedge ratio is appropriate.

- Some investors assert that there is higher positive correlation between asset and currency returns in bond portfolios than in equity portfolios. If that is true, then there is more reason to hedge currency risk in bond portfolios than in equity portfolios. In a bond portfolio, the riskiness of the asset and currency are more likely to reinforce each other.
- The hedge ratio (the percentage of currency exposure to hedge) varies by manager preference.

Strategic Cost Issues: Hedging is not free and benefits must be weighted versus costs.

- The bid/asked transaction cost on a single currency trade is generally small, but repeated transaction costs add up. Full hedging and frequent rebalancing can be costly.
- Purchasing options to hedge involves an upfront option premium cost. If the option expires out-of-the-money, the premium is lost.
- Forward currency contracts are often shorter term than the hedging period, requiring contracts be rolled over as they mature (an FX swap). The hedge lowers return volatility but the rollover can create cash flow volatility with realized gains and losses on the maturing contracts. Financing cash outflows when interest rates are high can be costly as the interest that would have been earned on the funds is lost.
- Overhead costs can be high. A back office and trading infrastructure are needed for currency hedging. Cash accounts in multiple currencies may have to be maintained to support settlements and margin requirements.
- One hundred percent hedging has an opportunity cost with no possibility of favorable currency movement. Some managers elect to "split the difference" between 0 and 100% hedging and adopt a 50% strategic hedge ratio.
- Hedging every currency movement is costly and managers generally chose partial hedges. They may hedge and rebalance monthly rather than daily or accept some amount of negative currency return rather than zero.

LOS 8.c: Formulate an appropriate currency management program given financial market conditions and portfolio objectives and constraints.

In conclusion, the factors that shift the strategic decision formulation toward a benchmark neutral or fully hedged strategy are:

- A short time horizon for portfolio objectives.
- High risk aversion.
- A client who is unconcerned with the opportunity costs of missing positive currency returns.
- High short-term income and liquidity needs.
- Significant foreign currency bond exposure.
- Low hedging costs.
- Clients who doubt the benefits of discretionary management.

MODULE QUIZ 8.1

Use the following information for Questions 1 and 2.

A Djiboutian (DJF) investor holds an international portfolio with beginning investments of USD 1,253,000 and EUR 2,347,800. Measured in the foreign currencies, these investments appreciate 5% and depreciate 7%, respectively.

Additional information:

Beginning Spot Exchange Rate	Beginning Forward Exchange Rate	Ending Spot Exchange Rate
DJF/USD 179.54	DJF/USD 185.67	DJF/USD 192.85
EUR/DJF 0.00416	EUR/DJF 0.00413	EUR/DJF 0.00421

1. The ending value of the USD investment is *closest* to:
   A. USD 1,150,000.
   B. DJF 236,200,000.
   C. DJF 253,700,000.
2. The unhedged return to the investor of the U.S. investment is *closest* to:
   A. –3%.
   B. +3%.
   C. +12%.
3. A European investor holds a diversified portfolio. From the euro perspective, the portfolio is weighted 60% and 40% in U.S. and U.K. investments.

Assets	Returns measured in foreign currency	Returns measured from investor's perspective	Standard deviation of asset's returns measured in foreign currency	Standard deviation of the foreign currency's returns
U.S.	5%	6%	4.5%	3.7%
U.K.	7%	8%	3.5%	4.7%

The correlation between the foreign-currency asset's returns and returns on the foreign currency are 0.81 and 0.67, respectively, for the U.S. and English assets. **Compute** the standard deviation for the investor in the U.S. assets. **Show** your work.

4. The strategic decision to hedge currency risk will be *least* affected by the:
   A. manager's market views.
   B. correlation between asset and currency returns.
   C. investor's time horizon, risk aversion, and liquidity needs.
5. Which of the following clients would *most likely* allow a manager to implement discretionary currency hedging?
   A. One with a shorter time horizon and higher liquidity needs.
   B. One with more confidence in the portfolio manager and high income needs.
   C. One very concerned with minimizing regret and higher allocation to equity investments.
6. Jane Simms manages a German portfolio and has a 1,000,000 long position in South Korean won (KRW) through a forward contract that is about to come due. The current spot exchange rate is EUR/KRW 0.00067/0.00068. The forward points for a three-month forward contract are –1.2/–1.1. She expects the KRW to depreciate significantly and has the authority to increase or decrease the contract size by 10%. **Explain** whether she will increase or decrease the size of the forward contract and the forward exchange rate at which she will contract.

7. Jane Archer manages a Swiss-based (CHF) hedge fund. A portion of the fund is allocated 60% and 40%, respectively, to EUR and AUD investments. She has collected the following information.

Estimates	Euro zone	Australia
Asset return in foreign currency	2.0%	2.5%
Change in spot exchange rate versus the CHF	–1.0%	3.0%
Asset risk measured in foreign currency (σ)	15.0%	25.0%
Currency risk (σ)	7.0%	9.0%
Correlation of asset and currency return	+0.85	+0.65
Correlation of returns (CHF/EUR, CHF/AUD)	+0.70	

The following questions are from the portfolio perspective, measured in CHF.

a. **Calculate** the expected return of the portfolio.

b. **Calculate** the standard deviation of the portfolio.

c. **Calculate** the expected return to the portfolio if Archer takes a leveraged position with a 150% positive weight in Australia and a 150% negative weight in the euro zone.

d. **Calculate** the expected standard deviation of returns to the portfolio if Archer takes a leveraged position with a 150% positive weight in Australia and a 150% negative weight in the euro zone.

MODULE 8.2: ACTIVE STRATEGIES: FUNDAMENTALS AND TECHNICAL ANALYSIS

Video covering this content is available online.

LOS 8.d: Compare active currency trading strategies based on economic fundamentals, technical analysis, carry-trade, and volatility trading.

The strategic decision sets the portfolio's normal currency hedging policy. If discretion is allowed, the manager can make active tactical decisions within defined boundaries, seeking to increase return. In all cases, active management requires that the manager have a view or a prediction of what will happen. Tactical decisions can be based on four broad approaches. Unfortunately, none of the approaches works consistently.

Economic Fundamentals

This approach assumes that, in the long term, currency value will converge to fair value. For example, a fundamental approach may assume purchasing power parity will determine long-run exchange rates. If the basket of goods and services produced in Country A costs 100 units of Country A's currency and that basket costs 200 units of Country B's currency in Country B, then the currency exchange rate of A to B is 100/200, a 0.50 A/B exchange rate.

Several factors will impact the eventual path of convergence over the short and intermediate terms. Increases in the value of a currency are associated with currencies:

- That are more undervalued relative to their fundamental value.
- That have the greatest rate of increase in their fundamental value.
- With higher real or nominal interest rates.
- With lower inflation relative to other countries.
- Of countries with decreasing risk premiums.

Opposite conditions are believed to be associated with declining currency values.

Technical Analysis

Technical analysis of currency is based on three principals:

1. Past price data can predict future price movement and because those prices reflect fundamental and other relevant information, there is no need to analyze such information.
2. Fallible human beings react to similar events in similar ways and therefore past price patterns tend to repeat.
3. It is unnecessary to know what the currency should be worth (based on fundamental value); it is only necessary to know where it will trade.

Technical analysis looks at past price and volume trading data. FX technical analysis focuses on price trends as volume data is generally less available. Technical analysis works best in markets with identifiable trends. Typical patterns that technicians seek to exploit are the following.

- An **overbought** (or **oversold**) market has gone up (or down) too far and the price is likely to reverse.
- A **support level** exists where there are substantial bids from customers to buy. A price that falls to that level is then likely to reverse and bounce higher as the purchases are executed.
- A **resistance level** exists where there are substantial offers from customers to sell. A price that rises to that level is then likely to reverse and bounce lower as the sales are executed.

At both support and resistance levels, the price becomes "sticky." However, if the market moves through the sticky resistance levels, it can then accelerate and continue in the same direction.

For example, assume technical traders have observed a support level for the GBP at 1.70 USD/GBP. The traders place limit orders to buy GBP at 1.70 USD/GBP. However, to limit their losses, the traders also enter stop loss orders to sell GBP at various prices between 1.70 and 1.69. If the GBP declines to the support level of 1.70, the buy orders are executed, supporting that price and explain the "sticky price behavior." However, if the GBP then declines lower, the stop loss sell orders are executed, driving the GBP lower as the GBP breaks its support level.

Moving averages of price are often used in technical analysis. A common rule is that if a shorter-term moving average crosses a longer-term moving average, it triggers a signal. The 50-day moving average rising above the 200-day moving average is a buy signal, falling below is a sell signal.

Video covering this content is available online.

MODULE 8.3: ACTIVE STRATEGIES: CARRY AND VOLATILITY TRADING

The Carry Trade

A **carry trade** refers to borrowing in a lower interest rate currency and investing the proceeds in a higher interest rate currency. Three issues are important to understand the carry trade.

1. **Covered interest rate parity (CIRP)** holds by arbitrage and establishes that the difference between spot (S_0) and forward (F_0) exchange rates equals the difference in the periodic interest rates of the two currencies.
   - The currency with the higher interest rate will trade at a **forward discount**, $F_0 < S_0$
   - The currency with the lower interest rate will trade at a **forward premium**, $F_0 > S_0$

2. The carry trade is based on a violation of **uncovered interest rate parity (UCIRP)**. UCIRP is an international parity relationship asserting that the forward exchange rate calculated by CIRP is an unbiased estimate of the spot exchange rate that will exist in the future. If this were true:
   - The currency with the higher interest rate will decrease in value by the amount of the initial interest rate differential.
   - The currency with the lower interest rate will increase in value by the amount of the initial interest rate differential.

   If these expectations were true, a carry trade would earn a zero return.
3. Because the carry trade exploits a violation of interest rate parity, it can be referred to as trading the forward rate bias. Historical evidence indicates that:
   - Generally, the higher interest rate currency has depreciated less than predicted by interest rate parity or even appreciated and a carry trade has earned a profit.
   - However, a small percentage of the time, the higher interest rate currency has depreciated substantially more than predicted by interest rate parity and a carry trade has generated large losses.

Generally, the carry trade is implemented by borrowing in the lower interest rate currencies of developed economies (**funding currencies**) and investing in the higher interest rate currencies of emerging economies (**investing currencies**). In periods of financial stress, the currencies of the higher risk emerging economies have depreciated sharply relative to the currencies of developed economies and such carry trades have generated significant losses. Given that periods of financial stress are associated with increasing exchange rate volatility, traders often exit their carry trade positions when exchange rate volatility increases significantly.

Reading 8

EXAMPLE: A carry trade

The spot exchange rate is BRL/USD 2.41. The interest rates in the two countries are 6% and 1%, respectively.

1. **Estimate** the one-year forward exchange rate for the Brazilian Real.
2. **State** the steps to initiate the carry trade and the theory on which it is based.
3. What is the profit on the trade if the spot exchange rate is unchanged and the trade is initiated by borrowing 100 currency units? **Show** your work.
4. What is the primary risk in this trade?

Answers:

1. The forward exchange rate for the Real should be approximately 5% below the current spot exchange rate to reflect the initial interest rate differential. The precise calculation is:

   BRL/USD $2.41 \times (1.06 / 1.01)^1$ = BRL/USD 2.529
2.
   - Borrow USD at 1%.
   - Convert USD to BRL at the spot exchange rate of BRL/USD 2.41.
   - Invest the BRL at 6%.

The carry trade is based on a violation of uncovered interest rate parity. It is profitable if the spot exchange rate of the higher interest rate currency declines less than predicted by the forward exchange rate.

3. It is 5%, reflecting the initial interest rate difference and unchanged spot exchange rate.
   - Borrow USD 100 creating a loan payable of USD 101.
   - Convert USD 100 to BRL 241 (= 100 × 2.41).
   - Invest the BRL 241 at 6% creating an ending value of BRL 255.46.
   - Convert the BRL 255.46 at the unchanged spot exchange rate back to USD 106.00 (= 255.46 / 2.41).
   - Pay off the USD loan for a profit of USD 5.00 on a USD 100 initial investment.
4. This is an unhedged trade and the profit or loss depends on the ending value of the BRL. If the BRL declines by more than 5%, the trade is unprofitable.

Figure 8.1: Summary of the Carry Trade

The Carry Trade:		
Is implemented by:	Borrowing and then selling in the spot market the lower yield currency.	To buy and invest in the higher yield currency.
Is trading the forward rate bias:	Selling in the spot market the currency trading at a forward premium.	And buying in the spot market the currency trading at a forward discount.

The carry trade is generally profitable under normal market conditions. But it can generate large losses in periods of financial distress and high volatility as investors flee high risk (yield) currencies.

PROFESSOR'S NOTE

You should notice this section does not support using the forward exchange rate as a prediction of how currency value will change, sometimes referred to as uncovered interest rate parity (UCIRP). Under IRP, the currency with the higher short-term interest rate will trade at a forward discount. UCIRP asserts that this calculated forward rate is a prediction of what will happen to the spot exchange rate and the higher rate currency will depreciate. This section has (1) noted that empirical evidence indicates the currency with the higher rate tends to appreciate, not depreciate, and (2) the carry trade is based on the higher rate currency appreciating or depreciating less than suggested by UCIRP. You should conclude that the Level III curriculum does not support using the forward exchange rate as a valid prediction of what will happen. The forward exchange rate can be and is used for hedging, but it just is not a good predictor of how the spot exchange rate will move, unless you want a very short career as a currency manager.

Volatility Trading

Volatility or "vol" trading allows a manager to profit from predicting changes in currency volatility. Recall from Level I and Level II that **delta** measures the change in value of an option's price for a change in value of the underlying and that **vega** measures change in value of the option for changes in volatility of the underlying. Vega is positive for both puts and calls because an increase in the expected volatility of the price of the underlying increases the value of both puts and calls.

Delta hedging entails creation of a **delta-neutral position**, which has a delta of zero. The delta-neutral position will not gain or lose value with small changes in the price of the underlying assets, but it will gain or lose value as the implied volatility reflected in the price of options changes. A manager can profit by correctly predicting changes in volatility.

A manager expecting volatility to increase should enter a **long straddle** by purchasing an at-the-money call and put. The manager is buying volatility. The two options will have equal but opposite deltas making the position delta neutral. If volatility increases, the options will rise in net value and the trade will be profitable.

A manager expecting volatility to decrease should enter a **short straddle** by selling both of these options. If volatility declines, the options will fall in net value. The options can be repurchased at lower prices for a profit.

PROFESSOR'S NOTE

Delta hedging will come up several times in the CFA curriculum. An important caveat is that the deltas will change and the positions must be continually rebalanced to maintain a delta-neutral position.

A **strangle** will provide similar but more moderate payoffs to a straddle. Out of-the-money calls and puts with the same absolute delta are purchased. The out-of-the-money options require larger movement in the currency value to create intrinsic value but will cost less. Both the initial cost and the likely profit are lower than for the straddle.

MODULE QUIZ 8.2, 8.3

1. A currency overlay manager will *most likely* implement a carry trade when the yield of investing currencies is:
   A. lower and volatility is falling.
   B. higher and currency volatility is rising.
   C. higher and currency volatility is stable.
2. Which of the following statements about volatility and interest rates is *most likely* true?
   A. Falling currency volatility leads traders to exit a carry trade.
   B. Rising currency volatility will increase the cost of a collar more than the cost of a protective put.
   C. A delta neutral hedging strategy is more likely to tilt to a net long position in the euro when the euro zone is experiencing rising real interest rates.

Reading 8

Video covering this content is available online.

MODULE 8.4: IMPLEMENTATION AND FORWARDS

LOS 8.e: Describe how changes in factors underlying active trading strategies affect tactical trading decisions.

Active trading strategies are, by definition, risky. An active manager forms market expectations and implements shorter term tactical strategies seeking to add value. If the manager is wrong or does not cover the transaction costs, return is reduced. Manager expectations that trigger tactical trading decisions include the following.

Expectation:		Action:
Relative currency:	Appreciation	Reduce the hedge (short position) on **OR** increase the long position in the currency
	Depreciation	Increase the hedge on or decrease the long position in the currency
Volatility:	Rising	Long straddle (or strangle)
	Falling	Short straddle (or strangle)
Market conditions:	Stable	A carry trade
	Crisis	Discontinue the carry trade

Subtle variations on these actions include the following.

- A carry trade may involve a bundle of funding and investment currencies and positions need not be equally weighted. For example, if the manager expects a particular currency to show greater relative increase in value, the trade would be structured with increased long (or decrease short) positions in that currency.
- Delta neutral positions can be "tilted" to net positive or negative based on the manager's view. A manager expecting a currency to appreciate (depreciate) could shift to a net positive (negative) delta.

Currency Management Tools

PROFESSOR'S NOTE

We now examine a variety of hedging techniques and tools plus special considerations that may arise in some situations. The CFA text includes the warning "rote memorization" is not advised. Instead think of basic "building blocks" that allow an infinite number of combinations; focus on the basic concepts and terminology.

Some useful tips to sort through the material include the following. Some of these may be repeated from other sections.

1. What is the currency exposure that needs to be hedged? A typical situation is a portfolio exposed to fluctuation in value of a foreign currency.
2. It is easier to work with FX quotes when the foreign currency is the base currency. If quotes are given as B/P, take the reciprocal to make it P/B.
3. Assume any statements or directions refer to the base currency unless otherwise indicated in the case. But be explicit in your answers and state the currency you are referring to.
4. Decide whether the case requires buying or selling the base currency.
   - Buying forwards (and futures) or buying call options on the base currency increases exposure to the base currency.
   - Selling forwards (and futures) or buying put options on the base currency decreases exposure to the base currency.
   - Remember that:
     - A call on the base currency is a put on the pricing currency.
     - A put on the base currency is a call on the pricing currency.
5. Hedging is not free.
   - Hedges using forwards have no or minimal initial cost but high opportunity cost because the potential upside of the hedged currency is eliminated.
   - Purchasing options has high initial cost but retains the upside of the hedged currency (the protective put strategy).
   - Lowering the cost of the hedge will require some combination of less downside protection or upside potential. Cost can be lowered through some combination of:
     - Writing options to generate premium inflow.
     - Adjusting the option strike prices.
     - Adjusting the size (notional amount) of the options.
     - Adding exotic features to the options.
6. Discretionary hedging allows the manager to deviate from a policy neutral hedge position. Allowing the manager discretion can lower hedging costs and enhance return but also increases the risk of underperformance.
7. The IPS (or question specifics) should define the strategic, policy neutral hedge position. Generally this is a 100% hedge to match the currency exposure of the portfolio's benchmark.

Reading 8

LOS 8.f: Describe how forward contracts and FX (foreign exchange) swaps are used to adjust hedge ratios.

Typically, **forward contracts** are preferred for currency hedging because:

- They can be customized, while futures contracts are standardized.
- They are available for almost any currency pair, while futures trade in size for only a limited number of currencies.
- Futures contracts require margin which adds operational complexity and can require periodic cash flows.
- Trading volume of FX forwards and swaps dwarfs that of FX futures, providing better liquidity.

A hedge can be a **static hedge**, which is established and held until expiration, or a **dynamic hedge**, which is periodically rebalanced.

Consider a EUR-based manager who must hedge an initial CHF 10,000,000 of asset exposure. One month later, the asset has appreciated to CHF 11,000,000. Assume the manager can initially sell a one- or three-month contract.

1. Initially sell 10,000,000 CHF in the forward market with a one-month forward contract. At contract expiration, roll over the hedge. At rollover, the change in initial contract price will produce a realized gain or loss and cash flow settlement consequences. At the rollover, the size of the new contract can be adjusted to match the new value of the position to be hedged. Over the initial month, the hedge is static but can be dynamic at the rollover.

   If desired, the rollover can be done using an FX swap so that cash flows occur on the expiration date of the initial contract. For an FX swap, the manager would, two days prior to initial contract expiration, buy CHF 10 million in the spot market to cover the short position in the forward and sell forward CHF 11 million to roll over the hedge. This is termed a "mismatched" FX swap because the "near" spot leg and "far" forward leg are not of equal size.

   Both the initial short forward contract and the spot market purchase of CHF are for CHF 10,000,000 and settle in two business days. Any difference between the EUR/CHF rate of the initial forward contract and the current spot price will produce a (positive or negative) cash flow in EUR. For example, if the CHF declined by EUR 0.01, the initial hedge (short forward) will produce a cash gain of EUR 100,000 (= EUR 0.01 × 10,000,000).

2. Initially sell 10,000,000 CHF in the forward market with a three-month forward contract. One month later, the manager is underhedged with a CHF 10,000,000 short position versus an asset now worth CHF 11,000,000.

   a. With a static hedge, the manager would do nothing even though CHF exposure has increased.

   b. With a dynamic hedge, the manager would increase the hedge to cover the additional exposure by selling an additional CHF 1 million forward for two months to create a total short position of CHF 11 million. Because no contracts are being closed on the rebalancing date, all realized gain and losses and cash flows are deferred until the end of the three-month period. A dynamic hedging strategy will specify periodicity of rebalancing the hedge.

The choice of hedging approach should consider:

- Shorter term contracts or dynamic hedges with more frequent rebalancing tend to increase transaction costs but improve the hedge results.
- Higher risk aversion suggests more frequent rebalancing.
- Lower risk aversion and strong manager views suggest allowing the manager greater discretion around the strategic hedging policy.

Roll Yield

Hedging also exposes the portfolio to **roll yield** or **roll return**. Roll yield is a return from the movement of the forward price over time toward the spot price of an asset. It can be thought of as the profit or loss on a forward or futures contract if the spot price is unchanged at contract expiration. Determining whether the roll yield produces a profit or a loss will depend on two factors: (1) whether the currency is trading at a forward premium or discount and (2) whether is it purchased or sold. Roll yield for a contract held to expiration is determined by initial forward minus spot price divided by initial spot price.

For example, consider an investor who sells CHF 1 million six-month forward for USD 1.05 when the spot rate is 1.04. The forward price is at a premium so the roll yield on a short position will be positive. Think of it as the investor sells at a high price and the price rolls down for a gain. The investor can deliver CHF 1 million for 1.05 USD when its initial cost in the market (at spot) is 1.04 USD, for a gain of USD 10,000. The unannualized roll yield is 0.01/1.04 = 0.96%.

Roll yield will affect the cost/benefit analysis of whether to hedge the currency risk. It is a cost of hedging. Positive roll yield will shift the analysis toward hedging and negative roll yield will shift the analysis away from hedging. The relationships of forward premium or discount, initial difference in interest rates, positive or negative roll yield, and impact on hedging cost are summarized in Figure 8.2.

Figure 8.2: Forward Premiums or Discounts and Currency Hedging Costs

Current position of foreign asset in Currency B	The hedge requires:	$F_{P/B} > S_{P/B}$, $i_B < i_P$ The forward price curve is upward-sloping.	$F_{P/B} < S_{P/B}$, $i_B > i_P$ The forward price curve is downward-sloping
Short the foreign asset	A long forward position in Currency B, the hedge earns:	Negative roll yield, which increases hedging cost and discourages hedging.	Positive roll yield, which decreases hedging cost and encourages hedging.
Long the foreign asset	A short forward position in Currency B the hedge earns:	Positive roll yield, which decreases hedging cost and encourages hedging.	Negative roll yield, which increases hedging cost and discourages hedging.

Reading 8

PROFESSOR'S NOTE

Suppose the initial forward price of the base currency is above its initial spot price. If the base currency is sold forward, F_T and S_T will converge at contract expiration and provide positive roll yield for the short position. The positive roll for the short position does not depend on whether the spot price increases or decreases. This is depicted in the following figure. It shows that the forward and spot price will converge at contract expiration regardless of whether the spot price increases or decreases. Suppose a manager sells the base currency forward when the initial forward price is above the spot price, $F_0 > S_0$. Convergence dictates that at contract expiration, $F_T = S_T$ and the roll return will be positive.

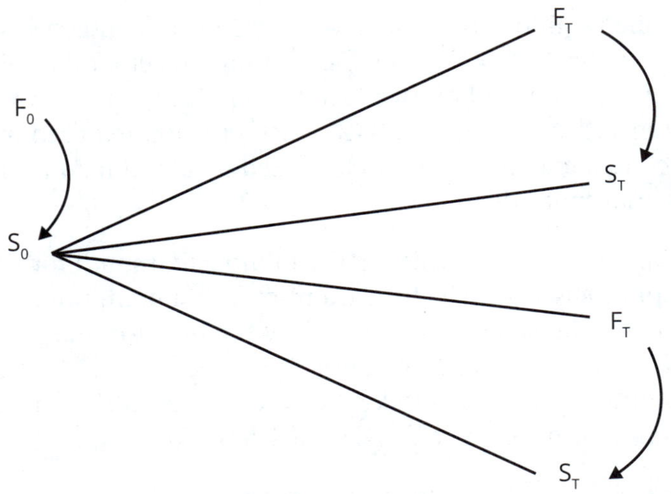

Note that the positive roll for the base currency short position is a negative roll for the long position. This discussion of roll and a contract on the base currency is equally true for contracts on any other assets such as stocks, bonds, and commodities.

Also note that the roll yield is not the total return from selling or buying the forward. The underlying spot price can increase or decrease. The forward price will converge to that unknown spot price at expiration of the forward. The total of the return to the forward position will be the change in price of the forward. That change in price of the forward has two components: 1) the unknown-in-advance change in the spot price, and 2) the known-in-advance roll yield.

EXAMPLE: Roll yield and interest rates

A USD-based investor has exposure to the South African rand (ZAR). The USD interest rate is 2.8% and the ZAR interest rate is 3.6%. **Determine** the roll yield for the investor if he hedges his ZAR exposure with a six-month forward.

Answer:

To hedge the long ZAR exposure, the investor sells the ZAR forward (buy the USD). IRP determines the premium or discount earned (roll yield) on the transaction. From IRP, the periodic risk-free rate of the currency purchased (USD) will be gained and the currency sold (ZAR) will be lost. Over a six-month period, this is approximately + 2.8% / 2 – 3.6% / 2 = –0.4%. The ZAR will trade at approximately a 0.4% forward discount.

A precise calculation of the discount requires first calculating the initial forward price using IRP:

$$F_{P/B} = S_{P/B}\left(\frac{1+i_P}{1+i_B}\right)$$

Then compare that forward price to the initial spot price to calculate the percentage roll yield (i.e., the forward premium or discount):

$$(F - S) / S$$

However by "assuming" an initial spot exchange rate between the two currencies of parity, a 1/1 exchange rate, this can be reduced to a single calculation:

% forward premium / discount = % roll yield
$= (1.00)(1.028 / 1.036)^{0.5} - 1 = -0.387\%$

Note that to analyze the ZAR, the ZAR is in the denominator of all terms.

PROFESSOR'S NOTE

The CFA text mentions but does not further apply a "similarity" between roll yield and trading the forward rate bias. Both depend on the initial interest rate differential between two currencies. In the previous example, the ZAR traded at a forward discount because it had an initially higher periodic interest rate.

- The forward rate bias trade (the carry trade) would buy the ZAR in the spot market to invest in and earn the higher interest rate.
- An investor who needs exposure to the ZAR would buy the ZAR in the forward market at a discount and earn positive roll yield.

The "similarity" is buying the higher yielding currency.

EXAMPLE: Hedging and roll yield

A portfolio's reporting currency is the Korean won (KRW) and the portfolio holds investments denominated in EUR, USD, and CHF. Current exchange rate information is provided below along with the manager's expectation for the spot rate in six months.

	Spot FX Rate	Six-Month Forward FX Rate	Manager's Forecast
KRW/EUR	1,483.99	1,499.23	1,450.87
KRW/USD	1,108.78	1,112.56	1,146.63
KRW/CHF	1,265.22	1,257.89	1,212.55

1. Which foreign currencies trade at a forward premium or discount?
2. Which foreign currency hedges would earn a positive roll yield?
3. Which foreign currencies would an active currency manager hedge?
4. **Comment** on how the roll yield affects the decision to hedge the EUR or USD.
5. **Calculate** the implied unannualized roll yield of a currency hedged for the portfolio's long exposure to CHF.

Answers:

1. The EUR and USD trade at a forward premium; forward price is above spot price.
2. The hedge will require a forward sale of the currency and sale at a forward premium will earn positive roll yield. Those are the EUR and USD.
3. An active manager will selectively hedge those currencies where the hedge is expected to improve return. The manager will compare expected unhedged with hedged returns. The manager is initially long each foreign currency so increases in the currency's value are a gain.

	Unhedged	**Hedged**
EUR	(1,450.87 / 1,483.99) –1 = –2.23%	(1,499.23 / 1,483.99) –1 = 1.03%
USD	(1,146.63 / 1,108.78) – 1 = 3.41%	(1,112.56 / 1,108.78) – 1 = 0.34%
CHF	(1,212.55 / 1,265.22) – 1 = –4.16%	(1,257.89 / 1,265.22) – 1 = –0.58%

   Comparing unhedged expected returns with hedged returns, the manager will hedge the EUR and CHF.

4. Selling forward the USD and EUR will result in positive roll yield which will reduce hedging costs. However, roll yield is only one factor to consider. The positive roll yield for selling the USD forward is not as attractive as the expected appreciation of leaving the USD unhedged.
5. The implied roll yield is the forward premium or discount. It is also the hedged currency return:

   $(F_0 - S_0) / S_0 = (F_0 / S_0) - 1 = (1{,}257.89 / 1{,}265.22) - 1 = -0.58\%$

This example demonstrates two issues involved with forward currency hedging. In essence, they are the same issue viewed from two different perspectives:

1. Positive (negative) roll yield will reduce (increase) hedging cost compared to the initial spot price.
2. Hedging locks in the forward price as an end of period exchange rate.

MODULE 8.5: IMPLEMENTATION AND OPTIONS

Video covering this content is available online.

LOS 8.g: Describe trading strategies used to reduce hedging costs and modify the risk–return characteristics of a foreign-currency portfolio.

The initial forward premium or discount is one cost factor to consider in analyzing the cost/benefit of a currency hedge. To reduce hedging cost, the manager can increase the size of trades that earn positive roll yield and reduce the size of trades that earn negative roll yield.

Forward hedging also incurs **opportunity cost**. Locking in a forward price to hedge currency risk will eliminate downside currency risk but also will eliminate any upside opportunity for gain from changes in exchange rates. Discretionary or option-based hedging strategies are designed to reduce opportunity cost.

Perfect hedging is expensive. If the manager wishes to insure against downside risk and retain upside potential, costs rise further. Reducing those hedging costs involves some form of less downside protection or less upside opportunity, moving the portfolio away from a 100% hedge ratio and/or toward more active decision making. The following discussion of strategies applies to a manager who wishes to hedge long exposure to the CHF (the base currency) and quotations are EUR/CHF.

1. **Over- or under-hedge with forward contracts** based on the manager's view. If the manager expects the CHF to appreciate, she can reduce the hedge ratio, hedging less than the full exposure to CHF risk. If the CHF is expected to depreciate, she can increase the hedge ratio, hedging more than the full exposure to CHF risk. If successful, this strategy creates "positive convexity"; gains will be increased and losses reduced. This is a relatively low cost strategy.

The rest of this discussion proceeds from roughly highest to lowest initial option cost.

2. **Buy at-the-money (ATM) put options** (also called **protective puts** or **portfolio insurance**). This strategy provides asymmetric protection, eliminating all downside risk and retaining all upside potential. But an at-the-money option is relatively expensive and has only time value (no intrinsic value). This strategy has the highest initial cost but no opportunity cost.
3. **Buy out-of-the-money (OTM) put options**. An ATM put would have a delta of approximately –0.50, called a 50-delta put because the sign of the delta is ignored with this terminology. Out-of-the-money puts have deltas that are smaller in magnitude than 0.50, so a 35-delta put is out of the money and a 25-delta put is further out of the money. Puts are less expensive the further they are out of the money, but also offer less downside protection. The manager will have downside CHF exposure down to the strike price of the puts. Compared to buying ATM protective puts, this strategy reduces the initial cost of the hedge but does not eliminate all downside risk.
4. **Collar**. The manager could buy the 35-delta puts on the CHF and sell 35-delta calls on the CHF. The OTM put provides some downside protection while costing less than an ATM put. The sale of the OTM call removes some upside potential (increasing opportunity cost) but generates premium income to further reduce initial cost. This strategy further reduces initial cost but also limits upside potential compared to buying out-of-the money put options only.

A counterparty who buys the OTM call and sells the OTM put has taken on a risk reversal. The risk reversal profits if the underlying rises above the OTM call strike price and loses if the underlying falls below the OTM put strike price. The seller of the call and buyer of the put (used in the collar) can be described as short the risk reversal.

5. **Put spread**. Buy OTM puts on the CHF and sell puts that are further out of the money, (e.g., buy a 35-delta put and sell a 25-delta put). There is downside protection, which begins at the strike price of the purchased puts, but if the CHF falls below the lower strike price of the put sold, that downside protection is lost. This strategy reduces the initial cost and also reduces downside protection compared to buying out-of-the money put options only.
6. **Seagull spread**. This is a put spread combined with selling a call (e.g., buy a 35-delta put, sell a 25-delta put, and sell a 35-delta call). Compared to the put spread, only this hedge has less initial cost and the same down side protection, but limits upside potential.

Further alternatives include varying the degree of upside potential and downside protection. The manager can vary the notional amounts of the options. For example, a 1 × 2 put spread would buy 100 40-delta puts and sell 200 30-delta puts. The sale of additional puts increases premium income, reducing the initial cost of the hedge, but doubles the downside risk if the currency value falls below the strike price on the 30-delta puts.

All of these strategies are considered "plain vanilla" in that they are combinations of standard options. **Exotic options** introduce features not found in standard options.

1. A **knock-in option** is a plain vanilla option that only comes into existence if the underlying first reaches some prespecified level.
2. A **knock-out option** is a standard option that ceases to exist if the underlying reaches some prespecified level.
3. **Binary** or **digital options** pay a fixed amount that does not vary with the difference in price between the strike and underlying price.

PROFESSOR'S NOTE

Clearly there are any number of combinations and odd names for hedging strategies that use combinations of options positions. The important thing is to recognize how the above strategies affect the tradeoff between the cost of a hedge, its downside protection, and its upside potential.

The issues involved with selecting a hedge are summarized in the following steps.

1. Determine the base currency in the P/B quote. In a USD/CHF quote, the CHF is the base and if the quoted price increases (decreases), the CHF appreciates (depreciates).
2. Determine whether the base currency will be bought or sold. If bought and the quoted price increases (decreases), there is a gain (loss). If sold and the quoted price increases (decreases), there is a loss (gain).

3. If buying the base currency is required to hedge the existing risk, buying forwards or calls can be used. Buying OTM calls or writing options will reduce the hedge cost but also reduce downside protection or upside potential.
4. If selling the base currency is required to hedge the existing risk, forwards are sold or puts are purchased. Buying OTM puts or writing options will reduce the hedge cost but also reduce downside protection or upside potential.
5. The higher the client's risk tolerance and the stronger the manager's views, the less likely a simple 100% hedge will be used.
6. Various combinations of options, strike prices, and position sizes can reduce initial hedging costs, even to zero, but only by reducing downside protection or upside potential.

Hedging Multiple Currencies

International portfolios will typically have exposure to more than one foreign currency. Generally, hedging each exposure individually is unnecessary, expensive, and time consuming. Consider a European investor who is underweight the AUD and overweight the NZD. The mechanical solution is a long position in AUD and a short position in NZD to reach neutral weights in both. Because the Australian and New Zealand economies are very similar, their currencies exhibit strong positive correlation. The two currencies are natural hedges for each other. If the initial over- and underweights were equal, there may be no need for any additional hedging.

MODULE 8.6: MORE ADVANCED IMPLEMENTATION ISSUES

Video covering this content is available online.

LOS 8.h: Describe the use of cross-hedges, macro-hedges, and minimum-variance-hedge ratios in portfolios exposed to multiple foreign currencies.

A **cross hedge** (sometimes called a **proxy hedge**) refers to hedging with an instrument that is not perfectly correlated with the exposure being hedged. Hedging the risk of a diversified U.S. equity portfolio with S&P futures contracts is a cross hedge when the portfolio is not identical to the S&P index portfolio. Cross hedges are generally not necessary in currency hedging because forward contracts for virtually all currency pairs are available but cross hedges may improve the efficiency of hedging.

Cross hedges also introduce additional risk to hedging. When the correlation of returns between the hedging instrument and the position being hedged is imperfect, the residual risk increases. The AUD and the NZD have a high positive correlation with each other so hedging an underweighting in the AUD with an overweighting in the NZD has little, but not zero, cross hedge risk.

The historical correlation is not a guarantee of the future. The future correlation may be different from historical correlation. If the correlation between two currencies moves toward zero, the (cross) hedge will not perform as expected. Portfolio performance could benefit or suffer from a change in correlation. The residual risk of the hedge is increased.

A **macro hedge** is a type of cross hedge that addresses portfolio-wide risk factors rather than the risk of individual portfolio assets. A bond portfolio might have interest rate risk, credit risk, and volatility risk exposures that the manager could hedge with bond futures (to hedge interest rate risk by modifying duration), credit derivatives (to hedge credit risk), and with volatility trading (to alter volatility risk).

One type of currency macro hedge uses a derivatives contract based on a fixed basket of currencies to modify currency exposure at a macro (portfolio) level. The currency basket in the contract may not precisely match the currency exposures of the portfolio, but it can be less costly than hedging each currency exposure individually. The manager must make a choice between accepting higher residual currency risk versus lower cost.

The **minimum-variance hedge ratio (MVHR)** is a mathematical approach to determining the hedge ratio. When applied to currency hedging, it is a regression of the past changes in value of the portfolio (R_{DC}) to the past changes in value of the hedging instrument to minimize the value of the tracking error between these two variables. The hedge ratio is the beta (slope coefficient) of that regression. Because this hedge ratio is based on historical returns, if the correlation between the returns on the portfolio and the returns on the hedging instrument change, the hedge will not perform as well as expected.

The practical implications of this are as follows:

1. Our forward hedging examples up to now have been "direct" hedges. For example, a USD portfolio that is long CHF 1,000,000 sells CHF 1,000,000 forward to hedge the risk, a simple one-for-one hedge ratio of the notional exposure. In technical terms, the portfolio is long CHF, the hedging vehicle is a forward contract on the CHF, and the CHF and its forward have a virtually 1.00 correlation; therefore, no MVHR analysis is needed, sell CHF 1,000,000 forward.
2. Cross hedges or macro hedges are considered "indirect" hedges, the correlation between the currency exposure in the portfolio and a currency contract may not be 1.00 and the minimum-variance hedge ratio may not be one-for-one.
3. The MVHR can be used to jointly optimize over changes in value of R_{FX} and R_{FC} to minimize the volatility of R_{DC}.

   To illustrate this use of the MVHR, consider the case of a foreign country where the economy is heavily dependent on imported energy. Appreciation of the currency ($+R_{FX}$) would make imports less expensive, which is likely to decrease production costs, increasing profits and asset values ($+R_{FC}$). **Strong positive correlation between R_{FX} and R_{FC} increases the volatility of R_{DC}. A hedge ratio greater than 1.0 would reduce the volatility of R_{DC}.**

   Consider the case of a foreign country where the economy is heavily dependent on exports. Appreciation of the currency ($+R_{FX}$) would make its exports more expensive, likely reducing sales, profits, and asset values ($-R_{FC}$). **Strong negative**

correlation between R_{FX} and R_{FC} naturally decreases the volatility of R_{DC}. A hedge ratio less than 1.0 would reduce the volatility of R_{DC}.

EXAMPLE: Determining and applying the MVHR

A U.S.-based portfolio is long EUR 2,000,000 of exposure. The portfolio manager decides to jointly hedge the risk of the asset returns measured in EUR and the risk of the currency return to minimize the volatility of the portfolio's returns measured in USD. The manager first adjusts all currency quotes to measure the value of the foreign currency by expressing the currency quotes as USD/EUR. He then calculates weekly percentage changes in value of the EUR (the R_{FX}) and unhedged percentage changes in value of the portfolio position measured in the portfolio's domestic currency (the R_{DC}). He performs a least squares regression analysis and determines based on the historical data that:

$$R_{DC} = 0.12 + 1.25(\%\Delta S_{USD/EUR}) + \varepsilon$$

With a correlation between R_{FX} and R_{FC} of 0.75

1. **Calculate** the size of and **state** the currency hedge to minimize expected volatility of the R_{DC}.
2. **Comment** on how effective the hedge is likely to be.

Answers:

1. EUR 2,000,000 × 1.25 = EUR 2,500,000; the manager will short EUR 2,500,000 to hedge a long EUR 2,000,000 exposure in the portfolio.
2. This is a cross hedge and is based on past correlation. The correlation can change and the hedge may perform better or worse than expected. In addition, a correlation of 0.75 is not perfect and there is random variation even in the past data.

Reading 8

Managing Emerging Market Currency

LOS 8.i: Discuss challenges for managing emerging market currency exposures.

The majority of investable asset value and FX transactions are in the six largest developed market currencies. Transactions in other currencies pose additional challenges because of: (1) higher transaction costs, "high markups" and (2) the increased probability of extreme events. Examples of these problems include the following.

- Low trading volume leads dealers to charge larger bid/asked spreads. The problem is compounded as the spreads tend to increase even further during periods of financial crisis.
- Liquidity can be lower and transaction costs higher to exit trades than to enter trades. Consider the carry trade that leads investors to gradually accumulate long positions in higher yield emerging market currencies. During periods of economic crises, the majority of those investors may attempt to exit a carry

trade at the same time, driving the value of the emerging market currency down below its fundamental value and disrupting normal trading activity.

- Transactions between two emerging market currencies can be even more costly. Few dealers have the expertise to directly make a market between the currencies of smaller markets. A dealer may quote a transaction between the Malaysian ringgit (MYR) and Hungarian forint (HUF) but would, in fact, execute component transactions in EUR/MYR and EUR/HUF with other dealers who have the expertise to trade only one of the two currencies.
- Emerging market currencies return distributions are non-normal with higher probabilities of extreme events and negative skew of returns. Many trading strategies and risk measures assume a normal distribution and are, therefore, flawed.
- The higher yield of emerging market currencies will lead to large forward discounts. This produces negative roll yield for investors who need to sell such currencies forward.
- Contagion is common. During periods of financial crisis the correlations of emerging markets with each other and with their currencies tend to converge toward +1.0. Both emerging markets and their currencies have declined as a group. At the very time diversification is most needed, it tends to disappear.
- There is *tail risk*; the governments of emerging markets tend to actively intervene in the markets for their currencies, producing long periods of artificial price stability followed by sharp price movements when market forces overwhelm the government's capacity to intervene. The "tail risk" refers to these negative events occurring more frequently than would be assumed in the normal distribution.

Non-deliverable forwards (NDFs): Emerging market governments frequently restrict movement of their currency into or out of the country to settle normal derivative transactions. Such countries have included Brazil (BRL), China (CNY), and Russia (RUB). NDFs are an alternative to deliverable forwards and require a cash settlement of gains or losses in a developed market currency at settlement rather than a currency exchange.

A benefit of NDFs is lower credit risk because delivery of the notional amounts of both currencies is not required. Only the gains to one party are paid at settlement.

An additional point to consider with NDFs is that they exist because the emerging market government is restricting currency markets. Changes in government policy can lead to sharp movements in currency values (i.e., there is tail risk).

EXAMPLE: Calculating cash settlement values for an NDF

A trader buys EUR 1,000,000 six months forward at RUB/EUR 39. Six months later, the spot exchange rate is RUB/EUR 40. **Calculate** the cash flows that will occur at settlement.

Answer:

The trader has agreed to "sell" RUB 39,000,000 for EUR 1,000,000. At settlement, the market value of EUR 1,000,000 is RUB 40,000,000 so the investor has a gain of RUB 1,000,000.

> However, NDF settlements are made in the developed market currency at the ending spot exchange rate so we must convert the gain of RUB 1,000,000 to EUR at RUB/EUR 40. The EUR value of RUB 1,000,000 at settlement is 1,000,000 / 40 = 25,000 euros and the trader will receive this payment from the counterparty. There is only a net exchange of gain.

MODULE QUIZ 8.4, 8.5, 8.6

1. Peter Perkins has a U.S.-based portfolio and decides to hedge his exposure to the Swiss franc (CHF) with a protective put strategy. However, he also decides he is willing to reduce the downside protection to lower the initial cost. Which of the following strategies will accomplish his objective?
   A. Buy 50-delta calls and puts on the CHF.
   B. Buy a 40-delta put and sell a 20-delta put on the CHF.
   C. Buy a 40-delta put and sell a 35-delta call on the CHF.
2. Jane Archer manages a Swiss-based (CHF) hedge fund. GBP 1,000,000 is currently invested in a diversified portfolio of U.K. stocks. Archer regresses the monthly returns of a diversified U.K. stock index (returns measured in CHF) versus the monthly change in value of the CHF/GBP. The regression coefficients are intercept = 0.11 and slope coefficient = 1.25. **Determine** the quantity of GBP Archer will short to implement a hedge of direct currency risk and a minimum-variance hedge.

	Direct currency hedge	Minimum-variance hedge
A.	GBP 1,000,000	GBP 1,000,000
B.	GBP 1,000,000	GBP 1,250,000
C.	GBP 1,250,000	GBP 1,250,000

3. A trader enters a short three-month non-deliverable forward on 2,000,000 CNY at CNY/USD 6.1155. At the end of the period, the spot exchange rate is USD/CNY 0.1612. The trader's gain or loss is *closest* to:
   A. USD 4,600 loss.
   B. USD 4,700 loss.
   C. USD 4,650 gain.

Reading 8

KEY CONCEPTS

LOS 8.a

An investment in assets priced in a currency other than the investor's domestic currency (a *foreign asset* priced in a *foreign currency*) has two sources of risk and return: (1) the return on the assets in the foreign currency and (2) the return on the foreign currency from any change in its exchange rate with the investor's *domestic currency*. These returns are multiplicative and an investor's returns in domestic currency can be calculated as:

Equation 1: $R_{DC} = (1 + R_{FC})(1 + R_{FX}) - 1 = R_{FC} + R_{FX} + (R_{FC})(R_{FX})$

$R_{DC} \approx R_{FC} + R_{FX}$

Equation 2: $R_{DC} = \sum_{i=1}^{n} w_i (R_{DC,i})$

Equation 3: $\sigma^2(R_{DC}) \approx \sigma^2(R_{FC}) + \sigma^2(R_{FX}) + 2\sigma(R_{FC})\sigma(R_{FX})\rho(R_{FC},R_{FX})$

Equation 4: $\sigma(R_{DC}) = \sigma(R_{FX})(1 + R_{FC})$

where for Equation 4:
R_{FC} = the return on a foreign currency denominated risk-free asset

LOS 8.b

Passive hedging is rule-based and typically matches the portfolio's currency exposure to the portfolio's benchmark in order to eliminate currency risk relative to the benchmark.

Discretionary hedging allows the manager to deviate modestly from passive hedging. The primary goal is currency risk reduction while seeking some modest value added return.

Active currency management allows wider discretion to selectively hedge or not hedge and to deviate substantially from the benchmark. The goal is value added, not risk reduction. At the extreme, an active manager can treat currency as an asset class and take positions independent of the portfolio assets. For example, a manager who is bearish on the Swedish krona (SEK) can short the SEK even if no SEK assets are owned.

Currency overlay management is a broad term referring to the use of a separate currency manager. The asset manager first takes positions in the markets considered most attractive, without regard to the resulting currency exposures. The overlay manager then adjusts the currency exposures. The overlay manager's mandate can be passive, discretionary, or active.

Arguments made for not hedging currency risk include the following:

- Avoid the time and cost of hedging or trading currencies.
- Currency effects are a "zero-sum game"; if one currency appreciates, another must depreciate.
- In the long run, currencies revert to a theoretical fair value.

Arguments for active currency management include the following:

- In the short run, currency movement can be extreme.
- Inefficient pricing of currencies can be exploited to add to portfolio return. Inefficient pricing of currency can arise as many foreign exchange (FX) trades are dictated by international trade transactions or central bank policies.

LOS 8.c

Factors that favor a benchmark neutral or fully hedged currency strategy are:

- A short time horizon for portfolio objectives.
- High risk aversion.
- High short-term income and liquidity needs.
- Significant foreign currency bond exposure.
- Low hedging costs.
- Clients who doubt the benefits of discretionary management.
- A client who is unconcerned with the opportunity costs of missing positive currency returns.

LOS 8.d

1. Economic fundamentals assumes that purchasing power parity (PPP) determines exchange rates in the very long run. In the shorter run, currency appreciation is associated with:
   - Currencies that are undervalued relative to fundamental value (based on PPP).
   - Currencies with a faster rate of increase in fundamental value.
   - Countries with lower inflation.
   - Countries with higher real or nominal interest rates.
   - Countries with a decreasing country risk premium.
2. Technical analysis:
   - Overbought (or oversold) currencies reverse.
   - A currency that declines to its support level will reverse upward unless it pierces the support level, in which case, it can decline substantially.
   - A currency that increases to its resistance level will reverse downward unless it pierces the resistance level, in which case, it can increase substantially.
   - If a shorter term moving average crosses a longer term moving average, the price will continue moving in the direction of the shorter term moving average.
3. The carry trade exploits the forward rate bias (i.e., forward exchange rates are not a valid predictor of currency market movement).
   - Borrow the lower interest rate currency (often a developed market).
   - Convert it to the higher rate currency (often an emerging market) at the spot exchange rate.
   - Invest and earn the higher interest rate.

This is a risky, not a hedged, trade. If the higher interest rate currency appreciates or depreciates less than "implied" by the forward rate, the trade will be profitable. In times of severe economic stress, the carry trade can be very unprofitable as the higher interest rate (and riskier) currency collapses.

4. Volatility trading profits from changes in volatility.
   - If volatility is expected to increase, enter a straddle (purchase a call and put with the same strike price, typically using at-the-money options). A strangle (buy an out-of-the-money call and put) can also be used. The strangle will cost less but will have less upside if volatility increases.
   - If volatility is expected to decline, enter a reverse straddle or strangle (i.e., sell the options).

LOS 8.e

Expectation:		Action:
Relative currency:	Appreciation	Reduce the hedge (short position) on **OR** increase the long position in the currency
	Depreciation	Increase the hedge on or decrease the long position in the currency
Volatility:	Rising	Long straddle (or strangle)
	Falling	Short straddle (or strangle)
Market conditions:	Stable	A carry trade
	Crisis	Discontinue the carry trade

LOS 8.f

Typically, forward contracts are preferred for currency hedging because:

- They can be customized, while futures contracts are standardized.
- They are available for almost any currency pair, while futures trade in size for only a limited number of currencies.
- Futures contracts require margin which adds operational complexity and can require periodic cash flows.
- Trading volume of FX forwards and swaps dwarfs that of FX futures, providing better liquidity.

A hedge can be a static hedge, which is established and held until expiration, or a dynamic hedge, which is periodically rebalanced.

The choice of hedging approach should consider:

- Shorter term contracts or dynamic hedges with more frequent rebalancing tend to increase transaction costs but improve the hedge results.
- Higher risk aversion suggests more frequent rebalancing.
- Lower risk aversion and strong manager views suggest allowing the manager greater discretion around the strategic hedging policy.

Hedging also exposes the portfolio to roll yield or roll return. Roll yield is a return from the movement of the forward price over time toward the spot price of an asset. It can be thought of as the profit or loss on a forward or futures contract if the spot price is unchanged at contract expiration.

Forward Premiums or Discounts and Currency Hedging Costs

Current position of foreign asset in Currency B	The hedge requires:	$F_{P/B} > S_{P/B}$, $i_B < i_P$ The forward price curve is upward-sloping.	$F_{P/B} < S_{P/B}$, $i_B > i_P$ The forward price curve is downward-sloping
Short the foreign asset	A long forward position in Currency B, the hedge earns:	Negative roll yield, which increases hedging cost and discourages hedging.	Positive roll yield, which decreases hedging cost and encourages hedging.
Long the foreign asset	A short forward position in Currency B the hedge earns:	Positive roll yield, which decreases hedging cost and encourages hedging.	Negative roll yield, which increases hedging cost and discourages hedging.

LOS 8.g

The cost of hedging a currency exposure:

- Positive roll will reduce and negative roll will increase hedging costs.
- Hedging with forward (or futures) has no explicit option premium cost, but it has implicit cost; it removes upside as well as downside.
- Active managers can selectively over- or under-hedge. Buy more or sell less of the currency expected to appreciate.
- An at-the-money (ATM) put (a protective put or portfolio insurance) is the most expensive (upfront premium cost) form of option hedging (e.g., buy a 50 delta put).

Option hedging costs can be reduced by decreasing upside potential or increasing downside risk. To hedge an existing currency exposure:

- Buy an out-of-the-money (OTM) put.
- Use a collar; buy an OTM put and sell an OTM call.
- Use a put spread; buy an OTM put and sell a further OTM put.
- Use a seagull spread; buy an OTM put, sell a further OTM put and sell an OTM call.
- Use exotic options that require additional conditions before they can be exercised or which can expire early.

LOS 8.h

A cross hedge (sometimes called a proxy hedge) uses a hedging vehicle that is different from, and not perfectly correlated with, the exposure being hedged.

A macro hedge is a type of cross hedge that addresses portfolio-wide risk factors rather than the risk of individual portfolio assets. One type of currency macro hedge uses a derivatives contract based on a fixed basket of currencies to modify currency exposure at a macro (portfolio) level.

The minimum-variance hedge ratio (MVHR) is a mathematical approach to determining the hedge ratio. Regress past changes in value of the portfolio (R_{DC}) to the past changes in value of the hedging instrument (the foreign currency) to find the hedge ratio that would have minimized standard deviation of R_{DC}. The hedge ratio is the beta (slope coefficient) of that regression.

- Positive correlation between R_{FX} and R_{FC}; MVHR > 1.
- Negative correlation between R_{FX} and R_{FC}; MVHR < 1.

LOS 8.i

A transaction in a lesser developed country's currency poses challenges because of: (1) higher transaction costs, and (2) the increased probability of extreme events. Examples of these problems include the following:

- Low trading volume leads dealers to charge larger bid/asked spreads.
- Liquidity can be lower and transaction costs higher to exit trades than to enter trades.
- Transactions between two emerging market currencies can be even more costly.
- Emerging market currencies return distributions are non-normal with higher probabilities of extreme events and negative skew of returns.
- The higher yield of emerging market currencies will lead to large forward discounts. This produces negative roll yield for investors who need to sell such currencies forward.
- Contagion is common during periods of financial crisis; the correlations of emerging markets with each other and their currencies tend to converge toward +1.0. At the very time diversification is needed most, it tends to disappear.
- *Tail risk* exists where the governments of emerging markets actively intervene in the markets for their currencies producing long periods of artificial price stability followed by sharp price movements when market forces overwhelm the government's capacity to intervene. These negative events occur more frequently than would be assumed with a normal distribution.

Non-deliverable forwards (NDFs) are forward contracts in which the exchange of the notional amounts of the currencies are not required. NDFs are an alternative to deliverable forwards and allow for the gains or losses of an emerging market's restricted currency to be settled in a developed market currency, which lowers credit risk. Only the gains to one party are paid at settlement.

ANSWER KEY FOR MODULE QUIZZES

Module Quiz 8.1

1. **C** The ending value in USD is: USD 1,253,000 × 1.05 = USD 1,315,650. The ending value in DJF is: USD 1,315,650 × DJF/USD 192.85 = DJF 253,723,103. (LOS 8.a)

2. **C** $(1 + R_{FC})(1 + R_{FX}) - 1$

   $(1.05)(192.85 / 179.54) - 1 = 12.78\%$

   (LOS 8.a)

3. It depends on the standard deviation of the asset returns measured in the foreign currency, the standard deviation of the currency, and the correlation between these two sources of return.

   Variance = $(1.0^2)(4.5^2) + (1.0^2)(3.7^2) + 2(1.0)(1.0)(0.81)(4.5)(3.7) = 60.913$

   Standard deviation = 7.8%

   (LOS 8.a)

4. **A** The manager's market views affect tactical decisions to vary away from the strategic decision. The portfolio and market circumstances determine the strategic decision. (LOS 8.b)

5. **C** Any of the following will shift the portfolio toward active currency management allowing greater manager discretion:
   - A long time horizon for portfolio objectives.
   - Low risk aversion.
   - Concern with regret at missing opportunities to add value through discretionary currency management.
   - Low short-term income and liquidity needs.
   - Little foreign currency bond exposure.
   - High hedging costs.
   - Clients who believe in the benefits of discretionary management.

   (LOS 8.b)

6. The case states that Simms must hold a long position in the KRW and her long futures position is coming due. She must roll it over with another long position. She does have the authority to increase or decrease the long hedge position by 10%. Because she believes the KRW will depreciate, she should reduce the hedge size 10% and will buy only 900,000 KRW rather than the existing 1,000,000 when she rolls over the hedge. The quotes are given in EUR/KRW so she must transact at the higher price of 0.00068 reflecting she is paying more EUR per KRW. The

Reading 8

spot quote is given in five decimal places so the forward points decimal must be moved five places to the left for a forward price of 0.00068 – (1.1 / 100,000) = 0.00068 – 0.000011 = 0.000669 EUR/KRW. (LOS 8.a)

7.

a. The expected returns measured in the investor's domestic currency (CHF) are:

EUR asset: (1.02)(0.99) – 1 = +0.98%

AUD asset: (1.025)(1.03) – 1 = +5.58%

The weighted average return is: 0.6(0.98%) + 0.4(5.58%) = 2.82%

b. The standard deviations of asset returns measured in the investor's domestic currency are:

EUR asset: $[(15.0^2) + (7.0^2) + 2(15.0)(7.0)(0.85)]^{1/2} = 21.27\%$

AUD asset: $[(25.0^2) + (9.0^2) + 2(25.0)(9.0)(0.65)]^{1/2} = 31.60\%$

The standard deviation of portfolio returns is:

$[0.6^2(21.27^2) + 0.4^2(31.60^2) + 2(0.6)(0.4)(0.70)(21.27)(31.60)]^{1/2} = 23.42\%$

c. The expected returns measured in the investor's domestic currency (CHF) are:

EUR asset: (1.02)(0.99) – 1 = +0.98%

AUD asset: (1.025)(1.03) – 1 = +5.58%

The weighted average return is: –1.5(0.98%) + 1.5(5.58%) = 6.90%

d. The standard deviations of asset returns measured in the investor's domestic currency are:

EUR asset: $[(15.0^2) + (7.0^2) + 2(15.0)(7.0)(0.85)]^{1/2} = 21.27\%$

AUD asset: $[(25.0^2) + (9.0^2) + 2(25.0)(9.0)(0.65)]^{1/2} = 31.60\%$

The standard deviation of portfolio returns is:

$[(-1.5)^2(21.27^2) + (1.5)^2(31.60^2) + 2(-1.5)(1.5)(0.70)(21.27)(31.60)]^{1/2} = 33.87\%$

(LOS 8.a)

Module Quiz 8.2, 8.3

1. **C** A carry trade should be more profitable in periods of economic stability (low, stable currency volatility) with lower interest rates in the borrowing currencies and higher interest rates in the investing currencies. (Module 8.3, LOS 8.d)

2. **C** Rising real interest rates in the euro zone would attract capital and be associated with a rising currency value, leading a manager to tilt to a long position in the euro. The other two answers are incorrect. Low volatility is favorable to a carry trade. Rising volatility increases the price of both calls and puts. It is likely to have a greater impact on the cost

of the protective put, which requires purchase of a put. In contrast, the collar cost is increased to purchase the put but offset by an increased receipt from selling the call. (Module 8.3, LOS 8.d)

Module Quiz 8.4, 8.5, 8.6

1. **B** This question requires you select the strategy that meets the objectives set by Perkins. He has three objectives and only one answer choice meets all three. He wants a protective put on the CHF; all three strategies buy a put on the CHF. He wants to lower the initial cost; one strategy buys a call, which will raise the cost, but it must be rejected. He is willing to reduce his downside protection in order to lower the initial cost; the only one strategy to do this is the buy a 40-delta put and sell a 20-delta put on the CHF. Note the strategy that sells an OTM call also lowers the initial cost but does so by limiting upside; this is not what Perkins specified. (Module 8.5, LOS 8.g)

2. **B** A direct currency hedge is a simple 1.0 hedge ratio; Archer will sell 1,000,000 GBP forward. A MVHR considers the correlation between returns of the foreign asset measured in the portfolio's domestic currency and change in value of the foreign currency. The hedge ratio is the beta (slope coefficient) of the regression. Archer will sell 1,250,000 GBP forward. (Module 8.6, LOS 8.h)

3. **C** An NDF settles in the developed market currency; however, the information is presented in a mixture of CNY/USD and USD/CNY which requires additional steps:

   Determine the size of the trade in USD at the forward exchange rate:

   CNY 2,000,000 / (CNY/USD 6.1155) = USD 327,037.85

   Determine the G/L on the USD position in CNY. The two exchange rates need to be in CNY/USD.

   Ending spot exchange rate USD/CNY 0.1612 is CNY/USD 6.20347.

   G/L = (CNY/USD 6.20347 – 6.1155) × 327,037.85 = CNY 28,769.52

   Determine the G/L in USD based on ending spot exchange rate is:

   G/L = CNY 28,769.52 × USD/CNY 0.1612 = USD 4,637.65

   The CNY was shorted at CNY/USD 6.1155 and declined in value to CNY/USD 6.20347 producing a gain on the trade of USD 4,637.65.

   (Module 8.6, LOS 8.i)

TOPIC QUIZ: DERIVATIVES AND CURRENCY MANAGEMENT

You have now finished the Derivatives and Currency Management topic section. On your Schweser online dashboard, you can find a Topic Quiz that will provide immediate feedback on how effective your study of this material has been. The test is best taken timed; allow three minutes per question. Topic Quizzes are more exam-like than typical QBank questions or module quiz questions. A score less than 70% suggests that additional review of the topic is needed.

FORMULAS

Put-call parity:

call premium (paid initially) – put premium (received initially) = initial stock price paid – PV(X) received

In symbols, $c_0 - p_0 = S_0 - PV(X)$, which can be rearranged to $S_0 + p_0 = c_0 + PV(X)$.

Notional principal of the interest rate swap:

$$NP_s = \left(\frac{MD_T - MD_p}{MD_s}\right)(MV_P)$$

where:

NP_S = notional swap principal

MD_T = target modified duration

MD_P = current portfolio modified duration

MD_S = modified duration of swap

MV_P = market value of portfolio

Identifying the CTD bond at delivery:

profit/(loss) on delivery = [(settlement price × CF) + AI_T] – (CTD clean price + AI_T)

To fully hedge (immunize) a portfolio's value against interest rate changes:

$\Delta P = HR \times \Delta$ futures price

where:

ΔP = change in portfolio's value

HR = hedge ratio = Number of futures contracts

$$\Delta P = HR \times \frac{\Delta CTD}{CF}$$

$$HR = \frac{\Delta P}{\Delta CTD} \times CF$$

Duration-based hedge ratio (BPVHR):

To achieve a target duration, the formula can be amended to:

$$BPVHR = \frac{-BPV_{portfolio}}{BPV_{CTD}} \times CF$$

BPVHR = number of short futures

$BPV_{portfolio} = MD_{portfolio} \times 0.01\% \times MV_{portfolio}$

MD = modified duration

$BPV_{CTD} = MD_{CTD} \times 0.01\% \times MV_{CTD}$

$MV_{CTD} = \text{CTD price} / 100 \times \$100{,}000$

$$BPVHR = \frac{BPV_{target} - BPV_{portfolio}}{BPV_{CTD}} \times CF$$

$BPV_{target} = MD_{target} \times 0.0001 \times MV_{portfolio}$

Number of futures contracts needed

$$= \frac{\text{monetary value of position to be hedged}}{\text{futures price} \times \text{multiplier}}$$

The hedge ratio for futures can be calculated as:

$$HR = \frac{\text{amount of currency to be exchanged}}{\text{futures contract size}}$$

$$\text{Number of futures required} = \left(\frac{\beta_T - \beta_P}{\beta_F}\right)\left(\frac{MV_P}{F}\right)$$

where:

β_T = target portfolio beta

β_P = current portfolio beta

β_F = futures beta (beta of stock index)

MV_P = market value of portfolio

F = futures contract value = futures price × multiplier

Variance over the life of the swap:

$\text{settlement amount}_T$ = (variance notional)(realized variance − variance strike)

Realized variance:

$R_i = \ln(P_t / P_{t-1})$

$$\text{daily variance} = \left[\frac{\sum_{i=1}^{N-1} R_i^2}{(N-1)}\right]$$

annualized variance = daily variance × 252; 252 = assumed trading days in a year

Variance notional:

$$\text{variance notional} = \frac{\text{vega notional}}{2 \times \text{strike price (K)}}, \text{ so profit/(loss)} = N_{VAR} \times (\sigma^2 - K^2)$$

$$= N_{vega} \times \left(\frac{\sigma^2 - K^2}{2K}\right)$$

$$\text{expected variance to maturity} = \left(\sigma_t^2 \times \frac{t}{T}\right) + \left(K_{(T-t)}^2 \times \frac{T-t}{T}\right)$$

where:

σ_t^2 = annualized realized volatility from initiation to valuation date squared

$K_{(T-t)}^2$ = annualized implied volatility from valuation date to swap maturity squared

Probability of a change in the Fed funds target rate:

percent probability of rate change

$$= \frac{\text{effective rate implied by futures} - \text{current Fed funds target rate}}{\text{Fed funds rate assuming a rate change} - \text{current Fed target funds rate}}$$

Note that this can be expressed as

$$\frac{\text{implied Fed funds effective rate} - \text{current target rate}}{\text{expected size of rate change}}$$

Foreign Asset Return and Risk:

$$R_{DC} = (1 + R_{FC})(1 + R_{FX}) - 1 = R_{FC} + R_{FX} + (R_{FC})(R_{FX})$$

$$R_{DC} \approx R_{FC} + R_{FX}$$

$$R_{DC} = \sum_{i=1}^{n} w_i (R_{DC,i})$$

$$\sigma^2(R_{DC}) \approx \sigma^2(R_{FC}) + \sigma^2(R_{FX}) + 2\sigma(R_{FC})\sigma(R_{FX})\rho(R_{FC},R_{FX})$$

$$\sigma(R_{DC}) = \sigma(R_{FX})(1 + R_{FC})$$

where:
R_{FC} = the return on a foreign currency denominated risk-free asset

INDEX

Notes

Notes

Kaplan SCHWESER™
2024 CFA® Notes 备考笔记三级

第三册（全五册）

SCHWESERNOTES™ 2024 CFA® PART III

BOOK 3

Fixed Income and Equity

美国开普兰公司 著

中信出版集团 | 北京

图书在版编目（CIP）数据

Kaplan SCHWESER 2024 CFA®; Notes 备考笔记 = SCHWESERNOTES™; 2024 LEVEL Ⅲ CFA®; 三级：全五册：英文 / 美国开普兰公司著 . -- 北京：中信出版社，2023.8

ISBN 978-7-5217-5649-4

Ⅰ . ① K… Ⅱ . ①美… Ⅲ . ①金融－分析－资格考试－自学参考资料－英文 Ⅳ . ① F83

中国国家版本馆 CIP 数据核字 (2023) 第 083168 号

Kaplan SCHWESER 2024 CFA® Notes 备考笔记三级第三册（全五册）
著者：　美国开普兰公司
出版发行：中信出版集团股份有限公司
（北京市朝阳区东三环北路 27 号嘉铭中心　邮编　100020）
承印者：　河北鹏润印刷有限公司

开本：889mm × 1194mm　1/16　　印张：74.5　　字数：2130 千字
版次：2023 年 8 月第 1 版　　印次：2023 年 8 月第 1 次印刷
书号：ISBN 978-7-5217-5649-4
定价：1599.00 元（全五册）

Book 3: Fixed Income and Equity

SchweserNotes™ 2024

Level III CFA®

KAPLAN SCHWESER

SCHWESERNOTES™ 2024 LEVEL III CFA® BOOK 3: FIXED INCOME AND EQUITY

Published in 2023 by Kaplan, Inc.

Printed in the United States of America.

ISBN: 978-1-0788-3754-5

CONTENTS

FIXED INCOME

READING 16

LEARNING OUTCOME STATEMENTS (LOS)

12. Fixed-Income Active Management: Credit Strategies

The candidate should be able to:

a. describe risk considerations for spread-based fixed-income portfolios. (page 99)
b. discuss the advantages and disadvantages of credit spread measures for spread-based fixed-income portfolios, and explain why option-adjusted spread is considered the most appropriate measure. (page 103)
c. discuss bottom-up approaches to credit strategies. (page 113)
d. discuss top-down approaches to credit strategies. (page 116)
e. discuss liquidity risk in credit markets and how liquidity risk can be managed in a credit portfolio. (page 119)
f. describe how to assess and manage tail risk in credit portfolios. (page 120)
g. discuss the use of credit default swap strategies in active fixed-income portfolio management. (page 122)
h. discuss various portfolio positioning strategies that managers can use to implement a specific credit spread view. (page 126)
i. discuss considerations in constructing and managing portfolios across international credit markets. (page 135)
j. describe the use of structured financial instruments as an alternative to corporate bonds in credit portfolios. (page 137)
k. describe key inputs, outputs, and considerations in using analytical tools to manage fixed-income portfolios. (page 138)

13. Overview of Equity Portfolio Management

The candidate should be able to:

a. describe the roles of equities in the overall portfolio. (page 151)
b. describe how an equity manager's investment universe can be segmented. (page 153)
c. describe the types of income and costs associated with owning and managing an equity portfolio and their potential effects on portfolio performance. (page 156)
d. describe the potential benefits of shareholder engagement and the role an equity manager might play in shareholder engagement. (page 159)
e. describe rationales for equity investment across the passive–active spectrum. (page 161)

14. Passive Equity Investing

The candidate should be able to:

a. discuss considerations in choosing a benchmark for a passively managed equity portfolio. (page 167)
b. compare passive factor-based strategies to market-capitalization-weighted indexing. (page 170)
c. compare different approaches to passive equity investing. (page 172)
d. compare the full replication, stratified sampling, and optimization approaches for the construction of passively managed equity portfolios. (page 173)
e. discuss potential causes of tracking error and methods to control tracking error for passively managed equity portfolios. (page 175)
f. explain sources of return and risk to a passively managed equity portfolio. (page 176)

15. Active Equity Investing: Strategies

The candidate should be able to:

a. compare fundamental and quantitative approaches to active management. (page 181)
b. analyze bottom-up active strategies, including their rationale and associated processes. (page 182)
c. analyze top-down active strategies, including their rationale and associated processes. (page 182)
d. analyze factor-based active strategies, including their rationale and associated processes. (page 187)
e. analyze activist strategies, including their rationale and associated processes. (page 192)
f. describe active strategies based on statistical arbitrage and market microstructure. (page 194)
g. describe how fundamental active investment strategies are created. (page 197)
h. describe how quantitative active investment strategies are created. (page 198)
i. discuss equity investment style classifications. (page 203)

16. Active Equity Investing: Portfolio Construction

The candidate should be able to:

a. describe elements of a manager's investment philosophy that influence the portfolio construction process. (page 213)
b. discuss approaches for constructing actively managed equity portfolios. (page 216)
c. distinguish between Active Share and active risk and discuss how each measure relates to a manager's investment strategy. (page 218)
d. discuss the application of risk budgeting concepts in portfolio construction. (page 224)
e. discuss risk measures that are incorporated in equity portfolio construction and describe how limits set on these measures affect portfolio construction. (page 230)
f. discuss how assets under management, position size, market liquidity, and portfolio turnover affect equity portfolio construction decisions. (page 232)
g. evaluate the efficiency of a portfolio structure given its investment mandate. (page 234)
h. discuss the long-only, long extension, long/short, and equitized market-neutral approaches to equity portfolio construction, including their risks, costs, and effects on potential alphas. (page 235)

READING 9

Overview of Fixed-Income Portfolio Management

EXAM FOCUS

This reading provides a good overview of issues covered in more detail in subsequent readings, so don't obsess about exact nuances of terminology. Take in what is said and move on to the rest of fixed income to see what we are going to do with these ideas and concepts. Do take the time to understand the model for projecting or decomposing bond return.

We make reference to historical results such as return, standard deviation, and correlation in this reading. They reflect results reported in the CFA reading. The numbers are to suggest typical relationships. They are not to be memorized and do not dictate what can happen in any specific period.

MODULE 9.1: ROLE OF FIXED INCOME

Video covering this content is available online.

LOS 9.a: Discuss roles of fixed-income securities in portfolios and how fixed-income mandates may be classified.

The fixed-income market is highly varied. It includes publicly traded securities such as bond and money market securities as well as nonpublic instruments such as loans and private placement securities. It varies by maturity and credit quality segments. There are structure differences such as straight bonds without embedded options, instruments with embedded prepayment options, variable coupon structures, and inflation adjustment features.

As an asset class used in a portfolio, fixed income may provide:

1. *Diversification*. In general, fixed income has low correlation to equity markets. Adding an asset class to an existing portfolio with a correlation of less than +1 improves its risk-adjusted return through diversification benefits. The lower the correlation, the greater the diversification benefit. Specific correlation numbers vary by time period and type of instrument used. For 2000 to 2019, the correlations of various fixed-income indexes to the S&P 500 equity index ranged from –0.30 for 10-year U.S. Treasury bonds to +0.63 for U.S. high-yield (credit-risky) bonds.

   Diversification can be achieved internally within the fixed-income asset class, primarily due to changes in credit spreads causing divergence in the performance of investment-grade securities versus credit-risky high-yield (below investment-grade) securities.

   These correlations are not always stable over time. A particular problem is flight to quality. During periods of market stress, all lower-quality and riskier assets, including high-yield bonds and equities, tend to decline together (correlation approaching +1) as investors sell these assets and buy high-quality developed-market government bonds for safety. Thus, correlation of these government bonds to riskier assets declines during periods of stress and may be negative.

   The volatility of bond market returns can also vary over time, increasing significantly for high-yield bonds in times of market crisis.

2. *Regular cash flow.* Most fixed income provides regular, predictable cash flow that investors can use to meet expected future obligations. This is convenient for an individual needing regular living expenses or specific periodic expenditures such as college tuition payments. Institutions such as insurance companies that must make periodic payments to policyholders could structure and dedicate a portfolio of bond assets to meet these payouts. Investors could also build a buy-and-hold laddered portfolio of bonds to provide regular cash flow. Buy and hold means no sales or trading are planned, and laddered means a somewhat equal amount of par comes due periodically. Implicit in this discussion is that there is no significant credit risk and that all payments will be made on the bonds.

3. *Inflation hedge.* While not the first thing most investors would think of, some types of bonds do provide forms of inflation protection. Standard fixed-coupon (nominal rate) bonds do not. For simplicity, assume the bonds are purchased at par so that initial yield is the coupon rate. The purchase yield and coupon reflect nominal compensation for an expected future rate of inflation and a real return above that rate of inflation. If inflation increases, the coupon cash flow is fixed and the investor suffers on an inflation-adjusted basis. Looked at another way, the yield a new investor would want increases and the price of the bond must decline.

   – Inflation-linked (also called real rate or real return) bonds provide direct protection for the effect of inflation. Like regular bonds, the coupon payment amount is the coupon rate × par. But unlike regular bonds, the par adjusts for inflation. If 1 million par is purchased and inflation is 5%, the par increases by 5% to 1.05 million. (For later comparison with floating-coupon bonds, assume the previous inflation rate was 3%, though this does not directly affect the calculations for the inflation-linked bond.) That leads the coupon payment amount to increase by 5% as well. For example, if the real rate were 0.5%, the first (annualized) coupon payment is 5,250 (1,050,000 × 0.005). This adjustment continues every period to compensate for cumulative inflation over the life of the bond. At expiration, inflation-adjusted par is paid to the investor. Thus, both coupon payments and par are inflation protected.

– Floating-coupon (floating-rate) securities also provide inflation protection. The coupon rate is set by a formula such as the market reference rate (MRR) + 100 basis points. If inflation and MRR are initially 3.0% and 3.5%, the first (annual) coupon payment on 1 million par would be 45,000 [1,000,000 (0.035 + 0.01)]. If inflation then increases by 2% to 5.0%, it is likely MRR will also increase by 2% to 5.5% and the next coupon payment will increase to 65,000 [1,000,000 (0.055 + 0.01)]. No adjustment is made to the par amount. Thus, it is said the coupons are inflation protected but not the principal.

PROFESSOR'S NOTE

It is easy to misunderstand this material. In theory, both inflation-linked and floating-coupon securities provide full inflation protection but do so in different ways. Imagine fixed-coupon nominal rate (NR), inflation-linked, and floating-coupon bonds from the same issuer with the same maturity. In a fully efficient market, all three would be priced to reflect the same consensus expectations for inflation and have the same expected return. (Because they respond to inflation risk differently, there could be small differences.) If the actual rates of inflation turn out to higher (lower) than initial consensus expectations, the actual returns for the inflation linked and floating coupon would be superior (inferior) to the NR bond. Between the inflation linked and floating coupon, one or the other may end up being best depending on the actual path of future inflation. Notice in the earlier example with inflation increasing from 3% to 5% the par and coupon payment amount for the inflation-linked bond increased by 5% while the par of the floating coupon was unchanged, but the coupon payment amount went from 45,000 to 65,000, an increase of 44.4%.

The bottom line is to accept the conclusions as presented in the reading; they are correct. You can come back and develop spreadsheet models to test various scenarios after you have the charter. If you like bonds, it is fun to do so.

Fixed-Income Mandates

Fixed-income investment mandates can be classified into two major types: liability-based mandates and total return mandates.

Liability-based mandates are portfolio assets that are managed solely to meet expected future liability payouts. All asset cash flows are reinvested until paid out to meet the liabilities. This is often referred to as immunization. There are several forms and variations of **immunization**.

- **Cash-flow matching** is the simplest form of immunization. The assets are selected so that cash flows occur when and in the size needed to meet the liability payouts.
- **Duration matching** matches the duration of the assets and liabilities so the two will fluctuate in a similar way as interest rates change, such that their ending values will remain matched.
- **Contingent immunization (CI)** is a hybrid of active management and immunization. The portfolio is initially funded with more money than required to meet the future liability payouts. The present value of the assets (PVA) exceeds the present value of the liabilities (PVL). The difference is the surplus. As long as the surplus is positive, the portfolio can be managed in any way the manager believes will add value. If CI succeeds, the surplus will grow and the ultimate cost of CI will be less than that of initially immunizing. If the active management is unsuccessful and the surplus declines to zero, the portfolio must be immediately immunized and the ultimate cost of CI will be more than that of initial immunization but by a known amount.
- **Derivatives overlays**, involving the use of futures or swaps contracts, can be used to implement duration matching or contingent immunization strategies.

Total return mandates do not seek to fund future liabilities but may target an absolute rate of return or, more commonly, seek to equal or outperform (relative return versus) a benchmark. The key metrics to evaluate such portfolios are **active return** (portfolio return less return of the relevant benchmark, also called value added or alpha) and volatility of that active return (standard deviation of active return, also called **active risk**, **tracking error**, or **tracking risk**). Total return mandates include the following:

- **Pure indexing**, which attempts to replicate the performance of a bond index. It targets zero active return and risk. Unlike the equity market, the large number of individual bonds in most indexes and their potential lack of liquidity makes literal duplication of the index (holding every issue in the same weight as in the index) impractical. Most pure bond indexing instead seeks to exactly match all the risk factors of the index (such as duration, credit or quality, sectors, and prepayment risks) while still allowing the manager some leeway on the individual bonds selected. The turnover (trading) in the portfolio should be low and similar to the turnover in the index.
- **Enhanced indexing** allows some additional flexibility in constructing the portfolio and seeks to add some modest active return. Typically, duration (interest rate risk) is still matched to the index, but some risk mismatches such as modest over- or underweighting of sectors and quality are allowed. Slightly higher portfolio turnover is likely.
- **Active management** allows much larger deviations from the risk factors of the index and seeks greater active return. Duration can also be mismatched and portfolio turnover can be much higher.

Fixed-Income Portfolio Measures

LOS 9.b: Describe fixed-income portfolio measures of risk and return as well as correlation characteristics.

PROFESSOR'S NOTE

This section reviews some fundamental definitions of fixed-income risk and return measures, almost all of which have been met at previous levels of the CFA program. Remember that the Level III exam will likely be less focused on the calculation of these measures than previous levels were and more focused on the interpretation and use of these measures in a portfolio management situation. Understanding what the measures are telling you is the key focus here.

Key bond risk and return measures are displayed here:

Name	Definition	Interpretation
Macaulay duration	Weighted average *time* to receive cash flows, where weights are the present value of the cash flows	A higher Macaulay duration means investors are waiting longer to receive cash flows and hence face higher price volatility when yields change.
Modified duration	Macaulay duration divided by one plus the periodic yield of the bond	This gives the approximate expected percentage change in bond price for a 1% change in yield. For example, a bond with a modified duration of 7 is expected to fall by approximately 7% when yields rise by 1%.
Effective duration	Sensitivity of a bond's price to a parallel shift change in a benchmark yield curve, based on directly modeling changes in prices due to changes in a benchmark curve	This gives the approximate expected percentage change in bond price for a 1% change in benchmark curve. Effective duration is used for complex bonds where cash flows are not certain, such as bonds with embedded options.
Key rate duration (or partial duration)	Sensitivity of a bond's price to a change in a benchmark yield *curve for a specific maturity, while other rates remain the same*	It helps to assess exposure to nonparallel changes in yield curves, where different maturity rates move by different amounts. For example, a bond with a 10-year key rate duration of 7 is expected to fall by approximately 7% when 10-year benchmark yields rise by 1% *while all other maturity rates stay the same.*

(*continued*)

Name	Definition	Interpretation
Empirical duration	A measure of interest rate sensitivity derived from regressing bond returns versus benchmark yield changes	This is the same interpretation as effective duration; however, it is based on past observed market behavior rather than derived through modeling.
Money duration (or dollar duration)	A measure of the monetary gain or loss expected due to a 1% change in yield, which is calculated as modified duration × market value	A higher money duration implies a larger absolute change in portfolio value (in currency terms) when yields change by 1%.
Price value of a basis point (PVBP) [or "dollar value of an 0.01" (DV01) or basis point value (BPV)]	Money duration × 0.0001	It measures the absolute change in portfolio value (in currency terms) when yields change by 1 basis point.
Convexity	The extent to which the bond's price behavior versus changes in yield is nonlinear (i.e., not a straight line). Convexity is positive for fixed-coupon bonds without embedded options.	Positive convexity implies that a bond price is expected to rise by *more* than that implied by duration alone when yields fall and fall by *less* than that implied by duration alone when yields rise.
Effective convexity	Measures the extent of a *nonlinear* relationship between a bond's price and changes in a benchmark yield curve, based on directly modeling changes in prices due to changes in a benchmark curve	Effective convexity is used for complex bonds where cash flows are not certain, such as bonds with embedded options.

Some key facts to consider include the following:

- Convexity is valuable to bondholders when yields are expected to change. This is because positive convexity, as just described, implies that a bond price is expected to rise by *more* than that implied by duration alone when yields fall and fall by *less* than that implied by duration alone when yields rise. Note that this will mean investors will pay higher prices for higher convexity bonds (and accept lower yields vs. yields of other less convex bonds).
- Convexity is often referred to as a second order measure—meaning that it measures how much the sensitivity of price versus yield *changes* as yields change. As a second order measure, it is approximately proportional to duration squared—in other words, a bond with a duration of 20 years will have approximately four times the convexity of a bond with a duration of 10 years (because 20 squared is four times 10 squared).
- Convexity is directly related to the *dispersion* of cash flows in time around the Macaulay duration of the bond. For a given Macaulay duration, the lowest convexity bond will be a zero-coupon bond with one cash flow at maturity.

Fixed-Income Portfolio Measures

When combining bonds together in a portfolio, the following apply:

- The Macaulay duration of a portfolio is the weighted average time to receive the cash flows of the portfolio. It is commonly estimated as the cash-weighed duration of the individual assets in the portfolio (note that this applies to all basic duration measures). For example, if 40% of a portfolio is invested in a bond with a duration of 10 and the remaining 60% of the portfolio is invested in a bond with a duration of 15, the portfolio duration is estimated as $(0.4 \times 10) + (0.6 \times 15) = 13$.
- The modified duration and convexity of a portfolio is estimated as the cash-weighted convexity of the individual assets in the portfolio, similar to the process for the Macaulay duration just described.
- The effective duration and effective convexity of a portfolio are calculated using the following formulas:

$$\text{effective duration} = \frac{(PV_{-}) - (PV_{+})}{2(\Delta\text{curve})(PV_0)}$$

$$\text{effective convexity} = \frac{(PV_{-}) + (PV_{+}) - 2(PV_0)}{(\Delta\text{curve})^2(PV_0)}$$

where:

PV_0 = current value of the portfolio
PV_{-} = value of portfolio when benchmark curve is shifted down
PV_{+} = value of portfolio when benchmark curve is shifted up
Δcurve = change in benchmark curve

- **Spread duration** measures a portfolio's percentage sensitivity to a 1% change in *credit spreads*.
- **Duration times spread (DTS)** is equal to spread duration multiplied by the bonds' credit spread. This measure adjusts spread duration to give a higher sensitivity to spread changes when spreads themselves are higher. This adjustment reflects the empirically observed behavior that bonds with higher spreads are expected to have higher spread *changes* (i.e., spread changes tend to be proportional to current spread levels, rather than the same in absolute term across bonds with different spreads).

Fixed-income managers would use these measures just listed to actively manage a fixed-income portfolio as follows:

- A manager expecting interest rates to fall would increase the duration of their portfolio in order to increase the amount by which their bond prices rise. Conversely, a manager who expected rates to rise would lower the duration of their portfolio.

- A manager who expects credit spreads to narrow would increase the spread duration of their portfolio in order to increase the amount by which their bond price rises. They may also lower the credit rating of the bonds held in the portfolio. Conversely, a manager who expects spreads to widen would decrease the duration of their portfolio or increase the average credit rating of their holdings.
- A manager can use **relative value** techniques to rank individual bonds based on valuation, issuer characteristics, and technical market conditions, so that they can select the best bond to reflect their market view. For example, a manager who expects spreads to narrow can use relative value techniques to select the best bonds (according to their selection criteria) with a DTS greater than that of the benchmark.

Correlations Between Fixed-Income Sectors

Correlations between bonds in the same market are likely to be high due to the similar overarching macroeconomic conditions that apply to all bonds in the market.

Returns on investment-grade bonds with low credit risk are likely to be primarily driven by changes in the benchmark sovereign yield curve. High-yield bonds, however, are more likely to be affected by changes in spread than benchmark rates. There is likely a negative relationship between benchmark rates and spreads, because in poor economic conditions, interest rates will likely be low but credit spreads high (and vice versa). For this reason, high-yield securities are likely to exhibit higher correlations with equity.

Bond Liquidity

LOS 9.c: Describe bond market liquidity, including the differences among market sub-sectors, and discuss the effect of liquidity on fixed-income portfolio management.

Liquidity is the ability to make transactions in relatively large size, quickly, and with minimal deviation from the market price of the asset. In the bond market, the most recently issued (on-the-run) developed-market government bonds are likely to be quite liquid and other bonds may be quite illiquid. Those other bonds may trade virtually never or at very wide bid-ask spreads. Issues leading to illiquidity include:

- The very large number of bond issues, each of which can be quite small, compared to the smaller number of stock issues in the equity market. A single issuer can have dozens or more separate bonds outstanding. Each can be unique in terms of maturity, coupon, and call features. Each issuer's bonds are heterogeneous (different), unlike the stock of the issuer, which is homogeneous. Most issuers have one class of common stock (and perhaps none, one, or a few issues of preferred stock).

- Bonds usually trade over the counter, which increases the search cost to find a counterparty to any transaction. This also makes transactions less transparent (it is harder to find information on past price and volume of transactions). Bond liquidity is usually higher for recently issued bonds as dealers may have an inventory of those bonds on hand. As time passes, the bonds are likely to become held in portfolios of investors with no plans to trade the bonds. When the issuer puts out a new issue of similar remaining maturity to a previous issue, the older issue becomes off-the-run and its liquidity decreases. The less liquid issues normally trade at a higher yield to maturity, offering a liquidity premium. These liquidity premiums can vary widely depending on specific circumstances.

PROFESSOR'S NOTE

Some authors refer to an illiquidity premium and others to a liquidity premium. They mean the same thing. The current Level III fixed-income readings call it a liquidity premium, meaning extra compensation in the form of higher yield for lack of liquidity. Remember that as liquidity and the ability to execute transactions at reasonable prices decrease, the liquidity (or illiquidity) premium and yield increase.

Liquidity varies widely by bond market subsector. Generally:

- Liquidity for on-the-run high-quality sovereign government debt is high and declines somewhat for older off-the-run issues. These sovereign government bonds are usually large in size, more homogeneous, and often used as benchmarks for pricing other bonds and as collateral in the repo market (an issue discussed later).
- Corporate bonds are far more varied in credit quality and size of issue. Liquidity typically declines with lower quality as the bonds become riskier and with smaller size of the issue. Size can be an important factor as it takes roughly the same commitment of resources to analyze a large or small issuer, but with smaller issuers it is more difficult to acquire a large holding for the portfolio. Small issuers may also be excluded from bond indexes.

Effects of Liquidity on Bond Portfolio Management

- *Pricing data*. Historically bonds trade over the counter with past price and value information not reported. This makes it difficult to find pricing information. Some countries have moved towards centralized collection and reporting of this trade information, increasing market transparency. In the absence of such reporting or with infrequent trading of a bond issue, pricing information may be based on out-of-date trade prices. Instead of using old prices, bond pricing is often based on **matrix pricing**. Information is gathered on recent trades of bonds with similar features (maturity, quality, and coupon). The YTM of those trades is used to calculate the inferred market price of similar bonds.
- *Portfolio construction*. Buy-and-hold investors have less need for liquidity as they have no plans to sell the bonds; thus, they may prefer to select less liquid bonds in exchange for higher yield. In contrast, active investors and traders will prefer more liquid bonds, reasoning their active management strategies will generate

additional return and compensate for lower initial yield. Other investors who anticipate the possibility of needing to sell bonds before maturity to meet unexpected needs may tend to avoid less liquid bonds such as longer maturity and smaller issuers or private placements. The cost of crossing a bid-ask yield spread can be approximated as bond duration × (ask yield – bid yield). For example, a manager trading in a bond with a duration of 10 and a bid-ask spread of 20 bps would suffer costs of 10 × 0.002 = 0.02, or 2%, if they bought the bond at the ask and immediately sold the bond at the bid.

- The fact that most bond trading is done in dealer markets leads less liquid bonds to trade at higher bid-ask spreads. Dealers will reason that if they purchase such bonds, it will take longer to then resell them. Thus, dealers will widen the bid-ask to earn greater expected compensation for holding less liquid bonds in inventory.

Alternatives to Direct Investment in Bonds

PROFESSOR'S NOTE

There is no direct LOS on this next section, but you will recognize topics that are covered elsewhere, so we include a brief summary. These indirect investments are typically more liquid than the underlying bonds.

- Fixed-income exchange-traded funds (ETFs) replicate many sectors of the fixed-income market. The shares are listed on an exchange and therefore easily traded throughout the trading day and have high liquidity.
- Open-end mutual funds offer the ability to subscribe to and redeem fund units on a daily basis and provide diversification and economies of scale that smaller investors would not be able to achieve directly in bond markets.
- Derivatives include exchange-traded bond futures and options and OTC instruments such as interest rate swaps and total return swaps (TRS). Under a TRS, one party (the *total return receiver*) pays an interest rate plus a spread in return for the total return on a reference bond portfolio. An investor might prefer to receive the total return of a bond portfolio under a TRS because the contract will likely only require a relatively small amount of capital to be posted as collateral versus fully funding an ETF position. Drawbacks of using a TRS to access bond market returns include facing the counterparty risk of the total return payer, the rollover risk of renewing contracts when reaching maturity, and potential regulatory reform requiring higher collateral and increasing the costs of such contracts.

Reading 9

MODULE QUIZ 9.1

1. A credit analyst is evaluating the potential for fixed-income securities to provide an inflation hedge. Which of the following types of securities protects both the bond coupon and notional principal amounts from inflation?
   A. Fixed-coupon bonds.
   B. Inflation-linked bonds.
   C. Floating-coupon bonds.
2. A fixed-income portfolio manager is seeking to outperform the Barclays Capital Aggregate Bond Index. Which of the following statements *most accurately* describes a pure indexing strategy for achieving the total-return mandate? Pure bond indexing:
   A. allows large deviations from the risk factors of the index and seeks a high active return.
   B. matches duration to the index, but some risk mismatches of sectors and quality are allowed.
   C. seeks to exactly match all the risk factors of the index while allowing the manager some leeway on the individual bonds selected.
3. Regarding the varying liquidity characteristics among bond market subsectors, which of the following bond issues would typically lead to higher levels of liquidity?
   A. Issuing a small corporate bond issue.
   B. Issuing on-the-run sovereign government debt.
   C. Issuing a corporate bond that is below investment grade.

MODULE 9.2: MODELING RETURN

Video covering this content is available online.

LOS 9.d: Describe and interpret a model for fixed-income returns.

Expected fixed-income return can be viewed as having five components. These components could be projected to calculate expected return or calculated after the fact to decompose sources of return actually earned. The following example explains this approach and the required calculations. While it appears formidable in aggregate, it is a combination of simple time value of money calculations and bond math concepts covered at earlier levels. For a bond portfolio, it uses aggregate portfolio data and that aggregation is provided. Otherwise, there is too much weighted average calculating to be practical without access to spreadsheets.

EXAMPLE: Expected return of a bond portfolio

A fixed-income strategist wishes to forecast the expected return of a bond portfolio for the next year. She gathers the following information and assumes no reinvestment of cash flow:

Par value (notional principal) in millions	50
Average coupon rate of portfolio	3.0%
Coupon frequency	Semiannual
Horizon analysis	1 year
Average bond price of portfolio	101.500
Projected bond price in one year if yield curve is unchanged	102.419
Average bond convexity (C) of portfolio	28
Average bond duration (modified duration or MD) of portfolio	5.60
Expected average benchmark YTM change	–0.54%
Expected change in spread	–0.06%
Expected gains or losses versus investor's currency (for 40% of portfolio allocated to foreign bonds)	+3.925%

Projected return:

Component 1, **coupon income**:

annual coupon payment / current bond portfolio price = 3.0 / 101.50 = 2.956%

Because this example assumes no cash-flow reinvestment, it does not matter that the coupons are paid semiannually. With a 3.0% annual coupon rate, 1.50 will be received in 6 and 12 months for total coupons collected of 3.00 per 100 par. Collected coupon amount divided by initial price is the coupon income of the portfolio, sometimes referred to as current yield.

Component 2, **rolldown return**:

This is a projection of the bond prices in the portfolio assuming the yield curve is unchanged. For example, suppose the portfolio were made up only of a 7-year bond priced to yield 2.76% with a price of 101.50. Further assume the initial yield curve is upward sloping and the 6-year bond yields 2.56%. A bond pricing model could be used to project the price of the 7-year bond in one year when it is a 6-year bond priced at a 2.56% yield. (Note that this is not necessarily a simple analysis for a portfolio of bonds and would have to be done bond by bond and then aggregated. That is why it is a given value in the data provided). The rolldown return is calculated as follows:

(end of horizon period projected price – beginning price) / beginning price = (102.419 – 101.50) / 101.50 = 0.905%

Note that if the yield curve is flat and a bond is initially priced at a premium (discount) to par, the projected price at end of period will be lower (higher) than the start-of-period price as the bond's price is pulled to par at expiration. With a sloped yield curve, that may not always be true in the shorter run (before maturity). It is true that if the yield curve is upward (downward) sloping, the rolldown return will be higher (lower) than the start-of-period YTM because the bond will decline in the remaining term to maturity over the horizon period and be priced at a lower (higher) YTM at the end of that period.

Components 1 and 2 are sometimes combined and called the **rolling yield**:

$$2.956 + 0.905 = 3.86\%$$

Component 3, **expected price change due to change in benchmark yield (ΔY)**:

Let's assume the projected price based on rolldown of 102.419 is in fact an aggregate portfolio benchmark yield (YTM) of 2.56%. The analyst then projects a 54-basis-point decline in yields versus the 2.56% yield used in the rolldown calculation. Expected price change is calculated from the investor's expected change in benchmark yield using the portfolio's duration and convexity:

$$(-MD \times \Delta Y) + (\tfrac{1}{2} \times C \times \Delta Y^2) = (-5.6 \times -0.0054) + [\tfrac{1}{2} \times 28 \times (-0.0054)^2] = 0.03024 + 0.00041 = 3.065\%$$

Notice that the convexity effect is very small and only adds 0.041% to the return. Convexity is a second-order effect and is often insignificant for option-free bonds unless the ΔY is very large. If the portfolio includes bonds with embedded options, then effective duration and effective convexity must be used. Floating-rate securities would also complicate the analysis, as their duration is low, but will still have a sensitivity to changes in spreads, as discussed next.

Component 4, **expected price change due to change in credit spreads (ΔS)**:

The analyst also projects a 6-basis-point narrowing of spreads over the investment horizon. This change in spread is assumed to flow through to change the bond's yield. The impact of this change in spread on the bond's price can be calculated in a similar way to the duration and convexity formula used in the previous component:

$$(-MD \times \Delta S) + (\tfrac{1}{2} \times C \times \Delta S^2) = (-5.6 \times -0.0006) + [\tfrac{1}{2} \times 28 \times (-0.0006)^2] = 0.00336 + 0.000005 = 0.337\%$$

Component 5, **expected gains or losses versus investor's currency**:

The portfolio is invested 40% in foreign denominated bonds, and the investor expects the foreign currencies (weight to reflect portfolio exposures) to appreciate 3.925%, giving the portfolio an expected gain of 3.925% × 0.40 = 1.570%.

In summary, the projected bond return is the sum of these:

1. Coupon income: annual coupon amount / current bond price
   3.0 / 101.50 = 2.956%
2. Rolldown return: (projected ending bond price (BP) – beginning BP) / beginning BP; based on no change in the yield curve
   (102.419 – 101.50) / 101.50 = 0.905%
3. Price change due to investor's benchmark yield change predictions: $(-MD \times \Delta Y) + (½ \times C \times \Delta Y^2)$
   $[-5.6 \times (-0.0054)] + [½ \times 28 \times (-0.0054)^2] = 3.065\%$
4. Price change due to investor's spread change predictions: $(-MD \times \Delta S) + (½ \times C \times \Delta S^2)$
   $[-5.6 \times (-0.0006)] + [½ \times 28 \times (-0.0006)^2] = 0.337\%$
5. Currency gain or loss: projected change in value of foreign currencies weighted for exposure to the currency
   3.925% × 0.40 = 1.570% = expected total return for the year = 8.833%

Note the rolling yield = #1 + #2 = 2.956% + 0.905% = 3.86%.

Except for yield income, this analysis is based on projections. Rolldown assumes the yield curve is unchanged. But techniques for plotting the yield curve vary. Plotting is often done using on-the-run government bond yields, and then the curve is interpolated between those points. At times, the curve may be based on off-the-run government bond yields. Such bonds are more numerous, but the yields usually include a liquidity premium. Predicted price change is based on only duration and convexity projection. It does not include how individual bonds may shift in relative valuation. Credit losses and currency G/L are pure predictions.

PROFESSOR'S NOTE

Technically, spread duration should be used in the calculation for Part 4, but our example follows the example as presented in the CFA curriculum. The assumption here seems to be that the spread duration of a fixed-coupon bond should be similar to the modified duration of the bond. While this is a fair approximation for a fixed-coupon bond, it is not a good assumption for floating-rate bonds where modified duration is likely to be low (because coupons move in line with benchmark rates), but spread duration is likely to be high (because increases in spread do not flow through to higher coupons). This is addressed more fully in a later reading on credit strategies. If given both effective duration and convexity and spread duration and convexity in a question, use effective duration for Part 3 and spread measures for Part 4.

This return decomposition is a framework that is used to analyze the returns from active strategies over the next two readings. This is a **very** important series of calculations!

MODULE 9.3: LEVERAGE AND TAX ISSUES

Video covering this content is available online.

Reading 9

LOS 9.e: Discuss the use of leverage, alternative methods for leveraging, and risks that leverage creates in fixed-income portfolios.

Leverage is a way to increase portfolio return and is particularly attractive in periods of lower interest rates (and expected return). (The return on the portfolio can also be called the return on investor's investment or equity in the portfolio.) As long as funds can be borrowed (B) at rates below the return earned on the investments made ($r_I > r_B$), leverage will enhance portfolio return. Leverage also increases the exposure of the portfolio to interest rate risk and losses if interest rates increase above the return on portfolio assets ($r_I < r_B$). Borrowing is normally done at shorter-term interest rates, and those costs can increase faster than return on assets if interest rates increase. Said another way, the asset duration normally exceeds the liability duration in a leveraged portfolio.

The leveraged portfolio's return (return on investor equity) can be calculated as:

r_p = portfolio return (amount) / portfolio equity

$r_I + [(V_B / V_E) \times (r_I - r_B)]$

where:

r_p = return on portfolio
r_I = return on invested assets
r_B = rate paid on borrowings
V_B = amount of leverage
V_E = amount of equity invested

There are multiple ways to achieve leverage.

Repurchase agreements (repos) are an explicit way to borrow funds that could be used for leveraging. A securities owner "sells" a security for cash and simultaneously agrees to "buy" it back at a specified future date. The repo is functionally a way to borrow money, and the assets are the collateral for the loan. The loan term is often overnight, though the repo could be renegotiated the next day at a new interest rate. Longer repo terms are also possible. The borrowing nature of the transaction is even more evident in the details of the transaction. A securities dealer might enter an overnight $100,000,000 repo at a 2.5% repo rate. This means the dealer receives 100,000,000 and pays back 100,000,000 × [1 + (0.025 / 360)] the next day. (This is the normal calculation methodology for repo rates.)

The actual securities "sold" are not typically specified, and the money borrower can deliver any types previously agreed to. This is called general collateral. For example, any domestic government bonds can be delivered, and their market value must equal 102% of the repo amount, in this case $102 million. The 2% is a haircut amount and provides additional security to the money lender. The lender now holds collateral worth more than the funds lent. The collateral is returned the next day (for an overnight repo) when the loan is repaid. Other kinds of collateral can also be allowed to secure the loan, and the haircut would be larger for riskier and less liquid securities. In other words, the repo rate may not need to be adjusted based on the quality of the collateral because the amount of collateral is adjusted.

The repo can be bilateral with cash and collateral securities directly exchanged between the two counterparties or tri-party. Tri-party repos use an intermediate third party (usually a bank) who holds the underlying collateral for the two counterparties and records the exchange of ownership. That is less costly than actually exchanging ownership between the two counterparties.

The above repo is cash driven and any collateral (previously agreed to by the parties to the repo) can be used. Repos can also be security driven. In a security driven repo, the money lender wants to have temporary possession of specific collateral. They may need it for some hedging or arbitrage reason and could offer a lower repo rate in exchange for delivery of a specific security. The repo is now a form of securities lending (and will be discussed later).

Futures contracts also provide leverage. Futures contracts can be purchased and require only a small initial margin deposit. The contract price times multiplier is the full price of the contract and the quantity of the underlying security now controlled. In other words, buying a bond contract at a full price of $105,607 requires only a small margin deposit but provides the upside and downside of buying that full amount of underlying bonds. The amount of leverage achieved can be calculated as:

leverage = (notional value of contract – margin amount) / margin amount

Swap agreements also provide leverage. Entering a 10 million notional 5-year receive 4% fixed versus pay LIBOR swap is equivalent to buying 10 million of 5-year 4% bonds and borrowing 10 million at a floating rate of LIBOR. A receive-fixed swap increases the portfolio's exposure to the bond market and its duration with no explicit investment of funds. A receive-floating versus pay-fixed swap would have the opposite effect. Traditionally, swaps did not require posting of collateral and were largely unregulated and unreported; the 2008–09 financial crisis has led many swap users to settle swaps through a central clearinghouse, providing some of the benefits of standardization and exchange trading.

Securities lending, as mentioned earlier, is closely related to the repo market, but the motivations are different. Securities lending often supports short selling. Short selling means selling a security that is not owned and receiving immediate payment for the security. In many cases, the security must be immediately delivered, so the short seller must borrow the security from someone else (and later return the security). A bilateral repo can be used to do this. The securities borrower specifies the desired security or securities to be received. The lender of the securities will specify the amount and types of collateral that the securities lender will receive back.

The lender of the securities can specify receiving cash in exchange for the securities lent. The securities lender can then invest the cash (which is typically greater than the value of the securities lent) to earn interest and compensation. The securities lender could also agree to accept back general, high-quality government bonds as collateral. Suppose the securities lender lends 10 million of a specific bond and receives back 10.5 million of various government bonds in exchange. The securities lender earns the interest on that collateral. If those earnings are higher than the fair compensation for the securities lent, a portion might be rebated to the securities borrower. The rebate rate equals:

rebate rate = collateral earnings rate − security lending rate

PROFESSOR'S NOTE

Think of it as I need 50 million of Bond X, you have it and will lend it to me if I compensate you. You will take back as collateral some larger amount (say 105%) of cash or general (not specific) government securities. You can use that collateral to find another way to make some money, and if I really needed Bond X, this could induce me to pay you other explicit fees. Obviously, this is a very specialized market used by a small number of large participants.

Unlike the repo market, security lending agreements are usually open ended. They do not have a specified maturity and continue until one counterparty requires settlement, reversing the transaction with return of the collateral. This can create additional risk if the other counterparty was not prepared to reverse his part of the transaction.

Ultimately, the earnings of the securities lender depend on how badly the securities borrower needs that specific collateral. If the need is high, the securities lender can demand an explicit fee. The securities lender can also demand more cash be posted as collateral or require more general collateral to be delivered. Either increases what the securities lender can earn.

Risks Created by Leverage

In addition to the obvious risk, if the costs of borrowing increase above the earnings on the portfolio assets, other risks are also created. If interest rates increase, the value of the leveraged portfolio and collateral will decline. This may induce money lenders to demand repayment and force liquidation of portfolio assets when they are down in value. This is referred to as a fire sale, selling under distressed conditions. If such liquidations are widespread, they can produce a vicious cycle as each round of sales drives down prices, leading other credit providers, repurchase participants, and securities lenders to demand repayment and/or stop lending.

Managing Taxable and Tax-Exempt Portfolios

LOS 9.f: Discuss differences in managing fixed-income portfolios for taxable and tax-exempt investors.

Both tax-exempt and taxable investors should seek the highest possible risk-adjusted return net of fees and transaction costs, consistent with their objectives and constraints. This is more complex for taxable investors because taxes must also be taken into account to determine after-tax return and risk. Different types of tax issues arise and differ by tax jurisdiction around the world. The following are some examples:

- The two sources of bond return are usually taxed differently. Income may be taxed at a different rate from capital gains (price change). Both are usually taxed only when realized, but there are exceptions. For zero-coupon bonds, imputed income (increase towards par) may be taxed each year as income even though there is no cash flow.
- In general, capital gains are only taxed at sale and at a lower tax rate than for interest income. Gains on securities held for a longer period may be taxed at a lower rate than on securities held for a shorter period.
- Capital losses may only be allowed to be used to offset capital gains, but not other income sources. But if capital losses exceed gains, they may be carried forward to offset future realized gains. (In some cases, the realized losses can be carried back to reduce taxes already paid for a previous year, generating a tax reduction or refund on the current tax return.)
- It may be possible to invest some portions of the portfolio in tax-sheltered or tax-advantaged accounts.

Strategies to use in managing taxable accounts include:

- Realize capital losses to offset gains. This can include selective tax loss harvesting for partial sales when the investment was acquired at multiple prices.
- Extend holding periods to realize long-term, rather than short-term, capital gains.
- Extend holding periods to defer taxes.
- Consider differentials in income versus gain tax rates when selecting investments.

PROFESSOR'S NOTE

The above is just a listing of issues from earlier readings. Review the earlier material if it seems unfamiliar.

Taxation of investments in mutual funds and other collective investment funds varies by country. Income on the underlying assets is usually taxable to the fund investors when it is earned by the fund, regardless of whether the income is paid out or reinvested in the fund. However, the taxation of gains realized within the fund varies.

- Some countries use pass-through taxation of gains. The fund investor is taxed when the fund realizes the gain and that tax payment subsequently reduces taxes on gains when the investor sells the fund shares.
- Other countries use deferred taxation of the gains realized within the fund and instead tax the investor on all gains when the fund shares are sold.

In contrast, when a client hires a manager to manage the client's portfolio directly (a separately managed account) all income, gains, and losses in the portfolio are normally reported on the client's tax return and taxable to the client.

EXAMPLE: Taxable vs. tax-exempt portfolios

A manager must raise EUR5,000,000 to meet a client's need for funds. The client's portfolio is separately managed, and all tax issues are passed through and immediately taxable to the client. Income and capital gains tax rates are 38% and 15%, respectively. The manager is looking at two bonds and will sell all of one or of the other. Both have market value of EUR5,000,000 and have the same remaining maturity, coupon, and credit quality. Any taxes owed due to the sale are to be ignored in the analysis and covered by other client funds. Bond A has a significant unrealized gain, while bond B has a significant unrealized loss. The manager believes the bonds are substantially identical except bond B has a slightly higher yield.

Select the bond the manager will sell and **explain** why if the investor is (1) taxable, or (2) tax-exempt.

Answer:

1. Taxable: Sell bond B to avoid realizing a gain and paying a tax now.
2. Tax-exempt: Sell bond A to retain bond B and its slightly better yield.

MODULE QUIZ 9.2, 9.3

1. Suppose that a bond portfolio has 25 million in notional principal and an average annual coupon rate of 5%. The average bond duration of the portfolio is computed as 8, and the average convexity of the portfolio is 0.5. If an investor in this portfolio expects the average yield change to be 0.35% with no change in spread, the expected portfolio price change due to the investor's forecast is *closest* to:
   A. –1.752%.
   B. –2.799%.
   C. –3.978%.
2. A credit investor is interested in using leverage in his portfolio to enhance return. Which of the following statements is *most correct* regarding the use of leverage and the risks that leverage creates when implemented in fixed-income portfolios?
   A. If interest rates increase, the value of the leveraged portfolio and collateral decline.
   B. Liability duration normally exceeds asset duration.
   C. As long as funds can be borrowed at rates above the return earned on the investments made, leverage will enhance portfolio return.
3. When managing fixed-income portfolios for taxable investors, which of the following strategies should *most likely* be applied?
   A. Realize capital gains to offset any losses.
   B. Shorten holding periods to realize long-term, rather than short-term, capital gains.
   C. Consider differentials in income versus gain tax rates when selecting investments.

KEY CONCEPTS

LOS 9.a

Fixed income as an asset class provides three major roles when added to an investment portfolio: diversification, regular cash flows, and inflation protection (in the form of floating-rate securities and inflation-linked securities).

There are two major classifications of fixed-income mandates: liability-based mandates, which invest to fund future liabilities, and total return mandates, which invest to track or beat a benchmark.

Types of liability-based mandates include cash-flow matching, duration matching, and contingent immunization strategies.

- Cash-flow matching funds liabilities with coupon and par amounts received on the dates the liabilities are paid.
- Duration matching matches asset and liability duration to achieve comparable results. Duration matching generally gives more flexibility in asset selection and, therefore, may meet the objective at a lower cost.
- Contingent immunization is a hybrid of active management with potential immunization. The portfolio must initially be overfunded and can be actively managed. If successful (unsuccessful), the surplus will grow (be lost) and the ultimate cost will end up being lower (higher) than from immunization.

Types of total return mandate include:

- Pure indexing, which exactly matches the holdings of the index.
- Enhanced indexing, which allows modest deviations (but matches duration to control interest rate risk).
- Active management, which does not restrict deviations versus the index and allows duration mismatches.

LOS 9.b

Bond risk and return measures include the following:

- Macaulay duration is the weighted average time to receive cash flows.
- Modified duration is the estimated percentage change in a bond price given a 1% change in yield [measured as Macaulay duration / (1 + the periodic yield of the bond)].
- Effective duration is the modeled estimated percentage change in a bond price given a 1% change in a benchmark curve. It is used for bonds with embedded options.
- Key rate duration (partial duration) is the estimated percentage change in a bond price given a 1% change in a key benchmark maturity yield while other yields remain the same.
- Empirical duration is the actual sensitivity of a bond's price relative to movements in a benchmark rate from a linear regression.
- Money duration (dollar duration) equals modified duration × market value. It gives a sense of size, as well as sensitivity.

- Price value of a basis point [DV01 or basis point value (BPV)] equals money duration × 0.0001. It measures the absolute currency sensitivity to a basis point move in rates.
- Convexity measures the curvature of the relationship of price and yield. More-convex bonds are expected to outperform less convex bonds when yields shift.
- Effective convexity models convexity when cash flows are not certain. It is used for bonds with embedded options.

Macaulay duration increases linearly with maturity.

Convexity is approximately proportional to duration squared.

Convexity is also directly related to the dispersion of cash flows in time around the Macaulay duration.

To aggregate duration and convexity measures for a portfolio of fixed-income assets, the cash-weighted average of the durations and convexities of the individual bonds is usually used.

Spread duration is the sensitivity of a bond's price to a unit change in spreads.

Duration times spread (DTS) = spread duration × credit spread. It reflects the fact that bonds with larger spreads tend to have larger movements in spread.

A manager who expects interest rates to rise (fall) will lower (increase) duration.

A manager who expects credit spreads to widen (narrow) will lower (increase) spread duration.

Relative value analysis involves the ranking of individual bonds according to fundamental value drivers in order to pick the best securities to express a top-down view on markets.

LOS 9.c

Liquidity in the bond market (ability to buy or sell on a timely basis at or near fair market value) is substantially lower than in equity markets.

Most bonds do not trade or trade infrequently after issuance (said to go "off-the-run").

The sheer number and variety of individual bond issues is immense.

The market is mostly over-the-counter with trade price and volume not reported.

Liquidity is highest for sovereign government, higher-quality, and most recently issued (on-the-run) bonds.

Smaller issues are generally less liquid.

Effects:

- Bond pricing data is more difficult to obtain.
- Portfolio managers have to choose between more-liquid bonds or less liquid bonds that may offer a liquidity premium.
- Derivatives and ETFs are generally more liquid and an alternative to direct investment in bonds.

LOS 9.d

Return can be projected (or actual return decomposed) as the sum of the following:

1. Coupon income: annual coupon amount / current bond price.
2. Rolldown return, assuming no change in yield curve: (projected ending bond price (BP) – beginning BP) / beginning BP.
3. Price change due to investor yield change predictions: $(-MD \times \Delta Y) + (\frac{1}{2}C \times \Delta Y^2)$.
4. Price change due to investor yield change predictions: $(-MD \times \Delta S) + (\frac{1}{2}C \times \Delta S^2)$.
5. Currency G/L: projected change in value of foreign currencies weighted for exposure to the currency.

Coupon income + rolldown return may be referred to as rolling yield.

LOS 9.e

- Leveraged portfolio return can be calculated as $r_I + [(V_B / V_E) \times (r_I - r_B)]$.
- If r_I exceeds (is below) r_B, the leverage enhances (reduces) portfolio return.
- Repurchase agreements (and securities lending), futures contracts, and swaps can all be used to leverage return.
- In addition to the detrimental effects if r_I is less than r_B, the lender of the funds can demand repayment, forcing liquidation of portfolio assets at fire sale prices, which can feed a financial crisis.

LOS 9.f

Taxes complicate portfolio management, as managers seeking to maximize return must consider the different tax effects of each portfolio decision.

ANSWER KEY FOR MODULE QUIZZES

Module Quiz 9.1

1. **B** Inflation-linked bonds provide direct protection for the effects of inflation. They protect coupon payments from inflation and adjust par (i.e., principal) for inflation. Floating-coupon securities also provide protection from change in inflation, but the adjustment mechanism is different and only affects the coupon. Fixed-coupon bonds do not protect coupons or principal from the effects of inflation. (LOS 9.a)

2. **C** Pure indexing attempts to replicate the performance of a bond index. It seeks to exactly match all of the risk factors of the index while still allowing the manager some leeway on the individual bonds selected. Enhanced indexing allows some additional flexibility in constructing the portfolio and seeks to add some modest active return. Active management allows much larger deviations from the risk factors of the index and seeks greater active return. (LOS 9.a)

3. **B** Liquidity for on-the-run high-quality sovereign government debt is high and declines somewhat for older off-the-run issues. These government bonds are usually large in size and have a high level of credit quality. Liquidity among corporate bonds typically declines with lower quality as the bonds become riskier and with the size of the issue (i.e., smaller issuers are less liquid). (LOS 9.c)

Module Quiz 9.2, 9.3

1. **B** Expected price change is calculated from the investor's expected change in yield using the portfolio's duration and convexity as follows: $(-MD \times Y) + (\frac{1}{2}C \times Y^2) = (-8 \times 0.0035) + (\frac{1}{2} \times 0.5 \times 0.0035^2) = -0.028 + 0.000003 = -2.7997\%$. Note that the expected change in spread is zero; hence, there is no impact on price from changes in spread. (Module 9.2, LOS 9.d)

2. **A** If interest rates increase, the value of the leveraged portfolio and collateral decline. As long as funds can be borrowed at rates *below* the return earned on the investments made, leverage will enhance portfolio return. Asset duration normally *exceeds* the liability duration in a leveraged portfolio. The other statements are false because a typical leverage transaction involves borrowing at lower shorter-term rates (and therefore in a liability with low duration) to invest at longer-term higher rates (and therefore in an asset with higher duration). (Module 9.2, LOS 9.d)

3. **C** Strategies to use when managing taxable accounts include:
   - Realize capital *losses* to offset *gains*.
   - *Extend* holding periods to realize long-term, rather than short-term, capital gains.
   - Consider differentials in income versus gain tax rates when selecting investments.

   (Module 9.3, LOS 9.f)

READING 10

Liability-Driven and Index-Based Strategies

EXAM FOCUS

We now turn to the substantive discussion of liability-based and index-based fixed-income management approaches.

MODULE 10.1: LDI, BASICS

Video covering this content is available online.

LOS 10.a: Describe liability-driven investing.

Broadly speaking, **liability-driven investing (LDI)** is used when there are definable future liabilities to be paid from portfolio assets. It is classified as passive total return, but in this context, that does not mean nothing should be done—as many of these strategies require continual monitoring and adjustments. (In contrast, active management generally means managing to outperform a specified index or benchmark.) The specific LDI approach used depends on the nature of the liabilities. LDI is mostly used for institutional portfolios. There are some commonly used terms:

- **Asset-liability management (ALM)** means strategies that consider assets in relation to liabilities. It is appropriate when both the present value (PV) of the assets and liabilities change with changing interest rates.
- **Liability-driven investing (LDI)** or liability-based investing takes the liabilities as a given and manages the assets to meet those future liability values—for example, there is an insurance company or defined benefit (DB) pension plan that must fund future liability payouts. (Note that LDI is now being used in a more specific way than in the initial paragraph. The focus of this reading is on

this more specific type of LDI investing, where the liabilities are taken as a given and the assets are managed in relation to those liabilities.)

- **Asset-driven investing (ADI)** takes the assets as a given and manages or adjusts the liabilities in relation to those assets. For example, a leasing company with specific types of floating- or fixed-rate financial assets may structure its liabilities to match the characteristics of those assets.

LDI can also apply to individuals, particularly when the goal is to accumulate sufficient funds to meet retirement. Consider a married individual who plans to retire in 12 years and is planning to use the value of his bond portfolio to fund the purchase of an annuity. He will reinvest any cash flows from the bonds and could also plan to add a regular amount to the bond position every year to meet the goal.

Four types of liabilities exist:

1. **Known future amount(s) and payout dates(s), called Type I**. The issuer of an option-free fixed-rate bond has this type of liability. We will see that these are the easiest type of liability to model.
2. **Known future amount(s) but uncertain payout dates(s), called Type II**. The issuer of a callable or putable bond has this type of liability. An insurance company selling term life insurance also fits here. The amount of payout is known, but the date of payout on any single policy is not. (However, actuaries can apply the law of large numbers to estimate likely payout amounts in any given period with considerable accuracy.)
3. **Uncertain future amount(s) but known payout dates(s), called Type III**. Floating rate instruments and real rate bonds such as Treasury Inflation Protection Securities (TIPS) fall in this category.
4. **Uncertain future amount(s) and uncertain payout dates(s), called Type IV**. Property and casualty as well as some DB plan liabilities fall in this category.

Simple duration (Macaulay or modified) is adequate to model Type I liabilities. The others require effective duration—modeled to reflect the initial shape of the yield curve plus assumed upward and downward shifts in the yield curve to estimate the potential amount and timing of liability payouts.

Immunizing a Single Liability

LOS 10.b: Evaluate strategies for managing a single liability.

Immunization is a fixed-income management process in which the portfolio is managed to minimize the variability of the rate of return earned over a specified time period. That means the future value (FV) of the portfolio can be confidently predicted, and if enough funds are invested initially, a known future liability can be funded.

Cash flow matching is the simplest but least flexible approach to immunizing. For a single liability, buy a zero-coupon bond with par and maturity matching the liability. With no cash flows to reinvest or bonds to sell, there is no cash flow or price risk. The bonds must also be default free.

Because a single liability is effectively a zero-coupon liability, its time to payment is also its Macaulay duration. Thus, a cash flow matched immunized portfolio will match the Macaulay durations of the assets and liabilities.

Macaulay duration is the weighted average time until the cash flows of an instrument are received. That is why Macaulay duration of a zero-coupon instrument is its maturity, but Macaulay duration of a non-zero-coupon instrument is less than its maturity. The weights are based on each cash flow's PV as a percentage of the total PV of the instrument's cash flows (the latter being the price of the instrument).

Macaulay duration is also a balance point where price and reinvestment risk offset each other:

- **Price risk** is the uncertainty of proceeds if a bond must be sold before maturity.
- **Reinvestment risk** is the uncertain FV of any cash flows received and reinvested before the end of the holding period.

If it is assumed interest rates change only once, immediately, in parallel fashion, and by a small amount, then:

- If rates increase, higher earnings from reinvesting all cash flows will offset a loss on price at the end of the horizon period.
- If rates decrease, lower earnings from reinvesting all cash flows will offset a gain on price at the end of the horizon period.

The unreasonable nature of the assumptions will be dealt with soon.

Modified duration is Macaulay duration divided by 1 plus the periodic interest rate used to compute the cash flow PVs:

- Modified duration is the (slightly) more accurate measure of immediate price change of the instrument.
- Macaulay duration is the (slightly) more appropriate measure of time for some immunization techniques.

Computing portfolio statistics: Portfolio yield (meaning YTM), duration, dispersion of cash flows, and convexity are commonly computed as weighted averages based on market value weighting of each holding in the portfolio. **For ALM, these average computations are less accurate than portfolio statistics computed directly from the portfolio's aggregate cash flows.**

PROFESSOR'S NOTE

There is no LOS or indication that you should try and make these portfolio statistic calculations. They are provided, and your challenge is to understand how to apply them in immunization situations. The actual process would require access to computer spreadsheet tools. The process is summarized here for those interested.

1. Project the time to receipt (starting with the nearest to most distant) of every portfolio cash flow.

2. Determine the aggregate portfolio cash flow in each period. The analysis uses six-month periods.
3. Determine the portfolio IRR that equates future cash flows with the current market value of the portfolio.
4. Use that IRR to determine the PV of each future cash flow from Step 2. (The sum of those PVs will be the current portfolio market value.)
5. Calculate the PV weight (*w*) to apply to each payment as its PV (Step 4) divided by the sum of the PVs.
6. For each cash flow, multiply its *(w)* by its time until receipt *(t)*. The sum of the *(w)(t)*s is the portfolio's Macaulay duration. Duration is normally expressed in years, so if the cash flow periods were in six-month increments, divide by 2 (two six-month periods in a year) for annual duration.
7. Portfolio dispersion is computed as the weighted average variance of when each cash flow is received around portfolio duration. (Remember, duration is just the weighted average of when all the cash flows are received).
8. Portfolio convexity can be computed by summing for each cash flow: $[(t)(t + 1)(w)]$ and then divide this sum by $(1 + \text{portfolio IRR}_{\text{periodic}})^2$.

Here is what to focus on:

Portfolio statistics should be used for ALM work rather than traditional weighted average calculations based on each bond. The difference in the two approaches is determined by the shape of the yield curve:

- With a flat yield curve, there is no difference.
- In an upward-sloping yield curve, portfolio duration and IRR will be higher-than-average duration and YTM of the bonds because portfolio statistics reflect all cash flows (and return) to be received and the longer maturity bonds will impact the portfolio for a longer time.
- (Downward sloping curves are unusual and not discussed. In such a situation, you would build a spreadsheet and calculate all the numbers to see what happens. You cannot make such spreadsheet calculations on the exam.)

The goal of the immunized portfolio is to earn the initial portfolio IRR, not the average YTM of the bonds. Earning the IRR means the portfolio will grow to a sufficient FV to fund the liability.

PROFESSOR'S NOTE

Although we have just made the point that portfolio-level statistics based on aggregate portfolio cash flow and IRR should be used, be aware that it is not unusual to use simple weighted average date (such as YTM and duration) as approximations. That would add some error to the analysis.

The dispersion will be important because it is related to convexity and the convexity effect. Convexity matters because, when combined with modified duration, it provides a more accurate measure of estimated price change. Recall that $\%\Delta$ in value = $(-MD \times \Delta Y) + (\frac{1}{2}C \times \Delta Y^2)$.

But more specifically, in relation to immunization:

$$\text{convexity} = \frac{\text{Macaulay duration}^2 + \text{Macaulay duration} + \text{dispersion}}{(1 + \text{periodic IRR})^2}$$

The dispersion and convexity will indicate the risk exposure of the immunization strategy to structural risk from shifts and twists in the yield curve.

Reading 10

Effects of Yield Curve Changes

Assume that the portfolio is being used to immunize a single liability (sometimes called a bullet) due in five years, the portfolio and liability D are initially matched at the 5.0 medium (M) duration of the liability, the initial value of the portfolio equals the discounted (at portfolio IRR) PV of the liability, and portfolio convexity exceeds convexity of the single cash flow liability. We can create an extreme situation to demonstrate the issues. Assume that the portfolio is made up of two bonds with a shorter (S) and longer (L) duration than the liability duration (M). This describes a barbell portfolio strategy, concentrating the assets in longer and shorter duration around the liability's single (bullet) duration.

If the yield curve shifts up or down in parallel fashion, the portfolio results will slightly exceed the amount required to pay the future liability. Duration matching alone would have led to meeting the future liability need, but the additional positive convexity of the assets will lead them to outperform duration results alone for large parallel shifts in the curve. (Recall the dispersion of cash flows and thus the convexity of the two-bond portfolio must exceed that of the single-point liability.)

- For a large parallel increase in the curve (Figure 10.1), the immediate decrease in portfolio value will be less than the decrease in the PVL due to the positive convexity effect. With the parallel increase, the new portfolio IRR will increase by basically the same amount as the increase in discount rate for the PVL. In other words, the future rate of increase in A and L are still the same, but starting from a new PVA that is relatively higher than the PVL, the FVA will exceed the FVL.
- For a large parallel decrease in the curve (Figure 10.2), the immediate increase in portfolio value will exceed the increase in the PVL due to the positive convexity effect. With the parallel decrease, the new portfolio IRR will decrease by basically the same amount as the decrease in discount rate for the PVL. In other words, the future rate of increase in A and L are still the same, but starting from a new PVA that is relatively higher than the new PVL, the FVA will exceed the FVL.

Figure 10.1: Parallel Yield Shift Up

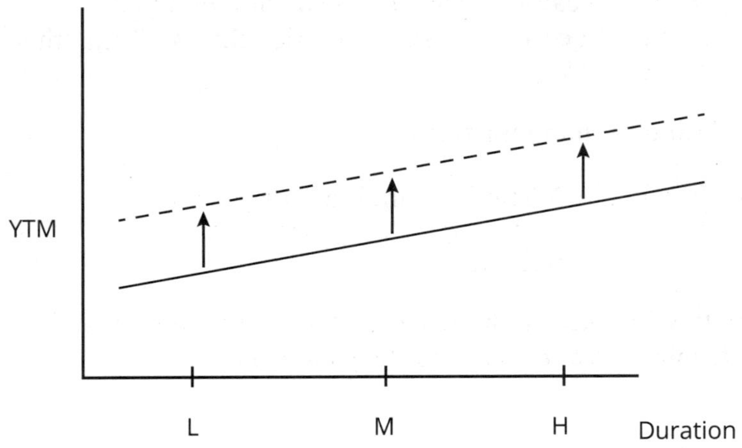

Figure 10.2: Parallel Yield Shift Down

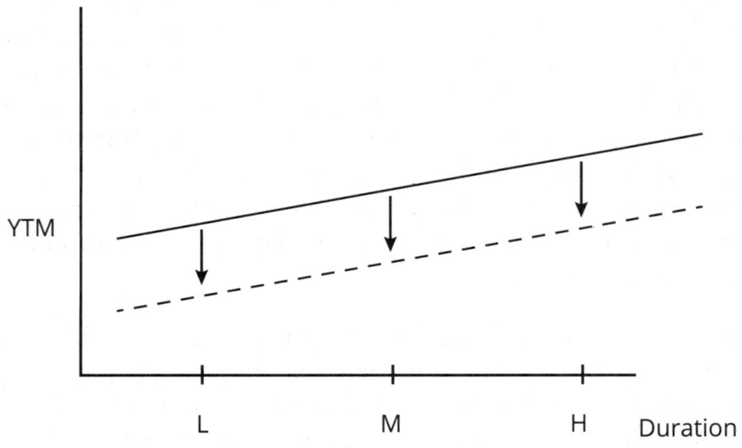

The parallel shift analysis indicates that the duration (rather than cash flow) matching immunization strategy does have **structural risk**. The structural risk is due to creating portfolio duration with a different allocation of asset durations (L and H) versus the allocation of liability durations (M only). That can lead to differing performance of the assets and liabilities as the yield curve shifts. Fortunately, most interest rate changes can be described as roughly parallel, and by building the portfolio with an asset dispersion (hence, convexity) that exceeds the single liability payout date, the portfolio benefits from the structural risk.

The parallel shift analysis:

- Indicates that immunization can be described as *zero replication*. A single zero-coupon bond could have been used for a no-risk, perfect cash flow match. The changes in portfolio value and IRR have replicated (or done better due to positive convexity) the changes in yield and value of that replicating zero-coupon bond. In general, if the change in portfolio IRR matches change in yield of the replicating zero, the risks for the strategy are low.
- Does not indicate the strategy is always structurally risk free. Other kinds of yield curve reshaping may or may not cause the strategy to fail in meeting the future payout. These other reshapings are discussed shortly.

- Does indicate the parallel shift assumption is sufficient to lead the strategy to succeed—but it is not a necessary assumption because the strategy may still be successful in other conditions. It is *sufficient,* but not *necessary*.
- Does not mean the strategy is buy and hold. Coupon-bearing bond duration declines more slowly than maturity, while the bullet liability duration will decline linearly with the approaching pay date. To maintain the immunization, the portfolio assets must be continually rebalanced to continually match portfolio to liability duration as time or market conditions change; otherwise, the strategy is at risk.

If the curve either steepens or flattens, the analysis becomes more complex and the structural risk increases. Assume for this discussion that rates do not change for the M duration liability, but move in roughly opposite directions for the L and H duration assets.

- Steepening twist (Figure 10.3): Yield L decreases while yield H increase relative to yield M. The portfolio market value will decrease because the decline in value of the longer duration bond will exceed the increase in the value of the shorter duration bond. PVL will be unchanged with no change in yield M. PVA is now below PVL. That, by itself, does not indicate the strategy will fail. If portfolio IRR increases sufficiently, the required FV might still be reached. (Recall that portfolio IRR would tend to increase above a single point M YTM with a steeper curve). This indicates that a steepening curve may create structural risk.

Figure 10.3: Steepening Twist

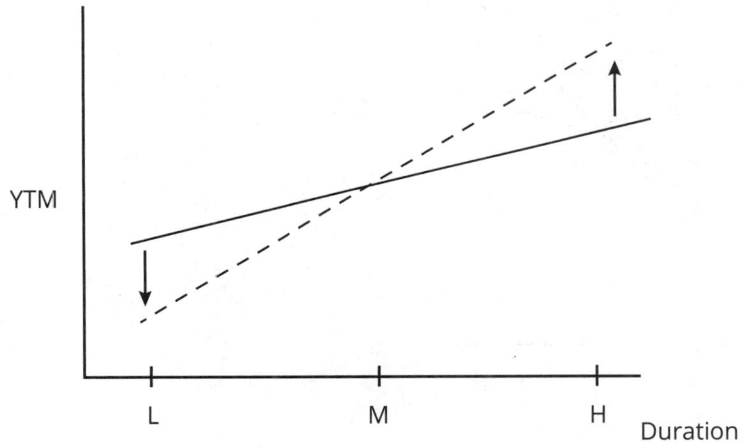

- Flattening twist (Figure 10.4): Yield L increases while yield H decrease relative to yield M. The portfolio market value will increase because the increase in value of the longer duration bond will exceed the decrease in the value of the shorter duration bond. PVL will be unchanged with no change in yield M. PVA is now above PVL. That, by itself, does not indicate the strategy will succeed. If portfolio IRR decreases sufficiently, the required FV of assets to meet the payout may not be reached. (Recall that portfolio IRR would tend to decrease below a single point M YTM with a flatter curve). This indicates that a flattening curve may create structural risk.

Figure 10.4: Flattening Twist

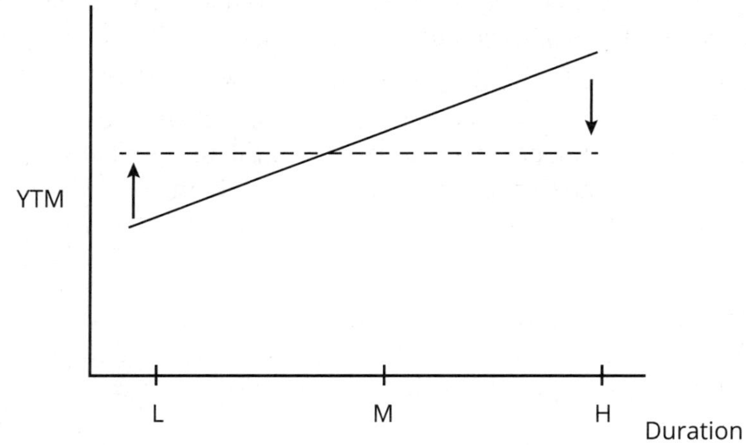

- Positive butterfly twist (Figure 10.5): Yield L and H increase while yield M decreases. The portfolio market value will decrease as both yield L and H increase. PVL will increase as yield M decreases. PVA is now below PVL. That is certainly detrimental, but it is possible the strategy could succeed if the portfolio IRR increases enough versus the decrease in liability discount rate. This indicates that the positive butterfly may create significant structural risk.

Figure 10.5: Positive Butterfly Twist

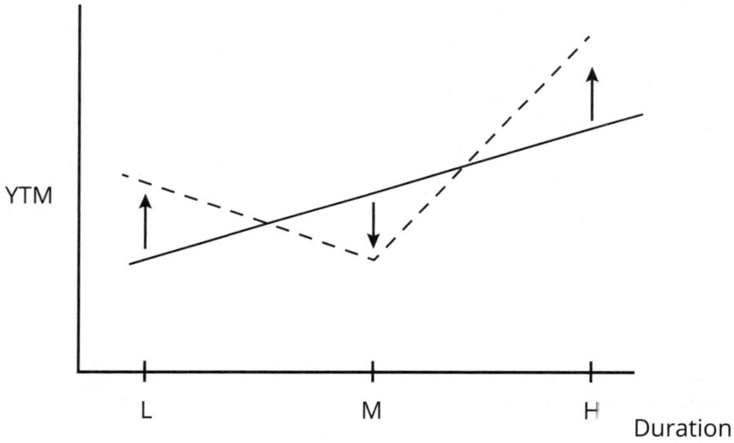

- Negative butterfly twist (Figure 10.6): Yield L and H decrease while yield M increases. The portfolio market value will increase as both yield L and H decrease. PVL will decrease as yield M increases. PVA is now clearly above PVL. That is certainly favorable, but does not guarantee the strategy will succeed if the portfolio IRR decreases too much in relation to the increase in liability discount rate. It again indicates the possibility of significant structural risk.

Figure 10.6: Negative Butterfly Twist

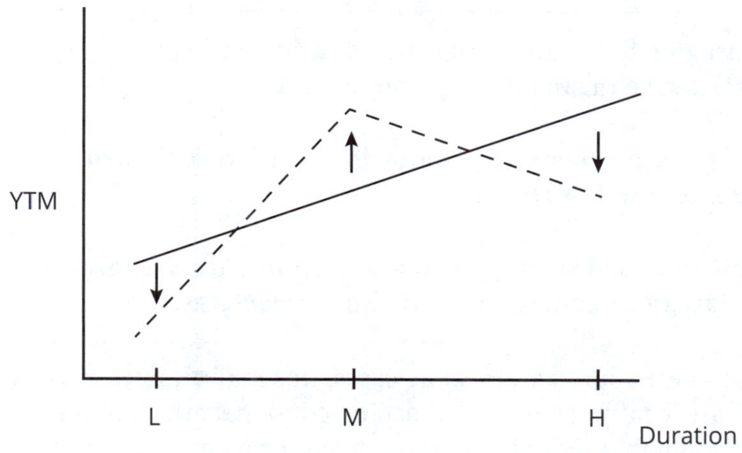

The risk in immunization is higher when the change in portfolio IRR does not match the change in yield of the replicating zero or is insufficient to fund the liability at the new level of rates. This structural risk can be reduced by reducing the dispersion of asset cash flows around the liability cash flow. This is not surprising because if you make dispersion 0, you have a zero-coupon bond and a perfect cash flow match to the single liability. Now, recall the earlier equation for determining convexity from duration and dispersion; reducing dispersion is directly related to reducing convexity. This leads to the rules for immunizing a single liability:

1. Initial portfolio market value (PVA) equals (or exceeds) PVL. (There are exceptions to this for more complex situations where the initial portfolio IRR differs from the initial discount rate of the liability.)
2. Portfolio Macaulay duration matches the due date of the liability ($D = D_L$).
3. Minimize portfolio convexity (to minimize dispersion of asset cash flows around the liability and reduce risk to curve reshaping).
4. Regularly rebalance the portfolio to maintain the duration match as time and yields change. (But also consider the tradeoff between higher transaction costs from more frequent rebalancing versus the risk of allowing durations to drift apart.)

PROFESSOR'S NOTE

It may seem strange to require minimizing convexity of assets when +C is good for immediate price change. But that ignores the real issue of immunization, failing to reach the FV needed to pay the liability.

Money duration: The first two conditions of immunization can be combined by matching money duration of the assets and liability. Money duration is the money change in value of the assets or liability for change in interest rates. It can be calculated as modified duration (MD) multiplied by the value of the item multiplied by a specified change in yield of the item. It is common to express it as **basis point value (BPV):**

$$BPV = MD \times V \times 0.0001 = \text{price value of a basis point}$$

BPV is also referred to as *price value of a basis point* (*PVBP*) or value of an 01, meaning a 1 BP change in rates.

Immunizing Multiple Liabilities

LOS 10.c: Compare strategies for a single liability and for multiple liabilities, including alternative means of implementation.

LOS 10.d: Describe construction, benefits, limitations, and risk–return characteristics of a laddered bond portfolio.

LOS 10.e: Evaluate liability-based strategies under various interest rate scenarios and select a strategy to achieve a portfolio's objectives.

Cash flow matching is the safest approach. In some cases, this may allow *accounting defeasance* where the assets are legally set aside and dedicated to meet the labilities—allowing both those assets and liabilities to be removed from the balance sheet of the organization responsible for paying the liability. The simplest cash flow match is to buy zero-coupon bonds in the amounts and due dates to meet each liability.

- Cash flow matching of a stream of liabilities may also be possible using coupon-bearing bonds. In concept, a bond is purchased due on and with par plus (+) final coupon to exactly fund the longest liability. Its earlier coupon payments can be used to partially meet the earlier liabilities. Then, in recursive fashion, the next-longest liability is funded by buying a bond due on and with par plus (+) final coupon to exactly fund that next-longest liability (after considering the coupon of the bond or bonds already purchased for the longer liability or liabilities).
- In practical terms, it is unlikely that the coupon-bearing bonds necessary for perfect cash flow matching will exist. A *cash-in-advance* constraint could be used, requiring the bond used to fund a specific liability to mature before the required payout date of the liability. This would expose the portfolio to reinvestment risk in an upward-sloping yield curve. The upward-sloping curve is anticipated to create reinvestment risk because as cash comes in to be reinvested for a short time period until payout, the reinvestment must be at the lower rates at the short end of the curve.

Laddered portfolios can be used in cash-flow matching multiple liabilities. A laddered portfolio has roughly equal par amounts purchased across different maturities. The same duration could also be achieved by concentrating all the holdings in a single middle duration (a bullet portfolio) or in a combination of shorter and longer duration holdings (a barbell portfolio). If all three portfolios have the same duration, they all have roughly the same price sensitivity to a parallel yield curve shift. The advantages of the laddered portfolio include the following:

1. The portfolio has regular liquidity, as some bonds come due each year. This is particularly significant if less liquid bonds such as corporates are used because the need to sell bonds at large bid-ask spreads to generate required cash flows is reduced. These near-to-maturity bonds would also be treated as less risky collateral and could be used to borrow at favorable interest rates.

2. There is broad diversification of cash flow across time and the yield curve and less concentrated exposure to nonparallel changes at specific maturities on the curve.
3. There is diversification between price risk on long-dated bonds and reinvestment risk on short-dated bonds. The bonds that mature each year can be reinvested at long-term, typically higher, rates, keeping the overall duration of the portfolio stable over time.
4. The laddered portfolio will have more convexity than the bullet, a benefit if there are large parallel shifts. Recall that convexity is directly related to the dispersion of cash flows across time. Note that the ladder, however, will not be as convex as a barbell portfolio.

- An alternative to building laddered bond portfolios with individual bonds is to use a laddered portfolio of **target-date** (fixed-maturity) bond ETFs. Each ETF has a designated year when it will mature and be paid off. It is passively managed to replicate the performance of a bond maturing in that year. For many investors, the ETF will offer cost advantages compared with purchasing individual bonds and have more liquidity if unanticipated sales are needed.
- Laddered portfolios do have some disadvantages. For some investors, an ongoing (no target date) passive index or active bond fund may be better. These ongoing funds are likely to be larger, provide greater diversification of credit risk, and be more liquid than directly investing in the underlying bonds.

Duration matching is a more flexible and generally practical approach to funding multiple liabilities. Like immunizing a single liability, there must be sufficient assets to fund the liability, and Macaulay durations of assets and liabilities (in this case, the average liability duration) must match. However, matching money durations is the more common approach. Money duration is more useful when initial amounts and discount rates of assets and liabilities differ. The rules for immunizing multiple liabilities become the following:

1. Initial portfolio market value (PVA) equals (or exceeds) PVL. (There are exceptions to this for some situations where the initial portfolio IRR differs from the initial discount rate of the liability.)
2. Portfolio and liability basis point values match ($BPV_A = BPV_L$).
3. Asset dispersion of cash flows and convexity exceed those of the liabilities. (But not by too much, in order to minimize structural risk exposure to curve reshaping).
4. Regularly rebalance the portfolio to maintain the BPV match of A and L as time and yields change.

EXAMPLE: U.K. bond company

A U.K.-based company has several option-free bond issues (liabilities) outstanding. The company would like to retire the bonds early, and has more than sufficient funds to do so. The company considers a bond tender offer (offer to repurchase the bonds from the public), but the bonds are widely distributed among buy-and-hold investors. The prices that would have to be paid are too high to make the tender desirable to the company.

The company could also establish a dedicated cash flow matched portfolio of U.K. government bonds and legally defease the bonds. In that case, both the company's bond liabilities and assets (the cash flow matching bond portfolio) could be removed from the company's balance sheet. The cost of the portfolio would be GBP475 million, and the company considers this too high.

The third alternative is to establish a duration matching portfolio; using high-quality corporate bonds, the cost will be less than for the government bond portfolio. While the portfolio will not qualify for defeasance, the company believes it will improve its credit rating and is the better choice.

The portfolio statistics for the company's liabilities and three proposed corporate bond portfolios are shown in the following table. All calculations are annualized and based on aggregate portfolio cash flows. Each portfolio is considered sufficient to pay the liabilities. Monetary amounts are in GBP:

Statistics	Company's Liabilities	Proposed Portfolios		
		A	B	C
Market value	457,780,900	Approximately 460,000,000		
Modified D	7.52	7.51	7.53	7.37
BPV	344,250	343,100	345,400	339,120
Convexity	45.12	35.14	46.29	65.97

1. **Select** the most appropriate portfolio (A, B, or C) to immunize the liabilities and **justify** your selection with *two* reasons.
2. If the company expects high volatility and the potential for very large parallel shifts in the yield curve, **select** the *one* other portfolio (A, B, or C) it would most likely consider and **explain** why.

Answers:

1. Portfolio B—because (1) its BPV closely matches, and (2) its convexity slightly exceeds that of the liabilities.
2. Portfolio C—while the BPV is not as good a match, it has much higher convexity, and this would increase return relative to change in liability values for large parallel shifts in the yield curve.

MODULE 10.2: MANAGING A DURATION GAP

Video covering this content is available online.

A **derivatives overlay** can be used to adjust the portfolio and maintain the duration match without the expense of adjusting the underlying assets. Futures contracts are often used.

In the United States, there are various Treasury futures contracts available based on the 30-year bond, as well as 2-, 5-, and 10-year Treasury notes. Each contract specifies a set of deliverable securities that the contract seller may deliver at contract expiration. The seller must deliver 100,000 par of a deliverable security [also called *most deliverable bond* or *cheapest-to-deliver* (CTD) bond]. The buyer must pay the seller the initial contract price multiplied by the conversion factor for that bond (CF_{CTD}) that the seller chooses to deliver. In recent years, an Ultra 10-year contract was developed that specifies a much narrower range of deliverable notes. The purpose of this was to limit the deliverable items to ones that have a duration much closer to that of the 10-year note. The issue of which bond the seller chooses to deliver is important because the duration of that CTD determines the duration (price volatility) of the contract—hence, its BPV. The exact calculation of contract BPV is complex (not covered by CFA material), but is approximately:

$$\text{futures BPV} \approx \frac{BPV_{CTD}}{CF_{CTD}}$$

Calculating the number of contracts required to adjust the portfolio assets is simply the desired change in BPV divided by the BPV of the contract:

$$N_f = \frac{\text{BPV of liability} - \text{BPV of current portfolio}}{\text{BPV of futures}}$$

EXAMPLE: U.K. bond company revised

Suppose the U.K.-based company seeking to immunize its bond liabilities had instead chosen to immunize only a portion of its debt. The company selected an asset portfolio with a BPV of 217,525 to immunize a portion of the liabilities with a BPV of 217,512—a duration gap of only 13. After a modest increase in rates with a significant positive butterfly twist, the asset and liability BPVs are now 203,456 and 218,517 for a duration gap of 15,061.

Assume that there are government bond–based futures contracts based on 5- and 10-year notes, with features similar to U.S. Treasury–based futures contracts. Each contract specifies a range of deliverable government notes that the contract seller may select for delivery at contract expiration. Each deliverable note requires the seller to deliver 100,000 par and the buyer to pay initial contract price multiplied by the conversion factor for that bond (CF_{CTD}).

Figure 10.7: Characteristics of the CTD Note for the 5- and 10-Year Contracts; Per 100,000 Par

CTD Characteristics	5-Year Contract	10-Year Contract
YTM	1.71%	2.51%
Modified D	4.75	8.67
BPV of CTD	48.1650	86.7001
Conversion factor	0.9237	0.9169

1. **Determine** and **justify** if contracts will be bought or sold, assuming:
   i. the 5-year contract is used.
   ii. the 10-year contract is used.
2. **Calculate** contracts to use, assuming:
   i. the 5-year contract is used.
   ii. the 10-year contract is used.
3. If the liability duration is 8.99, **state** which contract is most likely to minimize structural risk based only on the information provided. You must choose either the 5 or 10 year, and not a combination of both. **Justify** your answer.

Answers:

1. To increase asset BPV to match liability BPV, buy contracts regardless of which contract is used.
2.
   i. Contract BPV ≈ 48.1650 / 0.9237 = 52.1436
   (218,517 – 203,456) / 52.1436 = buy 289 contracts
   ii. Contract BPV ≈ 86.7001 / 0.9169 = 94.5579
   (218,517 – 203,456) / 94.5579 = buy 159 contracts
3. The only available, relevant information is the liability duration. The 10-year contract is the better duration match. This closer match would likely minimize structural risk to nonparallel yield curve shifts.

PROFESSOR'S NOTE

You should be noticing that the PVA = PVL requirement is a bit of a misstatement. It will be true initially if the portfolio yield and liability discount rate are equal. Even then, it need not hold true after initiation, as the path of portfolio yield and liability discount rate can diverge. The strategy can still succeed if the changes in portfolio market value and yield track the path an immunizing, replicating zero-coupon bond could have followed. In other words, if the change in portfolio market value reflects a new portfolio yield, that will still reach the FVL desired. But even at initiation, PVA need not equal PVL if the portfolio yield and liability discount rate differ.

In practice, initially overfunding the portfolio with more market value than the strictly required PVA is common. If the surplus is significant, contingent immunization can be considered.

Contingent immunization (CI) is a hybrid active/passive strategy and requires a significant surplus. As long as that surplus is of sufficient size, the portfolio can be actively managed. At the extreme, assets could be invested in equity, commodities, real estate, or any other assets. If the assets earn more than the initially available immunization rate, the surplus will grow, and can eventually be returned to the investor. If the strategy is unsuccessful, the surplus will shrink, and the portfolio must be immunized before the surplus declines below zero. For example:

- Invest the entire portfolio in stocks.
- Invest only the surplus in stocks or in long stock options. Use the balance of the assets to construct an immunized portfolio. This approach allows fewer funds for active management, but is in some ways safer because only the surplus amount is at risk of loss, and an immunized portfolio is already in place.
- Use active bond management techniques. Returning to the previous U.K. example that required buying 159 of the 10-year note contracts, the manager could overhedge or underhedge based on a view of interest rates. Consider the 159 contracts to be a 100% hedge.
  - If the manager believes rates will increase, underhedge (<100%) and the losses on the contracts will be reduced, improving portfolio performance and increasing the surplus.
  - If the manager believes rates will decrease, overhedge (>100%) and the gains on the contracts will be increased, improving portfolio performance and increasing the surplus.
  - Because the contract is based on 100,000 par, each 1/32 of change in price of 100 par will equate directly to a gain or loss on the contract of 31.25 [(1 / 32) × (100,000 / 100)].

CI approaches can be vulnerable to liquidity risk.

- If all of the assets (instead of just the surplus) are actively managed and the surplus declines, the assets must be quickly liquidated without further loss and converted to an immunizing portfolio before the surplus becomes negative.
- Even if only the surplus amount is actively managed, liquidity issues can still be a problem. If short option contracts were used, the downside risk is unlimited for calls and very large for puts (in excess of initial premiums received). Likewise, the potential losses on futures contracts are very large and could exceed the portfolio surplus.

MODULE QUIZ 10.1, 10.2

1. A bond issuer is reviewing the four main categories of liabilities. He is interested in issuing a liability that can be managed easily and has known future amounts and payout dates. Which of the following types of liabilities *most likely* meets the issuer's demands?
   A. Callable bonds.
   B. Option-free fixed-rate bonds.
   C. Treasury inflation-protected securities.

2. An investor is looking to immunize a single liability, but is concerned with the impact from yield curve shifts and twists. When attempting to immunize this liability, which of the following rules should the investor apply?
   A. The portfolio Macaulay duration should match the due date of the liability.
   B. The dispersion of asset cash flows around the liability should be maximized.
   C. The present value of liabilities should exceed the initial portfolio market value.
3. Which of the following statements correctly describes contingent immunization?
   A. It uses Treasury futures contracts to adjust the portfolio and maintain duration matching.
   B. It constructs a portfolio of zero-coupon bonds that provide enough cash inflows to meet liabilities.
   C. It uses active bond portfolio management, as long as the present value of assets exceeds the present value of liabilities.
4. A client at RBI Funds would like to build a laddered bond portfolio. In terms of the construction and advantages of a laddered portfolio, which of the following statements is *most correct*?
   A. With a laddered portfolio, the investor is diversified between price and reinvestment risk.
   B. A laddered portfolio has more reinvestment risk in any single year compared to a barbell portfolio.
   C. The more distributed cash flows of a ladder portfolio compared to a bullet portfolio will provide less convexity.

MODULE 10.3: ADVANCED STRATEGIES

Video covering this content is available online.

Pensión funds can include complex Type IV liabilities where both the amount and timing of payouts may be uncertain.

PROFESSOR'S NOTE

We include a brief description of the complexities of projecting these liabilities. There is no direct LOS or questions for that issue. I suggest you briefly skim this note and move to the discussion of the various LDI strategies and issues.

Pension plan rules normally base benefit payouts on years of service, wages, and some multiplier. LDI strategies require estimates of those liabilities. Actuaries can develop models to estimate those liabilities based on the following: initial years of service by employees to the company (G), current wage rate (W_0), wage growth rate and future wages (w and W_T), the multiplier (m), additional years of work until retirement (T), a discount rate (r) related to risk (a high-quality corporate bond rate is normally used), and an estimate of how many years the benefit will be paid (Z).

The liability projection can then be based on the accumulated benefit obligation (ABO), which is a lower number and represents the legal liability if the plan were closed now or a higher projected benefit obligation (PBO) of what is actually expected to be paid in an ongoing plan. Unless the plan is terminating, the higher PBO is generally the more realistic number.

The risk characteristics of the liability must also be estimated. This is normally done by assuming equal upward and downward shifts in the yield curve (Δcurve) to generate a lower PV_+ of the liabilities if rates move up, and higher PV_- if rates move down around the initial PV_0 of the liabilities. Such data can then be used to infer effective duration (and convexity, though that formula is not covered).

$$\text{effective D} = \frac{PV_- - PV_+}{2 \times \Delta\text{curve} \times PV_0}$$

More complex analysis may be needed to incorporate changing yield curve shape and path dependency issues such as effect on interest rate levels and time to retirement.

Typically, it is assumed there is no reliable, consistent relationship between other portfolio assets such as equity in the portfolio and interest rates. Their value may be affected by changing interest rates, but not in the same predictable way as fixed-income assets. In such cases, the duration of those other plan assets is assumed to be zero.

As an example, assume an ongoing DB pension plan has a PBO of USD2.57 billion. The effective duration has been modeled as 9.35. The BPV of the liabilities is:

$$2.57 \text{ billion} \times 9.35 \times 0.0001 = 2{,}402{,}950 \text{ BPV}_L$$

The plan assets of $3.07 billion are 60% equity and 40% bonds. The manager chooses to hold a laddered bond portfolio of 1-to-5-year Treasury and investment grade corporate bonds; his reasoning is that these can be used to fund nearer-term plan distributions. While there is no cash flow match, the bonds are highly liquid and can be sold to meet distributions. The duration of the bonds is only 2.85. The BPV of the assets is:

$$3.07 \text{ billion} \times 0.40 \times 2.85 \times 0.0001 = 349{,}980 \text{ BPV}_A$$

The duration gap is 2,402,950 − 349,980 = 2,052,970. The manager reasons he can use the Treasury bond contracts to eliminate the duration gap. The contract is based on 100,000 par. The CTD bond has a BPV of 128.98, duration of 13.53, and a conversion factor of 0.9436. The BPV of the contract is:

$$128.98 \;/\; 0.9436 = 136.6893 \text{ BPV}_{\text{futures}}$$

Reading 10

Assuming the manager has no view on interest rates, he could construct a 100% hedge to remove the duration gap. He will buy contracts to increase the asset duration:

$$N_f \text{ for 100\% hedge } = \frac{2{,}402{,}950 - 349{,}980}{136.6893} = 15{,}019 \text{ to buy}$$

Assume instead that the manager has discretion to overhedge or underhedge by 10%, and he believes that interest rates will decline. To profit by this, he will buy more contracts than required for a 100% hedge to set the asset duration above the liability duration. He will buy:

$$N_f \text{ for 110\% hedge} = 1.10 \times 15{,}019 = 16{,}521 \text{ to buy}$$

Now, assume instead that the manager believes that interest rates will increase. To profit by this, he will buy fewer contracts than required for a 100% hedge to set the asset duration below the liability duration. He would have bought:

$$N_f \text{ for 90\% hedge} = 0.90 \times 15{,}019 = 13{,}517 \text{ to buy}$$

Hedging with futures creates operational and practical risks. Margin must be posted and adjusted daily; that means all gains or losses on the contracts are posted in cash (or other securities) daily. Recall that each 1/32 change in price of the contract is a gain or loss on each contract of 31.25. If the hedge is successful, that G/L is an offset to changes in the value of the liability. But those are changes in unrealized value, not cash flow that must be posted in the margin account. In practice, these issues make 100% hedges rare in such situations. Partial hedges (< 100%) to reduce the duration gap are more common.

PROFESSOR'S NOTE

While not needed (and requiring data not provided in the discussion), the 1/32 value change of 31.25 per contract on an assumed starting par price and duration of 13.53 can be used to infer the change in rates needed to cause that percentage change in price: 31.25 / 100,000 = –13.53 Δr, making the Δr only about 0.2 basis points. Clearly, the margin cash flow issues can be substantial on some 15,000 contracts with even modest changes in rates.

Interest rate swaps are another way to adjust the duration gap. As OTC instruments, they may avoid the margin cash flow issues of futures. Recall that a receive-fixed swap is equivalent to buying more bond assets and will increase portfolio duration; it has positive (+) duration. A pay-fixed swap will reduce duration; it has negative (–) duration. The swap's net duration is calculated as the difference between fixed- and floating-rate bonds that would replicate the swap's future coupon flows.

Assume a 10-year swap is available and the manager has discretion to hedge 30%–70% of the duration gap, with a 50% hedge considered a neutral or normal position. The duration gap in BPV is still 2,402,950 – 349,980 = 2,052,970 with asset duration too low. The durations of the replicating fixed and floating sides of the swap are 9.18 and 0.25. The BPVs per 100 notional for each side of the net swap duration are:

fixed-side BPV = 100 × 9.18 × 0.0001 = 0.0918

floating-side BPV = 100 × 0.25 × 0.0001 = 0.0025

net swap BPV = +0.0918 – 0.0025 = 0.0893

The notional swap principal (NP) required to close the duration gap for a 100% hedge is the duration gap in BPV divided by the swap BPV per 1 NP. Note that the BPVs are per 100 NP and must be divided by 100 for BPV per 1 NP.

Enter a receive-fixed swap to increase asset duration:

$$\text{NP} = \frac{2{,}052{,}970}{(0.0893 \; / \; 100)} = 2.3 \text{ billion for a 100\% hedge}$$

Assuming the manager expects rates to increase and given the hedging constraints, what hedge would be used?

With increasing rates expected the manager will leave asset duration as low as permitted for a 30% hedge. He will enter a receive-fixed swap of 0.3 × 2.30 = 0.69 billion NP.

Assuming the manager just entered the 30% hedge and now believes rates will decline, what will he do?

He will want to increase asset duration to the max allowed, a 70% hedge. He would want a receive-fixed swap of 0.7 × 2.30 = 1.61 billion NP. That will require an additional receive-fixed swap of 1.61 – 0.69 = 0.92 billion NP.

While historically swaps have not required margin posting, that has been an evolving issue. Many swaps now require periodic marking to market and posting of the gain or loss in margin or as a direct cash settlement. That reduces counterparty and credit risk, but introduces the same practical cash flow complications of exchange-traded futures.

An alternative to the swap is a swaption. The plan pays an initial premium for the right to enter a swap. The plan that needs to increase BPV of assets would purchase a receiver swaption, giving the plan the *right* to initiate a receive-fixed swap at a prespecified **swap fixed rate (SFR)**; the swap's SFR may be called the *swaption strike rate*. The cost is limited to the initial premium paid. As time passes, comparing the SFR for new swaps (new SFR) to the SFR of the swaption determines if the swaption has value:

- If the new SFR declines, this right to receive a now above-market SFR has positive value and effectively increases the BPV of the assets. The value of the swaption is part of portfolio assets and increases the total value of plan assets.
- If the new SFR increases, this right to receive a now below-market SFR has no value, the swaption will not be exercised, and it would be allowed to expire worthless. Note that if a swap had been used instead of a swaption, the plan would suffer escalating losses on a receive-fixed swap.

EXAMPLE: Swap vs. swaption hedges

A U.S. pension plan has a 450,000 BPV duration gap with BPV of assets less than of liabilities. The plan uses a swap with a BPV per 100 notional of 0.2571 to construct a 50% hedge ratio. After setting up the 50% hedge, the manager forms the opinion that rates will increase, and would like to benefit if his view is correct, but be unaffected if he is wrong. The manager would be willing to adjust the hedge position by 15% to a 35% or 65% hedge. He checks and finds that both payer and receiver swaptions are available with a strike rate of 2.7%. The premiums for the payer and receiver swaptions are 55 and 75 basis points, respectively.

1. **State** the terms and **calculate** the notional principal of the 50% hedge ratio swap the manager would use.
2. **State** the terms and **calculate** the initial cost of the swaption the manager would buy or sell to adjust his hedge to a 35% hedge.
3. **Determine** the rate on new swaps and **state** whether new rates will have to be higher or lower than that rate to make exercising the swaption profitable.

Answers:

1. (450,000 × 0.50) / (0.2571 / 100) = 87.515 million NP of a receive-fixed swap.
2. 15% of the full hedge is (450,000 × 0.15) / (0.2571 / 100) = 26.254 million notional.

   The initial hedge is receive fixed, so to reduce the hedge, the manager will buy a payer swaption of 26.254 million NPl. The premium cost is 26.254 million × 0.0055 = 144,397.
3. If new SFRs are greater than the strike rate of 2.7%, the payer swaption and right to pay 2.7% is valuable and should be exercised.

PROFESSOR'S NOTE

This is hard material. You must know the terminology as well as be able to think clearly and logically to solve these questions.

Regarding Question 1, the assets have less BPV than the liabilities. If rates decline, the assets will increase less than the liabilities, and the plan will suffer. The correct swap is to receive fixed as that will increase duration and BPV of assets to reduce this loss if rates decline.

Regarding Question 2, if the manager wants the right to a smaller hedge position, he needs a pay-fixed swap to reduce his fixed inflow from the initial swap. Buying a payer swaption gives him the right to decide later if he wants to turn on the pay-fixed swap embedded in the swaption.

Regarding Question 3, economic logic dictates that his right to pay 2.7% and receive floating becomes valuable if new market conditions would require paying more than 2.7%. In that case, paying 2.7% is a bargain. The mechanics of how he captures this value are not covered, but there are a couple of possibilities: (1) He can exercise the swaption, pay the bargain SFR, and receive floating in this now higher interest rate environment. Of course, rates as well as the future floating rates received can change. (2) He could exercise the swaption and begin paying the 2.7% plus simultaneously enter into a new receive-fixed swap, receiving an SFR above the 2.7% he is paying. On each payment date, he will net the difference of 2.7% paid versus the higher SFR received for the life of the two swaps.

Note that the premium cost paid for the swaption is a sunk cost, and cannot be recovered. It does not affect the decision of whether the swaption is exercised. That premium is paid and gone regardless of whether the swaption is exercised.

The third alternative for the manager who needs to increase asset BPV is a swaption collar, which is a combination of buying one swaption and selling another.

- The manager would buy the receiver swaption to provide economic benefit if the SFR declines.
- To reduce the initial premium cost outlay, the manager sells a payer swaption. Note that this means the buyer of the payer swaption has the right to turn on a pay-fixed swap and the manager (seller) must accept that fixed rate. The buyer will do this if new SFRs exceed the payer swaption's strike rate. The sale of the payer swaption can limit the potential future benefits to the seller as the buyer will exercise and pay the SFR when rates increase (i.e., when unattractive to the seller of the swaption).

Choosing an Optimal Strategy

PROFESSOR'S NOTE

This material requires a solid understanding of terminology, swap diagrams, and the economic rationales of why swaptions are exercised. The discussion of *swaption seller* is tricky. The terms "payer swaption" and "receiver swaption" always refer to the fixed rate action of the *swaption buyer*. The *buyer of the payer swaption* will have positive value if new SFRs exceed the swaption strike rate the buyer would pay. That is negative value to the *seller of the payer swaption*, who must now accept and receive a below-market SFR.

But there is another issue here as well. The purpose of the hedge is to reduce risk. In this case, if rates go down, the assets—with lower BPV than the BPV of the liabilities—will increase in value less than the liabilities. In other words, hedging is to reduce or eliminate interest rate risk, which exists because no one can perfectly predict interest rates. But selecting the optimal hedge strategy will, as we'll see, require at least some ability to predict direction or magnitude of rate changes. Recognize that all three strategies work and reduce interest rate risk. But if you want optimal strategy, you need to predict interest rates to at least some degree.

The choice of optimal strategy will depend on the manager's view of interest rates. Consider the DB plan with a duration gap and a need to increase asset duration. In other words, the plan is currently at risk if interest rates decline because the assets would increase less than the liabilities increase, and the plan surplus would decline. The manager has three swap-based hedging choices:

1. Enter a receive-fixed swap versus pay MRR.
2. Buy a receiver swaption.
3. Enter a zero-cost collar composed of buying the receiver swaption and selling a payer swaption.

The swap notionals and payment frequency are the same. All floating payments are MRR. After consulting with the sponsor and the sponsor's accountants, the manager is instructed that all gain or loss on swaptions will be captured and reported on the sponsor's financial statements. In other words, she can evaluate the swaptions as if they are marketable securities for decision-making purposes. She is directed that she must use one of the hedges because the duration gap is too large and too risky to the plan surplus. All the hedges have the same effect on the duration gap. She cannot be unhedged. She gathers the following additional data:

	Premium Cost
2.5% fixed-rate swap	None
2.3% receiver swaption	75 bp
3.3% payer swaption	75 bp

The receive 2.5% SFR swap is optimal if the *manager expects the new SFR will be at or below 2.5%.*

- This is equivalent to buying 2.5% fixed-rate bonds (financed by borrowing at MRR), increasing asset duration and BPV. The plan will benefit from the decline in rates.
- Buying the 2.3% receiver swaption is suboptimal because there is an initial cost, and the 2.3% fixed rate received by the plan is lower.
- The collar (buy the 2.3% receiver swaption; sell the 3.3% payer swaption) is suboptimal because the 2.3% fixed rate received by the plan is lower. The payer swaption buyer has no rational reason to exercise his right with the new SFR below 3.3%.

Figure 10.8: Comparing Swap-Related Strategies

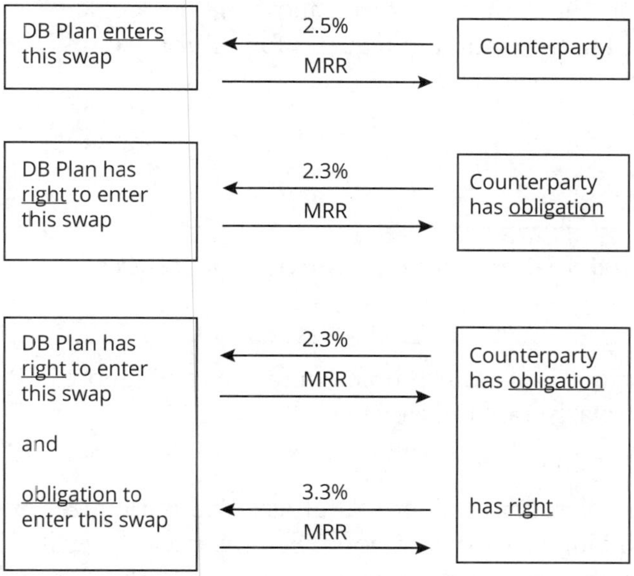

The collar is optimal if the *manager expects the new SFR will be above 2.5% but below 3.3%.*

- The collar (buy the 2.3% receiver swaption and sell the 3.3% payer swaption) has no intrinsic value, which is the best choice.
  - The right to receive 2.3% when rates are above 2.5% has no value.
  - The payer swaption buyer has no rational reason to exercise his right with new SFRs below 3.3%.
- The other hedges have negative value or zero value with an up-front cost.
  - The swap of receive 2.5% will have negative value when SFRs are above 2.5%.
  - The receiver swaption (right to receive 2.3%) has no value when new SFRs are above 2.5% and required an initial cost.

Buying the 2.3% receiver swaption is *optimal at some level of new SFRs above 3.3%.*

- The 2.3% receiver swaption has no intrinsic value with new SFRs above 3.3%. But there was an initial premium cost. This is the best case at some level of SFRs above 3.3%.
- The receive 2.5% swap has increasing negative value as new SFRs increase above 3.3%.
- The collar also begins to have increasing negative value as new SFRs increase above 3.3%.
  - The receive 2.3% swaption has no value.
  - The 3.3% payer swaption increases in value as SFRs increase above 3.3%, and this is negative value to the seller (the plan).
  - As SFRs increase, that negative value will at some point exceed the initial cost of the receiver swaption, and the receiver swaption would become optimal.
  - The breakeven rate to make the payer swaption optimal is above 3.3%.

PROFESSOR'S NOTE

Fortunately, the method of calculating breakeven above 3.3% is not even covered. We do not plan to respond to requests for, "But I just want to see how to do it."

Video covering this content is available online.

MODULE 10.4: RISKS

LOS 10.f: Explain risks associated with managing a portfolio against a liability structure.

- Hedge amounts are approximations based on assumed durations and ignore convexity. Convexity matters for large-rate movements.
- Duration assumes parallel shifts in the curve.
- Twists in the yield curve can create substantial structural risk, and immunization may fail to replicate the immunizing zero-coupon bond. Setting asset convexity (somewhat) higher than liability convexity creates net positive convexity (C of assets exceeds C of liabilities) while limiting the dispersion of asset cash flows in relation to liability flows to minimize structural risk.
- Model risk can be significant in some cases. See the earlier discussion of assumptions required to estimate DB plan liabilities, effective duration, and BPV.
- Measurement error when weighted average characteristics of the portfolio assets and liabilities are used instead of portfolio statistics based on portfolio cash flows and yield (IRR).
- Futures BPV calculations are based on an assumed CTD bond. That bond can change, changing the futures duration and BPV. Also, a more accurate estimate of futures BPV should adjust for accrued interest discounted at short-term rates (because accrued interest paid is recouped on the next coupon payment date).
- Portfolio yield and liability discount rate may differ, reflecting different risk levels. This creates spread risk (i.e., the risk the asset and liability discount rates and their PVs may shift in unexpected ways). Here are a few examples.
  - The liability discount rate may reflect corporate debt rates and assets government bond rates. Using Treasury contracts introduces this same potential spread risk.
  - Use of Treasury rates introduces a more subtle risk. The Treasury market is highly liquid and more likely to reflect frequent price change. That is reflected in higher reported volatility of Treasury rates. By definition, *higher volatility* means a higher rate of change in Treasury rates compared to other rates, (i.e., nonparallel shifts).
  - Using swaps also creates spread risk as swap rates directly reflect the MRR market.

- Traditionally, OTC derivatives have counterparty risk. The move toward requiring collateral reduces the counterparty risk, but creates cash flow risk. Counterparties must be prepared to meet the demands to post cash or other collateral. The same risks already exist for exchange-traded futures.
- Asset liquidity risk exists if positions cannot be quickly adjusted with reasonable transaction costs.

MODULE QUIZ 10.3, 10.4

1. Assume that the BPV duration gap of a defined benefit pension plan is equal to $300,000. The pension fund manager would like to hedge 100% of this duration gap with a 10-year swap. The manager finds that the duration of the fixed side of the swap is 8.25 and the duration of the floating side of the swap is 0.5. What is the notional swap principal required to fully close the duration gap?
   A. $125 million.
   B. $387 million.
   C. $495 million.
2. A risk analyst is discussing the risks associated with managing a bond portfolio against a liability structure. She makes three statements regarding liability-driven investment risks. Which of her statements is *most likely* an indicator of spread risk?
   A. "Bond positions cannot be adjusted with reasonable transaction costs in a timely manner."
   B. "Hedge calculations are approximated based on only the duration of the assets and liabilities."
   C. "The liability discount rate may reflect corporate debt rates, and the asset discount rate may reflect government bond yields."

MODULE 10.5: INDEX-BASED INVESTING

Video covering this content is available online.

LOS 10.g: Discuss bond indexes and the challenges of managing a fixed-income portfolio to mimic the characteristics of a bond index.

Many bond indexes exist—providing varying exposures to duration, credit, and other risk factors. Investing in a bond market index fund provides low cost diversification and an alternative to active fixed-income management. Their goal is to minimize tracking error. Tracking error also called *tracking risk* or *active risk*. It is the standard deviation of the portfolio's active return (portfolio return − benchmark return).

The **pure index** or **full replication approach** requires holding all the securities and weighting them as in the index. **Enhanced indexing** matches all the primary risk exposures of the index, but not all the holdings. The goal is more efficient tracking of the index by avoiding some of the overly costly transactions required for pure indexing.

Indexing for bonds is more difficult than for equity:

- Fixed-income markets are much larger, more bond issues are outstanding, and the characteristics of individual bonds vary widely. This generally makes full replication impractical.
- Any one issuer may have multiple bond issues outstanding. They may differ substantially in liquidity, making it appropriate to concentrate positions in the less-costly to trade, liquid issues.
- Most bond trading is done OTC through dealers, unlike stock traded on exchanges. Capital requirements have increased for dealers post-2008. The higher capital cost has reduced dealers' willingness to hold large bond inventories and increased the bid-ask spread charged by dealers. The result is that bond market liquidity has declined.
- Most individual bond issues do not trade in any given year. Many transactions that do occur are not publicly reported, making reliable price and volume data more difficult to obtain. This also leads to valuation challenges in existing portfolios. Bond pricing for nontrade securities is based on **matrix** or **evaluated pricing**. The price of similar, traded bonds is captured and used to calculate YTM. That YTM is then used to infer the price of nontraded bonds. The more unusual the features of a bond, the more difficult it is to find an appropriate traded bond to use as the basis of such pricing.
- Bond index composition and characteristics can change fairly quickly as new bonds are issued and old bonds approach maturity or change in credit quality and other characteristics.

Matching the primary risk characteristics of the bond index is generally more practical than full replication. Matching primary risk factors includes:

- Matching modified duration (MD) to minimize tracking error due to parallel shifts in the yield curve. For bonds with embedded options, effective duration must be used instead:

  $$\%\Delta \text{ value} = -\text{MD } \Delta y$$

- Matching key rate durations to minimize tracking error due to nonparallel changes in the yield curve. There are multiple key rate durations, and each simulates the expected change in value if one single point on the yield curve shifts. For example, the price change if five-year rates shift is as follows:

  $$\%\Delta \text{ value} = -\text{MD}_{\text{key rate } n} \, \Delta y_n$$

- Match weighting exposure to the various bond sector and quality ratings of the index. For nongovernment securities, it is useful to distinguish price change due to a general change in rates (i.e., government bond yields) from spread change. MD measures change due to the general change in rates, and spread duration measures how the nongovernment bonds perform relative to government bonds when (credit) spread changes:

  $$MD = \text{Macaulay duration} / (1 + YTM_{periodic})$$

  $$\%\Delta \text{ value} = -MD\ \Delta y$$

  $$\%\Delta \text{ relative value} = -D_S\ \Delta s$$

  $$\text{spread} = y_{higher\ yield} - y_{government}$$

- Matching sector/coupon/maturity cell weights of the index. For example, if the index is 1.7% in A-rated corporates of 2–3 duration, match that weight. When there are bonds with embedded options such as callable or mortgage-backed securities, match these weighting exposures as well. Doing so means effective duration and convexity will be matched.
- Matching issuer exposure weights to control for specific event risk affecting only that issuer, such as bankruptcy.

Another method of minimizing yield curve risk is matching **present value distribution of cash flows**. The following example demonstrates this and its relationship to bond price, duration, and key rate durations. They are all interrelated. The example is for a 4.0% semiannual pay three-year bond trading at par (4% YTM):

4.0% semiannual pay 3-year bond priced at 4% YTM*			**w = PV as % of total PV**	**Duration contribution = (t)(w)**
Cash flow due in time *t*	**Amount**	**PV**		
0.5	2.00	1.9608	0.0196	0.0098
1	2.00	1.9223	0.0192	0.0192
1.5	2.00	1.8846	0.0188	0.0283
2	2.00	1.8477	0.0185	0.0370
2.5	2.00	1.8115	0.0181	0.0453
3	102.00	90.5731	0.9057	2.7172
		100.0000	**1.0000**	**2.8567**
* for a periodic discount rate of:		2.00%		

- List the cash flows by six-month period (t). If there were embedded options, the cash flows would be the best estimates of amount and when the cash would be received.
- The bond's price is the discounted PV of its future cash flows using a 4%/2 semiannual periodic discount rate.
- Each weight (w) is computed as that PV as a percentage of total PV (the price).

- Each (t)(w) is the cash flow's contribution to duration and a key rate duration. The sum of the duration contributions (key rates) is the bond's duration.
- Matching the *w* of portfolio to the *w* of the index will also match their (t)(w). This matching of present value distribution of cash flows is also matching the duration contributions and key rate durations. These actions minimize exposure risk from changes in shape of the yield curve. They also match total duration and convexity.

The goal of matching all the risk factors is to minimize tracking error while avoiding some of the expense of full replication.

Alternative Methods of Obtaining Passive Bond Market Exposure

Passive index replication provides diversifying exposure to the fixed-income market without the expense of active management. As discussed earlier, the nature of the fixed-income markets generally makes full replication impractical. Enhanced indexing provides one acceptable alternative. **Stratified sampling (cell matching)** can be used to implement enhanced indexing. The manager first determines the most significant characteristics that need to be matched. For example, the manager could divide the index into three duration and sector groupings:

Index	Duration		
	1–5	5–10	10–15
Treasury	5.1%		
Corporate			
ABS			

In the cell grid for the index, only the data for 1–5 duration Treasuries is shown. To cell match, the manager will also hold 5.1% in bonds with these characteristics, but need not use all of the same bonds as in the index to do so. The manager will also need to collect and match the weights for the other eight cells.

Cell matching can incorporate **environmental, social, and corporate governance** (ESG) or socially responsible investing restrictions. ESG may prohibit or explicitly require securities with specific characteristics. For example, bonds of high carbon emission industries are prohibited, and bonds of clean energy industries are desired. The manager will seek to do both while still matching cell weights.

Relevant techniques to reduce the expense of pure indexing or add value include:

- Reducing fund expenses, including transaction costs.
- Overweighting undervalued and underweighting overvalued: securities, sectors, and portions of the yield curve; while still matching overall index characteristics. The basic principle is to avoid areas of spread widening and favor areas of spread narrowing.
- Over (under)weighting callable bonds for their typically higher yield when interest rate volatility is expected to be low (high) and impact of the call feature on price (and effective duration) is more (less) predictable.

LOS 10.h: Compare alternative methods for establishing bond market exposure passively.

Indirect exposure is an alternative to investing directly in bonds through full or enhanced indexing. Indirect exposure can be gained with funds or synthetically through derivative strategies. These indirect approaches usually avoid the higher initial costs of directly trading in bonds, but incur ongoing expenses and other possible risks.

Bond index **mutual funds** may be particularly well suited for smaller investors. They provide broad market exposure with one investment and economies of scale. Aggregating the capital of many investors typically gives these funds access to more securities at better prices.

Open-ended fund shares can be redeemed or purchased at **net asset value (NAV)** once per day. However, such funds charge ongoing management fees and may also charge fees at purchase (front load) or sale (back load). Unlike bonds, they do not typically mature, plus the holdings and income stream change over time.

Exchange-traded funds (ETFs) provide some advantages in that the shares trade continuously on exchanges and investors can buy or sell continuously, rather than once per day. The typical investor cannot purchase or redeem shares directly with the fund. However, **authorized participants** can redeem shares in kind with a pro rata distribution of the underlying fund assets. Those participants can also assemble a package of the underlying fund assets and trade them to the fund in exchange for new shares of the fund. This redemption and purchase in kind (with fund assets instead of cash) creates an arbitrage mechanism between the open-market price of fund shares and NAV. That benefits all investors in the fund. However, the arbitrage mechanism is less effective than in the equity market due to the illiquidity of many underlying bond assets; they are simply harder to buy or sell at the expected fair price.

Total return swaps (TRS): The manager enters a swap to receive a desired bond market index total return (both income and price change) in exchange for paying MRR + spread. TRS are equivalent to buying the index and borrowing the funds needed for purchase at MRR + spread. If the index has a negative return in a given period, the index receiver pays that return to the index payer to replicate the loss in value that would have occurred if the index receiver had actually invested in the index:

- If not fully collateralized, the TRS is effectively a leveraged investment in the index.
  - The user does not directly own the underlying securities. The TRS replicates the underlying return, but there is counterparty (credit) risk if the dealer cannot perform his side of the transaction.

Bond Benchmark Selection

LOS 10.i: Discuss criteria for selecting a benchmark and justify the selection of a benchmark.

Benchmark selection begins with defining the client's objectives and constraints, then determining the strategic asset allocation that will meet these requirements. The manager may be given tactical discretion to vary those asset class exposures.

Selecting suitable bond indexes can be more complicated than for equity. Here are examples:

- In a static (no changes) bond portfolio, duration will decline as the bonds age.
- New bond issuance may cause the characteristics of the index selected as a benchmark to change over time. For example, issuers may shift to shorter or longer security issuance, making a given index no longer appropriate for a given investor's desired duration.

A bond investor could start by defining the desired interest rate (duration) risk and sector exposures. That could lead to a custom index (instead of a broad market index) of desired sub-exposures, such as 50% in 5-to-10-year Treasuries and 50% in 1-to-3-year investment grade corporates as a benchmark. (See **credit barbell** in the next paragraph).

Smart beta rules could be used. This means identifying relatively simple, definable rules that can be followed to add value. The custom index explained previously is one such example, and is called a **credit barbell**. Longer-term Treasuries (with no credit or spread risk) are used to give the portfolio the desired duration exposure. Shorter-term corporate securities are used to add additional spread return. Those shorter-term securities will be less vulnerable to relative price underperformance if spreads widen.

MODULE QUIZ 10.5

1. Using a full replication approach for bond indexing may be impractical, given the large size of the bond market and the varying characteristics of individual bonds. Instead, it may be easier to match the primary risk characteristics of the selected bond index. When reviewing specific risk characteristics, the risk factor that minimizes tracking error due to nonparallel shifts in the yield curve is associated with matching:
   A. modified duration.
   B. key rate durations.
   C. issuer exposure weights.
2. A bond portfolio manager is looking to gain passive exposure to the bond market. Which of the following approaches would allow the manager to receive the return from a desired bond market index in exchange for paying MRR plus a spread?
   A. Total return swap.
   B. Exchange-traded funds (ETFs).
   C. Exchange-traded derivatives.
3. Which of the following statements regarding fixed-income benchmarks is *most likely* false?
   A. If a static bond index is used as a benchmark, the duration will remain the same as the bonds age.
   B. New bond issuance may cause the characteristics of the selected benchmark to change over time.
   C. Issuers may shift to shorter or longer security issuances, making a given benchmark no longer appropriate for a given investor.

KEY CONCEPTS

LOS 10.a

- Liability-driven investing is a form of asset-liability management (ALM) that manages the assets in relation to the characteristics of the liabilities. This is easier when the future liability payouts are known in amount and timing. The liabilities are essentially the benchmark for making decisions.
- Asset-driven investing is a less common form of ALM and adjusts the liabilities in relation to the characteristics of the assets.

LOS 10.b

Immunization can be used to fund liabilities with a high degree of certainty. The assets are dedicated to this purpose and all cash flows are reinvested until needed for payout.

Cash flow matching is without risk, assuming there are no defaults. Bonds are bought and held in sufficient amount and pay date to meet the liabilities. It is the most restrictive strategy, and so typically costs more (has lowest return).

Duration matching achieves similar results, but is less restrictive in the assets selected. Matching Macaulay duration of the assets to liabilities balances the exposure between price and reinvestment risk. Duration and other portfolio statistics should be based on portfolio yield (IRR). To immunize a single-period liability:

- Initial PVA equals (or exceeds) PVL. (There are exceptions to this for more complex situations where initial portfolio IRR differs from initial discount rate of the liability.)
- Match Macaulay durations ($D_A = D_L$).
- Minimize portfolio convexity.
- Rebalance the portfolio to maintain the duration match.

Immunization (duration matching) issues include the following:

- The assets have greater convexity than the single date liability; therefore, the portfolio benefits from large parallel shifts but is at risk from curve twists (nonparallel shifts). Minimizing convexity minimizes this structural risk.
- Immunization can be interpreted as zero replication, meaning a successful immunization will replicate the price and yield path of a zero-coupon bond that could have been used for a perfect cash flow match immunization.

LOS 10.c

Multiple liabilities can be cash flow matched with a portfolio of zero-coupon bonds or coupon-bearing bonds whose cash flows (P&I) most closely match the liability payouts. Duration matching can be done by matching the BPV of the assets and liabilities. The rules are as follows:

1. Initial PVA equals (or exceeds) PVL (see the caveat given under single liability rules).
2. $BPV_A = BPV_L$

3. Asset dispersion of cash flows and convexity exceed those of the liabilities. (But not by too much, in order to minimize structural risk exposure to curve reshaping).
4. Regularly rebalance the portfolio to maintain the BPV match.

Derivatives are often used to adjust the BPV of the assets and hedge or partially hedge the duration gap:

- Buying (selling) futures or receive (pay) fixed swaps increases (decreases) asset duration and BPV.
- Futures BPV ≈ BPV_{CTD} / CF_{CTD}
  - BPV = MD × V × 0.0001
- N_f = (BPV of liability – BPV of current portfolio) / BPV of futures.
- NP for swap = (BPV of liability – BPV of current portfolio) / BPV of 1 NP for the swap.
  - BPV_{swap} is the difference in BPV of fixed and floating side.

Contingent immunization (CI) requires the portfolio be overfunded with a positive surplus (PVA > PVL). If the surplus is positive, the portfolio can be actively managed (not immunized):

- If active management is successful, the return will exceed the initially available immunization rate, the surplus will grow, and ultimate cost of the strategy will be less than immunizing.
- If active management fails, the surplus will decline to zero and the portfolio must be immunized. The ultimate cost will exceed that of immunizing.

LOS 10.d

Laddered portfolios:

- Laddered portfolios can be useful in cash flow matching multiple liabilities.
- Provide diversification across the yield curve and natural liquidity as a portion of the bonds come due each year. In an upward sloping yield curve, this can also be desirable as each maturing bond is rolled over into the longest (and highest yielding) maturity used in the ladder.
- Have more convexity than a bullet portfolio because their cash flows are more distributed.
- Could be constructed with a sequence of target-date ETFs as an alternative to individual bonds.

LOS 10.e

A 100% hedge eliminates the duration gap (matches BPV of assets and liabilities). In the normal scenario of $BPV_A < BPV_L$, a manager who expects interest rates to:

- Increase will reduce the hedge size, leaving the BPV of assets less than of a fully hedged duration gap. Leaving the BPV of assets at a lower level means they will decline in value less as interest rates increase.
- Decrease will increase the hedge size, increasing the BPV of assets above that of a fully hedged duration gap. Increasing the BPV of assets means they will increase in value more as interest rates decrease.

Regarding the three swap methods of reducing a negative duration gap (increase BPV of assets):

- Entering a receive-fixed swap is generally optimal if interest rates in the future are below the swap's SFR.
- Using a zero-cost collar (buy receiver swaption and sell payer swaption) is generally optimal if interest rates in the future are moderately higher (i.e., between the swap and payer swaption SFRs).
- Buying a receiver swaption is generally optimal if interest rates in the future exceed the payer swaption SFR by some amount.

LOS 10.f

Risks include:

- Hedge amounts are approximations based on assumed durations and ignore convexity.
- Duration assumes parallel shifts in the curve.
- Twists in the yield curve can create structural risk (risk due to curve reshaping).
- Multiple assumptions (model risk) are required to model the characteristics of complex liabilities, such as those in DB plans.
- Measurement error issues occur when weighted average characteristics are used instead of portfolio statistics based on portfolio yield (IRR).
- Futures base calculations are approximations based on an assumed CTD bond, and that CTD can change.
- Spread risk exists if the relationship between asset yield and liability discount rate changes.
- Traditionally, OTC derivatives have counterparty risk.
- Cash flow risk for exchange-traded and OTC derivatives requiring cash settlement of gain/loss or margin.
- Asset liquidity risk if positions cannot be quickly adjusted at near fair market value.

LOS 10.g

Bond index funds offer low cost diversification. Their goal is to minimize tracking error. But there are challenges (compared to equity):

- A much larger number of bond issues with diverse characteristics exists. This generally makes full replication impractical.
- Liquidity has declined post-2008, is often low, and varies by bond issue.
- Trading is OTC, and dealers have become less able to supply liquidity.
- Most individual bonds rarely trade, and price must be estimated based on matrix pricing.
- Bond index composition and characteristics can change.

Enhanced indexing matches the primary risk factors of the index. To minimize tracking error:

- Match modified duration—and effective duration if there are option features.
- Match key rate durations.
- Match weighting exposure to the various bond sectors, quality ratings, issuers, and all other material factors. Cell matching is a common technique used to do this.

LOS 10.h

Passive bond market exposure can be achieved with:

- A separately managed account that replicates the index.
- Index mutual funds, either open ended or ETFs.
- Synthetic strategies, such as receiving a bond index return under a total return swap.

LOS 10.i

Determine the client's objectives and constraints before finalizing the strategic asset allocation. Then, select a bond index that matches the objectives and constraints as well as the desired asset class characteristics. Selecting a suitable index is complicated by:

- The possible decline in index duration as the bonds age.
- The changing characteristics of many indexes over time as the holdings change.

ANSWER KEY FOR MODULE QUIZZES

Module Quiz 10.1, 10.2

1. **B** Type I liabilities have known future amounts and payout dates. The issuer of an option-free fixed-rate bond has this type of liability. These are the easiest to manage liabilities because their sensitivity to interest rate movements can be modeled using modified duration. Callable bonds have known future amounts, but uncertain payout dates (Type II). Real rate bonds, such as Treasury inflation-protected securities, have uncertain future amounts, but known payout dates (Type III). (Module 10.1, LOS 10.a, 10.b)

2. **A** Rules for immunizing a single liability include the following:
   - Initial portfolio market value (PVA) equals (or exceeds) PVL.
   - Portfolio Macaulay duration matches the due date of the liability (DA = DL).
   - Minimize portfolio convexity (to minimize dispersion of asset cash flows around the liability and reduce risk to curve reshaping).

   (Module 10.1, LOS 10.b)

3. **C** Contingent immunization is a hybrid active/passive strategy. It requires initially overfunding the portfolio with more assets than needed to immunize and meet the future liability. As long as that surplus is of sufficient size, the portfolio can be actively managed. A derivatives overlay uses Treasury futures contracts to adjust the portfolio. Cash flow matching creates a portfolio of zero-coupon bonds to match cash inflows with cash outflows. (Module 10.2, LOS 10.b)

4. **A** With a laddered portfolio, the investor is diversified between price and reinvestment risk. Some bonds mature each year and can be reinvested if rates are high. This creates a form of dollar cost averaging over time. The ladder has less reinvestment risk in any single year versus the barbell (or bullet). The more distributed cash flows of the ladder compared to the bullet will provide greater convexity—benefiting performance for large changes in rates. (Module 10.1, LOS 10.d)

Module Quiz 10.3, 10.4

1. **B** The basis point values (BPVs) per 100 notional for each side of the swap and the net swap duration are computed as:

   fixed-side BPV = 100 × 8.25 × 0.0001 = 0.0825
   floating-side BPV = 100 × 0.5 × 0.0001 = 0.005
   net swap BPV = +0.0825 – 0.005 = 0.0775

   The notional swap principal required to close the duration gap for a 100% hedge is the duration gap in BPV divided by the swap BPV per 1 NP.

   NP = $300,000 / (0.0775 / 100) = $387 million

   Note that the case never said if BPV of assets or liability is larger. Thus, we can compute the size of the swap, as asked, but not if it is a pay- or receive-fixed swap. (Module 10.3, LOS 10.e)

2. **C** An example of spread risk occurs when the portfolio yield and liability discount rate differ, which reflects different risk levels. If the spread between the two rates changes, the change in rates of the two cannot match; their present values may not change in the expected ways. Using only duration will ignore convexity, which will result in some error. Not being able to adjust positions with reasonable transaction costs is an example of asset liquidity risk. (Module 10.4, LOS 10.f)

Module Quiz 10.5

1. **B** Matching key rate durations minimizes tracking error due to nonparallel twists in the yield curve. Matching modified duration minimizes tracking error due to parallel shifts in the yield curve. Matching issuer exposure weights controls for specific event risk that affects only that issuer, such as bankruptcy. (LOS 10.e)

2. **A** In a total return swap, a manager enters a swap to receive a desired bond market index total return (both income and price change) in exchange for paying MRR + spread. If the index has a negative return in a given period, the index receiver pays that return to the index payer to replicate the loss in value that would have occurred if the index receiver had actually invested in the index. (LOS 10.h)

3. **A** In a static (no changes) bond portfolio, duration will decline as the bonds age. New bond issuance may cause the characteristics of the selected benchmark to change over time. Issuers may shift to shorter or longer security issuance, making a given index no longer appropriate for a given investor. (LOS 10.i)

READING 11

Yield Curve Strategies

EXAM FOCUS

We now turn our attention to methods for adding value by positioning portfolio exposures along the yield curve. You will see many concepts already discussed, such as bullet versus ladder versus barbell, adjusting convexity, and PVBP (which a previous reading referred to as BPV). Think of this as positioning on a credit risk-free government yield curve to add value. The next reading will extend these ideas to focus on adding value through credit risk decisions.

MODULE 11.1: YIELD CURVE DYNAMICS, TRADES FOR A STATIC YIELD CURVE

Video covering this content is available online.

LOS 11.a: Describe the factors affecting fixed-income portfolio returns due to a change in benchmark yields.

Active management requires the investment manager to have a view of how the yield curve will behave over time. If the manager acts on this view, is correct, and the view was not already reflected in security prices, the actions can add value to the portfolio's performance.

A yield curve plots the yield of a certain type of fixed-income security as a function of its maturity. Yield curves are most typically plotted for credit risk-free government bonds to act as a benchmark for other, riskier, types of fixed-income securities. The "yield" could be yield to maturity (YTM), spot rates, or even forward rates. For our purposes, the yield will be YTM unless clearly indicated otherwise. Thus, in the United States, the typical benchmark yield curve will be for YTM as a function of maturity for U.S. Treasury securities.

While the concept of a yield curve is straightforward, its generation involves modeling and assumptions that are often not straightforward. Plugging gaps in maturity through the use of interpolation (i.e., averaging nearby available yields), differences in accounting or regulatory rules, and the choice of which existing bonds to use to construct the yield curve can affect the resulting curve. Yield curves are often constructed using more-liquid, more-recently issued on-the-run securities. The use of all securities, including less liquid off-the-run securities, would lead to a higher yield curve due to the liquidity premium.

Yield curves are generally not stable but change over time. To determine how to profit from expected changes in the yield curve, it is helpful to view yield curve changes as resulting from three sources, which are a change in the following:

1. *Level.* This is a parallel shift where all yields shift up (or down) by the same amount.

EXAMPLE: An upward parallel shift

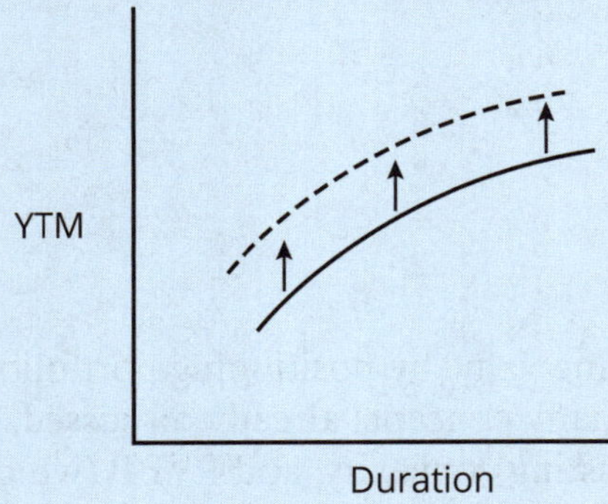

2. *Slope.* The slope is where the curve becomes flatter or steeper (a "twist").

EXAMPLE: A steepening

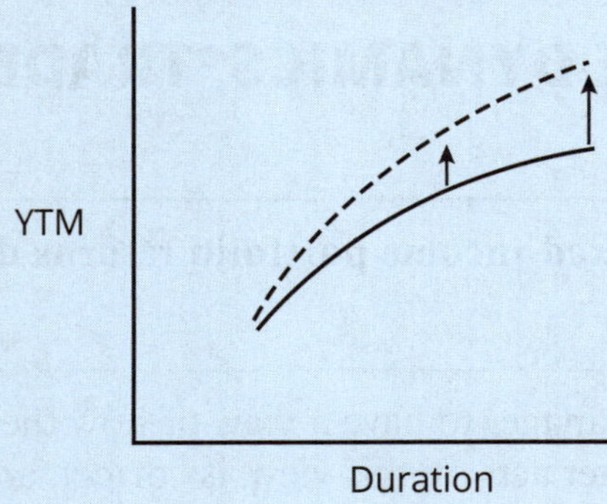

The slope of a curve can be measured by subtracting a short-term yield from a long-term yield. If this difference increases, then the curve is steepening.

3. *Curvature*. This is where the curve becomes more or less curved (a "butterfly movement").

EXAMPLE: Increased curvature

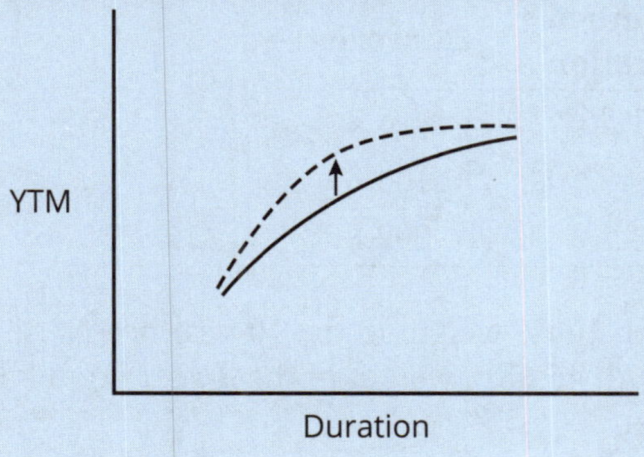

The curvature of the yield curve is measured through the butterfly spread:

butterfly spread = –(short-term yield) + (2 × medium-term yield) – long-term yield

If the butterfly spread is increasing, then medium-term yields are rising relative to short-term and long-term yields and the curvature of the yield curve is increasing.

In reality, most changes in the curve involve more than one source. However, by far the most important yield curve change in explaining changes in bond prices is a parallel shift in rates.

Recall from a previous reading, Overview of Fixed-Income Portfolio Management, the five-step return decomposition process:

1. Coupon income = annual coupon amount / current bond price
2. Rolldown return = (projected bond price (BP) assuming no yield curve change – beginning BP) / beginning BP
3. Price change due to investor yield change predictions: $(-MD \times \Delta Y) + (\frac{1}{2}C \times \Delta Y^2)$
4. Price change due to investor spread change predictions: $(-MD \times \Delta S) + (\frac{1}{2}C \times \Delta S^2)$
5. Currency G/L: projected change in value of foreign currencies weighted for exposure to the currency

The impact of changes in the benchmark yield curve (ΔY) is captured in Part 3 of the process just listed. Recall also some key facts regarding duration and convexity that we stated in an earlier reading but will be relevant in this reading also:

- Part 3 of the return decomposition shows that bonds with higher convexity outperform similar bonds with lower convexity in periods of high interest rate volatility (ΔY). This will likely lead to bonds with higher convexity trading at a premium and consequently offering lower yield to maturity.
- The higher the dispersion of cash flows in time around a bond's modified duration, the higher the convexity of the bond. This means that barbell portfolios, with highly dispersed cash flows, will have a higher convexity than bullet portfolios with the same duration.

EXAMPLE: Barbell vs. bullet

Consider the following hypothetical U.K. government bonds:

Maturity	Coupon	Modified Duration	Convexity
2y	2.25%	1.86	5.2
10y	0.25%	9.52	104.8
20y	1.25%	16.23	292.8

Portfolio 1 is a bullet portfolio with 100% weight in the 10-year bond. Portfolio 2 is a barbell portfolio with 46.68% weight in the 2-year bond and 53.32% weight in the 20-year bond.

Calculate the change in values of Portfolios 1 and 2 if the yield curve undergoes a parallel shift up of 50 basis points.

Answer:

Using Part 3 of the return decomposition process, the following are calculated:

price change of the 2-year bond = $(-1.86 \times 0.005) + (\frac{1}{2} \times 5.2 \times 0.005^2) = -0.0092$ or -0.92%

price change of the 10-year bond = $(-9.52 \times 0.005) + (\frac{1}{2} \times 104.8 \times 0.005^2) = -0.0463$ or -4.63%

price change of the 20-year bond = $(-16.23 \times 0.005) + (\frac{1}{2} \times 292.8 \times 0.005^2) = -0.0775$ or -7.75%

price change of Portfolio 1 = -4.63% because it is 100% invested in the 10-year bond

price change of Portfolio 2 = $(0.4668 \times -0.92\%) + (0.5332 \times -7.75\%) = -4.56\%$

Note how the higher convexity of Portfolio 2 (barbell) causes outperformance versus the lower convexity of Portfolio 1 (bullet). Note also that the weight of Portfolio 2 has been deliberately chosen to set Portfolio 2's duration to be equal to that of Portfolio 1, because $(0.4668 \times 1.86) + (0.5332 \times 16.23) = 9.52$.

Yield Curve Strategies

We now turn our attention to the trades an active manager can make to earn excess returns based on their view on the shape and level of the yield curve.

Static Yield Curve

LOS 11.b: Formulate a portfolio positioning strategy given forward interest rates and an interest rate view that coincides with the market view.

An active manager can earn excess return from the view that an upward-sloping yield curve will remain unchanged over time by either increasing maturity (and therefore also increasing duration) to earn higher yields or introducing leverage into the portfolio to magnify returns.

Cash-based static yield curve strategies include the following:

- **Buy and hold.** Extend the duration of the portfolio to be longer than that of the benchmark in order to earn higher returns, primarily through higher coupon income on longer-dated bonds. The buy-and-hold nature of the strategy keeps portfolio turnover and associated trading costs low.
- **Rolling down the yield curve.** This strategy is based on the fact that, as time passes, the bond's remaining maturity and duration decrease. In an upward-sloping curve, that means its yield will decline as time passes. It differs from buy and hold in that the manager aims to earn excess return from both higher coupon income and rolldown return from the bond's price changing over time. The manager will look to find a bond positioned next to a relatively steep portion on the curve such that as time passes and its yield declines, the bond will offer the greatest increase in price. Then, after the yield declines, the manager sells the bond and rolls out the curve to repeat the process by buying another bond at the end of a steep segment of the curve.
- **Repo carry trade.** A carry trade is just another form of leverage. Return is enhanced by borrowing at a lower rate to invest the funds in an asset that will generate a higher rate of return. In a stable upward-sloping curve, borrow at lower shorter-term rates to invest at higher longer-term rates.

Derivatives-based static yield curve strategies include the following:

- **Long futures positions.** Futures contracts provide implicit leverage into fixed-income positions because investors are required only to fund margin payments to open positions, which are usually a small fraction of the exposure gained through the futures contract.
- **Receive-fixed swap.** By receiving the fixed leg and paying the floating leg [a short-term market reference rate (MRR)] under an interest rate swap, the active manager can synthetically increase the duration of the portfolio. Recall from the derivatives material of the curriculum that the fixed leg of the swap carries the most duration because it is analogous to a fixed-coupon bond. A manager that receives the fixed leg increases their portfolio duration. They expect to earn the swap carry of the swap fixed rate – MRR, while also earning the profits and losses from marking the swap to market over time.

Reading 11

PROFESSOR'S NOTE

LIBOR was for a long time the benchmark floating rate for interest rate derivatives. This rate is now being phased out and replaced by different market reference rates (MRR) in different markets across the world (usually secured overnight interbank funding rates). So, instead of seeing LIBOR underlying interest rate derivatives, expect to see MRR in the future.

Note that the curriculum reading here revisits material that we saw in the liability-driven investing and derivative sections of the curriculum. As a reminder, the BPV of a Treasury futures contract is related to the BPV of the underlying cheapest-to-deliver (CTD) bond through the conversion factor (CF) of the CTD as follows:

$$\text{futures BPV} = \frac{BPV_{CTD}}{CF_{CTD}}$$

Then the number of futures contracts to go long = target BPV / futures BPV.

EXAMPLE: Extending duration (bond vs. swap)

An active manager has the view that the yield curve will remain static over the next six months. They are considering two different trades to exploit this view by extending the duration of the portfolio.

Trade A: Purchase a 10-year 3% semiannual coupon U.K. Treasury bond currently yielding 2.5%, priced at 104.3998.

Trade B: Enter a 10-year semiannual receive-fixed swap at 3%. Current floating MRR is 0.5%.

For a six-month horizon, a £50 million par value position, and a 25 bps fall in both Treasury yields and swap rates, **calculate**:

1. The coupon income and price appreciation for Trade A. Break the price appreciation down into rolldown and the change in price due to the change in rates.
2. The swap carry and MTM gain/loss on the swap.

Answers:

1. Coupon income for the bond in Trade A = 0.03 / 2 × £50,000,000 = £750,000

   Price of bond in six months: **19** N; **2.25** / 2 = 1.125 I / Y; 3 / 2 = 1.5 PMT; 100 FV; CPT PV: 106.3828

   Hence, the price appreciation for £50,000,000 par = (106.3828 – 104.3998) / 100 × £50,000,000 = £991,500.

   (Note that the price is a "percentage of par" quote. We divide the price by 100 here to scale down to £1 of par; then we multiply by £50 million to scale up to the full size of the bond).

In order to break the price appreciation into rolldown and impact of yield change, we price the bond in six months' time at its original yield (note that we are assuming here that the yield curve between 10 and 9.5 years is flat).

Price of bond in six months with unchanged yield: **19** N; **2.5/2** = 1.25 I/Y; 3/2 = 1.5 PMT; 100 FV; CPT PV: 104.2048

price appreciation due to rolldown = (104.2048 – 104.3998) / 100 × £50,000,000 = –£97,500

price appreciation due to yield change = (106.3828 – 104.2048) / 100 × £50,000,000 = £1,089,000

2. Swap carry = fixed-leg income – floating-leg outflow = [(0.03 – 0.005) / 2] × £50,000,000 = £625,000

In order to value the swap in six months' time, we view the swap as two separate bonds: the receive fixed position is viewed as a long position in a 3% fixed-coupon bond, and the pay floating position is viewed as a short position in a floating-rate note (FRN).

Value of £1 of par of the fixed leg in six months' time after fair swap rates have fallen by 25 bps: 19 N; 2.75 / 2 = 1.375 I/Y; 0.03 / 2 = 0.015 PMT; 1 FV; CPT PV: £1.020776346

value of fixed-leg side = 1.020776346 × £50,000,000 = £51,038,817

The floating side can be viewed as an FRN, which at a payment date will reset to par. Hence, the value of the swap in 6 months' time = £51,038,817 – £50,000,000 = £1,038,817.

MODULE QUIZ 11.1

1. Portfolio A is a bullet portfolio, Portfolio B is a barbell portfolio, and both are invested in risk-free government securities with the same portfolio modified duration. Under which of the following yield curve changes will Portfolio B outperform Portfolio A?
   A. A downward shift in yields only.
   B. An upward shift in yields only.
   C. Both a downward and an upward shift in yields.
2. A manager that expects a stable yield curve environment is likely to consider which of the following trades to profit from this view?
   A. Receive-fixed swap.
   B. Pay-fixed swap.
   C. Reverse repo carry trade.

3. Which of the following yield curve scenarios is the major risk to a manager engaging in a buy-and-hold strategy?
   A. A parallel shift up in yields.
   B. An inversion from a normal upward-sloping yield curve to a downward-sloping yield curve due to falling long-term rates.
   C. Yield curve remains unchanged.

MODULE 11.2: TRADES FOR A DYNAMIC YIELD CURVE

Video covering this content is available online.

LOS 11.c: Formulate a portfolio positioning strategy given forward interest rates and an interest rate view that diverges from the market view in terms of rate level, slope, and shape.

We now consider the scenarios where the manager has a view that the yield curve will change level, slope, or curvature. Note that the view that rates will fall is a *bullish* view, because this means fixed-income security prices will rise. Conversely, the view that interest rates will rise more than expected is a *bearish* view.

Divergent Rate Level View

An active manager can earn excess return from a bullish view that the benchmark yield curve will shift down by *increasing* the duration of their portfolio. Conversely, a manager with the bearish view that the yield curve will shift up would *lower* the duration of their portfolio.

Managers could use cash bonds, interest rate swaps, or futures contracts to alter the duration of the portfolio as follows:

Strategy	Increase Duration	Decrease Duration
Cash bond	Overweight longer-dated bonds	Short sell bonds/overweight shorter-dated bonds
Swap	Receive fixed	Pay fixed
Futures	Long contracts	Short contracts

Recall the three hypothetical U.K. government bonds used in a previous example:

Maturity	Coupon	Modified Duration	Convexity
2y	2.25%	1.86	5.2
10y	0.25%	9.52	104.8
20y	1.25%	16.23	292.8

A benchmark consisting of an equal weight in the three bonds would have a duration of (1.86 + 9.52 + 16.23) / 3 = 9.203 and a convexity of (5.2 + 104.8 + 292.8) / 3 = 134.3.

A manager expecting rates to rise could take an overweight position of 50% in the 2-year bond and 25% in both the 10-year and 20-year bonds. The portfolio would have a duration of (0.50 × 1.86) + (0.25 × 9.52) + (0.25 × 16.23) = 7.368 and a convexity of (0.50 × 5.2) + (0.25 × 104.8) + (0.25 × 292.8) = 102.0.

Now, if we assume that the manager's view was correct and that there is an immediate 40 bps increase in rates, we can use Step 3 of the return decomposition process to calculate the change in price for both the benchmark and the portfolio:

> price change of the benchmark = $(-9.203 \times 0.004) + (\frac{1}{2} \times 134.3 \times 0.004^2) =$ -0.0357 or -3.57%
>
> price change of the portfolio = $(-7.368 \times 0.004) + (\frac{1}{2} \times 102.0 \times 0.004^2) =$ -0.02866 or -2.87%

The manager correctly lowered the duration before a shift up in the level of the yield curve, leading to excess return of –2.87% – (–3.57%) = 0.7%.

Note that the manager could have achieved the same outcome through combining the benchmark portfolio with a pay-fixed swap with a modified duration of –8.354. The size of the swap required can be calculated here using basis point value (BPV) (recall that BPV = market value × modified duration × 0.0001). Assuming the manager has a portfolio value of $100 million:

> BPV of benchmark = $100 million × 9.203 × 0.0001 = $92,030
>
> target portfolio BPV = $100 million × 7.368 × 0.0001 = $73,680

Hence, the pay-fixed swap must have a BPV of $73,680 – $92,030 = –$18,350.

Using a swap with a duration given as –8.354, we use a notional principal (NP) that solves –8.354 × NP × 0.0001 = –$18,350. We can then solve for NP = –$18,350 / (–8.354 × 0.0001) = $21.98 million.

Divergent Yield Curve Slope View

Due to the inverse relationship between rates and bond prices, an active manager that expects a change in the *shape* of the yield curve should buy bonds with rates that are expected to fall relative to the rest of the curve (because prices will rise) and short sell bonds with rates that are expected to rise relative to the rest of the curve (because prices will fall).

Therefore, a manager expecting a steepening curve, where long-term rates are rising and short-term rates are falling, should short sell long-dated bonds and buy short-dated bonds. Conversely, a manager expecting a flattening curve where short-term rates are rising and long-term rates are falling should buy long-dated bonds and short sell short-dated bonds.

A manager might expect a change in the *level* of yields to occur simultaneously alongside a change in slope. Recall that a manager expecting a fall in the level of rates is referred to as bullish, and a manager expecting a rise in the level of rates is referred to as bearish. A bullish manager would position their overall portfolio duration to be positive, such that the portfolio increases in value as rates fall. A bearish manager would position their overall portfolio duration to be negative, such that the portfolio increases in value as rates rise. A manager that does not expect a change in the level of the curve would likely position their portfolio as duration neutral.

A **bull steepener** is the view that short-term rates will fall by more than long-term rates. This might occur when central banks cut short-term rates during an economic contraction.

A **bear steepener** is the view that long-term rates will rise by more than short-term rates. This might occur when central banks keep short-term rates too low for too long, increasing longer-term inflation expectations and the required return on longer-term bonds.

Figure 11.1: Steepening Yield Curve

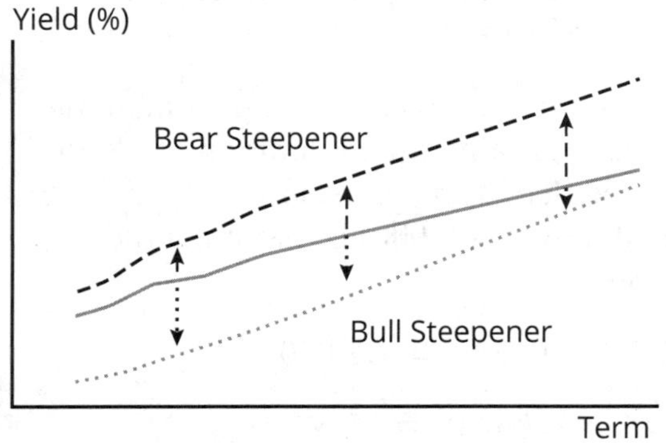

A **bear flattener** is the view that short-term rates will rise by more than long-term rates. This might occur when central banks begin to raise short-term rates in response to rising inflation expectations.

A **bull flattener** is the view that long-term rates will fall by more than short-term rates. This might occur when there is a flight to quality in uncertain markets as investors sell risky assets and purchase risk-free benchmark securities.

Figure 11.2: Flattening Yield Curve

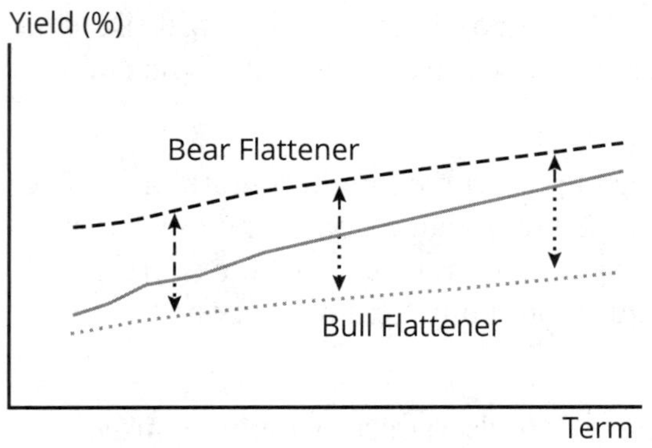

A summary of these curve changes and the associated strategies are displayed here:

<table>
<tr><th>View</th><th>Portfolio Duration</th><th>Short-Term Bonds</th><th>Long-Term Bonds</th></tr>
<tr><td>Steepener (no change in level)</td><td>Zero</td><td rowspan="3">Buy</td><td rowspan="3">Short sell</td></tr>
<tr><td>Bear steepener</td><td>Negative</td></tr>
<tr><td>Bull steepener</td><td>Positive</td></tr>
<tr><td>Flattener (no change in level)</td><td>Zero</td><td rowspan="3">Short sell</td><td rowspan="3">Buy</td></tr>
<tr><td>Bear flattener</td><td>Negative</td></tr>
<tr><td>Bull flattener</td><td>Positive</td></tr>
</table>

PROFESSOR'S NOTE

It is very difficult to digest this sort of information without picturing what is happening. Do not try to rote learn tables like the one here, but think logically about the definition of each view and how the manager should buy bonds where rates are falling relative to the rest of the market and sell bonds where rates are rising relative to the rest of the market. This, combined with maintaining a positive duration in a bull market and a negative duration in a bear market, unlocks the table without the need for memorization.

EXAMPLE: Bull steepening

A portfolio manager expects the yield curve to steepen and has collated the following information on government bonds:

Maturity	Coupon	Modified Duration	Convexity
2y	2.25%	1.86	5.2
10y	0.25%	9.52	104.8

The manager wishes to take a long position with market value of £100 million and an appropriately sized short position in order to take advantage of their view. They currently do not expect a change in the general level of rates.

1. **Describe** the trades the manager should make to profit from their view.
2. **Calculate** the total profit or loss of the portfolio if there is an immediate 20 bps decline in 2-year yields and 20 bp rise in 10-year yields.
3. **Discuss** how the manager would adjust the portfolio positions should they subsequently decide the yield curve will undergo a bull steepener (no calculations required).

Answers:

1. To profit from the view that the yield curve is going to steepen, the manager should buy short-dated bonds (2-year maturity) and short sell long-dated bonds (10-year maturity). It is stated that the manager wishes to take a long position with market value of £100 million. This implies a BPV of the long position in short-dated bonds of £100,000,000 × 1.86 × 0.0001 = £18,600.

Since the manager has no view on change in the level of rates, they should remain duration neutral. Hence, the BPV of the short position in the 10-year bonds must equal –£18,600 to cancel out the BPV of the long position in 2-year bonds. This means we require a market value for the short position in 10-year bonds (MVs) such that MVs × 9.52 × 0.0001 = –£18,600. This implies MVs = –£18,600 / (9.52 × 0.0001) = –£19,537,815.

2. We can use Step 3 of the return decomposition process to calculate the change in price for both bonds:

   price change of the 2-year bond = (–1.86 × –0.002) + (½ × 5.2 × 0.002^2) = 0.0037304 or 0.37304%

   resulting gain = 0.0037304 × £100 million = £373,040

   price change of the 10-year bond = (–9.52 × 0.002) + (½ × 104.8 × 0.002^2) = –0.01883 or –1.883%

   resulting gain = –0.01883 × –£19,537,815 = £367,897

   total increase in portfolio value = £373,040 + £367,897 = £740,937

3. If the manager believes the next yield curve change will be a bull steepener, then they believe that the steepening of the curve is going to take place in a generally falling-rate environment.

   The manager should adjust the portfolio to have a positive duration in order to profit from rates generally falling. This can be done by adding more to the long position in the 2-year bond or short selling less of the position in the 10-year bond.

Divergent Yield Curve Shape View—Change in Curvature

If a manager has the view that the curvature of the yield curve is likely to change, they can profit from this view by combining long and short positions in bullets and barbells (referred to as a **butterfly strategy**). Note that the bullet is referred to as the body and the barbell referred to as the wings in this trade.

If the manager believes that curvature will *increase*, they think that medium-term rates will rise relative to short- and long-term rates. In this scenario, the manager should short sell a medium-term bullet and buy a barbell ("short the body and long the wings"). Conversely, if the manager believes that curvature will *decrease*, they think that medium-term rates will fall relative to short- and long-term rates. In this scenario, the manager should buy a medium-term bullet and short sell a barbell ("long the body and short the wings").

Recall that the curvature of the yield curve can be measured through the butterfly spread:

butterfly spread = –(short-term yield) + (2 × medium-term yield) – long-term yield

An increase in the butterfly spread implies that medium-term rates are rising relative to short- and long-term rates, and, hence, curvature is increasing. Conversely, a fall in the butterfly spread implies that curvature is decreasing.

Recall also that an increase in curvature is referred to as a negative butterfly twist. A manager with a negative butterfly view expects the curvature of the yield curve to increase.

Note that while butterfly strategies are constructed to be duration neutral, they will not be convexity neutral due to the barbell having a higher convexity than the bullet.

PROFESSOR'S NOTE

This is a real minefield because a negative butterfly twist corresponds to an increase in the butterfly spread! Given this is fixed income, we shouldn't be surprised to see an inverse relationship; however, we need to tread very carefully when presented with information on curvature on the exam. A tip to remembering the negative/positive twist idea is to think that the curve actually "frowns" more after a negative butterfly twist (due to the increased curvature). A positive butterfly twist causes the curve to "frown" less—or even smile in a positive way!

EXAMPLE: Butterfly strategy

Recall the following three hypothetical U.K. bonds:

Maturity	Coupon	Modified Duration	Convexity
2y	2.25%	1.86	5.2
10y	0.25%	9.52	104.8
20y	1.25%	16.23	292.8

A manager wishes to construct a portfolio to profit from a positive butterfly view. They wish to set the total market value of any long position in the portfolio to £100 million, and they wish the wings of the trade to be of equal market value.

1. **Explain** how a manager should construct a duration neutral portfolio. **Show** your calculations.
2. **Calculate** the profit on the portfolio if 2- and 20-year yields rise by 10 bps and the 10-year yield falls by 25 bps.
3. **Discuss** the convexity exposure of the resulting portfolio and the impact on portfolio performance, should the manager's view be correct (note that no calculations are required for this part).

Answers:

1. A positive butterfly view implies the manager thinks that short-term and long-term rates will rise relative to intermediate rates. The manager should short sell the 2-year and 20-year bonds (the "wings") and buy the 10-year bonds (the "body").

Reading 11

If the manager wishes to take a long position of value £100 million, this implies a BPV from the 10-year bond of £100 million × 9.52 × 0.0001 = £95,200. It is stated in the question that the manager wishes the wings to have equal market value, MV_w. In order to be duration neutral, we require the total BPV of the short wings to equal the BPV of the long body:

$$(MV_w \times 1.86 \times 0.0001) + (MV_w \times 16.23 \times 0.001) = £95{,}200$$

Solving for MV_w:

$$0.000186MV_w + 0.001623MV_w = £95{,}200$$

$$0.001809MV_w = £95{,}200$$

$$= >MV_w = £95{,}200 / 0.001809 = £52{,}625{,}760$$

Hence, the manager should buy £100 million of the 10-year bond and short sell £52,625,760 of both the 2-year and the 20-year bond.

2. We can use Step 3 of the return decomposition process to calculate the change in price for each bond:

   price change of the 2-year bond = $(–1.86 \times 0.001) + (½ \times 5.2 \times 0.001^2) = –0.001857$ or –0.1857%

   resulting p/l = –0.001857 × –£52,625,760 = £97,747

   price change of the 10-year bond = $(–9.52 \times –0.0025) + (½ \times 104.8 \times –0.0025^2) = 0.0241275$ or 2.41275%

   resulting p/l = 0.0241275 × –£100,000,000 = £2,412,750

   price change of the 20-year bond = $(–16.23 \times 0.001) + (½ \times 292.8 \times 0.001^2) = –0.0160836$ or –1.60836%

   resulting p/l = –0.0160836 × –£52,625,760 = £846,412

   total increase in portfolio value = £97,747 + £2,412,750 + £846,412 = £3,356,909

3. The portfolio is short a high convexity barbell and long a lower convexity bullet. This implies that the overall portfolio is short convexity, which will decrease portfolio performance when yields move. (Note that if we summed the convexity adjustments from Part 2, we would see that the convexity effect of the bullet is in fact larger than that of the short wings. However, this is due to the fact that medium-term rates moved by more than the short-term and long-term rates. If medium-term rates had moved by the same amount as the short-term and long-term rates, the overall impact of convexity would have been negative.)

MODULE QUIZ 11.2

1. Which of the following trades is *most likely* to be executed by a manager that expects a downward shift in yields?
   A. Enter a pay-floating swap.
   B. Enter a receive-floating swap.
   C. A short futures position.
2. A manager positions their portfolio to have a negative overall duration with long positions in short-term bonds and short positions in long-term bonds. Which of the following yield curve changes is the manager *most likely* anticipating?
   A. Bear flattener.
   B. Bear steepener.
   C. Bull flattener.
3. A manager who buys the wings and sells the body in a butterfly trade is *most likely* expecting:
   A. a decrease in curvature.
   B. the butterfly spread to decrease.
   C. a negative butterfly twist.

MODULE 11.3: YIELD CURVE VOLATILITY STRATEGIES, KEY RATE DURATION

Video covering this content is available online.

LOS 11.d: Formulate a portfolio positioning strategy based upon expected changes in interest rate volatility.

We now turn our attention to bonds with embedded options and stand-alone option strategies in fixed-income markets.

In the underlying bond markets, the major types of bonds with embedded options are callable bonds and putable bonds.

A **callable** bond gives the issuer the right to buy the bond back from the investor before maturity. It can be viewed as a combination of an option-free bond and a short call option because this call has been granted to the issuer. The embedded short call option becomes more valuable as yields fall and underlying bond prices rise. This leads to negative convexity for callable bonds at low yields, as their prices will rise at a slower pace than option-free bonds due to the increase in the value of the call option.

Figure 11.3: Callable Bond

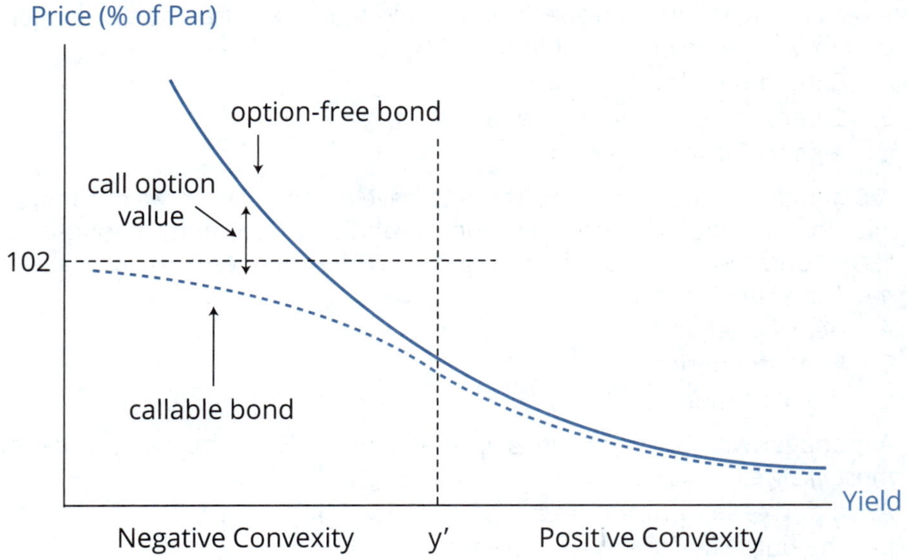

A **putable** bond gives the investor the right to sell the bond back to the issuer before maturity. It can be viewed as a combination of an option-free bond and a long put option because this put is owned by the investor. The embedded long put option becomes more valuable as yields rise and underlying bond prices fall. This leads to a floor underneath putable bond prices at high yields, as their prices fall at a slower pace than option-free bonds due to the increase in the value of the put option.

Figure 11.4: Putable Bond

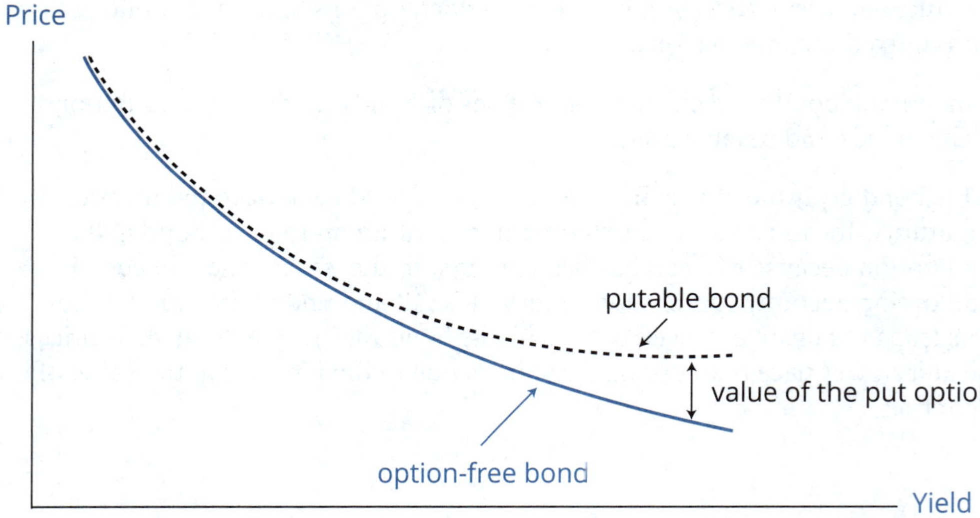

Recall that bonds with embedded options should be analyzed using *effective* duration and convexity measures, which incorporate the impact on the cash flows of changes in the benchmark yield in their calculation. Note that Macaulay duration/convexity and modified duration/convexity measures cannot be used for bonds with embedded options because they do not account for the uncertainty of the bond's cash flows due to the exercise of the embedded option.

The formulas for effective duration and convexity were stated in an earlier reading but are reprinted here for convenience:

$$\text{effective duration} = \frac{(PV_-) - (PV_+)}{2(\Delta\text{curve})(PV_0)}$$

$$\text{effective convexity} = \frac{(PV_-) + (PV_+) - 2(PV_0)}{(\Delta\text{curve})^2 (PV_0)}$$

where:

PV_0 = current value of the portfolio

PV_- = value of portfolio when benchmark curve is shifted down

PV_+ = value of portfolio when benchmark curve is shifted up

Δcurve = change in benchmark curve

A general rule for bonds with embedded options that is useful to keep in mind is that the option always *lowers* the duration of the otherwise option-free bond. This is because the short call and long put positions move inversely to the underlying bond (when the bond falls, the option position value increases and vice versa).

In the derivatives markets, the three major types of options available are options on bond prices, options on bond futures, and swaptions.

Adding **call options on either a bond price or a bond futures contract** will *increase* the duration of a fixed-income portfolio because the calls will increase in value as yields fall and bond prices rise.

Adding **put options on either a bond price or a bond futures contract** will *decrease* the duration of a fixed-income portfolio because the puts will increase in value as yields rise and bond prices fall.

Swaptions can also be used to alter the duration of a fixed-income portfolio.

A **payer swaption** gives the holder the right to enter a pay-fixed swap. This becomes valuable as rates rise; hence, a payer swaption *decreases* the duration of the portfolio.

A **receiver swaption** gives the holder the right to enter a receive-fixed swap. This becomes valuable as rates fall; hence, a receiver swaption *increases* the duration of the portfolio.

A summary of the different types of options and their impact on portfolio duration is displayed here:

Strategy	Impact on Duration
Long call on bond prices/bond futures prices	Increase
Long put on bond prices/bond futures prices	Decrease
Long payer swaption	Decrease
Long receiver swaption	Increase

Key Rate Duration

LOS 11.e: Evaluate a portfolio's sensitivity using key rate durations of the portfolio and its benchmark.

Recall that **key rate duration** (or partial duration) measures the sensitivity of a portfolio to a movement in a key maturity rate *while other rates remain constant*. Note that the sum of key rate durations for a portfolio will equal the effective duration of the portfolio because this sum represents the aggregate sensitivity of the portfolio to a move in all maturity yields at the same time (i.e., a parallel shift in the yield curve).

Key rate duration is used to identify which maturities a manager's portfolio has most sensitivity to and, in doing so, allows us to assess the manager's exposure to nonparallel changes in the yield curve (slope/curvature). Recall that this is not possible under modified or effective duration measures, which assume a parallel shift in yield curves.

A manager with a high positive key rate duration at a particular maturity has the view that this maturity rate is going to fall. Conversely, a manager with a high negative key rate duration at a particular maturity has the view that this maturity rate is going to rise.

Key rate duration can be calculated as follows:

$$\text{KeyRateDur} = -\frac{\text{change in portfolio value}}{\text{portfolio value} \times \text{change in key rate}}$$

PROFESSOR'S NOTE

When dealing with zero-coupon bonds, an easy way to get to key rate duration is to take the modified duration of each zero-coupon bond and multiply by its weight in the portfolio. This scales the bond's sensitivity to changes in rates down to represent the portfolio's sensitivity to a unit change in the key rate. Note that this would not work for coupon-paying bonds because part of their modified duration would come from cash flows that occur at other maturities (i.e., the coupons before maturity).

EXAMPLE: Key rate duration

An active fixed-income portfolio manager takes the following positions in the zero-coupon bonds displayed below:

Maturity	Annualized Yield	Position ($m)
2	2%	250
10	3%	–50
20	5%	100

The manager's benchmark is equally weighted across the three zero-coupon bonds.

1. **Calculate** the key rate durations and overall modified durations for both the manager and the benchmark.
2. **Determine** the most likely view of the manager on the next change in yield curve level, slope, and curvature.

Answers:

1. First, compute the modified durations of the zero-coupon bonds through the relationship:

    modified duration = Macaulay duration / (1 + yield)

    Using the fact that the Macaulay duration of a zero-coupon bond is its maturity, the following are calculated:

    modified duration of 2-year bond = 2 / (1.02) = 1.961

    modified duration of 10-year bond = 10 / (1.03) = 9.7087

    modified duration of 20-year bond = 20 / (1.05) = 19.0476

    Next, calculate the key rate duration of the portfolio by multiplying each zero-coupon bond by its weight in the portfolio:

    2-year key rate duration = 1.961 × (250 / 300) = 1.634

    10-year key rate duration = 9.7087 × (–50 / 300) = –1.618

    20-year key rate duration = 19.0476 × (100 / 300) = 6.349

    total portfolio modified duration = 1.634 – 1.618 + 6.349 = 6.365

    Doing the same for the benchmark gives the following:

    2-year key rate duration 1.961 × (100 / 300) = 0.654

    10-year key rate duration = 9.7087 × (100 / 300) = 3.236

    20-year key rate duration = 19.0476 × (100 / 300) = 6.349

    total benchmark modified duration = 0.654 + 3.236 + 6.349 = 10.239

Reading 11

2. Summarizing the result derived in part 1 results in the following:

Maturity	Portfolio	Index	Active Position (Difference)
2-year key rate duration	1.634	0.654	0.980
10-year key rate duration	–1.618	3.236	–4.854
20-year key rate duration	6.349	6.349	0.000
Overall modified duration	6.365	10.239	–3.874

At the overall portfolio level, the manager has a negative active duration of –3.875. This implies that the manager is bearish (i.e., believes that rates are generally going to rise).

From a slope perspective, the manager has a positive active exposure to short-term rates (0.980) but a zero active exposure to long-term rates (0.000). This suggests that the manager expects short-term rates to rise by *less* than long-term rates (i.e., the curve is going to steepen).

The manager also has a significant negative exposure to medium-term rates and overall a positive exposure to short-term and long-term rates. This implies that the manager has a negative butterfly view, where they expect medium-term rates to rise by more than short-term and long-term rates.

Overall, this manager is positioned for a combination of a negative butterfly and a bear steepener.

MODULE QUIZ 11.3

1. Given otherwise similar bond characteristics, a manager who is expecting an upward shift in rates is *least likely* to invest in:
   A. a callable bond.
   B. a putable bond.
   C. an option-free bond.
2. Which of the following positions would *most likely* be established by a manager expecting a downward shift in yields?
   A. Short a receiver swaption.
   B. Long a payer swaption.
   C. Long a call option on bond futures contracts.
3. A manager has created active key rate durations of 3, –0.5, and –3 at the 10-year, 20-year, and 30-year maturities, respectively, using only derivatives to create the active exposures. Which of the following derivatives positions is the manager *most likely* using?
   A. Receive-fixed 10-year swap, short 20-year futures, and pay-fixed 30-year swap.
   B. Pay-fixed 10-year swap, short 20-year futures, and receive-fixed 30-year swap.
   C. Short 10-year futures, long 20-year futures, and receive-fixed 30-year swap.

MODULE 11.4: ACTIVE MANAGEMENT ACROSS CURRENCIES, EVALUATING YIELD CURVE STRATEGIES

Video covering this content is available online.

LOS 11.f: Discuss yield curve strategies across currencies.

Unhedged Foreign Bond Position

A manager who invests in a foreign currency bond will earn the return of the bond in the foreign currency, R_{FC}, alongside returns due to changes in the exchange rate, R_{FX}. These two return components compound together to give a total domestic return, R_{DC}, given by the following:

$$R_{DC} = (1 + R_{FC})(1 + R_{FX}) - 1$$

A manager with several different foreign exposures should calculate the domestic returns, R_{DC}, individually for each foreign market, then weight these returns according to each foreign market's weight in the portfolio.

PROFESSOR'S NOTE

This equation mirrors the approach in the currency management reading in derivatives. Recall that the R_{FX} return here **must** be calculated as the change in the FX quote, with the domestic currency as the variable (price) currency and the foreign currency as the fixed (base) currency (referred to as a direct quote). This is required because the investor's domestic returns are driven by how much one unit of the foreign currency is worth in terms of their own domestic currency, which is what a direct quote displays. If this direct quote rises, the investor profits from an appreciating foreign currency and R_{FX} will be positive. If this direct quote falls, the investor suffers losses from a depreciating foreign currency and R_{FX} will be negative.

For example, if we had a U.K. portfolio manager investing in a Japanese bond, the domestic currency would be GBP and the foreign currency would be JPY. To calculate R_{FX}, we need to look at how the GBP/JPY (i.e., direct quote) quote has moved. The question might state that the JPY/GBP rate was 150 at the start of the period and 125 at the end of the period—this quote is the wrong way around for our purposes. We need to invert this quote and observe that the GBP/JPY quote at the start of the period was 1 / 150 = 0.006667 and ended the period at 1 / 125 = 0.0080. Then R_{FX} can then be calculated as (0.0080 – 0.006667) / 0.006667 = 20%. The U.K. manager has benefited from their JPY strengthening during the period—we can see this most easily from the GBP/JPY rate moving up during the period.

The Hedging Decision

EXAMPLE: Unhedged foreign bond investment

An Australian portfolio manager invests in a 2-year zero-coupon U.S. Treasury bond for one year. Details of the transaction are as follows:

- The U.S. bond is initially trading at a price of 96.374.
- The USD/AUD exchange rate was 0.90 at the start of the year and 0.80 at the end of the year.
- The U.S. bond ends the year at a price of 99.939.

Calculate the return of the investor in domestic currency terms.

Answer:

The foreign currency return of the U.S. Treasury bond, R_{FC}, is the return in the local U.S. market, ignoring any currency effects:

R_{FC} = (99.939 – 96.374) / 96.374 = 3.70%

The domestic currency here is AUD and the foreign currency is USD. In order to calculate R_{FX}, the impact of foreign exchange, we need to calculate the percentage change in the AUD/USD exchange rate, with the domestic currency as the variable currency. The quotes in the question, therefore, need to be inverted before calculations:

Opening AUD/USD = 1 / 0.90 = 1.1111
Closing AUD/USD = 1 / 0.80 = 1.2500

Now we can calculate R_{FX} as R_{FX} = (1.2500 – 1.1111) / 1.1111 = 12.5%.

The domestic return of the USD assets is therefore (1.037) × (1.125) – 1 = 16.66%.

A manager may choose to hedge their foreign currency exposure by selling the foreign currency forward, thereby locking in an exchange rate to convert the foreign funds back to their domestic currency.

Recall the fundamental no-arbitrage principal of **covered interest rate parity (CIRP),** which implies that, in efficient markets, a manager that hedges a foreign currency by selling the foreign currency forward should *not* earn excess returns. CIRP states that high interest rate currencies should trade at a forward *discount*, so that when a manager sells high interest rate currencies forward to remove currency risk, the forward discount offsets the interest rate differential earned from holding the higher interest rate currency. CIRP means that the manager fails to earn an overall higher return in their hedged foreign bond, instead only earning their *domestic* risk-free rate.

Recall that, according to CIRP, the fair forward rate is related to the spot rate by adjusting for interest rate differentials over the period of length *T* as follows:

$$\text{forward rate} = \text{spot rate} \times \frac{\left(1 + r_{DC}\right)^{T}}{\left(1 + r_{FC}\right)^{T}}$$

Notice how the foreign, fixed currency appears on the base of this relationship, just as it does for the currency quote itself.

EXAMPLE: The hedging decision

Following on from the previous example, assume the manager actually holds the U.S. bond for two years to its maturity when it redeems at par. Recall the following formation:

- The original price of the U.S. 2-year zero-coupon bond was 96.374.
- The original USD/AUD exchange rate was 0.90 at initiation of the trade.

An equivalent 2-year zero-coupon Australian government bond was yielding 5% at the initiation of the trade.

1. **Calculate** the fair 2-year forward rate.
2. **Demonstrate** that the manager would earn their domestic risk-free rate if they used this forward rate to hedge their USD foreign currency exposure. **Show** your work.

Answers:

1. The domestic risk-free rate implied by the 2-year zero-coupon Australian is 5%. The foreign risk-free rate based on the price of the U.S. Treasury is $(100 / 96.374)^{(1/2)} - 1 = 1.864\%$.

   Using the covered interest rate parity formula, the fair 2-year AUD/USD forward rate is as follows [note that we continue to work in direct quotes (DC/FC) here]:

$$\text{forward rate} = \text{spot rate} \times \frac{\left(1 + r_{DC}\right)^{T}}{\left(1 + r_{FC}\right)^{T}} = \frac{1}{0.90} \times \frac{(1.05)^{2}}{(1.01864)^{2}} = 1.1806$$

2. To hedge their receipt of USD 100 in two years' time, the manager should sell USD 100 forward at the fair forward rate of AUD/USD 1.1806 and receive in return 100 × 1.1806 = AUD 118.06.

   The original AUD cost of the U.S. bond was 96.374 / 0.90 = 107.0822.

   Therefore, the annualized domestic return to the Australian investor is $(118.06 / 107.0822)^{(1/2)} - 1 = 5.0\%$.

   This is the same annualized return as the domestic risk-free Australian government bond, as required by covered interest rate parity.

Reading 11

> **PROFESSOR'S NOTE**
>
> Note that the interest rate differential in the USD market here was actually negative: USD yield – AUD yield = 1.864% – 5% = –3.1%. Here, covered interest rate parity implies that the higher-yielding AUD will be at a forward discount and the lower-yielding USD will be at a forward premium.
>
> The forward rate of 1.1806 AUD/USD is higher than the spot AUD/USD rate of 1.1111 by an annualized $(1.1806/1.1111)^{(1/2)} - 1 = 3.1\%$. This is indeed a premium on the USD (don't forget that if the quote is higher, it is the base currency that is stronger).
>
> Observe how, in this case, the premium on the low interest rate currency offsets the lower interest rate earned in the foreign market, causing the investor to earn their domestic risk-free rate.

If the manager chooses *not* to hedge, they will earn a domestic return that depends on the actual movement of exchange rates over their investment horizon. The theory of **uncovered interest rate parity (UIRP)** states that high interest rate currencies should *actually* depreciate over time, such that all *unhedged* investors earn the same return, regardless of which currency they hold. This theory implies that spot rates should move toward the original forward rates set by CIRP. UIRP tends *not* to hold—high interest rate currencies on average tend *not* to depreciate over time according to their interest rate differential versus other currencies, which means the forward rate is not an unbiased predictor of future spot rates (called **forward rate bias**). This forward rate bias can be exploited by executing a carry trade, described later in this chapter.

> **PROFESSOR'S NOTE**
>
> In the example just listed, **uncovered** interest parity would forecast that the actual AUD/USD spot rate in two years' time should turn out to be 1.1806, (i.e., the original forward rate set by **covered** interest rate parity). This does not tend to happen. In practice, the exchange rate tends to move from 1.1111 today to some value between 1.1111 and 1.1806 in two years' time, but doesn't on average move all the way to the original forward rate. In other words, high interest rate currencies tend not to weaken as implied by their forward discount, which means the carry trade can earn excess returns.

Hedging Foreign Coupon-Paying Bonds

Now, let us consider an Australian investor who wishes to hedge their exposure to a *coupon-paying* U.S. Treasury bond.

In order to hedge their foreign USD exposure, the Australian investor must lock in a rate at the outset, which they can periodically exchange the regular foreign USD coupon payments received from the U.S. bond for domestic AUD over the life of the bond. They can achieve this by entering into a **fixed-fixed cross-currency swap**, agreeing to pay USD and receive AUD over the life of the swap. Note that the fixed-fixed cross-currency swap also involves an exchange of principal amounts at the start and the end of the swap's life, which can be used to finance the initial purchase of the foreign U.S. bond and convert back the foreign USD par proceeds in domestic AUD at maturity.

Assume that the current USD/AUD rate is 0.80 and that the manager wishes to hedge an investment in USD 100 million par of a 10-year U.S. Treasury bond currently trading at par. The manager enters into a fixed-fixed cross-currency swap to pay-fixed USD and receive-fixed AUD with principal sizes of USD 100 million and 100 million / 0.80 = AUD 125 million.

Position	At Initiation	Periodic Semiannual Payments for Next 10 Years	At the End
U.S. Treasury Bond	Pay out USD 100 million to purchase the U.S. bond	Receive-fixed USD bond coupon	Receive USD 100 million par at maturity of bond
Fixed-Fixed Cross-Currency Swap	Receive USD 100 million and pay AUD 125 million in exchange of principal amounts	Pay-fixed USD leg Receive-fixed AUD leg	Pay USD 100 million and receive AUD 125 million in exchange of principal amounts
Net Flow	*Pay AUD 125 million principal outflow*	*Receive-fixed AUD payment*	*Receive AUD 125 million principal inflow*

As can be seen from the net flow box, the resulting exposure for the Australian manager is the same as investing in a domestic Australian bond. This is analogous to the scenario with the zero-coupon bond—if parity relations hold, a manager that hedges a foreign exposure will earn their domestic return on the hedged position.

The pay USD, receive AUD fixed-fixed cross-currency swap just described is, in practice, generated through a combination of the three underlying swaps (swaps A, B, and C) listed here:

Swap	Description	Interest Paid	Interest Received	Principal Exchange at Outset	Principal Exchange at End
A	USD interest rate swap	USD Fixed	USD Floating	None	None
B	AUD interest rate swap	AUD Floating	AUD Fixed	None	None
C	Cross-currency basis swap	USD Floating	AUD Floating	Receive in USD principal, pay out AUD principal	Pay out USD principal, receive in AUD principal

The rationale is as follows:

- The fixed-fixed legs (pay USD, receive AUD) are provided by Swaps A and B.
- The floating legs of Swaps A and B cancel with the floating legs of the cross-currency basis swap, Swaps C.
- The cross-currency basis swap, Swap C, provides the exchange of principal amounts required to fund the investment in foreign U.S. bonds and convert the principal proceeds back into domestic AUD at the end.

Reading 11

PROFESSOR'S NOTE

We first met cross-currency basis swaps in the derivatives section of the curriculum. Recall that they are an exchange of floating rates in different currencies with an exchange of principal amounts at the outset and the end. A good rule of thumb regarding the direction of the principal payments is to think of the floating leg paid out as an interest rate paid on funds borrowed through the swap. In this case, we are paying out USD Floating; hence, we must be using the swap to borrow USD at the start (receive USD principal in) and repay this USD principal at the end (pay USD principal out).

Recall also that covered interest rate parity can be breached in cross-currency basis swaps due to an adjustment to the non-U.S. interest leg referred to as basis. If the basis is negative, this implies that the non-U.S. floating leg is below the fair rate implied by covered interest rate parity. This means that borrowers of U.S. funds through cross-currency basis swaps, like our Australian investor here, are willing to receive a lower interest rate on their domestic currency in order to borrow USD through the swap.

The decomposition of the fixed-fixed cross-currency swap into the three swaps gives an insight into ways an active manager might express an active view on interest rates or currencies. For example, if the manager chose not to initiate Swap A, this would leave them with a fixed USD coupon coming in from the bond and a floating USD payment going out under Swap C. Hence, the manager would be net receiving fixed and paying floating in USD and will therefore profit if USD rates fall (think: positive duration). Note, however, that currency is still fully hedged under the cross-currency swap.

Unhedged Cross-Currency Trade: The Carry Trade

To conclude this section on currency, we shall consider a classic *unhedged* cross-currency trade: the **carry trade**. The carry trade involves borrowing in a low interest rate currency and depositing in a high interest rate currency. The manager faces the risk that the high interest rate currency weakens and can also take a view on the relative yield curve changes in the two currencies by borrowing and depositing over different maturities, as per the example here.

EXAMPLE: INR carry trade

A manager is considering executing a carry trade with a 1-year horizon through borrowing U.S. dollars (USD) and investing in short-term Indian rupee (INR) securities. Details of the trade are as follows:

- The manager will borrow at the 1-year USD rate of 1%.
- The manager will roll 90-day INR securities, which currently offer a rate of 5% on an annualized basis.
- The current INR/USD spot rate is 70.

1. **Calculate** the approximate return from the carry trade if interest rates and exchange rates remain stable over the year.

2. **Calculate** the return from the carry trade based on if short-term 90-day INR rates evolve to be 5%, 6%, 4%, and 3% over the coming year, and the final INR exchange rate is 85.

Answers:

1. Foreign returns from rolling the INR securities every 90 days for a year $= (1 + 0.05 / 4)^4 - 1 = 5.1\%$.

   The cost of funds in USD for 1 year = 1%.

   With no change in exchange rates, there are no profits/losses from currency exposure; hence, total return = 5.1% – 1% = 4.1%.

2. Foreign returns from rolling the INR securities every 90 days for a year $= (1 + 0.05 / 4) \times (1 + 0.06 / 4) \times (1 + 0.04 / 4) \times (1 + 0.03 / 4) - 1 = 4.6\%$.

   The cost of funds in USD for 1 year = 1%.

   In order to measure the foreign exchange impact, we need to look at the percentage change in the value of the INR, since this is the currency the manager is depositing in. Hence, we need to look at the change in the USD/INR quote where the INR is the base currency. This quote started the year at 1 / 70 = 0.014286 and ends the year at 1 / 85 = 0.011765. Therefore, the p/l from fx is calculated as (0.011765 / 0.014286) – 1 = –17.6%.

   The total p/l from the carry trade = 4.6% – 1.0% – 17.6% = –14.0%.

PROFESSOR'S NOTE

While we said earlier that forward rate bias means that the carry trade can, on average, earn excess returns, it appears here that the major risk of the carry trade has crystallized in this example. A significant depreciation in the high interest rate currency has wiped out the interest rate differential many times over and caused significant losses. It is likely this trade occurred in a time of flight to quality in a market crisis, where the carry trade can suffer significant losses.

Note that swaps can also be used to profit from an active cross-currency view. Generally, a manager would use swaps to:

- Receive floating in markets where they expect floating rates to rise, and pay floating in markets where they expect rates to fall.
- Receive fixed in markets where they expect rates to fall and pay fixed in markets where they expect rates to rise.
- The manager would also be subject to foreign exchange risk. They should be careful to ensure that expected currency movements do not wipe out or exceed the expected interest rate advantage (as per the example just listed).

PROFESSOR'S NOTE

This is simply a basic duration comment. If we keep in mind that we wish to extend duration (receive fixed) when rates are expected to fall and lower duration (receive floating) when rates are expected to rise, with an exam question, logic should prevail.

A Framework for Evaluating Yield Curve Strategies

LOS 11.g: Evaluate the expected return and risks of a yield curve strategy.

Recall the five-step return decomposition process:

1. Coupon income = annual coupon amount / current bond price
2. Rolldown return = [projected bond price (BP) assuming no yield curve change – beginning BP] / beginning BP
3. Price change due to investor yield change predictions: $(-MD \times \Delta Y) + (\frac{1}{2}C \times \Delta Y^2)$
4. Price change due to investor spread change predictions: $(-MD \times \Delta S) + (\frac{1}{2}C \times \Delta S^2)$
5. Currency G/L: projected change in value of foreign currencies weighted for exposure to the currency

Steps 1–3 and 5 have been central to the discussions in this chapter (Step 4 is considered in the next reading on credit strategies). This reading concludes with some applications of Steps 1–3 and 5 of the process just listed.

PROFESSOR'S NOTE

There is nothing new here that we have not already seen in the chapter, and the examples in the curriculum become quite repetitive. It is really just an exercise in tying all of the information together in a scenario analysis. The important thing here is that this is likely how this material will be actually tested. We present one example for reference.

EXAMPLE: CAD bullet vs. barbell

A U.S.-based portfolio manager is considering investing in Canadian zero-coupon bonds. The manager collates the following information relating to the expected performance of a bullet portfolio relative to a barbell portfolio over the next year.

	Bullet	**Barbell**
Average bond price	96.75	97
Expected average price in 1 year assuming stable yield curve	98.75	98.95
Expected effective portfolio duration	4.89	4.92
Expected portfolio convexity	28.5	43
Expected change in CAD bond yields	0.25%	0.25%
Expected change in CAD versus USD	–0.50%	–0.50%

1. **Calculate** the expected return from the bullet and barbell portfolios over the next year.
2. **Discuss** reasons for the difference in performance of the bullet and barbell portfolios.

Answers:

1. Using the five-part return decomposition process:

   Step 1: Coupon income

   Since all bonds are zero-coupon bonds, there is no coupon yield for either the bullet or the barbell portfolios.

   Step 2: Rolldown return

   Bullet: (98.75 – 96.75) / 96.75 = 2.067%

   Barbell: (98.95 – 97) / 97 = 2.010%

   Step 3: Impact of changes in yield

   Bullet: Price change = $(-4.89 \times 0.0025) + (0.5 \times 28.5 \times 0.0025^2) =$ –0.01214 or –1.214%

   Barbell: Price change = $(-4.92 \times 0.0025) + (0.5 \times 43 \times 0.0025^2) =$ –0.01217 or –1.217%

   Step 4: Impact of changes in spread

   There is no information regarding changes in spread, so we assume this is zero for both the bullet and barbell.

   Step 5: Impact of currency

   Steps 1–3 have given us the foreign market returns in CAD. We can compound this with the expected currency return of –0.50% to get the expected domestic returns in USD.

   Bullet: $(1 + 0.02067 - 0.01214) \times (1 - 0.005) - 1 = 0.0035$ or 0.35%

   Barbell: $(1 + 0.02010 - 0.01217) \times (1 - 0.005) - 1 = 0.0029$ or 0.29%

2. The bullet outperforms the barbell by 6 bps. This primarily comes from the higher expected rolldown return of the bullet bond versus the two bonds that make up the barbell. It must be the case that the bullet bond lies on a steeper part of the yield curve than the average of the two bonds that make up the barbell leading to a slightly larger fall in yield and a slightly higher rolldown return for the bullet.

PROFESSOR'S NOTE

Notice that Step 5 here compounds currency return on the domestic return of the bond, whereas in the first example of this return decomposition process given in an earlier reading, we simply added Step 5 to the other components. So which is correct? Given that the section in this chapter that delves into detail on currency uses a multiplicative approach as just listed, we would recommend using the multiplicative approach. Chances are, though, that given the earlier example simply adds Step 5, it is unlikely that examiners could actually mark this approach wrong if it were used in the exam.

MODULE QUIZ 11.4

1. A U.S. investor buys a zero-coupon 1-year European bond denominated in EUR for EUR 99.01. At the same time, the 1-year U.S. interest rate is 3%. The manager chooses to hedge currency exposure through selling EUR forward against USD. If covered interest rate parity holds, the manager will *least likely*:
   A. sell EUR at a 2% premium against USD.
   B. sell USD at a 2% premium against EUR.
   C. buy USD at a 2% discount against EUR.
2. Excess returns from the unhedged carry trade imply that which of the following parity relationships is not holding?
   A. Covered interest rate parity only.
   B. Uncovered interest rate parity only.
   C. Both covered and uncovered interest rate parity.
3. A manager believes a foreign yield curve will undergo a bull steepening, while their higher-yielding domestic yield curve will remain stable and upward sloping. In order to maximize carry benefits according to their view, the manager should:
   A. pay-fixed in foreign currency, receive-fixed in domestic currency.
   B. pay-fixed in foreign market, receive-floating in domestic currency.
   C. pay-floating in foreign currency, receive-fixed in domestic currency.
4. A manager constructs a barbell portfolio using a 60% position in Bond A and a 40% position in Bond B, details of which are displayed here:

Bond	Maturity	Coupon	Modified Duration	Convexity
A	2y	2.25%	1.86	5.2
B	10y	0.25%	9.52	104.8

   If a bear flattening occurs through a 50 bps rise in the 2-year rate and a 30 bps rise in the 10-year rate, the change in price of the portfolio will be *closest* to:
   A. –1.68%.
   B. –1.71%.
   C. –1.97%.

KEY CONCEPTS

LOS 11.a

The three primary yield curve changes are changes in:

- Level, as measured by a parallel shift in yields across the curve.
- Slope, as measured by long-term yields – short-term yields.
- Curvature, as measured by the butterfly spread:

  – (short-term yield) + (2 × medium-term yield) – long-term yield

The five-step return decomposition process can be used to analyze the impact of changes in the yield curve on fixed-income securities:

1. Coupon income = annual coupon amount / current bond price
2. Rolldown return = [projected bond price (BP) assuming no yield curve change – beginning BP] / beginning BP
3. Price change due to investor yield change predictions: $(–MD \times \Delta Y) + (½C \times \Delta Y^2)$
4. Price change due to investor spread change predictions: $(–MD \times \Delta S) + (½C \times \Delta S^2)$
5. Currency G/L: projected change in value of foreign currencies weighted for exposure to the currency

The impact of changes in the benchmark yield curve (ΔY) is captured in Part 3 of the process.

LOS 11.b

Active strategies when the (upward-sloping) yield curve is expected to be stable:

- Buy and hold—extend duration to get higher yields.
- Rolling down the yield curve—weight the portfolio highest for securities at the long end of the steepest yield curve segments, which maximizes price gains on securities from declines in yield as time passes.
- Repo carry trade—buy a long-term bond using short-term repo financing.
- Long futures—increase the leverage of the portfolio through futures contracts.
- Receive-fixed swap—earn the swap carry of swap fixed rate – MRR.

LOS 11.c

Change in Yield Curve Level

A manager expecting a parallel shift down (up) in yields should increase (decrease) the duration of the portfolio.

Strategies to alter the duration of a portfolio are as follows:

Strategy	Increase Duration	Decrease Duration
Cash bond	Overweight longer-dated bonds	Short sell bonds/overweight shorter-dated bonds
Swap	Receive fixed	Pay fixed
Futures	Long contracts	Short contracts

Change in Slope

- Steepening curve: short sell long-dated bonds and buy short-dated bonds.
- Flattening curve: buy long-dated bonds and short sell short-dated bonds.

A manager with no view on overall level of yields should structure the trades just listed to be duration neutral. If a manager is bullish (bearish) on the yield level, they should position the portfolio to have positive (negative) duration.

Change in Curvature

- Increasing curvature (negative butterfly twist): short sell bullet (body), buy barbell (wings)
- Decreasing curvature (positive butterfly): short sell barbell (wings), buy bullet (body)

A manager with no view on overall level of yields should structure the trades just listed to be duration neutral. If a manager is bullish (bearish) on the yield level, they should position the portfolio to have positive (negative) duration.

LOS 11.d

A callable bond (option-free bond and short call option) will rise at a slower rate than an option-free bond as yields fall (exhibiting negative convexity).

A putable bond (option-free bond and long put option) will fall at a slower rate than an option-free bond as yields rise.

Option strategies:

Strategy	Impact on Duration
Long call on bond prices/bond futures prices	Increase
Long put on bond prices/bond futures prices	Decrease
Long payer swaption	Decrease
Long receiver swaption	Increase

LOS 11.e

Key rate duration (or partial duration) measures the sensitivity of a portfolio to a movement in a key maturity rate *while other rates remain constant*.

$$\text{KeyRateDur} = \frac{\text{change in portfolio value}}{\text{portfolio value} \times \text{change in key rate}}$$

A high positive (negative) key rate duration at a specific maturity implies that the portfolio will outperform if this maturity rate falls (rises) relative to other maturities.

LOS 11.f

The domestic return of a foreign bond with a foreign currency return, R_{FC}, and a return from the DC/FC exchange rate of R_{FX} is as follows:

$$R_{DC} = (1 + R_{FC})(1 + R_{FX}) - 1$$

In efficient markets, covered interest rate parity means that high interest rate currencies trade at a forward discount. This means that a hedged foreign bond position cannot earn excess returns because any interest rate advantage of the foreign bond is offset by the forward discount. Hence, a hedged foreign bond investor earns their domestic interest rate.

An unhedged manager in a foreign bond will earn the foreign currency return of the bond and any appreciation/depreciation of the foreign currency over the investment horizon (as per the formula just listed). Uncovered interest rate parity theorizes that high interest rate currencies should actually weaken over time. This theory tends not to hold and allows the unhedged manager to earn excess returns from the carry trade (borrow in a low interest rate currency, deposit in a high interest rate currency).

A manager wishing to hedge exposure to a foreign coupon-paying bond should enter a fixed-fixed cross-currency swap as the foreign currency payer and domestic currency receiver.

LOS 11.g

The five-step return decomposition process from LOS 11.a can be used to assess the relative performance of different portfolios under different yield curve change scenarios.

ANSWER KEY FOR MODULE QUIZZES

Module Quiz 11.1

1. **C** Portfolio B, being a barbell portfolio, will have higher convexity than Portfolio A, the bullet portfolio. Higher convexity bonds benefit from falling less in price when yields rise and rising more in price when yields fall. (LOS 11.a)

2. **A** A manager that expects a stable yield curve should increase risk to enhance returns by either extending the duration of the portfolio or using leverage. A receive-fixed swap will increase the duration of the portfolio and enhance returns. Answer B is incorrect because a pay-fixed swap would lower the duration of the portfolio. Answer C is incorrect because a reverse repo is a form of lending—a manager wishing to increase leverage should enter a repo carry trade, which is a form of collateralized borrowing. (LOS 11.b)

3. **A** A manager that is engaging in a buy-and-hold strategy is extending the duration of their portfolio in order to enhance returns when they forecast that the yield curve will not change. The risk to this strategy is that yields do move and rise, causing prices to fall. Answer B is incorrect because if the curve inverts and longer-term rates fall, the manager's bond prices will rise and they will outperform. Answer C is incorrect because the manager will successfully enhance returns as anticipated if the yield curve remains stable due to higher returns on higher duration bonds. (LOS 11.b)

Module Quiz 11.2

1. **A** A manager that expects a shift down in rates should increase the duration of their portfolio order to magnify price rises in their portfolio. Entering a receive-fixed (and pay-floating) swap will increase the duration of the portfolio. The other answers are incorrect because they will lower the duration of the portfolio. (LOS 11.c)

2. **B** The negative overall duration of the manager implies that they expect rates to rise; hence, this is a bearish trade (i.e., we expect fixed-income prices generally to fall). The fact that the manager is long short-term bonds implies that they expect short-term yields to rise by less than long-term rates. Similarly, the fact that the manager is short long-term bonds suggests that they expect longer-term yields to rise by more than short-term rates. This implies that the manager expects the curve to steepen. (LOS 11.c)

3. **C** A manager that is long the wings (short-term and medium-term bonds) and short the body (medium-term bonds) will outperform if medium-term rates increase relative to short-term and long-term rates. This would be an increase in curvature and a corresponding rise in the butterfly spread (recall the butterfly spread = –short-term rate + (2 × medium-term rate) – long-term rate). This increase in curvature is referred to as a negative butterfly twist. (LOS 11.c)

Module Quiz 11.3

1. **C** An upward shift in yields will cause option-free bonds to fall more than bonds with embedded options. The putable bond will fall by less than an option-free bond because the embedded long put option will increase in value and place a floor beneath the bond price. A callable bond will fall by less than an option-free bond because the embedded short call option will decrease in value, which will partially offset losses on the underlying bond. (LOS 11.d)

2. **C** Answer A is incorrect because receiver swaptions are profitable when rates fall because the holder can choose to exercise their right to receive a relatively high rate after the rate move. Answer B is incorrect because payer swaptions are profitable when rates rise because the holder can choose to pay a relatively low rate; however, in the scenario expected by the manager, they would expire worthless. Answer C is the correct option—as rates fall, bond futures prices will rise and a call on futures will increase in value. (LOS 11.d)

3. **A** A manager should use receive-fixed to increase duration and pay-fixed to lower duration. Buying futures increases duration and selling futures decreases duration. Note that there are other ways of altering the duration of the portfolio, but Answer A is the only option that corresponds with the active positions of the manager. (LOS 11.e)

Module Quiz 11.4

1. **B** The foreign EUR interest rate implied by the zero-coupon bond price is (100 / 99.01) – 1 = 0.01 or 1%. Covered interest rate parity states that high interest rate currencies will be at a forward discount. Here, the USD interest rate is 3% and, hence, is the high interest rate currency. Covered interest rate parity states that the USD will trade at a 2% discount to EUR in the forward market. (LOS 11.f)

2. **B** In order for the unhedged carry trade to earn excess profits, uncovered interest rate parity, which states that high interest rate currencies depreciate, must not hold. Covered interest rate parity relates to establishing a fair forward rate, which is not relevant for an unhedged carry trade. (LOS 11.f)

3. **C** A bull steepener occurs when rates fall and short-term rates fall faster than long-term rates. In order to maximize carry benefit, the manager should pay the foreign floating rate that is expected to fall by more than longer-term rates and receive the higher longer-term fixed domestic rate that is expected to remain stable. (LOS 11.f)

4. **A** Using the third step of the five-step return decomposition process, the following can be calculated:

   Price change of the 2-year bond = $(-1.86 \times 0.005) + (\frac{1}{2} \times 5.2 \times 0.005^2)$ $= -0.0092$ or -0.92%

   Price change of the 10-year bond = $(-9.52 \times 0.003) + (\frac{1}{2} \times 104.8 \times 0.003^2) = -0.0281$ or -2.81%

   Hence, the performance of the barbell portfolio = $(0.6 \times -0.92\%) + (0.4 \times -2.81\%) = -1.68\%$

   (LOS 11.g)

READING 12

Fixed-Income Active Management: Credit Strategies

EXAM FOCUS

This reading turns our attention to ways to earn excess return versus a benchmark by altering exposure to credit-risky positions. Recall the five-step return decomposition process introduced and applied repetitively in the previous two readings—this reading focuses on Step 4 of the process, which is the impact of changes in credit spreads. The reading begins with a discussion of the different types of spread used by fixed-income analysts—make sure you are comfortable with each type and that you can perform basic interpolation of benchmark yields based on maturity. After a discussion of bottom-up versus top-down techniques, there is a large section on using underlying bonds or CDS derivatives to express views on spreads, and another application of the five-step return decomposition to attribute any excess return of the portfolio versus the benchmark.

MODULE 12.1: CREDIT RISK AND CREDIT SPREAD

Video covering this content is available online.

LOS 12.a: Describe risk considerations for spread-based fixed-income portfolios.

A **spread** is defined as the excess return of a bond over a comparable benchmark security, which compensates investors for risks inherent in the bond that are not inherent in the benchmark. The two major risks that spreads primarily represent are credit risk (the risk the issuer fails to make payment as promised) and liquidity risk (the risk the investor is not able to trade in the security at a reasonable price). This reading focuses on credit risk and the associated credit spread of fixed-income securities.

The two crucial components of credit risk are as follows:

- **Probability of default (POD)**. This is the chance that the issuer fails to make payments on its obligation when due, usually expressed on an annualized basis.
- **Loss given default (LGD)** (or **loss severity**). This is the proportion of investment lost if a default occurs. It is calculated as 1 – recovery rate (RR), where *RR* is the percentage of exposure recovered in default.

Note that the total expected credit losses from a credit-risky security are equal to the sum of POD × LGD for all periods scaled up by the expected exposure at the time of default. The present value of these expected losses is called the credit valuation adjustment (CVA) and represents the discount that the credit-risky instrument should trade below an equivalent risk-free security in order to compensate investors for their expected credit losses.

Note that while an analyst will be interested in forecasting expected losses, a starting point for analysis is the historical realized percentage of value lost to default, referred to as the **credit loss rate**.

In terms of calculating the credit spread, a simplified approach is to assume that investors need to earn their periodic expected loss of POD × LGD:

$$\text{credit spread} \approx \text{POD} \times \text{LGD}$$

EXAMPLE: Credit spread, POD, and LGD

A credit analyst notes that an issuer has first lien bonds outstanding with a spread of 1.5%. The historical recovery rate for similar first lien bonds is 50%. The issuer is preparing to issue second lien bonds. The historical recovery rate of similar second lien bonds is 40%.

Calculate the fair credit spread for the second lien bonds.

Answer:

Solve for the POD for the issuer implied by the first lien bonds:

$$\text{spread} = \text{POD} \times \text{LGD}$$

$$\text{POD} = \text{spread} / \text{LGD} = 1.5\% / (1 - 0.50) = 3\%$$

Then, use this relationship again to find the fair credit spread for the second lien bonds:

$$\text{spread} = \text{POD} \times \text{LGD} = 3\% \times (1 - 0.4) = 1.8\%$$

PROFESSOR'S NOTE

"Lien" here is a legal term referring to the ranking of claim on collateral for a borrowing.

Recall that credit-risky securities are divided into high-quality *investment grade (IG)* (rated BBB and above) and *high yield (HY)*, or *speculative* (rated BB or below). Actual defaults in IG bonds are extremely rare; however, there remains the risk of a ratings downgrade, called a **credit migration**. For lower-quality bonds, default risk becomes a more significant risk than the risk of credit migration.

A plot of credit spreads versus maturity for a particular type of bonds is called the **credit spread curve**. An upward-sloping curve implies that POD is more likely in the long term versus the short term. A flat curve suggests that defaults are equally likely across maturities. The shape of the credit curve is primarily driven by changes in credit conditions over the **credit cycle**, summarized in the following table:

	Stage of Economic Cycle			
	Early Expansion (Recovery)	**Late Expansion**	**Peak**	**Contraction (Recession)**
Corporate defaults	Peak	Falling	Stable	Rising
Credit spread level	Stable	Falling	Rising	Peak
Credit spread slope	IG: Stable HY: Inverted	Upward sloping for both IG and HY	Upward sloping for both IG and HY	IG: Flat HY: Inverted

Figure 12.1: Economic Cycle

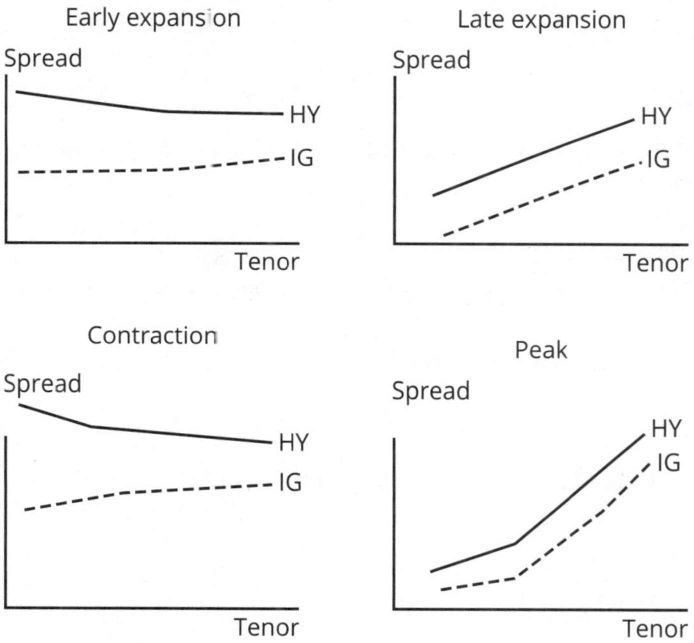

The major difference between IG and HY credit curves over the credit cycle is the inversion of the HY curve in an economic downturn, reflecting the fact that near-term POD and downgrade risk for HY names is elevated. Generally, HY securities experience sharper changes in level and slope over the cycle than IG-rated securities.

It has already been observed in a previous reading that risk-free rates and spreads often move in opposite directions (i.e., are negatively correlated). For example, strong economic conditions often lead to increasing benchmark risk-free rates as investors sell risk-free securities to move into riskier assets. However, at the same time, there is a decreasing risk of default and narrowing credit spreads. For lower-quality securities, the narrowing of spreads is likely to have a significant impact on price and result in a sensitivity to changes in risk-free benchmark rates that is *lower* than that predicted by modified duration. Conversely, weaker economic conditions often lead to decreasing risk-free rates but increasing risk of default and wider spreads. Once again, spreads moving in the opposite direction to benchmark yields will dampen the sensitivity of the low-quality bond's price versus changes in benchmark rates.

For example, consider a HY bond yielding 6% versus a Treasury of a similar maturity yielding 2%. The spread of the bond over the benchmark is 6% – 2% = 4%. Assume the bond is a 5-year bond with a modified duration of 4.4. Let's assume that a contraction in economic activity occurs and there is a flight to quality, forcing down the risk-free benchmark yield to 1%. Modified duration would imply that the bond should rise by 4.4%. However, let's assume that the credit spread widens due to the downturn to 5%. This implies a new yield of the bond of 1% + 5% = 6%. The yield of the bond hasn't changed; hence, the price of the bond will not have changed. The observed sensitivity of this bond to changes in benchmark rates is 0, a lot lower than the modified duration of 4.4.

This effect is captured in differences between analytical (i.e., modified) and *empirical* duration. **Empirical duration** is based on regression of market data of actual bond price returns and benchmark rate changes. Since the actual bond price is driven by both spreads and benchmark rates, empirical duration will be *lower* than analytical duration for low-quality securities.

MODULE QUIZ 12.1

1. At the peak of the economic cycle, the credit spread curve is *most likely*:
   A. rising and upward sloping.
   B. falling and downward sloping.
   C. rising and downward sloping.
2. Which of the following credit spread curves is *most likely* to invert during a recession?
   A. Both the IG curve and the HY curve.
   B. The IG curve only.
   C. The HY curve only.
3. Relative to its analytical duration, the empirical duration for a HY issuer is likely to be:
   A. lower.
   B. similar.
   C. higher.

MODULE 12.2: CREDIT SPREAD MEASURES

Video covering this content is available online.

LOS 12.b: Discuss the advantages and disadvantages of credit spread measures for spread-based fixed-income portfolios, and explain why option-adjusted spread is considered the most appropriate measure.

Fixed-Rate Bond Credit Spread Measures

The simplest measure of spread, the **yield spread** (or **benchmark spread**) of a bond is defined as the bond's YTM minus the YTM of the closest maturity on-the-run government bond.

The ***g*-spread** of a bond is defined as the bond's YTM minus an interpolated YTM of the two adjacent maturity on-the-run government bonds. The interpolation process is designed to estimate a government benchmark YTM that matches the maturity of the bond exactly and is demonstrated in the following example.

EXAMPLE: Yield spread and *g*-spread

A credit analyst collates the following information regarding a corporate bond and two adjacent maturity on-the-run government benchmark securities:

	Maturity (Years)	Coupon	Yield	ModDur
Corporate bond	12	4.30%	4.5%	11.1
Government	10	2.75%	3.0%	9.2
Government	20	5.25%	5.0%	17.5

1. **Calculate** the yield spread and *g*-spread for the corporate bond.
2. **Calculate**, using both the yield spread and the *g*-spread, the estimated change in price of the corporate bond under the following scenario:
   - The corporate bond's spread and the 10-year government bond yield remain unchanged.
   - The 20-year government bond yield falls by 10 bps.

Answers:

1. The yield spread of the corporate bond is its yield minus the nearest dated government bond yield (in this case, the 10-year government bond). Hence, the yield spread = 4.5% – 3.0% = 1.5%.

   To calculate the *g*-spread, we must interpolate the two adjacent government bond YTMs to estimate a 12-year government bond YTM. We do this by calculating the weights that would need to be held in the 10-year and 20-year bonds in order to have an average maturity of 12 years (i.e., the same as the corporate bond's maturity).

Reading 12

Assuming a weight of *w* in the 20-year bond and a weight, therefore, of (1 – w) in the 10-year bond, we need to solve for *w* such that:

$$12 = (1 - w) \times 10 + (w \times 20)$$
$$12 = 10 - 10w + 20w$$
$$2 = 10w$$
$$w = 0.2$$

Hence, a portfolio with 20% in the 20-year bond and 80% in the 10-year bond will have the same average maturity as the 12-year corporate bond. Such a portfolio would have a YTM of (0.8 × 3%) + (0.2 × 5%) = 3.4%. This is the benchmark government YTM for the *g*-spread.

Hence, the *g*-spread of the corporate bond = 4.5% – 3.4% = 1.1%.

PROFESSOR'S NOTE

The interpolation process used in this example is used multiple times in this reading. It is important that you know how to perform this process. It is worth noting that if the adjacent government securities have maturities *S* (shorter) and *L* (longer) versus the target maturity *M*, then to quickly calculate the weight in the longer-dated benchmark bond, we can use the following ratio:

$$(M - S) / (L - S)$$

For example, in this case, S = 10, M = 12, and L = 20, so we could calculate that the weight in the 20-year government bond should be (12 – 10) / (20 – 10) = 2 / 10 = 0.2.

We will use this more direct method for interpolation throughout the rest of this chapter.

2. Based on yield spread, the corporate bond's YTM is equal to the 10-year government bond YTM plus the yield spread. Since neither of these are expected to change, the yield of the bond is not expected to change; therefore, the price of the bond is not expected to change.

   The only change expected is a 10 bps fall in the 20-year government bond YTM from 5% to 4.9%. Using the same maturity weights as before, this implies that the interpolated 12-year government YTM will change to (0.8 × 3.0%) + (0.2 × 4.9%) = 3.38%.

   If the *g*-spread remains at 1.1%, this implies that the corporate bond yield will move to 3.38% + 1.1% = 4.48%. This implies a change in the corporate bond YTM of 4.48% – 4.5% = –0.02%. With a modified duration of 11.1, the expected price change of the bond is –11.1 × –0.02% = 0.222%.

The ***i*-spread (interpolated spread)** of a bond is defined as the bond's YTM minus the maturity interpolated swap fixed rate. The advantage of the *i*-spread is that it is based on a tradeable derivative that can be used to hedge duration or measure carry returns (i.e., measure the difference between the long-term fixed leg and the shorter-term floating leg).

The **asset swap spread (ASW)** is defined as the bond's fixed *coupon* minus the maturity interpolated swap fixed rate. This represents the spread that the bond is offering over the *floating* market reference rate (MRR) over its life (assuming the bond is trading close to par). For example, if a manager purchases a corporate bond close to par with a coupon of 6%, when the equivalent maturity swap fixed leg is 4%, the ASW is 6% – 4% = 2%. The manager could earn this 2% as a fixed spread above floating MRR by buying the bond and entering a pay-fixed swap. The net periodic receipt of the manager from this combination of the bond and the swap would be +6% bond coupon – 4% swap fixed leg + MRR swap floating leg = MRR + 2%.

EXAMPLE: *i*-spread and ASW

Recall the bonds from the previous example:

	Maturity (Years)	Coupon	Yield	ModDur
Corporate bond	12	4.30%	4.5%	11.1
Government	10	2.75%	3.0%	9.2
Government	20	5.25%	5.0%	17.5

Ten- and twenty-year swap spreads over similar maturity government bond YTMs are 20 bps and 30 bps, respectively.

Calculate the *i*-spread and the ASW for the corporate bond.

Answer:

The 10-year swap fixed rate = 3.0% + 0.2% = 3.2%.

The 20-year swap fixed rate = 5.0% + 0.3% = 5.3%.

We can use the same weights in the previous example to interpolate between the 10- and 20-year maturities to estimate the 12-year maturity, namely 20% in the 20-year maturity and 80% in the 10-year maturity.

The interpolated 12-year swap fixed rate = 0.8 × (3.2%) + 0.2 × (5.3%) = 3.62%.

The *i*-spread = corporate YTM – interpolated swap fixed rate = 4.50% – 3.62% = 0.88%.

The ASW = corporate bond coupon – interpolated swap fixed rate = 4.30% – 3.62% = 0.68%.

Recall that a YTM is a non-simple average of the spot rates that apply to the different cash flows of a bond. Similarly, a swap fixed rate is a non-simple average of the expected floating MRR rates over the life of the swap. The use of YTMs and swap fixed rates to derive spreads, therefore, ignores *how* spot rates change over different maturities (called the term structure of spot rates).

In order to respect the term structure of spot rates when calculating spreads, we turn to the **zero-volatility spread (*z*-spread)**. The *z*-spread uses a trial-and-error calculation to determine a single spread that, when added to risk-free spot rates, discounts the bond's future cash flows back to its current market value.

Later in this reading, we will be looking at excess returns from active trading of credit default swap (CDS) contracts. Recall that under such a contract, there is a protection buyer who makes a regular payment to the protection seller and, in return, receives a payment should a credit event occur on a reference bond. The protection buyer pays a standardized fixed coupon adjusted by an up-front payment/receipt to reflect the fair value of the protection, known as the **CDS spread**. This CDS spread should, in theory, be equal to the *z*-spread that is earned on the underlying bond, since both are essentially a risk premium paid to the party facing the credit risk of the bond. However, differences between the CDS spread and the *z*-spread can occur due to technical reasons, such as the underlying bond price trading away from par, accrued interest on the underlying bond, and idiosyncratic features of the CDS protection. The **CDS basis** is defined as the CDS spread minus the *z*-spread. This is a useful measure for those trading CDS contracts.

None of the spread measures introduced so far in this reading (yield spread, *g*-spread, *i*-spread, ASW, or *z*-spread) are appropriate for measuring the credit/liquidity risk of a bond with an embedded option.

The **option adjusted spread (OAS)** is the only spread measure appropriate for assessing the credit/liquidity risk of bonds with embedded options. It uses an assumption of interest rate volatility to build an interest rate tree of possible paths for forward risk-free interest rates. Future cash flows are adjusted for the optionality of the bond along each path (i.e., to reflect whether the option would be exercised). The OAS is then a trial-and-error calculation to determine a single spread that, when added to every node of the interest rate tree of risk-free rates, discounts the bond's adjusted future cash flows back to its current market value. By adjusting the cash flows of the bond to reflect expected interest rate volatility, the uncertainty of the cash flows due to the optionality of the bond has been removed, and the resulting OAS, therefore, does *not* include any impact of the option on the spread. The OAS measures the spread that is earned for facing the credit and liquidity risk of the issuer—the impact of the option has been removed from the spread.

The OAS is the best measure for consistent comparison of the spreads on bonds with embedded options (e.g., callable, putable) and bonds without embedded options.

PROFESSOR'S NOTE

Take care here—it would be better to call the OAS the option **removed** spread because the process of calculating it removes the impact of the option. You will not be required to calculate the OAS for the exam. However, you must keep an eye out for bonds that have a significantly different OAS to other spreads—this implies there is an embedded option in the bond and OAS **must** be used to compare the bond against other bonds. Take the hint here—OAS is best!

Floating-Rate Note Credit Spread Measures

A floating-rate note (FRN) pays a periodic coupon equal to a floating market reference rate (MRR) plus a fixed **quoted margin (QM)**. For example, a corporate FRN might pay MRR + 50 bps.

This coupon will change in line with change in MRR, so when benchmark interest rates rise, the coupon of the bond also rises and, therefore, the price of the bond will not fall like the price of a fixed-coupon bond would fall. This means that FRNs have lower rate duration, EffRateDur (i.e., price sensitivity to changes in benchmark yields), than fixed-coupon bonds.

Note, however, that the 50 bps QM is *fixed*. This means that if the credit quality of the issuer declines, leading to credit spreads widening, the corporate FRN *will* fall in price. Hence, the FRN will likely have an effective spread duration, EffSpreadDur, significantly higher that its rate duration. The required return of investors *above* the current MRR is called the **discount margin (DM)**. In the example just listed, if the DM is above 50 bps due to deteriorating credit conditions, the FRN will trade below par. If the DM falls below 50 bps due to improving credit conditions, the FRN will trade above par. When DM = QM, the FRN will trade at or close to par because the coupon paid is expected to be equal to the required return of investors. Note that in the calculation of the DM, the expected future coupons are based on the *current period's* MRR + QM, and the discount rate applied to these coupons is the *current period's* MRR + DM. As such, the calculation of DM assumes that the MRR is not expected to change over the life of the FRN (i.e., it assumes a flat MRR curve and does not reflect the term structure of the MRR).

PROFESSOR'S NOTE

DM is playing the role of yield here, and QM is playing the role of coupon. Think: Low coupon bonds trade below par (and vice versa).

The rate duration and spread duration of an FRN are given by the following formulas:

$$\text{EffRateDur}_{\text{FRN}} = \frac{(\text{PV}_-) - (\text{PV}_+)}{2(\Delta\text{MRR})(\text{PV}_0)}$$

$$\text{EffSpreadDur}_{\text{FRN}} = \frac{(\text{PV}_-) - (\text{PV}_+)}{2(\Delta\text{DM})(\text{PV}_0)}$$

where:

PV_0 = current value of the portfolio

PV_- = value of portfolio when benchmark curve is shifted down

PV_+ = value of portfolio when benchmark curve is shifted up

ΔMRR = change in benchmark curve

ΔDM = change in DM

PROFESSOR'S NOTE

Notice that these formulas are applications of the general effective duration formula introduced in an earlier reading. The difference is that Δcurve on the denominator has been replaced by the change in the rate (MRR) or spread (DM) against which we wish to measure price sensitivity.

EXAMPLE: Discount margin

A 1-year FRN pays 3-month MRR + 1.25% on a quarterly basis. The current MRR is 0.55% and is assumed to stay constant over time, and the discount margin is 1.55%.

1. **State** whether the FRN will be trading below, equal to, or above par. **Justify** your response.
2. **Calculate** the value of $1 million of par of the FRN.

Answers:

1. The FRN will trade *below* par. The DM of 1.55% is above the QM of 1.25%, which implies that investors require a higher margin above the MRR than that being paid by the FRN. This will cause the bond to trade below par because the future overall discount rate applied to bond cash flows will be higher than the coupon paid.
2. Assuming that the MRR doesn't change, the bond will pay a quarterly coupon of (MRR + QM) / 4 = (0.55% + 1.25%) / 4 = 0.45%. For a par amount of $1 million, this represents a $4,500 payment every quarter, along with par of $1 million paid in one year's time.

   The quarterly discount rate to apply to these cash flows is equal to (MRR + DM) / 4 = (0.55% + 1.55%) / 4 = 0.525%.

   Therefore, the value of $1 million of par is calculated as follows:

$$\text{value} = \frac{\$4{,}500}{(1.00525)} + \frac{\$4{,}500}{(1.00525)^2} + \frac{\$4{,}500}{(1.00525)^3} + \frac{\$1{,}004{,}500}{(1.00525)^4}$$

$$= \$997{,}039$$

As we have said, a drawback of the discount margin is that it assumes the MRR stays constant at its current level over the life of the bond, which effectively assumes that the term structure of interest rates is flat. The **zero-discount margin (Z-DM)** addresses this drawback by incorporating the term structure of interest rates into its calculation. The derivation of the Z-DM is similar to that of the DM; however, future coupon rates are equal to the relevant *MRR forward rate* plus the QM, and discount rates are equal to the *relevant spot MRR plus the Z-DM.* By respecting the term structure of MRR, the Z-DM is playing a similar role to floating-rate securities that the *z*-spread played to fixed-coupon bonds.

Note that the Z-DM will depend on the path of forward MRRs—if the MRR curve is upward sloping, the calculation of the Z-DM will use *higher* MRR spot rates for longer maturities when discounting cash flows, which will cause the Z-DM to be *lower* than the DM (which assumes the MRR remains unchanged in its calculation).

The Impact of Spreads on Portfolio Return

Recall from a previous reading, Overview of Fixed-Income Portfolio Management, the five-step return decomposition process:

1. Coupon income = annual coupon amount / current bond price
2. Rolldown return = (projected bond price (BP) assuming no yield curve change – beginning BP) / beginning BP
3. Price change due to investor yield change predictions: $(-MD \times \Delta Y) + (\frac{1}{2}C \times \Delta Y^2)$
4. Price change due to investor spread change predictions: $(-MD \times \Delta S) + (\frac{1}{2}C \times \Delta S^2)$
5. Currency G/L: projected change in value of foreign currencies weighted for exposure to the currency

While Step 4 of this process captures the impact of changes in spread on a manager's returns, Steps 1–3 are also important in explaining the excess return of corporate bonds versus benchmark securities, as demonstrated in the following example:

EXAMPLE: Corporate vs. government bond rolldown

A manager collates the following information regarding a corporate bond and a benchmark government security with a similar maturity:

	Maturity	Coupon	YTM
Corporate bond	5	4.00%	2.25%
Government	4.5	2.00%	1.20%

Both bonds have a semiannual coupon. **Calculate** the annualized excess rolling yield earned by the manager if they hold the corporate bond versus if they hold the government bond over the next six months.

Answer:

Pricing the corporate bond produces the following:

Starting price: 10 N; 2.25 / 2 = 1.125 I / Y; 2 PMT; 100FV; CPT PV: 108.232

Price in 6 months: 9 N, CPT PV: 107.450

Hence, 6-month coupon yield = (0.5 × 4) / 108.232 = 1.849%

6-month rolldown return = (107.450 / 108.232) – 1 = –0.723%

Total annualized rolling yield = (1.849% – 0.723%) × 2 = 2.25%

Doing the same for the government bond results in the following:

Starting price: 9 N; 1.2 / 2 = 0.6 I / Y; 1 PMT; 100 FV; CPT PV: 103.494

Price in 6 months: 8 N, CPT PV: 103.115

Hence, 6-month coupon yield = (0.5 × 2) / 103.494 = 0.966%

6-month rolldown return = (103.115 / 103.494) – 1 = –0.366%

Total annualized rolling yield = (0.966% – 0.366%) × 2 = 1.20%

The annualized excess rolling yield of the corporate bond = 2.25% – 1.20% = 1.05%

When applying Step 4 of the return decomposition process, credit managers focus on the sensitivity of the bond's price with respect to changes in yield *spread* rather than changes in benchmark yields. This is achieved through using **effective spread duration (EffSpreadDur)** and **effective spread convexity (EffSpreadCon)**, which play the same price sensitivity roles with regard to changes in spread as effective duration and effective convexity do with benchmark yields.

The effective spread duration and effective spread convexity of a portfolio are calculated using the following formulas:

$$\text{effective spread duration} = \frac{(PV_-) - (PV_+)}{2(\Delta\text{spread})(PV_0)}$$

$$\text{effective spread convexity} = \frac{(PV_-) + (PV_+) - 2(PV_0)}{(\Delta\text{spread})^2 (PV_0)}$$

where:

PV_0 = current value of the portfolio

PV_- = value of portfolio when benchmark curve is shifted down

PV+ = value of portfolio when benchmark curve is shifted up

Δspread = change in spread

Using these spread-specific sensitivity measures, the calculation of Step 4 of the return decomposition process becomes:

$$\%\Delta\text{price} = (-\text{EffSpreadDur} \times \Delta\text{spread}) + (\tfrac{1}{2} \times \text{EffSpreadCon} \times \Delta\text{spread}^2)$$

"Δspread" here is typically defined as the change in the *OAS*.

PROFESSOR'S NOTE

All these formulas are analogous to the effective duration and convexity measures based on yield curve changes with which we are already very familiar. Also remember our conclusion about the different types of spread—OAS is best for comparing valuations across different types of bonds.

A practical observation regarding changes in spread is that it tends to be proportional to the spread itself rather than an absolute measure. Put simply, we would expect greater *changes* in spread for bonds with higher spread levels than we would for bonds with lower spread levels.

This proportionate relationship between spread change and spread level is captured through measuring the **duration times spread (DTS)** of a bond portfolio, approximately defined as follows:

$$\text{DTS} \approx \text{EffSpreadDur} \times \text{spread}$$

PROFESSOR'S NOTE

We can multiply DTS through by an expected proportional change in index (i.e., average) OAS in order to derive the expected basis point change in portfolio value (in the other direction). To see why, consider how DTS × % change in index OAS = EffSpreadDur × spread × % change in index OAS. The second two terms in this expression represent the expected spread change for the bond, assuming the proportionate change in spread for the bond is the same as the proportionate change in spread for the index. The first term represents the price sensitivity relative to this change in spread as usual. The following example demonstrates this idea.

EXAMPLE: DTS

A portfolio manager collates the following information regarding their two-bond portfolio:

Issuer	OAS (bps)	EffSpreadDur	Weight
A-rated	180	9.0	70%
C-rated	400	9.5	30%

The current benchmark index OAS is 200 bps. **Calculate**:

1. The DTS of the portfolio.
2. The expected change in the value of the portfolio for a 20 bps increase in benchmark spread.

Answers:

1. DTS of the A-rated bond = 9.0 × 180 = 1,620

   DTS of the C-rated bond = 9.5 × 400 = 3,800

   Hence, the DTS of the portfolio = (0.70 × 1,620) + (0.30 × 3,800) = 2,274
2. The proportionate expected index spread widening is 20 / 200 = 10%.

   We can multiply the DTS of the portfolio through by this proportionate change in spreads to calculate the expected basis point *fall* in the value of the portfolio: 2,274 × 0.1 = 227.4 bps.

   The portfolio is expected to fall in value by 227.4 bps.

Excess Spread

The goal of any active manager is to earn excess return over fair market returns by finding mispriced securities. In the case of a fixed-income manager, they want to earn **excess spread**—spread in excess of the fair spread for suffering credit losses. If we view the credit losses as both changes in market value due to widening spread (EffSpreadDur × Δspread) and expected credit losses (POD × LGD), then the excess spread of the manager becomes the following:

$$\text{expected excess spread} = \text{spread} - (\text{EffSpreadDur} \times \Delta\text{spread}) - (\text{POD} \times \text{LGD})$$

PROFESSOR'S NOTE

This is an unannualized excess return over a specific holding period. If inputs are given as annualized figures, they need to be de-annualized to match the holding period. We are going to use this equation many times later in this reading to analyze the source of the manager's excess return. It's an important one!

EXAMPLE: Excess spread

A credit analyst collects the following information regarding a corporate bond:

- Effective spread duration: 4.5 years
- Current credit spread: 250 bps
- 1.5% annualized expected: POD
- Expected loss severity: 55%
- Expected credit spread in six-months' time: 270 bps

Evaluate the valuation of this corporate bond based on the estimates of the credit analyst and the bond's expected excess spread over a six-month holding period.

Answer:

expected excess spread over the next 6 months = spread – (EffSpreadDur × Δspread) – (POD × LGD) = (0.025 × 0.5) – (4.5 × (0.027 – 0.025)) – ((0.015 × 0.5) × 0.55) = –0.000625 or –6.25 bps

The bond is expected to earn a negative excess return over the next six months and is therefore currently *overvalued*.

PROFESSOR'S NOTE

The units of this equation are a bit of a minefield. There are decimals, basis points, and whole number percentages all going on at the same time and this often causes concern to students. Best advice when unsure about which units we should work in is to use decimals for everything. While the numbers may be small, their decimal value is their true size. If you put decimals in, you will get decimals out (as in this example).

MODULE QUIZ 12.2

1. A manager is calculating spread measures for a 12-year corporate bond using on-the-run Treasury bonds with 10 years and 15 years to maturity. In an upward-sloping yield curve environment, the manager will calculate a yield spread that is:
   A. lower than the *g*-spread.
   B. equal to the *g*-spread.
   C. higher than the *g*-spread.

2. For a corporate fixed-coupon bond trading below par, the *i*-spread will be:
   A. lower than the ASW.
   B. equal to the ASW.
   C. higher than the ASW.
3. A manager holds £1,000,000 face value in each of bonds X and Y. Bond X is priced at 102 with accrued interest of 1.0 per 100 par and an OAS of 120 basis points. Bond Y is priced at 94 with accrued interest of 1.5 per 100 par and an OAS of 140 basis points. The OAS of the portfolio is *most likely*:
   A. below 130 bps.
   B. equal to 130 bps.
   C. above 130 bps.
4. During an economic recovery, the Z-DM for an FRN is *most likely*:
   A. lower than the DM.
   B. equal to the DM.
   C. higher than the DM.

MODULE 12.3: BOTTOM-UP AND TOP-DOWN CREDIT STRATEGIES

Video covering this content is available online.

LOS 12.c: Discuss bottom-up approaches to credit strategies.

Bottom-Up Credit Strategies

Bottom-up managers engage in individual security selection to attempt to earn excess return. The focus here is on finding the best issuer or individual bond investment (rather than focusing on the best macro environment as a top-down manager would do).

The bottom-up manager starts by identifying the universe of bonds relevant to their mandate, then divides that universe into sectors such as industry and/or geography.

The manager then looks for relative misvaluation within each sector to determine individual securities to select.

Fundamentally, this credit analysis is an assessment of the likelihood of the issuer making scheduled principal and interest payments as they come due. Factors to consider here include the following:

- Operating history and competitive position of the issuer within its industry.
- Relevant financial ratios relating to profitability (e.g., EBITDA/total assets), leverage (e.g., debt/equity), and coverage ratios (e.g., EBITDA/interest).

Reading 12

Credit Risk Models

There are two major categories of credit risk models: **structural** models and **reduced form** models.

Structural models assume POD to be driven by the likelihood of the future value of the assets of a borrower falling below the threshold that would trigger default. These models are often referred to as "distance to default" models because the models are assessing how far away from defaulting an issuer currently is in terms of the volatility of their assets. Estimates for the volatility of the issuer's asset often come from equity market data such as market capitalization and equity price volatility. Examples of structural models include Moody's Expected Default Frequency (EDF) and Bloomberg's Default Risk (DRSK) models, which provide daily estimates of POD and implied fair credit spreads.

Reduced form models look for relationships between macroeconomic conditions and the individual characteristics of a borrower, such as financial ratios, to infer **default intensity** (or periodic POD) for a bond issuer. This default intensity and estimated LGD can then be used to estimate the fair credit spread of the bond.

An example of a reduced form model is **Altman's *z*-score**, which uses key financial ratios of companies as inputs to a regression-based equation, the output of which is used to classify the issuer in terms of likelihood of subsequent default. The *z*-score is calculated as follows:

$$z\text{-score model} = (1.2 \times A) + (1.4 \times B) + (3.3 \times C) + (0.6 \times D) + (0.999 \times E)$$

where:

A = working capital / total assets

B = retained earnings / total assets

C = EBIT / total assets

D = market value of equity / total liabilities

E = sales / total assets

The interpretation of the *z*-score is as follows:

$z\text{-score} > 3.0 \rightarrow$ low chance of default

$1.8 \leq z\text{-score} \leq 3.0 \rightarrow$ some risk of default

$z\text{-score} < 1.8 \rightarrow$ likely to default

PROFESSOR'S NOTE

A natural question to ask upon sight of a model like this is, "Do I have to memorize this?" While everything in the curriculum is examinable, it is noted that curriculum examples give the Altman model in the question body. This suggests that memorization of this should not be a first priority. Instead, focus on using the model given a list of components of the inputs and the model itself and interpreting the resulting *z*-score according to the bands just stated.

Bottom-Up Relative Value Analysis

The expected excess spread calculation introduced in the previous section can be used in a relative value analysis across different bonds to assess which bond would be the most attractive in a specific assumed spread change scenario. As a reminder, the expected excess spread is given by the following:

expected excess spread = spread – (EffSpreadDur × Δspread) – (POD × LGD)

Given a set of assumptions for changes in spread, POD, and LGD, the bond with the highest expected excess spread is considered to offer the best relative value.

The analyst should be careful to note any structural differences between the types of bonds being analyzed—for example, embedded options or seniority on capital structure. Liquidity is also an important concern because this will also affect the spreads offered by fixed-income securities. It should also be considered how other corporate events such as merger and acquisition activities impact spreads.

Credit spread curves can also be used for relative value analysis, as demonstrated in the following example:

EXAMPLE: Relative value analysis using spread curves

A corporate issuer has the option-free bonds outstanding displayed below:

Maturity (yr)	Coupon	YTM
2	0.5%	0.9%
5	2.0%	1.5%
15	3.5%	3.5%

On-the-run benchmark bonds have the following yields:

Maturity (yr)	YTM
2	0.2%
5	0.8%
10	2.0%
30	4.0%

The company plans on issuing a new bond with maturity of 10 years. Expectations are that the new bond will offer 5 bps more than the credit spread derived from interpolating the existing credit spread curve for the issuer.

Calculate the fair credit spread for the new 10-year bond issue.

Answer:

In order to derive a fair 10-year credit spread from the existing credit spread curve, we interpolate credit spreads of the two adjacent maturity credit spreads—namely the 5-year and 15-year maturities.

The 5-year credit spread is easily calculated from the data as 1.5% – 0.8% = 0.7%.

In order to calculate the 15-year credit spread, we need a 15-year benchmark yield. Since there is no 15-year benchmark yield given, we need to interpolate the two adjacent maturities benchmark YTMs, namely the 10-year maturity and the 30-year maturity. Recall from an earlier example, for the adjacent maturities *S* (shorter) and *L* (longer) versus the target maturity *M* to quickly calculate the weight in the longer-dated maturity, we can use the ratio (M – S) / (L – S). Here, M = 15, S = 10, and L = 30; hence, weight in the 30-year maturity = (15 – 10) / (30 – 10) = 25%, and weight in the 10-year maturity = 75%.

Therefore, the interpolated 15-year benchmark YTM = (0.75 × 2.0%) + (0.25 × 4.0%) = 2.5%.

The 15-year credit spread is then calculated as 3.5% – 2.5% = 1.0%.

Now we can interpolate between the 5-year and 15-year maturity credit spreads to find the 10-year credit spread:

- Weight in the 15-year maturity = (10 – 5) / (15 – 5) = 50%. Weight in the 5-year maturity is therefore 50%.
- The interpolated 10-year credit spread plus the new issue premium of 5 bps = (0.5 × 0.7%) + (0.5 × 1.0%) + 0.05% = 0.90%.

Top-Down Credit Strategies

LOS 12.d: Discuss top-down approaches to credit strategies.

The top-down approach focuses on macro factors that are likely to affect the credit portfolio. Relevant factors include strength of economic growth and corporate profits. Stronger growth and profits are associated with decreasing spreads and suggest moving down in credit quality for greater relative price gains. Top-down managers may use this relationship to identify when to focus on HY versus IG.

Top-down can also be used to identify sectors of the market most likely to improve (or deteriorate), and the manager can overweight (or underweight) those sectors. This analysis could also be used by the bottom-up manager to identify sectors for more-targeted individual security analysis.

Top-down analysis may focus on historical patterns such as the credit cycle and credit spread changes. The credit cycle refers to variations in real economic growth and default rates. The two are negatively correlated in general, though it is not a perfect relationship.

The default rate and spreads are also highly correlated, so the manager must generally be able to anticipate the next change in economic conditions to add value. For example, suppose real growth is very low, defaults are high, and OAS for HY bonds is well above average; there is no particular opportunity because the high spread is compensation for high default losses. But if the manager has insight that the economy and growth rate are going to improve, it is an opportune time to move into HY.

The top-down manager would likely vary the portfolio's average credit rating upward to a higher (or downward to a lower) rating in anticipation of weaker (or stronger) than consensus expectations for economic growth. The manager should consider how the portfolio's average quality is calculated. Often, a numeric sequence is assigned to each rating (e.g., AAA = 1, AA+ = 2, AA = 3, AA– = 4). The portfolio's market value weighted average rating is then calculated. This approach can understate exposure to credit risk because default rates and losses tend to increase rapidly as the rating declines. Other more weighted scales assign a number that increases much more rapidly than 1, 2, 3, 4 as credit rating declines (e.g., 1, 10, 20, 40 is used by Moody's). Portfolio averages of a weighted scale will show that exposure to credit risk increases at a faster than linear rate, as bond ratings decline.

As seen before in this reading, portfolio average OAS and spread duration are also calculated based on market value weighted average. A higher spread indicates that the portfolio has greater exposure to credit-risky assets. To reflect the empirical observation that assets with higher spreads exhibit higher spread changes, DTS should be used as per the example earlier.

Note that the excess spread equation introduced earlier can also be applied to a class of bond such as rating or sector in order to establish the most attractive macro area to invest. The manager could also use top-down analysis to form a view on changes in the shape of the credit curve for a particular sector or class of bonds.

Factor-Based Credit Strategies

Active fixed-income managers are increasingly deploying strategies that use style-based factors, similar to their counterparts in active equity portfolio management. Four factors that have been identified as offering a risk premium in corporate bond investing are as follows:

1. *Carry*. The expected return if conditions remain unchanged over time, measured by the OAS.
2. *Defensive*. Empirical observation that lower-risk assets offer higher *risk-adjusted* returns than higher risk assets.
3. *Momentum*. Bonds that have recently outperformed (underperformed) go on to outperform (underperform) in the future.
4. *Value*. Low market value versus fundamental value (or equivalently high excess return).

These factors are analogous to factors identified in equity markets, with some technical adjustments. However, they do provide diversification against common equity or credit-based risk premiums and are not fully explained by traditional risk exposures or mispricing.

Environmental, Social, and Governance (ESG) Factors

Similar techniques for ESG investing are used in fixed income as they are in other asset classes, namely:

- Negative **screening** to exclude industries, companies, or sovereigns with poor ESG records.
- Use of **ESG ratings** to target issuers with favorable ESG characteristics. ESG ratings play a similar role to credit ratings in that they attempt to classify investments based on key underlying features. ESG ratings tend to be more diverse than credit ratings; however, there is a positive relationship between the two due to (1) companies with poor ESG records being more likely to suffer financial distress and (2) credit rating agencies starting to incorporate ESG factors into credit ratings.
- Investing to *directly fund* ESG-specific initiatives. For example, **green bonds** are bonds issued to raise finances for projects that reduce air pollution, improve recycling, promote environmental remediation (i.e., reduce contamination of the environment), and improve the sustainability of building construction. Such bonds have shown very strong demand from investors in recent years.

MODULE QUIZ 12.3

1. Altman's *z*-score model is specified as follows:

   z-score model = (1.2 × A) + (1.4 × B) + (3.3 × C) + (0.6 × D) + (0.999 × E)

   where:

   A = working capital / total assets

   B = retained earnings / total assets

   C = EBIT / total assets

   D = market value of equity / total liabilities

   E = sales / total assets

   A corporate issuer has sales of $2,000, total assets of $3,500, working capital of $2,100, retained earnings of $1,900, EBIT of $600, total liabilities of $1,200, and the market value of the company's equity is $3,000. The Altman's *z*-score for this company implies that the issuer has:
   A. low default risk.
   B. some risk of default.
   C. high default risk.

2. An analyst is using a structural model to assess the credit risk of a corporate issuer. Which of the following changes to the inputs of the model will *most likely* decrease the probability of default of the issuer?
   A. A decrease in the interest coverage ratio of the issuer.
   B. A decrease in the volatility of the issuer's share price.
   C. An increase in the leverage ratio of the issuer.

3. A credit analyst collates the following information regarding two corporate issuers:

Rating	EffSpreadDur	YTM	OAS (bps)	POD	Recovery Rate
A	6	3.5%	150	0.25%	40%
B	8	6.0%	300	3.00%	40%

The manager expects spreads to widen by 15%. Based on excess spread, which of the following statements is accurate?
A. The A-rated bond is more attractive than the B-rated bond.
B. The A-rated bond and B-rated bond are both of similar attractiveness from a valuation perspective.
C. The A-rated bond is less attractive than the B-rated bond.

4. Which of the following fixed-income risk factors suggests that low duration bonds should have higher risk-adjusted returns?
A. Carry.
B. Defensive.
C. Value.

MODULE 12.4: LIQUIDITY AND TAIL RISK

Video covering this content is available online.

LOS 12.e: Discuss liquidity risk in credit markets and how liquidity risk can be managed in a credit portfolio.

Liquidity Risk

Liquidity levels in fixed-income markets range from extremely high for large issues of on-the-run (i.e., most-recently issued) bonds in developed market sovereign debt to very low for smaller corporate off-the-run securities, which may not even trade at all during a typical trading day. For illiquid bonds that trade infrequently, **matrix pricing** (or **evaluated pricing**) is often used, which estimates fair value through reference to the yields and prices of similar actively traded and government securities.

The bond market has historically been a dealer-quoted OTC market, although electronic trading and liquid ETF products are gaining in prominence. For bonds with an active quote, transaction costs can be measured through the effective spread, which measures the cost of paying above the midpoint of a spread as a buyer or receiving a price below the midpoint of a spread as a seller.

effective spread for a buy order = trade size × (trade price – midquote)

effective spread for a sell order = trade size × (midquote – trade price)

where:

midquote = (bid + ask) / 2

Transaction costs can also be measured through referencing market prices and volumes reported into the TRACE (Trade Reporting and Compliance Engine) system for U.S. corporate bonds.

To manage liquidity risk, managers can:

- Use more-liquid on-the-run securities for shorter-term strategies and less liquid securities for longer-term strategies.
- Use liquid fixed-income alternatives such as credit default swaps (CDS) (discussed in depth later in this reading) or exchange-traded funds (ETFs). Fixed-income ETFs have become increasingly popular in fixed income in recent years. While ETFs are traded by investors in the secondary market on an exchange, the creation and cancellation of ETF shares is a process that happens directly between an institutional investor with special status (referred to as the **authorized participant**) and the ETF manager, meaning that the end investors in the ETF never have to directly buy or sell the bonds underlying the ETF. ETFs never mature, nor do they have a duration that drifts lower over time (unless they are target maturity ETFs that aim to mature on a specified date).
- Use asset swaps to hedge exposure on illiquid bonds over the time it takes to transact. For example, a manager wishing to sell a large illiquid holding over a long period of time could enter a pay-fixed asset swap to hedge the fixed-coupon income received on the corporate bond. As the trade in the underlying bond is slowly executed, the swap should be concurrently unwound.

Tail Risk

LOS 12.f: Describe how to assess and manage tail risk in credit portfolios.

"Tail risk" refers to the risk of losses due to infrequent but high negative impact events.

Value at risk (VaR) is a measure of minimum expected loss occurring in a given time frame with a specified probability. For example, if the 1% daily VaR of a portfolio is $7 million, this means that there is a 1% chance that the portfolio could lose $7 million (or more) on any given trading day.

The VaR is a percentile in a return distribution—for example, if the 1% daily VaR is $7 million, we know that the probability of observing a loss of $7 million or worse on any given day is 1%, and the probability of not suffering this loss is 99%.

PROFESSOR'S NOTE

Think of VaR as the loss at the point of the return distribution where the tail (say bottom 1% of returns) begins.

There are three common methods used to derive the return distribution from which VaR is estimated:

1. **Parametric method.** This assumes returns are normal and uses the parameters (mean and standard deviation) to calculate the loss at a given percentile of the distribution. Recall that for a normal distribution, we identify the 5th percentile as 1.65 standard deviations below the mean and the 1st percentile as 2.33 standard deviations below the mean. The advantage of the parametric VaR method is that it is simple to apply. The disadvantage is that it does not perform

well for portfolios with non-normal distribution, such as those containing options.

2. **Historical simulation.** This applies historical movements in key risk factors (movements in rates, spreads, etc.) to the existing portfolio in order to generate a return distribution. The advantage of this historical VaR is that it uses actual market data and can handle portfolios with non-normal returns. The disadvantage is that it is heavily dependent on the historical sample used, and this history may not be a guide to the future.
3. **Monte Carlo analysis.** This generates return distribution through random simulations from a user-defined model. The advantage is that the user-defined model has the flexibility to incorporate non-normal distributions. The disadvantage is that there is high model risk (i.e., the VaR is highly dependent on model assumptions being sound).

An example of the parametric method applied to fixed-rate bonds follows.

EXAMPLE: Fixed-rate bond VaR

A fixed-income manager invests $100 million into a 15-year bond with a coupon of 2%, yield of 3%, and a modified duration of 12. If daily yield volatility is assumed to be 1.5%, what is the VaR for the position at 99% confidence (1% in the tail) for one month (assuming 20 trading days in the month and normally distributed yields)?

Answer:

First, scale up the daily yield volatility to 20-day volatility by multiplying the square root of 20 (recall that variance scales up with time; therefore, standard deviation, which is the square root of variance, scales up by multiplying through by the square root of time). Hence, the 20-day yield volatility is $1.5\% \times \sqrt{20} = 6.708\%$. This is a proportionate measure; hence, a single standard deviation move in yields = $0.06708 \times 3\% = 0.2012\%$. The 99% confidence level for yield changes, which corresponds to the 1% VaR for the portfolio value, is $2.33 \times 0.2012\% = 46.9$ bps.

The impact on the portfolio of a 46.9 bps move is $-12 \times 0.469\% = -5.63\%$. Given a portfolio value of $100 million, this implies a 20-day 1% VaR of $5.63 million.

VaR as a tail risk measure has the following drawbacks:

- Tail events tend to be more frequent and more severe than VaR forecasts.
- It fails to capture changes in correlation and liquidity during times of market stress.
- It fails to quantify the expected loss during a tail event.

Several extensions of VaR exist that are aimed at addressing these drawbacks:

- **Conditional value at risk (CVaR)** is the expected loss *given the portfolio is experiencing a loss in the tail*. It is a measure of the average loss in the tail and addresses the third drawback listed previously.

- **Incremental VaR (IVaR)** (or **partial VaR**) measures the change in VaR from adding or removing a position in a portfolio.
- **Relative VaR** measures the VaR of a portfolio's returns relative to a benchmark. It can be used to assess the minimum underperformance of an active manager relative to their benchmark in a given time frame with a specified probability.

When performing risk analysis, estimates for the volatility of benchmark rates can be taken from the implied volatility of option-based derivative contracts such as swaptions, while credit models can derive expected spread volatility from CDS and equity market prices.

Risk analysis should extend beyond quantitative estimates of loss to consider the consequences of experiencing large losses in times of stress. For example, managers using leverage should model the impact of margin calls, managers of DB plan assets should consider the ability of plan sponsors to meet extra contributions, and treasurers of banks should assess their ability to meet regulatory reserves in times of stress.

MODULE QUIZ 12.4

1. An active credit manager has a holding in a 5% coupon corporate bond, the size of which is 10 times the average daily trading volume according to historical TRACE data. In order to manage the interest rate risk of liquidating this position, the manager should enter:
   A. a pay-fixed swap and unwind the swap over time as the bond is sold.
   B. a pay-fixed swap and unwind the swap once the bond is fully sold.
   C. a receive-fixed swap and unwind the swap over time as the bond is sold.
2. An active credit manager can *best* assess the impact on the risk profile of a portfolio by increasing or decreasing an active position in the portfolio through using:
   A. relative VaR.
   B. incremental VaR.
   C. conditional VaR.

MODULE 12.5: CREDIT DEFAULT SWAPS AND SYNTHETIC STRATEGIES

Video covering this content is available online.

LOS 12.g: Discuss the use of credit default swap strategies in active fixed-income portfolio management.

Synthetic Credit Strategies

A credit default swap (CDS) is a derivatives contract that involves two parties—a protection buyer and a protection seller.

The protection buyer pays a regular fixed coupon to the protection seller periodically over the life of the contract in return for a payment upon a prespecified credit event on a reference issuer (or issuers). The protection seller suffers losses if a credit event occurs and is, therefore, referred to as being long risk (i.e., they face the credit risk of the reference issuer). The size of the CDS is specified at the outset and referred to as the notional principal.

Figure 12.2: CDS Mechanics

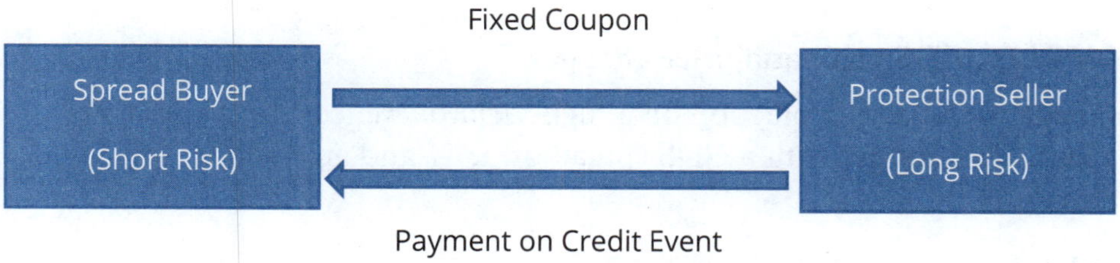

The fixed coupon paid periodically by the protection buyer is standardized to 1% for investment-grade (IG) issuers and 5% for high-yield (HY) issuers for operational reasons, since standardizing the regular payment in this way makes settlement and clearing of contracts more straightforward. It is important to note that this standardized coupon is *not* the fair premium that should be regularly paid by the protection buyer (referred to as the **CDS spread**) for the credit protection based on credit pricing models. If the fair CDS spread is above the standardized fixed coupon, the protection buyer needs to make an up-front premium payment to the protection seller at initiation of the contract. Conversely, if the fair CDS spread is below the standardized fixed coupon, the protection buyer will receive an up-front premium payment from the protection seller.

The upfront payment is calculated as follows:

Scenario	Upfront Premium
CDS spread = fixed coupon	None
CDS spread > fixed coupon	[(CDS spread – fixed coupon) × $\text{EffSpreadDur}_{\text{CDS}}$] paid to protection seller
CDS spread < fixed coupon	[(fixed coupon – CDS spread) × $\text{EffSpreadDur}_{\text{CDS}}$] paid to protection buyer

The up-front premium is used to approximate the price quotation of the CDS contract as a percentage of notional amount as follows:

$$\text{CDS price} \approx 1 + [(\text{fixed coupon} - \text{CDS spread}) \times \text{EffSpreadDur}_{\text{CDS}}]$$

This pricing convention conforms with the usual inverse price/yield relationship seen in fixed income because, when CDS spreads rise, the CDS price will fall and vice versa.

PROFESSOR'S NOTE

When it comes to the up-front premium, rather than rote learning these formulas, focus on the intuition that if the protection buyer pays a fixed coupon that is less than what is fair (the CDS spread), then they need to top up what they pay to the protection seller. The difference between the

CDS spread and the fixed coupon is multiplied through by the effective spread duration of the CDS to incorporate the percentage impact on value of this difference, which gives us the up-front premium. With regard to the CDS price formula, note this is simply adjusting "1," which represents 100% of par, for the up-front premium to create an inverse relationship between CDS prices and spreads. For higher-quality issuers, the CDS spread will be lower than the fixed coupon and the CDS price will be above par. For lower-quality issuers, the CDS spread will be higher than the fixed coupon and the CDS price will be below par.

EXAMPLE: CDS price and price changes

A manager purchases protection on a high-yield reference obligation using a 5-year CDS contract with a CDS spread of 5.5% and an effective spread duration of 4.5.

Calculate:

1. The up-front premium and the price of the CDS.
2. The mark-to-market gain or loss to the protection buyer if the CDS spread immediately falls to 5.4%.

Answers:

1. The reference obligation is a high-yield bond; hence, the fixed coupon on this contract will be 5%. The fair CDS spread of 5.5% is greater than the fixed coupon; hence, the protection buyer is going to have to pay an up-front premium equal to the following:

   up-front premium = (CDS spread – fixed coupon) × EffSpreadDur = (0.055 – 0.05) × 4.5 = 0.0225 or 2.25%

   The CDS price = 1 + [(fixed coupon – CDS spread) × EffSpreadDur] = 1 + [(0.05 – 0.055) × 4.5] = 0.9775 or 97.75%. Note that the quick way to derive the CDS price is to notice that the CDS spread is higher than the fixed coupon; hence, we deduct the up-front premium from par.
2. The price impact of a change in spread = –ΔCDS spread × EffSpreadDur = –(5.40% – 5.50%) × 4.5 = 0.45%. Note that the protection buyer would suffer a mark-to-market loss here of 0.45% due to the fall in spread.

PROFESSOR'S NOTE

Here, spreads have narrowed and hence the protection buyer is suffering losses. The protection buyer can be viewed as synthetically short the reference issuers bond (this is the reason they are called "short risk")—if spreads widen (and prices fall), they profit.

CDS contracts can reference an individual issuer (single name) or an index of names (index-based). For example, the Markit CDX North American Investment Grade Index comprises 125 equally weighted CDS contracts. Payer (receiver) options also exist on CDS contracts where the option holder pays a premium for the right to buy (sell) protection on a CDX index on a future date. The holder of a payer CDS option profits if fair CDS spreads are above the CDS strike at expiry. The holder of a receiver CDS option profits if fair CDS spreads are below the CDS strike at expiry.

Active CDS strategies include CDS long-short strategies and CDS curve trades.

A **CDS long-short strategy** involves buying protection on issuers, where credit spreads are expected to widen relative to other issuers, while simultaneously selling protection on issuers, where credit spreads are expected to narrow relative to other issuers.

EXAMPLE: CDS long-short strategy

A manager wishes to increase exposure to XYZ Corp and decrease exposure to ABC Corp in their credit portfolio. Details of CDS contracts on the two companies are displayed here:

	Tenor (Years)	CDS Spread (bps)	EffSpreadDur
ABC Corp	5	220	4.59
XYZ Corp	5	240	4.62

Describe the appropriate long-short CDS trade to meet the manager's objectives. **Calculate** the manager's return if ABC Corp spreads widen by 15 bps and XYZ Corp spreads narrow by 20 bps, based on $15 million notional principal for each contract.

Answer:

The manager should sell protection on XYZ Corp to increase exposure to XYZ Corp and profit if spreads narrow; they should buy protection on ABC Corp to decrease exposure to ABC Corp and profit if spreads widen.

Profits from ABC Corp's spread widening = $15,000,000 × 0.0015 × 4.59 = $103,275.

Profits from XYZ Corp's spread narrowing = $15,000,000 × 0.002 × 4.62 = $138,600.

Total profit/loss from the trade = $103,275 + $138,600 = $241,875.

PROFESSOR'S NOTE

Keep in mind the risk side of the contract—to increase exposure, we increase risk and sell protection. When we sell protection, we profit if spreads fall, just as if we were long the bonds of the issuer.

The CDS curve is a plot of CDS spreads versus maturity for a reference entity or index. An active manager can use **CDS curve trades** to profit on their view on changes in the CDS curve through buying protection at maturities where CDS spreads are expected to rise relative to other maturities and selling protection at maturities where spreads are expected to fall relative to other maturities.

EXAMPLE: Duration-neutral CDS curve flattener

An active credit manager expects the upward-sloping CDS curve for high-yield U.S. issuers to flatten. Details of the 5-year and 10-year CDS index contracts are displayed here:

Issuer	Tenor (Years)	CDS Spread (bps)	EffSpreadDur
HY CDS index	5	410	4.78
HY CDS index	10	490	9.18

1. **Describe** the appropriate long-short CDS to profit from the manager's view, assuming they wish to remain duration neutral and hold a $5,000,000 notional position in the 5-year contract.
2. **Calculate** the investor's return if 5-year spreads fall by 5 bps and 10-year spreads fall by 20 bps.

Answers:

1. The manager expects a flattening CDS curve; hence, they expect the 10-year CDS spread to fall relative to the 5-year CDS spread. The manager should, therefore, buy protection in the 5-year contract and sell protection in the 10-year contract.

   It is stated that the manager wishes to hold a notional principal of $5 million in the 5-year contract. The BPV of this position = notional principal × EffSpreadDur × 0.0001 = $5 million × 4.780 × 0.0001 = $2,390.

   In order to remain duration neutral, we require the position in the 10-year contract to have the same BPV as the position in the 5-year contract. Hence, the notional principal in the 10-year position must satisfy notional principal × 9.18 × 0.0001 = $2,390. Solving for the notional principal in the 10-year contract gives notional principal = $2,390 / (9.18 × 0.0001) = $2,603,486.

2. The manager has bought protection in the 5-year contract. Losses for a 5 bps fall in spread = –5 × $2,390 = –$11,950.

   The manager has sold protection in the 10-year contract. Gains for a 20 bps fall in spread = 20 × $2,390 = $47,800.

   The total profit/loss = $47,800 – $11,950 = $35,850.

Credit Spread Curve Strategies

LOS 12.h: Discuss various portfolio positioning strategies that managers can use to implement a specific credit spread view.

This section turns our attention to the strategies that active managers can employ to profit from a view on the shape or level of the credit spread curve.

Static Credit Spread Curve Strategies

A manager who believes that the current credit spread curve will remain unchanged can earn excess return in the cash market through either lowering the average credit rating of their bond portfolio or increasing the spread duration of the portfolio by buying and holding longer-dated bonds.

PROFESSOR'S NOTE

These two strategies are analogous to two of the strategies seen in an earlier yield curve reading for a static benchmark yield curve. There, the manager could increase risk through leverage (the equivalent strategy here is to increase risk through lowering the credit rating of the portfolio) or through a buy-and-hold strategy using higher-returning longer-dated bonds.

EXAMPLE: Credit spread curve buy-and-hold strategy for static credit curve

An active credit manager collates the following data regarding the bonds of a corporate issuer and comparable government benchmark bonds. All coupons are semiannual, and all government securities listed are trading at par.

	Corporate Bonds			
Maturity (Years)	Coupon	YTM	Price	Govt. Par Yields
5	2.00%	2.00%	100.0000	0.50%
10	2.40%	2.30%	100.8888	0.80%
15	3.10%	2.90%	102.4187	1.10%

The manager expects a stable credit spread curve over the next six months and consequently takes an overweight position of $10 million face value of the 15-year corporate bond versus the 10-year corporate bond in order to extend the credit duration of the portfolio.

1. **Calculate** the incremental coupon income and rolldown price appreciation earned by the manager from extending the credit duration of the portfolio.
2. **Determine** the attribution of this incremental return to benchmark yield versus credit spread. **Show** your calculations.

Answers:

1. First, solve for the incremental coupon income generated from overweighting the 15-year corporate bond versus the 10-year corporate bond over the next six months.

   total incremental coupon = [(15-year corporate coupon – 10-year corporate coupon) / 2] × $10 million

   = [(0.031 – 0.024) / 2] × $10 million = $35,000

Next, we need to calculate price appreciation due to rolling down the static curve. To price the bonds in six months' time with a static yield curve, we use interpolation of the existing data to estimate the YTM of the corporate bonds and the benchmark government bonds after six months have passed.

PROFESSOR'S NOTE

Recall that if the adjacent securities have maturities S (shorter) and L (longer) versus the target maturity M, then to quickly calculate the weight in the longer-dated bond, we can use the ratio (M – S) / (L – S). Here, when interpolating to get the 9.5-year yield (M) from the existing 5-year (S) and 10-year (L) yields, we have a weight in the 10-year security of (9.5 – 5) / (10 – 5) = 0.9 and therefore a weight in the 5-year security of 0.1. These are the same weights for the 15-year and 10-year yields, respectively, when interpolating for the 14.5-year yield.

The interpolated 9.5-year corporate yield = (0.9 × 2.3%) + (0.1 × 2.0%) = 2.27%.

Price of 10-year corporate bond in six months' time (with 9.5 years to go): 19 N; 2.27 / 2 = 1.135 I / Y; 2.4 / 2 = 1.2 PMT; 100 FV; CPT PV: 101.1053

Recall that the original price of the 10-year corporate bond was given as 100.8888.

Hence, the absolute rolldown return of the 10-year bond = [(101.1053 – 100.8888) / 100] × $10 million = $21,650.

The interpolated 14.5-year corporate yield = (0.9 × 2.9%) + (0.1 × 2.3%) = 2.84%.

Price of 15-year corporate bond in six months' time (with 14.5 years to go): 29 N; 2.84 / 2 = 1.42 I / Y; 3.1 / 2 = 1.55 PMT; 100 FV; CPT PV: 103.0726

Recall that the original price of the 15-year corporate bond was given as 102.4187.

Hence, the absolute rolldown return of the 15-year bond = [(103.0726 – 102.4187) / 100] × $10 million = $65,390.

Hence, the total incremental rolldown return due to price appreciation is $65,390 – $21,650 = $43,740.

Therefore, the total incremental return earned from overweighting the 15-year bond versus the 10-year bond is $35,000 + $43,740 = $78,740.

2. Recall that the incremental coupon income from Part 1 was $35,000.

   To attribute this extra coupon into an extra benchmark coupon versus an extra coupon related to credit, we calculate the incremental coupon earned from the government bond as [(15-year govt. coupon – 10-year govt. coupon) / 2] × \$10 million = [(0.011 – 0.008) / 2] × \$10 million = \$15,000.

Hence, the incremental coupon coming from the credit spread = \$35,000 – \$15,000 = \$20,000.

In order to attribute the incremental rolldown price appreciation to changes in benchmark yield versus credit spread, we first need to assess the change in credit spread due to the 10-year and 15-year bonds rolling down the credit curve.

Using the same methodology as Part 1, we interpolate the yields of the government securities as follows:

interpolated 9.5-year government yield = (0.9 × 0.80%) + (0.1 × 0.50%) = 0.77%

interpolated 14.5-year government yield = (0.9 × 1.10%) + (0.1 × 0.80%) = 1.07%

We now analyze the change in *g*-spread (corp. YTM – govt. YTM) over the six months:

Bond	Corp. YTM	Govt. YTM	*g*-Spread
10-year at initiation	2.30%	0.80%	1.50%
9.5-year in six months' time	2.27%	0.77%	1.50%
Change over the six months	**–0.03%**	**–0.03%**	**0.00%**
15-year at initiation	2.90%	1.10%	1.80%
14.5-year in six months' time	2.84%	1.07%	1.77%
Change over the six months	**–0.06%**	**–0.03%**	**–0.03%**

Recall from Part 1 that the total rolldown return of the 10-year corporate bond is \$21,650.

The table here shows that this rolldown return came from a 0.03% fall in corporate bond yield, which was all attributable to the change in the government YTM.

Recall from Part 1 that the total rolldown return of the 15-year corporate bond is \$65,390.

The table here shows that this rolldown return came from a 0.06% fall in corporate bond yield, which is split evenly between a 0.03% fall in govt. YTM and a 0.03% fall in *g*-spread. Therefore, half the rolldown return (\$65,390 / 2 = \$32,695) is attributable to changes in benchmark yields, and the other half (\$32,695) is attributable to changes in credit spread.

Reading 12

Price appreciation due to rolldown return is summarized in the following table (figures in $):

		Attributed To	
Bond	**Total Rolldown Return**	**Benchmark Yields**	**Credit Spreads**
10-year	21,650	21,650	0
15-year	65,390	32,695	32,695
Incremental (15-yr – 10-yr)	43,740	11,045	32,695

Total incremental return from holding the 15-year bond over holding the 10-year bond = total incremental coupon income + total incremental rolldown return = $35,000 + $43,740 = $78,740.

Incremental return from credit spreads = incremental coupon from credit spreads + incremental rolldown return from credit spreads = $20,000 + $32,695 = $52,695.

A manager expecting a static curve can also use CDS contracts to profit from this view. The manager may increase risk by selling protection on lower credit quality issuers or extend duration through selling protection on longer-dated CDS contracts.

EXAMPLE: CDS strategy for a static credit spread curve

A manager expects a static credit spread curve over the next 12 months and plans to increase the spread duration of the portfolio in order to enhance returns. They collect the following information regarding CDS contracts on a domestic HY index:

Reference Obligation	Tenor (Years)	CDS Spread (bps)	EffSpreadDur
HY index	5	450	4.8
HY index	10	550	8.9

The manager takes the appropriate position in $50 million notional of the 10-year CDS. Assume annual coupon payments and a 9-year effective spread duration of 8.1.

1. **State** whether the manager should buy or sell protection in the 10-year CDS.
2. **Calculate** the total coupon income and rolldown return from the position in the 10-year CDS.

Answers:

1. The manager wishes to extend the duration of the portfolio. They should take a long-risk position in the longer-dated 10-year CDS through selling protection.

2. Being a high-yield reference obligation, the fixed coupon on the CDS will be 5%. The manager will therefore receive 0.05 × \$50,000,000 = \$2,500,000 coupon income during the year.

   To calculate the rolldown return, we need to calculate the price of the 10-year CDS in 1 year's time when it has rolled down the curve to become a 9-year CDS. To find the 9-year CDS spread, we interpolate using the original 5-year and 10-year CDS spreads. Here, S = 5, L = 10, and M = 9; hence, the weight in the longer 10-year maturity = (9 – 5) / (10 – 5) = 0.8.

   Then the 9-year interpolated CDS spread = (0.8 × 550) + (0.2 × 450) = 530 bps.

   opening price of 10-year CDS

   = 1 + (fixed coupon – CDS spread) × EffSpreadDur

   = 1 + (0.05 – 0.055) × 8.9

   = \$0.9555

   The price of the 10-year CDS in one year's time on becoming a 9-year CDS = 1 + (0.05 – 0.053) × 8.1 = \$0.9757.

   The manager is long risk (sold protection); therefore, they profit as CDS spreads fall and prices rise. Profit from price appreciation = (\$0.9757 – \$0.9555) × \$50,000,000 = \$1,010,000.

   The total return = coupon income + price appreciation = \$2,500,000 + \$1,010,000 = \$3,510,000.

PROFESSOR'S NOTE

There was an important step toward the end of the last example where we used the change in price of the CDS contract to calculate overall P/L. We stated that the manager sold protection, was long risk, and therefore benefitted if spreads fell and prices rose. *When calculating profit or loss from change in CDS price, view the long risk position as being like a long bond position—it profits if prices rise and spreads fall.* It is important for this and subsequent examples that this is clear. The following is a useful summary:

	Profit if CDS Spreads	Profit if CDS Prices
Sell protection (long risk)	Fall	**Rise**
Buy protection (short risk)	Rise	**Fall**

Dynamic Credit Spread Curve Strategies

Recall from the opening section in this chapter that the credit cycle is a key driver of the credit spread curve. A summary of the appropriate strategies for an economic slowdown or economic recovery are displayed in the following table:

		Strategy	
Economic Stage	**Typical Curve Feature**	**Cash**	**CDS**
Economic recovery	HY spreads narrow more than IG spreads	Buy HY bonds Sell IG bonds	Sell HY protection Buy IG protection
	HY credit curve steepens	Buy short-term HY bonds Sell long-term HY bonds	Sell short-term HY protection Buy long-term HY protection
Economic slowdown	HY spreads widen more than IG spreads	Buy IG bonds Sell HY bonds	Sell IG protection Buy HY protection
	HY credit curve flattens/inverts	Buy long-term HY bonds Sell short-term HY bonds	Sell long-term HY protection Buy short-term HY protection

EXAMPLE: Dynamic credit curve cash strategy—economic slowdown

An active credit manager collects the following information on three corporate bonds in their investment universe:

Rating	Current OAS	Expected Loss (POD × LGD)	EffSpreadDur
A	1.30%	0.09%	6.00
BBB	1.72%	0.39%	6.60
BB	2.60%	0.79%	5.90

The manager's benchmark is equally weighted across the three zero-coupon bonds. The manager is expecting an economic slowdown causing divergence in the changes of HY spreads relative to IG spreads over the next 12 months. The manager intends to take a 100% long position in a single bond and a 100% short position in a single bond to profit from this view.

1. **Describe** the trades the manager should make to profit from their credit spread curve view.
2. **Calculate** the excess spread of the portfolio and the benchmark under an economic slowdown where both OAS and expected loss increase by 40% for IG bonds and 80% for HY bonds.

Answers:

1. In an economic slowdown, HY spreads will likely widen by more than IG spreads. The manager should therefore sell HY bonds and buy IG bonds (think: flight to quality). Their portfolio should therefore be positioned 100% long the A-rated bond and 100% short the BB-rated bond.

2. Recall the excess spread of an investment is given by this formula:

    expected excess spread = spread – (EffSpreadDur × Δspread) – (POD × LGD)

    Applying this to the three bonds with the stated changes in spread and yield gives the following:

    excess spread of A-rated bond = 0.013 – [6 × (0.4 × 0.013)] – (0.0009 × 1.4) = –0.01946 or –1.946%

    excess spread of BBB-rated bond = 0.0172 – [6.60 × (0.4 × 0.0172)] – (0.0039 × 1.4) = –0.03367 or –3.367%

    excess spread of BB-rated bond = 0.026 – [5.90 × (0.8 × 0.026)] – (0.0079 × 1.8) = –0.11094 or –11.094%

    excess spread of the equally weighted benchmark = (–1.946% – 3.367% – 11.094%) / 3 = –5.47%

    excess spread of the active portfolio = (+1 × –1.946%) + (–1 × –11.094%) = 9.15%

EXAMPLE: Dynamic credit curve synthetic strategy—economic slowdown

A credit analyst collates the following information regarding CDS contracts on an IG index and a HY index:

Reference Obligation	Tenor (Years)	CDS Spread (bps)	EffSpreadDur
IG index	5	100	4.65
HY index	5	250	4.63

The manager is expecting an economic slowdown causing divergence in the changes of HY spreads relative to IG spreads over the next 12 months. The estimated spread durations of the IG index and HY index in 12 months' time are 3.85 and 3.82, respectively. The manager intends to invest in a long-short CDS trade with notional of $50 million in each of the contracts listed to profit from this view.

1. **Describe** the trades the manager should make to profit from their credit spread curve view.
2. **Calculate** the total return of the strategy under an economic slowdown where CDS spreads increase by 40% for the IG index and 80% for the HY index.

Answers:

1. In an economic slowdown, HY spreads will likely widen by more than IG spreads. The manager should therefore buy protection on the HY index and sell protection on the IG index (think: flight to quality).

Reading 12

2. The total return of the portfolio will consist of coupon paid/received and price appreciation.

   The manager will pay a 5% coupon to buy the HY protection and receive a 1% coupon for selling the IG protection. Net coupon outflow = \$50 million × (0.05 – 0.01) = \$2 million.

   In order to calculate price appreciation, we need to calculate the price of the CDS contracts at initiation and after 12 months. We will use this formula:

   $$\text{CDS price} \approx 1 + [(\text{fixed coupon} - \text{CDS spread}) \times \text{EffSpreadDur}_{CDS}]$$

   We also recall once again that the standardized coupon on a CDS contract is 1% for IG and 5% for HY.

   price of the IG index CDS at initiation = 1 + (0.01 – 0.01) × 4.65 = 1

   price of the IG index CDS after 12 months = 1 + [0.01 – (0.01 × 1.4)] × 3.85 = 0.9846

   The manager has sold protection on the IG index and is therefore long risk: they benefit from rising prices. Therefore, p/l from selling IG protection = \$50 million × (0.9846 – 1) = –\$770,000.

   price of the HY index CDS at initiation = 1 + (0.05 – 0.025) × 4.63 = 1.11575

   price of the HY index CDS after 12 months = 1 + [0.05 – (0.025 × 1.8)] × 3.82 = 1.0191

   The manager has bought protection on the HY index and is therefore short risk: they benefit from falling prices. Therefore, p/l from buying HY protection = \$50,000,000 × (1.11575 – 1.0191) = \$4,832,500.

   total p/l from price appreciation = –\$770,000 + \$4,832,500 = \$4,062,500

   Subtracting the premium outflow gives a total p/l of \$4,062,500 – \$2,000,000 = \$2,062,500.

MODULE QUIZ 12.5

1. A CDS contract on a HY issuer has a CDS spread of 4.7% and effective spread duration of 4.5. The up-front premium on \$10 million notional of this contract is:
   A. \$135,000 and paid to the protection seller.
   B. \$135,000 and paid to the protection buyer.
   C. \$1,665,000 and paid to the protection seller.
2. An active credit manager expecting a stable credit curve is *least likely* to:
   A. sell protection in longer-dated CDS contracts.
   B. buy protection in shorter-dated CDS contracts.
   C. lower the credit rating of the portfolio.

3. An active credit manager who is expecting an economic recovery should *most likely*:
   A. lower exposure to HY securities.
   B. use CDS contracts to sell short-dated protection and buy long-dated protection.
   C. use CDS contracts to buy protection on HY issuers and sell protection on IG issuers.
4. An active credit manager decides to overweight exposure to an investment-grade company using $10 million notional of CDS contracts with tenor of 5 years, a CDS spread of 150 basis points, and a spread duration of 4.5. One year later, the CDS spread is 120 basis points and the spread duration is 3.5. The profit from the CDS trade is *closest* to:
   A. $100,000.
   B. $155,000.
   C. $255,000.

MODULE 12.6: GLOBAL CREDIT STRATEGIES, STRUCTURED CREDIT, AND FIXED-INCOME ANALYTICS

Video covering this content is available online.

LOS 12.i: Discuss considerations in constructing and managing portfolios across international credit markets.

Global Credit Strategies

A manager engaging in cross-border credit strategies has the following considerations when constructing their portfolio:

- Attempts to diversify through investing in different sectors (e.g., sovereign issuers vs. corporate issuers) in an emerging market that is heavily reliant upon a dominant industry or commodity export may yield little success, as all securities are likely to perform in a similar way.
- Significant sector differences may exist, even between developed markets. For example, a far higher proportion of the U.S. fixed-income market is related to mortgage and other asset-backed securities than are other developed markets.
- Differences in accounting standards across markets may affect the liquidity, profitability, and solvency ratios used in credit analysis.
- Differences in the magnitude and timing of the credit cycle across countries often present opportunities in yields, exchange rates, and credit spread curves.

Recall from an earlier reading that the domestic return of a foreign market investment can be calculated as follows:

$$R_{DC} = (1 + R_{FC})(1 + R_{FX}) - 1$$

where:

R_{DC} = domestic return

R_{FC} = foreign currency (local market) return

R_{FX} = appreciation/depreciation of foreign currency versus domestic currency

EXAMPLE: Cross-border credit strategy

A U.S.-based active credit manager has the view that an economic recovery will see European credit outperform U.S. credit over the next 12 months. They identify the following CDS contract based on a European HY index:

Reference Obligation	Tenor (Years)	CDS Spread (bps)	EffSpreadDur
EUR HY index	5	450	4.55

Calculate the price return (ignoring coupon) of the appropriate position in the above CDS contract if the European credit spreads fall by 20% and the EUR strengthens against the USD by 2%.

Answer:

Note that the high-yield index will have a standardized fixed coupon of 5%.

The initial price of the CDS = 1 + (0.05 – 0.045) × 4.55 = 1.02275.

After the fall in spreads, the new price of the CDS = 1 + [0.05 – (0.045 × 0.8)] × 4.55 = 1.0637.

Hence, the foreign price return, R_{FC} = (1.0637 – 1.02275) / 1.02275 = 0.04 or 4%.

Given an expected appreciation of the foreign currency of 2%, the domestic return of the U.S. investor is calculated as (1.04) × (1.02) – 1 = 0.0608 or 6.08%.

Managers investing in emerging markets often begin their credit analysis by assessing the willingness and ability of the government to meet their sovereign debt payments. Considerations here include the following:

- **Institutional considerations**. Consider the enforcement of property rights, contract law, and the level of political stability in the country. Geopolitical risk such as trade wars or conflicts, plus ESG factors, are also important.
- **Economic profile**. Tax revenues from economic activity, plus the level of debt and annual deficit as a percentage of GDP, all directly affect the ability of a country to meet its debt payments.

- **Exchange rate regime**. Fixed exchange rate regimes limit the flexibility and effectiveness of monetary policy. From a sovereign credit risk perspective, high external (foreign) debt/GDP implies a higher chance of financial distress, while a low currency reserves/GDP ratio suggests potential liquidity issues.

Investors in emerging market corporate bonds also need to consider the level of control/influence the government may exert on the running of business and the "sovereign ceiling" set by the government, whereby corporations are usually not assigned higher-quality credit ratings than the sovereign credit rating of their domicile.

Liquidity risk is a key concern for investors in emerging market bonds because often a relatively small number of bonds trade on a regular basis, resulting in investors demanding a liquidity premium. Currency risk is also a key concern for investors. The higher yields available in emerging markets could be interpreted under uncovered interest rate parity as a sign that the currency is expected to depreciate. However, as discussed in a previous reading, uncovered interest rate parity is not a theory that always holds, meaning that investors could earn excess returns from an international carry trade (called the forward rate bias).

Structured Credit

LOS 12.j: Describe the use of structured financial instruments as an alternative to corporate bonds in credit portfolios.

Structured credit instruments allow investors to purchase securities that are backed by debt-based collateral, such as a pool of mortgages or commercial loans.

There are two primary reasons for an investor to invest in structured credit:

1. The structured instrument issues different *tranches* of security, each with a different risk profile, allowing the investor to create risk exposures not available through investing directly in the collateral. For example, with credit tranching, credit losses in the underlying collateral will flow to the most junior tranche first. The most senior tranche will, therefore, have the lowest credit risk and receive the highest credit rating. Investors that are not be able to invest in the collateral due to their credit rating being too low will be able to invest in the higher-rated senior tranches of the structured product. Structured products that offer such tranching features include the following:
   - Collateralized debt obligations (CDOs)—with general debt obligations as collateral.
   - Collateralized loan obligations (CLOs)—with leveraged loans (i.e., loans to non-investment-grade companies) as collateral.
2. The structured instrument offers *exposure* to collateral that the investor cannot access directly. Examples include the following:
   - Mortgage-backed securities (MBSs) backed by mortgages.
   - Asset-backed securities (ABSs) backed by credit card, auto, or other types of loan.

Reading 12

- Covered bonds—senior debt obligations of a commercial bank backed by a pool of mortgages or loans made by the bank. The investor here has recourse to the other asset of the bank should the bank fail to make payments on the covered bond (this is not the case for other types of structured products that are issued by an off-balance sheet special purpose vehicle (SPV) with no recourse to the original lender of the collateral loans). This, along with the fact that a lender would substitute nonperforming loans in the collateral, makes the credit risk of a covered bond lower than that of other structured products.

PROFESSOR'S NOTE

Remember that Level III is all about application in an investment scenario rather than forensic focus on technical detail. Expect questions to test the understanding of how/why a manager would use these products in certain situations. For example, a manager expecting an economic recovery would sell senior tranches and buy junior tranches in anticipation of lower credit quality assets outperforming higher credit quality assets (just in the same way that a credit manager would lower the credit rating of their portfolio before an economic recovery in order to outperform).

Fixed-Income Analytics

LOS 12.k: Describe key inputs, outputs, and considerations in using analytical tools to manage fixed-income portfolios.

Fixed-income analytical tools perform important operational and investment tasks for a fixed-income investment manager. They comprise three major parts: inputs, user-defined parameters, and outputs.

- **Inputs** include portfolio position data, relevant market data (prices/yields, exchange rates, volatilities, etc.), credit and ESG ratings, and index data subscriptions for benchmarking purposes.
- **User-defined parameters** comprise models for term structure, risk (e.g., VaR), scenario analysis, and filters to include or exclude bonds by sector or ESG rating. The time horizon of the manager is also an important user-defined parameter, as is the overall objective of the manager (e.g., total return vs. liability-driven).
- **Outputs** include a summary of portfolio positions and risk exposures versus the benchmark index, position selection and portfolio construction tools, risk and scenario analysis, and trading and cash management tools.

The investment manager should consider the accuracy of model inputs, the appropriateness of assumption in the user-defined models, and how the outputs relate to the manager's overall objectives.

MODULE QUIZ 12.6

1. An active credit manager has exposure to two emerging markets, Market A and Market B, with the following economic profiles:

	Country A	Country B
Foreign debt/GDP	100%	60%
Budget deficit/GDP	4%	6%
Currency reserves/GDP	12%	21%

Based on these ratios, if the manager wishes to invest in the country with the greatest fiscal stability, they should increase exposure to:
A. Country A and reduce exposure to Country B due to the relative budget deficit/GDP ratios.
B. Country B and reduce exposure to Country A due to the relative foreign debt/GDP ratios.
C. Country B and reduce exposure to Country A due to the relative currency reserves/GDP ratios.

2. After recent central bank actions, an active credit manager expects an economic recovery and a strong rebound in residential housing prices. The portfolio position *most appropriate* to profit from this view is to sell:
A. the BB-rated tranche of a credit card ABS and buy the AA-rated tranche of the same structured product.
B. the AA-rated tranche of a CDO and buy the BB-rated tranche of the same structured product.
C. the AA tranche of an MBS and buy the BB tranche of the same structure product.

3. A manager performing risk analytics on their portfolio of MBS securities is *most likely* to increase the future value output of their portfolio relative to similar option-free bond holding through making which of the following input changes?
A. A downward parallel shift in the yield curve.
B. An increase in interest rate volatility.
C. A decrease in interest rate volatility.

Reading 12

KEY CONCEPTS

LOS 12.a

The two primary components of credit risk are probability of default (POD), usually expressed as an annualized probability, and loss given default (LGD) or loss severity calculated as 1 – recovery rate (RR). The credit valuation adjustment (CVA) of a credit-risky bond is the present value of expected credit losses, calculated as the sum of (POD × LGD × expected exposure) across the life of the bond. The credit-risky bond's fair value is equal to an equivalent risk-free bond's value minus the CVA.

The following is a simple approach to estimating the fair credit spread for the next period:

$$\text{spread} \approx \text{POD} \times \text{LGD}$$

A plot of credit spreads versus maturity for a class of bonds is called the credit spread curve. This curve is largely driven by the credit cycle linked to the general level of economic activity as follows:

	Stage of Economic Cycle			
	Early Expansion (Recovery)	**Late Expansion**	**Peak**	**Contraction (Recession)**
Corporate defaults	Peak	Falling	Stable	Rising
Credit spread level	Stable	Falling	Rising	Peak
Credit spread slope	IG: Stable HY: Inverted	Upward sloping for both IG and HY	Upward sloping for both IG and HY	IG: Flat HY: Inverted

Empirical duration is based on regression of market data of actual bond price returns and benchmark rate changes. Since the actual bond price is driven by both spreads and benchmark rates, empirical duration will be *lower* than analytical duration for low-quality securities.

LOS 12.b

Fixed-Rate Bond Credit Spread Measures

yield spread (benchmark spread) = bond's YTM – YTM of closest maturity on-the-run government bond

g-spread = bond's YTM – interpolated YTM of the two adjacent maturity on-the-run government bonds

i-spread (interpolated spread) = bond's YTM – the maturity interpolated swap fixed rate

asset swap spread (ASW) = bond's fixed *coupon* – the maturity interpolated swap fixed rate

zero-volatility spread (*z*-spread) = bond's spread over risk-free *spot rates*

The CDS spread is the fair value of the protection bought under a CDS contract, expressed as a periodic percentage of notional exposure.

CDS basis = CDS spread – *z*-spread

The option adjusted spread (OAS) is a bond's spread over an interest rate tree of potential future risk-free forward-rate paths. The OAS removes the impact of options on the spread and should be used to compare across different types of bond.

Floating-Rate Note (FRN) Credit Spread Measures

Quoted margin (QM) is the fixed margin above a floating market reference rate (MRR) making up an FRN coupon.

Discount margin (DM) is the constant spread above the current MRR rate offered by an FRN.

If DM is less (greater) than QM, then the FRN will trade above (below) par.

The rate duration and spread duration of an FRN are given by the following:

$$\text{EffRateDur}_{\text{FRN}} = \frac{(\text{PV}_{-}) - (\text{PV}_{+})}{2(\Delta\text{MRR})(\text{PV}_0)}$$

$$\text{EffSpreadDur}_{\text{FRN}} = \frac{(\text{PV}_{-}) - (\text{PV}_{+})}{2(\Delta\text{DM})(\text{PV}_0)}$$

Zero-discount margin (Z-DM) is the constant spread above the current term structure of MRR rates offered by an FRN.

The Impact of Spreads on Portfolio Return

The effective spread duration and effective spread convexity of a portfolio are calculated using the following formulas:

$$\text{effective spread duration} = \frac{(\text{PV}_{-}) - (\text{PV}_{+})}{2(\Delta\text{spread})(\text{PV}_0)}$$

$$\text{effective spread convexity} = \frac{(\text{PV}_{-}) + (\text{PV}_{+}) - 2(\text{PV}_0)}{(\Delta\text{spread})^2(\text{PV}_0)}$$

The sensitivity of a bond portfolio to changes in spread is given by:

$$\%\Delta \text{ price} = (-\text{EffSpreadDur} \times \Delta\text{spread}) + (\tfrac{1}{2} \times \text{EffSpreadCon} \times \Delta\text{spread}^2)$$

where Δ*spread* is typically defined as the change in the OAS.

Reading 12

The duration times spread (DTS) of a bond portfolio respects the fact that spread changes tend to be proportional to spread size, and is approximately defined as follows:

$$\text{DTS} \approx \text{EffSpreadDur} \times \text{spread}$$

The excess return over credit losses expected from a bond portfolio is defined as the *excess spread* and calculated as follows:

$$\text{expected excess spread} = \text{spread} - (\text{EffSpreadDur} \times \Delta\text{spread}) - (\text{POD} \times \text{LGD})$$

LOS 12.c

Bottom-up credit strategies aim to identify the most attractive individual bond investments by focusing on the operating history of the borrower and key financial ratios.

Credit risk models used on a bottom-up basis can be structural or reduced form. Structural models assess the probability of default as the probability of the assets of the borrower falling below the value of their liabilities. Reduced form models assess probability of default and the impact of credit losses through modeling the relationship between macroeconomic variables and the characteristic of the borrower.

An example of a reduced form model is the Altman's *z*-score, which maps key financial ratios to a *z*-score using linear regression. A *z*-score greater than 3 implies a low chance of default. A *z*-score between 1.8 and 3 indicates some chance of default, while a score below 1.8 indicates that default is likely.

LOS 12.d

Top-down credit strategies focus on macroeconomic factors that are likely to affect the credit portfolio. Managers attempt to form views on the timing of the credit cycle, lowering the credit rating of the portfolio prior to good economic conditions and increasing the credit rating of the portfolio prior to poor economic conditions.

Factor-based credit strategies focus on identifying factors in fixed-income securities that are rewarded with a risk premium. Four factors that have been identified are carry, defensive, momentum, and value.

ESG techniques in fixed income include negative screening, use of ESG ratings, and direct funding of ESG initiatives such as green bonds.

LOS 12.e

Fixed income has historically been an OTC market with low liquidity in off-the-run, smaller, emerging market corporate issues and higher liquidity for on-the-run, larger, developed market sovereign issues.

Transaction costs can be measured through the effective spread:

$$\text{effective spread for a buy order} = \text{trade size} \times (\text{trade price} - \text{midquote})$$

$$\text{effective spread for a sell order} = \text{trade size} \times (\text{midquote} - \text{trade price})$$

where:

$$\text{midquote} = (\text{bid} + \text{ask}) / 2$$

LOS 12.f

Value at risk (VaR) is a measure of minimum expected loss occurring in a given time frame with a specified probability.

The three common methods used to generate distributions for VaR calculations are the parametric method, which uses the parameters of the normal distribution; the historical method; and Monte Carlo simulation.

Extensions of VaR include the following:

- Conditional value at risk (CVaR) is the expected loss *given the portfolio is experiencing a loss in the tail.*
- Incremental VaR (IVaR) (or partial VaR) measures the change in VaR from adding or removing a position in a portfolio.
- Relative VaR measures the VaR of a portfolio's returns relative to a benchmark.

LOS 12.g

Under a credit default swap (CDS), a protection buyer pays a regular fixed coupon to the protection seller periodically over the life of the contract in return for a payment on a prespecified credit event on a reference issuer (or issuers).

If the fair value of the protection (the CDS spread) is different from the fixed coupon paid, then an up-front premium is paid/received by the protection buyer, as follows:

Scenario	Upfront Premium
CDS spread = fixed coupon	None
CDS spread > fixed coupon	[(CDS spread – fixed coupon) × $\text{EffSpreadDur}_{\text{CDS}}$] paid to protection seller
CDS spread < fixed coupon	[(fixed coupon – CDS spread) × $\text{EffSpreadDur}_{\text{CDS}}$] paid to protection buyer

The CDS price as a percentage of par is quoted as follows:

$$\text{CDS price} \approx 1 + [(\text{fixed coupon} - \text{CDS spread}) \times \text{EffSpreadDur}_{\text{CDS}}]$$

A *CDS long-short strategy* involves buying protection on issuers where credit spreads are expected to widen relative to other issuers, while simultaneously selling protection on issuers where credit spreads are expected to narrow relative to other issuers.

A *CDS curve trade* involves buying protection at maturities where CDS spreads are expected to rise relative to other maturities and selling protection at maturities where spreads are expected to fall relative to other maturities.

LOS 12.h

Static credit spread curve strategies when the (upward-sloping) credit spread curve is expected to be stable include the following:

- Lower the credit quality of the portfolio or extend the spread duration of the portfolio.
- Sell protection on lower-quality credit issuers or sell protection over longer maturities.

Reading 12

Dynamic credit spread curve strategies when the credit spread curve is expected to change include the following:

		Strategy	
Economic Stage	**Typical Curve Feature**	**Cash**	**CDS**
Economic recovery	HY spreads narrow more than IG spreads	Buy HY bonds Sell IG bonds	Sell HY protection Buy IG protection
	HY credit curve steepens	Buy short-term HY bonds Sell long-term HY bonds	Sell short-term HY protection Buy long-term HY protection
Economic slowdown	HY spreads widen more than IG spreads	Buy IG bonds Sell HY bonds	Sell IG protection Buy HY protection
	HY credit curve flattens/inverts	Buy long-term HY bonds Sell short-term HY bonds	Sell long-term HY protection Buy short-term HY protection

LOS 12.i

A manager engaging in cross-border credit strategies should consider whether foreign market reliance on an industry or commodity export limits diversification, any significant sector weight differences between markets, differences in accounting standards, and difference in the magnitude and timing of credit cycles between countries.

The domestic return of a foreign credit investment is given by the following:

$$R_{DC} = (1 + R_{FC})(1 + R_{FX}) - 1$$

Investors in emerging markets should consider institutional factors such as political stability and enforcement of the law, the economic profile of the country, and the exchange rate regime.

LOS 12.j

Structured credit instruments allow managers to access collateral they could not access directly (ABS, MBS, covered bonds), allow managers to tailor their risk exposure through the tranching of securities (CDO, CLO), or both.

LOS 12.k

Fixed-income analytical tools comprise three major parts: inputs (positions, market data, ratings, and index data), user-defined parameters (models, time horizon, and objectives), and outputs (risk summaries, portfolio construction, trading, and cash management tools).

ANSWER KEY FOR MODULE QUIZZES

Module Quiz 12.1

1. **A** At the peak of the economic cycle, lower defaults and increased profitability cause short-term credit spreads to remain low. Longer-term credit spreads will likely increase due to higher leverage, increased inflation expectations over the longer term, and the pricing in of higher defaults when a contraction begins. The curve will likely be rising and upward sloping in this stage of the economic cycle. (LOS 12.a)

2. **C** While the IG credit spread curve is likely to flatten during periods of economic downturn, it is only the HY curve that typically inverts (i.e., becomes downward sloping), due to the high level of defaults in the short term for HY issuers. (LOS 12.a)

3. **A** Analytical duration measures the theoretical sensitivity of a bond's price to a unit move in benchmark rates (think: modified duration). Empirical duration is derived through regressing a bond's actual returns relative to movements in benchmark rates. As benchmark rates rise in good economic times, credit spreads tend to fall (and vice versa in bad economic times). This inverse relationship between benchmark rates and spreads will cause bond yields to move by less than benchmark rates; hence, the bond price will empirically be less sensitive to changes in rates than analytical duration implies. Therefore, empirical duration will be lower than analytical duration. (LOS 12.a)

Module Quiz 12.2

1. **C** The yield spread compares the YTM of the 12-year corporate bond to the nearest maturity on-the-run Treasury YTM. In this case, the nearest maturity is the 10-year maturity. The *g*-spread compares the YTM of the corporate bond to the 12-year interpolated government YTM using the 10- and 15-year maturity Treasuries. Given that the yield curve is upward sloping, the 12-year interpolated Treasury YTM will be higher than the 10-year government YTM. This implies that the *g*-spread will be lower than the yield spread. (LOS 12.b)

2. **C** The *i*-spread is defined as the corporate YTM minus an interpolated swap rate. The asset swap spread (ASW) is defined as the bond's coupon minus the interpolated swap rate. Since the bond is trading below par, the YTM of the bond will be higher than its coupon; hence, the *i*-spread will be higher than the ASW. (LOS 12.b)

3. **A** First, solve for the market value of Bonds X and Y:

   market value of Bond X = £1,000,000 × (1.02 + 0.01) = £1,030,000

   market value of Bond Y = £1,000,000 × (0.94 + 0.015) = £955,000

   Therefore, the total portfolio value = £1,030,000 + £955,000 = £1,985,000.

Reading 12

The weight of Bond X = £1,030,000 / £1,985,000 = 0.51889.

The weight of Bond Y = 0.48111.

Given that we can see that Bond X has a higher weight than Bond Y in the portfolio, we will have a higher weight in the 120 bps bond than in the 140 bps bond; hence, the portfolio OAS will be less than 130 bps.

For completeness, the OAS of the portfolio = (0.51889 × 120) + (0.48111 × 140) = 129.6 bps. (LOS 12.b)

4. **A** The DM assumes that the yield curve is flat because it is the constant margin above the current MRR that is required by investors. The Z-DM reflects the term structure of the MRR curve in that it reflects the constant return in excess of MRR spot rates that is required by investors. In an upward-sloping MRR curve environment, the MRR spot rates will be higher than the current MRR as maturity increases, and so the Z-DM will be lower than the DM. (LOS 12.b)

Module Quiz 12.3

1. **A** First, we calculate the inputs to the Altman model:

   A = working capital / total assets = $2,100 / $3,500 = 0.60

   B = retained earnings / total assets = $1,900 / $3,500 = 0.54

   C = EBIT / total assets = $600 / $3,500 = 0.17

   D = market value of equity / total liabilities = $3,000 / $1,200 = 2.5

   E = sales / total assets = $2,000 / $3,500 = 0.57

   Using these inputs in the model, we calculate the following *z*-score:

   z-score model = (1.2 × 0.60) + (1.4 × 0.54) + (3.3 × 0.17) + (0.6 × 2.5) + (0.999 × 0.57) = 4.11

   This *z*-score of 4.11 is above the threshold of 3, so we are required to label the company as low default risk. (LOS 12.c)

2. **B** Under structural models, the probability of default is measured by how far the assets of the issuer are away from a level that would trigger a default in terms of standard deviations. A decrease in the interest coverage ratio and increase in leverage both imply the issuer has a lower ability to service its debt and, therefore, is closer to default and has a higher POD. A fall in the volatility (i.e., standard deviation) of equity will imply a fall in the standard deviation of the issuer's assets, which will increase the distance to default (in terms of standard deviations) and, therefore, lower the POD of the issuer. (LOS 12.c)

3. **A** Excess spread is calculated using this formula:

   expected excess spread = spread – (EffSpreadDur × Δspread) – (POD × LGD)

   Given a 15% increase in spreads:

   excess spread for A-rated bond = 0.015 – [6 × (0.15 × 0.015)] – [0.0025 × (1 – 0.4)] = 0%

   excess spread for B-rated bond = 0.03 – [8 × (0.15 × 0.03)] – [0.03 × (1 – 0.4)] = –0.024 or –2.4%

   With a higher excess spread, the A-rated bond offers a more attractive valuation than the B-rated bond. (LOS 12.c)

4. **B** The carry factor represents returns earned from holding fixed-income securities over time. The value factor represents returns available from investing in bonds with a low value relative to their fundamental value. The defensive factor suggests that risk-adjusted returns for less risky securities are superior to those of higher risk (longer duration) securities. (LOS 12.d)

Module Quiz 12.4

1. **A** It will take a significant amount of time to carefully liquidate such a large position. In the meantime, the manager should hedge the interest rate exposure of the fixed-coupon received on the bond by paying fixed under an interest rate swap. As the bond is sold over time, the swap should be unwound to match the remaining bond position. (LOS 12.e)

2. **B** Incremental VaR measures the impact of changing positions in the portfolio on overall VaR. Relative VaR measures VaR relative to a benchmark index, and conditional VaR measures the average loss given we are in the tail of the distribution. (LOS 12.f)

Module Quiz 12.5

1. **B** The up-front premium is calculated as follows:

   upfront premium = (fixed coupon – CDS spread) × EffSpreadDur × notional

   The standardized fixed coupon for a HY reference obligation is 5%. Hence, the up-front premium = (0.05 – 0.047) × 4.5 × $10,000,000 = $135,000. Since the fixed coupon that is actually paid is higher than the fair CDS spread, this up-front premium is paid from the protection seller to the protection buyer. (LOS 12.g)

2. **B** Managers expecting a static credit spread curve should enhance the return of the portfolio through lowering the credit rating of the portfolio (buy HY bonds, sell HY protection) or extending the spread duration of the portfolio (buy longer-dated bonds, sell longer-dated CDS contracts). (LOS 12.h)

3. **B** An economic recovery is likely to see HY spreads fall by more than IG spreads and credit curves steepening. A manager should therefore sell protection on HY issues versus buying protection on IG issuers or increase exposure to HY securities in order to benefit from HY bonds outperforming IG bonds. To profit from the steepening curve, they should sell short-term protection and buy longer-term protection. (LOS 12.h)

4. **C** The CDS contract is on an IG issuer; hence, the standardized fixed coupon is 1%.

   initial price of the CDS = 1 + [(0.01 – 0.015) × 4.5] = 0.9775

   price of the CDS after 12 months = 1 + [(0.01 – 0.012) × 3.5] = 0.993

   Since the manager wishes to overweight exposure to the issuer, they will sell protection to take a long risk position. A long risk position wins when prices rise.

   profit from price appreciation = (0.993 – 0.9775) × $10,000,000 = $155,000

   coupon income = 0.01 × $10,000,000 = $100,000

   total profit = $155,000 + $100,000 = $255,000

   (LOS 12.h)

Module Quiz 12.6

1. **A** If the manager wishes to invest in countries with the greatest fiscal stability, they should invest in countries with the lowest budget deficit/GDP ratios, since this ratio indicates how much borrowing the country needs to make each year to meet its spending requirements. The foreign debt/GDP ratio is used to assess external leverage, and the currency reserves/GDP ratio is used to assess the liquidity position of the countries. (LOS 12.i)

2. **C** In anticipation of an economic rebound, managers should lower the credit quality of investments since high-yield spreads will likely contract by more than IG spreads. The manager can incorporate their view on a housing market recovery by using MBS securities. (LOS 12.j)

3. **C** MBS securities contain a prepayment option held by the mortgage borrowers. This option, like a call option on a bond, will become more valuable as interest rate volatility increases. Since the prepayment option lies with the borrowers, the MBS securities have an embedded short position in the prepayment option. The MBS security will become more valuable if volatility assumptions fall and the embedded short prepayment option value falls. (LOS 12.k)

TOPIC QUIZ: FIXED INCOME

You have now finished the Fixed Income topic section. On your Schweser online dashboard, you can find a Topic Quiz that will provide immediate feedback on how effective your study of this material has been. The test is best taken timed; allow three minutes per question. Topic Quizzes are more exam-like than typical QBank questions or module quiz questions. A score less than 70% suggests that additional review of the topic is needed.

READING 13

Overview of Equity Portfolio Management

EXAM FOCUS

These introductory readings cover the role of equity in the portfolio, common approaches to equity investing, and shareholder engagement.

MODULE 13.1: EQUITY INVESTMENT ROLES

Video covering this content is available online.

LOS 13.a: Describe the roles of equities in the overall portfolio.

Within the overall investment portfolio, equity securities play several beneficial roles. These roles include capital appreciation, dividend income, diversification, and the potential to hedge inflation.

Capital Appreciation

The main driver of long-term equity returns is capital (or price) appreciation. Capital appreciation results from investing in companies that are experiencing growth in cash flows, revenues, and/or earnings. These companies range from small technology companies that are focused on growth opportunities to large, well-established companies that are focused on value-added acquisitions and minimizing costs.

In the last 50 years, equity returns on average have been higher than bonds and bills. In general, equities tend to outperform other major asset classes during periods of strong economic growth, and underperform during periods of weak economic growth.

Dividend income: This is an important component of equity return. When companies generate excess cash flows, they can decide to either reinvest those cash flows in value-added projects or distribute them to investors in the form of *dividends*. Well-established companies often pay dividends to investors and those dividends may increase over time. However, dividend payments are not guaranteed to increase or even continue into the future. Typical recent annual dividend yields have been 1%–3%. Dividend yield tends to be more stable than return due to price change.

Diversification: Equity securities offer diversification benefits due to less than perfect (i.e., less than +1.0) correlation with other asset classes. When assets are less than perfectly correlated, portfolio standard deviation will be lower than the weighted sum of the individual asset standard deviations.

However, the risk reduction is not constant. During a financial crisis correlations tend to increase, limiting the diversification benefit. In addition, asset class standard deviations could increase, further reducing the expected reduction in portfolio risk.

Inflation hedge: In some cases, individual equities or equity sectors may provide a hedge against inflation. A company that can charge its customers more when input costs increase (due to inflation), can provide an inflation hedge by increasing to cash flow and earnings as prices increase. Commodity-producing companies (e.g., oil producer) may also benefit directly from commodity price increases.

The general record for equities as an inflation hedge is mixed. Studies generally show positive correlation between equity real returns and inflation, but the relationship varies over time and by country. Other studies show that equities and inflation become negatively correlated during periods of hyperinflation. In addition, equity prices are typically a leading economic indicator while inflation is a lagging economic indicator; also suggesting a less than perfect correlation between equity return and inflation.

Client Investment Considerations

The decision to include equities or the kinds of equities to include in a portfolio also depends on client investment considerations as outlined in the investment policy statement (IPS). Clients with a high risk tolerance may prefer growth-oriented companies, while clients with a low risk tolerance may prefer stable, well-established companies that pay dividends.

Client constraints may include environmental, social, and governance (ESG) considerations and religious beliefs. Portfolio managers can address these constraints using the following:

- **Negative screening** (i.e., exclusionary screening), which excludes companies or sectors that do not meet client standards.
- **Positive screening** (i.e., best-in-class screening), which seeks to uncover companies or sectors that rank most favorably with clients.
- **Thematic investing**, which screens equities based on a specific theme, such as climate change. A related approach is **impact investing**, which aims to meet investor objectives by becoming more actively engaged with company matters and/or directly investing in company projects.

Equity Investment Segmentation

LOS 13.b: Describe how an equity manager's investment universe can be segmented.

The three main **segmentation** approaches include size and style, geography, and economic activity. Using these approaches provides a better understanding of how equity investments integrate into the overall portfolio and enhance diversification benefits.

Size and Style

- Size, typically measured by market capitalization, can be categorized by large-cap, mid-cap, or small-cap companies.
- Style can be categorized by growth or value companies, or a mix of these two styles (sometimes referred to as *blend* or *core*). Investment style can be determined by analyzing company metrics, such as price-to-earnings ratios, price-to-book ratios, dividend yield, and earnings and/or book value growth.

A style box can be used to rank (or *score*) companies or portfolios among these metrics. An example is shown in Figure 13.1.

Figure 13.1: Equity Investment Style Box

		Style		
		Value	Blend	Growth
Size	Large	Large-cap value	Large-cap blend	Large-cap growth
Size	Medium	Mid-cap value	Mid-cap blend	Mid-cap growth
Size	Small	Small-cap value	Small-cap blend	Small-cap growth

It may be beneficial for portfolio managers to analyze exactly where each company falls within the nine size/style boxes (e.g., create a scatterplot of each investment within an equity index). For example, when comparing two equities within the large-cap value box, a scatterplot may reveal that one of these companies has a higher market cap and is solidly valued while the other may be closer to medium-cap and a blend investment style. Managers can also break the nine boxes into additional equity style classifications such as micro-cap growth.

Advantages to segmenting by size and style include:

- Portfolio managers can better address client investment considerations in terms of risk and return characteristics.
- The potential for greater diversification benefits by investing across different sectors or industries.

- The ability to construct relevant benchmarks for funds that invest in a specific size/style category.
- The ability to analyze how company characteristics change over time. For example, as a small-cap growth company matures it may move into the mid-cap or large-cap categories and shift towards blended from pure growth.

The last advantage is also a disadvantage in that the categories are not stable over time.

Geography

This approach categorizes international markets by stage of economic development, such as developed markets, emerging markets, and frontier markets. Examples for each economic development stage include the following:

- *Developed markets*: United States, United Kingdom, Germany, Australia, and Japan.
- *Emerging markets*: Brazil, Russia, India, China, and South Africa.
- *Frontier markets*: Iceland, Estonia, Nigeria, Jordan, and Vietnam.

The main advantage to geographic segmentation is that investors with significant domestic market exposure can better understand how to diversify across international markets. One disadvantage to this approach is that investing in international equity markets may subject investors to currency risk. Another disadvantage is an overestimation of the diversification benefit. For example, a domestic investor from a developed market purchases stock in large companies in a foreign market to diversify. But the companies may have already diversified their business internationally and may even derive much of their income from the investor's country.

Economic Activity

This approach groups companies into sectors or industries by applying either a market-oriented or a production-oriented approach. A *market-oriented approach* segments companies by markets served, how products are used by consumers, and how cash flows are generated. A *production-oriented approach* segments companies by products manufactured and inputs required during the production process. Note that applying either approach may lead to slightly different classifications. For example, a market-oriented approach may classify a coal company in the energy sector, while a production-oriented approach may classify that same company in the basic materials sector.

The four primary classification structures for segmenting companies by economic activity are:

- Global Industry Classification Standard (GICS).
- Industrial Classification Benchmark (ICB).
- Thomson Reuters Business Classification (TRBC).
- Russell Global Sectors Classification (RGS).

The GICS applies a market-oriented approach, while the remaining structures apply a production-oriented approach. Each of these structures starts with a broad sector/industry classification and then divides further by subsector/sub-industry. As an example, consider the segmentation method shown in Figure 13.2 for the GICS Consumer Staples sector.

Figure 13.2: GICS Classification Example

Sector	Consumer Staples
Industry Group	Food, Beverage, and Tobacco
Industry	Beverages
Sub-Industry	Soft Drinks

PROFESSOR'S NOTE

The four classification structures differ on their application of sector versus industry. For example, GICS, TRBC, and RGS refer to their top level as sectors and then subdivide into industries. In contrast, ICB starts with industries and then subdivides into sectors.

An advantage to economic activity segmentation is that it allows portfolio managers to analyze, compare, and construct performance benchmarks based on specific sectors/industries. In addition, diversification benefits are enhanced when investments span different sectors/industries. The main disadvantage to this approach is that some companies, especially larger firms, may have business operations that are not easily assigned to one specific sector or industry.

Equity Indices and Benchmarks

Equity market indices and equity portfolio benchmarks can be constructed based on a combination of size/style and geographic segmentation. For example, the MSCI Europe Large Cap Value Index and the MSCI China Small Cap Index combine elements from both size/style and geographic classifications. Economic activity can also be used to subdivide equity indices by sector or industry. For example, the MSCI World Energy Index and the S&P Global Natural Resources Index track global companies categorized by sector/industry. Equity indices can also track unique client considerations, such as ESG practices.

MODULE QUIZ 13.1

1. Equities typically offer diversification benefits when combined with other major asset classes in a portfolio. **Discuss** *two* reasons an economic crisis may affect the ris< reduction archived through diversification.

2. Assume an investor is segmenting the equity investment universe by economic activity. **Describe** *two* advantages for applying this segmentation approach.

Video covering this content is available online.

MODULE 13.2: PORTFOLIO INCOME AND COSTS, SHAREHOLDER ENGAGEMENT, PASSIVE/ACTIVE MANAGEMENT

LOS 13.c: Describe the types of income and costs associated with owning and managing an equity portfolio and their potential effects on portfolio performance.

There are several ways to earn (current) income from an equity portfolio.

Dividend income is the most obvious and often the largest. One additional consideration is how the dividends are taxed; they may be subject to income and/or withholding tax. Note that investors with a growth-oriented focus are less likely to seek portfolio income from dividends.

Some companies pay an **optional stock dividend**, which allows investors to choose between cash payments or stock dividends (i.e., new shares). This "option" between cash and stock dividends has value for the investor and can even be sold to another investor to immediately monetize the "option." On occasion some companies pay a **special dividend**, a one-time cash payment to investors (as opposed to the more typical periodic regular dividend).

Securities lending is another way to generate current income. Securities lending is often part of short selling. A short sale is the sale of a security that is not owned. To make the short sale, the seller must typically borrow the security in order to deliver it to the buyer when the short sale is made. The lender of the security is typically paid a fee and may also receive collateral or cash on which they can also earn a return. The lender also receives back the security lent at a future date. Securities lending is not unusual in index funds large institutional portfolios such as pension funds and endowments.

Security or **stock lending** does introduce additional issues. Short selling (like any sale) tends to drive down the securities price, which is not particularly beneficial to the lender (who still owns) the security. This is more likely to concern an active manager who expects their holdings to outperform, as opposed to a passive index fund manager. The lender must also be concerned with the quality of the borrower and the borrower's ability to return the securities. The borrower must also compensate the lender for any dividend payments that occur during the period of the loan. The lender generally loses the right to vote the shares during the period of the loan.

Lenders typically collect a small fee, in the range of 0.2%–0.5% annually for developed markets. This fee can increase substantially for emerging market stock loans or stocks that are in high demand for borrowing, known as *specials*. As mentioned, lenders can also earn extra income by reinvesting the borrower's posted cash collateral. However, this reinvestment would be subject to various risks, such as market, credit, and operational risk. The reinvestment is likely to incur costs such as administration costs to keep track of everything.

Additional income strategies include:

- Writing options (i.e., selling options) to earn option premiums. A **covered call** strategy involves writing a call option on a stock owned. The writer then loses the upside of the security if the price increases above the strike price. Another option strategy is a **cash-covered put** (also known as a cash-secured put). This involves selling a put option on stock and setting aside sufficient cash equivalents to pay for the stock if the put option buyer exercises their right. The risk to the seller is the put buyer will only exercise the right if the stock declines in value.
- **Dividend capture** where an investor buys a stock right before its ex-dividend date, holds that stock through the ex-dividend date (entitling the investor to receive the dividend payment), and then sells the stock. The strategy is premised on and will be profitable if the stock price declines by less than the amount of the dividend. Theory says the stock should decline by the dividend amount but stock movements may differ from expectations given market forces (e.g., supply and demand) and/or income tax considerations.

Equity portfolios also incur fees and costs. These include:

- **Management** and **performance (incentive)** fees.
- **Administration** fees.
- **Marketing** and **distribution** fees.
- **Trading** costs.
- **Investment strategy** costs.

Management fees (i.e., ad valorem fees) compensate the manager and pay research and analysis, computer hardware and software, compliance, and processing trades. These fees are typically based on a percentage of assets under management and are due at regular time intervals (e.g., annually). The management fees vary and are usually higher for actively managed portfolios due to higher levels of investment analysis and portfolio turnover. The management fees are usually presented as a standard schedule of fees although they can be negotiated.

Some managers also earn **performance fees** (i.e., **incentive fees**) when the portfolio outperforms a stated return objective. These fees are more common for hedge funds and alternative managers. For example, suppose a portfolio exceeds a threshold return, the manager may earn a performance fee in the range of 10%–20% based on any capital appreciation above the threshold. Incentive fees are often one sided; the manager shares in outperformance but is not penalized for underperformance.

To protect an investor from paying for performance twice, there may be a **high-water mark**. For example, assume a hedge fund earns a performance fee for outperforming its return objective and then the portfolio declines in value. The manager will only earn an incentive fee on future appreciation above the previous level that was already compensated for.

PROFESSOR'S NOTE

We are about to briefly discuss various types of fees and costs associated with equity (and other) assets. Managers may charge one management fee that covers all of these. In other cases the manager may break out some or all of these and present them as separate fees. Other managers may not provide some of these services and a separate third party provides and charges for them. The bottom line is that services are not free and must be paid for. The way the bill is presented varies and investors need to consider all the costs in total.

Portfolios may be subject to **administration fees** associated with corporate activities, such as measuring risk/return and voting on company issues. The manager may include these services in the basic management fee; however, if these functions are conducted by external parties, administration fees will likely be separate from management fees. Additional administrative type fees include the following:

- *Custody fees*: charged for having a custodian hold assets independent of the portfolio manager.
- *Depository fees*: charged to assist custodians with segregating portfolio assets and for verifying portfolio compliance with investment limits, such as leverage and cash requirements.
- *Registration fees*: charged for registering ownership of mutual fund shares.

Some firms also charge separate **marketing** and **distribution** fees to cover:

- Employing marketing, sales, and client services teams.
- Advertising investment products and services.
- Sponsoring and presenting at relevant conferences.
- Developing and distributing marketing materials (e.g., brochures).
- Fees from online platforms that offer multiple fund options (i.e., platform fees).
- Sales commissions from financial intermediary services (e.g., financial planners or brokers).

Trading costs (i.e., transaction costs) refer to costs associated with buying and selling securities. These transaction costs can be either explicit or implicit. *Explicit costs* include broker commissions, stock exchange fees, and taxes. *Implicit costs* include bid-ask spreads, price impact from the transaction, and delay costs (i.e., slippage costs) from not completing an entire trade due to illiquidity.

Investment strategy costs are an implicit cost related to the chosen investment strategy. As mentioned earlier, actively managed funds that require more investment analysis and transactions will have higher fees/costs than passively managed funds. However passive funds like index funds may be subject to hidden costs from *predatory trading*. This additional cost stems from predatory traders purchasing (selling) shares that are soon to be added (removed) from an equity index. These transactions will create price impact costs for the fund and a profit for the predatory trader.

Strategies may demand or provide liquidity. For example, momentum strategies tend to demand liquidity by buying shares in an increasing market and selling shares in a decreasing market. This is likely to create high market impact costs. Contrarian strategies are the opposite and tend to supply liquidity by buying shares in a decreasing market and selling shares in an increasing market. This is likely to create low market impact costs. Passive index replication strategies are likely to fall in the middle.

Shareholder Engagement

LOS 13.d: Describe the potential benefits of shareholder engagement and the role an equity manager might play in shareholder engagement.

Shareholder engagement refers to investors and managers interacting with companies in ways to potentially favorably impact the stock price. Engagement also benefits the company with improved corporate governance. Engagement includes participating in calls with the company and/or voting on corporate issues at general meetings (i.e., general assemblies). Such meetings may discuss:

- *Corporate strategy*: Company objectives, constraints, growth opportunities, and resources. Additional items may include company research, culture, products, competitive environment, and sustainability. Prioritizing stakeholder interests and balancing short-term obligations with long-term goals may also be items of interest for shareholders.
- *Capital allocation*: Selection process for new projects that add value, and strategy for potential mergers and acquisitions. Shareholders may also be interested in capital expenditures, use of leverage, payment of dividends, and equity financing.
- *Corporate governance*: Internal controls and functions of the company's audit and risk committees. Additional items include how the company manages regulatory and political risks.

- *Compensation structures*: Top management remuneration, incentives, and alignment with shareholder interests. Larger shareholders may influence future compensation structures.
- *Composition of the board of directors*: The board's experience, competence, diversity, culture, and effectiveness. Additional items include succession planning to address departing board members.

Shareholder engagement is not free because it requires an investment of time and resources.

- Active managers are more likely to do so in order to influence the company in ways they expect will improve performance.
- Passive managers are more likely to focus on minimizing these costs for themselves and for the companies they invest in.
- Larger investors can more easily absorb these costs as they spread the costs over a large amount of assets.
- Successful engagement benefits all shareholders, including "free riders." Free riders do not engage but reap the same benefit from any increase in the stock price.
- Engagement can also be used to address nonfinancial concerns (e.g., ESG issues), though such benefits may be harder to quantify.
- Other stakeholders such as employees, customers, creditors, regulators, and governments are also impacted by shareholder engagement outcomes. After engagement activities, these stakeholders may have more or less influence on a given company. For example, decisions to reduce company costs may impact employee compensation. The act of shareholder engagement can also be influenced by external factors, such as academic research or media coverage.

Beyond the issues of time, cost, and free riders; shareholder engagement has other limitations. Engagement may:

- Focus on short-term goals such as increasing cash flows or stock prices at the expense of the company's long-term goals.
- Lead to the acquisition of material, nonpublic information; increasing the risk of insider trading.
- Create potential conflicts of interest. For instance, an engaged portfolio manager may support company management because the management also invests in the manager's fund.

Equity managers play a key role in engagement and may assign specific employees responsibility for this task. Firms may also consult with outside experts for advice on shareholder voting and monitoring corporate governance issues. Some countries set legal and regulatory requirements and require firms to establish written documentation for how to meet these obligations.

Activist investing takes engagement even further. Activist investors may:

- Propose shareholder resolutions and launch media campaigns to influence the vote.
- Seek representation on the company's board of directors.
- Launch proxy fights to achieve their goals. A proxy fight means seeking to persuade other shareholders to support their proposals.

Active/Passive Management for Equity Portfolios

LOS 13.e: Describe rationales for equity investment across the passive–active spectrum.

Passive investors seek to replicate an equity market index or benchmark. Active managers seek to outperform the benchmark and add value. While the distinction seems clear, the reality is strategies may blur this distinction, such as closely track the index with limited deviations allowed to add some value. Active investing is riskier as the manager could also underperform the benchmark. Rationales for shifting to active management include:

- Confidence the manager has the expert knowledge and skill to add value.
- Client preferences—unless enough investors are interested, the manager will not be able to attract enough funds to cover the costs of active investing. Growth strategies are often seen as more likely to benefit from active management while value style may be more passive.
  - Managers must also manage the investor's expectations for what to reasonably expect from the strategy; investors with unreasonable expectations are more likely to become dissatisfied.
  - However, strategies that become too popular can also be a problem. Too much capital flowing in may make it harder to find opportunities to add value.
  - Managers must also select an appropriate benchmark that investors will be interested in. The benchmark should contain a broad range of underlying equities with sufficient liquidity to support active management. Narrow limited benchmarks don't give the manager much room to deviate and are likely to support a more passive approach.
- Mandates from clients to invest in certain companies (e.g., ESG considerations) may require a more active approach as the manager may need to use screening and other techniques to meet the mandates.

The results of active management are less certain and the costs are higher. Active management is also subject to other potential risks:

- *Reputation risk* results from violations of rules, regulations, client agreements, or moral principles.

- *Key person risk* results from individuals who are essential to the success of the fund leaving the investment firm.
- *Higher portfolio turnover* which can lead to higher tax burdens. Active funds could be structured to limit tax consequences, but the techniques used to do this can themselves be costly and risky. Managers who use such techniques need additional knowledge to navigate the applicable tax regulations, which of course vary by country and situation.

MODULE QUIZ 13.2

1. **Explain** why actively managed portfolios are typically subject to higher fees and costs than passively managed portfolios.

2. **Explain** how shareholder engagement can benefit investors who are not actively involved in company issues.

3. **Identify** two disadvantages of shareholder engagement activities.

4. A client is concerned with low fees, seeks substantial value added versus their benchmark, has numerous ESG restrictions, and has selected a narrowly defined benchmark made up of large companies. Based on the client's concerns, **explain** *two* reasons the client should favor a passive approach and *two* reasons the client should favor an active approach.

5. Compared to passively managed funds, active funds tend to have higher research and trading costs. **Identify** and **describe** *two* additional types of risk for active managers and investors.

KEY CONCEPTS

LOS 13.a

The roles of equities in a portfolio include capital appreciation, dividend income, diversification benefits, and the potential to hedge inflation.

The allocation to equity must be consistent with the client's investment objectives and constraints. For investors with environmental, social, and governance (ESG) considerations, portfolio managers may apply negative or positive screening approaches to select appropriate companies or use thematic or impact investing techniques.

LOS 13.b

The equity investment universe can be segmented by:

- Size (market capitalization) and style (growth, value, or blended).
- Geographic segmentation (which includes developed markets, emerging markets, and frontier markets).
- Economic activity segmentation by sectors or industries. Classification can be based on a market-oriented or a production-oriented approach.
- Or combinations of the previous can be used.

LOS 13.c

Income can be generated from:

- Dividends, mostly in the form of regular dividends received.
- Lending securities for a fee and earning funds on cash collateral received.
- Writing options for the premium received.
- Dividend capture through buying a stock just before and selling it just after it goes ex-dividend.

Managers typically charge regular and some charge performance-based management fees. Some managers cover all services in the management fee. Others also charge additional fees for specific additional services, or coordinate with third-party providers who provide and charge fees for specific services. The bottom line is to determine the total fees regardless of how they are broken down.

Other costs to consider are:

- Transaction and trading costs, which may be explicit or implicit.
- Strategy costs—generally active strategies will have higher cost. Passive strategies may incur hidden costs such as predatory pricing when others anticipate and trade ahead of the passive investor.
- Liquidity demands—momentum strategies that buy in up or sell in down markets demand liquidity and typically pay high market impact costs. Contrarian strategies are the opposite.

LOS 13.d

Shareholder engagement refers to shareholders and managers seeking to influence the companies they invest in through calls and/or shareholder voting. Engagement benefits the company with improved corporate governance. It may benefit shareholders through higher stock price. Free riders who don't incur the costs of engagement also benefit.

Activist investors take this further and propose resolutions to be voted on and seek the support of others or engage in proxy fights to achieve their goals.

LOS 13.e

Equity portfolios are often characterized as being actively or passively managed. However, in practice, portfolios may exhibit characteristics from both investment strategies. Rationales for equity portfolios to span across the passive–active spectrum include manager confidence, client preferences, benchmark selection, client mandates, active management costs/risks, and taxes.

ANSWER KEY FOR MODULE QUIZZES

Module Quiz 13.1

1. Risk reduction is likely to be less than expected.
   - The correlations are likely to move upward towards 1.0.
   - The volatility of the assets is likely to increase.

   (LOS 13.a)

2.
   - It allows portfolio managers to analyze, compare, and construct performance benchmarks based on specific sectors or industries.
   - Diversification benefits are enhanced when investing across sectors or industries.

   (LOS 13.b)

Module Quiz 13.2

1. Such funds require more investment analysis and portfolio turnover than passively managed funds. (LOS 13.c)

2. They can earn a free ride, benefiting from the activities of others to increase the stock price without the time and cost of engagement. (LOS 13.d)

3. (1) The cost and time commitment from shareholders and management, (2) the desire to influence cash flows or stock prices in the short term, at the expense of long-term goals, (3) the potential for insider trading violations, and (4) the potential for conflicts of interest. (LOS 13.d)

4. Passive: (1) Passive managers can charge lower fees; (2) The narrowly *defined* benchmark of presumably efficient large cap stocks is not going to provide the opportunity for active managers to find ways to add value.

   Active: (1) Active management is required to meet the desired value added; (2) The ESG restrictions will require an active manager who uses various screening and other techniques to simultaneously meet this constraint *and* the overall objectives. This client sounds highly unrealistic in their objectives, but that was not the question asked. (LOS 13.e)

5.
   - Reputation risk results from violations to rules, regulations, client agreements, or moral principles.
   - Key person risk results from essential individuals leaving the investment firm.

   (LOS 13.e)

READING 14

Passive Equity Investing

EXAM FOCUS

This is the second of four equity readings. The first one is an introduction, the current reading discusses passive management, and the last two discuss active equity portfolio management. This reading starts by covering benchmarks and methods used in constructing indexes along with index rebalancing and reconstitution. The reading then shifts to discussing different approaches to investing passively (e.g., pooled investments such as ETFs). The focus then shifts to the construction of passively managed portfolios from full replication to optimization. The reading ends with a discussion on tracking error and attribution analysis.

MODULE 14.1: BENCHMARKS

Video covering this content is available online.

LOS 14.a: Discuss considerations in choosing a benchmark for a passively managed equity portfolio.

An equity index used as a benchmark for equity investment strategies must be (1) rules-based, (2) transparent, and (3) investable.

Rules-based: The rules for including and excluding stocks in the portfolio, the weighting scheme, and the rebalancing frequency must be consistent, objective, and predictable so investors can replicate the investment performance of the index.

Transparent: The rules underlying the index are public, clearly stated, and understandable to investors.

Investable: Investors can replicate the return and risk performance of the index.

Considerations in choosing a benchmark include (1) determining the desired market and risk exposures, and (2) identifying the methods used in constructing and maintaining the index.

Market and Risk Exposures

The choice of portfolio exposure includes the choice of which markets to invest in as well as the various risks the portfolio will be exposed to. Overall, these choices depend on the investor's risk and return objectives and portfolio constraints identified in the investment policy statement.

Some examples of **market exposure** choices are:

- Choosing between broad market exposure and focused exposure to certain sectors.
- Choosing between domestic or international exposure.
- Choosing among developed, emerging, or frontier markets.

The **risk factor exposure** of a passive portfolio refers to the expected sensitivity of portfolio returns to various risk factors. Recall that a multifactor model of returns uses multiple risk factors, while the CAPM is based on a single-factor market risk. Examples of risk factors used in portfolio construction include market risk (beta), firm size, style (e.g., growth vs. value), and prior returns (momentum). Other factors considered include the liquidity, volatility, and firm "quality." We examine portfolio risk factors in greater detail later in this review.

Identifying the Methods Used in Constructing and Maintaining an Index

The construction of an index starts with the method of identifying stocks to include; this method can be **exhaustive** (every stock in a defined universe; e.g., the CRSP U.S. Total Market Index) or **selective** (a subset of stocks within a universe; e.g., the S&P 500 Index or the Dow Jones Industrial Average [DJIA]).

Methods of index-weighting include (1) market-cap weighting, (2) price weighting, (3) equal weighting, and (4) fundamental weighting.

Market-cap weighting refers to weighting each portfolio stock by its total market capitalization as a percentage of the total capitalization of all the stocks in the index. The market portfolio in the CAPM and many indexes, such as the S&P 500, are market-cap weighted. The most common market-cap weighting method in practice is based on each stock's free-floating shares (i.e., outstanding shares that are not closely held and, therefore, available for trading by market participants).

Price weighting refers to weighting each portfolio stock by its price. This can be achieved with a portfolio that holds an equal number of shares of each index stock, which gives stocks with higher share prices larger index weights. The DJIA is an example of a price-weighted index.

Equal weighting refers to investing equal amounts in each portfolio stock. Equal weighting reduces concentration risk, especially compared to market-cap weighting for the large-cap segment where capitalizations vary widely. For example, the weight of the five largest firms in the S&P 500 Index in 2018 was greater than the weight of the 250 smallest firms in the index. Equal weighting also reduces changes in sector exposures as market prices change compared to market-cap weighting. Equal weighting is factor-indifferent; it randomizes factor mispricing and, because of its small-cap bias relative to market-cap weighting, returns are more volatile than for market-cap weighting. Equal weighting can produce marginally better returns before transaction costs when stock prices vary around their intrinsic values.

Fundamental weighting refers to weighting index stocks by their proportions of the total index value of a fundamental factor, such as sales, income, or dividends. For example, a stock of a firm that pays 3% of all the dividends paid by index companies will have a 3% weight in a dividend-weighted index.

Stock concentration is a key concern in the selection of the appropriate index. Concentration can be captured using the concept of "effective number of stocks," which can be measured using the **Herfindahl-Hirschman index (HHI)**. HHI is the sum of the squared weights of the individual stocks in the portfolio:

$$\text{HHI} = \sum_{i=1}^{n} w_i^2$$

where:

n = number of stocks in the portfolio

w_i = weight of stock *i*

HHI ranges from $\frac{1}{n}$ (an equally weighted portfolio) to 1 (a single stock portfolio), so as HHI increases, concentration risk increases.

The *effective number* of stocks is the reciprocal of the HHI:

$$\text{effective number of stocks} = \frac{1}{\text{HHI}}$$

For example, a market-cap weighted index with 500 stocks might have an HHI of 0.01 and, therefore, an effective number of stocks of $\frac{1}{0.01} = 100$. The fact that 100 is less than the number of stocks in the portfolio reflects the disproportionate effect of the largest capitalization stocks in the index. An *equal weighted* index of 500 stocks would have an HHI of 0.002 and an effective number of stocks of $\frac{1}{0.002} = 500$.

Rebalancing is the process of adjusting portfolio weights as index weightings change. For an equal weighted index, portfolio weights are no longer equal as soon as prices change. Price-weighted index weights change in response to stock splits and stock dividends. Market-cap-weighted portfolio weights require rebalancing when index firms issue new shares or repurchase shares in a significant amount. Rebalancing incurs trading costs (and possibly tax costs) and will decrease returns. To reduce such costs, rebalancing is often done only periodically, often quarterly.

Reconstitution is the process of removing and replacing stocks that no longer fit the desired market exposure of an index. For example, if a small-cap stock's capitalization increases, it may become a mid-cap stock and have to be removed from and possibly replaced in a small-cap index. Reconstitution will also reduce index portfolio returns as trading costs are incurred.

Two practices are used to reduce trading costs associated with migration of a stock between indexes on reconstitution dates. **Buffering** refers to the practice of establishing a threshold level for the change in a firm's capitalization rank that must be met before moving it from one index to another on a reconstitution date. Consider a large-cap index comprising the stocks of the 200 largest firms in a market and a mid-cap index of the next 300 stocks in capitalization rank. If a firm in the mid-cap index increases in capitalization so that it is one of the largest 200 firms, it is not actually moved into the large-cap index until its rank increases beyond the *buffer zone*—for example, until it has reached the size rank of 150 or higher at the next reconstitution date.

An alternative method of reducing the transaction costs of stock migration among indexes is termed **packeting**. With packeting, when a mid-cap company's capitalization increases so that it qualifies as large-cap stock, half of the portfolio position is moved to the large-cap index on the reconstitution date. If the stock still meets the criteria for inclusion in the large-cap index at the next reconstitution date, the remainder of the position is moved from the mid-cap to the large-cap index.

LOS 14.b: Compare passive factor-based strategies to market-capitalization-weighted indexing.

The CAPM is a single-factor model in which the only risk factor that drives returns is the return on the market portfolio, and the risk of individual securities is measured by their beta (market risk). Multifactor models consider multiple risk factors, and returns on individual securities are the result of their exposures to, and the returns to, these risk factors. Fama and French (2015) identify five risk factors that can be used to explain the variation in (total) returns across equity securities. These five factors are:

- Market risk (based on beta, standardized covariance of returns with the return on the market).
- Firm size (market value of equity).
- Book-to-market value (shareholders' equity divided by market value of equity).
- Operating profitability (operating income divided by beginning shareholders' equity).
- Investment intensity (growth rate of total assets).

Indexes with a high exposure to a specific risk factor are created to allow investors to augment or replace a market-cap-weighted index based on their beliefs about future returns to the various risk factors. Available indexes with greater or less exposure to a factor than broad-based index funds are typically structured as **exchange-traded funds (ETFs)**.

Factor-weighted portfolios are rules-based, so they have lower operating costs than traditional actively managed funds but typically have higher costs than large-cap-weighted index funds. Factor-based index funds themselves are considered passive, as they are rules-based and typically transparent and replicable. However, emphasizing some factors and de-emphasizing others relative to the overall market portfolio is a form of active portfolio management.

Returns-oriented indexes and strategies include the following:

- Momentum-based indexes typically overweight stocks that have outperformed a benchmark index over the most recent period of a specified length.
- Dividend yield strategies often overweight stocks with relatively high dividends, or dividend growth rates.
- Fundamental-weighted index strategies are based on company fundamentals such as dividends, sales, and income.

Passive factor-based strategies frequently involve an element of active decision-making by altering the risk factor exposures and exploiting out-of-favor factors in an attempt to increase returns relative to a market-cap-weighted portfolio. Decisions regarding factor selection, weighting, and rebalancing tend to be transparent, allowing other investors to mimic the strategy. This can reduce or eliminate the opportunity for higher returns. The buy-sell actions of investors may move prices and reduce or eliminate the opportunity for increased factor returns.

There are three types of passive factor-based strategies: (1) return oriented, (2) risk oriented, and (3) diversification oriented.

Return-oriented strategies include dividend yield, momentum, and fundamentally weighted strategies, as noted previously.

Risk-oriented strategies include volatility weighting (where the weights are the inverse of price volatility) and minimum-variance investing (using the traditional Markowitz framework), where portfolios are selected that minimize portfolio variance, subject to constraints (such as maximum or minimum sector or country weights). The advantages of risk-oriented strategies are that they are simple and provide risk reduction. However, they are based on past return data, and as such may not reflect future conditions and outcomes.

Diversification-oriented strategies include equally weighted portfolios (as discussed previously) and maximum diversification strategies (achieved by maximizing the ratio of the weighted average volatility of the individual stocks to the portfolio volatility).

Passive factor-based strategies often use multiple benchmarks, including both factor-based and market-cap-weighted indexes, which can increase tracking error.

The advantage of passive factor-based investing is that it is typically less costly than active management but still allows for different factor exposures based on the investor's view of future factor returns. A disadvantage is that, relative to passive cap-weighted investing, management fees and trading commissions are typically higher.

MODULE QUIZ 14.1

1. Which of the following is a necessary characteristic for an equity index to have in order to use it as a benchmark for a passively managed equity portfolio?
   A. Selective.
   B. Investable.
   C. Flexible.
2. A small-cap, high P/E factor-based investment strategy is *best* classified as:
   A. risk oriented.
   B. return oriented.
   C. diversification oriented.

MODULE 14.2: APPROACHES TO PASSIVE INVESTING

Video covering this content is available online.

LOS 14.c: Compare different approaches to passive equity investing.

Three common approaches to passive equity investing involve the use of (1) pooled investments, (2) derivatives-based strategies, and (3) separately managed index-based portfolios.

Pooled investments include open-end mutual funds and ETFs. The advantages of open-end mutual funds are low transaction costs and the convenience of the fund structure. The advantages of ETFs are that they trade intraday (not just at market close each day) and they do not have to sell stocks in response to shareholder redemption requests. This eliminates taxable gains from portfolio stock sales that shareholders are exposed to with open-end mutual funds. The disadvantages include higher transaction costs from commissions and the bid-ask spread, as well as possible illiquidity in some ETF secondary markets.

Derivatives-based strategies use derivatives (options, futures, and swap contracts) to recreate the risk/return performance of an index. Derivative positions used to adjust the existing portfolio risk and return exposures may be called *overlay positions*, reflecting that they are used to modify the underlying portfolio positions. *Completion overlays* can move the portfolio back to the risk exposure of the index, for example, by adjusting the portfolio's beta to match the index beta. *Rebalancing overlays* can efficiently and cheaply match the reconstitution of the index as securities are added and dropped. *Currency overlays* adjust the foreign exchange risk of portfolio holdings denominated in a foreign currency.

Advantages of using equity index derivatives (options, futures, and swaps) over cash-based portfolio construction techniques are that derivatives:

- Can be used to quickly adjust a portfolio's factor exposures at low cost.
- Trade in liquid markets.
- Make it easy to leverage the portfolio.

Disadvantages include:

- Derivative positions have finite expirations, so they must be rolled over at or near expiration.
- Some contracts have position limits.
- Specialty portfolio needs might not be met by the existing offerings of exchange-traded derivative contracts.
- OTC derivatives introduce counterparty risk.
- Basis risk can increase tracking error.

Separately managed equity index-based portfolios hold all the constituent stocks in the index or a representative sample. They require regularly updated data on the index; sophisticated trading and accounting systems; well-established broker relationships to facilitate program trading and lower trading commissions; and compliance systems to ensure compliance with laws, regulations, and internal company policies.

LOS 14.d: Compare the full replication, stratified sampling, and optimization approaches for the construction of passively managed equity portfolios.

Passively managed index-based equity portfolios can be constructed by (1) full replication (hold all of the securities in the index), (2) holding a sample of the securities based on stratified sampling, or (3) using more complex optimization to maximize desirable characteristics while minimizing undesirable characteristics. In practice, a blend of these approaches may be used.

Full Replication

Full replication can be costly when there are large numbers of stock and liquidity is limited. The portfolio must be regularly reconstituted and rebalanced. The advantage of full replication is that it closely matches the index return (before transaction costs).

Stratified Sampling

To reduce the costs of full replication but still approximate the factor exposures of the underlying index, a manager may use **stratified sampling**. With stratified sampling, index stocks are divided into strata (subsets) based on key risk characteristics. Random samples of stocks within each strata are selected for inclusion in the portfolio. The weight of the stocks selected for each strata are such that the portfolio risk factor exposures match those of the index portfolio.

The strata of the constituent stocks must be mutually exclusive and exhaustive. The strata are often formed across multiple dimensions; for example, one strata may contain large capitalization stocks that have high-dividend yields and low momentum. Industry sector and country of domicile are also candidates for the characteristics of strata. The more criteria used in constructing strata, the smaller the tracking error—the degree to which the portfolio performance deviates from the index.

The manager must consider size of the sample used (i.e., how closely to approach full replication). Initially, tracking error declines as the size of the sample is increased. The manager will naturally first purchase the largest, most liquid, lowest cost stocks. But as more stocks are added and the portfolio approaches full replication, the added stocks will be less liquid, increasing the effect of transaction costs on tracking error.

Optimization

Optimization uses mean-variance analysis to minimize tracking error. The optimization typically maximizes a desirable result (e.g., returns) or minimizes an undesirable characteristic (e.g., variance), subject to one or more constraints. For an index portfolio, optimization seeks to minimize tracking error relative to the underlying index, and constraints may include a minimum number of stocks, a style tilt that matches that of the underlying index, or a minimum capitalization, among other possibilities. Optimization can be combined with stratified sampling, with optimization performed on each strata of a stratified sample.

A drawback of optimization is that it is based on historical relationships, which will change over time. Maintaining the optimal weights as these relationships change can be costly. Additionally, minimization of tracking error can result in portfolios that are not mean-variance efficient.

The advantages of optimization techniques are reduction of tracking error relative to stratified sampling and that they explicitly account for the covariances of constituent stock returns, rather than relying on a characteristic, such as industry sector, in constructing the portfolio.

Blended Approach

Full replication is preferred for indexes with small numbers of similar liquid stocks, while stratified sampling or optimization is preferable for indexes with many heterogeneous, thinly traded, small-capitalization stocks. For indexes with a large number of stocks—ranging from large and liquid to small and thinly traded, such as the Wilshire 5000—the manager may use a blended approach, with full replication for large liquid index stocks and stratified sampling or optimization for index stocks that are thinly traded.

MODULE QUIZ 14.2

1. **Discuss** *two* advantages and *two* disadvantages of using equity index derivatives versus cash-based strategies for passive equity investing.

2. **Discuss** the advantages and disadvantages of using ETFs to implement a passive equity investing strategy.

3. As the number of constituent stocks in an index increases, the tracking error of a passively managed portfolio that uses the index as a benchmark will *most likely*:
   A. increase.
   B. decrease.
   C. first decrease and then eventually increase.

MODULE 14.3: TRACKING ERROR, RETURN, AND RISK

Video covering this content is available online.

LOS 14.e: Discuss potential causes of tracking error and methods to control tracking error for passively managed equity portfolios.

Causes of Tracking Error

Tracking error refers to the standard deviation of the differences between index portfolio returns and published index returns. Differences between portfolio returns and index returns are caused by:

- Management fees.
- Commissions on trades.
- Sampling—compared to full replication, sampling typically increases tracking error.
- Intraday trading because index returns are based on closing prices.
- Cash drag—portfolios may hold cash balances that reduce returns in rising markets and increase returns in falling markets, as cash returns differ from index returns.

Controlling Tracking Error

Reducing tracking error involves a tradeoff between the higher trading costs of full replication and the increased potential for tracking error that comes with sampling. Even a passive index fund must do some trading in response to cash inflows and outflows and to reinvest dividends. Derivative positions in index futures can be used to reduce cash drag.

LOS 14.f: Explain sources of return and risk to a passively managed equity portfolio.

Attribution Analysis

The manager of a passively managed equity portfolio needs to understand the sources of index returns in order to effectively manage a portfolio intended to replicate index returns. **Attribution analysis** can be used to help the manager identify the sources of tracking error and hopefully reduce them.

PROFESSOR'S NOTE

Attribution analysis is covered in more detail in a separate section of the curriculum.

Securities Lending

As discussed earlier, large passive portfolios can lend securities to generate additional income, which can offset management fees (and other costs as well if management fees are quite low), thereby reducing tracking error.

Proxy Voting

Even passive managers have a fiduciary duty to vote the proxies of portfolio stocks in the best interests of their investors. By voting in ways that improve operations, better manage risk, or provide better board oversight and corporate governance, returns to index stocks may be increased. Voting proxies effectively can be a costly undertaking for a passive manager who must research a myriad of corporate issues across a broad portfolio of companies. Because of that, many passive managers use proxy-voting services.

MODULE QUIZ 14.3

1. **Explain** what cash drag is and how it results in tracking error.

2. **Explain** why tracking error is a better measure of a passive equity manager's skill than excess return.

3. **Explain** how securities lending can reduce tracking error in passively managed index portfolios.

KEY CONCEPTS

LOS 14.a

An equity index as a benchmark for equity investment strategies must be (1) rules-based, (2) transparent, and (3) investable.

Considerations in choosing a benchmark include (1) determine the desired market exposures, (2) be consistent with the client's objectives and constraints, and (3) identify the method used for constructing the index.

Constructing and maintaining an index involves the following:

- The weighting method to construct the index: (1) market-cap weighting, (2) price weighting, (3) equal weighting, or (4) fundamental weighting.
- Considering the level of stock concentration. The effective number of stocks can be determined as the reciprocal of the Herfindahl-Hirschman index (HHI).

$$\text{HHI} = \sum_{i=1}^{n} w_i^2$$

$$\text{effective number of stocks} = \frac{1}{\text{HHI}}$$

- The frequency of rebalancing (updating the weights of the stocks in the index) and reconstitution (removing and replacing stocks that no longer fit the index market exposure).

LOS 14.b

The return/risk characteristics of an index can be replicated by creating a portfolio with the same exposures to a set of risk factors as the index. This strategy is called a passive factor-based strategy.

Common factors are growth, value, size, yield, momentum, quality, and volatility.

There are three types of passive factor-based strategies: (1) return oriented, (2) risk oriented, and (3) diversification oriented.

LOS 14.c

Three common approaches to passive equity investing involve the use of (1) pooled investments, such as open-end mutual funds and ETFs, (2) derivatives-based strategies, and (3) separately managed index-based portfolios.

LOS 14.d

The three methods of constructing passively managed index-based equity portfolios are (1) hold and match the weights of all the securities in the index (full replication), (2) select a more liquid sample of securities to replicate the index (stratified sampling, often based on cell matching), (3) use a more technical and quantitative approach (optimization) to maximize desirable characteristics, and/or minimize undesirable characteristics. Blended approaches using a combination of these methods are also common.

LOS 14.e

Tracking error initially declines as sample size increases but then increases as costs (transaction, management, and illiquidity) outweigh the gains of increasing sample size. Intraday trading and cash drag also create tracking error.

Reducing tracking error requires a continuing evaluation of the tradeoff between the benefits of larger sample size and increasing costs. Derivatives can be used to reduce the effects of cash drag.

LOS 14.f

Attribution analysis is a key tool in helping the manager identify the sources of tracking error.

Securities lending can generate fee income to offset some of the costs of managing the portfolio and reduce tracking error.

Corporate governance and investor activism are important for both passive and active investors.

ANSWER KEY FOR MODULE QUIZZES

Module Quiz 14.1

1. **B** An equity index that is suitable as a benchmark should be rules-based, transparent, and investable. (LOS 14.a)

2. **B** Fundamentally weighted factor exposure strategies are considered to be return oriented because such strategies focus on the factors that have determined differences in return. (LOS 14.b)

Module Quiz 14.2

1. Advantages: Derivatives are (1) a quick, efficient, and cheap way to adjust exposure and (2) trade in liquid markets.

   Disadvantage: Derivatives (1) have finite expirations and so have to be rolled over, (2) some contracts have position limits, (3) specialty portfolio needs might not be met by the existing offering of exchange-traded derivative contracts, (4) OTC derivatives have counterparty risk, and (5) basis risk can increase tracking error. (LOS 14.c)

2. Advantages: ETFs handle shareholder redemptions more cheaply and efficiently than open-end mutual funds through in-kind delivery of stock. This reduces taxable gains and losses that would otherwise be passed on to shareholders.

   Disadvantages: Transaction costs from commissions and the bid-ask spread as well as illiquidity in some ETF secondary markets. (LOS 14.c)

3. **C** Adding to the sample size with liquid stocks first reduces tracking error; but as less liquid stocks are added, the costs and tracking error increase. (LOS 14.d)

Module Quiz 14.3

1. Even passive portfolios have some cash flows and some cash holdings, while indexes represent theoretical fully invested performance. Over time the cash is a low return asset, reducing the passive portfolio's return. The underperformance increases tracking error. (LOS 14.e)

2. The goal is to consistently match the index's performance and zero (or low) tracking error indicates a perfect (or close) match. (LOS 14.e)

3. Passive portfolios can lend their portfolio stocks to generate fee income (or return on collateral) and cover portfolio expenses. This can produce a better match of index performance, lowering tracking error. (LOS 14.f)

READING 15

Active Equity Investing: Strategies

EXAM FOCUS

This reading focuses on active equity management strategies. It covers factor-based, activist, statistical arbitrage, fundamental, and quantitative strategies. It concludes with style classification based on holdings-based versus returns-based analysis. You will need to know the vocabulary and be able to understand the output, pros, and cons of the processes covered here.

MODULE 15.1: FUNDAMENTAL VS. QUANTITATIVE APPROACHES

Video covering this content is available online.

LOS 15.a: Compare fundamental and quantitative approaches to active management.

Active equity investing seeks to outperform a passive benchmark. At the broadest level, these approaches can be divided into two categories: *fundamental* and *quantitative*.

Fundamental approaches are *subjective in nature*, relying on analyst discretion and judgment. An analyst will carry out and collate research on companies, markets, and economies; then using their skill and experience to estimate the intrinsic value of securities. The research will typically use the company's financial statements as well as insight into its business model, management team and industry positioning to establish a valuation of the company's shares.

These fundamental insights are used to generate forecasts. Higher conviction ideas will receive a larger weight in the portfolio, subject to risk parameters set out in fund mandates. Compared to the quantitative approach, there are likely to be fewer positions in the portfolio and the allocation to each will be larger. Risks to the strategy lie at the individual company level if the analyst has misestimated intrinsic value, or that the market fails to recognize the mispricing and the security remains mispriced. The fundamental manager continuously monitors stock positions and rebalances at any time according to their current opinion.

Quantitative approaches are *objective in nature*, relying on models that generate systematic rules to select investments. Expertise is required in statistical modeling, typically using large amounts of data. Historical data is analyzed to identify relationships between equity returns and variables (called *factors*) that have predictive power. These variables could relate to valuation (e.g., P/E ratio), size (e.g., market capitalization), financial strength (e.g., debt-to-equity ratio), and industry sector or price related attributes (e.g., price momentum).

Quantitative managers focus on identifying relationships between returns and factors across a large group of securities, spreading their factor bets across smaller positions in a larger number of holdings. Portfolio optimization is used to set weights in the portfolio that maximize expected portfolio alpha or information ratio. Risks to the strategy lie at the portfolio level if the factors do not deliver the performance as predicted by the model. The quantitative manager automatically rebalances according to the systematic rules of the strategy at predetermined intervals such as monthly or quarterly.

PROFESSOR'S NOTE

Do not be overly rigid with these definitions. A fundamental manager could use quantitative techniques such as free cash flow modeling, screening, or regression to help establish their opinion. Likewise, quantitative models can be based on data relating to fundamental company information found in their financial statements. The key takeaway is that when it comes to the decision to invest, fundamental investing is based more on an opinion and quantitative investing is based more on rules derived from data driven modeling.

Types of Active Management Strategies: Bottom-Up vs. Top-Down

LOS 15.b: Analyze bottom-up active strategies, including their rationale and associated processes.

LOS 15.c: Analyze top-down active strategies, including their rationale and associated processes.

Both fundamental and quantitative managers can be further categorized as either bottom-up or top-down strategies.

Bottom-up strategies use information about individual companies such as profitability or price momentum to build portfolios by selecting the best individual investments. **Top-down strategies** use information about variables that affect many companies such as the macroeconomic environment and government policies to build portfolios by selecting the best markets or sectors.

Managers can use a blend of bottom-up and top-down approaches. For example, a top-down strategist sets target country or sector weights, and then bottom-up portfolio managers select the best investments consistent with these weights. Or the bottom-up managers could drive the portfolio construction process through selecting the best individual investments, with a top-down-based *derivatives overlay* added to remove unintended macro exposures.

Bottom-Up Strategies

Quantitative bottom-up managers look for quantifiable relationships between company-level information (e.g., P/E ratio) and expected return that will persist into the future.

Fundamental bottom-up managers incorporate both quantifiable and qualitative characteristics of individual companies into their analysis (e.g., business model and branding, competitive advantage, and quality of company management and corporate governance).

PROFESSOR'S NOTE

The key takeaway is that fundamental bottom-up managers are looking for companies with strong business models, high brand quality and loyalty, strong competitive advantage, and good management teams with solid corporate governance because these companies may be best positioned to outperform their peers in the future.

Types of bottom-up strategies include both value-based and growth-based approaches, the sub-styles of which are summarized below:

Value-based approaches attempt to identify securities that are trading below their estimated intrinsic value. Sub-styles of value investing include the following:

- **Relative value**: Comparing price multiples such as P/E and P/B to peers. An undervalued company has an inexplicably low multiple relative to the industry average.
- **Contrarian investing**: Purchasing or selling securities against prevailing market sentiment. For instance, buying the securities of depressed cyclical stocks with low or negative earnings.
- **High-quality value**: Equal emphasis is placed on both intrinsic value and evidence of financial strength, high quality management, and demonstrated profitability (the "Warren Buffet" approach).
- **Income investing**: Focus is on high dividend yields and positive dividend growth rates.
- **Deep-value investing**: Focus is on extremely low valuations relative to assets (e.g., low P/B), often due to financial distress.

- **Restructuring and distressed debt investing**: Investing prior to or during an expected bankruptcy filing. The goal is to release value through restructuring the distressed company or through the company having sufficient assets in liquidation to generate appropriate returns.
- **Special situations**: Identifies mispricings due to corporate events such as divestures, spin-offs, or mergers.

Growth-based approaches attempt to identify companies with revenues, earnings, or cash flows that are expected to grow faster than their industry or the overall market. Analysts will be less concerned about high valuation multiples and more concerned about the source and persistence of the growth rates of the company. Focus could be on:

- Consistent long-term growth.
- Shorter-term earnings momentum.
- **GARP** (growth at a reasonable price); looking for growth at a reasonable valuation. Often this strategy will use the P/E-to-growth (PEG) ratio, which is calculated as the stock's P/E ratio divided by expected earnings growth in percentage terms.

EXAMPLE: Bottom-up strategy securities selection

Company	Share Price	Price to Book Value Ratio	Price to 12-Month Forward EPS	5-Year EPS Growth Forecast	Dividend Yield	Sector Average P/E
TW	3	0.75	1.5	–10%	–0.00%	8
NB	15	7.50	15.0	10%	1.0%	12
SO	30	10.00	20.0	2%	2.0%	30
TO	12	3.00	13.6	4%	9.0%	14

Based on the information in the table, determine which bottom-up investment strategy would most likely select each security. You must choose from the following list and each choice must be used only once.

- Deep value (of assets) investing
- GARP
- Income investing
- Relative value investing

Answer:

TW has the lowest P/B ratio 0.75. This low valuation of assets suggests a deep value approach would be appropriate, provided the analyst addresses reasons for the low valuation.

NB has the lowest PEG ratio of 15 / 10 = 1.5, which is substantially lower than the PEG ratio of the other stocks with positive earnings. This suggests GARP strategies might select this security.

SO has the lowest P/E of 20 versus its sector average of 30; a ratio of only 0.67. This suggests a relative value strategy might select this security, provided there are no obvious reasons why the valuation discount might exist. Note that TW has an even lower P/E versus its sector average P/E at 1.5 / 8 and would also appeal to a relative value strategy. But TW is the only security trading at a P/B below 1 and would be the only security likely to appeal to a deep discount strategy. TW must be selected for deep discount to meet the direction to use each strategy only once.

TO has the highest dividend yield of 1.08 / 12 = 9% which is substantially higher than the other securities. This suggests this company is a good candidate for income investing approaches.

Top-Down Strategies

Both fundamental and quantitative managers could use a top-down approach focusing on the overall macroeconomic environment and broad market variables rather than information relating to individual investments.

Top-down managers typically use broad market ETFs and derivatives to overweight the best markets and underweight the least attractive markets according to the following dimensions:

- Country/geography.
- Industry sector.
- Volatility: Volatility trading can be conducted through VIX futures, variance swaps, or option volatility strategies such as straddles.
- Thematic investment strategies: Focus on opportunities presented by new technologies, changes in regulations, and economic cycles. Themes could be long term and structural such as the shift to cloud computing, blockchain technology, or clean energy. Themes might also be shorter term in nature such as the impact on the value of a currency of a major political vote.

PROFESSOR'S NOTE

Recognize that the CFA curriculum will often list terms with no further explanation. Unless a term is discussed in detail, you are not responsible for researching that term. On the other hand, straddles are discussed in derivatives, which has already been discussed in the Level III curriculum, so of course you will want to be familiar with the basics of how a straddle works, by exam day.

The top-down allocation to country/geography and industry sector could be complemented by further insights from a fundamental bottom-up approach, which values a market through aggregation of the individual companies.

The proliferation over recent years of structured products and focused ETFs has provided managers with greater flexibility in implementing passive factor investing (sometimes referred to as "smart beta" products), allowing the manager to target a specific style or sector at a time when they believe it will outperform.

PROFESSOR'S NOTE

Smart beta is just another example of a new term for an old idea. In original CAPM theory, beta is the systematic risk of the market, and investors should earn a return based on their level of systematic risk exposure. Then CAPM expanded to include other priced risk factors such as market cap and value/growth. Now, smart beta expands that idea by suggesting you identify factors (betas) that are related to systematic return and rotate your portfolio exposures into those betas (factors) that are expected to outperform. So, a smart beta approach is a form of top-down that identifies basic drivers of return as opposed to a bottom-up approach of identifying individual security misvaluations.

MODULE QUIZ 15.1

1. Screening stock markets to identify companies with low price-to-book ratios for subsequent in-depth analysis is a process that could be used by:
   A. quantitative managers only.
   B. fundamental manager only.
   C. both fundamental and quantitative managers.
2. An active bottom-up manager aims to identify companies that have securities that are undervalued relative to the amount that would likely be received in a bankruptcy liquidation situation. This manager's strategy can be *best* described as:
   A. relative value.
   B. restructuring and distressed debt investing.
   C. deep value.
3. Which of the following active equity fund managers is *least likely* following a top-down investment approach?
   A. A manager that uses generalized autoregressive conditional heteroskedasticity (GARCH) models to forecast the volatility of U.S. market with the aim of buying options in times of low implied volatility and selling options in times of high implied volatility.
   B. A manager that aims to identify growth at a reasonable price (GARP) for individual components of the S&P 500.
   C. A manager that aims to identify subsectors of the energy and industrial goods sector that are likely to suffer due to changes to global climate change regulation.

MODULE 15.2: TYPES OF ACTIVE MANAGEMENT STRATEGIES

Video covering this content is available online.

Factor-Based Strategies

LOS 15.d: Analyze factor-based active strategies, including their rationale and associated processes.

A *factor* is a variable or characteristic with which asset returns are correlated. Typical examples are the size and value factors introduced by Fama and French (1993) in their multifactor model. They noticed that smaller companies tend to offer higher returns than larger companies (the *size* factor), and stocks with higher book values relative to market values also tended to outperform (the *value* factor). When such factors are identified, they can be used to rank stocks for investment with the aim of predicting future returns or risks.

Factors that are shown to have a positive association with a long-term positive risk premium are referred to as *rewarded* factors. Care must be taken when identifying factors to avoid factors that do not offer a persistent return (so-called *unrewarded* factors). It is very important that a factor makes intuitive sense. If not, aggressive backtesting of historical data will likely find spurious relationships that will not persist into the future.

PROFESSOR'S NOTE

These factors are the raw ingredients of quantitative (rule-driven) strategies but are also key ideas behind fundamental (judgment based) approaches we have already discussed. Once again, remember that the difference between the fundamental and quantitative approaches is not the rationale for outperformance, but how the decision to invest is made: fundamental is more subjectively driven by the managers and analysts, while quantitative is driven more by rules derived from historical data.

Identifying Factor Performance: The Hedged Portfolio Approach

Pioneered by Fama and French, the hedged portfolio approach follows the following process:

- Rank the investable stock universe by the factor (e.g., for the size factor, rank by market capitalization).
- Divide the universe into quantiles. A quantile is a defined percentage proportion of the universe. For example, the top 10% quantile for the size factor comprise the smallest 10% companies. Typical quantiles are deciles (10%) or quintiles (20%).

- Form a long/short portfolio by going long the best quantile and shorting the worst quantile. For the size factor based on deciles, this portfolio would buy the smallest 10% of the stock universe and short sell the largest 10% of the stock universe.
- The performance of this long/short portfolio is tracked over time and represents the performance of the factor.

Drawbacks to the hedged portfolio approach include:

1. The information in middle quantiles is lost in this approach. It could be that the best performing companies are not in the top quantile, but in a middle quantile. By going long and short the extreme quantiles this would be overlooked in construction of the factor.
2. It is assumed that the relationship between the factor and stock return is linear. In other words, as the factor increases, expected returns increase by a constant amount. Any nonlinear relationship between factors and performance will not be captured by the approach.
3. Portfolios can appear diversified when the manager uses multiple factors to select securities. But if the factors are highly correlated with each other, the diversification is likely to be less than expected.
4. The approach assumes the manager can short stocks to create the hedged portfolio.
5. The hedged portfolio is not a "pure" factor portfolio because it will typically have significant exposures to other risk factors.

A *factor mimicking portfolio* is a theoretical long/short portfolio that is dollar neutral with a unit (i.e., one-for-one) exposure to a chosen factor and an exposure of zero to other factors. These theoretical portfolios tend to be spread across a broad array of stocks. Managers may encounter liquidity and short selling constraints when attempting to construct them.

Investors who are restricted to long-only positions can tilt the portfolio toward factors that are expected to outperform the overall benchmark. If the tilts are modest the portfolio will still have low tracking error and could be considered an enhanced indexing strategy.

Types of Style Factor

Remember that factors can be constructed in any way that the manager chooses. The real value added is in identifying which factors will be predictive of the future.

Factor	Construction	Rationale for Risk Premium
Size	Long: small cap stocks Short: large cap stocks	Small companies at more risk of failure than large established companies
Value	Long: cheap; stocks with high book values to market values, high cash flows and/or low-price multiples Short: expensive companies with the opposite attributes	Could be explained by cheaper companies being more likely to be in financial distress—could also be explained by behavioral biases of market participants
Price momentum	Long: stocks that have recently outperformed Short: stocks that have recently underperformed	Behavioral biases such as belief in momentum that lead to an expectation that recent performance trends will continue
Growth	Long: companies with high historical or expected growth rates in earnings, revenues, and/or cash flows Short: companies with the opposite low growth prospects	Higher than average growth considered an indicator for strong future stock price performance
Quality	Long: companies with high quality earnings, evidenced by low non-cash accrual earnings and/or measures relating to changes in debt levels, profitability, stability or management efficiency measures; market sentiment measures based on analyst revisions could also be used; recent developments include natural language processing (NLP), which gauges sentiment through analysis of the type of language used in news stories Short: companies with low earnings quality with the opposite attributes to the long portfolio	Companies with higher quality earnings or improvement in sentiment are likely to outperform those with low quality earnings and deteriorating sentiment
Unstructured data	Uses big data, which includes both conventional market data and new forms of alternative unstructured data (e.g., satellite images, textual data, credit card data, or social media comments)	Various rationales exist based on the nature of the big data used

Factor Timing

A common subcategory of factor investing is *equity style rotation*, where the manager believes that different factors work well at different times. These strategies allocate to portfolios that represent factor exposures when that particular style is expected to outperform.

Having constructed factors of interest, an analyst might want to investigate what market conditions lead to the factor outperforming. This could involve regressing factor performance against a variable, which is suspected to be a key driver of factor performance. This process is considered in the next example.

EXAMPLE: Establishing drivers of style factor performance

A quantitative manager is investigating whether central bank interest rate decision surprises are a key variable in driving equity style factor performance. They are particularly interested in the three factors of the Fama and French model: market risk, size, and value.

The manager collects monthly performance data for the three style factors and regresses these factor returns against a custom defined variable, $ISurprise_t$ that measures the extent of the surprise of an interest rate decision in a given month *t*. The variable is calculated by comparing the actual interest rate decision of the central bank with the expectations priced into Eurodollar futures contracts the day before the decision.

- A high value for ISurprise_t indicates that the central bank decision was to target rates that were higher than that expected by market participants.
- A low value of ISurprise_t indicates the central bank announced a target policy rate that was below market expectations.

The analyst explores possible contemporaneous and lagged relationships by performing two regressions using the current month's and the next month's factor returns respectively against the variable ISurprise_t:

$$f_{i,t} = \beta_{i,0} + \beta_{i,1}\text{ISurprise}_t + \varepsilon_{i,t}$$

and:

$$f_{i,t+1} = \beta_{i,0} + \beta_{i,1}\text{ISurprise}_t + \varepsilon_{i,t}$$

where $f_{i,t}$ is the return of style factor *i* at time *t* and $f_{i,t+1}$ is the subsequent (next) month's return for style factor *i*.

The regression coefficients are presented in Figure 15.1.

Figure 15.1: Interest Rate Surprises and Style Factor Returns

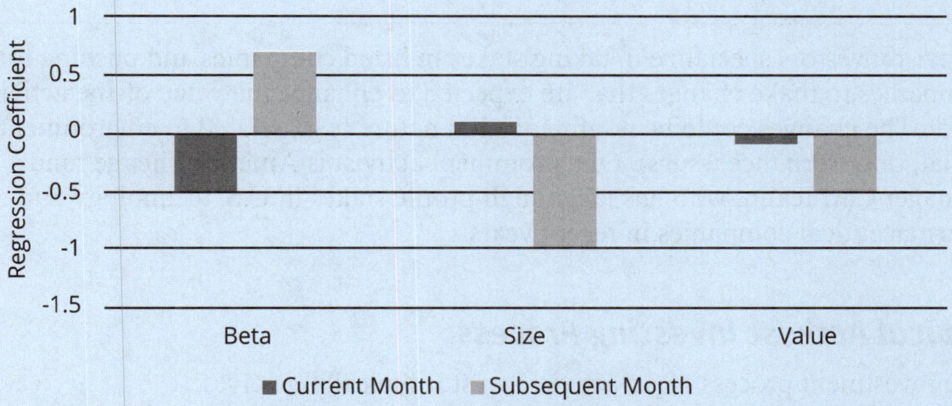

Based on the data in Figure 15.1, answer the following questions:

1. **Discuss** the main factor rotation timing implications from the regression.
2. **Discuss** practical issues in using the model to time factor rotation.

Answers:

1. For the current month:
   - The negative regression coefficient of 0.5 indicates that higher beta stocks underperform in the month of an upward surprise in interest rates, or outperform for a downward surprise.
   - Size and value provide no meaningful signal.

   For the subsequent month:
   - The strongest effect is the negative 1.0 regression coefficient indicating small companies underperform the month after higher than expected interest rates. Value companies also underperform for an upward surprise in rates while high beta stocks outperform with a roughly 0.7 positive regression coefficient.
2. Further analysis is needed in relation to the timing of the beta effect because the coefficient is negative for the current but positive for the subsequent month. For example, suppose there is a positive (upward surprise in rates) on the 20th of the month. How long will the negative effect on high beta stock performance last and when will it turn positive?

Activist Strategies

LOS 15.e: Analyze activist strategies, including their rationale and associated processes.

Activist investors specialize in taking stakes in listed companies and pushing for companies to make changes that are expected to enhance the value of the activist's stake. The changes could be nonfinancial in nature (e.g., related to environmental, social, or governance issues). One prominent activist is American hedge fund manager Carl Icahn, who has taken high-profile stakes in U.S. technology and pharmaceutical companies in recent years.

Typical Activist Investing Process

The investment process of an activist investor typically involves:

- Screening and analysis of activist opportunities.
- Buying an initial stake in the target company (typically less than 10% of voting rights).
- Submitting a public proposal for changes to the company, usually in the form of an open letter to the company.
- If no agreement, threatening a *proxy contest* (a proxy contest is a shareholder vote to force the proposed changes on the company).
- If no agreement, launching a proxy contest.
- Continuing to negotiate with management, but with no agreement eventually taking the matter to a proxy contest.

Popularity of Shareholder Activism

The foundations of activism go back to *corporate raiders* in the 1970s and 1980s who took large stakes in companies in order to influence operations and enhance value. Activist investing as a hedge fund style has seen assets under management more than double between 2007 and 2015. The number of public announcements of activist campaigns has increased four-fold in this period.

Tactics Used by Activists

These include:

- Seeking board representation (once attained this can be used to change management).
- Writing open letters to management detailing the changes, meeting with management, and engaging with other shareholders to court support in a proxy contest.
- Proposing changes at an annual general meeting (AGM).

- Proposing financial restructuring including increased dividends and share buybacks.
- Reducing extravagant management compensation.
- Launching legal proceedings against management for breach of fiduciary duties.
- Launching a media campaign against existing management.
- Breaking up a large inefficient conglomerate.

The typical defenses that are used by management resisting the activist's proposed changes include:

- Use of multi-class share structures, which grant multiple votes to founders.
- "Poison pill" clauses, which allow existing shareholders to purchase more shares in the target company at a discount, diluting the stake of the activist.
- Staggered board provisions, which mean the board is re-elected partially each year, and hence, cannot be replaced simultaneously.

Target Companies

Target companies tend to feature slower earnings and revenue growth than the market, negative share price momentum, and weak corporate governance. This poor track record is evidence that changes need to be made and makes it more likely the activist will garner support from other disgruntled shareholders in a proxy contest.

Impact

Studies show that activism does lead to improvements in growth, profitability, and corporate governance; however, it also leads to higher debt levels. The added performance of activist funds has been modest with hedge fund data showing Sharpe ratios slightly above the broad stock market.

Investors have generally reacted positively to activism announcements; data shows positive stock price outperformance for periods leading up to the announcement, with strongest outperformance on the day of the announcement, and modest outperformance over the following month.

MODULE QUIZ 15.2

1. An analyst is attempting to construct a hedged portfolio to represent the value factor in their domestic stock market. They use the following process:
   1. Rank securities in the domestic market in order of book value of equity in relation to market value of equity (book-to-market ratio).
   2. Purchase the quartile of securities with lowest book-to-market, short sell the quartile of securities with highest book-to-market ratio to create a dollar-neutral portfolio.
   3. Track the performance of the long/short portfolio over time.

   Which of the following statements *most accurately* describes an error in this process?
   A. Stage 1 is incorrect because price-to-book ratio should be used instead of book-to-market ratio.
   B. Stage 2 is incorrect because the top and bottom deciles of securities should be used to construct the dollar-neutral portfolio instead of the top and bottom quartile.
   C. Stage 2 is incorrect because the long/short portfolio should be constructed by purchasing the securities with the highest book-to-market and short selling the securities with the lowest book-to-market.

2. Which of the following strategies would *least likely* be used as part of the investment process of an activist investor?
   A. Buying a majority stake in the company to enforce value-enhancing changes on company management.
   B. Submit public proposal for changes to investee company, usually in the form of an open letter to the company.
   C. Launch a proxy contest against the current management team.

MODULE 15.3: OTHER STRATEGIES

Video covering this content is available online.

LOS 15.f: Describe active strategies based on statistical arbitrage and market microstructure.

Two other active equity strategies discussed are **statistical arbitrage** and **event-driven** strategies. Both are usually quantitative strategies, though they could incorporate judgment from a fundamental manager.

Statistical Arbitrage

Statistical arbitrage, or "stat arb" strategies, make extensive use of technical stock price and volume data to exploit pricing inefficiencies. Typically, they aim to profit from mean reversion in related share prices or by taking advantage of opportunities created by market microstructure issues.

Pairs trading is an example of a popular statistical arbitrage strategy. Pairs trading identifies two securities in the same industry that are historically highly correlated with each other and aims to profit from taking advantage of a temporary breakdown in this relationship. The strategy buys the underperforming security while shorting the outperforming securities. The strategy profits from mean reversion if the long (previous underperform) now outperforms, while the short (previous outperformer) now underperforms. The risk is that the breakdown of the observed previous relationship is long term in nature, there is no mean reversion, and in fact the long continues to underperform the short position in the pairs trade.

A simple pairs trading strategy might use the logarithm of the ratio of two related stock prices to generate trading signals, referred to as the *spread* (the logarithm is taken simply to make the signal more stable). This spread is deemed to be high when it is more than two standard deviations above its moving average, and low when it is more than two standard deviations below its moving average. The strategy would sell the spread when it is high, and buy the spread when it is low looking to profit from mean reversion.

PROFESSOR'S NOTE

Don't worry too much about the technical detail here. Converting the ratio to log value simply places more emphasis on the larger and presumably more profitable deviations in the ratio. The primary issue is that the spread generates a sell signal when it is high and a buy signal when it is low, and the strategy relies on the spread reverting to its mean.

Market microstructure-based arbitrage strategies take advantage of mispricing opportunities occurring due to imbalances in supply and demand that are expected to only last for a few milliseconds. Investors with the tools to analyze the limit order book of an exchange, and the capability for high-frequency trading are in a position to capture such opportunities.

Event-Driven Strategies

Even-driven strategies exploit market inefficiencies that may occur around corporate events such as mergers and acquisitions, earnings or restructuring announcements, share buybacks, special dividends, and spin-offs.

PROFESSOR'S NOTE

These events look a lot like the changes that activists may push for. The key difference here is that the event-driven manager simply tries to find pricing anomalies due to the event—the manager doesn't engage in activism to bring the event about.

The **risk arbitrage**, or "risk arb" strategy associated with merger and acquisition (M&A) activity is an example of an event-driven strategy.

In a cash merger, the risk arb manager will buy the shares of the target company after the deal has been announced. Due to the risk that the deal will be blocked for regulatory reasons or due to lack of shareholder approval, the stock price will be slightly below the deal price until the deal closes. The risk arb manager, therefore, will earn a profit when the deal closes. In a share-for-share transaction, the risk arb manager will simultaneously short sell the shares of the acquirer and purchase the shares of the target company in the same ratio as the proposed share exchange of the deal. Once again, the manager profits from the deal completing. The risk to the risk arb strategy is that the deal fails to close, which could cause large losses to the manager.

The key expertise of a risk arb manager is the ability to accurately estimate the risk of the deal failing and estimating deal duration and associated annualized premiums offered by stock prices.

EXAMPLE: Identifying opportunities

Jessica Nguyen, a portfolio analyst for Bridgeriver Associates, is reviewing several investment opportunities, as detailed in the following:

- Formby Corp is a large cap multinational technology company headquartered in the United States that designs consumer electronics and sells online computer services. After a decade of stellar growth, the company has accumulated significant cash balances, but growth in core markets has slowed and recent product launches have missed expectations. The company currently doesn't pay a dividend.
- Parmeon SA is a large French retailer with a well-known brand. Competition from the internet has been strong in recent years and the company has experienced slow growth and declining margins. Parmeon has recently announced its intent to acquire another well-known retailer. Parmeon will issue one share of its stock for one share of the acquired company. The deal is likely to attract the attention of regulators because it will create the largest retailer in the sector.
- Baron PLC is a commodity trading and services company based in the United Kingdom. Recent moves in commodity prices and tightening up of credit conditions has led to the company issuing several profit warnings, with management being replaced and the new team announcing a focus on selling assets to raise liquidity. Analysts are questioning whether the company can continue to service its debt. The correlation coefficient of Baron and the largest company in the sector has historically been very strong but has recently broken down.

For *each* investment opportunity (Formby, Parmeon and Baron), **identify** the active equity strategy you would *most likely* take an interest in. Your identification must be made from the following list:

- Activist investing.
- Distressed debt investing.
- Event-driven investing.
- Pairs trading.

For *each* opportunity **discuss** how the active equity strategy might be applied in that opportunity.

Answer:

Formby Corp: Activist investing—invest in the shares and advocate for cash payouts to shareholders rather than investing in projects with sub-par profitability. The payout could be in the form of regular or special dividends, or a share buyback program.

Parmeon: Event-driven investing—the high uncertainty around the approval of the deal by regulators could lead to misvaluation. For example, if the deal has a higher probability of completion than is assumed by the market, the target company's stock price is likely to be relatively undervalued. Buy the target company and short sell Parmeon in the same proportion as the share-for-share proposed exchange.

Baron: Distressed debt investing—if the manager believes the market is too pessimistic, buy the bonds. The company might recover and the bonds would increase in value or in a restructuring swapping it for equity. **Note that a pairs trade is not appropriate for Baron.** The breakdown in the historical correlation of Baron to its competitor appears to be based on fundamental changes in the management and strategy of Baron. It is not appropriate to assume mean reversion to the past relationship and mean reversion is the underlying assumption in a pairs trade.

Creating a Fundamental Active Investment Strategy

LOS 15.g: Describe how fundamental active investment strategies are created.

The fundamental active investment process will likely include the following steps:

1. Define the investment universe in accordance with the fund mandate.
   - Define the market opportunity (investment thesis) and explain why it is there.
2. Prescreen the investment universe to obtain a manageable set of securities for detailed analysis.
   - For example, a value manager might screen to remove stocks with high P/E multiples.
3. Analyze the industry, competitive position, and financial reports of the companies.
4. Forecast performance, most commonly based on cash flows or earnings.
5. Convert forecasts to valuations.
6. Construct a portfolio with the desired risk profile.
   - Incorporate any top-down views or constraints on sectors/markets.
7. Rebalance the portfolio as needed.

The process will most likely also include stock sell disciplines involving target prices to take profits and pre-defined stop loss levels to exit unsuccessful positions and mitigate behavioral biases that may bias the manager to hold on to losing positions.

Pitfalls in Fundamental Investing

Pitfalls in fundamental investing include the following.

Behavioral biases can affect the human judgment that fundamental strategies use for their insights into profitable investments. These biases include confirmation bias, the illusion of control, availability bias, loss aversion, overconfidence, and regret aversion bias.

PROFESSOR'S NOTE

Another discussion of behavioral biases that can lead generally rational people to, on occasion, make expensive mistakes.

A **value trap** where a stock that appears to be attractive because of a significant price fall, may in fact be overvalued and decline further. For example, a value manager who buys stocks based only on low P/E ratios risks buying securities of companies that are fundamentally deteriorating and may fail. Value managers need to also determine the stock is trading below intrinsic value given the company's future prospects and identify the trigger that will lead to upward revaluation of the stock.

A **growth trap** where the favorable future growth prospects are already reflected, or over-reflected, in the price. For example, the market price could reflect very aggressive growth of 15% and the price could decline if only above-average growth of 12% is realized. The trap is that growth stocks generally trade at a high P/E and even modest shortfalls in growth can lead to significant declines in P/E and stock price.

Creating a Quantitative Active Investment Strategy

LOS 15.h: Describe how quantitative active investment strategies are created.

The quantitative active investment strategy has a well-defined process:

1. Define the market opportunity.
2. Acquire and process data.
3. Back-test the strategy.
4. Evaluate the strategy.
5. Construct the portfolio.

Each one of these steps is discussed in more detail in the following paragraphs.

Define the Market Opportunity (Investment Thesis)

Quantitative managers use publicly available information to predict future returns of stocks, using factors to build their return-forecasting models. It is up to the manager to identify the opportunity.

Acquire and Process Data

This is the most time-consuming step. This involves building databases, mapping data from different sources, understanding data availability, cleaning up the data, and reshaping the data into a usable format. The categories of most commonly used data are:

- **Company mapping**: Tracking many companies over time and across data vendors. This will process company mergers, bankruptcies, and map different unique stock identifiers across different data vendors.
- **Company fundamentals**: Collect company demographic, price, and other financial data from vendors such as Bloomberg.
- **Survey data**: Details on corporate earnings and forecasts, macroeconomic variables, sentiment indicators, and information on fund flows.
- **Unconventional data**: Unstructured data including satellite images, measures of news sentiment, customer-supplier chains, corporate events, and many other types of information. Recent developments in *machine learning* have supported the ability to examine more and less conventional data, leading to improvements in strategy performance.

Backtesting the Strategy

This involves applying the strategy to historical data to assess performance. The correlation between factor exposures and subsequent portfolio returns for a cross section of securities is used as a measure of factor performance in back-tests. The idea is that if there is a strong relationship between factor exposure and subsequent performance then the factor has high predictive power. This correlation coefficient is known as the factor's information coefficient (IC). *There will be two variations on the IC calculation*: the Pearson IC and the Spearman Rank IC.

Earnings yield (E/P) is a type of valuation factor. An analyst who believes the market undervalues earnings yield could go long securities with high earnings yield and short securities with low earnings yield to gain exposure to, and earn returns from, the factor. Backtesting is used to determine if historical data supports the analyst's belief. To perform the back test, the analyst could:

1. Obtain a sample of historical data on a cross section of stocks.
2. Calculate earnings yield and subsequent performance of each stock.
3. Rank the stocks by earnings yield (factor score). Factor score is measured as a standardized distance away from the average earnings yield. Suppose the average earnings yield is 3% and the standard deviation of earnings yield across stocks is 5% then a stock with an earnings yield of 7% would have a standardized factor exposure of (7% – 3%) / 5% = 0.8.

4. Calculate the IC. Assuming a linear relationship between the factor exposure and holding period return, IC is the correlation between the factor exposure and holding period return. This is called the **Pearson IC**. Like any correlation, the IC will range between +1 and –1 or +100% and –100% if expressed as a percentage. A monthly value of even 5% to 6% is considered very strong.
5. The Pearson IC of the raw data is sensitive to even a few outliers (extreme high or low historical return). The **Spearman Rank IC** addresses this issue and is often considered more robust (superior). The Spearman Rank IC is the correlation of the rank of the factor scores and rank of subsequent performance.

PROFESSOR'S NOTE

This calculation of a standardized factor exposure is simply an application of the idea of *z*-values from basic quant. We are not interested in absolute earnings yield, but how far our earnings yields are away from the average earnings yield in terms of standard deviations. If this is related to the future performance of securities, then the factor has predictive power.

EXAMPLE: Pearson correlation coefficient IC and Spearman Rank IC

An analyst collects a cross section sample of nine stocks and calculates the E/P factor score for each stock. The factor scores and subsequent month's return are shown in the table.

Stock	Factor Score	Subsequent Month's Return (%)	Rank of Factor Score	Rank of Return
A	–1.57	10.06%	9	1
B	–1.01	–0.60%	8	9
C	–0.73	–0.50%	7	8
D	–0.40	–0.48%	6	7
E	–0.01	1.20%	5	6
F	0.65	3.00%	4	5
G	0.75	3.02%	3	4
H	0.90	3.05%	2	3
I	1.43	5.20%	1	2
Mean	0.00	2.66%		
Standard Deviation	1.00	3.43%		
Pearson IC		–0.99%		
Spearman Rank IC				40%

Based on the table:

1. **Discuss** whether the earnings yield factor exhibits predictive power for this dataset. In your discussion, **comment** on both the Pearson and Spearman Rank IC.
2. **Calculate** the performance of a long/short factor portfolio with an equal weighting of the three most extreme factor scores.
3. Based on these results, **discuss** what should be done next.

Answer:

1. The Pearson IC of –0.99% is very small. It suggests an insignificant negative relationship between E/P and return.

   However, the Pearson IC was distorted by a nonlinear relationship between factor and subsequent return. Stock A had a negative score and by far the highest positive return. Spearman Rank IC shows a strong +40% IC and does support that high E/P is associated subsequent strong performance.

2.
   - The long position will equal weight G, H, and I: (3.02% + 3.05% + 5.20%) / 3 = 3.76
   - Funded by an equal weighted short position in A, B and C: (10.06% – 0.6% – 0.5%) / 3 = 2.99%
   - Hence, the long/short factor portfolio would return 3.76% – 2.99% = 0.77%

3. A sample of nine stocks is not very large. The data supports the belief that high E/P is associated with favorable performance but also shows results can be significantly affected by outliers. Another larger sample, a different time period, and additional testing is appropriate.

Having considered individual factors, managers would then consider which factors to include in a **multi-factor model**. Managers can select and weight each factor using either a qualitative or systematic process. Factors could be treated like asset class weights and mean-variance optimization techniques used to decide optimal exposures. Investors should be aware that although factors appear effective individually, they may not add material value to a model if they are correlated with the other factors in the model.

Evaluating the Strategy

Out-of-sample testing, where the model is applied to data different to those that were used to build the model, is conducted to confirm model robustness. Managers would look at both returns generated and risk measures such as VaR and maximum drawdown.

Reading 15

Portfolio Construction

The following aspects are particularly relevant to quantitative investing when constructing portfolios:

- **Risk models:** Used to estimate the risk of the portfolio by considering individual variance of positions and correlation across positions. Managers generally rely on commercial risk model vendors for these data.
- **Trading costs:** Both explicit (e.g., commissions) and implicit (e.g., market impact cost) costs are considered. If two stocks have the same expected returns, the one with the lower trading costs will be selected.

Pitfalls in Quantitative Investing

Pitfalls in quantitative investing include the following:

- **Survivorship bias:** If back-tests are only applied to existing companies, then they will overlook companies that have failed in the past, and this will make the strategy look better than it actually is.
- **Look-ahead bias:** Results from using information in the model to give trading signals at a time when the information was not available. An example would be using December financial accounting data to generate trading signals for the following January. It is likely that the accounting data was not known by the market until the company issued its financial accounts well into the year, and therefore was not actually available to act as a trading signal in January.
- **Data-mining/overfitting:** Excessive search analysis of past financial data to find data that shows a strategy working. This should not be construed as proof that the strategy works because data was mined until data was found that suggested the strategy worked. This is not rigorous statistical testing, but simply testing lots of data until the analyst finds what they are looking for.
- **Turnover:** Constraints on turnover may constrain the manager's ability to follow a strategy.
- **Lack of availability of stock to borrow:** For short selling, this may also constrain a manager's ability to follow a strategy.
- **Transaction costs:** This can quickly erode the returns of a strategy that looked good in backtesting.

Another risk of quantitative strategies is *quant overcrowding*, which can occur if many quantitative managers are following similar strategies. Once a strategy becomes crowded, there is the risk that a period of poor performance could cause many managers attempt to exit their positions at the same time. This rush for the exit could exaggerate losses and lead to margin calls from lenders forcing managers to further liquidate their positions at unfavorable prices. This is the most likely explanation for a meltdown in equity quant strategies in the relatively serene market of August 2007. Indicators such as short interest and price momentum can be combined to estimate the potential overcrowding of markets. A high correlation between short interest (that is, number of declared short positions) and price momentum could indicate a short trade that could suddenly unwind aggressively.

MODULE QUIZ 15.3

1. High-frequency trading techniques are *most likely* used by:
   A. pairs-trading strategies.
   B. market microstructure strategies.
   C. event-driven strategies.
2. The *value trap* is *best* defined as:
   A. a stock that is trading at low multiples justified by deteriorating fundamental business conditions.
   B. a stock that is trading a low price multiples without justification.
   C. a stock that is trading at high price multiples justified by high expected earnings growth rates.
3. When backtesting a quantitative active investment strategy, a manager concerned about outliers in data is *most likely* to conclude that a factor has predictive power when:
   A. the information coefficient of factor scores versus contemporaneous returns is significantly different from zero.
   B. the Spearman Rank correlation coefficient of factor scores and subsequent returns is significantly different from zero and positive.
   C. the Pearson correlation coefficient of factor scores versus contemporaneous returns is significantly different from zero.

Reading 15

MODULE 15.4: EQUITY INVESTMENT STYLE CLASSIFICATION

Video covering this content is available online.

LOS 15.i: Discuss equity investment style classifications.

An investment style classification process is designed to split a stock universe into subgroups of stocks that represent the styles discussed in this reading (i.e., size, value, etc.). These groups should contain stocks that have a high correlation with each other (because they are part of the same style), but correlation between groups should be lower indicating that styles are distinct sources of risk and return. This process is useful for classifying the style of a portfolio and benchmarking managers.

Approaches to Style Classification

The two main approaches in style analysis are the **holdings-based** approach and the **returns-based** approach.

Holdings-Based Style Analysis

The holdings-based approach looks at the attributes of each individual stock in a portfolio and aggregates these attributes to conclude the overall style of the portfolio.

A common application of this idea is the *Morningstar Style Box*. In a style box, two factors—value and size—are each split into three groups, as shown in Figure 15.2.

Figure 15.2: Morningstar Fund Style Box

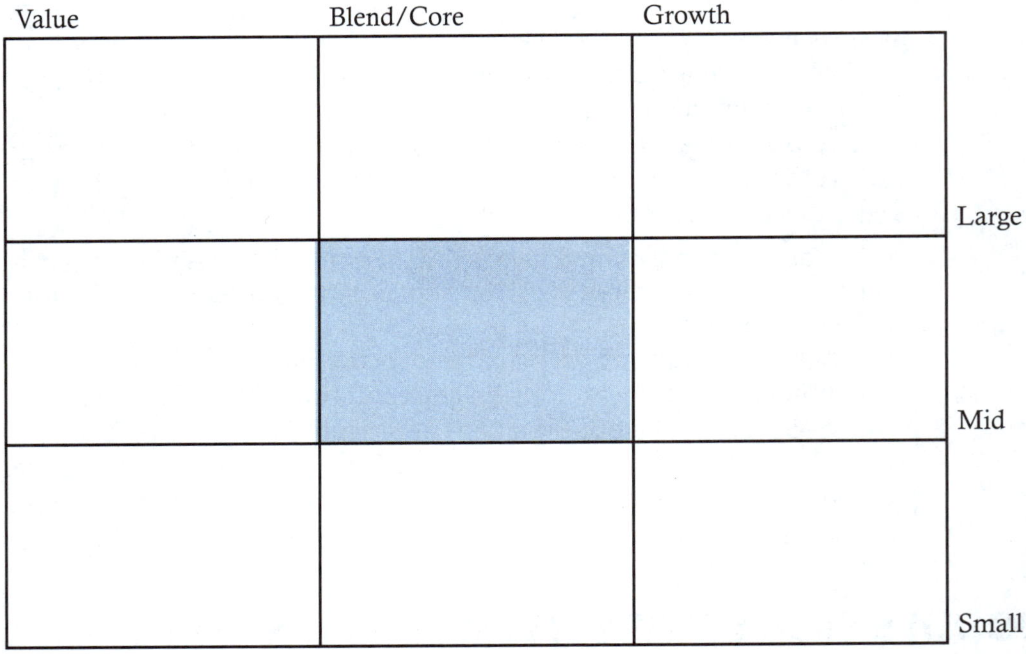

There is no consensus on the definition of large, mid, and small cap. One practice is to define large cap stocks as the top 70% of market capitalization of the universe, with mid-cap stocks represented by the next 20% of market capitalization, and small cap stocks the rest.

The style box approach aims to classify approximately the same number of stocks in each of the value, blend, and growth groups, essentially distributing the market value of each row evenly across the grid.

The classification of stocks into value/blend/growth involves assigning a *style score* to each individual stock. For example, to assign a value score, the dividend yield may be used. Stocks would be ranked according to their dividend yield and a score allocated to a stock based on their percentile of the market value of their particular group. If the stock is at the lower end of the dividend yield range, it will receive a low score close to 0, if it is at the high end of the dividend yield range, it will receive a high score close to 100. A comprehensive scoring model would use many indicators of value and combine them together in a pre-determined weighting.

PROFESSOR'S NOTE

The actual process of allocating a style score is complicated and omitted from the curriculum, and therefore, beyond the scope of the exam. The key takeaway here is that stocks are allocated a style score between 0 and 100 in a way designed to distribute rows evenly across the columns of the grid.

The same process can be done for growth attributes such as earnings growth, revenue growth and cash-flow growth to establish a growth factor score for each security. Once again, this score will be a number between 0 and 100. The indicators used by Morningstar and the weightings given to them in the value and growth style scores are displayed in Figure 15.3.

Figure 15.3: Morningstar Value and Growth Scoring Scheme

Value Score Components and Weights		**Growth Score Components and Weights**	
Forward-looking measures	**50.0%**	*Forward-looking measures*	**50.0%**
*Price to projected earnings		*Long-term projected earnings growth	
Historical measures	**50.0%**	*Historical measures*	**50.0%**
*Price to book	12.5%	*Historical earnings growth	12.5%
*Price to sales	12.5%	*Sales growth	12.5%
*Price to cash flow	12.5%	*Cash flow growth	12.5%
*Dividend yield	12.5%	*Book value growth	12.5%

Once a security has both a value score and a growth score, the difference can be taken as a net style score. If the net style score is strongly negative, the stock is classified as value. If the net style score is strongly positive then the stock is classified as growth. If the net style score is close to zero then the stock will be classified as core.

PROFESSOR'S NOTE

Morningstar classifies **stocks** without a strong value/growth bias as core. **Funds** without a strong value/growth bias are classified as blend. These are just two different technical terms for the same idea—an investment without a strong value/growth bias.

Once constructed for a stock universe, the grid can be used as a visual aid to help categorize and track managed investment portfolios. At a glance, an investor can see where a manager is positioned on the grid, and, if historical data exists, how this style has changed over time.

Note that the Morningstar Style Box approach acknowledges that a single security can exhibit both value and growth characteristics at the same time. A simpler classification system might assign a style score as a fraction of a stock's market cap to value and the complement to growth—for example, a system may assign a value score of 0.6 to a security indicating that 60% of the market cap of the company will be allocated to a value index and 40% allocated to a growth index.

Returns-Based Style Analysis

A returns-based style analysis aims to identify the style of a fund through regression of the funds returns against a set of passive style indices. By imposing a constraint on the regression that the sum of the slope coefficients should sum to a value of 1, the slope coefficients can be interpreted as the manager's allocation to that style during the period.

For example, a return-based style analysis might conduct a regression of fund returns versus four passive indices as follows:

$$R_p = a + b_1 SCG + b_2 LCG + b_3 SCV + b_4 LCV + \varepsilon$$

where:

R_p = returns on the manager's portfolio

a = a constant often interpreted as the value added by the fund manager

b_i = the fund exposure to style *i*

SCG = returns on a small-cap growth index

LCG = returns on a large-cap growth index

SCV = returns on a small-cap value index

LCV = returns on a large cap value index

ε = residual return not explained by styles used in the regression

giving an output of:

$b_1 = 0$, $b_2 = 0$, $b_3 = 0.15$, and $b_4 = 0.85$

From the values of the regression coefficients, we would conclude that the manager's portfolio has no exposure to growth stocks ($b_1 = 0$ and $b_2 = 0$), and that the manager is a value manager with primary exposure to large cap value ($b_4 = 0.85$) and a small exposure to small cap value ($b_3 = 0.15$).

Manager Self-Identification

The fund's investment strategy is usually self-described by the manager. Comparing that self-description with returns-based and holdings-based style analysis will either confirm a consistent identification or indicate a need for further investigation and analysis to explain the discrepancy. Some styles such as equity long/short, equity market neutral and short bias do not fit traditional style categories and the manager's description and fund prospectus becomes the key source of information on style of such funds.

Strengths and Limitations of Style Analysis

A summary of the advantages and disadvantages of returns-based versus holdings-based style analysis is displayed in the following:

Advantages of Returns-Based Analysis	Advantages of Holdings-Based Analysis
Does not require information on holdings.	Generally more accurate because it uses actual portfolio holdings.
Can be easily and universally applied.	Assesses each individual holding's contribution to style.
Disadvantages of Returns-Based Analysis	**Disadvantages of Holdings-Based Analysis**
Constraints on outputs can limit detection of extreme styles.	Requires the availability of all portfolio constituents and style attributes of each.
	Limited derivatives data may hinder analysis if derivatives are used.
	Different systems with different definitions of style will classify the same portfolio in different ways.

A holdings-based analysis pinpoints the current exposure of a fund. This is an advantage if the analyst wishes to know the most up-to-date positioning of a manager. However, if the analyst wishes to assess the average exposure a manager takes over time, then historical holdings-based analyses need to be available. A returns-based style analysis based on historical returns would capture this average exposure automatically through regressing historical returns.

MODULE QUIZ 15.4

1. The use of derivatives overlay strategies with limited information is *likely* to hinder style analysis performed by which of the following approaches?
   A. Holdings-based analysis only.
   B. Returns-based analysis only.
   C. Both holdings-based and returns-based analyses.

KEY CONCEPTS

LOS 15.a

Active equity managers can be broadly divided into two groups: fundamental managers, which use discretionary judgment and quantitative managers, which use rules-based (systematic) data-driven models. The main differences between the approaches are the following:

	Fundamental	Quantitative
Style	Subjective	Objective
Decision-making	Discretionary	Systematic
Primary resources	Human skill, experience, judgment	Expertise in statistical modeling
Information used	Research	Data and statistics
Analyst focus	Conviction of insight into small number of investments	Application of rewarded factors over large number of securities
Purpose of analysis	Forecast future corporate performance	Find historical relationships between factors and performance likely to persist
Portfolio Construction	Judgment and conviction within portfolio risk parameters	Optimization
Monitoring and Rebalancing	Continuous monitoring: rebalancing according to views	Automatic systematic periodic rebalancing

LOS 15.b

Bottom-up strategies analyze information at the company level to generate investment ideas. Bottom-up strategies can be divided into value and growth styles. Value sub-styles include relative value, contrarian, high-quality value, income investing, deep-value, restructuring and distressed debt, and special situations.

LOS 15.c

Top-down strategies focus on the macroeconomic environment, demographic trends, and government policies to make investment decisions. Top-down strategies could focus on geography, industry, equity style rotation, volatility-based strategies, or thematic investment ideas.

LOS 15.d

Quantitative strategies often use factor-based models, which aim to identify factors that drive performance historically and are likely to continue to do so in the future. Factors can be based on fundamental characteristics such as value and growth, and price momentum, or on unconventional data.

LOS 15.e

Activist investors specialize in taking meaningful stakes in listed companies and then publicly pushing for changes to the management, strategy, or capital structure of the company that they believe will enhance value.

LOS 15.f

Statistical arbitrage funds look to profit from anomalies in technical market data (i.e., prices and volumes), for example, pairs trading. Event-driven strategies exploit market inefficiencies that may occur around mergers and acquisitions, earnings announcements, bankruptcies, share buybacks, special dividends, and spin-offs.

LOS 15.g

The fundamental active investment process consists of the following steps:

1. Define the investment universe in accordance with the fund mandate.
   - Define the market opportunity (investment thesis) and explain why it is there.
2. Prescreen the investment universe to obtain a manageable set of securities for detailed analysis.
   - For example, a value manager might screen to remove stocks with high P/E multiples.
3. Analyze the industry, competitive position, and financial reports of the companies.
4. Forecast performance, most commonly based on cash flows or earnings.
5. Convert forecasts to valuations.
6. Construct a portfolio of profitable investments with the desired risk profile.
   - Incorporate any top-down view on sectors/markets at this stage.
7. Rebalance the portfolio with buy and sell disciplines.

Pitfalls in fundamental investing include behavioral biases, the value trap, and the growth trap. Behavioral biases include confirmation bias, illusion of control, availability bias, loss aversion, overconfidence, and regret aversion.

LOS 15.h

The quantitative active investment process includes the following steps:

- Define the market opportunity.
- Acquire and process data.
- Back-test the strategy.
- Evaluate the strategy.
- Portfolio construction.

Pitfalls in quantitative investing include look-ahead and survivorship biases, overfitting, data mining, unrealistic turnover assumptions, transaction costs, and short availability.

LOS 15.i

The two main approaches used in style analysis are holdings-based and returns-based. Holdings-based approaches aggregate the style scores of individual holdings, while returns-based approaches analyze the investment style of portfolio managers by regressing historical portfolio returns against a set of style indexes.

ANSWER KEY FOR MODULE QUIZZES

Module Quiz 15.1

1. **C** Screening is a process that can be used by both fundamental and quantitative active managers. It is how the final investment decision is made that determines whether the manager is classified as quantitative or fundamental. If the decision is made based on systematic rules rigidly applied to company data, then the manager would be classified as quantitative. If the investment decision is made based on the manager's opinion using their skill and experience, then the manager is deemed to be fundamental. (LOS 15.a)

2. **B** Identifying securities that are undervalued versus the amount received in bankruptcy liquidation is a form of distressed debt investing. Answer A is incorrect because a relative value manager would be searching for companies with low price multiples such as P/E without the need for a distressed situation that could lead to bankruptcy filing. Answer C is incorrect because a deep value manager looks for companies with low valuation relative to assets such as price-to-book, once again without the need for a distressed situation that could lead to bankruptcy filing. (LOS 15.b)

3. **B** A top-down investment approach focuses on broad macroeconomic variables to identify opportunities at the broad market level based on geography, industrial sector, or thematic investing data. Manager B is least likely to be classified a top-down manager because they are using data relating to individual components of the S&P 500 rather than looking at data relating to the aggregate market. Managers A and C are looking at broad market or sector data in order to identify investment opportunities, making them top-down managers. (LOS 15.c)

Module Quiz 15.2

1. **C** Stages 1 and 3 are correct. It is up to the analyst's discretion as to what proportion of the stock universe is bought and sold to create the dollar neutral portfolio, hence using quartiles is not an error. The error is in Stage 2 where high book-value to market-value companies should be purchased because these are cheap companies, and low book-value to market-value companies should be sold because these represent expensive companies. (LOS 15.d)

2. **A** Activist investors do not take controlling majority stakes (greater than 50%) in companies they invest in. They usually take a significant but minority position of less than 10% and look to garner support from other shareholders in a proxy context to enforce the value-enhancing changes they want to occur. (LOS 15.e)

Module Quiz 15.3

1. **B** Market microstructure-based arbitrage strategies take advantage of mispricing opportunities occurring due to imbalances in supply and demand that are expected to only last for a few milliseconds. Investors with the tools to analyze the limit order book of an exchange and the capability for high-frequency trading are able to capture such opportunities. (LOS 15.f)

2. **A** A value trap is a company that is trading with low price multiples due to deteriorating fundamental business conditions. This security looks cheap due to its low price multiple; however, the valuation comes from the market correctly anticipating a further deterioration in business conditions and hence an improvement in share price is unlikely. (LOS 15.g)

3. **B** A manager would conclude that a factor has predictive power when a cross section of securities' factor scores is positively correlated with subsequent returns. When based on the Pearson correlation coefficient this is referred to as the information coefficient, hence, answers A and C are saying the same thing. They are incorrect choices because the manager would need to see non-zero correlation between factor scores and *subsequent* market returns, not contemporaneous market returns. Answer B is the best choice here—a manager would use the Spearman Rank correlation coefficient when concerned about outliers in the data causing the Pearson correlation coefficient to be biased. (LOS 15.h)

Module Quiz 15.4

1. **A** A manager performing holdings-based analysis may come to erroneous conclusions about manager style if they do not have details regarding derivatives overlay strategies used to change the exposure of the fund. This is less likely to be a problem for returns-based analysis because the regression of historical returns carried out under this method will likely pick up the impact of any derivatives overlay strategies being used by the manager. (LOS 15.i)

Reading 15

READING 16

Active Equity Investing: Portfolio Construction

EXAM FOCUS

This reading focuses on issues related to the active management of equity portfolios. It begins with the building blocks of active equity portfolio construction and how they relate to the sources of active return. It covers Active Share, active risk, and how they are related to various strategies. Risk budgeting and associated calculations are covered, as are issues related to the scalability of asset management approaches. The reading concludes with issues related to the use of short positions.

MODULE 16.1: BUILDING BLOCKS OF ACTIVE EQUITY PORTFOLIO CONSTRUCTION

Video covering this content is available online.

LOS 16.a: Describe elements of a manager's investment philosophy that influence the portfolio construction process.

Active equity portfolios aim to outperform a benchmark after all costs. In the simplest terms, the excess return above a benchmark (**active return**) will be positive if the manager overweights securities that outperform the benchmark, and underweights securities that underperform the benchmark, because active returns are driven by differences in weights between the active and benchmark portfolios:

$$R_A = \sum_{i=1}^{N} \Delta W_i R_i$$

where:

R_i = return from security *i*

ΔW_i = active weight, the difference between portfolio and benchmark weight for security *i*

Sources of Active Returns

Active returns come from three sources:

1. The level of strategic long-term exposures to **rewarded factors**.
   - Rewarded factors are risks that are widely accepted as offering long-term positive risk premiums [market risk (beta), size, value, liquidity, etc.]
2. Tactical exposures to **mispriced** securities, sectors, and rewarded risks that generate *alpha* (return that cannot be explained by long-term exposure to rewarded factors). Alpha is directly related to manager *skill.*
3. **Idiosyncratic risk** (from concentrated active positions) that generates returns related to *luck*. It is labeled *luck* in the sense that it is not due to market risk exposure or value-added alpha.

Different managers will generate different proportions of their active returns from each source.

The decomposition of realized (*ex post*) active return can be seen in the next equation:

$$R_A = \sum\left(\beta_{pk} - \beta_{bk}\right) \times F_k + (\alpha + \varepsilon)$$

where:

β_{pk} = the sensitivity of the portfolio to each rewarded factor (k)

β_{bk} = the sensitivity of the benchmark to each rewarded factor

F_k = the return of each rewarded factor

$(\alpha + \varepsilon)$ = the return not explained by exposure to rewarded factors—alpha (α) is the active return attributable to manager skill, and ε is the idiosyncratic return—noise or luck (good or bad) (In practice it is very difficult to distinguish between α and ε)

Building Blocks Used in Portfolio Construction

The three main building blocks of portfolio construction are:

1. **Factor weightings.**
2. **Alpha skills.**
3. **Position sizing.**

These three building blocks are integrated into a successful portfolio construction process through a fourth component: **breadth of expertise**. Each component is considered in detail in the following.

First Building Block: Overweight/Underweight Rewarded Factors

This relates to the manager taking exposures to rewarded risks that differ from those of the benchmark. This can be thought of as active return due to differences in *beta*, where beta refers to sensitivity to a rewarded risk factor such as the market risk of CAPM, or the market, size, and value factors of the Fama and French model. With exposures to rewarded factors increasingly accessible via rules-based index products, simple static exposure to rewarded factors is no longer widely considered a source of alpha. Irrespective of the manager's approach, whether they explicitly target factor exposures or target individual securities, their performance can in part be attributed to sensitivity to these beta factors. This building block relates primarily to active return source number one: differences in exposures to long-term rewarded factors.

Second Building Block: Alpha Skills

Alpha skills are excess returns related to the unique skills and strategies of the manager. A manager can generate alpha through *factor timing*, which is skill in identifying when a factor might outperform/underperform its average return. This could apply to a rewarded factor, (e.g., correctly determining when value stocks will outperform growth stocks), but it could also apply to *unrewarded* factors, such as correctly timing geographical or industry sector exposures, commodity prices, or even security selection (a discretionary manager might refer to these as *thematic exposures*). This building block relates primarily to active return source number two: identifying mispricings.

Third Building Block: Sizing Positions

Position sizing balances managers' confidence in their alpha and factor insights while mitigating idiosyncratic risks coming from concentrated positions. Position sizing will affect all three sources of active risk, but the most dramatic impact will be on idiosyncratic risk. The general rule is that smaller positions in a greater number of securities will diversify away idiosyncratic risk and lead to lower portfolio volatility.

A factor-oriented manager who spreads their portfolio across many assets is likely to minimize the impact of idiosyncratic risk. A stock-picker is likely to hold more concentrated positions based on their insights into individual securities, and hence, deliberately assume a higher degree of idiosyncratic risk.

Integrating the Building Blocks: Breadth of Expertise

Success at combining the three building blocks is a function of a manager's breadth of experience. A manager with broader expertise is more likely to generate consistent active returns. This can be seen in the **fundamental law of active management**:

$$E(R_A) = IC\sqrt{BR}\,\sigma_{R_A}\,TC$$

where:

$E(R_A)$ = expected active return of the portfolio

IC = expected information coefficient of the manager, calculated as the correlation between manager forecasts and realized active returns

BR = breadth—the number of truly independent decisions made by the manager each year

TC = transfer coefficient, a number between 0 and 1 that measures the level to which the manager is constrained—TC will take a value of 1 if the manager has no constraints, and 0 if the manager is fully constrained

σ_{R_A} = the manager's active risk (the volatility of active returns)

This equation clearly shows that there is a direct link between breadth and expected outperformance—a larger number of independent decisions (higher breadth) should lead to higher active return.

A manager who considers a single factor defined by a single metric is unlikely to be making truly independent decisions, because all investment decisions are being driven by the same dimension, and therefore, are likely to have low breadth. A manager who uses multiple factors and multiple metrics for each factor is likely to make more independent decisions when constructing their portfolio, and hence, have higher breadth.

Approaches to Portfolio Construction

LOS 16.b: Discuss approaches for constructing actively managed equity portfolios.

The majority of investment approaches can be classified as:

- *Systematic or discretionary*: The degree to which the manager follows a set of systematic rules, rather than using discretionary judgment.
- *Bottom-up or top-down*: The degree to which the manager uses bottom-up stock-specific information, rather than macroeconomic information.

These approaches, and their use of the building blocks, are summarized in Figure 16.1.

Figure 16.1: Approaches and Their Use of Building Blocks

	Systematic	Discretionary
Top-Down	■ Emphasizes macro rewarded factors ■ Factor timing possible but rare ■ Diversified across broad universe ■ Formal portfolio optimization used ■ Few managers in this category	■ Emphasizes macro rewarded factors ■ Most likely to use factor timing ■ Diversified across broad universe or concentrated on smaller subset of securities ■ Less formal portfolio construction
Bottom-Up	■ Emphasizes security-specific factors ■ No factor timing ■ Diversified across broad universe ■ Formal portfolio optimization used	■ Emphasizes security-specific characteristics or factors ■ Potential factor timing ■ Diversified across broad universe or concentrated on smaller subset of securities ■ Less formal portfolio construction

(*Based on Exhibit 6 in CFA Institute Reading 18*)

Objectives and Constraints

Portfolio construction can be viewed as an optimization problem with a goal (the objective function) and a set of constraints. Objectives and constraints may be stated in absolute terms or relative to a benchmark; examples are given in Figure 16.2.

Figure 16.2: Objective Functions and Constraints of Portfolio Construction

	Absolute Framework	**Relative Framework**
Objective Function	Maximize Sharpe Ratio	Maximize Information Ratio
Constraints		
Sector/security weights	Maximum size in portfolio	Maximum deviation from benchmark
Risk	Maximum portfolio volatility specified as multiple (e.g., 0.9) of benchmark volatility	Maximum tracking error (active risk)
Market capitalization	Maximum/minimum set by mandate	Maximum/minimum set by mandate

Other approaches to optimization include:

- Specifying objectives in terms of *risk* (e.g., minimizing portfolio volatility, downside risk, or drawdowns).
- Maximizing exposure to rewarded factors (e.g., maximizing exposure to the size, value, and momentum factors).

- Maximizing exposure to securities having specific characteristics custom-defined by a discretionary manager [e.g., a custom-defined metric representing deep value (significant undervaluation)].
- Heuristic approaches that use less scientific methods, such as basing weighting on the ranking of securities with respect to a specified desired characteristic (e.g., low price to book).

MODULE QUIZ 16.1

1. An active equity manager makes 10 independent decisions per month with an information coefficient of 0.1, active risk of 5% and a transfer coefficient of 0.5. The expected active annual return of this manager is *closest* to:
   A. 0.8%.
   B. 2.5%.
   C. 2.7%.
2. Which of the following managers is *most likely* to use an approach which uses factor timing techniques?
   A. Systematic bottom-up.
   B. Discretionary bottom-up.
   C. Discretionary top-down.

Video covering this content is available online.

MODULE 16.2: ACTIVE SHARE AND ACTIVE RISK

LOS 16.c: Distinguish between Active Share and active risk and discuss how each measure relates to a manager's investment strategy.

In addition to the dimensions discussed previously, investment approaches can also vary according to whether the manager is highly *benchmark-aware* or is *benchmark-agnostic* (i.e., pays little attention to the benchmark). Each manager will specify the acceptable levels of deviation from the benchmark, and quantify this deviation in terms of *Active Share* and *active risk*.

Active Share measures the degree to which the number and sizing of the positions in a manager's portfolio are different from those of a benchmark, and is given by the following equation:

$$\text{Active Share} = \frac{1}{2}\sum_{i=1}^{n}\left|W_{p,i} - W_{b,i}\right|$$

where:

n = total number of securities in the benchmark or the portfolio

$W_{p,i}$ = weight of security i in the portfolio

$W_{b,i}$ = weight of security i in the benchmark

The vertical line brackets indicate that we take the absolute value of the weighting difference, irrespective of whether it is positive or negative.

Active Share takes a value between 0 and 1. If a manager holds a portfolio of stocks that are not in the benchmark, their Active Share equals 1, whereas if they hold the benchmark weights in their portfolio their Active Share will be 0. If a portfolio has an Active Share of 0.5, we can conclude that 50% of the portfolio is identical to that of the benchmark and 50% is not.

PROFESSOR'S NOTE

Some simple numerical illustrations may help clarify the interpretation of Active Share:

Assume a universe of six stocks—A through F, with 25% of the benchmark invested in each of A, B, C, D.

The extreme cases:

Extreme Case 1: Portfolio matches benchmark (100% overlap), Active Share = 0

	Weighting			
Stock	**Portfolio**	**Benchmark**	**Under**	**Over**
A	0.25	0.25	0	0
B	0.25	0.25	0	0
C	0.25	0.25	0	0
D	0.25	0.25	0	0
E	0	0	0	0
F	0	0	0	0
	1	1	0	0
		Active Share 0		

Extreme Case 2: No overlap between portfolio and benchmark, Active Share = 1

	Weighting			
Stock	**Portfolio**	**Benchmark**	**Under**	**Over**
A	0	0.25	0.25	0
B	0	0.25	0.25	0
C	0	0.25	0.25	0
D	0	0.25	0.25	0
E	0.4	0	0	0.4
F	0.6	0	0	0.6
	1	1	1	1
		Active Share 1		

Reading 16

Two cases that fall between the extremes:

		Weighting		
Stock	**Portfolio**	**Benchmark**	**Under**	**Over**
A	0	0.25	0.25	0
B	0.1	0.25	0.15	0
C	0.3	0.25	0	0.05
D	0.6	0.25	0	0.35
E	0	0	0	0
F	0	0	0	0
	1	1	0.4	0.4
		Active Share 0.4		

		Weighting		
Stock	**Portfolio**	**Benchmark**	**Under**	**Over**
A	0.05	0.25	0.2	0
B	0	0.25	0.25	0
C	0.3	0.25	0	0.05
D	0.2	0.25	0.05	0
E	0.35	0	0	0.35
F	0.1	0	0	0.1
	1	1	0.5	0.5
		Active Share 0.5		

Per the equation, Active Share $= \frac{1}{2}\sum_{i=1}^{n}\left|W_{p,i} - W_{b,i}\right|$. In words, it is the average of the total degree of overweighting and the total degree of underweighting (ignoring the minus sign for underweighting). Because, inevitably, total overweighting = total underweighting, Active Share = total overweighting or total underweighting (as seen previously).

(1 – Active Share) can be interpreted as the percent overlap between the portfolio and the benchmark. For example, in the upper example, the holdings in common are 0.1 in B, 0.25 in C, and 0.25 in D, a total of 0.6 (= 1 – 0.4). The lower example illustrates Active Share = 0.5 (50% overlap).

If two portfolios with the same benchmark invest only in benchmark securities, the portfolio with the *fewer* securities and therefore higher degree of concentration in positions will have a *higher* level of Active Share.

Active Share is used by many investors to assess the fees paid per unit of active management. For example, a fund with an Active Share of 0.2 would be considered expensive versus a fund with an Active Share of 0.5 if both funds were charging the same fees.

Active risk, also called *tracking error*, is the standard deviation of active returns (portfolio returns minus benchmark returns). As an equation:

$$\text{active risk}\left(\sigma_{R_A}\right) = \sqrt{\frac{\sum_{t=1}^{T}\left(R_{At}\right)^2}{T-1}}$$

where R_{At} is the active return at time *t*, and *T* is the number of return periods.

PROFESSOR'S NOTE

Simply put, active risk measures how consistent is/was the portfolio's performance relative to the benchmark.

There are two different measures of active risk: *realized* active risk, which depends on historical returns, and *predicted* active risk, which requires forward-looking estimates of correlations and variances.

Active risk is affected by the degree of cross-correlation between securities, whereas Active Share is not. For example, underweighting a pharmaceutical stock in order to overweight another pharmaceutical stock will certainly increase Active Share because the weights of the portfolio will be different to the weights in the benchmark. However, if the two pharmaceutical stocks are highly correlated, the portfolio will not behave markedly different from the benchmark, hence active risk is not likely to substantially increase. On the other hand, underweighting a pharmaceutical company and overweighting a security with a low correlation to the pharmaceutical company, such as a consumer discretionary company, will likely increase both Active Share and active risk.

A portfolio manager can completely control Active Share because they control the weights of the securities in the portfolio. However, a manager cannot completely control active risk because predicted active risk depends on estimations of correlations and variances of securities that may be different from those actually realized.

Decomposition of Active Risk

Given the earlier decomposition of active return into returns to factors, alpha, and idiosyncratic risk, it is possible to show that active risk is a function of the variance due to factor exposures and the variance due to idiosyncratic risk:

$$\sigma_{R_A} = \sqrt{\sigma^2\left(\Sigma\left(\beta_{pk} - \beta_{bk}\right) \times F_k\right) + \sigma_e^2}$$

PROFESSOR'S NOTE

The variance of the skill of the manager (alpha) is deemed to be part of the idiosyncratic risk component here.

Research conclusions on the composition of active return include:

- High net exposure to a risk factor leads to high level of active risk.
- A portfolio with no net factor exposure will have active risk attributed entirely to Active Share.

- Active risk attributable to Active Share is inversely proportional to the number of securities in the portfolio.
- Active risk increases as factor and idiosyncratic risk levels increase.

Distinguishing Between Different Portfolio Management Approaches

Active risk and Active Share can be used to discriminate between different portfolio management approaches, with respect to their factor exposures and level of diversification. The types of approaches, in order of increasing Active Share and active risk, can be broadly summarized as follows:

Investment Style	Description	Active Share and Active Risk
Pure indexing	No active positions: portfolio is equal to the benchmark	Zero Active Share and zero active risk
Factor neutral	No active factor bets—idiosyncratic risk low if diversified	Low active risk—Active Share low if diversified
Factor diversified	Balanced exposure to risk factors and minimized idiosyncratic risk through high number of securities in portfolio	Reasonably low active risk—high Active Share from large amount of securities used that are unlikely to be in the benchmark
Concentrated factor bets	Targeted factor bets—idiosyncratic risk likely to be high	High Active Share and high active risk
Concentrated stock picker	Targeted individual stock bets	Highest Active Share and highest active risk

This spectrum of manager styles and the approximate expected relationship with Active Share and active risk is displayed in Figure 16.3.

Figure 16.3: Approaches and Their Use of Building Blocks

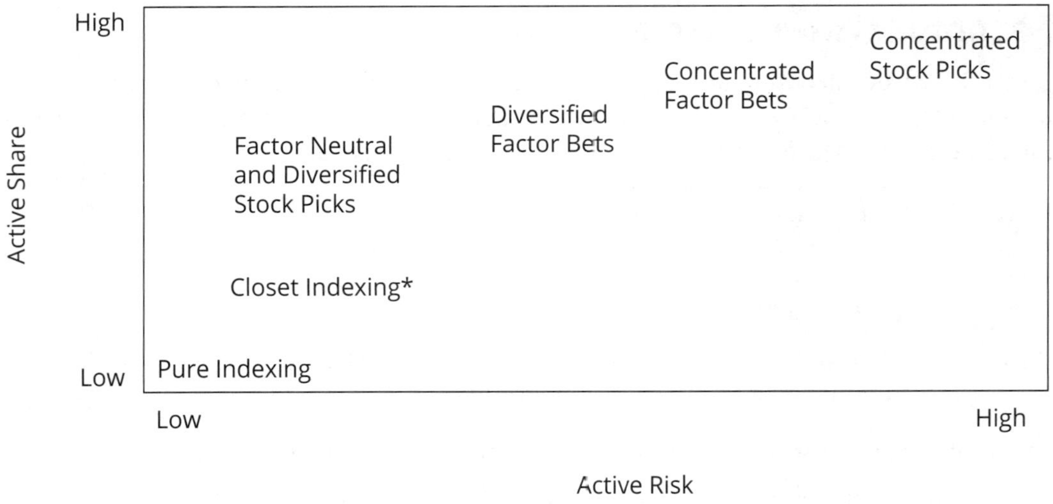

*A *closet indexer* is defined as a fund that advertises itself as being actively managed but is substantially similar to an index fund in its exposures.

PROFESSOR'S NOTE

It may be helpful to remind ourselves here of the differences between the three terms: Active Share, factor bets, and active risk.

Active Share (a number between 0 and 1) measures how similar the portfolio is to the benchmark in terms of its stock holdings; the lower the value of Active Share, the closer the portfolio is to the benchmark.

A manager makes **factor bets** when their portfolio's exposure to one or more risk factors differs from that of the benchmark. Taking factor bets necessarily involves increased Active Share, whereas a higher value of Active Share does not necessarily imply that factor bets have been taken (for example, a manager might hold Stock A instead of Stock B, but the two stocks may have identical factor exposures).

Active risk measures the extent to which the active return (portfolio return minus benchmark return) varies from period to period. It can be seen as a consequence of Active Share and factor bets.

Manager styles can also be identified through observing their sector and security-specific constraints. For example, a **sector rotator** would need to have large permitted deviations in sector weights, while a stock picker would need to have large permitted deviations in individual security weights. A diversified multi-factor investor would not need such large deviations from index weights, but would still need some flexibility in order to generate a moderate level of active risk and return.

EXAMPLE: Portfolio construction—approaches and return drivers

Based on the following information regarding four managers benchmarked against the same index, **identify** and **justify** the manager most likely to be:

- A concentrated stock picker.
- A diversified multi-factor investor.
- A closet indexer.
- A sector rotator.

Use each category *only once* in your answer.

Manager Constraints:	A	B	C	D
Target active risk	8%	5%	1%	9%
Maximum sector deviations	20%	8%	2%	0%
Maximum risk contribution, single security	3%	1%	1%	6%

Answer:

The key to this type of question is to start with the most obvious identification. Of course not everyone will agree which is most obvious. The point is start where you find the issue to be most clear-cut based on the data available.

Manager A is a sector rotator because large deviations in sector weight are allowed.

Manager D is concentrated stock selection with large risk contributions (deviation in weighting) allowed by security but no deviation in sector weight allowed.

Manager C is the closet indexer with low targeted active risk and low deviations allowed.

Manager B is the diversified multi-factor investor with moderate (neither very high nor low) active risk and sector deviations. The low single security risk likely indicates a large number of positions (reflecting the use of multiple factors to select the holdings).

MODULE QUIZ 16.2

1. A manager that substitutes a benchmark holding in their portfolio with a similar security not held in the benchmark will *most likely*:
   A. increase Active Share but not substantially increase active risk.
   B. increase active risk but not substantially increase Active Share.
   C. decrease Active Share and increase active risk.

MODULE 16.3: ALLOCATING THE RISK BUDGET

Video covering this content is available online.

LOS 16.d: Discuss the application of risk budgeting concepts in portfolio construction.

Risk budgeting is a process by which the total risk of a portfolio is allocated to constituents of the portfolio in the most efficient manner. It is an integral part of an effective risk management process. An effective risk management process has the following four steps:

1. Determine which *type* of risk measure is appropriate given the fund mandate.
   - **Absolute** risk measures are appropriate when the investment objective is expressed in terms of total returns (e.g., a long/short equity manager benchmarked against cash plus a margin).
   - **Relative** risk measures are appropriate when the investment objective is to outperform a market index.
2. Understand how each aspect of the strategy contributes to risk.
   - Does risk come from exposure to rewarded factors or allocations to sectors/securities?
3. Determine what level of *risk budget* is appropriate.
   - This is the overall level of risk targeted.
4. Properly allocate risk among individual positions/factors.

Causes and Sources of Absolute Risk

Absolute risk measures focus on the size and composition of absolute portfolio variance (i.e., without reference to any benchmark variance).

The contribution of Asset *i* to portfolio variance (CV_i) is given by the equation:

$$CV_i = \sum_{j=1}^{n} w_i w_j C_{ij} = w_i C_{ip}$$

where:

w_j = Asset *j*'s weight in the portfolio

C_{ij} = the covariance of returns between Asset *i* and Asset *j*

C_{ip} = the covariance of returns between Asset *i* and the portfolio $\left(= \sum_{j=1}^{n} w_j C_{ij}\right)$

The portfolio variance is the sum of each asset's contribution to portfolio variance.

EXAMPLE: Absolute risk attribution

A portfolio has the following characteristics:

	Portfolio Weight	Standard Deviation
Asset A	20%	22%
Asset B	30%	12%
Asset C	50%	10%
Portfolio	100%	8.6%

	Covariance		
	Asset A	**Asset B**	**Asset C**
Asset A	0.050000	0.006700	0.001300
Asset B	0.006700	0.014400	0.002000
Asset C	0.001300	0.002000	0.009800

1. **Calculate** the absolute contribution to portfolio variance of Asset A.
2. Given that the absolute contribution to portfolio variance of Assets B and C are 0.001998 and 0.002880 respectively, **calculate** the relative contribution to portfolio variance of Asset A.

Answers:

1. Asset A's contribution to total portfolio variance:

= weight of Asset A × weight of Asset A × covariance of Asset A with Asset A

+ weight of Asset A × weight of Asset B × covariance of Asset A with Asset B

+ weight of Asset A × weight of Asset C × covariance of Asset A with Asset C

= (0.20 × 0.20 × 0.050000) + (0.20 × 0.30 × 0.006700) + (0.20 × 0.50 × 0.001300)

= 0.002 + 0.000402 + 0.00013

= 0.002532

2. Portfolio variance is the sum of the absolute contributions to variance:

   = 0.002532 + 0.001998 + 0.002880 = 0.00741

   Thus the relative contribution of asset A to portfolio variance = 0.002532 / 0.00741 = 0.34 or 34%.

Portfolio variance can be attributed to sectors, countries, or pools of assets representing factors (e.g., value vs. growth), in a similar manner. Analogous to the contribution to total variance of a single asset, the contribution to portfolio variance of a sector can be calculated as its weight in the portfolio multiplied by the covariance of the sector with the portfolio.

Portfolio variance can also be separated into variance attributed to factor exposures and unexplained variance. A manager that generates most of her returns from exposure to rewarded factors (such as a multi-factor diversified manager) would expect to see a large contribution to risk explained by rewarded factors and a low contribution to risk from unexplained idiosyncratic risks. The contribution to portfolio variance of a factor is analogous to the contribution to portfolio variance of an asset, with weights replaced by beta sensitivities and assets replaced by factors. The contribution of Factor *i* to portfolio variance is given by the formula:

$$CV_i = \sum_{j=1}^{n} \beta_i \beta_j C_{ij} = \beta_i C_{ip}$$

where:

β_i = sensitivity of portfolio to Factor *i* (regression coefficient)

C_{ij} = the covariance of Factor *i* and Factor *j*

C_{ip} = the covariance of Factor *i* and the portfolio $\left(= \sum_{j=1}^{n} \beta_j C_{ij}\right)$

The portfolio variance is the sum of each factor's contribution to portfolio variance plus any unexplained variance.

EXAMPLE: Factor-based risk budgeting

The following table presents the risk-factor coefficients and variance/covariance matrix for a manager running a portfolio using a two-factor model (market and size).

		Variance/Covariance of Returns	
	Coefficients	**Market**	**Size**
Market	0.892	0.00178	0.00042
Size	–0.283	0.00042	0.00048

The standard deviation of the manager's return is 3.74%.

1. **Calculate** the proportion of the total portfolio variance explained by the market factor.
2. If the contribution to portfolio variance of the size factor is –0.00007, **calculate** the proportion of total portfolio variance that is unexplained.

Answers:

1. Variance attributed to the market factor (Factor 1):

   = coefficient of Factor 1 × coefficient of Factor 1 × covariance of Factor 1 with Factor 1

   + coefficient of Factor 1 × coefficient of Factor 2 × covariance of Factor 1 with Factor 2

   = (0.892 × 0.892 × 0.00178) + (0.892 × –0.283 × 0.00042)

   = 0.00131

   Total portfolio variance is 0.0374^2 = 0.0013988

   So, proportion of total portfolio variance explained by the market factor = 0.00131 / 0.0013988 = 93.7%

2. Total variance explained by the factors:

   = contribution to variance of Factor 1 + contribution to variance of Factor 2

   = 0.00131 + (–0.00007) = 0.00124

   Unexplained variance = total portfolio variance – variance explained by factors = 0.0013988 – 0.00124 = 0.00016

   Hence proportion of total portfolio variance that is unexplained = 0.00016 / 0.0013988 = 11.4%

PROFESSOR'S NOTE

Note that the answers to Parts 1 and 2 sum to more than 100%, because the size factor makes a negative contribution to total portfolio variance.

Causes and Sources of Relative/Active Risk

Relative risk is an appropriate measure when the manager is concerned with performance relative to a market index. Active variance, which is the variance of the differences between portfolio and benchmark returns, can be broken down in an analogous manner to absolute variance.

The contribution of Asset *i* to portfolio *active* variance (CAV_i) is given by the equation:

$$CAV_i = (w_{pi} - w_{bi})RC_{ip}$$

where:

w_{pi} = weight of Asset *i* in the portfolio

w_{bi} = weight of Asset *i* in the benchmark

RC_{ip} = the covariance between the active returns of Asset *i* and the active returns of the portfolio, which reflects the covariances between the active returns for Asset *i* and the active returns for each of the *n* assets in the portfolio:

$$RC_{ip} = \sum_{j=1}^{n}\left(w_{pj} - w_{bj}\right)RC_{ij}$$

Adding up the CAVs for all the assets in the portfolio will give the variance of the portfolio's active return (AV_p).

PROFESSOR'S NOTE

These formulas are analogous to those seen earlier for the contribution to absolute risk, but using active weight of the asset, and covariance of active returns. It is intuitively reasonable that an asset will contribute more to active variance if it has a higher active weight and if its active returns are related to overall portfolio active returns.

An example would be a benchmark composed of a 50/50 allocation to two equity indexes. The portfolio comprises allocations to these two indices and to a third asset, cash. Relevant information is displayed in Figure 16.4.

Figure 16.4: Relative Risk Attribution

	Benchmark Weight	Portfolio Weight	Standard Deviation	Active Risk	Correlation of Active Returns			Variance of Active Returns Attributed to Each Asset (%)
					Index A	Index B	Cash	
Index A	50%	35%	15%	6%	1.00	–1.00	–0.72	18%
Index B	50%	35%	9%	6%	–1.00	1.00	0.72	–18%
Cash	0%	30%	0.25%	12%	–0.72	0.72	1.00	100%
Total				3.60%	–0.72	0.72	1.00	100%

PROFESSOR'S NOTE

The formulas given have been used to compute $CAV_{\text{Index A}} = 0.000233$, $CAV_{\text{Index B}} = -0.000233$, and $CAV_{\text{Cash}} = 0.001296$, from which $AV_P = 0.001296$ and $\sigma_{AR} = \sqrt{0.001296} = 3.6\%$, as shown in the table. The rightmost column of the table gives each CAV as a percentage of AV_P. Note the calculation of CAV is not shown in the curriculum; thus, it will not be tested on the exam.

The $CAV_{\text{index A}}$ is calculated as follows:

$CAV_{\text{index A}} = -0.15 \times RC_{\text{A, portfolio}}$

where $RC_{\text{A, portfolio}} = (-0.15 \times RC_{A,A}) + (-0.15 \times RC_{A,B}) + (0.3 \times RC_{A,Cash})$

where $RC_{A,A} = (0.06 \times 0.06 \times 1) = 0.0036$

$RC_{A,B} = (0.06 \times 0.06 \times -1) = -0.0036$

$RC_{A,Cash} = (0.06 \times 0.12 \times -0.72) = -0.005184$

So $RC_{\text{A, port}} = (-0.15 \times 0.0036) + (-0.15 \times -0.0036) + (0.3 \times -0.005184) =$
$-0.00054 + 0.00054 - 0.0015552 = -0.0015552$

$CAV_{\text{index A}} = -0.15 \times -0.0015552 = 0.00023328$

The important points to note are:

- Contribution to active variance is a function of active risk not absolute standard deviation. While cash has a very low standard deviation, it has an active risk twice that of the indexes comprising the benchmark due to the low correlation of cash versus the benchmark. This leads to cash contributing to 100% of the active variance.

- The correlation of the active returns of index A and index B is –1. This is because the benchmark is an equally weighted average of the two indices—when one is outperforming the benchmark (so has positive active returns) then the other must be underperforming the benchmark (giving negative active returns).

Similar to the absolute risk attribution of the previous section, relative risk attribution can be conducted on a country, sector or factor level.

Active portfolio variance can also be segmented into variance explained by active factor exposures, and unexplained active variance associated with idiosyncratic risks.

Determining the Appropriate Level of Risk

Practical considerations when considering the appropriate level of portfolio risk include:

1. *Implementation constraints.* Constraints on short positions or on leverage may limit the manager's ability to under/overweight. Liquidity issues may increase costs as a manager increases active risk, which leads to a degradation of the information ratio as the extra costs weigh on active returns.
2. *Limited diversification opportunities.* We know from basic portfolio theory that increasing risk leads to decreasing marginal increases in expected returns (this gives rise to the concave efficient frontier of Markowitz). Portfolios with higher risk/return targets eventually run out of high-return investment opportunities and lose the ability to diversify efficiently, thereby reducing the Sharpe ratio.
3. *Leverage and its implications for risk.* While leverage could be used to solve issue number two in a single period (allowing the portfolio to move up the linear capital allocation line, rather than following the curved efficient frontier), too much leverage will eventually bring a reduction of expected compounded return in a multi-period setting. This comes from the fact that the geometric compounded returns (R_g) of a portfolio are approximately related to arithmetic non-compounded returns (R_a) and portfolio volatility σ as follows:

   $$R_g = R_a - \frac{\sigma^2}{2}$$

   Leverage increases both R_a and σ, but the squaring of σ in the expression means there will be a point where increasing leverage will lower expected geometric compounded returns over time.

PROFESSOR'S NOTE

Point three is related to the idea that geometric compounded returns over time fall as the volatility of a portfolio increases. For example, if a portfolio falls 2% and subsequently rises by 2% it will nearly return to its previous value (0.98 × 1.02 = 0.9996). However, if a portfolio falls by 20% and subsequently rises by 20% the portfolio value at the end of two periods will be lower (0.8 × 1.2 = 0.96). Both these portfolios have the same arithmetic uncompounded return of zero, yet the second has a lower compounded return over two periods because of its higher volatility.

Allocating the Risk Budget

An active manager should efficiently allocate their risk budget to sources that accurately represent their investment approach. Figure 16.5 compares sources of risk for a manager with balanced exposure to rewarded factors (Factor Diversified) versus a manager with concentrated sector and cash bets (Sector Rotator).

Figure 16.5: Comparative Sources of Risk, Drivers of Return

	Factor Diversified	Sector Rotator
Number of securities	High (in the hundreds)	Low (in the tens)
Position concentration	Low	High
Cash positions	Very low	High when allocated to cash
Market beta	Close to one (diversified)	Higher/lower than one depending on risk targets
Absolute risk	Lower	Higher, though tempered by large allocation to cash
Active risk	Lower	Higher due to large idiosyncratic risks coming from concentrated positions and sector bets
Active Share	Lower	Higher, consistent with higher security concentration
Average sector deviation	Lower	Higher, consistent with willingness to take sector bets
Source of risk: market	Higher	Lower, consistent with higher security concentration
Source of risk: sectors	Lower	Higher, consistent with sector bets
Source of risk: styles	Lower	Higher, consistent with concentrated positions
Source of risk: unexplained	Lower	Higher, consistent with sector rotation and concentrated positions

Additional Risk Measures

LOS 16.e: Discuss risk measures that are incorporated in equity portfolio construction and describe how limits set on these measures affect portfolio construction.

Risk constraints can be classified as *heuristic* or *formal*.

- **Heuristic risk constraints** are based on experience or general ideas of good practice. Examples include limits on exposure to individual positions, sectors or regions, limits on leverage, or measures designed to control the degree of illiquidity and turnover in the portfolio.

- **Formal risk constraints** are often statistical in nature. A key distinction between formal and heuristic risk measures is that formal risk measures require forecasts of return distributions, which introduces estimation error. Examples include limits on volatility, active risk, skewness, drawdowns, and VaR-based measures including:
  - Conditional VaR (CVaR)—the expected loss given VaR has been exceeded (also called expected tail loss or expected shortfall).
  - Incremental VaR (IVaR)—the change in VaR from adding a new position to a portfolio.
  - Marginal VaR (MVaR)—the impact of a very small change in position size on VaR.

Other points of note regarding risk constraints include:

- *Leverage* magnifies the negative impact of incorrect risk estimations. Infrequent but high impact negative "tail events" such as the market crashes seen in the early 2000s and 2008 can force a leveraged manager to liquidate all or part of his portfolio in an unfavorable environment, crystallizing significant losses.
- Unexpected increases in *volatility* can also derail investment strategies. Managers may tighten risk controls in more volatile periods to protect the portfolio from losses.
- Risk measures used depend on the style of management. A benchmark-agnostic manager with an absolute return philosophy is less likely to be concerned with statistical measures such as active risk and more concerned with more practical measures such as portfolio drawdown. A market-neutral equity manager is more likely to target keeping absolute volatility within a specific range in order to deliver the promised market-neutral low-volatility returns to investors.
- Portfolios with fewer positions will have higher estimation errors due to the random specific risks of concentrated positions, hence using formal risk measures is likely to be more difficult.

MODULE QUIZ 16.3

1. The contribution to total variance of a geographical country allocation is *best* defined as:
   A. the weight of the country in the portfolio multiplied by the covariance of the country returns with the global market portfolio returns.
   B. the weight of the country in the portfolio multiplied by the correlation of the country returns with the portfolio returns.
   C. the weight of the country in the portfolio multiplied by the covariance of the country returns with the portfolio returns.

2. Forecasting of return distributions is *most likely* required by:
   A. heuristic risk constraints only.
   B. formal risk constraints only.
   C. both heuristic and formal risk constraints.

Video covering this content is available online.

MODULE 16.4: IMPLICIT COST-RELATED CONSIDERATIONS IN PORTFOLIO CONSTRUCTION

LOS 16.f: Discuss how assets under management, position size, market liquidity, and portfolio turnover affect equity portfolio construction decisions.

The *market impact* cost of an investment strategy is an implicit cost related to the price movement caused by managers executing trades in the market. A manager buying securities may force security prices up, similarly a manager selling securities may force security prices down, thereby eroding the manager's alpha.

Factors that affect market impact costs include:

- Assets under management (AUM) versus market capitalization of securities:
  - The lower absolute level of trading volume for *smaller* cap securities can be a liquidity barrier to managers with *higher* AUM.
  - For example, assume a small cap investment has a market capitalization of \$5 billion and that 1% of its capitalization trades each day on average, implying daily turnover of 0.01 × \$5 billion = \$50 million. A manager of a \$1 billion fund may have a liquidity constraint of not holding more than 10% of the average trading volume of a security, which would limit the holding in the company to 0.1 × \$50 million = \$5 million. This implies the maximum position in the fund the manager can take in the investment is \$5 million / \$1 billion = 0.5%. This may not be a large enough position to allow the manager to execute their strategy, particularly if the strategy involves concentrated positions.
- Higher **portfolio turnover** and shorter **investment horizons** generally lead to higher market impact costs.
- Managers whose trades include "information" (where the trades act as a signal to the market that investment conditions have changed and encourage other market participants to carry out similar trades) will likely have higher market impact costs.

The market impact cost of a single trade is often measured by "slippage." **Slippage** is defined as the difference between the execution price and the midpoint of the quoted market bid/ask spread at the time the trade was first entered. Estimates of slippage based on recent empirical data lead to four notable conclusions:

1. Slippage costs are usually higher than explicit costs.
2. Slippage costs are greater for smaller-cap securities than for large-cap securities.

3. Slippage costs are not necessarily greater in emerging markets.
4. Slippage costs are substantially higher in times of high market volatility.

For successful small-cap focused strategies, the ability of the manager to continue implementing the strategy as AUM grow may be impaired by increasing slippage costs. In this case, the manager should either close their funds to contributions from new investors or inform investors that their strategy may have to change. Investors should be wary of managers raising new funds on the back of a track record that cannot be scaled for higher AUM.

Due to the higher impact costs of smaller-cap securities, a fund with a focus on large-cap stocks can support a higher level of AUM than a similar-strategy fund focused on small-cap stocks. A firm focused on small-cap stocks must either limit its AUM, diversify, limit turnover, or adapt its trading strategy to cap impact costs as AUM grow.

EXAMPLE: Issues of scale

A diversified multi-factor fund has a size of $200 million and 350 individual positions. The benchmark is a large/mid cap index with 1000 constituents and total market cap of approximately $20 trillion. The smaller securities in the index trade about 1.5% of shares outstanding daily. The strategy has the following constraints:

1. No investment can be made in any security that has an index weight of less than 0.02%.
2. The maximum fund position percentage holding is equal to the lesser of 10 × index weight or index weight plus 100 bps.
3. Absolute position sizes cannot exceed 5% of the security's average daily trading volume (ADV) over the trailing 12 months.

Based on the three constraints listed previously, **calculate** the level of AUM, which the fund's ability to execute this strategy is likely to be impaired.

Answer:

The limit on the absolute size of a stock that can be held in the fund for the smallest cap position is set by Constraints 1 and 3.

Constraint 1 indicates the manager cannot invest in stocks whose market cap is below approximately 0.0002 × $20 trillion = $4 billion.

The ADV of this smallest cap holding would be about 0.015 × $4bn = $60 million.

Constraint 3 implies the maximum absolute position size for this smallest cap holding is therefore 0.05 × $60 million = $3 million.

The strategy has a maximum position size set by Constraint 2.

Constraint 2 implies the maximum position for the smallest cap security is the lesser of 10 × 0.02% = 0.2% and 0.02% + 100 bps = 1.02%. This means the maximum position size in the fund is 0.2%.

Reading 16

> If the manager cannot hold up to 0.2% of the fund in the smallest capitalization position, then the ability to carry out the strategy is potentially impaired.
>
> Given that Constraints 1 and 3 imply the manager cannot hold more than \$3 million in the smallest capitalization holding, this means the ability to carry out the strategy is impaired by illiquidity when AUM reach \$3,000,000 / 0.002 = \$1.5 billion.
>
> If the fund size is higher than this, the manager is constrained by the liquidity of small cap positions and cannot hold the maximum weight allowed by the strategy.

MODULE QUIZ 16.4

1. All else equal, higher market impact cost is *most likely* associated with:
   A. lower AUM.
   B. investing in large cap securities.
   C. higher portfolio turnover.

MODULE 16.5: THE WELL-CONSTRUCTED PORTFOLIO

Video covering this content is available online.

LOS 16.g: Evaluate the efficiency of a portfolio structure given its investment mandate.

A **well-constructed portfolio** should deliver the characteristics promised to investors in a cost-efficient and risk-efficient way. This involves:

- A clear investment philosophy and a consistent investment process.
- Risk and structural characteristics as promised to investors.
- Achieving desired risk exposures in the most efficient manner.
- Reasonably low operating costs, given the strategy.

Funds aiming to deliver different required characteristics will have different well-structured portfolios. The following general points can be made about portfolios that have the same desired characteristics:

- Portfolios that can achieve desired risk exposures *with fewer positions* are likely to have more focus on risk management in the portfolio construction process. While this will not guarantee excess return, it does indicate risk efficiency is likely higher.
- If two portfolios have similar risk factor exposures, the product with the *lower absolute volatility and lower active risk* will likely be preferred (assuming similar costs).
- If two portfolios have similar active and absolute risks, similar costs, similar manager alpha skills, then the portfolio *with the highest Active Share* is preferable because this will leverage the alpha skill of the manager and have higher expected return.

- When selecting equity managers to create the equity allocation of a multi-asset fund, managers should be combined to create an overall equity allocation in the portfolio that is well-constructed. A risk factor exposure that is desired but not present in one manager could be compensated for by adding a different manager that specializes in generating exposure to that risk factor.

Long/Short, Long Extension, and Market-Neutral Portfolio Construction

LOS 16.h: Discuss the long-only, long extension, long/short, and equitized market-neutral approaches to equity portfolio construction, including their risks, costs, and effects on potential alphas.

Short selling securities is the process of borrowing securities and selling them in the market, with the intention of buying the securities back later at a lower price and returning them to the lender. Short sellers therefore make profits from security prices falling.

Introducing the ability to short sell securities allows investment managers to take advantage of negative insights gained through their investment research. **Long/short** is a general term used to describe any portfolio that can short sell securities.

The Merits of Long-Only Investing

An investor's choice between following long-only or long/short strategies is influenced by several factors:

- **Long-term risk premiums**, such as the market risk premium, are earned by investors going net *long* securities. Investors that short sell securities over the long term will therefore suffer negative returns. Investors that have *shorter* time horizons concerned about negative returns may prefer strategies that have short exposures.
- The **capacity and scalability** of a long-only strategy is set by the liquidity of the underlying securities. Capacity of short selling strategies is set by the availability of securities to *borrow* to facilitate short selling. This means the capacity of long/short strategies is likely to be lower than for long-only strategies, particularly those large-cap funds that face few long-only capacity issues.
- Due to **limited legal liability** laws, the maximum a long investor can lose is the amount they paid for the security (if the security falls to zero). The potential loss to a short seller is unlimited, however, as they lose as stock prices *rise*, and stocks prices have no price ceiling. This makes "naked" short selling with no hedging riskier than a long-only strategy.

- **Regulations** allow some countries to ban short selling in the interests of financial market stability.
- **Transactional complexity** is higher for a long/short fund. A long-only investor need only instruct a broker to buy shares and subsequently sell them. A short seller must source shares to borrow, provide collateral to the lender of the shares, and faces the risk the lender recalls the shares at an inopportune time. A short seller usually appoints a prime broker to deal with stock borrowing and collateral functions, which introduces an extra layer of counterparty risk, because if the prime broker goes bankrupt collateral may be lost.
- **Costs** are likely to be higher for long/short funds than long-only funds both in terms of management fees and operational expenses.
- The **personal ideology** of an investor might cause them to object to short selling. This may be because they find the concept of profiting from the failure of others morally wrong, or they believe the expertise to short sell is not consistently available from managers. Investors may find the leverage involved in some long/short strategies unacceptable.

Long/Short Portfolio Construction

There are many different styles of long/short strategies, defined by their *gross* and *net exposure*. Gross exposure is the sum of the value of the long positions plus the absolute value of the short position, expressed as a percent of investor's capital. Net exposure is the difference between the value of the long positions and the value of the short positions, again expressed as a percentage of investor's capital.

For example, a long/short fund raises $100 million of capital from investors. They invest $80 million in long positions and short sell $30 million of securities. Hence, the value of long positions is 80% and the value of short positions is 30%. Gross exposure is 110% (80% + 30%) and net exposure is 50% (80% – 30%). Note that this strategy will have a cash balance of $50 million comprising $20 million of uninvested capital on the long side ($100 million – $80 million), and $30 million of short sale proceeds.

Specific types of long/short funds include *long extension* and *market-neutral* funds.

Long extension portfolios are long/short strategies typically constrained to have a net exposure of 100%. For example, a long extension portfolio might have a long position of 130% and a short position of 30% (referred to as a 130/30 fund). This is a constrained form of long/short fund, in that the manager has no real discretion over gross/net exposure. This would be preferred by investors that want 100% net market exposure but also wish to allow the manager to engage in some level of short selling in order to benefit from negative views.

Market-neutral portfolios aim to remove market exposure through their long and short exposures. A simple example would be a fund that is long $200 million of assets with a market beta of 0.9 and short $150 million of assets with a market beta of 1.2, giving a net market beta of zero. If the long and short positions are of equal size (and thus have equal betas) then gross exposure will be twice the long position value and net exposure will be zero. These funds should have lower volatility than long-only strategies, and low correlation with other strategies. The objective will be to neutralize risks where the manager believes they have no comparative advantage in forecasting, allowing them to concentrate on their specific skills. Often market-neutral strategies are used for diversification purposes, rather than for the purpose of seeking high returns. Note that it is difficult in practice to maintain a zero beta, given that correlations between exposures change continually.

Market-neutral portfolios can be constructed through *pairs trading*, where the securities of similar companies are bought and sold to exploit perceived mispricings. Quantitative approaches to pairs trading are referred to as *statistical arbitrage* (stat arb).

PROFESSOR'S NOTE

Stat arb was previously discussed in detail in Reading 15.

The Benefits and Drawbacks of Long/Short Strategies

Long/short strategies offer the following *benefits*:

- Greater ability to express negative ideas than a long-only strategy. The most negative position a long-only manager can take is to not hold a security, meaning that maximum underweighting a long-only manager can take is set by the weight of the security in the benchmark. A long/short manager is not constrained in this way because they can short securities. This will increase the information ratio because lower constraints will increase the transfer coefficient of the manager (TC, measuring their ability to translate insights into investment decisions, as seen earlier in the fundamental law of active management).
- Ability to use the leverage generated by short positions to gear into high-conviction long ideas.
- Ability to remove market risk and act as a diversifying investment against other strategies.
- Greater ability to control exposure to risk factors. Because most rewarded factors (size, value, momentum, etc.) are obtained through a long/short portfolio, being able to short sell allows managers to better control their exposure to these factors.

PROFESSOR'S NOTE

Long/short portfolios that are constructed to represent rewarded factors were previously discussed.

Long/short strategies contain the following *drawbacks:*

- Unlike a long position, a short position will cause the manager to suffer losses if the price of the security increases. This means potential losses are unlimited because security prices are not bounded above. It also means the manager is reducing long-term exposure to the market risk premium.
- Some long/short strategies require significant leverage, which magnifies losses as well as gains.

Reading 16

- The cost of borrowing securities can become too high, particularly for securities that are difficult to borrow.
- Losses on the short position will increase collateral demands from stock lenders, particularly if leverage has been used. This may force the manager to liquidate positions at unfavorable prices. The manager may also be vulnerable to a *short squeeze*, where a sudden rise in the price of a heavily-shorted security forces short sellers to cover positions, buy back shares and potentially force the share price higher. Lenders of securities could also recall shares at inopportune times causing disruption to the manager's strategy.

MODULE QUIZ 16.5

1. If two portfolios have similar active and absolute risks, similar costs, and similar manager alpha skills, then:
   A. the portfolios must have equal Active Share.
   B. the portfolio with highest Active Share would be preferred.
   C. the portfolio with lowest Active Share would be preferred.
2. In general, which of the following statements *best* describes a benefit regarding long/short hedge fund strategies?
   A. The ability to use the leverage generated by short positions to gear into high conviction long ideas.
   B. The reduction of the long-term exposure to the market risk premium.
   C. The high leverage used by some market neutral strategies to generate investor returns.

KEY CONCEPTS

LOS 16.a

The three main building blocks of active return (excess return above a benchmark) for an active equity manager are:

- Active rewarded factor (beta) weightings (taking exposures that differ from the benchmark). Factor exposures include market, size, value, momentum, liquidity, et cetera.
- Alpha skills—timing rewarded and unrewarded factors, sectors, and securities. This primarily generates excess return through identifying mispricings.
- Position sizing—large positions affect all three sources of active returns, but will primarily generate high idiosyncratic risk (good/bad luck). It may be a required part of a concentrated manager's alpha-generating strategy.

Success at combining these building blocks comes from breadth of expertise, defined as the number of independent decisions the manager makes per year. Higher breadth implies higher ability to outperform benchmarks. We see this in the fundamental law of active management:

$$E(R_A) = IC\sqrt{BR}\,\sigma_{R_A}\,TC$$

LOS 16.b

Decision-making can be can be systematic (rule-driven) or discretionary (opinion-driven). Discretionary managers are more likely to engage in factor timing, hold concentrated portfolios, and are less likely to use formal portfolio optimization techniques. Information used can be top-down (relating to the macro environment) or bottom-up (relating to individual securities).

Objectives and constraints of managers can be absolute (e.g., maximize Sharpe ratio subject to maximum volatility) or relative (e.g., maximize information ratio subject to maximum active risk). Other constraints may focus on minimizing risk, maximizing exposures to desired factors, or heuristic approaches.

LOS 16.c

Active Share measures the degree to which the number and sizing of the positions in a manager's portfolio differ from those of a benchmark:

$$\text{Active Share} = \frac{1}{2}\sum_{i=1}^{n}\left|W_{p,i} - W_{b,i}\right|$$

Active Share falls between 0 and 1, and the lower the Active Share, the more similar are the portfolio's holdings to the benchmark. If a portfolio has an Active Share of 0.5, we can conclude that 50% of the portfolio is identical to that of the benchmark and 50% is not. A manager can completely control their Active Share because they completely control position sizes in the portfolio.

Active risk (tracking error), is the standard deviation of active returns (portfolio returns minus benchmark returns). A manager can not completely control active risk because it depends on estimates of covariances and variances of securities in the portfolio and the benchmark.

Active risk has two sources: active factor exposure (active beta) and idiosyncratic risk from concentrated positions (variance from both the skill and luck of the manager):

$$\text{Active risk}\left(\sigma_{R_A}\right) = \sqrt{\frac{\sum_{t=1}^{T}\left(R_{At}\right)^2}{T-1}} = \sqrt{\sigma^2\left(\Sigma\left(\beta_{pk}-\beta_{bk}\right)\times F_k\right)+\sigma_e^2}$$

LOS 16.d

Risk budgeting is the process by which the contribution to total risk of the portfolio is allocated to constituents of the portfolio in the most efficient manner. Contribution to portfolio variance can be calculated on an absolute or relative basis.

- The contribution of Asset *i* to absolute portfolio variance
$$= CV_i = \sum_{j=1}^{n} w_i w_j C_{ij} = w_i C_{ip}$$
- The contribution of Factor *i* to absolute portfolio variance
$$= CV_i = \sum_{j=1}^{n} \beta_i \beta_j C_{ij} = \beta_i C_{ip}$$
- The contribution of Asset *i* to relative portfolio variance
$$= CAV_i = \sum_{j=1}^{n}\left(w_{pi}-w_{bi}\right)\left(w_{pj}-w_{bj}\right)RC_{ij} = \left(w_{pi}-w_{bi}\right)RC_{ip}$$

Practical considerations when considering the appropriate level of portfolio risk include:

- Implementation constraints (e.g., limits on position sizes) causing information ratio degradation as active risk increases.
- Limited diversification opportunities in higher risk investments.
- Leverage increasing volatility and causing lower geometric average compounded returns over multiple periods.

LOS 16.e

Risk constraints can be classified as heuristic (based on experience like arbitrary position limits) or formal (based on statistical measures such as VaR). Formal constraints require the estimation of return distributions which introduces estimation error. This estimation error can be magnified by leverage and the idiosyncratic risk of concentrated positions.

LOS 16.f

The market impact cost of an investment strategy is an implicit cost related to the price movement caused by managers executing trades in the market. Managers with higher AUM, higher turnover and shorter time horizons, whose trades have a higher information content, dealing in smaller-cap less-liquid securities, will have higher market impact costs.

A firm focused on small-cap stocks must either limit its AUM, diversify, limit turnover, or adapt its trading strategy to cap impact costs as AUM grow.

LOS 16.g

A well-constructed portfolio should deliver the characteristics promised to investors in a cost-efficient and risk-efficient way. This involves:

- A clear investment philosophy and a consistent investment process.
- Risk and structural characteristics as promised to investors.
- Achieving desired risk exposures in the most efficient manner.
- Reasonably low operating costs given the strategy.

LOS 16.h

An investor's choice between following long-only or long/short strategies is influenced by several factors, including:

- Long-term risk premiums.
- Capacity and scalability.
- Limited legal liability.
- Regulation.
- Transactional complexity.
- Costs.
- Personal ideology.

Long extension portfolios guarantee investors 100% net exposure with a specified short exposure. A typical 130/30 fund will have 130% long and 30% short positions.

Market-neutral portfolios aim to remove market exposure through offsetting long and short positions. Pairs trading is a common technique in building market-neutral portfolios, with quantitative pair trading referred to as statistical arbitrage.

Benefits of long/short strategies include the ability to better express negative views, the ability to gear into high-conviction long positions, the removal of market risk to diversify, and the ability to better control risk factor exposures.

Drawbacks of long/short strategies include potential large losses because share prices are not bounded above, negative exposures to risk premiums, potentially high leverage for market-neutral funds, the costs of borrowing securities, and collateral demands from prime brokers. Being subject to a short squeeze on short positions is also a risk.

ANSWER KEY FOR MODULE QUIZZES

Module Quiz 16.1

1. **C** The manager will take 10 × 12 = 120 independent decisions per year. According to the fundamental law of active management the expected annual active return of the manager will be $0.1 \times \sqrt{120} \times 5\% \times 0.5 = 2.74\%$. (LOS 16.a)

2. **C** Factor timing techniques are difficult to use in a systematic rules-driven way and signals used to generate trading ideas are more often top-down verse bottom-up. (LOS 16.b)

Module Quiz 16.2

1. **A** By substituting a benchmark holding with a non-benchmark holding the manager will increase Active Share because Active Share measures the overall differences in weights between the portfolio and the benchmark. However, if the new security introduced into the portfolio behaves similarly to the benchmark security that has been substituted there may not be a significant increase in active risk of the portfolio because the substitution is unlikely to cause a major increase in the relative volatility of portfolio returns versus benchmark returns. (LOS 16.c)

Module Quiz 16.3

1. **C** Analogous to the contribution to total variance of a single asset, the contribution to portfolio variance of a geography can be calculated as its weight in the portfolio multiplied by the covariance of the country with the portfolio. (LOS 16.d)

2. **B** Heuristic risk constraints are rules of thumb that are deemed to be good practice but lack empirical evidence, such as maximum position size. Formal risk constraints are statistical in nature and usually involves statistical forecasting of return distributions. (LOS 16.e)

Module Quiz 16.4

1. **C** Answer A is incorrect; higher AUM will cause higher market impact costs because fund trades will be larger. Answer B is incorrect; larger cap securities are likely to be more liquid, and hence, offer lower impact costs. Higher portfolio turnover means the manager needs to trade more frequently, which implies a bigger market impact cost because some market impact cost will occur every time the manager trades. (LOS 16.f)

Module Quiz 16.5

1. **B** If two portfolios have similar active and absolute risks, similar costs, similar manager alpha skills, then the portfolio *with the highest Active Share* is preferable because this will leverage the alpha skill of the manager and have higher expected return. (LOS 16.g)

2. **A** The ability to use the leverage generated by short positions to gear into high conviction long ideas is a benefit of long/short investing which should improve the manager's ability to earn alpha on the long portfolio.

   With short positions, it means that that the manager is reducing long-term exposure to the market risk premium, which is a drawback of long/short strategies. The high leverage is a benefit in that it does magnify gains, however, it also magnifies losses so it is also a drawback. Therefore, it is not the best answer. (LOS 16.h)

TOPIC QUIZ: EQUITY

You have now finished the Equity topic section. On your Schweser online dashboard, you can find a Topic Quiz that will provide immediate feedback on how effective your study of this material has been. The test is best taken timed; allow three minutes per question. Topic Quizzes are more exam-like than typical QBank questions or module quiz questions. A score less than 70% suggests that additional review of the topic is needed.

FORMULAS

Expected Return is the sum of:

1. Coupon income: annual coupon amount / current bond price
2. Rolldown return: (projected ending bond price (BP) – beginning BP) / beginning BP; based on no change in the yield curve
3. Price change due to investor's benchmark yield change predictions: $(-MD \times \Delta Y) + (\frac{1}{2} \times C \times \Delta Y^2)$
4. Price change due to investor's spread change predictions: $(-MD \times \Delta S) + (\frac{1}{2} \times C \times \Delta S^2)$
5. Currency gain or loss: projected change in value of foreign currencies weighted for exposure to the currency

Rolling yield = coupon income + rolldown return

r_p = portfolio return (amount) / portfolio equity

Return for a leveraged portfolio: $r_I + [(V_B / V_E) \times (r_I - r_B)]$

where:

r_p = return on portfolio
r_I = return on invested assets
r_B = rate paid on borrowings
V_B = amount of leverage
V_E = amount of equity invested

leverage = (notional value of contract – margin amount) / margin amount

Rebate rate = collateral earnings rate – security lending rate

$$\text{convexity} = \frac{\text{Macaulay duration}^2 + \text{Macaulay duration} + \text{dispersion}}{(1 + \text{periodic IRR})^2}$$

BPV = MD × V × 0.0001 = price value of a basis point

$$\text{futures BPV} \approx \frac{BPV_{CTD}}{CF_{CTD}}$$

$$N_f = \frac{\text{BPV of liability} - \text{BPV of current portfolio}}{\text{BPV of futures}}$$

$$\text{effective D} = \frac{PV_- - PV_+}{2 \times \Delta\text{curve} \times PV_0}$$

In formulas that refer to MD, and if effective duration differs from MD, option positions are present and effective duration must be used instead of MD.

The notional swap principal (NP) required to close the duration gap for a 100% hedge is the duration gap in BPV divided by the swap BPV per 1 NP.

$$\text{effective duration} = \frac{(PV_-) - (PV_+)}{2(\Delta \text{curve})(PV_0)}$$

$$\text{effective convexity} = \frac{(PV_-) + (PV_+) - 2(PV_0)}{(\Delta \text{curve})^2 (PV_0)}$$

$\%\Delta \text{ value} = -MD_{\text{key rate n}}\ \Delta y_n$

$MD = \text{Macaulay duration} / (1 + YTM_{\text{periodic}})$

$\%\Delta \text{ value} = -MD\ \Delta y$

$\%\Delta \text{ relative value} = -D_S\ \Delta s$

$\text{spread} = y_{\text{higher yield}} - y_{\text{government}}$

$$\text{KeyRateDur} = -\frac{\text{change in portfolio value}}{\text{portfolio value} \times \text{change in key rate}}$$

butterfly spread = –(short-term yield) + (2 × medium-term yield) – long-term yield

credit spread ≈ POD × LGD

$$\text{EffRateDur}_{\text{FRN}} = \frac{(PV_-) - (PV_+)}{2(\Delta MRR)(PV_0)}$$

$$\text{EffSpreadDur}_{\text{FRN}} = \frac{(PV_-) - (PV_+)}{2(\Delta DM)(PV_0)}$$

where:

PV_0 = current value of the portfolio

PV_- = value of portfolio when benchmark curve is shifted down

PV_+ = value of portfolio when benchmark curve is shifted up

ΔMRR = change in benchmark curve

ΔDM = change in DM

$$\text{effective spread duration} = \frac{(PV_-) - (PV_+)}{2(\Delta \text{spread})(PV_0)}$$

$$\text{effective spread convexity} = \frac{(PV_-) + (PV_+) - 2(PV_0)}{(\Delta\text{spread})^2 (PV_0)}$$

$$\%\Delta\text{price} = (-\text{EffSpreadDur} \times \Delta\text{spread}) + (\tfrac{1}{2} \times \text{EffSpreadCon} \times \Delta\text{spread}^2)$$

$$\text{DTS} \approx \text{EffSpreadDur} \times \text{spread}$$

$$\text{expected excess spread} = \text{spread} - (\text{EffSpreadDur} \times \Delta\text{spread}) - (\text{POD} \times \text{LGD})$$

effective spread for a buy order = trade size × (trade price – midquote)

effective spread for a sell order = trade size × (midquote – trade price)

where:
midquote = (bid + ask) / 2

$$\text{CDS price} \approx 1 + [(\text{fixed coupon} - \text{CDS spread}) \times \text{EffSpreadDur}_{CDS}]$$

$$R_{DC} = (1 + R_{FC})(1 + R_{FX}) - 1$$

$$\text{forward rate} = \text{spot rate} \times \frac{(1 + r_{DC})^T}{(1 + r_{FC})^T}$$

Herfindahl-Hirschman index (HHI): $HHI = \sum_{i=1}^{n} w_i^2$

$$\text{effective number of stocks} = \frac{1}{HHI}$$

fundamental law of active management: $E(R_A) = IC\sqrt{BR}\,\sigma_{R_A}\,TC$

$$\text{Active Share} = \frac{1}{2}\sum_{i=1}^{n} \left| W_{p,i} - W_{b,i} \right|$$

$$\text{active risk}(\sigma_{R_A}) = \sqrt{\frac{\sum_{t=1}^{T}(R_{At})^2}{T-1}} = \sqrt{\sigma^2\left(\Sigma(\beta_{pk} - \beta_{bk}) \times F_k\right) + \sigma_e^2}$$

Contribution to portfolio variance calculated on an *absolute* or *relative* basis

- Contribution of Asset *i* to *absolute* portfolio variance

$$= CV_i = \sum_{j=1}^{n} w_i w_j C_{ij} = w_i C_{ip}$$

- Contribution of Factor *i* to *absolute* portfolio variance

$$= CV_i = \sum_{j=1}^{n} \beta_i \beta_j C_{ij} = \beta_i C_{ip}$$

- Contribution of Asset *i* to *relative* portfolio variance

$$= CAV_i = \sum_{j=1}^{n} (w_{pi} - w_{bi})(w_{pj} - w_{bj}) RC_{ij} = (w_{pi} - w_{bi}) RC_{ip}$$

INDEX

Notes

Notes

Kaplan SCHWESER™
2024 CFA® Notes 备考笔记三级

第四册（全五册）

SCHWESERNOTES™ 2024 CFA® PART III

BOOK 4

Alternative Investments, Private Wealth Management,
and Institutional Investors

美国开普兰公司 著

中信出版集团 | 北京

图书在版编目（CIP）数据

Kaplan SCHWESER 2024 CFA®; Notes 备考笔记 = SCHWESERNOTES™; 2024 LEVEL Ⅲ CFA®; 三级 : 全五册 : 英文 / 美国开普兰公司著 . -- 北京 : 中信出版社 , 2023.8

ISBN 978-7-5217-5649-4

Ⅰ . ① K… Ⅱ . ①美… Ⅲ . ①金融－分析－资格考试－自学参考资料－英文 Ⅳ . ① F83

中国国家版本馆 CIP 数据核字 (2023) 第 083168 号

Kaplan SCHWESER 2024 CFA® Notes 备考笔记三级第四册（全五册）
著者：　美国开普兰公司
出版发行：中信出版集团股份有限公司
（北京市朝阳区东三环北路 27 号嘉铭中心　邮编　100020）
承印者：　河北鹏润印刷有限公司

开本：889mm × 1194mm　1/16　　印张：74.5　　字数：2130 千字
版次：2023 年 8 月第 1 版　　印次：2023 年 8 月第 1 次印刷
书号：ISBN 978-7-5217-5649-4
定价：1599.00 元（全五册）

Book 4: Alternative Investments, Private Wealth Management, and Institutional Investors

SchweserNotes™ 2024

Level III CFA®

KAPLAN SCHWESER

SCHWESERNOTES™ 2024 LEVEL III CFA® BOOK 4: ALTERNATIVE INVESTMENTS, PRIVATE WEALTH MANAGEMENT, AND INSTITUTIONAL INVESTORS

Published in 2023 by Kaplan, Inc.

Printed in the United States of America.

ISBN: 978-1-0788-3756-9

CONTENTS

LEARNING OUTCOME STATEMENTS (LOS)

17. Hedge Fund Strategies

The candidate should be able to:

a. discuss how hedge fund strategies may be classified. (page 2)
b. discuss investment characteristics, strategy implementation, and role in a portfolio of equity-related hedge fund strategies. (page 3)
c. discuss investment characteristics, strategy implementation, and role in a portfolio of event-driven hedge fund strategies. (page 6)
d. discuss investment characteristics, strategy implementation, and role in a portfolio of relative value hedge fund strategies. (page 9)
e. discuss investment characteristics, strategy implementation, and role in a portfolio of opportunistic hedge fund strategies. (page 12)
f. discuss investment characteristics, strategy implementation, and role in a portfolio of specialist hedge fund strategies. (page 16)
g. discuss investment characteristics, strategy implementation, and role in a portfolio of multi-manager hedge fund strategies. (page 19)
h. describe how factor models may be used to understand hedge fund risk exposures. (page 24)
i. evaluate the impact of an allocation to a hedge fund strategy in a traditional investment portfolio. (page 25)

18. Asset Allocation to Alternative Investments

The candidate should be able to:

a. explain the roles that alternative investments play in multi-asset portfolios. (page 35)
b. compare alternative investments and bonds as risk mitigators in relation to a long equity position. (page 37)
c. compare traditional and risk-based approaches to defining the investment opportunity set, including alternative investments. (page 38)
d. discuss investment considerations that are important in allocating to different types of alternative investments. (page 40)
e. discuss suitability considerations in allocating to alternative investments. (page 44)
f. discuss approaches to asset allocation to alternative investments. (page 45)
g. discuss the importance of liquidity planning in allocating to alternative investments. (page 47)
h. discuss considerations in monitoring alternative investment programs. (page 48)

19. Overview of Private Wealth Management

The candidate should be able to:

a. contrast private client and institutional client investment concerns. (page 58)
b. discuss information needed in advising private clients. (page 60)
c. identify tax considerations affecting a private client's investments. (page 60)
d. identify and formulate client goals based on client information. (page 65)
e. evaluate a private client's risk tolerance. (page 67)
f. describe technical and soft skills needed in advising private clients. (page 63)
g. evaluate capital sufficiency in relation to client goals. (page 70)
h. discuss the principles of retirement planning. (page 72)
i. discuss the parts of an investment policy statement (IPS) for a private client. (page 76)
j. prepare the investment objectives section of an IPS for a private client. (page 76)
k. evaluate and recommend improvements to an IPS for a private client. (page 76)
l. recommend and justify portfolio allocations and investments for a private client. (page 85)
m. describe effective practices in portfolio reporting and review. (page 89)
n. evaluate the success of an investment program for a private client. (page 91)
o. discuss ethical and compliance considerations in advising private clients. (page 94)
p. discuss how levels of service and range of solutions are related to different private clients. (page 95)

20. Topics in Private Wealth Management

The candidate should be able to:

a. compare taxation of income, wealth, and wealth transfers. (page 107)
b. describe global considerations of jurisdiction that are relevant to taxation. (page 109)
c. discuss and analyze the tax efficiency of investments. (page 111)
d. analyze the impact of taxes on capital accumulation and decumulation in taxable, tax-exempt, and tax-deferred accounts. (page 114)
e. explain portfolio tax management strategies and their application. (page 118)
f. discuss risk and tax objectives in managing concentrated single-asset positions. (page 122)
g. describe strategies for managing concentrated positions in public equities. (page 124)
h. describe strategies for managing concentrated positions in privately owned businesses and real estate. (page 126)
i. discuss objectives—tax and non-tax—in planning the transfer of wealth. (page 128)
j. discuss strategies for achieving estate, bequest, and lifetime gift objectives in common law and civil law regimes. (page 130)
k. describe considerations related to managing wealth across multiple generations. (page 135)

21. Risk Management for Individuals

The candidate should be able to:

a. compare the characteristics of human capital and financial capital as components of an individual's total wealth. (page 151)
b. discuss the relationships among human capital, financial capital, and economic net worth. (page 151)
c. describe an economic (holistic) balance sheet. (page 154)
d. discuss risks (earnings, premature death, longevity, property, liability, and health risks) in relation to human and financial capital. (page 156)
e. describe types of insurance relevant to personal financial planning. (page 158)
f. describe the basic elements of a life insurance policy and how insurers price a life insurance policy. (page 160)
g. discuss the use of annuities in personal financial planning. (page 165)
h. discuss the relative advantages and disadvantages of fixed and variable annuities. (page 167)
i. discuss how asset allocation policy may be influenced by the risk characteristics of human capital. (page 172)
j. recommend and justify appropriate strategies for asset allocation and risk reduction when given an investor profile of key inputs. (page 173)

22. Portfolio Management for Institutional Investors

The candidate should be able to:

a. discuss common characteristics of institutional investors as a group. (page 181)
b. discuss investment policy of institutional investors. (page 183)
c. discuss the stakeholders in the portfolio, the liabilities, the investment time horizons, and the liquidity needs of different types of institutional investors. (page 186)
d. describe the focus of legal, regulatory, and tax constraints affecting different types of institutional investors. (page 186)
e. evaluate risk considerations of private defined benefit (DB) pension plans in relation to 1) plan funded status, 2) sponsor financial strength, 3) interactions between the sponsor's business and the fund's investments, 4) plan design, and 5) workforce characteristics. (page 189)
f. evaluate the investment policy statement of an institutional investor. (page 186)
g. evaluate the investment portfolio of a private DB plan, sovereign wealth fund, university endowment, and private foundation. (page 186)
h. describe considerations affecting the balance sheet management of banks and insurers. (page 210)

READING 17

Hedge Fund Strategies

EXAM FOCUS

This reading describes some of the most important categories of hedge fund strategies and examines their investment characteristics and how these strategies are implemented. First, we discuss some unique characteristics of hedge funds and consider how various strategies might be categorized. Then, investment characteristics and implementation strategies are presented for six major hedge fund strategy categories: equity-related, event-driven, relative value, opportunistic, specialist, and multi-manager strategies. Next, we introduce a model for understanding the risk exposures of each of these strategies. The final LOS assesses the contribution of each hedge fund strategy to the return and risk of conventional stock and bond portfolios.

MODULE 17.1: OVERVIEW OF HEDGE FUND STRATEGIES

Video covering this content is available online.

Introduction

Hedge funds represent an important subgroup of alternative investment opportunities; however, they do come with many advantages and disadvantages.

Key features that distinguish hedge funds from traditional investments include:

- Lower regulatory and legal constraints.
- Flexibility to use short selling and derivatives.
- A larger investment universe.
- Aggressive investment exposures.
- Comparatively free use of leverage.
- Liquidity constraints for investors.

- Lack of transparency.
- Higher cost structures.

Perhaps the largest question to be answered is whether the high expense levels of hedge funds is made worthwhile by the return and diversification that hedge funds are intended to deliver.

Some asset managers seek out hedge funds as a source of alpha, which is never easy to come by. Others see hedge funds as a way to access top investing talent.

LOS 17.a: Discuss how hedge fund strategies may be classified.

Classifications of Hedge Fund Strategies

Hedge fund strategies are categorized based on the kinds of securities they invest in, the trading strategy used, and the kinds of risk exposures taken.

There are numerous ways to classify hedge funds, but in this topic review, we use the following six strategy categories:

1. *Equity related.* These fund strategies focus on stocks, and hence the primary source of risk is equity risk. Amongst this category of strategies are several subtypes, including long/short equity, dedicated short bias, and equity market neutral.
2. *Event driven.* These hedge fund strategies relate to corporate actions such as governance activities, mergers, acquisitions, bankruptcies, and other major business events. The main risks of these strategies are event risk; the possibility that outcomes will not unfold as expected, including the failure of a merger, credit downgrades, or bankruptcy. In the following LOSs, the event-driven hedge fund strategies that we will examine are merger arbitrage and distressed securities.
3. *Relative value.* These hedge fund strategies seek to profit from the relative valuation differences between securities. Credit and liquidity risks often complicate these strategies, because the valuation differences being exploited often relate to securities with different credit quality or liquidity. Two relative value strategies that will be considered further are fixed income arbitrage and convertible bond arbitrage.
4. *Opportunistic.* These strategies employ a top-down approach, often consider multiple asset classes, and vary with market conditions. The two opportunistic strategies that will be considered here are global macro and managed futures.
5. *Specialist.* These hedge fund strategies often require specialized market expertise or knowledge. Often the risks of these strategies arise due to exposure to specific sectors or unusual securities. The two such specialist strategies we will consider in this topic review are volatility strategies and reinsurance strategies.
6. *Multi-manager.* These strategies use other hedge fund strategies as building blocks, combining different strategies together and rebalancing exposures over time. The two types of multi-manager hedge funds we will consider are multi-strategy funds and funds-of-funds.

MODULE QUIZ 17.1

1. A convertible bond arbitrage strategy is *most likely* classified as:
   A. a specialist strategy.
   B. an event-driven strategy.
   C. a relative value strategy.
2. A managed futures hedge fund strategy is *most likely* classified as:
   A. an opportunistic strategy.
   B. a specialist strategy.
   C. a relative value strategy.

MODULE 17.2: EQUITY, EVENT-DRIVEN, AND RELATIVE VALUE STRATEGIES

Video covering this content is available online.

LOS 17.b: Discuss investment characteristics, strategy implementation, and role in a portfolio of equity-related hedge fund strategies.

Equity-Related Hedge Fund Strategies

Equity-related hedge fund strategies focus primarily on stock markets, and the majority of their risk profiles involve equity-oriented risk. Within this equity-related category, long/short equity, dedicated short bias, and equity market neutral are the main strategies that will be discussed further.

Long/Short Equity

Long/short (L/S) equity hedge funds are straightforward to understand. The fund manager purchases (takes long positions in) stocks that they think will rise in value, and sells (takes short positions in) stocks that they believe will fall in value.

Investment Characteristics

When L/S equity managers combine long and short positions, the resulting portfolio has a beta (i.e., market exposure) equal to the sum of the positive and negative betas of the various long and short positions.

L/S equity hedge funds generally do not seek to *eliminate* market exposure entirely. L/S funds will typically have a 40%–60% net long exposure, which is beneficial considering that markets generally trend upward over time.

Many L/S equity managers aspire to provide returns comparable to that of a long-only fund but with half the amount of standard deviation.

Strategy Implementation

Because successful implementation of an L/S equity strategy requires managers to identify overpriced and underpriced stocks, the majority of L/S equity funds take a sector-specific focus, choosing stocks from a particular industry that they are familiar with. They may also use index funds to achieve a desired exposure. L/S funds that are comparatively market neutral may need to use leverage to achieve worthwhile returns.

Role in a Portfolio

The goal of most L/S equity managers is to attempt to source alpha from long and short exposures to single stocks, while also benefitting from a moderate overall long exposure.

When considering an investment in an L/S equity fund, one should consider whether the investment is worthwhile given the potentially high fees. Taking a traditional long-only equity position may be a more efficient way to achieve a comparable beta exposure.

Dedicated Short Selling and Short-Biased

As the name suggests, **dedicated short-selling** funds seek out securities that are overpriced in order to sell them short. These managers look for poorly managed companies, firms in declining market segments, or even firms with deceitful accounting. **Short-biased** managers use a similar strategy, except that the short position is somewhat offset by a long exposure.

One major challenge of being a short seller is that markets inevitably rise over time, which creates a tendency toward negative returns for shorts.

A notable subset of short selling is **activist short selling**, in which the fund manager not only takes a short position in a stock, but also presents research that contends that the stock is overpriced.

Investment Characteristics

Managers using short-biased strategies as well as dedicated short-selling strategies primarily aim to produce a negative correlation with conventional securities. Compared to other hedge fund strategies, expectations of return for short strategies tend to be lower. Compared to L/S equity hedge funds with their balanced beta exposures, short strategy funds tend to have greater volatility.

Strategy Implementation

Hedge fund managers go "short" a security by borrowing the security, selling it at the current market price, and then (ideally) profit by repurchasing the same security later at a lower price in order to return it to the lender.

The most challenging part of profiting from shorting stocks is finding securities that are going to lose value. Managers use a bottom-up approach to identify firms with unprofitable business models, bad management, too much debt, or even shady accounting.

A dedicated short seller takes on no long stock exposure; rather, they carefully select stocks for a pure short exposure, typically 60%–120% short. A dedicated short manager who wishes to temper the fund's market exposure will typically do this by holding cash.

Short-biased managers have a similar strategy; however, they may also take on some long exposure, while remaining net short, often 30%–60% net short.

For both dedicated short sellers and short-biased managers, relatively little leverage is used.

Role in a Portfolio

The primary goal of dedicated short-selling and short-biased funds is to produce returns that are uncorrelated (or negatively correlated) with the return of conventional portfolio assets. When successful, these negative correlations provide tremendous benefit to a portfolio.

However, this goal of negative correlation comes at a cost: expected returns for short strategies are relatively low. Historical performance of short strategies suggests that these strategies have produced returns that are unreliable and often underwhelming.

Equity Market Neutral

Equity market-neutral (EMN) strategies seek to attain a near-zero overall exposure to the stock market. They do this by taking long and short positions in various equities; the betas of these positions should sum to zero. The alpha of EMN strategies is intended to be derived from taking positions in securities that are temporarily mispriced.

Investment Characteristics

The overall goal of EMN funds is to create a portfolio that not only generates alpha, but is also relatively immune to movements in the overall market. Not surprisingly, without beta exposure, the returns of EMN funds tend to be modest. On the positive side, however, EMN funds can offer significant diversification and low volatility.

Strategy Implementation

Hedge fund managers for EMN funds take long positions in particular stocks thought to be temporarily undervalued and short positions in stocks seen as overvalued. When mean reversion eventually occurs, alpha should result.

While some EMN managers rely on intuition (i.e., discretionary managers), it is more common that they instead rely on a fixed set of rules to identify trade opportunities (i.e., quantitative managers).

Because EMN deliberately hedges away market beta, leverage is generally applied in order to achieve acceptable levels of return.

Popular subtypes of EMN funds include:

- **Pairs trading.** Two stocks with similar characteristics are identified that are respectively overvalued and undervalued. For example, the two securities might represent different share classes of the same firm, or one might be the stock of a firm and the other the stock of its holding company. In any case, the securities must be related but relatively mispriced.
- **Stub trading.** This EMN strategy involves going long and short shares of a subsidiary and its parent company. Generally the positions taken correspond to the percentage of the subsidiary owned by the parent.
- **Multi-class trading.** This strategy entails going long and short relatively mispriced share classes of the same firm, for example non-voting and voting shares. As the pricing of these shares reverts to their traditional valuations, profits can be made.

Besides investments in stocks, other instruments used to achieve a state of zero beta include options, stock index futures, or other kinds of derivatives.

Role in a Portfolio

EMN portfolios attempt to produce alpha without taking market beta risk. EMN strategies are of particular value in times when markets are volatile and performing poorly. The construction of EMN funds allows these funds to produce less volatility than funds that rely on beta as a source of return.

LOS 17.c: Discuss investment characteristics, strategy implementation, and role in a portfolio of event-driven hedge fund strategies.

Event-Driven Strategies

Event-driven hedge fund strategies are those that attempt to profit from predicting the outcome of corporate events, such as bankruptcies, mergers, restructurings, acquisitions, et cetera. To do this, these funds take positions in securities of these corporations or in related derivatives. A **soft-catalyst event-driven** approach is an investment made before an event is being announced, whereas a **hard-catalyst event-driven** approach is an investment made after a corporate event is being announced, taking advantage of security prices that have not fully adjusted. Soft-catalyst investing is generally more volatile and, thus, riskier than a hard-catalyst approach.

The main risk that impacts event-driven strategies is event risk. The chance that the outcome of the event will not be the one anticipated. For example, a merger arbitrage hedge fund may anticipate that a particular merger will be successful and then suffer a large loss when the merger fails.

In this topic review, we will consider two types of event-driven hedge fund strategies in detail: merger arbitrage and distressed securities.

Merger Arbitrage

Merger arbitrage strategies are investment schemes that attempt to earn a return from the uncertainty that exists in the market in the time between an acquisition being announced and when the acquisition is completed.

Hedge fund managers in the merger arbitrage space profit by correctly anticipating the outcome of various deals. One way to view merger arbitrage is to compare it to writing insurance on an acquisition. If the acquisition is completed as planned, the hedge fund earns an insurance premium. If the transaction fails, however, then the hedge fund stands to lose money, analogous to an insurance company making a payout.

Investment Characteristics

In the case of a merger deal that fails, the price movements that originally occurred when the merger was announced will reverse: the price of the target will fall, and the price of the acquirer will rise. A hedge fund that had taken a position based on the merger succeeding is likely to suffer a significant cost when the deal fails unexpectedly; possibly in the order of a 40% loss. This kind of potential outcome gives merger arbitrage significant left-tail risk.

Compared to typical hedge fund strategies, merger arbitrage is more liquid.

Strategy Implementation

In the most common merger arbitrage scenario, the portfolio manager takes positions in the securities of the companies involved, with the expectation of a successful deal. For example, in a stock-for-stock deal, the hedge fund manager will typically purchase the stock of the target company and *short* the stock of the acquiring company in anticipation of profiting when the deal is completed.

Less often, the hedge fund manager may have the opinion that the merger will fail (for example, the deal might be blocked by the government because it would stifle competition.) In this scenario, the fund would take the opposite position to those described above.

In order to generate a worthwhile level of return, hedge funds pursuing a merger arbitrage strategy will typically apply 300%–500% leverage in order to achieve low-double-digit returns.

One specific variety of merger arbitrage involves cross-border mergers and acquisitions (M&A) where two countries and two regulatory authorities are involved. Such mergers are seen as more risky.

Role in a Portfolio

The Sharpe ratios of merger arbitrage strategies tend to be high, as these strategies usually produce relatively steady returns. However, on top of these steady returns is significant left-tail risk.

Distressed Securities

Hedge funds that pursue a **distressed securities** strategy take positions in the securities of firms that are in financial distress, including firms that are in bankruptcy or near bankruptcy. Firms may find themselves in this position for a number of reasons, including too much leverage, difficulty competing in their sector, or accounting issues. The securities of such a firm will often trade at greatly depressed prices.

Compounding the discounting of the securities of distressed firms is the fact that institutions such as insurance companies and banks are often not permitted to hold non-investment-grade securities. The selling of such securities can create significant pricing inefficiencies and can open up opportunities for hedge funds seeking profit.

When a firm is liquidated, the assets of the company are sold and then the various investors are paid back *sequentially* depending on their seniority (e.g., senior secured debtholders first, then junior secured debt, unsecured debt, convertible debt, preferred stock, and lastly common stock).

As an alternative to liquidation, a firm may instead be able to reorganize, which may involve renegotiating the company's liabilities. Holders of debt may be asked to exchange that debt for new equity or to agree to an extension of the maturity.

Investment Characteristics

Considering the various event-driven hedge fund strategies, returns of distressed securities investing strategy tend to be somewhat greater, though generally with larger variability of outcomes.

The lock-up periods for investors in event-driven hedge funds tend to be comparatively long (often allowing no redemptions for the first two years), reflecting the fact that the outcome of distressed security investments generally takes an extended period of time to value and exit.

Strategy Implementation

Distressed investing can take different forms. Some managers may make only a passive investment in the distressed securities, while other managers will attempt to acquire the majority of a certain class of security in order to take creditor control during bankruptcy.

Successful distressed securities investing requires a particularly broad range of skills in order to navigate the various legal aspects of the strategy, including the bankruptcy and reorganization proceedings.

While shorting distressed securities is a possibility, the majority of distressed investing takes the form of long investments.

Distressed investing generally makes low use of leverage.

Role in a Portfolio

Distressed securities investing involves moderately high levels of illiquidity due to the nature of the assets being purchased. The returns of distressed securities investing is higher relative to other event-driven strategies, though it can be somewhat unpredictable and sensitive to declines in the overall market.

LOS 17.d: Discuss investment characteristics, strategy implementation, and role in a portfolio of relative value hedge fund strategies.

Relative Value Hedge Fund Strategies

As the name suggests, **relative value** strategies attempt to exploit valuation differences between securities. The most common securities used in relative value strategies are hybrid convertible debt, as well as fixed-income securities.

When successful, relative value strategies will earn various premiums over time, including liquidity, credit, and volatility premiums, reflecting differences in liquidity or credit quality between securities. However, in times of turbulent markets, losses can occur.

Two relative value hedge fund strategies that we will consider in detail are fixed-income arbitrage and convertible bond arbitrage.

Fixed-Income Arbitrage

The idea behind **fixed-income arbitrage** strategies is to take advantage of temporary mispricing of fixed-income instruments, by going long comparatively undervalued securities, and going short comparatively overvalued securities. Idiosyncrasies that might be exploited include yield curve kinks or anticipated changes in the shape of the yield curve.

The securities may be fixed-income instruments of many types, including consumer debt, bank loans, corporate bonds, or sovereign bonds. Hedge fund managers take positions in these securities under the assumption that prices will revert toward their fair values.

Fixed-income arbitrage strategies often make use of significant leverage, in pursuit of sufficient levels of return.

Strategy Implementation

Two subtypes of fixed-income arbitrage strategies that we will consider in further depth are (1) yield curve trades and (2) carry trades.

- **Yield curve trades.** In this strategy, the hedge fund manager has a view of how the shape of the yield curve will evolve over time based on macroeconomic forecasts. The portfolio manager makes long and short investments in fixed-income instruments in order to profit from the anticipated yield curve steepening or flattening. As usual, the portfolio manager will profit when the prices of the long securities rise and the prices of the short securities fall. If the positions taken are in securities of different firms, then liquidity, credit, and interest rate risks will be present. For positions in securities of the same issuer, interest rate movements would be the main source of risk.

- **Carry trades.** In a carry trade, the portfolio manager shorts a low-yielding security and goes long a high-yielding security. The source of return here is twofold; first, from the yield differential, and second from the price changes as mean reversion occurs.

Because fixed-income securities tend to be priced fairly efficiently, the amount of profit that can be earned by fixed-income arbitrage is somewhat limited. As a result, substantial leverage is often applied to fixed-income arbitrage strategies. (400% leverage is not uncommon; even 1500% leverage is not unheard of.)

Investment Characteristics

Generally, the return to fixed-income arbitrage strategies are relatively small, so significant levels of leverage are used to increase the amount of return.

The liquidity of fixed-income arbitrage depends on the particular strategy employed and the kinds of fixed income instruments used. Strategies involving U.S. Treasuries are very liquid, while strategies that make use of mortgage-backed securities or foreign instruments, for example, are less liquid.

Role in a Portfolio

Return distributions for a fixed income arbitrageur tend to be similar to writing puts. If the trade unfolds as expected, the investor will earn a return from the spread narrowing, plus a return from positive carry. However, if the spread between the two instruments widens unexpectedly, the return to the investor may become quite negative.

One drawback to fixed income arbitrage strategies is that their highly leveraged nature can cause modest price volatility to lead to a domino effect of margin calls and deleveraging. For example, the Asian Financial Crisis of 1997 and the Russian Ruble Crisis of 1998 led to the collapse of the renowned hedge fund Long-Term Capital Management.

Convertible Bond Arbitrage

Convertible bonds are fixed-income debt securities that make regular coupon payments but can additionally be exchanged for a prearranged number of common stock shares. The bond-to-stock conversion is at the bondholder's discretion, though it is only permitted at certain points in the bond's life.

One way to view convertible bonds is as a regular bond plus a long call option on the corresponding stock.

Analyzing convertible bonds is extremely complex due to impacts from a number of factors.

The primary goal of **convertible bond arbitrage** strategies is generally to profit from purchasing the implied volatility of convertible bonds, which is often underpriced. To do this without taking on excess risk, convertible bond arbitrageurs will take on other positions to try to hedge out the delta and gamma risk of the convertible bond holdings.

Investment Characteristics

Convertible bond arbitrage managers encounter two primary sources of liquidity issues; first, because the strategy requires the manager to borrow and then short sell the underlying equity and second, because the fixed income instruments being invested in are often complex niche products.

Strategy Implementation

Convertible arbitrage strategies generally exploit the fact that the options within convertible instruments usually exhibit low implied volatilities when compared to the historical volatilities of the equities that underlie the option. The challenge for the convertible bond arbitrage manager that invests in these convertibles is to hedge away the other sources of risk that are embedded in the convertible security including market risk, interest rate risk, and the credit risk of the bond issuer.

When a convertible bond's current conversion price is well above the current stock price, the OTM call (delta closer to zero) will cause the convertible bond to behave much like a straight bond and, therefore, conversion is not likely.

Conversely, when a convertible bond's current conversion price is well below the current stock price, the ITM call (delta closer to one) will cause the convertible bond to behave much like the corresponding stock and, therefore, conversion is likely.

Significant amounts of leverage are usually used to implement convertible bond strategies, often combining a three times long bond exposure with a two times short equity exposure. (The smaller short equity exposure stems from delta hedging the short stock exposure according to the delta of the long bond position.)

Role in a Portfolio

Convertible arbitrage strategies perform best during periods of normal market conditions, when liquidity is available, when volatility is modest, and when there is a good selection of convertible bonds being issued. Convertible arbitrage may not perform well in periods of illiquidity or weak credit.

MODULE QUIZ 17.2

1. Considering various equity-related hedge fund strategies, a strategy that is *most likely* to apply relatively high levels of leverage is:
   A. an EMN strategy.
   B. a dedicated short strategy.
   C. a short-biased strategy.
2. An equity-related hedge fund strategy with gross exposures of 80% long and 35% short is *most likely* to be classified as:
   A. a dedicated short strategy.
   B. a short-biased strategy.
   C. a long/short equity strategy.
3. Relative to other hedge fund strategies, EMN strategies are *most likely* to:
   A. exhibit relatively modest returns.
   B. be vulnerable to periods of market weakness.
   C. earn return from alpha and beta risk.
4. An investment in distressed securities is *most likely* to be characterized by:
   A. a long bias.
   B. a high level of liquidity.
   C. a large amount of leverage.
5. In a sequential payoff during a liquidation, the security holder that is *most likely* to be paid off first is the holder of:
   A. junior secured debt.
   B. convertible debt.
   C. preferred stock.
6. In implementing a convertible arbitrage strategy, the portfolio manager is *most likely* to take a position that is:
   A. long convertible bonds and short equity.
   B. long straight bonds and short convertible bonds.
   C. long convertible bonds and short straight bonds.

Video covering this content is available online.

MODULE 17.3: OPPORTUNISTIC, SPECIALIST, AND MULTI-MANAGER STRATEGIES

LOS 17.e: Discuss investment characteristics, strategy implementation, and role in a portfolio of opportunistic hedge fund strategies.

Opportunistic Hedge Fund Strategies

Opportunistic hedge fund strategies are a broad class of investing approaches that attempt to extract profits using a wide range of techniques in a broad range of securities markets. Rather than being focused on individual securities, these strategies take a top-down approach to make macro investments on a global basis across regions, sectors, and asset classes.

The returns of opportunistic hedge fund strategies are generally impacted by market cycles, global developments, and international interactions. The risks will depend on the particular strategy and asset classes involved.

The implementation of opportunistic hedge fund strategies can be based on a number of broad techniques. Technical analysis uses past price changes to forecast future price movements. Strategies based on fundamentals, on the other hand, attempt to analyze security prices, markets, sectors, and the relationships between markets, using economic data as the input.

Managers using a **systematic** implementation of their strategies use computer algorithms and rules to determine which trades to make. Managers using a **discretionary** process instead use their instinct to determine when to trade.

We will consider two opportunistic strategies in detail: global macro and managed futures.

Global Macro Strategies

Managers of **global macro** strategy funds attempt to profit from making correct assessments and forecasts of various global economic variables including inflation, currency exchange rates, yield curves, central bank policies, and the general economic health of different countries.

Global macro managers use a broad range of security types and global asset classes to take positions on these views.

A global macro manager that can identify a global trend early and take a position can profit.

Investment Characteristics

Global macro managers can take positions that are either **directional** (e.g., go long companies that are anticipated to benefit from expected interest rate hikes, and short companies that will be disadvantaged), or **thematic** (e.g., buy firms that will benefit from forthcoming free trade deals).

Unlike some hedge fund strategies, low-volatility-mean-reverting markets are not generally favorable for global macro returns.

Because global macro managers take investment positions based on their predictions of the future, there is significant potential for unsuccessful investments when global economies do not behave as expected or if unanticipated risks emerge. As a result, the returns of global macro funds tend to be uneven and volatile.

Strategy Implementation

Global macro strategies tend to be based on top-down analysis beginning with scrutiny of the global economy, then macro trends within economies, and so on, in order to identify potential opportunities.

Different global macro managers are likely to implement their strategies using very different techniques; for example, technical analysis vs. fundamental analysis, or discretionary implementation versus systematic implementation.

One commonality between global macro funds is that most tend to apply leverage, often representing 600% or 700% of fund assets.

A manager making directional predictions will generally use fundamental information to determine whether a particular asset is undervalued or overvalued on a historical basis. On the other hand, a manager using a relative value strategy will seek out securities that are overvalued or undervalued compared to one another.

Global macro managers tend to use discretionary approaches more than managed futures managers.

Role in a Portfolio

When added to a portfolio of traditional assets, a global macro hedge fund can bring a significant benefit (not only alpha, but also portfolio diversification).

A successful global macro manager will anticipate changes before other market participants and will then invest in a position and wait for the rest of the market to come around. This contrarian tendency can make an allocation to global macro strategies especially useful. For example, some global macro managers anticipated the United States' subprime mortgage crisis well before the housing bubble began to collapse in 2007.

During times of market stress, global macro funds have historically delivered right-tail skewed returns, which is extremely beneficial from a portfolio diversification perspective. However, this behavior cannot always be relied upon as such diversifying outcomes are not always realized.

Managed Futures

Hedge fund portfolio managers that pursue a **managed futures** strategy take long and short positions in a variety of derivatives contracts including futures, forwards, options on futures, swaps, and sometimes currencies and commodities.

Managed futures strategies can be as simple as trading index futures on a particular sector, or it can involve very exotic contracts such as futures on the weather.

Investment Characteristics

Managed futures funds do not buy and sell assets; rather, they enter into futures contracts in order to gain the desired exposures.

Because of the mechanics of futures contracts (requiring only a small amount of upfront collateral), managed futures funds can easily apply great amounts of leverage. Typically, a fund will use perhaps ⅛ of its capital as collateral on futures contracts. The other ⅞ or so will be invested in some highly liquid security (such as short-term government bonds) that will serve as collateral for the futures clearinghouse.

Managed futures funds are extremely liquid. The reason for this is that futures contracts themselves are highly liquid; they trade globally and continuously. Going long or short futures allows a hedge fund manager easy access to exposures across a range of asset classes.

One downside of the popularity of managed futures strategies is that **crowding** has occurred. Many market participants pursue the same trades and use similar signals, and execution slippage sometimes occurs.

Strategy Implementation

There are a number of ways to implement managed futures strategies.

In perhaps the most popular method, **time-series momentum (TSM)** trend following, portfolio managers simply follow momentum. They buy securities that have been rising in price and sell securities that have been falling.

Another similar methodology is **cross-sectional momentum (CSM)** strategies, which is carried out within a particular asset class (a *cross section* of assets). Again, the securities rising fastest are purchased and falling securities are shorted.

The high liquidity of futures contracts allows hedge fund managers to pursue a very wide selection of trading strategies. Generally, portfolio managers will rely on a signal trigger, most often based on volatility or momentum, to prompt the manager to trade.

In addition to using signals to indicate when to enter a trade, portfolio managers will also have rules for closing a position. Exit methodologies can be based on:

- Price target.
- Momentum reversal.
- Time.
- Trailing stop-loss.
- Some combination of these approaches.

The goal of managed futures strategies is to develop rules and signals that work well not only on historical data but also in real-world use. However, the more portfolio managers are using similar signals, the less effective these signals will become.

Managed futures strategies are typically implemented using systematic approaches, whereby the portfolio manager relies on signals produced by a computer program or model.

The size of positions taken are usually based on factors such as correlation and volatility.

Role in a Portfolio

Perhaps the most appealing feature of managed futures is their interaction with other investments. Overall, managed futures have very little correlation with traditional equity and fixed-income assets. The result is that when added to a portfolio, managed futures will generally improve the total risk-adjusted return.

This diversifying characteristic has proven its worth during times of market stress. While other strategies exhibit negative skewness during such periods, the positive right-tail skewness of managed futures provides a significant advantage.

LOS 17.f: Discuss investment characteristics, strategy implementation, and role in a portfolio of specialist hedge fund strategies.

Specialist Strategies

Portfolio managers for **specialist hedge fund strategies** use their knowledge of a particular market to pursue niche investment opportunities. The purpose of pursuing specialist strategies is to generate returns that are uncorrelated with traditional assets and produce high risk-adjusted returns. The risks of such strategies are often unique to the particular niche securities being invested in.

Two such strategies that we will consider in detail are volatility trading and reinsurance/life settlements.

Volatility Trading

Once an esoteric pursuit, **volatility trading** has evolved over recent years to become a recognized investable asset.

Volatility trading hedge fund managers will trade volatility-related assets globally, across countries and across asset classes, in order to exploit perceived differences in volatility pricing. The overall goal is to purchase underpriced volatility and sell overpriced volatility.

For example, the price of volatility in Asia has traditionally been lower than in other regions. Even though the Tokyo Stock Exchange traditionally has higher volatility than the New York Stock Exchange, implied volatility is usually cheaper in Tokyo than it is in New York.

Another volatility trade is to act as the counterparty to market participants that consistently seek long volatility. Because the negative correlation between stock market returns and equity volatility is high, equity investors seek to buy volatility as a hedge. A hedge fund that is willing to sell volatility will earn an insurance-like premium as compensation for taking on this risk; however, such a strategy can unravel in a dramatic fashion.

In the U.S. markets, the most common volatility futures are contracts on the **VIX index**, which tracks the 30-day implied volatility of the S&P 500 index. VIX contracts tend to be mean reverting because high volatility naturally tends to dissipate over time.

Strategy Implementation

Hedge fund managers wishing to pursue volatility trading have several options.

One possibility is to build various option strategies, such as straddles, calendar spreads, bull spreads, or bear spreads, using basic exchange-traded options.

A second possibility is to make use of over-the-counter (OTC) options, which are customized to meet the portfolio manager's specific needs. A drawback of this method, however, is that it introduces counterparty risk plus additional liquidity issues.

A more direct way to trade volatility is to use futures on the VIX index. An advantage of this method is that it is a very direct way to express a view on volatility, without the need for hedging. There are disadvantages though. First, the mean-reverting nature of the VIX index's price and second, many traders and investors crowd into the VIX futures in order to sell volatility and capture the associated premiums, making it difficult to profit from that strategy.

A fourth method of implementing a volatility trading strategy is to enter into an OTC **volatility swap** or alternatively a **variance swap**. These derivatives provide a relatively pure exposure to volatility. (Note that the name "swap" here is somewhat misleading. Volatility swaps and variance swaps are actually forward contracts with a payoff based on the difference between observed or realized variance multiplied by some notional amount).

Investment Characteristics

The investment characteristics of volatility trading will vary depending on the securities invested in and the positions taken.

Investors that take a short position in volatility will earn premiums and generally produce stable returns under average market conditions. A long position in volatility will display positive convexity, which can be valuable as a hedge.

The liquidity of a volatility trading strategy will depend on the instruments used. Futures and options based on VIX tend to be extremely liquid, and exchange-traded volatility options are liquid as well (especially when the tenor is short). OTC contracts on the other hand are generally less liquid.

The use of futures contracts makes it easy to apply leverage to a volatility trading strategy. The convexity of volatility derivatives means that sometimes large gains can be made from long volatility strategies while taking little risk.

Because of their unique nature, benchmarking of volatility trading strategy performance can be difficult.

Role in a Portfolio

In a portfolio, a long volatility strategy is a potent diversifier, because stock market volatility is highly negatively correlated with market returns. The downside of maintaining a long volatility position, however, is that a premium must be paid to the volatility seller.

Reinsurance/Life Settlements

In recent years, numerous hedge funds have formed to take advantage of attractive investment opportunities related to insurance policies. In a typical **life settlement** transaction, an insured person will sell (generally through a broker) their insurance policy to a hedge fund. After the investor pays the insured for the policy, the hedge fund then will be liable for the premium payments and will also receive the death benefit upon the passing of the insured.

Individuals will sell their life insurance contracts when they feel that they no longer benefit from the agreements. Individuals who purchased life insurance policies are incentivized to sell their policies to third-party brokers because those firms will oftentimes pay more for the policy than the issuing insurance company will pay for a surrendered policy.

Catastrophe risk **reinsurance** is another area where hedge funds are increasingly investing. **Catastrophe insurance** covers the holder against earthquakes, tornadoes, hurricanes, floods, and the like. In order to diversify and decrease risk, insurance companies in their normal course of business will sell off some of their risk to reinsurance companies, who may then lay these risks off on hedge funds in exchange for capital. Reinsurance can be a rewarding investment for a hedge fund if sufficient diversity can be obtained (e.g. vary by geography and types of insurance) if the insurance company provides sufficient loan loss reserves and if the policy premiums are adequate. When considering an investment in catastrophic insurance, the hedge fund considers both typical and worst-case outcomes and compares this to the insurance premiums to be received. Geographic diversity is important, as a specific catastrophic event will tend to affect only a particular part of the world.

Investment Characteristics

Strategies that involve investments in insurance contracts are illiquid because insurance policies are somewhat difficult to sell after initiation.

Strategy Implementation

The term "life settlement" refers to a secondary market transaction on an insurance policy. A hedge fund that invests in life settlements will analyze various pools of life insurance contracts that brokers offer, and invest in the ones that are predicted to offer an attractive return. After investing, the hedge fund then becomes the beneficiary of these contracts. The investment is successful if the present value of the future insurance payout exceeds the payments made by the hedge fund.

In selecting which insurance policies to invest in, a hedge fund will seek out policies with the following characteristics:

- The purchase price of the policy is low.
- The ongoing premium payments are low.
- The insured person is likely to die relatively soon.

One major prerequisite to profiting from life settlements is to develop an accurate alternative estimate of life expectancies. Appraising a life settlement requires a significant amount of skill and knowledge and requires comparing individual policyholders' outlooks to actuarial averages.

Role in a Portfolio

A very appealing feature of insurance investments in a portfolio is that the risk inherent in these strategies is almost entirely uncorrelated with market risks and business cycles. For example, floods and earthquakes have little or no correlation to the financial markets.

Thus, hedge funds that invest in such assets can add alpha to a portfolio while simultaneously adding return diversification.

LOS 17.g: Discuss investment characteristics, strategy implementation, and role in a portfolio of multi-manager hedge fund strategies.

Multi-Manager Hedge Fund Strategies

Up until this point in the topic review, we have been considering various individual hedge fund strategies. In reality, most investors invest not just in a single hedge fund strategy, but in a diverse set of strategies.

The notion behind multi-manager hedge funds is to assemble in a deliberate way a portfolio of diverse hedge fund strategies and to adjust the holdings strategically over time.

The best-known varieties of multi-manager hedge funds are funds-of-funds and multi-strategy funds.

Fund-Of-Funds

A **fund-of-funds (FoF)** takes capital from various individual investors and invests in a number of different hedge funds, generally each pursuing different strategies.

FoF can provide investors with a number of benefits:

- Diversification across hedge fund strategies.
- Expertise in individual manager selection.
- Strategic allocation and style allocation.
- Due diligence.
- Occasional value-added tactical decisions.
- Currency hedging.
- Leverage at the portfolio level.
- Better liquidity terms vs. individual hedge funds.
- Access to certain closed hedge funds.
- Economies of scale for monitoring.
- Research expertise.

- Potential liquidity efficiencies.
- Potentially valuable concessions from the underlying funds.

FoF also have the following disadvantages:

- A double layer of fees for the investor.
- Lack of transparency into individual hedge funds.
- No performance fees netting.
- Additional principal–agent issues.

Investment Characteristics

Individual hedge funds have traditionally charged a "**2 and 20**" fee structure, indicating management fees of 2% plus performance incentive fees of 20%. On top of this, FoF have historically added a 1% management fee, plus a further 20% incentive fee on the *total* FoF portfolio. (Though over time, these FoF fees have become negotiable and generally smaller.)

One important feature that FoF serve is making an investment in hedge funds practical for smaller investors, such as small institutions and for moderately wealthy individuals.

Hedge funds almost always require significant initial investments; typically $1 million. Achieving a diversified exposure to a number of such funds poses a difficulty for smaller investors, as an investment in 20 hedge funds might require a cumulative minimum investment on the order of $20 million. Furthermore, performing due diligence on 20 different hedge funds would require far more resources than most individual investors could muster. (Not to mention complications such as tax reporting on 20 investments.)

Using a FoF, on the other hand, a smaller investor can typically access a diversified hedge fund exposure for as little as $100,000. In this way, FoF serve as an entry point into hedge fund investing.

Aside from providing an accessible path into hedge funds, FoF provide a number of other advantages. For example, FoF may provide access to high-profile managers whose funds are otherwise closed to new investors. Also, the larger size of FoF may allow the fund to obtain valuable concessions from the underlying funds' management.

Liquidity can be a challenge for portfolio managers of funds-of-funds. Typically, a FoF will require a one-year initial **lock-up** for investors then will allow somewhat greater liquidity afterwards (e.g., monthly or quarterly). However, the underlying funds may have even stricter limits on liquidity, leaving a FoF manager in a potential squeeze.

Another drawback of funds-of-funds relates to potential netting risk, whereby investors could be required to make significant incentive payments to successful underlying funds, even if the overall performance of a FoF is poor.

Strategy Implementation

The fund-of-funds strategy is normally implemented as follows:

1. Use fund databases plus personal introductions to become familiar with hedge funds available for investment.
2. Choose an appropriate strategic allocation to different hedge fund strategies.
3. The manager selection process is initiated, using both top-down and bottom-up techniques.
4. For each hedge fund strategy, consider a number of candidates following that strategy.
5. Interview the candidate hedge fund managers.
6. Review relevant materials such as audit reports.
7. Examine the funds' personnel, operational processes, and risk management.
8. Negotiate with the individual fund managers for lower fees, improved liquidity, et cetera.
9. After the various funds are approved and included in the FoF, an ongoing monitoring process begins, intended to detect major personnel changes, style drift, et cetera.

The FoF's strategic allocation determines the percentage of total capital that will be invested in each hedge fund style. In addition to this strategic allocation is a tactical allocation, whereby the FoF manager will at various times underweight or overweight the various hedge fund strategies to reflect the FoF manager's perception of a changing market environment.

Role in a Portfolio

When a FoF manager takes a number of relatively uncorrelated hedge funds and combines them together in the same portfolio, a FoF should produce a number of advantages: greater diversification, steady returns, less concentrated exposure to risks, less volatility, and less exposure to the downside risk of any individual fund manager.

Multi-Strategy Hedge Funds

Like a FoF, **multi-strategy** hedge funds are funds that hold a number of other hedge funds where these various funds are pursuing diverse strategies. Also similar to a FoF, multi-strategy hedge funds are intended to use this diversification of strategy to produce steady low-volatility returns.

Unlike a FoF, the sub-funds in multi-strategy hedge funds are run by the same organization, rather than being managed by different hedge fund firms.

Investment Characteristics

The diversification of multi-strategy funds is intended to produce steady returns and low volatility.

Multi-strategy funds share some investment characteristics with funds-of-funds, but also there are significant differences. For example, the **operational risks** of a multi-strategy fund are not well-diversified as is with a FoF, because all of the operational processes of multi-strategy funds are performed under the same roof.

Furthermore, the diversity of strategies represented by the different funds in multi-strategy funds are often somewhat limited, because the managers employed by a specific multi-strategy fund tend to have somewhat similar investment viewpoints and methods.

A major advantage of multi-strategy funds over a FoF is the speed and relative ease with which **tactical** allocations can be made. Because each of the multi-strategy funds are managed in-house, it is relatively easy for the multi-strategy manager to reallocate investment from one strategy to another. The high internal transparency and fast response time makes tactical reallocations of multi-strategy funds practical, which could explain why multi-strategy funds have historically been seen as superior to funds-of-funds in protecting investments.

Investor fees for a multi-strategy fund are often more attractive than those of a FoF. While FoF investors are subject to netting risk (where hefty performance fees can be paid to some sub-fund managers, despite overall poor FoF performance), multi-strategy funds are more likely to absorb this netting risk internally. In this arrangement, the investor only pays an incentive fee on the total fund performance. (Some multi-strategy funds though do use a FoF-like "pass-through" fee model, which will expose investors to netting risk.)

Like a FoF, multi-strategy funds generally limit investor liquidity using redemption periods and initial lock-ups. Multi-strategy funds additionally often enforce limits on the amount of redemption each quarter.

Strategy Implementation

Multi-strategy funds carry out their approach by making investments in a number of varying hedge fund strategies.

One key advantage of multi-strategy funds is their ability to make tactical reallocations in addition to a fund's strategic allocation. Furthermore, the multi-strategy fund's internal teams are likely to be well informed about why and when capital and leverage should be reallocated, versus a FoF manager for whom the various funds are more opaque.

Risk management can also be more effective with a multi-strategy fund. Unlike FoF managers, multi-strategy managers should have an excellent view of correlations and common risks between the various funds.

Multi-strategy funds also enjoy efficiencies that come from multiple hedge fund teams sharing the same administrative resources.

Multi-strategy funds often will make greater use of leverage than the average FoF. Normally, leverage in multi-strategy funds does not pose much of a risk; however, during periods of market stress, small sources of danger can become significant left-tail risks that threaten the survival of the fund. (This kind of scenario lead to the demise of Ritchie Capital in 2005 and Amaranth Advisors in 2006.)

Multi-strategy funds generally have more varied performance than a FoF.

Role in a Portfolio

Multi-strategy funds are intended to improve an investment portfolio by adding diversification and steady, low-volatility returns.

Historically, multi-strategy funds have generally performed better than have funds-of-funds, due to a superior fee structure and greater ability to execute on tactical asset allocation. However, the leveraged nature of multi-strategy funds can sometimes lead to a left-tail blow-up during times of stress.

MODULE QUIZ 17.3

1. Considering global macro strategies and managed futures strategies, it would be *most accurate* to state that:
   A. managed futures strategies use more discretionary approaches.
   B. global macro strategies use more systematic approaches.
   C. both strategies tend to be highly liquid and use high leverage.
2. During periods of market stress:
   A. managed futures and global macro both exhibit right-tail skewness.
   B. managed futures strategies exhibit left-tail skewness.
   C. global macro strategies exhibit left-tail skewness.
3. Considering the correlation between equity volatility and equity market returns, the two measures are *most likely* to be:
   A. highly positively correlated.
   B. predominantly uncorrelated.
   C. highly negatively correlated.
4. A hedge fund is *most likely* to purchase a pool of life insurance policies that has high:
   A. surrender value.
   B. ongoing premium payments.
   C. likelihood of the insured person dying soon.
5. Compared to a multi-strategy fund, a fund-of-funds is *most likely* to offer the investor a more:
   A. effective tactical asset allocation.
   B. attractive fee structure.
   C. diverse strategy mix.
6. Compared to a multi-strategy fund, a fund-of-funds is *most likely* to offer an investor higher:
   A. transparency.
   B. netting risks.
   C. leverage.

Video covering this content is available online.

MODULE 17.4: FACTOR MODELS AND PORTFOLIO IMPACT OF HEDGE FUNDS

LOS 17.h: Describe how factor models may be used to understand hedge fund risk exposures.

Factor Models

Analysis of Hedge Fund Strategies

In this LOS, we will consider the use of a **conditional linear factor model** to quantify the risk exposures of various hedge fund strategies.

By conditional, we mean a model that takes into account that a fund may behave one way during normal market conditions and behave differently during a period of market turbulence (such as the global financial crisis of 2007–2009).

By determining a fund's actual risk exposures, events such as the widespread closure of hedge funds after the global financial crisis are less likely.

Conditional Factor Risk Model

Suppose we use the following conditional linear factor model to explain the return of Hedge Fund *i* in Period *t*:

$$\begin{aligned}(\text{Return on HF}_i)_t = {} & \alpha_i + \beta_{i,1}(\text{Factor 1})_t + \beta_{i,2}(\text{Factor 2})_t + \ldots + \beta_{i,K}(\text{Factor K})_t + \\ & D_t\beta_{i,1}(\text{Factor 1})_t + D_t\beta_{i,2}(\text{Factor 2})_t + \ldots + D_t\beta_{i,K}(\text{Factor K})_t \\ & + (\text{error})_{i,t}\end{aligned}$$

where:

α_i = intercept for Hedge Fund *i*

$\beta_{i,K}(\text{Factor K})_t$ = exposure during *normal* periods to Risk Factor *K*

D_t = dummy variable that equals zero during normal periods, and one during a financial crisis

$D_t\beta_{i,K}(\text{Factor K})_t$ = *incremental* exposure to Risk Factor *K* during financial crisis periods

$(\text{error})_{i,t}$ = random error with zero mean

Any returns not explained by the model's risk factors would be attributed to either omitted risk factors, alpha (i.e., hedge fund manager skill), or randomness (error).

Hasanhodzic and Lo (2007) used the following six factors:

1. *Equity risk (SNP500):* S&P 500 total return index.
2. *Interest rate risk (BOND):* Bloomberg Barclays Corporate AA Intermediate Bond Index.
3. *Currency risk (USD):* U.S. Dollar Index.
4. *Commodity risk (CMDTY):* Goldman Sachs Commodity Index (GSCI) total return.

5. *Credit risk (CREDIT):* Spread between Moody's Baa and Aaa corporate bond yields.
6. *Volatility risk (VIX):* CBOE Volatility Index (VIX).

A **stepwise regression** process is useful for creating linear conditional factor models that avoid multicollinearity problems, by avoiding the use of highly correlated risk factors. When this stepwise regression process was run by the authors of the original reading, the process resulted in the BOND and CMDTY factors being dropped due to multicollinearity issues. (CREDIT and SNP500 respectively produced higher adjusted R^2.)

This left the following four factors for measuring risk exposures:

1. Equity risk (SNP500).
2. Currency risk (USD).
3. Credit risk (CREDIT).
4. Volatility risk (VIX).

Each hedge fund strategy has different exposures to these various risk factors. These risk factors stem from taking long or short positions in financial instruments that are exposed to these risks.

For example, arbitrage strategies often are generally exposed to credit spread risk and market volatility risk. Event-driven strategies and L/S equity strategies generally have significant exposure to equity (market beta) risk.

LOS 17.i: Evaluate the impact of an allocation to a hedge fund strategy in a traditional investment portfolio.

In this LOS, we assess the effect of reallocating a portion of a traditional investment portfolio to a hedge fund strategy.

Specifically, we will consider what happens to the return and risk of the total portfolio when we add a 20% allocation to each of the hedge fund strategies discussed previously. The hedge fund allocation will be added to a conventional 60% stock/40% bond investment portfolio.

Portfolio Contribution of Hedge Fund Strategies

When the previously mentioned 20% allocation to hedge funds is added to a traditional 60% stock/40% bond investment portfolio, the resulting allocation is 48% stock, 32% bond, and 20% hedge fund.

Performance Contribution to a 60/40 Portfolio

When we add a 20% allocation to most hedge fund strategies to a traditional portfolio, the general result is the following:

- Total portfolio standard deviation decreases.
- Sharpe ratio increases.

- Sortino ratio increases.
- Maximum drawdown decreases in approximately one-third of portfolios.

The interpretation of these results is that hedge fund strategies generally increase risk-adjusted return and provide diversification to a traditional portfolio of stocks and bonds.

Risk-Adjusted Performance

The **Sharpe ratio** is one risk-adjusted measure of performance. The risk measure used to calculate the Sharpe ratio is standard deviation, so both downside and upside standard deviation result in a lower Sharpe ratio.

The **Sortino ratio** is a similar risk-adjusted measure of performance; however, only downside deviations are considered to reflect risk. Risk is measured as variability *below* a predefined level of return. Because of the left-tail risk present in many hedge fund strategies, the Sortino ratio is generally seen as a superior measure of the risk-adjusted performance of hedge funds.

When 20% allocations to various hedge fund strategies are added to the traditional stock/bond portfolio, notably high Sharpe ratios are also achieved from allocations to these strategies:

- Systematic futures hedge funds.
- Distressed securities.
- Fixed-income arbitrage.
- Global macro.
- Equity market neutral.

The highest Sortino ratios were attained via allocations to the following hedge fund strategies:

- Equity market neutral.
- Systematic futures.
- L/S equity.
- Event driven.

Allocations to the following strategies was found to be effective in generating superior risk-adjusted performance, based on the comparatively higher Sharpe and Sortino ratios:

- Systematic futures.
- Equity market neutral.
- Global macro.
- Event-driven hedge fund strategies.

On the other hand, it was observed that the following fund strategies do not significantly enhance risk-adjusted performance:

- Fund-of-funds.
- Multi-strategy.

While all of the hedge fund strategies expose the overall portfolio to various kinds of additional portfolio risks, allocating a portion of a stock/bond portfolio to hedge funds generally reduces risk and increases returns.

Risk Metrics

One key reason for investors to allocate a portion of their portfolio to hedge fund strategies is to reduce risk.

Standard Deviation

Perhaps not surprisingly, it was found that the following strategies resulted in the lowest standard deviations of returns for the overall portfolio:

- Dedicated short-biased.
- Bear market neutral.

These funds also produced notably low standard deviations:

- Systematic futures.
- FoF: macro/systematic.
- Equity market neutral.

The risk-reduction ability of these strategies has been found to be substantial. Not surprisingly, they are also some of the strategies that most improve risk-adjusted returns.

Funds that were found to have little positive impact on reducing standard deviations of the overall portfolio include:

- Event-driven: distressed securities.
- Relative value: convertible arbitrage.

An explanation for event-driven: distressed securities' lack of ability to reduce standard deviation is that these securities tend to take long positions in securities, and outcomes are either mild successes or grand failures.

Relative value: convertible arbitrage do little to improve standard deviation likely because their leveraged nature becomes a liability during times of market volatility.

Drawdown

Drawdown is defined as the peak-to-trough decline for a portfolio, generally quoted as the percentage drop between a peak and the subsequent trough. The **high-water mark** refers to the maximum value the portfolio has ever reached.

Drawdown is useful for quantifying the risk and past performance of various investment strategies, and for comparing one strategy's risk to another.

The hedge fund strategies that produced the smallest maximum drawdowns are various opportunistic strategies:

- Global macro.
- Systematic futures.
- Merger arbitrage.
- Equity market neutral.

Use of the conditional risk model can show that these strategies perform relatively well during periods of market crisis because they have minimal exposure to credit risk or equity. Furthermore, these strategies benefit from their liquid nature. These properties make opportunistic strategies useful diversifiers for traditional assets.

Other hedge fund strategies had entirely dissimilar drawdown performance. These strategies did little to mitigate the traditional portfolio's maximum drawdown:

- L/S equity.
- Event-driven: distressed securities.
- Relative value: convertible arbitrage.

These results are somewhat expected. Using the conditional risk model, we can demonstrate that these particular strategies have significant exposure to equity risk, and furthermore during crisis periods they have significant exposure to credit risk as well.

MODULE QUIZ 17.4

1. Conditional linear factor models used to understand hedge fund risk exposures are *most likely* to use factors including:
   A. liquidity risk, operational risk, valuation risk, and systemic risk.
   B. interest rate risk, commodity risk, margining risk, and concentration risk.
   C. equity risk, credit risk, currency risk, and volatility risk.
2. Adding a 20% allocation of a hedge fund strategy to a traditional 60%/40% portfolio is *most likely* to increase the total portfolio's:
   A. standard deviation.
   B. maximum drawdown.
   C. Sortino ratio.
3. The risk-adjusted performance of a traditional 60%/40% portfolio is *most likely* to be improved by adding an allocation to a hedge fund using the strategy of:
   A. equity market neutral.
   B. fund-of-funds.
   C. multi-strategy.

KEY CONCEPTS

LOS 17.a

Hedge fund strategies are classified based on the instruments they invest in, the philosophy followed, and the kinds of risk exposures taken.

This reading classifies hedge fund strategies into the following six categories:

1. Equity related.
2. Event driven.
3. Relative value.
4. Opportunistic.
5. Specialist.
6. Multi-manager.

LOS 17.b

Long/short equity. This strategy generates alpha via careful stock picking. L/S funds are typically liquid, and generally net long. Equity L/S managers aspire to the returns of a long-only approach but with lower standard deviations. The more market-neutral the approach, the more leverage is likely to be applied.

Dedicated short-selling and short-biased strategies. These two strategies have a negative correlations to traditional assets and modest return goals. The focus is on stock picking using minimal leverage. Dedicated short strategies are generally 60%–120% short at all times, while short-biased strategies are typically 30%–60% net short with some long exposure. Short-biased managers moderate short beta with some long exposure (and cash).

Equity market-neutral (EMN). These strategies attempt to profit from short-term mispricing between securities. Beta risk is minimal, making EMN strategies attractive in periods of market weakness. Most managers are quantitative (vs. discretionary). High leverage is usually used.

LOS 17.c

Merger arbitrage. This strategy attempts to profit by taking positions on a corporate takeover. Merger arbitrage returns are usually insurance-like with a high Sharpe ratio. However, left-tail risk is present. Negative returns can occur if a merger deals unexpectedly fails. Some leverage is usually applied to generate meaningful returns. It is a relatively liquid strategy.

Distressed securities. These strategies focus on firms in bankruptcy or facing other financial stress and seek out mispriced securities. Distressed securities strategies are usually long biased with high illiquidity and moderate or low leverage. Returns tend to be high compared to other event-driven strategies.

LOS 17.d

Fixed-income arbitrage. This strategy attempts to profit from the mispricing of bonds. Sub-strategies include yield curve trades and carry trades. Fixed-income arbitrage usually uses high leverage.

Convertible arbitrage. These strategies attempt to extract "underpriced" implied volatility from long convertible bonds. Convertible arbitrage works best when there is high convertible issuance, adequate market liquidity, and moderate volatility. Liquidity issues may arise from convertibles being somewhat illiquid. Convertible arbitrage managers generally run about 300% long versus 200% short.

LOS 17.e

Opportunistic strategies tend to be highly liquid and use high leverage.

Global macro. These strategies use discretionary approaches and a range of financial instruments to exploit trends in global financial markets. Global macro strategies offer diversification during periods of stress but with mixed outcomes.

Managed futures. In these strategies, a portfolio of futures contracts is actively managed using systematic approaches to provide portfolio and market diversification. Managed futures strategies often exhibit right-tail skew during market turmoil.

LOS 17.f

Specialist hedge fund strategies operate in market niches in order to generate uncorrelated returns. Success with these strategies usually requires specialized knowledge.

Volatility traders. These strategies seek to profit from changes in the term structure of volatility. OTC options can be used to create bull spreads, bear spreads, straddles, and calendar spreads. Alternatively, other instruments including VIX futures, volatility swaps, and variance swaps can be used.

Life settlements. In these strategies, pools of life insurance contracts are purchased, and the hedge fund becomes the beneficiary. The hedge fund manager looks for policies with low surrender value, low ongoing premium payments, and high probability that the insured person will die soon.

LOS 17.g

Multi-manager hedge fund strategies use strategy diversification in an attempt to produce low-volatility, steady returns.

Funds-of-funds. This strategy involves a hedge fund that invests in other hedge funds. Funds-of-funds can offer a very broad strategy mix but can suffer from a lack of transparency, slower tactical execution, and can also expose the FoF investor to netting risk.

Multi-strategy funds. In this hedge fund strategy, a single hedge fund pursues a combination of strategies all under one roof. Compared to funds-of-funds, multi-strategy funds offer a better fee structure and faster tactical asset allocation, though operational risks are less diversified.

LOS 17.h

Conditional linear factor models can be useful for analyzing hedge fund strategies in terms of their risk factor exposures. The curriculum makes use of a specific four-factor model (incorporating equity risk, currency risk, volatility risk, and credit risk factors) to quantify a strategy's exposures.

LOS 17.i

Hedge funds generally bring diversification to traditional stock/bond portfolios, and enhance risk-adjusted returns. The addition of a 20% hedge fund allocation to a traditional 60% stock/40% bond portfolio generally decreases the portfolio's total standard deviation, increases the Sharpe and Sortino ratios, and decreases maximum drawdown.

ANSWER KEY FOR MODULE QUIZZES

Module Quiz 17.1

1. **C** Convertible bond arbitrage strategies are generally classified as relative value strategies. (LOS 17.a)

2. **A** Managed futures strategies are generally classified as opportunistic strategies. (LOS 17.a)

Module Quiz 17.2

1. **A** EMN strategies usually apply somewhat high levels of leverage in order to produce meaningful levels of return. Neither dedicated short strategies nor short-biased strategies typically make significant use of leverage. (LOS 17.b)

2. **C** Equity L/S strategies typically have gross exposures of 70%–90% long and 20%–50% short. Dedicated short strategies are usually 60%–120% short at all times. Short-biased strategies are usually around 30%–60% net short. (LOS 17.b)

3. **A** Compared to various other hedge fund strategies, EMN strategies generally have relatively modest return profiles. EMN funds' primary source of return is alpha. They do not take on beta risk. Their lack of market exposure make EMN strategies attractive in periods of market weakness. (LOS 17.b)

4. **A** While short positions are possible in distressed securities investing, it is usually long biased. Illiquidity tends to be high, and the strategy generally uses moderate to low leverage. (LOS 17.c)

5. **A** When a firm's assets are sold off in liquidation, securities holders are paid sequentially depending on the priority of their claims: first senior secured debt, then junior secured debt, unsecured debt, convertible debt, preferred stock, and lastly common stock. (LOS 17.c)

6. **A** Convertible arbitrage managers generally attempt to extract underpriced implied volatility from holdings of long convertible bonds. To delta and gamma hedge these exposures, the managers will take *short equity* positions. (LOS 17.d)

Module Quiz 17.3

1. **C** Managed futures strategies usually are implemented via systematic approaches, while global macro strategies more often use discretionary approaches. Both strategies typically use high leverage and tend to be highly liquid. (LOS 17.e)

2. **A** Returns of managed futures and global macro strategies both typically exhibit right-tail (positive) skewness during times of market stress. Global macro strategies, however, generally deliver more heterogeneous outcomes. (LOS 17.e)

3. **C** Equity volatility is roughly 80% negatively correlated with equity market returns. Volatility levels rise when equity markets fall. This characteristic makes long volatility strategies useful diversifiers for long equity investments. (LOS 17.f)

4. **C** In implementing life settlement strategies, a hedge fund manager looks for policies with the following traits: low surrender value being offered to the insured individual, low ongoing premium payments required of the investor, and high probability that the insured person will die sooner than predicted by actuarial methods. (LOS 17.f)

5. **C** Funds-of-funds generally offer a more diverse strategy mix than do multi-strategy funds. Multi-strategy funds offer *quicker* tactical asset allocation and generally a *better* fee structure (for example, netting risk between strategies is often absorbed by the multi-strategy general partner). (LOS 17.g)

6. **B** Compared to multi-strategy funds, funds-of-funds offer an investor less transparency and higher netting risk. Multi-strategy funds have more variance due to less diverse strategies and use comparatively higher leverage. (LOS 17.g)

Module Quiz 17.4

1. **C** This reading uses a model that incorporates four factors: equity risk, credit risk, currency risk, and volatility risk. (The interest rate risk "BOND" and commodity risk "CMDTY" factors used by Hasanhodzic and Lo were dropped due to multicollinearity issues.) (LOS 17.h)

2. **C** Adding a 20% allocation of a hedge fund strategy to a traditional 60%/40% portfolio usually *decreases* total portfolio standard deviation while it increases Sharpe and Sortino ratios in the combined portfolios. An allocation to hedge funds often *decreases* maximum drawdown. (LOS 17.i)

3. **A** Adding allocations of equity market-neutral hedge fund strategies to a traditional portfolio has been shown to be effective in generating superior risk-adjusted performance, as evidenced by high Sharpe and Sortino ratios. (The same is true of systematic futures, global macro, and event-driven strategies). On the other hand, fund-of-funds and multi-strategy funds have been found not to enhance risk-adjusted performance significantly. (LOS 17.i)

READING 18

Asset Allocation to Alternative Investments

EXAM FOCUS

Candidates should understand the potential benefits of adding alternative investments to a portfolio of publicly traded equities and debt, and the factors that enter into the determination of an optimal allocation to alternative investments. Candidates will develop an understanding of the characteristics of different types of alternative investments that affect the asset allocation decision. They should able to contrast factor based optimization with mean-variance optimization. Candidates must pay special attention to liquidity concerns with alternative investments and how an investor's time horizon affects the suitability of specific types of alternative investments.

MODULE 18.1: ROLE OF ALTERNATIVE INVESTMENTS AND DEFINING THE INVESTMENT OPPORTUNITY SET

Video covering this content is available online.

LOS 18.a: Explain the roles that alternative investments play in multi-asset portfolios.

Alternative investments refers to various types of investments including hedge funds, private equity, private credit, commercial real estate, and real assets. There are also different types of investments, with somewhat different characteristics, within each of these categories. Real assets include agricultural commodities, precious metals, industrial metals, agricultural land, and oil. Hedge funds pursue a variety of strategies, including long-short hedging, short bias, risk arbitrage, and various quantitative investment strategies. Private equity funds might specialize in existing health care firms or venture capital investments. Each of these will have somewhat different risk and return characteristics as well as different correlations with the returns of traditional investments.

Overall, the goal of adding alternative investments to a portfolio is most often to improve the portfolio's risk and returns profile (e.g., increase the portfolio's **Sharpe ratio**). This can result from investing in assets that increase expected returns, have low risk, or, often, have low returns correlations with other portfolio assets so that diversification across asset classes reduces portfolio risk without sacrificing return. Additionally, investors may seek alternative investments that provide income, the potential for capital growth, or safety (preservation of value).

Private equity and private credit may be viewed primarily as return-enhancing (and risk-increasing) portfolio investments. Real assets may be viewed as risk-reducing (and thus, lower-return) investments. Hedge funds can fall anywhere along this spectrum, depending on the strategies pursued by their managers.

Equity investments, both public and private, typically provide capital growth. Investments in bonds or real estate may generate income. Real assets, and some hedge fund strategies, may diversify risk for an equity portfolio, while private credit may diversify the risk profile for a fixed-income portfolio that is primarily exposed to interest rate risk. Precious metals or government bonds may be seen as safe-haven asset classes.

Hedge funds. Some hedge fund strategies, such as equity long/short or short bias, may somewhat reduce a portfolio's overall equity beta but are mainly expected to increase returns through their managers' security selection skill. Other hedge fund strategies, such as merger arbitrage or global macro, may be less correlated with traditional asset classes.

Private equity. For a portfolio of public equity securities, an allocation to private equity has limited diversification potential because public and private companies face essentially the same risk factors. Thus, the main function of private equity in the portfolio is to increase expected returns.

Private credit. This class of alternative investments include both direct lending and distressed debt. Direct lending is primarily an income-producing investment. For a given range of credit quality, the risk-return profile tends to be similar for direct lending and publicly traded debt, except that direct lending has additional risk (and an expected return premium) due to its illiquidity. Distressed debt has a risk-return profile more like equity securities because factors specific to the issuer have a greater effect on the debt's performance than factors that affect fixed-income investments in general.

Commercial real estate. Real estate investments can hedge inflation risk. Both rental income and the value of properties owned may increase with inflation.

Real assets. Assets such as commodities, farm and timberland, and infrastructure also protect against inflation risk. Asset holdings can target particular subsets of inflation risk, such as energy, food, or building materials. Infrastructure investments require a longer time horizon and their correlation with inflation may be limited, for example, by utility rate regulations.

LOS 18.b: Compare alternative investments and bonds as risk mitigators in relation to a long equity position.

Are alternative investments or bonds the better choice for diversifying an equity portfolio? The answer may depend on the investor's investment horizon.

For a short investment horizon, the primary risk facing the investor is returns volatility. Reducing volatility is best achieved by allocating a portion of the portfolio to an asset class with a low correlation of returns with equities.

For alternative investments as an asset class, reported volatility of returns appears lower than the volatility of equity returns, and its correlation with equity returns also appears to be low. However, these statistics are likely to be biased downward for a number of reasons:

- **Appraisal-based** valuations of privately held investments result in smoothing of reported returns.
- Databases of alternative investment returns are subject to sampling biases, such as **survivorship bias** and **backfill bias**, which result in downside risk being understated in the reported data.
- Indexes of alternative investment returns reflect some degree of diversification because funds in an index may have low correlations of returns with each other. Thus, the volatility of returns on the index is less than the average volatility of returns on index components.

As a result, both the volatility of alternative investment returns and their correlation with equity returns may be higher than they appear to be in reported data.

By comparison, bonds as an asset class have had a lower correlation with equity returns than alternative investments. In fact, over the 20 years before 2017, their correlation with equity returns has been negative. (The correlation was positive in the two decades before that, when inflation was higher.) As a result, an allocation to bonds is likely to reduce the volatility of an equity portfolio's returns more than an equal allocation to alternative investments.

With a long time horizon, however, the primary risk is not returns volatility, but failing to achieve a minimum required rate of return over time. For example, an endowment must earn an average rate of return greater than the sum of inflation and its required annual distributions. Because bonds have a lower expected rate of return than equities, allocating assets to bonds may increase the risk of a portfolio failing to earn its needed rate of return.

In this case, alternative investments can be a better choice for diversification. Their returns correlation with equities, while higher than commonly reported, is still less than perfect even after adjusting for statistical biases. Therefore they offer a potential diversification benefit to an equity portfolio. Because the expected return on alternative investments is higher than that of bonds, over a long time horizon they reduce the risk of failing to meet the portfolio's return requirements.

Reading 18

LOS 18.c: Compare traditional and risk-based approaches to defining the investment opportunity set, including alternative investments.

Traditional approaches to defining the **investment opportunity set** include classifying asset groups by liquidity or by how they perform over economic cycles.

A portfolio manager using a liquidity-based approach would distinguish between alternative investments that are publicly traded, such as futures contracts or REITs, and those that are not publicly traded. Among alternative investments that are not publicly traded, the manager would further classify them by the length of the time commitment required. For example, private equity may be viewed as an asset class that requires a longer-term commitment than private credit, while both require a longer commitment than more liquid alternative investments.

Figure 18.1 shows how asset classes might be considered based on liquidity characteristics.

Figure 18.1: Liquidity-Based Investment Opportunity Set

	Fixed Income	Equity	Other Assets
More Liquid	Cash Bonds	Public Equity	Commodity Futures REITs
		Equity Hedge Funds	Private Real Estate
	Private Credit		Private Real Assets
Less Liquid		Private Equity	

Another traditional approach is to classify assets by how they are expected to perform under different scenarios for economic growth and inflation. Using this approach, a manager would distinguish among asset classes that provide growth in an expanding economy (primarily equities), asset classes that hedge inflation risk (such as real assets and inflation-linked bonds), and asset classes that hedge against deflation (primarily non-inflation-indexed government bonds). Figure 18.2 shows an example of an investment opportunity set that uses this approach.

Figure 18.2: Economic Environment-Based Investment Opportunity Set

	Negative/Low Growth	High Growth
Deflation	Non-Indexed Bonds	
↓		Public Equity Private Equity Private Credit
High Inflation	Indexed Bonds	Commodities Real Assets

A **risk factor based approach** to defining asset classes involves statistically estimating their sensitivities to risk factors identified by the manager. Examples may include economic growth and inflation, interest rates and credit spreads, or currency values. They may also include factors such as liquidity, capitalization, and value-versus-growth.

With respect to alternative investments, a risk factor analysis may show that some alternative investment classes are similar to traditional asset classes in terms of factor sensitivity. For example, private equity returns are sensitive to many of the same risks as public equity, while private credit has many of the same risk sensitivities as publicly traded high yield bonds.

Identifying sources of risk that are common across asset classes is one of the key advantages of a risk factor based approach. This mitigates a limitation of the traditional approaches, which may classify investments into different classes even when they face largely the same risk factors, leading a manager to believe the portfolio is more diversified than it actually is.

Another advantage of a risk-based approach is that by allowing a manager to analyze multiple dimensions of portfolio risk, this approach is useful for developing an integrated risk management framework. In this sense, it can be more useful than the traditional approaches for highlighting the primary drivers of portfolio risk.

Managers using a risk factor based approach must be aware that risk factor estimates can be sensitive to the period used for analysis. The results may also be more difficult to communicate to decision makers and to implement compared to traditional approaches.

MODULE QUIZ 18.1

1. Which of the following categories of alternative investments would be *most appropriate* for diversifying a portfolio of public equity?
   A. Private equity and short-bias hedge funds.
   B. Long-short hedge funds and distressed debt.
   C. Commercial real estate and global macro hedge funds.

2. For alternative investments as an asset class, appraisal-based valuations and sampling biases are believed to overstate:
   A. returns.
   B. risk measures.
   C. diversification benefits.

Video covering this content is available online.

MODULE 18.2: CONSIDERATIONS IN ALLOCATING TO ALTERNATIVE INVESTMENTS

LOS 18.d: Discuss investment considerations that are important in allocating to different types of alternative investments.

As with any asset allocation decision, an allocation to alternative investments must consider their risk, expected return, and returns correlation with the existing portfolio. An allocation to alternative investments also requires that investors consider a number of factors specific to this asset class. These include the choice of investment vehicles to be used, liquidity concerns, expenses and fees, the tax status of the investments, and the ability to obtain the expertise needed to invest successfully.

Setting return expectations for alternative investments is made more difficult by their short history relative to other asset classes and by the limited validity of the data that are available. A suggested approach to determining an expected return for a particular class of alternative investments is to estimate each of its risk factor exposures, and add the expected returns from these exposures to the risk-free rate. An analyst may add an assumed return for the fund manager's alpha and subtract fees and taxes, in order to refine this estimate.

Several characteristics of alternative investments limit the usefulness of mean-variance optimization as a tool for determining their appropriate portfolio allocations. Because of illiquidity and valuation issues, option-like return patterns, and the fact that returns from some strategies tend to be low or negative during a drawdown period and high in later years, we cannot assume returns are normally distributed. Additionally, for alternative investments for which committed capital is not immediately invested by the manager, a portfolio's effective allocation to the asset class might be less than its target.

Investment Vehicles

A typical structure for an alternative investment vehicle is a **limited partnership**. The investment manager is the **general partner** and investors in the fund are **limited partners**. With this structure, the liability of investors in the fund is limited to the amount they have committed. Often these limited partnerships are registered offshore for tax or reporting reasons.

Investing directly in a limited partnership is appropriate for large investors that have the expertise to evaluate managers and fund strategies. They typically invest in a variety of limited partnerships to diversify the specific risks that each general partner will take on as they pursue their strategies. Limited partners sometimes co-invest with a general partner, but they cannot be directly involved in fund operations.

For investors that lack the needed expertise, investing through a **fund-of-funds** may be appropriate. A fund-of-funds manager can pool capital from investors and use it to invest in limited partnerships. Typically, a fund-of-funds manager will specialize in a particular subset of alternative investment strategies. The benefit of a fund-of-funds is that it provides access to this asset class to investors who otherwise would not have it. The drawback is that they charge an additional layer of fees above those charged by the underlying limited partnerships.

Some investors that are large enough to demand favorable investment terms may establish **separately managed accounts (SMAs)** through which to access alternative investments. SMAs have requirements for both the investor and the fund manager that can make them challenging to implement. Another approach is to establish a limited partnership with a single client, known as a **fund of one**. A risk with SMAs or funds of one is that general partners, when allocating certain investment opportunities to investors, may favor limited partners who are paying the fund's standard fees.

Some open-ended mutual funds and "**undertakings for collective investment in transferable securities**" **(UCITS)** have developed to give smaller investors access to alternative investments. However, these structures are more regulated than the other investment vehicles and may constrain managers' choice of strategies. As a result, returns on investments through these structures might not achieve the returns realized by the asset class as a whole.

Liquidity Concerns

Liquidity risk is one of the distinguishing characteristics of alternative investments. Both the investment structures and the underlying investments themselves contribute to liquidity risk.

Limited partnerships for alternative investments are typically structured with subscription provisions for accepting capital, lock-up periods, and restrictions on redemptions. Hedge funds, for example, may accept new capital quarterly or monthly, impose lock-up periods (often six months or a year) during which limited partners may not make redemptions or may do so only with a penalty, and offer redemptions on a quarterly or annual schedule as well as requiring a notice period prior to redemptions. They may also impose "gates" or maximum amounts that can be redeemed at any one time.

For funds in the private equity, private credit, real estate, and real asset sectors, liquidity provisions are often more strict than is typical for hedge funds. Subscriptions are structured in "closes" for new investors, usually over a one-year period. Limited partners commit a stated amount of capital, and the general partner will "call" this capital over an investment period (such as 3 to 5 years) as they identify investment opportunities. Redemptions are typically not available. Instead, the fund will distribute capital over its life (often 10 to 12 years) as it exits its investments. A small secondary market exists for limited partnerships, but transactions often take place at significant discounts to funds' net asset values and may require approval from the general partner.

Figure 18.3 illustrates a time line of cash flows that might occur for a $10 million commitment to a private equity fund.

Figure 18.3: $10 Million Capital Commitment to a Hypothetical Private Equity Fund

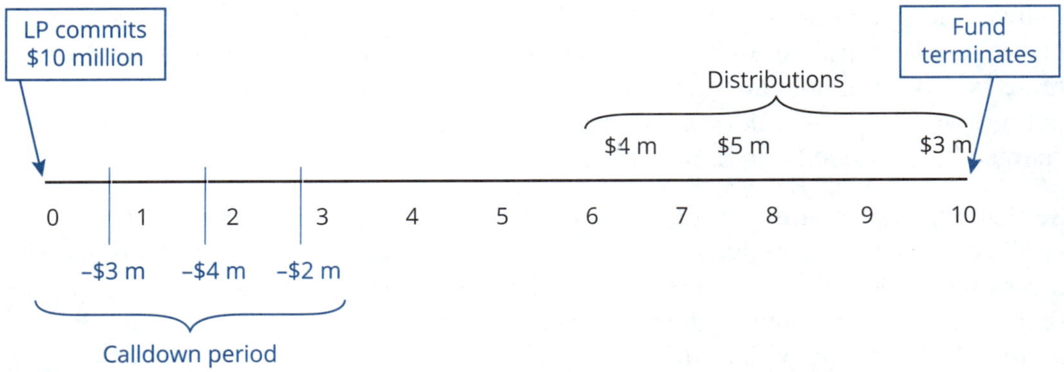

Note in the figure that only $9 million of the limited partner's capital was called. A general partner is not required to call the full amount of committed capital. This is an important consideration when estimating expected returns on a portfolio allocation to alternative investments. A fund may achieve an impressive rate of return, but a limited partner is only earning that return on the portion of committed capital that has been called.

Neither **capital calls** nor distributions occur on a predetermined schedule. Capital may be called (or not) at any time during the **calldown period**. Distributions can occur at any point in the fund's life, even during the calldown period. This, too, affects how much of a portfolio's allocation to alternative investments is actually invested at any point in time.

Limited partners must also consider the opportunity cost of their committed capital during the calldown period. Investing this capital in cash equivalents reduces returns. On the other hand, investing it in higher return but less liquid investments risks missing a capital call. Penalties for doing so can be severe, such as forfeiting all capital invested in the fund to date.

With respect to the liquidity of a fund's holdings, a potential issue is whether they are consistent with the fund's redemption terms. This is mostly a consideration for hedge funds; as noted previously, other types of private investment funds generally do not offer redemptions.

Hedge funds that pursue long-only equity strategies tend to hold relatively liquid investments that are consistent with offering redemptions monthly or quarterly. Short positions are less liquid, which can be a concern if funds that hold significant short positions also offer redemptions frequently. Investors should also note that general partners might designate some of a fund's less liquid holdings as not subject to the fund's ordinary redemption terms. This is referred to as a "**side pocket**." A fund's redemption terms may be misleading if a large portion of its holdings are side pocketed.

Frequent redemption periods may limit a general partner's flexibility to implement strategies with long time horizons or infrequent investment opportunities, such as event-driven strategies. This is particularly true for distressed assets and is the reason funds specializing in those tend to be private equity partnerships rather than hedge funds.

Funds that hold significant portions of illiquid investments, such as some relative value funds, may restrict redemptions under certain market conditions to avoid having to liquidate these assets during crisis periods. One effect of these restrictions is that during such periods, investors may demand redemptions from other hedge funds that have more liquid holdings.

Leverage is another important liquidity consideration because creditors have priority of claims over limited partners. Margin calls may force a leveraged fund to sell its most liquid holdings and be left with its less liquid investments, regardless of which holdings the general partner would otherwise prefer to keep.

Expenses, Fees, and Taxes

Many alternative investments involve significant fees and expenses, such as the "2 and 20" fee structure of many hedge funds (annual management fee 2% of assets under management, incentive fee 20% of gains). Administrative expenses of a fund may also be passed through to investors.

Funds with calldown structures charge management fees on the amount of committed capital, regardless of how much of it has been called down. This may generate negative returns in the early years of an investment when much of the committed capital is yet to be called.

Investors must ensure that their investments, and the investment vehicles used to invest, are consistent with their tax situations. Some fund strategies may result in short-term taxable income to investors, or may be subject to tax withholding. Investors who need to estimate their annual income for tax reporting may find it difficult to do so given the unpredictable nature of returns from many alternative investments. Tax-exempt organizations must ensure that income from a fund will not be considered to be unrelated to the organization's purpose, and therefore considered taxable.

Intermediaries or In-House Programs

Large investors may consider developing their own program for implementing alternative investments directly rather than using intermediaries such as funds of funds. An in-house program may be appropriate for an investor that needs highly customized solutions, desires close control over its investment program, or wishes to implement co-investments with general partners. The "build or buy" decision depends on whether the investor can produce similar results to those of an intermediary at lower cost or generate returns high enough to offset any costs in excess of the costs charged by an intermediary.

A successful program must be able to identify and invest with the best fund managers. Even if an investor is expert at choosing managers who will generate top returns, those managers may attract more capital than they can invest productively, and therefore close their funds to new investors. Managers may also decline capital from investors whose public reporting requirements they feel would be inconsistent with their proprietary strategies.

Investors must also be able to perform due diligence on managers with whom they wish to invest. This requires access to their key decision makers, both before and during the life of an investment. Without this level of access, an investor may be left in a troubled fund when better-informed investors have already demanded redemptions.

MODULE QUIZ 18.2

1. A limited partnership structure with a single client is known as:
   A. UCITS.
   B. a fund of one.
   C. a separately managed account.
2. Cash flows from investors into a private equity limited partnership:
   A. are at the discretion of the general partner.
   B. will be 100% invested after three to five years.
   C. are made only on the establishment date of the partnership.
3. Which of the following terms describes the practice of a hedge fund designating certain of its investment holdings as exempt from the fund's ordinary redemption terms?
   A. Gate.
   B. Lock-up.
   C. Side pocket.

Video covering this content is available online.

MODULE 18.3: SUITABILITY, APPROACHES, LIQUIDITY, AND MONITORING IN ALLOCATING TO ALTERNATIVE INVESTMENTS

LOS 18.e: Discuss suitability considerations in allocating to alternative investments.

In general, alternative investments are only suitable for large investors who have or can hire the specialized knowledge necessary to select profitable investments in this asset class. Because of the wide variety and complexity of alternative investment strategies that managers pursue, an investor needs a high level of expertise to understand the risks being undertaken and the market factors that drive the success of various fund strategies.

Alternative investment strategies are largely based on the premise that skilled managers can create value through active management. For this reason, alternative investments may not be suitable for investors whose philosophy is grounded in a belief in the price-efficiency of markets.

Time (investment) horizon is a key consideration in determining the suitability of alternative investments. Private equity and private real assets are generally suitable only for investors with long time horizons (15 years or more). For investors with shorter time horizons, hedge funds with short lock-up periods and strategies that can be exited relatively quickly may be suitable. Hedge funds that focus on liquid instruments such as publicly traded equities or commodity futures are examples.

A successful alternative investments program requires that the investor has a strong governance program. The investor should have a formal investment policy with clear objectives, put decision-making power in the hands of experts, and have a reliable reporting framework.

Investors in alternative investments must be comfortable with a lower level of transparency than is generally available with traditional investments. As private partnerships, the funds are not governed by the reporting requirements that apply to publicly traded companies. When they do issue reports to investors, the level of detail varies widely and reports often arrive with a significant time lag. Many hedge funds use independent administrators to calculate their net asset values, but private equity and private real asset funds typically do not, which gives them wider discretion in asset valuation. Furthermore, private equity and private real assets may be viewed as "blind pools" in that a fund does not begin acquiring assets until investors have already committed capital to the fund.

LOS 18.f: Discuss approaches to asset allocation to alternative investments.

A suggested approach to including alternative investments in an asset allocation decision is to do it in two stages, first with only the traditional asset classes and then also considering alternative investments. The process can be assisted by statistical tools such as:

- Monte Carlo simulation.
- Mean-variance optimization.
- Risk factor based optimization.

These approaches can be used individually or in combination. Regardless of the approach chosen, an investor must consider the statistical properties of alternative investment returns that distinguish them from traditional asset classes.

Modeling the risk and return properties of alternative investments is challenging. Because asset valuations for many alternative investments are based on appraisals, returns data are likely to be artificially smoothed and are often stale. As a result, using these data without adjustment would underestimate risk. Testing returns data for serial correlation is a suggested method for detecting this smoothing effect. If serial correlation is present, statistical techniques exist that can be used to unsmooth the data.

The distribution of returns is also known to be non-normal, exhibiting skew and excess kurtosis to a greater extent than traditional asset classes. Here, too, the data can be adjusted with statistical methods (such as stochastic volatility, regime switching, or extreme value theory) or by using observed returns instead of an assumed normal distribution of returns. A further limitation is the relatively short history of alternative investments, which may result in small-sample and time-period biases.

One method for modeling a distribution with fat tails (positive excess kurtosis) is to define risk and return properties for two or more distinct market environments, for example, a normal period and a high-volatility period. Returns for each of these can be described with a normal distribution with its own assumed mean and variance. Combining the distributions, using an assumed probability of each environment occurring, results in a non-normal distribution.

Monte Carlo simulation has been described elsewhere in the CFA curriculum. Its use with respect to optimizing an asset allocation can be summarized as follows:

1. Decide between asset class returns or risk factors as the variables to be simulated.
2. Define how the model should behave statistically, for example by accounting for properties like mean reversion, fat-tailed distributions, or unstable correlations.
3. If the model is based on risk factors, translate them to asset class returns.
4. Use the resulting asset class return scenarios to develop meaningful outputs, such as the probability of a shortfall to a portfolio's required or target rate of return.

We introduced **mean-variance optimization** in an earlier topic review and described its use with traditional asset classes. When using this technique with alternative investments, the results may produce an excessive allocation to this asset class, particularly to illiquid investments such as private equity, especially when the data are not properly adjusted for smoothed returns. An optimization model may be designed to constrain the allocation to alternative investments (or any asset class) to be within a minimum and maximum percentage, or to limit overall volatility or downside risk.

Investors should consider the asset allocations suggested by an optimization model to be a guideline rather than a prescription. They must consider the allocation in the context of their objectives and constraints, such as their liquidity requirements. They must also be aware of the limitations of mean-variance optimization. For example, small changes in the inputs may generate significant changes in optimal asset allocations.

Risk factor based optimization is similar to MVO, but instead of modeling asset classes by their return and risk characteristics, the investor models risk factors and factor return expectations. Exposures to risk factors are optimized with respect to an overall risk budget. As with mean-variance optimization, constraints can be included in the model. In this case, the constraints are limits on specific risk factor exposures.

A risk factor based approach requires the additional step of translating the optimized risk exposures into an asset allocation. For example, both public and private equity provide exposure to economic growth risk, but the allocation to each depends on the desired exposure to liquidity risk.

One of the limitations of this approach is that asset classes' return sensitivity to some risk factor exposures might not be stable over time. Another is that correlations among risk factors may behave like correlations among asset class returns and increase during periods of financial stress.

PROFESSOR'S NOTE

The curriculum reading provides extended examples of these portfolio optimization techniques. While we do not believe the authors' empirical results are required by the Level III LOS, reviewing these examples can provide useful insights into how the techniques may be applied to asset allocation in practice.

LOS 18.g: Discuss the importance of liquidity planning in allocating to alternative investments.

Managing liquidity is a crucial aspect of an alternative investments program, especially one that includes private investments with near-term capital calldown periods and long investment horizons. A portfolio must be managed in a way that meets its capital commitments while still providing required liquidity.

An investor can develop forecasting models to help manage liquidity. Examples of liquidity modeling include projecting cash flows to and from a fund and forecasting the annual capital commitments needed to reach and maintain the targeted allocation to alternative investments.

Cash flows for a typical private investment partnership are capital calls in the early years and distributions in the later years. An investor can make assumptions about how a fund will call its committed capital. A simple model might assign a percentage of remaining capital to each year of the calldown period. In this model the capital contribution in period *t* would be the following:

> percentage to be called in Period *t* × (committed capital – capital previously called)

Distributions from a fund can be modeled as percentages of its net asset value. The NAV increases with capital calls and investment returns, and decreases with distributions. To estimate distributions, an investor can assume an expected growth rate for the fund (that is, the IRR of its investments) and a percentage of NAV to be distributed in each period. Thus distributions in Period *t* would be the following:

> percentage to be distributed in Period *t* × [NAV in Period *t* – *1* × (1 + growth rate)]

and the NAV in Period *t* would be the following:

> NAV in Period *t* – *1* × (1 + growth rate)
>
> \+ contributions in Period *t*
>
> – distributions in Period *t*

Using models such as these, an investor can estimate the cash flows to and from a fund. The investor should understand a model's sensitivity to changes in model assumptions and how these affect cash flow forecasts.

Liquidity forecasting is also important for managing how a portfolio reaches and maintains its target asset allocations. Take for example a $15 billion portfolio that currently has no investments in private equity but wants to have a 10% allocation to that asset class. This is unlikely to be achievable all at once (and even if it could be, the private equity investments would not be diversified across vintage years as they should).

Instead, the allocation to private equity will need to increase toward its 10% target over a number of years. Importantly, that percentage will be based on the future values of both the overall portfolio and the private equity investments. Thus, reaching and maintaining the target allocation requires estimating these values.

Combined with the cash flow forecasting approach described previously for a particular fund, an investor can project the capital commitments needed over a span of years to reach the target allocation, and forecast the need to reinvest future distributions to maintain the target.

A crucial aspect of liquidity planning is having cash available to meet capital calls. Keeping these amounts in cash equivalents has significant opportunity costs. A suggested approach is to invest it in publicly traded securities that may be viewed as proxies for the private investments to which they are committed. For example, capital committed to private real estate but not yet called could be invested in publicly traded real estate investment trusts.

Capital calls, distributions, growth rates, and even fund lifetimes may turn out significantly different than expected. An investor should stress-test liquidity planning models against unexpected events such as delayed fund distributions when expected distributions have been earmarked to meet capital calls.

LOS 18.h: Discuss considerations in monitoring alternative investment programs.

An alternative investment program must be monitored to ensure that it is achieving its stated goals in terms of return, risk, income, and safety. Its performance should be evaluated in the context of these goals, rather than simply measured against a benchmark.

Even during the period when the allocation to alternative investments is building up to its target, monitoring is necessary to ensure the investments being made are consistent with the objectives of the program. Effective monitoring is particularly important with private and illiquid investments because these require considerable time to correct if they are out of line with the portfolio's objectives, or if the objectives have changed.

One reason that measuring against a benchmark or peer group can be misleading is the difficulty of selecting a representative one. Because many alternative investment strategies depend heavily on active management, any benchmark chosen is unlikely to be directly comparable to a portfolio's actual investments in the asset class. In addition, published indexes are often inconsistent with each other in the way they define various alternative investment strategies.

Monitoring of alternative investments can be challenging because their performance reporting can be infrequent and come with significant time lags. A further complication with private investments is that they often report internal rates of return rather than time-weighted rates of return. IRR is influenced by the timing of capital calls and distributions, and therefore, may be subject to manipulation. Investors may prefer to monitor a private fund's **multiple on invested capital (MOIC)**. MOIC is calculated by dividing the value of the fund's underlying investments, plus distributions, by total invested capital. Regardless of the metric used, investors should understand how any measure is affected by issues such as stale pricing and appraisal-based valuations. Understanding a fund's investment holdings qualitatively may be the best approach to judging whether a manager is adding value.

An investor should monitor these issues with respect to an alternative investment fund's management:

- A fund's "key persons" are typically specified in its documents. Limited partners may be able to exercise certain rights if a key person leaves, and should understand the circumstances that caused the departure.
- The manager's interests should be aligned with the investor's interests. Potential conflicts may exist if the manager raises a new fund that invests in some of the same underlying holdings. If a manager withdraws capital that he had invested alongside the limited partners, they should learn the reasons.
- Because managers have a great deal of discretion over how they invest capital, investors should monitor a fund's holdings over time for signs of style drift.
- Monitoring a fund's risk management framework is important, especially for leveraged strategies.
- An investor should observe the profile of a fund's other investors and judge whether they are likely to remain committed for the long term. An unexpected increase in redemptions by other investors may be a warning sign. This could potentially put the fund in a position of having to sell its more attractive holdings to raise cash, leaving the remaining investors with less liquid or more poorly performing assets. A manager may also exercise "gates" that block further redemptions.
- A large or unexpected increase in new investors may make more capital available to a manager than he has attractive opportunities to use. If this leads the manager to pursue lesser opportunities, the performance of the fund as a whole may suffer.
- A fund should have reliable auditors, custodians, and other third-party service providers. If these relationships change, an investor should understand whether it is for a positive reason (e.g., the fund outgrows the capabilities of a service provider and needs a larger one) or otherwise (e.g., an auditor quits a relationship because of a manager's actions).

MODULE QUIZ 18.3

1. Which class of publicly traded securities is *most likely* to be affected by similar risk factors to those that affect private credit?
   A. REITs.
   B. Equity securities.
   C. High yield bonds.
2. Alternative investments are *most likely* to be suitable for a portfolio investor that:
   A. has a strong governance program and insists on transparency.
   B. has a long time horizon and believes financial markets are efficient.
   C. believes active management can generate excess risk-adjusted returns over time.
3. When using optimization approaches to determine an allocation to alternative investments, recommended practices *least likely* include:
   A. using smoothed historical data as inputs.
   B. modeling normal and high-volatility periods separately.
   C. placing constraints on the allocations to various asset classes.
4. A $20 billion endowment has decided to increase its allocations to private equity and private credit from 5% each to 10% each. The endowment will *most likely* need to:
   A. forecast the timing of capital calls and hold enough capital in cash equivalents to meet them.
   B. account for the expected growth rate of the portfolio when planning the capital commitment.
   C. identify suitable investment vehicles for $100 million each of private equity and private credit.
5. Compared to an alternative investment partnership's reported internal rate of return, its multiple on invested capital is less affected by:
   A. stale pricing.
   B. timing of capital calls.
   C. appraisal-based valuations.

KEY CONCEPTS

LOS 18.a

Allocating portfolio assets to alternative investments can improve the risk-adjusted return of a portfolio that includes only traditional asset classes. Private equity and private credit may be viewed primarily as return-enhancing portfolio investments. Real assets may be viewed as risk-reducing investments. Hedge funds may serve either function in a portfolio, depending on the strategies they pursue.

LOS 18.b

Whether bonds or alternative investments are better risk mitigators for an equity portfolio depends on the investor's time horizon. Over short horizons, return volatility is the predominant risk, and bond returns have a lower correlation with equity returns than do alternative investment returns. Over long horizons, the main risk is failing to achieve the target return, so alternative investments may be more suitable than bonds because of their higher expected returns.

LOS 18.c

Traditional approaches to defining the investment opportunity set may be based on asset classes' liquidity or expected performance in different scenarios for economic growth and inflation.

A liquidity-based approach would distinguish among alternative investment classes that are publicly traded, such as REITs and commodity futures, and those that are not publicly traded, such as private equity.

An approach based on expected performance would distinguish alternative investment classes that are expected to outperform in a high-growth economy, such as private equity, from those that would be expected to provide an inflation hedge, such as indexed bonds or real assets.

A risk factor based approach to defining asset classes involves statistically estimating their sensitivities to risk factors. Its advantages compared to traditional approaches are that it can identify sources of risk that are common to different asset classes (such as public and private equity) and allow a manager to analyze multiple dimensions of portfolio risk. Its limitations are that it can be difficult to communicate to decision makers and implement, and that its results may be sensitive to the historical period used in the analysis.

LOS 18.d

In addition to risk, return, and correlation, important considerations for alternative investments include investment vehicles, liquidity, expenses and fees, taxes, and the need to obtain special understanding of the asset class.

Alternative investment funds are typically structured as limited partnerships, with the manager as general partner and investors as limited partners. Investors that are not large enough to invest directly in limited partnerships often invest in funds of funds to gain exposure to alternative investments.

Liquidity concerns include lock-up periods, redemption restrictions, the opportunity cost of committed capital, and the practice of "side pocketing" to exempt some assets from a hedge fund's redemption terms.

Alternative investment funds charge management fees and incentive fees. Management fees are based on committed capital rather than called capital. Investors must ensure that a fund's activities and distributions are consistent with their tax situations.

When deciding whether to invest through funds of funds or develop an in-house program, investors should consider the expense of developing and maintaining a program, their needs for customized solutions and close control, and whether they intend to make co-investments with general partners.

LOS 18.e

Alternative investments are suitable for large investors with long time horizons, the specialized knowledge to succeed in this asset class, strong governance frameworks, comfort with a lack of transparency, and a belief that active management can create value.

LOS 18.f

Asset allocation approaches such as Monte Carlo simulation, mean-variance optimization, and risk factor based optimization can be extended to include alternative investments. However, investors must take care to adjust the data for this asset class for smoothed returns that underestimate risk, and to include constraints in their asset allocation models. Otherwise these techniques are likely to over-allocate to alternative investments.

LOS 18.g

Liquidity planning for alternative investments must be managed such that the investor meets its capital commitments. An investor can develop forecasting models to project cash flows to and from a fund and forecast the capital commitments needed to reach and maintain the targeted allocation to alternative investments. These models should be tested for sensitivity to their assumptions about the timing of capital calls, distributions, growth rates, and lifetimes of the funds.

LOS 18.h

An alternative investment program must be monitored to ensure that it is achieving its stated goals. Its performance should be evaluated in the context of these goals, rather than measured against a benchmark. An appropriate benchmark is difficult to establish for an alternative investments program because its performance depends greatly on active management by the managers chosen.

Investors in private funds may choose *multiple on invested capital* as a metric to monitor, rather than the internal rates of return reported by the funds.

Investors should monitor an alternative investment fund's key persons, risk management framework, and third-party service providers, as well as the profile of the fund's other investors. They should be alert for signs of style drift or misalignment of a manager's interests with investors' interests.

ANSWER KEY FOR MODULE QUIZZES

Module Quiz 18.1

1. **C** Alternative investments that can diversify a public equity portfolio include commercial real estate, real assets, and hedge funds that pursue non-equity-oriented strategies. Private equity, distressed debt, and equity-oriented hedge funds are less appropriate because they are affected by many of the same risk factors as public equity. (LOS 18.a)

2. **C** Smoothing of returns and sampling biases are believed to understate the correlation of alternative investments with traditional asset classes and therefore overstate their diversification benefits. These data issues are believed to understate risk measures. Their effect on reported returns is not clear. (LOS 18.b)

Module Quiz 18.2

1. **B** A fund of one is a limited partnership structure that has only a single client. (LOS 18.d)

2. **A** Typically, in private equity limited partnerships, the limited partners commit a fixed amount of capital, which the general partner can call over a number of years as investment opportunities arise. Limited partners are responsible for having cash available to meet capital calls. General partners may call less than 100% of the committed capital. (LOS 18.d)

3. **C** Assets that are not subject to a fund's redemption terms are said to be held in a side pocket. A gate is a maximum amount an investor may redeem at one time. A lock-up is a restriction on redemptions during a period of time. (LOS 18.d)

Module Quiz 18.3

1. **C** High yield debt may be viewed as a proxy for private debt because they tend to be affected by the same risk factors. (LOS 18.c, 18.g)

2. **C** Allocating to alternative investments is most suitable for investors with long time horizons, strong governance programs, comfort with limited transparency, and a belief that active managers add value. (LOS 18.e)

3. **A** Because some alternative investments have relatively short histories of returns data, use of historical data alone may introduce time-period and small-sample biases. Unsmoothing is recommended because the data often reflect appraisal-based valuations. (LOS 18.f)

Reading 18

4. **B** To achieve a target allocation to alternative investments, an investor needs to account for the expected growth rate of the portfolio. Because the target will likely only be reached a number of years in the future, the commitment to the asset class will be larger than the target allocation as a percentage of today's portfolio value. Immediately investing the targeted percentage, even if enough suitable investments can be found, would lack diversification across vintage years. To reduce the opportunity cost of committed capital, cash that needs to be available if called can be invested in liquid public securities that have similar risk characteristics as their intended private investments. (LOS 18.g)

5. **B** Multiple on invested capital is less subject to manipulation of cash flow timing by a manager than IRR, but may sill reflect stale pricing and appraisal-based valuations. (LOS 18.h)

TOPIC QUIZ: ALTERNATIVE INVESTMENTS

You have now finished the Alternative Investments topic section. On your Schweser online dashboard, you can find a Topic Quiz that will provide immediate feedback on how effective your study of this material has been. The test is best taken timed; allow three minutes per question. Topic Quizzes are more exam-like than typical QBank questions or module quiz questions. A score less than 70% suggests that additional review of the topic is needed.

READING 19

Overview of Private Wealth Management

EXAM FOCUS

The essay questions have traditionally been heavily weighted toward investment policy statement (IPS) questions for individuals and institutions.

To answer IPS questions successfully, you must:

1. Be familiar with and understand a large number of potential issues that might apply in a given situation. These are covered in the SchweserNotes and CFA readings. There is no substitute for reading the material.
2. Carefully read and understand the facts of the case to determine which issues from Item 1 are relevant. Because each case is unique, you cannot expect to pass just by repeating what you saw as the answer to a previous question. CFA Institute says that the Level III exam is unique in requiring a high level of judgment—it is these questions where that most comes into play. You will have the opportunity to practice this as you go forward in the Schweser material.
3. Recognize that there is a process at work in developing an IPS and constructing a portfolio for a client. As the exam has required candidates to construct an IPS and then use it, we focus on this in our material.
4. The last stage is to construct a written answer that reflects Items 1, 2, and 3. This has not been required on other levels of the exam. The morning session is generally referred to as essay; however, the more precise term is constructed response. The key points that should appear in your answer have been decided, and your answer is evaluated strictly in terms of how well it makes and supports those points in a coherent fashion. Practice writing an effective constructed response answer many times before the exam.
5. A significant percentage of Level III candidates find this section frustrating because it does not meet their personal sense of consistency. Past answers are quite consistent on the main important issues, but they also include a range of random unimportant comments. The random comments are frustrating to

candidates who try to repeat what they have seen in past answers. Try to move past that and learn what is expected. Up until now, the CFA exam process has primarily focused on precise mathematical techniques. The Level III material will continue to draw on those skills. However, this exam will likely test your ability to find what another trained professional would have been expected to find and write when confronted with sometimes contradictory issues.

The next pages will lay out a variety of issues with which you are expected to be familiar. They may or may not be relevant to a given portfolio question. The exam will likely test the ability to determine what is relevant to a particular case and then apply it.

Video covering this content is available online.

MODULE 19.1: INVESTMENT CONCERNS OF PRIVATE CLIENTS AND INSTITUTIONS

LOS 19.a: Contrast private client and institutional client investment concerns.

Private clients, such as individuals and families, have different investment concerns from institutional investors, such as pension funds, endowments, banks, and insurance companies. These investment concerns include investment objectives and constraints as well as other considerations, such as governance structure, investment sophistication, regulatory environment, and investor uniqueness and complexity.

Investment Objectives

Private clients have a *wide range of investment objectives*, such as maintaining the real value of the investment portfolio, being financially secure in retirement, and providing financial support to family members. However, *these objectives may not be precisely defined*, as the private client may not be able to quantify the size of the investment portfolio required at the start of retirement or the annual cash flows required to fund the college expenses of dependents. The investment objectives of a private client *can change over time* due to life events and/or the performance of the client's investment portfolio. In addition, certain investment objectives *may be difficult to reconcile*, such as financial security in retirement and the ability to generously fund charitable projects at the same time.

Institutional clients, on the other hand, are more likely to have *clearly defined objectives* that are usually focused on funding liabilities (e.g., defined benefit pension plans and insurance companies). The investment objectives of institutional clients also tend to remain *stable over time.*

Constraints

Private clients have different constraints from institutional clients with respect to the following:

- **Time horizon.** Private clients have *shorter* time horizons compared to institutional clients, whose time horizons can theoretically be infinite.

The shorter time horizons limit the liquidity and risk-taking ability of private clients. A private client may also specify *different time horizons* for different investment objectives. In contrast, institutional clients typically have a single time horizon for a clearly defined objective.

- **Scale (or size).** Private client portfolios are usually *smaller* compared to those of institutional clients. As a result, certain asset classes, such as real estate and hedge funds, may be deemed unsuitable for private client portfolios as these investments may lead to an overly concentrated portfolio.
- *Taxes.* Taxes are an important consideration for private clients and can impact asset allocation and manager selection. In contrast, some institutional clients, such as endowments and foundations, may benefit from significant tax exemptions.

Other Considerations

Apart from investment objectives and constraints, the following investment concerns impact private clients and institutional investors in different ways:

- *Governance structure.* Institutional clients are likely to have a *formal investment governance structure*, with a board of directors and investment committee responsible for overseeing investment strategy and monitoring performance. On the other hand, private clients tend to have less formal investment governance, with a private wealth manager responsible for formulating the IPS, implementing the investment strategy, and reporting performance.
- *Investment sophistication.* Due to their formal governance structure and greater access to investment resources, institutional investors tend to be *more sophisticated* than private clients. Private clients are also more likely to display *emotional biases* in their investment decision-making, which may cause them to make suboptimal decisions.
- *Regulatory environment.* The regulatory environment for private clients and institutional investors varies greatly by jurisdiction. Some countries, like Australia and India, have the same regulator for these two investor groups, whereas other countries, like the United States, employ different regulators for each investor group.
- *Investor uniqueness and complexity.* Due to their uniqueness and complexity, individuals with similar investment objectives may choose very different investment strategies because of their different concerns and backgrounds. This is less likely to be observed with institutional investors.

MODULE QUIZ 19.1

1. Which of the following statements is *most accurate* with respect to the difference between private and institutional clients?
   A. Private clients are more likely to have clearly defined investment objectives compared to institutional clients.
   B. Private clients are likely to have shorter investment horizons and smaller portfolio sizes compared to institutional clients.
   C. Private clients are likely to have a more formal governance structure and a lower degree of investment sophistication compared to institutional clients.

2. Which of the following investments is *most likely* to be appropriate for a private client with a short investment horizon and high liquidity needs?
   A. Global bonds.
   B. Hedge funds.
   C. Private equity.

Video covering this content is available online.

MODULE 19.2: INFORMATION AND SKILLS NEEDED WHEN ADVISING PRIVATE CLIENTS

LOS 19.b: Discuss information needed in advising private clients.

LOS 19.c: Identify tax considerations affecting a private client's investments.

Private wealth managers need to gather relevant client information to develop an understanding of their clients prior to formulating their investment objectives and assessing their risk tolerance.

Personal Information

Relevant personal information that a private wealth manager should determine in discussions with a client include:

- Family circumstances, including marital status and the number and age of dependents.
- Proof of client identification.
- Employment information, including future career aspirations.
- Retirement plans.
- Sources of wealth.
- Specific return or investment objectives.
- Risk tolerance.
- Investment preferences (e.g., liquidity or unique concerns).

The formulation of a client's investment objectives and risk tolerance are discussed in more depth later in the reading.

Financial Information

Wealth managers can construct a *net worth statement* of a private client to obtain a comprehensive understanding of the client's financial profile in terms of assets and liabilities.

A private client's assets on a net worth statement include:

- Cash and deposit accounts.
- Brokerage/investment accounts.
- Retirement accounts (e.g., defined contribution plan account or the present value of defined benefit pension).

- Other employee benefits (e.g., stock options).
- Stock/ownership of private companies.
- Life insurance policies with a cash value.
- Real estate.
- Other personal assets (e.g., cars, jewelry).

Liabilities on a net worth statement include:

- Consumer debt and credit card balances.
- Mortgage loans.
- Other types of debt (e.g., car loans and student loans).
- Margin debt in brokerage accounts.

Figure 19.1 illustrates a sample net worth statement for a private client.

Figure 19.1: Net Worth Statement

Assets (in thousands):		Liabilities (in thousands):	
Cash and bank deposits	500	Credit card debt	175
Brokerage account	1,500	Home mortgage	500
DC plan balance	1,450		
Home	750		
Other personal property	125		
Total Assets	**4,325**	**Total Liabilities**	**675**
		Total Net Worth	**3,650**

In addition to a client's assets and liabilities, wealth managers should seek an understanding of a client's annual income and expenses. Sources of income cash flows include a client's salary, pension income, business profits, and investment income. An analysis of income versus expenses is especially important for private clients who need to carefully budget in order to save toward their retirement goals.

PROFESSOR'S NOTE

The *economic* net worth statement extends an individual's assets to include *human capital* (present value of expected future labor income), while liabilities are extended to include *consumption* and *bequest* goals. This is covered in more detail in Reading 21.

Tax Considerations

Taxes on individuals vary by jurisdiction and must be considered in the IPS. Some general classifications of taxes are as follows:

- **Income tax.** Taxes paid on any form of income (e.g., wage, rental, dividend, interest, and capital gains).

- **Wealth-based taxes.** These include taxes paid on the value of certain types of assets (e.g., real estate) and taxes paid on the value of assets transferred to another individual through inheritance, gifts, etc.
- **Consumption tax.** These include sales taxes and value-added taxes.

Tax planning can be complex because the tax environment varies by jurisdiction. For example, some countries, like the United States, tax short-term capital gains on securities at the individual's highest marginal tax rate, while long-term capital gains on securities are usually taxed at a lower rate.

The effects of taxes must be considered when formulating the investment strategy and portfolio asset allocation for a private client. The following strategies can be used to reduce the adverse impact of taxes:

- **Tax avoidance.** This is not to be confused with illegal tax evasion. The private client can minimize taxes by utilizing investment accounts that are legally exempt from taxes on income and capital gains (e.g., Individual Savings Accounts in the United Kingdom). Some jurisdictions also allow limited gift amounts to be transferred without incurring wealth-based taxes.
- **Tax reduction.** The private client can invest in tax-free securities and/or securities that are more tax efficient (e.g., in jurisdictions where capital gains are taxed at a lower rate than income, securities that generate returns mainly as price appreciation offer the private client a lower effective tax rate).
- **Tax deferral.** The private client can minimize the compounding effect of taxes on portfolio returns by deferring the recognition of these taxes into the future. Strategies that fall under this category focus on long-term capital gains and low turnover. Tax deferral is also offered by retirement plans such as 403(b) retirement savings accounts. These retirement plans permit tax-free contributions and earnings accumulation but require taxes to be paid on withdrawals.

> **For the Exam:** Calculations quantifying the benefits of utilizing the tax strategies previously discussed are covered in Reading 20.

Other Client Information

Additional information that a private wealth manager typically gathers for financial planning purposes includes:

- Wills and trust documents for estate planning.
- Insurance policies that the private client has taken out (e.g., life, disability).
- Service guidelines (e.g., whether the wealth manager is authorized to modify investment strategy and make trading decisions).
- Portfolio reporting requirements.
- Periodic liquidity requirements.
- Communications and information to share with other financial services professionals on behalf of the private client.

LOS 19.f: Describe technical and soft skills needed in advising private clients.

Private wealth managers need a combination of technical skills and soft skills to gather and utilize the information about their clients to formulate an investment strategy that will effectively address the goals, objectives, and constraints of their clients.

Technical skills include proficiency in financial planning; capital markets and asset classes; portfolio construction and monitoring; technology skills; and, in some situations, fluency in multiple languages.

Soft skills are essential for the interpersonal aspects of a client-advisor relationship and include communication and social skills, education skills, and business development and sales skills.

MODULE QUIZ 19.2

1. Ray McPherson, CFA, is meeting with a new private client, Henrietta Gove, to plan her investment strategy. McPherson has already established that Gove is 40 years old and works in internal audit for a publicly listed company. Gove mentioned several financial objectives during their last conversation and stated that she prefers low investment volatility. Gove's income more than adequately covers her expenses, and she would like to understand how her portfolio can fund a comfortable retirement lifestyle.

   List *five* additional pieces of personal information that McPherson should gather from Gove in order to prepare Gove's IPS.

2. A private wealth manager is educating her client on the importance of tax-efficient strategies. She makes the following three statements:

   Statement 1: I recommend that you change the asset location of your investment in high-coupon corporate bonds from a taxable account to a retirement account that allows tax-free earnings and withdrawals.

   Statement 2: You should reduce your exposure to dividend-paying equities in favor of a more tax-efficient asset class.

   Statement 3: If required, you should use an account that allows tax-free earnings but requires taxes to be paid on withdrawals.

   Identify the tax strategy (tax avoidance, tax deferral, or tax reduction) associated with each statement and give *one* reason for each answer.

3. Joan Cheong, CFA, just completed a portfolio review meeting with one of her private clients. Which of the following statements describes a soft skill that Cheong utilized in managing her client's portfolio?
   A. Cheong rebalanced her client's portfolio in accordance with the guidelines in her client's IPS.
   B. Cheong updated capital market expectations for the asset classes that are suitable for her client's portfolio.
   C. Cheong explained her client's portfolio performance in easy-to-understand terms and in her client's regional dialect.

MODULE 19.3: FORMULATING CLIENT GOALS AND EVALUATING RISK TOLERANCE

Video covering this content is available online.

LOS 19.d: Identify and formulate client goals based on client information.

Private wealth managers help their clients formulate and prioritize their financial goals. A private client's financial goals can be categorized into *planned goals* and *unplanned* goals.

Planned Goals

These are goals that can be *reasonably estimated* within a *specified time horizon*. Planned goals may include:

- Retirement goals (e.g., funding a comfortable existence post-retirement).
- Specific purchases (e.g., primary or secondary residence).
- Funding the education of dependents.
- Funding significant family events (e.g., wedding celebrations).
- Charitable giving.
- Wealth transfer during a private client's lifetime or at death.

Unplanned Goals

These goals are related to *unexpected financial expenditures*. Unplanned goals by their nature are more difficult to deal with because of the *uncertainty* associated with the *amount of expenditure* and/or *timing*. Examples of unplanned goals include unforeseen expenditures related to property repairs and unexpected medical expenses that are not covered by health insurance.

The Private Wealth Manager's Role in Formulating Client Goals

Private wealth managers can assist their clients in formulating their financial goals in the following ways:

- *Quantifying goals.* A private client may need assistance to formulate specific and realistic goals when these are difficult to quantify (e.g., funding a comfortable retirement).
- *Prioritizing goals.* When a private client has goals that are difficult to reconcile (e.g., purchasing a vacation property in retirement versus providing for the education of a client's dependents), the wealth manager can help the client identify the goals that have higher priority. Note that these may not necessarily be the ones that occur earlier in the client's time horizon.
- *Changing goals.* Private clients may decide to reevaluate their financial goals after a change in their financial circumstances. Wealth managers can assist clients in this process and in modifying their investment strategy.

Reading 19

EXAMPLE: Formulating client goals

Bonnie DuBois, a 60-year-old U.S. citizen, has just retired after a 35-year career in the fashion industry. Through a modest lifestyle, disciplined saving, and the help of a private wealth manager, she has accumulated a $2,000,000 diversified portfolio.

DuBois resides in a house that has been paid off for several years. She estimates she will need $60,000 per year, with annual increases for inflation, to fund her lifestyle in retirement. One of the benefits of DuBois's past employment is comprehensive health insurance in retirement, but she is concerned that she might need long-term care in the future.

In a recent conversation with her wealth manager, she mentions her desire to help support her son Barry, his wife Betty, and their three children (ages 14, 12, and 10). Barry's and Betty's combined salaries barely meet their living expenses currently as they hold relatively junior roles in their respective employment. DuBois expects to provide them with $30,000 per year for the next five years and states that supporting her son and his family is the most important priority for her because of its proximity timewise.

She also wishes to purchase a vacation property in five years, although she is unsure how she will fund the purchase. She has informed Barry and her wealth manager that, at her death, her estate will be gifted to a local museum.

1. Identify DuBois's planned and unplanned goals.
2. Discuss how DuBois's private wealth manager can assist her with quantifying and prioritizing her financial goals.

Answer:

1. DuBois's *planned* goals are (1) funding her lifestyle in retirement, (2) supporting her son and his family for the next five years, (3) purchasing a vacation property in the Caribbean, and (4) gifting her estate to a local museum at her death.

   Her *unplanned* goals are her long-term care costs if her health deteriorates in retirement and the property repairs that may be required for her house and the vacation property in the Caribbean if purchased.

2. DuBois has quantified the retirement funding goal and the support of her son and his family. She should work with her wealth manager to quantify her goal of purchasing a vacation property and to decide on the best way to fund the purchase. She and her wealth manager should also work to quantify her goal of gifting her estate to a local museum at her death.

   DuBois states that supporting her son and his family is her most important priority. Note that the timing of a financial goal should not be the primary reason for determining the priority of goals. DuBois's wealth manager needs to help her determine which of her goals are most important. If DuBois's support for her son and his family competes with her desire to purchase a vacation property and her ability to make a meaningful bequest to a local museum at her death, she should consider reevaluating her priorities.

LOS 19.e: Evaluate a private client's risk tolerance.

A private wealth manager needs to understand a client's risk tolerance in order to formulate an appropriate investment strategy for the client. A private client's risk orientation can be described in several ways:

- **Risk tolerance.** This reflects both the client's *willingness* and ability to take risks. The opposite of risk tolerance is *risk aversion*.
- **Risk capacity.** This addresses a private client's *ability* to take financial risks, based on the client's wealth, income, investment horizon, liquidity requirements, importance of goals, and other relevant considerations. The *higher* the risk capacity, the *greater* the ability of the client's portfolio to sustain losses without putting the client's goals in jeopardy. Risk capacity is a *more objective* measure compared to risk tolerance, which can be viewed as more of an attitude toward risk.

> **For the Exam:** Generally, the ability to bear risk is decreased by:
> - A shorter time horizon.
> - Large critical goals in relation to the size of the portfolio.
> - Goals that are important to the client or those that cannot be deferred.
> - High liquidity needs.
> - Situations where the portfolio is the sole source of support or there is an inability to losses in value.

- **Risk perception.** This is defined as a *subjective* measure of investment risk (e.g., whether a private client thinks of investment losses in absolute or percentage terms). Risk perception varies from one private client to the next; a wealth manager can play a part in influencing a client's risk perception.

Private wealth managers can evaluate the risk tolerance of their clients using a combination of *questionnaires* and *conversations*. Conversations can yield additional information about a private client's risk tolerance (e.g., the client's past investment successes and failures; risk perception; and financial background and experiences) that may be difficult to obtain from questionnaires as well as enable the wealth manager to educate clients about investment risk.

When private clients have *multiple* financial goals, the wealth manager should determine the client's risk tolerance for each goal (e.g., a client may have a low risk tolerance for more important goals but higher risk tolerance for lower priority goals).

MODULE QUIZ 19.3

1. Vivian Collins is a client of ESP Financial Advisors. She presents her personal circumstances as follows:
   - Collins is 45 years old, divorced, and has a daughter, Daija, aged 15 years.
   - Collins has worked at her current job with the government for the last 23 years and assumes that she will remain there until retirement in 20 years when she will collect her pension. Currently, her employment income comfortably covers her living expenses.
   - She wants to be able to send Daija to the college of her choice and states that this is her highest priority goal as it will happen in the next 3–6 years.
   - Collins expects her daughter to eventually marry and have children, and she would love to be able to leave something to her future grandchildren.
   - Collins expects her pension to cover most of her retirement expenses and thinks she will need $20,000 per year from her modest investment portfolio to fund her retirement lifestyle.

   Identify the issues relating to Collins's goal quantification and goal prioritization.

2. As a client of ESP Financial Advisors, Vivian Collins, age 45, expects to retire in 20 years. Her financial advisor is evaluating her risk tolerance level associated with each of the following financial goals:

Retirement:	Collins views retirement as a long-term goal and is prepared to accept a 10%–15% drop in expected retirement spending. However, she is concerned that she might face unexpected health-related expenses in retirement.
College fees:	Collins wants to be able to pay for her daughter's college education in the next 3–6 years. Currently, this is her highest priority goal.
Gifting:	Collins would like to leave a gift to her grandchildren at her death.

Describe Collins's risk tolerance level associated with each of her financial goals as either *lower* or *higher*, and **justify** each answer.

Reading 19

Video covering this content is available online.

MODULE 19.4: CAPITAL SUFFICIENCY ANALYSIS FOR CLIENT GOALS

LOS 19.g: Evaluate capital sufficiency in relation to client goals.

Capital sufficiency (or capital needs) analysis enables private wealth managers to determine the likelihood of their clients being able to meet their financial objectives. This analysis can be performed using deterministic forecasting and Monte Carlo simulation.

Deterministic Forecasting

A traditional, deterministic, linear return analysis assumes that a private client's portfolio will achieve a *single compound annual growth* rate across the client's investment horizon. When using this approach, the wealth manager needs to establish the following inputs:

- Current value of the investment portfolio.
- Investment horizon.
- Annual return assumption (this should be based on forward-looking capital market assumptions rather than the simplistic use of historical returns).
- Contributions into the portfolio and cash flows out of the portfolio over the investment horizon.
- Impact of taxes, inflation, and investment management fees.

While deterministic forecasting is *easy to understand* and implement, its main disadvantage is that the use of a *single return assumption is not representative of the actual market volatility*.

Monte Carlo Simulation

While deterministic forecasting focuses on a single rate of return, Monte Carlo simulation allows input variables (which are similar to the inputs used with the deterministic approach) to be given a *probability distribution* to allow for real world uncertainty. If required, each asset class can be modeled with its own return and risk assumptions and the asset class's correlation with the returns of other asset classes instead of using a single portfolio return assumption. The Monte Carlo simulation then generates *a large number of independent trials*, consistent with the assumed probability distributions, with each trial showing one potential outcome at the end of the investment horizon. A wealth manager can then aggregate all the outcomes to *determine the probability that a client will achieve a financial goal* over the investment horizon. A key consideration when using Monte Carlo simulation is the *quality of the underlying assumptions* because, like any complex model, the output of a Monte Carlo simulation will only be as good as its inputs.

For the Exam: Monte Carlo simulation is also discussed in other readings. You do not know how to actually do it, so the questions are likely to focus on interpreting the results of a simulation, as illustrated in the following example.

EXAMPLE: Interpreting Monte Carlo simulation results

A private wealth manager has performed a Monte Carlo simulation for a client who wants to gift $1,000,000 to a local art museum in 20 years. The results of the simulation for specific time intervals and percentiles are shown in Figure 19.2.

Figure 19.2: Monte Carlo Simulation Results for Client's Portfolio (Inflation Adjusted)

Percentile	Year 15 Portfolio Value	Year 20 Portfolio Value	Year 25 Portfolio Value
25th	$890,931	$1,339,655	$1,977,523
50th	$779,809	$1,103,982	$1,592,294
75th	$669,433	$883,247	$1,204,454
Successful trials	8%	61%	89%

From Figure 19.2, the wealth manager can conclude that 61% of trials met the client's financial objective after 20 years (i.e., the probability of success is 61%). Over the same time period, 50% of trials achieved a portfolio value in excess of $1,103,982 (the portfolio value at the 50th percentile), while 25% of trials achieved a portfolio value in excess of $1,339,655 (the portfolio value at the 25th percentile).

Wealth managers tend to use a *75%–90% probability of success* as a rule of thumb when advising private clients. If the probability of success is considered unacceptably low, a wealth manager could propose one or more of the following courses of action:

- Increase contributions over the investment horizon.
- Reduce the financial goal amount.
- Increase the time horizon for the financial goal.
- Pursue an investment strategy with higher expected returns while remaining within the client's risk tolerance.

While capital sufficiency analysis is a useful tool in financial planning, wealth managers should be careful not to pursue an investment strategy based only on its conclusions (it may not always be feasible to extend the time horizon for a financial goal in order to increase the probability of success).

Reading 19

MODULE QUIZ 19.4

1. A private wealth manager has performed a Monte Carlo simulation for a client who wants to make a $2 million charitable donation in 25 years. The results of the simulation for the charitable donation (adjusted for inflation) are shown in the following table.

Percentile	Year 20 Portfolio Value	Year 25 Portfolio Value	Year 30 Portfolio Value
25th	$1,933,318	$2,907,062	$4,291,225
50th	$1,692,188	$2,495,637	$3,455,269
75th	$1,452,663	$2,116,646	$2,613,665
95th	$1,308,705	$1,751,233	$2,196,357

The probability that the client's goal will be met is *closest* to:

A. 25%.
B. 50%.
C. 75%.

Video covering this content is available online.

MODULE 19.5: PRINCIPLES OF RETIREMENT PLANNING

LOS 19.h: Discuss the principles of retirement planning.

The principles underpinning retirement planning include the retirement stage of a private client's life, the analysis of the client's financial goals in retirement, and behavioral considerations.

Retirement Stage of Life

Private wealth managers work with their clients to establish how much they should save toward their financial goals and to determine when they will be financially able to retire. Since private clients do not always have a clear idea of their financial goals in retirement, a wealth manager has a role to play in influencing the retirement plans of their clients.

PROFESSOR'S NOTE

The financial stages of a private client's life are covered in more detail in Reading 21. We reproduce some of that material later to demonstrate how a private client's *human capital* (present value of expected future labor income) and *financial capital* (all the other assets of the private clients, such as financial savings and assets and tangible assets predominantly) change over the client's lifetime.

The following overview of the financial stages of life illustrates how retirement planning should start relatively early in the private client's adult life:

Education. The private client gains knowledge and skills through formal and informal education and apprenticeships. The emphasis in this stage of life is on *developing human capital* rather than saving for retirement.

Early career. The individual enters the workforce, often starts a family, and assumes other personal responsibilities. *Saving for retirement usually begins at this stage*, although there are many other competing financial goals.

Career development. After becoming established in a career, job skills can continue to expand and upward mobility increases. Financial obligations often increase to fund the college education of children. Successful individuals generally build financial capital and retirement savings over time.

Peak accumulation. Financial capital accumulation is typically greatest in the decade before retirement as human capital is converted into financial capital. Earnings and the need to accumulate funds for retirement (including pension benefits) are high. The private client also reduces liabilities, such as mortgage debt.

Preretirement. Emphasis continues to be on accumulating financial capital for retirement and reducing liabilities.

Early retirement. Private clients depend on cash flows from pension income (and part-time employment income in some cases) and their investment portfolio to fund their retirement lifestyle.

Late retirement. Expenses on leisure activities generally decrease, but uninsured health care expenses could increase, putting more pressure on financial resources.

One of the key challenges for a private wealth manager in the retirement stages of a client's life is *determining a rate at which distributions can be made* from the client's investment portfolio that can be maintained for the remaining lifetime of the client. This needs to be an ongoing process during the client's retirement in order to ensure that the investment portfolio can fully meet the client's financial goals in retirement.

Analysis of Retirement Goals

A private client's retirement goals can be analyzed using mortality tables, annuities, and Monte Carlo simulation.

Mortality tables. A mortality table shows *life expectancy for an individual at different ages* and enables a private wealth manager to determine the probability that a client will survive to a given age.

PROFESSOR'S NOTE

The probabilities of survival change every year. They are based on the individual's current age and show the probability for the *average individual* who has attained that age.

Figure 19.3 shows a sample mortality table for a client currently aged 72 with a life expectancy of 12 years. The table shows that the client has a 44% probability of living to 85 years and a 21% probability of reaching 90 years. These probabilities can be used to weight the expected annual cash flows of a client in retirement to estimate the present value of the client's retirement spending needs. It should be noted that, since mortality tables provide survival probabilities for an average individual, they might understate the actual probability of a given private client reaching a specified age, meaning that the client is faced with *longevity risk* (i.e., the risk of outliving one's financial resources).

Figure 19.3: Sample Mortality Table

Client Age	Life Expectancy	Survival Probability
72	12.0	100%
73	11.4	97%
74	10.8	93%
75	10.2	90%
76	9.7	86%
77	9.1	82%
78	8.6	77%
79	8.1	73%
80	7.6	68%
81	7.2	64%
82	6.7	59%
83	6.3	54%
84	5.8	49%
85	5.5	44%
86	5.1	39%
87	4.7	34%
88	4.4	29%
89	4.1	25%
90	3.8	21%

Reproduced from Level III CFA Curriculum Reading "Overview of Private Wealth Management," Example 6, with permission from CFA Institute.

For the Exam: While no explicit calculations using mortality tables are required in this reading, they are used to calculate *core capital* in the retirement stage of life in a later reading.

Annuities. The present value of the client's retirement spending needs can be determined by pricing an annuity. The buyer of an annuity makes an upfront payment in exchange for receiving a series of specified payments over time. An *immediate annuity* guarantees specified monthly payments for a predetermined period, with payments beginning immediately. Other types of annuities include a *deferred annuity*, where monthly payments begin at a specified time in the future, while a *life annuity* makes monthly payments for as long as the annuity holder is alive. If a private client's retirement spending needs are expected to be relatively stable over the client's life expectancy (from mortality tables), *a life annuity can be used to reduce longevity risk* and the price of a life annuity can be used as an estimate of the amount of financial resources required to fund the client's retirement goals.

Monte Carlo simulation. Monte Carlo simulation can be used to determine the probability that a private client's investment portfolio will meet the client's financial goals in retirement. The simulation can be *tailored to the client's actual portfolio asset allocation* and *used to explore different retirement scenarios*. This flexibility is important to private wealth managers because a client's retirement spending needs are usually *more complex than fixed monthly cash flows* (e.g., the client may wish to make a charitable donation before or at death).

As previously discussed, the output of a Monte Carlo simulation will only be as good as its input assumptions. Furthermore, *while the simulation provides the probability of success, it does not usually consider the amount by which the investment portfolio falls short of the client's retirement goals*. This *shortfall magnitude* is an important consideration for retirement planning, as the client will need to resolve this shortfall (e.g., reevaluate spending needs or other financial goals in retirement).

Behavioral Considerations When Advising Retirees

Private wealth managers need to consider the following behavioral biases associated with retirees:

- **Increased loss aversion.** Compared to younger investors, retirees are likely to be more loss-averse, affecting their return assumptions and asset allocation decisions in retirement.
- **Consumption gaps.** Consumption spending by retirees tends to be *lower* than what economic studies forecast. This can be attributed to *loss aversion* and *uncertainty about future retirement spending*.
- **The annuity puzzle.** As discussed previously, life annuities can be used to reduce longevity risk. However, individuals tend to avoid buying annuities to meet their spending needs in retirement. Possible explanations for this annuity puzzle include (1) clinging on to the hope of funding a better retirement lifestyle, (2) a desire to keep control of assets, and (3) the high cost of annuities.
- **Lack of self-control.** Retirees prefer to *meet their spending needs from investment income rather than by liquidating securities*. This preference for investment income over capital appreciation can be attributed to a lack of self-control when it comes to spending.

MODULE QUIZ 19.5

1. When analyzing a client's retirement goals, a private wealth manager considers the probability that the client will live to a certain age and then predicts the client's retirement spending requirements using the probability that the client will still be living in a given year. When combined with the client's expected annual cash flows in retirement, this approach enables the wealth manager to estimate the present value of the client's retirement spending requirements. The approach that the wealth manager is *most likely* using is:
   A. the annuity method.
   B. Monte Carlo simulation.
   C. mortality tables.
2. The behavioral bias exhibited by retirees who prefer to meet their spending needs from investment income rather than by liquidating securities in their investment portfolio is *most likely* related to:
   A. consumption gaps.
   B. self-control bias.
   C. heightened loss aversion.

Video covering this content is available online.

MODULE 19.6: THE INVESTMENT POLICY STATEMENT

LOS 19.i: Discuss the parts of an investment policy statement (IPS) for a private client.

LOS 19.j: Prepare the investment objectives section of an IPS for a private client.

LOS 19.k: Evaluate and recommend improvements to an IPS for a private client.

The IPS documents a private client's investment objectives, risk tolerance, investment time horizon, liquidity preferences, and any other preferences or constraints. The private wealth manager uses this information to construct the client's investment portfolio given the prevailing capital market conditions.

An IPS for a private client usually covers the following areas:

- Client background and investment objectives.
- Key investment parameters.
- Portfolio asset allocation.
- Portfolio management and implementation.
- Duties and responsibilities of the private wealth manager.

Client Background and Investment Objectives

A private client's background details are obtained from *personal*, *financial*, and *tax* information that the wealth manager has gathered on the client (discussed earlier in the reading). As part of the client's background, the private wealth manager should determine all the components of a client's investment portfolio as well as any other financial assets that the client may be holding outside the portfolio (e.g., with a different wealth manager) and cash flows from external sources (e.g., defined benefit pension).

We have already seen that clients may have *planned* and *unplanned* financial goals and objectives, which may be *ongoing* or *one-off* in nature. The private wealth manager should work with a client to *quantify* investment objectives wherever possible and reconcile *competing* objectives should they arise. Where a client has *multiple* objectives, the wealth manager can help the client *prioritize* these objectives into *primary* and *secondary* objectives.

As already discussed, a wealth manager can use *capital sufficiency* (or capital needs) *analysis* to determine the likelihood of their clients being able to meet their financial objectives and, where necessary, help clients revise these objectives to make them more realistic.

For the Exam: Past exam questions have required candidates to specify risk and return objectives when preparing an IPS. In this reading, you are required to prepare investment objectives separately from risk tolerance, which is considered under investment parameters.

EXAMPLE: Preparing client investment objectives

William Elam recently inherited $750,000 in cash from his father's estate and has come to Alan Schneider, CFA, for investment advice. Both William and his wife, Elizabeth, are 30 years old. William is employed as a factory worker and has an annual salary of $50,000. Although he receives total health care coverage for himself and his family, he makes no contributions to his firm's defined benefit pension plan and is not yet vested in any of the company's other retirement benefits. Elizabeth is an early childhood teacher with a salary of $38,000. She has only very recently opened a tax-deferred 403(b) retirement savings account. They have three children, aged eight, five, and three. They have a small savings account, no investments other than Elizabeth's retirement account, and credit card debt of $20,000.

When interviewed, William makes the following statements:

- "With a family of five, our combined salaries just meet our living expenses. It would be safe to assume that both our salaries and expenses will grow only at the rate of inflation."
- "We do not want to use our new wealth to improve our current lifestyle. Instead, we would like to grow the investment portfolio so that we can send our children to college and fund our retirement lifestyle when we stop working in 30 years."
- "We also want to set up a trust fund in the future for our children."

What are the key issues that Schneider should consider when preparing the investment objectives section of William's IPS?

Reading 19

Answer:

The purpose of William's investment portfolio is to pay for his children's college education, fund the retirement of him and Elizabeth, and set up a trust fund for his children. William has stated they do not want to use his inheritance to improve their current lifestyle. Since William and Elizabeth earn an income that covers their living expenses on an inflation-adjusted basis, distributions from the investment portfolio will begin when their children commence their college education in approximately 10 years (apart from paying off their credit card immediately). After paying for their children's college education, the couple will require distributions from the investment portfolio to set up the trust fund for their children and to fund their retirement.

Schneider should help the Elams *quantify* and *prioritize* their multiple investment objectives. He could use capital sufficiency analysis to determine the likelihood of these competing objectives being met given the size of the investment portfolio. He should also help them reevaluate and revise their current objectives if these objectives are not supported by capital sufficiency analysis.

Key Investment Parameters

A client's risk tolerance, time horizon, investment preferences, and constraints are covered in this section.

Risk tolerance. As discussed previously, risk tolerance considers a client's willingness *and* ability to accept investment risk. Generally, a client has a *low risk tolerance for more important goals* but higher risk tolerance for lower priority goals. An additional consideration is the proximity of the client's goals, with *near-term goals associated with lower risk tolerance* compared to longer-term goals. The process of evaluating a client's risk tolerance (e.g., questionnaires and/or conversations) is also covered in this section.

Time horizon. The investment horizon is often described as a *range* (e.g., in excess of 15 years for a long investment horizon or less than 10 years for a short horizon) rather than a specific length of time. Clients with multiple objectives can also have a different time horizon for each objective.

EXAMPLE: Time horizon

How should Schneider describe William's time horizon in the previous example?

Answer:

William has multiple objectives with different time horizons. The time horizon related to funding his children's college education exceeds 10 years. Assuming a trust fund is set up for his children after their college education, this time horizon is likely to exceed 20 years. Finally, the time horizon associated with retirement funding exceeds 30 years.

Asset class preferences. This section should list the *acceptable* asset classes for the client's portfolio (or alternatively asset classes that are unsuitable for the client), together with the risk-return characteristics of each asset class.

Liquidity preferences. Liquidity needs that have not been specified in the *Client Background and Objectives* section should be included here (e.g., the need for a cash reserve). A private wealth manager should also include liquidity preferences that may restrict investment in certain asset classes (e.g., a client's preference for dividend income may preclude investment in the stock of small, growth companies).

Other investment preferences. Some unique preferences include a concentrated position in a single stock (due to past employment or inheritance) and ethical investing.

Constraints. These client constraints restrict a private wealth manager's choice of investments or strategies for the client's portfolio (e.g., a client's preference for ethical investing).

> **For the Exam:** Past exam questions have required candidates to analyze a private client's time horizon, liquidity needs, taxes, legal and regulatory considerations, and unique preferences as investment constraints. *In this reading, risk tolerance, time horizon, liquidity preferences, other investment preferences, and constraints are analyzed as investment parameters, while taxes are included as part of the client's financial background information.*
>
> For the most part, you are provided with all the relevant information for a client's investment parameters in the story. A typical question might require you to address all the previously mentioned investment parameters in 10–12 minutes. You should give a brief factual answer for each parameter, supported by relevant facts from the story. If there are no issues to address for a particular parameter, say so in the answer rather than leaving it blank.
>
> Alternatively, a question may only ask you to address specific investment parameters and assign more minutes for each parameter. In this case, only address what is requested and provide more detail in your answer.

Portfolio Asset Allocation

This section describes the asset allocation approach that the private wealth manager will use for the client's investment portfolio. *Strategic* asset allocation indicates a long-term target allocation for each asset class, with the portfolio being rebalanced periodically to maintain the target allocation. *Tactical* asset allocation is an active management strategy that normally specifies a range for each asset class rather than a specific target allocation percentage.

Portfolio Management and Implementation

In order to effectively manage a client's investment portfolio on an ongoing basis, the private wealth manager needs clear guidance on the following issues:

Discretionary authority. This specifies the ability of the private wealth manager to take investment actions without first seeking the client's approval. Some clients give their wealth managers *full* discretion, whereas others prefer to *limit* discretionary authority to prespecified actions (such as rebalancing the portfolio in line with the agreed range for each asset class). A wealth manager providing a *nondiscretionary* service can make investment recommendations but is unable to act on the recommendation without client approval.

Rebalancing. The approach to rebalancing a client's investment portfolio should be clearly specified in the IPS. A *time-based* rebalancing (e.g., quarterly, semiannual, or annual rebalancing) does not consider deviations between actual and target asset class percentages, whereas a *threshold-based* rebalancing approach means that the portfolio is rebalanced once actual asset class weights deviate from target weights by a prespecified amount.

Tactical changes. The IPS should clearly state if a private wealth manager is given discretionary authority to undertake tactical asset allocation changes. The IPS should clearly state the acceptable range of weights for each asset class as well as the extent to which the manager is allowed to go beyond the upper or lower bounds when making tactical changes.

Implementation. This section covers information about acceptable investment vehicles (e.g., the use of in-house and/or external money managers, ETFs, mutual funds) and the due diligence process for making investment decisions.

Duties and Responsibilities of the Private Wealth Manager

The general responsibilities of a private wealth manager in helping a client meet their investment objectives are detailed in this section. These responsibilities include:

- Formulating and reviewing the IPS, including frequency of review.
- Recommending or selecting investment options and constructing the investment portfolio's asset allocation.
- Monitoring and rebalancing the portfolio.
- Monitoring portfolio implementation costs.
- Monitoring the third-party service providers.
- Reporting portfolio performance.
- Reporting taxes and financial statements.
- Voting proxies.

IPS Appendix

This section includes details of items that typically change more frequently than other sections of the IPS, such as the following:

- *Modeled portfolio performance.* This typically describes a range of possible portfolio outcomes over different investment horizons as well as a distribution of returns at specific percentiles.
- *Capital market expectations.* This covers the expected return, risk, and correlations of the asset classes that the private wealth manager can include in a client's portfolio.

The following example illustrates how you could be tested on an IPS for a private client. The nature of constructed response questions gives you some latitude in developing an acceptable answer and, in some cases, there may be more than one acceptable answer. You will be graded on whether you answer the questions in a way that is consistent with what is taught in the curriculum.

EXAMPLE: Evaluating an IPS for a private client

Bonnie DuBois, a 65-year-old U.S. citizen, has been retired for 5 years. Over that period, she has helped to support her son, Barry, and his family. DuBois's son and his wife, Betty, have both received significant promotions, so they no longer require her support.

DuBois is meeting with her financial advisor, Begren Knutsen, CFA, to determine if and how her IPS should be altered. She does not intend to change her modest lifestyle, and since she no longer needs to provide financial support to her son and his family, DuBois will instead plan bequests. She also specifies that the portion of the portfolio allocated to equities should use only domestic equities.

When Knutsen reviewed DuBois's IPS a year ago, she did not recommend any changes to the IPS or investment strategy. The value of DuBois's portfolio remains unchanged at $2 million. DuBois and Knutsen estimate her investment horizon will exceed 15 years. DuBois's highest priority is to be able to withdraw $75,000 per year on an inflation-adjusted basis to cover her living expenses. As unexpected expenses are likely to increase, she states the portfolio's cash reserve should be raised to $25,000. She also plans to leave a bequest of $1.2 million each to her son and to a local museum ($2.4 million in total) at her death.

Knutsen and DuBois have agreed to review her objectives, investment parameters, and asset allocation considerations at this meeting so that Knutsen can model DuBois's portfolio behavior with updated capital market assumptions. The sections of DuBois's current IPS that will be discussed at the meeting are shown in Figure 19.4. DuBois does not require any changes to be made to the *Portfolio Management, Responsibilities, and Review* sections of her IPS.

Discuss the changes that Knutsen should make to DuBois's original IPS to incorporate her *new retirement objectives* and *investment preferences*. You are *not* required to provide any specific asset class weights for the portfolio asset allocation as part of your answer.

Figure 19.4: Excerpts From Bonnie DuBois's Original Investment Policy Statement

Background and Investment Objectives

This investment policy statement (IPS) has been created for Bonnie DuBois for the purpose of meeting her financial objectives. It outlines her objectives and investment parameters, recommends an investment strategy for achieving these objectives, and details ongoing duties and responsibilities.

Reading 19

The objectives of this portfolio are to support the retirement lifestyle of DuBois, support her son and his family for one year, and gift her estate to a local museum at her death. The financial support for her son and his family is her primary objective, followed by the maintenance of her current lifestyle and her charitable donation at death. In order to achieve these objectives, DuBois anticipates needing her portfolio to distribute $90,000 per year on an inflation-adjusted basis. DuBois has not specified a specific monetary amount that she intends to gift to a local museum at death. The wealth manager will work with DuBois on an ongoing basis to quantify this objective.

DuBois's current portfolio of $2 million is held in a taxable account and a tax-deferred account. Expected cash distributions have been given due consideration when constructing her portfolio asset allocation. As her investment horizon is relatively long-term, she is seeking to achieve a higher rate of return commensurate with her risk tolerance.

Investment Parameters

Risk tolerance. DuBois is able and willing to accept volatility in the short and medium term. She acknowledges that this risk tolerance has been reflected in her current asset allocation.

Investment horizon. DuBois has an investment horizon that exceeds 15 years.

Asset class preferences. DuBois and her wealth manager have determined that the following asset classes are appropriate for her portfolio:

- Cash and money market instruments.
- Domestic government bonds.
- Domestic corporate bonds.
- Global government bonds.
- Domestic equities.
- Global equities.
- Domestic real estate securities.
- Commodities.

Other investment preferences. DuBois wishes to maintain her position in Chic Apparel, Inc., where she spent most of her 35-year career in the fashion industry before retiring. This position does not represent a significant concentration risk in her portfolio and stocks of Chic Apparel are actively traded on the domestic stock exchange.

Liquidity preferences. DuBois wishes to maintain a $10,000 cash reserve within her portfolio.

Constraints. DuBois's position in Chic Apparel has significant embedded capital gains.

Portfolio Asset Allocation (Strategic Allocation With Rebalancing Limits Provided in Brackets)

Cash and money market instruments	5% (4%–6%)
Domestic government bonds	10% (8%–12%)
Domestic corporate bonds	10% (8%–12%)
Global government bonds	10% (8%–12%)
Domestic equities	40% (35%–45%)
Global equities	10% (8%–12%)
Domestic real estate securities	10% (8%–12%)
Commodities	5% (4%–6%)

Answer:

DuBois's IPS needs to be modified to reflect her new investment objectives and parameters. These changes are detailed later.

Background and Investment Objectives

Since DuBois no longer needs to support her son and his family, her primary objective is now her retirement lifestyle. She also plans to leave a bequest of $1.2 million each to her son and to a local museum.

The second paragraph of the *Background and Investment Objectives* section of her current IPS should be modified as follows:

> The objectives of this portfolio are to support the retirement lifestyle of DuBois and to leave a bequest of $1.2 million each to her son and a local museum ($2.4 million in total) at her death. The financial maintenance of her retirement lifestyle is her primary objective, followed by the bequests to her son and a local museum at death. DuBois anticipates needing her portfolio to distribute $75,000 per year on an inflation-adjusted basis to cover her living expenses. The wealth manager will work with DuBois to ensure that her portfolio distribution rate is sustainable throughout retirement and reevaluate her other financial objectives if these are not supported by capital sufficiency analysis.

Investment Parameters

Risk tolerance. No changes required.

Investment horizon. No changes required, as it is still reasonable to expect her investment horizon to exceed 15 years.

Asset class preferences. DuBois states that her portfolio allocation to equities should only consist of domestic equities. Her wealth manager should advise her on the potential return and diversification implications of her decision. Mean-variance optimization of DuBois's portfolio should incorporate the constraint on investment in foreign equities.

Reading 19

The wording for asset class preferences should be modified as follows:

> DuBois and her wealth manager have determined that the following asset classes are appropriate for her portfolio:
>
> – Cash and money market instruments.
> – Domestic government bonds.
> – Domestic corporate bonds.
> – Global government bonds.
> – Domestic equities.
> – Domestic real estate securities.
> – Commodities.

Other investment preferences. No changes required.

Liquidity preferences. DuBois wishes to increase the cash reserve from $10,000 to $25,000. This change should be clearly stated as follows:

> DuBois wishes to maintain a $25,000 cash reserve within her portfolio.

Constraints. This section should be modified as follows to incorporate the constraint on investment in foreign equities:

> DuBois's portfolio allocation to equities should consist only of domestic equities. DuBois's position in Chic Apparel has significant embedded capital gains.

MODULE QUIZ 19.6

1. A private wealth manager has gathered the following information from a new client:

Risk tolerance:	Low
Liquidity needs:	$2 million for purchase of holiday apartment in 2 years
Asset class preferences:	No investment in commodities and hedge funds

   What information is *most likely* to be included in the *Investment Objectives* section of the client's IPS?
   A. Low risk tolerance.
   B. $2 million purchase of holiday apartment in 2 years.
   C. Investments in commodities and hedge funds have not been approved by client.

2. Which of the following investment considerations is *most likely* to be included as a constraint in a client's IPS?
   A. ESG investing.
   B. Time horizon.
   C. Liquidity preferences.

3. Which of the following items is *most likely* to be included in the *Portfolio Management* section of a client's IPS?
   A. Capital market expectations.
   B. Modeled portfolio behavior.
   C. Portfolio rebalancing methodology.
4. The requirement for a client's investment portfolio to hold a cash reserve and/or constraint on asset class selection because of the need to sell the portfolio relatively quickly is *most likely* to be included in:
   A. the *Liquidity Preferences* section of the client's IPS.
   B. the *Other Investment Preferences* section of the client's IPS.
   C. the *Portfolio Asset Allocation* section of the client's IPS.
5. Vivian Collins is a client of ESP Financial Advisors. She is 45 years old and expects to retire in 20 years. Her financial advisor has determined that Collins has the following financial goals:

Retirement:	Collins views retirement as a long-term goal and is prepared to accept a 10%–15% drop in expected retirement spending. However, she is concerned that she might face unexpected health-related expenses in retirement.
College fees:	Collins wants to be able to pay for her daughter's college education in the next 3–6 years. Currently, this is her highest priority goal.
Gifting:	Collins would like to leave a gift to her grandchildren at her death.

   Which of the following descriptions of Collins's investment time horizon is her financial advisor *most likely* to include in her IPS?
   A. Collins has a long horizon of 35 years, as she would expect to survive until 80 years old.
   B. Collins has multiple time horizons: the college fees goal has a time horizon of 3 years, the retirement goal has a time horizon of 20 years, and the gifting goal has a time horizon of 35 years.
   C. Collins has multiple time horizons: the college fees goal has a time horizon exceeding 3 years, the retirement goal has a time horizon exceeding 20 years, and the gifting goal has a time horizon exceeding 35 years.

Reading 19

MODULE 19.7: PORTFOLIO CONSTRUCTION

Video covering this content is available online.

LOS 19.1: Recommend and justify portfolio allocations and investments for a private client.

After developing a private client's IPS, a wealth manager constructs the client's investment portfolio to implement the client's investment strategy. A traditional approach and a goals-based investing approach to portfolio construction are discussed next.

Traditional Approach to Portfolio Construction

The traditional approach to constructing a private client's portfolio views risk in an *overall portfolio* context and consists of the following steps:

- Identify appropriate asset classes for the client's portfolio.
- Develop capital market expectations (i.e., expected returns, standard deviations, and correlations of asset classes).
- Determine asset class weights for the portfolio, consistent with the client's risk tolerance for the *overall* portfolio.

> **For the Exam:** Asset allocation approaches, such as mean-variance optimization (MVO) and Monte Carlo simulation, are covered in an earlier reading. A private wealth manager can use these approaches to establish an *optimal* portfolio that maximizes expected return for a specified level of risk consistent with a client's risk tolerance. As the optimal portfolio may include asset class allocations that are impractical to implement, the wealth manager may need to specify *asset class constraints* in the optimization process. The wealth manager *may also need to modify the optimal asset class weights to incorporate client preferences* (while remaining within acceptable risk limits) in the recommended portfolio allocation.

- Assess investment constraints (e.g., a client's preference for ethical investing) that may limit the wealth manager's choice of investments.
- Implement the portfolio.

> **For the Exam:** Key considerations when implementing the portfolio include:
>
> - Use of active or passive management (or a combination) for each asset class.
> - Degree of focus on specific sectors of each asset class (e.g., style factors for equity and credit quality for fixed income).
> - Manager selection.
> - Use of individual securities or pooled investment vehicles.
> - Degree of hedging required (e.g., for currency exposure).
> - Choosing asset location (e.g., placing investments that generate significant levels of taxable income into accounts that offer tax exemption).

> **EXAMPLE: Traditional approach to portfolio construction**
>
> Max Davidson is a 45-year-old heart surgeon who plans to retire in 15 years. Davidson is generally conservative with his investments and does not like portfolio volatility. His private wealth manager, Janine Becker, CFA, has determined that a portfolio standard deviation of 8% would be acceptable to Davidson. Davidson has stated a preference for bonds and large-cap equities in his investment portfolio.

Becker decides to use MVO to determine the optimal asset allocation for Davidson's portfolio based on the capital market expectations that she has developed. She specifies a minimum weight of 5% for real estate in the optimization because of its potential diversification benefits. She then modifies the optimal portfolio allocation to take into account Davidson's preferences. The optimal and recommended asset allocations for Davidson's portfolio are shown in Figure 19.5.

Figure 19.5: Asset Allocation for the Davidson Portfolio (Traditional Approach)

Asset Class	Allocation From MVO	Recommended Allocation
U.S. government bonds	32.5%	32.5%
Other investment-grade bonds	22.5%	25.0%
Large-cap equities	20.2%	25.0%
Other equities	14.8%	12.5%
Real estate	10.0%	5.0%
Total	**100.0%**	**100.0%**
Expected return	6.0%	5.9%
Volatility (in terms of standard deviation)	8.0%	8.0%

Goals-Based Investing

Goals-based investing essentially follows the same steps as the traditional approach to portfolio construction, the critical difference being that instead of constructing a single portfolio, the private wealth manager creates *separate portfolios for each of the client's goals*. Mean-variance optimization, which can be structured to maximize expected returns for a given level of risk or to meet a specified probability of success, is carried out for each goal portfolio rather than for the entire portfolio.

With goals-based investing, clients may find it *easier to specify their risk tolerance*, as this is expressed for each goal portfolio rather than for the client's entire portfolio. A key *disadvantage* of this approach is that the client's entire portfolio may not be mean-variance efficient. This is because the overall allocation of the entire portfolio will depend on the aggregated asset class allocations of the goal portfolios and is unlikely to be as well diversified as the optimal portfolio obtained using the traditional approach.

EXAMPLE: Goals-based investing

Suppose that, in addition to the information from the previous example, Davidson tells Becker that he has two important goals:

- Funding his daughter's college education in 5 years.
- Purchasing an annuity in 15 years to supplement the pension income that he will receive when he retires.

Davidson's current portfolio is valued at $4 million. He estimates that he will need $400,000 to fund his daughter's college education and wants low volatility for this goal. He is prepared to accept higher volatility for his other goal.

Becker uses a goals-based investing approach to construct two goal portfolios for Davidson, as shown in Figure 19.6. In this example, using a goals-based approach has the advantage of enabling Davidson to express his risk tolerance for the college education goal directly.

Figure 19.6: Asset Allocation for the Davidson Portfolio (Goals-Based Investing)

Asset Class	Allocation for College Education Portfolio	Allocation for Annuity Portfolio	Overall Portfolio Allocation
U.S. government bonds	46.0%	31.0%	32.5%
Other investment-grade bonds	34.0%	24.0%	25.0%
Large-cap equities	11.5%	26.5%	25.0%
Other equities	3.5%	13.5%	12.5%
Real estate	5.0%	5.0%	5.0%
Total	**100.0%**	**100.0%**	**100.0%**
Expected return	4.5%	6.0%	5.9%
Volatility (in terms of standard deviation)	4.7%	8.5%	8.0%

MODULE QUIZ 19.7

1. Rayyan Patel, CFA, has performed MVO to determine the optimal asset allocation for a client's portfolio, having determined that the maximum portfolio volatility that the client can tolerate is 9%. The MVO portfolio allocation together with three alternative portfolio allocations that Patel is considering are shown in the following table.

Asset Class	Allocation from MVO	Alternative 1 Allocation	Alternative 2 Allocation	Alternative 3 Allocation
Investment-grade bonds	30.5%	35.0%	32.0%	30.0%
High-yield bonds	15.0%	12.0%	10.0%	15.0%
U.S. equities	38.2%	38.0%	30.0%	20.0%
Other (non-U.S.) equities	12.8%	10.0%	20.0%	25.0%
Commodities	3.5%	5.0%	8.0%	10.0%
Total	**100.0%**	**100.0%**	**100.0%**	**100.0%**
Expected return	6.5%	6.1%	6.4%	6.6%
Volatility (in terms of standard deviation)	9.0%	8.7%	8.9%	9.2%

If Patel wants to adjust the portfolio allocation to incorporate his client's preference for non-U.S. equities and alternative investments, which of the following portfolio allocations is he *most likely* to recommend to his client?

A. Alternative 1.
B. Alternative 2.
C. Alternative 3.

MODULE 19.8: PORTFOLIO REPORTING AND REVIEW, AND EVALUATING AN INVESTMENT PROGRAM

Video covering this content is available online.

LOS 19.m: Describe effective practices in portfolio reporting and review.

Portfolio reporting enables private clients to understand how their investment portfolio is performing and whether their financial goals are likely to be achieved. It provides a basis for a private wealth manager to review a client's IPS and investment strategy with the client to determine if changes are required to achieve the client's goals.

Portfolio Reporting

A portfolio report for a private client typically includes the following items:

- Performance summary for the current period.
- Market commentary for the current period to provide context for the portfolio's performance.
- Portfolio asset allocation at the end of the current period, including strategic asset allocation weights or tactical asset class target ranges.
- Detailed performance of asset classes and individual securities.
- Benchmark report comparing asset class and overall portfolio performance to appropriate benchmarks.
- Historical performance of client's investment portfolio since inception.
- Transaction details for the current period (e.g., contributions, withdrawals, interest, dividends, and capital appreciation).
- Purchase and sale report for the current period.
- Impact of currency exposure and exchange-rate fluctuations.
- Progress toward meeting goal portfolios when using a goals-based investing approach.

> **For the Exam:** Be prepared to identify three or four items from the preceding list that could be added to a client's portfolio report to improve the client's understanding of portfolio performance.

Note that the *horizon mismatch* between quarterly (or annual) portfolio reports and the significantly longer investment horizon of a client can potentially distort a client's perception of the portfolio's long-term effectiveness. The portfolio reporting and review process enables the private wealth manager to provide context to investment performance for the current period and to manage a client's expectations appropriately.

Portfolio Review

A portfolio review enables the private wealth manager to reassess a client's IPS and investment strategy in light of recent performance to determine if changes are required. A portfolio review typically addresses the following areas:

- Appropriateness of client's existing goals and investment parameters and if any changes are required.
- Rebalancing of portfolio asset allocation to target allocation or ranges.
- Any changes to the wealth manager's ongoing management of the portfolio (e.g., degree of discretionary authority).
- Any changes or updates in the wealth manager's duties and responsibilities.
- Any changes to IPS and portfolio review frequency.

LOS 19.n: Evaluate the success of an investment program for a private client.

The degree to which a private client's investment program is considered a success is measured in terms of three criteria: goal achievement, process consistency, and portfolio performance.

Goal Achievement

An investment program is considered a success if it *fulfills a client's goals within the specified risk parameter*. Due to the ongoing nature of the investment program, the criteria for success should be whether it is *still likely to meet the client's longer-term goals* (e.g., using capital sufficiency analysis) *without a significant change in the original strategy*. For example, an investment program that now requires a client to contribute a much larger amount per year (compared to the original investment plan) toward a goal of achieving a lump sum target at retirement is unlikely to be considered a success.

Process Consistency

The success of an investment program depends on the consistency of processes that the manager uses. The following issues are typically considered in evaluating process consistency:

- Has the wealth manager implemented an investment strategy that is consistent with the client's goals and investment preferences?
- Is the wealth manager maintaining regular communications with the client to assess the need for changes to the IPS?
- How have recommended third-party investment managers performed relative to their benchmarks?
- What is the impact of recommended fund manager switches on portfolio performance?
- How has the use of tactical asset allocation affected portfolio performance (if applicable)?
- Has the rebalancing process followed IPS guidelines?
- What tax-efficient strategies have been employed for the portfolio?
- How has the wealth manager tried to reduce portfolio costs and expenses?

Portfolio Performance

Portfolio performance can be measured against an *absolute* performance benchmark (e.g., 5% fixed return) or *relative* to a passive benchmark (e.g., return on a domestic stock index). The impact of investment risk can be evaluated by comparing the *risk-adjusted return* (e.g., Sharpe ratio) of the client's portfolio and an appropriate benchmark and by comparing the portfolio's *downside risk* with the client's risk tolerance. Private wealth managers need to recognize that clients generally prefer to evaluate portfolio performance against benchmarks that they are familiar with (such as domestic equity indexes) and take this preference into consideration in the portfolio construction, reporting, and review process.

Reading 19

Definition of success. Private wealth managers and their clients should ideally agree on the measures of success at the inception of the investment program (e.g., whether to measure portfolio performance in absolute or relative terms) to avoid misunderstandings further down the line.

For the Exam: Questions are likely to ask you to evaluate a client's investment program against the three criteria previously discussed. An investment program can be said to be successful only if it achieves success on *all* three criteria.

EXAMPLE: Evaluating an investment program

Jamie George, CFA, has worked as a private wealth manager for Susan Montana for the last 15 years. Montana's goals have not changed over time, and she expects to retire in five years. The primary goals for her investment portfolio are to support her retirement lifestyle and to make an annual donation to her favorite charity in retirement.

Montana's portfolio has outperformed its benchmark by 0.2% over this period, while portfolio volatility has been slightly lower than the benchmark. The portfolio's return has also exceeded the rate of return that George used in the capital sufficiency analysis of Montana's portfolio 15 years ago. The output of his most recent capital sufficiency analysis indicates that the current portfolio and investment strategy are very likely to meet Montana's future goals.

After reviewing her IPS, Montana concludes that George has followed the process stated in the IPS. George has maintained an ongoing dialog with Montana, followed rebalancing guidelines, and reduced trading costs over time.

Evaluate the success of Montana's investment program under George's management.

Answer:

Montana's investment program has been successful when assessed against the following criteria:

- *Goal achievement*—Montana's portfolio return has exceeded the rate of return that George used in the original capital sufficiency analysis, and the output of his most recent capital sufficiency analysis indicates that the investment strategy is very likely to meet her future goals without the need for any meaningful changes.
- *Process consistency*—George has followed a consistent process in managing Montana's portfolio. This includes maintaining an ongoing dialog with Montana, following rebalancing guidelines, and reducing trading costs over time.
- *Portfolio performance*—Montana's portfolio has outperformed its benchmark over the last 15 years, with lower volatility compared to the benchmark.

MODULE QUIZ 19.8

1. Zach Bond, CFA, provides quarterly portfolio reports to his clients. Each portfolio report contains the following information:
   - Performance summary for the current quarter.
   - Portfolio asset allocation at the end of the quarter, including strategic asset allocation weights or tactical asset class target ranges.
   - Detailed performance of asset classes and individual securities.
   - Benchmark report comparing asset class and overall portfolio performance to appropriate benchmarks.

   List *four* additional items that Bond could provide to improve the quality of the portfolio reports that he prepares for his clients.

2. Christine Tan is preparing to meet Zach Bond, CFA, who has acted as her wealth manager for the last 20 years. Over this period, her portfolio has earned a 6% compound annual return, matching the annual return modeled by Bond in his capital sufficiency analysis of Tan's portfolio 20 years ago. The output of his most recent capital sufficiency analysis indicates that the current portfolio and investment strategy are very likely to meet Tan's future financial objectives. Tan's portfolio return has underperformed its benchmark by 0.3% over this period, while matching the benchmark's volatility. Tan notes that Bond has followed the guidelines laid out in her IPS in relation to ongoing communications, rebalancing methodology, tax strategies, and implementation costs.

   Tan is *most likely* to conclude that her investment program has:

   A. failed because it has not met all three criteria of a successful investment program.
   B. been a success because it has met two out of the three criteria of a successful investment program.
   C. been a success because it has met all three criteria of a successful investment program.

Reading 19

Video covering this content is available online.

MODULE 19.9: ETHICAL AND COMPLIANCE CONSIDERATIONS, AND PRIVATE CLIENT SEGMENTS

LOS 19.o: Discuss ethical and compliance considerations in advising private clients.

Private wealth managers need to fulfill many ethical and compliance requirements when advising their clients and managing their investment portfolios. These requirements are briefly discussed in the following sections.

Ethical Considerations

A private wealth manager should use the CFA Institute Code of Ethics and Standards of Professional Conduct as a basis for managing and resolving ethical issues and conflicts. Some of the more relevant ethical considerations are listed here:

Fiduciary duty and suitability. Assessing the suitability of potential investments for a private client is an important component of a wealth manager's fiduciary duty. Fiduciary duty and suitability considerations are covered in the following Standards of Professional Conduct:

- Standard I(B) *Independence and Objectivity*.
- Standard III(A) *Loyalty, Prudence, and Care*.
- Standard III(C) *Suitability*.
- Standard V(A) *Diligence and Reasonable Basis*.

Know your customer. The know your customer (KYC) rule requires private wealth managers to obtain relevant personal and financial information about their clients for portfolio management purposes as well as for regulatory compliance (e.g., money laundering investigations). KYC requirements are covered in Standard III(C) *Suitability*.

Confidentiality. Client confidentiality is a key tenet of a wealth manager–client relationship and can be a challenge when a private wealth manager's clients are known to each other (e.g., business associates). Standard III(E) *Preservation of Confidentiality* deals with the main considerations in client confidentiality.

Conflicts of interest. Private wealth managers may face potential conflicts of interest if their fee- or commission-based compensation structure influences the provision of investment advice and recommendations to their clients. Relevant considerations are covered in Standard I(B) *Independence and Objectivity* and Standard VI(A) *Disclosure of Conflicts*.

EXAMPLE: Ethical considerations

Jacob Windfall, CFA, is a portfolio manager for Fastrack Advisors, Inc. Fastrack has recently introduced a bonus system that rewards portfolio managers if their client portfolios outperform the benchmark each quarter. In order to enhance the short-term performance of his client portfolios, Windfall is considering purchasing a significant amount of stock in smaller companies with high betas for these portfolios even though he has not recommended any changes in investment strategy for his client portfolios this year.

Are there potential ethical considerations for Windfall's investment actions?

Answer:

Windfall faces a potential conflict of interest if the stock purchases are inconsistent with the IPSs of his clients and, therefore, are unsuitable for their portfolios. He should analyze his intended course of action objectively and disclose this potential conflict of interest to his clients.

Compliance Considerations

Regulatory requirements for private wealth managers vary by jurisdictions. For example, the *Markets in Financial Instruments Directive (MiFID II)* requires investment advisors to demonstrate the suitability of investment advice and meet threshold competence levels.

For the Exam: You are not required to be a compliance expert, but be prepared to state that private wealth managers must fulfill regulatory requirements as part of their responsibilities to clients if an exam question asks you to identify compliance considerations.

LOS 19.p: Discuss how levels of service and range of solutions are related to different private clients.

Private wealth management firms tailor their levels of service and range of solutions to the different private client segments that they serve. Typical categories of private clients include the mass affluent, high net worth, and ultra-high net worth segments.

Mass Affluent Segment

The mass affluent segment requires a *wide range of wealth management services*, such as portfolio construction, risk management, and retirement planning. It is characterized by a *larger number of clients per wealth manager* and *greater use of technology* in delivering services such as account creation and portfolio reporting. Due to the larger client-to-wealth-manager ratio, wealth managers do not tend to tailor their portfolio management approach for each client. Compensation for wealth managers in this segment can be based on *commissions* from investment transactions for the client (brokerage model) or *fees* linked to assets under management.

High-Net-Worth (HNW) Segment

The HNW segment exhibits a *smaller number of clients per wealth manager* compared to the mass affluent segment. Wealth management services provided in this segment are more likely to concentrate on *tailored investment solutions*, *tax planning*, and *estate planning*. The portfolios of HNW clients are more likely to contain *sophisticated* strategies (e.g., derivatives-based) and *alternative investments*. Estate planning considerations may also result in *longer investment horizons* and *greater risk capacity*.

Ultra-High-Net-Worth (UHNW) Segment

This segment is likely to have *multigenerational investment horizons*, *complex tax and estate planning*, and a *more comprehensive range of service requirements*, including ancillary services (e.g., travel planning) and advice on luxury investments (e.g., art and automobiles). The UHNW segment has a relatively *low client-to-manager ratio* because of the need to provide a *highly customized service* to clients.

A UHNW wealth manager typically manages the portfolios of multigenerational family members, requiring consideration of *family governance and inheritance issues*. UHNW clients are more likely to be serviced by a *client relationship team* that includes legal, tax, and investment experts in addition to a relationship manager. Some UHNW individuals may also choose to employ a *family office* of financial experts to manage their assets.

Robo-Advisors

Robo-advisors are *automated* wealth management advisors that assist private clients with their portfolio management needs. Robo-advisors gather client information using *online questionnaires* and recommend an appropriate asset allocation for the client's portfolio using mean-variance optimization or alternative techniques. The client's portfolio is constructed using *exchange-traded funds* or *mutual funds* and monitored on an ongoing basis. Periodic rebalancing and online performance reporting are also provided to the client.

Because of the automated client interface, the *costs associated with using robo-advisors are lower* than the fees charged by traditional private wealth managers. The *scalable* technology associated with robo-advisors also enables their services to be provided to clients with small portfolios in a cost-effective manner.

Robo-advisors are increasingly being employed by private clients for *more sophisticated* purposes (e.g., to fulfill unique investment preferences and for tax-efficient investing). They can also be used in combination with traditional private wealth managers to lower fees and to reach new private client segments.

EXAMPLE: Private client segments

List *three* key differences between the mass affluent and HNW private client segments.

Answer:

Three key differences between the mass affluent and HNW segments are as follows:

- The mass affluent segment has a larger client-to-manager ratio than the HNW segment.
- The portfolios of HNW clients are more likely to contain sophisticated investment strategies and alternative investments.
- Wealth managers are more likely to develop customized investment solutions for HNW clients rather than for clients in the mass affluent segment.

MODULE QUIZ 19.9

1. Shane Long, CFA, works as a wealth manager for the London branch of a prestigious Swiss private bank. Long is meeting a prospective client, Anna Bradescu, for the first time. In a telephone conversation with Bradescu two days ago, she mentioned that she owns penthouse apartments in Paris, New York, Hong Kong, and Tokyo. At the meeting, she provides Long with her personal calling card that includes an address in one of the most exclusive residential areas of London. Long politely asks Bradescu for her passport and bank account details and enquires about her family circumstances and sources of wealth. The ethical consideration that Long is *most likely* concerned about is:
   A. KYC.
   B. confidentiality.
   C. conflicts of interest.
2. Shane Long, CFA, has just concluded his first meeting with a prospective client, Anna Bradescu. Based on the information that Bradescu has provided, Long believes that Bradescu should be classified as an ultra-high net worth (UHNW) client. Which of the following is *most likely* a characteristic of the UHNW segment?
   A. High client-to-manager ratio.
   B. Complex tax and estate planning considerations.
   C. Greater use of technology in providing wealth management services.
3. The growth of robo-advisors in the wealth management industry is *most likely* driven by:
   A. cost considerations.
   B. the superior ability of robo-advisors to develop sophisticated investment strategies.
   C. the desire to have primarily human interaction for wealth advice coupled with automated portfolio construction, rebalancing, and reporting services.

Reading 19

KEY CONCEPTS

LOS 19.a

Investment Objectives

Private clients have a wide range of investment objectives that (1) may not be precisely defined, (2) can change over time, and (3) may be difficult to reconcile.

Institutional clients have more stable, clearly defined objectives.

Constraints

- Private clients have shorter time horizons compared to institutional clients. Private clients may also have different time horizons for different objectives compared to a single time horizon for institutional clients.
- Private client portfolios tend to be smaller than those of institutional clients, meaning that some types of alternative investments may be unsuitable for private client portfolios.
- Tax planning is an important consideration for private clients.

Other Considerations

Institutional clients tend to have a more formal governance structure and higher investment sophistication compared to private clients.

The regulatory environment and investor uniqueness and complexity are additional considerations for private clients.

LOS 19.b

Personal information that should be gathered for a private client includes family circumstances, employment, retirement plans, sources of wealth, investment objectives, risk tolerance, investment preferences, wills and trust documents, insurance policies, service guidelines, and portfolio reporting requirements.

Financial information gathering should include the client's personal balance sheet, annual income and expenses, and sources of cash flows.

LOS 19.c

Taxes on individuals include income tax, wealth-based taxes, and consumption tax.

Tax-efficient strategies include legal tax avoidance, tax reduction, and tax deferral.

LOS 19.d

Planned goals are those that can be reasonably estimated within a specified time horizon.

Unplanned goals are related to unexpected financial expenditures.

Private wealth managers can assist their clients in quantifying, prioritizing, and reevaluating or changing goals.

LOS 19.e

Risk tolerance is dependent on both the willingness and ability to take risk.

Risk capacity is based on the ability to take financial risks and is a more objective measure of risk compared to risk tolerance.

Risk perception is a subjective measure of risk and is affected by the way risk questions are framed.

LOS 19.f

Technical skills include proficiency in financial planning; capital markets and asset classes; portfolio construction and monitoring; technology skills; and in some instances, multiple languages.

Soft skills include communication and social skills; education skills; and business development and sales skills.

LOS 19.g

Capital sufficiency analysis is used to determine the likelihood of clients being able to meet their objectives.

Deterministic forecasting assumes that a private client's portfolio will achieve a single compound annual growth rate across the investment horizon.

Monte Carlo simulation allows for real world uncertainty and determines the probability of success for a client's objective.

LOS 19.h

Saving for retirement usually begins at the early career stage and continues through the preretirement stage. Private clients depend on cash flows from pension income and their investment portfolio to fund their retirement. A key challenge in retirement planning is determining a sustainable rate at which distributions can be made from a client's portfolio for the rest of the client's lifetime.

A client's retirement goals can be analyzed using mortality tables, annuities, and Monte Carlo simulation. A life annuity can be used to reduce longevity risk. Monte Carlo simulation provides the probability of success for a client's retirement goals but does not consider shortfall magnitude.

Behavioral biases exhibited by retirees include increased loss aversion, consumption gaps, the annuity puzzle, and lack of self-control (preference for spending income over capital appreciation).

LOS 19.i, 19.j, 19.k

Client Background and Investment Objectives

A client's background details are obtained from relevant personal, financial, and tax information.

Investment objectives may be planned, unplanned, ongoing, or a one-off. Multiple objectives should be prioritized into primary and secondary objectives.

Key Investment Parameters

Low risk tolerance is usually associated with high-priority goals and near-term goals.

Time horizon is described as a range (e.g., in excess of 15 years for a long horizon and less than 10 years for a short horizon). When a client has multiple objectives, there may be different time horizons for each objective.

Other investment parameters include asset class preferences, liquidity preferences (including a cash reserve), unique investment preferences, and constraints restricting investments for a client's portfolio.

Asset Allocation

Strategic asset allocation indicates a long-term target allocation for each asset class, with the portfolio being rebalanced periodically to maintain the target allocation.

Tactical asset allocation is an active management strategy that normally specifies a range for each asset class rather than a specific target allocation percentage.

Portfolio Management and Implementation

This covers wealth manager guidelines in relation to discretionary authority, portfolio rebalancing, tactical asset allocation changes, and acceptable investment vehicles that can be used to implement a client's investment strategy.

Wealth Manager Duties and Responsibilities

These include formulating and reviewing the client's IPS; constructing the portfolio; monitoring and rebalancing the portfolio; monitoring portfolio costs and third-party providers; and reporting portfolio performance.

IPS Appendix

This section includes modeled portfolio performance and capital market expectations.

LOS 19.l

The traditional approach to portfolio construction consists of identifying appropriate asset classes, developing capital market expectations, determining asset class weights, assessing constraints, implementing the portfolio, and choosing asset location.

Goals-based investing follows the same steps as the traditional approach but creates separate portfolios for each of the client's goals. This makes it easier for the client to specify risk tolerance as this is done for each specific goal.

LOS 19.m

Portfolio reports should include a performance summary for the current period; market commentary for the current period; portfolio asset allocation; detailed performance of asset classes and individual securities; benchmark report; historical performance of the client's investment portfolio; transaction details for the current period; purchase and sale report for the current period; and the impact of currency exposure and exchange rate fluctuations.

Portfolio reviews should cover the appropriateness of the client's existing goals and investment parameters; rebalancing of portfolio asset allocation to target allocation or ranges; any changes to the wealth manager's ongoing management of the portfolio; any changes or updates in the wealth manager's duties and responsibilities; and any changes to IPS and portfolio review frequency.

LOS 19.n

The success of an investment program should be evaluated in terms of goal achievement, process consistency, and portfolio performance. The investment program is successful only if it achieves success on all three criteria.

LOS 19.o

Ethical considerations include fiduciary duty and suitability, know your customer requirements, client confidentiality, and conflicts of interest.

Compliance considerations for private wealth managers vary by jurisdiction.

LOS 19.p

The mass affluent private client segment is characterized by a wide range of management services, larger client-to-wealth-manager ratio, and noncustomized portfolio management approach.

The HNW segment exhibits a smaller client-to-wealth-manager ratio, tailored investment solutions, and portfolios with sophisticated strategies and alternative investments.

The UHNW segment often has multigenerational investment horizons, complex tax and estate planning, and comprehensive service requirements that go beyond investment planning.

Robo-advisors are automated wealth management advisors that offer portfolio management services at a lower cost compared to traditional wealth managers. The scalable technology of robo-advisors allows them to service clients with small portfolios.

ANSWER KEY FOR MODULE QUIZZES

Module Quiz 19.1

1. **B** Private clients are likely to have a wide range of investment objectives that may not be precisely defined, whereas institutional clients are more likely to have clearly defined objectives. Private clients are likely to have a less formal governance structure and a lower degree of investment sophistication compared to institutional clients. (LOS 19.a)

2. **A** Bonds typically provide a regular income, meeting the private client's liquidity needs. Hedge funds and private equity often have a lock-up period, making these investments unsuitable for a private client with a short investment horizon and/or high liquidity needs. (LOS 19.a)

Module Quiz 19.2

1. McPherson has already established Gove's age, current employment, risk preference, interest in meeting several financial objectives, and low liquidity needs.

   McPherson should gather the following additional personal information about Gove's personal and investment background in order to prepare Gove's IPS (any five points from the following list would be acceptable):

   - Family circumstances, including marital status, and number and age of family members.
   - Proof of client identification (e.g., passport).
   - Future career aspirations.
   - Retirement plans.
   - Sources of wealth.
   - Specific return or investment objectives.
   - Unique investment preferences.
   - Further discussion of risk tolerance.
   (LOS 19.b)

2. Statement 1 is a tax avoidance strategy as the coupons and/or capital gains will not be taxed in the retirement account.

   Statement 2 is a tax reduction strategy because the new asset class recommended by the private wealth manager would attract lower taxes.

   Statement 3 is a tax deferral strategy. Since earnings accumulate tax free, taxes are deferred until withdrawals are made. (LOS 19.c)

3. **C** Portfolio rebalancing and updating capital market expectations demonstrate Cheong's technical skills. Cheong displayed interpersonal and language skills when explaining her client's portfolio performance. (LOS 19.f)

Module Quiz 19.3

1. In relation to goal quantification, Collins has quantified her retirement spending requirements. Her financial advisor needs to assist her in quantifying her daughter's college education expenses and the amount she would like to gift to her future grandchildren.

   In relation to goal prioritization, even though Collins has stated that her highest priority goal is meeting her daughter's college expenses, the proximity of that goal should not be the sole factor determining its priority. Collins's financial advisor needs to assist her in prioritizing her financial goals and, if necessary, reevaluating her goals if the financial support of her daughter's college education and/or the desire to leave a gift to her grandchildren adversely impact her ability to fund her retirement lifestyle. (LOS 19.d)

2. Collins has a *higher* risk tolerance associated with her retirement goal. This is because she views retirement as a long-term goal and is willing to accept a 10%–15% drop in expected retirement spending. Since she expects to retire in 20 years, Collins is also likely to have a higher risk tolerance for the funding of unexpected health-related expenses.

   Collins is likely to have *lower* risk tolerance associated with her college fees goal. This is a near-term and her highest priority goal.

   Collins is likely to have *higher* risk tolerance associated with the goal of leaving a gift to her grandchildren at her death due to the long-term nature of this goal. (LOS 19.e)

Reading 19

Module Quiz 19.4

1. **C** The simulation results show that the client has a 75% probability of having a portfolio value in excess of $2,116,646 in Year 25. Since the client's charitable donation is $2 million, the probability of success of meeting or exceeding that goal is slightly higher than 75%. (LOS 19.g)

Module Quiz 19.5

1. **C** The probabilities from mortality tables are used to weight the expected annual cash flows of a retiree in order to estimate the present value of the retiree's retirement spending needs. (LOS 19.h)

2. **B** A possible explanation for retirees preferring to spend investment income rather than liquidate securities is that retirees consider this a self-control mechanism. (LOS 19.h)

Module Quiz 19.6

1. **B** The purchase of a holiday apartment is a financial goal and should be included in the *Investment Objectives* section of the IPS. Risk tolerance and asset class preferences are considered under *Investment Parameters*. (LOS 19.j)

2. **A** ESG investing may require restrictions on investment in certain sectors or securities. These restrictions should be included as *Constraints* in the *Investment Parameters* section of an IPS. Time horizon and liquidity preferences are included as *Investment Parameters* in an IPS. (LOS 19.i)

3. **C** Rebalancing methodology, discretionary authority, tactical asset allocation changes, and implementation are covered in the *Portfolio Management* section of a client's IPS. Modeled portfolio behavior and capital market expectations are covered in the *IPS Appendix*. (LOS 19.i)

4. **A** A cash reserve and/or constraint on asset class selection because of liquidity needs is covered in the *Liquidity Preferences* section of an IPS. *Other Investment Preferences* might include a concentrated asset position. The *Portfolio Asset Allocation* section describes the asset allocation approach used for the client's portfolio (e.g., strategic or tactical asset allocation). (LOS 19.i)

5. **C** As each of Collins's financial goals has a different time horizon, Collins will have multiple time horizons. Time horizons should generally be expressed as a range because of the uncertainty associated with each goal (e.g., it is not possible to predict exactly how long Collins's retirement will last). (LOS 19.k)

Module Quiz 19.7

1. **B** Patel should recommend Alternative 2 as it correctly incorporates his client's preference for non-U.S. equities and alternative investments (as represented by commodities in this question) while staying within the portfolio volatility limit of 9%. Alternative 1 does not incorporate his client's preference for non-U.S. equities, while the portfolio volatility of Alternative 3 exceeds 9%. (LOS 19.l)

Module Quiz 19.8

1. Bond could provide the following additional items to improve the quality of his portfolio reports (any four points from the following list would be acceptable):
   - Market commentary for the current period to provide context for the portfolio's performance.
   - Historical performance of the client's portfolio since inception.
   - Transaction details for the current period showing contributions, withdrawals, interest, dividends, and capital appreciation.

- Purchase and sale report for the current period.
- Impact of currency exposure and exchange rate fluctuations.
- Progress toward meeting goal portfolios when using a goals-based investing approach.
(LOS 19.m)

2. **A** Tan's investment program has met the goal achievement criteria (her portfolio has matched the modeled return in Bond's capital sufficiency analysis and no meaningful changes are required to her investment strategy) and the process consistency criteria (guidelines were followed in relation to ongoing communications, rebalancing, etc.). However, the portfolio performance criteria has not been met because her portfolio has underperformed the benchmark's return over the period. A successful investment program is one that achieves success on *all* three criteria. (LOS 19.n)

Module Quiz 19.9

1. **A** Given that Bradescu appears to be very wealthy, Long will most likely want to satisfy KYC requirements (e.g., to fulfill anti-money laundering checks). (LOS 19.o)

2. **B** Characteristics of the UHNW segment include the provision of highly customized services (low client-to-manager ratio), including complex tax and estate planning. Greater use of technology in providing wealth management services is a characteristic of the mass affluent segment. (LOS 19.p)

3. **A** Robo-advisors offer a cost advantage in the provision of wealth management services compared to traditional wealth management firms. Robo-advisors offer a primarily digital interface and typically implement investment strategies using mutual funds and ETFs. (LOS 19.p)

READING 20

Topics in Private Wealth Management

EXAM FOCUS

This lengthy reading covers a wide and integrated range of topics beginning with taxation and leading to more specialized topics such as estate planning and family governance. Both an understanding of the terminology and the ability to perform calculations are required in this reading. Exam questions may explain you to calculate the maximum after-tax value or how to structure investments in such a way to achieve maximum after-tax value. Additionally, you may see questions where facts are sufficient to indicate the optimal strategy but insufficient details are provided to perform a calculation. Always remember that specific tax laws and regulations will be provided to you on exam questions, and you are not required to memorize laws and regulations specific to a country.

MODULE 20.1: APPROACHES TO TAXATION

Video covering this content is available online.

LOS 20.a: Compare taxation of income, wealth, and wealth transfers.

Main Categories of Taxes

1. Income tax (earnings): Paid by individuals, corporations, and other legal entities on various types of income including wages, rents, interest, and dividends.
2. Capital gains tax (earnings): Calculated on the price appreciation (e.g., proceeds minus cost) upon disposition of an asset. Tax rates of capital gains often differ from income.
3. Wealth/property tax (ownership): Paid annually on the value of assets held (frequently real estate). Has lower rates than income or capital gains taxes because wealth/property tax is assessed on the asset value.

4. Stamp duties (purchases): Tax on purchase price of real estate or financial assets.
5. Wealth transfer tax: Examples include inheritance, estate, or gift taxes. May be imposed on the transferee or the transferor.

Investment Income

Fixed-income instruments generate interest income, which is taxed at regular income tax rates in most jurisdictions.

Double taxation occurs when earnings are taxed first in the corporation, followed by some or all of the after-tax corporate earnings being paid out to investors as dividends, which are then taxed as well. As a result of the double taxation, many jurisdictions have provisions to reduce the level of taxation of the dividends (second level). **Qualified dividends** are an example of dividends taxed at a lower rate. Qualified dividends are dividends from shares in local and certain foreign corporations where the investor has owned the shares for a certain amount of time (e.g., 60 days) on an unhedged basis.

When investing internationally, **withholding taxes** by the country where the investment occurs must be considered. Withholding taxes usually apply to investment income and are based on the gross (and not net) income. In many cases, the withholding taxes may be applied against the tax otherwise assessed by the investor's home country.

Capital Gains

The general equation is as follows:

net sales price – tax (cost) basis = capital gain/loss

The net sales price is the price after deduction of commissions and trading costs. Often, the tax basis is simply the original cost of the asset. In some jurisdictions, there could be a "step-up" in basis to fair market value on the date of death with no capital gains taxes owing. In other jurisdictions, the step-up occurs upon death or departure in residency, but any unrealized gains would be taxed.

Realized capital gains occur upon the actual disposition of an asset. Unrealized capital gains are "paper gains," which represent appreciation on unsold items. In situations where there is a realized capital loss, most jurisdictions allow the realized capital loss to reduce any realized capital gains.

Depending on the holding period of the investments, the capital gains may be subject to a short-term (usually higher) rate or a long-term (usually lower) rate. The rationale behind the rate differentials is to encourage long-term investment and discourage short-term speculation. If countries have low long-term capital gains tax rates, this means that stocks are more tax-efficient investments than bonds, the latter of which are taxed at regular rates.

Some countries also differentiate between investment gains (lower or no tax on capital gains) and trading gains (taxed at regular rates).

Real Estate Tax

When considering real estate as an investment (and not as a principal residence), only the net income is taxable in most cases. This means items such as interest, depreciation, and repairs are deductible against the gross income of the property. In the case of depreciation (e.g., straight line or declining over a specified number of years), the annual expense would reduce the cost base. Upon the ultimate sale of the property, there may be a recapture of depreciation if the proceeds of the sale exceed the property's depreciated cost base. Finally, some jurisdictions allow for an exchange of "qualifying" properties that essentially delays the incurrence of capital gains to the time when the new property is disposed of.

Types of Investment Accounts

A **taxable account** (e.g., individual brokerage account) is taxed at the relevant rates for each type of investment income.

A **tax-deferred account** (e.g., individual retirement account) allows for pretax contributions and tax-free accumulation, but all amounts are taxed at withdrawal as regular income.

A **tax-exempt account** (e.g., Roth IRA in the United States) allows for after-tax contributions to accumulate on a tax-free basis and with no taxes upon withdrawal.

From an institutional investor perspective, foundations/endowments, sovereign wealth funds, and pension funds are usually tax exempt. In contrast, insurance companies are usually taxable.

LOS 20.b: Describe global considerations of jurisdiction that are relevant to taxation.

Types of Tax Systems

A **tax haven** is a jurisdiction with very low or no tax rates for residents and foreign investors (e.g., Bermuda).

A **territorial tax system** taxes only income that is earned locally (e.g., Hong Kong SAR).

A **worldwide tax system** will impose taxes on all sources of income, which inevitably leads to double taxation on the same income by more than one jurisdiction. However, relief may be provided in the form of tax credits by the home jurisdiction for tax already paid in the source jurisdiction or bilateral tax treaties. Often, taxes are imposed on only residents of the jurisdiction, so it is crucial to determine the jurisdiction in which one is a resident. It is usually based on the amount of time spent in the jurisdiction (e.g., considered resident if living there for 183 of 365 days of the year). Tie-breaker rules exist so that individuals are not in the onerous position of being a resident in two jurisdictions simultaneously.

Only a handful of countries (e.g., United States) impose a tax based on citizenship. For example, a U.S. citizen living and earning income in Singapore would be subject to income taxes in both Singapore and the United States. In that case, an equitable resolution would require some double taxation relief.

EXAMPLE: Cross border investing issues

Cecile is a citizen of the Philippines and lives in the Philippines. She is thinking of investing in property in the United States. Outline the various implications to Cecile of the various options based on U.S. taxation.

Option 1: Owning property directly in nonresident individual name

- Disadvantage: Withholding tax may apply to gross, not net, rental income.
- Disadvantage: U.S. estate tax must be paid upon death.

Option 2: Owning property indirectly via U.S. corporation (U.S. corporation is owned by Cecile or a non-U.S. corporation)

- Advantage: Withholding tax may apply to net rental income.
- Advantage: Upon death, U.S. corporation shares go directly to Cecile's beneficiaries.
- Disadvantage: Upon death, if U.S. corporation is liquidated, any capital gains are subject to higher corporate taxes than individual taxes.

Option 3: Owning property indirectly via non-U.S. corporation

- Advantage: Income is generally not subject to U.S. taxation.
- Advantage: Upon death, not subject to U.S. estate tax. Shares go directly to Cecile's beneficiaries.

EXAMPLE: Examining taxes under territorial vs. worldwide investment portfolios

Home country investment portfolios

- With both tax regimes, investment portfolios in the home country are subject to taxes in the home country.
- Check relative tax rates on capital gains, dividends, and interest and reallocate more (less) investments to those types with lower (higher) tax rates.

Foreign country investment portfolios

- If there is no tax treaty, withholding taxes on gross income may be required.
- If there is a tax treaty, there may be a reduction in withholding tax rates for one or more types of investment income (e.g., interest and dividends).
- Whether there is a treaty or not, to maximize after-tax return, check for any advantageous provisions in the foreign country where:
  - Investment income (e.g., capital gains) on investments held by foreign investors is not taxed in the foreign country, and

- Investment income (e.g., interest, dividends) is not subject to withholding taxes.

Wealth and estate taxes

- Check for any estate taxes and what items are included/excluded as that may impact investment allocations and/or investment holding structure (e.g., establish a non-U.S. company to hold U.S. investments to avoid U.S. estate tax).
- Check for any estate tax treaties that may allow for an estate tax exemption in the foreign country. However, in some instances, obtaining the exemption may require disclosure of full net worth to the foreign country tax authorities.

EXAMPLE: The Common Reporting Standard and Foreign Account Tax Compliance Act

To avoid tax leakage arising from tax evasion, automated tax information exchange between countries is becoming much more widespread. The focus is on banks, investment managers, and wealthy families with international investments.

The Common Reporting Standard (CRS) was facilitated by the OECD and involves information exchange between more than 100 jurisdictions. The CRS is also referred to as the Standard for Automatic Exchange of Financial Account Information.

The Foreign Account Tax Compliance Act (FATCA) originated in the United States as a means for U.S. taxpayers to pay tax on investment income earned outside of the country. The FATCA applies to all financial institutions who have U.S. investors.

LOS 20.c: Discuss and analyze the tax efficiency of investments.

Tax Efficiency

A **tax-efficient strategy** results in relatively high after-tax returns compared to pretax returns. Frequently, equities have greater tax efficiency versus fixed income and real estate, for example. Common reasons include (1) lower tax rates on dividends and capital gains in many countries and (2) the ability to time securities dispositions to maximize tax benefits.

Often, alternative assets are selected because of low correlations to traditional assets such as stocks and bonds. However, the tax laws pertaining to alternative assets (e.g., hedge fund strategies, partnerships) are usually far more complex than for traditional assets. As a result, the impact of alternative assets on portfolio risk and return should always be viewed from an after-tax and after-fee perspective.

Investments that emphasize high-yield (interest income) and/or high turnover are often tax inefficient. At the same time, timing must also be considered, and in that regard, a momentum strategy with higher turnover might initially be viewed as tax inefficient. However, momentum strategies are quite tax efficient in that they hold winners longer (thereby deferring tax on gains) and sell losers sooner (thereby realizing losses earlier to offset against any gains). As a general note, investment constraints that require managers to sell securities (and realize gains) and rebalance portfolios more frequently result in less tax efficiency (e.g., in some jurisdictions, short-term capital gains are taxed higher than long-term capital gains).

There are four common metrics used in examining tax efficiency:

1. After-tax holding period return
   - Relevant taxes are computed and deducted when investments are disposed of
   - Accounts for interest income, dividend income, and realized gains/losses but not unrealized gains/losses
2. After-tax post-liquidation return
   - An extension of what was just listed but there is an assumption of overall portfolio disposition after a specific period (e.g., 5 or 10 years)
   - This measure accounts for unrealized gains/losses
3. After-tax excess returns
   - Either of the metrics just listed compared to a benchmark value
4. Tax-efficiency ratio
   - After-tax annualized total return versus pretax annualized total return

After-Tax Holding Period Return

$$R' = [(\text{value}_1 - \text{value}_0) + \text{income} - \text{tax}] / \text{value}_0$$

Alternatively, $R' = R - (\text{tax} / \text{value}_0)$

Tax is estimated based on interest and dividends received plus capital gains/losses realized, each multiplied by the relevant tax rate. Any capital losses are assumed to be offset by capital gains but the absence of any gains may result in a higher after-tax return compared to a pretax return.

EXAMPLE: Calculating monthly after-tax return

Assume the portfolio value is $825,000 on April 1 and $5,000 of interest is received on April 15. Assume that the tax rate on interest income is 25% and the monthly pretax overall portfolio return is 1.20%.

Approximate the portfolio after-tax return.

Answer:

$1.20\% - [0.25(5{,}000)] / [825{,}000 + (5{,}000(30 - 15) / 30)] = 1.05\%$

After-Tax Post-Liquidation Return

The post-liquidation return (R_{PL}) involves deducting the implied tax as shown here:

$$R_{PL} = [(1 + R'_1)(1 + R'_2)\ldots(1 + R'_n) - (\text{liquidation tax / final value})]^{1/n} - 1$$

liquidation tax = (final value – tax basis) × tax rate on capital gains

EXAMPLE: After-tax post-liquidation return

A portfolio has the following returns:

	Pretax	After-Tax
Year 1	5.3%	4.8%
Year 2	–3.3%	–2.7%
Year 3	6.9%	6.0%
Cumulative	8.85%	8.09%
Annualized	2.87%	2.63%

The portfolio has embedded gains equal to 5% of the ending value with capital gains taxes paid at a rate of 15%.

Compute the annualized post-liquidation return of the portfolio over three years.

Answer:

Portfolio value after tax (from above) = 1.0809

Tax liability from unrealized gains from liquidation = 15% × 5% = 0.75% = 0.0075

Portfolio value net of tax on unrealized gains = 1.0809 – 0.0075 = 1.0734

Annualized post-liquidation return = $1.0734^{1/3} - 1$ = 2.39% (versus 2.87% if no taxes payable)

After-Tax Excess Return

The after-tax excess return (x') is computed as the after-tax return of the portfolio (R') minus the after-tax return of the benchmark (B').

$$x' = R' - B'$$

In the case of passive management, the benchmark could be an index. In the case of active management, it could be a specific portfolio that is consistent with the manager's investment style.

In this regard, the **tax alpha** would be defined as after-tax excess return (x') minus the pretax excess return (x).

$$\alpha_{tax} = x' - x$$

Tax-Efficiency Ratio (TER)

The TER is calculated as after-tax return (R′) divided by pretax return (R).

$$TER = R' / R$$

For positive returns in taxable accounts, the higher the TER, the better. A higher TER means that relatively less return is lost to taxes. Obviously, the TER is not relevant for tax-exempt or tax-deferred accounts.

The TER does not work so well for negative returns, and in such instances, using an absolute comparison between after-tax and pretax returns or looking at tax alpha could be useful measurement alternatives.

MODULE QUIZ 20.1

1. An investor is evaluating various assets and strategies for her portfolio. Based solely on tax effects, which type of investment would *most likely* be favored in a country with high tax rates on interest, dividend, and realized gains?
   A. Growth stocks with moderate turnover.
   B. Bonds with periodic payment of interest.
   C. Value stocks held for a moderate period of time.
2. A portfolio generates a total return of 15%. The tax rates on interest, dividend, and capital gains are 35%, 20%, and 20%, respectively. The proportions of the portfolio return from interest, dividends, and realized capital gains are 10%, 25%, and 35%, respectively. Using the information provided, the net return after all taxes is *closest* to:
   A. 11.25%.
   B. 11.50%.
   C. 12.68%.

MODULE 20.2: TAX LOCATION

Video covering this content is available online.

LOS 20.d: Analyze the impact of taxes on capital accumulation and decumulation in taxable, tax-exempt, and tax-deferred accounts.

So far, the coverage of tax has focused on financial planning decisions (e.g., after-tax growth assumptions for taxable accounts) and asset allocation (e.g., after-tax return and volatility). The focus in this section will be on asset location, retirement income planning, and charitable giving.

Taxable, Tax-Exempt, and Tax-Deferred Accounts

Many countries offer accounts that allow funds to be deposited and invested in a tax-advantaged manner. There are generally specified limits on how much can be invested in such accounts, and they are typically restricted to specified purposes such as retirement or health care. Two such accounts, tax-exempt and tax-deferred, will be discussed next.

Taxable accounts involve one or more tax rates on income (e.g., interest, dividends) or returns (e.g., realized capital gains) to determine R′. The taxes per period are paid and represent a cash outflow. The after-tax future value (R′) of the portfolio is then determined as follows, where *n* is the number of years:

$$FV_{AT} = (1 + R')^n$$

With tax-exempt accounts (TEAs), after-tax funds are deposited so no tax is due on the returns earned or on withdrawals. In other words, the after-tax future value does not explicitly depend on the tax rate and is calculated as follows:

$$FV_{AT} = (1 + R)^n$$

With tax-deferred accounts (TDAs), pretax funds are deposited, and the investor may take a tax deduction for the amount contributed, thereby reducing taxable income and taxes due. All tax is deferred until withdrawal, allowing tax-deferred compounding. Because no tax was paid on the funds deposited, tax is due on the full amount of withdrawals. The tax rate (t) will be the rate at the end of time *n* and the after-tax future value is calculated as follows:

$$FV_{AT} = (1 + R)^n(1 - t)$$

EXAMPLE: Comparing future after-tax amounts in different accounts

Assume that an investor lives in a country with a 35% flat tax rate on all investment income and returns. $100,000 is invested in each of three accounts:

1. A taxable account earning 9%, subject to annual tax.
2. A tax-deferred account (TDA) earning 9%.
3. A tax-exempt account (TEA) earning 9%.

Compute the after-tax amounts for each account at the end of 30 years on the assumption of full liquidation.

Answer:

1. $FV_{AT} = (1 + R')^n = \$100{,}000 \times [1 + (0.09)(1 - 0.35)]^{30} = \$550{,}460$.
2. $FV_{AT} = (1 + R)^n(1 - t) = \$100{,}000 \times [(1 + 0.09)^{30}(1 - 0.35)] = \$862{,}399$.
3. $FV_{AT} = (1 + R)^n = \$100{,}000 \times (1 + 0.09)^{30} = \$1{,}326{,}768$.

PROFESSOR'S NOTE

Superficially, it appears the TEA is superior to the TDA because there is no tax due on withdrawals. However, this ignores that TEA contributions are made with after-tax funds and TDA contributions are made with pretax funds. Suppose an investor has $100 pretax available for savings and is in the $30 tax bracket. The full $100 can be contributed to a TDA and invested. If that contribution is not made, the investor will owe $30 in taxes now and have only $70 for contribution to the TEA.

Asset Location

The concept of asset location refers to whether to place assets in taxable, tax-exempt, or tax-deferred accounts. In general, tax-efficient assets (e.g., equities that generate capital gains, which are often subject to lower tax rates) should be placed in taxable accounts and tax-inefficient assets (e.g., taxable bonds that generate taxable interest, which is often subject to higher tax rates) should be placed in tax-exempt or tax-deferred accounts. However, exceptions may apply if equities held for the long term or subject to high turnover could avoid the negative and compounding effects of short-term taxes by being held in tax-exempt accounts and generating a comparatively higher after-tax return.

Taxable accounts have the advantage of allowing losses incurred to be offset against gains earned (similar to tax loss harvesting). As well, in determining whether equities should be included in taxable versus tax-deferred accounts, consider the capital gains tax rate for the former and the tax rate upon withdrawal for the latter. For example, an overly low capital gains tax rate or an overly high marginal income tax rate at retirement would favor equities inclusion in taxable accounts. A low marginal income tax rate would generally favor equities inclusion in tax-deferred accounts.

For equity strategies, there is often the trade-off between passive strategies (more tax efficient due to low turnover and fewer transaction costs) versus active strategies (less tax efficient due to high turnover and more transaction costs) in that passive strategies often have lower returns than active strategies. In other words, there is a choice between (1) more tax efficiency and lower return and (2) less tax efficiency and higher return.

EXAMPLE: Tax location

Assume there are four asset classes:

1. Equity
2. Tax-managed equity (lower tax rate)
3. Fixed income (higher tax rate)
4. Tax-exempt fixed income

Portfolio composition:

- Asset class: 50% equity and 50% fixed income
- Account type: 50% in taxable accounts and 50% in tax-exempt accounts

Three possible asset location allocations:

- Tax-indifferent
- Tax-aware
- Asset location–sensitive

The *tax-indifferent* allocation considers only asset class 1 (equity) 50% and class 3 (fixed income) 50% and does not take any tax minimization strategies (e.g., asset classes 2 and 4) into consideration. The result is the lowest after-tax portfolio return of the three possibilities.

The *tax-aware* allocation takes away from asset classes 1 and 3 and adds to asset classes 2 (tax-managed equity) and 4 (tax-exempt bonds) so that it is 25% in each. Here, tax minimization strategies are used to try to increase after-tax portfolio returns.

The *asset location–sensitive* allocation follows the general rule of placing tax-efficient assets (50% in asset class 2: tax-managed equity) in taxable accounts and tax-inefficient assets (50% in asset class 3: fixed income) in tax-exempt accounts to generate the highest after-tax portfolio return of the three possibilities. The allocation ignores asset classes 1 and 4, as compared to asset classes 2 and 3, they are not so tax efficient and not so tax inefficient, respectively.

Any asset location strategy must retain flexibility given that goals and time horizons may vary between account types and given that multiple goals may exist. Using the previous example with tax-managed equities in taxable accounts, should there be a need for liquidity, a large allocation to equities may not be desirable and a larger allocation to bonds may be preferable despite the tax inefficiency of bonds.

Decumulation Strategies

The natural progression is from capital accumulation during the working years to tax-efficient decumulation during the retirement years to cover a retiree's spending needs.

The advantageous tax impacts on returns for tax-exempt and tax-deferred accounts over taxable accounts means that withdrawals should occur from taxable accounts first until they are exhausted. This is certainly true for a flat tax at all levels of income. In contrast, for a progressive tax system where marginal tax rates increase with income, it would make sense to "use up" the lower tax brackets with withdrawals from tax-deferred accounts first. After that, the withdrawals could come from the taxable accounts.

Charitable Giving Strategies

Charitable gifting has several key potential advantages:

- For the giver, the capital gains upon transfer to a qualifying charity of appreciated assets is deemed to be nil in some countries; in such instances, it is best to gift low-basis assets from taxable accounts.
- For the giver, the fair market value of the gifted assets would qualify for a tax deduction/credit in some countries and that lowers personal taxes payable.
- For the giver, if the assets are shares from a concentrated asset position, then the gift will lower the risk associated with the concentrated position.
- For the receiver, because the charity is tax exempt, it will not pay tax on any investment income or gains related to the gifted assets.

LOS 20.e: Explain portfolio tax management strategies and their application.

In using strategies to reduce taxes, it is necessary to distinguish between tax avoidance and tax evasion, the latter of which is illegal and involves deception and/or fraud to conceal income sources that would otherwise be subject to tax. In contrast, tax avoidance allows investors to minimize taxes by utilizing investment accounts that are legally exempt from taxes on income and capital gains (e.g., individual savings accounts in the United Kingdom). Some jurisdictions also allow limited gift amounts to be transferred without incurring wealth-based taxes.

Tax Management Strategies

The strategies can be classified in the following section.

Investments held in a manner to minimize taxes

- Allocating more to tax-exempt accounts than taxable accounts
- Holding certain investments (e.g., equities) for sufficient time to be subject to lower capital gains tax rates

Deferring income recognition

- Limiting dispositions to allow investments to earn more from tax-free compounding
- For progressive tax structures, waiting for marginal tax rates to fall when income levels are lower (e.g., retirement)
- Tax loss harvesting—offsetting capital gains by deliberately selling investments that have embedded capital losses; this is an example where greater turnover may create a tax benefit

Investment Vehicles

Four common vehicles include partnerships, mutual funds, exchange-traded funds (ETFs), and separately managed accounts (SMAs).

Partnership

Hedge funds and private equity funds are often structured as partnerships. Here, the partnership has no tax liability and taxes are usually allocated to the partners in the form of capital gains distributions, the latter of which are often taxed at lower rates.

Mutual Fund

Investment income (e.g., dividends, interest) is allocated to the investors and tax is paid by the investors based on when the income was received. Capital gains tax arises if the investor disposes of the fund shares based on the excess of proceeds and tax basis.

In some countries, investors must pay their proportion of taxes for realized capital gains that occur within the fund. The fund net asset value (NAV) is lowered by the amount of the capital gains distribution.

New mutual fund shareholders may become liable for unrealized capital gains of prior periods. Consider an example of a fund that is established with 10 investors and assets of $20 million. Over time, with no trading nor change in investors, the assets have increased in value to $24 million, so there is a $4 million embedded gain. Therefore, each investor has a tax basis of $2 million and a share investment worth $2.4 million. Assuming one new investor comes in and invests $2.4 million, the fund's total tax basis is $22.4 million and the fund's NAV is $26.4 million. The new investor has a $\frac{1}{11}$ ownership interest and the tax basis is $2,036,364 ($22.4 million / 11). If the fund were immediately liquidated, the new investor would have a capital gains distribution of $363,636 ($2,400,000 – $2,036,364) upon which there would be a tax liability. Therefore, the new investor is liable for taxes for which the investor did not benefit in terms of capital appreciation.

Measures such as the **potential capital gain exposure (PCGE)**, calculated as net gains (losses) divided by total net assets, may provide some clues as to the extent of embedded capital gains or untaxed capital appreciation in the fund that may become future tax liabilities for the investors. A high (low) PCGE suggests a high (low) likelihood of future capital gain distributions.

ETF

The ETF creation and redemption process is tax efficient because it allows managers the choice to transfer shares with a low cost basis to intermediaries (e.g., banks and brokerage firms). That will leave the ETF issuer with only the higher cost basis shares, which reduces the embedded capital gains and increases investors' after-tax returns.

SMA

SMAs have the greatest potential for tax management because everything can be customized for only one investor. For example, losses within the SMA can always be offset against any of the investor's gains separate from the SMA. In contrast, losses within a mutual fund are restricted in use to gains within that fund only.

Tax Loss Harvesting

The concept of tax loss harvesting involves the sale of securities with embedded losses to offset gains, which will lower the tax liability for the current year. Some jurisdictions have no restrictions on tax loss harvesting transactions, while others require a legitimate business reason that is not tax related.

One consideration for tax loss harvesting is the timing of sales in relation to the tax year-end. If a sale is being considered near the tax year-end, make the sale:

- Before year-end if it is a loss in order to place the loss in the current tax year and offset gains this year. That will lower taxes payable this year but increase taxes payable in the following year.
- After year-end if it is a gain. That will defer the gain and tax until the following year.

Watch out for situations where *wash sale* (or *superficial loss*) rules exist whereby, for example, losses may be denied if the same security is purchased 30 days before or after its sale at a loss. Circumventing the wash sale rules would require holding cash, an ETF, or a placeholder security for 31 days, which may be inconsistent with the desired exposures. Also, the subsequent repurchase of the security after 31 days, likely at a lower cost, means that there will be higher future capital gains. This is an example of how tax loss harvesting is a form of tax deferral.

Many tax authorities allow a form of **tax lot accounting**. When an investor makes a partial sale and has acquired the stock on different dates, each at a different cost, the investor may select which tax lots applied to the sale (the *specified-lot method*). In that case, the tax lots that produce the lowest tax bill should be designated as sold. Consider an investor who bought 100 shares of stock on three different dates for $10,000, $12,000, and $15,000. In this example, the investor just sold 100 shares.

Highest in, first out (HIFO) is generally optimal and the 100 shares with a cost basis of $15,000 should be designated as sold. If the sales price is higher than $15,000, that will minimize the gain and capital gains tax due now. If the sales price is less than $15,000, that will maximize the realized loss and the immediate tax benefits.

In case future tax rates are expected to be *higher* than current tax rates, **first in, first out (FIFO)** may be better and the 100 shares with a cost basis of $10,000 should be designated as sold. It will create a higher immediate tax bill (but at lower tax rates) and it defers the higher tax lots for sale in the future. This will lower the realized gain now or increase the realized loss at a future date. In other words, it will maximize the loss later, during a period of higher tax rates, resulting in greater tax benefits.

In case future tax rates are expected to be *lower* than current tax rates, **last in, first out (LIFO)** may be better and the 100 shares with a cost basis of $15,000 should be designated as sold. It will maximize the loss in the current period (at a higher tax rate) and defer the gains to the future where they will be taxed at a lower rate.

Because equity markets tend to appreciate over time, using LIFO is generally the most tax-efficient strategy. Here, the highest tax basis shares are sold first, which results in the lowest tax liability in the current period and defers the higher tax liabilities to future periods.

In some jurisdictions, tax lot accounting doesn't exist and other alternatives, such as average cost, are used to determine the tax cost basis.

Quantitative Tax Management

Risk and return are the basic principles in portfolio evaluation. In that regard, tracking error is used as a measure of the risk of introducing tax management and quantitative methods are used to maximize tax efficiency.

The general idea behind quantitative tax management is to minimize tracking error and trading costs as well as to minimize realized gains and maximize realized losses. The goal is to manage all that while meeting any other portfolio constraints (e.g., sector, country).

For new clients who transfer in appreciated securities, there is a delicate balance between the tax cost (e.g., realized gains) of selling those securities versus potential underperformance of holding those securities for too long. Those appreciated securities may not be consistent with the new investment objective.

Tax-optimized loss harvesting refers to looking for opportunities during the year as opposed to doing so only once near the end of the year. The assets that are sold during the process must be replaced, and therefore, the process uses quantitative methods to determine appropriate replacement assets that would be consistent with the portfolio's investment objectives.

Gain-loss matching optimization can be used to achieve the goals of minimizing capital gains and ensuring risk exposures are in line with portfolio objectives. In other words, it is possible to have zero capital gains by not selling securities with embedded gains, but that may result in excessive concentration risk, for example.

Many tax authorities impose a higher capital gains tax rate on shorter-term versus longer-term holdings. While it is generally desirable to extend the holding period to defer the tax, it is particularly desirable to extend the holding period when it also lowers the tax rate. Additionally, when there are short-term losses to apply, they should be used to offset short-term gains first because the latter are usually taxed at a higher rate than long-term gains.

MODULE QUIZ 20.2

1. An investment of $1,000 earns an annual interest of 5% (no capital gains). Assuming annual taxation at a 30% rate, the expected after-tax value of the investment in 10 years is *closest* to:
   A. $1,035.
   B. $1,140.
   C. $1,411.
2. Assume $100,000 is invested in a tax-deferred account. The expected after-tax balance that can be withdrawn from the account after 20 years, assuming a tax rate of 30% and a pretax return of 10%, is *closest* to:
   A. $386,968.
   B. $470,925.
   C. $672,750.
3. Assume $100,000 is invested in a tax-exempt account. The expected after-tax balance that can be withdrawn from the account after 20 years, assuming a tax rate of 30% and a pretax return of 10%, is *closest* to:
   A. $386,968.
   B. $500,925.
   C. $672,750.
4. An investor has $800,000 of equity securities in a tax-deferred account and $600,000 in bonds in a tax-exempt account. Assuming a tax rate of 40%, the after-tax asset allocation is *closest* to:
   A. 44.4% equity; 55.6% bonds.
   B. 57.1% equity; 42.9% bonds.
   C. 31.0% equity; 69.0% bonds.

5. Which of the following assets would be the *most appropriate* asset to locate in a tax-deferred account rather than a taxable account?
   A. Tax-exempt bonds.
   B. High-growth stocks.
   C. Corporate bonds.
6. An investor has a realized capital gain of $80,000 and is subject to a capital gains tax rate of 30%. The investor can sell another stock with a cost basis of $140,000 and a current market value of $90,000. The tax savings from harvesting the loss is *closest* to:
   A. $9,000.
   B. $10,000.
   C. $15,000.
7. For the previous question, assume the investor may either:

   Strategy 1: Sell the stock now and recognize the loss in the current year.

   Strategy 2: Hold the stock now and sell it at the end of the second year.

   In either case, the old or new stock is sold at the end of the second year after earning a 10% return for that year. Any current tax savings is immediately reinvested in a very similar stock (ignore any wash sale rules). Which of the strategies provides the highest future accumulation?
   A. Strategy 1.
   B. Strategy 2.
   C. The strategies provide the same future after-tax accumulation.

MODULE 20.3: CONCENTRATED POSITIONS

Video covering this content is available online.

Through work, inheritance, entrepreneurship, or for other reasons, individuals may come to hold concentrated positions in a single asset. Concentrated positions in a publicly traded single-stock position, a privately held business, or a real estate investment (not the primary residence) are covered in this module. A concentrated position may lead to inefficient asset allocation. An investment manager often works with the client to sell or otherwise monetize the asset. Such decisions often involve illiquidity, tax, legal, and emotional (behavioral finance) issues.

LOS 20.f: Discuss risk and tax objectives in managing concentrated single-asset positions.

A narrower definition of "concentrated position" will be used here, referring to the inability to create a diversified and efficient portfolio resulting from low tax basis (e.g., large capital gains tax liability to be avoided) or emotional attachment. Having a concentrated position in public equity could occur for several reasons, including an initial public offering or the accumulation of employee stock compensation over the years.

Concentrated single-asset positions also have company-specific risk, which is the nonsystematic risk of an investment that can be diversified away. It would be derived from adverse events that affect a specific company or industry but not the overall market.

Finally, concentrated positions could be subject to illiquidity and high transaction costs even if there is no tax due. A public company trading with insufficient volume may require a price discount to sell. The time and expense of finding a buyer for a private business can be substantial, so there cannot be any reliance on the proceeds to fund unexpected cash outflows.

In choosing a strategy to manage the concentrated position, the following factors should be considered:

- Level of concentration—the higher it is, the timelier the response needs to be to reduce the risk.
- Tax basis—the lower, the greater the taxes due.
- Tax rate—the higher, the greater the taxes due.
- Liquidity—the more illiquid, the greater the costs of risk reduction.
- Time horizon—more time may allow the concentration to be reduced gradually, which lowers the overall cost.
- Investor restrictions—may prevent an outright sale.
- Nonfinancial matters—emotional attachments may hinder the risk-reduction process.

Various strategies are available to manage concentrated positions, including:

- Sell the entire position—incur the tax liability and use the after-tax proceeds to invest in a more diversified manner.
- Sell the entire position gradually over time—same as what was just listed but reduces risk of doing so at a suboptimal time.
- Hedge and monetize—use derivatives to hedge (e.g., limit downside risk) and then borrow against its value and use the loan proceeds to accomplish client objectives.
- Tax-free exchange funds—one example involves investors combining their concentrated positions with other investors to create diversification but avoid triggering capital gains.
- Charitable gifts—assets can be transferred to private foundations and donor-advised funds where such assets can be sold and not incur any tax liabilities. Those funds could be used to achieve the donor's charitable objectives. The same can be done using charitable trusts that would also provide the donor with current income for living expenses.
- Tax minimization strategies—some tax laws allow a tax-free step-up in basis if one holds an asset to death, which is a legal form of tax avoidance. A gradual disposition of a concentrated position spreads the tax liability out over a period of time and is an example of a tax deferral strategy.

LOS 20.g: Describe strategies for managing concentrated positions in public equities.

Staged Diversification Strategy

Here, the disposition of the concentrated position is not done all at once but is done over multiple years to spread out the tax liability accordingly. But it means that the concentrated position is maintained for a longer time (although it is gradually being reduced). However, the after-tax funds could then be used to invest in a diversified asset (e.g., broad-based ETF).

Completion Portfolio

Here the other portfolio assets are structured for greatest diversification benefit to complement/complete the concentrated position. For example, if the concentrated position is an automobile stock, then the rest of the assets are selected to have a low correlation to automobile stocks such that the resulting total portfolio better tracks the return of the chosen benchmark. The selection of those assets (e.g., stocks, ETFs) is based on quantitative techniques.

On the tax side, quantitative techniques are used to determine how much rebalancing is required. There is both minimization of tracking error and maximization of after-tax return. Both objectives conflict because selling less shares at a time will reduce taxes but increase tracking error. In general terms, maximizing after-tax returns is achieved by realizing more capital losses and those capital losses are used to offset capital gains on the sale of the concentrated stock.

Equity Monetization, Collars, and Call Writing

Monetization generally involves receiving cash for a position without triggering a tax event. In other words, there is no disposition of the appreciated securities, and the investor still owns them. Monetization is a two-step process:

Step 1: Hedge a large part of the risk in the position. This can be achieved with a short sale, forward sale contract, forward conversion with options, or a total return equity swap. The underlying assumption here is a robust or liquid derivatives market.

Step 2: Borrow using the hedged position as collateral. The more effective the hedge, the higher the loan-to-value (LTV) ratio. For example, if a highly effective hedge can be established that limits the decline in value of a $10 million position to 5% (a $9.5 million ending value), it may now be possible to borrow $9.5 million (95% of initial LTV). The client can then use the $9.5 million to invest in a diversified portfolio.

Zero-cost collars are a common way to lower initial cost by giving up some stock upside. A put is purchased and a call is sold with different strike prices selected so the premiums are equal. For example, assuming a stock is currently trading at $50 per share, an investor could buy a 48 put for a $2.98 cash outflow and, as an offset, sell a 53 call for a $2.98 cash inflow. The investor has a net expenditure of zero. The investor is protected if the stock price falls below $48 but gives up some upside because the stock will be called at only $53 if its price rises to that level. Therefore, there is some risk reduction but not complete risk elimination. Also, for tax purposes, if the buy and sell premiums can be combined into one integrated transaction, it would be desirable, as it avoids any cash outflow associated with the taxation of the call premium income.

In terms of hedging, if a perfect hedge is used and removes all risk, it may be taxed as a sale (e.g., constructive sale). Therefore, the hedge must be structured to eliminate as much risk (and retain as little risk) as possible without the tax liability coming due. Using the information from the previous example, the investor would have to bear the risk of loss between $50 and $48. In that regard, the constructive sale rules are not likely to apply, and a taxable event could be avoided.

Covered call writing is a profitable strategy in stable markets if the stock price remains within a specific range, as the investor will simply keep the call option premiums received. An investor may hold a stock currently trading at $50 per share and does not want to sell at any price below $60. The strategy could be to sell call options with a strike price of $60 so that if the share price does manage to reach $60, the investor will receive $60 per share upon exercise of the call options. Covered call writing could be viewed as a form of staged diversification but will only work if the share price appreciates sufficiently.

Tax-Free Exchanges

With an **exchange fund**, consider 10 investors, each of whom has a concentrated position in a single stock with a low cost basis. Each investor's position is in a different stock. The investor contributes a holding into a newly formed exchange fund and each investor now owns a pro rata share of the new fund. If investor H had a position worth EUR 5 million with a cost basis of EUR 0.5 million and the total value of the new fund is EUR 100 million, investor H now owns 5% of the new fund with a cost basis of EUR 0.5 million. Investor H now participates in a diversified portfolio and defers any tax event until shares of the fund are sold.

Charitable Remainder Trust

Here, the individual makes an irrevocable donation of the shares to a charitable remainder trust (CRT) and receives a tax deduction for the donation. From the donation (capital), the CRT as a tax-exempt entity could sell those shares for no tax consequences and reinvest the proceeds into a more diversified portfolio. From the portfolio, the CRT pays out income amounts to the designated beneficiaries and, upon the passing of the last beneficiary, the remainder of the capital goes to the designated charity.

LOS 20.h: Describe strategies for managing concentrated positions in privately owned businesses and real estate.

Privately Owned Businesses

Private companies are usually smaller, less established, and have fewer sources of financing compared to public companies. As a result, for a given amount, a concentrated position in a privately held business is significantly riskier than a publicly traded firm. The owner of the company usually has much of the personal wealth invested in the business, and the desire for liquidity must be balanced with dilution of ownership interest and possibly even loss of control.

Besides an initial public offering (IPO), direct sale to another investor (e.g., strategic buyer, financial buyer, management/key employees), or sale of non-essential business assets, three main strategies are considered here.

Personal Line of Credit Secured by Company Shares

The owner can borrow from the company and pledge company stock as collateral. If the company does not have the financial resources to make the loan, the company could borrow to obtain the cash for the loan to the owner. Interest paid by the company could be a tax-deductible business expense. Alternatively, the line of credit (loan to the owner) could be from a third-party lender. The company may offer the lender a put, allowing the lender to transfer the loan to the company for cash. That increases the lender's assurance of repayment in exchange for more favorable loan terms to the owner.

Leveraged Recapitalization

The owner may retain 20%–40% of the equity capital and sell 60%–80% of the shares back to the company. The owner continues to manage the business with a significant financial stake. A private equity firm (PEF) could arrange the financing for the company to purchase the owner's stock. In exchange, the PEF receives equity in the company. This can be part of a phased exit strategy; the owner will sell and receive cash for a portion of equity in the initial transaction and then participate in and sell remaining shares when the PEF resells their position in a few years. Taxes are owed on the cash received in the initial recapitalization but additional taxes are deferred until the owner's remaining stock is sold. If tax rates are expected to increase in the future, the transaction can be structured with more cash in the initial transaction.

Employee Stock Ownership Plan (ESOP)

The owner sells stock to the ESOP, which in turn, sells the shares to company employees. In a leveraged ESOP, the company borrows money to finance the stock purchase. In the United States (subject to additional restrictions), the owner's sale of shares may not trigger a capital gains tax.

Real Estate

Property-specific risk for real estate is the direct counterpart to company-specific risk for a company. It is the additional, diversifiable risk associated with owning a specific property. It might arise, for example, from the discovery of environmental pollution on the site or the loss of a key tenant and rental income.

A single investment in a real estate asset can be large and constitute a significant portion of an investor's assets, bringing a high level of concentrated, property-specific risk. Real estate is generally illiquid and, if held for a long time, may have a significant unrealized capital gain. A seller considering the sale or monetization of a property should consider its current value relative to historical and expected value in the future, taxes on any transaction, availability of credit, and interest rate levels.

Two key strategies to consider include mortgage financing and a donor-advised fund or charitable trust.

Mortgage Financing

Normally, a sale of an income-producing property to an external party results in the immediate payment of capital gains taxes, loss of control, and no ability to benefit from future appreciation. Therefore, mortgage financing can be an attractive strategy to raise funds without suffering from any of those three negative effects.

With a nonrecourse loan, the lender's only recourse is to seize the property if the loan is not paid. The borrower effectively has a put option on the property. If the property value falls below the loan amount, the borrower could simply default on the loan, keep the loan proceeds, and "put" the property to the lender. A loan on income-producing property could have zero cash flow and zero tax effects on the borrower if the property's income covers the interest on the loan and other property expenses. The concentration risk is reduced because the loan proceeds could presumably be invested in liquid and diversified investments.

In effect, the borrower can still participate in future property appreciation but has a leveraged investment position. The borrower obtains a similar amount of funds that would have been received from an outright sale and still benefits from future appreciation.

Donor-Advised Fund (DAF) or Charitable Trust

A DAF can allow the property owner to take a tax deduction, gift more money to the charity, and influence the use of the donation. For example, an investor owns property worth $5 million and would like to make a $5 million contribution to a local hospital in exchange for having a new children's clinic named after his mother. The property was originally purchased for $3 million, and the investor has deducted $1.3 million of depreciation expense, making the current tax basis $1.7 million. If sold for $5 million, the investor would owe capital gains taxes on a $2 million capital gain and recapture taxes on $1.3 million ($3 million – $1.7 million). Instead, the investor could contribute the property to a DAF for the hospital and take a $5 million tax deduction, and the tax-exempt hospital could sell or retain the property with no tax due. Therefore, the gains and depreciation recapture are never taxed.

MODULE QUIZ 20.3

1. For which individual would reducing specific risk be *most appropriate*?
   A. An owner who holds 100% of a private business and the position is 40% of his total assets.
   B. An executive who owns shares of her employer's company and the position is 40% of her total assets.
   C. A spouse who inherited a real estate investment and the position is 10% of the spouse's total assets.
2. Which of the following owners of a concentrated position would *most likely* wish to retain control of the position as part of a monetization strategy?
   A. The owner of a rental apartment property.
   B. The owner of a warehouse who leases the building to a private company he owns.
   C. Young children who inherit a concentrated position in private stock of the company founded by their father.
3. The primary issue for a manager advising the holder of a concentrated position in a private company versus a public company is:
   A. determining the investment's value.
   B. determining the relevant tax rates to apply.
   C. evaluating the impact of currency values.

MODULE 20.4: GIFT AND ESTATE PLANNING

Video covering this content is available online.

LOS 20.i: Discuss objectives—tax and non-tax—in planning the transfer of wealth.

Gift and Estate Planning

An individual's **estate** is everything that is owned by the individual, including financial assets, real estate (immovable property), collections (e.g., art, stamps, coins), businesses, and intangible assets (e.g., trademarks, copyrights, patents).

Estate planning is the planning process associated with transferring the estate to others during an individual's lifetime or at death so that the assets go to the intended individuals or entities in the most efficient way (e.g., tax minimization).

Key objectives in gift and estate planning include the following.

Ensuring Adequate Liquidity and Ongoing Income

Funds are required to ensure the donors and beneficiaries meet their lifestyle goals and to ensure potential estate taxes are covered.

Control Over Assets

It is possible for the individual to provide beneficial ownership of the assets to the beneficiaries but not provide them with control of the assets, which is the same with charities—the individual donor may maintain control over the assets donated and direct how the funds are to be spent.

Asset Protection

In some cases, trusts may shield assets from creditors as well as jurisdictions that provide statutory ownership that effectively gives one person the right to the assets of another. If the system has **forced heirship** rules, for example, children have a right to a portion of a parent's estate, regardless of the location of the child vis-à-vis the parent, the relationship that exists between the parent and child, or even the relationship between the parents.

EXAMPLE: Forced heirship

Hope and Larry have been married for 40 years. They have two married children, Emma, age 32, and Toby, age 34. The forced heirship regime under which the family lives entitles a surviving spouse to 30% of the total estate, and the children are entitled to split 30% of the total estate. Assume Larry passes away with a total estate of €1,800,000.

Under the forced heirship rules, **determine** the amount Hope and each child will inherit. Will Larry be able to leave his sister €800,000?

Answer:

Under the forced heirship rules, Hope is entitled to 30% of the total estate or (0.30)(€1,800,000) = €540,000.

Under the forced heirship rules, the children are entitled to split 30% of the total estate or (0.30)(€1,800,000) = €540,000 in total, meaning there is €270,000 for each child.

In total, only €540,000 + €540,000 = €1,080,000 of the total €1,800,000 is distributed according to forced heirship rules. The remaining €720,000 may be left to Larry's sister. Therefore, it would not be possible to leave her €800,000.

Laws across the globe can vary dramatically. Many of the differences are due to the foundations upon which the legal systems are based. For example, a civil law system is based on old Roman law. In such a system, laws are handed down (i.e., a top-down system) by a legislative body. In contrast, a common law system, based primarily on old English law, is more "bottom up." Judges play very important roles in common law systems by refining any existing laws to meet particular situations. Once made by a judge, the decisions become precedent to be applied in future cases.

Tax-Effective Transfer of Assets

The two primary means of transferring assets are through gifts and bequests. Gifts transferred during one's lifetime may be subject to **gift tax**, and bequests (transfers after death) may be subject to estate taxes paid by the grantor/transferor or inheritance taxes paid by the recipient. In many countries, there are tax-free allowances applying to gifts and transfers that would allow for the reduction of gift, estate, and inheritance taxes. A prudent financial plan would ensure all the available tax-free allowances are used as much as possible. Asset transfers before death are sometimes preferable, especially if the capital gains can be taxed at lower rates (e.g., beneficiaries).

In the absence of **generation-skipping transfer taxes (GSTT)**, transferring assets directly to a third generation (e.g., grandparent directly to grandchild, bypassing the parent) avoids possible double taxation. Therefore, some countries have a GSTT that is often subject to a lifetime GSTT exclusion amount, so only transfers above the exclusion amount would attract GSTT.

Maintain Family Wealth

A family governance system may reduce or eliminate family disputes regarding investment and philanthropic objectives. The governance process is long term in nature, as it is meant to apply to the current and future generations. Items included in governance include trusts, foundations, and life insurance.

Business Succession

Transferring control and ownership to the next generation of the family is done through gifts and bequests. Depending on family circumstances and interest, the existing owner must decide whether to pass on the business to the next generation and to whom or to simply sell the business to an external party.

Charity

Charitable donations may be tax effective when they fall under gift and/or estate tax exemptions. As well, charitable donations may allow for a current tax deduction to the donor. Finally, establishing a private foundation may allow a family to maintain a long-term or permanent legacy.

LOS 20.j: Discuss strategies for achieving estate, bequest, and lifetime gift objectives in common law and civil law regimes.

General Estate Planning

The most common tool used to transfer assets is a **will** (or a **testament**). A will is the legal document that states the rights that others will have to your assets at your death. The person transferring assets through a will is known as a **testator**.

Probate is a legal process that takes place at death, during which a court determines the validity of the decedent's will, inventories the decedent's property, resolves any claims against the decedent, and distributes remaining property according to the will. Probate involves considerable paperwork and court appearances, and all costs associated with the probate process, which can be significant, are borne by the decedent's estate. If the decedent leaves no will or the will is deemed invalid, the decedent is said to have died **intestate**, and the distribution of the assets will be determined by the court.

Forced heirship rules, as mentioned before, caused some to try to get around such rules in the past. For example, they may transfer assets to an offshore trust in a different jurisdiction or give away assets before death.

Trusts are a common estate planning tool whereby the settlor establishes the trust by contributing assets and a trustee is assigned to maintain the assets for the beneficiaries designated by the settlor. Testamentary trusts are established when the settlor dies and inter vivos trusts are established while the settlor is still alive. Although the assets are held "in trust," legal ownership of the assets may be with the settlor or the trustee. In contrast, a foundation is able to hold assets in its own name.

Lifetime Gifts and Testamentary Bequests

As discussed previously, giving away assets before death is often a good estate planning technique and is known as a lifetime gratuitous transfer. Such gifts may or may not be subject to tax; for example, in some countries, transfers to spouses are tax free.

If assets are transferred upon death, the process is known as a **testamentary bequest** or a **testamentary gratuitous transfer** (or an inheritance from the perspective of the beneficiary). Estate or inheritance taxes may be due and set on a flat rate basis or **progressive tax rate schedule**, with increasing rates for greater wealth transferred. There is sometimes an allowance or threshold amount for which no transfer tax applies; it could be periodic (e.g., annual gift tax exclusion) and/or lifetime.

EXAMPLE: Inheritance tax (flat rate)

Ernestine, a widower, recently died. She was a resident in the country of Mosario at the time of her death and had a total estate valued at MOS 5 million. Her children are the beneficiaries of her estate. Mosario imposes an inheritance tax on estates worth over MOS 2 million at a flat rate of 25%. How much inheritance tax must be paid by the children?

Answer:

(MOS 5 million – MOS 2 million) × 25% = MOS 0.75 million

EXAMPLE: Estate tax (progressive rates)

Martin, who was single, recently died. He was a resident in the country of Karene at the time of his death and had a taxable estate of KAR 1.8 million. Martin was eligible for KAR 0.4 of exemptions.

An excerpt from Karene's progressive estate tax rates is as follows:

Taxable estate (KAR)	Tax rate (%)
Up to 500,000	5
500,001 to 1,000,000	7
1,000,001 to 1,500,000	12
1,500,001 to 2,000,000	15

How much estate tax is payable upon Martin's death?

Reading 20

Answer:

The taxable estate is KAR 1.8 million – KAR 0.4 million = KAR 1.4 million.

Tax on first 500,000 (5%)	KAR 25,000
Tax on next 500,000 (7%)	KAR 35,000
Tax on remaining 400,000 (12%)	KAR 48,000

Total estate tax is KAR 108,000.

A client with excess capital may gift the capital now or bequeath it at death. Doing so now and making use of the tax-free exemptions is generally considered prudent because, had the gift not been made during the lifetime, the appreciated amount would be subject to future estate or inheritance tax. By gifting earlier, there are less amounts subject to future estate or inheritance tax. As well, assuming the giver's tax rate is higher than the receiver's tax rate, the resulting and periodic income generated by the gift (e.g., interest, dividends) would be subject to a lower tax rate.

Charitable Gratuitous Transfers

There are three benefits of charitable gifts (e.g., appreciated securities):

1. The donor usually does not have to pay gift tax.
2. The donor receives an immediate tax deduction for the gift, which reduces the donor's current year tax liability.
3. The charity is usually tax exempt so it can invest the funds and there would be tax-free compounding.

Efficiency of Lifetime Gifts vs. Testamentary Bequests

This approach calculates a ratio of a gift now versus bequest at death. A ratio above/below 1 indicates that from a tax perspective, it is favorable/unfavorable to gift now. The calculations are based on the FV after tax to the receiver. Any FV after-tax calculations require assumptions, and the conclusions are only as good as the assumptions.

The basic form of the ratio is as follows:

FV after tax to the receiver if gifted now / FV after tax to the receiver if bequeathed at death

$$RV_{\text{tax-free gift}} = FV_{\text{gift}} / FV_{\text{bequest}}$$

There are two tax scenarios to consider.

1. The gift now is tax free to both the receiver and the donor.
2. The gift is taxable with tax paid by the receiver.

The relevant tax factors to consider are:

- r_g and t_g are the pretax return earned and the applicable tax rate on those earnings for assets held by the gift receiver,

- r_e and t_e are the pretax return earned and the applicable tax rate on those earnings for assets held by the gift giver,
- T_e is the estate tax rate and would be paid from the estate, and
- T_g is the gift tax rate and is assumed to be paid by the receiver.

$$FV_{gift} = [1 + r_g(1 - t_g)]^n$$

$$FV_{bequest} = [1 + r_e(1 - t_e)]^n(1 - T_e)$$

The two potential RV ratios are as follows:

1. RV of a tax-free gift, $T_g = 0$

$$RV_{\text{tax-free gift}} = RV_{\text{tax-free gift}} = \frac{FV_{gift}}{FV_{bequest}} = \frac{\left[1+r_g\left(1-t_g\right)\right]^n}{\left[1+r_e\left(1-t_e\right)\right]^n\left(1-T_e\right)}$$

2. RV of a taxable gift, T_g, paid by receiver

$$RV_{\text{taxable gift}} = RV_{\text{taxable gift}} = \frac{FV_{gift}}{FV_{bequest}} = \frac{\left[1+r_g\left(1-t_g\right)\right]^n\left(1-T_g\right)}{\left[1+r_e\left(1-t_e\right)\right]^n\left(1-T_e\right)}$$

RV of a tax-free gift, $T_g = 0$: The numerator projects FV after tax of the investment if held by the receiver. The denominator projects the FV after tax if held by the giver and then subject to estate taxes.

RV of a taxable gift, T_g, paid by the receiver: This is a variation on the tax-free gift formula with a subtraction in the numerator of $-T_g$ to reflect that the receiver of the gift must pay a tax and has less to invest. All else the same, it now makes gifting less attractive.

EXAMPLE: Gifting now vs. a bequest

Mary Jane is considering making a gift now or a bequest upon death. The assumptions are:

1. Life expectancy is an additional 20 years.
2. The pretax return and investment tax rate are 8% and 35%, respectively, for both Mary Jane and the receiver.
3. The gift tax rate and estate tax rate are 25% and 40%, respectively.

Scenario 1: Assuming the gift is not subject to gift taxes, **compute** the relative attractiveness of a gift or bequest and recommend the best approach.

Scenario 2: Assuming the gift is subject to gift taxes and the taxes are paid by the receiver, **compute** the relative attractiveness of a gift or bequest and recommend the best approach.

Reading 20

Answer:

Scenario 1:

$$[1 + 0.08(1 - 0.35)]^{20} / [(1 + 0.08(1 - 0.35))^{20} (1 - 0.40)] =$$
$$2.756 / ((2.756)(0.60)) = 2.756 / 1.654 = 1.67$$

Gifting now is more attractive.

Scenario 2:

$$[(1 - 0.25)(1 + 0.08(1 - 0.35))]^{20} / [(1 + 0.08(1 - 0.35))^{20} (1 - 0.40)] =$$
$$((0.75)(2.756)) / ((2.756)(0.60)) = 2.067 / 1.654 = 1.25$$

Gifting now is not as favorable, but still best.

MODULE QUIZ 20.4

1. The main objectives of estate planning are to minimize taxes and:
   A. achieve effective diversification.
   B. transfer assets to heirs or others.
   C. maximize returns.
2. When investors make charitable gifts of appreciated securities, they are usually able to:
   A. avoid capital gains taxes but are not able to take a deduction for the gift.
   B. take a deduction in an amount designed to exactly offset the capital gains tax.
   C. deduct the market value of the gift and avoid capital gains taxes.

3. Jan Jones has excess capital and is only concerned with maximizing the value of funds passed onto her heirs. She has an assumed after-tax return of investments of 8.5% with a tax rate on investments of 33%. Her heirs have an assumed pretax return on investments of 8% with a tax rate on investments of 25%. Gift and estate tax rates are 40% and 30%, respectively.
   A. If the gift would fall within the gift tax exclusion amount, **discuss** whether it is better to gift now or make a bequest.

   B. If the gift would exceed the gift tax exclusion amount, **discuss** whether it is better to gift now or make a bequest.

   C. **Discuss** any nonmonetary considerations in deciding whether to make a gift versus a bequest.

MODULE 20.5: ESTATE PLANNING AND FAMILY GOVERNANCE

Video covering this content is available online.

LOS 20.k: Describe considerations related to managing wealth across multiple generations.

Trusts

Trusts are a means by which a settlor (grantor) can transfer assets to beneficiaries outside of the probate process. The trustee (manager of the trust) holds the assets and manages them in the best interests of the beneficiaries according to the constraints of the trust documents. Trusts are recognized by, and are most prevalent in, common law countries.

Asset ownership can be a fuzzy concept with trusts. It might help to think of the assets as being placed in limbo somewhere between the settlor and the beneficiary. A trustee actually has possession of and manages the assets for the benefit of the settlor and/or beneficiaries and may be considered the owner of the assets for tax purposes only. Legal ownership of the assets may be held by the settlor or transferred to the trustee or beneficiaries, while ownership for tax purposes may reside with the settlor or the trustee. Therefore, the legal owner and the owner for tax purposes may be two different entities, depending on the structure of the trust.

In a **revocable trust**, the settlor can rescind (revoke) the trust and resume ownership of the assets. The settlor is considered the legal owner of the assets for tax and reporting purposes, and persons such as creditors and divorcing spouses may make claims against the trust assets.

In an **irrevocable trust**, the settlor relinquishes ownership and control. The trustee is considered the owner of the assets for tax purposes and is responsible for reporting and paying taxes on income generated by the trust. The irrevocable trust protects the trust assets from claims against the settlor. Note that a trust will not protect assets if it is deemed to have been created in anticipation of a claim.

The trustee may be responsible for distributing assets to the beneficiaries. In a **fixed trust**, the pattern of distributions to the beneficiaries is predetermined by the settlor and incorporated into the trust documents. When setting up a trust for a minor, for example, the settlor may wish the trustee to distribute a fixed portion of the assets when the minor reaches 21 years of age and then distribute a given percentage each year until the assets are depleted.

With a **discretionary trust**, the trustee determines how the assets are to be distributed. The primary concern is that the assets are distributed to produce the greatest benefit to the beneficiary. The settlor may convey general wishes through the trust documentation or through a letter of wishes. Beneficiaries have no legal right to either the income or the assets of the discretionary trust. Therefore, the trust assets are protected from claims against the beneficiaries.

There are several reasons for using a trust:

- Avoid giving control of assets to beneficiaries who would not be able to properly manage them.
- Allows the settlor to direct the assets for specific uses.
- Avoid dilution of ownership interest in a private business in countries where there is joint ownership and division of assets acquired during marriage.
- Avoid probate.
- There may be potentially lower tax rates. For example, the trust or the beneficiaries may be subject to a lower tax rate than the settlor. Or the trust could be set up in a country with a low tax rate.

Foundations

Foundations are most prevalent in civil law countries and maintain assets to fund charitable causes. Types of foundations include private and family. Foundations generally provide the donor with control in managing the assets. In many jurisdictions, private foundations are often bound by annual spending rules (e.g., 5% of investment assets) to maintain tax-free status. Additionally, the donor receives a tax deduction for the assets gifted to the foundation. It is becoming more common for foundations to have a fixed life rather than a perpetual one.

Life Insurance

As the only assets transferred by the grantor (policyowner) are the premiums paid, life insurance policies represent a very efficient means for transferring assets or even helping beneficiaries pay inheritance taxes. In many jurisdictions, the premiums are not usually considered part of the grantor's estate for tax purposes. In most jurisdictions, life insurance proceeds pass to beneficiaries without tax consequences. Depending on the jurisdiction, the policy might provide tax-free accumulation of wealth and/or loans to the policyholder on beneficial terms.

Life insurance can be used in combination with a trust. By establishing a trust on behalf of the beneficiaries and making that trust the direct beneficiary of the life insurance policy, the policyholder may transfer assets to young or disabled beneficiaries outside of the probate process.

Companies

A **controlled foreign corporation (CFC)** is set up in a country outside of the investor's home country for which the investor may hold assets. The investor would have a controlling interest in the company. It may be possible for the investment income earned in the CFC to escape taxation until the dividends are paid to the shareholder(s) or when the shares are sold.

Family Governance

Family enterprises often go through the following cycle: first generation generates wealth, next generation holds onto the wealth, and the last generation spends it. This reduction in wealth is caused by one or more of the following reasons: wealth dilution over many family members, no interest in continuing the family business, and poor financial literacy and planning. Therefore, a robust system of family governance could reduce the negative outcomes.

Family governance can be thought of as the mechanism for families to maintain and increase their wealth over the long term. The family values, mission, and vision must be determined as a group and there should be the appropriate legal documents and family agreements (binding and nonbinding) to allow for proper implementation of plans. Proper family governance will pay sufficient attention to the family's human capital (e.g., special skills with income-earning ability), intellectual capital, and social capital (e.g., philanthropy). Ultimately, proper communication within the family and teaching the younger members how to manage the family wealth will ensure maintenance of the wealth over the long term.

Governing Bodies Within the Family

Board of Directors (BOD)

A BOD is applicable at a much more advanced phase of the family business and may start out as an "advisory board" before evolving to a more formal BOD. Here, external expertise is brought in to assist in mitigating overconfidence bias, particularly with the business founder. The BOD is usually comprised of family members active in the business plus the external experts, and together, they must determine the business focus and objectives as well as make decisions in the best interests of the shareholders.

Family Council

Certain family members are selected to liaise directly with the BOD. Details of the family council are included in the family constitution, the latter of which would have been formulated with the input of the whole family.

Family Assembly

The family assembly is an annual (or more frequent) meeting of the family members to review the direction of the family business. One of the objectives of the family assembly is to promote transparency and minimize family conflicts in the process.

Family Office

The family office is an investment management hub but also fulfills other administrative duties such as accounting and legal.

Family Foundation

The family foundation is the philanthropic arm of the family, which is usually long term in nature. It is important to determine and agree upon the philanthropic goals.

Family Conflict Resolution

As conflicts are inevitable within families, it is important to have a clear **family constitution** in place. The family constitution is usually nonbinding but would normally contain sufficient detail to allow for the process of conflict resolution to begin. With conflict resolution, some or all of the issues discussed may become binding in the process.

Business Succession

Succession planning is usually focused on passing on the business to the next generation or simply selling it.

Passing the Business on to the Next Generation

The founder may do a direct transfer or use a trust to pass on the shares to the next generation. It could be done before death or upon death. If done before death, the founder could elect to maintain ownership of the voting shares to maintain control and only transfer the nonvoting shares. Another possibility is to transfer the voting shares only to the active members of the business and transfer nonvoting shares to the nonactive members.

During the transition, having both a BOD and family council in place could make the process more transparent and fairer to all family members. Ideally, the BOD will have sufficient external expertise and the family council will include members of each generation. Given that the family members will want to have access to funds to support their lifestyles, having a family council in place could help with satisfying the cash flow needs of the family members with the capital needs of the business.

Additionally, it is important that both the BOD and family council consist of members with diverse viewpoints to avoid social proof bias; it is the bias of "going with the flow" without being completely informed of the important details that could impact the decision.

Disposition of the Business

Assuming there is no appropriate person(s) in the next generation to pass on the business, a sale of the business may be necessary. As discussed earlier in the behavioral finance section, endowment bias is likely to be an issue, which could overinflate the seller's expectations. The seller may need to be counseled as to what is most realistic. Furthermore, key issues such as taxation, liquidity, and philanthropy issues (amongst others) must be addressed during the transition, as they will likely have a significant impact on proceeds from the sale.

Timing of the Disposition

An estate freeze, establishing a limited partnership and gifting, or transferring to a trust may reduce taxes on future appreciation. Furthermore, the value of a nonpublicly traded family business should be reduced to reflect lack of liquidity/marketability as well as reflect a minority interest discount if the ownership percentage sold does not provide control. The value reduction could result in lower gift and estate taxes.

Choosing Trustees

Appointed trustees could be individual or institutional. The former may have a more "personal touch" and know the parties personally, which may allow the trustee to make more informed decisions. The latter may work well from a long-term perspective over several generations combined in lower fees and a wider skill set. It may be prudent to have an ongoing dialogue between trustees and beneficiaries to allow for the trustees to make decisions that would be consistent with the settlor's desire while at the same time ensuring that the beneficiaries' needs are met.

If a family is large enough or has a sufficiently large amount of assets, a private trust company (PTC) that is tailored specifically for that family may be useful.

After the Disposition

The sale proceeds will give rise to a sudden liquidity inflow. Those funds could be used to finance the next business venture or be donated to charitable causes. Regarding the latter, the family should be able to agree on the next steps in terms of charitable goals and maximizing its social capital. In some cases, the family may desire to be less broad with its philanthropy and specify which charities to donate to and how much.

Planning for the Unexpected

Divorce

Some countries may recognize the rights of those involved in long-term domestic arrangements while others only recognize rights when there is a formal marriage in place.

The division of financial assets in the event of a marriage breakdown should be addressed in advance—that is often done through a prenuptial agreement (before marriage). Postnuptial agreements occur after the marriage is over and deal with financial matters after the marriage. Depending on the country, such agreements may or may not be binding.

If a prenuptial agreement is not in place, then the courts may need to get involved and could end up making decisions that may not be acceptable by one or both parties.

Finally, some jurisdictions do not consider marital assets to consist of only those that were acquired as part of the marriage. For example, inherited assets (before or during the marriage) by one spouse only, such as a family business, may be considered joint marital assets. In such a situation, trusts and other vehicles could be used to place the family business in a separate entity that would not be subject to division between the former spouses upon divorce.

Incapacity

Living wills and durable powers of attorney can be used to address potential incapacity in the future. A living will addresses an individual's medical care upon becoming incapacitated and is usually a legally binding document. A durable power of attorney allows a guardian to act on behalf of the grantor even after the grantor becomes incapacitated. The power of attorney often covers financial and medical matters.

Having a living will and/or durable power of attorney far in advance is potentially important in managing family wealth, as it allows decisions to be made by a guardian without delay upon the wealth owner becoming incapacitated. Furthermore, advance planning allows a suitable and qualified guardian to be appointed, likely one who is familiar with the business and family matters.

MODULE QUIZ 20.5

1. For estate planning purposes, investments in privately held companies are usually:
   A. tax efficient because gains realized are usually taxed at long-term rates.
   B. tax inefficient because it is difficult to determine fair market value; therefore, the correct amount to be taxed cannot be determined.
   C. tax efficient because they can be transferred from an estate using a valuation discount.
2. Jim Johnson is a widower and has a large amount of excess capital. He can either (1) make a very large gift now or bequest at death to his children or (2) make a gift now or bequest at death to his grandchildren.
   A. **Discuss** any financial or nonfinancial considerations that will determine if he disposes of the assets directly to his children or his grandchildren.

   B. **Discuss** how a trust might be used if he has reservations about the ability of his grandchildren to manage the money. **Recommend** and **explain** why a fixed or discretionary trust is likely to be best.

KEY CONCEPTS

LOS 20.a

The main categories of taxes are income tax, capital gains tax, wealth/property tax, stamp duties, and wealth transfer tax.

The general equation for capital gains is as follows:

net sales price – tax (cost) basis = capital gain/loss

Realized capital gains occur upon the actual disposition of an asset. Unrealized capital gains are "paper gains," which represent appreciation on unsold items. Depending on the holding period of the investments, the capital gains may be subject to a short-term (usually higher) rate or a long-term (usually lower) rate. Some countries differentiate between investment gains (lower or no tax on capital gains) and trading gains (taxed at regular rates).

There are three main types of investment accounts is taxable, tax deferred (TDA), and tax exempt (TEA).

LOS 20.b

A tax haven is a jurisdiction with very low or no tax rates for residents and foreign investors.

A territorial tax system taxes only income that is earned locally (e.g., Hong Kong SAR).

A worldwide tax system will impose taxes on all sources of income, which inevitably leads to double taxation, i.e., taxation on the same income by more than one jurisdiction. However, relief may be provided in the form of tax credits by the home jurisdiction for taxes already paid in the source jurisdiction or bilateral tax treaties.

LOS 20.c

A tax-efficient strategy results in relatively high after-tax returns compared to pretax returns.

There are four common metrics used in examining tax efficiency:

- After-tax holding period return.
- After-tax post-liquidation return.
- After-tax excess returns.
- Tax-efficiency ratio.

LOS 20.d

Taxable accounts involve one or more tax rates on income (e.g., interest, dividends) or returns (e.g., realized capital gains) to determine R′.

$$FV_{AT} = (1 + R')^n$$

With TEAs, after-tax funds are deposited so no tax is due on the returns earned or on withdrawals.

$$FV_{AT} = (1 + R)^n$$

With TDAs, pretax funds are deposited and the investor may take a tax deduction for the amount contributed, thereby reducing taxable income and taxes due. All tax is deferred until withdrawal, allowing tax-deferred compounding.

$$FV_{AT} = (1 + R)^n(1 - t)$$

In general, tax-efficient assets (e.g., equities that generate capital gains, which are often subject to lower tax rates) should be placed in taxable accounts and tax-inefficient assets (e.g., taxable bonds that generate taxable interest, which is often subject to higher tax rates) should be placed in tax-exempt or tax-deferred accounts.

LOS 20.e

Tax management strategies can be classified as follows:

- Investments held in a manner to minimize taxes (e.g., tax-exempt accounts, lower long-term capital gains tax rate)
- Deferring income recognition (e.g., limiting dispositions, waiting for tax rates to fall, tax loss harvesting)

Four common investment vehicles include:

- Partnerships
- Mutual funds
- Exchange-traded funds (ETFs)
- Separately managed accounts (SMAs)

Tax loss harvesting involves the sale of securities with embedded losses to offset gains, which will lower the tax liability for the current year.

Many tax authorities allow a form of tax lot accounting. When an investor makes a partial sale and has acquired the stock on different dates, each at a different cost, the investor may select which tax lots applied to the sale. There are some possibilities:

- Highest in, first out (HIFO) is generally optimal.
- In case future tax rates are expected to be *higher* than current tax rates, first in, first out (FIFO) may be better.
- In case future tax rates are expected to be *lower* than current tax rates, last in, first out (LIFO) may be better.

LOS 20.f

In choosing a strategy to manage the concentrated position, the following factors should be considered:

- Level of concentration—the higher it is, the timelier the response needs to be to reduce the risk.
- Tax basis and tax rate—the lower and the higher, respectively, the greater the taxes due.

- Liquidity—the more illiquid, the greater the costs of risk reduction.
- Time horizon—more time may allow the concentration to be reduced gradually, which lowers the overall cost.
- Investor restrictions—restrictions may prevent an outright sale.
- Nonfinancial matters—emotional attachments may hinder the risk reduction process.

LOS 20.g

Strategies for managing a concentrated position in public equities include the following:

- Staged diversification strategy over multiple years to spread out tax liability
- Completion portfolio using other assets to complement/complete the concentrated position
- Equity monetization by hedging a large part of the risk in the position using derivatives and then borrow using the hedged position as collateral
- Zero-cost collars used to lower initial cost by giving up some stock upside, the put premium paid and call premium received are equal
- Covered call writing can be a staged diversification assuming the share price appreciates sufficiently
- Exchange fund with a pooling of investments on a tax-free basis
- Charitable remainder trust to benefit both beneficiaries and a designated charity

LOS 20.h

Strategies for managing concentrated positions in privately owned businesses include the following:

- IPO
- Direct sale to another investor
- Sale of non-essential business assets
- Personal line of credit secured by company shares (owner borrows from company or from a third-party lender)
- Leveraged recapitalization (e.g., private equity firm)
- Sale to employee stock ownership plan

Strategies for managing concentrated positions in real estate include the following:

- Mortgage financing (e.g., nonrecourse loan)
- Donor-advised fund or charitable trust (e.g., avoid tax on gains and depreciation recapture)

LOS 20.i

An individual's estate is everything that is owned by the individual. Estate planning is the planning process associated with transferring the estate to others during an individual's lifetime or at death so the assets go to the individuals or entities intended and in the most efficient way.

Key objectives in gift and estate planning include the following:

- Ensuring adequate liquidity and ongoing income
- Control over assets
- Asset protection
- Tax-effective transfer of assets
- Maintain family wealth
- Business succession
- Charity

LOS 20.j

Computing estate and/or inheritance taxes may involve a flat tax rate or a progressive tax rate schedule.

There are three benefits of charitable gifts:

- The donor usually does not have to pay gift tax.
- The donor receives an immediate tax deduction for the gift, which reduces the donor's current year tax liability.
- The charity is usually tax exempt, so it can invest the funds and there will be tax-free compounding.

In looking at the relative value of a tax-free gift, consider the following equations:

- $RV_{\text{tax-free gift}} = FV_{\text{gift}} / FV_{\text{bequest}}$
- $FV_{\text{gift}} = [1 + r_g(1 - t_g)]^n$
- $FV_{\text{bequest}} = [1 + r_e(1 - t_e)]^n(1 - T_e)$

LOS 20.k

Trusts, foundations, life insurance, and companies are common estate planning tools. It is important to distinguish between testamentary versus inter vivos trusts, revocable versus irrevocable trusts, and fixed versus discretionary trusts. Trusts are used mainly for control, asset protection, and tax management reasons.

Family governance can be thought of as the mechanism for families to maintain and increase their wealth over the long term. Governing bodies may include a board of directors, a family council, a family assembly, a family office, and a family foundation. Conflict resolution begins with the family constitution.

Other important issues to anticipate include business succession/disposition, divorce, and incapacity.

ANSWER KEY FOR MODULE QUIZZES

Module Quiz 20.1

1. **A** Some of the gain will be deferred each year and such stocks pay low dividends. Bonds and value stocks will pay more of their return in the more heavily taxed interest and dividends. (LOS 20.a)

2. **C** The return after taxes on interest income, dividends, and realized capital gains factors in the proportions of the return sources and the respective taxes on each is calculated as follows:

   $0.15[1 - 0.10(0.35) - 0.25(0.20) - 0.35(0.20)] = 0.15(0.845) = 0.12675 = 12.68\%$

   (LOS 20.c)

Module Quiz 20.2

1. **C** The expected future value after paying annual taxes:

   $\$1{,}000[1 + 0.05(1 - 0.30)]^{10} = \$1{,}410.60$

   (LOS 20.d)

2. **B** The expected after-tax balance in the account in 20 years:

   $\$100{,}000[(1.10)^{20}(1 - 0.30)] = \$470{,}925$

   (LOS 20.d)

3. **C** The expected balance in the account in 20 years (no taxes need to be paid for a TEA):

   $\$100{,}000(1.10)^{20} = \$672{,}750$

   (LOS 20.d)

4. **A** The investor has $480,000 [$800,000 × (1 – 0.40)] after tax invested in equity. The bonds in the tax-exempt account are not subject to taxation and, therefore, are not adjusted. On an after-tax basis, the investor has 44.4% in equities [$480,000 / ($480,000 + $600,000)] and the other 55.6% in bonds [$600,000 / ($480,000 + $600,000)]. (LOS 20.d)

5. **C** Some countries exempt the interest income for some types of bonds from taxation. Because most of the return from bonds is interest income, there is no benefit in placing such tax-exempt bonds in a TDA because no tax is owed. The after-tax return from standard (taxable) corporate bonds would benefit from locating them in the TDA because their income return is generally taxed. High-growth stocks pay small dividends and provide most of their return from capital gains. By extending the holding period, tax deferral will be possible even in a taxable account. In turn, the greatest benefit is from locating the corporate bonds in the TDA. (LOS 20.e)

6. **C** If the stock is sold, there is a capital loss of $50,000 ($90,000 – $140,000), so combined with the $80,000 capital gain, there is a net capital gain of $30,000. The tax is 30% × $30,000 = $9,000.

   If the stock is not sold, the taxes on the full gain are $80,000 × 30% – $24,000. The recognition of the capital loss would result in a tax savings of $15,000 ($24,000 – $9,000). In that case, the benefit from harvesting the loss can also be calculated as the capital loss times the tax rate: $50,000 × 30% = $15,000. (LOS 20.e)

7. **A** The appreciation rate is the same in both cases, and assuming future tax rates do not change, there is a benefit to the tax deferral inherent in tax loss harvesting. Tax loss harvesting changes the pattern of tax payments (e.g., the payments are pushed into the future). However, if the stock is sold in the current year, the tax savings of $15,000 can be immediately reinvested and earn the 10% return. Therefore, strategy 1 will provide the higher future accumulation. (LOS 20.e)

Module Quiz 20.3

1. **A** A 10% position is not that concentrated and the contribution to portfolio-specific risk is not that great. Of the two 40% positions, the owner has more reason to diversify and reduce specific risk because a privately held business contains much more risk than a publicly traded company. (LOS 20.f, 20.h)

2. **B** Using the building for a business the warehouse owner also owns gives him a reason to retain control. (LOS 20.f, 20.h)

3. **A** With a public company, the share price (value) should be relatively easy to determine. In contrast, with a private company, the value is more difficult to determine and is subject to the intended use of the buyer and other factors. Currency and tax issues would have to be analyzed in either situation. Taxation might be more straightforward in selling the stock of a public company, but determining value is the most significant and time-consuming issue in valuing a private company. (LOS 20.h)

Module Quiz 20.4

1. **B** The primary objectives of estate planning are to minimize taxes and to facilitate the tax-efficient transfer of assets to heirs or recipients of charitable bequests. Diversification and maximizing returns are usually not the objectives of estate planning and are part of the grantor's/settlor's investment policy statement while accumulating assets throughout working years and throughout retirement. (LOS 20.i)

2. **C** When an investor makes a charitable gift of appreciated securities, the investor is usually able to avoid gift transfer taxes and can take an income tax deduction equal to the current fair market value of the gift. The appreciated securities continue to avoid capital gains taxes once transferred to the tax-exempt organization. (LOS 20.j)

3. **A** The giver can earn a higher after-tax return of 8.5% versus 6% for the receiver (8%(1 – 0.25) = 6%). *Note the return for the giver is in after-tax terms while the return for the receiver is given in pretax terms.* That favors waiting to make a bequest at death if the investment is held in the estate long enough and compounding at the higher rate of 8.5%. But giving now avoids any estate tax that could lower the return to less than 6%, making giving now more beneficial assuming that the gift tax is avoided. The relevant equation is as follows:

   $FV_{gift} / FV_{bequest} = [1 + r_g(1 - t_g)]^n / [1 + r_e(1 - t_e)]^n(1 - T_e)$

   Until the time period (*n*) is known, the optimal solution of gifting now versus making a bequest is unknown.

   B The giver can earn a higher after-tax return, and waiting to make a bequest will be subject to a lower transfer tax of 30%. Therefore, wait and make a bequest.

   C Gifting now gives up control and the assets cannot be recovered if the giver changes their mind or needs the funds. That may create a reason to wait and make a bequest. (LOS 20.j)

Module Quiz 20.5

1. **C** Investments in privately held companies are usually tax efficient from an estate planning perspective because they can be transferred after taking a valuation discount, which reduces the basis on which the transfer tax is calculated. The discount relates to uncertainty of true value as well as lack of liquidity and sometimes control. It is true that they are also tax efficient from the standpoint that any gains realized are usually taxed at favorable long-term rates but that pertains to liquidating the assets that would normally not be done before transferring them in an estate. (LOS 20.k)

2. **A** The primary financial consideration for Johnson would be whether he is subject to generation-skipping transfer tax (GSTT). In the absence of GSTT, transferring assets directly to his grandchildren avoids possible double taxation. However, he must check whether his country has a GSTT and whether it might have a lifetime GSTT exclusion amount so that only transfers above the exclusion amount would attract GSTT.

   The primary nonfinancial issue to consider is whether his children need some of the funds, in which case, some of the money will need to go to them.

   B Place the funds in a trust that will be managed for the benefit of the grandchildren. Discretionary is almost certainly best because the trustee can then make decisions to best meet Johnson's intent for how to take care of the grandchildren. (LOS 20.i, 20.k)

READING 21

Risk Management for Individuals

EXAM FOCUS

Be sure you recognize insurance is a risk management and transfer mechanism that in aggregate reduces the expected wealth of the users. Its primary purpose is to protect against adverse financial consequences. Life insurance can insure against premature death and annuities against living too long. Hence, they are risk management tools for the total wealth of the user.

Not every risk warrants the use of insurance. If a risk can be reduced or avoided, that is often the simplest and least expensive way to deal with it. In other cases, it may be best to just accept the risk. If neither of those approaches is acceptable, it may be possible to purchase insurance that will provide monetary compensation if the risk occurs. An investment manager may be able to help clients determine the best approach to a given situation and advise how that solution can change over the client's stages of life.

MODULE 21.1: HUMAN AND FINANCIAL CAPITAL

Video covering this content is available online.

LOS 21.a: Compare the characteristics of human capital and financial capital as components of an individual's total wealth.

LOS 21.b: Discuss the relationships among human capital, financial capital, and economic net worth.

An investor's **total wealth** is composed of both human capital and financial capital. **Human capital (HC)** is the discounted present value of expected future labor income. **Financial capital (FC)** is the sum of all the other assets of an individual. This includes financial items such as stocks, bonds, and alternative investments as well as personal items such as a home, car, and other physical assets.

Expected defined benefit (DB) plan benefits for an individual have elements of both HC and FC. DB benefits are deferred labor income, which suggests treating them as HC, but they have already been earned and paid for with past labor to provide future cash flow. This is more analogous to buying a financial asset (FC) and receiving future cash flows. An individual's expected DB plan benefits are best considered as part of the individual's FC.

Human Capital

Valuing **human capital** is analogous to valuing a stock or bond. Value is the discounted PV of future cash flows. The discount rate applied to the future cash flows is related to the riskiness of the cash flows. Higher risk employment requires a higher discount rate and all else the same reduces the value of the HC. Examples include high yield bond managers and downhill ski racers. Lower risk employment is discounted at lower discount rates. Examples include union employment and tenured college professors.

While the valuation is simple in theory, HC can only be estimated. The estimate requires multiple assumptions: projected future earnings and their rate of growth, mortality rates to determine the probability the earnings will be realized, nominal risk-free discount rates, and income volatility to determine the discount rate. All of these variables are subject to change over time.

EXAMPLE: Estimating HC

Alex Hamilton is 62 and expected to retire in 3 years. His current annual wage is 100,000 and expected to increase 4% per year. The risk-free discount rate is 3%, and his continued employment is considered very risky. A 10% risk premium is assumed. Using this information and the survival probabilities in the table, calculate his HC.

Increase earnings by 4% per year for the 3 years of employment, probability weight the earnings, and discount to the present value (PV) at 13% per year. 13% is the risk-free rate plus the risk premium.

Year	Probability of Life	Projected Wage	Probability Weighted	PV
1	98%	104,000	101,920	90,195
2	98%	108,160	105,997	83,011
3	97%	112,486	109,111	75,619
4	97%	0		
5	96%	0		
			HC =	248,825

Financial capital is the value of all other assets owned by the individual. It includes current assets such as money market assets that may be consumed within the next year, personal assets such as a car or furniture that are likely to be consumed over time, and investment assets that may appreciate over time. Some assets such as real estate may have both consumption and investment characteristics. Investment assets include both publicly traded marketable assets, which are relatively easy to value, and non-publicly traded. The latter include:

- Real estate (other than publicly traded REITs). A home is often an individual's largest single asset and may also be highly leveraged. If leveraged with recourse, default on the loan allows the lender to claim other assets of the individual as well. On a non-recourse loan, the lender can only seize the mortgaged property.
- Annuities (see further discussion later) are economically equivalent to a private defined benefit plan in that they pay a continuing income stream. Their value should include some discount of future cash flows to reflect the potential the payer may default.
- Cash-value life insurance (see further discussion later) is life insurance with a provision to borrow or take some present value portion of the future payout prior to death (which reduces the ultimate payout).
- Business assets or private equity may represent a substantial portion of wealth for some self-employed individuals. This can lead to concentrated risk exposures in the investor's wealth.
- Collectables (such as paintings and book collections) often involve substantial transaction costs and can have elements of personal consumption and utility as well as investment value.
- Pensions can be a significant non-marketable financial asset for some. The pension could be from a private or government entity. The vested portion of the pension already belongs to the individual and can be valued as the discounted value of benefits to be received (PV). The discounting must also include a mortality projection if payments are contingent on the beneficiary being alive (which is typical). The discount rate will reflect the riskiness of the plan portfolio and sponsor as well as any other guarantees or insurance of payment. Future payments of the pension may be indexed for inflation. Typically government pensions will be less risky.

Financial Stages of Life

Economic net worth is the sum of the individual's FC and HC less any liabilities owed by the individual. A typical individual might start an employment career with high HC and low FC. As remaining work career decreases with age, HC generally declines over time while FC increases as the individual saves and invests.

Education. The individual gains knowledge and skills through formal and informal education and apprenticeship. There is minimal emphasis on saving or risk management.

Early career. The individual enters the workforce, often starts a family, and assumes other personal responsibilities. Saving may be difficult and life insurance may be needed to insure substantial HC against death and the cessation of work income to meet continuing financial obligations to the family.

Career development. After becoming established in a career, job skills can continue to expand and upward mobility increases. Financial obligations often increase to fund the college education of children. Successful individuals generally build FC and retirement savings over time.

Peak accumulation. FC accumulation is typically greatest in the decade before retirement. Earnings and the need to accumulate funds for retirement are high. Financial obligations to educate the children are ceasing. Investment risk may start being reduced in anticipation of retirement. Career risk can also be high as it can be more difficult to find equivalent employment in the event of unplanned job loss.

Preretirement. Emphasis continues to be on accumulating FC for retirement, beginning to reduce investment risk, and tax planning for retirement.

Early retirement. Individuals adjust to a new lifestyle. For those with FC and good health, expenses could increase as they make use of the free time. The portfolio emphasis is on managing the portfolio so it will last for the remaining lifetime.

Late retirement. This stage is highly unpredictable. Individuals face longevity risk (out living their assets), increasing health care expenses could be an issue, and cognitive functions used to make decisions can decline.

In all stages, there can be unpredicted needs for health care and/or to care for family members.

The Individual's Balance Sheet

LOS 21.c: Describe an economic (holistic) balance sheet.

The **economic (holistic) balance sheet** extends the traditional balance sheet assets to include HC. Liabilities are extended to include consumption and bequest goals. This more complete economic view allows better planning of resource consumption to meet remaining lifetime goals as seen in the following example of an economic balance sheet. Note that a defined contribution plan balance with an explicit balance would likely have been included in the traditional balance sheet, but DB plan estimated PV likely would not.

EXAMPLE: Holistic balance sheet

(The items in bold italics are those not found on a traditional balance sheet.)

Assets (in thousands):		Liabilities (in thousands):	
Financial		Short-term debt	175
Current assets	500	Home mortgage	500
Investment assets	1,500		
Non-marketable		***Primary capital to fund lifetime expenses***	***3,500***
Home	750		
DC plan balance	1,450		
Private pension	***40***	***Planned bequests***	***1,000***
Government pension	***450***		
Human			
Future labor income	***250***		
Total Assets	4,940	Total Liabilities	5,175

Based only on the traditional balance sheet, the assets of 4,200,000 well exceed explicit debts of 675,000, while the holistic balance sheet shows negative net worth of 235,000. This suggests consumption and bequest plans are unrealistic. However, it is generally more difficult to value the additional items on the economic balance sheet, and the negative net worth could be an estimation error. There could also be missing economic assets such as expected inheritance that need to be included. If net worth is actually negative, it indicates ultimate spending plans will eventually have to change. The relatively low amount of HC (not pension benefits) suggests the individual is near retirement.

For many individuals, total wealth (HC + FC) as well as FC will peak near retirement. Both will then be drawn down in retirement.

The composition of the balance sheet is likely to change over the individual's life cycle. HC is likely the dominant asset for younger individuals. Over time, HC will decline as remaining work life shortens. FC should increase as the individual saves and invests in FC. Net worth can be positive or negative based on the adequacy of savings versus projected needs. Early in the life cycle assets such as real estate and other tangible assets may dominate the balance sheet. Other FC is then likely to increase in the later stages of life as funds are saved and invested. In early retirement, pension benefits are the dominant asset for many. For wealthier individuals pension benefits may be relatively smaller and FC may be relatively larger.

Video covering this content is available online.

MODULE 21.2: RISKS AND INSURANCE

Risk management for individuals requires:

- Specifying the objective, which is to maximize household welfare (utility).
- Identifying the risks to FC and HC.
- Evaluating and managing those risks through:
  - Risk avoidance: choose actions to avoid the chance of the loss occurring.
  - Risk reduction: choose actions that reduce the likelihood or amount of the loss.
  - Risk transfer: use insurance products to transfer the loss to others.
  - Risk retention (self-insurance): maintain sufficient assets to absorb the loss.
- Monitoring results and adjusting as needed.

LOS 21.d: Discuss risks (earnings, premature death, longevity, property, liability, and health risks) in relation to human and financial capital.

The typical risks for individuals include:

- **Earnings risk** (insure with disability insurance) refers to loss in HC. Job loss and other career disruptions can reduce HC and may even lead to the need to consume FC prematurely. Some jobs are inherently more risky than others. A logger has a higher probability of death or injury and resulting loss of HC. A high risk security manager may have a higher risk of job termination. Other jobs are at risk of a location transfer, which could disrupt the HC of a spouse whose job is less mobile and reduce the household's total wealth. Other jobs are cyclical, and income for the self-employed can be less certain.
- **Premature death risk** (insure with life insurance) can be a serious risk early in the career when substantial HC could be lost. In addition, it may cause unexpected expenses that consume limited FC of the survivors.
- **Longevity risk** (insure with annuities) is the opposite of premature death risk as individuals who live too long are at risk of outliving their FC. The determination of how much capital is required for retirement is complicated and risky. A given individual's lifespan is highly uncertain. The return on portfolio assets, rate of inflation, the inclusion or exclusion of inflation adjustment in DB payouts, distribution needs, and other income sources must be estimated. Mortality tables and Monte Carlo simulations are generally used to quantify longevity risk.
- **Property risk** (insure with property insurance) refers to sudden loss in value of physical property (FC). A house or car can be damaged or lost in a flood, a direct loss. This can also trigger unexpected needs such as temporary living or transportation expense or lost income such as rental income, leading to consumption of FC and reduction in total wealth. The loss of business property could reduce FC and also HC of the owner if the property is necessary to generate business income.
- **Liability risk** (insure with liability insurance) refers to being legally responsible for damages and a reduction in FC. The driver of a car may be responsible for damages or loss of life caused by an accident.

- **Health risk** (insure with health insurance) can lead to direct loss of FC to pay illness or injury related expenses. It can reduce HC through diminished or inability to work. It can also affect future expense needs and life expectancy. Coverage for health risk varies widely by country. Government and/or private insurance may provide for short-term but not for long-term care.

MODULE QUIZ 21.1, 21.2

1. An individual's present value of future defined benefit payments will *most likely* be classified as:
   A. financial capital.
   B. human capital.
   C. financial capital and total wealth.
2. Financial capital is *least likely* to peak at retirement for:
   A. the very wealthy.
   B. those with a pension.
   C. those who purchase an annuity.
3. Individuals are *most likely* to need substantial amounts of life insurance in which stage of life?
   A. Education.
   B. Career development.
   C. Early retirement.
4. An individual with negative net worth on a traditional balance sheet:
   A. should reduce expenses.
   B. should increase risk in their investment portfolio.
   C. may have positive net wealth.
5. An individual with a large alternative investment holding in art work is *most likely* to need:
   A. property insurance.
   B. life insurance.
   C. liability insurance.
6. An individual is about to retire. She will receive her first annual pension payment of $25,000 immediately upon retirement and immediately spend it on a lavish vacation. Then, one year later, she will receive another payment. Each payment will increase by 5% from the previous payment amount. Given her life expectancy, she expects to receive a total of 11 payments.

   The risk-free discount rate is 3%, and the risk premium for the pension is 8%. Ignoring the first payment, which she will immediately spend, the pension asset of 10 payments to include on the individual's holistic balance sheet is *closest* to:
   A. 170,000.
   B. 185,000.
   C. 200,000.

Video covering this content is available online.

MODULE 21.3: LIFE INSURANCE

Basic Life Insurance Terminology

- *Benefits or face amount.* The future payout (e.g., $1,000,000). The terms may specify payout as a lump sum or an annuity.
- *Premium.* The cost of the insurance.
- *Cash value.* What the owner can withdraw before payout, which reduces or terminates final payout.
- *Paid up.* A date when the insurance is fully paid for and no additional premiums are required.
- *Limitations.* Restrictions on the payout of the insurance amount (e.g., misrepresentation of the health status of the insured leading to no payment).
- *Contestability period.* Time period for the insurance company to investigate or deny payment of the claim.
- *Identity of the insured.*
- *Policy owner.* Responsible for making premium payments, often the insured. If the owner is not the insured, he must have an insurable interest in the insured. In other words, the owner must have a vested interest in the continued life of the insured and not simply be speculating on the insured's death.
- *Beneficiaries.* Receivers of the payout.
- *Premium schedule.* Amount and frequency of payments.
- *Riders.* Additional provisions included in the policy.
- *Modifications.* Allowable changes that can be made to the policy.

LOS 21.e: Describe types of insurance relevant to personal financial planning.

Life insurance protects the survivors from the adverse financial consequences of the insured's premature death. The optimal amount of insurance depends on the cost of the insurance and the loss in value to the survivors caused by the death. The insurance can also provide liquidity to meet death and estate expenses. This is more important if the other estate assets are illiquid. Some life insurance provides tax benefits by accumulating cash value on a tax-sheltered basis.

Life insurance can be grouped in two main types: temporary and permanent. Both require continuing payment of premiums to remain in effect. The premium is often paid annually or on some other designated basis.

PROFESSOR'S NOTE

Insurance terminology is not mutually exclusive. Think of term insurance as pure insurance. What is the cost to charge all members of a large group today such that the funds will cover the payout on those who die this year? In simple terms, if the group includes 100 people, probability of death for any one is 1%, and the payout on death is

GBP100,000, charge each individual GBP1,000. For permanent insurance, start with a premium today (higher than GBP1,000) that, if held constant and invested, will for the life of the group provide sufficient funds to pay the death benefit for all members of the group. A 5-year level payment term policy will have some of the characteristics of permanent insurance, but the price will be closer to pure annual insurance. First we discuss the general differences in life insurance type and then we get further into the pricing issue.

Temporary (term) insurance covers only a designated period such as 1, 5, or 20 years. The cost can be fixed or increasing over the designated period. The policy then ceases at the end of the period unless it includes a provision to renew the policy. Term insurance is less costly than permanent insurance because the mortality risk is lower for the insurance company as the individual's risk of dying increases later in life (after the insurance ceases). The mortality risk also means term insurance for younger individuals and for shorter time periods will cost less than for older individuals and longer periods, all other factors the same.

Permanent insurance is more costly and lasts for the life of the insured. The premium (cost) per period is usually fixed, and the policy builds value as the premium exceeds the pure cost of insurance in the initial years. In later years, this built up value covers the increasing cost that would be paid for pure (term) insurance. Permanent insurance can be categorized as whole life or universal insurance.

Whole life typically has a fixed annual premium payment. The policy continues and the policy cannot be canceled by the insurance company as long as premiums are paid. The non-cancelability makes purchase at a young age more desirable as new insurance may be unavailable or much more expensive if the insured person's health deteriorates. The policy may also reach a fully paid status in later years and require no further premiums. Participating whole life shares in company profits and may increase in value more quickly.

Universal life is similar in concept but with more flexibility. The premium payment can be increased or decreased to increase or decrease the amount of insurance and/or the rate at which cash value grows. There may be investment choices for where the premiums are invested. Premium payments can be discontinued and the insurance continues (a non-forfeiture clause) as long as the cash value and earnings on the cash value are sufficient to pay the pure (term) cost of insurance each period.

Life insurance policies can include riders, which provide additional benefits. Accidental death and dismemberment (AD&D) increases the payout if the insured dies or is dismembered in an accident. Accelerated death benefits (ADB) pay part or all of the insurance amount if the insured is terminally ill. A viatical settlement allows the sale of the policy to a third party. This provides immediate funds to the beneficiaries. The third party becomes the policy beneficiary and is responsible for future premium payments. Guaranteed insurability allows the purchase of more insurance regardless of future health. Waiver of premium keeps the insurance in force without premium payments if the insured becomes disabled.

LOS 21.f: Describe the basic elements of a life insurance policy and how insurers price a life insurance policy.

Life insurance pricing is simple in concept but complex in application. It is a large time value of money problem. The insurance company must charge sufficient premiums such that the money after investing the premiums is sufficient to pay the policy benefits, cover the company's costs, and leave a profit. The company is applying the law of large numbers. The remaining term of life for any one individual is highly uncertain, but predictable in aggregate for a large group. The pricing model can be broken down into three issues:

- **Mortality estimates.** Mortality tables are built to reflect past experience and future projections of mortality. Probability of death (1 − probability of life) can be refined and based on age, health, gender, and lifestyle choices. An 80-year-old male smoker in poor health who sky dives will pay more than a 40-year-old healthy woman with safer hobbies. The insurance company will gather information regarding the insurability of the applicant and may employ third party investigators and medical professionals to assess the risk factors. The company's goal is to avoid adverse selection and undercharging for the risks assumed.
- **Net premium.** Based on the assumed mortality rates, the company estimates the net premiums to charge for insurance based on an assumed discount rate. The discount rate is also the assumed rate of return on investing the premiums. At that discount rate, the premiums must be sufficient such that the PV of the premiums and payouts are equal (i.e., the premiums must be sufficient to pay future benefits).
- **Load.** The load plus net premium is the **gross premium** charged for the insurance. The load must cover the company's operating cost and expenses for writing the policy. This can include a sales commission to sell the policy and cost of any medical tests to determine insurability. Stock companies are owned by shareholders and must include a planned profit to provide a return to shareholders. Mutual companies are owned by the policyholders but must also charge more than the net premium to cover risk. If costs are eventually less than expected, some policies allow the policyholders to receive a dividend (which is technically a return of premium).

For a simple one-year term insurance policy, the application is relatively simple. Risk is limited as only one year of variables must be considered to estimate the net premium for pure insurance. Load will also be fairly simple to estimate. If the policy is renewed the following year, a new gross premium will be calculated. For a level payment multi-year term policy, the process is slightly more complex. The level premium will be higher than the Year 1 and less than the Year 5 premium for annual term. The premium is conceptually a weighted average of five sequential one-year term premiums. In reality, it should be higher as the company is at greater risk; it must project the relevant variables for the five-year period and cannot change the premium each year. See Figure 21.1 and Figure 21.2.

Figure 21.1: Annual Term Insurance for $100,000

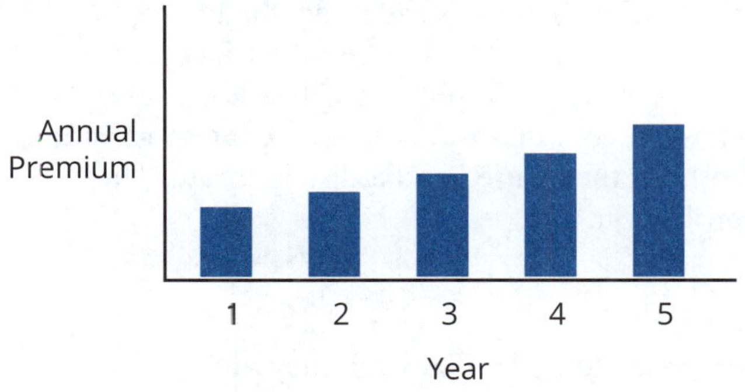

Figure 21.2: 5-Year Term Insurance for $100,000

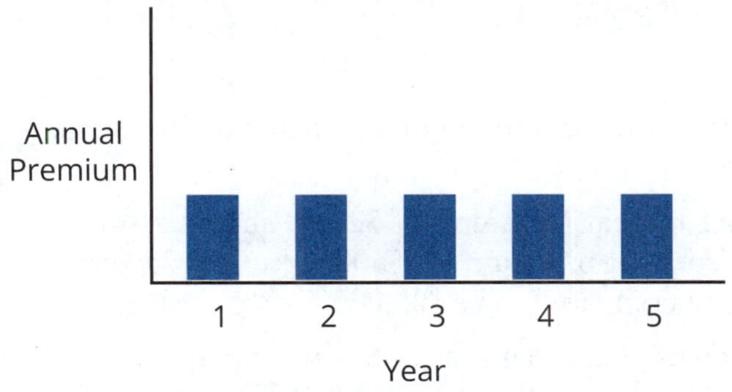

Permanent insurance pricing extends the same concepts, but with more uncertainty as the ultimate life expectancy of the insured individual has to be considered. The longer time period puts the insurance company at greater risk in correctly estimating mortality rate, discount rate (return on invested premiums), and expenses. These factors will make the initial premium higher. In addition, many such policies include a buildup of cash value that the policyholder can access before policy payout. The cash buildup is created by charging an even higher premium. Such policies typically include a paid up date when return on cash value is sufficient to pay future costs of insurance and premiums cease. See Figure 21.3.

Figure 21.3: Insurance Versus Cash Value in Permanent Insurance for $100,000

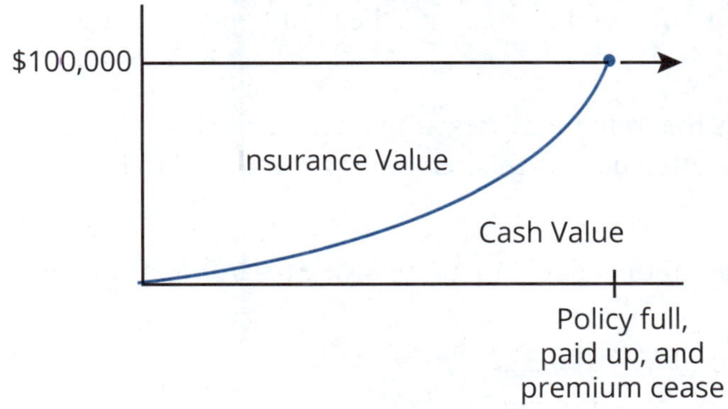

Comparing cost between insurance policies becomes more difficult as policy complexity increases. For annual term, when all else is the same, the lowest premium is lowest cost. For permanent insurance, the number of variables makes comparison complex as it is highly unlikely any two policies will be the same. Two common approaches are the **net payment cost index** and **net surrender cost index**. Both require an assumed age of death for the insured and a discount rate. The second also requires a cash value projection.

PROFESSOR'S NOTE

There is no direct LOS for these methods. However, they are a direct application of time value of money concepts. They are not unreasonable questions. You should also be able to reason through implications if a case clearly favors one policy over another, such as lower premium payment and higher dividend payment, or a lower index value.

To illustrate the issues, assume a 25-year time horizon till death and a 5% discount rate on a $100,000 insurance policy.

- Policy XX has annual beginning of year premiums of $2,000 and an assumed annual end of year dividend (return of premium) of $500. Terminal 25 year cash value projected (by the insurance company) to be $25,000.
- Policy YY has annual beginning of year premiums of $2,200 and an assumed annual end of year dividend (increase in cash value) of $550. Terminal 25 year cash value projected (by the insurance company) to be $27,500.

PROFESSOR'S NOTE

Be careful with the following calculations. Some steps require use of the **ordinary annuity (payments at end of period)** settings for your calculator. Other steps require the **annuity due (payments at start of period)** setting. If you do not use the proper setting at each step, your answer will be wrong.

Most CFA calculations use ordinary annuity. I keep my calculator set on ordinary annuity and only reset it to annuity due if required for a specific calculation. Then I reset it back to ordinary annuity. Many calculators show a small note on the screen of "beg" or "end" to show the mode.

Net payment cost index assumes the individual dies at the end of the horizon and cash value is not considered. It is often used if the insurance is projected to be paid up at that point:

Step 1: Compute the FV of the premiums paid, an annuity due (premiums paid at start of year).

XX: 2,000 PMT, 5 i_P, 25 n, FV = 100,227

YY: 2,200 PMT, 5 i_P, 25 n, FV = 110,250

Step 2: Compute the FV of the dividends, an ordinary annuity (dividends at end of year).

XX: 500 PMT, 5 i_P, 25 n, FV = 23,864

YY: 550 PMT, 5 i_P, 25 n, FV = 26,250

Step 3: The 25-year FV cost of insurance is Step 1 – Step 2.

XX: 100,227 – 23,864 = 76,363

YY: 110,250 – 26,250 = 84,000

Step 4: Annuitize this FV difference for the annual cost. Use an annuity due to match the requirement to pay premiums at the start of the year.

XX: 76,363 FV, 5 i_P, 25 n, PMT = 1,524

YY: 84,000 FV, 5 i_P, 25 n, PMT = 1,676

Step 5: Divide by $1,000 of insurance policy amount to index the annual cost ($100,000 / $1,000 = 100 units of insurance).

XX: $1,524 / 100 = $15.24 per $1,000 of insurance per year.

YY: $1,676 / 100 = $16.76 per $1,000 of insurance per year.

Net surrender cost index assumes the individual terminates the policy (insurance ceases) at the end of the horizon and the cash value is received. Step 1 and Step 2 are the same. Step 3 will be different and have consequences for Step 4 and Step 5.

Step 1: Compute the FV of the premiums paid, an annuity due (premiums paid at start of year).

XX: 2,000 PMT, 5 i_P, 25 n, FV = 100,227

YY: 2,200 PMT, 5 i_P, 25 n, FV = 110,250

Step 2: Compute the FV of the dividends, an ordinary annuity (dividends at end of year).

XX: 500 PMT, 5 i_P, 25 n, FV = 23,864

YY: 550 PMT, 5 i_P, 25 n, FV = 26,250

Step 3: The 25-year FV cost of insurance is Step 1 – Step 2 less the projected cash value.

XX: 100,227 – 23,864 – 25,000 = 51,363

YY: 110,250 – 26,250 – 27,500 = 56,500

Step 4: Annuitize this FV difference for the annual cost. Use an annuity due to match the requirement to pay premiums at start of year.

XX: 51,363 FV, 5 i_P, 25 n, PMT = 1,025

YY: 56,500 FV, 5 i_P, 25 n, PMT = 1,127

Step 5: Divide by $1,000 of insurance policy amount to index the annual cost ($100,000 / $1,000 = 100 units of insurance).

XX: $1,025 / 100 = $10.25 per $1,000 of insurance per year.

YY: $1,127 / 100 = $11.27 per $1,000 of insurance per year.

PROFESSOR'S NOTE

Many insurance regulators require companies to provide such standardize cost comparisons. Even then, the estimate of true cost depends on the assumptions. Of course, if you can precisely plan when you will die, this would be easier, but that's not a very practical solution.

Estimating the amount of insurance needed is another task. The starting point is estimating the remaining HC (PV of future earnings) of the insured plus expenses associated with the death and the PV of any other legacy goals (financial objectives that would have been met in the absence of premature death). The need may be lower as only expenses of the survivors, not the insured, are relevant.

Other Types of Insurance

- **Disability income insurance** provides partial replacement of the insured's job income if the job is lost.
- **Property insurance** provides compensation for losses in value of real property. **Homeowners insurance** covers the home, and **automobile insurance** covers the car.
- **Health and medical insurance** covers health care expense.
- **Liability insurance** covers losses if the insured is found legally responsible for damages to another.

MODULE QUIZ 21.3

1. The volatility of human capital and the demand for life insurance are:
   A. uncorrelated.
   B. positively correlated.
   C. negatively correlated.
2. Which of the following statements regarding the pricing of life insurance policies is *most accurate?*
   A. Mortality tables are built to reflect past experiences of mortality.
   B. For a level payment five-year term policy, the level premium should be higher than the Year 5 premium for an annual term policy.
   C. Based on the assumed mortality rates, the insurance company estimates the net premiums to charge for insurance based on the assumed rate of return on investing the premiums.

3. Consider the following policy:

Insurance amount	=	$250,000
Annual premium	=	$4,850
Expected annual dividend	=	$1,190
Time to maturity	=	30 years
Expected surrender value	=	$70,000

Based on a discount rate of 8%, the net surrender cost index per 1,000 of insurance is *closest* to:
A. $12.70.
B. $13.10.
C. $13.80.

MODULE 21.4: ANNUITIES

Video covering this content is available online.

A basic annuity is a one-time premium payout in exchange for fixed payouts received for the life of the annuitant. The initial premium is the investment. When the annuity ends, the payouts cease. The initial investment is not returned at the end. The overly simple analogy is to a level payout amortizing mortgage, the payouts are interest and a return of principal. The complication in an annuity is how long the insured's life will last. Basic terminology includes:

- The **insurer** collects the premium and makes the future payouts. (The insurer is often an insurance company, the company.)
- The **annuitant** receives the **annuity payouts** in the future.
- The contract **owner** pays the premium to purchase the annuity and is usually the annuitant.
- The **beneficiary** receives any remaining value of the contract at death of the annuitant. In many cases, there is no beneficiary as payouts cease at death of the annuitant.
- The **premium**, which is normally paid once at purchase, could also be referred to as the value of the contract. **The premium paid to the company is the price of the annuity**. However, the convention is to keep the premium constant and adjust the stated annual payout. This means that a **lower/higher quoted payout to the annuitant is equivalent to a higher/lower price for the annuity**.

LOS 21.g: Discuss the use of annuities in personal financial planning.

Annuities are the economic opposite of life insurance: for life insurance, pay an annual premium and receive one payoff at death to insure against premature death; for annuities, pay once and receive payouts back for life to insure against longevity risk. Both products spread the risk of when any one individual will die across a large pool of individuals.

Annuities take many forms. A DB pension plan from a private company or government that pays for the life of the retiree is a form of annuity. Annuities can also be purchased and used to supplement or replace DB plan payouts. While the potential permutations and features are not limited, annuities can generally be classified as deferred versus immediate and fixed versus variable. Usually, the annuity is illiquid once purchased, though it is possible there can be provisions to liquidate early or sell the future payout stream to a third party.

In a **deferred annuity**, the annual receipts start at a deferred future date. **Deferred variable annuities** are common and allow the owner to select from a list of investment options. Higher/lower investment returns will increase/decrease the future payouts to be received. While often compared to mutual funds, the investment choices are more limited and expenses are high. The annuity can also include an insurance feature with a guarantee of some minimum payouts received back. Otherwise, the payouts would just cease at death of the recipient. The investor may also be able to cash out the value and terminate the annuity at a future date (subject to a surrender charge that reduces what they receive). Unless the individual pays for additional features, the variable annuity does not guarantee any minimum future payouts.

Deferred fixed annuities pay a fixed benefit for life that starts at a defined future date. The longer the delay between initial premium paid and start of payouts received, all else the same, the lower the cost of the annuity, as the company can invest and increase the funds available before making payouts on the annuity.

An **advanced life deferred annuity** is a relatively lower cost way to hedge the longevity risk of the annuitants outliving their other assets. Like most fixed and variable annuities, they require an immediate premium payout at purchase. Like deferred fixed annuities, the payouts are fixed, but the delay period before they start is long, often age 80 or 85 for the annuitant. The low premium reflects three factors. First, the long delay before payouts begin allows the company a longer period to invest and grow the premium's value. Second, the period of payouts will be shorter as the life expectancy of the older annuitant will be shorter when payouts do begin. Third, a greater proportion of the annuitants will die before they receive any payouts.

Immediate variable annuities start payouts immediately, but the amount of the future payouts is indexed to the performance of some reference asset, such as a stock index. As the reference asset increases/decreases, the payouts increase/decrease. **Immediate fixed annuities** begin payout immediately and the payout amount does not change.

The features of the annuity and the annuitant's status will affect the payout. Typical features include:

- Life annuity with payouts for the life of the annuitant.
- Period certain annuity with payouts for a specified time period.
- Life annuity and period certain with payouts for the longer of the two periods.
  - Life annuity with refund is similar in concept but specifies a refund amount if a specified minimum payout amount has not been received before death of the annuitant.
- Joint life annuity specifies payout continues as long as at least one of the annuitants is alive.

Consider an initial $100,000 investment in (premium paid for) an annuity.

- A 60-year-old female might receive 5,900 per year for life on an immediate fixed annuity, while a 60-year-old male might receive 6,300. The higher payout for the male reflects the statistical probability he will not live as long, and total payouts made by the company will be less.
- Annual payouts for an 80-year-old female or male will be higher, say 14,300 and 15,200 respectively. This reflects that their remaining life expectancy is shorter, reducing the number of payouts the insurance company is likely to make.
- A rider specifying payouts be made for at least 10 years reduces the annual payout, reflecting higher cost to the insurance company. It no longer benefits from cessation of payouts to annuitants that live less than 10 years.
- A joint life provision that payouts continue as long as either member of a couple is alive will lower the annual payout on any of the previous annuities. Statistically, this increases the total number of payouts as the company pays as long as at least one member is alive.
- Adding a, or increasing the deferral period until start of payouts would increase the annual payout, as the company can keep the premium invested longer and it reduces the number of payouts expected to be made.
- Generally, in any of the previous policies, the initial annual payout on a variable annuity will be lower than a fixed annuity, but the expected total payout amount can be higher for the variable annuity based on the performance of the reference asset. Of course, there is no guarantee of this; it depends on the performance of the reference asset.

PROFESSOR'S NOTE

It should be occurring to you that the number and combination of features on insurance products is infinite. Why would that surprise you? Think product proliferation. The companies have every incentive to offer a vast menu of options to attract customers. Do not imagine the CFA material can produce a comprehensive analysis model. It does not exist. That does not mean a question cannot be written that can be solved by applying the basic economic and time value of money concepts being discussed; just think the case facts through logically.

LOS 21.h: Discuss the relative advantages and disadvantages of fixed and variable annuities.

The **volatility** of future benefits is obviously different. Lower risk investors may prefer the certainty of fixed payouts, and higher risk investors may prefer the potential for increasing variable payouts.

Flexibility often differs. Fixed annuities are generally irrevocable and payouts cannot be changed. In variable annuities the future value of the annuity and payouts are linked to the performance of a reference asset. Variable annuities are more likely to allow withdrawal of the funds at subsequent market value (after surrender fees for withdrawal).

Future market expectations will affect the choice. Payouts on a fixed annuity are largely determined by initial bond market interest rates. If rates are expected to increase, delay in purchase can lead to higher payouts on annuities purchased later.

However, the choice is not so simple and requires a consideration of **mortality credits**. Some individuals will die before, and some after, their expected lifespan. Annuitants who die earlier collect fewer payouts, effectively subsidizing those who die later. That is why insurance is called risk sharing or transfer. This concept is called mortality credits. All other factors the same, mortality credits make annuities less costly to purchase at a younger age. (Think of it as the annuitants who live longer earn a mortality credit paid by those who do not live as long and collect fewer payouts). However, the effect of mortality credits is difficult to see directly because other factors are also often changing.

As a simple example, consider a 60 year old who pays $100,000 for a lifetime annual payout of $5,000. Waiting to age 65 for the purchase might produce an annual payout of $6,000. Waiting appears to be economically beneficial, but this is deceptive. If market conditions are unchanged, the payout amount is reduced by mortality credits but increased by the fact the older individual who waits to purchase will statistically receive fewer payouts.

An easier way to see the effect of the mortality credit is to look at a deferred annuity for the 60 year old, which would start payouts at age 65. The initial payout could be $6,450. This is clearly better than if the individual waits until age 65 to purchase and immediately start receiving $6,000. It is the same individual, so the total payouts to be made are the same. Even here, two factors are at work. The annual payout amount, if purchased at age 60 to start payouts at age 65, is higher because the company can invest the premium for 5 years before making payouts at 65, and it is also higher because some of the annuitants will not live to age 65 to collect anything. Those who die earlier have subsidized and paid a mortality credit to those who live longer than age 65 and collect payouts.

PROFESSOR'S NOTE

While the effect of mortality credits can be difficult to see directly, the concept is fundamental to insurance risk sharing and pricing.

- Just remember that for life insurance the ultimate cost is lower if you die and the beneficiaries collect the one-time fixed payout sooner, while those who live longer end up paying more for the same payout. Admittedly, who wants to die sooner! (Be careful that your beneficiaries want you around for a long time.)
- For annuities, the issue reverses; annuitants who live longer end up collecting more and are subsidized by those who die sooner and collect less.

While this is a bit morbid, rest assured the insurance company is not stupid and fully understands all the implications of mortality tables, future payouts, and how they affect insurance pricing. The industry invented mortality tables.

Market expectations also affect variable annuity versus fixed annuity payouts because variable annuities shift risk to the annuitant from the company. The payout is based on the future performance of the risky reference asset. The annuitant earns both a mortality credit and a risk premium. The net effect is the total expected value of the payouts is higher, reflecting the higher expected return on the reference asset (although the initial annual payout is generally lower). The variable annuity is also more likely to allow cashing out, but at a value linked to the reference asset. There is a downside; fees for variable annuities tend to be higher. Variable annuities are also more complex and difficult to analyze. This difficulty tends to reduce price competition and further increase the price of variable annuities (i.e., lowers the annual payout received for premium invested compared to fixed annuities).

Inflation is also a factor. Variable annuities that link payout to an appreciating asset like the stock market are more likely to provide long-term inflation protection. Conventional fixed annuities that pay a constant nominal amount offer no inflation protection. (In contrast many DB plan benefits are indexed to inflation.) A fixed annuity with a rider to increase payments with inflation can be purchased, but at a higher cost. Alternatively, fixed annuities can be designed with payments that increase by predetermined amounts for some inflation protection. The prespecified increases may or may not match actual inflation.

Taxes are a factor, but they are complex and vary by jurisdiction. Consult a qualified advisor before making decisions. Typically, increases in value of an insurance product are not taxed before payouts. At payout, tax may or may not be due on the increase in value.

PROFESSOR'S NOTE

This tax comment is more cautionary than comments in some other Level III insurance readings. The bottom line in all the readings is taxation of insurance products is complex, you need more than the CFA curriculum will provide, and there can be some tax advantages. Do not send emails saying the statements in the different readings are not identical. The bottom line is consistent among readings.

The alternative to purchase of an annuity is to **self-insure** longevity risk. In other words, invest in financial assets and set a withdrawal amount that lasts to an assumed life expectancy. The life expectancy should be high because the alternative is running out of money. The decision is complex because the annuity payment reflects three components:

- Return of the principal (premium).
- Interest on the principal.
- Mortality credits as annuitants who die sooner are subsidizing (receiving fewer payouts) the annuitants who live longer (receive more payouts).

Self-insurance can earn the first two, but not the third. This favors use of the annuity. However, use of annuities reduces aggregate wealth of the users as the insurance companies invest rather conservatively and must cover costs plus profit (which is just the cost of invested capital). The decision becomes how much risk for the retiree to take versus cost. Factors that favor use of annuities rather than self-insurance include:

- A longer than average life expectancy.
- A desire for lifetime income.
- Less desire to leave an estate for the benefit of others.
- Conservative investors (high risk aversion).
- An absence of other guaranteed income sources such as pensions.

MODULE QUIZ 21.4

1. Insured individuals who live longer than the statistical average are *most likely* to earn a positive (benefit from the) mortality credit with:
   A. life insurance.
   B. an annuity.
   C. both life insurance and an annuity.
2. In which of the following situations would an individual be *most likely* to purchase a variable rather that a fixed annuity?
   A. They need a more certain income stream.
   B. They want to avoid higher fees.
   C. They want the flexibility to redeem the annuity in the future.
3. An individual should *most likely* purchase insurance for a risk that:
   A. poses high standard of living risk and is infrequent.
   B. poses high standard of living risk and is frequent.
   C. is smaller in amount and infrequent.

MODULE 21.5: COMPREHENSIVE EXAMPLE AND REVIEW

Video covering this content is available online.

PROFESSOR'S NOTE

This example is typical of Level III. A question can describe facts and ask for an answer that may draw on any of the relevant material covered in the readings. Don't panic, the case facts and taught material will provide the answer; just keep your cool and think it through.

Risk management involves multiple techniques. Some risks can be avoided (risk avoidance) (e.g., don't own expensive cars that are costly to repair). Avoiding the risk is a pure form of loss control. Loss prevention involves reducing the probability of the loss (e.g., keep the car in secure storage). Loss reduction involves taking actions to reduce the amount of the loss [e.g., installing fire suppression devices (the fire may still occur, but the likely damages are reduced)]. Risk management also involves risk transfer (buying insurance) and risk retention (self-insurance).

One approach to risk management involves categorizing the severity and frequency of the loss. Severity refers to the size of the loss in relationship to the financial resources of the individual. A $50,000 loss could be trivial to some but devastating to others. Likewise, if the loss is infrequent, it is less burdensome than if it occurs frequently. The matrix classification in Figure 21.4 can indicate the appropriate risk management technique to use.

Figure 21.4: Risk Management Decision Matrix

Characteristic of the Loss	Occurs Regularly	Infrequent
Very severe	Risk avoidance	Risk transfer
Not severe	Risk reduction	Risk retention

EXAMPLE: Analyze an individual's insurance program

Case facts:

- A couple in their early 40s has 3 dependent children.
- The husband earns $200,000 annually and is employed in a low risk profession. The employer provides life insurance equal to 2 years of salary. The health insurance plan is generous and covers the family. The employer provides short-term disability insurance to cover 75% of the earnings of the husband, but the benefits last for only 3 months.
- The wife works part time and earns $10,000. Her primary responsibility is care of the children and home. She expects to return to the workforce in the next few years. Her job skills are current, in high demand, and highly compensated.
- Their home was purchased a few years ago at the bottom of a severe real estate collapse and has appreciated 150%. The original loan balance was 90% of purchase price has been only slightly reduced. The couple has been collecting valuable antiques to furnish the home. Property insurance on the home and contents has not been changed since the purchase.
- The couple has a $2,000,000 investment portfolio. A wealthy friend of the couple recently suffered a severe financial loss due to her negligence when she caused a car accident. Her auto insurance only covered liability claims up to $50,000. The couple has a similar auto policy.
- The wife's mother died recently and her 65-year-old father is still alive. The father is in average health and has a large, secure, inflation indexed pension. The father's parents and both sets of grandparents died at relatively young ages.

A. **Discuss** the insurance needs of the couple with regard to life, health, long-term disability, auto, other property, and liability insurance.

B. **Comment** on factors that may increase and decrease their ability to self-insure.

C. **Discuss** *two* reasons why the wife's father is likely a poor candidate for purchase of an advanced life deferred annuity that would begin payment at age 85.

Answer:

A.

- It is unlikely life insurance equal to 2 years of the husband's salary would cover the family's loss in value if he dies. He needs more life insurance. While the wife's current income is low, her HC is high and she provides substantial value to the family now. Her services would be costly to replace. Some life insurance is needed on her to protect the family's standard of living.
- Employer health insurance is good and covers the family.
- Long-term disability is needed as the family is at risk if the husband cannot work for an extended period of time. This is mitigated by the potential for the wife to return to work.
- Auto insurance and or liability insurance need to be increased. The couple has substantial assets that are at risk if they were responsible for damages to another.
- Property insurance on the home and contents needs to be increased to match their current value.

B. They have substantial assets that increase their ability to absorb losses and self-insure. It is also likely they have substantial explicit liabilities in the form of a mortgage and implicit liabilities in the need to care for the children. These decrease their net wealth and ability to self-insure.

C.

- With a family history of below average life expectancy, the cost versus benefit is relatively low as the father may end up collecting no or only a small number of payments.
- With a large, secure, inflation indexed pension, the father will have less need for increased additional payments from an annuity starting in the future.

Human Capital and the Implications for Asset Allocation

LOS 21.i: Discuss how asset allocation policy may be influenced by the risk characteristics of human capital.

Asset allocation should consider the investor's total economic wealth, FC and HC. The characteristics of the HC are relatively hard to change, so the adjustment is likely to be in the FC. The nature of the HC may affect both the overall risk taken in the FC, and the assets and asset classes selected. For example, an individual employed in a high-risk profession would, all else the same, choose lower risk FC. If the HC is positively correlated with the stock market, then it will be best to select asset classes other than equity for any risky assets that are used. Of course, the individual should try and avoid FC tied directly to her employer.

EXAMPLE: Asset allocation

Sally is an MBA with high-risk HC that is 90% stock like. Her sister, Hellen, is a tenured college professor with HC that is 10% stock like. Based on these and all other considerations, they have both selected a 70/30 asset allocation (stock to bond) of total wealth. Sally has HC of 1.9 million and FC of 2.5 million. Hellen's HC and FC are 0.8 and 1.1 million, respectively. Based only on this information, **calculate** the target equity amount that each would hold in her FC.

Sally:

- Total desired equity amount = (1.9 + 2.5) × 0.7 = 3.08 million.
- Equity exposure from HC = 1.9 × 0.9 = 1.71 million.
- For her 2.5 million FC, she should allocate 1.37 million to equity.

Hellen:

- Total desired equity amount = (0.8 + 1.1) × 0.7 = 1.33 million.
- Equity exposure from HC = 0.8 × 0.1 = 0.08 million.
- For her 1.1 million FC, she would have to allocate 1.25 million to equity to reach her total wealth allocation goal. Most likely she will allocate all 1.1 million and be somewhat below her desired total allocation goal for equity.

The characteristics of HC can be complex. For example:

- For a couple, the HC of each member is not likely to be perfectly correlated (+1) with the other, making the couple's HC in aggregate less risky. Likewise, if both are employed, the couple's HC is less risky than if the same amount were earned but only by one member of the couple.
- If one member of the couple has less geographically mobile career skills, the couple's HC is at risk if the other member must move.
- If one member of the couple is not working but could return to work if needed, that lowers the risk of the couple's HC.
- Generally, HC is less risky than many forms of FC, and, all else the same, the asset allocation in FC is tilted toward riskier assets.

LOS 21.j: Recommend and justify appropriate strategies for asset allocation and risk reduction when given an investor profile of key inputs.

PROFESSOR'S NOTE

This is another cumulative LOS that can lead to a question and facts that draw on any of the relevant material covered in the readings.

The reading terms idiosyncratic and systematic risk are analogous to more general terms in portfolio theory. Idiosyncratic is specific or diversifiable risk that can be reduced through diversification or use of insurance products. Insurance is just a pooling and diversification of risk through the insured group. For example, life insurance pools the risk of those who die sooner and later than expected. Systematic risk is market risk for which the holder should be compensated. More/less risk tolerant individuals may choose more/less systematic risk.

Risk management strategies include:

- Determining and taking the appropriate amount of systematic (market) risk through an asset allocation of total wealth.
- Reducing where appropriate idiosyncratic (non-market) risks:
  - Through asset diversification.
  - Use of insurance to transfer risks.

For example:

- A young MBA with large debts and high expenses may skip saving for retirement in the early years of her career. If there is any need for life insurance, it should be low-cost, temporary insurance. Security portfolio diversification is relatively unimportant while HC dominates FC.
- A financially well off couple nearing retirement must be more concerned with FC diversification. Outliving the FC becomes of greater concern and longevity risk can be hedged with annuities. HC shrinks and the need for life and disability insurance diminishes or ceases. Health, long-term care, and liability insurance are more important priorities. The more affluent may choose to self-insure as long as it does not imperil standard of living.

Conclusion

The risk management process for individuals is complex and must consider risk and return to total wealth. At different stages of life, the relative importance of and risks to human and financial capital will shift. Market risks to FC can be largely addressed with standard portfolio tools. Adding insurance tools provides more comprehensive risk management of HC and total wealth.

MODULE QUIZ 21.5

1. An individual in a high-risk job will *most likely*:
   A. increase their allocation to industries that are highly correlated with their wage income.
   B. increase their allocation to risk-free assets.
   C. reduce their savings.
2. The need for retirement savings is *most likely* higher for:
   A. a recent college graduate with very young children.
   B. a young couple who has recently received a large inheritance.
   C. an older couple in their peak earnings years but employed in a declining industry.

KEY CONCEPTS

LOS 21.a

Total wealth is composed of both human capital and financial capital. Human capital (HC) is the discounted present value of expected future labor income. Estimation includes the future amount, the probability the individual will be alive to earn it, and a discount rate related to the riskiness of the amounts. Financial capital (FC) is the sum of all the other assets of an individual.

LOS 21.b

Net wealth is the sum of the individual's FC and HC less any liabilities owed by the individual. A typical individual might start an employment career with high HC and low FC. As the individual's remaining work career decreases with age, HC generally declines over time while FC increases as the individual saves and invests.

Generally, HC is highest in early career and declines until retirement. FC is likely to peak at retirement. The life stages are Education, Early Career, Career Development, Peak Accumulation, Preretirement, Early Retirement, and Late Retirement.

In all stages, there can be unpredicted needs for health care and/or to care for family.

LOS 21.c

The economic (holistic) balance sheet extends the traditional balance sheet assets to include HC. Liabilities are extended to include consumption and bequest goals. This more complete economic view allows better planning of resource consumption to meet remaining lifetime goals.

LOS 21.d

- Earnings risk. Job loss and other career disruptions can reduce HC and may even lead to the need to consume FC prematurely.
- Premature death risk. Can be a serious risk early in the career when substantial HC could be lost and cause unexpected expenses that consume limited FC.
- Longevity risk. Individuals who live too long are at risk of outliving their FC.
- Property risk. Loss in value of physical property (FC).
- Liability risk. If legally responsible for damages, leading to a reduction in FC.
- Health risk. Direct loss of FC to pay illness or injury related expenses and may reduce HC through diminished or inability to work.

LOS 21.e

- Life insurance protects the survivors from the adverse financial consequences of the insured's premature death.
- Disability income insurance provides partial replacement of the insured's job income if the job is lost.

- Property insurance provides compensation for losses in value of real property. Homeowners insurance covers the home and automobile insurance covers the car.
- Health and medical insurance covers health care expense.
- Liability insurance covers losses if the insured is found legally responsible for damages to another.

LOS 21.f

Temporary life insurance is for a set period of time. Permanent insurance builds up value sufficient to pay for insuring the remaining lifetime of the insured. Pricing reflects mortality estimates that determine how many in the group are expected to die during the insurance period and allow calculating the net premium to charge to make those payouts. Load is an estimate of company expenses and profit that is added to determine the gross premium charged for the insurance.

LOS 21.g

Annuities are the economic opposite of life insurance, pay once and receive payouts back for remaining life to insure against longevity risk. Immediate annuities begin payout immediately and deferred at a future time. Fixed annuity payouts do not change in amount, and variable payouts are linked to change in a reference asset.

LOS 21.h

Fixed versus variable annuities:

- Fixed provide a known future payout, while variable have a better chance of keeping up with inflation.
- Fixed will be priced to reflect bond market rates at the time of purchase, while variable will perform in line with changes in the reference asset and are more likely to allow withdrawals.
- Fees for variable are generally higher.
- Both may be subject to some taxes.
- Both earn a mortality credit:
  - For life insurance, the ultimate cost is lower if you die and the one-time fixed payout occurs sooner, while those who live longer end up paying more for the same payout.
  - For annuities, the issue reverses; annuitants who live longer end up collecting more and are subsidized by those who die sooner and collect less.

Risk Management Techniques

Characteristic of the loss:	Occurs regularly	Infrequent
Very severe	Risk avoidance	Risk transfer
Not severe	Risk reduction	Risk retention

LOS 21.i

Asset allocation should consider the investor's total economic wealth, FC and HC. For example, an individual employed in a high-risk profession would, all else the same, choose lower risk FC. If the HC is positively correlated with the stock market, then it will be best to select asset classes other than equity for any risky assets that are used. Of course, the individual should try and avoid FC tied directly to her employer.

LOS 21.j

A cumulative LOS, expect questions that draw on the entire reading.

- Determine and take the appropriate amount of systematic (market) risk through an asset allocation of total wealth.
- Reduce where appropriate idiosyncratic (non-market) risks:
  - Through asset diversification.
  - Use of insurance to transfer risks.

ANSWER KEY FOR MODULE QUIZZES

Module Quiz 21.1, 21.2

1. **C** While DB plan benefits have elements of both FC and HC, they are best categorized as FC. They are also part of total wealth, making C the best answer. (Module 21.1, LOS 21.a)

2. **A** The very wealthy may spend less than the total return earned on their assets and see FC increase over time. All others are more likely to spend more than their return and see FC decline. The value of both pensions and annuities is the PV of expected future payments and so declines with age and the reduction in number of future payments. (Module 21.1, LOS 21.a)

3. **B** HC and the need for life insurance is likely at its peak in the early career stage, followed by the career development stage when the expected work career and HC remain high. (Module 21.1, LOS 21.b)

4. **C** Making changes based only on the traditional balance sheet analysis would be premature because it fails to consider all economic variables affecting the individual. The holistic balance sheet with all variables included could show positive net wealth. On the traditional balance sheet, negative balance may mean little. Individuals who are early in their career with college debt could have negative net worth. Even if both balance sheets show a negative balance, it does not mean immediate changes must be made, only that long-term plans may need revision. (Module 21.1, LOS 21.c)

5. **A** While it is true they may be wealthy and may also need the other two, the direct need is for property insurance. (Module 21.2, LOS 21.d)

6. **B** The first pension receipt is offset by a liability, a planned expenditure, so it has zero value in our calculations.

   The long (and unrealistic under exam conditions) way to solve this question is to set up a spreadsheet to project the payments at end of Year 1 to 10 with the first payment on the spreadsheet being 5% higher than the 25,000, and all subsequent payments increasing by 5% annually. Each FV payment would be discounted to PV at 3% + 8% = 11%. The more realistic way to solve the question is to realize the starting 25,000 is growing 5% each year and is then discounted at 11%. This can be reduced to a net discount rate (including the effect of growth) each year of [1 + (0.03 + 0.08)] / 1.05 – 1 = 5.7%.

   The question is then an ordinary annuity calculation of 10 payments: 10 n, 25,000 PMT, 5.7 i, PV = 186,646.

   Variations on this calculation such as [(1.03)(1.08)] / 1.05 – 1 or 3 + 8 – 5 are also likely to be acceptable but less consistent with the CFA text. (Module 21.1, LOS 21.c)

Module Quiz 21.3

1. **C** Human capital volatility and demand for life insurance are negatively correlated. Life insurance acts as a substitute for human capital, so its face value depends on the perceived value of the human capital it replaces. If the human capital has high volatility (equity-like), a higher discount rate is used to estimate its present value. Thus, human capital with high volatility has a smaller present value than human capital with low volatility. (LOS 21.f)

2. **C** Based on the assumed mortality rates, the insurance company estimates the net premiums to charge for insurance based on an assumed discount rate. The discount rate is also the assumed rate of return on investing the premiums. At that discount rate, the premiums must be sufficient such that the present value of the premiums and payouts are equal so that the premiums are sufficient to pay future benefits. The level premium will be higher than the Year 1 and *lower* than the Year 5 premium for annual term. The premium is conceptually a weighted average of five sequential one-year term premiums. Mortality tables are built to reflect both past experiences *and future projections* of mortality. (LOS 21.f)

3. **A** The CFA convention is premiums are paid at the start of the year as is the annuitized cost (annuity due) and dividends are received at the end of the year (ordinary annuity).

   $FV_{premiums}$ = $593,377.46 (annuity due: $4,850 annual payment, 30 years, 8%)

   $FV_{dividends}$ = $134,807.02 (ordinary annuity: $1,190 annual payment, 30 years, 8%)

   FV_{net} = $388,570.44 (future value of premiums less dividends and surrender value)

   $Annual_{net}$ = $3,176.00 (annuity due payment: $388,570.44 future value, 30 years, 8%)

   NSCI = $12.70 per $1,000 per year (net annual cost divided by 250 [$250,000 / $1,000])

   (LOS 21.f)

Module Quiz 21.4

1. **B** With a long life, the individual will collect more payouts than the average annuitant and benefit (earning the positive mortality credit). In contrast, the payout on life insurance will be further in the future, and they are effectively subsidizing (earning a negative credit) those with a shorter life whose beneficiaries are paid the policy amount sooner. (LOS 21.h)

2. **C** Variable annuities are more likely to allow cashing out (at the market value with surrender fees). Fixed annuities have more certain income and generally lower fees but are generally not redeemable. (LOS 21.g)

3. **A** This is the most likely situation to use insurance. It will be difficult to recover if the risk is realized, and because it is infrequent, the cost of insurance will be relatively lower. B is something to avoid, and C is a good case for self-insurance (risk retention). (LOS 21.h)

Module Quiz 21.5

1. **B** Higher risk HC will, all else the same, reduce the allocation in FC to risky assets in favor of lower risk assets. The risky job makes savings more important and investing in assets with positive correlation to HC should generally be avoided in order to provide diversification within total wealth. (LOS 21.i)

2. **C** This is typically the period of maximum savings for retirement, and the risk of early job loss makes this even more important. While it is always good to start saving for retirement, the other two likely have more immediate needs. Answer choice A probably needs low-cost term life insurance and liquidity. B is likely in good financial shape and could benefit from advice on what to do with the inheritance. B can certainly consider retirement savings, but C has the greatest need. (LOS 21.j)

READING 22

Portfolio Management for Institutional Investors

EXAM FOCUS

This reading addresses the investment policy statement (IPS) of the major types of institutional investors. As seen in the reading on individual investors, the IPS contains a formal statement of investment objectives (i.e., return and risk tolerance) and constraints applying to the client. The exam is likely to present a case study with one or more of these types of institutional clients, and you will be asked to prepare or evaluate parts of the IPS, effectively advising the institutional client on how to structure their investment portfolio. It is crucial that you approach this material from this perspective. The key to scoring well on this portion of the exam is to understand what the various institutions are trying to achieve with their investment portfolios and which risk considerations and constraints apply when meeting these goals.

MODULE 22.1: OVERVIEW OF INSTITUTIONAL INVESTORS

Video covering this content is available online.

Common Characteristics

LOS 22.a: Discuss common characteristics of institutional investors as a group.

Types of institutional investors considered in this reading include defined benefit and defined contribution pension plans, sovereign wealth funds (SWFs), university endowments, private foundations, banks, and insurance companies. Before discussing the details of the IPS for each type of institution, we note the following five common characteristics that cause institutional investors to differ from individual investors:

1. **Scale (size).** Institutions tend to be larger than individual investors. The largest institutions may be too large for investments or managers with low capacity, such as small-cap equity or venture capital. These large institutions may therefore choose to directly access investments and manage them in-house. Smaller institutions may have issues diversifying across asset classes that have high minimum investment sizes (e.g., private equity or real estate). They may also face issues with hiring skilled investment professionals and instead choose to outsource to external managers and consultants.
2. **Long-term investment horizon.** With some exceptions, institutional investors tend to have longer time horizons than individual investors because institutional investors are driven by the need to meet specific liabilities that are relatively low.
3. **Regulatory framework.** Institutions are subject to different legal, regulatory, accounting, and tax rules than individual investors with the differences among institutional investors based on national jurisdiction. Regulations have been tightened since the 2007–2009 global financial crisis in an attempt to lower leverage, increase centralized clearing, and improve reporting transparency.
4. **Governance framework.** Institutions typically operate under a formal governance structure, whereas governance structures for individuals tend to be less formal. Governance structures are typically composed of a *board of directors* and an *investment committee*, which may be a subcommittee of the board. The board often sets the long-term strategic asset allocation of the institution, with the board and/or investment committee establishing the IPS and monitoring investment performance. The investment committee oversees investment policy. Investment strategy is implemented by an investment office typically headed by a chief investment officer; the investment management takes place either in-house by internal investment staff or is outsourced to external asset managers.
5. **Principal-agent issues.** The principal-agent conflict occurs when a principal (i.e., the owner of assets) appoints an agent to act on their behalf and the agent's interests are not aligned with the principal's interests. For institutions, this conflict occurs internally through the appointment of the investment committee and investment staff and occurs externally through the use of outsourced investment managers. The classic example of an external principal-agent conflict is a high management fee paid to third-party investment managers regardless of performance.

Investment Policy Statement

LOS 22.b: Discuss investment policy of institutional investors.

The IPS should include:

- The institution's *mission* and *investment objectives* (i.e., return and risk tolerance).
- Discussion of the *investment horizon* and *liabilities* that need to be paid by the institution.
- *External constraints* that affect the asset allocation (legal, regulatory, tax, and accounting).
- An asset allocation policy (i.e., portfolio weights) with ranges and asset class benchmarks.
- A rebalancing policy.
- Reporting requirements.

The IPS should be reviewed annually, and revisions should be made when necessary due to material changes in investor circumstances and/or market environment.

While each institution has unique features, four models have evolved as different general approaches to asset allocation. Three of these models are named after approaches used by Norway's sovereign wealth fund, the Yale University endowment, and the Canada Pension Plan, while the fourth model is liability driven. Details of the four models are outlined in Figure 22.1.

Figure 22.1: General Asset Allocation Approaches

Model	Description
Norway's sovereign wealth fund	*Asset allocation:* ■ Passively managed allocation to public equities and bonds (with traditional 60% equity/40% bonds base case allocation) ■ Little or no exposure to alternative assets ■ Tight tracking error limits *Advantages*: ■ Low costs and fees ■ Easy for board to comprehend *Disadvantages*: ■ No opportunity for outperformance of markets
Yale University endowment	*Asset allocation:* ■ High allocation to alternatives ■ Significant active management ■ Externally managed assets *Advantages*: ■ Potential for outperformance of markets *Disadvantages*: ■ Difficult for small institutions without expertise in alternatives ■ May also be difficult for large managers due to capacity issues of external managers ■ High fees/costs
Canada Pension Plan	*Asset allocation:* ■ High allocation to alternatives ■ Significant active management ■ Internally managed assets ■ Uses a reference portfolio of passive public assets as benchmark that can be easily understood/communicated *Advantages*: ■ Potential for outperformance of markets and development of internal capabilities *Disadvantages*: ■ Potentially expensive and difficult to manage
Liability driven	*Asset allocation:* ■ Focus is on maximizing expected surplus (assets − liabilities) return and managing surplus volatility *Advantages*: ■ Explicitly recognizes liabilities as part of investment process *Disadvantages*: ■ Certain risks of liabilities (e.g., longevity) are difficult to hedge

PROFESSOR'S NOTE

The liability-driven investing (LDI) model is the same as the model discussed in detail in the asset allocation section of the curriculum.

MODULE QUIZ 22.1

1. Eris Private Wealth, Inc., (EPW) provides investment advice to high-net-worth individuals. After a recent merger, EPW acquired some institutional clients. The board of EPW has asked the post-merger management team to prepare a report detailing the key differences between institutional clients and individual clients. The report makes the following two statements:

   Statement 1: It is likely that the different scale of institutional clients versus individual clients will narrow the available investment universe.

   Statement 2: The governance structure of institutional clients is likely to be more formal than the governance structure of the investment account of an individual client.

   How many of the post-merger management team's statements are correct?

   A. Only one statement is correct.
   B. Neither statement is correct.
   C. Both statements are correct.

2. The board of the SJT Foundation has specified the following objectives:
   - Make an aggressive allocation to alternative investments in order to diversify and hedge against long-term inflation risk.
   - Outsource investment management to external managers due to the lack of experience by internal investment staff in investing in alternative investments.
   - Pursue actively managed strategies to generate long-term outperformance of benchmarks.

   The investment approach *most likely* to meet these objectives is:

   A. the Canada Pension Plan model.
   B. the Yale University endowment model.
   C. the Norway sovereign wealth fund model.

LOS 22.c: Discuss the stakeholders in the portfolio, the liabilities, the investment time horizons, and the liquidity needs of different types of institutional investors.

LOS 22.d: Describe the focus of legal, regulatory, and tax constraints affecting different types of institutional investors.

LOS 22.f: Evaluate the investment policy statement of an institutional investor.

LOS 22.g: Evaluate the investment portfolio of a private DB plan, sovereign wealth fund, university endowment, and private foundation.

The remainder of this reading addresses the details of IPSs of different types of institutional investors. The general outline for each type of institution will be as follows:

- The main features/mission of the institution.
- The stakeholders (i.e., parties impacted by the success/failure of the institution).
- The key elements of the IPS, usually in the following order:
  - Liabilities and investment horizon.
  - Liquidity needs.
  - External constraints.
  - Investment objectives.
  - Asset allocation.

MODULE 22.2: PENSION FUNDS

Video covering this content is available online.

Main Features/Mission

Pension funds are plans designed to save and invest in order to provide income for plan beneficiaries upon retirement. The entity that sets up the plan is referred to as the plan sponsor and is usually an employer. There are two major types of pension plans: (1) **defined benefit (DB)**, in which a plan sponsor defines the *benefit* that will be paid to beneficiaries upon retirement in the future and (2) **defined contribution (DC)**, in which *contributions* to plan assets today are defined, but there is no guarantee of ultimate benefits paid to beneficiaries.

While the exact nature of plans varies depending on jurisdiction, the main differences between DB and DC plans are displayed in Figure 22.2.

Figure 22.2: Defined Benefit vs. Defined Contribution

Feature	Defined Benefit	Defined Contribution
Benefit payments	Contractually defined (usually dependent on final salary) Creates a measurable **liability** for the plan sponsor	Depends of the performance of investments Once promised contributions have been met, there is no liability for the plan sponsor
Contributions	Primarily by employer (employee may contribute also)	Primarily by employee (employer may contribute also)
Investment decision-making	Pension fund (sponsor and investment staff)	Sponsor provides suite of available investment funds Employee decides level of investment and asset allocation
Investment risk	Faced by sponsor	Faced by beneficiary
Mortality/ longevity risk	Pooled at the fund level—beneficiaries who live longer than expected are funded by those who die earlier than expected Risk of general increases in life expectancy faced by sponsor	Employee faces the longevity risk of outliving their own savings

Over recent decades, there has been a move from DB to DC plans driven by the plan sponsors' preference for lower financial risk and the fact that DC plans are portable (i.e., they can move with beneficiaries when they change jobs).

Hybrid plans also exist that exhibit features of both DB and DC plans. For example, a cash balance plan involves a sponsor defining contributions to assets, which are then pooled; the sponsor faces some of the investment risk, as per a DB plan.

We will now focus on DB plans and DC plans individually.

DB Pension Plan

Stakeholders

The following are stakeholders in a DB pension scheme:

- *Plan sponsors (employers)* must make contributions to plan assets. Poor investment performance will result in sponsors having to make extra contributions to an underfunded plan (i.e., when assets are lower than liabilities).
- *Plan beneficiaries (employees and retirees)* face the ultimate risk that an employer defaults on contributions to plan assets.
- *The investment staff, the investment committee, and/or the board* are directly impacted by the success or failure of the plan.

- *Governments* are stakeholders in that they provide tax incentives for employees to save for retirement, and taxpayers will ultimately face the costs of providing welfare for those that have failed to adequately save for retirement.
- *Shareholders* in the corporate employer are stakeholders since an underfunded plan will cause a balance sheet liability and lower income for the company. It will also lead to higher financial risk, which will likely increase share price volatility.

Liabilities and Investment Horizon

The liabilities of a DB pension plan are the present value of the future benefits promised to plan participants. Employees usually only qualify to receive these benefits after meeting certain requirements called *vesting* conditions—typically a required minimum number of years of service.

The funded status of the plan can be measured using the funded ratio, or vested benefit index:

funded ratio = fair value of plan assets / PV of DB obligations

The major factors affecting the size of the liability are summarized in Figure 22.3.

Figure 22.3: DB Pension Plan Liability Factors

Factor	Impact of *Increase* in Factor	Rationale
Service/tenure (years worked)	Increases liability	Benefits are usually linked directly to years of service by the employee.
Salary	Increases liability	Benefits are usually linked to final salary.
Longevity	Increases liability	Plan participants are paid benefits for every year they live in retirement. If they live longer in retirement, they will receive more years of benefits.
Employee turnover	Lowers liability	Higher employee turnover means fewer employees are likely to work the number of years of service required for vesting of benefits.
Additional/ matching contributions	Increases liability	Additional/matching contributions usually increases the benefits promised to employees.
Expected investment return	Potentially lowers liability	In some cases, an increase in expected returns increases the discount rate used for liabilities, lowering liabilities.
Discount rate	Lowers liability	A higher discount rate will give a lower present value of benefits, hence a lower liability.

The plan beneficiaries can be split into *active lives* (those still employed and earning benefits) and *retired lives* (those receiving benefit payments). The higher the proportion of retired lives in the plan, the shorter the investment horizon of the plan, which lowers the risk tolerance of the plan. Plans that are frozen (i.e., closed to new participants) will also have shorter investment horizons due to the lack of new active lives joining the plan.

Risk Considerations

LOS 22.e: Evaluate risk considerations of private defined benefit (DB) pension plans in relation to 1) plan funded status, 2) sponsor financial strength, 3) interactions between the sponsor's business and the fund's investments, 4) plan design, and 5) workforce characteristics.

Key considerations that drive the risk tolerance of the DB pension plan are summarized in Figure 22.4.

Figure 22.4: DB Pension Plan Risk Considerations

Consideration	Rationale
Plan funded status	Higher funded status potentially increases risk tolerance since the plan will have the ability to absorb short-term losses
Sponsor financial status	Lower debt ratios and higher profitability of sponsor increase risk tolerance since sponsor will have capacity to make contributions in the event of losses in plan assets
Size of plan compared to sponsor	Smaller plans (relative to the size of the sponsor) have greater risk tolerance since the sponsor can tolerate more volatility in contributions should plan assets underperform
Common risk exposures	The lower the correlation of sponsor operating results and the returns of pension assets, the greater the risk tolerance of the plan because the low correlation implies that in times of plan underperformance, the sponsor is likely to be profitable and able to increase plan contributions
Provision for early retirement/ lump-sum distributions	Such plan features generally imply a lower risk tolerance, as the shorter investment horizon means the plan has less time to recover from short-term losses
Workforce characteristics	The younger the workforce and the higher the proportion of active lives, the greater the duration of plan liabilities—increases risk tolerance since the plan has time to recover from short-term losses

PROFESSOR'S NOTE

While a general comment about a higher funded status implying a greater ability to take risk is true, it might still be the case that willingness to take risk remains low for the plan. For example, if the plan is in surplus and the sponsor wishes to remain in surplus to minimize contributions to the plan, then minimization of surplus volatility through LDI would be most appropriate. On the exam, make sure you read the information in the question and respond to it in the most appropriate way. In recent years, the factors discussed in Figure 22.4 have been a source of institutional IPS questions in the essay questions of the exam.

EXAMPLE: Viewpoint Research Corporation (defined benefit plan)

Viewpoint Research is a leading U.K. producer of polling and survey-based market research. Viewpoint is a relatively new company that has taken advantage of new online methods of collecting research data. Viewpoint's costs are largely related to wages and technological support in the U.K., while revenues are generated from clients across Europe. Five years ago, the company introduced a DB pension plan. All participants of the plan are currently either still working for the company or have left the company for alternative employment. The plan currently has a small deficit. While similar plans often offer early retirement and lump-sum distributions as options to plan participants, Viewpoint's plan does not offer such options.

The company has seen rapid growth in earnings over the previous year, with return on equity being higher than the industry average. The company employs significant leverage, with a debt-to-assets ratio 50% higher than that of established industry competitors.

Based solely on the information provided, **discuss** *two* factors that increase the plan's ability to take risk and two factors that decrease the plan's ability to take risk.

Answers:

Two factors that *increase* the plan's ability to take risk are:

1. The plan has zero retired lives, since all participants are either still working for the company or are working in alternative employment. This means the plan liabilities have a relatively long duration; hence, the plan has time to recover from short-term underperformance, which increases the ability of the plan to take risk.
2. The plan does not offer early retirement or lump-sum distribution options to plan participants. This increases the duration and predictability of liabilities, increasing the ability of the plan to take risk since it has time to recover from short-term falls in funded status.

Two factors that *decrease* the plan's ability to take risk are:

1. The company has higher debt levels than the industry average. This lowers the ability of the sponsor to increase contributions to the plan if investment performance is poor, which in turn lowers the risk tolerance of the plan.
2. The plan is running at a deficit. All else equal, this lowers the ability of the plan to take risk since further underperformance of plan liabilities may have a significantly negative impact on the ability of the plan to meet its future liabilities (i.e., make pension payments as required).

PROFESSOR'S NOTE

It might be tempting to simply copy the curriculum and say that the company has a high return on equity and, therefore, has good profitability, which increases the plan's ability to take risk. This is not a good response, since this high profitability is stated for the last year only and it has come at a time when the company has high debt levels; hence, it may simply be a reflection of the leverage of the company. There is no guarantee this short-term profitability can be maintained over the long term—the two answers previously given are better answers based on the case facts.

Liquidity Needs

Pension plans must maintain enough liquidity to pay their liabilities (i.e., pension benefits) as they come due. It is important to remember that the liquidity needs of the pension plan are a function of both the benefits being paid to retired lives *and* the sponsor contributions being made to the plan. Liquidity needs are generally *higher* when:

- The proportion of retired lives in the plan is higher, since retired lives are receiving benefit payments. Frozen plans will have higher liquidity needs than nonfrozen plans due to benefits exceeding contributions.
- The workforce of the employer is older, since the time to pay benefits will be shorter.
- The plan has higher funded status, since this will likely lead to lower sponsor contributions and more benefit payments will need to be met from existing plan assets.
- The plan participants have the ability to switch or withdraw from the plan, an event that usually triggers payments to participants.

A plan with lower liquidity needs can generally invest larger amounts in more risky asset classes.

External Constraints

Regulations vary by country; however, there are similar themes in global regulation. Many regulators now require extensive reporting on fees and costs incurred by plans both internally and externally. Personal liability for pension trustees has been increased to ensure they act in the best interests of plan beneficiaries. In Europe, updates to the Institutions for Occupational Retirement Provision (IORP II) Directive is introducing enhanced requirements regarding governance, risk management, and disclosure. In the United States, the Employee Retirement Income Security Act of 1974 (ERISA) regulates investing, funding requirements, and payouts of corporate pension plans. ERISA established the Pension Benefit Guaranty Corporation, a U.S. government agency that protects beneficiaries of terminated plans. The U.S. Pension Protection Act of 2006 established minimum funding ratios for DB plans, and a later revision of the act raised the rates corporations could use to discount their liabilities by using an average high-grade bond yield over 25 years rather than the existing market yield. While this has led to lower liabilities, it may also lead to higher risk taking in order to generate the higher returns needed to maintain funded status, since the value of liabilities will grow at this higher discount rate over time.

From a *tax* perspective, rules once again vary by country; however, pension funds are often treated favorably by governments in order to encourage individuals to save for retirement. Funds that are subject to taxation should consider the tax implications of their investment decisions. For example, lower longer-term capital gains tax rates may incentivize lower turnover strategies. Higher tax rates on profits from derivatives versus rates of returns from the underlying securities may preclude the use of derivatives. When investing internationally, funds should be aware of when and how to benefit from double-taxation treaties between countries, which may offer domestic tax credits when withholding taxes are suffered in foreign markets.

Accounting rules, again, differ by country. In the United States, corporate DB pension plans must follow GAAP, particularly Accounting Standards Codification (ASC) 715, Compensation—Retirement Benefits, which requires that funded status be shown as an asset or liability on the balance sheet. Public pension plans must follow Governmental Accounting Standards Board (GASB) rules, which require assets to be reported at market values and liabilities to be reported using a blended approach. The blended approach for liabilities uses the expected return on plan assets as the discount rate for the funded portion of the liability, and a lower discount rate—the yield on tax-exempt municipal bonds—for the unfunded portion. Using a higher discount rate for the funded liabilities could incentivize plans to take more risk in order to maintain the funded status of the plan over time.

PROFESSOR'S NOTE

The focus on the exam is on portfolio management rather than a forensic discussion of regulations, taxation, and accounting. Take away the broad points here and be led by the case study in the question in the exam. It is likely that if there is a significant external constraint that needs to be addressed, it will be referenced in the case.

Investment Objectives

For DB pension plans, the primary objective is to achieve a target return over a specified long-term horizon, while assuming a level of risk that is consistent with meeting its contractual liabilities. A secondary objective could be to minimize (in present value terms) the cash contributions the sponsor will be required to provide.

The target return of the plan should reflect the fact that plan assets need to grow through contributions and investment returns in line with the growth in liabilities of the plan (i.e., the discount rate applied to these liabilities). If a plan is in deficit, then plan assets need to grow faster than the liabilities—how much of this growth in plan assets comes from investment return and how much comes from extra contributions by the company is driven by the plan's ability to take risk and the sponsor's ability to make further contributions to the plan.

We will now focus on DC plans.

DC Pension Plan

Stakeholders

The stakeholders in a DC pension scheme include the following:

- *Plan sponsors (employers)*, while not facing the investment risk or longevity risk of the assets, retain important fiduciary responsibilities. These include contributing to the plan, overseeing the investment of plan assets, and offering suitable investment options to plan participants.
- *Plan beneficiaries (employees and retirees)* face the investment risk of contributions and investment returns not meeting retirement needs. They also face the longevity risk of living longer than expected and outliving their savings.
- *The board* must communicate with participants to keep them well informed, and these communications must consider the participants' level of sophistication. The board may be required to select a default investment option when participants are *disengaged* (i.e., do not make an explicit investment choice with their contributions).
- *Governments* are stakeholders in that they provide tax incentives for employees to save for retirement, and taxpayers will ultimately face the costs of providing welfare for those that have failed to adequately save for retirement.

Liabilities and Investment Horizon

The liabilities of a DC plan sponsor are the required contributions to plan assets; hence, unlike under a DB scheme, there is no liability associated with future benefits. Through pooling and increased scale, the DC plan may invest in alternative investments not usually available directly to retail investors. The DC plan sponsor bears the liquidity risk of any event that causes participants to exit the plan.

Individuals in a DC plan have an investment horizon linked to their age—older participants will have a shorter investment horizon because they will be retiring and drawing benefits sooner. Many DC plans offer a default *life-cycle option* (also called *target date option*) where asset mix is managed according to a desired retirement date. These life-cycle options can be either **participant-switching options**, which automatically switch members to a more conservative asset allocation as they age, or a **participant/cohort option**, which involves pooling the participant with other investors with a similar retirement date and the fund being managed more conservatively as the retirement date is approached.

Liquidity Needs

The primary drivers of liquidity needs are the age of the workforce and ability of participants to switch or withdraw from the plan. As is the case for DB schemes, if these factors are high, then liquidity needs of the fund will be high.

External Constraints

As per DB schemes, *regulations* vary by country. Regulators typically recognize that many DC plan participants have low levels of understanding about investments;

therefore, there is a requirement that plan sponsors educate participants on saving for retirement, particularly with regard to default options for disengaged participants. In Australia and the United States, there is a requirement for the plan to offer a diversified default option for participants. This, however, does not absolve the DC plan trustees of their fiduciary duties to run the plan in the best interests of participants.

From a *tax* perspective, DC plans in the United States (referred to as 401(k) plans) are *tax deferred*. This means participants make pretax contributions and investment earnings are not taxable; however, benefits are taxed as ordinary income. Withdrawals before age 59½ are penalized with an additional 10% tax. A similar tax-deferral system operates in the U.K., with the first 25% of benefits being tax-free.

PROFESSOR'S NOTE

As introduced in the DB section, ERISA in the United States and IORP II in Europe are relevant to both DB and DC plans.

Investment Objectives

The main objective of DC plans is to prudently grow assets to meet spending needs in retirement. As already discussed, there is an onus on the plan sponsor to provide cost-efficient default options for disengaged participants. If the plan offers funds with active management, a secondary objective may be to outperform the passive asset class returns of the default option's strategic asset allocation. In environments where participants can voluntarily switch between competing DC plan providers, outperforming other DC plans may be an investment objective.

Asset Allocation by DB and DC Pension Plans

Aggregate data for both DB and DC plans together show:

- Asset allocation varies by region, largely driven by differences in external constraints, risk appetite, and stakeholder preferences.
- Over the past decade, there has been a rotation from equities into alternative assets and fixed income to try to lower the volatility of funded ratios. Within equities, there is some evidence of home bias to domestic equity markets.

MODULE QUIZ 22.2

1. An increase in which of the following factors will *most likely* lead to a decrease in the liabilities of a DB pension plan?
   A. Life expectancy.
   B. Years of service.
   C. Expected employee turnover.

2. Which of the following changes would *most likely* increase the risk tolerance of a DB pension plan?
   A. An increase in the average age of the workforce.
   B. Poor investment performance causing the plan to move from overfunded to underfunded status.
   C. An increase in allocation to asset classes that have a low correlation with the operating results of the sponsor.

MODULE 22.3: SOVEREIGN WEALTH FUNDS

Video covering this content is available online.

Main Features/Mission

Sovereign wealth funds (SWFs) are investment funds owned by a government. The International Monetary Fund defines five broad categories of SWF, each with different missions:

1. **Budget stabilization funds.** These are set up when a nation's revenues are heavily linked to a natural resource or other cyclical industries to insulate government budgets from commodity price volatility or economic cycles.
2. **Development funds.** This investment prioritizes national socioeconomic projects, usually infrastructure or supporting key industries.
3. **Savings funds.** These funds invest revenues from nonrenewable assets for the benefit of future generations.
4. **Reserve funds.** These are designed to earn returns on excess foreign reserves held by central banks. Typically, foreign exchange reserves held by central banks are low-yielding assets relative to the yields offered by bonds issued by central banks that make up their liabilities. Reserve funds aim to reduce this negative cost of carry through boosting returns on reserves.
5. **Pension reserve funds.** These are used to save and invest to meet future pension liabilities of governments.

Stakeholders

The stakeholders in an SWF are as follows:

- *Current and future citizens* benefit from the fund's success either directly through receiving payments or indirectly through lower taxation or increased investment in the domestic economy.
- *Investment offices* invest SWF assets either directly in-house or appoint external managers.
- *The board* has a fiduciary duty to the ultimate beneficiaries of the fund.
- *Governments* are stakeholders in that they may rely on SWF returns to balance budget deficits.

Liabilities and Investment Horizon, and Liquidity Needs

The liabilities of SWFs are linked to their overall mission and generally are less well defined than other types of institutions. The liabilities and investment horizons of the five broad types of SWFs are listed in Figure 22.5.

Figure 22.5: SWF Liabilities and Time Horizons

SWF Type	Liabilities and Investment Horizon
Budget stabilization	■ Uncertain liabilities linked to commodity prices/cyclical industries ■ Short-term investment horizon because budget support required on a short-term basis
Development	■ Nature of liabilities linked to socioeconomic investments made by the fund ■ Some long-term horizons (e.g., infrastructure), some medium-term horizons (e.g., medical research)
Savings	■ Liabilities are linked to future generations; therefore, long term
Reserve	■ Liabilities are technically the yield promised on bonds issued by governments/central banks; however, funds will target higher returns ■ Investment horizons are very long, typically with no near-term liabilities
Pension reserve	■ Liabilities are linked to future pension payments; therefore, long term ■ Fund may have an *accumulation stage* in which contributions are made and a *decumulation phase* where benefits are drawn; time horizon will depend on when these stages occur

Liquidity Needs

- **Budget stabilization funds.** These must maintain the *highest* liquidity level and invest in assets with low risk of significant loss in the short term, in order to meet short-term deficits caused by negative economic- or commodity-related events.
- **Development funds.** Because infrastructure and research and innovation investments are long term, funds established to develop such projects generally have *low* liquidity needs.
- **Savings funds.** The main objective is to accumulate wealth for future generations; hence, liquidity needs are *lowest*. Liquidity needs increase as the nation's natural resources become depleted and the government withdraws from the fund to meet budgetary needs.
- **Reserve funds.** Liquidity needs are lower compared to stabilization funds but higher compared to savings funds. Liquid fixed-income securities are usually held that can be readily sold if there is a dramatic change in the reserves of the central bank.
- **Pension reserve funds.** Liquidity needs vary, being lower during the accumulation stage and higher during the decumulation stage.

External Constraints

From a *legal and regulatory* perspective, SWFs are typically established by laws that give the SWF its mission and structure. This may involve clear rules of asset allocation, particularly in the case of a development fund with a specific socioeconomic mission. In order to avoid political influence, high-quality governance, independence, transparency, and accountability are crucial. The Santiago Principles, a best-practices framework established by the International Forum of SWFs (IFSWF), addresses such concerns alongside other key elements expected of a high-quality SWF, such as ethics, risk management, and regular monitoring for compliance with the principles.

SWFs are generally *tax exempt*. This may void the SWF's ability to claim withholding taxes or tax credits that are normally available to taxable investors. Care should be taken when investing internationally to ensure double-taxation treaties exist when subject to withholding taxes abroad. SWFs should take care not to be perceived as using their status to avoid paying taxes in foreign jurisdictions in which they invest.

Figure 22.6: SWF Investment Objectives

SWF Type	Investment Objectives
Budget stabilization	■ Capital preservation ■ Aims to earn returns above inflation with a low probability of losses ■ Should avoid assets correlated with the source of government revenues
Development	■ Support a nation's economic development and increase long-run economic growth ■ Implicit objective is to earn a real rate of return greater than real domestic GDP growth or productivity growth
Savings	■ Maintain purchasing power of the assets over time while making ongoing spending on government budgetary needs
Reserve	■ Earn a rate of return in excess of the yield the government/central bank pays on bonds it has issued
Pension reserve	■ Earn returns to meet future unfunded pension and social care payments promised by the government

PROFESSOR'S NOTE

As will be discussed in the next section, savings funds share very similar objectives to endowments and foundations.

Asset Allocation by Sovereign Wealth Funds

Typical asset allocations differ by type of SWF as follows:

- **Budget stabilization funds.** The majority of fixed income and cash is due to the defensive nature of the fund.
- **Development funds.** These are driven by the socioeconomic mission of the fund (e.g., investment in local infrastructure projects).

- **Savings funds.** A long investment horizon means relatively high allocations toward equities and alternative investments, such as private equity and real assets.
- **Reserve funds.** Allocations are similar to those of savings funds, but with lower allocation to alternatives due to the potentially higher liquidity needs.
- **Pension reserve funds.** These have high allocations to equities and alternatives due to a long investment horizon and low liquidity needs in the accumulation phase.

As mentioned, savings funds and pension reserve funds typically follow the endowment model. Some may also adopt the Canadian model. Another general theme that drives asset allocation is fewer constraints leading to a broader investment mandate and longer time horizons than most institutional investors (e.g., pension funds) allowing for a higher allocation to alternative assets.

MODULE QUIZ 22.3

1. A strategic asset allocation of 10% equities, 60% fixed income, and 30% cash is *most appropriate* for which type of SWF?
   A. Savings funds.
   B. Development funds.
   C. Budget stabilization funds.
2. To boost its foreign currency (FX) reserves, the Bank of Canada (BoC) buys USD currency from domestic Canadian exporters that received USD for their export products. In the context of reserve funds, which of the following statements is *most accurate*?
   A. The BoC's excess FX reserves are invested in riskier, higher yielding assets.
   B. The BoC's financing of its purchase of USD can cause deflationary pressures.
   C. The BoC's issuance of monetary stabilization bonds result in a positive carry.

Video covering this content is available online.

MODULE 22.4: UNIVERSITY ENDOWMENTS AND PRIVATE FOUNDATIONS

While university endowments and private foundations have many similarities in their investment policies, they also have some key differences. We will consider these institutions individually, beginning with university endowments.

University Endowments

Main Features/Mission

University endowments are funds set up by gifts and donations, which are invested to earn returns that provide ongoing support to the university's operating budget. The main objective is to balance the needs of the university today against its needs in the future (i.e., to provide intergenerational equity).

One of the largest endowments is that of Harvard University with assets in excess of \$30 billion in 2016.

Stakeholders

The stakeholders of a university endowment are current and future students, alumni who contribute gifts and donations, and university employees whose livelihoods depend on the university. Stakeholders often have representation on the endowment's board or investment committee, such as alumni who may be investment professionals.

Liabilities and Investment Horizon

The need to maintain intergenerational equity and the unlimited life of the university mean endowments have a *perpetual* investment horizon.

The endowment's liabilities are the future payouts promised to the university, presented in an official spending policy. The endowment's spending policy should ensure intergenerational equity while smoothing payouts to insulate the university from market volatility. To achieve this, the dollar amount of spending each year can be stated as a weighted average of the previous year's spending (adjusted for inflation) and a spending rate (usually between 4% and 6%) applied to a moving average of assets under management (AUM). This can be formulated as:

$$\text{spending}_{t+1} = w \times [\text{spending}_t \times (1 + \text{inflation})] + \{(1 - w) \times (\text{spending rate} \times \text{average AUM})\}$$

where:
w = weight of the prior year's spending amount

Three different types of spending policies result from different values of *w*:

1. **Constant growth rule (w = 1).** The endowment provides a fixed (real) annual payout to the university once adjusted for inflation by the Higher Education Price Index (HEPI). While this method gives more certainty to the university of the payouts that will be received, this means the percentage of endowment value paid out periodically will fluctuate with the endowment value. This spending rule often contains caps and floors representing maximum and minimum percentage values of AUM over one or three years that can be paid out in any period.
2. **Market value rule (w = 0).** Annual payouts are a prespecified percentage (the *spending rate*, usually between 4% and 6%) of the three-to-five-year moving average of asset values. Payouts under this method are procyclical in that spending will fluctuate in line with the moving average of asset values.
3. **Hybrid rule (0 < w < 1).** Spending is a weighted average of the previous two rules.

Other liability-related factors that need to be considered are as follows:

- **Fundraising from donors.** Gifts and donations coming into the endowment mean that the net spending rate is closer to 2% to 4% of assets rather than the 4% to 6% spending rate applied.

- **Reliance of the university on the spending from the endowment.** All else equal, if the endowment spending comprises a larger proportion of the university's operating budget, then the risk tolerance of the endowment is lower.
- **Capability of the endowment or university to issue debt.** Access to debt markets increases the risk tolerance of the endowment because the institution can borrow to meet spending in times of poor investment performance.

Liquidity Needs

As noted previously, the endowment's annual spending net of gifts and donations is usually very low (around 2% to 4% of assets). Low liquidity needs plus the perpetual time horizon mean endowments usually have a high risk tolerance and absorb relatively high volatility in the short term in pursuit of longer-term returns.

External Constraints

From a *legal and regulatory* perspective, regulation varies by jurisdiction; however, endowments are typically subject to laws that require:

1. Investment on a total return basis (i.e., earning returns from both income and capital gains, not simply generating spending through income returns) and diversification according to modern portfolio theory (MPT).
2. Investment committees or boards and staff who have a fiduciary duty of care in overseeing investments.

In the United States, the Uniform Prudent Management of Institutional Funds Act 2006 (UPMIFA) allows flexibility in spending decisions and enforces the adoption of MPT. In the U.K., the Trustee Act (2000) plays a similar role (relevant to endowments since they are often structured as trusts in the U.K.). The shift to MPT principles has allowed endowments to allocate to a broad range of asset classes.

PROFESSOR'S NOTE

UPMIFA and the Trustee Act also apply to private foundations as discussed in the next section.

Endowments typically have *tax-exempt* status when generating investment returns. Universities are not typically taxed on payouts from the endowment, and donors to endowments usually can deduct gifts from their taxable income.

Investment Objectives

The investment objective is to preserve the purchasing power of the assets in perpetuity (i.e., grow in line with inflation) while achieving returns adequate to maintain the level of spending. As discussed previously, spending policy can be formulated in different ways; however, a typical spending rate target is 5% of average assets.

In practice, this means the university endowment has a primary objective to generate a real return (i.e., after inflation measured using the HEPI) of about 5% on average over a three-to-five-year period. A reasonable volatility limit is typically 10% to 15%. There may be a secondary objective of outperforming a passive benchmark or even a tertiary objective of outperforming a peer group of similar endowments. An issue with the objective of outperforming a peer group is that it may lead to decisions becoming dislocated from the core mission of funding unique liabilities and may lead to *herding* by investment managers into similar investments.

Given endowments need to beat inflation, they tend to have a significant allocation to real assets with expected returns that meet or beat inflation. One lesson from the 2007–2009 financial crisis is that the *liquidity risk* of endowments' portfolios should be analyzed with detailed cash flow modeling. Some endowments use a liquidity *risk band* representing an upper bound for the fund's exposure to illiquid investments, including the endowment's uncalled commitments in illiquid alternative asset funds.

Asset Allocation by University Endowments

Most large U.S. university endowments follow the endowment model, which involves a majority (>50%) allocation to alternative investments, an allocation that has increased over the past two decades. Smaller U.S. university endowments tend to allocate less to alternatives and more to domestic equities and fixed income, with some evidence of home bias causing U.S. equities to be overweighted in these portfolios relative to non-U.S. equities.

EXAMPLE: The Capital University endowment

The Capital University endowment supports 10% of the university's operating budget. The investment office of the endowment is relatively small, and the endowment has an annual spending policy to pay out 4% of the five-year average asset value to the university.

The endowment has historically allocated 30% to public U.S. equities and 70% of the portfolio to fixed income. The board has historically set the objective that annualized volatility should be no more than 15%, and this is not expected to change. A recent review of the endowment's investment policy yielded the following assumptions for expected asset class returns and recommended strategic asset allocation for the endowment:

Asset Class	10-Year Nominal Expected Return	Recommended Strategic Asset Allocation
Fixed income	3%	25%
U.S. equities	6%	35%
International equities	7%	20%
Real estate	8%	10%
Private equity	10%	10%

Expected consumer price inflation over the next 10 years is 1% per year. Higher education price inflation, as measured by the HEPI, is expected to be 100 basis points per year above consumer price inflation.

1. **Formulate** the investment objectives for the Capital University endowment's IPS. **Calculate** the nominal required return of the endowment that is consistent with this objective.

2. **Discuss** whether the recommended shift in strategic asset allocation weights should be accepted based on the expected return.
3. **Discuss** *one* factor that could make the recommended strategic asset allocation inappropriate for the endowment.

Answers:

1. The mission of the Capital University endowment is to maintain the purchasing power of the endowment's assets while financing 10% of the operating budget of the university in perpetuity. The nominal required return consistent with this object is a return that meets the spending rate of 4% plus the relevant rate of inflation, namely the HEPI, which is expected to be 1% + 100 basis points = 2%. Hence, the nominal required return of the endowment is 4% + 2% = 6%. The annual volatility of returns should not exceed 15%.
2. Based on expected return alone, the recommended strategic asset allocation weights should be accepted since the current asset allocation fails to meet the nominal required return objective, but the new asset allocation does meet the objective.

   The current asset allocation is expected to earn a nominal return of (0.3 × 6%) + (0.7 × 3%) = 3.9%. This falls far short of the required nominal return of 6%.

   The new asset allocation is expected to earn a nominal return of:

   $(0.25 \times 3\%) + (0.35 \times 6\%) + (0.2 \times 7\%) + (0.1 \times 8\%) + (0.1 \times 10\%) = 6.05\%$

   This meets the nominal required return objective of 6%.
3. Concerns regarding the new strategic asset allocation include the following:
   - The current investment office is described as small and appears to have no experience investing in alternative assets. The board should ensure that the investment staff have the skills, experience, and contacts to perform due diligence on the new asset classes—in particular, the alternative investment allocations to private equity and real assets.
   - The new strategic asset allocation must adhere to the risk objective of a maximum annual volatility of 15%. The investment staff should analyze whether the new asset allocation is going to meet this objective.

We now turn our attention to private foundations.

Private Foundations

Main Features/Mission

Foundations are nonprofit institutions set up to make grants to support specified charitable causes.

The focus of this reading is on *private* foundations set up by individual donors and their families, an example of which is the Bill & Melinda Gates Foundation, with focuses on global health and poverty. Foundations can also be *community* foundations set up by and for the good of the local community, *operating* foundations set up to fund a specific not-for-profit business, or *corporate* foundations set up from the profits of an existing company.

The main objective of private foundations is typically to maintain purchasing power in perpetuity and earn returns sufficient to support the grant-making activities of the foundation (similar to a university endowment's objective).

Stakeholders

The stakeholders of a private foundation may include the founding family, donors to the foundation, recipients of grants from the foundation, and the wider community that the foundation's activities may benefit. Intergenerational tensions may exist like those of an endowment where the needs of current recipients and future recipients of spending from the foundation need to be balanced. The government could also be considered a stakeholder due to the favorable tax treatment of foundations.

Board members of foundations are less likely to have professional investment experience than alumni on endowment boards. This difference in experience may result in less rigorous board oversight or greater delegation to investment staff. This may affect the quality of investment decisions, particularly in more sophisticated markets such as alternative investments.

Mission-related investing (also known as *impact investing*) is a technique increasingly adopted by foundations whereby investments are made into projects that promote the foundation's mission. The challenge with such investments is maintaining a sufficient return on assets to meet the foundation's long-term objectives.

Liabilities and Investment Horizon

Foundations typically have an investment horizon that is perpetual. There is a trend toward limited-life foundations that are mandated to spend down assets within a limited time frame of the founder's death, which would shorten the investment horizon.

In the United States, tax laws require private grant-making foundations to pay out *a minimum of 5% of assets (on a 12-month trailing basis) plus investment expenses.* Foundations must also spend any donations in the year the donation is received (known as flow through).

Unlike universities, which have other sources of revenue outside the spending of their endowment, foundations are relied upon almost exclusively to meet budgets. This, along with the higher liquidity requirements of foundations, means they typically have a lower risk tolerance than university endowments.

Liquidity Needs

As mentioned previously, U.S. foundations are legally required to spend 5% of assets. Foundations should maintain sufficient liquidity to meet near-term spending, capital calls from private limited partnership fund investments, and any margin calls on derivatives employed by the investment portfolio.

External Constraints

From a *legal and regulatory* perspective, foundations are subject to similar laws, such as UPMIFA in the United States and the Trustee Act in the U.K., which demand investment on a total return basis, diversification, and a duty of care from the board and investment staff.

Foundations typically have similar *tax-exempt* status to endowments, but this status depends on the minimum spending rules mentioned in the previous section. Failing to meet the spending requirement results in a 30% tax on undistributed income. Most U.S. foundations are also subject to a 2% tax on net investment income.

Investment Objectives

The investment objective is to generate a real return over consumer price inflation of the spending rate (minimum 5%) plus investment expenses, with expected annual volatility in a reasonable range (approximately 10% to 15%) over a three-to-five-year period.

There may be a secondary objective of outperforming a policy benchmark based on a tracking error budget.

Asset Allocation by Private Foundations

As mentioned, foundations have a lower risk tolerance than university endowments due to higher liquidity requirements and the heavy reliance on the foundation's spending. However, their overall risk tolerance remains high and, with a long-term objective of beating inflation, larger U.S. foundations allocate about half of the portfolio to alternative investments. Smaller foundations tend to have a higher allocation to domestic equities and fixed-income securities.

MODULE QUIZ 22.4

1. A university endowment has an annual spending policy of 5% of the three-year rolling asset value. Consumer price inflation is expected to be 3% per annum, while the Higher Education Price Index (HEPI) is expected to be 2.5% per annum. The investment objective of the endowment should be to achieve a total real rate of return of at least:
   A. 5.0%.
   B. 7.5%.
   C. 8.0%.

MODULE 22.5: BANKS AND INSURERS

Video covering this content is available online.

We now turn our attention to banks and insurers; these institutions are different from other institutions in that they are financial intermediaries that are run *for profit*. It is important to remember throughout this discussion that we are advising the institution on *its investment portfolio*, not on its core business of being a bank or an insurance company (however, as we shall see, these two activities are interlinked with each other).

Banks

Main Features/Mission

The primary function of a bank is to earn profits by taking deposits from savers and making loans to borrowers. Other functions carried out by a bank are safeguarding assets, executing transactions in securities and derivatives, and advising and investing in securities.

Stakeholders

Most major large international banks are publicly listed, making shareholders a key external stakeholder with an interest in maximization of profits. Customers of a bank, such as depositors and borrowers, are also key external stakeholders. Depositors expect the bank to protect their assets over time, and they make up a majority of the liabilities of the bank. Retail borrowers rely on the bank to finance home purchases, and commercial borrowers rely on the bank to fund their operations. These loans make up a majority of the assets of the bank. Other external stakeholders include creditors, credit rating agencies, regulators, and communities where the bank operates.

Internal stakeholders include the bank's employees, managers, and directors.

Liabilities and Investment Horizon

Deposits constitute the majority of a bank's liabilities. This includes *demand deposits*—which can be withdrawn without notice and are therefore deemed short term in duration—and *time/term deposits* that require advance notice before withdrawal.

Other liabilities include short-term wholesale funding from other financial institutions, long-term debt, and trading/securities payables and repo finance payables.

The majority of the assets of a bank are comprised of longer-term illiquid mortgage and commercial loans.

The investment horizon for a bank portfolio is influenced by the difference between the long-term illiquid assets and the short-term liquid liabilities of the bank. Although banks are perpetual organizations, the instruments held in the investment portfolio of a bank are likely to be very short in nature, such that the bank can manage the volatility of shareholder capital on a medium- to short-term basis.

Liquidity Needs

With deposits as short-duration liabilities and the potential need to raise liquidity in adverse market conditions, liquidity management is a key focus for banks. Since the 2007–2009 financial crisis, regulations have been introduced that require banks to have sufficiently liquid assets to cover near-term expected cash outflows (liquidity coverage ratios, or LCRs) and to have adequate levels of capital from stable sources (net stable funding ratios, or NSFRs). This has led to the investment portfolios of banks being more liquid and banks relying less on the wholesale interbank funding markets.

Banks lending to commercial markets still tend to use wholesale funding markets more than banks lending to retail markets. Retail banks use a higher level of retail deposits in their funding, which have lower costs and tend to be more stable than wholesale funds, giving retail banks a better liquidity position than commercial banks.

External Constraints

From a *legal and regulatory* perspective, the risks that a systemic bank failure pose to critical economic functions such as payment processing and extension of credit mean that regulators are intensely focused on capital adequacy, liquidity, and leverage levels.

The main goal of regulators is to make sure that banks have adequate capitalization to absorb losses rather than the losses having to be faced by customers, creditors, or taxpayers. This can be achieved through requiring diversification, asset quality–based reserves, and diverse and stable sources of funding. As seen in the section on liquidity, regulators require that banks maintain LCRs and NSFRs.

PROFESSOR'S NOTE

When considering the impact of investment decisions on required regulatory reserves, it is important to understand that a quality-based reserves system will require that a bank provide for higher reserves when they hold more risky assets. For example, if a bank switched from less-risky investment-grade bonds to riskier high-yield bonds, the risk-weighted assets of the bank would increase in the eyes of the regulator, and required reserves would consequently be higher.

Economies of scale and the benefits of diversification encourage banks to increase their size, with the largest banks regarded by regulators as *systemically important financial institutions (SIFIs)*. Since the global financial crisis, regulations for these SIFIs have:

- Increased capital required to absorb losses on assets.
- Placed limits on the amount of dividends and share buybacks since these payouts to shareholders effectively increase the leverage of the institution.

- Restricted the ability of subordinated debtholders and preferred shareholders to exert their claims in a bankruptcy, forcing them to bear more of the risk of the bank's activities.
- Restricted the use of derivatives, proprietary trading, and the use of off-balance sheet liabilities and guarantees.

From an *accountancy* perspective, three different accounting systems apply to financial institutions:

1. Standard financial reporting (GAAP or IFRS) is used to communicate results to shareholders. Due to the accruals process of accounting, this provides the smoothest reporting of income.
2. Statutory accounting is utilized by regulators and is comprised of a series of adjustments to make the accounts more conservative—for instance, removing intangible assets from the balance sheet, accelerating certain expenses and costs, and the recognition of reserves against unexpectedly large losses on assets or payments under guarantees.
3. True economic accounting uses market value for all assets and liabilities. This is likely to give the most volatile measure of income.

Banks typically are fully *taxable* entities; hence, they must consider the after-tax returns of their investment programs.

PROFESSOR'S NOTE

As will be seen later, this high-level discussion of regulation, accountancy, and tax also applies to insurance firms as well as banks.

Investment Objectives

The primary objective of a bank's investment portfolio is to manage liquidity and reduce risk mismatches between the bank's noninvestment assets and liabilities.

Banks establish an asset and liability management committee (ALMCo) to oversee investment activities. The ALMCo will set the IPS, monitor performance, and set risk limits regarding market, credit, liquidity, and solvency risks, with the authority to require changes on the asset and liability sides of the balance sheet. Having established these objectives, the investment team sets policy benchmarks, monitors performance, and reports to the bank's management and board.

We now turn our attention to the other major type of financial intermediary: insurers.

Insurers

Main Features/Mission

Insurers can be divided into the following two broad categories:

- **Life insurers.** They write insurance relating to whole life or term insurance with fixed payments, variable life insurance (with payouts linked to returns of investment funds chosen by the policyholder), annuity products, health insurance, and universal life insurance (with flexible premiums and benefit payouts).

- **Property and casualty (P&C) insurers.** They write insurance relating to commercial property and liability, home ownership, marine insurance, surety, and legal liabilities.

Stakeholders

Insurers tend to be organized as either publicly listed companies or mutual companies. For publicly listed companies, key external stakeholders are *shareholders* who require long-term maximization of the value of their capital while simultaneously honoring obligations to policyholders. Mutual companies are owned by their *policyholders*, either retaining profits as a surplus against potential losses or distributing them to policyholders through dividends or premium reductions. Other external stakeholders include derivatives counterparties, creditors, regulators, and rating agencies.

For traditional life insurance (including universal life) and fixed annuity policies, life insurers maintain a *general account* to fund the liabilities because the insurer bears the investment risk associated with meeting claims under these contracts. For variable life policies and variable annuities, the insurer operates a *separate account* in which assets are invested according to the investment choices of policyholders. For these policies, the policyholder bears the investment risk.

Internal stakeholders include an insurer's employees, management, and board of directors.

Liabilities and Investment Horizon

Insurance companies manage their investments with a focus on asset and liability management; therefore, the nature of the liabilities is crucial to the investment horizon of the investment portfolio.

Life insurers generally face a long duration liability stream through their contract payouts, although this can vary by product line. Because of this, life insurance companies have historically set investment horizons of 20 to 40 years.

P&C insurers generally face a liability stream with a shorter duration and higher uncertainty because claims are related to unlikely, unpredictable events with high payouts, such as natural disasters.

In a similar way to banks, while the institution has a perpetual time horizon, the nature and timing of policy claims will strongly affect the time horizon of investments held. A key consideration for both life and P&C insurers is the frequently occurring underwriting cycle, which causes fluctuations in profitability driven by changes in the level of competition at different points of the insurance business cycle. For example, at times of intense competition and low profits from underwriting insurance contracts, insurers will be inclined to bear less underwriting risk, which may increase their appetite for investment risk, all else equal.

Liquidity Needs

An insurer needs to manage both *internal* liquidity (cash from operations and investing activities) and *external* liquidity (ability to borrow in debt markets). Liquidity needs are affected by the level of interest rates. In times of high interest rates, policyholders with historically low-yielding contracts may surrender (i.e., cash in) their policies in order to invest at higher yields in other investments, thereby increasing the net cash outflows of the life insurer.

As noted previously, P&C insurers face significant cash flow uncertainty due to the nature of their liabilities; hence, portfolios require the ample liquidity of high proportions of cash or cash equivalents and short-term fixed-income securities.

Insurers divide general account investments into two major components: the *reserve* portfolio and the *surplus* portfolio. Regulations require the insurer to maintain a reserve portfolio capable of meeting policy liabilities, and this is therefore managed conservatively. The surplus portfolio is used to generate higher returns, often by assuming liquidity risk and allocating to alternative investments.

External Constraints

From a *legal and regulatory* perspective, insurers, like banks, carry out crucial financial intermediary roles and can become large enough to be classified by regulators as SIFIs. Similar to banks, regulators will aim to ensure that insurers have sufficient capital to absorb losses in the business and losses from investments.

In the United States, the *National Association of Insurance Commissioners (NAIC)* is an association of state regulators that set accounting and reporting policies. In Europe, *Solvency II* is a framework being used to standardize regulation across member states.

From an *accountancy* perspective, standard financial reporting, statutory reporting, and true economic accounting rules apply to insurers just as they do to banks.

Insurers typically are fully *taxable* entities and must run their investment programs with consideration of after-tax returns.

PROFESSOR'S NOTE

The high-level discussion of regulation, accountancy, and tax in the section on external constraints for banks is also relevant to insurers. Once again, keep in mind that a switch into riskier investments will increase the regulatory required reserves of the institution.

Investment Objectives

Similar to banks, the primary objective of an insurer's *investment* portfolio is to manage liquidity and reduce risk mismatches between the institution's assets and liabilities. This process must therefore consider the general business conditions of the insurer and the expected external economic conditions.

The investment oversight function of an insurer is typically carried out by a board committee that is responsible for all investment policies and procedures and reports to regulators and external stakeholders.

Video covering this content is available online.

MODULE 22.6: BANKS AND INSURERS; BALANCE SHEET MANAGEMENT AND INVESTMENT CONSIDERATIONS

LOS 22.h: Describe considerations affecting the balance sheet management of banks and insurers.

For both banks and insurance companies, the primary overall objective of the company is to maximize the market value of the institution's equity capital with a high level of assurance that the claims of depositors, creditors, and policyholders can be met.

An expression that captures how changes in the market value of assets, liabilities, and leverage levels affect the change in the market value of equity is:

$$\%\Delta E = \%\Delta A(M) - \%\Delta L(M - 1)$$

where:
$\%\Delta E$ = percentage change in the value of equity
$\%\Delta A$ = percentage change in the value of assets
$\%\Delta L$ = percentage change in the value of liabilities
M = leverage multiplier, A / E

PROFESSOR'S NOTE

This equation makes intuitive sense—the first term on the right-hand side (A) reflects how asset returns are magnified by the leverage (M) used by the firm. The second term relates to the liabilities of the company—the negative sign reflects the fact that increases in liabilities cause equity levels to fall, all else equal. The $M - 1$ term represents the size of liabilities relative to equity. For example, $M = 4$ means that for every \$4 of assets, the company has \$1 of equity. Since assets are funded by equity and liabilities, liabilities must be \$3 (i.e., M − 1).

EXAMPLE: Percentage change in the value of equity

A bank has an equity-to-assets ratio of 5%. **Calculate** the estimated percentage change in the market value of equity if liabilities rise by 1.5% and assets remain stable.

Answer:

With an equity-to-assets ratio of 5%, this means the bank has a leverage multiplier *M* of 1 / 0.05 = 20x.

If liabilities rise by 1.5% and assets do not change, then using the equation, the percentage change in the market value of equity is estimated to be:

$$\%\Delta E = (0\% \times 20) - (1.5\% \times 19) = -28.5\%$$

The previous equation can be tweaked slightly to assess the sensitivity of the institution's equity capital to a unit change in the reference yield, *y*, of the assets (i.e., the modified *duration* of the equity capital). This equation is:

$$D_E = D_A(M) - D_L(M-1)\left(\frac{\Delta i}{\Delta y}\right)$$

where:
D_E = modified duration of the institution's equity capital
D_A = modified duration of the institution's assets
D_L = modified duration of the institution's liabilities
M = leverage multiplier, A / E
$\frac{\Delta i}{\Delta y}$ = estimated change in yield of liabilities, *i*, relative to a unit change in yield of assets, *y*

PROFESSOR'S NOTE

Recall that modified duration measures the percentage change in the value of an asset or liability versus a 1% change in yield. This formula is analogous to the previous formula—the only extra term is the $\frac{\Delta i}{\Delta y}$ term, which reflects the expected movement in the yield of liabilities (i) relative to the expected move in the yield of assets (y). The measures of *M* and *M – 1* are playing exactly the same role as in the previous equation.

EXAMPLE: Computing duration for life insurer

WellLife Holdings is a life insurer with equity capital to financial assets of 12.5%. In a recent report to the board by the investment committee, the duration of assets was listed as 3, with the duration of liabilities listed as 2. It is also estimated that the yield on the liabilities of the insurer is likely to move by 70 basis points for every 1% move in the yield of the asset portfolio.

1. **Calculate** the duration of the insurer's shareholder capital.
2. **Estimate** the impact of a 25-basis-point fall on the value of shareholder capital in yields of the asset portfolio.
3. Management of the insurer is considering changing the ratio of equity-to-assets to 10%. Assuming all else stays the same, **discuss** the resulting impact on the duration of shareholder capital.

Answers:

1. If equity-to-assets is 12.5%, then the leverage multiplier M = 1 / 0.125 = 8x. As per the information in the question, $D_A = 3$, $D_L = 2$, and $\frac{\Delta i}{\Delta y} = 0.70$.

   The modified duration of shareholders' equity is therefore calculated as:

   $$D_E = (3 \times 8) - (2 \times 7 \times 0.70) = 14.2$$

2. A modified duration of 14.2 implies that a 1% change in the level of yield of the asset portfolio will lead to approximately a 14.2% change in the value of equity. Hence, if the yield of the asset portfolio falls by 25 basis points, then the value of equity will increase by approximately 0.25 × 14.2 = 3.55%.

3. An equity-to-assets ratio of 10% implies a leverage multiplier, *M*, of 1 / 0.1 = 10x. If all other variables stay the same, then the new modified duration of shareholders' equity will be:

   $$D_E = (3 \times 10) - (2 \times 9 \times 0.70) = 17.4$$

This framework can be extended to consider the expected volatility (i.e., standard deviation) of the percentage changes in the market value of equity capital using the following formula:

$$\sigma_E^2 = M^2\sigma_A^2 + (M-1)^2\sigma_L^2 - 2(M)(M-1)\sigma_A\sigma_L\rho_{AL}$$

where:

σ_E = standard deviation of percentage change in the market value of equity

σ_A = standard deviation of percentage change in the value of assets

σ_L = standard deviation of percentage change in the value of liabilities

M = leverage multiplier, A / E

ρ_{AL} = correlation of percentage value changes in assets and liabilities

PROFESSOR'S NOTE

Recall the two-asset variance formula that has been used many times over the course of the CFA curriculum—namely when combining Assets 1 and 2 with weights w_1 and w_2, standard deviations σ_1 and σ_2, and correlation ρ_{12}. The resulting variance of the portfolio is given by:

$$\sigma_{1+2}^2 = w_1^2\sigma_1^2 + w_2^2\sigma_2^2 + 2w_1w_2\sigma_1\sigma_2\rho_{12}$$

The equation for σ_E^2 is a simple application of this familiar formula to a *portfolio* with a weight, *M*, in the assets of the institution and a weight of *–(M – 1)* in the liabilities of the institution.

EXAMPLE: Computing volatility for life insurer

WellLife Holdings maintains a common equity-to-assets ratio of 12.5% and estimates that the annualized volatilities of assets and liabilities are 7% and 4% respectively. The investment committee estimates that the correlation between asset and liability returns is 0.3.

1. **Calculate** the standard deviation of changes in the value of shareholder capital.
2. New regulations are being introduced that will force WellLife to increase its equity-to-assets ratio to 20% and lower the volatility of its assets to 5%. **Calculate** the expected volatility of shareholder capital after the new regulations come into force, assuming all else stays the same.

Answers:

1. The leverage multiplier is 1 / 0.125 = 8x. With $\sigma_A = 0.07$, $\sigma_L = 0.04$, and $\rho_{AL} = 0.3$, the variance of shareholders' equity is given by:

   $$\sigma_E^2 = (8^2 \times 0.07^2) + (7^2 \times 0.04^2) - (2 \times 8 \times 7 \times 0.07 \times 0.04 \times 0.3)$$
   $$= 0.298$$

   The standard deviation of shareholders' equity is therefore $\sqrt{0.298}$ = 0.546, or 54.6%.

2. The new leverage multiplier is 1 / 0.2 = 5x. Using a new figure of σ_A = 0.05, the variance of shareholders' equity is given by:

   $$\sigma_E^2 = (5^2 \times 0.05^2) + (4^2 \times 0.04^2) - (2 \times 5 \times 4 \times 0.05 \times 0.04 \times 0.3)$$
   $$= 0.0641$$

   The standard deviation of shareholders' equity is therefore $\sqrt{0.0641}$ = 0.253, or 25.3%.

There are many strategies that the management of a bank or an insurance company can use to change the factors driving the volatility of shareholders' equity. These strategies could relate to the investment portfolio assets or the nature of the liabilities created by the operations of the company. A summary of these strategies is displayed in Figure 22.7.

Figure 22.7: Strategies for Changing Volatility

Strategy	Impact on Factor	Impact on σ_E	Comments
Hold diversified fixed-income investments	Lowers σ_A	Falls	Diversified fixed income has a lower standard deviation than other riskier asset classes.
Hold high-quality fixed-income investments	Lowers σ_A	Falls	There's a lower chance of significant loss in asset value.
Maintain similar asset and liability durations, and match asset/liability exposure to borrower and claimant options	Increases ρ_{AL}	Falls	Regulators penalize institutions with high asset/liability mismatches.
Hold common stock investments	Increases σ_A Lowers ρ_{AL}	Rises	Most regulators require reserves of 100% to be held against investments in common stock.
Derivatives transparency and collateralization	Lowers σ_A and σ_L Increases ρ_{AL}	Falls	The more understood and protected against counterparty default the institution is, the less chance there is of unexpected losses.
Hold more liquid portfolio investments	Lowers σ_A	Falls	
Surrender penalties for insurance contracts	Lowers σ_L	Falls	Penalties cushion losses when policyholders cash in after interest rates have risen.
Prepayment penalties on debt investments	Increases ρ_{AL}	Falls	Prepayments will occur in a low interest rate environment. Penalties on prepayments help offset rising liabilities in a falling rate environment.
Catastrophic insurance risk	Increases σ_L	Rises	Such losses are large and unpredictable and will cause regulators to demand higher reserves, investment in more liquid assets, and more robust reinsurance agreements.
Predictability of underwriting losses	Decreases σ_L	Falls	Total insurance liabilities are less uncertain.
Diversifying insurance business	Decreases σ_L	Falls	Total insurance liabilities are less uncertain.
Variable annuities	Increases ρ_{AL}	Falls	Asset investment gains and losses are passed through to policyholders due to the nature of the contract.

Asset Allocation for Banks and Insurers

In the case of banks and insurers, optimal investment management simultaneously focuses on the investment portfolio and the liabilities of the business, all within the context of external economic conditions and regulatory reserve requirements. The investment manager also needs to be conscious of the factors that affect the volatility of shareholders' equity and optimal levels of leverage as discussed previously.

PROFESSOR'S NOTE

While it might seem daunting that so many factors need to be considered when drafting an investment policy for banks and insurers, keep in mind that exam questions are likely to be very focused on a particular scenario. Often, a very basic knowledge of duration, credit risk, and liquidity of fixed-income securities—as well as the impact a change in these factors will most likely have on earnings, volatility of shareholder capital, and regulatory required reserves—is enough to answer the case study–related questions in the curriculum, as evidenced by the next example.

EXAMPLE: Switching to riskier investments

The ALMCo of SJT Bank recently conducted a quarterly review of business and investment conditions. The main findings are as follows:

- There is evidence that current corporate spreads are significantly below historical norms. It is expected that economic conditions are likely to deteriorate with corporate spreads widening.
- The bank expects disruption in the securitization and secondary loan markets to lower the liquidity of the bank's loan book. They also expect that withdrawals from depositors are likely to become larger and less predictable as economic conditions worsen.

As a result of these findings, the investment management team plans to switch a large portion of its investment portfolio from high-yield corporate floating-rate securities into investment-grade fixed-rate government securities. The team also plans to enter a plain vanilla pay-fixed/receive-floating interest rate swap under standard mark-to-market collateral terms with counterparties.

1. **Discuss** how the planned investment switch addresses the two main findings of the quarterly review conducted by the ALMCo.
2. **Discuss** the likely impact of the switch on required regulatory risk-based reserves.
3. **Describe** how the switch, including the swap position, likely affects the asset and liability duration mismatch of the bank.
4. What is the effect on expected earnings and expected volatility of earnings?

Answers:

1. The first finding of the ALMCo states that credit spreads are expected to widen. This will cause high-yield corporate bond prices to fall by more than investment-grade government bond prices. The proposed switch from high-yield corporate bonds to investment-grade government securities will therefore lower the bank's exposure to widening credit spreads.

   The second finding of the ALMCo states that the liquidity position of the bank is likely to worsen. Assets in the loan book are expected to become more difficult to sell, while demands for liquidity from depositors are expected to increase. The investment-grade government bonds are likely to be more liquid than the high-yield corporate bonds; hence, the switch will improve the liquidity position of the investment portfolio of the bank. This should help offset the deterioration in liquidity conditions in the bank's business.
2. The regulatory risk-based capital the company is required to hold is likely to fall. The government securities are investment grade, while the corporate bonds are high yield, or below investment grade, and as such will have higher credit risk than the government securities. Hence, the risk weighting of the government securities is going to be lower than the risk weighting of the corporate bonds. This means the regulator will view the company as having lower risk-weighted assets and, hence, will require it to hold less equity capital.
3. The switch, including the swap, will not affect the duration of the assets of the company. The switch from floating-rate securities to fixed-rate securities increases the duration of the bond portfolio since fixed-rate assets have higher durations than floating-rate assets. However, the pay-fixed/receive-floating swap will create a synthetic liability increasing the duration of the liabilities since the fixed-leg payments made under the swap will have a higher duration than the floating-leg payments received under the swap. If tailored correctly, this increase in liability duration will counterbalance the increase in asset duration, and the asset and liability profile of the bank will remain unchanged.
4. The government securities are likely to have a lower yield than the corporate securities because they do not offer a credit spread. This will lower the earnings of the bank. The volatility of the more liquid investment-grade government securities should also be lower than the volatility of the corporate bonds. This will lower the volatility of changes in the value of shareholders' equity capital.

MODULE QUIZ 22.5, 22.6

1. Capital requirements for banks and insurance companies are typically set with reference to:
   A. statutory reporting.
   B. true economic reporting.
   C. standard financial reporting.
2. SAJ Assurance (SAJ) is a life insurance company that underwrites a diverse range of life assurance and annuity products. The following is an excerpt from the IPS of SAJ:

   SAJ splits the firm's general account into two components: the reserve portfolio and the surplus portfolio. The objective of the reserve portfolio is to provide liquidity to pay policyholder claims in the normal course of insurance operations. The objective of the surplus portfolio is to hedge interest rate mismatches that occur between the reserve portfolio and the liabilities of the firm.

   This excerpt is *best* described as:
   A. correct.
   B. incorrect because it is the separate account of the life insurer that is broken down into the reserve and surplus portfolios, not the general account.
   C. incorrect with respect to the objective of the surplus portfolio. The surplus portfolio should be run with the objective of taking higher risk in order to earn higher returns to grow the surplus over the long term.
3. A bank has an equity capital ratio of 20%. Assets are expected to have a standard deviation of 7%, and liabilities are expected to have a standard deviation of 5%. The correlation of assets and liabilities is estimated to be 0.5. The volatility of shareholder capital for the bank is *closest* to:
   A. 9.3%.
   B. 16.3%.
   C. 30.4%.

KEY CONCEPTS

LOS 22.a

The five common characteristics of institutional investors are their larger size, long-term investment horizons, regulatory frameworks, governance frameworks, and principal-agent issues.

LOS 22.b

The investment policy statement (IPS) of an institution formally sets out the institution's mission and objectives, liabilities, investment horizon, external constraints (regulatory, accounting, and tax), asset allocation, and rebalancing and reporting policies.

Four common models used in institutional investing are the Norway model, the endowment model, the Canada model, and the liability-driven investing (LDI) model.

LOS 22.c, 22.d, 22.f

The stakeholders and key elements of the IPS for defined benefit (DB) pension plans versus defined contribution (DC) pension plans are described in the following table.

	DB Plan	**DC Plan**
Stakeholders	Employers, plan beneficiaries, investment staff, investment committee/board, governments, shareholders	Employers, plan beneficiaries, investment staff, investment committee/board, governments
Liabilities	Present value of future benefits promised to plan participants Higher when: ■ Employees work longer ■ Salaries are higher ■ Participants live longer ■ Lower employee turnover leads to higher vesting ■ Discount rate is low	No liability to plan sponsor once required contribution to plan has been met
Investment time horizon	Longer if proportion of active lives is higher	Dependent on the age of participant (longer if younger)
Liquidity needs	Higher with: ■ More retired lives ■ Older workforce ■ Higher funded status (may reduce contributions) ■ Flexibility of participants to switch plans	Higher with: ■ Older workforce ■ Flexibility of participants to switch plans

	DB Plan	DC Plan
External constraints	■ Regulations vary by country: IORP II in Europe, ERISA in United States ■ Tax treatment favorable ■ Accounting rules: ASC 715 requires funded status to be shown on balance sheet (U.S. GAAP); public pension plans follow GASB	■ Regulations vary by country: IORP II in Europe, ERISA in United States ■ Sponsor must offer appropriate default option to disengaged participants ■ Plans are tax deferred
Investment objectives	Achieve a long-term target return over a specified horizon with appropriate risk to meet contractual liabilities	Prudently grow assets to meet spending needs in retirement

The stakeholders and key elements of the IPS for the five types of SWFs are described in the following table.

	Budget Stabilization	Development	Savings	Reserve	Pension Reserve
Stakeholders	Country's citizens, the government, external and internal investment management				
Liabilities	Uncertain: linked to commodity prices/ economic cycle	Linked to socioeconomic investments	Spending on future generations	Yield promised on central bank/ government bonds	Future pension payments
Investment time horizon	Short term	Long/medium term depending on investment projects	Long term	Long term	Long term
Liquidity needs	Highest	Generally low	Lowest	Intermediate	Varies: low during accumulation stage, higher during decumulation stage
External constraints	Established by national legislation. Best practice set by IFSWF's Santiago Principles. Generally tax exempt.				
Investment objectives	Capital preservation	Real growth higher than real GDP growth	Maintain real perpetual spending	Grow faster than yield on central bank/ government bonds	Earn returns to meet future unfunded government pension payments

The following table describes the stakeholders and key elements of the IPS for university endowments and private foundations.

	University Endowments	Private Foundations
Stakeholders	Current and future students, alumni, university employees	Founding family, donors, grant recipients, broader community, governments
Liabilities	■ Set by the future spending promised to the university ■ Spending policy should consider: – Ongoing donations – Reliance of university on spending – Ability to issue debt ■ Spending may use a rule that takes a weighted average of last period's spending (adjusted for inflation) and a fixed spending rate applied to average AUM	■ U.S. tax rules require minimum spending of 5% of assets plus investment expenses ■ Must also spend donations in the same year they are received
Investment time horizon	Perpetual	Typically perpetual, but shortened for limited-life foundations
Liquidity needs	■ Spending rate net of donations is very low at 2%–4% of assets	■ Higher than endowments—legally required to spend 5% of assets ■ Reliance on spending by foundation is usually higher than the reliance of a university on endowment spending
External constraints	Typically tax exempt. Regulation varies by jurisdiction but generally requires a total return approach and prudence in investing (UPMIFA in United States, the Trustee Act in the U.K.).	
Investment objectives	Generate a total real return (after inflation measure by the HEPI) of about 5% on a three-to-five-year rolling basis, with reasonable annual volatility in the range of 10%–15%	Generate a real return over consumer price inflation of the spending rate (minimum 5%), plus investment expenses, on a three-to-five-year rolling basis, with reasonable annual volatility in the range of 10%–15%

The stakeholders and key elements of the IPS for banks and insurers are described in the following table.

	Banks	Insurers
Stakeholders	■ External: shareholders, depositors, borrowers, creditors, credit rating agencies, regulators, communities ■ Internal: employees, management, board	■ External: shareholders, policyholders, derivatives counterparties, creditors, regulators, credit rating agencies ■ Internal: employees, management, board
Liabilities	■ Primarily deposits that are short term	■ Life Insurers: long duration contract payouts ■ P&C insurers: shorter and less certain contract payouts
Investment time horizon	While perpetual organizations, investments are run on a short- or medium-term LDI basis.	
Liquidity needs	■ Driven by deposit withdrawals and potential need to raise liquidity in adverse market conditions. ■ Regulators apply liquidity coverage ratios and net stable funding ratios	■ Varies by product line: P&C liquidity needs generally higher than life ■ Liquidity needs will increase in times of high interest rates due to policyholders surrendering in search of high yields elsewhere
External constraints	Highly regulated due to importance to real economy and systemic risk, particularly SIFIs. Main goal of regulators is to ensure the institution holds sufficient risk-based capital to absorb losses. Three different types of accounting systems apply: 1. Standard financial reporting (GAAP or IFRS) 2. Statutory accounting for regulators (more conservative than financial reporting) 3. True economic accounting (marked-to-market) Banks and insurers are fully taxable.	
Investment objectives	Manage liquidity and risk mismatches between the institution's noninvestment assets and liabilities. This needs to be done in the context of the institution's overall profit maximization objective.	

LOS 22.e

The risk tolerance of a defined benefit pension plan is generally higher when:

- Funded status is higher.
- The sponsor has lower debt levels and is more profitable.
- The plan is small relative to the size of the sponsor's business.
- The correlation between the plan assets and the business of the sponsor is low.
- The plan has no provisions for early retirement or lump-sum options.
- The workforce is young and the plan has a high level of active lives.

LOS 22.g

Aggregated data of both DB and DC plans show that asset allocation varies by country due to differences in regulation, tax constraints, investment objectives, risk appetite, and demographics.

Typical asset allocation by SWF type include:

- Budget stabilization funds (mainly bonds and cash).
- Development funds (depends on socioeconomic causes supported).
- Savings and pension reserve funds (higher levels of equities and alternatives).
- Reserve funds (equities, alternatives with significant allocation to bonds).

Typical asset allocation for endowments and private foundations include the following:

- **University endowments.** Large U.S. endowments use the endowment model with a majority allocation to alternatives. Smaller U.S. endowments tend to hold more domestic equities and fixed income, with a lower allocation to alternatives.
- **Private foundations.** Large foundations allocate approximately 50% to alternatives. Smaller foundations allocate more to public equities and fixed income.

LOS 22.h

The change in the market value of equity is given by:

$$\%\Delta E = \%\Delta A(M) - \%\Delta L(M - 1)$$

where:
$\%\Delta E$ = percentage change in the value of equity
$\%\Delta A$ = percentage change in the value of assets
$\%\Delta L$ = percentage change in the value of liabilities
M = leverage multiplier, A / E

The duration of the equity of a bank or insurer is given by:

$$D_E = D_A(M) - D_L(M - 1)\left(\frac{\Delta i}{\Delta y}\right)$$

where:
D_E = modified duration of the institution's equity capital
D_A = modified duration of the institution's assets
D_L = modified duration of the institution's liabilities
M = leverage multiplier, A / E
$\frac{\Delta i}{\Delta y}$ = estimated change in yield of liabilities, *i*, relative to a unit change in yield of assets, *y*

The expected volatility (i.e., standard deviation) of the percentage change in the market value of equity capital is given by:

$$\sigma_E^2 = M^2\sigma_A^2 + (M - 1)^2\sigma_L^2 - 2(M)(M - 1)\sigma_A\sigma_L\rho_{AL}$$

where:

σ_E = standard deviation of percentage change in the market value of equity
σ_A = standard deviation of percentage change in the value of asset holdings
σ_L = standard deviation of percentage change in the value of liabilities
M = leverage multiplier, A / E
ρ_{AL} = correlation of percentage value changes in assets and liabilities

The volatility of equity of a bank or insurer can be lowered by:

- Reducing the volatility of assets.
- Reducing the volatility of liabilities.
- Lowering leverage.
- Increasing the correlation of assets and liabilities.
- Diversifying assets and liabilities.
- Increasing the liquidity and quality of investment assets.
- Accessing stable funding sources.

ANSWER KEY FOR MODULE QUIZZES

Module Quiz 22.1

1. **A** The first statement is incorrect. Institutional clients are generally larger in scale than individual clients. While this may cause some smaller asset classes or strategies to be inaccessible due to capacity issues, generally, the larger scale of institutional clients opens up more asset classes (e.g., private equity and real estate) that are not generally available to individual investors.

   The second statement is correct. Institutional investment programs tend to have more formal governance structures than the investment programs of individual investors, including an investment committee, board, and investment staff. (LOS 22.a)

2. **B** The endowment model is the approach most likely to meet the objectives of the foundation because it involves a large allocation to alternative investments and uses externally managed investment funds that employ active management. The Norway model is inappropriate because it uses largely passive strategies and provides little or no allocation to alternatives. The Canada model is inappropriate because it relies on internally managed assets rather than outsourcing to external managers. (LOS 22.b)

Module Quiz 22.2

1. **C** An increase in expected employee turnover would reduce the expected vesting of benefits with plan participants, since fewer employees are likely to complete minimum service conditions required to become eligible to receive benefits. This will lower the liabilities faced by the pension plan. An increase in years of service would lead to higher liabilities because benefits are usually linked directly to years of service. An increase in the life expectancy of plan participants will increase the liabilities of the plan because benefits are paid in every year of retirement. (LOS 22.c)

2. **C** Allocating to asset classes with returns that have a low correlation with the operating performance of the sponsor increases the plan's ability to take risk because it is more likely that the sponsor will be able to make contributions in times of poor investment performance. The fund moving from overfunded to underfunded status is most likely to lower the risk tolerance of the plan since continued underperformance may jeopardize the ability of the plan to meet future benefit payments. An increase in the average age of the workforce will shorten the time before benefits need to be paid. This is likely to lower the risk tolerance of the plan assets since there is less time to recover from any short-term poor performance. (LOS 22.e)

Module Quiz 22.3

1. **C** Budget stabilization funds are defensive in nature and are therefore largely fixed income and cash. Development funds would be expected to investment in projects and investments that promote the socioeconomic goals of the fund, while savings funds would allocate a higher weight to alternative investments and equities in order to meet their objective of beating inflation over the long term. (LOS 22.g)

2. **A** A country always needs FX reserves for global trade and for paying its foreign currency debt.

   In this example, the BoC invests the USD in very liquid but low yielding U.S. Treasuries. The BoC finances its purchase of USD by printing CAD currency. However, flooding the Canadian market with more CAD currency can cause *inflationary* pressures, therefore, answer choice B is incorrect.

   The BoC counters those inflationary pressures by issuing monetary stabilization bonds to "absorb" the excess CAD currency. The stabilization bonds are issued at a higher yield than the yield received from the U.S. Treasury investments. That results in a cost called "negative carry" (e.g., issue debt at higher yield, invest at lower yield), therefore, answer choice C is incorrect.

   The BoC periodically determines and updates how much in USD currency it needs in its FX reserves. Excess FX reserves not needed can then be transferred to a reserve fund and invested in riskier, higher yielding assets to offset the negative carry, therefore, answer choice A is correct. (LOS 22.g)

Module Quiz 22.4

1. **A** In order to preserve the purchasing power of the endowment, the real required rate of return (i.e., excluding inflation) should be equal to the spending rate of 5%. Note that the nominal required rate of return would include inflation as measured by the HEPI, totaling 5% + 2.5% = 7.5%. (LOS 22.g)

Module Quiz 22.5, 22.6

1. **A** Statutory reporting is required by regulators, which involves a series of adjustments to standard financial reporting that remove low-quality assets and accelerate certain expenses in order to set the level of required reserves. (Module 22.5, LOS 22.d)

2. **C** The excerpt is incorrect with regard to the objective of the surplus portfolio. The surplus portfolio represents investment funds of the company in excess of those required to meet the expected claims of policyholders. As such, the usual objective with the surplus portfolio is to take higher risk to earn higher returns in order to grow the surplus, maximize value for shareholders, and remain competitive as a life insurance company from a pricing perspective. (Module 22.5, LOS 22.f)

3. **C** The expected variance of the percentage changes in the market value of equity capital is given by:

$$\sigma_E^2 = M^2\sigma_A^2 + (M - 1)^2\sigma_L^2 - 2(M)(M - 1)\sigma_A\sigma_L\rho_{AL}$$

where:

σ_E = standard deviation of percentage change in the market value of equity

σ_A = standard deviation of percentage change in the value of assets

σ_L = standard deviation of percentage change in the value of liabilities

M = leverage multiplier, A / E

ρ_{AL} = correlation of percentage value changes in assets and liabilities

In this case, $\sigma_A = 0.07$, $\sigma_L = 0.05$, and $\rho_{AL} = 0.5$. The equity capital ratio of 20% implies that E / A = 0.20; hence A / E = 1 / 0.2 = 5x. Using the formula:

$$\sigma_E^2 = 5^2(0.07)^2 + (5 - 1)^2(0.05)^2 - 2(5)(5 - 1)(0.07)(0.05)(0.5)$$

$$= 0.1225 + 0.04 - 0.07 = 0.0925$$

Then, $\sigma_E = \sqrt{0.0925} = 0.304$ or 30.4%. (Module 22.6, LOS 22.g)

TOPIC QUIZ: PRIVATE WEALTH MANAGEMENT AND INSTITUTIONAL INVESTORS

You have now finished the Private Wealth Management and Institutional Investors topic sections. On your Schweser online dashboard, you can find a Topic Quiz that will provide immediate feedback on how effective your study of this material has been. The test is best taken timed; allow three minutes per question. Topic Quizzes are more exam-like than typical QBank questions or module quiz questions. A score less than 70% suggests that additional review of the topics is needed.

FORMULAS

conditional factor risk model:

$$(\text{Return on HF}_i)_t = \alpha_i + \beta_{i,1}(\text{Factor 1})_t + \beta_{i,2}(\text{Factor 2})_t + \ldots + \beta_{i,K}(\text{Factor K})_t + D_t\beta_{i,1}(\text{Factor 1})_t + D_t\beta_{i,2}(\text{Factor 2})_t + \ldots + D_t\beta_{i,K}(\text{Factor K})_t + (\text{error})_{i,t}$$

where:

α_i = intercept for Hedge Fund *i*

$\beta_{i,K}(\text{Factor K})_t$ = exposure during *normal* periods to Risk Factor *K*

D_t = dummy variable that equals zero during normal periods, and one during a financial crisis

$D_t\beta_{i,K}(\text{Factor K})_t$ = *incremental* exposure to Risk Factor *K* during financial crisis periods

$(\text{error})_{i,t}$ = random error with zero mean

after-tax holding period return:

$$R' = [(\text{value}_1 - \text{value}_0) + \text{income} - \text{tax}] / \text{value}_0$$

Alternatively, $R' = R - (\text{tax} / \text{value}_0)$

after-tax post-liquidation return:

$$R_{PL} = [(1 + R'_1)(1 + R'_2)\ldots(1 + R'_n) - (\text{liquidation tax} / \text{final value})]^{1/n} - 1$$

liquidation tax = (final value – tax basis) × tax rate on capital gains

after-tax excess return:

The after-tax excess return (x′) is computed as the after-tax return of the portfolio (R′) minus the after-tax return of the benchmark (B′).

$$x' = R' - B'$$

In this regard, the tax alpha would be defined as after-tax excess return (x′) minus the pretax excess return (x).

$$\alpha_{tax} = x' - x$$

tax-efficiency ratio (TER):

The TER is calculated as after-tax return (R′) divided by pretax return (R).

$$TER = R' / R$$

after-tax future value (R′) of the portfolio:

$$FV_{AT} = (1 + R')^n$$

tax-exempt account (TEA):

$$FV_{AT} = (1 + R)^n$$

tax-deferred account (TDA):

$$FV_{AT} = (1 + R)^n(1 - t)$$

The two potential RV ratios are as follows:

1. RV of a tax-free gift, $T_g = 0$

$$RV_{\text{tax-free gift}} = RV_{\text{tax-free gift}} = \frac{FV_{\text{gift}}}{FV_{\text{bequest}}} = \frac{\left[1 + r_g\left(1 - t_g\right)\right]^n}{\left[1 + r_e\left(1 - t_e\right)\right]^n\left(1 - T_e\right)}$$

2. RV of a taxable gift, T_g, paid by receiver

$$RV_{\text{taxable gift}} = RV_{\text{taxable gift}} = \frac{FV_{\text{gift}}}{FV_{\text{bequest}}} = \frac{\left[1 + r_g\left(1 - t_g\right)\right]^n\left(1 - T_g\right)}{\left[1 + r_e\left(1 - t_e\right)\right]^n\left(1 - T_e\right)}$$

The change in the market value of equity for banks and insurers:

$$\%\Delta E = \%\Delta A(M) - \%\Delta L(M - 1)$$

where:

$\%\Delta E$ = percentage change in the value of equity

$\%\Delta A$ = percentage change in the value of assets

$\%\Delta L$ = percentage change in the value of liabilities

M = leverage multiplier, A / E

The duration of the equity of a bank or insurer:

$$D_E = D_A(M) - D_L(M - 1)\left(\frac{\Delta i}{\Delta y}\right)$$

where:

D_E = modified duration of the institution's equity capital

D_A = modified duration of the institution's assets

D_L = modified duration of the institution's liabilities

M = leverage multiplier, A / E

$\frac{\Delta i}{\Delta y}$ = estimated change in yield of liabilities, i, relative to a unit change in yield of assets, y

The expected volatility (i.e., standard deviation) of the percentage change in the market value of equity capital for a bank or insurer:

$$\sigma_E^2 = M^2\sigma_A^2 + (M - 1)^2\sigma_L^2 - 2(M)(M - 1)\sigma_A\sigma_L\rho_{AL}$$

where:

σ_E = standard deviation of percentage change in the market value of equity

σ_A = standard deviation of percentage change in the value of assets

σ_L = standard deviation of percentage change in the value of liabilities

M = leverage multiplier, A / E

ρ_{AL} = correlation of percentage value changes in assets and liabilities

INDEX

Kaplan SCHWESER™
2024 CFA® Notes 备考笔记三级

第五册（全五册）

SCHWESERNOTES™ 2024 CFA® PART III

BOOK 5

Trading, Performance Evaluation, Manager Selection, Case Studies, and Ethical and Professional Standards

美国开普兰公司 著

中信出版集团 | 北京

图书在版编目（CIP）数据

Kaplan SCHWESER 2024 CFA®; Notes 备考笔记 = SCHWESERNOTES™; 2024 LEVEL Ⅲ CFA®; 三级 : 全五册 : 英文 / 美国开普兰公司著 . -- 北京 : 中信出版社 , 2023.8

ISBN 978-7-5217-5649-4

Ⅰ . ① K… Ⅱ . ①美… Ⅲ . ①金融－分析－资格考试－自学参考资料－英文 Ⅳ . ① F83

中国国家版本馆 CIP 数据核字 (2023) 第 083168 号

Kaplan SCHWESER 2024 CFA® Notes 备考笔记三级第五册（全五册）

著者：　美国开普兰公司

出版发行：中信出版集团股份有限公司

（北京市朝阳区东三环北路 27 号嘉铭中心　邮编　100020）

承印者：　河北鹏润印刷有限公司

开本：889mm × 1194mm　1/16　　印张：74.5　　字数：2130 千字

版次：2023 年 8 月第 1 版　　印次：2023 年 8 月第 1 次印刷

书号：ISBN 978-7-5217-5649-4

定价：1599.00 元（全五册）

Book 5: Trading, Performance Evaluation, Manager Selection, Case Studies, and Ethical and Professional Standards

SchweserNotes™ 2024

Level III CFA®

KAPLAN SCHWESER

SCHWESERNOTES™ 2024 LEVEL III CFA® BOOK 5: TRADING, PERFORMANCE EVALUATION, MANAGER SELECTION, CASE STUDIES, AND ETHICAL AND PROFESSIONAL STANDARDS

Published in 2023 by Kaplan, Inc.

ISBN: 978-1-0788-3758-3

CONTENTS

TRADING, PERFORMANCE EVALUATION, AND MANAGER SELECTION; AND CASE STUDIES

LEARNING OUTCOME STATEMENTS (LOS)

23. Trade Strategy and Execution

The candidate should be able to:

a. discuss motivations to trade and how they relate to trading strategy. (page 1)
b. discuss inputs to the selection of a trading strategy. (page 3)
c. compare benchmarks for trade execution. (page 6)
d. recommend and justify a trading strategy (given relevant facts). (page 7)
e. describe factors that typically determine the selection of a trading algorithm class. (page 9)
f. contrast key characteristics of the following markets in relation to trade implementation: equity, fixed income, options and futures, OTC derivatives, and spot currency. (page 13)
g. explain how trade costs are measured and determine the cost of a trade. (page 15)
h. evaluate the execution of a trade. (page 19)
i. evaluate a firm's trading procedures, including processes, disclosures, and record keeping with respect to good governance. (page 21)

24. Portfolio Performance Evaluation

The candidate should be able to:

a. explain the following components of portfolio evaluation and their interrelationships: performance measurement, performance attribution, and performance appraisal. (page 32)
b. describe attributes of an effective attribution process. (page 33)
c. contrast return attribution and risk attribution; contrast macro and micro return attribution. (page 33)
d. describe returns-based, holdings-based, and transactions-based performance attribution, including advantages and disadvantages of each. (page 34)
e. interpret the sources of portfolio returns using a specified attribution approach. (page 36)
f. interpret the output from fixed-income attribution analyses. (page 46)
g. discuss considerations in selecting a risk attribution approach. (page 49)
h. identify and interpret investment results attributable to the asset owner versus those attributable to the investment manager. (page 37)
i. discuss uses of liability-based benchmarks. (page 53)
j. describe types of asset-based benchmarks. (page 53)
k. discuss tests of benchmark quality. (page 56)
l. describe the impact of benchmark misspecification on attribution and appraisal analysis. (page 60)
m. describe problems that arise in benchmarking alternative investments. (page 58)
n. calculate and interpret the Sortino ratio, the appraisal ratio, upside/downside capture ratios, maximum drawdown, and drawdown duration. (page 62)
o. describe limitations of appraisal measures and related metrics. (page 62)
p. evaluate the skill of an investment manager. (page 67)

25. Investment Manager Selection

The candidate should be able to:

a. describe the components of a manager selection process, including due diligence. (page 79)
b. contrast Type I and Type II errors in manager hiring and continuation decisions. (page 81)

c. describe uses of returns-based and holdings-based style analysis in investment manager selection. (page 83)
d. describe uses of the upside capture ratio, downside capture ratio, maximum drawdown, drawdown duration, and up/down capture in evaluating managers. (page 84)
e. evaluate a manager's investment philosophy and investment decision-making process. (page 86)
f. evaluate the costs and benefits of pooled investment vehicles and separate accounts. (page 88)
g. compare types of investment manager contracts, including their major provisions and advantages and disadvantages. (page 90)
h. describe the three basic forms of performance-based fees. (page 91)
i. analyze and interpret a sample performance-based fee schedule. (page 93)

26. Case Study in Portfolio Management: Institutional

The candidate should be able to:
a. discuss tools for managing portfolio liquidity risk. (page 101)
b. discuss capture of the illiquidity premium as a long-term investment strategy. (page 105)
c. analyze asset allocation and portfolio construction in relation to liquidity needs and risk and return requirements and recommend actions to address identified needs. (page 106)
d. demonstrate the application of the Code of Ethics and Standards of Professional Conduct regarding the actions of individuals involved in manager selection. (page 113)
e. analyze the costs and benefits of derivatives versus cash market techniques for establishing or modifying asset class or risk exposures. (page 114)
f. demonstrate the use of derivatives overlays in tactical asset allocation and rebalancing. (page 114)
g. discuss ESG considerations in managing long-term institutional portfolios. (page 117)

27. Case Study in Risk Management: Private Wealth

The candidate should be able to:
a. identify and analyze a family's risk exposures during the early career stage. (page 133)
b. recommend and justify methods to manage a family's risk exposures during the early career stage. (page 134)
c. identify and analyze a family's risk exposures during the career development stage. (page 141)
d. recommend and justify methods to manage a family's risk exposures during the career development stage. (page 142)
e. identify and analyze a family's risk exposures during the peak accumulation stage. (page 148)
f. recommend and justify methods to manage a family's risk exposures during the peak accumulation stage. (page 151)
g. identify and analyze a family's risk exposures during the early retirement stage. (page 156)
h. recommend and justify a plan to manage risks associated with an individual's retirement lifestyle goals. (page 156)

28. Case Study in Risk Management: Institutional

The candidate should be able to:

a. discuss financial risks associated with the portfolio strategy of an institutional investor. (page 167)
b. discuss environmental and social risks associated with the portfolio strategy of an institutional investor. (page 178)
c. analyze and evaluate the financial and non-financial risk exposures in the portfolio strategy of an institutional investor. (page 185)
d. discuss various methods to manage the risks that arise on long-term direct investments of an institutional investor. (page 185)
e. evaluate strengths and weaknesses of an enterprise risk management system and recommend improvements. (page 185)

29 & 30. Code of Ethics and Standards of Professional Conduct, Guidance for Standards I–VII

The candidate should be able to:

29a. describe the structure of the CFA Institute Professional Conduct Program and the disciplinary review process for the enforcement of the CFA Institute Code of Ethics and Standards of Professional Conduct. (page 216)
29b. explain the ethical responsibilities required by the Code and Standards, including the sub-sections of each standard. (page 217)
30a. demonstrate a thorough knowledge of the CFA Institute Code of Ethics and Standards of Professional Conduct by interpreting the Code and Standards in various situations involving issues of professional integrity. (page 222)
30b. recommend practices and procedures designed to prevent violations of the Code and Standards. (page 222)

31. Application of the Code and Standards: Level III

The candidate should be able to:

a. evaluate practices, policies, and conduct relative to the CFA Institute Code of Ethics and Standards of Professional Conduct. (page 255)
b. explain how the practices, policies, or conduct does or does not violate the CFA Institute Code of Ethics and Standards of Professional Conduct. (page 255)

32. Asset Manager Code of Professional Conduct

The candidate should be able to:

a. explain the purpose of the Asset Manager Code and the benefits that may accrue to a firm that adopts the Code. (page 279)
b. explain the ethical and professional responsibilities required by the six General Principles of Conduct of the Asset Manager Code. (page 280)
c. determine whether an asset manager's practices and procedures are consistent with the Asset Manager Code. (page 280)
d. recommend practices and procedures designed to prevent violations of the Asset Manager Code. (page 280)

33. Overview of the Global Investment Performance Standards

The candidate should be able to:

a. discuss the objectives and scope of the GIPS standards and their benefits to prospective clients and investors, as well as investment managers. (page 293)
b. discuss requirements of the GIPS standards with respect to return calculation methodologies, including the treatment of external cash flows, cash and cash equivalents, and expenses and fees. (page 297)

c. explain the recommended valuation hierarchy of the GIPS standards. (page 318)
d. explain requirements of the GIPS standards with respect to composite return calculations, including methods for asset-weighting portfolio returns. (page 303)
e. explain the meaning of "discretionary" in the context of composite construction and, given a description of the relevant facts, determine whether a portfolio is likely to be considered discretionary. (page 306)
f. explain the role of investment mandates, objectives, or strategies in the construction of composites. (page 308)
g. explain requirements of the GIPS standards with respect to composite construction, including switching portfolios among composites, the timing of the inclusion of new portfolios in composites, and the timing of the exclusion of terminated portfolios from composites. (page 309)
h. explain requirements of the GIPS standards with respect to presentation and reporting. (page 314)
i. explain the conditions under which the performance of a past firm or affiliation may be linked to or used to represent the historical performance of a new or acquiring firm. (page 314)
j. discuss the purpose, scope, and process of verification. (page 322)

READING 23

Trade Strategy and Execution

EXAM FOCUS

This topic review evaluates the trade execution component of the portfolio management process. Understand trade motivations, trade characteristics, and how these—in conjunction with market conditions—determine the most appropriate approach for a trade. Crucial to determining the optimal trading approach are the costs of trading, which are both explicitly observable (i.e., commissions and fees) and implicitly part of the trading strategy (i.e., execution cost and opportunity cost). It is vital that you can calculate the total costs of trading using the implementation shortfall metric and decompose trading costs into component parts due to delay, trading, opportunity, and fixed fees. Finally, understand the areas addressed by the formal trade policy of an asset manager.

MODULE 23.1: TRADE MOTIVATIONS

Video covering this content is available online.

LOS 23.a: Discuss motivations to trade and how they relate to trading strategy.

The four categories of trade motivation include the following:

1. **Profit seeking.** Active portfolio managers seek to outperform their benchmark (i.e., generate alpha) trading securities they believe to be mispriced.
   - Managers need to act on their insight before the rest of the market; hence, a key consideration is the rate of **alpha decay**. Alpha decay is deterioration in alpha once an investment decision has been made. Managers with higher rates of alpha decay (e.g., managers trading on daily news flow) need to trade in shorter time frames; therefore, they have greater trade *urgency*.

Other managers (e.g., managers with insights based on long-term company fundamentals) will have lower rates of alpha decay and therefore a lower trade urgency.

- To minimize **information leakage** (i.e., alert the market to the security mispricing through their trading activity), managers may execute their trade in multiple venues. This may include less transparent venues called **dark pools**, which are trading systems with low pretrade transparency. Orders entered into a dark venue cannot be seen by other market participants before the trade occurs; hence, users know that there is no risk of information leakage. The disadvantage of dark pools is that traders can't see orders on the other side of the trade, so they do not know the pretrade likelihood of execution. Dark pools are referred to as alternative trading systems (ATSs) in the United States. In Europe, dark pools may be multilateral trading facilities (MTFs) bringing together buyers and sellers, or systematic internalizers (SIs), which are single-dealer liquidity pools. An execution venue with high pretrade transparency is called a lit venue. National stock exchanges are examples of lit venues.

2. **Risk management and hedging needs.** Portfolios need to be traded to maintain targeted risk exposures. This may be simply rebalancing the portfolio after a change in market conditions (e.g., a fixed income manager targeting a fixed duration level), or hedging to remove a risk factor from a portfolio (e.g., an equity manager hedging foreign exchange exposure). Derivatives trades may be used to facilitate risk management; however, this does require that appropriate liquid derivative contracts exist and that the fund mandate permits their use. When these conditions are not satisfied, trades in underlying securities will be required. Funds that use leverage need to monitor risk levels closely, since leverage magnifies risk.
3. **Cash flow needs.** These trades are primarily caused by investor subscriptions into, and redemptions out of, the fund.
   - The urgency of the trades depends on the nature of the cash flow, the liquidity of fund investments, and the liquidity terms promised to fund investors. For example, a manager investing in listed securities might promise daily liquidity to investors, whereas a hedge fund manager using less liquid securities might require a one-month notice for redemptions.
   - Funds with less liquid holdings will find it difficult to invest new client funds in a short time frame. This may lead to *cash drag*, where the low returns of cash cause the fund to underperform the benchmark. To avoid cash drag, a manager may engage in *equitization* strategies where liquid securities such as exchange-traded funds (ETFs) or derivatives are used to gain market exposure while the investment in underlying securities occurs over time.
   - Client redemptions are usually based on the fund's net asset value (NAV) using the closing prices of securities. Liquidating securities at closing prices, therefore, eliminates the risk of selling at prices different to those needed to meet redemptions. When determining which securities to sell to meet redemption requests, managers should consider both liquidity and tax implications.

4. **Corporate actions, margin calls, and index reconstitution.**
   - Corporate actions on portfolio holdings such as mergers, acquisitions, or spinoffs may require portfolio trading. Income-related corporate actions such as dividends or coupons income may need reinvesting. Funds that make regular distributions to investors may have to sell securities when income from investments is insufficient to meet these distributions.
   - Margin calls on leveraged positions as well as derivatives positions that are suffering losses may require urgent sales of portfolio holdings.
   - When the benchmark index is reconstituted, managers may need to execute trades to reflect the change. This is particularly important for index-tracking funds. Since the value of the index benchmark usually is based on closing prices, trading at closing prices minimizes the fund's tracking error to the benchmark.

Trading Strategy Inputs

LOS 23.b: Discuss inputs to the selection of a trading strategy.

Once the decision to invest has been made by the portfolio manager, the executing trader and the portfolio manager must work together to identify the optimal trading strategy given the manager's objectives. Key factors that dictate the appropriate trading strategy are (1) order characteristics, (2) security characteristics, (3) market conditions, and (4) individual risk aversion. These factors are discussed as follows:

1. **Order characteristics.** These include side, absolute size, and relative size.
   - **Side** refers to the direction of the order (buy, sell, short buyback (cover), or short sell). This is particularly important when there is price momentum expected where securities are moving in one direction. For example, it will be more costly to purchase securities in a rising market than to sell them. A list of only buy orders or only sell orders will have greater market risk exposure compared to a list of buys and sells with offsetting market risk exposures.
   - **Absolute size** refers to the number of securities being traded. Larger orders will have a higher *market impact cost* than smaller orders. Market impact cost is the adverse effect of the order on prices—the act of buying (selling) puts upward (downward) pressure on prices. Managers will generally trade larger orders with less urgency (if possible) to mitigate the market impact of the order.
   - With **relative size**, managers will often consider order size as a percentage of **average daily volume (ADV)**. Orders that constitute a higher percentage of ADV are expected to have higher market impact costs.
2. **Security characteristics.** These include security type, short-term alpha, price volatility, and security liquidity.
   - **Security type.** Different security types [e.g., underlying securities, ETFs, American depositary receipts (ADRs), global depositary receipts (GDRs),

derivatives, and foreign exchange (FX) contracts] trade in different markets with different costs, regulations, and liquidity.

- **Short-term alpha.** For active managers, a high rate of alpha decay requires a more urgent trade strategy. A manager will also have higher urgency in adverse market conditions (i.e., buying into a rising market or selling into a falling market).
- **Price volatility.** High price volatility implies high *execution risk*, defined as the risk that an adverse price movement will occur over the trading horizon.
- **Security liquidity.** Greater liquidity decreases execution risk and market impact cost. Narrow bid-ask spreads and large volume available for trading (i.e., market depth) are two key indicators of high liquidity.

3. **Market conditions.** Key market conditions that affect trading cost are volatility and liquidity levels. These can both change adversely (increased volatility and lower liquidity) in times of market crisis, such as the credit crisis of 2008. This can also occur for individual strategies. For example, quantitative equity fund managers experienced a liquidity shock in August 2007 due to managers, having herded into similar trades, attempting to liquidate at the same time. Even in normal market times, volatility and liquidity will be dynamically changing, and traders need to reflect this in their expectations. Lower liquidity suggests longer trading horizons; however, higher volatility might cause investors to speed up trades and incur higher costs to avoid execution risk of adverse price movements.
4. **Individual risk aversion.** A portfolio manager/trader with higher risk aversion is typically more concerned about the market risk of adverse movements in security prices than market impact costs and therefore will trade with more urgency.

These trade strategy inputs are key factors driving the two major costs of trading: market impact and execution risk. Market impact comes from trading too quickly, causing adverse price movements and information leakage as the market notices the liquidity imbalance in the market. On the flip side, execution risk, the risk of adverse price movements over the trading horizon, is caused by trading too slowly. Therein lies the **trader's dilemma**—alleviating market impact causes execution risk, and vice versa. Skillful traders will use their experience and judgment to balance these costs of trading.

EXAMPLE: Trading costs

A portfolio manager is discussing a list of buy and sell orders with the firm's head trader. The trader is specifically interested in how order size, security liquidity, and rate of alpha decay affects market impact risk and execution risk, respectively.

1. For each of the factors listed (order size, security liquidity, and rate of alpha decay), briefly **describe** how the factor affects the *market impact cost* of the trade. (Note: Consider each factor in isolation.)
2. The portfolio manager makes the following two statements:

   Statement 1: High market impact costs could be mitigated by executing the order over a longer trading horizon.

   Statement 2: If done correctly, this will not lead to an increase in any other types of trading cost.

   Discuss whether the two statements are true or false. Briefly **justify** your response.

Answers:

1. A larger order size will most likely lead to a higher market impact cost; the trader will have to trade at more adverse prices to execute a larger transaction.

   Higher liquidity results in narrower bid-ask spreads and higher market depth, both contributing to lower market impact cost; the trader will likely be able to execute the trade close to current market prices.

   Higher alpha decay prompts traders to trade quickly, leading to a higher market impact cost.
2. Statement 1 is true. Executing the order over a longer trading horizon will mean the manager can break the order up into smaller parts and therefore lower the market impact cost of the trade.

   Statement 2 is false. Executing a trade over a longer time horizon will lead to higher execution risk; the risk of an adverse price movement increases with the trading horizon.

MODULE QUIZ 23.1

1. Which of the following motivations to trade is *most likely* to require the executing trader to target closing prices?
   A. Margin calls.
   B. Profit seeking.
   C. Cash flow needs (redemption).
2. An increase in security liquidity is *most likely* to decrease:
   A. execution risk only.
   B. market impact only.
   C. both execution risk and market impact.

Video covering this content is available online.

MODULE 23.2: REFERENCE PRICE BENCHMARKS FOR TRADE EXECUTION

LOS 23.c: Compare benchmarks for trade execution.

Reference prices are used to determine expected trading costs, which enables managers/traders to select the optimal strategy for a trade. Reference prices are also a key input in the calculation of the actual cost of trading for posttrade evaluation.

Reference prices can be categorized as pretrade, intraday, posttrade, or price target. Details of these categories are as follows.

- **Pretrade benchmarks** are known before the start of trading. These include:
  - *Decision price*. This is the price at the time the portfolio manager made the investment decision.
  - *Previous close*. This is the closing price on the previous day (often used as a proxy for decision price by quantitative managers using systematic rules-based, data-driven strategies).
  - *Opening price*. This is the opening price on the day (often used as a proxy for decision price for subjective fundamental managers investing in securities for a long-term alpha, since it does not punish or reward traders for news released overnight when markets were closed). Note that if a trade is to be entered into an opening auction, which sets the day's opening price of a security at a trading venue, then this opening auction price is *not* a good benchmark since it can be affected by the trade.
  - *Arrival price*. This is the price of the security when the order is sent to the market for execution. Active portfolio managers trying to generate alpha will often specify a benchmark for an arrival price.
- **Intraday benchmarks** are based on prices during the trading period. These are used by managers who trade passively over a day or funds that may be rebalancing or minimizing risk. Intraday benchmarks include:
  - *Volume-weighted average price (VWAP)*. This is defined as the average price of all trades, weighted by volume, over the trading horizon. Managers may use the VWAP benchmark when they want to participate with volume patterns over a day (e.g., when rebalancing a portfolio over a day). Managers specify VWAP to help achieve the objective of using the cash received from sell orders to fund buy orders of the rebalancing.
  - *Time-weighted average price (TWAP)*. This is the equal-weighted average price of all trades executed over the trading horizon (i.e., TWAP ignores volume). TWAP may be appropriate for managers who wish to remove the impact of outliers (i.e., large trades that occur at the highs or lows of the day) since they believe they are less able to participate in these extreme trades. It is also appropriate in market environments with highly fluctuating volume throughout the day.

- **Posttrade benchmarks** are determined after trading has been completed. The most frequently used posttrade benchmark is the closing price, often used by managers who wish to execute at the closing price to reduce the tracking error of the fund. A drawback of this benchmark is that since the closing price is not known until after the trading is completed, a manager cannot assess trading performance during the trading horizon.
- **Price target benchmarks** are prices used by profit-seeking managers aiming to earn short-term alpha, related to the manager's view of the fair value of the security. For example, a manager may believe that a security that is currently priced at $10 has a true fair value of $10.50. This manager could use a price target benchmark of $10.50 in a strategy that purchases as many shares as possible below this level.

Trading Strategy Selection

LOS 23.d: Recommend and justify a trading strategy (given relevant facts).

The trading strategy selected by the manager and trader should reflect the costs and risks discussed in the previous section and be consistent with the manager's objectives. Examples of some common trade types and their most appropriate trading strategy are shown here:

Trade Type	Description
Short-term alpha	**Objective:** Trade short-term mispricing in a liquid equity market (e.g., overreaction to news flow). **Urgency:** High **Reference prices:** Price target benchmark linked to the manager's estimate of fair value combined with an *arrival price benchmark* for orders when placed in the market **Execution method:** Computer algorithm (discussed later)
Long-term alpha	**Objective:** Trade over the long term due to changes in fundamental conditions (e.g., sell average-sized positions in illiquid bonds that are expected to experience deteriorating credit conditions over the next year). **Urgency:** Low **Reference prices:** Difficult to use in practice **Execution method:** Sell securities gradually over a few weeks in small parts to avoid information leakage and pressure on dealer's prices.

Trade Type	Description
Risk rebalance	**Objective:** Rebalance or hedge risk exposure (e.g., reduce risk levels in liquid FX markets by liquidating long and short positions to bring fund volatility down to a target level). **Urgency:** It is low, since the trader is both buying and selling, which lowers execution risk. Execution risk would be higher for trades on only one side of the book since then the trader has directional exposure. **Reference prices:** TWAP **Execution method:** Algorithmically target TWAP over the next couple of days.
Cash flow driven **(client redemption)**	**Objective:** Liquidate the holding to meet client redemptions (e.g., liquidate small-cap fund to meet redemptions, which will be calculated using the closing prices of securities in the portfolio). The fund bears the risk that liquidations are not made at the closing prices used to calculate the redemption. **Urgency:** The trade needs to be completed by the end of the trading day. **Reference prices:** Closing price **Execution method:** Execute a reasonable amount of liquidity in the closing auction; execute the remainder before the close of trading (e.g., at VWAP).
Cash flow driven **(new trade mandate)**	**Objective:** Invest new client funds (e.g., invest large amount with a mandate to track a small-cap index with a 3% tracking error). Performance measurement will begin at the current day's closing price. **Urgency:** Liquidity is too low to execute in underlying securities by the end of the day, but immediate exposure is required by the client. Liquid index futures contracts exist. **Reference prices:** Closing price **Execution method:** Obtain immediate exposure to index through a long position in index futures to eliminate cash drag. Build underlying stock positions over time to reduce market impact, while simultaneously unwinding the futures position. There are two issues with this method: ■ There may not be a closing auction for the futures contract, in which case the futures trade would need to be done as close to the market close as possible. ■ The mandate must allow derivatives positions.

MODULE QUIZ 23.2

1. A portfolio manager who wishes to execute a trade passively over a trading day and mitigate the impact of outliers should use which of the following reference prices as a benchmark?
   A. TWAP.
   B. VWAP.
   C. Arrival price.
2. A quantitative U.S. sector-focused equity fund is mandated to have a low tracking error. The benchmark index is undergoing a reconstitution at the end of the trading day, and the fund's NAV is calculated daily using closing market prices. The portfolio manager has generated a list of trades that need to be executed to reflect the index reconstitution. The appropriate execution strategy for these trades is *most likely*:
   A. VWAP.
   B. arrival price.
   C. market on close.

MODULE 23.3: TRADE EXECUTION AND STRATEGY IMPLEMENTATION

Video covering this content is available online.

LOS 23.e: Describe factors that typically determine the selection of a trading algorithm class.

Once an appropriate trading strategy has been identified, the trade must be implemented. Trade implementation choices are described as follows:

High-touch approaches involve high levels of human involvement. This is usually required for large trades (known as block trades), since finding the other side to larger trades is more difficult, or in less liquid markets. High-touch approaches include:

- **Principal trades (broker risk trades).** This is where dealers or market makers assume all or some of the risk relating to executing the order, which is priced into their spread. **Quote-driven**, **over-the-counter (OTC)**, or **off-exchange markets** are primarily principal trade markets. Principal trades also include **request-for-quote (RFQ)** markets where market makers do not provide continuous quotes, but only do so on request.
- **Agency trades.** This is where the broker finds the other side of the trade, and risk for order execution remains with the portfolio manager/trader.

Electronic trading involves trading via computer and is used in more liquid markets. Trading here is typically *order driven* in that electronic systems allow buyers and sellers to advertise their limit orders in a central limit order book. A limit order is an order to trade at a certain (limit) price or better. For example, a trader may execute a buy order with a limit of $20. This means the trader will buy the security for any price up to $20, but not pay more than $20. Similarly, a seller limited at $20 will sell at any price above $20, but not lower. Electronic trading generally involves **direct market access (DMA)** and/or **algorithmic trading** (defined next). DMA allows buy-side portfolio managers/traders to access the order book of the exchange directly through a broker's technology infrastructure.

Algorithmic trading is the use of programmed rules to electronically trade orders, primarily used for two purposes: *profit seeking and trade execution*.

Profit-seeking algorithms use real-time market data to determine which securities to buy and sell, and are employed by electronic market makers, quantitative funds, and high-frequency traders.

Execution algorithms trade according to the rules specified by the manager to meet their objectives. Types of execution algorithms include the following:

- *Scheduled algorithms—percent-of-volume (POV), VWAP, and TWAP algorithms.* These execute trades using rules driven by historical volumes or specified time periods.
  - *POV algorithms* (a.k.a. participation algorithms) send orders according to a volume participation schedule (e.g., "participate as 5% of traded volume").
    - Advantage: They automatically exploit increased liquidity when available.
    - Disadvantage: They continue to trade at any (potentially adverse) price, and may not fill the order in a specified time if there is a lack of trading.
  - VWAP and TWAP algorithms are *time-slicing algorithms*. VWAP algorithms attempt to match the VWAP price for the period by carving up the trade and sending orders based on *historical* intraday volumes. The usual intraday volume profile is to trade more at the open and close and less in the middle of the day. TWAP algorithms perform a similar task; however, they ensure an equal number of shares is traded in each time period (e.g., each hour).
    - Advantage: They ensure that a specified number of shares are executed in a specified time period.
    - Disadvantage: They may force trades in times of low liquidity or trade too little in times of high liquidity.
- *Liquidity-seeking algorithms* (a.k.a. opportunistic algorithms) aim to take advantage of favorable liquidity conditions when offered by the market. For example, for a buyer, this algorithm would wait until a large seller appeared and then enter a market order. These orders use both lit and dark venues.
- *Arrival price algorithms* seek to trade close to market prices prevailing at the time the order is entered. These algorithms will trade more aggressively (i.e., faster) than other algorithms to trade more shares at close to the arrival price.
- *Dark strategies/liquidity aggregators* execute trades in dark pools, with aggregator algorithms attempting to optimize trading across multiple dark venues.
- *Smart order routers (SORs)* are algorithms that determine the best destination (either lit or dark) to route an electronic order to get the best result. SORs focus on getting the best price for market orders, or the highest probability of execution for limit orders.

PROFESSOR'S NOTE

While the descriptions just listed are important, the LOS requires you to select which algorithm is most appropriate for a given order or set of orders. We will discuss this exam-critical information next.

Which Algorithm?

Scheduled algorithms are appropriate for relatively small orders in liquid markets for managers with less urgency (i.e., greater risk tolerance for longer execution periods) and/or who are concerned with minimizing the market impact (e.g., a risk rebalancing trade executed over a trading day).

Liquidity-seeking algorithms are appropriate for larger orders in less liquid markets with higher urgency while trying to mitigate the market impact. They are also appropriate when a manager is concerned that displaying limit orders may lead to information leakage, or when liquidity is typically thin with sporadic episodes of high liquidity.

Arrival price algorithms are appropriate for relatively small orders in liquid markets for managers who believe prices are likely to move against them during the trade horizon, and therefore wish to trade more aggressively (e.g., a profit-seeking manager). They are also appropriate for more risk-averse managers who want to minimize execution risk.

Dark strategies/liquidity aggregators are appropriate for large orders in illiquid markets, and arrival price or scheduled algorithms would likely lead to high market impact. Since there is a lower chance of execution in dark pools, these strategies are for managers that do not need to execute the full order immediately.

SORs are appropriate for small market orders with low market impact where the market can move quickly, or for small limit orders with low information leakage where there are multiple potential execution venues.

EXAMPLE: Selection of appropriate algorithm

A portfolio manager wishes to execute three trades as follows:

Stock	Side	Share Price	Order Size (Shares)	Average Daily Volume	Urgency
SFDL	Buy	$8.50	10,000	20,000	High
TWEL	Buy	$32.31	5,000	100,000	Low
UDSL	Sell	$2.05	1,000,000	1,000,000	Low

The manager considers executing the orders using the following strategies:

- Scheduled algorithm.
- High-touch principal approach.
- Liquidity-seeking algorithm.

Recommend the most appropriate implementation strategy for each order. (Note: Each strategy should only be used once.)

Answer:

SFDL should be purchased using a liquidity-seeking algorithm. The low liquidity in the market and the high order size make minimization of market impact a key consideration, which a liquidity-seeking algorithm will achieve since it only trades when liquidity is offered by the other side of the market. The high urgency of the trade also makes a liquidity-seeking algorithm appropriate since execution should occur relatively quickly.

TWEL should be purchased using a scheduled algorithm. The low urgency of the trade suggests that concerns about longer trading horizons and adverse price movements are low. With low order size and relatively high liquidity, a scheduled algorithm such as POV, VWAP, or TWAP is most appropriate. These strategies trade passively throughout the day, which minimizes market impact costs.

UDSL should be sold using a high-touch principal approach. This order represents 100% of the ADV; hence, using an algorithm is not appropriate due to the high possibility of information leakage and high market impact cost. Discretion is required to find the other side of the trade; hence, a human intermediary is required, making the high-touch principal approach the most appropriate choice.

Recent developments in algorithmic trading include **clustering** and **high-frequency market forecasting**.

Clustering is a machine learning technique whereby a computer learns to identify which algorithm is optimal for different types of trades based on the key features of trades. The term *clustering* refers to the technique of grouping trades together with similar attributes (e.g., order size as a fraction of the ADV). Note this is similar to the approach used in the previous example to select optimal order; however, the difference is that clustering will quantitatively test factors for their impact on the performance of different algorithms. The machine learning nature of the process means clustering attempts to *identify* features of trades that determine optimal algorithm type that a human manager had not previously considered important.

High-frequency market forecasting attempts to model short-term market direction. One issue with this process is the (large) number of variables that could potentially explain market movements. The least absolute shrinkage and selection operator (LASSO) is a machine learning technique that helps to reduce the number of explanatory variables to a manageable number of significant variables.

Characteristics of Key Markets

LOS 23.f: Contrast key characteristics of the following markets in relation to trade implementation: equity, fixed income, options and futures, OTC derivatives, and spot currency.

Equities are usually traded on stock exchanges (lit markets) and dark pools. Equity markets are the most technologically advanced, with most of the trading executed electronically, and the use of algorithms is commonplace.

Fixed-income markets tend to trade in a large number of heterogeneous securities, as many issuers have multiple issues outstanding. While the fixed-income markets tend to have low liquidity, typical order size is large. Due to these characteristics, trading is mostly conducted in dealer-based, quote-driven markets. Electronic RFQ systems are becoming more common; however, algorithmic trading is largely limited to only the most liquid on-the-run (most recently issued) U.S. Treasuries and futures contracts. Electronic trading, while growing for corporate bonds, remains relevant for only a small fraction of the universe. Other fixed-income securities markets generally use high-touch execution methods—urgent trades would require a principal broker risk trade, while less urgent trades would use a broker-agent approach.

Electronic trading is common for exchange-traded derivatives. Algorithmic trading is not as common as for equities markets, and is used more for futures than for options. Buy-side traders generally use DMA.

OTC derivatives trading takes place in a dealer quote-driven market, usually implemented through high-touch approaches. Since the credit crisis of 2008, there has been a move by regulators to increase transparency and central clearing of basic OTC derivatives such as interest rate swaps (e.g., the Dodd-Frank Act of 2010 in the United States).

Spot foreign exchange trading takes place in OTC markets that use both electronic trading and high-touch broker approaches. The market works in three tiers: interbank, interdealer, and bank-to-client, with decreasing trade sizes and increasing spreads, respectively. For large urgent trades, RFQs are used with brokers. For large non-urgent trades, scheduled algorithms or high-touch agency approaches are used. Small trades are usually implemented using DMA.

EXAMPLE: Trade approach by market

The trading desk of a large multiasset buy-side firm has received the following three orders:

Market	Size	Urgency
Futures	Small	High
Agency MBS	Medium	Low
Equity	Large	Low

The trading desk is considering executing the trades using DMA, scheduled algorithms, or high-touch broker risk approaches.

Recommend the most appropriate approach for each order. (Note: Each approach should only be used once.)

Answer:

The most appropriate approach for the futures trade is DMA. Futures markets have well evolved electronic trading, and it is likely that an urgent small trade in futures can be executed most effectively through accessing exchange systems directly. There is no need to employ the high-touch approach of a broker since the order size is small and can be executed on the exchange easily. Algorithmic trading is not well developed in derivatives markets, and scheduled algorithms would likely take too long to execute a high-urgency trade.

The most appropriate approach for the agency MBS trade is a high-touch brokered approach. Fixed-income markets outside of Treasuries and corporate bonds typically use high-touch brokered execution methods. There is unlikely to be algorithmic or DMA available for agency MBS.

The most appropriate approach for the equity trade is a scheduled algorithm. It is likely that the trade, being large, would have too much market impact if executed through DMA. It is unlikely that a high-touch broker trade would be appropriate since the trade is not urgent (hence, does not need immediate execution), and most trading in equity markets is conducted electronically.

MODULE QUIZ 23.3

1. A trading desk has had the following orders submitted by the firm's portfolio managers:

Stock	Execution Risk Aversion	Market Impact	Order Size (% ADV)
PQR	Low	High	50%
STU	High	Low	10%
VWX	Low	Medium	20%

   For which order is an arrival price strategy *most likely* to be most appropriate?
   A. PQR.
   B. STU.
   C. VWX.

2. Request-for-quote (RFQ) systems are *most likely* to be used to implement trading strategies in which of the following markets?
   A. Equities.
   B. Fixed income.
   C. Exchange-traded derivatives.

MODULE 23.4: TRADE COST MEASUREMENT

Video covering this content is available online.

LOS 23.g: Explain how trade costs are measured and determine the cost of a trade.

Trading costs are either explicit in that they are easily visible (e.g., commissions and fees) or implicit in that they are embedded in the transaction (e.g., market impact/ execution risk). Total costs of trading can be measured using **implementation shortfall (IS)**. At the highest level, the absolute value of IS is calculated as:

$$IS = \text{paper return} - \text{actual return}$$

The paper return is the return a hypothetical portfolio would have had if the trade were executed at the original decision price *with zero cost.* The actual portfolio return of the portfolio is net of all costs. The difference between these two amounts is the total cost of executing the trade.

Usually, IS is expressed as basis points of the total cost of the paper portfolio.

EXAMPLE: Implementation shortfall

A portfolio manager decides to buy 50,000 shares of stock SJB at 9:00 am when the stock price is $20.00 (this is the decision price for the trade) and submits instructions to the firm's trader. The trader uses a limit price of $20.50 and in total manages to purchase 40,000 shares at an average price of $20.34. The fund is charged a commission of $0.02 per share, and there are no other fees. At the end of the day, SJB closes at $20.55.

Calculate (*in basis points*) the total IS for this trade.

Answer:

The paper portfolio is hypothetically assumed to fill the full order at the original decision price ($20.00). Hence, the paper return = 50,000 × ($20.55 – $20.00) = $27,500.

The actual return of the portfolio reflects that the trader purchased 40,000 shares at $20.34, and paid 40,000 × $0.02 = $800 for the execution.

Hence, the actual return = 40,000 × ($20.55 – $20.34) – $800 = $7,600.

Therefore, in absolute value terms, IS = $27,500 – $7,600 = $19,900.

The initial cost of the paper portfolio is 50,000 × $20 = $1,000,000, so IS in basis points is calculated as $19,900 / $1,000,000 = 0.0199, or 199 basis points.

PROFESSOR'S NOTE

Recall that a basis point is 1/100th of 1%. A decimal number is multiplied by 10,000 to convert it to basis points.

IS can be decomposed into the following parts:

- **Execution cost** occurs due to executing shares at a less favorable price than the original decision price. Execution cost can be further broken down into delay cost and trading cost.
  - **Delay cost** is due to adverse price movements in the time between the portfolio manager submitting the order to the trader and the time the trader releases it to the market. This delay is usually due to the time it takes the trading desk to determine the optimal execution strategy for the trade.
  - **Trading cost** is due to the market impact of executing the trade.
- **Opportunity cost** is the cost of *not* trading any unfilled part of the order. Recall that the paper portfolio assumes that all shares are executed immediately at the original decision price—the actual trade may have only filled part of the order, and the lost profit on the unfilled portion is the opportunity cost.
- **Fixed fees** are any explicit commissions or fees incurred in executing the trade.

To demonstrate this decomposition, let us return to the previous example, which had a total IS of $19,900. Recall that the trader received the order at 9:00 am, when the stock price was at $20.00. Assume that the trader placed the order 30 minutes later in the market by which time the stock price had moved to \$20.10 (\$20.10 is referred to as the arrival price of the order). The decomposition of IS in dollar terms is as follows:

- *Delay cost* is the adverse movement from \$20.00 to \$20.10 for the 40,000 shares that were executed during the day:

  delay cost = 40,000 × (\$20.10 – \$20.00) = \$4,000

- *Trading cost* is the difference between the execution price, \$20.34, and the arrival price, \$20.10, for 40,000 shares traded during the day:

  trading cost = 40,000 × (\$20.34 – \$20.10) = \$9,600

- *Opportunity cost* is the paper profit on the 10,000 shares *not* purchased, which relates to the paper profit from buying these shares at \$20.00 and the stock closing at \$20.55:

  10,000 × (\$20.55 – \$20.00) = \$5,500

- *Fixed fees* are the explicit commission paid on the execution of 40,000 shares:

  40,000 × \$0.02 = \$800

Then, the total IS value = \$4,000 + \$9,600 + \$5,500 + \$800 = \$19,900.

PROFESSOR'S NOTE

All of the components of IS can be expressed (and usually are) in terms of basis points (bps) of the original cost of the paper portfolio, which in this case is \$1,000,000. Hence, delay cost would be expressed as \$4,000 / \$1,000,000 = 0.004, or 40 bps. Similarly, the trading cost is 96 bps, the opportunity cost is 55 bps, and fixed fees are 8 bps—for a total IS of 199 bps.

Improving Execution Performance

Delay costs arise due to adverse price movement during the interval between the trader receiving an order from the portfolio manager and passing it on to a broker/market. Delay costs can be minimized with efficient trading practices that give traders the pretrade and posttrade analysis they need to make a swift decision on an optimal trading strategy.

A detailed analysis of opportunity cost can help managers deploy unused cash into the next-most attractive investment, thereby reducing the impact of opportunity cost on the portfolio. For example, a manager who recognizes that only 80% of an order is likely to be transacted due to a lack of liquidity can invest the remaining 20% of the order into the next-most attractive trade and avoid cash drag on uninvested funds.

Analysis of trading (market impact) costs can also help traders establish proper price benchmarks and appropriate urgency of trade.

EXAMPLE: Implementation shortfall detailed analysis

A portfolio manager decides to sell 100,000 shares of Future Recreation (FTRB) at 1:05 pm when the share price is £2.56. The trading desk of the firm receives the order and conducts a review of the trade details to determine the optimal trade strategy. Due to the low market volume, it is decided that a high-touch agency broker approach is optimal with a limit price of £2.50. The trader submits the order to a broker at 1:13 pm when the share price is £2.59. By the end of the day, the broker had executed 70,000 shares at an average price of £2.60. Commission for the trade is £400. At the end of the day, the stock closes at a price of £2.54 per share.

1. **Calculate** the total IS for the trade in basis points.
2. **Decompose** IS into the delay, trading, opportunity, and fixed-fee costs.

Answers:

1. Note that because this is a sell order, positive returns are earned when the actual trading price rises above the decision price.

    Return of the paper portfolio = 100,000 × (£2.56 – £2.54) = £2,000

    Return of actual portfolio = 70,000 × (£2.60 – £2.54) – £400 = £3,800

    IS = paper return – actual return = £2,000 – £3,800 = –£1,800

    Original cost of paper portfolio = 100,000 × £2.56 = £256,000

    IS in basis points = –£1,800 / £256,000 = –0.00703, or –70.3 basis points

    A negative cost is a benefit; it means that the trader's actions added value relative to the paper portfolio. If the trader had immediately executed the sell order (with no costs), the portfolio would be worse off than the actual portfolio (because prices subsequently rose, and the executions were made at higher prices). Negative IS indicates that the trader's actions benefited the portfolio.

2. Delay cost = 70,000 × (£2.56 – £2.59) = –£2,100

    Delay cost (bps) = –£2,100 / £256,000 = –82.0 basis points

    Negative delay cost represents value added since the price movement during the time the trading desk received the order and submitted it to the market worked in favor of the seller.

    Trading cost = 70,000 × (£2.59 – £2.60) = –£700

    Trading cost (bps) = –£700 / £256,000 = –27.3 basis points

    Negative trading cost indicates that the execution price improved on the arrival price of the order.

    Opportunity cost = 30,000 × (£2.56 – £2.54) = £600

    Opportunity cost (bps) = £600 / £256,000 = 23.4 basis points

    Fixed fees = £400 (given)

    Fixed fees (bps) = £400 / £256,000 = 15.6 basis points

    Total IS = –82.0 – 27.3 + 23.4 + 15.6 = –70.3 bps

MODULE 23.5: EVALUATING TRADE EXECUTION

Video covering this content is available online.

Reading 23

LOS 23.h: Evaluate the execution of a trade.

Trade cost analysis is vital for portfolio managers to be able to assess the effectiveness of brokers, algorithms, and other strategies. Costs are evaluated versus specified price benchmarks, which vary depending upon the objectives of the manager/nature of the order. This benchmark price could be an arrival price, VWAP, TWAP, or the closing market price. There can even be more than one relevant benchmark if the strategy has several objectives.

In general, buyers incur costs if they execute trades above relevant benchmark prices, while sellers incur costs if they execute below relevant benchmark prices. Trade costs are calculated such that a positive value represents underperformance against the benchmark, and can generally be formulated as follows:

$$\text{absolute cost (\$)} = \text{side} \times (\text{execution price} - \text{benchmark price}) \times \text{shares executed}$$

where:
side = +1 for a buy order, –1 for a sell order

PROFESSOR'S NOTE

This is a general formulation of the cost idea that was used in IS in the previous section. Keep in mind the intuition that we suffer costs (i.e., underperformance) when we buy high (execution price > benchmark price), or sell low (execution price < benchmark price).

These costs are often expressed in *basis points* of the original benchmark price, using the following expression:

$$\text{trade cost (bps)} = \text{side} \times \frac{(\text{execution price} - \text{benchmark price})}{\text{benchmark price}} \times 10{,}000$$

EXAMPLE: Trade cost

A portfolio manager is executing a buy order using a market on close (MOC) benchmark. The manager purchases at \$25.50, and the closing price of the stock is \$25.60. **Calculate** the cost (in basis points) based on the closing price benchmark.

Answer:

Since this is a buy order, side = +1. Using the formula for the absolute cost (per share), we find the following:

$$\text{absolute cost per share} = +1 \times (\$25.50 - \$25.60) = -\$0.10$$

In basis points, this cost is –\$0.10 / \$25.60 = –0.00391, or –39.1 basis points. The negative sign indicates that the trader's actions added value (*a negative cost is a benefit*). This can clearly be seen since the buy trade has been executed below the benchmark price, and buying low is adding value from a trading perspective.

Regardless of the skill of the trader, buy orders in a rising market and sell orders in a falling market incur positive trading costs due to adverse price movements. To remove the impact of market movements on trade cost, traders can use **market-adjusted cost**. The market-adjusted costs ensure a trader is not penalized or rewarded for general market movements over the trade horizon by subtracting the *index cost* adjusted for the security's beta. The index cost is a representation of the costs due to general market index movements, and is calculated as follows:

$$\text{index cost (bps)} = \text{side} \times \frac{(\text{index VWAP} - \text{index arrival price})}{\text{index arrival price}} \times 10{,}000$$

PROFESSOR'S NOTE

Index cost is simply a measurement of how much VWAP has increased over the trading period versus the original arrival price of the index. Recall that the arrival price is the price of a security when an order is first submitted to a market. This is expressed in basis points as a proportion of the index arrival price.

The market-adjusted cost of the trade is given by the following expression:

$$\text{market-adjusted cost (bps)} = \text{arrival cost (bps)} - \beta \times \text{index cost (bps)}$$

where:
arrival cost = the arrival cost of the trade based on an arrival price benchmark
β = beta of the security versus the index used to calculate index cost

EXAMPLE: Market-adjusted cost

A trader submits a buy order to a market when the security price is €10.00 and a relevant index price is €3,500. The order is executed over the next hour at an average price of €10.15. VWAP for the index over this period is €3,507, and the beta of the security is 1.5.

Calculate the market-adjusted cost of this trade in basis points.

Answer:

Since the order is a buy, side = +1. The index cost in basis points is given by:

$$\text{index cost (bps)} = +1 \times \frac{(€3{,}507 - €3{,}500)}{€3{,}500} \times 10{,}000 = 20 \text{ bps}$$

The arrival cost of the trade is given by:

$$\text{arrival cost (bps)} = +1 \times \frac{(€10.15 - €10.00)}{€10.00} \times 10{,}000 = 150 \text{ bps}$$

Then, the market-adjusted cost is given by:

$$\text{market-adjusted cost (bps)} = 150 \text{ bps} - (1.5 \times 20 \text{ bps}) = 120 \text{ bps}$$

Added Value

A different method of trade cost analysis is comparing the arrival cost to the estimated pretrade cost. The estimated pretrade cost is calculated using a model that incorporates key trade cost variables such as order size, liquidity of the market, and so on. If a fund executes at less than the pretrade cost estimate, then the trader has added value. More formally:

added value (bps) = arrival cost (bps) − estimated pretrade cost (bps)

In the previous example, the arrival cost of the trade was 150 bps. If the pretrade cost estimate was 160 bps, then the added value for the trade is 150 bps − 160 bps = −10 bps. Again, be careful with signs here—*remember that a negative cost is a benefit*, and this trader has added value through his trading decisions.

Trade Governance

LOS 23.i: Evaluate a firm's trading procedures, including processes, disclosures, and record keeping with respect to good governance.

It is both a good practice, and is usually required by regulation, that an asset manager has a formal written trade policy that clearly spells out trade procedures. Trade policy has four key areas: (1) the meaning of *best execution*, (2) the factors that determine the optimal trading approach, (3) a listing of approved brokers and execution venues, and (4) details of the monitoring processes used by the asset manager. These areas are further discussed as follows:

1. **Meaning of best execution.** *Best execution* is a general term used by regulators to describe the duty of asset managers to seek the best possible *result* for clients when trading their assets. Trade policy should define *best execution* within the applicable regulatory framework. Generally, the factors that determine best execution include:
   - Execution price.
   - Trading costs.
   - Speed and likelihood of execution and settlement.
   - Order size and liquidity.
   - Nature of the trade (e.g., urgency of the trade).

   Note that best execution does *not* simply mean seeking the best price or trading at the lowest cost. For example, a manager with a large stake in a company that the manager is confident is going to file for bankruptcy would likely achieve a better *result* for clients if the manager sold a block with a trusted dealer at a significantly discounted price, even if there were higher bids for small quantities at other lit execution venues. This could be justified as *best execution* because of the execution risk of adverse market movements and the risk of information leakage if the manager began hitting the bids at the execution venues (though these prices are initially higher than the broker price).

2. **Factors that determine the optimal execution approach.** The trade policy needs to communicate these criteria, which usually include:
   - Urgency and size of order.
   - Liquidity of security (ADV) and the nature of security (e.g., standardized vs. customized).
   - Characteristics of available execution venues.
   - Investment strategy objectives (e.g., long term vs. short term in nature).
   - Reason for the trade.

   These factors will need to reflect both the relevant regulations and market trading conventions for different asset classes used by the manager. For example, new regulations called MiFID II (Markets in Financial Instruments Directive) have effectively prohibited the use of soft-dollar arrangements in Europe. Soft-dollar arrangements are arrangements whereby an asset manager can pay for goods or services using rebates from client commissions offered in return for executing a high amount of volume with the broker, which may jeopardize the best execution if the manager uses the client's soft dollars for the manager's own benefit.

   As discussed earlier, different asset classes have different methods of trading. For example, equities and exchange-traded derivatives are more likely to be traded using algorithms than fixed-income products, which are likely to be traded using a more high-touch approach.
3. **List of eligible brokers and execution venues.** Trade policy should include a list of approved brokers and a description of the process used to create it. The best practice is to establish a **best execution monitoring committee (BEMC)** consisting of portfolio execution, compliance, and risk personnel that is responsible for maintaining, updating, and distributing the list to parties involved in trade execution. Due diligence of brokers is particularly important for OTC trades where there is no protection of exchange rules, low transparency, and no central clearing to mitigate counterparty risk. General principles for approval to the list include:
   - High quality of service in terms of competitive execution price or speed of service/trade size capacity.
   - Financial stability to mitigate counterparty risk.
   - Good reputation for ethical behavioral.
   - Adequate settlement facilities.
   - Competitive explicit costs such as commissions.
   - Willingness to commit capital to principal trades when required for less liquid securities.
4. **Process for monitoring execution arrangements.** The approved broker list should be constantly monitored for reputational issues, trading error frequency, criminal actions, and financial stability. Any brokers who fail to meet the required standard should be removed promptly. Execution quality should also be monitored on an ongoing basis. Trading records should be kept in order to facilitate this analysis and to address any client or regulator concerns regarding the executions or trade allocations made by an asset manager to her clients.

MODULE QUIZ 23.4, 23.5

1. A portfolio manager submits an order to sell 10,000 shares of stock STU to the trading desk when the price is $32.50. After careful analysis of the trade details, the trading desk submits the order to the market when the price is $32.60 with a limit of $32.60. The trader executes 4,000 shares at a price of $32.65 and commissions are $0.03 per share. The stock closes at the end of the trading day at $32.35. The total implementation shortfall (IS) for this trade, in basis points, is *closest* to:
   A. 9.23 bps.
   B. 12.92 bps.
   C. 33.23 bps.
2. A portfolio manager executes a sell order at an average price of $8.38. The arrival price of the order was $8.40. The relevant index value at the time of order entry was 3,000 and the VWAP for the index over the trading period was 3,050. If the stock has a beta of 1.3, the market-adjusted cost of the trade is *closest* to:
   A. –142.5 bps.
   B. 23.8 bps.
   C. 240.5 bps.
3. The trade policy of an investment firm makes the following two statements:

   Statement 1: The head trader is exclusively responsible for firm-wide trade execution monitoring and implementation of sound trade governance.

   Statement 2: A list of eligible brokers used by the firm is created and maintained by the BEMC of the firm. This committee ensures that only brokers who execute with the lowest implicit and explicit trading costs are admitted to the list.

   How many of the statements are in line with trade governance best practice?
   A. Zero.
   B. One.
   C. Two.

KEY CONCEPTS

LOS 23.a

The four motivations for a portfolio manager to trade are as follows:

Motivation	Impact on Trading Strategy
Profit seeking	■ High alpha decay → high urgency ■ Low alpha decay → low urgency ■ May use dark pools to mitigate information leakage
Risk management/ hedging	■ Derivatives could be used if contracts exist and mandate permits
Cash flow needs	■ Cash drag on inflows into funds with illiquid holds could be mitigated through *equitization* strategies ■ Client redemptions are usually based on closing NAV (hence, managers will typically target closing prices as execution benchmarks)
Corporate actions/ index reconstitutions/ margin calls	■ Income may need reinvesting ■ Index reconstitutions are usually based around closing prices (hence, managers will typically target closing prices as execution benchmarks) ■ Margin calls will likely require high urgency

LOS 23.b

Key factors that dictate the appropriate trading strategy are as follows:

- Order characteristics: These are side, quantity, and percentage of ADV.
  - Larger trades are normally executed over longer time horizons to lower market impact.
- Security characteristics: These are type, short-term alpha, volatility, and liquidity.
  - Higher volatility implies a higher urgency to lower execution risk.
- Market conditions: A crisis can adversely impact volatility and liquidity.
- Individual risk aversion: Higher risk aversion implies higher urgency to lower execution risk.

The trader's dilemma is balancing the market impact cost of trading too quickly versus the execution risk of trading too slowly.

LOS 23.c

Reference price benchmarks include the following:

Reference Price	Examples
Pretrade	■ Decision price ■ Previous close: often used by quantitative managers ■ Opening price: often used by longer-term fundamental managers ■ Arrival price: used by profit-seeking managers
Intraday	■ VWAP: used when managers want to participate with volume ■ TWAP: used when managers want to trade evenly and mitigate the impact of outliers, and for markets with unpredictable trading volumes
Posttrade	■ Closing price: used by index-tracking managers ■ Price target benchmarks: usually based on the manager's view of fair value
Price target	■ Usually based on the fair value estimate of an active manager

LOS 23.d

The primary goal of a trading strategy is to balance expected costs, risks, and alpha decay in line with the manager's objectives, risk aversion, and other constraints.

LOS 23.e

Trade implementation choices include the following:

Approach	Appropriate For
Higher touch—principal	Large urgent trades in illiquid securities
Higher touch—agent	Large trades in illiquid securities that are less urgent
DMA	Small trades in liquid electronic markets
Profit-seeking algorithms	Used by electronic market makers, quantitative funds, and high-frequency traders
Scheduled algorithms: POV, VWAP, TWAP	Relatively small orders in liquid electronic markets for managers with less urgency (e.g., portfolio rebalancing)
Liquidity-seeking algorithms	Larger orders in less liquid electronic markets with higher urgency, or when liquidity is sporadic
Arrival price algorithms	Relatively small orders in liquid electronic markets with high urgency (e.g., profit-seeking managers)
Dark strategies	Large orders in illiquid markets and arrival price or scheduled algorithms would likely lead to high market impact
SORs	Small market orders with low market impact where the market can move quickly, and small limit orders with low information leakage where there are multiple potential execution venues

LOS 23.f

The main characteristics of key markets are as follows:

- Equities are mostly traded electronically on lit exchanges and dark pools. Algorithmic trading is common.
- Fixed-income securities are typically traded in dealer-driven, high-touch principal markets. Clients use electronic RFQ systems to access quotes from dealers. Algorithmic trading is limited to the most liquid on-the-run U.S. Treasuries.
- Exchange-traded derivatives are largely traded electronically, though algorithmic trading is less common than for equity markets. Buy-side traders generally use DMA.
- OTC derivatives historically have been traded in high-touch dealer markets. Since the credit crunch, there has been a move to increase transparency and force basic OTC derivatives to be centrally cleared.
- Spot foreign exchange trading takes place in OTC markets that use both electronic (algorithms and DMA) and high-touch approaches for larger trades.

LOS 23.g

The total implicit and explicit costs of trading are measured by the implementation shortfall (IS):

$$\text{IS} = \text{paper return} - \text{actual return}$$

Usually, IS is expressed as basis points of the total cost of the paper portfolio.

IS can be decomposed into the following parts:

- Execution cost is when the execution price is worse than the decision price and comprises:
  - Delay cost, which is when the arrival price is worse than the decision price.
  - Trading cost, which is when the execution price is worse than the arrival price.
- Opportunity cost occurs on unexecuted shares when the closing price is worse than the decision price.
- Fixed fees are any explicit commissions or fees incurred in executing the trade.

LOS 23.h

When performing trade cost analysis:

$$\text{trade cost (bps)} = \text{side} \times \frac{(\text{execution price} - \text{benchmark price})}{\text{benchmark price}} \times 10{,}000$$

where:
side = +1 for a buy order, and –1 for a sell order

Benchmark price could be the arrival price, VWAP, TWAP, or closing price of the stock.

To not reward or punish a manager for the market movement over the trading horizon, market-adjusted cost removes the cost associated with the market move as follows:

$$\text{market-adjusted cost (bps)} = \text{arrival cost (bps)} - \beta \times \text{index cost (bps)}$$

where:

$$\text{index cost (bps)} = \text{side} \times \frac{(\text{index VWAP} - \text{index arrival price})}{\text{index arrival price}} \times 10{,}000$$

When a pretrade estimate of cost is available, the added value of the trader's actions is given by:

$$\text{added value (bps)} = \text{arrival cost (bps)} - \text{estimated pretrade cost (bps)}$$

LOS 23.i

An asset manager should have a formal written trade policy which clearly sets out its procedure. Trade policy has four key areas: (1) the meaning of best execution, (2) the factors that determine the optimal trading approach, (3) a listing of approved brokers and execution venues, and (4) details of the monitoring processes used by the asset manager.

ANSWER KEY FOR MODULE QUIZZES

Module Quiz 23.1

1. **C** Client redemptions from investment funds are usually based on the fund's net asset value, which is calculated using closing prices of securities. In this case, trading at the closing price eliminates the risk to the fund of executing liquidating sales at price different to those used to calculate the redemption proceeds required for investors. The target price for a profit-seeking trade will depend on the urgency of the trade. Trades with a high rate of alpha decay will require immediate execution; trades with a low rate of alpha decay will require less urgent execution. Trades to meet margin calls usually need to be executed immediately. (LOS 23.a)

2. **C** Market impact is the adverse movement in price caused by submitting an order to the market and forcing prices up as a buyer, or down as a seller. For a given order size, impact is higher in less liquid markets than it is in more liquid markets. Hence, an increase in security liquidity will lower market impact costs. Execution risk is the risk of an adverse movement in a share price in the time it takes to execute an order. In a more liquid market, a given order size can be executed in a shorter time horizon; hence, execution risk is also lower. (LOS 23.b)

Module Quiz 23.2

1. **A** A manager who wishes to trade passively over a trading day will want to execute at the average price over the day (hence, will choose TWAP or VWAP). If a manager wants to minimize the impact of outliers, the manager should use TWAP as a benchmark since this will not overweight large buy or sell orders at extreme prices over the day. Arrival price benchmarks are relevant for managers trading short-term alpha opportunities (hence, not relevant for a manager wishing to trade passively). (LOS 23.c)

2. **C** Executing the trading list as close to the closing market prices of the securities on the trading day is the most appropriate strategy, since this will best align the trade execution prices with the closing prices used to calculate fund NAV and reconstitute the benchmark. This will minimize the tracking error of the fund versus the benchmark as per the low tracking error mandate of the fund. (LOS 23.d)

Module Quiz 23.3

1. **B** Arrival price strategies will execute orders with high urgency, or when the manager has high risk aversion against the execution risk associated with longer execution time periods. They are not appropriate for orders with high market impact or relatively illiquid markets. Therefore, the best answer choice here is STU because it is an order with high execution risk aversion, low market impact, and the order size is a small percentage of average daily volume (ADV). An arrival price strategy is not appropriate for orders in PQR or VWX due to the lower risk aversion, higher market impact, and higher order sizes. (LOS 23.e)

2. **B** RFQ systems are systems used by investors to request prices from dealers in less liquid quote-driven markets. Fixed-income markets are most likely to use RFQ systems since these markets are less liquid and driven by dealer quotes. Due to higher liquidity levels and more advanced technology, equity markets and exchange-traded derivatives markets are more likely to be electronic and order driven rather than quote-driven markets using RFQ systems. (LOS 23.f)

Module Quiz 23.4, 23.5

1. **B** The paper portfolio assumes that all the shares are immediately sold at the original decision price with no trading costs. The paper return is as follows:

   paper return = 10,000 × ($32.50 – $32.35) = $1,500

   The actual portfolio return reflects the actual P/L generated by the trading of the order, after commissions of 4,000 × 0.03 = $120. In this case, the actual return is as follows:

   actual return = 4,000 × ($32.65 – $32.35) – $120 = $1,080

   Hence, the IS in dollars is $1,500 – $1,080 = $420. As a proportion of the initial paper portfolio, this is $420 / (10,000 × $32.50) = 0.0012923, or 12.92 basis points. (Module 23.4, LOS 23.g)

2. **C** The market-adjusted cost of an execution is given by:

   market-adjusted cost (bps) = arrival cost (bps) – β × index cost (bps)

   The arrival cost of the trade is given by:

   $$\text{arrival cost (bps)} = \text{side} \times \frac{(\text{execution price} - \text{arrival price})}{\text{arrival price}} \times 10{,}000$$

   Since this order is a sale, 'side' = –1 and the arrival cost is:

   $$\text{arrival cost (bps)} = -1 \times \frac{(\$8.38 - \$8.40)}{\$8.40} \times 10{,}000 = 23.8 \text{ bps}$$

   The index cost is given by:

   $$\text{index cost (bps)} = \text{side} \times \frac{(\text{index VWAP} - \text{index arrival price})}{\text{index arrival price}} \times 10{,}000$$

   For this order:

   $$\text{index cost (bps)} = -1 \times \frac{(3{,}050 - 3{,}000)}{3{,}000} \times 10{,}000 = -166.7 \text{ bps}$$

   Then, the market-adjusted cost is:

   market-adjusted cost (bps) = 23.8 – (1.3 × –166.7) = 240.5 bps

   (Module 23.5, LOS 23.h)

3. **A** Neither statement is best trade governance practice.

   Statement 1 is not best practice since a firm should establish a BEMC, which should collaborate with portfolio managers, risk management, and legal/compliance to enact trade governance.

   Statement 2 is not best practice since best execution does not simply relate to the lowest-cost broker. Best execution needs to consider the overall result from executing trades, which goes beyond prices and costs; it also needs to consider factors such as speed of execution, likelihood of execution and settlement, order size, and the nature of trades. (Module 23.5, LOS 23.i)

READING 24
Portfolio Performance Evaluation

EXAM FOCUS

Performance evaluation of a portfolio is important to managers, sponsors, and clients who need to quantify performance and understand key drivers of both risk and return. Some of the calculations in the reading, if done in full, can be extremely tedious and are best left to spreadsheets and software programs. For the exam, expect the calculations to be reasonable. Also expect a fair balance of testing on both the calculations and the qualitative concepts. There is a sizable amount of material in the reading that overlaps with previous readings as well as the subsequent reading on investment manager selection.

MODULE 24.1: PERFORMANCE EVALUATION

Video covering this content is available online.

In a large institutional portfolio, it is common to have multiple investment managers where decisions are made by both the fund sponsor as well as by individual managers within the fund that affect portfolio performance. Performance evaluation can deconstruct returns to quantify which decisions added or subtracted value for the fund.

The fund sponsor's perspective will capture all value added or lost, while the manager's perspective will focus only on what a manager did to add or lose value for the fund. The material presupposes a large investor (e.g., a pension fund, endowment, or foundation) selects several investment managers to meet their investment goals and objectives.

The objective of the reading is to provide the tools necessary to evaluate active investment decisions made by plan sponsors and portfolio managers.

Components of Performance Evaluation

LOS 24.a: Explain the following components of portfolio evaluation and their interrelationships: performance measurement, performance attribution, and performance appraisal.

Performance evaluation consists of three interrelated components that build upon each other:

- **Performance measurement** serves as the initial foundation phase and calculates both the return and the risk of the fund over specified time periods. It is imperative to determine, before any performance evaluation analysis, if the portfolio will be compared to a benchmark (relative performance) or to a target return percentage that is specified in advance by the portfolio manager (absolute performance).
- **Performance attribution** determines the key drivers that generated the account's performance. Performance attribution expands upon the risk and return that was quantified through performance measurement and explains how the return was achieved given the risk taken by the portfolio manager. Also, performance attribution can explain both relative and absolute returns.
- **Performance appraisal** determines whether the performance was affected primarily by investment decisions, by the overall market, or by chance. Performance appraisal combines output from both performance measurement and performance attribution to render a professional judgment on the quality of the performance. If a fund's performance is attributed to luck, we cannot expect the portfolio manager to exhibit similar returns in the future.

In summary, performance evaluation answers three questions regarding a portfolio's performance:

1. What performance did the fund achieve during the period (performance measurement)?
2. How did the fund manager achieve their performance (performance attribution)?
3. Did the fund manager achieve their performance via skill or luck (performance appraisal)?

Performance Attribution

It is crucial to analyze the results of performance attribution as part of the portfolio evaluation process. As data is becoming more readily available, performance attribution has become more frequently used by many types of industry practitioners, including individual clients, who want to better understand the portfolio manager's investment process. For performance attribution to be a useful tool, it is imperative that the attribution process account for all aspects of the fund's risk and return. An attribution that does not account for the total risk and return of the fund is misleading and cannot be relied upon for any meaningful analysis.

LOS 24.b: Describe attributes of an effective attribution process.

An effective performance attribution process includes:

- A reflection of 100% of the portfolio's return or risk exposure.
- The portfolio manager's current decision-making process.
- The active investment decisions taken by the portfolio manager.
- A full explanation of the portfolio's excess return and risk.

The attribution analysis must account for 100% of the portfolio's risk and return and adequately represent the portfolio manager's current investment process. If the fundamental investment process of the fund has recently changed, then that attribution analysis must be updated to reflect those changes in the investment process.

Performance Attribution—Return Attribution & Risk Attribution

LOS 24.c: Contrast return attribution and risk attribution; contrast macro and micro return attribution.

Return attribution evaluates the impact of the active portfolio management decisions on the fund's investment returns.

Risk attribution is the parallel of return attribution but analyzes the impact of the portfolio manager's active investment decisions on portfolio risk.

Risk is generally compared to the portfolio's appropriate benchmark, but it can also be calculated in absolute terms, independent of a benchmark. For example, a relative-based risk attribution analysis would not be appropriate for a portfolio manager who has predetermined an absolute target return investment goal. Unfortunately, many investors often compare their portfolio's performance to a widely quoted passive index such as the S&P 500. A widely quoted index may or may not be an appropriate benchmark for their portfolio.

After a 10-year bull market in the S&P 500, performance attribution is likely to become even more important as portfolio managers justify their performance and fees during periods of negative returns. An additional benefit of performance attribution is its function as a form of quality control when reviewing an active portfolio. Basically, did the fund manager do what they said they were going to do?

Micro Attribution vs. Macro Attribution

Performance attribution is extremely flexible and can be analyzed at both the fund sponsor and the individual portfolio manager level.

Micro attribution analyzes the portfolio at the portfolio manager's level and seeks to verify that the portfolio manager did what they said they would and to understand the drivers of the portfolio's return.

Macro attribution analyzes investment decisions at the fund sponsor's level; it's commonly used with institutional investing. Macro attribution quantifies the fund sponsors' decisions to deviate from their strategic asset allocation and the timing when they made those decisions.

Performance Attribution—Returns-Based, Holdings-Based, and Transactions-Based

LOS 24.d: Describe returns-based, holdings-based, and transactions-based performance attribution, including advantages and disadvantages of each.

The three main approaches to conducting performance attribution are returns-based, holdings-based, and transactions-based methods.

Returns-based attribution regresses total portfolio returns against major risk factors (for example, systematic risk, size, value) to identify the active bets of the manager and their impact on active returns.

Holdings-based attribution uses beginning-of-period portfolio holdings to assess the active sector/stock selection bets of the manager and their contribution to active return. This method does not adjust for portfolio changes made during the evaluation period; hence, the output may not fully reconcile to overall portfolio returns for a manager with high turnover. This mismatch is referred to as a "timing" or "trading" effect, which can be reduced by using shorter evaluation periods.

Transactions-based attribution improves upon the holdings-based attribution by including the impact of any trades executed during the evaluation period.

The selection of attribution method will be driven by the nature of the data available, the investment process of the manager, and the need for accuracy by the analyst. A summary of the advantages and disadvantages of the three methods is displayed in Figure 24.1.

Figure 24.1: Advantages and Disadvantages of Performance Attribution Methods

Method	Advantages	Disadvantages
Returns-based	■ Easy to implement ■ Does not require holdings data (useful for private funds—e.g., hedge funds)	■ Least accurate because does not consider underlying holdings ■ Returns data can be manipulated
Holdings-based	■ More accurate than returns-based because considers underlying holdings	■ Needs data on fund holdings ■ Mismatch due to trading effect—not appropriate for high turnover active funds with long evaluation periods
Transactions-based	■ Most accurate method	■ Highest data requirements ■ Highest complexity

PROFESSOR'S NOTE

Note that the returns-based and holdings-based attribution methods are analogous to the returns-based and holdings-based style analysis methods discussed in the Equity section of the Level III curriculum. For the exam, make sure you can recommend the most appropriate method, given the advantages/disadvantages of each.

An example of a returns-based attribution is the fundamental factor-based model, and an example of a holdings-based approach is the Brinson model, both of which are discussed later in this reading.

MODULE QUIZ 24.1

1. Which component of performance evaluation attempts to determine whether performance was affected primarily by chance?
   A. Performance appraisal.
   B. Performance attribution.
   C. Performance measurement.
2. Which method of performance attribution is the *most* reliable?
   A. Returns-based.
   B. Holdings-based.
   C. Transactions-based.

Video covering this content is available online.

MODULE 24.2: APPROACHES TO RETURN ATTRIBUTION

LOS 24.e: Interpret the sources of portfolio returns using a specified attribution approach.

Arithmetic Attribution and Geometric Attribution

Arithmetic attribution calculations focus on the active return of a portfolio in a single period by subtracting the benchmark return, *B*, from the portfolio return, *R*. A problem with this approach is that single-period arithmetic active returns do not compound to equal active returns over multiple periods without a "smoothing" adjustment.

To demonstrate, consider the following returns data for a portfolio and a benchmark over two periods:

	Period 1	Period 2
Portfolio Return (*R*)	5%	5%
Benchmark Return (*B*)	3%	3%

If you invested \$100 in the portfolio over these two periods, you would end up with a portfolio worth $\$100 \times 1.05^2 = \$110.25$ and a two-period performance of 10.25%. Comparing this to the benchmark ending wealth of $\$100 \times 1.03^2 = \$106.09$, and its two-period performance of 6.09%, implies a two-period active return of 10.25% – 6.09% = 4.16%.

Note that an arithmetic attribution would calculate an active return of 5% – 3% = 2% for each period. These arithmetic active returns of 2% do not compound to equal the two-period active return of 4.16%, because $(1.02^2 - 1) = 4.04\%$.

A solution to this problem is to use *geometric* attribution, which defines the periodic excess return of the portfolio, *G*, as a ratio rather than a subtraction:

$$G = \frac{1 + R}{1 + B} - 1$$

In our previous example, the two-period geometric active return is 1.1025/1.0609 – 1 = 3.92%, while each single-period geometric active return is 1.05/1.03 – 1 = 1.94%. These single-period geometric returns *do* compound across two periods because $(1.0194)^2 - 1 = 3.92\%$.

PROFESSOR'S NOTE

All the attribution models that follow in this reading are arithmetic models, which is representative of the fact that a vast majority of performance appraisal practitioners use arithmetic attribution.

Equity Return Attribution—the Brinson Model

LOS 24.h: Identify and interpret investment results attributable to the asset owner versus those attributable to the investment manager.

The Brinson Model comprises two different, but very similar, performance attribution methods, referred to as the Brinson-Hood-Beebower (BHB) method and the Brinson-Fachler (BF) method.

The Brinson-Hood-Beebower (BHB) Method

We shall illustrate the **BHB method** through application to the following portfolio and benchmark data, relating to an institutional fund that has allocated to two external managers—a growth manager and a value manager. We will assess the value added/lost by the decision to allocate to these external managers in terms of how the manager's style performs relative to the overall benchmark, and how well the managers perform relative to their style.

PROFESSOR'S NOTE

As we shall see later in this reading, attribution of the value added by a fund sponsor's decision to allocate to asset classes, styles, and individual styles is referred to as a macro attribution.

Figure 24.2: BHB Model Example

Style	Fund Weight	Fund Return	Benchmark Weight	Benchmark Return
Growth Equity Style	75%	13%	60%	10%
Value Equity Style	25%	19%	40%	20%
Total	**100%**	**14.5%**	**100%**	**14.0%**

First, note some basic calculations. The total portfolio return is given by:

$$\text{portfolio return, } R = \sum_{i=1}^{n} w_i R_i$$

where:
w_i = portfolio weight of the *i*th segment (usually style, sector, or geography)
R_i = portfolio return in the *i*th segment
n = number of segments in the portfolio

In this case, the total portfolio return is calculated as (0.75 × 13%) + (0.25 × 19%) = 14.5%.

Similarly, the total benchmark return is given by:

$$\text{benchmark return, } B = \sum_{i=1}^{n} W_i B_i$$

where:
W_i = benchmark weight of the *i*th segment
B_i = benchmark return in the *i*th segment

In this case, the total benchmark return is calculated as (0.60 × 10%) + (0.40 × 20%) = 14.0%.

Note that the total active return of the portfolio is R – B = 14.5% – 14.0% = 0.5%.

The BHB method breaks the total active return of the portfolio (0.5%) into three components: the allocation effect, the selection effect, and the interaction effect.

The **allocation effect** measures the value added/subtracted through the decision to overweight/underweight a segment versus the benchmark. It is calculated by multiplying the active weight in the segment by the passive benchmark segment return.

The allocation effect for segment *i*, A_i, can be formulated as:

$$A_i = (w_i - W_i) \times B_i$$

In this example:

- growth allocation effect = (0.75 – 0.60) × 10% = 1.5%
- value allocation effect = (0.25 – 0.40) × 20% = –3.0%
- total allocation effect = 1.5% – 3.0% = –1.5%

Note how the total allocation effect here is negative, indicating that the decision to overweight growth and underweight value was an incorrect decision in a period where the value style outperformed growth.

The **selection effect** measures the value added/subtracted through selecting investments in the portfolio different from those of the benchmark. It is calculated by multiplying the passive benchmark weight of the segment by the active return generated in the segment.

The selection effect for segment *i*, S_i, can be formulated as:

$$S_i = W_i \times (R_i - B_i)$$

In this example:

- growth selection effect = 0.60 × (13% – 10%) = 1.8%
- value selection effect = 0.40 × (19% – 20%) = –0.4%
- total selection effect = 1.8% – 0.4% = 1.4%

Note how the selection effect is positive in the growth style where the manager selected outperformed the growth benchmark; however, the selection effect was negative in the value segment due to poor performance of manager selected versus the value benchmark.

The **interaction effect** measures the impact on active return of the allocation and selection effects acting *together*.

The interaction effect for segment i, I_i, can be formulated as:

$$I_i = (w_i - W_i) \times (R_i - B_i)$$

In this example:

- growth interaction effect = (0.75 – 0.60) × (13% – 10%) = 0.45%
- value interaction effect = (0.25 – 0.40) × (19% – 20%) = 0.15%
- total interaction effect = 0.45% + 0.15% = 0.60%

Note that the interaction effect is positive in the growth segment because the portfolio was overweight a style where the manager selected by the portfolio outperformed. The interaction effect was also positive in the value segment because the portfolio was underweight a style where manager selection was poor.

Reading 24

PROFESSOR'S NOTE

It might not be immediately obvious as to what role the interaction effect is playing. It is required because the allocation effect is **purely** looking at the impact of going overweight/underweight segments (in this case style)—it ignores any selection ability. The selection effect is **purely** looking at the impact of picking the right investments (in this case allocating to outperforming managers)—it ignores any impact of overweighting/underweighting segments. The interaction effect is required because there will be a "compounding" together of the impact of selection and segment weighting. For example, a portfolio that is overweight a style in which superior managers were selected will outperform by more than the sum of the allocation and selection effects.

While the interaction effect might be the least intuitive of the three effects, it is worth noting that it is simply derived from the first term of the allocation effect multiplied by the second term of the selection effect.

A summary of the output of the BHB model is displayed in the following:

Style	Allocation	Selection	Interaction
Growth Equity Style	1.50%	1.80%	0.45%
Value Equity Style	–3.00%	–0.40%	0.15%
Total	–1.50%	1.40%	0.60%

Note the total value added = –1.50% + 1.40% + 0.60% = 0.50%, which matches the figure calculated at the beginning of the analysis for total active return.

The Brinson-Fachler (BF) Method

The BF method addresses a minor drawback in the way the BHB method calculates the allocation effect for individual segments of the portfolio. The allocation effect for segment *i* under the BHB method is potentially problematic because the sign of the resulting allocation effect does not automatically indicate whether the decision to overweight/underweight a particular segment of the portfolio was correct.

In the previous example, it should be obvious that it was a bad decision to overweight the growth style during the period because the style performed worse than the benchmark as a whole (the passive return for the growth style was 10%, while the overall benchmark return was 14%).

However, under the BHB method, the growth-style allocation effect was calculated as (0.75 – 0.60) × 10% = +1.5%. This positive allocation effect is potentially misleading because the decision to overweight the growth style was a bad decision and detracted from the active return of the portfolio. This can only be seen when we calculate the allocation effect for the value style to be (0.25 – 0.40) × 20% = –3.0% and aggregate to a total allocation effect of +1.5% – 3.0% = –1.5%.

The BF model tweaks the way the allocation effect is calculated to address this drawback of the BHB model. Under the BF model, the allocation effect looks at the active weight in the segment multiplied by the passive benchmark return of the segment *relative to the overall benchmark*. This can be formulated as:

$$A_i = (w_i - W_i) \times (B_i - B)$$

Under the BF method, the allocation effect is calculated as:

- growth allocation effect = (0.75 – 0.60) × (10% – 14%) = –0.60%
- value allocation effect = (0.25 – 0.40) × (20% – 14%) = –0.90%
- total allocation effect = –0.60% – 0.90% = –1.50%

Under the BF method, we can see more clearly that the decision to overweight growth was a bad decision. Note that the aggregate allocation effect of –1.50% remains the same under both the BHB and the BF approaches.

The selection effect and the interaction effect are calculated in exactly the same way under both the BHB and the BF methods.

A summary of the output of the BF model is displayed in the following:

Style	Allocation	Selection	Interaction
Growth Equity Style	–0.60%	1.80%	0.45%
Value Equity Style	–0.90%	–0.40%	0.15%
Total	–1.50%	1.40%	0.60%

Note that the only difference between the BF output and the BHB output is the individual growth and value allocation effects.

PROFESSOR'S NOTE

In practice, the BF model tends to be the more popular model.

Macro Attributions vs. Micro Attribution

Investment decisions for an institutional fund, such as a university endowment fund, will have investment decisions being made on many different levels.

It will have an investment committee at the top of its investment decision-making structure responsible for setting overall strategic asset allocation weights and overseeing internal investment staff. The internal investment staff of the endowment would be responsible for tactical deviations from strategic asset allocation and the selection of external portfolio managers. Together, the investment committee and the internal investment staff would be referred to as the fund sponsor. Conducting a performance attribution on the decisions made by the fund sponsor is called a **macro attribution**.

The BHB and the BF model attributions in the previous section were macro attributions. They looked at the value added through the decisions made by the sponsor to overweight/underweight different styles of *manager* versus the benchmark and the value added by the sponsor's ability to select good *managers* in these styles.

Further down the investment decision-making structure are individual portfolio managers (either internal or external to the endowment) making decisions to overweight/underweight segments (e.g., substyle/sector/geography) of their portfolio to generate an active return. A performance attribution applied to these decisions made at the individual investment-manager level is called **micro attribution**.

For example, an expansion of the previous example might show that the managers made active bets on size (small-cap vs. large-cap stocks) as follows:

Figure 24.3: Micro Attribution Example

Style	Fund Weight	Fund Return	Benchmark Weight	Benchmark Return
Growth Equity Style	75%	13%	60%	10%
Large-cap growth equities	50%	15%	30%	8%
Small-cap growth equities	25%	9%	30%	12%
Value Equity Style	25%	19%	40%	20%
Large-cap value equities	25%	19%	40%	20%
Total	**100%**	**14.50%**	**100%**	**14.00%**

Using the BF model, the allocation effect for a micro attribution calculates the allocation effect of the *size* bets made by the growth and value managers. Recall that the allocation effect is calculated as:

$$A_i = (w_i - W_i) \times (B_i - B)$$

Applying this calculation to the active bets of the growth manager made with respect to size gives:

- large-cap growth allocation effect = (0.50 – 0.30) × (8% – 14%) = –1.20%

- small-cap growth allocation effect = (0.25 – 0.30) × (12% – 14%) = 0.10%
- total growth allocation effect = –1.20% + 0.10% = –1.10%

The key takeaway from these calculations is that the growth manager allocated poorly by overweighting large-cap growth stocks when large-cap growth stocks underperformed the general benchmark.

Recall that the selection effect is formulated as:

$$S_i = W_i \times (R_i - B_i)$$

Applying this calculation to the active bets of the growth manager made with respect to size gives:

- large-cap growth selection effect = 0.30 × (15% – 8%) = 2.10%
- small-cap growth selection effect = 0.30 × (9% – 12%) = –0.90%
- total growth selection effect = 2.10% – 0.90% = 1.20%

These calculations show that good stock picking in the large-cap growth segment more than outweighed poor stock picking in the small-cap growth segment.

Recall that the interaction effect is formulated as:

$$I_i = (w_i - W_i) \times (R_i - B_i)$$

Applying this calculation to the active bets of the growth manager made with respect to size gives:

- large-cap growth interaction effect = (0.50 – 0.30) × (15% – 8%) = 1.40%
- small-cap growth interaction effect = (0.25 – 0.30) × (9% – 12%) = 0.15%
- total growth interaction effect = 1.40% + 0.15% = 1.55%

These calculations show that the growth manager benefited from overweighting large-cap stocks where they exhibited good stock-picking ability, and likewise benefitted from underweighting small-cap stocks where they exhibited poor stock-picking ability.

Applying similar calculations to the value manager yields the following results:

Figure 24.4: Micro Attribution Output

Style	Allocation	Selection	Interaction
Growth Equity Style	–1.10%	1.20%	1.55%
Large-cap growth equities	–1.20%	2.10%	1.40%
Small-cap growth equities	0.10%	–0.90%	0.15%
Value Equity Style	–0.90%	–0.40%	0.15%
Large-cap value equities	–0.90%	–0.40%	0.15%
Total	**–2.00%**	**0.80%**	**1.70%**

Some important points to note here:

- The total allocation + selection + interaction effect is –2.00% + 0.80% + 1.70% = 0.5%, which is the total active return of the portfolio. Note that this is the same as the macro-attribution output.
- The total growth equity style effects are calculated by summing the individual effects for large-cap growth and small-cap growth segments. These totals are not the same as the numbers calculated for the growth manager under the macro attribution; however they do aggregate to the same overall active return across all effects. (The sum of the growth manager effects under the macro analysis was –0.60% + 1.80% + 0.45% = 1.65%. The sum of the growth manager effects under the previous micro analysis is –1.10% + 1.20% + 1.55% = 1.65%.)

Micro attribution can be conducted on many different types of portfolio segments—for example, style, industrial sector, or geography. As the previous macro/micro attributions show, a manager's allocation and selection effects can be different if the attribution is performed along different types of segments. For example, a manager may have negative aggregate selection effect with respect to industrial sector and positive aggregate selection effect with regard to geography. This begs the obvious question: is the manager a good stock picker? The answer to that question lies in the decision-making process. If the manager constructs the portfolio along geographical lines, then the data show the manager to be a good stock picker. If sector selection is central to the manager's decision process, then the data are showing that the manager is a poor stock picker.

PROFESSOR'S NOTE

The curriculum goes on to apply the BF model to a portfolio segmented by sector, geography, and even individual security. In each case, the attribution is performed by applying the BF formulas in the same way as previously demonstrated to each segment of the portfolio. Some points to note:

1. In later attributions, the reading presents the selection and interaction effect together rather than individually. A shortcut to lumping together the selection and interaction effects is to use the formula for the previous selection effect with portfolio weights instead of benchmark weights: $w_i \times (R_i - B_i)$.

   For example, in the large-cap growth equity segment in the previous micro attribution, the selection effect was calculated to be 2.10% and the interaction effect was calculated to be 1.40%. The sum of selection and interaction (3.50%) could be calculated quickly by basing selection effect on actual portfolio weights using the formula $w_i \times (R_i - B_i) = 0.5 \times (15\% - 8\%) = 3.50\%$.
2. When the micro attribution is conducted on a single stock, the allocation effect actually represents the selection effect (because an allocation to a single security is really a stock-selection decision), and the selection effect represents the market timing and transaction costs of the manager with respect to the individual security.

Equity Return Attribution—Factor-Based Return Attribution

In the previous section, we demonstrated that the BHB model calculates the attribution of security selection, asset allocation, and their interaction effects. It is common to analyze additional investment manager decisions to better understand an investment strategy. A frequently used attribution model is the **fundamental factor model**, where a portfolio's sensitivity to additional factors can be tested.

The **Carhart model** calculates the excess return from active portfolio management investment decisions by determining the impact on the portfolio due to the following factors: (1) market index (RMRF), (2) market capitalization (SMB), (3) book value to price (HML), and (4) momentum (WML). For more in-depth analysis, the Carhart model allows practitioners to remove the effects of known market factors to quantify the excess returns from active management decisions that are not accounted for in the Carhart model.

$$R_p - R_f = a_p + b_{p1}RMRF + b_{p2}SMB + b_{p3}HML + b_{p4}WML + E_p$$

where:

R_p = portfolio return

R_f = risk-free rate

a_p = alpha or return above the expected return for the portfolio's level of systematic risk

b_p = various portfolio factor sensitivities

RMRF = return on a value-weighted equity index above that of the one-month T-bill rate

SMB = small minus big, a size (market-capitalization) factor; equal to the difference between the average return on three small-cap portfolios and the average return on three large-cap portfolios

HML = high minus low, a value factor; equal to the difference between the average return on two high-book-to-market portfolios and the average return on two low-book-to-market portfolios

WML = winners minus losers, a momentum factor; equal to the difference between the return on a portfolio of the past year's winners and the return on a portfolio of the past year's losers

E_p = error term to capture the part of the portfolio return unexplained by the model

In applying the Carhart factor model, consider the attribution results for a portfolio manager's investment decisions.

Figure 24.5: Sample Carhart Factor Model Attribution

	Factor Sensitivity				Contribution to Active Return	
	Portfolio	Benchmark	Difference	Factor Return	Absolute	Proportion of Total
Factor	1)	2)	3)	4)	3) × 4)	Active
RMRF	0.98	1.00	–0.02	4.62%	–0.09%	–5.59%
SMB	–1.10	–1.00	–0.10	–2.06%	0.21%	12.46%
HML	0.30	0.00	0.30	4.30%	1.29%	78.01%
WML	0.09	0.05	0.04	8.75%	0.35%	21.17%
				Factor tilts return	1.75%	106.05%
				+ Security selection	–0.10%	–6.05%
				Active return	**1.65%**	100%

Analyzing attribution analysis results is important in determining the manager's ability to consistently add value. To start the analysis, one can review either the portfolio or its benchmark. Looking at the benchmark (Figure 24.5, Column 2) the sensitivity to RMRF of 1 suggests that the benchmark is a diversified index. The negative coefficient of the benchmark's sensitivity to SMB indicates the benchmark has a large-cap focus tilt. We can summarize the benchmark as large-cap blend (no tilt toward growth or value) that does not use momentum.

To analyze the investment decisions by the portfolio manager, review Column 1 (portfolio) and Column 3 (difference between portfolio and benchmark). The portfolio exhibits a value tilt but closely resembles the benchmark on the other factors.

The next step in the attribution analysis is to determine if the value tilt taken by the portfolio manager added or detracted value from the portfolio. From the factor sensitivities table, the value tilt contributed 1.29%, or over 78% of the total realized active return for the portfolio. The other effects were minor compared to the value tilt taken by the portfolio manager. Finally, the portfolio manager's effectiveness at stock picking (security selection) detracted slightly (–0.10%) from the portfolio's returns.

It is important to check if the portfolio manager's prospectus indicates that they follow a value-based strategy. If the prospectus indicates the manager is a growth investor, this was not demonstrated in the model attribution and further due diligence is required.

Fixed-Income Return Attribution

LOS 24.f: Interpret the output from fixed-income attribution analyses.

Three common methods of fixed-income attribution include:

- Exposure decomposition—duration based.
- Yield curve decomposition—duration based.
- Yield curve decomposition—full-repricing based.

PROFESSOR'S NOTE

For the exam, candidates are not responsible for fixed-income attribution calculations but are responsible for interpreting the results from any of the fixed-income attribution methods.

Exposure Decomposition—Duration Based

The major active bets that a fixed-income manager could take to generate active return versus the benchmark are the following:

- Duration—for example, a manager that expects the yield curve to shift *down* would *increase* the duration of the portfolio versus the benchmark.
- Curve shape—a manager could position the portfolio to outperform by correctly anticipating a change in the shape of the yield curve—for example a steepening of the curve
- Sector selection—a manager that believes that corporate spreads will narrow, leading to corporate bonds outperforming government bonds, would increase exposure to the corporate bond sector.
- Bond selection—a manager could overweight individual bonds that are expected to outperform the benchmark.

An exposure decomposition partitions both the portfolio and the benchmark by weight into duration "buckets" (e.g., short/mid/long). For each duration bucket, the portfolio and the benchmark are also partitioned by weight into sectors (e.g., government/corporate). From here, the attribution analysis decomposes the active return of the manager into the sources previously listed for each duration bucket and each sector.

Figure 24.7 shows the breakdown of a hypothetical portfolio and its benchmark by weights, which would act as an input to an exposure decomposition attribution. The buckets are segmented into short and medium durations.

Figure 24.6: Fixed-Income Exposure Decomposition Analysis

Bucket	Duration
Short	2 or less
Medium	Greater than 2 up to and including 8

Figure 24.7: Exposure Decomposition Example

	Portfolio Weights			Portfolio Duration			Portfolio Contribution to Duration		
	Short	Medium	Total	Short	Medium	Total	Short	Medium	Total
Corporate	20%	45%	65%	1.20	7.30	5.42	0.24	3.29	3.53
Government	20%	15%	35%	1.40	6.90	3.76	0.28	1.04	1.32
Total	40%	60%	100%	1.30	7.20	4.84	0.52	4.32	4.84

	Benchmark Weights			Benchmark Duration			Benchmark Contribution to Duration		
	Short	Medium	Total	Short	Medium	Total	Short	Medium	Total
Corporate	25%	20%	45%	1.20	7.30	3.91	0.30	1.46	1.76
Government	31%	24%	55%	1.40	6.90	3.80	0.43	1.66	2.09
Total	56%	44%	100%	1.31	7.08	3.85	0.73	3.12	3.85

	Portfolio Weights			Portfolio Return			Portfolio Contribution to Return		
	Short	Medium	Total	Short	Medium	Total	Short	Medium	Total
Corporate	20%	45%	65%	2.10%	2.18%	2.16%	0.42%	0.98%	1.40%
Government	20%	15%	35%	3.00%	2.76%	2.90%	0.60%	0.41%	1.01%
Total	40%	60%	100%	2.55%	2.33%	2.42%	1.02%	1.40%	2.42%

	Benchmark Weights			Benchmark Return			Benchmark Contribution to Return		
	Short	Medium	Total	Short	Medium	Total	Short	Medium	Total
Corporate	25%	20%	45%	2.10%	2.18%	2.14%	0.53%	0.44%	0.96%
Government	31%	24%	55%	3.00%	2.76%	2.90%	0.93%	0.66%	1.60%
Total	56%	44%	100%	2.60%	2.50%	2.56%	1.46%	1.10%	2.56%

Note: Figures are rounded for presentation.

Key points to note here:

- The total return of the portfolio was 2.42%. The total return of the benchmark was 2.56%. The purpose of this attribution is to explain why the active return of the portfolio was 2.42% – 2.56% = –0.14%.
- The overall portfolio duration was 4.84, versus an overall benchmark duration of 3.85. This implies that the portfolio would outperform if the yield curve experienced a parallel shift down. The manager achieved this higher duration through having a higher total weight in the medium duration bucket (60%) versus the benchmark (44%).
- The manager was overweight corporate bonds in the portfolio (65%) versus the benchmark (45%). This implies that the manager expected corporate bond spreads to narrow, leading to corporate bonds outperforming government bonds.

From the inputs displayed previously, an attribution can be performed, the results of which are summarized in Figure 24.8.

Figure 24.8: Hypothetical Decomposition—Attribution Results

Duration Bucket	Duration Effect	Curve Effect	Total Interest Rate Allocation	Sector Allocation	Bond Selection	Total
Short	–0.15%	–0.16%	–0.31%	0.05%	0.00%	–0.26%
Medium	0.48%	–0.23%	0.25%	–0.13%	0.00%	0.12%
Total	0.33%	–0.39%	–0.06%	–0.08%	0.00%	–0.14%

Key points to note here:

- The higher duration active position of the manager generated positive outperformance of 0.33%. The manager was correct to extend the duration of the portfolio, which implies that the yield curve did indeed fall.
- 39 bps of active return was lost due to changes in the shape of the yield curve. Because the manager was overweight higher duration assets, this suggests that medium yields rose and short yields fell. This implies a steepening of the yield curve.
- 8 bps were lost because the manager overweighed the corporate sector. This implies that, contrary to the manager's expectations, corporate spreads widened during the period. This is also evidenced by the lower returns in the benchmark for corporate bonds than for government bonds.
- The manager did not engage in active bond selection during the period.

The duration-based exposure decomposition method allows simple presentation of the output of the attribution with relatively low data requirements. The model is usually used for marketing and client reporting where there is a high need to present results in a clearly understandable way.

PROFESSOR'S NOTE

Remember that the important thing here is to interpret the output of the attribution, not to perform calculations to derive the figures.

Yield Curve Decomposition—Duration Based

The total return of a bond can be decomposed into several different sources. These sources include the following:

- Yield or income—the return earned through collecting the coupon income
- Roll—the impact of time passing and the bond "rolling down" a stable yield curve
- Shift—the impact of a parallel shift in the yield curve estimated through duration and convexity
- Shape—the impact of a change in the yield curve, such as a change in slope or curvature

- Spread—the impact of a change in spread for either a sector, a specific security, or both
- Residual—unexplained movements due to the estimation involved in assessing the components previously addressed (in particular, duration and convexity)

PROFESSOR'S NOTE

The first three of these sources of return: yield, roll, and shift were calculated for an individual bond in the total return decomposition performed in the fixed-income section of the curriculum.

The duration-based yield curve decomposition decomposes the *active* return of a portfolio manager to these sources of return. For example, a manager with an overweight position in high-coupon, high-yield corporate bonds will expect to have a positive contribution to active return from the yield component due to the high coupon and the spread component due to a presumed expected narrowing of the credit spread. Note that should their holdings default on coupons, or spreads in fact widen, then these effects would be negative, indicating that the manager lost value versus the benchmark due to the overweight position in high-yield corporate bonds.

Duration-based yield curve decomposition requires more data showing that the exposure decomposition method and the calculations involve more operational complexity. As such, these models tend to be used by analysts and portfolio managers rather than for marketing or client communication.

Yield Curve Decomposition—Full Repricing

A full repricing yield curve decomposition is the most comprehensive form of fixed-income attribution. Instead of estimating the impact of active bets using duration and yields to maturity, the full repricing approach breaks down the active return of the manager using individual *spot rates* for cash flows occurring at different maturities. Recall that a spot rate is a rate of return earned by a single cash flow at a specified maturity.

The full repricing approach breaks the active returns of the manager down to the individual cash flows that generated the active returns. As such, it is the most precise of the three fixed-income attribution methods and can accommodate the broadest range of instruments and yield curve changes. The drawback of the full repricing method is that it is the most complex method and, therefore, is least likely to be easily understood by the recipient of the output.

Risk Attribution

LOS 24.g: Discuss considerations in selecting a risk attribution approach.

Selecting the most appropriate risk metric for attribution analysis requires an in-depth understanding of the investment process of the portfolio manager. It is critical to identify whether the portfolio manager follows a top-down or bottom-up investment process and to define the portfolio's appropriate benchmark.

While performance attribution is important in the overall portfolio analysis process, only looking at returns is insufficient to evaluate the complete investment process. The risk taken by the portfolio manager must also be analyzed to fully evaluate the investment management process. Risk attribution identifies the sources of risk taken by the investment manager that resulted in the fund's returns.

The following table summarizes investment process (row) and type of attribution analysis (column). The correct approach to risk attribution occurs at the intersection of the relevant row and column in the following table.

Investment Process	Type of Attribution Analysis	
	Relative	Absolute
Bottom up	Security's marginal contribution to tracking risk (tracking error)	Security's marginal contribution to total risk
Top down	Attribute tracking error to relative allocation and selection	Factor's marginal contribution to total risk and specific risk
Factor based	Factor's marginal contribution to tracking error and active specific risk	

Tracking risk (or tracking error) is the relevant risk measure to consider for relative attribution analysis, and the general objective is to determine the returns generated from active management and compare them to the amount of tracking risk assumed. For the bottom-up approach, each security in the portfolio has a marginal contribution to tracking risk, and that amount is multiplied by its active weight to determine the contribution to tracking risk. In contrast, the top-down approach takes a more macro approach and attributes active return to allocation; then it attributes tracking error to allocation and selection.

Absolute attribution analysis quantifies general risk arising from market, size, and style exposures and specific risk arising from stock picking. A common risk measure to use is standard deviation. For example, a bottom-up approach could be focused on selection decisions. Therefore, it would be necessary to obtain each security's marginal contribution to total risk—in other words, the change in portfolio standard deviation resulting in a small increase of the security holding in the portfolio. Taking the sum of the marginal contributions to total risk for all the securities and dividing by total portfolio risk will provide the overall risk contribution due to selection decisions.

Risk attribution provides insight into the amount of risk that was introduced into the fund. Risk attribution must be combined with return attribution to fully understand the portfolio manager's active investment decisions.

MODULE QUIZ 24.2

1. The following is an extract from a micro attribution analysis of one of the investment managers of the Hiatus fund:

Economic Sectors	Portfolio Weight (%)	Sector Benchmark Weight (%)	Portfolio Return (%)	Sector Benchmark Return (%)
Energy	8.38	7.72	3.55	3.32
Financial	15.48	13.42	1.66	1.10
Technology	17.89	22.01	3.21	3.18

*The overall benchmark return was 2.32%.

Using the previous table, **calculate** and **evaluate**:

(i) The allocation effect for the energy sector using the Brinson-Fachler model.

(ii) The selection effect for the financial sector.

(iii) The interaction effect for the technology sector.

Use the following information for Questions 2 through 4.

Patty McDaniel and Peggy Peterson are consultants to Sigma Advisors. Sigma manages funds for wealthy individuals and small institutions. McDaniel and Peterson have been asked by Sigma to develop a plan to evaluate investment manager performance.

As part of McDaniel's and Peterson's task, Sigma asks them to perform micro performance attribution on one of its managers, Frank Matson. Matson invests primarily in large-cap value stocks. Matson's performance relative to the appropriate benchmark is shown in the following table.

	Portfolio Sector Weight	Benchmark Sector Weight	Portfolio Sector Return	Benchmark Sector Return
Agricultural	4.00%	6.00%	–2.00%	–1.00%
Capital goods	8.00%	9.00%	–4.00%	–5.00%
Consumer durables	32.00%	35.00%	2.00%	3.00%
Energy	6.00%	6.00%	8.00%	2.00%
Financial	20.00%	18.00%	6.40%	4.00%
Technology	16.00%	16.00%	2.60%	–2.00%
Utilities	12.00%	10.00%	4.00%	–2.00%
Cash	2.00%	0.00%	0.20%	
Total	100.00%	100.00%		
Portfolio plus cash return			2.90%	0.86%

2. From the data in the table, does Matson demonstrate an ability to wisely allocate funds to the capital goods and/or financial sectors?
   A. Yes, but only in the capital goods sector.
   B. Yes, but only in the financial sector.
   C. Yes, in both capital goods and financial sectors.
3. Does Matson demonstrate an ability to select stocks in the consumer durables and/or technology sectors?
   A. Yes, in both technology and consumer durables sectors.
   B. Yes, but only in the technology sector.
   C. No, he does not demonstrate the ability to select stocks in either sector.
4. Does Matson demonstrate an ability to generate a positive return from interaction effect in the agricultural and/or utilities sectors?
   A. Yes, but only in the agricultural sector.
   B. Yes, in both agricultural and utilities sectors.
   C. Yes, but only in the utilities sector.

MODULE 24.3: BENCHMARKING INVESTMENTS AND MANAGERS

Video covering this content is available online.

Liability-Based Benchmarks

LOS 24.i: Discuss uses of liability-based benchmarks.

A more frequent benchmark in institutional investing is the **liability-based benchmark**, which is likely to be used by fund sponsors and portfolio managers when a firm has a specific liability to pay in the future (e.g., a defined benefit plan). A liability-based benchmark focuses on the cash flows necessary to satisfy the liability and frequently limits the investment choices available to the portfolio manager (e.g., equity and fixed income only). Frequently used assets within a liability-based benchmark include nominal bonds, inflation-adjusted bonds, and high-quality stocks.

As an example of a liability, consider a defined benefit plan that requires future cash flows to fund future liabilities. Some of the plan features will likely impact the structure of the liability and therefore impact which assets the portfolio manager should select to meet those cash flows.

Such features include:

- How many years until the average number of workers will retire in the plan.
- How many workers have already retired and are drawing cash from the plan.
- The impact of inflation on the liabilities.
- The correlation between the company's operating profit (EBIT) and the plan assets.
- If the plan is frozen or has a terminal life.
- Any actuarial assumptions, including life expectancy and required discount rate for the plan.

Asset-Based Benchmarks

LOS 24.j: Describe types of asset-based benchmarks.

The *seven primary types of benchmarks* are as follows:

1. **Absolute.** An **absolute benchmark** is a return objective that aims to exceed a minimum target return. An example would be the minimum acceptable return (MAR) that is used in computing the Sortino ratio.
   - Advantage:
     - Simple and straightforward benchmark.

Reading 24

- Disadvantage:
  - Absolute return objective is not an investable benchmark.

2. **Broad market indexes.** There are several well-known broad market indexes that are used as benchmarks (e.g., S&P 500 for U.S. common stocks).
   - Advantages:
     - Well recognized, easy to understand by clients, and widely available.
     - Unambiguous, generally investable, measurable, and may be specified in advance.
     - Appropriate to use if it reflects the current investment process of the manager.
   - Disadvantage:
     - Manager's style may deviate from the style reflected in the index (e.g., it is not appropriate to use the S&P 500 for a small-capitalization U.S. growth stock manager).
3. **Style indexes.** Investment-style indexes represent specific portions of an asset category. Four well-known U.S. common stock style indexes are (1) large-capitalization growth, (2) large-capitalization value, (3) small-capitalization growth, and (4) small-capitalization value.
   - Advantages:
     - They are widely available, widely understood by clients, and widely accepted.
     - If the index reflects the manager's style and it is investable, it is an appropriate benchmark.
   - Disadvantages:
     - Some style indexes can contain weightings in certain securities and sectors that may be larger than considered prudent.
     - Differing definitions of investment style can produce quite different benchmark returns, making them inappropriate benchmarks.
4. **Factor-model-based. Factor models** involve relating a specified set of factor exposures to the returns on an account. A well-known one-factor model (CAPM) is the market model where the return on a portfolio is expressed as a linear function of the return on a market index. A generalized factor model equation would be:

$$R_P = a_p + b_1F_1 + b_2F_2 + \ldots + b_KF_K + \varepsilon$$

where:
R_P = periodic return on an account
a_p = "zero factor" term, representing the expected value of R_P if all factor values were zero
F_i = factors that have a systematic effect on the portfolio's performance; i = 1 to K
b_i = sensitivity of the returns on the account to the returns generated from factor i
ε = error term; portfolio return not explained by the factor model

Some examples of factors are the market index, industry, growth characteristics, a company's size, and financial strength. The benchmark portfolio (normal portfolio) is the portfolio with exposures to the systematic risk factors that are typical for the investment manager.

The manager's past portfolios are used as a guide.

- Advantages:
  - It is useful in performance evaluation.
  - It provides managers and sponsors with insight into the manager's style by capturing factor exposures that affect an account's performance.
- Disadvantages:
  - Focusing on factor exposures is not intuitive to all managers or sponsors.
  - The data and modeling are not always available and may be expensive to obtain.
  - It may be ambiguous because different factor models can produce different outputs, leading to misspecification.

5. **Returns-based. Returns-based benchmarks** are constructed using (1) the managed account returns over specified periods and (2) corresponding returns on several style indexes for the same periods. Those return series are submitted to an allocation algorithm that solves for the combination of investment-style indexes and most closely tracks the account's returns.
   - Advantages:
     - Generally easy to use and intuitive.
     - Meets the criteria of a valid benchmark.
     - Useful where the only information available is account returns.
   - Disadvantages:
     - The style indexes may not reflect what the manager owns or what the manager or client would be willing to own.
     - Enough monthly returns would be needed to establish a statistically reliable pattern of style exposures.
     - Will not work when applied to managers who change style.
6. **Manager universes.** The **median manager** or fund from a broad universe of managers or funds (that follows a similar investment process) is used as the benchmark. The median manager is the fund that falls at the middle when funds are ranked from highest to lowest by performance.
   - Advantage:
     - It is measurable.
   - Disadvantages:
     - Manager universes are subject to "survivor bias," as underperforming managers often go out of business and their performance results are then removed from the universe history.

- Fund sponsors who choose to employ manager universes must rely on the compiler's representations that the universe has been accurately compiled.
- They cannot be identified or specified in advance, so it is not investable; thus, it's not an acceptable benchmark.

7. **Custom security-based. Custom security-based benchmarks** are designed to reflect the manager's security allocations and investment process.
   - Advantages:
     - Meets all the required benchmark properties and all the benchmark validity criteria.
     - Allows continual monitoring of investment processes.
     - Allows fund sponsors to effectively allocate risk across investment management teams.
   - Disadvantages:
     - It can be expensive to construct and maintain.
     - A lack of transparency by the manager (e.g., hedge funds) can make it impossible to construct such a benchmark.

Benchmark Quality Evaluation

LOS 24.k: Discuss tests of benchmark quality.

It's important to understand the properties that constitute a valid benchmark. A valid benchmark should possess the following seven characteristics, which should align the benchmark's style and risk with that of the manager and provide the manager with an appropriate management objective:

1. **Specified in advance.** The benchmark is known to both the investment manager and the fund sponsor. It is specified at the start of an evaluation period.
2. **Appropriate.** The benchmark is consistent with the manager's investment approach and style.
3. **Measurable.** Its value and return can be determined on a reasonably frequent basis.
4. **Unambiguous.** There are clearly defined identities and weights of securities constituting the benchmark.
5. **Reflective of the manager's current investment opinions.** The manager has current knowledge and expertise of the securities within the benchmark.
6. **Accountable.** The manager(s) should accept the applicability of the benchmark and agree to accept differences in performance between the portfolio and benchmark as caused only by their active management.
7. **Investable.** It is possible to replicate the benchmark and forgo active management.

A portfolio return can be broken up into three components: market, style, and active management.

$$P = M + S + A$$

where:
P = investment manager's portfolio return
M = return on the market index
S = B − M = excess return to style; difference between the manager's style index (benchmark) return and the market return—S can be positive or negative
A = P − B = active return; difference between the manager's overall portfolio return and the style benchmark return

This relationship recognizes first that the manager's style benchmark can earn more or less than the market. Had the manager taken a passive position in a broad market index, the return on that index, *M*, would be an appropriate benchmark, and S = 0. Because the manager might specialize in a particular style, however, we add (if B > M, S > 0) or subtract (if B < M, S < 0) the difference between the benchmark and market returns. Finally, the return to active management, *A*, is the difference between the manager's portfolio return and the benchmark return and is attributed to active management.

EXAMPLE: Test of Benchmark Quality

A large-cap growth portfolio fell 11% in the first six months of the year. In the same period, a relevant large-cap growth index fell by 12% and the broad domestic equity index fell by 10%.

A client has expressed concern about the active return of the manager during the period, stating that they would have expected a skillful growth manager to outperform the broad market during the period.

Evaluate the validity of the concern of the client.

Answer:

The concern of the client is not valid, because the manager has performed well for a growth-style manager, even though underperforming the broad market during the period.

The incremental return to the large-cap growth style, *S*, for the period is equal to the return of the large-cap growth index (*B*) minus the return of the broad market index (*M*) = −12% − (−10%) = −2%. This indicates that the growth style has been out of favor during the period and has underperformed the general market.

> The return due to active management, A, is the return of the portfolio (P) minus the growth index return (B) = –11% – (–12%) = +1%. This indicates that the manager has outperformed the style-specific benchmark and therefore has positive returns to active management. This implies that the client's comment regarding active return is not valid. It is the style of the manager that has caused the portfolio to underperform the market, not the active return of the manager.

Benchmarking Alternative Investments

LOS 24.m: Describe problems that arise in benchmarking alternative investments.

Hedge Funds

Three general types of benchmarks could be considered for hedge funds: (1) broad market indexes, (2) risk-free rate, and (3) hedge fund peer universes. However, they present some problems.

Broad market indexes are not appropriate to use as a benchmark for hedge funds because hedge funds cover a wide range of investment strategies. In addition, hedge funds differ significantly from each other and can have wide asset allocation fluctuations in the long term, which makes the use of broad market indexes problematic. With hedge funds using leverage, short positions, and derivatives—plus their overall lack of liquidity, transparency, ability to monitor, and low or no correlation of returns with the broad market index—broad market indexes should not be used as a benchmark for hedge funds.

The risk-free rate with an added spread could be used for some hedge fund strategies that focus on arbitrage. The idea here is that the risk-free nature of arbitrage strategies should be matched with the risk-free rate as the appropriate benchmark. Any additional spread would take into account the incremental returns due to active management net of costs. Unfortunately, the vast majority of hedge funds will carry some systematic risk, and the use of leverage will only exacerbate the risk. As a result, the spread would need to be increased accordingly. Finally, as with broad market indexes, the lack of correlation of hedge fund returns and the risk-free rate makes the risk-free rate an unsuitable benchmark.

Hedge fund peer universes are not suitable because a specific peer group's risk and return objectives are not likely to match those of a specific hedge fund. Additionally, peer universes are subject to backfill and survivorship bias. Finally, because of the frequent illiquidity of underlying assets in hedge funds, current pricing may not be exact and may be based on an appraisal or prior period price. As a result, there may be a smoothing effect, which reduces the reported standard deviation, thereby increasing the Sharpe ratio and the allocation to hedge funds.

Real Estate

Many real estate benchmarks exist but they are not all suitable for real estate investments:

- The benchmarks are derived from a sample of the real estate universe, which means they are not completely representative of the real estate asset class.
- The performance of the index probably bears a very high correlation to the largest investments.
- Benchmark returns are self-reported, so some subjectivity and/or bias may be present.
- Benchmarks that are value-based could be biased toward the most expensive properties or geographical areas.
- The use of appraisal data (e.g., infrequent pricing) leads to a smoothing effect and understated volatility or risk.
- There is a lack of comparability with benchmark returns given that some benchmarks use leverage while others do not.
- The indexes assume no transaction costs, full transparency, and normal liquidity, which is usually not the case; those factors would impact actual real estate returns.

Additionally, there is lack of consistency in the use of return measures. For example, the cash inflows and outflows for open-end funds are controlled by the investor, so time-weighted returns would be used. In contrast, the cash inflows and outflows for closed-end funds are controlled by the manager, so an internal rate of return (IRR) would be used.

Private Equity

Benchmarks exist to allow for performance comparisons specific private equity funds and that of a relevant peer group. The metric used is usually IRR, taking into account all investment cash flows since inception plus the ending investment value. Key problems with such benchmarks include managers using different methods of valuation, which makes comparison more difficult. In addition, IRR may be biased by losses or gains occurring near the beginning of an investment. Finally, all the results are reported at one common point in time, even though the firms are likely in varying stages of development.

Commodities

Benchmarks for commodity investments are usually based on futures as opposed to actual assets. This may result in significant differences between the benchmark and the commodity investments portfolio, which reduces the comparability. Similar to other alternative investments, the different amounts of leverage employed by portfolios versus benchmarks—as well as the different weightings of exposures between portfolios and benchmarks—make the benchmarking process problematic for commodities.

Managed Derivatives

Managed derivatives funds, often referred to as managed futures funds, use specific derivatives trading strategies to generate returns. Benchmarks are either strategy-specific or peer group-based. An example of a strategy-specific benchmark is the Mount Lucas Management Index, which follows a basic momentum trading strategy. Peer-group benchmarks are similar to those used for hedge funds and will potentially exhibit the same issues as hedge fund peer-group-based benchmarks such as survivorship bias.

Distressed Securities

Given the illiquidity and severe lack of marketability of distressed securities, it is almost impossible to determine an appropriate benchmark. Should the financial state of a distressed company become better, it may become more liquid. However, it is likely to require a significant amount of time to occur (if it even does) and that creates valuation problems (e.g., stale pricing).

Market indexes do exist such as the Barclay Distressed Securities Index; however, they may take into account numerous strategies so the suitability of indexes for a specific strategy is questionable. As well, the indexes may perform valuations at erratic intervals so the issue of stale pricing may not be solved.

Appropriate Choice of Benchmark

LOS 24.1: Describe the impact of benchmark misspecification on attribution and appraisal analysis.

The phrase *garbage in, garbage out* is appropriate to use regarding the impact of benchmark misspecification on attribution and appraisal analysis. Useful performance evaluation (and any of its three components) requires an appropriate fund benchmark. When an incorrect benchmark is used in the performance evaluation process then performance measurement, which comprises attribution and appraisal analysis, will not be useful or provide valid information on understanding the investment process. Misspecified benchmarks will result in misfit active return.

To illustrate active return, suppose a manager invests in large and liquid French stocks. The sponsor assesses the manager's performance using the Euronext 100 Index. Although French stocks comprise the majority of the Euronext 100 Index, the Euronext 100 does include stocks from the Netherlands, Belgium, Portugal, and Luxembourg. As a result, the CAC 40 (large and liquid French stocks) would be more appropriate to label as the manager's normal portfolio. Assume the manager's portfolio return is 10%, the Euronext 100 (investor benchmark) return is 9% and the CAC 40 (normal portfolio) return is 12%.

Based on the returns provided, the manager outperformed the investor benchmark (10% versus 9%) but underperformed its proper benchmark (10% versus 12%). In other words, the misfit active return is +3% and the *true* active return is –2%.

MODULE QUIZ 24.3

1. Rhombus Asset Management (Rhombus) runs a U.S. small-cap equity portfolio. The portfolio generated an 8.9% return during 2005. Rhombus uses the Russell 2000® Index as the most appropriate benchmark. The Russell 2000® Index yielded 9.1% over the same evaluation period. The Wilshire 5000, a broad U.S. equity market index, yielded 8.5% over the same evaluation period.

   Calculate Rhombus's return due to style and due to active management. **Assess** Rhombus's performance compared to the benchmark and to the market.

2. Hexagon PLC is an investment management company based in London. It manages portfolios consisting of European equities only. It states that its benchmark is to beat the median manager. **Discuss** the validity of the median manager benchmark approach.

MODULE 24.4: PERFORMANCE APPRAISAL

Video covering this content is available online.

LOS 24.n: Calculate and interpret the Sortino ratio, the appraisal ratio, upside/downside capture ratios, maximum drawdown, and drawdown duration.

LOS 24.o: Describe limitations of appraisal measures and related metrics.

The final stage of the performance evaluation process is performance appraisal. Performance appraisal is designed to assess whether the investment results are more likely due to skill or luck.

Should we hire or fire the manager? Risk-adjusted performance measures are one set of tools to use in answering such questions. Active investment management skill is evident when the portfolio manager's investment process adds value on a risk-adjusted basis. In other words, can the fund manager outperform their appropriate benchmark on a risk-adjusted basis consistently?

PROFESSOR'S NOTE

Unfortunately, many investment managers have only a few years of performance to evaluate, which makes it extremely difficult to differentiate between luck and skill through the appraisal process. It is recommended to have many years of observations to determine at an appropriately high confidence level that the manager truly possesses superior investment skill.

The following seven appraisal measures will be discussed (the first five are risk-adjusted measures):

1. Sharpe ratio.
2. Treynor ratio.
3. Information ratio.
4. Appraisal ratio.
5. Sortino ratio.
6. Capture ratios (upside and downside).
7. Drawdown (maximum drawdown, drawdown duration).

Sharpe Ratio

$$S_A = \frac{\overline{R}_A - \overline{r}_f}{\hat{\sigma}_A}$$

The Sharpe ratio is calculated as the incremental or excess return over the risk-free rate (numerator) divided by standard deviation (denominator). A key drawback with the ratio is that the denominator does not differentiate between volatility that is upside versus downside. Therefore, with the Sharpe ratio, there is a penalty for all volatility, even if it is "good" volatility.

Treynor Ratio

$$T_A = \frac{\overline{R}_A - \overline{r}_f}{\hat{\beta}_A}$$

The Treynor ratio is similar to the Sharpe ratio, but the denominator for the former is measured by beta, so it only considers systematic risk rather than total risk like the latter. Therefore, with the Treynor ratio, the universe of appropriate benchmarks is limited to only those that assume efficient markets. The Treynor ratio is only useful in evaluating portfolios that have systematic risk and do not have unsystematic risk; in other words, such portfolios are well diversified.

Information Ratio

$$IR = \frac{E(r_p) - E(r_B)}{\sigma(r_p - r_B)}$$

The information ratio (IR) is used to measure a portfolio's performance against the benchmark but accounts for differences in risk. The numerator is the difference between the mean returns of the portfolio and the benchmark, respectively. The denominator is known as the tracking risk, or the variability in the portfolio performance with that of its benchmark.

Appraisal Ratio

The appraisal ratio measures the ratio of active return, α, to the volatility of the residual term, σ_ε, both derived from a factor-based regression.

$$AR = \frac{\alpha}{\sigma_\varepsilon}$$

A manager with a higher AR is generating more active return per unit of active risk (as represented by residual risk σ_ε also referred to as the "standard error of the regression") and is therefore a superior active manager according to this measure.

PROFESSOR'S NOTE

The "standard error of the regression," σ_ε is the volatility of the error term in a factor-based regression. As such, it represents the component of the volatility of manager returns that is not explained by the regression model factors. This component of volatility is generated by the manager taking active bets relative to the factors in the model, hence σ_ε here is playing the role of active risk. You should not concern yourself with the direct calculation of σ_ε however, it can be deduced from basic portfolio and benchmark performance data as per the following example.

The AR is analogous to the information ratio—it looks at active return per unit of active risk. The only difference to the information ratio is that the AR uses a factor-based regression to estimate active return and active risk.

A common single-factor application is the capital asset pricing model (CAPM). Recall that under the CAPM, the fair return of Manager *i* is given by:

$$E(R_i) = R_f + \beta_i[E(R_m) - R_f]$$

where:
R_i = return of Manager *i*
R_f = risk-free rate
β_i = relative systematic risk
R_m = market return

Under the CAPM framework, α can be calculated as the difference between the forecasted return of the security and the CAPM fair return. It can also be shown that the variance of the manager, σ_i^2, is driven partly by the systematic variance of the manager related to market variance, and partly by residual variance specific to the manager as follows:

$$\sigma_i^2 = \beta^2 \sigma_m^2 + \sigma_\varepsilon^2$$

This implies that σ_ε can be deduced from:

$$\sigma_\varepsilon^2 = \sigma_i^2 - \beta^2 \sigma_m^2$$

PROFESSOR'S NOTE

If required to calculate residual risk in this way, be sure to remember to take the square root of σ_ε^2 before using it in the denominator of the appraisal ratio.

EXAMPLE: Appraisal ratio

Annualized data relating to the performance of an investment manager is presented in the following:

Portfolio return	8%
Portfolio standard deviation	20%
Portfolio beta	1.2
Market index return	6%
Market standard deviation	16%
Risk-free rate	1%

Calculate the appraisal ratio of the manager.

Answer:

The fair return of the manager according to CAPM is calculated as:

$$E(R_i) = R_f + \beta_i[E(R_m) - R_f]$$
$$= 1\% + 1.2(6\% - 1\%)$$
$$= 7\%$$

The alpha of the manager is equal to the portfolio return less the CAPM fair return = 8% – 7% = 1%.

Nonsystematic variance of the manager is calculated as:

$$\sigma_\varepsilon^2 = \sigma_i^2 - \beta^2\sigma_m^2$$
$$= 0.20^2 - (1.2^2 \times 0.16^2) = 0.003136$$

The appraisal ratio is calculated as:

$$AR = \frac{0.01}{\sqrt{0.003136}} = 0.18$$

Sortino Ratio

The Sortino ratio only considers the standard deviation of the downside risk. That is in contrast to the Sharpe ratio, which considers all risk (e.g., both upside and downside). Positive volatility associated with the upside can be considered "good" volatility.

In practice, however, clients tend to be more concerned about volatility associated with negative returns. As a result, the Sortino ratio can provide a more meaningful view of a portfolio's risk-adjusted performance than the Sharpe ratio.

$$SR_D = \frac{E(r_p) - r_T}{\sigma_D}$$

$$\widehat{SR}_D = \frac{\bar{r}_p - \bar{r}_T}{\hat{\sigma}_D}$$

In the previous equation, the r_T refers to a target rate of return—sometimes called the minimum acceptable return (MAR)—and σ_D refers to target semideviation. Semideviation measures the standard deviation of returns *below the target return*. In other words, the Sortino ratio penalizes managers only for "bad" volatility by considering only returns below the MAR; it ignores "good" volatility generated by returns above the target return. To calculate the semideviation of a series of returns, an analyst would sum the squares of the distances of returns below the target return, *ignoring those returns that beat the target return*. Dividing by the *total* number of observations (*including* those above the target return) gives semivariance. The square root of this number is the semistandard deviation.

Therefore, assuming an average portfolio return of 7%, MAR of 3%, and semi-standard deviation of 5%, the Sortino ratio is calculated as (7% – 3%) / 5% = 0.80. Similar to the Sharpe ratio, the higher the Sortino ratio, the better the risk-adjusted performance.

The Sortino ratio is more appropriate for investments with non-normal (nonsymmetrical) return distributions. Positively skewed and negatively skewed investment strategies would both result in lower Sharpe ratios (e.g., higher standard deviation in the denominator), but only the negatively skewed investment strategy would result in a lower Sortino ratio (e.g., higher semi-standard deviation in the denominator). Therefore, for investments that have nonsymmetrical or skewed return distributions, such as hedge funds or options, the Sortino ratio appears to be a more appropriate performance metric. However, a comparability problem exists with the Sortino ratio because the determination of MAR is subjective and specific to each investor.

Capture Ratios

Capture ratios determine the manager's relative performance when markets are up or down. Consider an up market where the index or benchmark return is positive. The question is whether the manager's portfolio return is also positive and if it is above or below the benchmark return. For example, if the benchmark return is 4% and the portfolio return is 5%, the upside capture ratio is 125% (5% / 4% = 1.25) and there is outperformance during a period of positive returns. Assuming the same benchmark return but a portfolio return of only 3%, the upside capture ratio is 75% (3% / 4% = 0.75) and there is underperformance during a period of positive returns.

Similarly, consider a down market where the index or benchmark return is negative. For example, if the benchmark return is –4% and the portfolio return is –5%, the downside capture ratio is 125% (–5% / –4% = 1.25) and there is underperformance during a period of negative returns. Assuming the same benchmark return but a portfolio return of –3%, the downside capture ratio is 75% (–3% / –4% = 0.75) and there is outperformance during a period of negative returns.

One can now calculate the capture ratio (upside capture divided by downside capture). Using the previous examples with benchmark returns of +4% and –4% and portfolio returns of +5% and –5%, the capture ratio is 1.25 / 1.25 = 1. A capture ratio of 1 is indicative of a symmetrical return profile. Therefore, if the capture ratio > 1, then there is a positively asymmetrical (convex) return profile in that there is greater upside capture than downside capture. Correspondingly, if the capture ratio < 1, there is a negatively asymmetrical (concave) return profile in that there is greater downside capture than upside capture.

For example, during an up market, if the manager earns 7% and the benchmark earns 8%, the upside capture is 87.5%. If, during a down market, the manager earns –6% and the benchmark earns –10%, the downside capture is 60%. Therefore, the capture ratio is about 1.46 (87.5% / 60%), which indicates a positively asymmetrical (convex) return profile. Ideally, the manager would capture as much of the upside as possible and capture as little of the downside as possible to maximize the capture ratio.

Drawdown

Drawdown is a measure, based on past performance, that calculates the maximum loss incurred if an investor had invested at a peak valuation and subsequently liquidated at a trough valuation. Drawdown duration is the total time required to fully recover a drawdown; it is from when the drawdown commences up to when the cumulative drawdown is zero. Drawdown duration can be subdivided into a drawdown phase and a recovery phase. Maximum drawdown occurs at the very end of the drawdown phase and at the very start of the recovery phase; it is the point at which the cumulative drawdown is at its highest (in absolute terms).

To illustrate and calculate drawdown duration and maximum drawdown, consider the following data pertaining to the monthly returns of a stock for a 12-month period.

Month	Monthly Return	Drawdown	Cumulative Drawdown	Comments
01/2018	3.14%		0.00%	
02/2018	–2.55%	–2.55%	–2.55%	Drawdown phase begins
03/2018	–2.71%	–2.71%	–5.26%	
04/2018	–4.66%	–4.66%	–9.92%	
05/2018	–4.91%	–4.91%	–14.83%	
06/2018	–0.73%	–0.73%	–15.56%	Maximum drawdown
07/2018	2.18%		–13.38%	Recovery phase begins
08/2018	3.11%		–10.27%	
09/2018	2.45%		–7.82%	
10/2018	3.65%		–4.17%	
11/2018	4.03%		–0.14%	
12/2018	4.14%		0.00%	Drawdown recovered

Based on the data provided, the maximum drawdown was calculated as –15.56% and the drawdown duration was approximately 10 months (from beginning of drawdown in 02/2018 to full recovery of drawdown in 12/2018).

Manager Skill Evaluation

LOS 24.p: Evaluate the skill of an investment manager.

The skill of an investment manager can be evaluated through attribution analysis as well as appraisal analysis. An example of each type of analysis is provided next.

Example of Attribution Analysis

Manager X has a benchmark of the Euronext 100. The following summary information states that Manager X underperformed the benchmark by 67 bps. The question is whether the underperformance is due to lack of skill or bad luck.

	Manager X		Euronext 100		Attribution Effects		
Market	**Weight**	**Annualized Return**	**Weight**	**Annualized Return**	**Allocation**	**Selection + Interaction**	**Total**
France	60%	10.14%	63%	11.49%	–0.04%	–0.81%	–0.85%
Netherlands	15%	8.78%	19%	7.65%	0.09%	0.17%	0.26%
Belgium	15%	9.12%	11%	8.12%	–0.07%	0.15%	0.08%
Portugal	6%	4.35%	5%	4.99%	–0.05%	–0.04%	–0.09%
Luxembourg	4%	7.14%	2%	7.92%	–0.04%	–0.03%	–0.07%
Total	**100%**	**9.32%**	**100%**	**9.99%**	**–0.12%**	**–0.56%**	**–0.67%**

The manager underperformed the benchmark by 12 bps due to country weighting decisions. Although the manager made a good decision in underweighting the Netherlands by 4% because it underperformed the total benchmark by 2.34%, the manager made bad decisions in all of the other countries. For example, the manager underweighted France by 3% when it outperformed the total benchmark by 1.50% and overweighted Belgium by 4% when it underperformed the total benchmark by 1.87%. Overall, the manager was not successful with country weighting decisions.

The manager underperformed the benchmark by 56 bps due to stock picking decisions. Although the manager selected outperforming stocks in the Netherlands and Belgium that earned a total of 32 bps, there was significant underperformance in France that lost 81 bps. Overall, the manager was not successful with picking stocks. Additionally, the selection effect was significantly greater than the allocation effect.

In the next example, the level of risk taken to achieve the manager's performance will be considered by comparing performance to other managers.

Example of Appraisal Analysis

In this section, performance appraisal measures for the same period will be analyzed for Managers X, Y, and Z. All managers will be compared to the same benchmark; return and standard deviation percentages are all expressed on an annualized basis.

Appraisal Measure	Manager X	Manager Y	Manager Z	Benchmark
Return	9.32%	11.42%	8.12%	9.99%
Standard deviation	11.65%	13.76%	10.11%	11.98%
Sharpe ratio	0.63	0.68	0.61	0.67
Treynor ratio	0.07	0.08	0.06	0.08
Information ratio	(0.22)	0.41	(0.72)	–
Sortino ratio (MAR = 4%)	0.75	0.78	0.63	0.87

Manager X's volatility of returns (as measured by standard deviation) is only slightly below that of the benchmark. Manager X's volatility of returns is between that of Manager Z (Z is lower by about 1.5%) and Manager Y (Y is higher by about 2.1%). Those observations are confirmed by the Sharpe ratios for all three managers and the benchmark (using an assumed risk-free rate of 2%). Therefore, although Manager X took on less total risk and earned less return than the benchmark and Manager Y, Manager X's return was relatively lower than both of them on an excess return (annualized return less risk-free rate) per unit of risk basis. Manager X did perform better than Manager Z on a risk-adjusted basis.

The conclusions based on the Sharpe ratio are consistent with those for the Treynor ratio and IR. Given that both Manager X and Manager Z underperformed the benchmark, it makes sense that their IRs are negative. Therefore, on the basis of systematic risk only, Manager X did not perform as well as Manager Y or the benchmark.

Manager X's Sortino ratio of 0.75 is higher than its Sharpe ratio of 0.63, which suggests that Manager X should be able to earn greater returns in relation to the 4% threshold for measuring downside risk.

Conclusion

Overall, Manager X was not able to demonstrate sufficient skill in investing as demonstrated by losses incurred due to poor country allocation and poor stock selection decisions, relative to the benchmark.

Additionally, on a risk-adjusted basis, Manager X did outperform Manager Z but fell short when compared to Manager Y and the benchmark.

Consideration may need to be given to replacing Manager X with a suitable manager who is able to outperform the benchmark in terms of country allocation and stock selection as well as outperform its peers on a risk-adjusted basis.

MODULE QUIZ 24.4

1. One of your portfolio managers, Mort Van Sleet, has recently complained that by measuring risk-adjusted returns using the Sharpe ratio, he is placed at an unfair disadvantage. He has stated flatly that the standard deviation of his portfolio returns is artificially inflated. **Explain** how this can be true, and **offer** and **explain** a potential solution to the problem.

2. During an up market, assume a manager earns 4% and the benchmark earns 3%. Then, in a down market, the same manager earns –4% and the benchmark earns –8%. Which of the following amounts is *closest* to the manager's capture ratio?
   A. 0.25.
   B. 0.38.
   C. 2.67.

KEY CONCEPTS

LOS 24.a

Performance evaluation answers three questions regarding a portfolio's performance:

1. What performance did the fund achieve during the period (performance measurement)?
2. How did the fund manager achieve their performance (performance attribution)?
3. Did the fund manager achieve their performance via skill or luck (performance appraisal)?

LOS 24.b

An effective performance attribution process includes:

- A reflection of 100% of the portfolio's return or risk exposure.
- The portfolio manager's current decision-making process.
- The active investment decisions taken by the portfolio manager.
- A full explanation of the portfolio's excess return and risk.

LOS 24.c

Return attribution evaluates the impact of the active portfolio management decisions on the fund's investment returns. Risk attribution is the parallel of return attribution but analyzes the impact of the portfolio manager's active investment decisions on portfolio risk.

Micro attribution analyzes the portfolio at the portfolio manager's level and seeks to verify that the portfolio manager did what they said they were going to do and to understand the drivers of the portfolio's return. Macro attribution analyzes investment decisions at the fund sponsor's level and quantifies the decisions made by the fund sponsors to deviate from their strategic asset allocation and the timing when they made those decisions.

LOS 24.d

Returns-based attribution uses regressions to analyze the portfolio returns over some period and isolates the asset class components through indexes that would have generated these returns. There is no attempt to determine the actual holdings of the portfolio.

Holdings-based attribution uses beginning-of-period portfolio assets; the accuracy of analysis improves as the time interval for the analysis becomes smaller (e.g., annual to monthly, to weekly). Since holdings-based attribution does not adjust for any portfolio changes that are made after the initial period, this analysis frequently does not match the actual portfolio returns.

Transactions-based attribution improves upon the holdings-based attribution by updating the attribution of the beginning-of-period holdings of the portfolio with any subsequent trades. Both the weights and the returns of the portfolio will reflect the actual transactions, including any transaction costs.

LOS 24.e

The Brinson-Hood-Beebower (BHB) and Brinson-Fachler models quantify the portfolio returns into three attribution effects: the allocation effect, the security selection effect, and the interaction effect.

- The allocation effect refers to the portfolio manager's decision to overweight or underweight specific sector weightings in the portfolio versus the portfolio benchmark.
- The security selection refers to the value the portfolio manager either added or detracted from the portfolio by selecting individual securities within the sector and weighting the portfolio differently compared to the benchmark's weightings.
- The interaction effect refers to the residual amount that ensures the arithmetic return minus the relative benchmark is fully accounted for in attribution analysis.

The Carhart model calculates the excess return from active portfolio management investment decisions by determining the impact on the portfolio due to the following factors: (1) market index (RMRF), (2) market capitalization (SMB), (3) book value to price (HML), and (4) momentum (WML).

LOS 24.f

Exposure decomposition is a top-down approach that utilizes duration to quantify active portfolio manager decisions regarding interest rate decisions relative to its benchmark.

Yield decomposition (duration) can be either top-down or bottom-up and utilizes both duration and yield to maturity (YTM) in computing price return (as one component in calculating total return).

Yield decomposition (full repricing) involves repricing based on zero-coupon curves, or spot rates. The full-repricing method is the most accurate measure of price changes in securities.

LOS 24.g

There are two general methods of risk attribution: relative and absolute.

For relative attribution analysis, tracking risk (or tracking error) is the relevant risk measure to consider and the general objective is to determine the returns generated from active management and compare them to the amount of tracking risk assumed.

Absolute attribution analysis quantifies general risk arising from market, size, and style exposures and specific risk arising from stock picking. A common risk measure to use is standard deviation.

LOS 24.h

Macro attribution analysis looks at the impact of fund sponsor decisions. Micro attribution analysis looks at the impact of portfolio manager decisions. Both types of analysis utilize the BHB and Brinson-Fachler model computations to determine allocation, selection, and interaction effects.

LOS 24.i

A liability-based benchmark focuses on the cash flows necessary to satisfy the liability and frequently limits the investment choices available to the portfolio manager (e.g., equity and fixed income only). Frequently used assets within a liability-based benchmark include nominal bonds, inflation-adjusted bonds, and high-quality stocks.

LOS 24.j

There are seven types of benchmarks:

1. An absolute benchmark is a return objective that aims to exceed a minimum target return.
2. Broad market indexes, such as the S&P 500 for U.S. common stocks, can be used as benchmarks.
3. Investment-style indexes represent specific portions of an asset category and can be used as a benchmark. Four well-known U.S. common stock style indexes are (1) large-capitalization growth, (2) large-capitalization value, (3) small-capitalization growth, and (4) small-capitalization value.
4. Factor models involve relating a specified set of factor exposures to the returns on an account. Some examples of factors are the market index, industry, growth characteristics, a company's size, and financial strength. The benchmark portfolio (the normal portfolio) is the portfolio with exposures to the systematic risk factors that are typical for the investment manager. The manager's past portfolios are used as a guide.
5. Returns-based benchmarks are constructed using (1) the managed account returns over specified periods and (2) corresponding returns on several style indexes for the same periods. Those return series are submitted to an allocation algorithm that solves for the combination of investment-style indexes that most closely tracks the account's returns.
6. A manager universe looks at a wide group of managers that have a similar investment process. The median manager or fund from that universe is used as the benchmark. The median manager is the fund that falls at the middle when funds are ranked from highest to lowest by performance.
7. Custom security-based benchmarks are designed to reflect the manager's security allocations and investment process.

LOS 24.k

A portfolio return can be broken up into three components: market, style, and active management.

$$P = M + S + A$$

where:
P = investment manager's portfolio return
M = return on the market index
S = B − M = excess return to style; difference between the manager's style index (benchmark) return and the market return—S can be positive or negative
A = P − B = active return; difference between the manager's overall portfolio return and the style benchmark return

LOS 24.l

When an incorrect benchmark is used in the performance evaluation process then performance measurement, which comprises attribution and appraisal analysis, will not be useful. Misspecified benchmarks will result in "misfit" active return.

LOS 24.m

Three general types of benchmarks could be considered for hedge funds: (1) broad market indexes, (2) risk-free rate, and (3) hedge fund peer universes. However, broad market indexes are not appropriate to use as a benchmark for hedge funds because hedge funds cover a wide range of investment strategies and differ significantly from each other. The risk-free rate is not appropriate because the vast majority of hedge funds will carry some systematic risk and the use of leverage will only exacerbate the risk. Hedge fund peer universes are not suitable because a specific peer group's risk and return objectives is not likely to match that of a specific hedge fund.

With the many real estate benchmarks that could be used, they may not be suitable for all real estate investments for reasons including: small sample size, bias toward larger investments, use of appraisal data, lack of consistency regarding use of leverage, and unrealistic assumptions of no transaction costs, full transparency, and normal liquidity.

Private equity benchmarks usually use internal rate of return (IRR) measures but managers may be using different methods of valuation. Also, IRR may be biased by losses or gains occurring near the beginning of an investment. Finally, all the results are reported at one common point in time even though the firms are likely in varying stages of development.

Benchmarks for commodity investments are usually based on futures as opposed to actual assets. That may result in significant differences between the benchmark and the commodity investments portfolio, which reduces the comparability.

Managed derivatives use specific benchmarks because of the lack of market indexes. As a result, such benchmarks may be too specific or not specific enough for a given investment strategy and therefore not suitable.

Given the illiquidity and severe lack of marketability of distressed securities, it is almost impossible to determine an appropriate benchmark.

LOS 24.n, 24.o

The Sharpe ratio is calculated as the incremental or excess return over the risk-free rate (numerator) divided by standard deviation (denominator). A key drawback with the ratio is that the denominator does not differentiate between volatility that is upside versus downside.

The Treynor ratio is similar to the Sharpe ratio but the denominator for the former is measured by beta so it only considers systematic risk rather than total risk like the latter.

The information ratio (IR) is used to measure a portfolio's performance against the benchmark but accounting for differences in risk. The numerator is the difference between the mean returns of the portfolio and the benchmark, respectively. The denominator is known as the tracking risk, or the variability in the portfolio performance with that of its benchmark.

The appraisal ratio (AR) is calculated as alpha divided by the standard deviation of the residual/unsystematic risk (or otherwise known as the standard error of regression). Alpha is excess return, calculated as the return earned by the portfolio minus the return suggested by CAPM.

The Sortino ratio only considers the standard deviation of the downside risk. It uses a minimum acceptable return (MAR, or target rate of return) and target semi-standard deviation (target semideviation). The Sortino ratio penalizes managers only for "bad" volatility by considering only returns below the MAR.

Capture ratios determine the manager's relative performance when markets are up or down. Consider an up market where the index or benchmark return is positive. The question is whether the manager's portfolio return is also positive and if it is above or below the benchmark return (upside capture). Similarly, consider a down market where the index or benchmark return is negative. The question is whether the manager's portfolio return is negative and if it is above or below the benchmark return (downside capture). Using those amounts, the capture ratio is calculated as upside capture divided by downside capture.

Drawdown duration is the total time required to fully recover a drawdown; it is from when the drawdown commences up to when the cumulative drawdown is zero. Maximum drawdown occurs at the very end of the drawdown phase and at the very start of the recovery phase.

LOS 24.p

The skill of an investment manager can be evaluated through attribution analysis as well as appraisal analysis.

ANSWER KEY FOR MODULE QUIZZES

Module Quiz 24.1

1. **A** Performance appraisal determines whether the performance was affected primarily by investment decisions, by the overall market, or by chance. Performance appraisal combines output from both performance measurement and performance attribution to render a professional judgment on the quality of the performance.

   Performance measurement serves as the initial foundation phase and calculates both the return and the risk of the fund over specified time periods. Performance attribution determines the key drivers that generated the account's performance. (LOS 24.a)

2. **C** Transactions-based attribution improves upon the holdings-based attribution by updating the attribution of the portfolio's beginning-of-period holdings with any subsequent trades. Transactions-based attribution is the most reliable of the measures.

   Returns-based attribution uses regressions to analyze the portfolio returns over some period and isolates the asset class components through indexes that would have generated these returns. There is no attempt to determine the actual holdings of the portfolio. It is the least reliable of the three methods but the easiest to implement.

   Holdings-based attribution uses beginning-of-period portfolio assets; the accuracy of analysis improves as the time interval for the analysis becomes smaller. Holdings-based attribution frequently offers a higher level of quality of attribution analysis than the returns-based attribution. (LOS 24.d)

Module Quiz 24.2

1. (i) energy sector allocation effect = [(0.0838 – 0.0772) × (3.32% – 2.32%)] = 0.0066%

   This shows that the decision to overweight a sector that performed better than the overall benchmark resulted in a positive contribution to portfolio performance.

   (ii) financial sector security selection effect = 0.1342 × (1.66% – 1.10%) = +0.0752%

   The positive contribution shows that the Hiatus portfolio held financial stocks that performed better than the financial stocks contained in the sector benchmark.

   (iii) technology sector interaction effect = [(0.1789 – 0.2201) × (3.21% – 3.18%)] = –0.0012%

   Underweighting the portfolio in the technology sector when the fund performed better than the sector benchmark has led to a negative contribution. (LOS 24.h)

2. **C** To answer this question, we must first examine the return for the overall benchmark versus the return for the benchmark in both sectors. The overall return for the benchmark is given at 0.86%. The capital goods sector return in the benchmark was –5.00%. For the financial sector, it was 4.00%. Thus, relative to the overall benchmark return of 0.86%, the capital goods sector was an underperforming sector and the financial sector outperformed. Now determine whether Matson overweighted or underweighted each sector. He underweighted the weak capital goods sector (8.00% allocation for the manager versus 9.00% for the benchmark), and he overweighted the strong financial sector (20.00% allocation for the manager versus 18.00% for the benchmark). Because Matson underweighted a weak sector and he overweighted a strong sector, he made correct decisions for both.

   No calculations are needed to reach these conclusions. However, the allocation effect can be calculated by multiplying the difference between the portfolio and benchmark allocation by the difference in sector benchmark return and overall benchmark return for each sector. For the capital goods sector, it is (8.0% – 9.0%) × (–5.00% – 0.86%) = 0.0586%. For the financial sector, it is (20.0% – 18.0%) × (4.00% – 0.86%) = 0.0628%. (LOS 24.h)

3. **B** To answer this question, examine the return for the manager against the return for the benchmark in each sector. Matson's return in the consumer durables sector was 2% versus 3% for the benchmark, so he did not outperform the benchmark for security selection in this sector. However, the return for the manager in the technology sector was 2.6% versus –2% for the benchmark, so he did outperform the benchmark for security selection in this sector.

   No calculations are needed to reach the conclusions just listed. However, the selection effect can be calculated by multiplying the difference between the portfolio and benchmark return in each sector by the benchmark's weight. For the consumer durables sector, it is (2.0% – 3.0%) × 35% = –0.35%. For the technology sector, it is (2.6% + 2.0%) × 16% = 0.736%. (LOS 24.h)

4. **B** To answer this question, multiply the difference in weightings for the manager and the benchmark by the difference in returns for the manager and the benchmark in each sector. In the agricultural sector, this is (4% – 6%) × (–2% + 1%) = 0.02%. In the utilities sector, this is (12% – 10%) × (4% + 2%) = 0.12%. (LOS 24.h)

Reading 24

Module Quiz 24.3

1. style return = B – M = 9.1% – 8.5% = +0.6%

   active management return = P – B = 8.9% – 9.1% = –0.2%

   The positive style return tells us small-cap stocks outperformed the market as a whole.

   However, the negative active management return tells us Rhombus has underperformed its benchmark for the evaluation period in question. Consistently underperforming the benchmark would bring Rhombus's investment management skills under question. (LOS 24.k)

2. The median manager is not a valid benchmark because that manager cannot be specified in advance and is not investable. It is not a passive alternative to active management. The only benchmark characteristic it meets is it can be measured after the fact. (LOS 24.j)

Module Quiz 24.4

1. In calculating the traditional standard deviation, all returns for the measurement period are used (e.g., all the positive and negative alphas). This is like looking at the entire normal distribution, with the benchmark return as the center of the distribution. Negative alphas would fall to the left of the benchmark return, and positive alphas would fall to the right.

   The manager is arguing that only negative alphas are relevant for measuring risk. This would be analogous to using only the left half of that normal distribution. Using the Sortino ratio compensates for this by only using returns below a designated level.

   Excess return for the Sortino ratio (the numerator) is calculated as the portfolio return less the minimum acceptable portfolio return (MAR). The denominator of the ratio is the standard deviation of returns calculated using only returns below the MAR. The motivation behind the downside measure of volatility utilized in the Sortino ratio is the sense that very good performance (high returns) can unfairly inflate the volatility measure (the standard deviation used as the risk measure). (LOS 24.o)

2. **C** If, during an up market, the manager earns 4% and the benchmark earns 3%, the upside capture is 133.3%. If, during a down market, the manager earns –4% and the benchmark earns –8%, the downside capture is 50%. Therefore, the capture ratio is about 2.67 (133.3% / 50%). (LOS 24.n)

READING 25

Investment Manager Selection

EXAM FOCUS

The investment manager selection process involves both quantitative and qualitative considerations, although the focus in the reading is primarily qualitative. Some topics in the reading (e.g., returns-based and holdings-based style analysis, and pooled investment vehicles) are covered in other areas of the curriculum or were covered in previous levels (e.g., Type I and II errors), which should allow for more efficient coverage of the material. Key areas of focus for the exam include Type I and II errors, capture ratios and drawdowns, and computing performance-based fees.

MODULE 25.1: MANAGER SELECTION PROCESS

Video covering this content is available online.

LOS 25.a: Describe the components of a manager selection process, including due diligence.

Due diligence is the analysis and investigation in support of an investment decision, action, or recommendation. Due diligence on investment managers must emphasize the sources and reasons behind the actual returns generated in the past. Then there must be an evaluation on the probability of repeatedly earning sufficient or better returns in the future using the same investment process. Overall, due diligence must consist of manager universe, quantitative analysis, and qualitative analysis.

Manager Universe

The manager universe consists of only those managers who are *suitable* for the portfolio in terms of the objectives and constraints of the IPS, invest in the relevant *style* (e.g., value, growth, mixed) desired by the client, and will manage the portfolio with the appropriate balance between *active versus passive* approaches.

This is a process of elimination that must carefully balance having too many or too few managers in the candidate pool from which to make a selection. The purpose of the manager search is crucial. For example, the desire for a specific new strategy or risk exposure will involve trying to find the best manager for that strategy or exposure. Or the inclusion of a new manager to diversify an existing portfolio would require a manager who could complement the existing holdings. The terms "best" and "complement," for example, have an aspect of subjectivity that must be looked at in the context of the IPS.

The search usually begins by establishing the role for the potential manager within the portfolio and that is defined by the benchmark. The benchmark can be determined using one or more of: third-party categorization, returns-based style analysis, holdings-based style analysis, and manager experience. With third-party categorization of managers provided by database or software providers, the problem is that the provider's definition may not be the same as that definition for the purposes of the role within the portfolio. Manager experience can be ascertained by analyses of holdings within the manager's portfolios as well as past returns. Returns-based and holdings-based style analyses will be examined in greater detail later.

At the manager universe stage, there should not be any performance assessment; that will occur later during quantitative analysis. Instead, there must be an emphasis on the manager's risk profile and whether or not it is a good fit for the portfolio's requirements. The universe of managers is constantly changing as strategies change and as managers come and go.

Quantitative Analysis

The manager's performance should be evaluated objectively in terms of the distribution of past returns. Through performance **attribution and appraisal**, one can distinguish between managerial skills versus luck (e.g., external market factors). The **capture ratio** would examine performance in both good and weak market conditions. Finally, one must check for any significant **drawdowns** (i.e., peak-to-trough decline in percentage terms for a specific time period).

Qualitative Analysis

Two important issues arise in qualitative analysis: (1) What is the likelihood that the same level of returns will continue in the future? (2) Does the manager's investment process account for all the relevant risks? Those two issues will be elaborated somewhat here.

Continuity of returns can be assessed by looking at the four Ps—philosophy, process, people, and portfolio. In short, the *philosophy* focuses on a specific area of market inefficiency to earn excess returns. Then the *process* and *people* will determine whether the strategy is feasible and if it is possible to execute the strategy with the given knowledge and skills of the employees. Finally, the *portfolio* must be built in a way that is congruent with the philosophy and process.

Risk assessment considers the *firm* and whether it is robust and performing well, and its likelihood of remaining a going concern. Examining the *process and procedures* of the firm involves aspects such as the quality of the back office, the ability to safeguard assets, and the ability to prepare useful reports on a timely basis. Going into such detail with operational due diligence is meant to determine any risks not evident in the firm's past returns and to determine the firm's sustainability. The proposed *investment vehicle* must be assessed for suitability within the portfolio and the *terms* of the manager contract must be reasonable and relevant in context of the investment strategy and vehicle. Finally, continual *monitoring* of the manager is needed to ensure the manager continues to be the appropriate one for the portfolio.

LOS 25.b: Contrast Type I and Type II errors in manager hiring and continuation decisions.

Type I and II Errors

In making decisions on whether to hire a new manager or to keep or fire an existing manager, hypothesis testing can be used. The null hypothesis (H_0) is that there is no value added, therefore, to demonstrate that it is value added on a statistically significant basis, the calculated test statistic would have to be large enough so that the null hypothesis would be rejected.

As a result, there could be a Type I error whereby the null hypothesis is rejected, when in fact, there was no value added. In other words, the hired or kept manager did not demonstrate sufficient skill. Alternatively, there could be a Type II error whereby the null hypothesis is not rejected, when in fact, there was value added. In other words, the manager who was not hired or the manager who was fired did demonstrate sufficient skill. Figure 25.1 summarizes Type I and II errors.

Figure 25.1: Type I and Type II Errors

		Realization	
		Below expectations (no skill)	At or above expectations (skill)
Decision	Hire/Retain	Type I	Correct
	Not Hire/Fire	Correct	Type II

Type I errors receive much more attention than Type II errors. One reason may relate to the notion of regret aversion by the decision maker, which is linked to an error of commission (a Type I error). Errors of commission are active decisions that result in explicit (or visible) costs. In contrast, Type II errors are errors of omission, so they result in implicit or opportunity (less visible) costs. Another reason is that Type I errors are easier to determine; for example, a manager's relative performance can be measured against a benchmark. Such performance also impacts the decision maker's compensation so additional care would be taken to reduce the risk of a Type I error. In contrast, Type II errors are difficult to determine; for example, how can one objectively determine how a manager (who was not hired) would have performed? Finally, Type I errors are much more visible to clients who can easily determine that their investments have underperformed the benchmark over a specific time period, for example. In contrast, clients are less likely to follow or monitor managers who are not hired or who are fired to determine if such managers would have added value over the same time period.

Preventing Type II Errors

An excessive number of Type II errors would be indicative of a problem with the hiring and firing of managers. The obvious solution to minimizing Type II errors would be to track the subsequent performance of managers who were not hired as well as those who were fired. For example, what are the characteristics of the managers who are selected versus those who are not selected and are those characteristics of the selected managers consistent with the portfolio investment objectives? As well, what are the characteristics of the managers who are retained versus fired, and again, are the characteristics of the retained managers consistent with the portfolio investment objectives? Ultimately, it is important not to hire or fire managers because of short-term performance or because of behavioral biases.

Costs of Type I and II Errors

Type I errors result in costs associated with retaining managers who are weak, while Type II errors result in costs associated with not retaining managers who are strong. Therefore, assuming two separate groups of managers (e.g., strong and weak), the greater the differences in sample size and mean, the greater the costs of Type I and II errors. The wider the dispersion of returns between strong and weak managers, the easier it is to distinguish between their relative skills. Therefore, it makes it less likely to have a Type I or II error which results in a lower expected cost of a Type I or II error.

In an efficient market, the dispersion of return distributions between the two groups is probably smaller due to greater difficulty in achieving alpha through active management, which would lessen the costs of hiring or retaining weak managers (Type I error).

If markets are mean-reverting, then Type I errors may occur when firing a poor performer, only to have performance improve subsequently or hiring a strong performer only to have performance deteriorate subsequently (Note: That is not a Type II error because the assumption is that the poor and strong performers have been accurately determined initially but it is the mean-reversion of the markets that leads to the Type I error). Type II errors occur in mean-reverting markets when strong managers are fired or not hired (e.g., they subsequently underperform when the market goes down) or managers who have weaker short-term performance (but have sufficiently strong long-term performance) are fired or not hired and they subsequently outperform when the market goes up.

MODULE QUIZ 25.1

1. Quantitative analysis of the manager selection process includes:
   A. defining the universe.
   B. evaluating a performance appraisal.
   C. performing investment due diligence.
2. The difference in expected cost between Type I and Type II errors is:
   A. higher the lower the perceived difference between the distribution of skilled and unskilled managers.
   B. lower the greater the perceived difference between the distribution of skilled and unskilled managers.
   C. higher the greater the perceived difference between the distribution of skilled and unskilled managers.
3. A return distribution of skilled managers that is not distinct from the return distribution of unskilled managers, *most likely* implies a:
   A. highly inefficient market.
   B. low opportunity cost of not hiring a skilled manager.
   C. high opportunity cost of not hiring a skilled manager.

MODULE 25.2: APPROACHES TO MANAGER ANALYSIS

Video covering this content is available online.

Reading 25

LOS 25.c: Describe uses of returns-based and holdings-based style analysis in investment manager selection.

Style Analysis

Style analysis examines the manager's risk exposures (e.g., industry, concentration, capitalization) in relation to an appropriate benchmark and the changes in those exposures over time. The risk exposures allow for the classification of managers (e.g., value, growth) by style for selection purposes and to perform returns-based style analysis (RBSA) and holdings-based style analysis (HBSA). Once RBSA and HBSA have been performed, congruence between the output and the investment process is crucial to ensure the process can be replicated consistently in the future. Monitoring the RBSA and HBSA output over time can help to detect style drift, whereby the manager's actions are deviating from the manager's stated style.

Style analysis is relevant when comparisons can be made over time and between different managers, when it is done on a timely basis, when the risks analyzed are the key sources of the manager's risk and return, and when the reported amounts are consistent with the manager's actual risk exposures. Style analysis works best for publicly traded investments with frequent pricing data. For less liquid investments, style analysis can still be used to generate questions in the due diligence process. In sum useful style analysis must be *meaningful*, *accurate*, *consistent*, and *timely*.

RBSA

RBSA estimates the portfolio's sensitivities to security market indexes for a set of key risk factors. One complication of RBSA is that the risk factors are estimated rather than using predetermined style categories. However, the approach is top-down in nature and little additional data is needed to perform the analysis so the computational approach is relatively easy. RBSA can determine the key risk factors and return drivers for basic and complex strategies. Also, RBSA uses objective data and allows for comparability between managers and through time. Finally, RBSA can be performed on a timely basis (e.g., right after the data is released).

RBSA lacks precision since it essentially assumes that there is a static portfolio for the period. As a result, it makes it difficult to ascertain the impact of multiperiod investment decisions for a given period, and could alter the breakdown of the sources of value added. The portfolio may also contain illiquid securities, so stale prices could understate risk exposure. When performance is computed based on appraisals of ongoing projects and the internal rate of return of cash distributions (e.g., venture capital and private equity), the short-term volatility may be understated. A manager's true return standard deviation is best gauged over a longer time period. Finally, reporting timeliness will decrease in the presence of illiquid or nontraded securities due to the longer time required for pricing.

HBSA

HBSA looks at the actual securities included in the portfolio at one time. That allows one to estimate the current risk exposures using a more security-specific (bottom-up) approach. Many of the advantages are the same as for RBSA (e.g., determine key risk factors and return drivers, comparability between managers and through time, performed on a timely basis). Overall, HBSA is most appropriate for equity-based strategies.

A key drawback of HBSA is the increased computational requirement as complexity increases and transparency decreases. HBSA uses a point in time analysis format that may not be useful in projecting into the future or if the portfolio has high turnover. Similar to RBSA, the presence of illiquid and nontraded securities results in stale pricing and that could understate risk exposure as well as decrease reporting timeliness.

LOS 25.d: Describe uses of the upside capture ratio, downside capture ratio, maximum drawdown, drawdown duration, and up/down capture in evaluating managers.

Capture Ratios

Capture ratios determine how suitable a manager is with respect to the investor's risk tolerance and time horizon. The **upside capture ratio (UC)** looks at capture when the benchmark has a positive return. Based on the benchmark return, UC that is higher (lower) than 100% is indicative of outperformance (underperformance).

Conversely, the **downside capture ratio (DC)** looks at capture when the benchmark has a negative return. Based on the benchmark return, DC that is lower (higher) than 100% is indicative of out- (under-) performance.

The **capture ratio (CR)** = UC ratio / DC ratio. The CR is a measure of return asymmetry, > 1 = positive asymmetry (convex shape), and < 1 = negative asymmetry (concave shape).

In examining positive asymmetry (convex shape), the question is whether the investment strategy is naturally convex or if the convexity occurs because of manager skill. With the former, consider an example of a hedging strategy that involves buying a series of out-of-the-money puts prior to severe market downturns. The result is positive asymmetry with many small losses (low DC ratio) due to the puts expiring worthless with far fewer large gains in this scenario (high UC ratio). With the latter, consider an example of a long-only equity strategy requiring active management to minimize losses and maximize gains. That requires manager skill, but may not result in consistent positive asymmetry.

When betas are increasing (decreasing), momentum-driven strategies should have higher (lower) UC than value-driven strategies. A low-beta (high-beta) strategy will have lower (higher) UC and DC. Therefore, CRs can be used to confirm the investment strategy.

Drawdown

Drawdown is the total peak-to-trough loss for a specified time period; maximum drawdown is the largest peak-to-trough loss during that time period. Large drawdowns are not appropriate for investors approaching the end of their investment horizon. **Drawdown duration** is the total time from when the drawdown begins to when the total drawdown recovers to zero (the latter achieved with offsetting gains).

In comparing a long-only strategy (100% invested in S&P TR Index) versus a low-beta strategy (50% in S&P TR Index, 50% in 90-day T-bills), it is quite possible for the low-beta strategy to outperform the long-only strategy on a risk-adjusted returns basis. In other words, a low-beta strategy may have lower absolute returns but the lower risk in the form of lower drawdowns may result in better risk-adjusted returns.

Drawdowns are useful for identifying poor or poorly executed investment strategies, weak internal controls, and operational problems. Significant or extended drawdowns could cause a manager to utilize self-preservationist tactics that could harm the investors.

There is a fine line between risk management versus self-preservation. For example, it may be prudent to immediately sell assets with unrealized losses in a market downturn, because those losses may become worse later due to a fundamental change in the asset. It might be risky to sell assets in a market downturn should there be a subsequent reversal. The question is whether the manager acted properly in accordance with the IPS, acted for self-preservation reasons, or had a sudden overreaction.

In applying the concept of drawdown to the IPS, those investors with shorter time horizons and lower risk tolerance with less time to recover from losses should invest with managers with smaller and less extended drawdowns.

MODULE QUIZ 25.2

1. Which of the following statements is *least likely* an advantage of HBSA over RBSA?
   A. HBSA is a more precise tool.
   B. HBSA is generally easier for equity strategies.
   C. The data required for HBSA is generally easier to obtain.
2. A manager whose relative performance is better during market upturns *most likely* has a capture ratio that is:
   A. equal to one.
   B. less than one.
   C. greater than one.

MODULE 25.3: EVALUATING MANAGERS

Video covering this content is available online.

LOS 25.e: Evaluate a manager's investment philosophy and investment decision-making process.

Investment Philosophy

The entire investment process should be driven by a succinct and precise investment philosophy. Some managers believe that markets are very efficient and that active management will underperform after considering all related costs. Therefore, those managers will execute passive strategies and attempt to earn risk premiums instead. These **risk premiums** are the returns that are earned above the risk-free rate for bearing undiversifiable risks, also referred to as systematic or market risk. To earn risk premiums, passive strategies will target one or more specific systematic risk factors including equity risk, credit risk, liquidity risk, and volatility risk.

In contrast, active strategies take the position that markets are inefficient and can allow for those inefficiencies to be exploited when market prices of securities deviate from their intrinsic values.

There are two broad types of inefficiencies to be considered: behavioral and structural. **Behavioral inefficiencies** are mispricings caused by other investors and their behavioral biases (e.g., trend-following). The mispricings are very short-term in nature and therefore, must be quickly exploited (sometimes within seconds) prior to the market correction. **Structural inefficiencies** occur because of laws and regulations, which can make them long-term in nature. Active strategies often believe in the value of diversification for risk management purposes and believe in the notion of market prices converging to intrinsic value. With the latter, the idea is to exploit the incongruence prior to convergence.

Whatever the investment philosophy, it is necessary for the manager to be able to convey the underlying assumptions in a clear manner. Going deeper, do the assumptions make sense and are they congruent with the investment process? For example, the belief of inefficient markets would not be congruent with a passive approach. Furthermore, has the philosophy remained constant over time, thereby making it repeatable? If not, have the changes in philosophy been logical in view of market changes or have they merely been reactionary based on short-term performance? The former would support the repeatability of the process while the latter would not. Finally, is the inefficiency being exploited more of an informational advantage or more of a *structural inefficiency*? The former is more short-term in nature and likely less repeatable, while the latter is more long-term in nature and likely more repeatable.

Assuming there is a valid inefficiency to exploit, there is the related issue of capacity. Capacity refers to the amount, repeatability, and sustainability of the inefficiency. For example, the inefficiency must provide enough excess returns to cover transaction costs and fees. If leverage is required, then borrowing costs must be considered. Also, is the inefficiency repeatable or just a one-time opportunity? Finally, what minimum asset level is required in order to earn a sufficient return from the inefficiency? Therefore, sustainability depends on market depth and liquidity and the amount of capital that can be set aside to exploit the inefficiency.

Investment Decision-Making Process

Idea Generation

An investment signal may be a piece of information that can be used to establishing an investment position to exploit an inefficiency. To effectively exploit inefficiencies, investment strategies must utilize unique information to have an informational advantage over other market participants. Additionally, that information must be obtained and used on a very timely basis as it is frequently the case that the window of opportunity to exploit is very short. Finally, the investment manager must have superior cognitive or interpretive skills with regards to utilizing the information.

Idea Implementation

Here the investment idea is transformed into an investment position (i.e., signal capture). Two key concerns include the repeatability of process and its congruence with the investment philosophy plus the determination and approval of the investment position.

Portfolio Construction

A fundamental question is what kinds of securities are used to construct the portfolio. For example, if derivatives are used, then is the manager sufficiently knowledgeable and experienced with derivatives to adapt to changing markets?

The portfolio allocations may be done quantitatively or qualitatively. Either way, the allocations must make sense in view of the investment philosophy. For example, a passively managed portfolio should not have excessive turnover. The allocations should also account for the manager's views, therefore, performance maximization would occur by overweighting the expected outperformers and underweighting the expected underperformers. A related issue is the allocation of long and short positions—they may be paired or determined separately. If they are paired, then proper position sizing will eliminate market risk. At the same time, it will allow for the exploitation of inefficiencies prior to the convergence of market prices with intrinsic values.

Assets under management (AUM) will likely increase over time, therefore, the underlying positions may need to be adjusted (e.g., liquidity constraints) to allow for greater AUM.

Stop losses are orders to sell a security once it reaches a certain price and can be an important risk management tool. Hard or soft stop losses may be used. The former involve automatic dispositions when a specific loss threshold is met and the latter involve subjective evaluations when a specified loss threshold is met. As well, hedges are used to manage risk so information about how they are implemented, the financial instruments used to hedge, and the determination of hedge ratios, is necessary.

With liquidity, it should be determined whether the manager is a net supplier or demander of liquidity. Either way, care must be taken to ensure that the portfolio can react appropriately to changing market conditions or investor liquidity requirements. A portfolio that has too many illiquid securities may be faced with high exit costs in addition to the usual high transaction costs. There is also the risk of having to sell securities at depressed prices if funds are suddenly required by the investor. Therefore, in assessing liquidity, there should be an analysis of how much of the portfolio can be liquidated in five days or less (more liquid and therefore, greater flexibility) and well as how much needs more than 10 days to liquidate (less liquid and therefore, subject to higher transaction costs). A calculation of average daily volume (weighted by portfolio position size) is also necessary. Finally, there should be the determination of any security where the firm owns more than 5% of its total market capitalization as that would suggest some liquidity problems if the entire position needed to be disposed of suddenly.

Portfolio Monitoring

The monitoring process looks at external factors such as the general economy and financial markets and their impact on how the manager may exploit relevant inefficiencies. It also looks at internal factors such as historical returns, risk level, and allocations. There is a check for any significant deviations from the investment process (e.g., style drift) and to ensure that investment decisions are congruent with the most up-to-date client objectives.

LOS 25.f: Evaluate the costs and benefits of pooled investment vehicles and separate accounts.

Separately managed accounts (SMAs) and pooled investment vehicles are used to execute investment strategies. Pooled vehicles bring together the funds from all investors into one portfolio (e.g., mutual funds, ETFs, hedge funds) and there is no customization for any specific investor. SMAs hold the funds of one investor in a separate account so a key analysis is the cost-benefit trade-off of holding investments in a SMA. As well, one must ensure the manager has the capability and resources to manage the SMA.

Compared to pooled investments, SMAs have higher transaction costs but provide control, customization, tax efficiency, separate reporting, and greater transparency. The *control* is in the form of direct and legal ownership of the underlying securities by the investor. Therefore, there is extra protection given to the investor in case of a liquidity event or bankruptcy of the manager. As well, unlike pooled investments, the investor is not impacted by the redemption demands of other investors. In terms of *customization*, SMAs allow for the tailoring of client-specific objectives and constraints. *Tax efficiency* could be higher in SMAs because there is only payment of realized capital gains required; for pooled investments, payment of accrued taxes on unrealized gains may be required. Investing strategies for SMAs can be tailored to minimize taxes paid by the individual investor. In terms of transparency, SMAs can provide an instantaneous snapshot or dashboard view of the investment holdings at any given point. Pooled investments may be able to do so but probably with a delay.

Customized SMAs require an extra layer of due diligence to evaluate security selection, portfolio construction, and operational issues. Cost-wise, SMAs have fixed costs that must be borne entirely by the one investor and cannot be spread amongst multiple investors in the case of pooled investments. For pooled investments, the incremental costs of adding additional investors are relatively low (e.g., custody, reporting) whereas SMAs require a separate account for each investor. Trading costs are relatively higher for SMAs because trades cannot be aggregated (e.g., buy and sell trades amongst multiple investors) to reduce trading volumes. A customized SMA will differ from the benchmark so it creates tracking risk due to investor constraints instead of manager actions. Customized SMAs are subject to micromanagement risk on the part of the investor and that makes it difficult to determine the true value added by the manager (if any). Investors may be subject to trend chasing, avoidance of unfamiliar investments, and not understanding the benefits of hedging (which often involve sacrificing some returns).

MODULE QUIZ 25.3

1. Passive strategies earn risk premiums based on bearing:
   A. systematic risk only.
   B. unsystematic risk only.
   C. both systematic and unsystematic risk.
2. Which step in the investment decision-making process focuses on the attributes of information in exploiting inefficiencies?
   A. Signal capture.
   B. Signal creation.
   C. Portfolio construction.
3. One reason for an investor to choose a separately managed account over a pooled investment vehicle would *most likely* include the investor:
   A. is tax exempt.
   B. desires lower costs and fees.
   C. desires real-time details on investment positions.

Video covering this content is available online.

MODULE 25.4: MANAGER CONTRACTS AND FEES

LOS 25.g: Compare types of investment manager contracts, including their major provisions and advantages and disadvantages.

Although investment contracts cover a wide variety of terms, the focus here will be on liquidity and management fees, in context of what is most suitable for the investor's needs.

Liquidity

Closed-end funds and ETFs have the highest liquidity because they are traded intra-day. Open-end funds offer almost as much liquidity in that they are traded based on end-of-day NAV only.

Investments held in limited partnership structures (e.g., hedge funds, private equity, and venture capital) usually involve investment capital that is tied up for more time. For example, hedge fund liquidity involves redemption frequency, lockup periods, notification periods, and gates. Redemption frequency refers to how often the investor may withdraw funds, and the notification period refers to the amount of advance notice required by the investor for a redemption. The lockup period refers to the period immediately following the initial investment, where funds may not be withdrawn. A hard lock does not permit redemptions, while a soft lock permits redemptions for a fee. Gates provide for a limit in the redemption amount for any given redemption.

Private equity and venture capital funds have the lowest liquidity because of capital calls; investors only receive returns after about five years into the 10-year average life of the funds. The manager may extend the life of the fund for up to two one-year periods, which further lowers liquidity.

Key advantages of limited partnership terms include ability to have a long investment horizon, thereby not allowing investors to overreact to short-term aberrations. As well, allowing for the earning of illiquidity premiums by investing in illiquid assets and not being forced to sell assets at depressed prices due to redemption requests.

Key disadvantages of limited partnership terms include the impaired ability to change portfolio allocations in response to changes in the market. As well, the impaired ability to meet sudden liquidity demands.

With SMAs, the liquidity is determined by the liquidity of the underlying assets, as the securities can be sold at any time.

LOS 25.h: Describe the three basic forms of performance-based fees.

Management Fees

Managers charge fees to cover their fixed and variable costs as well as to earn a profit. The average asset-weighted expense ratio paid by mutual investors has declined substantially over the years as investors have increasingly allocated to no-load mutual funds and index funds which have lower fees.

Mutual fund fees are often based on AUM. In some cases, minimum balances are required. Fees can be structured as a fixed dollar amount or on the basis of a percentage of assets. The fee structure (e.g., AUM, performance-based) is important to ensure that managers work to the advantage of the investors. It could be argued, however, that even in the absence of incentives, managers will still work to the advantage of the investors to retain them and potentially gain new investors. However, the fee structure may result in a misalignment of the principal and the agent's interests. For example, the investor does not always see the full extent of all the work the manager is doing; or the investor and manager may have different opinions on how to interpret time horizons or investment losses. Additionally, overall investment performance has a strong element of luck, so in theory, the manager should not be rewarded for it.

An advantage of the investor paying fees based on AUM is that it rewards based on the manager's skill and ability to grow the asset base. Many managers have declining percentage fees for larger accounts, so the AUM fee percentage is reduced with increased asset size, which reduces investors' fees. Unfortunately, luck may play a significant role in the short-term growth of assets. Another disadvantage is that once the assets are attained by the managers, there is more incentive to retain the assets and earn the AUM fees (e.g., engage in safe strategies, such as indexing) rather than take risks for the benefit of the investor.

Basic Forms

Performance-based fees are a form of risk sharing between the investor and the manager in order to align their interests. They are computed on the basis of total or relative return. The fees (using a sharing percentage) could be based on total performance or performance in excess of a base.

There are three basic forms of performance-based fees:

- Symmetrical structure with full upside and downside exposures.
  - Fee = base + performance sharing
  - The greatest alignment between investor and manager incentives but increased risk to manager due to the full downside exposure
- Bonus with full upside and limited downside exposures.
  - Fee = Greater of: (1) base, (2) base + sharing of positive performance
- Bonus with limited upside and downside exposures.
  - Fee = Greater of: (1) base, (2) base + sharing of positive performance (within limit)

Performance-based fee structures transform symmetrical gross active return distributions into asymmetrical net active return distributions. The result is lower relative variance on the upside versus the downside. Therefore, by using a symmetrical risk measure such as standard deviation, there could be an underestimation of downside risk.

Performance-based fees benefit investors since they will pay relatively lower performance-based fees (rather than relatively higher standard fixed fees) in the case of low active returns. Such fees benefit managers, as they may incentivize them to increase their efforts to benefit the investor's portfolio and to increase their own compensation. However, all three structures have in common the fact that base fees are paid even when the manager underperforms.

Some investments have no limits on performance fees. In some cases, performance fees could be tempered to include high-water or clawback provisions (e.g., hedge funds) that will offset prior period negative returns from current period positive returns, for example. For private equity partnerships, the investors are structured as limited partners and the manager as the general partner. A beneficial term for the investors is one that stipulates the repayment of principal and share of profits to the limited partners prior to any payment of performance fees to the general partner.

In negotiating fee agreements, only the most successful managers or the ones with limited capacity can command the highest base fees and/or the highest sharing percentages.

Call Option

The previous bonus fee structures are analogous to a manager having a long position in a call option on the portfolio active return. The exercise price would be the base fee. See Figure 25.2 for a graphical representation. The payoff to the manager is theoretically unlimited.

Figure 25.2: Payoff Line of Sample Performance-Based Fee Schedule 1

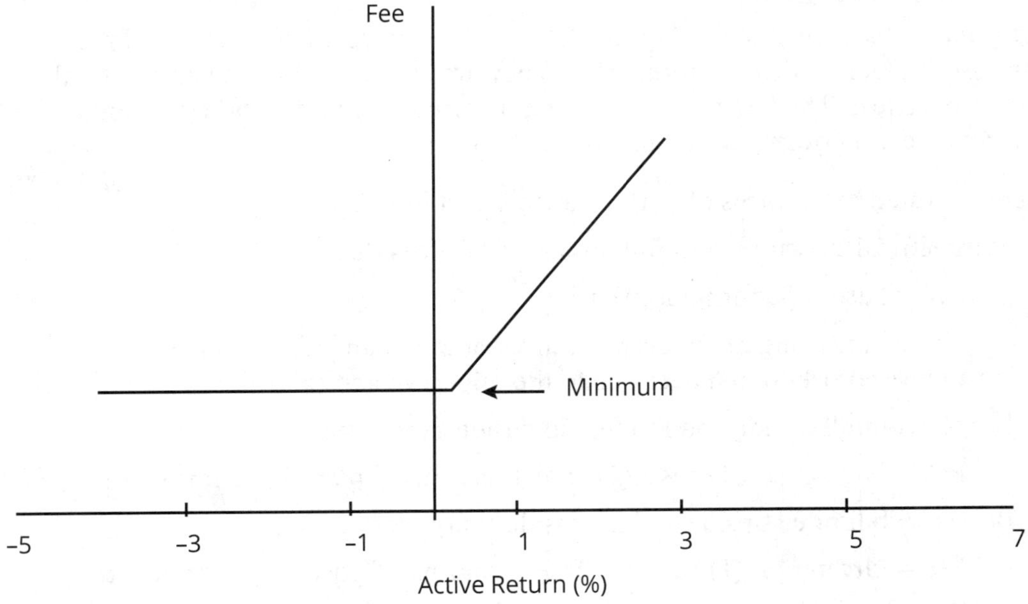

In Figure 25.3, there is the addition of a short position in a less valuable call option with an exercise price equal to the maximum fee (assuming such a provision is applicable).

Figure 25.3: Payoff Line of Sample Performance-Based Fee Schedule 2

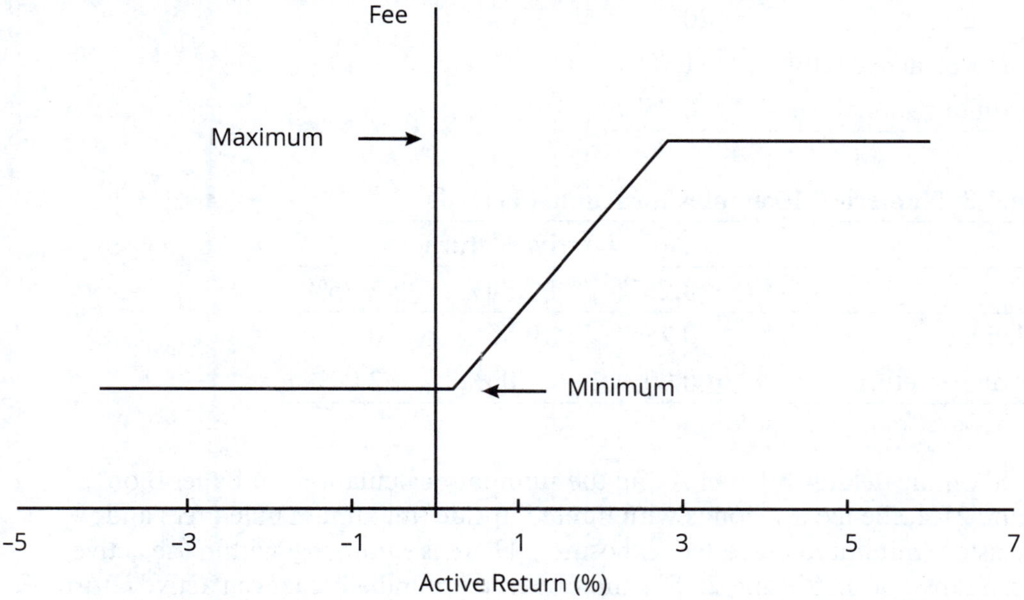

Based on this discussion, a net long position in a call option on portfolio active return, would cause a manager to take more risk since option pricing theory states that higher volatility increases option value. Therefore, it is recommended that managers be both penalized for taking too much risk and rewarded for earning higher risk-adjusted returns.

Other Issues

LOS 25.i: Analyze and interpret a sample performance-based fee schedule.

A sample performance-based fee schedule is illustrated in Figure 25.4.

Figure 25.4: Sample Performance-Based Fee Schedule

Panel A. Sample Fee Structure

Standard fee	0.50%
Base fee	0.25%
Sharing*	20%
Breakeven active return	1.50%
Maximum annual fee	0.75%

Panel B. Numerical Examples for Annual Periods

	Active Return		
	≤ 0.25%	**1.50%**	**≥ 2.75%**
Billed fee	0.25%	0.50%	0.75%
Net active return	≤ 0.00%	1.00%	≥ 2.00%

* On active return, beyond base fee.

Based on the details in Panel A and the summary calculations in Panel B of Figure 25.4, the fee is a bonus with limited upside (maximum billed fee) and downside (minimum billed fee) exposures. There is symmetry within the active return range of 0.25% and 2.75% and centered around a breakeven active return of 1.50%. In calculating the breakeven return, we have the following:

(1.50% – 0.25%) × 20% = 0.25% performance fee

Adding the performance fee to the base fee of 0.25% results in a total billed fee of 0.50%, which is the same as the standard fee of 0.50%.

At an active return of 0.25% or less, the performance fee is zero (the nonnegativity constraint frequently encountered in practice prevents the performance fee from being negative).

In that case, the billed fee is simply the base fee of 0.25%. At an active return of 2.75% or more, the performance fee is maximized at 0.50%, and so the billed fee is a maximum of 0.75%.

MODULE QUIZ 25.4

1. Which investment fund generally has the *least* amount of liquidity?
   A. Hedge fund.
   B. Closed-end fund.
   C. Private equity fund.
2. Which of the following fee structures *most likely* has no impact on the volatility of a portfolio's net returns?
   A. Incentive fees only.
   B. Management fees only.
   C. Neither incentive fees nor management fees.

3. Fund X earns a –3% gross return for the year. The computed management fee is equal to a base fee of 2% plus a 20% sharing of both positive and negative performance. The sharing is based on return net of the base fee. What is Fund X's total management fee for the year?
   A. 1.0%.
   B. 1.4%.
   C. 2.0%.
4. Fund Y earns a gross return of 12% for the year, while the relevant benchmark earns 3%. The computed management fee is equal to the higher of either a base fee of 0.4%, or base plus a 20% sharing of positive performance, up to a maximum annual fee of 2.9%. The sharing is based on active return. What is Fund Y's total management fee for the year?
   A. 2.2%.
   B. 2.8%.
   C. 2.9%.

Reading 25

KEY CONCEPTS

LOS 25.a

In the context of investment manager selection, due diligence consists of manager universe, quantitative analysis, and qualitative analysis.

The manager universe consists of only those managers who are *suitable* for the portfolio in terms of the objectives and constraints of the IPS, invest in the relevant *style* (e.g., value, growth, mixed) desired by the client, and will manage the portfolio with the appropriate balance between *active versus passive* approaches.

Quantitative analysis focuses on performance attribution and appraisal as well as the analyses of CR and significant drawdowns.

Two important issues arise in qualitative analysis:

- What is the likelihood that the same level of returns will continue in the future?
- Does the manager's investment process account for all the relevant risks?

LOS 25.b

Type I errors occur when the null hypothesis is rejected, when in fact, there was no value added. In other words, the hired or kept manager did not demonstrate sufficient skill. Type II errors occur when the null hypothesis is not rejected, when in fact, there was value added. In other words, the manager who was not hired or the manager who was fired did demonstrate sufficient skill.

Type I errors receive much more attention than Type II errors since the former are errors of commission (more visible) while the latter are errors of omission (less visible). Also, Type I errors are easier to determine than Type II errors.

LOS 25.c

Style analysis examines the manager's risk exposures in relation to an appropriate benchmark and the changes in those exposures over time. The risk exposures allow for the classification of managers by style for selection purposes and to perform RBSA and HBSA.

RBSA is a top-down approach that estimates the portfolio's sensitivities to security market indexes for a set of key risk factors. HBSA is a bottom-up approach that looks at the actual securities included in the portfolio at one time. Many of the advantages of RBSA are the same as for HBSA (e.g., determine key risk factors and return drivers, comparability between managers and through time, performed on a timely basis).

LOS 25.d

The capture ratio (CR) = UC ratio / DC ratio. The CR is a measure of return asymmetry; > 1 = positive asymmetry (convex shape) and < 1 = negative asymmetry (concave shape).

Drawdown is the total peak-to-trough loss for a specified time period; maximum drawdown is the largest peak-to-trough loss during that time period. Drawdown duration is the total time from when the drawdown begins to when the total drawdown recovers to zero (the latter achieved with offsetting gains).

LOS 25.e

The entire investment process should be driven by a succinct and precise investment philosophy. Some managers believe markets are very efficient and will execute passive strategies. Other managers believe markets are inefficient and can allow for those inefficiencies to be exploited when market prices of securities deviate from their intrinsic values; they will execute active strategies. Active managers will look at behavioral inefficiencies (shorter-term; caused by other investors and their behavioral biases) and structural inefficiencies (longer-term; caused by laws and regulations).

The investment decision-making process consists of four steps:

1. Idea generation
2. Idea implementation
3. Portfolio construction
4. Portfolio monitoring

Within portfolio construction, the key issues to consider include allocation, risk management, and liquidity.

LOS 25.f

SMAs and pooled investment vehicles are used to execute investment strategies. Pooled vehicles bring together the funds from all investors into one portfolio and there is no customization for any specific investor. SMAs hold the funds of one investor in a separate account; the cost-benefit trade-off of holding investments in a SMA must be evaluated.

Compared to pooled investments, SMAs have higher transaction costs but provide control, customization, tax efficiency, separate reporting, and greater transparency. Customized SMAs require an extra layer of due diligence to evaluate security selection, portfolio construction, and operational issues.

LOS 25.g

Closed-end funds and ETFs have the highest liquidity because they are traded intra-day. Open-end funds offer almost as much liquidity in that they are traded based on end-of-day NAV only.

Investments held in limited partnership structures (e.g., hedge funds, private equity, venture capital) usually involve investment capital that is tied up for more time.

Private equity and venture capital funds have the lowest liquidity because of capital calls; investors only receive returns after about five years into the 10-year average life of the funds. There may be the possibility to extend by the manager for up to two one-year periods, which further lowers liquidity.

With SMAs, the liquidity is determined by the liquidity of the underlying assets.

LOS 25.h, 25.i

There are three basic forms of performance-based fees:

- Symmetrical structure with full upside and downside exposures
  - Fee = base + performance sharing
  - The greatest alignment between investor and manager incentives but increased risk to manager due to the full downside exposure
- Bonus with full upside and limited downside exposures
  - Fee = Greater of: (1) base, (2) base + sharing of positive performance
- Bonus with limited upside and downside exposures
  - Fee = Greater of: (1) base, (2) base + sharing of positive performance (within limit)

ANSWER KEY FOR MODULE QUIZZES

Module Quiz 25.1

1. **B** Quantitative analysis includes attribution and appraisal (as well as an analysis of the capture ratio and drawdown). Defining the universe is a separate step in the manager selection process, and investment due diligence is a component of qualitative analysis. (LOS 25.a)

2. **C** The greater the difference in the distribution between skilled and unskilled managers, the greater the opportunity cost of retaining and cost of hiring an unskilled manager. (LOS 25.b)

3. **B** When two distributions are not distinct, the unskilled managers are not expected to significantly underperform the skilled managers, implying a low opportunity cost of not hiring skilled managers. Inefficient markets are likely to exhibit larger differences of returns between skilled and unskilled managers. (LOS 25.b)

Module Quiz 25.2

1. **C** The data required for HBSA is likely to be more difficult to find than the data required for RBSA.

   HBSA is more precise than RBSA; RBSA is a relatively imprecise tool that does not require a thorough computational effort but that may sacrifice accuracy. HBSA is typically easier for equity strategies. (LOS 25.c)

2. **C** A capture ratio (upside capture divided by downside capture) greater than one indicates the upside capture is greater than downside capture and reflects greater participation in rising markets than in falling markets. (LOS 25.d)

Module Quiz 25.3

1. **A** Passive strategies assume markets are efficient enough that active management does not add value that exceeds its transaction costs and fees. Therefore, the risk premiums being sought are only for bearing risk that is not easily diversified away, which is systematic risk.

   Unsystematic risk is relevant for active strategies only. (LOS 25.e)

2. **B** Signal creation (idea generation) focuses on how investment ideas are generated and information is viewed in context of the efficient market hypothesis to determine whether it can be used to exploit inefficiencies. (LOS 25.e)

3. **C** SMAs can provide an instantaneous snapshot or "dashboard view" of the investment holdings at any given point. Pooled investments may be able to do so, but probably with a delay.

   The tax benefits of a SMA would only accrue to investors who are taxable and would not benefit those who are tax exempt. SMAs generally have higher costs and fees than pooled investment vehicles. (LOS 25.f)

Module Quiz 25.4

1. **C** Private equity funds have the lowest liquidity because of capital calls. Closed-end funds have the highest liquidity because they are traded intra-day. (LOS 25.g)

2. **B** Management fees are charged as a fixed percentage based on assets, which results in a lower net return but no impact on the standard deviation of the returns.

   Because incentive fees are charged as a percentage of returns (reducing net gains or reducing net losses), incentive fees lower the standard deviation of returns. (LOS 25.h)

3. **A** $2\% + [20\% \times (-3\% - 2\%)] = 1\%$.

   (LOS 25.i)

4. **A** Higher of: (1) 0.4%, or (2) $0.4\% + [20\% \times (12\% - 3\%)] = 2.2\%$

   (LOS 25.i)

READING 26

Case Study in Portfolio Management: Institutional

EXAM FOCUS

This case study covers the following issues: capturing the illiquidity premium, managing liquidity, asset allocation, using derivatives or cash for tactical asset allocation, and portfolio rebalancing. There is also some coverage of potential ethical violations in the process of manager selection. Some of the material covered in this reading assumes prior knowledge of alternative investments and other basic portfolio management concepts.

MODULE 26.1: MANAGING LIQUIDITY RISK

Video covering this content is available online.

LOS 26.a: Discuss tools for managing portfolio liquidity risk.

Liquidity risk refers to a portfolio having to dispose of illiquid securities at a deep discount during troubled markets. Four key methods to manage liquidity risk include (1) liquidity profiling and time-to-cash tables, (2) rebalancing and commitments, (3) stress testing, and (4) derivatives.

Liquidity Profiling and Time-to-Cash Tables

For an endowment, the potential cash inflows and outflows must be determined. Taking the example of a university endowment with sizable holdings of illiquid assets, cash outflows would have to account for distributions to the university as well as capital call requests for certain types of investments such as hedge funds or private equity. Cash inflows would typically include donations and investment income earned from the portfolio.

The next step is to establish a timeline that involves constructing a liquidity classification schedule (time-to-cash table). That schedule would have three distinct components: (1) amount of time needed to convert assets to cash, (2) liquidity classification level, and (3) liquidity budget. An example is provided in Figure 26.1.

Figure 26.1: Time-to-Cash Table

Time to Cash	Liquidity Classification	Liquidity Budget (% of portfolio)
< 1 week	Highly liquid	At least 5%
< 1 quarter	Liquid	At least 25%
< 1 year	Semi-liquid	At least 40%
> 1 year	Illiquid	Up to 40%

The liquidity classification is closely linked to the amount of time it takes to liquidate an investment without having a major impact on markets. The latter would be demonstrated by a minimal differential in the expected market price immediately before and after a sell transaction. In addition, an investment that takes over one year to exit would likely be considered illiquid.

The time to cash may include a full range of periods beyond those illustrated in Figure 26.1, depending on whether they correspond to the investor's cash outflows. The liquidity budget will then provide minimum or maximum percentage allocations for the different time periods. For example, the three more liquid groups state minimum allocations, while the illiquid group states a maximum. Those requirements apply in all market situations, including times when liquidity is constrained; hence, the results of any stress tests are useful in determining the requirements.

To develop the liquidity budget, there must be preliminary work performed in observing the liquidity traits of the investments over a reasonable time period. Within a specific asset class, the various investments could have very diverse liquidity characteristics [e.g., exchange-traded funds (ETFs) may be more liquid than commingled funds]. Additionally, the same type of investment (e.g., commingled fund) may offer different levels of liquidity; one may offer semiannual liquidity because it is focused on small-cap foreign stocks, while the other may offer monthly liquidity because it is focused on large-cap foreign stocks. That is why it is important to analyze the investments in greater detail. An excerpt of a liquidity profile is provided in Figure 26.2.

Figure 26.2: Liquidity Profile

Asset Class	Asset Class Allocation (% of portfolio)	Investment Allocation (% of overall portfolio)	Investment Vehicle	Liquidity Classification			
				Highly Liquid	Liquid	Semi-Liquid	Illiquid
Fixed income	12%	4%	Separate account	100%	0%	0%	0%
		6%	Commingled fund	100%	0%	0%	0%
		2%	Futures	100%	0%	0%	0%
Domestic equity	20%	9%	Commingled fund	0%	50%	50%	0%
		9%	Separate account	0%	100%	0%	0%
		2%	ETF	100%	0%	0%	0%

Rebalancing and Commitments

Rebalancing

In addition to managing liquidity, it is necessary to maintain the overall risk profile within a desired (quantitative) range because over time and during times of market stress, asset values will change—sometimes very dramatically—thus greatly altering the desired balances in each asset class. With rebalancing costs for illiquid investments being very high, it is therefore crucial to maintain enough liquid assets to execute any necessary rebalancing transactions.

Systematic rebalancing policies are designed to maintain the long-term (strategic) asset allocation as much as possible. Examples include calendar and percent-range rebalancing with predetermined acceptable ranges for various asset classes. In attempting to reduce transaction costs, a wider range would be required for more volatile investments. In contrast, a narrow range would incur frequent transaction costs each time the allocation percentage for a given asset class falls outside of its (narrow) range.

Automatic adjustment mechanisms assist in keeping the portfolio risk profile relatively constant if there is a change from the target. For example, assume the portfolio has exposure to market risk relating to private companies and public companies, and that we can use public companies as a proxy for private companies. If the private equity has a beta of 1, and if the private equity allocation falls by 2% relative to the target, then there would be an automatic adjustment to increase the public equity allocation by 2%. That is intended to maintain the level of systematic risk, but of course, it means the level of unsystematic risk (which we can also think of as illiquidity risk) has decreased. The same methodology can be extended to other illiquid asset classes, where the public market can be a reasonable proxy for the private market.

Reading 26

Commitments

Investing in private market funds makes it more difficult for the portfolio to keep a stable or specific allocation level in the long term because within a given fund, the timing and frequency of when the committed capital is drawn and the return of capital distributions are beyond the control of the investor. By investing in multiple funds, however, the timing and frequency becomes more stable.

A multiyear funding strategy tries to determine the right level of annual commitments (investments) from the portfolio to arrive at a long-term optimal exposure to the asset class. That annual amount is derived from extensive quantitative analysis that considers, amongst other things, the estimated rate in which committed capital is drawn, the rate in which distributions are made, and the rate of change of asset size. In the end, there should be a determination of the asset class exposure as a percentage of the total portfolio for several hypothetical commitment levels. Additionally, the use of scenario analysis can take the analysis further to account for various market conditions (e.g., regular vs. stressed). Over time, the level of annual commitments will need to be adjusted as needed.

Stress Testing

Stress testing explicitly considers how the liquidity needs of a portfolio will change during a period of market stress. The idea is to conduct analysis to assume "worst case" or very extreme market conditions and the impact on both assets and liabilities at the same time. For example, for assets, one could make extreme assumptions on volatility (high), returns (low), correlation of returns between assets (high), and liquidity (low). For liabilities, one could assume that the distributions suddenly increase significantly during a period of market stress.

The stress tests can be based on any combination of the following: history, statistical models, and scenario analysis.

Derivatives

Derivatives require far less cash than investing in underlying assets, which makes derivatives an ideal method for rebalancing. In addition, a futures overlay allows for rebalancing of many (but not all) asset classes without altering any of the asset allocations determined by the external active managers.

With leverage, taking a long futures position requires only minimal cash requirements for margin, for example. Therefore, any cash not required for margin can be used to invest in other assets with differing levels of liquidity, or to meet other liquidity requirements. Options can be purchased at premiums that are often only a fraction of the cost of the underlying asset, thereby serving as a form of leverage. Or, options can be sold to earn premium income that helps to generate liquidity.

LOS 26.b: Discuss capture of the illiquidity premium as a long-term investment strategy.

It is often the case that relatively illiquid investments such as private equity and real estate will earn an additional return (over the market return) for taking on the risk of holding up capital for an unknown amount of time. This is known as the illiquidity (or liquidity) premium earned. Studies have shown that the illiquidity premium increases with the amount of time (think of an upward-sloping yield curve, for example).

A different way to model the illiquidity premium is to think of it as the value of a put option where the strike price is the marketable price (a theoretically estimated price, as if it were freely traded) of the illiquid asset when it was purchased. That leads to the computation of the price of the illiquid asset as follows:

illiquid asset price = marketable asset price – put price

Using the marketable and the illiquid prices, we can derive the expected returns for both, and the difference in expected returns would be the illiquidity premium in percentage terms as follows:

illiquidity premium (%) = expected return on illiquid asset (%) – expected return on marketable asset (%)

There are a substantial number of studies to support the positive correlation between illiquidity and expected returns for publicly traded stocks.

In practice, the illiquidity premium is challenging to accurately determine given all the other factors that interact in determining equity returns. In addition, broad market indexes are used to estimate illiquidity premiums, even though the typical investor is not likely to have such a breadth of investment exposure. As a result, the typical investor faces exposure to more unsystematic risk, which means that liquidity budgeting is essential in the balancing act of simultaneously earning excess returns through the illiquidity premium and managing risk.

MODULE QUIZ 26.1

1. A portfolio analyst makes the following two statements:

   Statement 1: The illiquidity premium is relatively easy to determine accurately.

   Statement 2: Calendar and percent-range rebalancing are examples of automatic adjustment mechanisms.

   How many of the analyst's statements are correct?

   A. Zero.
   B. One.
   C. Two.

2. **Describe** how futures and options can be used for leverage and liquidity purposes.

MODULE 26.2: ADDRESSING LIQUIDITY NEEDS

Video covering this content is available online.

LOS 26.c: Analyze asset allocation and portfolio construction in relation to liquidity needs and risk and return requirements and recommend actions to address identified needs.

Quadrivium University (QU) Endowment[1]

The Quadrivium University (QU) endowment was set up many years ago with the purpose of offering financial assistance to undergraduate students. The current value of the endowment is $8 billion, and about 75% of that amount has unrestricted use, with the other 25% being subject to donor-specified use restrictions.

QU's annual operating budget is $583 million, and more than two-thirds of that amount covers the remuneration of faculty and administrative staff. The remainder is to cover debt payments, maintenance costs, and provide funds related to research and financial aid. The endowment makes annual distributions to fund about 60% of QU's operating budget, and the dollar amounts have been increasing for each of the past five years. Greater stability in the distributions has been requested by the board of the university, so in that regard, the spending rule was changed after the financial crisis over 10 years ago. Formerly, a simple spending rule existed based on 5% of the market value of the endowment at the beginning of the year. Now, the spending rule incorporates geometric smoothing and is expressed as follows:

(66% × spending for the previous fiscal year) + 34% × (5% × endowment value at the end of the previous fiscal year)

To compute the QU endowment's spending for the current year, the previous year's spending was $358.1 million and the endowment's market value at the end of the previous fiscal year was $7,002.3 million.

(66% × $358.1 million) + 34% × (5% × $7,002.3 million) = $355.4 million

[1] Reproduced from Level III CFA Curriculum reading "Case Study in Portfolio Management: Institutional," with permission from CFA Institute.

The QU endowment's investment objective is to earn a sufficient return over the long term to cover the annual spending and to maintain the real value of the endowment. At an annual 5% spending rate and 2%–3% annual inflation applicable to universities, the endowment has an annual nominal return requirement of 7%–8%. The risk objective is between a 12% and 14% annual standard deviation of portfolio returns.

Quadrivium University Investment Company (QUINCO)

A board of trustees ("the Trustees") oversees the activities of QU. The Quadrivium University Investment Company (QUINCO) is the university investment office and is responsible for managing the QU endowment. Aaron Winter is the president of QUINCO, and he reports to the university president and to the QUINCO board of directors ("the Board"). The Board consists of 11 individuals appointed by the Trustees, and the Board deals with approving investment policy and guidelines. QUINCO staff are charged with implementing the investment policy.

QUINCO's 13 investment professionals are officially employed by QU. QUINCO's investment model involves implementation of investment strategy by external managers instead of having in-house investment management. Instead, internal staff deal with asset allocation, risk management, manager selection, and continuation decisions regarding the external managers.

Assets are invested in (1) fixed income, (2) public equity, (3) private equity, (4) real assets (e.g., private real estate, natural resources), and (5) diversifying strategies (e.g., hedge funds). The last three categories comprise alternative investments. Each of the five categories is managed by a senior portfolio manager and an analyst. The other three investment professionals are a portfolio strategist and analyst, who are responsible for asset allocation and risk management, and the president, who serves as the chief investment officer (CIO). The portfolio strategist has ongoing duties involving rebalancing, overlays, and tactical asset allocation (TAA) tilts. Any decisions made by external investment managers and TAA deviations require the approval of the internal investment committee. Winter leads that committee, which includes all senior portfolio managers and the portfolio strategist. Finally, the Board must provide final approval for the hiring of any external managers.

QUINCO Investment Strategy

QUINCO's investment strategy is concerned primarily with the long term. Its connections with QU alumni networks in the industry has allowed the endowment to benefit from the knowledge of the best-in-class managers.

Initially, its investment universe was confined to traditional publicly traded stocks and bonds. With growth of the endowment, the long-term strategy began to include alternative investments (e.g., private equity, real estate, commodities, hedge funds), which may allow for greater diversification and higher risk-adjusted returns. Alternative investments have helped to boost the endowment's returns over the past 20 years, although QU's allocation to alternative investments is still below average compared to other comparable endowments. Over a long time span, the alternative investments portion of the portfolio has become more established and diversified with respect to managers and strategies, for example.

Spanning over a 20-year period from 1996 to 2017, the QU endowment asset allocation has changed as follows:

- Cash allocation has remained constant at 1%.
- Traditional stocks (domestic) and bonds initially accounted for almost 70% of assets but have been reduced to about 30%.
- International equity (developed markets) initially accounted for almost 25% of assets but have been reduced to 10%.
- Emerging market equity initially accounted for 0% and has increased to 10%–15%.
- Private equity initially accounted for less than 5% and has increased to 15%–20%.
- Real assets (e.g., real estate, commodities) initially accounted for less than 5% and have increased to 10%–15%.
- Diversifying strategies (e.g., hedge funds) initially accounted for 0% and have increased to 10%–15%.

During the most recent strategic asset allocation (SAA) review by the QUINCO Board two years ago, they resolved to increase the allocation to alternative investments and decrease the allocation to developed market equities (domestic and international).

Winter has worked at QUINCO for five years and became the president and CIO one year ago. He will be performing his first asset allocation review. Winter has a portfolio strategy team to assist him with the review. The team includes Julia Thompson, the team lead, as well as her asset allocation analysis plus the senior portfolio managers for fixed income and public equities. After consulting with the Board, Winter advises the team to deal with the following matters pertaining to the review:

- An optimal liquidity profile and liquidity management plan for the endowment.
- The SAA in context of the investment outlook; there is an expectation of lower future returns in most traditional asset classes.
- The use of TAA as a complement to SAA to improve risk-adjusted returns.
- The QU endowment's underperformance compared to its peers.

Strategic Asset Allocation (SAA)

The strategy team have finished the work requested and will be making a presentation to the Board. As part of their economic analysis, they used unsmoothing methods for private equity (a relatively illiquid asset class) due to the smoother reported returns resulting from the lack of frequency of pricing data, for example. The unsmoothing methods resulted in an upward adjustment to the reported volatility of private equity. Figure 26.3 summarizes the results of the team's analysis.

Figure 26.3: Risk/Return Analysis[2]

Asset Class	Expected Real Return (annual geometric mean, next 10 years)	Expected Nominal Return (annual geometric mean, next 10 years)	Standard Deviation of Returns (annual)	Sharpe Ratio
Cash	0.9%	3.4%	1.7%	
Fixed income	1.8%	4.3%	6.3%	0.14
Domestic equity	5.0%	7.6%	18.1%	0.23
International developed equity	4.8%	7.4%	19.7%	0.20
Emerging market equity	6.0%	8.7%	26.6%	0.19
Private equity	8.5%	11.2%	24.0%	0.32
Real assets	4.5%	7.1%	13.3%	0.27
Diversifying strategies	4.0%	6.6%	10.0%	0.31

Note: Inflation assumed to be 2.5% p.a.

With some research, it was determined that the primary reasons for the QU endowment's underperformance relative to its peers was the lower amount of risk taken and the lower allocation to illiquid investments, especially private equity. Therefore, the current and proposed allocations are as follows:

	Current	Proposed
Cash	1%	1%
Fixed income	14%	9%
Domestic equity	17%	15%
International developed equity	10%	9%
Emerging market equity	12%	12%
Private equity	18%	23%
Real assets	13%	16%
Diversifying strategies	15%	15%

Some metrics are provided in Figure 26.4 that suggest increasing the allocation to private equity and real assets would raise the Sharpe ratio. Thompson realizes that there are higher investment management and performance fees for private equity and real assets compared to public equity and fixed income, so the returns in Figure 26.4 are on a net-of-fees basis. There is also some reporting of Monte Carlo simulation results to bring attention to the potential erosion in purchasing power. The Board is willing to accept an annualized standard deviation of returns between 12% and 14%.

2 Reproduced from Level III CFA Curriculum reading "Case Study in Portfolio Management: Institutional," Exhibit 7, with permission from CFA Institute.

Figure 26.4: Current and Proposed Risk/Return Data[3]

Portfolio Characteristic	Current SAA	Proposed SAA
Expected nominal return (annual average, geometric, next 10 years)	7.5%	7.8%
Expected real return (annual average, geometric, next 10 years)	5.0%	5.3%
Standard deviation of returns (annual)	12.5%	13.2%
Sharpe ratio	0.33	0.34
Probability of 25% erosion in purchasing power over 20 years with 5% spending rate	35%	30%

Note: The probability of erosion in purchasing power was derived based on a Monte Carlo simulation with a 20-year investment horizon, assuming expected return and volatility characteristics will be the same as for the next 10 years.

Thompson argues that the higher Sharpe ratio is sufficient reason to amend the SAA. She knows that the standard deviation of returns increases by 0.7% if the proposed asset allocation is accepted. Her reasons for taking on more stand-alone risk include the following:

- Lower future returns expected for all asset classes will necessitate taking on more risk to maintain the same level of returns.
- QU's endowment takes on less risk than its peers.
- The estimated Sharpe ratio for fixed-income investments (less risky) means that there should not be as much allocation to less risky assets.
- Monte Carlo simulations have indicated that in the long term, the proposed asset allocation has a better chance of earning the desired real return and preserving purchasing power.

Liquidity Management

Managing liquidity is paramount for the endowment given QU's need for cash flows from the endowment. As part of their management duties, Thompson's team performs cash flow modeling over several time horizons and under normal and stressed market conditions. Thompson is worried that liquidity may deteriorate significantly during stressed market conditions. Three reasons why deterioration may occur include the following:

- For private equity, capital calls are greater than capital distributions, resulting in a greater concentration of private equity (a more illiquid investment) in the portfolio.
- Certain investments made by portfolio managers may restrict investors from withdrawing their funds during stressed market conditions, which decreases the portfolio's overall liquidity.
- Private equity investments are not valued as frequently as public equity, for example. The resulting lagged valuations mean there is a relative increase as a percentage of the portfolio and a relative decrease in liquid assets as a

[3] Reproduced from Level III CFA Curriculum reading "Case Study in Portfolio Management: Institutional," Exhibit 10, with permission from CFA Institute.

percentage of the portfolio during stressed market conditions (e.g., the liquid assets fall in value "faster" because they are valued more frequently). The percentage of assets available for meeting liquidity needs is reduced when it could be needed most during periods of market stress.

Accordingly, Thompson's team has prepared a summary of liquidity profiles as follows:

- Existing portfolio liquidity profile:
  - Normal conditions: highly liquid (19%), liquid (26%), semi-liquid (22%), illiquid (33%)
  - Stress conditions: highly liquid (15%), liquid (26%), semi-liquid (20%), illiquid (39%)
- Proposed portfolio liquidity profile:
  - Normal conditions: highly liquid (14%), liquid (24%), semi-liquid (23%), illiquid (39%)
  - Stress conditions: highly liquid (11%), liquid (25%), semi-liquid (21%), illiquid (43%)

MODULE QUIZ 26.2

1.

A. **Discuss** *three* reasons why the QU endowment should increase its allocation to illiquid investments.

B. **Discuss** *one* concern with increasing the allocation to illiquid assets and **describe** how that concern can be mitigated.

2.

A. Using the information in Figure 26.4, **discuss** *two* reasons that support Thompson's proposed asset allocation.

B. **Discuss** *two* tradeoffs involved with implementing the proposed asset allocation.

C. **State** *two* items that Thompson should confirm before implementing the proposed asset allocation.

3. **Discuss** how a current spending policy, based on a combination of prior year spending and prior year market value, could impact liquidity needs when market conditions deteriorate.

4. **Discuss** *three* tools for QUINCO to use for liquidity management—specifically, (1) cash flow forecasting and commitment pacing models, (2) liquidity budgets, and (3) stress tests.

5. **Describe** the impact on QU's liquidity resulting from the proposed asset allocation. **Describe** any follow-up actions Thompson needs to take with respect to the proposed asset allocation.

MODULE 26.3: MODIFYING ASSET ALLOCATION

Video covering this content is available online.

LOS 26.d: Demonstrate the application of the Code of Ethics and Standards of Professional Conduct regarding the actions of individuals involved in manager selection.

Asset Manager Selection

Several months later, the process of hiring more external managers to implement the proposed asset allocation changes has begun. A request for proposal (RFP) for a private equity manager was issued, and one of the responses came from Genex Venture Capital (GVC) with a proposal to invest in its venture capital fund called "GVC Fund II." GVC is owned and operated by Virginia Hall, CFA, who is on the QU endowment board and has been a long-time and highly supportive donor to the university. Therefore, both the university treasurer and president are strongly in support of GVC's proposal and have indicated so to Winter. Winter, on the other hand, believes that Hall asked the two individuals in advance to support her proposal. Through the process of elimination, the two finalists are GVC and another venture capital fund that is a direct competitor of GVC, called Beacher Venture Investments (Beacher).

GVC and Beacher are requested to present to QUINCO's investment committee. Jason Allen, a former colleague of Winter, is GVC's managing director, and he gives the GVC presentation. However, Winter knows that the presentation contains confidential information that is not publicly available, which was possibly obtained from the university treasurer. In addition, GVC's historical returns are presented with amounts materially greater than those reported elsewhere by third parties. Beacher is the more established pick of the two firms, despite some problems with the performance of its previous fund. But some concerns were raised about GVC's short existence to date. Ultimately, Bud Davis, one of QUINCO's top portfolio managers in private equity, is asked to make a recommendation on which firm to go with.

Davis states that GVC is finding it difficult to raise the targeted $300 million for Fund II since Fund I only raised $100 million. Investors are worried about the threefold expansion and the uncertainty whether GVC can achieve its goal. However, Davis tempers that point with strong, positive comments about GVC's manager and GVC's investment approach. In addition, Davis confirms that GVC's investment management fee will be lowered. Based on Davis's comments, the investment committee agrees with Davis's recommendation to go with GVC.

Afterward, Winter speaks with Allen to convey the news. During the conversation, Allen states that Davis's spouse, Andrea, is Hall's daughter. When Winter confronted Davis with that knowledge, Davis simply stated that it was well known and assumed that everyone on the investment committee already knew of the relationship.

LOS 26.e: Analyze the costs and benefits of derivatives versus cash market techniques for establishing or modifying asset class or risk exposures.

LOS 26.f: Demonstrate the use of derivatives overlays in tactical asset allocation and rebalancing.

The Board has approved a much larger active risk budget for QUINCO's proposed TAA plan. The annual tracking error limit was specifically increased from 100 bps to 250 bps to try to increase overall portfolio returns. Winter and his staff are completely responsible for implementing the new TAA plan, and they have the authority to use 150 bps of the 250 bps budget to do so. Additionally, because the use of derivatives in the implementation would result in increased leverage, the Board approved a maximum leverage position of 5% of the portfolio value.

Winter thinks that the TAA plan will allow for overweight and underweight positions in acceptable asset classes and allow for investing in assets beyond the policy portfolio benchmark universe that are still consistent with the investment policy. In implementing the plan, Winter began with fair value and mean reversion by creating fair value models for the portfolio assets. Relevant economic and financial data known to have predictive power were gathered and used to estimate future risk and return for periods ranging from one to three years. The output from the models (i.e., theoretically correct fair value) is then compared to actual prices to assess whether any variances are significant enough to be exploited, after considering the costs involved in doing so. Subsequent and thorough backtesting revealed that the models worked well.

Specifically, large-cap U.S. equities were priced far below their fair value and mean reversion would occur in about a year. Thompson uses that information and proposes to overweight U.S. equities by 1% using either a total return swap, equity futures, or ETFs. The objective is to minimize use of cash and transaction costs.

Her team comes up with the following summary, shown in Figure 26.5.

Figure 26.5: Comparing Investment Costs[4]

Cost Component	ETF	Futures	Total Return Swap
Commission (round trip)	4.00	2.00	5.00
Management fee (annual)	9.50	0.00	0.00
Bid/offer spread (round trip)	2.50	2.00	6.00
Price impact (round trip)	15.00	10.00	0.00
Mispricing (tracking error, annual)	4.00	8.00	0.00
Cost to roll the futures contract	0.00	20.00	0.00
Funding cost	0.00	0.00	40.00
Total cost	**35.00**	**42.00**	**51.00**

Notes: The exhibit shows the team's cost comparison for the three implementation options—ETFs, futures, and total return swaps—for an $80 million notional exposure to the S&P 500 Index (assuming a fully funded mandate) over a one-year investment horizon. All numbers are in basis points (bps) unless otherwise indicated.

Thompson feels that ETFs require too much up-front cash (100% of the value) or that the 50% permitted margin would provide only limited leverage opportunities ($80 million investment with $40 million provided in cash and $40 million borrowed). She realizes that using futures and total return swaps to obtain $80 million exposure would require far less cash than the $40 million required if using ETFs.

On the other hand, ETFs and futures are more liquid—they are widely traded and have low transaction costs. Both instruments allow for early termination, should market conditions warrant it, and Thompson has made it known that the flexibility is important to her. Total return swaps are traded over the counter (OTC) in that the terms are negotiated and features are customized between the counterparties. However, with futures, Thompson does not like the daily margin monitoring tasks. Additionally, she has concerns over interest rate and counterparty credit risk.

The overlay will be performed on the assumption of a leverage level of 4, meaning 25% of the investment is provided in cash and 75% borrowed. Financing costs are based on a 2% 3-month market reference rate (MRR) for futures and swaps, with an additional 0.5% financing cost for ETFs.

Reading 26

4 Reproduced from Level III CFA Curriculum reading "Case Study in Portfolio Management: Institutional," Exhibit 15, with permission from CFA Institute.

Asset Allocation Rebalancing

It is now three months after the overweight position in U.S. equities, and the position has done well. Fixed income has not performed well due to a large rise in interest rates. As a result, there has been noticeable drift in the QU endowment asset allocation. Rebalancing of the portfolio is performed quarterly for cost control reasons; however, the portfolio drift from the SAA is checked on a monthly basis. At the end of each quarter, if a relatively liquid asset class moves outside the rebalancing corridor, then it is systematically rebalanced back to either the target allocation or to the edge of the corridor. For more illiquid asset classes, high transaction costs mean that rebalancing is done more implicitly by altering the commitments and reinvestments when allocations drift to the either end of the corridor.

Pertinent asset allocation information on the QU endowment is presented in Figure 26.6.

Figure 26.6: Asset Allocation Information[5]

	Target Allocation (SAA)	Corridor	Min/Max Target	Current Allocation
Cash	1%	±1%	0%–2%	0.8%
Fixed income	9%	±3	6%–12%	6.5%
Domestic equity	15%	±2.5	12.5%–17.5%	17.3%
International developed equity	9%	±2%	7%–11%	11.5%
Emerging market equity	12%	±2%	10%–14%	13.9%
Private equity	23%	±5%	18%–28%	19.2%
Real assets	16%	±3%	13%–19%	13.8%
Diversifying strategies	15%	±3%	12%–18%	17.1%
Total	**100.0%**			**100.0%**

Based on her analysis of Figure 26.6, Thompson notices the following:

- International developed equity at a current allocation of 11.5% has exceeded the top end of the corridor (11%) by 0.5%.
- Fixed income at a current allocation of 6.5% is off significantly from the target of 9% but still within the acceptable range of 6%–12%.
- Private equity at a current allocation of 19.2% is near the low end of the corridor (18%).
- Real assets at a current allocation of 13.8% is near the low end of the corridor (13%).

As an immediate action, Thompson wishes to reduce the international developed equity allocation and increase the fixed income allocation by 0.5%. That will take the former back to the top edge of its corridor. The question is whether to perform

[5] Reproduced from Level III CFA Curriculum reading "Case Study in Portfolio Management: Institutional," Exhibit 17, with permission from CFA Institute.

the transaction through the cash market or the derivatives market. She is aware that implementation will take more time in the cash market but is necessary for larger or more important adjustments.

Upon further research, Thompson finds out that the 0.5% rebalancing transaction over a three-month investment horizon will incur 30 bps of transaction costs in the cash market (bid/offer spread of 5 bps, price impact of 5 bps, and cash drag of 20 bps). The cash drag includes the impact of timing delays and disruptions to active manager portfolios. The same rebalancing transaction will incur 24 bps of transaction costs in the futures market (bid/offer spread of 3 bps, price impact of 4 bps, and mispricing of 17 bps).

With additional consultations within the team, Thompson then opts to rebalance international developed equity back to the 9% allocation, so that involves a 2.5% decrease to equity as well as a 2.5% increase to fixed income. Now, the investment horizon is one year and will incur 60 bps of transaction costs in the cash market (bid/offer spread of 5 bps, price impact of 5 bps, and cash drag of 50 bps). For the futures market, there will be 82 bps of transaction costs (bid/offer spread of 4 bps, price impact of 4 bps, cash drag of 68 bps, and cost of rolling futures contracts of 6 bps).

ESG Integration

LOS 26.g: Discuss ESG considerations in managing long-term institutional portfolios.

Nine months later, Winter is informed by the president of the university of a student protest planned against the endowment and the university over a U.S.-based apparel manufacturer, Portro, Inc. (Portro). Portro clothing is sold at the university store and is included as a holding in the endowment. A recent report published by the International Labor Organization (ILO) outlined social issues in two of Portro's largest suppliers involving allegations of child labor, health and safety issues, and poor working conditions. One of the suppliers is also used for QU-branded clothing sold at the university store. The students are expected to demand the endowment divest its holdings of Portro and the university drop the supplier.

An ESG investing policy has been in place for the past seven years at QUINCO, which is based upon the following:

- Acknowledging the risk and return of the investments are affected by ESG and traditional financial factors.
- Transparency on material ESG issues impacting investment activities.
- Long-term sustainability for companies and markets the endowment invests in.

QUINCO's investing approach focuses on considering all material ESG and traditional financial factors in the investment process. Because external asset managers are used, the endowment relies on these managers to integrate the ESG factors into their investment processes.

Reading 26

To address how the endowment assesses ESG manager implementation, Winter recently hired Natalya Long, CFA, as an ESG integration specialist. Long has been updating the investment policy to include the following:

- Enhanced due diligence in monitoring ESG investing and manager selection regarding:
  - If a formal ESG integration policy exists.
  - How ESG factors are incorporated into the investment process.
  - The manager's commitment to disclosing material ESG issues in a timely manner.
  - The consistency between QUINCO's ESG responsible investing policy and the manager's ESG integration approach.
- Key components of the ESG responsible investing policy include responsible ownership, reporting, and communication. Responsible ownership is implemented through proxy voting and corporate engagement on ESG issues (e.g., human capital, climate change, and reporting and disclosure).
- Monitoring of ESG metrics for the QUINCO portfolio includes: metrics comparing ESG ratings or scores for portfolio companies from industry providers with peer companies and the policy benchmark; assessing portfolio sensitivities to a range of climate-related risks by developing an analytical framework; and aggregate data on the carbon footprint of endowment portfolio companies. The metrics are monitored over time for changing trends.
- Demonstrating a commitment to responsible investing by being a signatory to the internationally recognized UN Principles for Responsible Investment (PRI).

The enhancements made to the ESG policy by Long provide a framework for Winter's response to the Portro situation.

Winter was not aware of the relationship between the supplier and the university store but had known about the ILO report on Portro. He also knew the endowment had two sources of potential exposure: (1) Portro as a constituent in the benchmark index for the U.S. public equity allocation and (2) a large holding of Portro Inc. in a concentrated portfolio strategy run by one of QUINCO's U.S. equity managers.

Winter is asked by the university president to prepare a formal response to the students' grievances by explaining the endowment's ESG responsible investing policies.

Investment Response

The issues with Portro's suppliers had been identified for some time through the ESG metrics monitoring system along with Portro's poor ESG ratings versus its peers. At the most recent quarterly review meeting, several weeks before the ILO report was published, these issues had been brought up as part of the team's systematic manager engagement strategy. At that meeting, the QUINCO team asked the external manager of the U.S. equity portfolio to explain the risks arising from the supply chain issues and how they would be managed in a timely and transparent manner. The meeting revealed that she routinely takes into consideration ESG factors in the investment analysis even though there was no formal ESG integration policy in place. She remained confident in the company's long-term potential even after accounting for the negative impact to Portro's valuation in the short-term due to the costs of fixing its supply chain problems. She also mentioned she would be monitoring Portro's management response to the issues in the coming months to determine whether to reduce the size of the position. Although the QUINCO team concluded the external manager followed an adequate due diligence process in considering ESG and traditional financial factors, they still felt further manager and corporate engagement was necessary to address the situation.

As part of its responsible ownership strategy, the QUINCO team prepares to engage with Portro on specific issues highlighted in the ILO report. This includes joining with other institutional investors in a dialogue with Portro's management and proxy voting to support shareholder resolutions increasing the company's transparency regarding reporting human capital management in the supply chain.

Winter prepares his formal response to share with the QU Student Association by summarizing QUINCO's responsible investing policy and how this applies to the endowment's Portro holdings. He highlights the endowment's long-term commitment to sustainability of the markets and companies the endowment invests in and to integrate relevant ESG factors into the endowment's investment process. He also stresses that, under the endowment's responsible investing strategy, divestment of the investment is to be considered only as a last resort because it is a suboptimal risk mitigation strategy. He highlights the plan to maintain awareness of Portro's company management on the specific issues at hand and to focus discussion on possible mitigating actions using tools, such as proxy voting and manager and corporate engagement. Winter then asks the head of the University Administration Office to immediately remove the supplier's apparel being sold in the university store and plans to revisit this decision at a later time.

MODULE QUIZ 26.3

1. **Discuss** ethical issues and potential violations of the Code and Standards by Winter, Hall, the QU president and QU treasurer, Allen, and Davis. (Note: The citation of specific standard numbers and names is not necessary.)

2. On the assumption of no leverage employed, **identify** the *most appropriate* method for Thompson to use to implement the overweight to U.S. equities. **Justify** your response with *three* reasons, including cost, logistical, and risk considerations.

3. Assuming a leverage level of 4, **determine** whether Thompson would change her mind in terms of investment vehicle for implementation purposes. **Identify** *one* issue unrelated to cost. (Note: Ignore any additional return that could be earned by investing the 75% of cash that is not required for the investment.)

4. **Discuss** the issues of cash drag in rebalancing in the cash market and tracking error in rebalancing in the derivatives market.

5. **Discuss** how implementation speed and rebalancing size would impact the method of implementation.

6. Assuming the 2.5% reallocation is performed, **evaluate** the implementation options and **select** the *most appropriate* one for Thompson to use.

7. **Describe** how an ESG investment could be monitored.

KEY CONCEPTS

LOS 26.a

Four key methods to manage liquidity risk include (1) liquidity profiling and time-to-cash tables, (2) rebalancing and commitments, (3) stress testing, and (4) derivatives.

A liquidity classification schedule (time-to-cash table) has three distinct components: (1) amount of time needed to convert assets to cash, (2) liquidity classification level, and (3) liquidity budget.

To maintain the overall risk profile within a desired (quantitative) range, both systematic rebalancing policies and automatic adjustment mechanisms are used.

A multiyear funding strategy tries to determine the right level of annual commitments (investments) from the portfolio to arrive at a long-term optimal exposure to the asset class. Over time, the level of annual commitments will need to be adjusted as needed.

Stress testing explicitly considers how the liquidity needs of a portfolio will change during a period of market stress. The idea is to conduct analysis to assume "worst case" or very extreme market conditions and the impact on both assets and liabilities at the same time.

Derivatives require far less cash than investing in underlying assets, which makes derivatives an ideal method of rebalancing (e.g., by their nature, derivatives have significant leverage possibilities).

LOS 26.b

The illiquidity (or liquidity) premium refers to the additional return (over the market return) for taking on the risk of holding up capital for an unknown amount of time. Studies have shown that the illiquidity premium increases with the amount of time.

$$\text{illiquidity premium (\%)} = \text{expected return on illiquid asset (\%)} - \text{expected return on marketable asset (\%)}$$

In practice, the illiquidity premium is challenging to accurately determine given all the other factors that interact in determining equity returns.

LOS 26.c

With some research, it was determined that the primary reasons for the QU endowment's underperformance relative to its peers was the lower amount of risk taken and the lower allocation to illiquid investments, especially private equity. Therefore, the current and proposed allocations are as follows:

	Current	Proposed
Cash	1%	1%
Fixed income	14%	9%
Domestic equity	17%	15%
International developed equity	10%	9%
Emerging market equity	12%	12%
Private equity	18%	23%
Real assets	13%	16%
Diversifying strategies	15%	15%

Managing liquidity is paramount for the endowment given QU's need for cash flows from the endowment. There should be cash flow modeling over several time horizons and under normal and stressed market conditions. Liquidity may deteriorate significantly during a stressed market condition.

- For private equity, capital calls are greater than capital distributions, resulting in a greater concentration of private equity in the portfolio.
- Certain investments made by portfolio may restrict investors from withdrawing their funds during stressed market conditions, which decreases the portfolio's overall liquidity.
- Private equity investments are not valued as frequently as public equity. The resulting lagged valuations mean there is a relative increase as a percentage of the portfolio and a relative decrease in liquid assets as a percentage of the portfolio during stressed market conditions.

LOS 26.d

Potential violations of the Code and Standards with respect to the process of asset manager selection include:

- Standard I(B): Independence and Objectivity.
- Standard I(C): Misrepresentation.
- Standard III(D): Performance Presentation.
- Standard III(E): Preservation of Confidentiality.
- Standard IV(A): Loyalty.
- Standard V(A): Diligence and Reasonable Basis.
- Standard VI(A): Disclosure of Conflicts.

LOS 26.e

Because changes in the market will often result in asset allocation drifts, the endowment portfolio will need to be periodically rebalanced. Derivatives are both cash efficient and quite liquid, so their role is threefold: (1) rebalancing, (2) changes in TAA, and (3) meeting short-term liquidity requirements.

Rebalancing with derivatives is most likely to be implemented more quickly, and with no impact on the active managers. That is on the assumption of reasonably high levels of liquidity in the equity futures market, for example.

If the rebalancing transaction is larger, then the transaction is likely to be more permanent or long term in nature. That makes rebalancing with cash more desirable despite the associated cash drag.

LOS 26.f

Derivatives overlays would allow the endowment to periodically rebalance exposures to asset classes without impacting the existing allocations to external active managers. That makes overlays more desirable for making smaller, short-term adjustments that could easily be reversed later.

LOS 26.g

An ESG investment policy should include the following:

- Enhanced due diligence in monitoring ESG investing and manager selection regarding:
  - If a formal ESG policy exists.
  - How ESG factors are incorporated into the investment process.
  - Disclosing material ESG issues in a timely manner.
- Key components of an ESG responsible investing policy include responsible ownership, reporting, and communication. Responsible ownership is implemented through proxy voting and corporate engagement on ESG issues (e.g., human capital, climate change, sustainability, and reporting and disclosure).
- Monitoring of ESG investments includes: metrics comparing ESG ratings or scores for portfolio companies from industry providers with peer companies and the policy benchmark; assessing portfolio sensitivities to a range of climate-related risks by developing an analytical framework; and aggregate data on the carbon footprint of portfolio companies. Metrics should be monitored over time for changing trends.

ANSWER KEY FOR MODULE QUIZZES

Module Quiz 26.1

1. **A** Statement 1 is incorrect. In practice, the illiquidity premium is challenging to accurately determine given all the other factors that interact in determining equity returns. In addition, broad market indexes are used to estimate illiquidity premiums, even though the typical investor is not likely to have such a breadth of investment exposure.

   Statement 2 is incorrect. Calendar and percent-range rebalancing are examples of systematic rebalancing policies.

   (LOS 26.a, LOS 26.b)

2. Taking a long futures position requires only minimal cash requirements for margin, which is a form of a leveraged investment. Therefore, any cash not required for margin can be used to invest in other assets with differing levels of liquidity, or to meet other liquidity requirements.

   Options can be purchased at premiums that are often only a fraction of the cost of the underlying asset, thereby serving as a form of leverage. Or, options can be sold to earn premium income that helps to generate liquidity.

   (LOS 26.a)

Module Quiz 26.2

1.

   A. The QU endowment has a long-term investment focus, which increases its ability to invest in illiquid investments. Therefore, the addition of such assets to the QU endowment's investment opportunities may allow the efficient frontier to be shifted upward so that it achieves a higher return for a stated level of risk.

   The QU endowment has consistently earned positive returns with its illiquid (alternative) investments over the past 20 years. After such a long time period, the illiquid investments portion of the portfolio is clearly established and diversified. With a team of industry experts at their disposal, including best-in-class managers, the endowment should expect to continue earning strong returns in the future, which justifies increasing the allocation to illiquid investments.

   Compared to its peers, the QU endowment is underinvested in illiquid investments. Therefore, an increased allocation is justified to overcome its past underperformance compared to its peers.

Reading 26

B. The increased allocation to illiquid assets (especially private equity and real assets) introduces more unsystematic risk. Therefore, placing smaller amounts in a larger number of investments will reduce much of that unsystematic risk.

Alternate answer: The increased allocation to illiquid assets (especially private equity and real assets) can result in liquidity being reduced during periods of market stress. To reduce this risk, perform cash flow modeling to determine the level of illiquid assets under stressed conditions.

(LOS 26.c)

2.

A. The proposed asset allocation has a better risk-return relationship than the existing SAA, as illustrated in Figure 26.4 by the increase in Sharpe ratio from 0.33 to 0.34.

The proposed asset allocation has a higher chance of earning the target return in the long term. Using the Monte Carlo simulation results, there is a 70% probability of having at least 75% of the purchasing power for the next 20 years; the result in Figure 26.4 explicitly states 30% probability of a 25% erosion. Under the existing SAA, there is only a 65% probability of having at least 75% of the purchasing power.

B. One tradeoff of the proposed asset allocation is the increase in portfolio volatility—annual standard deviation rises 0.7% to 13.2%. However, given the expectation of lower returns for all asset classes, greater risk must be taken to earn the same level of returns.

Another tradeoff is the transaction costs, since private equity and real assets are most likely to have higher investment management and performance fees than traditional public stock and bond investments. However, the return amounts in Figure 26.4 are on a net-of-fees basis, so they account for the increased fees.

C. She should confirm that the metrics in Figure 26.4 such as the standard deviation of returns (increased from 12.5% to 13.2%) and the 30% probability of a 25% erosion in purchasing power are acceptable within the endowment's risk appetite.

She should confirm that after increasing the illiquid assets allocation, the new asset allocation continues to meet all the portfolio liquidity requirements.

(LOS 26.c)

3. Spending policies have a built-in countercyclical impact, so spending rates end up being less than 5% during stronger market conditions and more than 5% during weaker market conditions. As a result, the endowment's liquidity needs are amplified during stressed market conditions.

(LOS 26.c)

4. Cash flow forecasting and commitment pacing models can be used to estimate the increased allocation to private equity and real assets. For example, cash outflows need to be estimated for future commitments in private equity; capital calls are legal obligations. Also, during market downturns, such cash outflows may become more onerous as inflows from prior investments could be curtailed or completely stopped due to a lack of cash as investments may not be liquidated due to low valuations.

   Liquidity budgets can be created after accounting for the endowment's cash inflows and outflows.

   Stress tests can be performed using both historical information and hypothetical assumptions within the framework of sensitivity analysis to determine how much variance in liquidity may occur and still be within the liquidity budget constraints.

   (LOS 26.c)

5. There will be a noticeable increase in more illiquid investments and a noticeable decrease in highly liquid investments. For example, in normal conditions, highly liquid assets will decrease by 5% (from 19% to 14%) and illiquid assets will increase by 6% (from 33% to 39%). In stressed conditions, highly liquid assets will decrease by 4% (from 15% to 11%) and illiquid assets will increase by 4% (from 39% to 43%). QU's overall liquidity profile will become more illiquid due to the increased investment in private equity and real assets, both of which are the most illiquid asset classes.

   Thompson must be certain that the endowment will be able to meet all its liquidity needs (e.g., distributions and rebalancing) for the proposed allocation and do so in stressed market conditions. Monitoring at key times when there is increased risk of not being able to meet its liquidity needs, as well as regular stress tests, would be suitable follow-up items to perform.

   (LOS 26.c)

Module Quiz 26.3

1. Aaron Winter, QUINCO CIO
   - Standard VI(A): Disclosure of Conflicts. Winter should have disclosed to the Board that the owner of GVC is already very closely associated with the university.
   - Standard I(B): Independence and Objectivity. Winter is under pressure from some members of the university to award the position to GVC, which would impact his independence and objectivity. Winter should have disclosed that GVC's managing director is a former colleague as that it could potentially impair Winter's independence and objectivity.
   - Standard III(E): Preservation of Confidentiality. Winter suspected that GVC used confidential information in its presentation, and he should have disclosed his concerns to the university.

- Standard I(C): Misrepresentation and Standard III(D): Performance Presentation. Winter is suspicious as to the precision of the historical results provided.
- Standard V(A): Diligence and Reasonable Basis. Winter did not confirm or dispel his suspicions by doing any subsequent research or probing with GVC.

Virginia Hall, QU trustee, owner of GVC

- Standard VI(A): Disclosure of Conflicts. If Hall is trying to influence the hiring decision in favor of her company, then there is a conflict of interest. Hall's position as a QU trustee and her ownership of GVC is also a conflict as GVC is one of the finalists to be considered for hiring as an external portfolio manager for the QU endowment.
- Standard IV(A): Loyalty. By potentially putting her own business interests ahead of the best interests of the university (she is a QU trustee), Hall would be in violation of her duty of loyalty.
- Standard III(E): Preservation of Confidentiality. Hall may have obtained confidential information and used it in GVC's presentation to improve GVC's chances of being hired.

QU president and QU treasurer (both are members of the QU Board)

- Standard IV(A): Loyalty. Both the president and treasurer must act in the university's best interests by hiring only the best portfolio manager. They are violating Standard IV(A) by pressuring Winter to hire GVC given Hall's close association with the university.
- Standard III(E): Preservation of Confidentiality. They may also be in violation of Standard III(E) if they were the culprits who provided the confidential information in the GVC presentation.
- Standard VI(A): Disclosure of Conflicts and Standard I(B): Independence and Objectivity. For example, they should have disclosed their bias toward Hall given her past generosity to the university. Furthermore, they should have abstained from any voting decisions on the external manager given their lack of independence and objectivity.

Jason Allen, GVC's managing director

- Standard I(C): Misrepresentation and Standard III(D): Performance Presentation. Allen may have used incorrect information, unknowingly or knowingly, in his presentation.

Bud Davis, QUINCO senior portfolio manager

- Standard VI(A): Disclosure of Conflicts and Standard I(B): Independence and Objectivity. Davis needs to make an objective evaluation of GVC in context of a hiring decision. The fact that his spouse is the daughter of GVC's owner presents a serious impairment to his independence and objectivity, and he should have disclosed the relationship.

(LOS 26.d)

2. With respect to costs, the ETF is the lowest at 35 bps, with 70% of it due to price impact (buying and selling the position) and the management fee. Futures are more costly at 42 bps, with rolling costs (due to upward-sloping yield curve) constituting about half of the costs. Price impact and tracking error constitute most of the remaining costs. The total return swap is the highest at 51 bps. On cost considerations alone, the ETF should be chosen.

   Logistically, futures require quarterly rollover and daily monitoring of margin, so in that regard, futures are less appealing for Thompson. ETFs are managed by the ETF manager. There are no real logistical issues for total return swaps. On logistical considerations, either the ETF or the total return swap should be chosen.

   From a tracking error (risk) perspective, ETFs face tracking error for reasons such as cash drag and mandatory diversification. Futures face tracking error for reasons such as liquidity and interest rate differentials. Total return swaps have no tracking error since the receipt is the S&P 500 Index return. On tracking error considerations, the total return swap should be chosen.

   Furthermore, Thompson worries about interest rate risk, which would be prevalent with futures and the total return swap. She also worries about counterparty credit risk, which would occur with swaps. On risk considerations, the ETF should be chosen.

   Overall, the best choice is the ETF because it has the lowest cost, no logistical issues, and no exposure to interest rate and counterparty credit risks.

   (LOS 26.e)

3. ETF financing cost = \$80 million × 75% × 2.5% = \$1.5 million = 1.875%

   futures financing cost = \$80 million × 75% × 2% = \$1.2 million = 1.5%

   swaps financing cost = \$80 million × 75% × 2% = \$1.2 million = 1.5%

   Taking into account the costs from Figure 26.5:

   ETF total cost = 0.35% + 1.875% = 2.225%

   futures total cost = 0.42% + 1.5% = 1.92%

   swaps total cost = 0.51% + 1.5% = 2.01%

   On the basis of costs with the assumption of a leverage level of 4, Thompson may change her mind and elect to implement using futures because it is the lowest-cost option by 9 bps.

   However, Thompson must consider the incremental work to be performed with monitoring the futures (e.g., margin) and rolling over the contracts every quarter.

   (LOS 26.f)

4. In the cash market, cash drag (in the form of timing delays and disruptions to active manager portfolios) comprises two-thirds of the total costs. A sufficient amount of investments from international developed equity managers would need to be liquidated, and the cash would be taken from those managers and transferred to existing or new fixed income managers. Doing so results in transaction costs as well as cash drag, since there will be some delay in getting the funds to the fixed income managers and having the funds invested.

   In the derivatives market, tracking error comprises more than 70% of the total costs. The transaction would involve a short position in equity futures to reduce exposure and a long position in fixed-income futures to increase exposure. The use of multiple futures contracts will increase tracking error; it is 17 bps for two contracts compared to 8 bps for one contract, as noted earlier in Figure 26.5.

   (LOS 26.e)

5. Rebalancing with derivatives is most likely to be implemented more quickly, and with no impact on the active managers. That is on the assumption of reasonably high levels of liquidity in the equity futures market, for example.

   If the rebalancing transaction is larger, then the transaction is likely to be more permanent in nature rather than merely a short-term adjustment that could easily be reversed later.

   (LOS 26.f)

6. From a cost perspective, transacting in the cash markets is preferable given the savings of 22 bps compared to transacting in the derivatives markets.

   Should a faster implementation time be required, transacting in the derivatives market is preferable.

   Given the larger size of the rebalancing (2.5% now vs. 0.5%, discussed earlier), there is an implied longer time horizon that supports transacting in the cash markets.

   Overall, with a 2.5% reallocation, the most appropriate option would be to transact in the cash markets.

   (LOS 26.e)

7. Monitoring of an ESG investment could be done through an ESG metrics monitoring system. An ESG metrics monitoring system could compare ESG ratings or scores for portfolio companies from industry providers with peer companies and the policy benchmark, assess portfolio sensitivities to a range of climate-related risks by developing an analytical framework, and aggregate data on the carbon footprint of portfolio companies. The metrics are then monitored over time for changing trends.

   (LOS 26.g)

READING 27

Case Study in Risk Management: Private Wealth

EXAM FOCUS

Risk management is a vital piece of putting together a personal financial plan. By understanding a client's full situation, and taking a holistic view of their circumstances, we have the best opportunity to offer advice tailored to their goals and needs.

This reading will focus on identifying a family's risk exposures throughout different stages of their lives. We will be following the same family members through four stages of their careers: early career, career development, peak accumulation, and early retirement. Each stage comes with new variables and new challenges. We must find ways to help mitigate or remove any risks the family might face.

Keep in mind, each stage provides a snapshot in time, with multiple variables. Focus on the information that is being presented for that stage; resist the temptation to use external variables to justify a risk management recommendation.

PROFESSOR'S NOTE

For the purposes of this reading, we will focus on the Learning Outcome Statements. The original reading provides further detail regarding local regulations, current economic conditions, and tax laws. While this provides a more holistic view, it is very likely that a case on the exam will forgo multiple pages of background information and will instead provide a narrower list of things you need to consider.

Video covering this content is available online.

MODULE 27.1: EARLY CAREER STAGE[1]

Jessica and Paul Schmitt, both age 28, were recently married. They are in the early phase of their careers. Both Jessica and Paul graduated with master's degrees three years ago in computer science and mathematics, respectively.

Paul took a teaching position at a local school upon graduation. He earns a gross annual salary of €45,600, which translates to a take-home pay of €33,670, after social security and tax deductions.

After graduating university, Jessica joined an IT startup. Jessica's gross annual salary is €24,000, which after taxes and social security contributions becomes €20,490. Though Jessica's current salary is low, the potential exists for a significant increase. She also expects to receive a bonus if the startup becomes successful; this bonus is likely to represent a significant share of her compensation. Were she to move to a different employer, Jessica could earn a much better salary; however, she believes strongly that the startup will succeed and prefers this potential upside that her current position offers.

The couple combined have savings of €15,000. Aside from their participation in their government's pension scheme (to which they have contributed since beginning work three years ago), the Schmitts have no other financial assets. Their only other asset of note is their car (which they use only occasionally). The Schmitts have an automobile insurance policy in place, protecting them from liability for other parties' repair costs or injury compensation.

The Schmitts are debt-free because their parents covered their expenses when they were students, and tuition costs were relatively low at the university they attended. The Schmitts' monthly expenses are €2,900, which includes rent of €1,000.

The following table is a summary of the Schmitts' finances:

Figure 27.1: Summary of the Schmitts' Circumstances in the Early Career Stage (€)[2]

	Jessica	Paul	Combined
Annual Gross Income	24,000	45,600	69,600
Annual Net Income	20,490	33,670	54,160
Source of income	IT Startup	Teacher	
Annual living expenses			34,800
Financial assets			15,000
Debt			0
Car			7,000

After further discussion, you identify the following objectives for the couple:

- Ensure long-term financial security
- Ensure a comfortable retirement

1 Portions of the case reproduced from Level III CFA Curriculum reading "Case Study in Risk Management: Private Wealth," with permission from CFA Institute.

2 Reproduced from Level III CFA Curriculum reading "Case Study in Risk Management: Private Wealth," Exhibit 2, with permission from CFA Institute.

- Start a family soon
- Purchase a condominium

The Schmitts have toured a home that costs €270,000 located in a popular neighborhood that has seen considerable property value appreciation recently. A 25-year mortgage would be 3.6% per year, fixed for five years, and floating thereafter.

LOS 27.a: Identify and analyze a family's risk exposures during the early career stage.

Identify the Risks

At this point, we have identified the Schmitts' financial objectives as well as their financial assets and liabilities. Because the couple are early on in their career, the majority of their economic balance sheet consists of their **human capital**. Notice that Paul and Jessica's human capital differs in the following ways:

- **Paul's human capital** is very bond-like as long as he continues his career as a teacher. This is because (1) he has high job security, which limits earnings risk, (2) Paul's job may not be portable to other countries due to licensing requirements, and (3) his income is expected to increase as he gains seniority but otherwise has very limited upside potential.
- **Jessica's human capital** is very equity-like in her current industry role. This is because (1) there are significant unknowns related to her future employment cash flows, though she can also earn considerable rewards if she excels at her job and the firm performs well, (2) unemployment is a much greater worry for Jessica because, unlike Paul, Jessica's job does not have significant job security, (3) her discretionary bonus payments are uncertain, and (4) Jessica's human capital is portable across countries.

As a result, Jessica and Paul's marriage creates a diversified mix of human capital.

Next, we must turn to actually identifying and analyzing the couple's risk exposures. Despite being young and in good health, they still face the following risks:

Earnings Risk

The couple face earnings risk from either unemployment or disability. Because both are young and have little in the way of financial capital, their largest asset on their economic balance sheet is their human capital.

The two big drivers of earnings risk at this career state are the risk of unemployment and risk of a health event or disability.

Unemployment: Jessica, more than Paul, faces a significant risk of unemployment because the firm where she works is a startup, while Paul's career has more job security. The probability of Jessica losing her job is difficult to estimate, but we can be confident it is higher than the likelihood of Paul becoming unemployed. Because they have been paying into the social security system for a few years, they would be

Reading 27

entitled to an unemployment benefit, which would partially replace each of their salaries.

Disability: Despite the fact that Jessica and Paul are young and fit, the risk of a health event or disability is still present. Again, the couple would be entitled to disability payments from the state social security system, but the monthly income from that source would not be enough to cover their current salary.

Premature Death Risk

The case suggests the likelihood of a premature death is low, as both Paul and Jessica are in good health. In the unlikely event of premature death, there would be a few implications for the surviving spouse at this stage of life:

- One-time costs such as the funeral expenses would need to be paid. Additionally, the surviving spouse would need to establish a fund to deal with emergencies alone.
- The surviving spouse's lifestyle would be affected because of the need to assume sole responsibility for household costs, such as rent.

Car Accident and/or Repair Costs

The Schmitts own an older car. They have an insurance policy in place that should protect them in case they need to pay compensation or repair costs to other motorists. However, they are not covered for repair or replacement of their own car.

Home Purchase

At this stage of their lives, the Schmitts do not have a lot of cash flow to support short-term expenditures. While they would be able to finance a house purchase through a mortgage, making a substantial down payment would leave them with little liquid assets. This could become an issue if some of the previously mentioned risks were to arise (e.g., their old car needs to be replaced, one or both of them suddenly lose their job, etc.).

Other Liabilities

Most of the couple's assets are covered by insurance at this point. There are not any other apparent major liability risks.

LOS 27.b: Recommend and justify methods to manage a family's risk exposures during the early career stage.

Earnings Risk

We previously identified two drivers of earnings risk: sudden unemployment and a health/disability event. Methods of mitigating these risks are different.

Unemployment: Earnings risk resulting from unemployment can be problematic to insure against. In some countries, supplemental income provided by government assistance is available to aid the unemployed, but one of the best ways to protect against sudden job loss is to accumulate a savings "buffer" of several months of normal expenditures. Six months is generally an appropriate recommendation.

Disability: **Disability insurance** can address earnings risk from serious illness or disability. We should recommend that each of them purchase a policy that would supplement their net income from disability benefits provided by the state. Because the Schmitts' salaries are expected to increase over time, we should recommend they choose a policy that allows them to purchase additional coverage going forward.

To determine the amount of disability insurance needed, we calculate the present value (PV) of net earnings that would need to be replaced. For the Schmitts, inputs required for this calculation are shown in Figure 27.2.

Figure 27.2: Disability Insurance Calculation (€)[3]

	Jessica	Paul
Net income to be replaced	20,490	33,670
Annual disability coverage by the social security system	18,000	18,000
Shortfall	2,490	15,670
Benefit period (until retirement)	37 years	37 years
Assumed annual benefit adjustment	2%	2%
Discount rate	3%	3%
PV of future earnings replacement required (annuity due)	77,700	489,000

The future earnings replacement required is a *growing* annuity due. While the TVM keys of the calculator are usually used to calculate the present value of a *constant* annuity due, they can also be used for a growing annuity due if we make an adjustment to the discount rate to reflect the growth in the payments. This can be done by using a "growth-adjusted discount rate" defined as follows:

$$\text{growth} - \text{adjusted discount rate} = \frac{(1 + r)}{(1 + g)} - 1$$

where:
r = annual discount rate
g = annual growth rate

In this case, the growth-adjusted discount rate of the payment = (1.03/1.02) – 1 = 0.0098 or 0.98%.

We can now use the growth-adjusted discount rate to calculate the present value of an annuity due in the usual manner, as follows:

- Set the calculator to annuity due mode (BGN) using the keystrokes 2nd PMT 2nd ENTER.

[3] Reproduced from Level III CFA Curriculum reading "Case Study in Risk Management: Private Wealth," Exhibit 5, with permission from CFA Institute.

Reading 27

- The PV of future earnings replacement for Jessica is calculated using the TVM keys: 37 N; 0.98 I/Y; 2490 PMT, CPT PV = –77,717.
- The PV of future earnings replacement for Paul is calculated using the TVM keys: 37 N; 0.98 I/Y; 15,670 PMT; CPT PV = –489,087.
- Note that numbers in the table are rounded to the nearest €100.

PROFESSOR'S NOTE

To see how the growth-adjusted discount rate works, consider a single future cash flow at time *n* (CF_N) which has grown by a growth rate *g* in every period from the cash flow today at time zero (CF_0). The present value of this cash flow can be written as:

$$PV(CF_N) = \frac{CF_0(1+g)^n}{(1+r)^n}$$

Dividing both the numerator and denominator by a factor of $(1 + g)^n$ gives:

$$PV(CF_N) = \frac{CF_0}{(1+r)^n/(1+g)^n}$$

From here we could view the denominator simply as $[(1 + r) / (1 + g)]^n$. Writing $(1 + r) / (1 + g) = 1 + r^*$ this expression becomes:

$$PV(CF_N) = \frac{CF_0}{(1+r^*)^n}$$

Now we can see that we can view the present value of a growing cash flow (CF_n) as the present value of a constant cash flow (i.e., the same as CF_0 today) discounted at a growth-adjusted discount rate r^* where:

$$(1+r^*) = \frac{(1+r)}{(1+g)}$$

The expression for the growth-adjusted discount rate, r^*, follows:

$$r^* = \frac{(1+r)}{(1+g)} - 1$$

Premature Death Risk

To protect against premature death risk, the couple should take on **life insurance**. If one of the Schmitts were to die prematurely, life insurance would help support the other's loss of future income. As a reminder, there are two methods for calculating the amount of coverage necessary.

- **Human life value:** estimates the amount of future earnings that must be replaced

- **Needs analysis:** estimates the amount needed to cover living expenses for the surviving spouse

PROFESSOR'S NOTE

Both of these methods were introduced in the reading on Risk Management for Individuals in the Private Wealth Management section of the curriculum.

At this stage of the couple's lives, we determine the amount of coverage using the needs analysis method because of uncertainty about the level of future earnings life insurance would need to replace.

Figure 27.3: Life Insurance Calculation (€)[4]

	Paul	Jessica
Total cash needs (funeral, emergency fund, debts)	30,000	30,000
Capital needs (PV of surviving spouse's 25,000 annual living expenses – PV of survivor's income until retirement)	411,000	–77,000
Total financial needs	**441,000**	**–47,000**
Less capital available (savings)	15,000	15,000
Less PV of vested retirement accounts (attributable to surviving spouse)	12,000	21,000
Additional life insurance needs	**414,000**	**–83,000**

The capital needs figures in the previous table warrant some discussion. In the event of the death of either spouse, it is assumed that the surviving spouse has ongoing expenses of €25,000 per year until death, assumed to be at age 90. Note that, given a current age of 28 for both spouses, this implies a time horizon of 90 – 28 = 62 years. These expenses are assumed to grow at 2% and are discounted at a rate of 3%, implying a growth-adjusted discount rate of 1.03/1.02 – 1 = 0.98%. We can then calculate the present value of this growing annuity due using the TVM keys (with the calculator in BGN mode): 62 N; 0.98 I/Y; 25,000 PMT; CPT PV = –1,168,818 rounded to a value of €1,169,000.

Now, recall from earlier in the reading Jessica's net salary is currently €20,490. If we assume this will grow at 6% and use a risk-adjusted discount rate of 6%, then the growth-adjusted discount rate becomes 1.06/1.06 – 1 = 0%. This means that the task of calculating the present value of her income until she is 65 becomes the simple calculation of (65 – 28) × €20,490 = €758,130, rounded to €758,000. Then the capital needs should Paul die are €1,169,000 (PV of Jessica's expenses) – €758,000 (PV of Jessica's income) = €411,000.

An analogous calculation can be done for capital needs should Jessica die. We assume the same expenses, but the present value of Paul's income is assumed

Reading 27

4 Reproduced from Level III CFA Curriculum reading "Case Study in Risk Management: Private Wealth," Exhibit 6, with permission from CFA Institute.

to grow at 3% and is discounted at 3% (recall Paul's income is less risky than Jessica's income). This means that the risk-adjusted discount rate is once again 0% (1.03/1.03 – 1) and the present value of Paul's income can be easily calculated to be (65 – 28) × €33,666 = €1,245,642, rounded to €1,246,000. Hence the capital needs should Jessica die are €1,169,000 – €1,246,000 = –€77,000. The message here is that should Jessica die, Paul can still fund his expected future expenses through his expected future income.

Note that Paul's life insurance coverage needs are much higher than Jessica's. We should recommend purchasing a life insurance policy covering Paul's life. We should also mention to the couple that this will need to be reevaluated once the couple decides to start a family.

Car Accident and/or Repair Costs

The Schmitts' existing car insurance plan covers costs associated with other parties in the case of an accident, but it does not cover the Schmitts. The couple has mentioned they rarely use the car, so we should advise them to self-insure by means of a sufficient savings buffer, rather than spending money on additional coverage.

Liability Risk

Because the couple has minimal liability risk, there is nothing to recommend at this stage.

House Purchase

Because the couple has little financial capital, we should advise them against purchasing the home at this time. While there are many long-term benefits of home ownership, they can decrease their risk exposures by delaying the house purchase.

Instead of the house purchase, we should recommend that the Schmitts develop a plan to increase their savings and other financial assets. Should they purchase a home in the near future, they would be left virtually without other financial assets.

The Schmitts should create a substantial savings buffer, at least six months of expenses in total. Furthermore, once the savings buffer is in place, the couple should draw up an investment plan.

PROFESSOR'S NOTE

In the original reading, the couple purchases the home against the advisor's recommendation. This slightly changes the couple's risk exposures in a few ways:

- It would require that their life insurance coverage be reevaluated, because any mortgages or loans taken on would still need to be paid in the event of premature death.
- While the couple currently has very little liability risk, purchasing a home would introduce this risk into their situation. Upon purchase of a home, taking on homeowner's insurance would be prudent.

MODULE QUIZ 27.1

1. For a family that is in the early career stage, the largest asset on their economic balance sheet is *most likely* to be:
   A. a mortgage.
   B. human capital.
   C. their savings account.
2. One reason that supports investors in their early career stage investing in their portfolio aggressively is that:
   A. human capital is equity-like.
   B. they have time to recoup losses.
   C. they still need to build up a sufficient safety net.
3. Which of the following is the *most appropriate* argument against purchasing new home while in the early career stage of life?
   A. Local real estate prices have been on the decline for two consecutive years and don't appear to be turning around any time soon.
   B. Families in the early career stage have little experience with real estate and should wait until they observe a full market cycle.
   C. The family has little financial capital available to cover short-term expenses, and purchasing a new property could present unexpected expenses.

MODULE 27.2: CAREER DEVELOPMENT STAGE

Video covering this content is available online.

We continue the Schmitts' case 17 years later. They have developed significantly in their careers and remain healthy. Both of their incomes are greater now, Jessica's significantly so. With their increased incomes, they have repaid the entire loan from Jessica's parents and most of their mortgage, while accumulating a liquidity buffer of just under €80,000.

Based on their understanding of the IT industry, the Schmitts have assembled a portfolio of shares in 10 local IT companies. They now own residential property in the area where these companies are located and are considering investing in additional residential property there.

Jessica and her employer each contribute €3,000 annually to a defined-contribution pension plan. Paul's employment benefits as a teacher include life insurance coverage equal to three times his salary, as well as disability benefits that would equal €2,520 per month.

The couple has two children: Roxane, age 12, and Peter, age 7. Peter requires extra support at school to accommodate mental development issues. The family's annual living expenses have increased to €65,000. After Roxane was born, the Schmitts increased their life insurance coverage, but they have not adjusted it since.

The two following tables provide a summary of the Schmitts' financial circumstances and annual budget.

Figure 27.4: Summary of the Schmitts' Circumstances in the Career Development Stage (€)[5]

	Jessica	Paul	Combined
Annual gross income	80,000	66,000	146,000
Annual net income	53,650	46,510	100,160
Source of income	Department head, IT	Teacher	
Annual living expenses			65,000
Pension provisions	Government pension as mandated by law *and* Employer's DC plan with a total annual contribution of 3,000 from Jessica + employer	Government pension as mandated by law; no separate private pension	
Employer-provided insurance		Life insurance coverage of 3 × 66,000 = 198,000	
Private life insurance	200,000 life policy taken out after birth of first child	Life policy of 440,000	
Disability insurance	Government insurance coverage of 25,200 per year Private coverage of a lump sum of 112,200 (the original 80,000 policy taken out at 28, plus 2% annual benefit adjustment)	Government insurance covering 30,245 per year Private coverage producing a lump sum of 686,100 (the original 490,000 policy taken out at age 28, plus 2% annual benefit adjustment)	

5 Reproduced from Level III CFA Curriculum reading "Case Study in Risk Management: Private Wealth," Exhibit 8, with permission from CFA Institute.

Reading 27

Figure 27.5: Summary of the Schmitts' Annual Budget in the Career Development Stage (€)[6]

Combined annual gross salary	146,000
Less taxes and social security contributions	45,800
Net pay	**100,200**
Less living costs (including mortgage payments)	65,000
Less miscellaneous costs (house repair, maintenance, etc.)	3,500
Cash available for insurance and savings	**31,700**
Insurance premiums	3,500
Funds available to save or invest	**28,200**
Currently used primarily to:	
Fund investment portfolio	22,000
Add to savings accounts	3,200
Contribute to Jessica's employer's pension plan	3,000

LOS 27.c: Identify and analyze a family's risk exposures during the career development stage.

Earnings Risk

As in the early stage of the couple's careers, the same two earnings risks apply.

- *Unemployment:* Jessica continues to be at greater risk of unemployment than Paul does. Furthermore, because Jessica's salary is now substantially higher than it was before, the amount of income at stake is much greater.
- *Disability:* Should one of them become disabled, the rest of the family would suffer from lost earnings. The nondisabled spouse could be limited in their opportunity set, impacting income and costs.

Premature Death Risk

Having children increases the adverse financial consequences for the family of early death of one of the parents. Not only would the cost of raising the children no longer be met, the surviving spouse could suffer a reduction in income after becoming a single parent.

Investment Portfolio

The couple has built up their main investment vehicle, but the account is concentrated in a volatile sector. Additionally, because Jessica works in IT, the portfolio's performance is likely to be highly correlated with her human capital. If the IT sector underperforms, their investment portfolio and Jessica's career prospects are likely to suffer simultaneously.

6 Reproduced from Level III CFA Curriculum reading "Case Study in Risk Management: Private Wealth," Exhibit 10, with permission from CFA Institute.

The residential property in which the Schmitts are considering a speculative investment is located in the area where Jessica's offices and many other IT companies are located. It is comparable to their existing property.

Retirement Goals

The Schmitts' retirement funds could turn out to be inadequate for the lifestyle they desire if the couple's contributions to the retirement plans are inadequate or if the funds do not perform well. In addition to their state pension income in retirement, Jessica is participating in her employer's defined contribution company pension, which will help increase the probability of reaching their retirement goals.

By your calculations, if Paul and Jessica remain employed until their retirement age of 65, they will have a total gross retirement income of €76,000 (inclusive of pension and DC pension income), which is roughly half of their current income.

It is likely the couple's living expenses will be less than their current living expenses, but at this point there is a risk that their retirement income will be insufficient.

Other Risks

Other risks could include property risks or other liabilities.

LOS 27.d: Recommend and justify methods to manage a family's risk exposures during the career development stage.

Earnings Risk

Disability Insurance

Both Paul and Jessica already have disability insurance policies. However, the current level of coverage no longer matches the present value of future earnings, as demonstrated in the following table:

Figure 27.6: Disability Insurance Coverage Calculation in the Career Development Stage (€)[7]

	Jessica	Paul
Net income to be replaced	53,650	46,510
Annual disability coverage by the social security system	25,200	30,245
Shortfall	28,400	16,265
Benefit period (until retirement)	20 years	20 years
Assumed annual benefit adjustment	2%	2%
Discount rate	3%	3%
PV of future earnings replacement required (annuity due)	519,000	297,000

7 Reproduced from Level III CFA Curriculum reading "Case Study in Risk Management: Private Wealth," Exhibit 11, with permission from CFA Institute.

The PV of future earnings replacement can be calculated for both spouses using TVM keys and a growth-adjusted discount rate of 1.03/1.02 – 1 = 0.98%, as in same calculation in the earlier stage of life.

For Jessica, this would be: 20 N; 0.98 I/Y; 28,400 PMT; CPT PV: –518,560, rounded to €519,000, and a similar calculation with PMT set to 16,265 is required for Paul. Remember the calculator needs to be in "BGN" mode for these calculations because the payments are an annuity due.

Over the course of 20 years, assuming an annual benefit adjustment of 2% and a discount rate of 3%, the present value of Jessica's required futures earnings replacement is €519,000. For Paul, the same calculation results in a value of €297,000.

Currently, Jessica's level of disability coverage is €112,200 and Paul's is €686,100. We should recommend that Paul and Jessica adjust the level of coverage to reflect their current present values of future earnings replacement. Jessica's coverage should be increased to €520,000, and Paul's reduced to €300,000.

PROFESSOR'S NOTE

You might be tempted to simply look at the total coverage between both parties. Remember, the purpose of this coverage is to help supplement income for the other party involved.

Life Insurance

To protect against the risk of Jessica or Paul's untimely death, each purchased life insurance at age 28. However, both of their salaries have increased and they now have children, so it is likely the amount of coverage needs to be changed. To determine the new coverage amount, we can use the *human life value* and *needs analysis* methods.

Human Life Value

The human life value method takes the view that should a spouse die, the resulting life insurance payout needs to replace the present value of the income lost, net of any reduction in expenses that would have been directly attributable to the deceased.

We will use the following information to apply this method. You should assume this information would be provided to you in the exam.

Figure 27.7: Inputs Required for Human Life Value Method at Age 45 (€)[8]

	Paul	Jessica
Annual after-tax income	46,510	53,650
Annual expenses directly attributable to individual	10,000	10,000
Annual employee benefits	10,000	4,000
Annual expected growth in income	2%	5%
Discount rate	3%	3%
Existing life insurance	638,000	200,000

8 Reproduced from Level III CFA Curriculum reading "Case Study in Risk Management: Private Wealth," Exhibit 12, with permission from CFA Institute.

This process can be summarized for Paul as follows:

- Start with the current after-tax income for Paul of €46,510.
- Subtract the €10,000 annual expenses attributable to Paul, which would not be incurred should he die: €46,510 – €10,000 = €36,510.
- Add the €10,000 employee benefits (such as contributions to pension plans) that would not be earned should Paul die: €36,510 + €10,000 = €46,510.
- Gross up to a required pretax payout to meet this shortfall in contribution to family finances. Assuming a tax rate of 30%, this is equal to €46,510/(1 – 0.3) = €66,443.
- Use the growth-adjusted discount rate of 0.98% (1.03/1.02 – 1) to calculate the present value of this pretax annuity due: 20 N; 0.98 I/Y; 66,443 PMT; CPT PV = –1,213,193, rounded to a value of €1,213,000.
- Subtracting the existing life insurance in place of €638,000 gives a life insurance requirement of €1,213,000 – €638,000 = €575,000.

A similar process can be carried out for Jessica to produce a life insurance requirement of €1,444,000.

PROFESSOR'S NOTE

This is the same process as that introduced in the reading on Risk Management for Individuals in the Private Wealth Management section of the curriculum.

Investment Portfolio

Concentrated Stock Positions

The couple should hold an investment portfolio that has low correlation to their human capital. They should also find a way to diversify the portfolio, rather than holding concentrated positions in only 10 companies.

In order for the couple to achieve better diversification, we should recommend that, at a minimum, no new contributions be made in shares of IT companies. Rather, contributions should be directed into pooled investment vehicles—specifically funds that are well diversified by region, sector, and security selections.

Real Estate

Reasons that the couple should avoid investing in speculative real estate include the following:

- The local property's value is highly correlated to the strength of the local IT sector, which is highly correlated to the value of Jessica's human capital.
- Funding for the purchase would need to come from their investment portfolio and a loan because the couple has limited resources available.
- If they opt for funding the purchase with their investment portfolio, they would further decrease their diversification.

- An investment property would be a large, illiquid, and concentrated holding.
- They would incur ongoing costs to own and manage rental property.

Retirement Savings Plans

We can identify a substantial shortfall in the Schmitts' projected income in retirement relative to their retirement goals. To mitigate the risk of having inadequate funds to support their lifestyle in retirement, the Schmitts should consider dedicating a greater amount to their retirement needs.

According to their budget, the couple's after-tax monthly €8,350 income is greater than their monthly expenditures by approximately €2,700. Even after insurance premium payments, this should leave the couple with €2,350 per month (€28,200 per year) to invest. The Schmitts have built up a substantial liquidity buffer (€80,000) and should consider redirecting further contributions towards Jessica's pension or the investment portfolio to fund future retirement income.

Outcome

Suppose that the Schmitts accept your recommendations: they set aside the idea of buying a property near the IT district and they stop adding to their savings buffer, instead increasing their contributions to the pension plan from Jessica's employer. Furthermore, the Schmitts will continue their contributions to their investment portfolio but will begin moving away from investing in individual securities, instead putting funds into diversified equity funds.

MODULE QUIZ 27.2

1. The risk of unemployment is *most likely* to be mitigated by:
   A. life insurance.
   B. savings buffers.
   C. disability insurance.
2. In the career development stage of an investor's life, the *most appropriate* method of allocating an investment portfolio is to use:
   A. a few securities from the same sector in which the investor currently works and is knowledgeable about.
   B. a mix of pooled investment vehicles that are low cost and diversified across region, sector, and securities.
   C. a basket of 20–25 individual securities that are representative of the different sectors of the global stock market.
3. Which of the following is the *least appropriate* reason for a client to reevaluate their life insurance policy in the career development stage?
   A. The client's spouse gives birth to their first child.
   B. The client's parents die in a car accident and the funeral costs came as a surprise.
   C. The client has been promoted multiple times in last five years and now his earnings are twice what they were.

Reading 27

Video covering this content is available online.

MODULE 27.3: PEAK ACCUMULATION STAGE

It is 10 years later, and Jessica and Paul are now in their peak accumulation phase at age 55 years old. Over the past decade, they have progressed in their careers and have seen their incomes continue to increase.

Jessica's employer is now making significantly-increased contributions to the company pension plan. Jessica too has also been aggressively contributing to the firm's pension plan and to her new private pension, partly to benefit from tax breaks.

The segment of the technology sector that Jessica's company competes in is facing challenges arising from the ever-changing market environment. Paul's job remains steady. He too has been contributing consistently to a private pension plan.

The Schmitts' investment portfolio has grown substantially thanks to regular contributions and investment returns. Currently, the portfolio is invested in a number of diversified funds, and comprises 70% stocks (primarily global equity, plus some Eurolandian stocks) and 30% fixed income (divided approximately evenly between domestic government bonds and high-quality corporate bonds).

The value of the home has seen a decline in real terms, as a result of general softness in Eurolandia's real estate market, plus as a result of the local area losing its previous appeal.

Though the Schmitts have paid down their mortgage, they are still supporting Roxane, who only recently completed her undergraduate degree and is now pursuing graduate studies. The couple is also providing for the special needs of Peter, who is now age 17. Peter has made progress but will probably need assistance for his entire life. The Schmitts estimate that they spend €13,000 per year to support Peter.

The Schmitts recognize that retirement planning has become an important issue now that they plan to retire in 10 years (at age 65). They maintain a healthy lifestyle. Together, they compile a summary of their current financial circumstances, shown in the following table.

Figure 27.8: Summary of the Schmitts' Circumstances in the Peak Accumulation Stage (€)[9]

	Jessica	Paul	Combined
Annual gross income	120,000	80,000	200,000
Annual net income	77,888	53,888	131,776
Source of income	Department head, IT	Teacher	
Annual living expenses			75,000
Property			340,000

9 Reproduced from Level III CFA Curriculum reading "Case Study in Risk Management: Private Wealth," Exhibit 13, with permission from CFA Institute.

Figure 27.8: Summary of the Schmitts' Circumstances in the Peak Accumulation Stage (€) (continued)

	Jessica	Paul	Combined
Bank accounts			80,900
Investment portfolio			611,400
Pension provisions	Government pension as mandated by law, *and* Employer's DC plan with a total annual contribution of 3,000 from Jessica + employer *and* Private pension savings of 15,000	Government pension as mandated by law *and* Private pension savings of 47,500	
Private life insurance	1 million private policy	900,000 private policy plus 3× salary insurance coverage of 240,000 provided by the employer	
Disability insurance	Government insurance coverage of 30,805 per year Private coverage that would provide a lump sum of 633,900 (the original 520,000 policy taken out at 45, plus 2% annual benefit adjustment)	Government insurance coverage of 36,966 per year Private coverage that would provide a lump sum of 365,700 (the original 300,000 policy taken out at age 45, reflecting 2% annual benefit adjustment)	

Financial Objectives

The couple develops the following financial objectives:

- Deliver financial security over the next decade while continuing in full-time employment.
- Have an agreeable retirement.
- Be able, both before and after they retire, to provide Peter with lifelong support and assistance.
- Leave a substantial inheritance for Roxane.

Once again, we analyze these objectives and assess where the couple may be exposed to risks.

Reading 27

LOS 27.e: Identify and analyze a family's risk exposures during the peak accumulation stage.

Earnings Risks

- *Unemployment:* Profitability is volatile in Jessica's industry. Should she lose her job at her current age, it might be difficult for her to find equivalent employment (at her current well-above-average salary and level of seniority).
- *Disability:* Despite the couple maintaining a healthy lifestyle, the risk of losing future earnings due to disability remains. We should examine their current earnings situation to identify how much would be covered by social security.

Figure 27.9: Disability Insurance Coverage Calculation in the Peak Accumulation Stage (€)

	Jessica	Paul
Net income to be replaced	77,900	53,900
Annual disability coverage by the social security system	30,720	36,870
Shortfall	47,180	17,030
Benefit period (until retirement)	10 years	10 years
Assumed annual benefit adjustment	2%	2%
Discount rate	3%	3%
PV of future earnings replacement required (annuity due)	452,000	163,000

Once again, there is a shortfall between the Schmitts' net income and what is covered by the social security system. However, the couple has more than adequate supplementary insurance coverage to handle this shortfall, with the adjustments they made to their coverage 10 years ago. Jessica and Paul have disability coverage of €633,900 and €365,700, respectively.

PROFESSOR'S NOTE

Keep in mind, the period over which the Schmitts would rely on such benefit payments has decreased to 10 years instead of 20. This means that a lower present value of the disability protection will now be adequate.

Premature Death Risk

One of the couple's objectives is providing financial security for the family over the next 10 years, and an early death could easily derail this objective. Both Jessica and Paul have life insurance, so we will consider the current coverage to see if adjustments need to be made.

Figure 27.10: Life Insurance Coverage Calculation in the Peak Accumulation Stage (€)

	Jessica	Paul
Recommended additional life insurance using the human life value method	–17,000	–403,000
Recommended additional life insurance using the needs analysis method	–782,500	–1,000,500

Regardless of the method used, it is apparent that the couple's current life insurance coverage is more than enough to cover the surviving spouse's financial needs.

PROFESSOR'S NOTE

The calculations performed for the life insurance needs during the peak accumulation stage are the same as in the previous stages of life using updated inputs.

Retirement Lifestyle Goals

The couple has continued to contribute to the mandatory government pension. Upon their retirement in 10 years' time at age 65, the Schmitts expect to immediately purchase a fixed annuity (with an assumed 5.0% annuity yield). Further assumptions are in Figure 27.11.

Figure 27.11: Schmitts' Retirement Assets and Main Risks (Excluding their Investment Portfolio) (€)[10]

Assets	Type and Current Value	Expected Growth Rate	Expected Value at Age 65	Expected Annual Gross Pension Benefit	Risks
Paul's mandatory government pension plan	DB pension plan	-	-	48,950 (55% of estimated final salary)	Government may reduce retirement benefits due to fiscal pressures
Jessica's mandatory government pension plan	DB pension plan	-	-	28,191	As above
Jessica's company pension	DC plan, current value 113,500 in a balanced fund	14,000 annual contributions, increasing at 2% 4% annual investment returns	350,000	17,515	Investment risk and interest rate risk that could result in lower annuity income yield
Paul's private pension plan	DC plan currently valued at 47,500 in a balanced fund	6,000 annual contributions, increasing at 2%, 3% investment returns	135,900	6,795	As above
Jessica's private pension savings plan	DC plan opened recently Valued at 15,000 Uses aggressive, actively managed investment strategy with high risk	10,000 annual contributions, increasing at 2% 8% investment returns	201,600	10,080	As above
			Total income	**111,531**	

[10] Reproduced from Level III CFA Curriculum reading "Case Study in Risk Management: Private Wealth," Exhibit 19, with permission from CFA Institute.

Excluding the investment portfolio, the couple's estimated total pension income will amount to approximately €111,500 before taxes, or approximately €84,000 after taxes. The couple believes they will need to live on approximately €75,000 (in real terms) in retirement. While this is encouraging news, risks to these assumptions are a loss of employment, solvency of the state pension systems, or poor returns in the DC plans in the years before the couple retires.

Investment Portfolio

The investment portfolio has two objectives: supporting Peter and leaving an inheritance for Roxane. According to the couple, the required probability of success for supporting Peter is 100%, while the required probability of success for leaving an inheritance to Roxane is 60%.

Goal #1: Support Peter. Based on average life expectancy, Peter is expected to survive his parents by 40 years (to age 90). The couple estimates it costs them €13,000 to care for Peter each year, and it would be €30,000 per year to care for Peter if outside help is used.

You find the present value of these costs to be €500,000, after considering the Schmitts' plan to assist their son up until their retirement. Fortunately, this amount is less than the current portfolio of €611,000.

Goal #2: Inheritance for Roxane. The Schmitts want to leave money to Roxane. The probability of success they require for this goal is lower than that of supporting Peter, with a much longer time horizon because this inheritance will be left upon the couple's death. When asked about a dollar amount, the couple said they want to leave "as much as possible."

Asset Allocation

The couple's asset allocation within the investment portfolio should first address the objective of supporting Peter, while leaving the remaining balance as an inheritance for Roxane. The Schmitts' multiple objectives span multiple time periods.

LOS 27.f: Recommend and justify methods to manage a family's risk exposures during the peak accumulation stage.

Earnings Risk

- *Unemployment:* While it is almost impossible to formally insure against job loss, the Schmitts have continued to build up their savings and are effectively self-insuring against loss of employment.
- *Disability:* Earlier, we calculated the present value of earnings not covered by social security to be €452,000 for Jessica and €163,000 for Paul. Currently, the couple have more than sufficient coverage through their disability insurance (€633,900 and €365,700, respectively). We should recommend actually decreasing this coverage for both of them to lower the premiums being paid every month.

Premature Death

As in the case of disability insurance, the couple also has higher life insurance than what is necessary. We would recommend decreasing this coverage to lower the premiums paid.

Retirement Savings

The Schmitts are in a position to retire comfortably. The current projected income (assuming they continue to contribute the maximum amount) from their pension assets in retirement is in excess of their projected spending needs. The couple should continue to contribute the legal maximum to their pension plans.

Investment Portfolio Asset Allocation

Because the couple's first retirement goal, to live comfortably, is already covered through their retirement plans, we can focus on the other two objectives: supporting Peter and leaving an inheritance to Roxane.

The current balance of the investment portfolio is €611,000. We know the couple has been contributing €33,000 to this portfolio on an annual basis, and we should recommend that the Schmitts continue making these contributions. The higher the contributions, in addition to capital gains and dividends, the higher the probability of meeting the couple's objectives.

Because the couple has multiple objectives that span multiple time periods, we should follow a goals-based investing approach. Using this approach, we recommend creating two sub-portfolios that correspond to supporting Peter and leaving an inheritance to Roxane.

- *Peter's sub-portfolio:* Assets devoted to the goal of Peter's care, currently €500,000 allocated 70% equity/30% fixed-income, should be reallocated gradually toward an increasing proportion of inflation-protected government bonds. Allocating to inflation-protected bonds will help make sure the portfolio maintains its real value over time. Because the portfolio will not be touched for almost 20 years, realized gains should be managed in a way that maximizes the benefit of any capital gain tax exemptions.
- *Roxane's sub-portfolio:* Most of the portfolio is allocated to Peter's long-term care objectives, leaving only €111,000 in investable assets available for Roxane's sub-portfolio. This objective has an even longer time horizon (30+ years), so this sub-portfolio should initially be 100% allocated to diversified global equity funds to benefit from the high expected returns from equities.

Bear in mind the importance of reviewing whether the allocation stays in line with these goals as the Schmitts continue to save and accumulate assets. The portfolio allocations should be monitored regularly.

MODULE QUIZ 27.3

Brandon and his wife, Eileen, are 55 years old and are in the peak accumulation stage of their careers. They meet with John Davis, CFA, a family friend, to begin to prepare for retirement, which they expect will occur in 10 years. Eileen, who is chief marketing officer at a small marketing firm, makes an annual salary of $100,000 per year and expects her compensation to increase at 4% annually, somewhat above the current inflation rate of 2%, for the next 10 years. Brandon, having just left his job as a computer programmer, recently took a part-time consulting position with a small technology firm and is making $60,000 per year. He expects his compensation to rise with the current rate of inflation. Currently, the government provides non-taxable disability assistance of 30% of gross income. Assume that the current tax rate is 20% and the discount rate is 3%.

1. Assuming that both Brandon and Eileen will qualify for government disability assistance, **calculate** the amount of additional disability insurance they should each take out individually, rounded to the nearest $100.

2. Five years later, Eileen receives a large raise of $50,000 per year. She believes her future compensation will continue to rise at 4% until retirement. Despite a large increase in salary, **discuss** why it may not be necessary to take out additional disability insurance. Note: There are no calculations necessary to answer this question.

Reading 27

3. Brandon and Eileen will have to fund their retirement income solely from their retirement accounts and investment portfolio. They also have three children, ages 30, 20, and 15, all three of whom, upon Brandon and Eileen's death, their parents would like to receive a substantial inheritance. The total value of their investment assets is currently valued at $2.5 million. Which of the following is *least appropriate* justification for Davis to use a goals-based investment strategy when making recommendations to Brandon and Eileen?
   A. Brandon and Eileen's goals have multiple time horizons associated with them.
   B. Brandon and Eileen have multiple goals they are trying to accomplish upon retirement.
   C. A strategy based on Brandon and Eileen's goals will maximize the portfolio's return for given measure of risk.

MODULE 27.4: EARLY RETIREMENT STAGE

Video covering this content is available online.

We close the Schmitts' case study with the couple about to turn 65 and retire. They are generally in excellent health, though they infrequently make use of the government's medical system.

They currently spend less than they did in previous stages of life, and their investments now amount to approximately €1.5 million. Even with the gradual transition from equity funds to fixed-income funds, equities still account for 50% of the total portfolio, as a result of vigorous returns from this asset class. The rest is divided evenly between inflation-protected government bonds and high-quality corporate bonds.

Jessica's earnings have diminished because she decided to withdraw from her management role and enter IT consulting. The Schmitts' expenditures have also decreased because Roxane is now living independently.

In a meeting, the couple describes some of their goals as they enter this new stage of their career:

- **Retire soon** with a comfortable income level for their lifetimes and avoid a scenario in which they live longer than their money. The Schmitts consider themselves to be in good physical shape and expect to live beyond the typical life expectancy. They also want to ensure that they preserve the purchasing power of their income in retirement.
- **Provide financial support for Peter.** The Schmitts estimate that in 10 years the cost of their son's care will be €35,000 per year before inflation.
- **Leave an inheritance to Roxane** in a still-undefined amount.
- **Help Roxane buy her first property** by providing her with up to €150,000.

The couple's financial circumstances and pension assets are summarized in Figures 27.12 and 27.13.

Figure 27.12: Summary of the Schmitts' Circumstances in the Early Retirement Stage (€)[11]

	Jessica	Paul	Combined
Annual Gross Income	90,000	89,000	179,000
Source of income	Senior IT Consultant	Teacher	
Annual living expenses			70,000
Property			420,000
Investment portfolio			1,511,000

Figure 27.13: Summary of the Schmitts' Retirement Assets in the Early Retirement Stage (€)[12]

Paul's mandatory government pension plan	Annual pension of 48,950 (55% of final salary of 89,000)
Jessica's mandatory government pension plan	Annual pension of 28,190
Jessica's company pension	DC plan; Fund value of 350,000 corresponding to an annual pension of 17,500
Paul's private pension savings plan	135,000 corresponding to annual pension of 6,750
Jessica's private pension savings plan	175,000 corresponding to annual pension of 8,750

Note: The annual pension amounts assume that the fund value at retirement is used to purchase a fixed payment annuity at a 5% yield.

Prior to assessing the couple's risk exposures, we establish the following:

- With the Schmitts' retirement imminent, there is no longer a need for disability or life insurance coverage.
- The government pension income that they will soon begin to receive is now known with certainty.

A strategy should be established for the pension schemes the Schmitts have. Their financial advisor explains that the options for the couple are as follows:

1. Create a stream of income for the remainder of their lives by purchasing annuities. The current nominal rate is 4.5% after costs.
2. Withdraw lump sums. Up to one-third of the employer pension can be withdrawn, while the private pension offers more flexibility. Current law states that 25% of a lump sum distribution is tax-free.
3. Keep the monies invested in the retirement plans schemes.

Reading 27

[11] Reproduced from Level III CFA Curriculum reading "Case Study in Risk Management: Private Wealth," Exhibit 22, with permission from CFA Institute.

[12] Reproduced from Level III CFA Curriculum reading "Case Study in Risk Management: Private Wealth," Exhibit 23, with permission from CFA Institute.

LOS 27.g: Identify and analyze a family's risk exposures during the early retirement stage.

At this point, the couple's risks look slightly different than they have in previous stages. They do not need to keep their life or disability insurance because they are no longer employed and earnings risk is no longer an issue. Additionally, saving for retirement through their public or private pensions no longer incurs risk because the amount of pension income in retirement is known.

Instead, there are two big risks at the early retirement stage.

Retirement Income Risk

One of the risks the Schmitts face is outliving their assets in retirement. Because the couple will receive pension income from the mandatory government pension plan, we know that part of their retirement income is already covered. However, both Jessica and Paul have private and employer pension plans, which do not provide known income in retirement.

Investment Portfolio Goals

- Provide economic support for Peter (this is a top priority).
- Give an inheritance to their children, chiefly Roxane.
- Offer Roxane a deposit on her house purchase in coming years.
- Maintain the ability to draw on their investments to cover unexpected expenses—for example, if their retirement income does not increase as much as the cost of living. Or if an unexpected expense arises, for example, related to their health care needs.

LOS 27.h: Recommend and justify a plan to manage risks associated with an individual's retirement lifestyle goals.

Retirement Income Objectives

The Schmitts have an objective of making sure their after-tax retirement income covers their €70,000 of living expenses. Their combined government pension plan income will yield €77,150 before taxes, so the couple will have to supplement the rest of this income with their employer and private pensions.

Current law says the couple can withdraw up to 25% of their company pension plans tax-free. If we withdraw 25% from Jessica's largest account and Paul's only pension account, and use the remaining balance to purchase an inflation-protected annuity at 4.5% after all fees, the couple would receive a total of €93,600 in pre-tax income, or €72,000 after tax. This is greater than the €70,000 in annual living expenses.

Figure 27.14: Summary of the Schmitts' Retirement Income Proposal in Early Retirement Stage (€)[13]

Jessica's state pension	28,200
Paul's state pension	48,950
Total pretax income from state pension	**77,150**
Annuity (4.5% after all fees) purchased using 75% of Jessica's company pension plan	11,800
Annuity (4.5% after all fees) purchased using 75% of Paul's private pension plan	4,600
Total pretax income from pensions and annuities	**93,600**
Less tax	21,600
After-tax income	**72,000**

The remaining one-quarter of the two pension plans could be taken as a tax-free lump sum (creating a total of €121,250). Jessica's remaining, untouched, private pension plan, would not be needed as a source of retirement income. You suggest withdrawing that 25% of that plan as a tax-free lump sum of €43,750, leaving the remainder invested in the plan.

The end result of this is the couple's living expenses are covered by pension income and inflation-protected annuities, while the couple is able to withdraw €165,000 tax-free (€121,250 + €43,750).

Investment Portfolio Asset Allocation

Suppose that the Schmitts ask you to advise them about their investment portfolio, which currently stands at €1,511,000. The couple will additionally receive a pension lump sum of €165,000 tax-free, which will leave €131,250 in Jessica's private pension plan, and bring the total value of resources available to about €1.8 million.

We must address the couple's top priority objective: supporting Peter. At the moment, the couple is taking care of their son from their current living expenses. However, they estimate the annual cost of supporting Peter will be €35,000 in nominal terms in 10 years, at which point they believe they will no longer be able to provide for him. This amount is expected to remain relatively constant in real terms. Using some assumptions around life expectancy, we estimate that the present value of these costs amounts to €800,000.

Next, we inquire about the couple's investment preferences, to which they respond with the following:

- They do not want to experience more than a 20% drop in the overall value of their investment portfolio.
- The Schmitts like to feel "in control" and wish to invest in instruments they can liquidate easily.

Reading 27

13 Reproduced from Level III CFA Curriculum reading "Case Study in Risk Management: Private Wealth," Exhibit 24, with permission from CFA Institute.

- Despite Eurolandia's stability, they worry about inflation.
- They do not want to make investments in real estate funds.

Because the Schmitts' income needs are being met by their pension income and annuities, their ability to take risk in their investment accounts is much higher than that of other couples that may need to use such accounts to supplement their pension income. However, based on Jessica's comments about not wanting to see their portfolio value decrease more than 20% in any year, their willingness to take risk is lower.

Because there are multiple objectives, it is appropriate to use a goals-based asset allocation approach. Using a combination of a goals-based investing techniques and capital market assumptions for the major asset classes (including Eurolandian equities), we come up with the following proposal:

Figure 27.15: Investment Portfolio and Goals as the Schmitts Enter Retirement[14]

Existing Asset Allocation	Current Allocation (€)	Goals	Time Horizon	Recommended Asset Allocation
Liquid funds (cash proceeds from pension lump sum)	165,000	Help Roxane with property purchase deposit	<1 year	Keep funds in cash
Inflation-protected government bond funds	380,000	Care for Peter	10 years	Inflation-protected bonds 45% (739,000)
Corporate bond funds	370,000	Inheritance for Roxane (amount undefined) and funding for unexpected expenses	Up to 25 years	Corporate bond funds 10% (164,000)
Passively managed equity funds	750,000			Global equities 35% (575,000), including actively managed equity funds in Jessica's private pension plan; Eurolandian equities 10% (164,000)
Jessica's private pension plan (actively managed equities)	131,250			
Total	**Approximately 1.8 million**			

14 Reproduced from Level III CFA Curriculum reading "Case Study in Risk Management: Private Wealth," Exhibit 26, with permission from CFA Institute.

We justify this recommendation using the following comments:

- To help Roxane with a down payment on a new home, we recommend keeping the funds received from the pension lump sum in cash.
- We calculated the present value of Peter's care costs to be €800,000. In the investment portfolio, we should allocate this amount to inflation-protected government bonds to maintain purchasing power.
- The majority of the remaining balance should be allocated to global equities to allow the investment portfolio to benefit from long-term stock returns.

Notice the portfolio is already invested in various asset classes, so a transition will require the couple to realize capital taxes. Therefore, we should recommend these moves are made in a matter that takes advantage of capital gains tax exemptions, if applicable.

MODULE QUIZ 27.4

Lynn and Michael are 65 years old and have reached the early retirement stage of their careers. They currently have no debt outstanding and, over the course of their lives, have built up a combined investment portfolio value of $5 million. They meet with their advisor, Jamie Rodriguez, CFA, to discuss the following objectives in retirement:

- Live a comfortable retirement with their annual expenses covered. Starting next year, they estimate their annual living expenses will be $100,000 before tax.
- Set aside $1 million (in today's dollars) to leave to their three children, Kyle, Jacob, and Grant, in 30 years.
- Go on vacation twice a year, the total cost of which should amount to roughly $20,000 per year.

Throughout the conversation, Jamie inquires about the couple's risk tolerance. Lynn explains that she made a few bad investments earlier in her career and doesn't think she could stomach a drawdown of more than 20% in any given year. Michael shares that he wants more upside potential in their portfolio and wants to invest a significant portion of it in the stock market.

1. **Describe** and **justify** Lynn's ability and willingness to take risk.

Reading 27

2. Based on the couple's objectives, **describe** and **justify** which asset allocation technique Jamie should follow, and what kind of asset allocation recommendation (conservative, moderate, or aggressive) he should make across the different objectives.

   a. Asset allocation technique

   b. Asset allocation

      i. Live a comfortable retirement

      ii. Leave $1 million (in today's dollars) to their three children

      iii. Go on vacation twice a year

KEY CONCEPTS

LOS 27.a

Risk exposures during the early career stage:

A family in the early career stage will have little financial assets, and economic assets will be primarily human capital.

Earnings risk: There is a risk of earnings loss from unemployment and/or disability.

Premature death risk: Spouses and children need protection against an untimely death of a spouse and the subsequent loss of income.

LOS 27.b

Managing risk exposures during the early career stage:

Earnings risk: A family should accumulate a savings reserve to protect against unemployment, as well as take out disability insurance.

Premature death risk: A family should purchase life insurance. The amount can be determined using the *human life value* and/or *needs analysis* methods.

LOS 27.c

Risk exposures during the career development stage:

Earnings risk: There is a risk of earnings loss from unemployment and disability. Risk increases with rising income, as well as if there is an increase in the number of dependents.

Premature death risk: Early passing can set surviving family members back in lifestyle, plus there may be an additional decrease in income if the surviving spouse becomes the primary caregiver for children.

Investment portfolio: Even if the family has built up investment savings, the portfolio may not be properly diversified or may be too correlated to human capital.

Retirement goals: Retirement income objectives must be met.

LOS 27.d

Managing risk exposures during the career development stage:

Earnings risk: To protect against unemployment, three to six months of expenses should be accumulated. To protect against disability, disability insurance should be purchased (and updated to reflect revised salary projections).

Premature death risk: Families should purchase and/or update their life insurance policy to reflect expenses and salary projections.

Investment portfolio: This should be properly allocated and diversified against human capital.

Retirement goals: Proper savings goals should be developed. Asset allocation in retirement and savings accounts should match the objectives of these goals.

LOS 27.e

Risk exposures during the peak accumulation stage:

Earnings risk: There is a risk of earnings loss from unemployment and disability. Risk increases with rising income, as well as if there is an increased number of dependents.

Premature death risk: Premature death can set surviving family members back in lifestyle. Employment income may be impacted if the spouse takes on additional childcare duties.

Investment portfolio: Investment portfolios may not be appropriately allocated for current life stage and/or for the objectives to be met in retirement.

Retirement goals: Income objectives in retirement should be identified.

LOS 27.f

Managing risk exposures during the peak accumulation stage:

Earnings risk: As a hedge against unemployment, three to six months of expenses should be built up. To protect against disability, disability insurance should be purchased and/or updated to reflect updated salary projections. It may be appropriate to decrease insurance coverage at this stage to reflect the shortened time horizon.

Premature death risk: Life insurance should be updated. It is likely that the appropriate amount of insurance will decrease because the time horizon has been shortened.

Investment portfolio: This should be reallocated and rebalanced to reflect shortened time to retirement. It may be appropriate to reallocate to a balanced fund.

Retirement goals: Savings goals and asset allocation recommendations should reflect income objectives in retirement.

LOS 27.g

Risk exposures during the early retirement stage:

Retirement income: The retiree is no longer contributing to a retirement account, so income is known. The family must be able to match expenses with a reasonable income objective.

Investment portfolio: The investment portfolio may not match family goals for this life stage.

LOS 27.h

Managing risks to an individual's retirement lifestyle goals:

Retirement income: The family should consider purchasing annuities and/or taking lump sum distributions from pension plans (if applicable) to maximize potential income and tax benefit.

Investment portfolio: The investment portfolio should be allocated to match objectives and the time horizons of those objectives.

ANSWER KEY FOR MODULE QUIZZES

Module Quiz 27.1

1. **B** In their early career stage, people have many working years ahead of them, and thus tend to be richly endowed with human capital—especially if they are trained in fields that are in high demand. (LOS 27.a)

2. **B** People that are young and rich in human capital can afford to take more investment risk because they have ample time to recoup investment losses, plus they will have opportunities to invest labor income ahead of them during their working career. The other two reasons are reasons for someone in their early career stage to not invest in their portfolio aggressively. (LOS 27.b)

3. **C** In the early career stage of life, a home purchase will increase a person's vulnerability to unexpected short-term outlays: their ability to pay unexpected bills will be limited if they use their limited savings as a down payment or to cover transaction costs. (LOS 27.b)

Module Quiz 27.2

1. **B** It is difficult to directly insure against earnings risk arising from loss of employment. Financial advisors typically recommend that their clients build up a savings "buffer" amounting to approximately six months' worth of normal expenditures. This allows employees to self-insure themselves to be able to cope with job loss. (LOS 27.c)

2. **B** Individuals should hold an investment portfolio with as low as possible correlation to their human capital. They should also steer clear of concentrated holdings in favor of diversification. Financial advisors generally recommend low-cost pooled investment vehicles, specifically funds that are diversified across a broad range of regions, sectors, and securities. (LOS 27.d)

3. **B** If the client has children, his level of insurance coverage will need to be reviewed and potentially increased significantly. Under the *human life value* method, the amount of coverage that a life insurance policy should provide is estimated as the amount of future earnings that must be replaced, which is based on current and future salary. (LOS 27.d)

Module Quiz 27.3

1. **Disability Insurance Coverage for Brandon and Eileen**

	Eileen	Brandon
Post-tax income to be replaced (salary × (1 – 0.2))	80,000	48,000
Annual disability coverage from government assistance (salary × 0.3)	30,000	18,000
Shortfall	50,000	30,000
Benefit period (until retirement)	10 years	10 years
Assumed annual benefit adjustment	4%	2%
Discount rate	3%	3%

Calculating the present value of future earnings replacement required for Eileen:

- Growth-adjusted discount rate = 1.03/1.04 – 1 = –0.96%.
- Set the calculator to annuity due mode (BGN) using the keystrokes 2nd PMT 2nd ENTER.
- The PV of future earnings replacement is calculated using the TVM keys: 10 N; –0.96 I/Y; 50,000 PMT; CPT PV = –522,383.

The amount of additional disability insurance coverage Eileen should take out is **$522,400**.

Calculating the present value of future earnings replacement required for Brandon:

- Growth-adjusted discount rate = 1.03/1.02 – 1 = 0.98%.
- With calculator in BGN mode, using the TVM keys: 10 N; 0.98 I/Y; 30,000 PMT; CPT PV = $287,232.

The amount of additional disability insurance coverage Brandon should take out is **$287,200**.

(LOS 27.e)

2. Even though Eileen received such a large salary increase, the time horizon until retirement has shortened. Therefore, the present value of future earnings not covered by the government assistance program may now actually be less than the current disability coverage. (LOS 27.e)

3. **C** The idea behind goals-based investing is to disaggregate an investor's portfolio into multiple sub-portfolios, each designed to fund a goal that has its own probability of success and time horizon. (LOS 27.f)

Module Quiz 27.4

1. a. Willingness

   Lynn's willingness to take risk is low. She mentions making a few bad investments earlier in her career, which has made her cautious. Additionally, Lynn said she doesn't think she could stomach a 20% drawdown in any given year.

   b. Ability

   Lynn's ability to take risk is high. She and Michael currently have a portfolio of $5 million, and their income needs are $120,000 next year. Even though they wish to set aside $1 million, that's still 3% ($120,000 / $4,000,000) of income needs per year.

   (LOS 27.g)

2. a. Asset allocation technique

   Jamie should follow a goals-based asset allocation technique. Lynn and Michael have multiple objectives that span multiple time periods. Jamie should recommend dividing their portfolio into sub-portfolios.

   b. Asset allocation

   i. Live a comfortable retirement

   This sub-portfolio will represent the largest allocation. Because the income needs are small relative to the total portfolio, the asset allocation can be aggressive. However, given Lynn's low willingness to take risk, this sub-portfolio should be more conservative so as to keep her invested.

   ii. Leave $1 million (in today's dollars) to their three children

   Because this objective culminates 30 years in the future, this sub-portfolio should be invested aggressively (in asset classes like stocks) to grow as much as possible.

   iii. Go on vacation twice per year

   Because this annual income goal is covered by the first objective, the answer should be the same as i.

   (LOS 27.h)

READING 28

Case Study in Risk Management: Institutional

EXAM FOCUS

The focus of this reading is risk considerations associated with the portfolio strategy of an institutional investor. A fictional sovereign wealth fund is the case study for the reading, which illustrates the risks associated with direct investments in illiquid assets. The case study also has a strong focus on environmental, social, and governance (ESG) risks. As a Level III candidate, you will be required to analyze and quantify a wide variety of risks as the case study develops over time.

This reading also includes a variety of risk management and measurement approaches and introduces the components of an enterprise risk management (ERM) system. It is important to be able to recognize the strengths and weaknesses of an ERM system in exam questions and be able to recommend improvements.

MODULE 28.1: FINANCIAL RISKS FACED BY INSTITUTIONAL INVESTORS

Video covering this content is available online.

LOS 28.a: Discuss financial risks associated with the portfolio strategy of an institutional investor.

Risk Management for Institutional Investors

Risk management is concerned with the impact of events and exposures to risk factors that may prevent an organization from achieving its long-term objectives. Risks explored in this reading include financial risks such as market and liquidity risk, and non-financial risks such as operational and reputational risk.

Investors are increasingly interested in **environmental**, **social, and governance (ESG) issues** and want to engage with portfolio companies ever more closely to monitor business plans and activities. Global issues such as climate change, sustaining the environment, fair treatment of labor, employee health and safety, and addressing standards of living in the poorest nations are becoming important considerations when choosing investment assets. How might these ESG issues impact investors?

Investors are keen to avoid being associated with any adverse publicity and potential **reputational damage** from investing in companies with negative environmental, social, and governance impacts, sometimes referred to as **headline risk**. The investment strategy of aligning portfolio assets to benefit from the ongoing ESG transition to a more sustainable world is attracting a lot of interest as a medium to long-term investment strategy.

Institutional Investor Risk Objectives

Pension funds provide retirement income to plan members. The key risk is the inability to meet contractual pension payouts to beneficiaries when due.

Endowments and foundations aim to provide financial support to current and future beneficiaries, so maintaining *intergenerational equity* (i.e., being fair to current and future generations). The key risk is the inability to provide sufficient financial support to the budget of the institution, preventing the institution from fulfilling its mission and purpose.

Sovereign wealth funds have varying objectives but, in general, provide government funding in either the short, medium, or long term. The case study later in this reading is a fictitious sovereign wealth savings fund set up to transfer wealth to future generations over the long term. Typically, the proceeds from the discovery and sale of valuable natural resources forms the capital invested in sovereign wealth savings funds.

Banks and insurance companies focus mainly on asset-liability management. Banks borrow short term and lend long term, creating an inherent duration mismatch, which introduces liquidity risk and interest rate risk. Banks aim to earn the spread between lending rates and funding rates, known as the net interest margin.

Insurance companies also need to fund the products they sell, which may be a contingent claim many years in the future (e.g., a life insurance policy). Both banks and insurance companies are required to hold minimum levels of solvency capital and are not the focus of this reading.

Risk Consideration: Illiquid Assets

The **endowment model** assumes a long, often perpetual time horizon. Institutions such as university endowments aim for real long-term growth to fund their future spending, yet also need to be fair and equitable to current students.

To achieve long-term growth, institutions turn up the risk dial and include high allocations to illiquid asset classes such as private equity, real estate, hedge funds, natural resources, and infrastructure. However, this creates a dilemma for the institution. With large allocations to illiquid assets, how does an organization meet its current liquidity spending needs, both in normal market conditions and in a crisis? There is a saying, "You can't eat an illiquid asset."

This leads to the risk that an organization is unable to make the very payments that the institution was set up to provide. It is important to find the right balance between liquid and illiquid assets and to carefully plan sources of contingency funding.

PROFESSOR'S NOTE

Before the financial crisis in 2008, the Harvard Endowment held approximately 55% of its portfolio in private equity, hedge funds, and real assets. Between July 1 and October 31, 2008, the endowment fell 22%, a drop of $8 billion. Harvard faced a liquidity crisis. How do you fund current spending with illiquid assets? Ultimately, Harvard chose to borrow to secure the funding needed rather than suffer losses by selling illiquid assets at deep discounts.

Risk Consideration: Types of Liquidity Risk

Liquidity risk has different dimensions and definitions. **Market liquidity** (a.k.a. asset liquidity) refers to how quickly an asset can be sold at a fair price. The relative size of a holding versus the market volume is an important factor, as is market turnover and current trading conditions. For example, selling 500 shares will be easier than selling 500,000. Selling in normal trading conditions will be very different from selling in a crisis, when many investors are heading for the exits at the same time.

Funding liquidity risk is the risk of being unable to meet financial obligations when due. The Harvard Endowment in 2008 is a good example to illustrate both types of liquidity risk. Being unable to sell a large proportion of portfolio assets, except at fire sale prices, illustrates asset illiquidity. However, being able to raise funds via borrowing to meet spending obligations illustrates that Harvard had available sources of funding liquidity.

Risk Consideration: Liquidity in a Crisis

In normal market conditions, portfolios may perform in line with long-term expectations, liquidity is plentiful, and market sentiment is positive. In crisis conditions, many markets react negatively to uncertainty and liquidity disappears as investors run for the exits.

Notice how funding liquidity and market liquidity are connected. In a crisis, sources of funding often dry up or become expensive (such as securitizations). At the same time, market liquidity can also fall, leaving investors with illiquid assets and liquidity funding shortages.

Liquidity Needs and Sources for Institutional Investors

Liquidity outflows will vary considerably depending on the contractual obligations of each institutional investor. Pensions have contractual payments to retirees due today and promised future payments to active plan members. Endowments and foundations may have more discretion over their current and future spending plans. Sovereign wealth funds may have long-term multigenerational time horizons or be required to support a government budget deficit today.

Liquidity outflows can also be in the form of **capital calls**. Private equity investments call for investor capital in stages, with investors receiving capital calls, often at short notice, making liquidity planning more difficult. Capital calls are a good reason not to overcommit to this asset class and to provision the required liquidity funding. The **denominator effect** is the risk that portfolio allocations to illiquid assets increase due to capital calls.

Liquidity inflows include pension contributions and donations for endowments and foundations. Inflows also include investment distributions received from illiquid investments such as private equity. Donations can fluctuate, especially in economic downturns, as donors may be less able to contribute.

Portfolio rebalancing is more difficult to implement with illiquid assets. Rebalancing a portfolio back to the agreed strategic asset allocation requires selling and buying portfolio assets. This will be more costly to achieve with substantial illiquid holdings in normal market conditions and may not be possible at all in a crisis. Portfolio assets held for liquidity include cash and fixed income; however, the endowment model aims for long-term growth with lower allocations to these liquid assets.

Risk Consideration: Illiquid Assets and Return Smoothing

Return smoothing results from investments in illiquid assets, such as private equity and real estate, held for long time periods in private markets. The lack of transactions in these illiquid private markets creates a valuation problem. How do we value the assets with no recent transactions? Portfolio valuations are, instead, based on appraisal estimates that lag "true" values. Smoothing creates a false picture of volatility by applying a downward bias.

The **impact of smoothing** in a rising market is that asset values and return estimates are too low, leading to falsely low return volatility. In a falling market, asset values and return estimates are too high, leading again to a false picture of low volatility. The common impact of smoothing on return volatility is that it appears low, creating a false impression of lower risk.

Using **smoothed data** results in poor decision-making in asset allocation. Assets with smoothed returns appear to have lower correlations with the rest of the portfolio. A consequence may be to overallocate to illiquid assets aiming for increased portfolio diversification. In reality, the assets have higher "true" volatility and higher correlations with portfolio assets, so relying on smoothed data is misleading.

Public market equivalents are an effective proxy for returns in private markets. Using small-cap equities as a proxy for private equity is an example of this approach. A second approach is to unsmooth the illiquid asset returns (i.e., bring back the true volatility by removing the first- and higher-order serial correlations in observed returns).

PROFESSOR'S NOTE

A model to estimate volatility from smoothed returns is included in the Volatility Forecasting section of Reading 2: Capital Market Expectations, Part 2: Forecasting Asset Class Returns.

Risk Consideration: Direct vs. Indirect Investments in Illiquid Assets

Direct investments in illiquid asset classes, such as private equity and infrastructure, are in the form of sole or co-ownership (co-investing) of a private company.

Advantages of direct investments in illiquid assets are:

- Control over individual investment assets.
- Increased portfolio liquidity due to control over the timing of exits.
- Access to more detailed firm information and business plans.
- Avoids paying fund management fees (e.g., 2% per annum (pa) and 20% profit sharing over a hurdle return).

Disadvantages of direct investments in illiquid assets are:

- Portfolio concentration risk results given the challenge to diversify across enough projects.
- Attracting and retaining in-house expertise is challenging and expensive.
- Directly owning a business can lead to additional liabilities (e.g., products, customers, legal, health and safety, employee welfare, and environmental).
- Being a direct owner increases reputational risk due to being closely associated with a firm should problems occur.

Indirect investments in illiquid asset classes, such as private equity and infrastructure, are in the form of investment funds via a third-party investment manager.

Advantages of indirect investments in illiquid assets are:

- Increased diversification across individual projects reduces idiosyncratic risks. It is common to also diversify across project vintage years (the year an investment is first made).
- Specialized fund management expertise can be outsourced, so there is no need to recruit, retain, and compensate an internal team.
- Liability is limited to only the funds invested.

Disadvantages of indirect investments in illiquid assets are:

- Little control over choice of portfolio assets.
- Less information available on individual assets.
- Lower portfolio liquidity, as no control over the timing of exits.
- Payment of fund management fees, typically 2% annual management and 20% share of profits above a hurdle return.
- Uncertain timing of capital calls, which creates liquidity risks.

Managing Liquidity Risk

Institutional investors use various tools to estimate and manage their liquidity needs.

A five-step liquidity management process is as follows:

Step 1: Establish liquidity risk parameters (policy guidelines, escalation triggers).

Step 2: Assess the liquidity of the current portfolio (measure vs. guidelines; monitor).

Step 3: Develop a cash flow model (project future expected cash flows).

Step 4: Stress test liquidity needs (and cash flow projections).

Step 5: Plan for emergencies (a.k.a. a contingency funding plan; what to liquidate, other funding options).

MODULE QUIZ 28.1

1. You are reviewing indirect investments in private equity. Which of the following is *most accurate* of this investment approach?
   A. Indirect investments decrease portfolio liquidity.
   B. Indirect investments incur annual fund management fees and avoid profit sharing.
   C. Indirect investments have higher asset concentrations.
2. Which of the following is *least accurate* of unsmoothed returns?
   A. Volatility is biased downward.
   B. Market transactions are plentiful.
   C. Appraisals are rarely used.
3. **Identify** *two* disadvantages of direct investments in private asset classes.

MODULE 28.2: ENTERPRISE RISK MANAGEMENT

Video covering this content is available online.

LOS 28.e: Evaluate strengths and weaknesses of an enterprise risk management system and recommend improvements.

Perspectives of Risk Management

Top-down perspective is set by the board of directors and the chief investment officer (CIO). It defines the overall risk tolerance, return objectives, and overall investment guidelines for the institution. It also establishes an enterprise risk management framework to optimize risk and return decisions, coordinate risk planning and actions, and help make better strategic business decisions.

Bottom-up perspective is taken by the investment team tasked with implementing the investment strategy. This involves measuring, monitoring, and reporting risk exposures of individual portfolios and asset classes. An internal investment team could be in place or hire external asset managers and monitor progress toward the overall return and risk objectives.

Portfolio-level risk is a function of the correlations and covariances of the assets in the portfolio. Assets, risk factors, and correlations will likely behave very differently in crisis periods.

Asset class-level risk requires detailed information that may be challenging to obtain. For public securities, such as equities, detailed information will likely be readily available, whereas for privately held investments, such as private equity or hedge funds, information may be less detailed and available less frequently.

Returns-based risk systems focus on the analysis of an investment manager's historic returns for a fund or strategy. Note the assumption that past performance is helpful in estimating future performance and evaluating manager skill.

Holdings-based risk systems have access to the details of the underlying assets held in the fund. Access to this granular level of data may not be available, especially for hedge funds aiming to maintain confidentiality over proprietary investment strategies. Holdings-based systems are more costly and time consuming to analyze and implement.

Absolute risk measures risk on a stand-alone basis.

Relative risk compares risk and return to a suitable benchmark.

Short-term risk metrics focus on estimating short-term losses. Calculations of volatility, value at risk, and conditional value at risk focus on relatively short time periods (all discussed later in this reading).

Long-term risk metrics, including Monte Carlo simulation, provide estimates of asset values and cash flow spending over longer time periods. Monte Carlo simulation is a powerful tool for exploring various assumptions, portfolio allocations, and spending strategies and is able to incorporate the effects of rebalancing strategies.

Quantitative models are a useful resource in risk management (e.g., value at risk, stress testing, and Monte Carlo simulation). Behind every model are assumptions such as distributions, data periods, time horizons, growth, inflation, and default rates that drive future estimates and values. Rather than predict the future, these models aim to show a range of possible futures.

Qualitative risk assessments are also important in risk management. Risks such as reputational risk and operational risk are very difficult to quantify. The **four eyes** principle (two heads are better than one) is an important resource in risk (i.e., discussing risks, sharing experience, and cross-functional investment committees).

Human biases from personal experience and beliefs influence both quantitative and qualitative approaches in the assumptions chosen. For example, many U.S. credit practitioners had not experienced real estate price declines until 2008.

Due Diligence and Ongoing Risk Monitoring

Investing in alternative assets such as hedge funds, private equity, and real assets requires considerable due diligence to assess financial, operational, and investment risks prior to investing.

Due diligence evaluating an investment team, its operations, risk management practices, custodians, safekeeping of assets, and the business ethics of a firm is essential. A growing component of due diligence covers environmental, social, and governance issues, discussed later in this reading.

Applying a Enterprise Risk Management Framework to Institutional Investors

Enterprise risk management (ERM) is a top-down approach in which an organization decides which risks to take and which to avoid or transfer to achieve its purpose and objectives.

ERM typically includes all risks faced by an organization, including major risks such as:

- Credit risk.
- Market risk.
- Operational risk.
- Liquidity risk.
- Reputational risk.
- Environmental, social, and governance risks.

ERM starts with strong governance from the board of directors and clearly defines risk tolerances and return objectives creating a coordinated risk management framework with clear accountabilities throughout the organization.

A typical risk management process involves the following steps:

Step 1: Identify risks.

Step 2: Measure risks.

Step 3: Perform risk mitigation and management.

Step 4: Monitor risks.

Step 5: Report risks.

Step 6: Use analysis and strategic planning.

Enterprise Risk Management Framework

The **board of directors** sets the overall risk tolerance and return objectives for the organization. The risk framework will usually include an internal investment committee and CIO. The investment committee will include senior leaders across the organization to leverage strategic experience and risk expertise.

An **investment policy statement (IPS)** is the investment plan specifically tailored to the organization's objectives and constraints, acting as a route map toward achieving the required return objectives.

Risk tolerance is defined within the IPS. Specific risk tolerances can be set for the following:

- Volatility.
- Maximum drawdown.
- Value at risk and conditional value at risk.
- Leverage, derivatives, and short positions.
- Limits on illiquid holdings.
- Maximum tracking error budgets.

The objective is not to minimize or eliminate risk but instead to optimize the compensation for taking the risk (i.e., take the right level of risk for the institution).

Risk Measurement Methodologies

Value at risk (VaR) is an estimate of an unexpected loss of an asset or portfolio, at a given confidence level, for a given holding period. Unexpected losses are low frequency, high severity events.

- Expected losses (high frequency, low severity)
- Unexpected losses (low frequency, high severity)
- Catastrophic losses (very low frequency, very high severity)

VaR defines unexpected losses at a chosen confidence level, typically 95%, 99%, or 99.9%.

Consider an example of a 1-day, 95% VaR estimate of $1 million.

- The confidence level is 95%, meaning we assume that 95% of the time, the maximum loss will be $1 million.
- The significance level is 5%, also known as the error rate, meaning that 5% of the time the loss will be larger than the $1 million estimate.

A common misconception is that VaR describes the maximum possible loss. In the previous example, there is a 5% chance that the losses will exceed the VaR estimate of $1 million and fall into the catastrophic loss category.

When selecting a VaR holding period, it is important to consider the *liquidity of the asset* or portfolio. For many years, regulators assumed a 10-day VaR holding period for market risk, assuming that most assets can be liquidated in 10 days. The 2008 crisis showed that, for many assets, 10 days is insufficient, and so regulation now requires the consideration of longer holding periods.

While VaR is a useful tool to explore unexpected losses, consideration must also be given to *catastrophic losses* that lie in the tail of the distribution *beyond the VaR estimate*.

Conditional VaR is defined as the *average loss beyond a VaR estimate*. Conditional VaR is also widely referred to as expected shortfall and expected tail loss.

Consider an example of a 1-day, 95% VaR estimate of $1 million.

- Conditional VaR focuses on the tail of the loss distribution, beyond the VaR estimate.
- It explores the potential for losses to be higher than the VaR scenario (i.e., explores catastrophic losses).
- It takes an average of the losses beyond the VaR estimate.
- It is a useful complement to VaR to explore non-normal market conditions.

Stress testing and scenario analysis are also important risk tools to explore the uncertainty of the future. Business models estimate future revenues, costs, and earnings using realistic assumptions today. Stress testing explores how *changes in assumptions* affect business revenues, costs, and earnings. A business model may look attractive in normal market conditions; however, conditions may change.

Stress testing identifies *critical factors* driving the success and profitability of a business and explores how unexpected changes in critical factors impact revenues, costs, and earnings. Stress testing is a form of *"what if" analysis*, helping to understand critical vulnerabilities and aiding contingency planning.

Scenario analysis explores historical, current, and hypothetical events that may affect a business. For example, climate scenario analysis is currently a hot topic trying to explore the potential impacts of climate change over time.

Maximum drawdown is the greatest drop in net asset value measured from a high to a low over a specific time period (e.g., the maximum daily drawdown). This is an intuitive risk measure because it is easier to relate to the concepts of declines in value (i.e., drawdowns as opposed to complex calculations).

It is common to use maximum drawdown as a risk-adjusted return measure, such as return over the maximum drawdown, so that the risk taken is in context with the returns earned, and then used as a comparable ratio.

Portfolio factor analysis indicates common drivers and correlations within portfolio assets. It is essential to *look through* portfolio assets to understand common factor exposures.

Examples of portfolio risk factors include the following:

- Growth, value, and momentum.
- Volatility and credit.
- Liquidity.
- Currency.
- Equity.
- Environmental, social, and governance.

Strategically selecting **factor exposures** and **required levels of diversification** across factors are important risk and return considerations.

Tools to explore factor exposures include these:

- Returns-based analysis (analyzing a manager or fund's past returns).
- Holdings-based analysis (analyzing the holdings within a fund).
- Scenario analysis (historic and forward looking).
- Stress testing (of critical risk factors).

Strategic asset allocation (SAA) is the long-term policy asset allocation that sets the optimum course toward achieving an organization's investment objectives. The SAA is implemented internally by an in-house investment team, or externally via third-party investment managers. The portfolio is regularly monitored, reviewed, and rebalanced, in line with the investment policy statement.

Appropriate benchmarks are selected for public equity investments to allow the measurement and assessment of active return (alpha) and active risk (tracking error). To be effective, benchmarks should reflect the manager's style and fulfill the **SAMURAI criteria** contained in the CFA LIII Evaluation Readings (originally defined by Bailey & Tierney 1998).

Characteristics of a valid benchmark are as follows:

- **S**pecified in advance.
- **A**ppropriate and consistent with the manager's investment style.
- **M**easurable.
- **U**nambiguous, able to clearly identify the securities.
- **R**eflective of current investment opinions.
- **A**ccountable, accepted by the manager.
- **I**nvestible, possible to replicate passively.

Currency risk exposures are aligned to risk tolerances and monitored carefully because they can have a large impact on domestic returns when foreign returns are converted back to the reporting currency. The IPS will specify passive, semiactive, or active currency approaches, depending on risk tolerance, experience, and expertise in this area.

Currency hedging can be costly and more difficult to achieve in emerging markets due to the lower availability of derivative instruments.

Allocation drift is the drift away from the desired strategic asset allocation. Regular rebalancing strategies are agreed on to bring the portfolio back in line with the strategic asset allocation.

Reporting to stakeholders means reporting to bodies such as to the internal investment committee and the board of directors.

MODULE QUIZ 28.2

1. A risk analyst estimates a 95%, 10-day VaR of $1.25 million. The investment committee asks the analyst to change the VaR model assumptions. Which of the following is correct?
   A. An increase in the significance level will increase the VaR estimate.
   B. A decrease in the holding period will reduce the VaR expected loss.
   C. An increase in the confidence level will increase the conditional VaR.
2. Which of the following is *least accurate* of an enterprise risk management system?
   A. Risk tolerance is set by the chief investment officer.
   B. Maximum drawdown provides short-term risk estimates.
   C. Returns-based risk systems are more likely to be preferred to holdings-based risk systems with hedge fund risk analysis.
3. **Identify** *three* steps in the enterprise risk management process.

Video covering this content is available online.

MODULE 28.3: ENVIRONMENTAL AND SOCIAL RISKS FACED BY INSTITUTIONAL INVESTORS

LOS 28.b: Discuss environmental and social risks associated with the portfolio strategy of an institutional investor.

Externalities, Responsible Investing, and Universal Ownership

Externalities are costs or benefits received resulting from the actions of third parties. For example, during the COVID-19 pandemic, enforced lockdowns led to commercial winners and losers. Sectors such as hospitality and retail were negatively affected; however, the enforced switch to online business also brought new opportunities for growth and innovation.

Principles for responsible investing (PRI) is a voluntary framework developed in 2006 by the United Nations in collaboration with the investment community, to incorporate ESG issues into investment analysis and decision-making. A key theme of the framework is for investors to be **active owners** engaging with portfolio firms and seeking ESG disclosures. The aim is to understand current ESG exposures (e.g., carbon dependencies from fossil fuels) and review adaption plans and revised business models for those businesses needing to change to a zero-carbon world.

Universal ownership is a concept that applies to large institutional investors such as pension funds and sovereign wealth funds that create large well-diversified portfolios. The concept of being a universal owner is that, in large portfolios, these investors have their share of both winners and losers from externalities.

For example, a portfolio firm that pollutes a river to save costs may well be increasing costs for other firms in the portfolio that rely on the availability of natural resources, such as clean water. The universal owner does not benefit from investing in firms following such practices. Instead, the universal owner benefits from raising ESG standards overall across society.

Environmental and Social Factors

Institutional investors are increasingly incorporating environmental and social factors into investment decisions alongside traditional financial factors. A common strategy is to align portfolio exposures to sectors, industries, and firms, which are likely to prosper in transitioning to a more sustainable society. Conversely, it is important to avoid investing in firms with poor management practices in the treatment of their workforce, health, and safety or with environmental issues.

Environmental Issues

- Air and water pollution.
- Carbon emissions and climate change.
- Energy efficiency.
- Water scarcity and waste management.
- Deforestation and biodiversity.

Social Issues

- Human rights and labor standards.
- Gender and diversity.
- Occupational health and safety.

- Customer satisfaction and product responsibility.
- Data security and privacy.
- Community relations and charities.

Climate Risks and Opportunities

The **2015 Paris Climate Agreement** encouraged countries and companies to reduce or eliminate carbon emissions, in order to limit global temperature increases to 2 degrees Celsius (+2DC) above pre-industrial levels. Individual countries determine their own nationally determined contributions (NDCs), which are pledges toward reducing their national carbon emissions.

While this was a positive step in the right direction, current levels of global NDC pledges to reduce carbon emissions are insufficient. To achieve the Paris Agreement goal, carbon emissions need to fall 25% by 2030 and reach net zero carbon by 2070, according to the Intergovernmental Panel on Climate Change.

The world needs to transition toward a low carbon future, but how easy or difficult will this be, and how fast or slow will the transition happen? Aligning portfolio assets and exposures to those sectors, technologies, and firms likely to benefit from this transition over the medium to long term is a popular ESG strategy. Conversely, there should be a push toward avoiding sectors, technologies, and firms with earnings linked to fossil fuels and outdated unworkable business plans in a future zero-carbon economy.

Stranded assets are resources that are no longer viable and difficult to monetize due to new regulatory restrictions, outdated technology, or shifts in consumer demand (e.g., coal mines, black and white TVs, tape decks, etc.). Firms that fail to adapt may find outdated assets stranded.

The **Inevitable Policy Response (IPR)** is research estimating *when* (not if) governments and policymakers will make the necessary regulatory changes to deliver the climate change needed, to meet the objectives set in the Paris Agreement.

The research uses the term **inevitable**, meaning governments will be forced to act more decisively, as the longer the delay in taking action, the more abrupt the policy changes will need to be in the future, and the greater the economic shocks in transitioning to a zero-carbon world.

The research conducted by Vivid Economics and Energy Transition Advisers, explores the impacts of transition risk on the macroeconomy, sectors, regions, asset classes, and on the implications for land use. The research forecasts that policy responses are required by 2025, which could be abrupt, forceful, and disorderly, and would bring considerable transition risks and economic shocks.

Adapting to climate change will bring winners and losers. Firms that invest in new low carbon technology and that can adapt to new business models will become the early winners. Firms relying on fossil fuels and outdated practices may find higher taxes and limits on activities, and changes to customer preferences could find existing business models are no longer viable. For example, the switch to electric vehicles is already underway and it is accelerating as countries change policies and the regulation of fossil fuels.

Climate Risks: Transition Risk and Physical Risk

Climate transition risk is the risk of being too slow to transition to the new zero-carbon world, effectively left behind with an outdated business model. While it widely accepted that the physical climate risks are the gradual impacts zero-carbon transition is inevitable, the speed that this transition will happen is uncertain.

Drivers of transition risk are as follows:

- Future changes in carbon regulation (e.g., carbon limits, carbon taxes, and bans).
- Higher input costs (of fossil fuels) reducing profit margins.
- Development of new clean technologies (e.g., transition to electric vehicles).
- Shifts in consumer preferences (e.g., transition away from fossil fuels).
- Increased environmental concerns and increased global coordination (e.g., Paris Agreement 2015).

Climate transition risk is systemic in nature, affecting whole sectors, regions, and cities. Systemic impacts from transition risk also include customers, suppliers, distribution channels, transportation, and vital infrastructure. The interconnectedness of local economies to climate risk factors results in the modeling of climate risk scenarios being highly complex.

Physical climate risk has two dimensions:

- Acute physical risks.
- Chronic physical risks.

Acute physical climate risks are *one-off weather events*. Examples include the following:

- Wildfires.
- Hurricanes.
- Storms.
- Droughts and heat waves.

Climate change is increasing the frequency and intensity of these weather events.

For example, the devastation of a hurricane or a wildfire, to human life, as well the potential for damaging businesses, property, and portfolio assets, has been increasing. Hurricane Katrina in the United States in 2005 resulted in 1,800 deaths and $125 billion in damage. In 2020, there were numerous global wildfires, notably in Australia, California, and Oregon, resulting in loss of life and billions of dollars of damage.

Chronic physical climate risks are the *gradual impacts of climate change*. Examples include:

- Rising sea levels.
- Rising temperatures from global warming.

Coastal areas are affected by rising sea levels, with real asset values falling and properties becoming uninsurable. Towns and cities near water may find that the changing climate means having to relocate.

Rising temperatures affect infrastructure, such as roads and railways, leading to the accelerated depreciation of these assets and increased costs. In warm climates, rising temperatures disrupt working conditions and the ability to provide products and services in heat waves.

New Risk Factors: Location and Temperature

Physical climate risks illustrate the importance of the *location of portfolio assets* and the resulting risks of flooding due to sea level rises and one-off weather events such as storms, hurricanes, heat waves, and droughts. Portfolio assets may also be impacted by *increases in local temperatures* in certain locations (e.g., droughts, heat waves, and wildfires).

PROFESSOR'S NOTE

Location and temperature are important risk factors in the case study later in this reading. Be sure to read the background due diligence case study notes carefully.

The **Task Force on Climate-Related Financial Disclosures (TCFD)** encourages organizations, including banks, asset managers, and asset owners, to make climate related disclosures within existing reporting requirements. The TCFD, established in 2015, is a voluntary disclosure framework that encourages organizations to make disclosures in the following areas:

- Governance.
- Strategy.
- Risk management.
- Metrics and targets.

Firms have access to climate-related scenarios to estimate the future impacts to their business models and firm assets, from both physical and transition climate risks.

Climate Risk Responses: Mitigation and Adaptation

Climate risk mitigation and adaptation strategies reduce the vulnerability to both physical and transition climate risks. **Mitigation strategies** reduce the reliance on fossil fuels and carbon intensive resources. Increases in carbon regulation, restrictions on usage, and carbon taxes will likely increase input costs.

Adaptation strategies look to prosper in the zero-carbon world, investing in markets, companies, and technologies that are likely to benefit from the transition. Climate change brings many new opportunities aligned to future decarbonization policy and regulation, and it aligns to changing consumer preferences and the opening of new zero-carbon markets, products, and services.

New opportunities include the following:

- Clean energy (providers and manufacturers of clean energy: solar, wind, hydro).
- Energy efficiency (products and services to improve energy efficiency, such as recycling).

- Batteries and storage (products improving storage capacity; impacts for electric vehicles).
- Smart grids (digitally enhanced electricity grids; integration of clean energy sources).
- Materials (lithium and copper are needed for batteries in clean energy technologies).

Material Social Issues for an Institutional Investor

Outsourcing and Labor Practices

International outsourcing aims to reduce costs and increase efficiency to increase profit margins. Outsourcing partners take over workloads in manufacturing, operational roles, and customer service functions, usually in low-cost labor countries.

Social issues for institutional investors include the following:

- Exploitation of workers.
- Lax employment regulation.
- A lack of unions to protect employees.
- Forced employee overtime.
- Poor working conditions.
- Health and safety practices.
- Equality and human rights.

The **reputational damage** from being associated with the exploitation of local workers is an important risk, sometimes termed **headline risk**. This is especially important with direct international investments in such countries where the institutional investor is both an owner and managing the business. This reputational damage can be costly, leading to consumer boycotts, aggressive action groups, fines, and the enforced switching of supply chains.

Manufacturing and technology brands such as Nike, Apple, and Samsung have all been accused of labor management issues.

Fair and Just

Respecting and protecting the rights of employees in all countries is termed the **"just" transition**. In developed countries, laws and regulations exist to ensure fairness and justice for all, and to prevent the exploitation of the vulnerable. These formal protections often do not exist in developing countries.

As economies transition to low and zero carbon, industries such as coal mining may see the displacement of workers and negative impacts to local communities. In this context, a "just transition" will encourage a dialogue between workers, employers, and policymakers to minimize the human impact and to provide support to those affected.

Sustainable Development

The term "sustainable development" means meeting the needs of the current generation while protecting resources for future generations. This is a familiar concept at Level III as we discuss intergenerational equity [i.e., being fair to both current and future generations (endowments and foundations)]. The context here is sustainability for society as a whole.

The United Nations introduced 17 sustainable development goals in 2005 as part of its 2030 agenda for sustainable development. The goals include commitments to meeting 169 targets across the following areas:

1. No poverty, zero hunger, good health and well-being, quality education.
2. Gender equality, clean water and sanitation, affordable clean energy.
3. Decent work, industry and infrastructure, reduced inequalities, sustainable cities.
4. Responsible consumption and production, climate action, life below water, life on land.
5. Peace, justice, and strong institutions, partnerships for the goals.

Transition to Sustainable Economies

Since the industrial revolution, carbon-intensive industries have developed and expanded, having negative impacts on the world's natural capital.

The world's natural capital includes:

- Air and water.
- Soil geology.
- All living things.

These carbon-intensive industries have been a key driver of climate change.

Transitioning to a sustainable economy aims to protect the world's natural capital, limiting negative impacts on the environment and confronting social inequities. Creating a "just transition" in the change that lies ahead will help people, regions, and countries adapt to a zero-carbon future.

Institutional investors are increasingly engaging with firms on ESG issues, assessing transition plans, reviewing business models, considering climate scenarios, and identifying the firms that are best and worst placed to prosper in the change that lies ahead.

MODULE QUIZ 28.3

1. Which of the following is *least accurate* of the 2015 Paris Agreement on climate risk?
   A. Agreed to limit global temperature rises to +2 degree Celsius versus 2015 levels.
   B. Voluntary pledges from countries to reduce carbon emissions.
   C. Insufficient current reductions in emissions to meet the Paris Agreement targets.
2. Which of the following is *least likely* to be an example of climate transition risk?
   A. Insurers refuse to renew insurance on a coastal property.
   B. Carbon regulation bans the sale of fossil fuel–powered automobiles from 2030.
   C. Carbon taxes increase the cost of goods sold for a manufacturer.
3. **Explain** the concept of a "just" transition, and **identify** the type of risk associated with this concept.

MODULE 28.4: CASE STUDY

Video covering this content is available online.

LOS 28.c: Analyze and evaluate the financial and non-financial risk exposures in the portfolio strategy of an institutional investor.

LOS 28.d: Discuss various methods to manage the risks that arise on long-term direct investments of an institutional investor.

LOS 28.e: Evaluate strengths and weaknesses of an enterprise risk management system and recommend improvements.

Case Study Introduction and Background Information

You work as an analyst for a small sovereign wealth fund in Ruritania (R-SWF), reporting to the head of risk. The R-SWF investment committee is considering new **direct investments** in **private equity** and **infrastructure**. As part of your role, you are evaluating these potential investments and will have the responsibility for monitoring and reviewing any investments made moving forward. The committee has tasked you to review the R-SWF risk management system and recommend improvements.

Republic of Ruritania and the Discovery of Natural Resources

Twenty years ago, Ruritania found large deposits of valuable rare metals used in the manufacturing of computers and technology. Ruritania formed a sovereign wealth fund (R-SWF) to provide growth for future generations. A key goal of the "savings" sovereign wealth fund is to transform nonrenewable assets into diversified financial assets to **share wealth across generations**.

R-SWF Assets

R-SWF contains a diversified portfolio of fixed income, equities, and alternatives. R-SWF has both **direct investments** and investments made via **investment funds**. The alternative investments include private equity, real estate, and infrastructure.

Case Study Sections

The case study is broken down into three sections (referred to as scenes):

- *Scene 1*: **Today**. An investment committee meeting to discuss **two potential new investments**.
- *Scene 2*: **Three years later**. Investment committee meeting to discuss the investment performance of the two investments.
- *Scene 3*: **Two years after Scene 2** (i.e., 5 years from today). Additional information is provided on investment performance.

Scene 1: Investment Committee Meeting Today

Initial Case Facts (1.0)

- The investment committee is considering **two new direct investments** in **private equity** and **infrastructure**. You are supporting the head of risk in discussing the risks of the potential investments at the meeting.
- Investment 1—A **direct infrastructure investment** in an airport.
- Investment 2—A **direct private equity investment** in a beverage manufacturer.

The investment committee participants (and CFA Level III candidates) have the following background information.

- Memo 1A—Background on R-SWF's performance and asset allocation.

- Memo 1B—Details on the proposed **direct infrastructure investment**.
- Memo 1C—Details on the proposed **direct private equity investment**.

PROFESSOR'S NOTE

The background information that follows is part of the R-SWF due diligence process to evaluate these two new investment proposals. This due diligence data is available in advance of the upcoming investment committee meeting that you will be attending. All the case study documents contain many clues that link to the risk concepts and theory covered earlier in the reading. Remember your task is to identify the risks of the two investment proposals and review the strengths and weaknesses of the R-SWF risk management process.

Memo A—Investment Committee Meeting Memo 1.0

TO:	**R-SWF Investment Committee members**
FROM:	**R-SWF Chief Investment Officer**
RE:	**Investment Committee Meeting Agenda**
Distribution:	**Head of Risk, Head of PE, Head of Equities, Head of Infrastructure, and LIII Candidates**

MEETING AGENDA

Review of Asset Allocation:	**Chief Investment Officer**
Review of Infrastructure Investment Opportunity:	**Head of Infrastructure**
Review of Private Equity Investment Opportunity:	**Head of Private Equity**
Risk review—Infrastructure Opportunity:	**Head of Risk + All**
Risk review—Private Equity Opportunity:	**Head of Risk + All**
Summary and Actions:	**Chief Investment Officer**

MEMO 1A—ASSET ALLOCATION BACKGROUND DATA

R-SWF Summary Data

- The Ruritanian Sovereign Wealth Fund was created 25 years ago.
- Latest AUM is $50 billion.
- Over the 25-year time horizon, R-SWF has outperformed its benchmark by 150 bp net of fees.
- Since inception, the fund has experienced some short-term periods of underperformance.

R-SWF Current Asset Allocation

Equities	40%
Fixed Income	9%
Alternatives	50%
Cash	1%

Funding for the **two new direct investments** in **private equity** and **infrastructure** will come from a mix of cash, fixed income, dividends. and receivables. The asset/liability committee (ALCO) will determine the funding mix.

R-SWF Allocation: Alternatives

Real estate	15%
Hedge funds	10%
Infrastructure	10%
Private capital	10%
Natural resources	5%

R-SWF Allocation: Private Capital

Private equity funds	5%
PE direct & co-investments	3%
Private debt funds	1%
Private debt direct	1%

R-SWF Allocation: Infrastructure

Infrastructure funds	7%
Infrastructure direct	3%

MEMO 1B—PROPOSED DIRECT INFRASTRUCTURE INVESTMENT

Overview of Investment Opportunity—Sunnyland Airport

Sunnyland is a frontier market, island nation, with beautiful beaches and a range of hotels. Tourism is currently constrained due to the small airport that can only support light aircraft carrying up to 10 passengers. The local government plans to expand the airport with a new terminal and runway, which will open up tourism to larger aircraft carrying up to 150 passengers. The terminal and runway will be located 2 km and 1 km from the sea, respectively.

R-SWF Sunnyland Airport Investment

- R-SWF is considering a **$100 million investment** in a public-private partnership with the Sunnyland Airport Authority (SAA), on a build-operate-transfer (BOT) basis.
- This potential infrastructure investment of $100 million **represents 0.2%** of the latest R-SWF AUM of $50 billion.
- The Sunnyland Airport infrastructure investment (if undertaken) would represent **approximately 2% of total infrastructure assets** (i.e., $100 million / $5,100 million = 1.96%).
- The expected investment term is 25 years.
- The expected IRR over the full investment term is 15%.
- The R-SWF head of infrastructure believes the potential return on investment in the Sunnyland Airport infrastructure project far outweighs the potential risks.

Sunnyland Airport Project Costs and Funding

- Total project cost of $500 million for the airport terminal (estimated to carry 5 million passengers per annum).
- **Airport operating group (AOG)** providing $33 million of funding and will operate the airport under a fixed fee plus or minus a performance incentive.
- Nonrecourse project finance of $300 million (70/30 debt/equity) with a 15-year term and 3-year grace period.
- **Two-year construction period** with a fixed price construction contract via tender process.
- A **25-year concession** in place with an investor consortium, with entitlements to collect commercial revenue (car parking, duty free, retail), as well as all regulated airport charges (passenger departure and landing charges). The terms of the concession require a payment of a quarterly concession fee of 35% of all revenue to the Sunnyland Airport Authority (SAA).
- Concession agreement requirement that the construction of the airport terminal meet quality and performance standards.

MEMO 1C—PROPOSED DIRECT PRIVATE EQUITY INVESTMENT

Overview of Investment Opportunity—Atsui Beverage Company (ABC)

The Atsui Beverage Company (ABC) is located in the tropical frontier market of Atsui. ABC is the only local manufacturer and seller of carbonated beverages in Atsui; all other beverages are imported. ABC is an unlisted company and is keen to raise funds to modernize its plant.

It is important to the founder of ABC to keep control of the company, and so it is only willing to sell a minority stake in the company to raise private equity capital.

ABC Financial Information

- Revenue for the last 12 months of $50 million, and EBITDA of $7 million. The R-SWF head of PE is optimistic about the **potential for significant improvement in revenue and efficiency** once the plant modernization is completed. **Modernization** will allow ABC to **expand the business** into noncarbonated sports drinks and juices.
- ABC estimates show that productivity will increase significantly once the plant is modernized. Central to the modernization plans is an estimated **40% reduction** in **the labor head count** from 500 to 300 local employees. This reduction in head count will bring **large cost savings** and future higher EBITDA margins.

Atsui Local Information

- Atsui is a landlocked nation, meaning that access to the nearest port is in another nation state via river transportation.
- ABC is located near a river and uses this method of transportation to the port. The **nearby river** is well known for its **unique biodiversity** that flourishes in the tropical climate of Atsui.

R-SWF Atsui Beverage Company (ABC) Investment

- The founder of ABC is offering R-SWF a **minority 35% stake** in the company in return for **$25 million**.
- The ABC investment of $25 million **represents 0.05% of R-SWF total assets** of $50 billion and **0.4% of R-SWF total private equity assets** of $6,025 million (including ABC).
- R-SWF is an experienced private equity investor in both direct and indirect forms of private equity investments. R-SWF is planning to increase its allocation to direct private equity investments, including co-ownership over the next 5 years.
- R-SWF has **two seats on the board of ABC**, which will expand from **five to seven members**. The head of PE plans to take one of these board positions on behalf of R-SWF and no decisions taken as to the second board member.
- The R-SWF head of PE recommends the proposed investment in ABC on the basis that the **potential returns far exceed the potential risks**.

Minutes of the Investment Committee Meeting 1.0

Participants:

- Chief Investment Officer
- Head of Infrastructure
- Head of Private Equity
- Head of Risk
- Head of Equities
- Analysts

Meeting Minutes

Meeting Key Purpose—Chief Investment Officer

To consider the proposed R-SWF infrastructure and PE investments in Sunnyland Airport and the Atsui Beverage Company and specifically discuss the risks of each

Sunnyland Airport Overview—Head of Infrastructure

- Summary of the proposition and background data provided to everyone in the background notes.
- The recent **build-operate-transfer (BOT)** analyst training received excellent feedback.
- Recap of the project financials: Overall airport project cost of $500 million and a 2-year construction period. Our investment commitment would be $100 million, representing 0.2% of AUM.
- The experienced airport operator, **AOG,** will be running the operation and contributing $33 million of its own private equity.
- Balance of project capital (approx. $300 million) from the local government in nonrecourse 15-year debt capital, with a 3-year grace period.

- Expected return on the R-SWF $100 million investment over **25-year investment horizon** is estimated to be 15% IRR.
- Head of infrastructure has visited Sunnyland and noted the lack of natural resources to diversify its economy. **Sunnyland is heavily reliant on tourism,** hence, the need for the airport expansion project.

Atsui Beverage Company (ABC) Overview—Head of Private Equity

- Summary of the proposition and background data provided to everyone in the background notes.
- Head of PE discussed the recent trips to Atsui as part of the due diligence process. Of note was the discovery of a potentially strong product, the **"Mango Special,"** one of a series of **new noncarbonated drinks and juices** that can be expanded once the plant is modernized.
- Recap of the project financials: ABC is offering a **35% ownership stake** in return for a **$25 million investment**. ABC advises that $20 million of the R-SWF $25 million investment will be used for modernization of its plant.
- Head of private equity recapped the efficiency savings from the planned reduction in head count and the potential increases in EBITDA from modernizing the plant, discussed in the background notes. In addition, the opening of the noncarbonated drinks markets, bringing in new revenue streams for ABC.

Risk Discussions on the Atsui ABC Investment: Clarifications from the Head of Private Equity

- **Risk to the cost savings.** Head of private equity clarified that the cost savings are contingent on reducing the workforce from 500 to 300. The chief investment officer suggested there is a risk that local unions and/or local politicians may oppose this reduction in headcount.
- **Reputational risk.** Such an adverse reaction to the modernization could lead to reputational risk for R-SWF and bring conflicts in Ruritania's relations with the Atsui government. Head of private equity explained the plans for community relations with both impacted employees and with the local community in Atsui. ABC will be investing heavily in staff training and development to help the transition.
- **Risk of local and foreign competition.** Question raised about the extent of local competition and the ability of foreign competitors to enter the Atsui beverage marketplace. Head of PE clarified that ABC is the sole beverage manufacturer in Atsui and that the local government applies high import tariffs that have been effective in limiting foreign competitors.
- **Risk of a change of government in Atsui.** Question raised about the upcoming elections in Atsui. Head of risk highlighted the risk that a change in administration may end import tariffs, bringing in foreign competition. The chief investment officer agreed that it is likely that Atsui will reduce import tariffs in the future.

- **Risk of a price war with foreign competitors.** Point made that if tariffs are reduced, large foreign beverage competitors could enter the Atsui beverage market and start a price war. Head of PE suggested ABC has **unique local beverages** such as the **Mango Special** that are popular in the local market. The foreign competitors do not compete with these product lines.
- **Question about exports.** Head of equities asked if ABC is planning to start exporting its products as part of its expansion plans. Chief investment officer advised that the neighboring markets are also tropical frontier countries, where beverages are still a luxury item. Transport to the nearest port is via a river, which does have the potential to open up sales to neighboring markets.
- **Risk of ABC management.** Head of risk raised a question about the **experience, skills, and education** of the **founder,** bearing in mind that R-SWF will only have a minority stake in the business with limited control. The risk of corruption was a follow-on point raised as a potential issue. Head of PE advised that R-SWF will be tracking progress carefully and directly involved in the modernization process. R-SWF has had **lots of co-investing experience** in working with management teams. R-SWF has two seats on the board. Also, extensive due diligence has been carried out with management, suppliers, and customers. Plans are also in place to **incentivize management** to ensure alignment to growth plans and strong oversight.

General Risk Discussions on Both Investments

- **Currency risk.** Head of risk raised the issue of currency risk in frontier markets in general. Volatility of the local currency against the dollar could lead to large losses from currency risk alone. Head of Infrastructure advised that the revenues from the Sunnyland Airport project would be largely in dollars, as customer pricing is geared toward international travel markets. Head of PE advised that dollars are widely used by visitors in Atsui.
- **Local borrowing.** Question raised about the **currency of local borrowing** for both frontier market organizations. Head of infrastructure advised that the $300 million debt in the Sunnyland Airport project is denominated in dollars, as local banks do not have the lending capacity yet.
- **Default risk.** Head of risk raised the question of default risk on the borrowings of each organization to complete their respective capital projects. Head of infrastructure advised that the $300 million debt raised in Sunnyland was **nonrecourse financing**, and the detailed concession agreement clearly outlined the terms of default.
- **Climate risk.** Head of equities identified the **medium to long-term climate risk impact** of **sea level rise** on the 25-year Sunnyland Airport investment, which is less than a kilometer from the sea. Over time and especially at high tides, airport operations may be impacted. Head of Infrastructure advised that drainage systems have been designed to handle projected climate impacts, and the engineers are confident of mitigation plans, based on 1-in-50-year and 1-in-100-year flood scenarios.
- **Local government relations.** Question raised about local relationships between Ruritania and the frontier markets, as both projects will need the support of local administrations. Both the head of PE and of infrastructure advised the projects had the support of the local governments.

- **Sunnyland Airport stress testing.** Head of risk asked about stress testing the assumed 15% IRR returns over the 25-year investment horizon. Risks identified included construction delays, penalties, budget overruns, and variances in revenues. Head of infrastructure discussed research completed of airport traffic scenarios, including **low, base case, and high customer traffic scenarios**. The low case 25-year IRR was in the region of 10%, and the high case was toward 20%. For cost overrun scenarios, a +/– 10% sensitivity has been factored in, which translates to a 25-year 13% IRR. The contracts pass any liabilities for delays or substandard work to the contractor.
- **Risk of a global recession.** Question raised from the head of equities about the impacts on tourism to frontier markets from a prolonged global recession. Sunnyland relies heavily on tourism and would be impacted by a downturn in discretionary spending. Head of infrastructure advised that historically during downturns, airlines have cut prices to stimulate demand and recovered relatively quickly.
- **Coronavirus pandemic and future pandemics.** Head of risk recapped the experience from the COVID-19 pandemic, especially the inability to travel due to restrictions from some locations. The risk of new variants leading to future pandemics and further travel restrictions would have the potential to limit or even halt all revenue for an extended period. Head of infrastructure advised that COVID-19 has resulted in updated contract terms with more emphasis on restructuring and rescheduling finance agreements to allow all parties time to recover from temporary travel restrictions.
- **Tourism portfolio correlation.** Head of PE asked for clarification of R-SWF portfolio exposures to tourism to avoid excessive concentration and sector correlations.

VOTING ON THE SUNNYLAND INFRASTRUCTURE INVESTMENT

- Head of Infrastructure YES
- Head of Risk YES
- Head of PE YES
- Head of Equities YES
- Chief Investment Officer YES

VOTING ON THE ATSUI ABC PRIVATE EQUITY INVESTMENT

- Head of Infrastructure YES
- Head of Risk YES
- Head of PE YES
- Head of Equities YES
- Chief Investment Officer YES

The investment committee approved investments in both projects.

Case Study Questions Based on Investment Committee Meeting 1.0

Question 1:

Evaluate the impact of adding *each* of the proposed investments to the liquidity risk of the R-SWF portfolio. **Justify** your answer.

Question 2:

A key risk in the Sunnyland airport investment is changing volumes of customer traffic. **Explain** and **describe** a form of analysis that you would implement to explore this risk and increase confidence prior to investing.

Question 3:

Explain the financial risks of the upcoming election in Atsui to the proposed private equity investment in ABC.

Answer 1:

The Sunnydale Airport investment of $100 million represents 0.2% of R-SWF total assets and 2% of total infrastructure assets. The Atsui ABC investment of $35 million represents 0.05% of R-SWF total assets and 0.4% of total private equity assets. The conclusion is that both proposed investments are relatively small and so will not affect overall portfolio liquidity.

In addition, both investments are direct investments providing a greater degree of control and discretion over investment exit plans. R-SWF also has a long time horizon and is a "savings sovereign wealth fund" with few contractual needs for income instead structured for growth.

The nature of the planned 25-year investment term in Sunnyland and in growing the business in ABC in Atsui makes each investment relatively illiquid in the short and medium term. However, at the R-SWF portfolio level, due to its relatively small size, liquidity risk is not affected by the addition of these two investments.

Answer 2:

The Sunnyland Airport project depends on attracting an increased number of tourists. Although airport capacity will increase from supporting only light aircraft able to carry a maximum of 10 passengers to supporting larger aircraft carrying up to 150 passengers, there is a key risk in the variability of customer traffic numbers.

A global recession leading to reductions in discretionary spending as well as travel restrictions resulting from future variants in a pandemic are risk factors impacting customer traffic. Scenario analysis will explore the impacts of changes to customer traffic resulting from a range of realistic scenarios. This scenario analysis should incorporate appropriate assumptions affecting frontier markets, as well as data from previous regional downturns and local data from the pandemic.

Each scenario should aim to quantify the financial impacts of variations in traffic on revenues, costs, and earnings, incorporating specific risks and local/regional contagion impacts on Sunnyland. Stress testing is recommended to explore breakeven points and critical customer number levels to maintain viable business models in the short, medium, and longer term.

Answer 3:

The approach is not sufficient to manage the financial risks resulting from a change of government in the upcoming elections. Under the current administration, heavy tariffs on foreign imports protect ABC from foreign competition, allowing it a virtual local monopoly. The CIO estimated that a relaxing of tariffs after the election is a fair assumption. Should this occur, ABC will find new larger entrants into its local market better able to compete on price. ABC does currently have unique local beverages; however, there is the risk of competitors creating similar alternatives once tariffs are reduced.

Scenario analysis is recommended to explore the impacts of a change in tariff, future relations with a changed local administration, and the impacts on regional and international competition prior to investing.

Scene 2: R-SWF Investments 2.0—Extension of Case Facts

Three years have passed since R-SWF made the two direct investments in Sunnyland and Atsui. The investment committee now **plans an investment review of the two projects**. Last month, the first stage of the review focused on financial performance, with the upcoming second stage of the review focusing on **current and potential future risks**.

The following data and updated project information is provided to all investment committee members and CFA Level III candidates.

- **Memo 2A:** Current R-SWF asset allocation and performance
- **Memo 2B:** Update on the Sunnyland Airport infrastructure project and risk discussion
- **Memo 2C:** Update on the Atsui ABC private equity project and risk discussion

Memo 2A—Investment Committee Meeting Memo 2.0

TO:	**R-SWF Investment Committee members**
FROM:	**R-SWF Chief Investment Officer**
RE:	**Investment Committee Meeting 2.0 Agenda**
Distribution:	**Head of Risk, Head of PE, Head of Equities, Head of Infrastructure, and LIII Candidates**

MEETING AGENDA

■ **Review of Asset Allocation:**	**Chief Investment Officer**
■ **Review of the Sunnyland Infrastructure Project:**	**Head of Infrastructure**
■ **Review of the Atsui ABC Private Equity Project:**	**Head of Private Equity**
■ **Risk review – Infrastructure Opportunity:**	**Head of Risk + All**
■ **Risk review – Private Equity Opportunity:**	**Head of Risk + All**
■ **Other Risks:**	**Head of Equities**
■ **Summary and Actions:**	**Chief Investment Officer**

MEMO 2A—ASSET ALLOCATION AND PERFORMANCE DATA

R-SWF Summary Data:

- 28 years since R-SWF inception.
- Latest AUM $56 billion USD (previously $50 billion).
- Over the 28-year time horizon, R-SWF has outperformed its benchmark by 130 bp net of fees (previously 150 bp).
- Since inception, the fund has experienced some short-term periods of underperformance.

R-SWF Updated Asset Allocation:

■ Alternatives	51%
■ Equities: Emerging & Frontier	17%
■ Equities: Developed	12%
■ Fixed Income	9%
■ Cash	1%

A detailed breakdown and analysis of the current asset allocation was provided for the financial review last month.

Memo 2B—Sunnyland Airport Infrastructure Project—Update

Project Update

The **construction of the airport is complete,** with no material cost overruns. The Sunnyland government and airport authority are happy with the quality of the new terminal and its potential to increase tourism.

A **grand opening** of the new terminal is planned for September, just before the start of the October to May tourist season. The airport operating group (AOG) managing the terminal is looking to renegotiate its management contract and raise management fees.

Climate Change

The new runway is only 1 km from the ocean, and concerns are increasing about the medium- to long-term **risk of a rise in sea level** due to climate change. **One-off weather events** such as storms are also increasing in frequency and intensity in the region.

In addition, Sunnyland has experienced hotter temperatures in recent years because of climate change. Previously, the local tourist season was October through May, with tourists avoiding the baking hot summer months. However, hotter May temperatures in recent years risk shortening the Sunnyland tourist season even further.

Risk Discussions on the Sunnyland Infrastructure Investment

Risks Identified:

- **Revenue risk** that airport traffic may be lower than previously estimated.
- **Service quality risk** of underperforming service quality standards, impacting customer experience and reputational risk.
- **Risk of higher than estimated operating and maintenance costs.**
- **Risk of default of AOG**, the operator of the Sunnyland Airport terminal.
- **Expropriation risk** of airport assets by the Sunnyland government.
- **Currency risk** when translating profits back to the reporting currency.
- **Interest rate risk** of future increases in borrowing costs.
- **Other risks** (e.g., climate risks).

Memo 2C—Atsui ABC Private Equity Project—Update

The modernization of the ABC plant is complete.

Economic Recession

Unfortunately, Atsui and the wider region are suffering from an economic recession that started last year. Because beverages are a luxury item, ABC revenues are down.

New Government and Lower Import Tariffs

The elections brought in a **change of government,** which has reduced foreign import tariffs from **100% to 20%**. Speculation is that the new government wants to attract foreign loan finance and reduce barriers to local markets.

Cost Savings and Efficiency

The original plan to **decrease headcount by 40%** has increased to **50%** due to lower revenues in the current recession. Cost savings are slow to realize due to the **strict employment laws in Atsui**, requiring 2-year notice periods. In a drive to cut costs, the ABC management recently **cut employee breaks** from 1 hour to 30 minutes and **removed soap from the restrooms,** asking employees to bring in their own.

Dumping Waste in the Local River

To cut costs, ABC management has been **dumping waste in the nearby river** rather than paying for transport down river to the waste treatment plant. The local river has beautiful fishing and biodiversity, but the dumping of waste is starting to spoil the area.

Risk Discussions on the Atsui ABC Private Equity Investment

Risks Identified:

- **Elimination of import tariffs** no longer providing any protection against foreign competitors.
- **Shifts in market preferences** away from carbonated beverages to healthier alternatives.
- **Quality control** risks of products, services, and compliance with local regulations.
- **Local management risks,** as we are not in control of the operation, being a minority shareholder.
- **Expropriation risk** from the Atsui government.
- **Currency risk** when translating profits to the reporting currency.
- **Other risks** (e.g., climate risks).

Minutes of the Investment Committee Meeting 2.0

Participants:

- Chief Investment Officer
- Head of Infrastructure
- Head of Private Equity
- Head of Risk
- Head of Equities
- Analysts

Meeting Minutes

Meeting Key Purpose—Chief Investment Officer

Following last month's financial review of the Sunnyland Airport and Atsui ABC projects, we agreed to have an updated risk review based on our updated risk analysis.

R-SWF assets have grown by $6 billion to $56 billion over the last 3 years; however, the fund outperformance above benchmark fell from 150 bp to 130 bp due to recent difficulties in real estate markets.

CIO emphasized the growing importance of environmental and social risks and the **increased scrutiny on the fund** from outside observers.

Sunnyland Airport Project Update—Head of Infrastructure

New Airport Terminal

- The new Sunnyland Airport terminal is fully completed and has had great reviews both locally and internationally.
- The construction phase experienced delays beyond the estimated 2-year construction plan, resulting in cost overruns, which according to the contract are liabilities for the contractor. To date, some of the delay penalties are still to be paid and discussions continue with the contractor, the airport operator (AOG), and the government over cost allocations moving forward.

- The official launch of the new terminal is late August, ready for the October through May visitor season. Early bookings are in line with our expectations for Year 1.

Climate Change

- Head of risk made the point that **concerns about the effects of climate change** directly impacting Sunnyland Airport **have increased in the last 3 years**.
- Head of infrastructure advised that the **assumptions used** in the original environmental impact assessment scenarios **have changed**. The original assumptions provided some comfort that rising sea levels and the impact of severe on-off weather events would be at a manageable level. Current discussions with the government in Sunnyland are that the island may need to construct flood barriers, where the cost and effectiveness is still largely unknown.
- Head of equities suggested that **all businesses on the Island** would require **protection from flooding** from sea level rise. This may lead to many joint funding projects and government intervention.
- Head of infrastructure suggested that **new climate taxes** might need be imposed in Sunnyland to cover the costs of constructing flood barriers.

Higher Airport Terminal Management Costs

- Head of infrastructure advised that AOG, the airport operator, has signaled it wants to **negotiate an increased fee** to operate the terminal. Important to have a concession agreement that aligns all interests when the airport traffic begins to rise. Risk that AOG wants out of the contract and leaves us with the problem of finding a new operator.

Atsui ABC Project Update

Modernized Plant but Many Challenges—Update From Head of PE

- The modernization of the ABC plant is now completed. Atsui is in the **middle of a recession**, which has resulted in a devaluation of its currency and **drop in the demand** for ABC beverage products.
- Following the recent elections, the new administration plans to **reduce tariffs on imports** from 100% to 20%, taking away ABC's competitive price advantage
- The planned efficiency savings from reducing head count are slow to materialize, as Atsui employment rights require up to a 2-year notice period for employees. Because of the recession, ABC management plans to lay off up to 50% of its workforce rather than 40% as originally planned. This brings **reputational risk** for R-SWF being associated with significant layoffs in frontier markets.
- ABC has been **dumping waste in the nearby river**, rather than paying transportation for waste treatment, as a way to cut costs. The river has a **unique natural biodiversity,** including a very rare reptile. The actions of ABC are beginning to attract the attention of locals and environmental scientists who are noticing changes to the river.
- ABC management, in an effort to cut costs, has **restricted employee breaks** from 1 hour to 30 minutes and has **removed soap from the restrooms**, requiring employees bring their own soap to work.

Is It Time to Exit the ABC Investment?

- Head of risk raised concerns over reputational risk. While the investment in ABC is not significantly large, the **reputational risks** of being associated with health and safety, social justice, and environmental pollution issues are very significant and potentially very damaging. It is time to exit!
- Head of PE acknowledged the risks raised but suggested retaining the ABC investment.
- CIO discussed the role of educating ABC management in environmental, social, and reputational risks.
- Head of equities also outlined that it is necessary to change the focus of the ABC management incentives, **away from cost cutting**, to instead **incentivize quality management practices**. The question remains as to whether the founder and majority shareholder will be open to changing their management practices if this increases costs.
- Head of equities suggested that if the investment is retained, discussions must open up with the Atsui government. The Atsui government policies of reducing tariffs on imports and mandatory 2-year redundancy periods may lead to the ultimate closure of the ABC factory unless a workable rescue plan can be established.
- CIO acknowledged the **headline risk** of Ruritania being widely reported as associated with the mistreatment of Atsui ABC employees, environmental pollution, and social injustice in this current recessionary environment.

Atsui ABC Investment—Head of Risk Summary

- Engage with ABC management; change the mindset away from just cost cutting to measures of quality that incorporate the ESG risks we have discussed.
- Lobby the Atsui government on the tariffs and 2-year notice period to see if they will help ABC.
- Review progress in 1 year. If no progress, time to look for the exits.
- CIO thanked the head of risk for this summary.

Sunnyland Airport Investment—Head of Equities Summary

- Engage with the Sunnyland government about its plans to adapt to climate change.
- This is a long-term investment; the effects of climate change will intensify with rising sea levels and warmer summers.
- Engaging with the government and the wider community, including the local business leaders and local people, is the way forward.

Case Study Questions Based on Investment Committee Memo 2.0

Question 4:

You are asked by the chief investment officer to **describe** how the following risks will be managed for each investment.

- Shift in market demand toward healthier foods and the reduction in demand for carbonated drinks in Atsui
- Risk that future interest rates will be higher than expected, resulting in higher borrowing costs for the Sunnyland airport project

Question 5:

Identify the primary environmental risk for the investments in Sunnyland Airport and in the Atsui Beverage Company. **Recommend** how each risk can be managed by R-SWF.

Question 6:

Identify a material social risk that applies to both investments that was not identified by the investment committee. **Discuss** how the risk should be managed.

Answer 4:

Shift in customer preferences

ABC can hedge this risk by continuing to diversify its product range to include healthier alternatives. The popular Mango Special is a good example of a locally developed, successful, healthy, noncarbonated beverage. ABC should leverage its experience in beverage product development using natural ingredients and widen its range of natural, healthy product offerings. Investing in research and development, trialing new products, and working closely with customers will help ABC anticipate changes in consumer tastes and market demand.

Protect against rising interest rates

R-SWF should consider hedging its interest rate exposure in the Sunnyland project. Both up-front and opportunity costs of hedging should be incorporated into the analysis, along with any cash flow impacts of hedges. The choice of financial instruments to hedge interest rate exposures in frontier markets is likely to be more limited.

Answer 5:

Sunnyland Airport

The primary environmental risk affecting the investment in Sunnyland Airport is the impact of climate change. First, a rise in sea level (chronic physical climate risk) may affect the airport runway and terminal, potentially disrupting operations, as the airport is less than 1 km from the sea.

This risk of flooding and disruption will increase at high tides. Bearing in mind the long-term nature of this R-SWF investment in Sunnyland, there is a risk that if the rise in sea level is significant over time, the airport could no longer operate safely; worst-case scenario is that the airport would need to close. The Sunnyland data also acknowledges an increasing frequency and severity of one-off (acute physical climate risks) weather events such as storms. Planes are not able to take off and/or land in severe storms, so the airport traffic disruptions will likely increase due to climate change over time.

Recommended that R-SWF engage with the key stakeholders in Sunnyland, such as the local government, the airport operator, and business and community leaders, to understand Sunnyland plans to combat climate change. It is likely that a number of large-scale government-led adaption initiatives such as building flood barriers will be needed. Recommended that R-SWF use scenario analysis to explore the impacts of climate change. The rising sea level can't be mitigated by R-SWF, but plans can be put in place to adapt working with the government and the local community.

Atsui ABC

The primary environmental risk affecting ABC is its dumping of waste into the river. This recent management-led cost-cutting practice is already changing the river, known for its unique biodiversity, beauty, and rare wildlife. ABC is already attracting the attention of scientists and other environmental groups concerned about the river, bringing potentially damaging reputational risk for R-SWF being associated with polluting the river and destroying the environment. Potentially, any cost savings may be soon be lost if ABC is charged with cleanup costs, potential fines, and reputational damage.

Recommended that R-SWF engage with ABC management to stop this practice. Important to find alternative environmentally friendly ways to deal with waste. To minimize the environmental and reputational damage, assess the cost/benefit of a cleanup operation to restore the river. Educate ABC management in sustainable development and a "just" transition in environmental and social working practices. Discuss with ABC management the introduction of positive management incentives to align interests and reward sustainability in ABC. As R-SWF only has a 35% minority stake in ABC, there is a risk that the founder does not buy in to these concepts. R-SWF must communicate the previously mentioned risks to ensure that the waste dumping stops. By engaging with ABC to make these changes, R-SWF will align with its own ESG investment objectives.

Answer 6:

Reputational risk

Reputational risk is significant for both investments. Reputational risk may be easy to identify but very difficult to quantify and manage.

ABC reputational risk

ABC management's cost-cutting practices are introducing significant reputational risk, both for ABC and R-SWF. First, dumping waste into the river, polluting the local environment, damaging an area of unique biodiversity home to rare wildlife is already attracting the attention of locals, environmental scientists, and other groups. The ABC actions could well damage relations with the community, which uses the river as a popular fishing spot, and attract fines, penalties, and cleanup costs.

The potential reputational damage from negative publicity to both ABC and R-SWF is far greater. ABC relies on customers from its local markets. There is a risk of negative reactions to ABC from polluting the local environment, repercussions from the local people who buy their products, and from community groups and from the government. Second, there is risk of reputational damage to R-SWF from being associated with environmental pollution and destroying the habitat of rare wildlife.

A second area of reputational risk for both ABC and R-SWF is social issues connected to the treatment of the ABC workforce. Cutting 50% of the workforce will have a major impact on the local community. ABC does not have any plans in place for a "just" transition to engage with staff and community leaders to help minimize disruption.

Management practices, such as cutting lunch breaks and removing soap from restrooms, bring reputational risk for both ABC and, especially, R-SWF. The R-SWF CIO termed this "headline risk," making the headlines for the wrong reasons (i.e., being associated with social injustice, health and safety and/or human rights issues would be extremely damaging). The focus instead should be on retraining staff and introducing incentives to ensure quality sustainable management practices.

Sunnyland reputational risk

The impact of sea level rise due to climate risk can be damaging to the reputation of R-SWF in a number of ways. First, R-SWF must be actively engaging with the local stakeholders, such as the government, the airport operator, and local communities, to show R-SWF is willing to participate in finding and implementing solutions. Failure to engage may bring reputational damage to these vital ongoing business relationships. The island as a whole needs to work together to find ways to adapt to climate change, and R-SWF, as an owner of the airport, needs to be actively involved.

A second aspect of reputational risk is for tourism in Sunnyland as a whole. If summers are becoming too hot, storms becoming more frequent and intense, and flights potentially becoming less reliable, will this impact the island's reputation with foreign visitors. These longer-term impacts of climate change may change tourist traffic. Finally, the quality of service standards, efficiency, and overall customer service experience at the new airport terminal will affect the reputation of Sunnyland as a tourist destination.

Scene 3: R-SWF Case Continues

Two years have passed since the 3-year review meeting, which means five years have now passed since the initial investments in Sunnyland and ABC.

Update on the Sunnyland Airport Infrastructure Investment

Revenues are down due to fewer tourists. Airport traffic has fallen to 50% below the base case forecast.

Costs have been rising due to commencing climate adaptation programs in Sunnyland. Costs are 50% higher than the base case forecast.

The outlook for the medium and long term is unfavorable.

Update on the Atsui ABC Private Equity Investment

R-SWF sold its 35% stake in ABC for $27 million to an international beverage company.

R-SWF avoided any adverse reputational damage resulting from the investments in ABC.

Question 7:

Using evidence from the R-SWF case study, **evaluate** the strengths and weaknesses of R-SWF enterprise risk management processes. **Recommend** and **justify** improvements.

Answer 7:

R-SWF ERM strengths

Enterprise risk management requires a coordinated approach across an organization involving the senior managers to make strategic risk and return decisions.

R-SWF has successfully created this coordinated risk framework via its investment committee structure, involving all the heads of each asset class, together with the head of risk. The R-SWF committee members were all involved in identifying key risks and assessing the strategic risk and return of each investment proposition. In fact, all committee members had a vote on proceeding with each project. Further evidence of the strong risk focus, is the investment committee meeting 2.0, which was specifically to review updated risks of both investments.

As part of ERM, it is essential to have a strong independent risk function that challenges the business to consider key risks. Clearly, R-SWF has this in place, as the head of risk raised many risk issues at each meeting and strongly cautioned against the rising reputational risks of the ABC investment.

R-SWF was effective in providing relevant data and additional training to committee members to enable participants to make informed decisions. The meetings themselves welcomed contributions from all attending; even heads of other asset classes had their say. For example, the head of equities made some valuable contributions to the climate risk discussions, illustrating the benefits for R-SWF of pooling risk expertise at the committee meetings.

R-SWF ERM weaknesses

First, environmental and social risks were not evaluated prior to investing. The due diligence background data for both projects did provide important clues to signal further investigations, which were not followed up. For example, plans to significantly cut employee head count in ABC brought issues of labor fairness, health, and safety, as well as social justice. The unique biodiversity of the local river and environment were identified in the initial briefing notes but were not recognized as risks at the pre-investment meeting.

These ESG issues were not considered in negotiations with ABC management about working practices and incentives. R-SWF should have engaged with the founder and agreed on sustainable management practices for the workforce and the environment. R-SWF should have avoided incentivizing cost cutting and rewarded quality in building a sustainable business model.

The Sunnyland Airport investment is highly dependent on tourist numbers. The scenario analysis exploring the impacts of scenarios was inadequate. In reality, tourist traffic was 50% down and costs were 50% up from base case assumptions in just 5 years. More detailed scenario analysis was needed, incorporating realistic assumptions. In addition, stress testing is recommended to explore the impacts of low frequency but high impact downturns in airport traffic. This would have helped R-SWF better understand the risks and make better decisions.

The due diligence to climate risk was also inadequate. Realizing the new airport terminal will be within 1 km of the sea and Sunnyland being a tropical island nation should have prompted further investigation. The initial engineering impact assessments relied upon by R-SWF proved to be inaccurate only 3 years later. R-SWF should have expanded its climate risk due diligence to include climate scenario analysis and stress testing prior to investing.

While the investment committee did identify many risks, there was little evidence of robust action plans to mitigate risks. The action plan should incorporate controls, as well as hedging and other risk transfer strategies. Finally, the plan should incorporate the environmental, social, and reputational risks mentioned previously.

MODULE QUIZ 28.4

1. **Identify**, for each investment, the *earliest* evidence that signaled potential environmental risks. **Explain** for each investment why the evidence selected signaled potential environmental risks.

   (Only one example of evidence is required for each investment.)

2. **Identify**, for each investment, the *earliest* evidence that signaled potential social risks. **Explain** for each investment why the evidence selected signaled potential social risks.

   (Only one example of evidence is required for each investment.)

KEY CONCEPTS

LOS 28.a

Focus on events that could prevent an organization from meeting its long-term objectives.

Financial risks: (1) market losses, (2) liquidity risk

Nonfinancial risks: (1) reputational, (2) operational risks, (3) environmental, social, and governance risks

Dimensions of risk: top-down and bottom-up analysis, returns-based and holdings-based, absolute and relative risk, long-term and short-term risk metrics, quantitative and qualitative techniques

Liquidity risks: define needs and sources for liquidity, in normal and crisis conditions

Illiquid assets: private equity, real estate, infrastructure

Appraisal valuations result in smoothed returns and volatility.

LOS 28.b

Universal owners are holders of large diversified portfolios. Universal owners are impacted both negatively and positively by externalities.

Physical climate risks arise from one-off weather events (acute physical risks—e.g., storms, floods, and heat waves) and gradual effects of climate change (chronic physical risks—e.g., rise in sea levels and temperatures).

Transition climate risks are driven by: (1) new carbon policy and regulation; (2) advances in clean technologies; (3) higher input costs; and (4) shifts in consumer preferences.

Portfolio assets can be adversely impacted by physical climate risk in vulnerable locations (e.g., sea level rise, increased heat waves). Businesses are also impacted by rises in temperatures affecting business models.

Climate change brings winners and losers: (1) winners profit in a zero carbon economy; and (2) losers with old business models may find assets stranded.

Climate transition strategies: (1) mitigation (avoid, withdraw from fossil fuels); (2) adaption (to zero-carbon business models).

Social risks: community relations, health and safety, labor standards, equality, and human rights.

"Just" transition: being fair and just to people affected by transition changes.

LOS 28.c

A key focus of the case study is the environmental and social risks for institutional investors. The case study background notes will provide important clues to signal a variety of risks. Another risk associated with portfolio firms with alleged social or environmental issues is reputational risk.

LOS 28.d

Long-term direct investments in illiquid assets have both advantages and disadvantages:

Advantages: (1) control over assets (e.g., exits); (2) increased portfolio liquidity due to control of exits; (3) avoids paying fund management fees; and (4) access to more detailed information as a business owner

Disadvantages: (1) concentrated positions; (2) additional liabilities; (3) attracting, retaining, and compensating in-house expertise

Long-term indirect investments in illiquid assets also have advantages and disadvantages:

Advantages: (1) no need for in-house team and costs; (2) limited liability of funds invested.

Disadvantages: (1) pay fund management fees; (2) no control over portfolio assets; (3) lower liquidity due to no control over the timing of exits.

Managing liquidity risk requires a 5-step process: (1) establish liquidity parameters; (2) assess current liquidity; (3) develop a cash flow model to project future cash flows; (4) stress test liquidity needs; and (5) develop an emergency plan.

LOS 28.e

ERM framework includes: (1) board of directors; (2) chief investment officer; (3) investment committee; (4) risk function.

ERM risk management process includes: (1) identify risks; (2) measure risks; (3) manage and mitigate risks; (4) monitor risks; (5) risk reporting; and (6) strategic analysis and planning.

Investor policy statement contains the risk and return objectives and constraints of the investment plan.

Risk tolerance is set by the board and defined by: volatility, maximum drawdown, value at risk, and conditional value at risk, a.k.a. expected tail loss.

Quantitative risk methodologies include: (1) returns-based analysis; (2) holdings-based analysis; (3) scenario analysis; and (4) stress testing.

Other risk metrics include: liquidity risk parameters, active risk budgets, restrictions on leverage, and the use of derivatives.

Strategic asset allocation is implemented either internally or via third-party investment managers.

Recommend a suitable benchmark for public investments to measure relative returns and active risk.

Have regular portfolio monitoring, reviews, and implementation of agreed rebalancing strategies.

Based on what was previously listed, identify strengths and weaknesses in an enterprise risk management system and recommend improvements.

ANSWER KEY FOR MODULE QUIZZES

Module Quiz 28.1

1. **A** Indirect investments are via investment funds that provide no direct control of the timing of exits. Therefore, indirect forms of investment in private equity reduce portfolio liquidity. Indirect investments incur both annual management and profit-sharing fees (carried interest). Indirect forms of investment achieve higher levels of diversification and lower levels of concentrations from investing in a larger number of projects. (LOS 28.a)

2. **A** *Unsmoothed returns* have plentiful transactions, have no need for appraisals, and reflect accurate levels of volatility. *Smoothed returns* have few transactions, a need for appraisals, and put a downward bias on volatility. (LOS 28.a)

3. Direct investments in private asset classes require a dedicated and experienced in-house team. It is challenging and expensive to attract and retain the high-quality, in-house talent needed.

   Direct investments in private asset classes may have higher concentration of risks due to challenges in scaling up portfolio investments to achieve higher levels of diversification. Higher concentration risks increase the idiosyncratic risks associated with each individual investment. (LOS 28.a)

Module Quiz 28.2

1. **C** The VaR significance level is 5%. An increase in the significance level, say to 10%, changes the VaR confidence level to 90%. The lower confidence level reduces the VaR estimate.

   A decrease in the holding period will decrease the VaR estimate. However, VaR is an estimate of an unexpected loss rather than an expected loss, making that answer option inaccurate.

   An increase in the confidence level, say from 95% to 99%, will increase the VaR estimate, as more extreme tail losses will be incorporated. Conditional VaR will also increase because this represents the average loss beyond the VaR. (LOS 28.e)

2. **A** The board of directors sets the risk tolerance, not the chief investment officer.

   Maximum drawdown, value at risk, and conditional value at risk are all short-term risk metrics. Monte Carlo simulation is a long-term risk methodology.

Returns-based risk systems analyze the historic returns of investment managers. Holdings-based risk systems have access to all the portfolio holdings as part of the analysis. Hedge funds often prefer to maintain confidentiality of portfolio holdings to protect proprietary investment strategies. As a result, returns-based risk systems will likely be preferred. (LOS 28.e)

3. The enterprise risk management process includes the following steps: (1) identify risks, (2) measure risks, (3) mitigate and manage risks, (4) monitor risks, (5) report risks, and (6) do strategic analysis and planning. (LOS 28.e)

Module Quiz 28.3

1. **A** The 2015 Paris Agreement agreed to limit global temperature rises to +2 degrees Celsius based on pre-industrial levels (not 2015 levels). The Paris Agreement has voluntary pledges to reduce carbon emissions called nationally determined contributions. Current levels of nationally determined contributions (voluntary pledges) are insufficient to meet the target set in the Paris Agreement (limiting global warming to +2DC). (LOS 28.b)

2. **A** Physical climate risk results from one-off weather-related weather events (acute physical risks) and gradual impacts of climate risk, such as rising sea levels (chronic physical risks). An insurer refusing to insure a coastal property is an example of chronic physical climate risk. Transition climate risk is failing to adapt or mitigate to the zero-carbon economy. Transition risk results in an outdated business model and possibly stranded assets (unable to monetize). Transition risk is driven by changes in carbon regulation (carbon taxes, carbon limits), new clean technologies, and shifts in consumer demand. (LOS 28.b)

3. A "just transition" relates to social risks. Fairness, justice, and equality are important principles for everyone. Business decisions can have impacts on employees, local communities, and entire towns and cities. "Just transitions" ensure that support and communication is provided to assist people impacted and minimize the negative impacts of transitions. (LOS 28.b)

Module Quiz 28.4

1. Memo 1B provided initial details of the Sunnyland Airport investment that contained important environmental risk signals.

   The Sunnyland Airport and runway being located so close to the sea (2 km and 1 km) were important signals of the risk of sea level rise due to climate change. The chosen 25-year time horizon is also shown in Memo 1B. This signals the need for detailed climate scenario analysis to explore the chronic physical climate risk of sea level rises and the uncertainty that surrounds the scale, timing, and costs of impacts to mitigate such risks.

Memo 1C provided important environmental signals for the Atsui Beverage Company Investment. The due diligence information in this memo included the details that ABC is a landlocked country, relying upon a river that allows for transport to the port. The river has unique biodiversity, which immediately should trigger environmental discussions. Investing directly brings the potential for additional liabilities. Further investigations were necessary to identify potential risks and the local regulations that may exist. Discussions should have taken place with the founder based upon this risk signal. (LO 28.c)

2. Memo 1B also signaled social risks present in the Sunnyland Airport project.

Local government and community relations are at the center of such an important infrastructure project. Memo 1B shows a wide range of parties being involved in the project (e.g., the government, the airport operator, the construction contractors, and R-SWF). This illustrates the social risks of working with multiple stakeholders, agreeing on approaches, and finding solutions when things go wrong. Later in the case, tensions did start to appear as the airport operator wanted to renegotiate its fee.

With the airport being so important to so many businesses, local people, industry groups, and investors, there is considerable social risk with the project. Worst case, if R-SWF falls out with the airport operator, who replaces them? Alternatively, if relations worsen between R-SWF and the local government, investment assets could be expropriated or heavy local taxes introduced.

Memo 1C signals social risks connected with the ABC private equity investment.

First, the founder is worried about giving up control. This signals a need for discussions with the founder about agreeing to a business model, working practices, and the design of sustainable incentive programs. R-SWF should have ensured that ABC management practices are aligned to sustainable development standards, in the treatment of the workforce and the environment. It was later discovered that management practices were not aligned, and exploitation of the workforce and the dumping of waste illustrates R-SWF did not adequately explore these social risks when co-investing.

A second signal of social risks also contained in Memo 1C is the proposed dramatic reduction in the ABC head count from 500 to 300. This should have signaled further investigations into employee contract law, which would have revealed the required very generous 2-year notice period. R-SWF did not follow up on this, and the resulting delays caused considerable problems in capturing efficiencies. In addition, the scale of the planned reduction in head count in such a small local community will result in considerable social impacts to individuals and the wider community. The loss of local jobs, relationship with the community, brand reputation, and relationship with the government are all important social considerations. Planned changes should follow a “just transition,” where communities are consulted and supported throughout periods of change.

Note that only one piece of evidence to signal each risk was required.

(LOS 28.c)

TOPIC QUIZ: TRADING, PERFORMANCE EVALUATION, AND MANAGER SELECTION; AND CASE STUDIES

You have now finished the Trading, Performance Evaluation, and Manager Selection; and Case Studies topic section. On your Schweser online dashboard, you can find a Topic Quiz that will provide immediate feedback on how effective your study of this material has been. The test is best taken timed; allow three minutes per question. Topic Quizzes are more exam-like than typical QBank questions or module quiz questions. A score less than 70% suggests that additional review of the topic is needed.

READINGS 29 & 30 Code of Ethics and Standards of Professional Conduct, Guidance for Standards I–VII

EXAM FOCUS

Ethics will most likely be 10%–15% of the exam with two or three item set questions. While the CFA Institute has never specifically said they will not use constructed responses for ethics, they have not done so for over 10 years. The content and what you need to know will be the same regardless of the question format.

Level III questions tend to focus on compliance, portfolio management issues, and questions on the Asset Manager Code. Prepare properly and ethics can be an easier section of the exam. That is a big advantage when you move to the questions in other topic areas.

Just like Level I and Level II, ethics requires that you know the principles and be able to apply them to specific situations to make the expected decision. Some ethics questions can be vague with unclear facts so be prepared to make a "best guess" on a few of the questions. As you read the material, pay particular attention to the numerous examples (the application). As soon as you finish reading the Ethics material, work the Schweser and CFA end of reading practice problems. Reading principles without practicing questions for application or vice versa will not be sufficient and you need to do both. Be prepared and make this an easier part of the exam.

Video covering this content is available online.

MODULE 29.1: CODE AND STANDARDS

LOS 29.a: Describe the structure of the CFA Institute Professional Conduct Program and the disciplinary review process for the enforcement of the CFA Institute Code of Ethics and Standards of Professional Conduct.

The CFA Institute Professional Conduct Program is covered by the CFA Institute Bylaws and the Rules of Procedure for Proceedings Related to Professional Conduct. The Program is based on the principles of fairness of the process to members and candidates and maintaining the confidentiality of the proceedings. The Disciplinary Review Committee of the CFA Institute Board of Governors has overall responsibility for the Professional Conduct Program and enforcement of the Code and Standards.

The CFA Institute Professional Conduct staff conducts inquiries related to professional conduct. Several circumstances can prompt such an inquiry:

1. Self-disclosure by members or candidates on their annual Professional Conduct Statements of involvement in civil litigation or a criminal investigation, or that the member or candidate is the subject of a written complaint.
2. Written complaints about a member or candidate's professional conduct that are received by the Professional Conduct staff.
3. Evidence of misconduct by a member or candidate that the Professional Conduct staff received through public sources, such as a media article or broadcast.
4. A report by a CFA exam proctor of a possible violation during the examination.
5. Analysis of exam materials and monitoring of social media by CFA Institute.

Once an inquiry has begun, the Professional Conduct staff may request (in writing) an explanation from the subject member or candidate and may: (1) interview the subject member or candidate, (2) interview the complainant or other third parties, and/or (3) collect documents and records relevant to the investigation.

The Professional Conduct staff may decide: (1) that no disciplinary sanctions are appropriate, (2) to issue a cautionary letter, or (3) to discipline the member or candidate. In a case where the Professional Conduct staff finds a violation has occurred and proposes a disciplinary sanction, the member or candidate may accept or reject the sanction. If the member or candidate chooses to reject the sanction, the matter will be referred to a disciplinary review panel of CFA Institute members for a hearing. Sanctions imposed may include condemnation by the member's peers or suspension of candidate's continued participation in the CFA Program.

LOS 29.b: Explain the ethical responsibilities required by the Code and Standards, including the sub-sections of each standard.

Code of Ethics

Members of CFA Institute [including Chartered Financial Analyst® (CFA®) charterholders] and candidates for the CFA designation ("Members and Candidates") must:[1]

- Act with integrity, competence, diligence, respect, and in an ethical manner with the public, clients, prospective clients, employers, employees, colleagues in the investment profession, and other participants in the global capital markets.
- Place the integrity of the investment profession and the interests of clients above their own personal interests.
- Use reasonable care and exercise independent professional judgment when conducting investment analysis, making investment recommendations, taking investment actions, and engaging in other professional activities.
- Practice and encourage others to practice in a professional and ethical manner that will reflect credit on themselves and the profession.
- Promote the integrity and viability of the global capital markets for the ultimate benefit of society.
- Maintain and improve their professional competence and strive to maintain and improve the competence of other investment professionals.

The Standards of Professional Conduct

I. Professionalism

II. Integrity of Capital Markets

III. Duties to Clients

IV. Duties to Employers

V. Investment Analysis, Recommendations, and Actions

VI. Conflicts of Interest

VII. Responsibilities as a CFA Institute Member or CFA Candidate

Standards of Professional Conduct[2]

I. PROFESSIONALISM

A. **Knowledge of the Law.** Members and Candidates must understand and comply with all applicable laws, rules, and regulations (including the CFA Institute *Code of Ethics* and *Standards of Professional Conduct*) of any government, regulatory organization, licensing agency, or professional association governing their professional activities. In the event of conflict, Members and Candidates must comply with the more strict law, rule, or regulation. Members and Candidates must not knowingly participate or assist in any violation of laws, rules, or regulations and must disassociate themselves from any such violation.

B. **Independence and Objectivity.** Members and Candidates must use reasonable care and judgment to achieve and maintain independence and objectivity in their professional activities. Members and Candidates must not offer, solicit, or accept any gift, benefit, compensation, or consideration that reasonably could be expected to compromise their own or another's independence and objectivity.

C. **Misrepresentation.** Members and Candidates must not knowingly make any misrepresentations relating to investment analysis, recommendations, actions, or other professional activities.

D. **Misconduct.** Members and Candidates must not engage in any professional conduct involving dishonesty, fraud, or deceit or commit any act that reflects adversely on their professional reputation, integrity, or competence.

II. INTEGRITY OF CAPITAL MARKETS

A. **Material Nonpublic Information.** Members and Candidates who possess material nonpublic information that could affect the value of an investment must not act or cause others to act on the information.

B. **Market Manipulation.** Members and Candidates must not engage in practices that distort prices or artificially inflate trading volume with the intent to mislead market participants.

III. DUTIES TO CLIENTS

A. **Loyalty, Prudence, and Care.** Members and Candidates have a duty of loyalty to their clients and must act with reasonable care and exercise prudent judgment. Members and Candidates must act for the benefit of their clients and place their clients' interests before their employer's or their own interests.

[2] Copyright 2014, CFA Institute. Reproduced and republished from "The Code of Ethics," from *Standards of Practice Handbook, 11th Ed.*, 2014, with permission from CFA Institute. All rights reserved.

B. **Fair Dealing.** Members and Candidates must deal fairly and objectively with all clients when providing investment analysis, making investment recommendations, taking investment action, or engaging in other professional activities.

C. **Suitability.**

1. When Members and Candidates are in an advisory relationship with a client, they must:

    a) Make a reasonable inquiry into a client's or prospective clients' investment experience, risk and return objectives, and financial constraints prior to making any investment recommendation or taking investment action and must reassess and update this information regularly.

    b) Determine that an investment is suitable to the client's financial situation and consistent with the client's written objectives, mandates, and constraints before making an investment recommendation or taking investment action.

    c) Judge the suitability of investments in the context of the client's total portfolio.

2. When Members and Candidates are responsible for managing a portfolio to a specific mandate, strategy, or style, they must make only investment recommendations or take investment actions that are consistent with the stated objectives and constraints of the portfolio.

D. **Performance Presentation.** When communicating investment performance information, Members or Candidates must make reasonable efforts to ensure that it is fair, accurate, and complete.

E. **Preservation of Confidentiality.** Members and Candidates must keep information about current, former, and prospective clients confidential unless:

1. The information concerns illegal activities on the part of the client or prospective client,

2. Disclosure is required by law, or

3. The client or prospective client permits disclosure of the information.

IV. DUTIES TO EMPLOYERS

A. **Loyalty.** In matters related to their employment, Members and Candidates must act for the benefit of their employer and not deprive their employer of the advantage of their skills and abilities, divulge confidential information, or otherwise cause harm to their employer.

B. **Additional Compensation Arrangements.** Members and Candidates must not accept gifts, benefits, compensation, or consideration that competes with, or might reasonably be expected to create a conflict of interest with, their employer's interest unless they obtain written consent from all parties involved.

C. **Responsibilities of Supervisors.** Members and Candidates must make reasonable efforts to ensure that anyone subject to their supervision or authority complies with applicable laws, rules, regulations, and the Code and Standards.

V. INVESTMENT ANALYSIS, RECOMMENDATIONS, AND ACTIONS

A. **Diligence and Reasonable Basis.** Members and Candidates must:

1. Exercise diligence, independence, and thoroughness in analyzing investments, making investment recommendations, and taking investment actions.

2. Have a reasonable and adequate basis, supported by appropriate research and investigation, for any investment analysis, recommendation, or action.

B. **Communication with Clients and Prospective Clients.** Members and Candidates must:

1. Disclose to clients and prospective clients the basic format and general principles of the investment processes used to analyze investments, select securities, and construct portfolios and must promptly disclose any changes that might materially affect those processes.

2. Disclose to clients and prospective clients significant limitations and risks associated with the investment process.

3. Use reasonable judgment in identifying which factors are important to their investment analyses, recommendations, or actions and include those factors in communications with clients and prospective clients.

4. Distinguish between fact and opinion in the presentation of investment analysis and recommendations.

C. **Record Retention.** Members and Candidates must develop and maintain appropriate records to support their investment analysis, recommendations, actions, and other investment-related communications with clients and prospective clients.

VI. CONFLICTS OF INTEREST

A. **Disclosure of Conflicts.** Members and Candidates must make full and fair disclosure of all matters that could reasonably be expected to impair their independence and objectivity or interfere with respective duties to their clients, prospective clients, and employer. Members and Candidates must ensure that such disclosures are prominent, are delivered in plain language, and communicate the relevant information effectively.

B. **Priority of Transactions.** Investment transactions for clients and employers must have priority over investment transactions in which a Member or Candidate is the beneficial owner.

C. **Referral Fees.** Members and Candidates must disclose to their employer, clients, and prospective clients, as appropriate, any compensation, consideration, or benefit received from, or paid to, others for the recommendation of products or services.

VII. RESPONSIBILITIES AS A CFA INSTITUTE MEMBER OR CFA CANDIDATE

A. **Conduct as Participants in CFA Institute Programs.** Members and Candidates must not engage in any conduct that compromises the reputation or integrity of CFA Institute or the CFA designation or the integrity, validity, or security of CFA Institute programs.

B. **Reference to CFA Institute, the CFA Designation, and the CFA Program.** When referring to CFA Institute, CFA Institute membership, the CFA designation, or candidacy in the CFA Program, Members and Candidates must not misrepresent or exaggerate the meaning or implications of membership in CFA Institute, holding the CFA designation, or candidacy in the CFA Program.

MODULE QUIZ 29.1

1. In the case of a complaint about a member's professional conduct, CFA Institute Professional Conduct Program staff are *least likely* to:
   A. review documents and records related to the complaint.
   B. request an interview with the member or with the party making the complaint.
   C. suspend the member's right to use the CFA designation while an investigation is in progress.
2. Which of the following requirements for members and candidates is one of the six components of the Code of Ethics?
   A. Maintain and improve their professional competence.
   B. Do not act or cause others to act on material nonpublic information.
   C. Distinguish between fact and opinion when presenting investment analysis.

Readings 29 & 30

3. If a member or candidate is offered an additional compensation arrangement by a client, which of the seven Standards of Professional Conduct states the requirements the member or candidate must follow?
   A. Duties to Clients.
   B. Conflicts of Interest.
   C. Duties to Employers.

LOS 30.a: Demonstrate a thorough knowledge of the CFA Institute Code of Ethics and Standards of Professional Conduct by interpreting the Code and Standards in various situations involving issues of professional integrity.

LOS 30.b: Recommend practices and procedures designed to prevent violations of the Code and Standards.

PROFESSOR'S NOTE

You should be prepared for questions that require you to apply the Standards in specific case situations. In such questions, you must recognize the case facts described and then decide which Standards are directly relevant. This is primarily a test of critical thinking, not of memorization. To prepare you, we will in this section focus on a review of the key points for each Standard and the recommended procedures. If you know the main issues, you are more likely to successfully apply them. You should review the recommended procedures several times between now and exam day because they fit the Level III emphasis on the bigger picture and managing the business as well as portfolios and assets. Once you complete our review and understand the basic principles that you must know, then move to application and practice. For practice, complete our sample questions. The CFA reading includes many examples of applying the Standards, and you should read all the examples as well as complete the CFA end of chapter questions for this reading.

It is important you know the basic principles before you move to the specific examples and questions. Those examples and questions can only be a sample of possible applications. When you try to learn by practice only, without first knowing the principles that are being applied, you generally get the wrong ideas. Prepare and practice are two different steps. The combination is what leads to success. Do both.

In many cases the actions that members and candidates must not take are explained using terms open to interpretation, such as "reasonable," "adequate," and "token."

Some examples from the Standards themselves are:

...use reasonable care and judgment to achieve...

...accept any gift, that reasonably could be expected to compromise...

…act with reasonable care and exercise prudent judgment…

…deal fairly and objectively with all clients…

…make a reasonable inquiry into…

…make reasonable efforts to ensure…

…might reasonably be expected to create a conflict of interest with…

…Have a reasonable and adequate basis…

…Use reasonable judgment in…

…matters that could be reasonably expected to impair…

The requirement of the LOS is that you know what constitutes a violation, not that you draw a distinction between what is "reasonable" and what is not in a given situation. We believe the exam writers take this into account and that if they intend, for example, to test whether a recommendation has been given without reasonable care and judgment, it will likely be clear either that the care and judgment exhibited by the analyst did not rise to the level of "reasonable," or that it did.

No monetary value for a "token" gift is given in the Standards, although it is recommended that a firm establish such a monetary value for its employees. Here, again, the correct answer to a question will not likely hinge on candidate's determination of what is a token gift and what is not. Questions should be clear in this regard. A business dinner is likely a token gift, but a week at a condominium in Aspen or tickets to the Super Bowl are likely not. Always look for clues in the questions that lead you to the question-writer's preferred answer choice, such as "lavish" entertainment and "luxury" accommodations.

Next, we present a summary of each subsection of the Standards of Professional Conduct. For each one, we first detail actions that violate the Standard and then list actions and behaviors that are recommended within the Standards. We suggest you learn the violations especially well so you understand that the other items are recommended. For the exam, it is not necessary to memorize the Standard number and subsection letter. Knowing that an action violates, for example, Professionalism, rather than Duties to Employers or Duties to Clients, should be sufficient in this regard. Note that some actions may violate more than one Standard.

One way to write questions for this material is to offer a reason that might make one believe a Standard does not apply in a particular situation. In most, if not all, cases the "reason" does not change the requirement of the Standard. If you are prohibited from some action, the motivations for the action or other circumstances simply do not matter. If the Standard says it's a violation, it's a violation. An exception is when intent is key to the Standard, such as intending to mislead clients or market participants in general.

Video covering this content is available online.

MODULE 30.1: GUIDANCE FOR STANDARDS I(A) AND I(B)

STANDARD I: PROFESSIONALISM[3]

Standard I(A) Knowledge of the Law

Members and Candidates must understand and comply with all applicable laws, rules, and regulations (including the CFA Institute Code of Ethics and Standards of Professional Conduct) of any government, regulatory organization, licensing agency, or professional association governing their professional activities. In the event of conflict, Members and Candidates must comply with the more strict law, rule, or regulation. Members and Candidates must not knowingly participate or assist in and must dissociate from any violation of such laws, rules, or regulations.

The Standards begin with a straightforward statement: Don't violate any laws, rules, or regulations that apply to your professional activities. This includes the Code and Standards, so any violation of the Code and Standards will also violate this subsection.

A member may be governed by different rules and regulations among the Standards, the country in which the member resides, and the country where the member is doing business. Follow the most strict of these, or, put another way, do not violate any of the three sets of rules and regulations.

If you know that violations of applicable rules or laws are taking place, either by coworkers or clients, you must approach your supervisor or compliance department to remedy the situation. If they will not or cannot, then you must dissociate from the activity (e.g., not working with a trading group you know is not allocating client trades properly according to the Standard on Fair Dealing, or not using marketing materials that you know or should know are misleading or erroneous). If this cannot be accomplished, you may, in an extreme case, have to resign from the firm to be in compliance with this Standard.

Recommendations for Members

- Establish, or encourage employer to establish, procedures to keep employees informed of changes in relevant laws, rules, and regulations.
- Review, or encourage employer to review, the firm's written compliance procedures on a regular basis.
- Maintain, or encourage employer to maintain, copies of current laws, rules, and regulations.
- When in doubt about legality, consult compliance personnel or a lawyer.

3 Copyright 2014, CFA Institute. Reproduced and republished from "The Code of Ethics," from *Standards of Practice Handbook, 11th Ed.*, 2014, with permission from CFA Institute. All rights reserved.

- When dissociating from violations, keep records documenting the violations, encourage employer to bring an end to the violations.
- There is no requirement in the Standards to report wrongdoers, but local law may require it; members are "strongly encouraged" to report violations to CFA Institute Professional Conduct Program.

Recommendations for Firms

- Have a code of ethics.
- Provide employees with information on laws, rules, and regulations governing professional activities.
- Have procedures for reporting suspected violations.

Standard I(B) Independence and Objectivity

Members and Candidates must use reasonable care and judgment to achieve and maintain independence and objectivity in their professional activities. Members and Candidates must not offer, solicit, or accept any gift, benefit, compensation, or consideration that reasonably could be expected to compromise their own or another's independence and objectivity.

Analysts may face pressure or receive inducements to give a security a specific rating, to select certain outside managers or vendors, or to produce favorable or unfavorable research and conclusions. Members who allow their investment recommendations or analysis to be influenced by such pressure or inducements will have violated the requirement to use reasonable care and to maintain independence and objectivity in their professional activities. Allocating shares in oversubscribed IPOs to personal accounts is a violation.

Normal business entertainment is permitted. Members who accept, solicit, or offer things of value that could be expected to influence the member's or others' independence or objectivity are violating the Standard. Gifts from clients are considered less likely to compromise independence and objectivity than gifts from other parties. Client gifts must be disclosed to the member's employer prior to acceptance, if possible, but after acceptance, if not.

Members may prepare reports paid for by the subject firm if compensation is a flat rate not tied to the conclusions of the report (and if the fact that the research is issuer-paid is disclosed). Accepting compensation that is dependent on the conclusions, recommendations, or market impact of the report, and failure to disclose that research is issuer-paid, are violations of this Standard.

Recommendations for Members

Members or their firms should pay for their own travel to company events or tours when practicable and limit use of corporate aircraft to trips for which commercial travel is not an alternative.

Recommendations for Firms

- Establish policies requiring every research report to reflect the unbiased opinion of the analyst and align compensation plans to support this principle.
- Establish and review written policies and procedures to assure research is independent and objective.
- Establish restricted lists of securities for which the firm is not willing to issue adverse opinions. Factual information may still be provided.
- Limit gifts from non-clients to token amounts.
- Limit and require prior approval of employee participation in equity IPOs.
- Establish procedures for supervisory review of employee actions.
- Appoint a senior officer to oversee firm compliance and ethics.

Video covering this content is available online.

MODULE 30.2: GUIDANCE FOR STANDARDS I(C) AND I(D)

Standard I(C) Misrepresentation

Members and Candidates must not knowingly make any misrepresentations relating to investment analysis, recommendations, actions, or other professional activities.

Misrepresentation includes knowingly misleading investors, omitting relevant information, presenting selective data to mislead investors, and plagiarism. Plagiarism is using reports, forecasts, models, ideas, charts, graphs, or spreadsheets created by others without crediting the source. Crediting the source is not required when using projections, statistics, and tables from recognized financial and statistical reporting services. When using models developed or research done by other members of the firm, it is permitted to omit the names of those who are no longer with the firm as long as the member does not represent work previously done by others as his alone.

Actions that would violate the Standard include:

- Presenting third-party research as your own, without attribution to the source.
- Guaranteeing a specific return on securities that do not have an explicit guarantee from a government body or financial institution.
- Selecting a valuation service because it puts the highest value on untraded security holdings.
- Selecting a performance benchmark that is not comparable to the investment strategy employed.
- Presenting performance data or attribution analysis that omits accounts or relevant variables.
- Offering false or misleading information about the analyst's or firm's capabilities, expertise, or experience.
- Using marketing materials from a third party (outside adviser) that are misleading.

Recommendations for Members

- Understand the scope and limits of the firm's capabilities to avoid inadvertent misrepresentations.
- Summarize your own qualifications and experience.
- Make reasonable efforts to verify information from third parties that is provided to clients.
- Regularly maintain web pages for accuracy.
- When using social media, only distribute the same information that is allowed to be distributed using traditional forms of communication.
- Avoid plagiarism by keeping copies of all research reports and supporting documents and attributing direct quotes, paraphrases, and summaries to their source.

Standard I(D) Misconduct

Members and Candidates must not engage in any professional conduct involving dishonesty, fraud, or deceit or commit any act that reflects adversely on their professional reputation, integrity, or competence.

The first part here regarding professional conduct is clear: no dishonesty, fraud, or deceit. The second part, while it applies to all conduct by the member, specifically requires that the act, "reflects adversely on their professional reputation, integrity, or competence." The guidance states, in fact, that members must not try to use enforcement of this Standard against another member to settle personal, political, or other disputes that are not related to professional ethics or competence.

Recommendations for Firms

- Develop and adopt a code of ethics and make clear that unethical behavior will not be tolerated.
- Give employees a list of potential violations and sanctions, including dismissal.
- Check references of potential employees.

MODULE 30.3: GUIDANCE FOR STANDARD II

Video covering this content is available online.

STANDARD II: INTEGRITY OF CAPITAL MARKETS

Standard II(A) Material Nonpublic Information

Members and Candidates who possess material nonpublic information that could affect the value of an investment must not act or cause others to act on the information.

Information is "material" if its disclosure would affect the price of a security or if a reasonable investor would want the information before making an investment decision. Information that is ambiguous as to its likely effect on price may not be considered material.

Information is "nonpublic" until it has been made available to the marketplace. An analyst conference call is not public disclosure. Selective disclosure of information by corporations creates the potential for insider-trading violations.

The prohibition against acting on material nonpublic information extends to mutual funds containing the subject securities as well as related swaps and options contracts. It is the member's responsibility to determine if information she receives has been publicly disseminated prior to acting or causing others to act on it.

Some members and candidates may be involved in transactions during which they are provided with material nonpublic information by firms (e.g., investment banking transactions). Members and candidates may use this information for its intended purpose, but must not use the information for any other purpose unless it becomes public information.

Under the so-called **mosaic theory**, reaching an investment conclusion through perceptive analysis of public information combined with non-material nonpublic information is not a violation of the Standard.

Recommendations for Members

- Make reasonable efforts to achieve public dissemination by the firm of information they possess.
- Encourage their firms to adopt procedures to prevent the misuse of material nonpublic information.

Recommendations for Firms

- Issue press releases prior to analyst meetings to assure public dissemination of any new information.
- Adopt procedures for equitable distribution of information to the market place (e.g., new research opinions and reports to clients).
- Establish firewalls within the organization for who may and may not have access to material nonpublic information. Generally, this includes having the legal or compliance department clear interdepartmental communications, reviewing employee trades, documenting procedures to limit information flow, and carefully reviewing or restricting proprietary trading whenever the firm possesses material nonpublic information on the securities involved.
- Ensure that procedures for proprietary trading are appropriate to the strategies used. A blanket prohibition is not required.
- Develop procedures to enforce firewalls with complexity consistent with the complexity of the firm.
- Physically separate departments.
- Have a compliance (or other) officer review and authorize information flows before sharing.
- Maintain records of information shared.

- Limit personal trading, require that it be reported, and establish a restricted list of securities in which personal trading is not allowed.
- Regularly communicate with and train employees to follow procedures.

Standard II(B) Market Manipulation

Members and Candidates must not engage in practices that distort prices or artificially inflate trading volume with the intent to mislead market participants.

Member actions may affect security values and trading volumes without violating this Standard. The key point here is that if there is the *intent to mislead,* then the Standard is violated. Of course, spreading false information to affect prices or volume is a violation of this Standard as is making trades intended to mislead market participants.

Readings 29 & 30

MODULE QUIZ 30.1, 30.2, 30.3

1. In situations where the laws of a member or candidate's country of residence, the local laws of regions where the member or candidate does business, and the Code and Standards specify different requirements, the member or candidate must abide by:
   A. local law or the Code and Standards, whichever is stricter.
   B. the Code and Standards or his country's laws, whichever are stricter.
   C. the strictest of local law, his country's laws, or the Code and Standards.
2. According to the Standard on independence and objectivity, members and candidates:
   A. may accept gifts or bonuses from clients.
   B. may not accept compensation from an issuer of securities in return for producing research on those securities.
   C. should consider credit ratings issued by recognized agencies to be objective measures of credit quality.
3. Bill Cooper finds a table of historical bond yields on the website of the U.S. Treasury that supports the work he has done in his analysis and includes the table as part of his report without citing the source. Has Cooper violated the Code and Standards?
   A. Yes, because he did not cite the source of the table.
   B. Yes, because he did not verify the accuracy of the information.
   C. No, because the table is from a recognized source of financial or statistical data.
4. Which of the following statements about the Standard on misconduct is *most accurate*?
   A. Misconduct applies only to a member or candidate's professional activities.
   B. Neglecting to perform due diligence when required is an example of misconduct.
   C. A member or candidate commits misconduct by engaging in any illegal activity, such as a parking ticket offense.

5. Ed Ingus, CFA, visits the headquarters and main plant of Bullitt Company and observes that inventories of unsold goods appear unusually large. From the CFO, he learns that a recent increase in returned items may result in earnings for the current quarter that are below analysts' estimates. Bullitt plans to make this conclusion public next week. Based on his visit, Ingus changes his recommendation on Bullitt to "Sell." Has Ingus violated the Standard concerning material nonpublic information?
   A. Yes.
   B. No, because the information he used is not material.
   C. No, because his actions are consistent with the mosaic theory.
6. Green Brothers, an emerging market fund manager, has two of its subsidiaries simultaneously buy and sell emerging market stocks. In its marketing literature, Green Brothers cites the overall emerging market volume as evidence of the market's liquidity. As a result of its actions, more investors participate in the emerging markets fund. Green Brothers *most likely*:
   A. did not violate the Code and Standards.
   B. violated the Standard regarding market manipulation.
   C. violated the Standard regarding performance presentation.

Video covering this content is available online.

MODULE 30.4: GUIDANCE FOR STANDARDS III(A) AND III(B)

STANDARD III: DUTIES TO CLIENTS

Standard III(A) Loyalty, Prudence, and Care

Members and Candidates have a duty of loyalty to their clients and must act with reasonable care and exercise prudent judgment. Members and Candidates must act for the benefit of their clients and place their clients' interests before their employer's or their own interests.

Client interests always come first. Although this Standard does not impose a fiduciary duty on members or candidates where one did not already exist, it does require members and candidates to act in their clients' best interests and recommend products that are suitable given their clients' investment objectives and risk tolerances. Members and candidates must:

- Exercise the prudence, care, skill, and diligence under the circumstances that a person acting in a like capacity and familiar with such matters would use.
- Manage pools of client assets in accordance with the terms of the governing documents, such as trust documents or investment management agreements.
- Make investment decisions in the context of the total portfolio.
- Inform clients of any limitations in an advisory relationship (e.g., an adviser who may only recommend her own firm's products).
- Vote proxies in an informed and responsible manner. Due to cost-benefit considerations, it may not be necessary to vote all proxies.

- Client brokerage, or "soft dollars" or "soft commissions," must be used to benefit the client.
- The "client" may be the investing public as a whole rather than a specific entity or person.

Recommendations for Members

Submit to clients, at least quarterly, itemized statements showing all securities in custody and all debits, credits, and transactions. Disclose where client assets are held and if they are moved. Keep client assets separate from others' assets.

If in doubt as to the appropriate action, what would you do if you were the client? If still in doubt, disclose and seek written client approval.

Encourage firms to address these topics when drafting policies and procedures regarding fiduciary duty:

- Follow applicable rules and laws.
- Establish investment objectives of client.
- Consider suitability of a portfolio relative to the client's needs and circumstances, the investment's basic characteristics, or the basic characteristics of the total portfolio.
- Diversify unless account guidelines dictate otherwise.
- Deal fairly with all clients in regard to investment actions.
- Disclose conflicts of interest.
- Disclose manager compensation arrangements.
- Regularly review actions for consistency with documents.
- Vote proxies in the best interest of clients and ultimate beneficiaries.
- Maintain confidentiality.
- Seek best execution.
- Put client interests first.

Standard III(B) Fair Dealing

Members and Candidates must deal fairly and objectively with all clients when providing investment analysis, making investment recommendations, taking investment action, or engaging in other professional activities.

Do not discriminate against any clients when disseminating recommendations or taking investment action. "Fairly" does not mean "equally." In the normal course of business, there will be differences in the time emails, faxes, and other communications are received by different clients.

Different service levels are acceptable, but they must not negatively affect or disadvantage any clients. Disclose the different service levels to all clients and prospects, and make premium levels of service available to all those willing to pay for them.

Readings 29 & 30

Give all clients a fair opportunity to act on every recommendation. Clients who are unaware of a change in the recommendation for a security should be advised of the change before an order for the security is accepted.

Treat clients fairly in light of their investment objectives and circumstances. Treat both individual and institutional clients in a fair and impartial manner. Members and candidates should not take advantage of their position in the industry to disadvantage clients (e.g., taking shares of an oversubscribed IPO).

Recommendations for Members

- Encourage firms to establish compliance procedures requiring proper dissemination of investment recommendations and fair treatment of all customers and clients.
- Maintain a list of clients and holdings—use to ensure that all holders are treated fairly.

Recommendations for Firms

- Limit the number of people who are aware that a change in recommendation will be made.
- Shorten the time frame between decision and dissemination.
- Publish personnel guidelines for pre-dissemination—have in place guidelines prohibiting personnel who have prior knowledge of a recommendation from discussing it or taking action on the pending recommendation.
- Disseminate new or changed recommendations simultaneously to all clients who have expressed an interest or for whom an investment is suitable.
- Establish systematic account review—ensure that no client is given preferred treatment and that investment actions are consistent with the account's objectives.
- Disclose available levels of service and the associated fees.
- Disclose trade allocation procedures.
- Develop written trade allocation procedures to:
  - Document and time stamp all orders.
  - Bundle orders and then execute on a first come, first fill basis.
  - Allocate partially filled orders.
  - Provide the same net (after costs) execution price to all clients in a block trade.

MODULE 30.5: GUIDANCE FOR STANDARDS III(C), III(D), AND III(E)

Video covering this content is available online.

Standard III(C) Suitability

1. When Members and Candidates are in an advisory relationship with a client, they must:
   a. Make a reasonable inquiry into a client's or prospective client's investment experience, risk and return objectives, and financial constraints prior to making any investment recommendation or taking investment action and must reassess and update this information regularly.
   b. Determine that an investment is suitable to the client's financial situation and consistent with the client's written objectives, mandates, and constraints before making an investment recommendation or taking investment action.
   c. Judge the suitability of investments in the context of the client's total portfolio.
2. When Members and Candidates are responsible for managing a portfolio to a specific mandate, strategy, or style, they must make only investment recommendations or take only investment actions that are consistent with the stated objectives and constraints of the portfolio.

In advisory relationships, members must gather client information at the beginning of the relationship, in the form of an investment policy statement (IPS). Consider clients' needs and circumstances and, thus, their risk tolerance. Consider whether or not the use of leverage is suitable for the client.

If a member is responsible for managing a fund to an index or other stated mandate, he must select only investments that are consistent with the stated mandate.

Unsolicited Trade Requests

An investment manager may receive a client request to purchase a security that the manager knows is unsuitable, given the client's investment policy statement. The trade may or may not have a material effect on the risk characteristics of the client's total portfolio and the requirements are different for each case. In either case, however, the manager should not make the trade until he has discussed with the client the reasons (based on the IPS) that the trade is unsuitable for the client's account.

If the manager determines that the *effect on the risk/return profile of the client's total portfolio is minimal*, the manager, after discussing with the client how the trade does not fit the IPS goals and constraints, may follow his firm's policy with regard to unsuitable trades. Regardless of firm policy, the client must acknowledge the discussion and an understanding of why the trade is unsuitable.

If the trade would have a *material impact on the risk/return profile of the client's total portfolio*, one option is to update the IPS so the client accepts a changed risk profile that would permit the trade. If the client will not accept a changed IPS, the manager may follow firm policy, which may allow the trade to be made in a separate client-directed account. In the absence of other options, the manager may need to reconsider whether to maintain the relationship with the client.

Recommendations for Members

- Establish a written IPS, considering the type of client and account beneficiaries, the objectives, constraints, and the portion of the client's assets managed.
- Review the IPS annually and update for material changes in client and market circumstances.
- Develop policies and procedures to assess suitability of portfolio changes. Consider the impact on diversification, risk, and meeting the client's investment strategy.

Standard III(D) Performance Presentation

When communicating investment performance information, Members and Candidates must make reasonable efforts to ensure that it is fair, accurate, and complete.

Members must not misstate performance or mislead clients or prospects about their investment performance or their firm's investment performance.

Members must not misrepresent past performance or reasonably expected performance, and must not state or imply the ability to achieve a rate of return similar to that achieved in the past.

For brief presentations, members must make detailed information available on request and indicate that the presentation has offered only limited information.

Recommendations for Members

- Encourage firms to adhere to Global Investment Performance Standards.
- Consider the sophistication of the audience to whom a performance presentation is addressed.
- Present the performance of a weighted composite of similar portfolios rather than the performance of a single account.
- Include terminated accounts as part of historical performance and clearly state when they were terminated.
- Include all appropriate disclosures to fully explain results (e.g., model results included, gross or net of fees, etc.).
- Maintain data and records used to calculate the performance being presented.

Standard III(E) Preservation of Confidentiality

Members and Candidates must keep information about current, former, and prospective clients confidential unless:

1. The information concerns illegal activities on the part of the client;
2. Disclosure is required by law; or
3. The client or prospective client permits disclosure of the information.

If illegal activities by a client are involved, members may have an obligation to report the activities to authorities.

The confidentiality Standard extends to former clients as well.

The requirements of this Standard are not intended to prevent members and candidates from cooperating with a CFA Institute Professional Conduct Program (PCP) investigation.

Recommendations for Members

- Members should avoid disclosing information received from a client except to authorized coworkers who are also working for the client. Consider whether the disclosure is necessary and will benefit the client.
- Members should follow firm procedures for storage of electronic data and recommend adoption of such procedures if they are not in place.
- Assure client information is not accidentally disclosed.

Readings 29 & 30

MODULE QUIZ 30.4, 30.5

1. Cobb, Inc., has hired Jude Kasten, CFA, to manage its pension fund. The client(s) to whom Kasten owes her primary duty of loyalty is:
   A. Cobb's management.
   B. the shareholders of Cobb, Inc.
   C. the beneficiaries of the pension fund.
2. Which of the following actions is *most likely* a violation of the Standard on fair dealing?
   A. A portfolio manager allocates IPO shares to all client accounts where it is suitable, including her brother's fee-based retirement account.
   B. An investment firm routinely begins trading for its own account immediately after announcing recommendation changes to clients.
   C. After releasing a general recommendation to all clients, an analyst calls the firm's largest institutional clients to discuss the recommendation in more detail.
3. The Standard regarding suitability *most likely* requires that:
   A. an adviser must analyze an investment's suitability for the client prior to recommending or acting on the investment.
   B. a member or candidate must decline to carry out an unsolicited transaction that she believes is unsuitable for the client.
   C. when managing an index fund, a manager who is evaluating potential investments must consider their suitability for the fund's shareholders.
4. Which of the following is *most likely* a recommended procedure for complying with the Standard on performance presentation?
   A. Exclude terminated accounts from past performance history.
   B. Present the performance of a representative account to show how a composite has performed.
   C. Consider the level of financial knowledge of the audience to whom the performance is presented.

5. The CFA Institute Professional Conduct Program (PCP) has begun an investigation into Chris Jones, a Level II CFA candidate, and a number of his CFA charterholder colleagues. Jones has access to confidential client records that could be useful in clearing his name and wishes to share this information with the PCP. Which of the following *most accurately* describes Jones's duties with regard to preservation of confidentiality?
   A. Sharing the confidential information with the PCP would violate the Standards.
   B. The Standards encourage, but do not require, that Jones support the PCP investigation into his colleagues.
   C. Jones may share confidential information about former clients with the PCP but may not share confidential information about current clients.

Video covering this content is available online.

MODULE 30.6: GUIDANCE FOR STANDARD IV

STANDARD IV: DUTIES TO EMPLOYERS

Standard IV(A) Loyalty

In matters related to their employment, Members and Candidates must act for the benefit of their employer and not deprive their employer of the advantage of their skills and abilities, divulge confidential information, or otherwise cause harm to their employer.

This Standard is applicable to employees. If members are independent contractors, rather than employees, they have a duty to abide by the terms of their agreements.

Members must not engage in any activities that would injure the firm, deprive it of profit, or deprive it of the advantage of employees' skills and abilities.

Members should always place client interests above interests of their employer, but consider the effects of their actions on firm integrity and sustainability.

There is no requirement that the employee put employer interests ahead of family and other personal obligations; it is expected that employers and employees will discuss such matters and balance these obligations with work obligations.

There may be isolated cases where a duty to one's employer may be violated in order to protect clients or the integrity of the market, when the actions are not for personal gain. This may be referred to as whistle-blowing.

Independent practice for compensation is allowed if a notification is provided to the employer fully describing all aspects of the services, including compensation, duration, and the nature of the activities and the employer consents to all terms of the proposed independent practice before it begins.

PROFESSOR'S NOTE

The distinction between an employee and contractor is important in applying this and other standards. Think of it as employee status conveys an implication of an exclusive work relationship with the employer and contractor does not. To engage in outside practice or accept additional compensation requires disclosure and approval from the employer. But consider an individual who directly offers services to various clients. The manager is self-employed. With no inference of exclusivity, there is no need to notify or receive approval to add another client. This still leaves other responsibilities in place. If the clients expected or were told the manager is full time self-employed and goes to part time or also becomes an employee at another firm, that is almost certainly material to any reasonable client and must be disclosed.

When leaving an employer, members must continue to act in their employer's best interests until their resignation is effective. Activities that may constitute a violation include:

- Misappropriation of trade secrets.
- Misuse of confidential information.
- Soliciting employer's clients prior to leaving.
- Self-dealing.
- Misappropriation of client lists.

Employer records on any medium (e.g., home computer, tablet, cell phone) are the property of the firm.

When an employee has left a firm, simple knowledge of names and existence of former clients is generally not confidential. There is also no prohibition on the use of experience or knowledge gained while with a former employer. If an agreement exists among employers (e.g., the U.S. "Protocol for Broker Recruiting") that permits brokers to take certain client information when leaving a firm, a member may act within the terms of the agreement without violating the Standard.

Members and candidates must adhere to their employers' policies concerning social media. When planning to leave an employer, members and candidates must ensure that their social media use complies with their employers' policies for notifying clients about employee separations.

Recommendations for Members

- Keep personal and professional social media accounts separate. Business-related accounts approved by the firm constitute employer assets.
- Understand and follow the employer's policies regarding competitive activities, termination of employment, whistleblowing, and whether you are considered a full- or part-time employee, or a contractor.

Recommendations for Firms

Employers should not have incentive and compensation systems that encourage unethical behavior.

- Establish codes of conduct and related procedures.

Standard IV(B) Additional Compensation Arrangements

Members and Candidates must not accept gifts, benefits, compensation, or consideration that competes with or might reasonably be expected to create a conflict of interest with their employer's interest unless they obtain written consent from all parties involved.

Compensation includes direct and indirect compensation from a client and other benefits received from third parties.

Written consent from a member's employer includes email communication.

Understand the difference between an additional compensation arrangement and a gift from a client:

- If a client offers a bonus that depends on the *future performance* of her account, this is an additional compensation arrangement that requires written consent in advance.
- If a client offers a bonus to reward a member for her account's *past performance,* this is a gift that requires disclosure to the member's employer to comply with Standard I(B) Independence and Objectivity.

Recommendations for Members

Make an immediate written report to the employer detailing any proposed compensation and services, if additional to that provided by the employer. It should disclose the nature, approximate amount, and duration of compensation.

Members and candidates who are hired to work part time should discuss any arrangements that may compete with their employer's interest at the time they are hired and abide by any limitations their employer identifies.

Standard IV(C) Responsibilities of Supervisors

Members and Candidates must make reasonable efforts to ensure that anyone subject to their supervision or authority complies with applicable laws, rules, regulations, and the Code and Standards.

Members with employees subject to her control or influence must have in-depth knowledge of the Code and Standards. Those members must make reasonable efforts to prevent employees from violating laws, rules, regulations, or the Code and Standards, as well as make reasonable efforts to detect violations.

An adequate compliance system must meet industry standards, regulatory requirements, and the requirements of the Code and Standards.

Members with supervisory responsibilities have an obligation to bring an inadequate compliance system to the attention of firm's management and recommend corrective action.

A member or candidate faced with no compliance procedures or with procedures he believes are inadequate must decline supervisory responsibility in writing until adequate procedures are adopted by the firm.

Recommendations for Members

A member should recommend that his employer adopt a code of ethics. Members should encourage employers to provide their codes of ethics to clients.

Once the compliance program is instituted, the supervisor should:

- Distribute it to the proper personnel.
- Update it as needed.
- Continually educate staff regarding procedures.
- Issue reminders as necessary.
- Require professional conduct evaluations.
- Review employee actions to monitor compliance and identify violations.
- Respond promptly to violations, investigate thoroughly, increase supervision while investigating the suspected employee, and consider changes to prevent future violations.

Recommendations for Firms

Do not confuse the code with compliance. The code is general principles in plain language. Compliance is detailed procedures to meet the code.

Compliance procedures should:

- Be clearly written.
- Be easy to understand.
- Designate a compliance officer with authority clearly defined.
- Have a system of checks and balances.
- Establish a hierarchy of supervisors.
- Outline the scope of procedures.
- Outline what conduct is permitted.
- Contain procedures for reporting violations and sanctions.

The supervisor must then:

- Disseminate the compliance program to appropriate personnel and periodically update the program.
- Continually educate and remind personnel to follow the program.
- Make professional conduct review part of employee review.
- Review employee actions to identify and then correct violations.

When a violation is detected, the supervisor must:

- Respond promptly and investigate thoroughly.
- Supervise the accused closely until the issue is resolved.
- Consider changes to minimize future violations.

Ethics education will not deter fraud, but when combined with regular compliance training, it will establish an ethical culture and alert employees to potential ethical and legal pitfalls.

Incentive compensation plans must reinforce ethical behavior by designing them to align employee incentives with client best interests (e.g., don't incent inappropriate risk taking or other actions detrimental to the client).

MODULE 30.7: GUIDANCE FOR STANDARD V

Video covering this content is available online.

STANDARD V: INVESTMENT ANALYSIS, RECOMMENDATIONS, AND ACTIONS

Standard V(A) Diligence and Reasonable Basis

Members and Candidates must:

1. Exercise diligence, independence, and thoroughness in analyzing investments, making investment recommendations, and taking investment actions.
2. Have a reasonable and adequate basis, supported by appropriate research and investigation, for any investment analysis, recommendation, or action.

The application of this Standard depends on the investment philosophy adhered to, members' and candidates' roles in the investment decision-making process, and the resources and support provided by employers. These factors dictate the degree of diligence, thoroughness of research, and the proper level of investigation required.

The level of research needed to satisfy the requirement for due diligence will differ depending on the product or service offered. A list of things that should be considered prior to making a recommendation or taking investment action includes:

- Global and national economic conditions.
- A firm's financial results and operating history, and the business cycle stage.
- Fees and historical results for a mutual fund.
- Limitations of any quantitative models used.
- A determination of whether peer group comparisons for valuation are appropriate.

Evaluate the quality of third-party research. Examples of criteria to use in judging quality are:

- Review assumptions used.
- Determine how rigorous the analysis was.
- Identify how timely the research is.
- Evaluate objectivity and independence of the recommendations.

When **using** quantitative research such as computer-based models, screens, and rankings, members need not be experts. However, they must understand the basic assumptions and risks and consider a range of input values and the resulting effects on output. When **creating** such models, a higher level of knowledge and understanding is required.

Develop standardized criteria to evaluate external advisers and subadvisers, such as considering:

- The advisers' code of ethics plus their compliance and control procedures.
- The quality of their return information and process to maintain adherence to intended strategy.

When participating in group research or decision-making, members who disagree need not dissent or disassociate from the final conclusion, as long as the conclusion was based on a reasonable and adequate basis and was independently and objectively developed.

Recommendations for Members

Members should *encourage their firms to consider* these policies and procedures supporting this Standard:

- Have a policy requiring that research reports and recommendations have a basis that can be substantiated as reasonable and adequate.
- Have detailed, written guidance for proper research, supervision, and due diligence.
- Have measurable criteria for judging the quality of research, and base analyst compensation on such criteria.
- Have written procedures that provide a minimum acceptable level of scenario testing for computer-based models and include standards for the range of scenarios, model accuracy over time, and a measure of the sensitivity of cash flows to model assumptions and inputs.
- Have a policy for evaluating outside providers of information that addresses the reasonableness and accuracy of the information provided and establishes how often the evaluations should be repeated.
- Adopt a set of standards that provides criteria for evaluating external advisers and states how often a review of external advisers will be performed.

Standard V(B) Communication with Clients and Prospective Clients

Members and Candidates must:

1. Disclose to clients and prospective clients the basic format and general principles of the investment processes they use to analyze investments, select securities, and construct portfolios and must promptly disclose any changes that might materially affect those processes.
2. Disclose to clients and prospective clients significant limitations and risks associated with the investment process.
3. Use reasonable judgment in identifying which factors are important to their investment analyses, recommendations, or actions and include those factors in communications with clients and prospective clients.
4. Distinguish between fact and opinion in the presentation of investment analyses and recommendations.

All means and types of communication with clients are covered by this Standard, not just research reports or other written communications.

Members must distinguish between opinions and facts and always include the basic characteristics of the security being analyzed in a research report. Expectations based on statistical modeling and analysis are not facts.

Members must explain to clients and prospects the investment decision-making process used.

In preparing recommendations for structured securities, allocation strategies, or any other nontraditional investment, members must communicate those risk factors specific to such investments.

Members must communicate significant changes in the risk characteristics of an investment or investment strategy.

Members must update clients regularly about any changes in the investment process, including any risks and limitations that have been newly identified.

When using projections from quantitative models and analysis, members may violate the Standard by not explaining the limitations of the model and the assumptions it uses, which provides a context for judging the uncertainty regarding the estimated investment result.

Members and candidates must inform clients about limitations inherent to an investment. Two examples of such limitations are liquidity and capacity. Liquidity refers to the ability to exit an investment readily without experiencing a significant extra cost from doing so. Capacity refers to an investment vehicle's ability to absorb additional investment without reducing the returns it is able to achieve.

Recommendations for Members

Selection of relevant factors in a report can be a judgment call so members should maintain records indicating the nature of the research, and be able to supply additional information if it is requested by the client or other users of the report.

Encourage the firm to establish a rigorous method of reviewing research work and results.

Standard V(C) Record Retention

Members and Candidates must develop and maintain appropriate records to support their investment analyses, recommendations, actions, and other investment-related communications with clients and prospective clients.

Members must maintain research records that support the reasons for the analyst's conclusions and any investment actions taken. Such records are the property of the firm. All communications with clients through any medium, including emails and text messages, are records that must be retained.

A member who changes firms must re-create the analysis documentation supporting her recommendation using publicly available information or information obtained from the company and must not rely on memory or materials created at her previous firm.

Recommendations for Members

Maintain notes and documents to support all investment communications.

Recommendations for Firms

If no regulatory standards or firm policies are in place, the Standard recommends a seven-year minimum holding period.

MODULE QUIZ 30.6, 30.7

1. Connie Fletcher, CFA, works for a small money management firm that specializes in pension accounts. Recently, a friend asked her to act as an unpaid volunteer manager for the city's street sweep pension fund. As part of the position, the city would grant Fletcher a free parking space in front of her downtown office. Before Fletcher accepts, she should *most appropriately*:
   A. do nothing because this is a volunteer position.
   B. inform her current clients in writing and discuss the offer with her employer.
   C. disclose the details of the volunteer position to her employer and obtain written permission from her employer.
2. Sarah Johnson, a portfolio manager, is offered a bonus directly by a client if Johnson meets certain performance goals. To comply with the Standard that governs additional compensation arrangements, Johnson should:
   A. decline to accept a bonus outside of her compensation from her employer.
   B. disclose this arrangement to her employer in writing and obtain her employer's permission.
   C. disclose this arrangement to her employer only if she actually meets the performance goals and receives the bonus.
3. A member or candidate who has supervisory responsibility:
   A. should place particular emphasis on enforcing investment-related compliance policies.
   B. is responsible for instructing those to whom he has delegated authority about methods to detect and prevent violations of the law and the Code and Standards.
   C. has complied with the Standards if she reports employee violations to upper management and provides a written warning to the employee to cease such activities.
4. Which of the following actions is a *required*, rather than *recommended*, action under the Standard regarding diligence and a reasonable basis for a firm's research recommendations?
   A. Compensate analysts based on a measure of the quality of their research.
   B. Review the assumptions used and evaluate the objectivity of third-party research reports.
   C. Have a policy requiring that research reports and recommendations have a basis that can be substantiated as reasonable and adequate.

Readings 29 & 30

5. Claire Marlin, CFA, manages an investment fund specializing in foreign currency trading. Marlin writes a report to investors based on an expected appreciation of the euro relative to other major currencies. Marlin shows the projected returns from the strategy under three favorable scenarios: if the euro appreciates less than 5%, between 5% and 10%, or more than 10%. She clearly states that these forecasts are her opinion. Has Marlin violated the Standard related to communication with clients?
   A. Yes.
   B. No, because she disclosed the basic characteristics of the investment.
   C. No, because she distinguished fact from opinion and discussed how the strategy may perform under a range of scenarios.
6. If regulations do not specify how long to retain the documents that support an analyst's conclusions, the Code and Standards recommend a period of at least:
   A. 5 years.
   B. 7 years.
   C. 10 years.

MODULE 30.8: GUIDANCE FOR STANDARD VI

Video covering this content is available online.

STANDARD VI: CONFLICTS OF INTEREST

Standard VI(A) Disclosure of Conflicts

Members and Candidates must make full and fair disclosure of all matters that could reasonably be expected to impair their independence and objectivity or interfere with respective duties to their clients, prospective clients, and employer. Members and Candidates must ensure that such disclosures are prominent, are delivered in plain language, and communicate the relevant information effectively.

Members must fully disclose to clients, prospects, and their employers all actual and potential conflicts of interest in order to protect investors and employers. These disclosures must be clearly stated.

The requirement that all potential areas of conflict be disclosed allows clients and prospects to judge motives and potential biases for themselves. Disclosure of broker-dealer market-making activities would be included here. Board service is another area of potential conflict.

The most common conflict that requires disclosure is actual ownership of stock in companies that the member recommends or that clients hold.

Another common source of conflicts of interest is a member's compensation/bonus structure, which can potentially create incentives to take actions that produce immediate gains for the member with little or no concern for longer-term returns for the client. Such conflicts must be disclosed when the member is acting in an advisory capacity and must be updated in the case of significant change in compensation structure.

Members must give their employers enough information to judge the impact of a conflict, take reasonable steps to avoid conflicts, and report them promptly if they occur.

Recommendations for Members

Any special compensation arrangements, bonus programs, commissions, performance-based fees, options on the firm's stock, and other incentives should be disclosed to clients. If the firm refuses to allow this disclosure, document the refusal and consider disassociating from the firm.

Standard VI(B) Priority of Transactions

Investment transactions for clients and employers must have priority over investment transactions in which a Member or Candidate is the beneficial owner.

Client transactions take priority over personal transactions and over transactions made on behalf of the member's firm. Personal transactions include situations where the member is a beneficial owner.

Personal transactions may be undertaken only after clients and the member's employer have had an adequate opportunity to act on a recommendation. Note that family member accounts that are client accounts should be treated just like any client account; they should not be disadvantaged.

Members must not act on information about pending trades for personal gain. The overriding considerations with respect to personal trades are that they do not disadvantage any clients.

When requested, members must fully disclose to investors their firm's personal trading policies.

Recommendations for Members

Members should encourage their firms to adopt the procedures listed in the following recommendations for firms and disclose these to clients.

Recommendations for Firms

All firms should have basic procedures in place that address conflicts created by personal investing. The following areas should be included:

- Establish limitations on employee participation in equity IPOs and systematically review such participation.
- Establish restrictions on participation in private placements. Strict limits should be placed on employee acquisition of these securities and proper supervisory procedures should be in place. Participation in these investments raises conflict of interest issues similar to those of IPOs.
- Establish blackout/restricted periods. Employees involved in investment decision-making should have blackout periods prior to trading for clients—no front running (i.e., purchase or sale of securities in advance of anticipated client or employer purchases and sales). The size of the firm and the type of security should help dictate how severe the blackout requirement should be.

- Establish reporting procedures, including duplicate trade confirmations, disclosure of personal holdings and beneficial ownership positions, and preclearance procedures.
- Disclose, upon request, the firm's policies regarding personal trading.

Standard VI(C) Referral Fees

Members and Candidates must disclose to their employer, clients, and prospective clients, as appropriate, any compensation, consideration, or benefit received from or paid to others for the recommendation of products or services.

Members must inform employers, clients, and prospects of any benefit received for referrals of customers and clients, allowing them to evaluate the full cost of the service as well as any potential partiality. All types of consideration must be disclosed.

Recommendations for Members

Members should encourage their firms to adopt clear procedures regarding compensation for referrals.

Recommendations for Firms

Have an investment professional advise the clients at least quarterly on the nature and amount of any such compensation.

Video covering this content is available online.

MODULE 30.9: GUIDANCE FOR STANDARD VII

STANDARD VII: RESPONSIBILITIES AS A CFA INSTITUTE MEMBER OR CFA CANDIDATE

Standard VII(A) Conduct as Participants in CFA Institute Programs

Members and Candidates must not engage in any conduct that compromises the reputation or integrity of CFA Institute or the CFA designation or the integrity, validity, or security of CFA Institute programs.

Members must not engage in any activity that undermines the integrity of the CFA charter. This Standard applies to conduct that includes:

- Cheating on the CFA exam or any exam.
- Revealing anything about either broad or specific topics tested, content of exam questions, or formulas required or not required on the exam.
- Not following rules and policies of the CFA Program.
- Giving confidential information on the CFA Program to candidates or the public.

- Improperly using the designation to further personal and professional goals.
- Misrepresenting information on the Professional Conduct Statement (PCS) or the CFA Institute Professional Development Program.

Members and candidates are not precluded from expressing their opinions regarding the exam program or CFA Institute but must not reveal confidential information about the CFA Program.

Candidates who violate any of the CFA exam policies (e.g., calculator, personal belongings, Candidate Pledge) have violated Standard VII(A).

Members who volunteer in the CFA Program may not solicit or reveal information about questions considered for or included on a CFA exam, about the grading process, or about scoring of questions.

Standard VII(B) Reference to CFA Institute, the CFA Designation, and the CFA Program

When referring to CFA Institute, CFA Institute membership, the CFA designation, or candidacy in the CFA Program, Members and Candidates must not misrepresent or exaggerate the meaning or implications of membership in CFA Institute, holding the CFA designation, or candidacy in the CFA Program.

Members must not make promotional promises or guarantees tied to the CFA designation, such as over-promising individual competence or over-promising investment results in the future (i.e., higher performance, less risk, etc.).

Members must satisfy these requirements to maintain membership:

- Sign the PCS annually.
- Pay CFA Institute membership dues annually.

If they fail to do this, they are no longer active members.

Do not misrepresent or exaggerate the meaning of the CFA designation.

There is no partial CFA designation. It is acceptable to state that a candidate successfully completed the program in three years if, in fact, he did, but claiming superior ability because of this is not permitted.

Recommendations for Members

Members should be sure that their firms are aware of the proper references to a member's CFA designation or candidacy, as errors in these references are common.

MODULE QUIZ 30.8, 30.9

1. Daniel Lyons, CFA, is an analyst who covers several stocks, including Horizon Company. Lyons's aunt owns 30,000 shares of Horizon. She informs Lyons that she has created a trust in his name into which she has placed 2,000 shares of Horizon. The trust is structured so that Lyons will not be able to sell the shares until his aunt dies, but may vote the shares. Lyons is due to update his research coverage of Horizon next week. Lyons should *most appropriately*:
   A. update the report as usual because he is not a beneficial owner of the stock.
   B. advise his superiors that he is no longer able to issue research recommendations on Horizon.
   C. disclose the situation to his employer and, if then asked to prepare a report, also disclose his beneficial ownership of the shares in his report.
2. Kate Wilson, CFA, is an equity analyst. Wilson enters two transactions for her personal account. For cash flow reasons, Wilson sells 500 shares of Tibon, Inc., a stock on which she currently has a "Buy" recommendation. Wilson buys 200 shares of Hayfield Co. and the following day issues a research report on Hayfield with a "Buy" recommendation. Has Wilson violated the Code and Standards?
   A. No.
   B. Yes, both of her actions violate the Code and Standards.
   C. Yes, but only one of her actions violates the Code and Standards.
3. Hern Investments provides monthly emerging market research to Baker Brokerage in exchange for prospective client referrals and European equity research from Baker. Clients and prospects of Hern are not made aware of the agreement, but clients unanimously rave about the high quality of the research provided by Baker. As a result of the research, many clients with non-discretionary accounts have earned substantial returns on their portfolios. Managers at Hern have also used the research to earn outstanding returns for the firm's discretionary accounts. Hern has *most likely*:
   A. not violated the Code and Standards.
   B. violated the Code and Standards by using third-party research in discretionary accounts.
   C. violated the Code and Standards by failing to disclose the referral agreement with Baker.
4. After writing the Level III CFA exam, Cynthia White goes to internet discussion site *CFA Haven* to express her frustration. White writes, "CFA Institute is not doing a competent job of evaluating candidates because none of the questions in the June exam touched on Alternative Investments." White *most likely* violated the Standard related to conduct as a candidate in the CFA program by:
   A. publicly disputing CFA Institute policies and procedures.
   B. disclosing subject matter covered or not covered on a CFA exam.
   C. participating in an internet forum that is directed toward CFA Program participants.

5. After passing all three levels of the CFA exams on her first attempts and being awarded her CFA charter, Paula Osgood is promoting her new money management firm by issuing an advertisement. Which of these statements would *most likely* violate the Standard related to use of the CFA designation?
   A. "To earn the right to use the CFA designation, Paula completed the relevant amount of work experience and passed three exams covering ethics, financial statement analysis, asset valuation, and portfolio management."
   B. "Paula passed the three levels of the CFA exams on her first attempts and is a member of her local investment analyst society."
   C. "Because of her extensive training, Paula will be able to achieve better investment results than managers who have not been awarded the CFA designation."

ANSWER KEY FOR MODULE QUIZZES

Module Quiz 29.1

1. **C** The process for enforcing the Code and Standards does not include suspending a member or candidate while an inquiry is in progress. If CFA Institute Professional Conduct staff receive information that prompts an inquiry, the staff may request information from the member or candidate, interview parties who initiated a complaint, or review relevant records and documents. (LOS 29.a)

2. **A** One of the six components of the Code of Ethics requires members and candidates to "maintain and improve their professional competence and strive to maintain and improve the competence of other investment professionals." The other two answer choices are required by the Standards of Professional Conduct but are not components of the Code of Ethics. (LOS 29.b)

3. **C** The Standard related to additional compensation arrangements is a subsection of Standard IV Duties to Employers. (LOS 29.b)

Module Quiz 30.1, 30.2, 30.3

1. **C** To comply with Standard I(A) Knowledge of the Law, a member must always abide by the strictest applicable law, regulation, or standard. (Module 30.1, LOS 30.a, 30.b)

2. **A** Gifts from clients are acceptable under Standard I(B) Independence and Objectivity, but the Standard requires members and candidates to disclose such gifts to their employers. Standard I(B) allows issuer-paid research as long as the analysis is thorough, independent, unbiased, and has a reasonable and adequate basis for its conclusions, and the compensation from the issuer is disclosed. Members and candidates should consider the potential for conflicts of interest inherent in credit ratings and may need to do independent research to evaluate the soundness of these ratings. (Module 30.1, LOS 30.a, 30.b)

3. **C** According to Standard I(C) Misrepresentation, members and candidates must cite the sources of the information they use in their analysis, unless the information is factual data (as opposed to analysis or opinion) from a recognized financial or statistical reporting service. The U.S. Treasury is one example of a recognized source of factual data. (Module 30.2, LOS 30.a, 30.b)

4. **B** Failing to act when required by one's professional obligations, such as neglecting to perform due diligence related to an investment recommendation, violates Standard I(D) Misconduct. Acts a member commits outside his professional capacity are misconduct if they reflect poorly on the member or candidate's honesty, integrity, or competence

(e.g., theft or fraud).Violations of the law that do not reflect on the member or candidate's honesty, integrity, or competence (e.g., an act related to civil disobedience or minor civil offenses) are not necessarily regarded as misconduct. (Module 30.2, LOS 30.a, 30.b)

5. **A** The statement from the CFO about the current quarter's earnings is material nonpublic information. Ingus violated Standard II(A) Material Nonpublic Information by acting or causing others to act on it. (Module 30.3, LOS 30.a, 30.b)

6. **B** The intent of Green Brothers' actions is to manipulate the appearance of market liquidity in order to attract investment to its own funds. The increased trading activity was not based on market fundamentals or an actual trading strategy to benefit investors. It was merely an attempt to mislead market participants in order to increase assets under Green Brothers' management. The action violates Standard II(B) Market Manipulation. (Module 30.3, LOS 30.a, 30.b)

Module Quiz 30.4, 30.5

1. **C** Standard III(A) Loyalty, Prudence, and Care specifies that for the manager of a pension or trust, the duty of loyalty is owed to the beneficiaries, not to the individuals who hired the manager. (Module 30.4, LOS 30.a, 30.b)

2. **B** The firm must give its clients an opportunity to act on recommendation changes. Firms can offer different levels of service to clients as long as this is disclosed to all clients. The largest institutional clients would likely be paying higher fees for a greater level of service. The portfolio manager's brother's account should be treated the same as any other client account. (Module 30.4, LOS 30.a, 30.b)

3. **A** According to Standard III(C) Suitability, a member or candidate who is in an advisory relationship with a client is responsible for analyzing the suitability of an investment for the client before taking investment action or making a recommendation. If a member or candidate believes an unsolicited trade is unsuitable for a client, the appropriate action is to discuss the trade with the client. The adviser may follow her firm's policies for obtaining client approval if the requested trade would not affect the risk and return of the client's portfolio materially. If the trade would have a material effect, the adviser should discuss with the client whether the IPS needs to be updated. When managing a fund to an index or stated mandate, the manager is responsible for ensuring that potential investments are consistent with the fund's mandate. Suitability for individuals would be a concern for an adviser who recommends the fund to clients, but not for the manager of the fund. (Module 30.5, LOS 30.a, 30.b)

4. **C** Recommendations stated in Standard III(D) Performance Presentation include considering the sophistication and knowledge of the audience when presenting performance data. Other recommendations are to

include terminated accounts in past performance history; to present the performance of a composite as a weighted average of the performance of similar portfolios, rather than using a single representative account; and to maintain the records and data that were used to calculate performance. (Module 30.5, LOS 30.a, 30.b)

5. **B** Members and candidates are required to cooperate with PCP investigations into their own conduct and encouraged to cooperate with PCP investigations into the conduct of others. Sharing confidential information with the PCP is not a violation of Standard III(E) Preservation of Confidentiality. Any client information shared with the PCP will be kept in strict confidence. Standard III(E) states that members and candidates are required to maintain confidentiality of client records even after the end of the client relationship. (Module 30.5, LOS 30.a, 30.b)

Module Quiz 30.6, 30.7

1. **C** According to Standard IV(A) Loyalty, members and candidates are expected to act for the benefit of their employer and not deprive the employer of their skills. Fletcher is performing work similar to the services that her employer provides. Although the position is a volunteer position, Fletcher will receive compensation in the form of a free parking space. In light of the circumstances, Fletcher must disclose the details of the position to her employer and get written permission before accepting the volunteer position. (Module 30.6, LOS 30.a, 30.b)

2. **B** Johnson should disclose her additional compensation arrangement in writing to her employer and obtain her employer's written consent before accepting this offer, in accordance with Standard IV(B) Additional Compensation Arrangements. (Module 30.6, LOS 30.a, 30.b)

3. **B** Members or candidates may delegate supervisory duties to subordinates but remain responsible for instructing and supervising them. Reporting the violation and warning the employee are not sufficient to comply with Standard IV(C) Responsibilities of Supervisors. The supervisor must also take steps to prevent further violations while she conducts an investigation, such as limiting the employee's activity or increasing her monitoring of the employee. Supervisors should enforce investment-related and non-investment related policies equally. (Module 30.6, LOS 30.a, 30.b)

4. **B** Standard V(A) Diligence and Reasonable Basis requires analysts who use third-party research to review its assumptions and evaluate the independence and objectivity of the research. The other choices are recommended procedures for compliance with the Standard. (Module 30.7, LOS 30.a, 30.b)

5. **A** Standard V(B) Communication with Clients and Prospective Clients requires that members and candidates communicate the risk associated with the investment strategy used and how the strategy is expected to

perform in a range of scenarios. Marlin should have also discussed how her strategy would perform if the euro depreciates instead of appreciating as she expects. (Module 30.7, LOS 30.a, 30.b)

6. **B** When no other regulatory guidance applies, Standard V(C) Record Retention recommends that records be maintained for a minimum of seven years. (Module 30.7, LOS 30.a, 30.b)

Module Quiz 30.8, 30.9

1. **C** Even though the shares are held in trust, Lyons is considered a beneficial owner under Standard VI(A) Disclosure of Conflicts because he has a pecuniary interest in the shares and because he has the power to vote the shares. Lyons is obligated to inform his employer of the potential conflict. If Lyons's employer permits him to continue issuing investment recommendations on the company, Lyons must disclose the existence of a potential conflict in his reports. (Module 30.8, LOS 30.a, 30.b)

2. **C** Only one of these transactions is a violation. Standard VI(B) Priority of Transactions requires members and candidates to give clients an adequate opportunity to act on a recommendation before trading for accounts in which the member or candidate has a beneficial ownership interest. Members and candidates may trade for their own accounts as long as they do not disadvantage clients, benefit personally from client trades, or violate any regulations that apply. The Standard does not prohibit members and candidates from entering personal transactions that are contrary to what their firms are recommending for clients, as long as the transaction does not violate any of these criteria. (Module 30.8, LOS 30.a, 30.b)

3. **C** According to Standard VI(C) Referral Fees, Hern must disclose the referral arrangement between itself and Baker so that potential clients can judge the true cost of Hern's services and assess whether there is any partiality inherent in the recommendation of services. (Module 30.8, LOS 30.a, 30.b)

4. **B** Standard VII(A) Conduct as Participants in CFA Institute Programs prohibits candidates from revealing which portions of the Candidate Body of Knowledge were or were not covered on an exam. Members and candidates are free to disagree with the policies, procedures, or positions taken by the CFA Institute. The Standard does not prohibit participating in CFA Program-related internet blogs, forums, or social networks. (Module 30.9, LOS 30.a, 30.b)

5. **C** Standard VII(B) Reference to CFA Institute, the CFA designation, and the CFA Program prohibits members and candidates from implying superior performance as a result of being a CFA charterholder. Concise factual descriptions of the requirements to obtain the CFA charter are acceptable. Osgood's statement that she passed the exams on her first attempts is acceptable because it states a fact. (Module 30.9, LOS 30.a, 30.b)

READING 31

Application of the Code and Standards: Level III

EXAM FOCUS

The cases are not intended to teach new material, but to provide additional examples of applying the Code and Standards. There are five cases and within each case are multiple-choice questions (47 total). Prior to reviewing the summary here, you should read each of the cases contained in the Level III curriculum readings and answer the multiple-choice questions. All 47 multiple-choice questions contain valuable explanations for the correct answer as well as explanations for the incorrect answers.

MODULE 31.1: CASES

Video covering this content is available online.

LOS 31.a: Evaluate practices, policies, and conduct relative to the CFA Institute Code of Ethics and Standards of Professional Conduct.

LOS 31.b: Explain how the practices, policies, or conduct does or does not violate the CFA Institute Code of Ethics and Standards of Professional Conduct.

Case Outline: Sovereign Investment Corporation

Victoria Adebayo has recently returned to her home country to become the chief financial officer of Sovereign Investment Corporation (SIC). Before this new role, Adebayo had worked for a U.K. hedge fund, HFI.

The objectives of SIC are to develop the country's economy by financing local projects that generate a positive return on investment and attract international investors. A secondary objective is to develop the country's capital markets.

SIC controls an investment company, National Investments (NI), which offers domestically listed stock to international investors in return for overseas finance.

A regional governor, who is also the leader of the country's main opposition party, is lobbying for a major investment in a mining project in a remote area. The project will bring development benefits to the region and a positive ROI but requires significant capital investment. The current government's minister of finance advocates for a smaller urban infrastructure project. This project requires less initial investment than the mining project and will create hundreds of jobs for the supporters of the incumbent government. The minister of finance was involved in the hiring of Adebayo.

Adebayo believes that undertaking both projects simultaneously would place too great a strain on NI's resources. She quickly decides to invest in the smaller infrastructure project first and then later to invest in the larger mining project. Adebayo believes that this project sequence would have the benefits of supporting the current governmental regime and that the opposition party may have gained power by the time the mining project is undertaken. She also believes that the infrastructure project will generate a higher return in the short run, which will be beneficial for attracting investors, which in turn will help to finance the mining project.

DISCUSSION: Diligence and Reasonable Basis, Suitability

Standard V(A): Diligence and Reasonable Basis requires members making investment decisions to have a reasonable and adequate basis to support their decisions. This includes exercising independence, thoroughness, and diligence. Adebayo has violated this standard as she acted quickly based on political considerations rather than proper financial analysis. Additionally, while she faces political pressure, she must remain independent and avoid conflicts of interest.

The political pressure causing a conflict of interest could have been mitigated if NI had developed a strong governance framework for investment decisions. This framework should be focused on allowing staff to perform sufficient due diligence and to make decisions free from bias. Simple disclosure of the conflict of interest per Standard VI(A): Disclosure of Conflicts would be insufficient to avoid a violation because it does not remove the requirement to make objective, independent investment decisions. The case also considers whether Adebayo could discharge her duties by requiring investment decisions to be authorized by a higher governmental authority. In this case, this would lead to greater political bias, not less, and still result in decisions lacking objectivity, which would still breach Standard V(A).

Standard III(C): Suitability requires members to make investment decisions that are consistent with a funds mandate. Adebayo has a dual mandate to invest in projects that will boost her country's economic development while generating positive ROI. Adebayo has not breached this standard as both projects considered are consistent with this mandate.

Anthony Corrales, a previous colleague of Adebayo at HFI, contacts Adebayo about a potential investment in NI. Corrales requests information on NI's financial condition and both current and future projects. Adebayo provides him with the standard investor disclosure package.

Corrales decides that NI is an excellent investment and complies with HFI's mandate. To convince his partners at the hedge fund of the strength of his convictions, he immediately invests 25% of his personal portfolio in NI. After several days of deliberation, the partners at HFI decide to invest in NI. At the same time, the HFI partners ask for assurance that NI will maintain its aggressive strategy, targeting high returns. Adebayo, in response, assures HFI that NI is committed to generating a high ROI for investors. Once HFI's investment is publicly announced, the shares of NI rise on the exchange. Corrales requests regular updates on NI's performance, funding plans, and financial status directly from Adebayo.

DISCUSSION: Suitability, Communication with Clients and Prospective Clients, Fair Dealing

Standard III(C): Suitability requires members to make investment decisions that are consistent with a funds mandate. Adebayo violates the standard by not disclosing that NI has a dual mandate to promote economic development and positive ROI. Investors must be made aware that investment returns are not the only factor driving NI's investment decisions.

Sharing information on NI's financial position and projects is not a violation of standards, providing it is not confidential or material non-public information. Transparency is an important element of Standard V(B): Communication with Clients and Prospective Clients. Providing this information to potential investors is both reasonable and appropriate to support their due diligence. By providing the standard investor disclosure package, Adebayo is not showing any favoritism to HFI and therefore has not violated Standard III(B): Fair Dealing.

The request for regular updates directly from Adebayo is not a violation of Standard III(B): Fair Dealing, provided that all NI investors are fairly treated and are provided with the same information. No evidence is included in the case study that suggests the information supplied to Corrales by Adebayo is not provided to all NI investors.

DISCUSSION: Priority of Transactions, Conflicts of Interest

Standard VI(B): Priority of Transactions requires that investment transactions for clients and employers must have priority over transactions where a member is a beneficial owner. Corrales purchases his stake in NI before his employer. Trading for Corrales's personal account in advance of trading for clients or an employer is referred to as front running and is not only a violation of the standard but also illegal in many jurisdictions and, therefore, may also violate Standard I(A): Knowledge of the Law. Corrales's position in NI benefits directly from the price appreciation after the announcement of HFI's investment. Regardless of whether HFI is disadvantaged by Corrales's personal investment, Corrales should wait until after his employer (or clients) has traded before trading for his account.

Investing in the same stock as an employer or client does not automatically create a conflict of interest per Standard VI(A): Conflicts of Interest,

Reading 31

> provided that the ownership is disclosed. Reportable situations include conflicts that may interfere with the provision of unbiased investment advice or cause the employee not to act in the employer's best interest. In this scenario, it is implied that Corrales's employer is aware of his investment.

Corrales recruits overseas subadvisors to identify private market investments for HFI and to aid with local laws and regulations. The subadvisors are paid directly from the fund's assets and have connections with high-ranked local government officials but have minimal or no experience as financial advisors. The subadvisors make payments on behalf of the fund to cover "deal fees" aimed at gaining government support for investments. The subadvisors are not required to detail their actions or list what specific expenses the fees cover. The fees are reported as operating expenses in HFI's accounts.

> **DISCUSSION: Subadvisors**
>
> The use of subadvisors to provide specialist expertise outside of the scope of a member's experience or ability does not automatically violate Standard V(A): Diligence and Reasonable Basis. Corrales has breached the standard because members must review subadvisors as diligently as they review funds or securities, including their knowledge and expertise. In this case, the subadvisors have limited advisory experience. Additionally, members who are directly involved with the use of external advisors need to ensure that their firm has standardized criteria for reviewing external advisors.
>
> Corrales's reporting of the "deal fees" as legitimate operating expenses breaches Standard I(C): Misrepresentation. The true nature of the payments appears to be to bribe overseas government officials. Additional suspicion is raised by the lack of supporting documentation. While subadvisors can be legitimately used to aid the investment process, the subadvisors' limited advisory experience would indicate that this is not their primary purpose. Bribery of government officials is likely to breach local anti-bribery laws, resulting in the violation of Standard I(A): Knowledge of the Law.

Ani Mehrotra is hired by Adebayo to promote NI globally to potential investors. Adebayo discloses to Mehrotra that she has not paid her CFA Institute membership dues but continues to use the designation on her business card. When questioned on this, Adebayo claims that the use of the designation is like a degree from a university and cannot be taken away. When asked by a potential client, in a meeting at which Mehrotra is present, whether all of NI's senior investment professionals are CFA charterholders, she claims that they are, which is not contradicted by Mehrotra.

Mehrotra leads an exam prep class offered by his local society for local candidates. After the exam, his students describe their experience of the examination experience, including the relative difficulty of the exam and areas of the syllabus that were not tested. Mehrotra asks his students for their opinion on the most difficult exam questions. Mehrotra aims to use the feedback to ensure future candidates taking his course are better prepared.

DISCUSSION: Reference to the CFA Designation and Conduct of Participants in CFA Institute Programs

Adebayo has violated Standard VII(B): Reference to the CFA Institute, CFA Designation, and the CFA Program. Adebayo is incorrect in that the designation is like a university degree. To use the designation, members must satisfy the CFA Institute membership requirements, which include both annual payment dues and submission of the Professional Conduct Statement. Adebayo may refer to herself as a previous CFA Institute member but must not use the designation or present herself as a charterholder until her membership is reactivated.

Mehrotra violates Standard I(A): Knowledge of the Law by remaining silent while Adebayo claims all senior investment professionals at NI hold the charter. This standard makes members responsible for violations in which they knowingly participate or assist. A member who believes an activity is either unethical or unlawful must dissociate from the violations of others. Inaction is not sufficient to comply with the standard. To comply with the standard, Mehrotra should discuss the issue with Adebayo and ask her to correct the statement made to the client. If Adebayo refuses, Mehrotra should raise the issue with SIC's compliance department and dissociate by not attending any new sales meetings with Adebayo.

Mehrotra breaches Standard VII(A): Conduct as Participants in CFA Institute Programs, which prevents candidates from engaging in or members soliciting any conduct that compromises the integrity of CFA Institute Programs, including discussing the specifics of the examination. By soliciting information on specific questions, Mehrotra violates the standard. If Mehrotra informs future candidates of specific questions tested in the past or in areas that were not tested, this would also be a violation even if Mehrotra had not solicited the information. Discussing how candidates perceived the difficulty of the examination would not violate the standard as this is non-specific subjective information.

Case Outline: Marcia Lopez

During the same month, Marcia Lopez obtained a master's degree in finance, wrote the Level I CFA exam, and accepted a position in the wealth management department of a large financial institution, BankGlobal. Two months later, upon passing the Level I exam, she begins working at the firm. Her supervisor, David Hockett, CFA, is reviewing Lopez's business card request that states the following: "CFA, Level I." He adds that she should also include the year in which she expects to be granted the CFA charter.

DISCUSSION: Referencing Participation in the CFA Program

According to Standard VII(B) Reference to CFA Institute, the CFA Designation, and the CFA Program, Lopez must be explicit that she is a CFA candidate and may not suggest that she has a partial designation. Furthermore, stating an expected date for receipt of the CFA charter is not acceptable because it is not possible to verify uncertain future events.

Reading 31

Hockett then has Lopez meet other members of his wealth management team. Hockett's team has a very strong rapport with BankGlobal's research department. Due to technical problems with the firm's computer systems, there is about a 45-minute delay between the time when the research analysts submit their changes in recommendations and the time when they are uploaded to BankGlobal's website and sent to their clients. As a courtesy to Hockett's team, the analysts usually inform them verbally about their changes prior to the information going live on the website. Right after they hear the information, the team uses that information to ensure that their discretionary accounts are not negatively impacted when the changes are made public.

DISCUSSION: Fair Dealing

According to Standard III(B) Fair Dealing, Hockett's team members must not use the information verbally obtained from the analysts for the benefit of their discretionary clients' accounts until the information has been made public. By doing so, they are not treating all of the firm's clients in a fair and impartial manner. In fact, they are giving preferential treatment to the discretionary accounts and in the process, clients who have nondiscretionary accounts may be unfairly disadvantaged.

Although the information may be perceived by the general public to be material, the information was created by external analysts, who are assumed not to be in possession of material nonpublic information (unless otherwise stated). Therefore, there is no violation of Standard II(A) Material Nonpublic Information.

With a few months of work experience, Lopez is given the opportunity to meet with potential new clients, Marty and Mary Kochanski. The Kochanskis were referred to Hockett by Gary White, a business banker at BankGlobal. The only information that White provided to Hockett about the Kochanskis was that they were both 61 years old, retired, and wanted to invest the $7.4 million of proceeds from the sale of Mary's business. Based solely on the information provided by White, Hockett tells Lopez to devise a "balanced portfolio" investment for the Kochanskis.

In preparing the portfolio, Lopez selects two equity and two fixed income funds. For those four funds, she makes a few simplifying assumptions in presenting the returns. For example, she averages the funds' five-year annualized rates of return and excludes terminated accounts. As well, she provides comparative numbers with five-year annualized rates of return for a "composite portfolio" that includes discretionary accounts of similar size to the Kochanskis' and that have a balanced objective.

DISCUSSION: Know Your Client and Performance Presentation

Hockett and Lopez did not perform sufficient due diligence on their prospective clients *prior* to recommending the balanced portfolio. That is in violation of Standard III(C) Suitability. They should have taken the time to meet with the clients to find out relevant information such as their risk and return objectives and their investment experience prior to recommending any investments.

> Lopez excluded the performance of terminated accounts, which violates Standard III(D) Performance Presentation. The requirement to include terminated accounts is meant to prevent an upward bias in reporting returns due to survivorship bias.

The Kochanskis invest their $7.4 million of funds in a balanced portfolio with BankGlobal. In a conversation with White, Hockett discusses his incentive and quarterly bonus program. Hockett acknowledges that the vast majority of his clients have low risk tolerances and have a long-term approach to investing. However, he has been earning excess returns in those accounts in the short-term by investing portions of their portfolios in high beta stocks. Because those stocks have the appearance of low risk, Hockett does not need to amend the client investment policy statement.

Lopez sends a message to her close friends that she has taken on the Kochanskis as new clients.

> **DISCUSSION: Suitability and Confidentiality**
>
> Hockett violated Standard III(C) Suitability because he has placed his client funds in unsuitable investments (e.g. high beta stocks with a short-term focus) that are inconsistent with their investment objectives (e.g. low risk tolerance with a long-term focus). Clearly, high beta stocks are not low risk. Changing the investment strategy requires the input and approval of the clients, which was not obtained by Hockett.
>
> Lopez violated Standard III(E) Preservation of Confidentiality by revealing their identity as clients to her friends. All information about former, current, or prospective clients must be kept confidential and remain within the firm.

Reading 31

Case Outline: Castle Biotechnology

Castle Biotechnology (Castle) operates a biopharmaceutical company and controls nine other subsidiary biopharmaceutical companies. Last year, Castle acquired a controlling interest in Global Capital Management (Global), an investment banking and asset management firm. Two of Castle's subsidiary companies, Street Pharmaceuticals (STRX) and Appaloosa Biotech (APBX) went public recently although Castle maintains voting control of each of them.

David Plume, PhD, CFA, is a biopharmaceutical analyst for Global. Previously, he was a biochemist at Castle for many years and during that time, he developed close relationships with both the president and the chief executive. Plume's remuneration at Global includes an annual bonus of 0.10% of the gross proceeds raised for each initial public offering (IPO) with which he is involved.

Shortly after STRX's and APBX's respective IPOs, Plume wrote highly favorable research reports on both companies and rated them both a *buy*. Several months after the APBX report was issued, he sold short APBX and did not disclose the transaction given that he had never been a beneficial owner of APBX.

In his research reports, Plume does not disclose that Castle controls Global, STRX, and APBX since that information is already disclosed in STRX's and APBX's offering prospectuses. He also does not disclose that he owns Class A preferred shares of Castle and options on Castle's common stock, both of which he acquired while employed at Castle.

DISCUSSION: Conflicts of Interest and Professionalism

Plume violated Standard VI(A) Disclosure of Conflicts by not disclosing in his research report that Global is controlled by Castle. That fact would have been important in allowing the users of the report to assess the conflict of interest and determine how it may have impacted Plume's independence and objectivity in writing his research reports. The risk of impairment of his independence and objectivity was high given that he developed close relationships with two key members of Castle's management team.

Because of his ownership of preferred shares of Castle and options on Castle's common stock, Plume should have disclosed that Global is controlled by Castle. By not doing so, he violated Standard VI(A). Additionally, because he owns shares of Castle, he has a material beneficial ownership interest in both STRX and APBX (and he issued 'buy' recommendations on them). That is a conflict of interest that he should have disclosed.

Plume's nondisclosure in his research report of his annual bonus is a violation of Standard I(B) Professionalism, Independence and Objectivity because he is being compensated based on a deal amount. Standard I(B) states, "Compensation arrangements should not link analyst remuneration directly to investment banking assignments in which the analysts may participate as a team member." Additionally, the bonus is calculated on the gross proceeds of the IPO, which makes it an additional compensation arrangement. As a result, the nondisclosure would be a violation of Standard VI(A).

Plume's short sale transaction of APBX violates Standard VI(A) because of the conflict of interest arising when he had previously issued a 'buy' recommendation. That conflict should have been disclosed.

Sandra Benning, CFA, was previously employed as an investment adviser at Kodiak Securities (Kodiak) and resigned from there recently to join Global in the same role. Immediately upon resignation from Kodiak, she used social media and personal email to encourage her clients to move with her to Global. Global paid Benning a substantial signing bonus calculated on the percentage of her clients from Kodiak who transferred their accounts to Global. Global's annual bonus for its investment advisers is calculated on the amount of their clients' IPO participation. Neither bonus was disclosed to Benning's clients.

DISCUSSION: Duties to Employers and Conflicts of Interest

Because there was not a noncompete agreement in place with Kodiak and her solicitation of her clients from Kodiak occurred after she resigned, Benning's actions do not constitute a violation of Standard IV(A) Loyalty.

Benning's signing bonus was based on the percentage of her former clients who switched over to Global. Clearly there is an actual or potential conflict of interest that should have been disclosed to her former clients. Knowing that Benning would be compensated for the percentage of clients switched over would have allowed her former clients to recognize that her independence and objectivity may be impaired. In short, it would have allowed them to make a more informed decision on whether they should switch their accounts over or not. Because she did not disclose the signing bonus to her former clients, Benning violated Standard VI(A) Disclosure of Conflicts.

Benning's annual bonus that is based on the level of her clients' participation in IPOs results in a conflict of interest because it brings into question whether she is recommending the IPOs because they are suitable for her clients or because she is trying to maximize her bonus. As a result, she was required to disclose the annual bonus to her former clients and by not doing so, Benning once again violated Standard VI(A).

Global is underwriting an upcoming IPO for Frontier Therapeutics (FTSX), one of the companies controlled by Castle. Global's IPO allocation policy is to allocate IPO shares only to those institutional clients who indicate they will buy more shares on the first day of trading.

DISCUSSION: Tie-In Agreement

A tie-in agreement exists when an underwriter requires the investing client to purchase additional shares of the new issue in the secondary market in exchange for the ability to purchase the IPO shares. The effect is to artificially increase demand and increase the share price on day one of trading. That is in direct violation of Standard II(B) Market Manipulation. It is also in violation of Standard III(B) Fair Dealing because Benning is not treating all her institutional clients fairly when she is only allocating IPO shares to those clients who will buy more shares once trading commences.

Benning's new client, Claris Deacon, makes a series of visits to Benning's office to open a series of accounts, including a brokerage account and a checking account. As well, Deacon signed an Option Account Application and Agreement on her final visit but subsequent to that visit, Benning amended some of the wording in the agreement regarding Deacon's suitability. Benning decides to initial the agreement for Deacon to save Deacon the time from having to make another visit.

Later Deacon contacts Benning to advise her that she cannot transfer funds between her brokerage and checking accounts. Benning investigates and determines that the links between the accounts were not activated. She calls Deacon and obtains her verbal authorization to sign the Account Linking form on her behalf.

Benning subsequently receives a call from Deacon's husband, Steve. He advises that his wife is having major health problems and requests that Benning redeem some mutual fund shares and transfer the proceeds over immediately. In response, Benning processes several redemptions and withdrawals from Deacon's account at Steve's request in the coming weeks.

DISCUSSION: Professionalism and Loyalty, Prudence, and Care

Changing the language and initialing the form on behalf of Deacon is a violation of Standard I(D) Misconduct in that there may have been elements of dishonesty or deceit in doing so. Although there was verbal approval from Deacon, it would have been necessary for her to provide written authorization.

Benning is also in violation of Standard III(A) Loyalty, Prudence, and Care when she redeemed shares and processed withdrawals in Deacon's account without Deacon's written consent. Benning did not demonstrate loyalty, prudence, or care with those actions. Deacon's husband was not listed as a joint account holder on any of the accounts and was not given any prior written authorization by Deacon to transact in any of her accounts.

Case Outline: Lionsgate Limited and Bank of Australia

Lionsgate Limited (LL) is a fund manager and its strongest fund is an equity mutual fund, the Victory Capital Fund (VCF) that is managed by Tony Hill and his group of analysts. In LL's marketing materials, statements include VCF being the best performing Australian equity fund for a 10-year period, earning returns of 28.7% gross of fees over the most recent 1-year period, and 13.2% annually since inception in 2005.

Hill often appears on talk shows to discuss the VCF and in lieu of any financial remuneration, the show sponsors offer him nonmonetary items such as wine, retail gift cards, and travel discounts. Hill does not disclose the receipt of those items to LL.

Nicole Martin, CFA, is an analyst on Hill's team. When Hill became less involved with VCF, Martin picked up more of the duties associated with VCF including security selection and investment decision-making. Over the past three years, VCF's performance was attributable only to Martin and the other analysts. However, Martin and Hill maintain publicly that he is the one in charge of all investment decision marking for the VCL.

During LL's most recent quarterly board meeting, Hill announced his resignation to the board and informed them that he will be establishing his own fund management firm. To minimize the negative impacts of his departure, the board requests that he not disclose his departure to anyone for the next two weeks while they attempt to search for his replacement. Hill promises not to do so. After the board meeting, Hill has a private meeting with his team to announce his departure and establishment of his own firm. He asks his team to join him and 10 of his 16 analysts agree to do so. To those 10 analysts, he advises that they will have to use their time after work and on weekends to lease office space and register with the government authorities. Furthermore, he advises them that because there was no noncompetition agreement signed with LL, they are able to begin soliciting their clients from LL as soon as the new firm commences operations.

DISCUSSION: Duties to Clients, Communication With Clients and Prospective Clients, Duties to Employers

Hill's statements about the performance of VCF are statements of fact and not opinions so there is no violation of Standard III(D) Performance Presentation. He is specific in stating that the performance is gross of fees or "pre-fees" and that complies with Standard III(D).

Hill's appearance on the talk shows is meant presumably to promote the interests of the VCF (and LL) so there is no conflict of interest with VCF and LL. Therefore, the acceptance of the nonmonetary items is not a violation of Standard IV(B) Additional Compensation Arrangements.

Both Martin and Hill violated Standard V(B)1: Communication with Clients and Prospective Clients because they did not disclose that Hill no longer has primary responsibility for the fund's performance. In other words, their public statement about Hill is false. The fact that Hill still worked at LL is not sufficient on its own.

Hill violated Standard IV(A) Loyalty. The board (and indirectly his employer) requested a two-week period of confidentiality on his pending departure and after promising such confidentiality, he immediately reneged on his promise when he met with his team to announce his departure from LL. Had Hill not made the promise to the board, it would have been acceptable for him to announce his departure to his team without violating Standard IV(A).

Simply asking his team to move with him away from LL is not a violation of Standard IV(A). The team members are free to make their own decisions; there is no breach of loyalty to LL by Hill.

Leasing space and registering with the government authorities prior to resigning from LL is not a violation of Standard IV(A) or Standard III(A) Loyalty, Prudence, and Care so long as the activities are performed outside of work hours (e.g. weekends and evenings).

In the absence of a noncompete agreement with LL, Hill does not violate Standard IV(A) when telling his team to solicit their former clients with LL only after his team ceases employment with LL.

Rob Portman, CFA, works at LL as a salesperson for the VCF and has set up a major event for prospective clients in hopes of meeting his annual sales targets. To clients and prospective clients he emphasizes Hill's stock-picking skills and Hill's role as the VCF's primary investment decision maker. Hill is always invited to important client meetings and when necessary, clients are directed to Martin (who is referred to as Hill's "assistant"). Portman speaks with LL's chief investment officer (CIO) to inquire about rumors regarding Hill and members of his team departing LL. The CIO advises him to disregard the rumors. However, Portman checks "Sky News Business Channel" and discovers that the CIO and some board members recently sold their shares in LL and in the VCF. In response, Portman does the same thing.

DISCUSSION: Misrepresentation and Integrity of Capital Markets

Portman has misrepresented the VCF by inviting Hill to important client meetings and making his clients believe that Hill is in charge of stock selection and investment decision-making for the VCF. In fact, those activities are performed by Martin and the other team members. Furthermore, with clients he refers to Martin as Hill's "assistant". Therefore, Portman is in violation of Standard I(C) Misrepresentation.

LL's CIO and the board members sold their shares prior to the public announcement of Hill's departure. Hill's departure would be considered material nonpublic information in that reasonable investors would want to know such information prior to making an investment decision. By acting on the information, they violated Standard II(A) Material Nonpublic Information.

Portman does not have material nonpublic information about Hill's departure from LL and the VCF. Portman merely used a public source of information to determine the sale of the shares by the CIO and the board members. Therefore, Portman did not use material nonpublic information and did not violate Standard II(A).

LL is owned in part by Bank of Australia (BOA). Kirk Graeme, CFA, works as a financial adviser in BOA's wealth management group and is well-regarded for his work on new issues. He receives additional compensation for new issue purchases that are paid by the issuer. BOA has a capital markets group and the group is a member of the syndicate for the new issues purchased by Graeme. BOA's policy does not require disclosure of commissions on new issues since clients already receive such information in their prospectuses when they purchase new issues. However, Graeme discloses his new issue commissions to those clients who request it. In 2016 and 2017, Graeme and BOA earned commissions of $477,000 and $1,908,900, respectively, on the same transactions.

DISCUSSION: Disclosure of Conflicts

Graeme violated Standard VI(A) Disclosure of Conflicts by only informing those clients who asked about his commissions earned on new issues. In fact, Standard VI(A) requires him to advise all of his clients about the commissions in order for them to have all the information needed to determine the objectivity of the investment advice or actions taken by him on their behalf. It does not matter that the information is already included in the prospectuses of the new issues. The size of the commissions earned by Graeme is reasonably large (about 25% of the amount earned by BOA) so it is large enough to potentially impair his objectivity.

Graeme opened a $250,000 joint account for Melissa and Rodney Delaney. The Delaneys mentioned that the account comprised most of their investable assets. They further stated that they had a long investment time horizon in excess of 15 years and a low risk tolerance. For the next 10 months, 50% Graeme's purchase recommendations were new issues and 75% of the dollar value of the purchases in the account were new issues. Five months was the longest holding period for any new issues in their account. During the same time, he conducted similar activities in many of his other client accounts.

At year end, his supervisor, Jane Balmer, met with him to discuss her concerns over his handling of his accounts over the past year. She referred her concerns to BOA's director of compliance. Graeme substantially curtailed the activity in his client accounts after the meeting with Balmer.

DISCUSSION: Suitability and Responsibility of Supervisors

The Delaneys have low risk tolerance. Graeme's handling of their account with the frequent purchases of the new issues and short holding periods was inconsistent with the Delaneys' risk tolerance. As a result, Graeme is in violation of Standard III(C)1: Suitability in that the new issues were not suitable for his clients because of their low risk tolerance.

Balmer was not thorough enough in her duties as a supervisor in relation to Graeme's behavior. As a result, she is in violation of Standard IV(C) Responsibilities of Supervisors. Merely referring the situation to the director of compliance was insufficient; instead, she should have opened up a full investigation to determine the full severity of Graeme's violations. As well, she should not have relied on his subsequent curtailing of activity as an indication of the nonrecurrence of the violations.

Graeme opened an account for David Milgram five years ago. The investment policy statement (IPS) was drawn up together and has not been updated since. Recently, Milgram complained to Balmer about the decline in value of his account. Immediately afterwards, Balmer meets with Graeme to discuss the complaint and the account. Nothing is reported to the BOA's director of compliance. Graeme, Balmer, and Milgram meet the next day at BOA's offices to review the account and update the IPS. Graeme emphasizes the need to look at the nature of the investments and to focus on other factors in addition to the value of holdings.

DISCUSSION: Suitability and Responsibilities of Supervisors

Standard III(C)1: Suitability requires that the IPS be updated at least annually. Because it was not updated for five years, then Graeme has violated Standard III(C)1.

Balmer immediately began an investigation as soon as she received the complaint by Milgram. She met with Graeme to discuss the complaint and the account as well as meeting with Graeme and the Milgram to review the account and IPS. As a result, Balmer was in compliance with Standard IV(C) Responsibilities of Supervisors. There was no requirement for her to report the complaint to the director of compliance as long as she began the investigation promptly, which she did.

Case Outline: Gabby Sim

Gabby Sim began working at Global Harvest Bank (GHB), an independent private bank offering a wide range of services. She first meets with her supervisor, Ahmad Yousoff, who is also the chief investment officer (CIO). Then she meets with the president, Irene Wong, and two board members, David Tan and Audrey Chuong, CFA. The four of them discuss a memorandum of understanding (MOU) signed with MGM2, a new institutional client. MGM2 is owned by the government of

Sasparia and has the objective of promoting Sasparian economic development. Yousoff and Wong paid Tan and Chuong some of the advisory fees earned from MGM2 in recognition of the latter's efforts in assisting to bring MGM2 on as a client. Yousoff did not disclose the fee-sharing agreement to MGM2. Chuong then encourages Yousoff to meet Boe Hie, a businessman in Sasparia who was one of the founders of MGM2. Chuong did not disclose to Yousoff that Hie has given her son an executive position in MGM2.

DISCUSSION: Conflicts of Interest

The compensation paid to Tan and Chuong is a reward to them for helping to bring MGM2 on as a client. It is not a referral fee since they did not refer MGM2 to GHB as a client. Therefore, it does not need to be disclosed to MGM2 and the lack of disclosure is not a violation of Standard VI(C) Referral Fees.

There is a potential impairment of Chuong's independence and objectivity when Hie hired her son into an executive position at MGM2. Her conflict situation could lead to her acting against her employer, GHB's, best interests. As a result, she should have disclosed to her employer that her son is an employee of the potential client. Therefore, her lack of disclosure is a violation of Standard VI(A) Disclosure of Conflicts.

Sim has been assigned by Yousoff to open an account for Hie in the name of Bad Moon Rising Ltd. (Bad Moon). Hie is the sole beneficial owner and authorized signatory on the account. Sim is not given the chance to ask Hie about his investment experience, objectives, and risk tolerance. Instead, Hie refuses to answer those questions and that for confidentiality reasons, he asks her to destroy all notes of their meeting and replace them with the following information: *Self-employed consultant with a net worth of $110 million. Long-term investment objective with annual return goal between 5% and 10% and a conservative risk profile.*

Hie advises Sim that there will be many large deposits going into his account from MGM2 in the coming months and some of those funds may need to be wired to his other accounts around the world. He requests that she process those transactions expediently and will pay her a year-end bonus for doing so. Hie advises that if Sim has any further questions about the account or its transactions, she should contact board members Tan and Chuong.

After the meeting, Sim uses the information provided by Hie to prepare his investment policy statement and destroys the meeting notes as requested by Hie. She later meets with Yousoff to discuss the meeting with Hie and makes no mention of the year-end bonus from Hie. Sim opens the account.

DISCUSSION: Record Retention, Additional Compensation Arrangements, and Suitability

By destroying all meeting notes with Hie, Sim is not maintaining appropriate records to support her investment actions and therefore is in violation of Standard V(C) Record Retention. Supporting documents under Standard V(C) include notes from clients from meetings to review investment policy statements. Although Hie has stated that he requires confidentiality, keeping meeting notes would not be a violation of

> Standard III(E) Preservation of Confidentiality or Standard III(A) Loyalty, Prudence, and Care.
>
> The bonus promised by Hie is considered additional compensation, therefore Sim violated Standard IV(B) Additional Compensation Arrangements when she failed to disclose the bonus to Yousoff. It is possible that processing Hie's transactions expediently may cause Sim to favor Hie over GHB's other clients. The existence of the bonus could likely impair her independence and objectivity, therefore she also violated Standard I(B) Professionalism, Independence and Objectivity by not disclosing the bonus. Standard I(B) states that bonuses from clients are permissible if they are disclosed to the employer. It is then up to the employer to determine if the bonus is acceptable and will not disadvantage the other clients.
>
> Opening the account for Hie violates Standard III(C) Suitability because Sim was not provided with sufficient information by Hie to develop a reasonable IPS. The information provided was vague and would not have allowed Sim to formulate a proper IPS that consists of items such as risk tolerance, return requirements, time horizon, liquidity needs, and tax concerns.

Very shortly after the Bad Moon account is opened, a large sum is wired to the account from MGM2. Sim contacts Hie about the deposit and he faxes her a copy of an investment agreement between MGM2 and Bad Moon to support the deposit. However, Sim is not completely satisfied with the amount and description in the agreement, so she raises her concerns with Yousoff. Sim explains to Yousoff that she would like to meet with Hie and a representative from MGM2 to provide her with assurance over the validity of the deposit. Yousoff says the copy of the investment agreement is sufficient and that she should contact Tan and Chuong instead. Sim contacts them and they both confirm the validity of the investment agreement and Hie's interactions with MGM2.

> **DISCUSSION: Responsibilities of Supervisors and Confidentiality**
>
> Yousoff has responsibilities as a supervisor and merely asking Sim to contact Tan and Chuong is a violation of Standard IV(C) Responsibilities of Supervisors. As part of his duties as a supervisor, he should have agreed with Sim's idea to meet with Hie and a representative from MGM2 rather than telling her to contact Tan and Chuong instead. Contacting the latter is not as direct as obtaining firsthand knowledge of the transaction. As well, he should not have simply declared the agreement to be acceptable since Sim specifically raised concerns about it. Yousoff should have investigated it further to fulfill his supervisory duties to detect violations of the laws, rules, and the Code and Standards.
>
> Because Yousoff specifically told Sim to contact Tan and Chuong with any further questions about the Bad Moon account, Sim is not in violation of Standard III(E) Preservation of Confidentiality.

In the subsequent months, MGM2 wires a substantial amount of money into the Bad Moon account over several transactions. Hie provides Sim with documentation in the form of agreements signed by Yousoff in his role as GHB's CIO. Most of the funds eventually end up in Hie's various personal bank accounts around the world. Sim continues to be suspicious of the account activity and again contacts Yousoff. She tells him that she suspects money laundering. Yousoff tells her to ignore her suspicions and merely focus on getting the transactions executed in an expedient manner.

DISCUSSION: Professionalism

It is clear that Sim's repeated concerns about the account have produced inaction on the part of Yousoff in his role as a supervisor. Therefore, under Standard I(A) Knowledge of the Law, Sim must escalate the matter and obtain advice from compliance personnel or legal counsel.

Hie had recommended that Sim meet with his mother-in-law, Madam Tan Swee Neo. Sim meets with her and finds out that she is 70 years old and made her money through real estate although she has since moved that money into fixed deposits and low risk energy utility stocks. However, she has recently decided that she wants to earn more income from her investments and tells Sim that she wants to invest in more conservative equities with the return objective of paying for her grandchildren's educational expenses. She heard from her friends about oil-linked structured notes issued by GHB even though she does not know anything about oil futures. Sim provides Neo with a brochure on the structured note written in English, which Neo cannot read. Therefore, Sim verbalizes the summary of the product to Neo in Chinese. Sim does not translate all the fine print for Neo but does warn her that there is no guarantee of the 10% annual coupon and there is a penalty for early redemption. Sim does state that the coupon payments have been made for all three years of the product's existence. Neo invests $50,000 (half of her life savings) in the notes and Sim processes the transaction.

DISCUSSION: Suitability

In purchasing the structured notes for Neo, Sim violated Standard III(C) Suitability. Because Neo does not know anything about oil futures and such investments are inconsistent with her current investment portfolio of fixed deposits and low risk energy utility stocks, Sim should not have purchased the structured notes. Sim does not meet the requirements of Standard III(C) by merely providing Neo with a brochure in English (which Neo cannot read) and warning Neo that the annual 10% coupon is not guaranteed.

One year later, Neo does not receive any coupon payment from her investment. She also hears that oil prices are likely to continue falling in the coming years. As a result, she calls Sim to request that Sim promptly redeem her investment and move the funds into a fixed deposit. Sim advises Neo about the penalties involved with redemption, but Neo is impatient, does not want to hear the details, and tells Neo to get the redemption done as soon as possible. Sim executes the redemptions. Because of the redemptions, the investment has decreased from $50,000 to $30,000 and Neo wants to know why. Sim reminds her of the penalty for early redemption and that Neo was warned about it. However, Neo says she did not expect the penalty to be so large and thought her investment would be low risk since coupon payments have been made every year for the three years the product has been in existence. Dissatisfied, Neo launches a complaint against Sim.

DISCUSSION: Prudence and Care

Sim must demonstrate reasonable care or prudent judgment in dealing with her clients' requests. By executing the redemptions immediately and not fully explaining the penalties to Neo and not further researching the impact of the falling oil prices on the risk of the investment, Sim is in violation of Standard III(A) Loyalty, Prudence, and Care. Despite Neo's impatience, Sim should have insisted on thoroughly explaining to Neo the penalties involved with redemption. Sim should have also performed sufficient due diligence to determine if the falling oil prices would indeed increase the risk of the investment in oil futures.

Additionally, Sim could be in violation of Standard III(C) Suitability because Neo's request for immediate redemption indicated her lack of investment experience. The substantial redemption penalties would jeopardize Neo's return objective of providing sufficient funds for her grandchildren's education and Sim should have considered that prior to the redemption.

MODULE QUIZ 31.1

1. Marcia Lopez, private wealth manager at BankGlobal, has several high net worth clients that have told her they would like to receive information about the overall economic and financial market outlook through her social media platform; this is in addition to the quarterly written reports they already receive from BankGlobal. With approval from the bank's technology and compliance departments, she establishes her social media group and requests her clients to join the group to receive the information. The platform makes it clear to all clients that if they post any comments, the comments will be public, so the platform is not the right place to communicate personal or confidential information. Nevertheless, one of her clients posts on the group page that he personally lost a lot of money in the stock market recently, and he proceeds to provide very personal and confidential details in the process. All clients in the group were able to view the client's comment until Lopez discovered it a few hours later, and promptly removed the comment. Did Lopez violate the Code and Standards in her conduct with the social media platform?
   A. Yes, because Lopez should have screened the client's comment before it was posted.
   B. Yes, because Lopez should not have set up such a group in the first place because of the high risks to client confidentiality.
   C. No, because Lopez took reasonable steps to maintain client confidentiality by telling clients that all posts would be public, and she promptly deleted inappropriate posts.

2. Sandra Benning, CFA, is an investment adviser at Global Capital Management (Global) and has a client, Claris Deacon, who is recovering from health issues. Benning earns a portfolio return that is far superior to the target previously established with Deacon. As a result, Deacon offers to have Benning join her and her husband on an all-expense paid trip to the Bahamas for two weeks. It is a common occurrence for investment advisers at Global to receive gifts from clients, ranging from modest to substantial values. What should Benning do regarding the gift from Deacon?
   A. Disclose Deacon's gift to her supervisor.
   B. Thank Deacon for the gift, but politely decline it because it is too lavish.
   C. Accept the gift as it is a common occurrence to receive gifts from clients.
3. Tony Hill was employed as an equity mutual fund manager at Lionsgate Limited and played a key role in developing a highly successful quantitative model used within the Victory Capital Fund. Hill developed the model while working overtime hours into the late evenings, but was not paid for the work because his compensation is based solely on management and incentive fees. After Hill left the firm, Hill's former supervisor continues to authorize the use of Hill's model without his permission and without providing any attribution to him. By allowing the continued use of Hill's model after his departure from the firm, is there a violation of the Code and Standards?
   A. Yes, because the firm did not provide any attribution to Hill after Hill left the firm.
   B. Yes, because the firm is no longer allowed to use the model after Hill leaves the firm.
   C. No, because the model is the property of Lionsgate, and so they can continue using it and need not provide attribution to Hill.
4. Ahmad Yousoff is a supervisor at Global Harvest Bank (GHB) where Gabby Sim works. Sim has a client, Boe Hie, who has made some questionable transactions in his account. Being dissatisfied with Yousoff's response to her concerns with the suspicious transactions in Hie's account, Sim escalates her concerns to the firm's compliance department. They concur with Yousoff and advise her that she should do as he instructs since he is her supervisor. Sim is dissatisfied with the compliance department's response. What is the appropriate course of action for Sim to take at this point?
   A. Request that the firm disclose the information publicly.
   B. Notify legal counsel at GHB or resign from her position.
   C. Take no action since she has already escalated her concerns to the highest level within the firm.

KEY CONCEPTS

LOS 31.a, 31.b

Sovereign Investment Corporation

- Standard I(A): Knowledge of the Law makes members responsible for violations in which they knowingly participate or assist. A member who believes an activity is either unethical or unlawful must dissociate from the violations of others. Inaction is not sufficient to comply with the standard. Bribery of government officials is likely to breach local anti-bribery laws, resulting in a violation.
- Standard I(C): Misrepresentation requires not knowingly making any misrepresentations, which includes the reporting of the "deal fees" as legitimate operating expenses.
- Standard III(B): Fair Dealing provides that all investors be fairly treated and be provided with the same information (e.g., a standard investor disclosure package or regular investor updates).
- Standard III(C): Suitability requires members to make investment decisions that are consistent with the stated objectives and constraints of the portfolio, including a funds' mandate.
- Standard V(A): Diligence and Reasonable Basis requires members making investment decisions to have a reasonable and adequate basis to support their decisions, including exercising independence, thoroughness, and diligence. Members must review subadvisors as diligently as they review funds or securities, including their knowledge and expertise. Additionally, members who are directly involved with the use of external advisors need to ensure that their firm has standardized criteria for reviewing external advisors.
- Standard V(B): Communication with Clients and Prospective Clients includes transparency as an important element. Providing information for an investor's due diligence is considered reasonable and appropriate.
- Standard VI(A): Disclosure of Conflicts requires members to make full and fair disclosure of all matters that could reasonably be expected to impair their independence and objectivity with respect to their clients, prospective clients, and employer.
- Standard VI(B): Priority of Transactions requires that investment transactions for clients and employers have priority over transactions where a member is a beneficial owner.
- Standard VII(A): Conduct as Participants in CFA Institute Programs prevents candidates from engaging in or members from soliciting any conduct that compromises the integrity of CFA Institute Programs, including discussing the specifics of the examination. Discussing how candidates perceived the difficulty of the examination would not violate the standard because it is non-specific subjective information.
- Standard VII(B): Reference to the CFA Institute, CFA Designation, and the CFA Program required that one must not refer to the designation as a university degree. To use the designation, members must satisfy the CFA Institute membership requirements, which include both annual payment of dues and submission of the Professional Conduct Statement.

Marcia Lopez

- Standard III(B) Fair Dealing requires all clients to be treated in a fair and impartial manner. For example, investment advisers cannot favor their discretionary accounts over their other accounts.
- Standard III(C) Suitability requires:
  - One to develop an investment policy statement for a client prior to making any investment recommendations for the client.
  - Investments to be consistent with the client's long-term objectives.
- Standard III(D) Performance Presentation does not allow the exclusion of the performance of terminated accounts.
- Standard III(E) Preservation of Confidentiality requires all information about a current, former, or prospective client to be kept confidential, including the name of the client.
- Standard VII(B) Reference to CFA Institute, the CFA designation, and the CFA Program, does not permit one to state he has earned a partial designation or to state an expected date of receipt of the CFA charter.

Castle Biotechnology

- Standard I(B) Independence and Objectivity, requires the disclosure of a bonus or any compensation arrangement by a researcher (e.g., in a relevant research report).
- Standard I(D) Misconduct does not permit an investment adviser to sign a form on behalf of a client.
- Standard II(B) Market Manipulation does not permit the use of tie-in agreements because of their intention to artificially increase demand and support a higher share price.
- Standard III(A) Loyalty, Prudence, and Care, requires a client to provide written authorization in order to allow another party to transact in the client's account.
- Standard IV(A) Loyalty does not prohibit former employees from contacting clients of their previous firm as long as there is no noncompete agreement.
- Standard VI(A) Disclosure of Conflicts requires:
  - The disclosure to clients of full ownership details of a related group of companies when there are potential conflicting activities, such as investment banking and research.
  - The disclosure of beneficial ownership interests where one is a researcher making investment recommendations.
  - Full disclosure where a researcher makes a personal investment decision that is contrary to what is stated publicly.
  - The disclosure of any bonuses received that were based on the level of client participation in investments.
- Standards VI(A) Disclosure of Conflicts and VI(C) Referral Fees requires one to disclose to clients the receipt of any signing bonuses related to bringing them in as new clients.

Lionsgate Limited and Bank of Australia

- Standard I(C) Misrepresentation does not allow for any misrepresentations of one's role in the investment process to clients.
- Standard II(A) Material Nonpublic Information does not:
  - Allow one to act on material nonpublic information; acting on such information before its public dissemination is a violation.
  - Prohibit one from acting on publicly reported information and on information that one does not reasonably believe is material nonpublic information.
- Standard III(C)1: Suitability requires:
  - The management of client accounts in a manner consistent with the clients' risk tolerances.
  - At least an annual updating of the client IPS.
- Standard III(D) Performance Presentation requires one to make only statements of fact when presenting performance and does not permit false or opinion-based statements.
- Standard IV(A) Loyalty*:*
  - Requires an employee to honor all requests made by the employer that were agreed upon by the employee; the employee must not be disloyal to the employer, even upon the announcement of resignation and before departure.
  - Allows a departing employee to solicit colleagues of the same firm to also depart with the employee to go into a competitive business.
  - Requires all activities related to the new competing business to be conducted outside of work hours.
  - Allows the solicitation of former clients as long as there is no noncompete agreement and that the solicitation occurs only after departure from the former firm.
- Standard IV(B) Additional Compensation Arrangements does allow for the receipt of a gift by an employee as long as it does not create a conflict with her employer's interest.
- Standard IV(C) Responsibilities of Supervisors requires:
  - That the supervisor do more than merely escalate concerns to the director of compliance.
  - Supervisors to initiate an investigation to ascertain the extent of any wrongdoing by employees when there is reasonable suspicion of a violation of the law or the Code and Standards.
- Standard V(B)1: Communication With Clients and Prospective Clients requires proper and accurate disclosure of who is primarily responsible for the investment decision-making duties.
- Standard VI(A) Disclosure of Conflicts requires one to make full disclosure to clients of commissions received from investments made by those clients.

Gabby Sim

- Standard I(A) Knowledge of the Law, requires one to escalate one's concerns to compliance personnel or legal counsel if the initial reporting of the concerns to the supervisor does not result in any resolution.
- Standard III(A) Loyalty, Prudence, and Care, requires one to use reasonable care or prudent judgment in executing transactions for clients. Sufficient prior research and explanation to the client is necessary as opposed to merely executing a transaction immediately upon request by the client.
- Standard III(C) Suitability requires:
  - Full information of a potential client's investment experience, objectives, and risk tolerance before an account is opened.
  - Investments to be made that are consistent with the risk and return objectives noted in a client's IPS.
- Standard III(E) Preservation of Confidentiality allows a lapse in confidentiality if specific permission was granted by the client.
- Standards IV(B) Additional Compensation Arrangements and I(B) Professionalism, Independence and Objectivity, require the disclosure to the employer of any bonuses or other payments received from a client to prevent any preferential treatment of that client to the detriment of other clients.
- Standard IV(C) Responsibilities of Supervisors requires supervisors to make reasonable efforts to ensure compliance with laws, rules, regulations, and the Code and Standards when faced with a query from a subordinate. Merely accepting statements at face value without further investigation is not sufficient.
- Standard V(C) Record Retention does not permit the destruction of meeting notes with a client that support investment actions, even if the destruction if requested by the client.
- Standard VI(A) Disclosure of Conflicts requires the disclosure to one's employer of a potential conflict such as a family member being an employee of a potential client.
- Standard VI(C) Referral Fees specifically covers referral fees only and does not cover all fee-sharing arrangements.

ANSWER KEY FOR MODULE QUIZZES

Module Quiz 31.1

1. **C** Lopez is not in violation of Standard III(E) Preservation of Confidentiality. She took reasonable steps to maintain client confidentiality in the use of the social media platform. She specifically stated that all comments posted to the platform would be public so it was not the appropriate place to communicate personal or confidential information. Therefore, if a client discloses confidential information through a comment, then it is beyond Lopez's control. The fact that she promptly removed the comment once she found out about it further supports her compliance with Standard III(E). (LOS 31.a, 31.b)

2. **A** Under Standard I(B) Independence and Objectivity, members and candidates may accept bonuses or gifts from clients as long as they disclose them to their employer because gifts in a client relationship are deemed less likely to affect one's independence and objectivity than gifts in other situations. However, disclosure is required to allow supervisors to monitor such situations to prevent against employees favoring a gift-giving client over non-gift-giving clients. It is not necessary for Benning to decline the gift; it is her employer's prerogative to decide whether or not Benning should accept the gift. (LOS 31.a, 31.b)

3. **C** Research and models developed while employed at the firm are the property of the firm. The firm still has the right to use Hill's work after he leaves and need not provide any attribution to him. The firm has paid Hill for his work. It does not matter that he was not paid explicitly for working overtime to perform the work because he is implicitly paid for it through the management and incentive fees that he earns from his employer. Therefore, there is no violation of Standard I(C) Misrepresentation regarding plagiarism. (LOS 31.a, 31.b)

4. **B** Informing the firm's compliance department produced no action toward resolving the concerns of Sim; therefore, under Standard I(A) Knowledge of the Law, the next step for Sim is to seek the advice of legal counsel regarding her concerns. Another possibility would be to report the violation to governmental or regulatory organizations. The Guidance to Standard I(A) states, "Although the Code and Standards does not compel members and candidates to report violations to their governmental and regulatory organizations unless such disclosure is mandatory under applicable law . . . such disclosure may be prudent under certain circumstances." That was not one of the choices provided. The issue does not pertain to Standard II(A) Material Nonpublic Information; therefore, attempting to have her firm disclose the information publicly is not relevant. Although extreme, CFA members must dissociate from the activity which may result in her resigning from her position. (LOS 31.a, 31.b)

READING 32

Asset Manager Code of Professional Conduct

EXAM FOCUS

The Asset Manager Code is specific to Level III. It applies to investment firms, not individuals. It largely duplicates and, in some cases, extends portfolio management-related requirements of the Standards of Professional Conduct.

MODULE 32.1: THE ASSET MANAGER CODE

Video covering this content is available online.

LOS 32.a: Explain the purpose of the Asset Manager Code and the benefits that may accrue to a firm that adopts the Code.

The Asset Manager Code (AMC) is global, voluntary, and applies to investment management firms. Firms are encouraged to adopt the AMC as a template and guidepost to ethical business practice in asset management. Adoption demonstrates that the firm is placing client interests first. The AMC is flexible and firms must develop their own policies and procedures, tailored to their business and clients, to ensure compliance with the AMC. The AMC provides guidance on risk management. Adoption benefits the firm as a step in gaining the trust and confidence of its clients.

LOS 32.b: Explain the ethical and professional responsibilities required by the six General Principles of Conduct of the Asset Manager Code.

LOS 32.c: Determine whether an asset manager's practices and procedures are consistent with the Asset Manager Code.

LOS 32.d: Recommend practices and procedures designed to prevent violations of the Asset Manager Code.

PROFESSOR'S NOTE

These three LOS are inseparable. We will cover the six general principles of the AMC. Meeting the principles and requirements puts the firm in compliance.

Under each principle, we will also list the recommended practices and procedures (P&P). The recommendations provide guidance on the type of policies and procedures the firm could use to meet the requirements and then claim compliance with the AMC. Adopting the recommended P&P (if relevant) will assist the firm in preventing violations of the AMC. The firm is still responsible for determining the specific P&P needed for their business. Not all sections of the AMC have recommendations.

There are many references to issues such as the client IPS, best execution, firm-wide risk management, and soft dollars that are covered elsewhere in the curriculum, so do not bog down on those.

Once you read the material and/or watch our related videos, you should immediately work our questions and the end of chapter questions in the CFA reading for the AMC.

There are six components to the Asset Manager Code of Professional Conduct[1]:

A) Loyalty to Clients.

B) Investment Process and Actions.

C) Trading.

D) Risk Management, Compliance, and Support.

E) Performance and Valuation.

F) Disclosures.

1 Reading 32, CFA Program Curriculum, Volume 6, Level III (CFA Institute, 2022).

Related to these components are six general principles of conduct:

- Always act ethically and professionally.
- Act in the best interest of the client.
- Act in an objective and independent manner.
- Perform actions using skill, competence, and diligence.
- Communicate accurately with clients on a regular basis.
- Comply with legal and regulatory requirements regarding capital markets.

A) Loyalty to Clients

1. Place the client's interest ahead of the firm's.

   Recommendations: Align manager compensation to avoid conflict with client best interests, such as avoiding an incentive for excessive risk taking in order to increase manager compensation.
2. Maintain client confidentiality.

   Recommendations: Create a privacy policy to document how such information is gathered, stored, and used. Include an anti-money laundering policy (if needed) to prevent the firm's involvement in illegal activities.
3. Refuse business relationships and gifts that would compromise independence, objectivity, and loyalty to clients.

   Recommendations: Refuse gifts and entertainment of more than minimal value from service providers. Establish written P&P to define appropriate limits for gifts from both service providers and clients. Require employees to disclose such gifts. Prohibit cash gifts. Managers may maintain other (significant) business relationships with clients as long as potential conflicts are managed and disclosed.

B) Investment Process and Actions

1. Use reasonable care and judgment in managing client assets. Managers should act as other knowledgeable professionals would act to balance risk and return for the client.
2. Do not manipulate price and volume in an effort to mislead market participants as this damages the integrity of markets to the detriment of all investors. Actions such as establishing large positions to distort prices or spreading false rumors are violations.
3. Deal fairly with all clients when providing information, advice, and taking actions. Managers may offer higher levels of service to some clients for higher compensation if the service levels are disclosed and available to all clients willing to pay for them. Managers can engage in secondary investment opportunities (that are offered as a result of other business activities) if the opportunity is fairly allocated to all suitable clients.
4. Have a reasonable and adequate basis for recommendations. The due diligence required will vary based on the complexity and risks of the strategy. Third-party

Reading 32

research can be used if there is a reasonable basis to support it. Managers must be knowledgeable of the securities they recommend. This is particularly true for complex strategies and such strategies must be explained in understandable ways to the client.

5. For portfolios **managed to a specific style or strategy**, managers do not have to evaluate the suitability to a given client. Managers must provide suitable disclosure so clients can determine if the portfolio is suitable for their needs. The portfolio must then be managed in the manner intended. Flexibility and deviations from that intent must be expressly agreed to by clients.

   Recommendations: Disclose permitted deviations from intent as they occur (or in normal reporting). If the strategy or style of the portfolio changes, allow clients to redeem the investment without undue penalty.

6. When **managing portfolios of a specific client**, understand the client's objectives and constraints in order to take suitable actions for that client.

   Recommendations: Establish and update a written IPS for that client at least annually and as circumstances warrant. The IPS will specify the roles and responsibilities of the manager, and those will vary by situation. A performance benchmark to evaluate portfolio performance should be specified. Ideally, each investment decision will be made in the context of the client's total situation (but recognizing the client decides what information to share with the manager).

C) Trading

1. Do not act or cause others to act on material nonpublic information that could affect the value of public securities. Such actions are frequently illegal and damage the integrity of markets. Managers must adopt compliance procedures to segregate information between those with reasons to have such information and the rest of the firm.

   Recommendations: Managers can use procedures such as firewalls between those with reasons to have such information and the rest of the firm. They should develop procedures to evaluate whether company-specific information is material and nonpublic. Information on pending trades or holdings may be material nonpublic information.

2. Give clients priority over the firm. Managers cannot execute ahead of clients or to the detriment of clients' interests. Managers may invest their own capital along with clients if clients do not suffer.

   Recommendations: Develop P&P to monitor and limit personal trading by employees, require prior approval of investment in private placements and IPOs, and provide the compliance officer with employee personal transaction and holdings information. Establish a watch list of companies in which employees may not personally trade without approval.

3. Use client commissions only to pay for investment-related products and services that directly benefit the client, not for the management of the firm.

   Recommendations: Some managers have eliminated soft dollars. If soft dollars are used, disclose this to clients and adopt industry best practices such as the CFA Institute Soft Dollar Standards.

4. Seek best execution for all client trades.

   Recommendations: If clients direct trading, advise the clients it may compromise the manager's ability to seek best execution and seek written acknowledgment of this from the client.

5. Establish policies for fair and equitable trade allocation. All clients for whom the trade is suitable should be given the opportunity to participate.

   Recommendations: Group suitable accounts and trade as a block (all participate at the same price) and allocate partial trades pro rata. Specifically address how IPOs and private placements are handled.

D) Risk Management, Compliance, and Support

1. Develop detailed P&Ps to comply with the AMC and all legal/regulatory requirements.
2. Appoint a competent, knowledgeable, credible compliance officer with authority to implement the P&Ps.

   Recommendations: The officer is independent of the investment and operations personnel. The officer reviews all firm and employee transactions. Require all employees to acknowledge they understand and comply with the AMC.

3. Use an independent third party to verify that information provided to clients is accurate and complete. Verification may be based on audit or reviews of pooled funds and account statements and transaction reports from the custodian bank for individual accounts (i.e., not just on internal records of the firm).
4. Maintain records to document investment actions.

   Recommendations: Retain compliance records and documentation of violations and corrective actions. Retain for at least seven years or as required by law and regulations.

5. Employ sufficient and qualified staff to meet all AMC requirements. Managers must have (pay for) the resources to deliver the services promised and to assure compliance with the P&Ps.
6. Establish a business continuity plan to deal with disasters or market disruptions. At minimum this should include:
   - Backup (preferably offsite) of account information.
   - Plans to monitor, analyze, and trade investments.
   - Communication plans with key vendors and suppliers.
   - Employee communication and coverage of key business functions when normal communications are out.
   - Client communication plans.
7. Establish a firm-wide risk management plan to measure and manage the risks taken. It must be objective and independent of the influence of the portfolio managers.

   Recommendations: Consider outsourcing this process if needed. It may include stress and scenario testing. Be prepared to describe the process to clients.

E) Performance and Valuation

PROFESSOR'S NOTE

See the GIPS reading.

1. Present performance data that is fair, accurate, relevant, timely, and complete. Do not misrepresent performance of accounts or the firm.

   Recommendations: Adopt GIPS.

2. Use fair market prices when available and fair valuation in other cases.

   Recommendations: Independent third parties should be responsible for valuation to avoid conflicts of interest as manager fees are normally based on account value.

F) Disclosures

1. Ongoing, timely communication with clients using appropriate methods.
2. Ensure truthful, accurate, complete, and understandable communication. Use plain language. Determine what to disclose and how.
3. Include any (all) material facts regarding the firm, personnel, investments, and the investment process.
4. Disclose:
   - Any conflicts of interest such as those arising from relationships with brokers and other clients, fees, soft dollars, bundled fees, directed brokerage, manager or employee holdings in the same securities as clients, and any other material issues.
   - Regulatory and disciplinary actions related to professional conduct by the firm or employees.
   - Investment process information including strategy, risk factors, lock-up period, derivatives, and leverage.
   - Management fees and client costs including the method of their determination. Provide gross- and net-of-fee returns. Disclose any unusual expenses. Use plain language to explain how all fees are calculated. Disclose all fees charged and provide itemized charges if requested. Disclose average or expected fees to prospective clients.
   - All soft dollar and bundled fees, what is received in return, and how they benefit the client.
   - Regular and timely client investment performance reporting. Quarterly performance within 30 days of quarter end.
   - Valuation methods used to make investment decisions and value client assets. Typical disclosure is by asset class.
   - The P&Ps used for shareholder voting. These must address how controversial and unusual issues are handled, provide guidance for further actions when voting against corporate management recommendations, and disclose any delegation of voting. Provide clients details on votes cast for their holdings if requested.

- Trade allocation policies.
- Review and audit results of the client's funds and accounts.
- Significant personnel and organizational changes including mergers and acquisitions involving the firm.
- The firm's risk management process and changes to the process. Disclose what risk metrics the client will receive. Regular disclosure of client specific risk information is recommended.

MODULE QUIZ 32.1

1. Terillium Traders is a small stock brokerage firm that specializes in buying and selling stocks on behalf of client accounts. Several of Terillium's brokers have recently been placing both a bid and an offer on the same security about two hours before the market opens for trading. This allows their trades to be one of the first ones made after the markets open. Just before the markets open, these brokers would then cancel one of the orders in anticipation that the market would move in favor of the other order. Which component, if any, of the Asset Manager Code of Professional Conduct has *most likely* been violated?
   A. The component dealing with investment process and actions related to market manipulation.
   B. The Trading section of the Code because this is an example of "front-running" client trades.
   C. Loyalty to Clients, the section pertaining to placing client interests before their own.
2. Harriet Fields, an investment adviser specializing in selling municipal bonds, advertises on television explaining the safety and security of these bonds. The bonds she is currently selling are limited obligation bonds backed only by the revenue generated from the projects they fund, which include a housing project and a golf course. Fields tells her prospective clients that the bonds are safe, secure, and offer generous interest payments. Which of the following statements is *most correct* regarding Fields's actions?
   A. Fields did not violate the Code because municipal bonds are generally regarded as being safe investments.
   B. Fields violated the part of the Code dealing with performance and valuation.
   C. Fields violated the Code when she misrepresented the bonds by not explaining their inherent risks.

Reading 32

3. World Investment Advisers (WIA) is a large sales force of registered investment representatives which has affiliations with many firms that produce investment-related products. One of the affiliated firms is a mutual fund company called Life Investors, which has a special agreement with WIA in which WIA has identified Life Investors as a "preferred product provider" in their internal marketing materials to their investment representatives. In return for this preferential treatment by WIA, Life Investors has reimbursed WIA for the cost of these marketing materials out of the trading commissions generated from the sale of Life Investors mutual funds by WIA sales representatives. Which of the following statements regarding any violations of the Code is *most correct*? WIA violated the Code relating to:
   A. accepting gifts of minimal value because Life Investors is paying for the marketing materials that could influence WIA's representatives.
   B. having a reasonable and adequate basis for making investment decisions.
   C. soft commissions by using client brokerage to pay for marketing materials.

4. Liz Jenkins, CFA, is an asset manager for Gray Financial, a financial services firm that has adopted the Asset Manager Code in managing client accounts. Jenkins has a client who has recently been depositing into his account bearer bonds (coupon bonds) issued by Gas Tech, a natural gas exploration company. Shortly after depositing the bonds, the client has then been requesting disbursement of funds from these bonds. Jenkins suspects this client may be using the firm in an illegal money laundering scheme. Which of the following items regarding how the firm should act is *most correct*?
   A. The firm must monitor the suspicious activity without the client knowing he is being investigated.
   B. The firm must disassociate from the client.
   C. A report must be filed with the appropriate legal authorities.

5. Kendall Asset Managers has branch offices in several different geographical locations spread out by hundreds of miles, and in some instances, located in remote areas. Due to their remote locations and small staffs, some offices do not have a compliance officer, and brokers working in these offices have sometimes had to take on the responsibility of hiring the branch manager. Some brokers work out of their homes and use their own personal email to contact clients. Some branches only keep records in electronic form for seven years. Which of the following is *least likely* a breach of the Code regarding Kendall Asset Managers?
   A. Keeping records in electronic form for seven years.
   B. Communicating with clients via personal email.
   C. Having the brokers in a remote office hire the branch manager.

6. As part of the Asset Manager Code, the firm must adopt policies that:
   A. prohibit managers from engaging in outside business interests with clients separate from the portfolio management relationship.
   B. establish guidelines for when confidential client information will be disclosed to others.
   C. prohibit managers from accepting lavish gifts from clients and service providers.

KEY CONCEPTS

LOS 32.a

The purpose of AMC is to assist the firm in developing ethical business and risk management practices while gaining the trust of clients.

LOS 32.b

The AMC covers:

1. Loyalty to Clients.
2. Investment Process and Actions.
3. Trading.
4. Risk Management, Compliance, and Support.
5. Performance and Valuation.
6. Disclosures.

General principles of conduct:

- Always act ethically and professionally.
- Act in the best interest of the client.
- Act in an objective and independent manner.
- Perform actions using skill, competence, and diligence.
- Communicate accurately with clients on a regular basis.
- Comply with legal and regulatory requirements regarding capital markets.

LOS 32.c

Review the cases and work the questions in the Schweser and CFA material to practice applying the ethics requirements.

LOS 32.d

Loyalty to Clients

- Always put the client's interests before your own by designing appropriate compensation arrangements for managers.
- Determine how confidential client information should be collected, utilized, and stored.
- Determine the amount of which token gifts can be accepted.

Investment Process and Actions

- Take reasonable care when dealing with client accounts.
- Don't engage in market manipulation.
- Deal fairly with all clients.
- Have a reasonable basis for all investment recommendations.

Trading

- Do not trade on material nonpublic information.
- Always place client trades before your own.
- Use soft dollars to aid the manager in the investment decision-making process.
- Seek best execution and allocate trades equitably among all clients.

Risk Management, Compliance, and Support

- Ensure compliance with the Asset Manager Code and legal and regulatory requirements.
- Appoint a compliance officer.
- Disseminate portfolio information in an accurate manner.
- Have an independent third party review client accounts.
- Appropriately maintain records.
- Hire qualified staff with sufficient resources.
- Have a contingency plan in place.

Performance and Valuation

- Report results in an accurate manner using fair market values.

Disclosures deal with any kind of material information disclosed to the client, such as conflicts of interest, regulatory disciplinary actions, the investment decision-making process, and strategies including inherent risks, fee schedules, calculation of performance results, proxy voting issues, allocating shares of stock, and the results of any audits.

ANSWER KEY FOR MODULE QUIZZES

Module Quiz 32.1

1. **A** This is an example of trying to manipulate price and/or volume. There is no indication of trying to execute for personal or firm benefit ahead of clients, making the other two choices not relevant. (LOS 32.d)

2. **C** Fields violated the Disclosures section of the Code by misrepresenting the bonds as being safe and secure. She must provide a more balanced discussion of reward and risk. Performance and valuation deals with presenting the track record of the manager and disseminating client account values to the client. Fields violated at least two of the ethical responsibilities related to the Code, which are (1) to always act in an ethical manner and (2) to act for the benefit of your clients. (LOS 32.b)

3. **C** This is a violation of the Code dealing with trading, specifically related to the use of soft dollar commissions, also referred to as client brokerage, which are trading commissions paid to WIA by Life Investors. Soft commissions are assets of the client and should only be used to purchase goods or services to aid in the investment decision-making process (e.g., purchasing research) and should not be used to pay for marketing materials. (LOS 32.d)

4. **A** Potential illegal or unethical activity cannot be ignored. The firm must take action, such as investigating. There is no requirement to disassociate merely due to suspicion and no requirement to go to the authorities. (LOS 32.d)

5. **A** Record retention for seven years is only a suggestion if no other regulations or laws exist, but it is the least likely violation here. Using personal emails for client communication would compromise the ability to maintain and review records. Allowing the brokers to hire their supervisor would compromise any effective supervision. Communicating with clients using personal email is not acceptable because this type of communication may be difficult to monitor as mandated by the Compliance and Support part of the Code. Part of an effective compliance system is to have a designated compliance officer who can develop and implement written compliance policies. Allowing the brokers in an office to hire and presumably fire the person who is responsible for supervising them does not allow for effective internal controls, which need to be present to prevent fraudulent behavior. (LOS 32.d)

6. **B** The firm must develop policies and procedures to maintain client information, including how to deal with the rare cases it must disclose. Lavish gifts from service providers are prohibited, but not from clients. Gifts from clients are a disclosure issue. Outside business relationships with clients are not prohibited, but are another potential for conflicts of interests (like lavish client gifts), which require disclosure to the employer. (LOS 32.d)

READING 33

Overview of the Global Investment Performance Standards

EXAM FOCUS

GIPS is now considered part of ethics, which is 10–15% of the exam. Historically, GIPS was 0–5% of the exam and tested in the item set format. On rare occasions, it has been tested as a constructed response question.

GIPS falls pretty far down the list of favorite topics for most candidates. Like ethics, you must know the concepts and principles, then apply them to specific situations to identify compliance or non-compliance. There are a surprising number of calculation issues. To prepare for GIPS:

- **It is strongly advised you watch the videos that go with each module for this reading.**
- **Work practice questions.**

There are a couple of pitfalls to watch out for:

- This reading reflects the revised GIPS reading based on the 2020 edition of the GIPS standards, which have been updated from the 2010 standards.
- CFA Institute indicates that candidates are required to have knowledge from two CFA Institute readings: the curriculum reading, as well as a separate document on its website. This SchweserNotes reading provides the key components from both in a single reading.
- A popular myth is to read the actual GIPS document from the CFA Institute website instead of the assigned material. It will not provide the end-of-chapter questions you are expected to have worked and can mislead you on what is actually in the assigned material.
- Like ethics, it is easy to make up questions that cannot be answered. Exam questions are designed to test your understanding of the assigned material and not hypothetical real-world situations that would require additional research or delve into the sub-issues that can arise in GIPS.

Read the assigned material, work the practice questions, and there is every reason to do well on this section of the exam.

MODULE 33.1: GIPS OVERVIEW

Video covering this content is available online.

The GIPS Standards

The Global Investment Performance Standards (GIPS®) contain ethical and professional standards for the presentation of investment performance results. The GIPS are a *voluntary* set of standards. They are based on the fundamental principles of full disclosure and fair representation of performance results. When investment management firms comply with the GIPS, clients, prospective clients, and consultants are better equipped to fairly assess historical investment performance.

The GIPS are not all-encompassing because there is no practical way for a set of standards to address every possible situation a firm may face. The GIPS should, therefore, be viewed as a *minimum* set of investment performance presentation standards. Investment management firms should always include additional information in their performance presentations that would help current and prospective clients better understand the reported performance results.

The 2020 edition of the GIPS standards is delineated into three sections: standards for investment management firms, for asset owners, and for verifiers. Asset owners who manage assets for an organization, participants, or beneficiaries and *compete for business* would use the GIPS standards for firms. Asset owners who *do not compete for business* would use the GIPS standards for asset owners. Verifiers are third parties who provide **verification** that an investment firm is in compliance with GIPS standards. The LOS focus on the standards for investment management firms.

The GIPS standards provide a globally accepted method for calculating and presenting investment results to **prospective clients** and **prospective investors**. The definition includes those clients or investors who currently have funds at the firm, as well as those who don't. Clients are those that invest in a firm's strategies via a segregated account, whereas investors are those that invest in a firm's pooled funds. In the discussion of the GIPS standards, the terms *client* and *investor* are often used interchangeably.

When a firm claims compliance with the GIPS standards, the firms must calculate and present compliant returns in a **GIPS report**, which must be provided to all, not just some, of its prospective clients and investors. The GIPS report provides the firm's previous investment performance, as well as required and additional disclosures. It should be up to date and comparable to reports from other firms with similar strategies that also claim compliance.

Objectives, Scope, and Benefits of the GIPS

LOS 33.a: Discuss the objectives and scope of the GIPS standards and their benefits to prospective clients and investors, as well as investment managers.

Objectives

The objectives of GIPS are as follows:

- Advance the interests of investors and increase their confidence in the investment industry.
- Provide accurate and comparable data to investors.
- Create a globally accepted standard for the determination and presentation of investment performance.
- Facilitate fair competition among global investment managers.
- Encourage self-regulation in the global investment industry.

Scope

Only investment management firms and asset owners who compete for business may claim compliance to the GIPS standards for firms. With respect to the terminology used to refer to a firm's assets under management, a **composite** is a collection of portfolios with similar investment mandates, objectives, or strategies. A **segregated account** is a portfolio owned by a single investor and is sometimes referred to as a separately managed account (SMA). A **pooled fund** is also a portfolio, but it is not owned by a single investor. Whereas broad distribution pooled funds are subject to regulation and are available to the general public (e.g., mutual funds), **limited distribution pooled funds** are not available to the general public (e.g., hedge funds).

The scope of the GIPS standards is as follows:

- GIPS compliance can only be claimed on a firm-wide basis.
  - GIPS compliance cannot be claimed for just some of an investment firm's products.
  - GIPS compliance cannot be claimed for only specific composites, pooled funds, or portfolios.
- To claim GIPS compliance, a firm must comply with all, not just some, of the applicable GIPS standards requirements.
  - The GIPS standards also include recommendations, which are optional but following them is consistent with best practices.
  - The GIPS standards will evolve over time as strategies and technologies change.

Reading 33

- A claim of GIPS compliance indicates, among other things, that:
  - A firm's data inputs, processes, and return calculations are compliant.
  - All the firm's fee-paying segregated accounts have been assigned to at least one composite.
  - All the firm's limited distribution pooled funds are included in a composite appropriate to their characteristics.
  - *Note:* Broad distribution pooled funds are only required to be in a composite if their strategy is also offered in separate accounts.

PROFESSOR'S NOTE

One way of thinking about the scope of the GIPS is that it can't be halfway. To be GIPS compliant, all customers should be provided a report, all the firm's products must be compliant, and all GIPS standards must be followed. Compliance with GIPS can't be halfway.

The exception to this is broad distribution pooled funds, which often do not have to be included in a composite, as previously noted. Why are they different? Think of it this way: Broad distribution pooled funds are typically government regulated such that investor protections have already been established.

Benefits to Prospective Clients and Investors

GIPS helps investors make sound decisions when choosing an investment manager because:

- GIPS compliance standardizes the determination and presentation of investment results, thereby making manager performance more comparable.
- Manager performance is more reliable when the firm is GIPS compliant.
- The **benchmark** requirements of GIPS can facilitate a discussion with the manager about the proposed investment strategy's past and targeted future performance.

Benefits to Investment Managers

Firms incur costs to ensure GIPS compliance. In return, GIPS may provide the following benefits:

- GIPS increase investor confidence in both the investment industry and the firm.
  - This is especially true if the firm is verified by a third party.
- GIPS compliance helps attract new investors who prefer or require their managers to be GIPS compliant.
- GIPS helps firms compete internationally because firm performance is comparable across borders.
- GIPS helps firms strengthen and maintain internal controls due to the recordkeeping and reporting required by GIPS.
- Firms may gain additional information about their operations due to the technology often adopted by firms to comply with GIPS.

MODULE 33.2: COMPLIANCE FUNDAMENTALS

Video covering this content is available online.

Definition of the Firm[1]

A **firm** is defined as:

> "an investment firm, subsidiary, or division held out to clients or potential clients as a distinct business entity."

A **distinct business entity** is defined as:

> "a unit, division, department, or office that is organizationally or functionally separated from other units, divisions, departments, or offices and that retains discretion over the assets it manages and that should have autonomy over the investment decision-making process."

What are some characteristics for identifying a distinct business entity? An organization is more likely to be characterized as a distinct business entity if it has a distinct:

- Legal organization (e.g., as a separate subsidiary).
- Market.
- Client base.
- Investment process.
- Investment strategy.
- Investment staff such as portfolio managers and analysts.
- Physical location.
- Chain of command.

PROFESSOR'S NOTE

Why is the delineation of the firm and a distinct business entity important? Recall from LOS a that compliance with GIPS can't be halfway. Consider a national bank with two investment management divisions: one for high net worth investors (HNWI) and another for retail investors (RI). If the RI division wishes to become GIPS compliant but the HNWI division does not, the RI can only claim GIPS compliance if RI is held out to the public as a distinct business entity and could be characterized as a separate firm.

[1] CFA Program 2024. Curriculum, Volume 6, Level III.

Reading 33

Note, however, that judgment is required to make the determination as to whether an organization should be characterized as a distinct business entity. Suppose a firm has two separate divisions but they use the same trading desk to execute their order. If all the desk does is buy and sell securities, then an argument could be made that both divisions are distinct business entities. If however, the trading desk helps value securities, then it is less likely that the divisions could be characterized as distinct business entities.

The definition of the firm affects the initial implementation of GIPS compliance and continuing compliance activities. It is also used to determine the **fair value of total firm assets**, which for the defined firm:

- Include discretionary and nondiscretionary assets.
- Include fee-paying and non-fee-paying assets.
- Are net of leverage used.
- Are only actual (not simulated) assets.
- Exclude advisory-only assets.
- Exclude uncalled, **committed capital** (i.e., capital that investors have pledged but which the firm has not yet drawn).

Fair value is defined as the value at which willing and knowledgeable parties would exchange an asset. It is most easily determined as the market value of identical assets in liquid markets. Discretionary assets are those where the manager has control of the investment strategy and include those assets managed by a subadvisor if the manager selects the sub-advisor. Nondiscretionary assets are those where client constraints materially affect the manager's ability to execute the strategy.

Note, however, that when calculating *composite* assets, not total *firm* assets, nondiscretionary assets are **not** included. Logically, this makes sense because when calculating composite performance, performance not controlled by the manager should not be attributed to the manager.

In the case of the excluded advisory-only client assets, the firm only offers investment advice and does not have trading authority for the assets.

Other Compliance Fundamentals

In addition to these basic concepts regarding compliance, there are also the following fundamentals.

- To initially claim compliance with the GIPS standards, the firm must attain compliance for a minimum of five years or for the period since firm inception if the firm has been in existence for less than five years.
- Firms must establish, update on a timely basis, and document policies and procedures for meeting GIPS. This includes policies for any GIPS recommendations voluntarily adopted and any error corrections.
- If the GIPS standards conflict with local laws and regulations, the firm must comply with local laws and regulations and disclose the conflict.
- The firm must not present performance-related information that is false or misleading, whether the information pertains to GIPS or not.

- The firm must provide an annual GIPS-compliant report to all existing clients for the composites in which that client's performance is included.
- Benchmarks must reflect the corresponding investment strategy and must be total return benchmarks, not price-only benchmarks.
- The firm must disclose all **material errors** and disclose corrected reports to current clients and verifiers.
- The firm must maintain data needed for GIPS compliance and must maintain a list of composites for the last five years.

MODULE 33.3: RETURN CALCULATIONS

Video covering this content is available online.

LOS 33.b: Discuss requirements of the GIPS standards with respect to return calculation methodologies, including the treatment of external cash flows, cash and cash equivalents, and expenses and fees.

GIPS requires comparable calculation methods by all firms to facilitate comparison of results. For non-private market investment portfolios, returns must be calculated monthly. Portfolio returns must be calculated on a total return basis using beginning (BV) and ending fair value (EV). If there are no interim external cash flows, the return (R_t) during a time period is simply:

$$R_t = \frac{EV - BV}{BV}$$

In many cases, however, there are interim external cash flows (ECF), such as client withdrawals (outflows) or additional client contributions (inflows). Large interim ECFs can distort return calculations because the EVs are affected and it would be unclear how much of the return is due to client cash flows and how much is due to manager performance.

Ideally, to eliminate the potential distortion in returns due to ECFs, the investment would be valued each time an interim ECF occurs. The sub-period returns must then be geometrically linked to create a time-weighted rate of return (TWRR):

$$R_{TWRR} = (1 + R_1) \times (1 + R_2) \times (1 + R_3) \times \ldots \times (1 + R_t)$$

This computation is illustrated in the following example.

EXAMPLE: Time-weighted rate of return

The Rooney account was $2,500,000 at the start of the month and $2,700,000 at the end. During the month, there was a cash inflow of $45,000 on day 7 and $25,000 on day 19. The values of the Rooney account are $2,555,000 and $2,575,000 (inclusive of the cash flows for the day) on day 7 and day 19, respectively. **Calculate** the time-weighted rate of return (assuming 30 days in the month).

Answer:

First, calculate three subperiod returns using the rate of return calculation when external cash flows occur at the end of the evaluation period:

Subperiod 1 (days 1–7)

$$r_{t,1} = \frac{[(\$2{,}555{,}000 - 2{,}500{,}000) - 45{,}000]}{\$2{,}500{,}000} = 0.004 = 0.4\%$$

Subperiod 2 (days 8–19)

$$r_{t,2} = \frac{[(\$2{,}575{,}000 - 2{,}555{,}000) - 25{,}000]}{\$2{,}555{,}000} = -0.002 = -0.2\%$$

Subperiod 3 (days 20–30)

$$r_{t,3} = \frac{(\$2{,}700{,}000 - 2{,}575{,}000)}{\$2{,}575{,}000} = 0.049 = 4.9\%$$

Second, compound the returns together (chain-link) to calculate an overall time-weighted rate of return:

$$\text{TWRR} = (1 + 0.004)(1 - 0.002)(1 + 0.049) - 1 = 0.051 = 5.1\%$$

In the previous example, the account was valued every day there was an interim ECF. Calculating a TWRR this way is referred to as a true or exact TWRR because, due to the interim valuations, the TWRR is not distorted by the ECFs.

However, sometimes a firm does not value its portfolios every day. Furthermore, if the ECFs are relatively small, then approximations of the monthly return will provide a close estimate of the true TWRR. The methods of calculating an approximate return under the GIPS standards are as follows.

Approximations

Modified Dietz Return

The Modified Dietz return method adjusts the simple return formula as follows:

$$R_{MD} = \frac{\text{EV} - \text{BV} - \text{ECF}}{\text{BV} + \text{adjusted ECF}}$$

For example, assume a portfolio experienced cash inflows from client contributions. The cash inflows are subtracted from the ending value and adjusted cash inflows are added to the beginning value. The numerator's logic is that a manager should not get credit for a client's contribution while in the denominator it is recognized that the manager had use of that cash inflow for part of the period, as demonstrated in the following.

In the previous Rooney account example, the adjusted ECFs are calculated using partial month weightings (W) as follows:

ECF	Weight (W)	Adjusted ECF
\$45,000	(30 – 7) / 30 = 23 / 30	23 / 30 × \$45,000 = \$34,500
\$25,000	(30 – 19) / 30 = 11 / 30	11 / 30 × \$25,000 = \$9167

The 1st ECF was received on Day 7, meaning that the manager had use of it for 23 days. The manager had use of the 2nd ECF for 11 days. Using these in the formula for the Modified Dietz return (R_{MD}):

$$R_{MD} = \frac{\$2{,}700{,}000 - \$2{,}500{,}000 - \$45{,}000 - \$25{,}000}{\$2{,}500{,}000 + \$34{,}500 + \$9{,}167} = 5.1\%$$

In the example, if the ECFs were cash outflows such as client withdraws, they would have been denoted with a negative sign.

MIRR

A second approximation is the modified internal rate of return (MIRR). It is simply an internal rate of return (IRR) that adjusts for the timing of the ECFs. It can be solved for by trial and error or spreadsheet to find the interest rate (r) that equates the EV to the future value of the BV and ECFs. Like Modified Dietz, each ECF is weighted by the days of the month.

In the calculation that follows, the ending three zeros (000) are dropped to simplify, and the remainder-of-month periods are calculated to two decimal places.

$$2{,}700 = 2{,}500(1 + r) + 45(1 + r)^{0.77} + 25(1 + r)^{0.37}$$

$$\text{MIRR} = 5.1\%$$

Since both the Modified Dietz and MIRR use the number of days in the month, they are said to be methods that adjust for daily-weighted ECFs. The Modified Dietz and MIRR typically provide similar values.

Regardless of whether the exact method or the approximations (Modified Dietz or MIRR) are used, GIPS requires that the monthly returns be geometrically linked to calculate an annual return. The larger the ECFs and the more volatile the market, the greater the discrepancy will be between the true TWRR and the approximations.

PROFESSOR'S NOTE

The previously calculated exact TWRR was 5.1%, making the approximations very close. This is not surprising, given that the ECFs were relatively small. If the ECFs are relatively small and the path of returns does not vary significantly by subperiod, the methods will produce similar results.

Solving for the MIRR by trial and error is not an LOS and not covered in the CFA reading. Note that the MIRR defined here is not the same as the MIRR you may have encountered in a corporate finance class. Although they are both IRRs, they differ in how they "modify" the IRR.

To recap, under the GIPS requirements:

- Firms must calculate monthly returns for non-private market investment portfolios.
- If a firm calculates daily valuations and returns, the daily return must be geometrically linked to create a monthly true TWRR.

- If a firm does not calculate daily returns and the ECFs are not large, approximations to the true TWRR that do not require an interim valuation can be used.
- If the ECFs are large, the portfolio must be valued at the time of the ECFs to calculate a subperiod return.
- Regardless of how the monthly return is calculated, the monthly return must be geometrically linked to create an annual return.

For portfolios other than non-private market investment portfolios, what are the GIPS requirements?

- Private market investment portfolios values and returns must be calculated quarterly (e.g., real estate, private equity, and other illiquid, not publicly traded, investments).
- Pooled funds not in a composite must be valued and returns calculated at least annually.
  - The fund must also be valued and a subperiod return calculated at the time of subscriptions or redemptions.

What constitutes a **large cash flow**?

- The definition of a large ECF is determined by each firm for each composite.
- Generally, a large ECF is that which is large enough to affect the return calculation.
- The firm's policy for the determination of a large cash flow must be documented.

Other Return Calculation Topics

In addition to the return calculations discussed previously, the GIPS standards have other requirements.

There are some investment strategies where the firm controls the timing and size of the ECFs. In these cases, a money-weighted return (MWR) will be more representative of the manager's skill than the TWRR. MWRs can be used instead of TWRRs if:

- The firm has control of the timing of ECFs.
- The portfolios are closed-end, or fixed life, or fixed commitment, or have a significant amount of illiquid assets.

The MWR (which is an IRR calculation) must be calculated and the portfolios valued at least annually.

Other return calculation requirements are as follows.

- Trade date, not settlement date, prices must be used to calculate returns.
- Partial year returns cannot be annualized.
  - This would be equivalent to representing simulated returns as actual returns, which is not allowed under GIPS.
- Total returns, which include income and capital gains/losses, must be used.
  - For investments that generate income, such as bonds, accrual accounting must be used.
  - Returns must reflect the manager's allocations to cash and cash equivalents.
    - This is true even if the firm uses an outside firm to manage the cash.
    - Cash equivalents include money market instruments and fixed-income securities with maturities less than a year.

PROFESSOR'S NOTE

Once again, we can think of GIPS as not being half- or partway. Total, not just price, returns must be used and one can't assume that a partial-year return would continue for the entire year (i.e., it can't be annualized). Also, it makes sense that returns must reflect cash returns. A manager may not want to, given the low returns to cash, but this would not be consistent with the fair representation of the manager's returns.

- Under GIPS, the presented **gross-of-fees** return must have been calculated after the deduction of transactions costs.
- **Transactions costs** reflect the costs of buying and selling securities.
  - Examples include brokerage commissions, spreads, exchange fees.
  - For private market investments, they can also include legal, advisory, and other fees.
  - **Custody fees** should not be included.
  - Transactions costs can be estimated but only if they are unknown.
- In some cases, portfolios pay **bundled** or **all-in-fees**, which can include trading costs, as well as **investment management**, custody, **administrative**, and other fees.
  - In this case, the presented gross-of-fees return must be reduced by:
    - the portion of the bundled fee due to transactions costs; or
    - the entire bundled fee if the transactions costs cannot be separated out.

PROFESSOR'S NOTE

The emphasis here on returns that are reduced by trading costs but not investment management costs might seem surprising, given that management fees reduce investors' returns. However, it is recommended that net-of-fees returns, reflecting management fees (4.B.1), are also presented. It is also the case that different investors pay different fees. For example, those with more assets often pay lower management fees in percentage terms. Not surprisingly, then, it is required that investors be provided with a fee schedule (4.C.11).

MODULE QUIZ 33.1, 33.2, 33.3

1. Assume that Firm Z is the investment manager for 15 retail clients and has full discretion over the investment of the clients' assets. At the end of each day, any excess cash in the portfolios is swept into a money market fund. Firm Z does not manage the money market fund, so it does not include the cash portion of the portfolio in its total return performance calculation. **Discuss** whether it is an acceptable practice for Firm Z to claim compliance with the GIPS.

2. Consider the total quarterly returns for the growth and income composite of the investment firm ADA: Q1 = 3.00%, Q2 = 4.15%, Q3 = 3.75%, and Q4 = 3.15%. **Calculate** the appropriate total annual return under the calculation methodology under the GIPS.

3. For promotional purposes, the Jaspre Investment Management firm (JIM) wants to take advantage of the prestige associated with presenting performance results that are in compliance with the GIPS. To save time and expense, JIM decides to create five composites for marketing purposes. These portfolios represent 60% of the firm's fee-paying discretionary portfolios. Recognizing that the firm cannot claim compliance for all of its portfolios, JIM plans to include the following compliance statement with its performance presentation: *"The investment results presented in this report have been prepared and presented in compliance with the Global Investment Performance Standards (GIPS®) for the majority of the assets under management by Jaspre Investment Management, Incorporated."* **Discuss** whether JIM's claim of compliance is acceptable under the GIPS.

4. Kenzo Fund Managers (KFM) manages a fund that has the following cash flows and valuations (in U.S.$ millions) for the month of September:

Date	Value (Before Cash Flow)	Cash Flow	Value (After Cash Flow)
1 September	50.0	N/A	50.0
10 September	51.5	5.0	56.5
20 September	59.0	–2.0	57.0
30 September	55.0	N/A	55.0

(a) **Calculate** the approximate TWRR for September using the Modified Dietz method.

(b) **Calculate** the exact TWRR for September revaluing the portfolio at every ECF.

5. It would be *most likely* that the money-weighted returns could be used instead of time-weighted returns if:
   A. the account is large.
   B. the account is non-discretionary.
   C. the manager can control the timing of external cash flows into and out of the portfolio.

MODULE 33.4: COMPOSITES

Video covering this content is available online.

LOS 33.d: Explain requirements of the GIPS standards with respect to composite return calculations, including methods for asset-weighting portfolio returns.

Global Investment Performance Standards (GIPS®) for Firms, page 13

Composites are groupings of one or more portfolios with similar investment mandates, objectives, or strategy. Because composite returns are an essential part of the firm's communication with investors, the GIPS standards require that composite return calculations be calculated at least monthly, except for private market investments and pooled funds not in a composite, which must be calculated at least quarterly and annually, respectively. Composite returns must be calculated in one of three ways:

1. Asset-weighting portfolio returns by beginning-of-period values
2. Asset-weighting portfolio returns by both beginning-of-period values and ECFs
3. The aggregate method

The first method is perhaps the simplest as each portfolio return is just multiplied by its beginning of period weight. The second method is similar except that we also adjust for the ECFs. The third method uses total composite values at the beginning and end of period. The weighting of ECFs in the second and third methods will look familiar to you from the Modified Dietz method covered previously.

EXAMPLE: A U.S. manager's equity composite contains three portfolios. The following values for the month of October show the external cash flows and the beginning and ending portfolio values. The values are in $ millions.

Portfolio	30-Sep	3-Oct	13-Oct	19-Oct	31-Oct
A	$110.00			–$10.10	$109.20
B	$167.80		–$11.10		$166.90
C	$344.20	$22.00			$345.10
Total	$622.00	$22.00	–$11.10	–$10.10	$621.20

Questions:

a) **Calculate** the Modified Dietz return for each portfolio.

b) **Calculate** the composite return using beginning of period portfolio values.

c) **Calculate** the composite return using beginning of period portfolio values with external cash flows.

d) **Calculate** the composite return using the aggregate return method.

Answers:

a) Positive signs for the ECF denote cash inflows such as client contributions, and negative signs denote cash outflows such as client withdraws. The adjustments to the ECFs result in partial month weightings (W) of each cash flow as follows:

Portfolio	ECF	Weight (W)	Adjusted ECF
A	–$10.10	(31 – 19) / 31 = 12 / 31	12 / 31 × –$10.10 = –$3.91
B	–$11.10	(31 – 13) / 31 = 11 / 31	18 / 31 × –$11.10 = –$6.45
C	$22.00	(31 – 3) / 31 = 28 / 31	28 / 31 × $22.00 = $19.87

Using these in the formula for the Modified Dietz return (R_{MD}):

$$\text{Portfolio A: } R_{MD} = \frac{\$109.20 - \$110 - -\$10.10}{\$110 - \$3.91} = \frac{\$9.30}{\$106.09} = 8.77\%$$

$$\text{Portfolio B: } R_{MD} = \frac{\$166.90 - \$167.80 - -\$11.10}{\$167.80 - \$6.45} = \frac{\$10.20}{\$161.35} = 6.32\%$$

$$\text{Portfolio C: } R_{MD} = \frac{\$345.10 - \$344.20 - \$22}{\$344.20 + \$19.87} = \frac{\$21.10}{\$364.07} = -5.80\%$$

Notice that for Portfolio A, even though the ending value of \$109.20 was lower than the beginning value of \$110.00, the return was positive because the client withdrew \$10.10 from the portfolio during the month. The same pattern holds for Portfolio B.

The opposite is true for Portfolio C. Although the ending value was greater than the beginning value, the return is negative. The client had contributed additional capital of \$22.00 during the month, and once we factor this additional contribution in, the return is negative.

b) To calculate the composite return using beginning of period values, first find the weights of each portfolio in the composite:

$$\text{A: } \frac{110.00}{622.00} = 17.68\%\text{; B: } \frac{167.80}{622.00} = 26.98\%\text{; C: } \frac{344.20}{622.00} = 55.34\%$$

The composite return is the sum of the weights times the returns:

$$= 0.1768 \times 8.77\% + 0.2698 \times 6.32\% + 0.5534 \times -5.80\%$$

$$= 1.5505\% + 1.7051\% + -3.2097\% = 0.05\%$$

c) To calculate the composite return using beginning of period portfolio values with external cash flows, first find the weights of each portfolio in the composite. Since the denominator of the Modified Dietz formula for each portfolio factors in the beginning values and weighted cash flows, it can be used to obtain the weightings. Using the previously noted figures, the total for the composite is \$106.09 + \$161.35 + \$364.07 = \$631.51. The weights are then:

$$\text{A: } \frac{106.09}{631.51} = 16.80\%\text{; B: } \frac{161.35}{631.51} = 25.55\%\text{; C: } \frac{364.07}{631.51} = 57.65\%$$

The composite return is the sum of the weights times the returns:

$$= 0.1680 \times 8.77\% + 0.2555 \times 6.32\% + 0.5765 \times -5.80\%$$

$$= 1.4734\% + 1.6148\% + -3.3437\% = -0.25\%$$

Notice that under this method, the composite return is slightly negative, whereas in the previous method, the return was positive. This is because under this method, the weighted cash flows are figured in and Portfolio C's early in the month cash flow results in a larger Portfolio C weighting. Thus, Portfolio C's negative return has more influence in the composite's return than under the previous method.

d) In the aggregate return method, the composite is treated as a single portfolio of its constituents and the return is calculated using the Modified Dietz formula. In the numerator, we use the total of the portfolio values and cash flows from the bottom of the table. In the denominator, the total of the portfolios' Modified Dietz values from the previous method are used.

$$R_{MD} = \frac{\$621.20 - \$22 - - \$11.10 - - \$10.10 - \$622}{\$631.51} = \frac{-\$1.60}{\$631.51} = -0.25\%$$

In many cases, the second and third method for calculating the composite return will produce the same result.

Reading 33

Discrition and Composite Construction

LOS 33.e: Explain the meaning of "discretionary" in the context of composite construction and, given a description of the relevant facts, determine whether a portfolio is likely to be considered discretionary.

Global Investment Performance Standards (GIPS®) for Firms, page 18

As mentioned previously, composites are groupings of similar portfolios. The GIPS standards specify requirements for composite construction so that investors are provided a fair and accurate representation of manager performance. The intent of the requirements is to, in part, prevent managers from excluding poorly performing portfolios from composites.

A key determinant in whether a portfolio is included in a composite is whether the manager has discretion. Whether a portfolio is discretionary hinges on the manager's ability to implement the investment strategy. If the performance of a portfolio does not reflect a manager's decisions (i.e., the portfolio is nondiscretionary), then that portfolio would be excluded from the calculation of composite returns.

Generally speaking, the requirements for what *must* be included in at least one composite are as follows:

- All actual, fee-paying, discretionary segregated accounts.
- Pooled funds that are also offered as segregated accounts.
  - These include limited distribution pooled funds, as well as broad distribution pooled funds that have strategies also offered to individuals through a separate account.

In general, the requirements for what must **not** be included in a composite are as follows:

- Nondiscretionary accounts.
- Pooled funds that are not also offered as segregated accounts (e.g., a broad distribution pooled fund—which is typically government regulated).
- Simulated portfolios.

Non-fee-paying, discretionary segregated accounts may be included with additional disclosures.

While these general guidelines are succinctly stated, their implementation is subject to judgment, which necessitates the discussion that follows.

PROFESSOR'S NOTE

It might seem strange that a portfolio could be in more than one composite. However, consider a value portfolio. The portfolio must be included in both the value composite and the small cap value composite (assuming that the portfolio meets the inclusion criteria for both composites). Note, however, that the firm should be careful to not double count the portfolio's assets when determining total firm value.

Discretion

- Given its importance, a firm must maintain and apply a clear, written definition of discretion.
- A client's investment policy statement (IPS) will specify risk preferences and constraints.
  - These include:
    - The benchmark the manager is measured against.
    - Risk controls such as limits on equity sector weights, bond credit quality, and the use of derivatives.
    - Environmental, social, and governance (ESG) preferences.
    - Restrictions on the sale of company stock.
    - Limits on the sale of low basis stocks to avoid high taxation.
    - Legal restrictions (e.g., a government fund can only hold domestic securities).
  - However, none of these *automatically* make a portfolio nondiscretionary (i.e., there are degrees of discretion).
  - Guidance is based on whether the manager's ability to use professional judgment is materially constrained.
    - For example: If an IPS constraint limits the use of derivatives and the manager does not normally use derivatives anyway, the portfolio would likely be deemed discretionary.
  - If the constraint is deemed immaterial, the manager can:
    - Place the portfolio in a composite with similar, unconstrained portfolios.
  - If the constraint is deemed material, the manager should:
    - Group the portfolio with similar, constrained portfolios.
    - Exclude the portfolio from all composites.
  - In some cases, there may be restrictions for particular assets (as in the sale of low basis stock mentioned previously). In these cases, a manager may:
    - Consider the entire portfolio nondiscretionary; or
    - Remove these assets and place the remainder of the portfolio in a composite; or
    - Consider the entire portfolio discretionary if the restricted assets value is below a certain percentage of the portfolio, as stated in their policy.
- In some cases, its ECFs might indicate that a portfolio is nondiscretionary.
  - For example: A client makes large withdraws that necessitates a large cash balance, restricting the manager's ability to invest in equity positions to the degree as with other portfolios in the composite.

Model Portfolios

- Simulated portfolios cannot be in a composite.
- These portfolios are called hypothetical, model, or **theoretical** portfolios.
- They are often based on the backtesting of data.
- Their performance can be provided in **supplemental** information, but not in composite results.
  - Note that any information the firm provides that is supplemental to the GIPS requirements must be labeled as such and must not contradict or conflict with required GIPS disclosures.
- However, sometimes a firm will use its own funds (seed money) to create a new strategy.
  - The performance for these actual portfolios can be included in existing or new composites.
  - These portfolios would be subject to the disclosure requirements for non-fee-paying portfolios.

Non-Fee-Paying Portfolios

- Non-fee-paying portfolios may be included in a composite, but the firm is not required to.
- If included, firms are required to disclose the percentage of composite assets represented by non-fee-paying portfolios.

Composite Construction

LOS 33.f: Explain the role of investment mandates, objectives, or strategies in the construction of composites.

Global Investment Performance Standards (GIPS®) for Firms, page 18

A critical step in achieving an accurate and comparable representation of a firm's performance is the defining and construction of composites. As per the GIPS standards, composites must:

- Be determined by investment mandate, objective, or strategy.
- Contain all portfolios that match the composite definition.
- Be based on criteria that is documented in the firm's policies and procedures.
- Be defined such that clients are able to compare the performance of one firm to another.
- Be representative of the firm's products and be consistent with the firm's marketing strategy.

The list just described is straightforward, but applying the list items in practice is more difficult. A starting point in composite construction might be competitors' composite classifications and/or the styles requested by potential investors. A composite's construction will have lasting presentation consequences and should thus be constructed carefully. A composite definition too narrow (e.g., small cap value frontier market stocks) results in too few portfolios in each, creates unnecessary costs, and potentially jeopardizes client confidentiality. A composite definition that is too broad results in disparate performance among composite portfolios.

The following are examples on which to base composite construction:

- Equity style.
- The benchmark.
- Equity or bond sector.
- Risk/return profile using measures such as tracking error.
- Whether active, passive, or core plus management is used.
- Investment strategy such as sector rotation, fundamental analysis, etc.

The Inclusion and Exclusion of Composite Portfolios

LOS 33.g: Explain requirements of the GIPS standards with respect to composite construction, including switching portfolios among composites, the timing of the inclusion of new portfolios in composites, and the timing of the exclusion of terminated portfolios from composites.

Global Investment Performance Standards (GIPS®) for Firms, page 18

Over time, a portfolio manager will gain new clients, lose others, and have clients who change their objectives. The treatment of these portfolios will affect the composite's return. Because unethical managers may be tempted to move their best-performing portfolios to a particular composite, the GIPS standards specify requirements regarding the movement of portfolios in and out of composites. As such, the GIPS standards require firms to have policies for:

- When portfolios are included in composites.
- When portfolios are excluded from composites.
- Switching a portfolio from one composite to another.
- Cash flows from new investments or liquidations.
- The minimum asset level for a composite.

The firm's policy should be established on a composite-by-composite basis and applied in a timely, consistent manner. We discuss each of these as follows.

Portfolio Inclusion

- New portfolios should be included in a composite at the beginning of the next full measurement period.
  - For example: If a portfolio is funded with cash on July 6 and the firm calculates composite returns monthly, the new portfolio should be included in the composite on August 1.
- However, the firm has discretion on the timing of portfolio inclusion because it may take time to invest new funds. This is often the case when:
  - The investment is made in illiquid securities such as in emerging markets; or
  - The investment is funded with other securities that must be sold before new securities are bought.
- Thus, the firm's documented policy may vary by composite, with some composites allowing for longer periods prior to portfolio inclusion.

Portfolio Exclusion

- Terminated portfolios should be included in a composite through the last full measurement period in which the firm had discretion.
- Clients sometimes direct a firm to stop trading an account or transfer control to a new manager before the portfolio is fully liquidated.
  - For example: Suppose on June 4 a client notifies a firm to stop trading because they will be leaving the firm on July 9. In this case, the portfolio should be included in the composite only through May 31.

Switching Portfolios

- A portfolio can be switched to a new composite due to actions by the client or by the firm.
  - A client may change the portfolio's mandate, objective, or strategy.
    - For example: A client now allows the use of derivatives, so the portfolio is switched to a composite that allows such.
  - The firm may redefine the composite such that the portfolio is no longer appropriate for the composite.
    - Redefining a composite by a firm should be highly unusual.
    - In most cases, a firm should create a new composite instead.
- When a portfolio is switched to a new composite, the portfolio's performance must remain in the old composite's historical performance.

Significant Cash Flows

- **Significant cash flows** are those large enough such that it impedes the firm from implementing the strategy on a timely basis.
  - For example: A client contribution/withdrawal may be so large that it can't be invested/divested quickly in an illiquid market.

- The firm should document what constitutes "significant" in its policies.

- To prevent composite performance from being affected by cash inflows/outflows in the event of significant cash flows, a firm can:
  - Temporarily exclude the portfolio from the composite; or
  - Create and report on a **temporary new account** (outside of the composite), which would contain:
    - Cash contributions until they can be invested; or
    - Securities until they can be divested.

Minimum Asset Levels

- A portfolio may be excluded from a composite if its size is so small that it can't be invested appropriately by a firm.
- As portfolios change in size, they must be added to or removed from a composite as per firm policy regarding the size limits for adding and removing portfolios.
  - For example: A portfolio must be added to a composite if its size rises above €5 million but removed if it falls below €4.5 million.
- The minimum asset level must be specified in advance and portfolios that are removed cannot have their prior performance removed from the composite's historical record.

EXAMPLE: Account #207 invests in illiquid, fixed income securities. The account receives a large cash infusion on April 12 that cannot be invested quickly at reasonable prices. It is expected to take 60 days for the funds to be reasonably invested.

Best Solution:

Place the funds in a new, temporary, subaccount (call it 207T) until the funds are invested. Continue to report results for 207 in its appropriate composite. Results for 207T will not be reported in any composite. Once 207T is invested in accord with account objectives, 207T will be merged into 207 and affect future results for 207. (Note that the client will need to receive reports showing the results of 207T and 207 to comply with general reporting requirements under the Standards of Professional Conduct. Subaccount 207T is only excluded from GIPS reporting.)

Alternative Solution:

The funds could be placed directly into 207 and 207 results would be excluded from the composite results until the funds are invested in accord with client objectives. GIPS composite results are based on monthly results so if the investments are completed by June 15, account 207 will be excluded from the composite for months April, May, and June. (Note that the client will need to receive reports showing the results of 207 to comply with general reporting requirements under the Standards of Professional Conduct. Account 207 is temporarily excluded from GIPS reporting.)

Reading 33

MODULE QUIZ 33.4

1. The investment management firm of Rangan, Rollins, and Cramer (RRC) manages portfolios using a long-short strategy. However, RRC does not ever intend to market this strategy and, thus, does not include the performance of these portfolios in any of the firm's composites. **Discuss** whether this practice is acceptable if RRC claims that its performance presentation results are compliant with the GIPS.

2. The Teletron Investment Management firm (TIM) plans to market an aggressive growth investment strategy using a newly developed proprietary prediction model. To test the model, TIM created an aggressive growth composite and produced a years of returns history using hypothetical assets and a back-tested asset allocation strategy. TIM intends to show the model composite results in its performance presentation. **Discuss** whether this practice is acceptable under the GIPS.

3. For each of the following client portfolio characteristics choose, according to the GIPS requirements, whether the characteristic *may be included* or *must be excluded* from a composite and **explain** your decision.

   i. Client has significant liquidity needs with an accompanying significant cash position.

   A. May be included.

   B. Must be excluded.

   Explain your decision.

   ii. Client does not pay fees.

   A. May be included.

   B. Must be excluded

   Explain your decision.

   iii. Client requests strictly following an index.

   A. May be included.

   B. Must be excluded

   Explain your decision.

4. Johnson Investment Management (JIM) uses monthly valuation. Assuming the general provisions of GIPS apply, **discuss** when it would be appropriate to remove a portfolio from JIM's composite if the portfolio is terminated on July 15, 2015.

Reading 33

5. A U.K. manager's composite contains two portfolios. The following values for April show the external cash flows and the beginning and ending portfolio values. The values are in £ millions.

Portfolio	31-Mar	12-Apr	20-Apr	22-Apr	30-Apr
A	£400.00	£25.00		£10.00	£467.00
B	£200.00		–£13.00		£224.00
Total	£600.00	£25.00	–£13.00	£10.00	£691.00

(a) **Calculate** the Modified Dietz return for each portfolio.
(b) **Calculate** the composite return using beginning of period portfolio values.
(c) **Calculate** the composite return using beginning of period portfolio values with external cash flows.
(d) **Calculate** the composite return using the aggregate return method.

Video covering this content is available online.

MODULE 33.5: GIPS PRESENTATION AND REPORTING

LOS 33.h: Explain requirements of the GIPS standards with respect to presentation and reporting.

LOS 33.i: Explain the conditions under which the performance of a past firm or affiliation may be linked to or used to represent the historical performance of a new or acquiring firm.

Global Investment Performance Standards (GIPS®) for Firms, page 21

GIPS requires that, when marketing a particular investment strategy, firms must make every reasonable effort to provide a GIPS report to prospective clients and limited distribution pooled fund investors. There are two types of GIPS reports, **GIPS Composite Reports** and **GIPS Pooled Fund Reports**. The curriculum focuses specifically on the requirements for Composite Time-Weighted Return Reports. As such, that should be your focus too. The requirements for Composite Time-Weighted Return Reports include the following.

Performance History

Upon GIPS adoption, firms are required to present GIPS compliant annual performance for:

- At least 5 years.
  - Unless the composite has been in existence for less than 5 years.
- And then extended each year until the firm builds a 10-year GIPS compliant history.

Returns and Size Measures

The report must include the following:

- Time-weighted returns for the composite and benchmark.
- The amount of firm assets.
- The amount of composite assets.
  - The number of portfolios in the composite if there are six or more.
  - Note that there is no minimum number of portfolios for a composite to be formed.

Risk

The report must include annual measures of internal composite dispersion, benchmark dispersion, and composite dispersion as a whole. **Internal dispersion** measures the variability of portfolio returns within the composite, whereas the latter two measures allow the client to compare the composite's historical risk against a benchmark. It might be useful to think of the first as a micro measure and the latter two as macro measures.

Internal dispersion

- This allows the client to determine how consistent portfolio performance is within the composite.
- A very large internal dispersion may indicate that:
  - The firm was not successful in consistently implementing the composite strategy; and/or
  - The composite definition is too broad.
- Only portfolios in existence for the entire year can be included in internal dispersion calculations.
- Acceptable methods of calculating internal dispersion include:
  - High and low returns.
  - Range.
  - Equal-weighted standard deviation.
  - Asset-weighted standard deviation.
  - Or another measure chosen by the firm that fairly represents the composite's internal dispersion.

EXAMPLE: Internal dispersion

The following figure illustrates the structure of a composite during 2020. An *X* indicates that the portfolio was included in the composite for the quarter. If a cell is blank, the portfolio was not included in the composite for the entire quarter. **Determine** which portfolios should be contained in the internal dispersion measure for 2020.

Figure 33.1: Composite Structure, 2020

Portfolio	Quarter 1	Quarter 2	Quarter 3	Quarter 4
A	X	X	X	X
B	X	X	X	
C	X	X	X	X
D		X	X	X
E	X	X	X	X
F			X	X

Answer:

Based on the information contained in the previous figure, Portfolios A, C, and E would be included in the internal dispersion measure for 2020. Portfolios B, D, and F should be excluded from the calculation of the composite's 2020 internal dispersion because they do not have an entire year of performance results. Note that this is only three portfolios to include in the dispersion calculation. Unless there are other portfolios with a full year of data to include in the calculation, no dispersion will be reported. Six or more are required to report dispersion.

The measures of dispersion suggested by the reading include the following:

- The range of annual returns.
- The high and low annual returns.
- The standard deviation of equal-weighted annual return.
- The asset-weighted standard deviation of annual returns.

The **range** of annual returns and the **high and low** annual returns are the simplest and most easily understood measures of dispersion. The advantages of these measures include simplicity, ease of calculation, and ease of interpretation. Disadvantages include the fact that an extreme value can skew the data, and they do not stand alone as adequate risk measures.

The **standard deviation** across equally weighted portfolios is the most widely accepted measure of dispersion within a composite. It is calculated as:

$$\sigma_C = \sqrt{\frac{\sum_{i=1}^{n}[R_i - \text{MEAN}(R)]^2}{n-1}}$$

where:
R_i = return on portfolio i
MEAN(R) = equal-weighted mean (composite) return
n = number of portfolios

PROFESSOR'S NOTE

The use of either n or n – 1 in the denominator can be supported, and firms are encouraged to disclose how they calculate standard deviation.

The *standard deviation with asset-weighted composite* returns is calculated in the following manner:

$$\text{dispersion} = \sqrt{\sum_{i=1}^{n} w_i (R_i - C_{ASSET})^2}$$

where:

R_i = unweighted return on portfolio *i*

w_i = market weight of portfolio *i* relative to the market value of the composite

C_{ASSET} = composite's asset-weighted return, or $C_{ASSET} = \sum w_i R_i$

Composite and benchmark dispersion

The firm should also present the historical dispersion for the benchmark and the composite as a whole, using the *ex post* standard deviation.

The standard deviation must be presented:

- For each annual period.
- For the composite and benchmark.
- Using the previous three years of data on an annualized basis.

Portability

When one firm acquires or joins with another firm, group of managers, or manager, the new firm can link their performance to the previous firm's historical performance if:

1. Substantially all the investment decision makers are retained by the new firm.
2. The decision-making process remains substantially intact and independent within the new firm.
3. The new firm has records that document the previous firm's historical performance.
4. There is no break in the performance record between the new and previous firm.

If only the first three conditions are met, then the previous firm's historical performance can be used to represent that of the new firm, but the records may not be linked. For example, if the previous firm's employees take a garden (temporary) leave at the time of acquisition, the composite assets will not be managed for that period and there will be a break in the presented performance for that time period.

Last, if the new firm is GIPS compliant but the previous firm is not, then the new firm has one year to bring the assets into compliance for future reporting.

Advisory-Only Assets and Uncalled, but Committed Capital

As previously mentioned, advisory-only assets and uncalled, but committed, capital cannot be included in total firm assets. However, the firm can report information on them on a separate basis or combined with composite or firm assets. If reported on a combined basis, the firm must also report on that for the advisory only and for the uncalled, but committed, assets. In any case, the firm must clearly label the assets that are advisory-only and uncalled, but committed.

MODULE 33.6: THE VALUATION HIERARCHY

Video covering this content is available online.

LOS 33.c: Explain the recommended valuation hierarchy of the GIPS standards.

Global Investment Performance Standards (GIPS®) for Firms, page 16

Fair value is the amount an asset would be sold in an arm's-length transaction between willing and knowledgeable parties. The GIPS standards provide a recommended valuation hierarchy for determining fair value. Fair value should include accrued income for bonds and other income-generating assets. In the case of cash, income may be accounted for on a cash or accrual basis. Firms must document their valuation process and methodologies, which should be composite—or pooled fund specific.

The GIPS recommended valuation hierarchy is in descending order of usage. A method lower in the hierarchy is used only when all methods higher in the hierarchy are unavailable. The fair value hierarchy is as follows:

1. The quoted price for an identical asset in a liquid market on the same day.
2. The quoted price for a similar asset in a liquid market on the same day.
3. The quoted price for identical or similar assets in markets that are not active.
    a. For example: A stock trades infrequently such that the last available price is days old.
4. A value based on market inputs.
    a. For example: Applying the P/E ratio for comparable securities to the firm's earnings.
5. A subjective value that is unobservable.
    a. This is a last resort and should only be used to measure fair value when observable inputs and prices are not available or appropriate.
    b. If used, the firm must disclose the assets valued this way as a percentage of composite assets.

MODULE QUIZ 33.5, 33.6

1. Alan Tribon, compliance officer at Frankfurt Investment Management, has scheduled a meeting with one of Frankfurt's portfolio managers, Ashon Guptar, to discuss an investment performance presentation that he recently prepared.

   The following are excerpts from the conversation between Tribon and Guptar:

   Excerpt 1

   Tribon: "I see that the returns in the presentation are reported gross of return of investment management fees. I seem to recall that the GIPS require firms to present performance on a net of management fees basis."

   Guptar: "You are correct, and I will promptly see that the performance results are recalculated and the presentation is changed to reflect net-of-fees performance."

   Excerpt 2

   Tribon: "I notice that there is disclosure of total firm assets for each period. I know this has always been a GIPS requirement, but must we disclose the assets that we direct to sub-advisers under client mandate?"

   Guptar: "Yes, unfortunately, the GIPS require that the firm include as total assets under management those assets managed by client-appointed sub-advisers."

   i. Regarding Excerpt 1 is Tribon correct or incorrect? If incorrect, **explain** why.

   ii. Regarding Excerpt 2 is Guptar correct or incorrect? If incorrect, **explain** why.

2. In July 20X7, Edith Poloski, Jason Masserelli, and Rajesh Granta formed PMG Investment Management (PMG). Poloski has considerable experience in the area of security analysis, and Masserelli and Granta have expertise in fixed income and equity portfolio management, respectively.

   Initially, PMG exclusively managed the portfolios of high-net-worth individuals with a minimum investment requirement of $3 million. However, recently, PMG has decided to broaden its client base by lowering its minimum investment requirement. To attract new clients and improve the information that its current clients receive, PMG has prepared a performance presentation that reflects the results of its major investment styles. Performance results are presented for a fixed income, an equity, and a balanced composite. The following list contains the actions that PMG took when preparing its current performance presentation. For each of the actions, choose whether the action is in compliance (Choice A) or not in compliance (Choice B) with the GIPS standards. If not in compliance with the GIPS standards, **explain** why.

Action 1: The S&P 500 index was used as the benchmark for comparison with all three composite styles.

A. In compliance with the GIPS standards.

B. Not in compliance with the GIPS standards.

If not in compliance with the GIPS standards, **explain** why.

Action 2: PMG used accrual accounting, and book values are used for computations of fixed-income returns.

A. In compliance with the GIPS standards.

B. Not in compliance with the GIPS standards.

If not in compliance with the GIPS standards, **explain** why.

Action 3: For fixed-income return calculations, accrued income is included.

A. In compliance with the GIPS standards.

B. Not in compliance with the GIPS standards.

If not in compliance with the GIPS standards, **explain** why.

Action 4: Due to the change in the firm's client base, PMG did not include its fee schedule.

A. In compliance with the GIPS standards.

B. Not in compliance with the GIPS standards.

If not in compliance with the GIPS standards, **explain** why.

Action 5: Asset-weighted composite returns were calculated using end-of-period weightings.

A. In compliance with the GIPS standards.

B. Not in compliance with the GIPS standards.

If not in compliance with the GIPS standards, **explain** why.

Action 6: All composites included only assets under management and were not linked with simulated or model portfolio performance.

A. In compliance with the GIPS standards.

B. Not in compliance with the GIPS standards.

If not in compliance with the GIPS standards, **explain** why.

Action 7: Equal-weighted rates of return that adjust for cash flows are used for portfolio returns.

A. In compliance with the GIPS standards.

B. Not in compliance with the GIPS standards.

If not in compliance with the GIPS standards, **explain** why.

Action 8: Performance calculations were made after the deduction of actual trading expenses.

A. In compliance with the GIPS standards.

B. Not in compliance with the GIPS standards.

If not in compliance with the GIPS standards, **explain** why.

3. If a security does not have an observable, quoted market price available from an active market, the next *best* valuation basis, according to the GIPS valuation hierarchy, is:
   A. subjective, unobservable inputs.
   B. observable market-based inputs other than quoted prices.
   C. quoted prices from an inactive market for the same or a similar security.

Video covering this content is available online.

MODULE 33.7: GIPS VERIFICATION

LOS 33.j: Discuss the purpose, scope, and process of verification.

Verification can be characterized as the process whereby an independent, outside party assesses the firm's:

- Policies and procedures for composite or pooled fund construction and maintenance.
- Performance calculation.
- Performance presentation.
- Distribution of performance.

The purpose of verification is to provide greater confidence to investors and to the firm in its claim of GIPS compliance. Verification is based on the GIPS principle of fair presentation and full disclosure. Verification, however, does not assure that the construction, calculation, and presentation for any particular portfolio or composite is accurate. Although not required, verification is recommended and consistent with best practices.

The Benefits of Verification to the Firm

Besides providing confidence in its claim of GIPS compliance, other benefits to the firm from GIPS verification include:

- Increased knowledge of performance presentation personnel.
- Better quality presentations.
- Better internal processes and procedures.
- Possible marketing benefits.

Selecting a GIPS Verifier

A firm should consider its operations, products, and needs when choosing a verifier. For example, the needs of the following pairs of firms will differ and as a result, the best verifier for each may differ:

- A large global firm versus a small local firm.
- A tax exempt investor (e.g., a pension fund) versus a firm that focuses on managing portfolio taxes.
- A quantitative manager utilizing derivatives versus a direct real estate investor.

A firm should request that potential verifiers provide the following information:

- A description of the verifier including its personnel and organizational structure.
- Services offered and previous projects completed.
- The verifier's project management, sampling, and testing procedures.
- References from previous clients.
- Fees, proposal, and timeline.

The Scope of GIPS Verification

Verification must be carried out in accordance with the GIPS Standards for Verifiers and must be issued firmwide. Verification cannot be provided for just a single portfolio, composite, or pooled fund. A firm cannot say that a portfolio, fund, or strategy is "in compliance." Verification can only be claimed for the entire firm. A firm must meet all the requirements of GIPS, it cannot claim that it is in compliance "except for."

PROFESSOR'S NOTE

Once again, as in the reading earlier, we see that GIPS can't be halfway or partway. Verification can only be claimed for an entire firm, not just part of it.

However, a firm can have the verifier perform a detailed **performance examination** on one or more composites or pooled funds and then state that a performance examination has been issued on that specific composite or fund.

The GIPS Verification Process

The GIPS Standards for Verifiers provides the various procedures that verifiers must follow. The reading focuses on the planning, sample selection, and testing components of verification. In planning for the verification process, the verifier must gather information about the firm, including all the firm's products, calculation methodologies, and GIPS policies and procedures.

Although verification must be asserted on a firmwide basis, verifiers often use samples of the firm's products to do so. When choosing samples, the verifier must consider the size of the firm and composites, the firm's internal controls and methods, the number of years being verified, and other factors. If the verifier discovers deficiencies, larger samples or additional verification procedures may be necessary.

Verifiers should also perform testing to determine if the firm satisfies requirements in areas including the following:

- Recordkeeping.
- Policies and procedures.
- Firm definition.
- The thoroughness of the firm's list of composites and limited distribution pooled funds.
- Calculation of total firm assets.
- Input data such as portfolio inflows and outflows.
  - These can often be verified with custodial statements and other third party documents.
- The construction and maintenance of composites including:
  - The classification of portfolios as discretionary or nondiscretionary.
  - The assignment of portfolios to appropriate composites.
    - Portfolios with outlier returns may indicate calculation errors or a misassignment to a composite.
- The content of the firm's GIPS Report and any marketing material.

MODULE QUIZ 33.7

1. Which of the following statements regarding verification is *least accurate*? Verification is:
   A. voluntary.
   B. recommended as part of best practices.
   C. a requirement and noted as part of a GIPS compliant presentation.
2. Which of the following statements regarding verification is *most accurate*?
   A. The verification process includes a detailed analysis of all the firm's products.
   B. Verification can be provided for a single portfolio, composite, or pooled fund.
   C. Verification does not assure that the construction, calculation, and presentation for any particular portfolio or composite is accurate.

KEY CONCEPTS

LOS 33.a

The Global Investment Performance Standards (GIPS®) contain ethical and professional standards for the presentation of investment performance results. The GIPS are a voluntary set of standards.

The LOS focus on the standards for investment management firms.

Asset owners who manage assets for an organization, participants, or beneficiaries and compete for business would also use the GIPS standards for firms.

The objectives of GIPS are to:

- Advance the interests of investors and increase their confidence in the investment industry.
- Provide accurate and comparable data to investors.
- Create a globally accepted standard for the determination and presentation of investment performance.
- Facilitate fair competition among global investment managers.
- Encourage self-regulation in the global investment industry.

The scope of the GIPS standards is as follows:

- GIPS compliance can only be claimed on a firmwide basis.
- To claim GIPS compliance, a firm must comply with all, not just some, of the applicable GIPS standards requirements.
- A claim of GIPS compliance indicates, among other things, that:
  - A firm's data inputs, processes, and return calculations are compliant.
  - All the firm's fee-paying segregated accounts and limited-distribution pooled funds have been assigned to at least one composite.

Definition of the Firm

- A firm is held out to clients or potential clients as a distinct business entity.
- A distinct business entity is that which is separated from other parts of the firm and retains discretion over asset management.
- Judgment is required to determine what qualifies as a distinct business entity.

The definition of the firm is used to determine the fair value of total firm assets, which for the defined firm:

- include discretionary and nondiscretionary assets.
- include fee-paying and non-fee-paying assets.
- are net of leverage used.
- are only actual (not simulated) assets.
- exclude advisory-only assets.
- exclude uncalled, but committed, capital.

Other Compliance Fundamentals

- When calculating composite assets (not total firm assets), nondiscretionary assets are not included, (i.e., only include discretionary assets when calculating composite performance).
- To initially claim compliance with the GIPS standards, the firm must attain compliance for a minimum of five years or for the period since firm inception if the firm has been in existence for less than five years.
- Firms must establish, update, and document GIPS policies and procedures.
- If the GIPS standards conflict with local laws and regulations, the firm must comply with local laws and regulations and disclose the conflict.
- The firm must not present performance-related information that is false or misleading.
- The firm must provide an annual GIPS compliant report to all existing clients for relevant composites.
- Benchmarks must reflect the corresponding investment strategy and be total return benchmarks.
- The firm must disclose all material errors and disclose corrected reports to current clients and verifiers.
- The firm must maintain GIPS compliance data and a list of composites for the last five years.

LOS 33.b

GIPS requires comparable return calculation methods to facilitate comparison of results. In many cases, there are interim external cash flows (ECF), such as client withdrawals (outflows) or additional client contributions (inflows) that can distort return calculations.

Ideally, to eliminate these potential distortions, the investment would be valued each time an interim ECF occurs. The subperiod returns must then be geometrically linked to create a true time-weighted rate of return (TWRR):

$$R_{TWRR} = (1 + R_1) \times (1 + R_2) \times (1 + R_3) \times \ldots \times (1 + R_t)$$

The methods of calculating an approximate return that do not require interim valuations are the Modified Dietz and MIRR methods.

$$\text{Modified Dietz return: } R_{MD} = \frac{EV - BV - ECF}{BV + \text{adjusted ECF}}$$

The modified internal rate of return (MIRR) is simply an internal rate of return (IRR) that adjusts for the timing of the ECFs.

Since both the Modified Dietz and MIRR use the number of days in the month, they are said to be methods that adjust for daily-weighted ECFs. The Modified Dietz and MIRR typically provide similar values.

Under the GIPS requirements:

- Firms must calculate monthly returns for non-private market investment portfolios.

- If a firm calculates daily valuations and returns, the daily return must be geometrically linked to create a monthly true TWRR.
- If a firm does not calculate daily returns and the ECFs are not large, approximations to the true TWRR that do not require an interim valuation can be used.
- If the ECFs are large, the portfolio must be valued at the time of the ECFs to calculate a subperiod return.
- Regardless of how the monthly return is calculated, the monthly return must be geometrically linked to create an annual return.

For portfolios other than non-private market investment portfolios, the GIPS requirements are as follows:

- Private market investment portfolios values and returns must be calculated quarterly.
- Pooled funds not in a composite must be valued and returns calculated at least annually.
  - The fund must also be valued and a subperiod return calculated at the time of subscriptions or redemptions.

Large Cash Flows

- The definition of a large ECF is determined by each firm for each composite.
- Generally, a large ECF is large enough to affect the return calculation.
- The firm's policy for the determination of a large cash flow must be documented.

There are some investment strategies where the firm controls the timing and size of the ECFs. In these cases, a money-weighted return (MWR) will be more representative of the manager's skill than the TWRR. MWRs can be used instead of TWRRs if:

- The firm has control of the timing of ECFs.
- The portfolios are closed-end, or fixed life, or fixed commitment, or have a significant amount of illiquid assets.

The MWR (which is an IRR calculation) must be calculated and the portfolios valued at least annually.

Other return calculation requirements are as follows.

- Trade date, not settlement date, prices must be used to calculate returns.
- Partial-year returns cannot be annualized.
- Total returns, which include income and capital gains/losses, must be used.
  - For investments that generate income, such as bonds, accrual accounting must be used.
  - Returns must reflect the manager's allocations to cash and cash equivalents.
- Under GIPS, the presented gross-of-fees return must have been calculated after the deduction of transactions costs.
- Transactions costs reflect the costs of buying and selling securities.
  - Examples include brokerage commissions, spreads, exchange fees.
  - For private market investments, they can also include legal, advisory, and other fees.

Reading 33

  - Custody fees should not be included.
  - Transactions costs can be estimated but only if they are unknown.
- In some cases, portfolios pay bundled or all-in fees, which can include trading costs, as well as investment management, custody, administrative, and other fees.
  - In this case, the presented gross-of-fees return must be reduced by:
    - The portion of the bundled fee due to transactions costs; or
    - The entire bundled fee if the transactions costs cannot be separated out.

LOS 33.c

Fair value is the amount an asset would be sold in an arm's-length transaction between willing and knowledgeable parties.

- Fair value should include accrued income for bonds and other income-generating assets.
  - For cash, income may be accounted for on a cash or accrual basis.
- Firms must document their valuation process and methodologies, which should be composite- or pooled fund-specific.
- A method lower in the GIPS recommended valuation hierarchy is used only when all methods higher in the hierarchy are unavailable. The fair value hierarchy is:
  1. The quoted price for an identical asset in a liquid market on the same day.
  2. The quoted price for a similar asset in a liquid market on the same day.
  3. The quoted price for identical or similar assets in markets that are not active.
  4. A value based on market inputs.
  5. A subjective value that is unobservable.

LOS 33.d

Composite returns must be calculated in one of three ways:

1. Asset-weighting portfolio returns by beginning-of-period values.
2. Asset-weighting portfolio returns by both beginning-of-period values and ECFs.
3. The aggregate method.

The first method is perhaps the simplest as each portfolio return is just multiplied by its beginning of period weight. The second method is similar except that we also adjust for the ECFs. The third method uses total composite values at the beginning and end of period.

LOS 33.e

Composites must be constructed so that investors are provided a fair and accurate representation of manager performance. The requirements should prevent managers from excluding poorly performing portfolios from composites.

A key determinant in whether a portfolio is included in a composite is whether the manager has discretion. If the performance of a portfolio does not reflect a manager's decisions (i.e., the portfolio is nondiscretionary), then that portfolio would be excluded from the calculation of composite returns.

Generally speaking, the requirements for what must be included in at least one composite are as follows:

- All actual, fee-paying, discretionary segregated accounts.
- Pooled funds that are also offered as segregated accounts.

In general, the requirements for what must not be included in a composite are as follows:

- Nondiscretionary accounts.
- Pooled funds that are not also offered as segregated accounts.
- Simulated portfolios.

Non-fee-paying, discretionary segregated accounts may be included with additional disclosures.

Discretion

- Given its importance, a firm must maintain and apply a clear, written definition of discretion.
- A client's investment policy statement (IPS) will specify risk preferences and constraints.
  - However, none of these *automatically* make a portfolio nondiscretionary.
  - Guidance is based on if the manager's ability to use professional judgment is materially constrained.
  - If the constraint is deemed immaterial, the manager can:
    - Place the portfolio in a composite with similar, unconstrained portfolios.
  - If the constraint is deemed material, the manager should:
    - Group the portfolio with similar, constrained portfolios.
    - Exclude the portfolio from all composites.
  - In some cases, there may be restrictions for particular assets. In these cases, a manager may:
    - Consider the entire portfolio nondiscretionary; or
    - Remove these assets and place the remainder of the portfolio in a composite; or
    - Consider the entire portfolio discretionary if the restricted assets are below a certain percentage of the portfolio, as stated in their policy.
- In some cases, its ECFs might indicate that a portfolio is nondiscretionary.

Model Portfolios

- Simulated portfolios cannot be in a composite.
- These portfolios are called hypothetical, model, or theoretical portfolios.
- They are often based on the backtesting of data.
- Their performance can be provided in supplemental information, but not in composite results.
- However, sometimes a firm will use its own funds (seed money) to create a new strategy.
  - The performance for these actual portfolios can be included in existing or new composites.

Non-Fee-Paying Portfolios

- Non-fee-paying portfolios may be included in a composite but, if included, firms are required to disclose the percentage of composite assets represented by non-fee-paying portfolios.

LOS 33.f

A critical step in achieving an accurate and comparable representation of a firm's performance is the defining and construction of composites. As per the GIPS standards, composites must:

- Be determined by investment mandate, objective, or strategy.
- Contain all portfolios that match the composite definition.
- Be based on criteria that is documented in the firm's policies and procedures.
- Be defined such that clients are able to compare the performance of one firm to another.
- Be representative of the firm's products and be consistent with the firm's marketing strategy.

Regarding composite construction:

- A starting point in composite construction might be competitors' composite classifications and/or the styles requested by potential investors.
- A composite definition that is too narrow results in too few portfolios in each, creates unnecessary costs, and potentially jeopardizes client confidentiality.
- A composite definition that is too broad results in disparate performance among composite portfolios.
- Examples on which to base composite construction include:
  - Style; sector, strategy, benchmark, risk/return profile, etc.

LOS 33.g

Regarding the movement of portfolios in and out of composites, the GIPS standards require firms to have policies for:

- When portfolios are included in composites.
- When portfolios are excluded from composites.
- Switching a portfolio from one composite to another.
- Cash flows from new investments or liquidations.
- The minimum asset level for a composite.

The firm's policy should be established on a composite-by-composite basis and applied in a timely, consistent manner.

Portfolio Inclusion

- New portfolios should be included in a composite at the beginning of the next full measurement period.
- However, the firm has discretion on the timing of portfolio inclusion because it may take time to invest new funds if the funding is other securities or if illiquid markets are being invested in.

- Thus the firm's documented policy may vary by composite, with some composites allowing for longer periods before portfolio inclusion.

Portfolio Exclusion

- Terminated portfolios should be included in a composite through the last full measurement period in which the firm had discretion.
- Clients sometimes direct a firm to stop trading an account or transfer control to a new manager before the portfolio is fully liquidated.

Switching Portfolios

- A portfolio can be switched to a new composite due to actions by the client or by the firm.
  - A client may change the portfolio's mandate, objective, or strategy.
  - The firm may redefine the composite such that the portfolio is no longer appropriate for the composite.
    - Redefining a composite by a firm should be highly unusual.
- When a portfolio is switched to a new composite, the portfolio's performance must remain in the old composite's historical performance.

Significant Cash Flows

- Significant (as defined in the firm's documentation) cash flows are those large enough such that it impedes the firm from implementing the strategy on a timely basis.
- To prevent composite performance from being affected by cash inflows/outflows in the event of significant cash flows, a firm can temporarily exclude the portfolio from the composite or create and report on a temporary new account (outside of the composite).

Minimum Asset Levels

- As portfolios change in size, they may be added to or removed from a composite as per firm policy.
- The minimum asset level must be specified in advance, and portfolios that are removed cannot have their prior performance removed from the composite's historical record.

LOS 33.h, 33.i

GIPS requires that firms must make every reasonable effort to provide a GIPS report to prospective clients and limited-distribution pooled fund investors.

The requirements for Composite Time-Weighted Return Reports include the following.

- At least 5 years of performance history upon GIPS adoption:
  - Unless the firm has been in existence for less than 5 years.
  - And then extended each year until the firm builds a 10-year GIPS compliant history.
- Time-weighted returns for the composite and benchmark.

Reading 33

- The amount of firm assets.
- The amount of composite assets.
- The number of portfolios in the composite if there are six or more.
- Internal composite dispersion to show how consistent portfolio performance is within the composite.
  - The firm can choose which measure to use as long as it fairly represents the composite's internal dispersion.
- Historical dispersion for the benchmark and the composite as a whole, using the *ex post* standard deviation, which must be:
  - For the previous three years of data on an annualized basis.

Portability

When one firm acquires or joins with another firm, group of managers, or manager, the new firm can link their performance to the previous firm's historical performance if:

1. Substantially all the investment decision makers are retained by the new firm.
2. The decision-making process remains substantially intact and independent within the new firm.
3. The new firm has records that document the previous firm's historical performance.
4. There is no break in the performance record between the new and previous firm.

If only the first three conditions are met, then the previous firm's historical performance can be used to represent that of the new firm, but the records may not be linked.

If the new firm is GIPS compliant but the previous firm is not, then the new firm has one year to bring its assets into compliance for future reporting.

Advisory-Only Assets and Uncalled, But Committed, Capital

- The firm can report information on advisory-only assets and uncalled, but committed, capital on a separate basis or combined with composite or firm assets.
- If reported on a combined basis, the firm must also report on that for the advisory-only and for the uncalled, but committed, assets.

LOS 33.j

The purpose of verification is to provide greater confidence to investors and to the firm in its claim of GIPS compliance. Verification is based on the GIPS principle of fair presentation and full disclosure. Although not required, verification is recommended and consistent with best practices.

Verification can be characterized as the process whereby an independent, outside party assesses the firm's:

- Policies and procedures for composite or pooled fund construction and maintenance.
- Performance calculation.

- Performance presentation.
- Distribution of performance.

Verification must be carried out in accordance with the GIPS Standards for Verifiers and must be issued firmwide.

- Verification cannot be provided for just a single portfolio, composite, or pooled fund.
- A firm must meet all the requirements of GIPS; it cannot claim that it is in compliance "except for."
- However, a firm can have the verifier perform a detailed performance examination on one or more composites or pooled funds and then state that a performance examination has been issued on that specific composite or fund.

The GIPS Standards for Verifiers provides the various procedures that verifiers must follow, which include planning, sample selection, and testing.

In planning for the verification process, the verifier must gather information about the firm, including all the firm's products, calculation methodologies, and GIPS policies and procedures.

Although verification must be asserted on a firmwide basis, verifiers often use samples of the firm's products to do so.

- When choosing samples, the verifier must consider the size of the firm and composites, the firm's internal controls and methods, the number of years being verified, and other factors.
- If the verifier discovers deficiencies, larger samples or additional verification procedures may be necessary.

Verifiers should also perform testing to determine whether the firm satisfies requirements in areas including the following:

- Recordkeeping.
- Policies and procedures.
- Firm definition.
- The thoroughness of the firm's list of composites and limited distribution pooled funds.
- Calculation of total firm assets.
- Input data such as portfolio inflows and outflows.
- The construction and maintenance of composites, including:
  - The classification of portfolios as discretionary or nondiscretionary.
  - The assignment of portfolios to appropriate composites.
    - Portfolios with outlier returns may indicate calculation errors or a misassignment to a composite.
- The content of the firm's GIPS Report and any marketing material.

ANSWER KEY FOR MODULE QUIZZES

Module Quiz 33.1, 33.2, 33.3

1. GIPS require the returns from cash and cash equivalents held in portfolios must be included in total-return calculations as long as the portfolio manager has control over the amount of the portfolio allocated to cash. This requirement stands even if the manager does not actually invest the cash, as is the case when it is held in a money market sweep account. This would not be an acceptable practice. (Module 33.3, LOS 33.b)

2. GIPS require periodic returns to be geometrically linked. Thus, the annual return is computed as follows:

   $R_{annual} = [(1 + R_{Q1}) \times (1 + R_{Q2}) \times (1 + R_{Q3}) \times (1 + R_{Q4})] - 1 =$
   $[(1.0300)\ (1.0415)(1.0375)(1.0315)] - 1 = 14.8\%.$

   (Module 33.3, LOS 33.b)

3. JIM may not claim compliance with the GIPS. A firm must be in full compliance with the GIPS in order to claim GIPS compliance. There is no such thing as *partial* compliance under the GIPS. (Module 33.1, LOS 33.a)

4. (a) The Modified Dietz method is calculated as:

   $$R_{MDietz} = \frac{EMV - BMV - CF}{BMV + \sum_{i=1}^{n} W_i \times CF_i}$$

   $$= \frac{55 - 50 - 3}{50 + \left(\frac{20}{30} \times 5\right) + \left(\frac{10}{30} \times (-2)\right)}$$

   $$= 3.80\%$$

   (b) The exact TWRR values the portfolio at every ECF.

   The month divides into three periods:

   period 1 return = (51.5 – 50.0) / 50 = 1.5 / 50 = 3.00%

   period 2 return = (59.0 – 56.5) / 56.5 = 2.5 / 56.5 = 4.42%

   period 3 return = (55.0 – 57.0) / 57.0 = –2 / 57.0 = –3.51%

   geometric linking for the month = (1.0300 × 1.0442 × 0.9649) – 1 = 3.78%

   (Module 33.3, LOS 33.b)

5. **C** It is most likely that money-weighted returns could be used instead of time-weighted returns if the manager has control of the timing of ECFs. The portfolios must also be closed-end, or fixed life, or fixed commitment, or have a significant amount of illiquid assets. (LOS 33.b)

Module Quiz 33.4

1. All actual fee-paying discretionary portfolios must be included in at least one composite. This requirement prevents firms from *cherry-picking* their best performing portfolios for presentation purposes. It does not matter if the firm ever plans to market the particular strategy to which a portfolio is being managed; if the portfolio is fee-paying and discretionary, it must be included in a composite. (LOS 33.e)

2. TIM cannot include model performance results in its presentation and claim compliance with the GIPS. Composites must include only assets under management and may not link simulated or model portfolios with actual performance. Simulated, back-tested, or model portfolio results do not represent the returns of actual assets under management and, thus, may not be included in the composites' GIPS-compliant performance results. The model results must be presented as simulated rather than real assets. (LOS 33.e)

3.

Characteristic	A. May Be Included in a Composite B. Must Be Excluded From Composite	Explanation*
i. Client has significant liquidity needs with an accompanying significant cash position.	B. Must be excluded	With both a significant liquidity requirement and cash position, *the manager's actions are limited to the point that the portfolio would probably not qualify as discretionary and thus should not be included.*
ii. Client does not pay fees.	B. May be included	Fee-paying portfolios are required to be in a composite. *Non-fee-paying portfolios that are discretionary may be included.*
iii. Client requests strictly following an index.	B. Must be excluded	*If the client significantly restricts a manager's ability to implement their investment strategy, then the portfolio is likely nondiscretionary and must be excluded from a composite.*

*Italics indicate an answer that would be sufficient for the exam.
(LOS 33.e)

Reading 33

4. The GIPS require terminated portfolios to be included in the historical record of the appropriate composite(s) through the last full reporting period that the portfolio was under management. This prevents the inclusion of the returns from a terminated portfolio for partial periods in a composite's return. Also, retaining the performance of a terminated portfolio in a composite's historical performance avoids survivorship bias. In the case of JIM, the terminated portfolio should be included in the composite until June 30 (i.e., the end of the month preceding July 15). (LOS 33.f)

5. (a) The adjustments to the ECFs result in partial month weightings (W) of each cash flow as follows:

Portfolio	ECF	Weight (W)	Adjusted ECF
A	£25	(30 – 12) / 30 = 18/30	18 / 30 × £25 = £15
A	£10	(30 – 22) / 30 = 8/30	8 / 30 × £10 = £2.67
B	–£13	(30 – 20) / 30 = 10/30	10 / 30 × –£13 = –£4.33

Using these in the formula for the Modified Dietz return (R_{MD}):

$$\text{Portfolio A: } R_{MD} = \frac{£467 - £400 - £25 - £10}{£400 + £15 + £2.67} = \frac{£32}{£417.67} = 7.66\%$$

$$\text{Portfolio B: } R_{MD} = \frac{£224 - £200 - -£13}{£200 - £4.33} = \frac{£37}{£195.67} = 18.91\%$$

(b) To calculate the composite return using beginning of period values, first find the weights of each portfolio in the composite:

$$A{:}\frac{400}{600} = 66.67\%$$

$$B{:}\frac{200}{600} = 33.33\%$$

The composite return is the sum of the weights times the returns:

= 0.6667 × 7.66% + 0.3333 × 18.91%

= 5.1069% + 6.3027% = 11.41%.

(c) To factor in the beginning values and weighted cash flows, the total for the denominators of the Modified Dietz formula is:

£417.67 + £195.67 = £613.34

Using these figures, the weights are:

$$A{:}\frac{417.67}{613.34} = 68.1\%$$

$$B{:}\frac{195.67}{613.34} = 31.9\%$$

The composite return is the sum of the weights times the returns:

$= 0.681 \times 7.66\% + 0.319 \times 18.91\%$

$= 5.2165\% + 6.0323\% = 11.25\%$

Notice that under this method, the composite return is slightly lower than in the previous method. This is because Portfolio A had a lower return (7.66%) than Portfolio B (18.91%). The larger ECFs for Portfolio A gave it a larger weight in this method and hence this reduced the overall composite return to 11.25%.

(d) In the aggregate return method, the numerator uses the total of the portfolio values and cash flows from the bottom of the table. In the denominator, the total of the portfolios' Modified Dietz values from the previous method are used.

$$R_{MD} = \frac{£691 - £25 - -£13 - £10 - £600}{£613.34} = \frac{£69}{£613.34} = 11.25\%$$

(Module 33.3, LOS 33.b; Module 33.4, LOS 33.d)

Module Quiz 33.5, 33.6

1. Part i

Excerpt 1 Tribon: I seem to recall that the GIPS require firms to present performance on a net of management fees basis.

Incorrect. Under the GIPS, firms may present performance net or gross of fees. The GIPS do require firms to disclose whether performance results are calculated gross or net of investment management and other fees paid by clients to the firm or to the firm's affiliates.

Part ii.

Excerpt 2 Guptar: GIPS require that the firm include as total assets under management those assets managed by client-appointed sub-advisers.

Incorrect. Total firm assets include all discretionary and non-discretionary assets under management within the defined firm. They do not include assets assigned to a sub-adviser unless the firm has discretion over the selection of the sub-adviser. (Module 33.5, LOS 33.h)

2.

Action Numbers not in compliance, Answer Choice B.	Explanation of Why Action is Not GIPS Compliant
1	The total return for the benchmark (or benchmarks) that reflects the investment strategy or mandate represented by the composite must be presented for the same periods for which the composite return is presented. The S&P 500 Index should not be used as a benchmark for the fixed-income and balanced composites.
2	Portfolio valuations must be based on fair values (not cost basis or book values).
4	The GIPS requires the disclosure of an appropriate fee schedule.
5	Composites must be asset-weighted using beginning-of-period weightings or another method that reflects both beginning market value and cash flows.
7	Time-weighted rates of return that adjust for cash flows must be used. Periodic returns must be geometrically linked.

Actions 3, 6, and 8 are in compliance with GIPS, Answer Choice A. (LOS a–d, h)

3. **C** The GIPS valuation hierarchy is as follows:

   1. Quoted prices from an active market for the same or a similar security.
   2. Quoted prices from an inactive market for the same or a similar security.
   3. Observable market-based inputs other than quoted prices.
   4. Subjective, unobservable inputs.

   Based on this hierarchy, if observed market prices from an active market are not available, the next best valuation basis is to use quoted prices from an inactive market. (Module 33.6, LOS 33.c)

Module Quiz 33.7

1. **C** Verification is voluntary and recommended as part of best practices. If verification were performed, it would be noted as part of the GIPS compliant performance presentation report. (LOS 33.j)

2. **C** Verification does not assure that the construction, calculation, and presentation for any particular portfolio or composite is accurate. Verifiers often use samples of the firm's products to determine if the firm is following the GIPS Standards. Verification must be issued firmwide and cannot be provided for a single portfolio, composite, or pooled fund. A detailed *performance examination* can be done on one or more composites or pooled funds with the firm issuing a statement indicating a performance examination has been issued on that specific composite or fund. (LOS 33.j)

TOPIC QUIZ: ETHICAL AND PROFESSIONAL STANDARDS

You have now finished the Ethical and Professional Standards topic section. On your Schweser online dashboard, you can find a Topic Quiz that will provide immediate feedback on how effective your study of this material has been. The test is best taken timed; allow three minutes per question. Topic Quizzes are more exam-like than typical QBank questions or module quiz questions. A score less than 70% suggests that additional review of the topic is needed.

FORMULAS

Implementation shortfall (IS)—at the highest level, the absolute value is:

IS = paper return – actual return

IS can be decomposed into the following parts:

- Execution cost:
  - Delay cost = shares executed × (arrival price – decision price)
  - Trading cost = shares executed × (average purchase price – arrival price)
- Opportunity cost = portion of order not filled × (closing price – decision price)
- Fixed fees = shares executed × commission per share

total IS value ($) = delay cost + trading cost + opportunity cost + fixed fees

All of the components of and total IS can be expressed in terms of basis points (bps) of the original cost of the paper portfolio. A basis point is 1/100th of 1%. A decimal number is multiplied by 10,000 to convert it to basis points.

Trade costs represent costs relative to the benchmark; a positive value represents underperformance:

absolute cost ($) = side × (execution price – benchmark price) × shares executed

$$\text{trade cost (bps)} = \text{side} \times \frac{(\text{execution price} - \text{benchmark price})}{\text{benchmark price}} \times 10{,}000$$

where:
side = +1 for a buy order, –1 for a sell order

Market-adjusted cost is used to remove the impact of market movements on trade cost, which ensures a trader is not penalized or rewarded for general market movements over the trade horizon.

$$\text{index cost (bps)} = \text{side} \times \frac{(\text{index VWAP} - \text{index arrival price})}{\text{index arrival price}} \times 10{,}000$$

market-adjusted cost (bps) = arrival cost (bps) – β × index cost (bps)

where:
arrival cost = the arrival cost of the trade based on an arrival price benchmark
β = beta of the security versus the index used to calculate index cost

Added value is a different method of trade cost analysis comparing the arrival cost of the trade with the estimated pretrade cost calculated using a model that incorporates key trade cost variables such as order size and liquidity of the market. If a fund executes at a cost *lower* than the pretrade cost estimate, then the trader has added value.

added value (bps) = arrival cost (bps) – estimated pretrade cost (bps)

A negative cost is a benefit—this trader has added value through their trading decisions.

Allocation effect BHB model—the contribution to the *i*th sector is equal to the portfolio's sector weight minus the benchmark's sector weight, times the benchmark sector return: $A_i = (w_i - W_i)B_i$

Allocation effect Brinson-Fachler model—the contribution to the *i*th sector is equal to the portfolio's sector weight minus the benchmark's sector weight, times the benchmark sector return minus the overall benchmark return: $A_i = (w_i - W_i)(B_i - B)$

Security selection—the contribution to selection in the *i*th sector is equal to the benchmark sector weight times the portfolio's sector return minus the benchmark's sector return: $S_i = W_i(R_i - B_i)$

Interaction effect—the contribution to the *i*th sector is equal to the portfolio sector weight minus the benchmark sector weight, times the portfolio sector return minus the benchmark sector return: $I_i = (w_i - W_i)(R_i - B_i)$

Carhart model:

$$R_p - R_f = a_p + b_{p1}RMRF + b_{p2}SMB + b_{p3}HML + b_{p4}WML + E_p$$

where:
RMRF = portfolio's sensitivity to a market index
SMB = market capitalization factor
HML = book-to-price factor
WML = momentum factor

For fixed income:

% total return = % income return + % price return

where:
% price return ≈ –duration × change in YTM

Factor-model-based benchmark:

$$R_P = a_p + b_1F_1 + b_2F_2 + \ldots + b_KF_K + \varepsilon$$

where:
R_P = periodic return on an account
a_p = "zero factor" term, representing the expected value of R_P if all factor values were zero
F_i = factors that have a systematic effect on the portfolio's performance; i = 1 to K
b_i = sensitivity of the returns on the account to the returns generated from factor *i*
ε = error term; portfolio return not explained by the factor model

Benchmark quality of a portfolio:

$$P = M + S + A$$

where:
P = investment manager's portfolio return
M = return on the market index
S = B – M = excess return to style; difference between the manager's style index (benchmark) return and the market return—S can be positive or negative
A = P – B = active return; difference between the manager's overall portfolio return and the style benchmark return

Sharpe ratio:

$$S_A = \frac{\overline{R}_A - \bar{r}_f}{\hat{\sigma}_A}$$

Treynor ratio:

$$T_A = \frac{\overline{R}_A - \bar{r}_f}{\hat{\beta}_A}$$

Information ratio:

$$IR = \frac{E(r_p) - E(r_B)}{\sigma(r_p - r_B)}$$

Appraisal ratio:

$$AR = \frac{\alpha}{\sigma_\varepsilon}$$

Sortino ratio:

$$SR_D = \frac{E(r_p) - r_T}{\sigma_D}$$

$$\widehat{SR}_D = \frac{\bar{r}_p - \bar{r}_T}{\hat{\sigma}_D}$$

Capture ratios are calculated as portfolio return divided by benchmark return. The capture ratio is calculated as upside capture divided by downside capture.

$$R_{TWRR} = (1 + R_1) \times (1 + R_2) \times (1 + R_3) \times \ldots \times (1 + R_t)$$

$$R_{MD} = \frac{EV - BV - ECF}{BV + \text{adjusted } ECF}$$

INDEX

O

P

Q

R

S

T

U

V

Notes

Notes